Koren Talmud Bavli

THE NOÉ EDITION

SHABBAT • PART SEVEN

Steinsaltz Center

KOREN

תלמוד בבלי

KOREN TALMUD BAVLI

THE NOÉ EDITION

שבת

SHABBAT

Daf 137b through Daf 157b

COMMENTARY BY

Rabbi Adin Even-Israel Steinsaltz

EDITOR-IN-CHIEF

Rabbi Dr Tzvi Hersh Weinreb

SENIOR CONTENT EDITOR

Rabbi Dr Shalom Z Berger

EXECUTIVE EDITOR

Rabbi Joshua Schreier

•

STEINSALTZ CENTER

KOREN PUBLISHERS JERUSALEM

Supported by the Matanel Foundation

Koren Talmud Bavli, The Noe Edition
Vol. 2.7: Tractate Shabbat, Daf 137b through Daf 157b
Paperback, ISBN, 978-965-7765-32-6

First Hebrew/English paperback edition, 2019

Koren Publishers Jerusalem Ltd.
PO Box 4044, Jerusalem 91040, ISRAEL
PO Box 8531, New Milford, CT 06776, USA
www.korenpub.com

Steinsaltz Center

Steinsaltz Center is the parent organization of institutions established by Rabbi Adin Even-Israel Steinsaltz

PO Box 45187, Jerusalem 91450 ISRAEL
Telephone: +972 2 646 0900, Fax +972 2 624 9454
www.steinsaltz-center.org

Hardcover design by Ben Gasner

This book was published in cooperation with the Israel Institute for Talmudic Publications.

הִנֵּה יָמִים בָּאִים, נְאֻם אֲדֹנָי יֱהֹוִה, וְהִשְׁלַחְתִּי רָעָב בָּאָרֶץ,
לֹא־רָעָב לַלֶּחֶם וְלֹא־צָמָא לַמַּיִם, כִּי אִם־לִשְׁמֹעַ אֵת דִּבְרֵי יהוה.

Behold, days are coming – says the Lord God – I will send a hunger to the land, not a hunger for bread nor a thirst for water, but to hear the words of the Lord. (AMOS 8:11)

The Noé edition of the Koren Talmud Bavli
with the commentary of Rabbi Adin Even-Israel Steinsaltz
is dedicated to all those who open its covers
to quench their thirst for Jewish Knowledge,
in our generation of Torah renaissance.

This beautiful edition is for the young, the aged,
the novice and the savant alike,
as it unites the depth of Torah knowledge
with the best of academic scholarship.

Within its exquisite and vibrant pages,
words become worlds.

It will claim its place in the library of classics,
in the bookcases of the Beit Midrash,
the classrooms of our schools,
and in the offices of professionals and business people
who carve out precious time to grapple with its timeless wisdom.

For the Student and the Scholar

DEDICATED BY LEO AND SUE NOÉ

Steinsaltz Center

Executive Director, Steinsaltz Center
Rabbi Meni Even-Israel

Managing Editor
Rabbi Jason Rappoport

Senior Content Editor
Rabbi Dr. Shalom Z. Berger

Translators
Amy Fay Kaplan Benoff
Betzalel Philip Edwards
Rabbi Elli Fischer
Gila Hoch
Stephen Lauber
Elie Leshem
Rabbi Eli Ozarowski
Gavriel Reiss
Yosef Rosen
Jay Shapiro
Rabbi Ami Silver
Eliana Kinderlehrer Silver
Avi Steinhart
Amiel Vick
Rabbi Abe Y. Weschler
Rabbi Yaakov Komisar
Rabbi Adin Krohn
Rabbi Jason Leib
Sally Mayer
Rabbi Jonathan Mishkin
Rabbi Noam Shapiro
Rabbi Michael Siev
Rabbi David Strauss

Editors
Mali Brofsky
Rabbi David Jay Derovan
Rabbi Dov Karoll

Copy Editors
Aliza Israel, *Coordinator*
Bracha Hermon
Shira Finson
Ita Olesker
Nechama Unterman

Language Consultants
Dr. Stephanie E. Binder, *Greek & Latin*
Rabbi Yaakov Hoffman, *Arabic*
Dr. Shai Secunda, *Persian*
Shira Shmidman, *Aramaic*

KOREN

Design & Typesetting
Raphaël Freeman, *Design & Typesetting*
Dena Landowne Bailey, *Typesetting*
Tani Bayer, *Jacket Design*

Images
Eliahu Misgav, *Illustration*
Yehudit Cohen, *Image Acquisition*

Digital Edition
Raphaël Freeman, *Team Leader*
Eliyahu Skoczylas, *Senior Architect*
Tani Bayer, *User Interface Design*
Dena Landowne Bailey, *Concept*
Rabbi Hanan Benayahu, *Concept*
Laura Messinger, *Commercial Liaison*

Introduction by the Publisher

The Talmud has sustained and inspired Jews for thousands of years. Throughout Jewish history, an elite cadre of scholars has absorbed its learning and passed it on to succeeding generations. The Talmud has been the fundamental text of our people.

Beginning in the 1960s, Rabbi Adin Even-Israel Steinsaltz שליט"א created a revolution in the history of Talmud study. His translation of the Talmud, first into modern Hebrew and then into other languages, as well the practical learning aids he added to the text, have enabled millions of people around the world to access and master the complexity and context of the world of Talmud.

It is thus a privilege to present the *Koren Talmud Bavli*, an English translation of the talmudic text with the brilliant elucidation of Rabbi Steinsaltz. The depth and breadth of his knowledge are unique in our time. His rootedness in the tradition and his reach into the world beyond it are inspirational.

Working with Rabbi Steinsaltz on this remarkable project has been not only an honor, but a great pleasure. Never shy to express an opinion, with wisdom and humor, Rabbi Steinsaltz sparkles in conversation, demonstrating his knowledge (both sacred and worldly), sharing his wide-ranging interests, and, above all, radiating his passion. I am grateful for the unique opportunity to work closely with him, and I wish him many more years of writing and teaching.

Our intentions in publishing this new edition of the Talmud are threefold. First, we seek to fully clarify the talmudic page to the reader – textually, intellectually, and graphically. Second, we seek to utilize today's most sophisticated technologies, both in print and electronic formats, to provide the reader with a comprehensive set of study tools. And third, we seek to help readers advance in their process of Talmud study.

To achieve these goals, the *Koren Talmud Bavli* is unique in a number of ways:

- The classic *tzurat hadaf* of Vilna, used by scholars since the 1800s, has been reset for great clarity, and opens from the Hebrew "front" of the book. Full *nikkud* has been added to both the talmudic text and Rashi's commentary, allowing for a more fluent reading with the correct pronunciation; the commentaries of *Tosafot* have been punctuated. Upon the advice of many English-speaking teachers of Talmud, we have separated these core pages from the translation, thereby enabling the advanced student to approach the text without the distraction of the translation. This also reduces the number of volumes in the set. At bottom of each *daf*, there is a reference to the corresponding English pages. In addition, the Vilna edition was read against other manuscripts and older print editions, so that texts which had been removed by non-Jewish censors have been restored to their rightful place.
- The English translation, which starts on the English "front" of the book, reproduces the *menukad* Talmud text alongside the English translation (in bold) and commentary and explanation (in a lighter font). The Hebrew and Aramaic text is presented in logical paragraphs. This allows for a fluent reading of the text for the non-Hebrew or non-Aramaic reader. It also allows for the Hebrew reader to refer easily to the text alongside. Where the original text features dialogue or poetry, the English text is laid out in a manner appropriate to the genre. Each page refers to the relevant *daf*.

- Critical contextual tools surround the text and translation: personality notes, providing short biographies of the Sages; language notes, explaining foreign terms borrowed from Greek, Latin, Persian, or Arabic; and background notes, giving information essential to the understanding of the text, including history, geography, botany, archaeology, zoology, astronomy, and aspects of daily life in the talmudic era.
- Halakhic summaries provide references to the authoritative legal decisions made over the centuries by the rabbis. They explain the reasons behind each halakhic decision as well as the ruling's close connection to the Talmud and its various interpreters.
- Photographs, drawings, and other illustrations have been added throughout the text – in full color in the Standard and Electronic editions, and in black and white in the Daf Yomi edition – to visually elucidate the text.

This is not an exhaustive list of features of this edition, it merely presents an overview for the English-speaking reader who may not be familiar with the "total approach" to Talmud pioneered by Rabbi Steinsaltz.

Several professionals have helped bring this vast collaborative project to fruition. My many colleagues are noted on the Acknowledgements page, and the leadership of this project has been exceptional.

RABBI MENACHEM EVEN-ISRAEL, DIRECTOR OF THE STEINSALTZ CENTER, was the driving force behind this enterprise. With enthusiasm and energy, he formed the happy alliance with Koren and established close relationships among all involved in the work.

RABBI DR. TZVI HERSH WEINREB שליט״א, EDITOR-IN-CHIEF, brought to this project his profound knowledge of Torah, intellectual literacy of Talmud, and erudition of Western literature. It is to him that the text owes its very high standard, both in form and content, and the logical manner in which the beauty of the Talmud is presented.

RABBI JOSHUA SCHREIER, EXECUTIVE EDITOR, assembled an outstanding group of scholars, translators, editors, and proofreaders, whose standards and discipline enabled this project to proceed in a timely and highly professional manner.

RABBI MEIR HANEGBI, EDITOR OF THE HEBREW EDITION OF THE STEINSALTZ TALMUD, lent his invaluable assistance throughout the work process, supervising the reproduction of the Vilna pages.

RAPHAËL FREEMAN, EDITOR OF KOREN, created this Talmud's unique typographic design which, true to the Koren approach, is both elegant and user friendly.

It has been an enriching experience for all of us at Koren Publishers Jerusalem to work with the Steinsaltz Center to develop and produce the Koren Talmud Bavli. We pray that this publication will be a source of great learning and, ultimately, greater *avodat Hashem* for all Jews.

Matthew Miller, Publisher
Koren Publishers Jerusalem
Jerusalem 5772

Contents

For the vocalized Vilna Shas layout, please open as a Hebrew book.

Introduction to **Perek XX**

This chapter addresses a variety of issues related to rabbinical prohibitions on food preparation on Shabbat: Is it permitted to suspend a wine strainer on Shabbat, what food may one strain and how may he do it, and other questions related to food preparation for humans as well as the handling of hay and other types of animal feed. The chapter clarifies the various details of the prohibited labors that may be relevant to these activities. However, this connection is merely external and associative and explains only the reason why these different topics have been combined in one chapter. On the other hand, this chapter, as those that precede and follow it, addresses a range of fundamental halakhic problems.

One of these problems addressed here is a continuation of the laws of building on Shabbat. Chapter Twelve was devoted to the laws of building a permanent structure, which is prohibited by Torah law. This chapter, on the other hand, discusses additional aspects of the labor of building, based upon an expanded definition of the labor that includes erecting a tent. This broadened definition includes the construction of any building or even the combination of different parts into any whole which could in any way be considered a structure. The construction of a tent can also mean combining parts of utensils or even attaching different fabrics together.

Another topic addressed in this chapter is food preparation. The Torah forbade performing any of the prohibited labors on Shabbat even for the purpose of food preparation. This chapter examines at length various methods of food preparation to determine if they are permitted or if they constitute a violation of Torah law or rabbinic law, and establishes guidelines and boundaries for making these determinations.

מתני׳ רַבִּי אֱלִיעֶזֶר אוֹמֵר: תּוֹלִין אֶת הַמְּשַׁמֶּרֶת בְּיוֹם טוֹב, וְנוֹתְנִין לַתְּלוּיָה בְּשַׁבָּת. וַחֲכָמִים אוֹמְרִים: אֵין תּוֹלִין אֶת הַמְּשַׁמֶּרֶת בְּיוֹם טוֹב, וְאֵין נוֹתְנִין לַתְּלוּיָה בְּשַׁבָּת, אֲבָל נוֹתְנִין לַתְּלוּיָה בְּיוֹם טוֹב.

MISHNA **Rabbi Eliezer says: One may suspend** and stretch over a base **the strainer**[B] through which sediment is filtered from wine, **on a Festival. And one may place** wine **through** a strainer that was already **suspended** the day before; however, one may not suspend the strainer **on Shabbat. And the Rabbis say: One may not suspend the strainer on a Festival, and one may not place** wine for filtering **through a suspended** strainer **on Shabbat; however, one may place** wine **through a suspended** strainer[NH] **on a Festival.**

גמ׳ הָשְׁתָּא רַבִּי אֱלִיעֶזֶר, אוֹסוּפֵי אֹהֶל עֲרַאי לָא מוֹסְפִינַן, לְמִיעֲבַד לְכַתְּחִלָּה שָׁרֵי?!

GEMARA The Gemara raises a difficulty with regard to Rabbi Eliezer's position: **Now, Rabbi Eliezer** holds that **we may not** even **add** to **a temporary tent** on Shabbat; could it be that **to make** a tent **is permitted** ***ab initio***? Stretching a strainer over a base, which Rabbi Eliezer permits, is comparable to making a tent.

מַאי הִיא – דִּתְנַן, פְּקָק הַחַלּוֹן, רַבִּי אֱלִיעֶזֶר אוֹמֵר: בִּזְמַן שֶׁקָּשׁוּר וְתָלוּי – פּוֹקְקִין בּוֹ, וְאִם לָאו – אֵין פּוֹקְקִין בּוֹ. וַחֲכָמִים אוֹמְרִים: בֵּין כָּךְ וּבֵין כָּךְ – פּוֹקְקִין בּוֹ.

The Gemara explains the question: **What is** this opinion of Rabbi Eliezer's? **As we learned** in a mishna: With regard to **a window shutter** used to cover a skylight, **Rabbi Eliezer says: When it is tied** to **and hanging** from the window, i.e., it is not touching the ground, **one may shutter** the window **with it, and if not, one may not shutter** the window **with it. And the Rabbis say: Both** in **this** case **and** in **that** case **one may shutter with it.**

וְאָמַר רַבָּה בַּר בַּר חָנָה אָמַר רַבִּי יוֹחָנָן: הַכֹּל מוֹדִים שֶׁאֵין עוֹשִׂין אֹהֶל עֲרַאי בַּתְּחִלָּה בְּיוֹם טוֹב, וְאֵין צָרִיךְ לוֹמַר בַּשַּׁבָּת. לֹא נֶחְלְקוּ אֶלָּא לְהוֹסִיף, שֶׁרַבִּי אֱלִיעֶזֶר אוֹמֵר: אֵין מוֹסִיפִין בְּיוֹם טוֹב, וְאֵין צָרִיךְ לוֹמַר בַּשַּׁבָּת. וַחֲכָמִים אוֹמְרִים: מוֹסִיפִין בַּשַּׁבָּת, וְאֵין צָרִיךְ לוֹמַר בְּיוֹם טוֹב.

And Rabba bar bar Ḥana said that **Rabbi Yoḥanan said: Everyone agrees that one may not construct a temporary tent on a Festival** for the **first time, and needless to say,** one may not do so **on Shabbat.** The *tanna'im* **disagree only** with regard to **adding** to an existing tent, **as Rabbi Eliezer says: One may not add** to an existing structure **on a Festival, and needless to say,** one may not do so **on Shabbat. And the Rabbis say: One may add** to the temporary structure **on Shabbat, and needless to say,** one may do so **on a Festival.**

רַבִּי אֱלִיעֶזֶר סָבַר לָהּ כְּרַבִּי יְהוּדָה, דְּתַנְיָא: אֵין בֵּין יוֹם טוֹב לַשַּׁבָּת אֶלָּא אוֹכֶל נֶפֶשׁ בִּלְבַד, רַבִּי יְהוּדָה מַתִּיר אַף מַכְשִׁירֵי אוֹכֶל נֶפֶשׁ.

The Gemara answers: Rabbi Eliezer indeed holds that the suspension of a strainer constitutes a prohibited labor. However, **Rabbi Eliezer holds in accordance with** the opinion of **Rabbi Yehuda** with regard to actions that facilitate preparation of food on a Festival, **as it was taught** in a *baraita*: **The only** difference **between a Festival and Shabbat** is with regard to the preparation of **food alone.** It is permitted to perform labors for the purpose of food preparation on a Festival, but not on Shabbat. **Rabbi Yehuda permits even actions that facilitate food preparation** on a Festival, e.g., fixing utensils with which food is prepared on the Festival. Similarly, Rabbi Eliezer permits the suspension of a strainer, which would otherwise constitute a prohibited labor, in order to prepare wine for use on the Festival.

אֵימַר דִּשְׁמַעִינַן לֵיהּ לְרַבִּי יְהוּדָה – בְּמַכְשִׁירִין שֶׁאִי אֶפְשָׁר לַעֲשׂוֹתָם מֵעֶרֶב יוֹם טוֹב, בְּמַכְשִׁירִין שֶׁאֶפְשָׁר לַעֲשׂוֹתָם מֵעֶרֶב יוֹם טוֹב מִי שָׁמְעַתְּ לֵיהּ?!

The Gemara asks: **Say that we heard** that **Rabbi Yehuda** permits labors that are otherwise prohibited if they **pertain to actions that facilitate** food preparation **that cannot be performed on the eve of the Festival;** however, **with regard to actions that facilitate** food preparation **that can be performed on the eve of the Festival, did you hear** that **he** permits doing so?

דְּרַבִּי אֱלִיעֶזֶר עֲדִיפָא מִדְּרַבִּי יְהוּדָה.

The Gemara answers: The leniency **of Rabbi Eliezer exceeds that of Rabbi Yehuda.** Unlike Rabbi Yehuda, Rabbi Eliezer does not distinguish between actions that facilitate food preparation that can and those that cannot be performed on the eve of the Festival.

״וַחֲכָמִים אוֹמְרִים״. אִיבַּעְיָא לְהוּ: תָּלָה מַאי? אָמַר רַב יוֹסֵף: תָּלָה – חַיָּיב חַטָּאת.

We learned in the mishna: **And the Rabbis say:** One may not suspend the strainer on a Festival. **A dilemma was raised before** the Sages: If **he suspended** a strainer unwittingly, **what** is the *halakha*? **Rav Yosef said:** If **he suspended** it, **he is liable** to bring **a sin-offering,** like anyone who unwittingly performs a labor prohibited by Torah law on Shabbat.

BACKGROUND

Strainer – מְשַׁמֶּרֶת: In talmudic times, a strainer consisted of a rim with a handle above it. Straining was accomplished by fabric that was stretched over the rim of the container and tied at the bottom.

Strainer used in talmudic times

NOTES

Suspending a strainer – תְּלִיַּית מְשַׁמֶּרֶת: In the Jerusalem Talmud it is stated that if a new strainer is suspended, one is also liable for completing production of a vessel, since he renders it fit for use.

HALAKHA

Suspending a strainer of wine – תְּלִיַּית מְשַׁמֶּרֶת יַיִן: On Shabbat or a Festival, it is prohibited to stretch a cloth strainer over a base in order to filter sediment from wine. One who does so performs the prohibited labor of making a tent. On Shabbat, it is also prohibited to place wine with sediment into a strainer that was suspended before Shabbat. However, it is permitted to do so on a Festival, in accordance with the opinion of the Rabbis (*Shulḥan Arukh, Oraḥ Ḥayyim* 315:9, 319:9, 510:4).

אֲמַר לֵיהּ אַבַּיֵּי: אֶלָּא מֵעַתָּה, תְּלָא כּוּזָא בְּסִיכְתָּא הָכִי נַמִי דְּמִיחַיַּיב?!

Abaye said to him: But if that is **so,** that an action of that sort constitutes performance of the prohibited labor of building by Torah law, then if **one suspended a jug on a peg, is he also liable** for building a tent?

Perek **XX**
Daf **138** Amud **a**

אֶלָּא אָמַר אַבַּיֵּי: מִדְּרַבָּנַן הִיא, שֶׁלֹּא יַעֲשֶׂה כְּדֶרֶךְ שֶׁהוּא עוֹשֶׂה בְּחוֹל.

Rather, Abaye said: It is a rabbinic decree issued so **that one will not conduct** himself on Shabbat **in the manner that he conducts** himself **during the week.**[N]

מַנְקִיט אַבַּיֵּי חוּמְרֵי מַתְנִיתָא, וְתָנֵי: הַגּוֹד וְהַמְשַׁמֶּרֶת כִּילָּה וְכִסֵּא גַּלִּין – לֹא יַעֲשֶׂה, וְאִם עָשָׂה – פָּטוּר אֲבָל אָסוּר. אֹהֳלֵי קֶבַע – לֹא יַעֲשֶׂה, וְאִם עָשָׂה – חַיָּיב חַטָּאת. אֲבָל מִטָּה וְכִסֵּא טַרְסְקָל וְאִסְלָא – מוּתָּר לְנוֹטְתָן לְכַתְּחִילָּה.

Abaye would consolidate the principles of the ***baraitot*** pertaining to the construction of a tent on Shabbat **and teach:** With regard to **a large wineskin, a wine strainer,**[H] **a canopy** hung over a bed, **and a folding chair** whose cover is detached from its legs, **one may not assemble** them due to the prohibition against making a temporary tent. **If one did** so unwittingly, **he is exempt** by Torah law from bringing a sin-offering, **but** it is **prohibited** by rabbinic decree. With regard to **permanent tents,**[H] **one may not make** them, **and if he did** so, **he is liable to** bring **a sin-offering** for performing the prohibited labor of building. **However,** with regard to **a bed, and a folding chair** [***teraskal***][LH] whose cover is attached to its legs, **and a** collapsible **toilet,**[B] **it is permissible to open them *ab initio*,** since they are prepared for use from before Shabbat.

״וְאֵין נוֹתְנִין לַתְּלוּיָה בַּשַּׁבָּת״. אִיבַּעְיָא לְהוּ: שִׁימֵּר מַאי? אָמַר רַב כָּהֲנָא: שִׁימֵּר – חַיָּיב חַטָּאת.

We also learned in the mishna: **One may not place** wine for filtering even **into a suspended** strainer **on Shabbat. A dilemma was raised before** the Sages: If **one strained** wine, **what** is the *halakha*? **Rav Kahana said:** If **one strained** wine, **he is liable to** bring **a sin-offering.**

מַתְקִיף לַהּ רַב שֵׁשֶׁת: מִי אִיכָּא מִידֵּי דְּרַבָּנַן מְחַיְּיבִי חַטָּאת, וְרַבִּי אֱלִיעֶזֶר שָׁרֵי לְכַתְּחִילָּה?!

Rav Sheshet strongly objects to this: Is there something for which the Rabbis render one liable to bring **a sin-offering**[N] **and Rabbi Eliezer permits** its performance ***ab initio***? Extreme differences of opinion of that kind are rarely found in one mishna.

מַתְקִיף לַהּ רַב יוֹסֵף: אַלְמָה לָא?! הֲרֵי עִיר שֶׁל זָהָב, דְּרַבִּי מֵאִיר מְחַיֵּיב חַטָּאת וְרַבִּי אֱלִיעֶזֶר שָׁרֵי לְכַתְּחִילָּה!

Rav Yosef strongly objects to this question: **Why not? Isn't** there an analogous dispute with regard to a woman who wears **a city of gold** ornament from one domain to another on Shabbat, **as Rabbi Meir renders** her **liable** to bring **a sin-offering, and Rabbi Eliezer permits** it even ***ab initio***?

LANGUAGE

Teraskal chair – כִּסֵּא טַרְסְקָל: From the Greek τρισκελής, *triskelès*, meaning a three-legged chair. *Teraskal* has a different meaning here than it does in other places in the Talmud.

BACKGROUND

Toilet – אִסְלָא: The toilet was typically a metal frame over which they would stretch out a leather hide with a hole.

Stone toilets from the talmudic period

NOTES

That one will not conduct himself on Shabbat in the manner that he conducts himself during the week – שֶׁלֹּא יַעֲשֶׂה כְּדֶרֶךְ שֶׁהוּא עוֹשֶׂה בְּחוֹל: According to the Ramban, Abaye rules that suspending a strainer violates the rabbinic prohibition against constructing a tent. It is permitted to do so for pomegranates (139b, p. 322), because the strainer need not be firmly suspended for the pomegranates. Since the strainer is suspended in an atypical manner, the rabbinic decree was not issued for that case. Rabbeinu Yona explains that a tent is defined as anything constructed to cover the space beneath it. When one places pomegranates on a strainer, he does not utilize the space underneath the fabric. Therefore, the strainer does not function as a tent at all.

Is there something for which the Rabbis render one liable to bring a sin-offering, etc. – מִי אִיכָּא מִידֵּי דְּרַבָּנַן מְחַיְּיבִי חַטָּאת וכו׳: This question stems from the Talmud's objective throughout to minimize the scope of disputes. It is difficult to assume that one Sage would render one liable by Torah law while the other would rule the act entirely permitted. In cases like that, the position of one of the disputants is usually emended in order to render the opinions more compatible. Other commentaries explain that this type of question arises only in cases where the Rabbis rule one liable and an individual Sage disagrees with them and rules one entirely exempt. In other cases, the Gemara is not troubled by disputes of this kind (Rashba).

HALAKHA

A large wineskin, a wine strainer, etc. – הַגּוֹד וְהַמְשַׁמֶּרֶת וכו׳: It is prohibited to suspend a canopy, a strainer, and the like in their usual manner on Shabbat. Rather, one should spread them in an unusual manner. For instance, one should first attach the upper section and only then attach the lower section. One who suspended a canopy in its usual manner is exempt from bringing a sin-offering; however, it is prohibited by rabbinic law. This ruling is in accordance with the opinion of Abaye (Rambam *Sefer Zemanim, Hilkhot Shabbat* 21:17, 22:28; *Shulḥan Arukh, Oraḥ Ḥayyim* 315:3).

Permanent tents – אֹהֳלֵי קֶבַע: One who establishes a permanent tent on Shabbat is liable to bring a sin-offering for having performed the prohibited labor of building. A temporary tent is prohibited by rabbinic decree, in accordance with the opinion of Abaye (Rambam *Sefer Zemanim, Hilkhot Shabbat* 22:27).

Folding beds and chairs – מִטּוֹת וְכִסְּאוֹת מִתְקַפְּלִים: It is permitted to open folding beds and chairs on Shabbat *ab initio* because they were already attached and completed entities before Shabbat. This ruling is in accordance with the opinion of Abaye (Rambam *Sefer Zemanim, Hilkhot Shabbat* 22:28; *Shulḥan Arukh, Oraḥ Ḥayyim* 315:5).

מַאי הִיא – דְּתַנְיָא: לֹא תֵּצֵא אִשָּׁה בְּעִיר שֶׁל זָהָב, וְאִם יָצְאָה – חַיֶּיבֶת חַטָּאת, דִּבְרֵי רַבִּי מֵאִיר. וַחֲכָמִים אוֹמְרִים: לֹא תֵּצֵא, וְאִם יָצְאָה – פְּטוּרָה. רַבִּי אֱלִיעֶזֶר אוֹמֵר: יוֹצְאָה אִשָּׁה בְּעִיר שֶׁל זָהָב לְכַתְּחִילָּה.

What is that dispute? **As it was taught** in a *baraita*: **A woman may not go out** into the public domain on Shabbat **with a city of gold** ornament. **And if she did go out** with it into the public domain, **she is liable to bring a sin-offering;** this is **the statement of Rabbi Meir. And the Rabbis say: She may not go out** with it *ab initio*, **and if she went out, she is exempt. And Rabbi Eliezer says: A woman may go out with a city of gold** ornament ***ab initio***. Apparently, there is precedent for a dispute in which one opinion maintains that an action incurs liability to bring a sin-offering, while another opinion rules that it is permitted *ab initio*.

אֲמַר לֵיהּ אַבָּיֵי: מִי סָבְרַתְּ רַבִּי אֱלִיעֶזֶר אַדְּרַבִּי מֵאִיר קָאֵי, דְּאָמַר ״חַיֶּיבֶת חַטָּאת״? אַדְּרַבָּנַן קָאֵי, דְּאָמְרִי ״פָּטוּר אֲבָל אָסוּר״, וְאָמַר לְהוּ אִיהוּ: מוּתָּר לְכַתְּחִילָּה.

Abaye said to Rav Yosef: **Do you hold that Rabbi Eliezer is relating to** the statement of **Rabbi Meir, who said** that **she is liable** to bring **a sin-offering? He is relating to** the statement of **the Rabbis, who said one is exempt but it is prohibited, and he said to them** that he holds that it is **permitted *ab initio*.** Had there not been the intermediate opinion of the Rabbis, an argument with such extreme opinions would not have been possible.

מִשּׁוּם מַאי מַתְרֵינַן בֵּיהּ? רַבָּה אָמַר: מִשּׁוּם בּוֹרֵר, רַבִּי זֵירָא אָמַר: מִשּׁוּם מְרַקֵּד.

The Gemara asks: One is liable to bring a sin-offering for straining. **Due to** performance of **what** category of prohibited labor **do we forewarn him? Rabba said:** It is **for** the category of **selecting,** as one is selecting the wine from the sediment. **Rabbi Zeira said:** It is **for** the category of **sifting,**[N] as straining is similar to sifting flour in a sifter, which is a form of selecting.

אָמַר רַבָּה: כְּווֹתִי דִּידִי מִסְתַּבְּרָא, מָה דַּרְכּוֹ שֶׁל בּוֹרֵר – נוֹטֵל אוֹכֶל וּמַנִּיחַ הַפְּסוֹלֶת, אַף הָכָא נַמִי – נוֹטֵל אֶת הָאוֹכֶל וּמַנִּיחַ אֶת הַפְּסוֹלֶת.

Rabba said: According to my opinion, it is reasonable. What is the manner of one who selects? He **takes the food and leaves the refuse; here too,** when straining wine, **one takes the food and leaves the refuse.**

אָמַר רַבִּי זֵירָא: כְּווֹתִי דִּידִי מִסְתַּבְּרָא, מָה דַּרְכּוֹ שֶׁל מְרַקֵּד – פְּסוֹלֶת מִלְמַעְלָה וְאוֹכֶל מִלְּמַטָּה, אַף הָכָא נַמִי – פְּסוֹלֶת מִלְמַעְלָה וְאוֹכֶל מִלְּמַטָּה.

Rabbi Zeira said: According to my opinion, that this is not typical selection but rather a specific type of selection, **it is reasonable,** as **what is the manner of sifting?** The **refuse** remains **atop** the sifter **and the food is below. Here too,** when straining wine, the **refuse** remains **atop** the strainer **and the food is below.**

תָּנֵי רָמֵי בַּר יְחֶזְקֵאל: טַלִּית כְּפוּלָה – לֹא יַעֲשֶׂה, וְאִם עָשָׂה – פָּטוּר אֲבָל אָסוּר. הָיָה כָּרוּךְ עָלֶיהָ חוּט אוֹ מְשִׁיחָה – מוּתָּר לִנְטוֹתָהּ לְכַתְּחִילָּה.

Rami bar Yeḥezkel taught: With regard to **a doubled cloak,**[NH] **one may not make** a covering on Shabbat by taking the cloak and placing it over a rope and extending the two sides in order to form something similar to a canopy beneath which one could lie (*ge'onim*; Rif). **And if one made it, he is exempt** from bringing a sin-offering by Torah law, **but it is prohibited** by rabbinic decree. **If there was a string or a cord wrapped around it** before Shabbat, and the cloak was attached to the string while folded, **it is permitted to** spread it and **stretch it *ab initio*.**

בְּעָא מִינֵּיהּ רַב כָּהֲנָא מֵרַב: כִּילָּה מַהוּ? אֲמַר לֵיהּ: אַף מִטָּה אֲסוּרָה. מִטָּה מַהוּ? אֲמַר לֵיהּ: אַף כִּילָּה מוּתֶּרֶת. כִּילָּה וּמִטָּה מַהוּ? אֲמַר לֵיהּ: כִּילָּה אֲסוּרָה, וּמִטָּה מוּתֶּרֶת.

On a related issue, **Rav Kahana raised a dilemma before Rav:** In the case of **a canopy, what** is the *halakha*? Is it permitted to spread it on Shabbat? **He said to him: Even a bed is prohibited.** Rav Kahana asked: With regard to **a bed, what** is the *halakha*? **He said to him: Even a canopy is permitted.** Rav Kahana again asked: In the case of **a bed and a canopy, what** is the *halakha*? **He said to him: A canopy is prohibited, and a bed is permitted.**[N]

וְלָא קַשְׁיָא; הָא – דְּקָאָמַר ״אַף מִטָּה אֲסוּרָה״ – כְּדְקַרְמָנַאי, הָא דְּקָאָמַר לֵיהּ ״אַף כִּילָּה מוּתֶּרֶת״ – כִּדְרָמֵי בַּר יְחֶזְקֵאל. ״כִּילָּה אֲסוּרָה וּמִטָּה מוּתֶּרֶת״ – כְּדִידַן.

The Gemara comments: **And this is not difficult,** as the responses do not in fact contradict one another. Rather, **when he said: Even a bed is prohibited,** this is referring to folding beds **like those of the Carmanians.**[B] Unfolding them is considered like making a tent. **When he said: Even a canopy is permitted,** this is referring to spreading the canopy in the manner explained by **Rami bar Yeḥezkel.** The canopy was bound by a string from before Shabbat. When he said: **A canopy is prohibited, and a bed is permitted,** this is referring to beds and canopies **like ours,** which do not fold. A bed of that kind involves no building. However, spreading canopies is performed in a manner similar to constructing a tent.

NOTES

For the category of selecting…for the category of sifting – מִשּׁוּם בּוֹרֵר...מִשּׁוּם מְרַקֵּד: Rashi, along with other commentaries, explains that these two opinions are not mutually exclusive. Rather, both Sages agree that if one was forewarned against straining lest he perform the other category of labor, the warning is valid (Rambam). Other commentaries assert that these opinions indeed differ. According to Rabba, if one who was warned not to sift failed to heed the warning and strained, he is exempt from punishment because he may have not taken the warning seriously, due to the disparity between the warning and his action (*Tosafot*). In the Jerusalem Talmud, both of these opinions are rejected. The opinion of Rav Sheshet, that there is a separate, rabbinic prohibition applicable to straining, is adopted.

Doubled cloak – טַלִּית כְּפוּלָה: Some of the *ge'onim* and the Rosh explain that this is a cloak suspended in a corner between two walls to provide cover so one can sleep.

Rav's answers to Rav Kahana – תְּשׁוּבוֹת רַב לְרַב כָּהֲנָא: This series of questions and answers seems quite unusual. See *Tosafot*, who explain it. *Tosafot* elsewhere explain that these three questions were not asked at the same time. Rather, each was posed on a different occasion, in reference to a different case.

HALAKHA

Doubled cloak – טַלִּית כְּפוּלָה: On Shabbat, it is permitted to spread a cloak that was folded, placed on a pole, or suspended on strings before Shabbat, in accordance with the opinion of Rami bar Yeḥezkel, as explained by the Rif (Rambam *Sefer Zemanim, Hilkhot Shabbat* 22:29; *Shulḥan Arukh, Oraḥ Ḥayyim* 315:10).

BACKGROUND

Carmanians – קַרְמָנַאי: The Carmanians were the inhabitants of the province of Carmania, northeast of Persia. The ancient name of the province, Carmania, remains in use even today, as it is now known as the Kerman province of Iran (*ge'onim; Arukh*).

NOTES

Curtain – **וִילוֹן**: Some commentaries explain, as Rashi does elsewhere, that a curtain may be spread because it is neither a fixed structure nor an actual tent. Other authorities state that spreading a curtain is not considered building, because the curtain is not intended to serve as a partition. It is spread for privacy (*Me'iri*).

HALAKHA

Curtain – **וִילוֹן**: It is permitted to spread and open a curtain on Shabbat. It does not constitute a tent, as stated by Rav (*Shulḥan Arukh, Oraḥ Ḥayyim* 315:10).

אָמַר רַב יוֹסֵף: חֲזֵינָא לְהוּ לְכִילֵּי דְּבֵי רַב הוּנָא דְּמֵאוּרְתָּא נְגִידוּ, וּמִצַּפְרָא חֲבִיטָא רַמְיָא.

Rav Yosef said: I saw the canopies of the house of Rav Huna that were spread out in the evening, and in the morning they were cast off and lying on the ground. This indicates that it is permitted to dismantle and spread them on Shabbat.

אָמַר רַב מִשּׁוּם רַבִּי חִיָּיא: וִילוֹן, מוּתָּר לְנוֹטְתוֹ וּמוּתָּר לְפוֹרְקוֹ.

Rav said in the name of Rabbi Ḥiyya: With regard to **a curtain,**[NH] **it is permitted to spread it, and it is permitted to dismantle it.** Since a curtain has no roof, neither action constitutes establishing a tent.

וְאָמַר שְׁמוּאֵל מִשּׁוּם רַבִּי חִיָּיא:

And Shmuel said in the name of Rabbi Ḥiyya:

Perek **XX**
Daf **138** Amud **b**

NOTES

A bridegroom's canopy – **כִּילַּת חֲתָנִים**: Some question how is it possible for a canopy to satisfy all the conditions stipulated by Rav Sheshet, son of Rav Idi (*Tosafot*). The variant reading of *Tosafot* and the Rambam omits the statement that inclines of tents are considered tents. Rashi comments that the bridegroom's canopy was not designated for sleeping. Rather, it was a tall, narrow canopy that served decorative purposes. In tractate *Eiruvin*, Rashi explains that the bridegroom's canopy consisted of several small canopies, each of which satisfied the conditions stipulated with regard to a canopy.

HALAKHA

A bridegroom's canopy – **כִּילַּת חֲתָנִים**: On Shabbat, it is permitted to assemble and dismantle a bridegroom's canopy whose roof is less than a handbreadth wide and that does not reach the width of a handbreadth within three handbreadths of its roof. The reason it is permitted is that it is prepared for use, which the *Magen Avraham* interprets to mean designated for this purpose from before Shabbat. However, if it was not prepared for use, it is prohibited to spread the canopy on Shabbat (Rambam *Sefer Zemanim, Hilkhot Shabbat* 22:30; *Shulḥan Arukh, Oraḥ Ḥayyim* 315:11).

It is prohibited to wear a felt hat – **סִיאָנָא אָסוּר**: It is prohibited on Shabbat to wear a hat with a brim that is a handbreadth wide and is firm (*Magen Avraham*), even inside a house, because this act constitutes establishing a tent. The later commentaries discussed at length the hats worn in their times, some of which had brims that were wider than a handbreadth, and they raised several rationales to justify leniency in places where it was customary to wear them (see *Taz*; *Magen Avraham*; *Be'er Heitev*; and others; Rambam *Sefer Zemanim, Hilkhot Shabbat* 22:31; *Shulḥan Arukh, Oraḥ Ḥayyim* 301:40).

כִּילַּת חֲתָנִים מוּתָּר לְנוֹטְתָהּ וּמוּתָּר לְפוֹרְקָהּ.

With regard to **a bridegroom's canopy,**[NHB] which has no roof but is entirely sloped, **it is permitted to spread it and it is permitted to dismantle it** on Shabbat.

אָמַר רַב שֵׁשֶׁת בְּרֵיהּ דְּרַב אִידִי: לָא אֲמַרַן אֶלָּא שֶׁאֵין בְּגַגָּהּ טֶפַח, אֲבָל יֵשׁ בְּגַגָּהּ טֶפַח – אֲסוּרָה. וְכִי אֵין בְּגַגָּהּ טֶפַח נַמִי לָא אֲמַרַן אֶלָּא שֶׁאֵין בְּפָחוֹת מִשְּׁלֹשָׁה סָמוּךְ לְגַגָּהּ טֶפַח, אֲבָל יֵשׁ בְּפָחוֹת מִשְּׁלֹשָׁה סָמוּךְ לְגַגָּהּ טֶפַח – אָסוּר. וְלָא אֲמַרַן אֶלָּא שֶׁאֵין בְּשִׁיפּוּעָהּ טֶפַח, אֲבָל יֵשׁ בְּשִׁיפּוּעָהּ טֶפַח – שִׁיפּוּעֵי אֹהָלִים כְּאֹהָלִים דָּמוּ. וְלָא אֲמַרַן אֶלָּא דְּלָא נָחִית מִפּוּרְיָא טֶפַח, אֲבָל נָחִית מִפּוּרְיָא טֶפַח – אָסוּר.

Rav Sheshet, son of Rav Idi, said: We only said that it is permitted in a case where **its roof is not a handbreadth** wide; **however, if its roof is a handbreadth** wide, **it is prohibited.** Furthermore, even **when its roof is not a handbreadth** wide, **we only said** that it is permitted **where there is not** the width of a **handbreadth within three** handbreadths **of its roof; however, if it** expands to the width of **a handbreadth within three** handbreadths **of its roof, it is prohibited. And we only stated** that it is permitted **where there is not in its incline** the width of **a handbreadth; however,** if **there is in its incline** the width of **a handbreadth, it is prohibited.** This *halakha* is in accordance with the principle that **the inclines of tents,** even though they are not actual roofs, **are considered like tents. And we only said** that this canopy is permitted **where** no part of the canopy **descends** to **a handbreadth** below the bed; **however,** if part of the canopy **descends** to **a handbreadth** below the bed, **it is prohibited,** as the bed itself becomes a roof, and the curtain is considered a wall.

וְאָמַר רַב שֵׁשֶׁת בְּרֵיהּ דְּרַב אִידִי: הַאי סִיאָנָא שָׁרֵי. וְהָאִיתְּמַר: סִיאָנָא אָסוּר! לָא קַשְׁיָא, הָא – דְּאִית בֵּיהּ טֶפַח, הָא – דְּלֵית בֵּיהּ טֶפַח.

And Rav Sheshet, son of Rav Idi, also **said:** Wearing **this felt hat is permitted** on Shabbat, even though it has a wide brim and is similar to a tent. The Gemara raises a difficulty: **Wasn't it stated** elsewhere that **it is prohibited** to wear **a felt hat**[H] on Shabbat? The Gemara answers: This is **not difficult: This** latter statement, which prohibited wearing the hat, is referring to a case **where its** brim **has** the width of **a handbreadth** wide and is similar to a tent. **That** statement by Rav Sheshet, which permits wearing the hat, is referring to a case **where its** brim **does not have** the width of **a handbreadth.**

BACKGROUND

A bridegroom's canopy – **כִּילַּת חֲתָנִים**:

Bridegroom's canopy with several small inclines at the top, each less than a handbreadth, in accordance with Rashi's version of the text and explanation

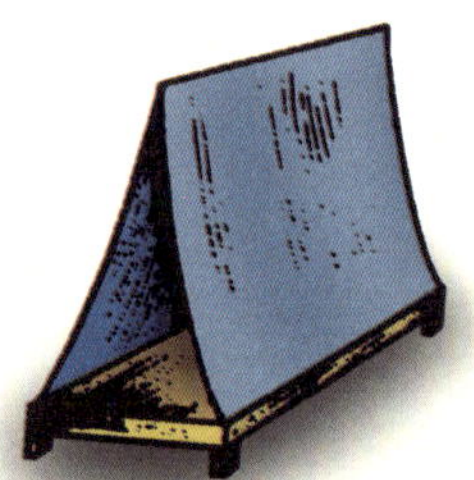

Narrow and tall bridegroom's canopy suspended on a single pole and positioned over the middle of a bed, in accordance with the opinion of *Tosafot* and the accepted halakhic ruling

אֶלָּא מֵעַתָּה, שַׁרְבֵּיב בִּגְלִימָא טֶפַח הָכִי נַמִי דְּמִיחַיַּיב?! אֶלָּא לָא קַשְׁיָא, הָא – דְּמִיהֲדַק, הָא – דְּלָא מִיהֲדַק.

The Gemara asks: **But if** that is so, if **one extended** his **cloak a handbreadth** beyond his head, would you **also** say **that he is liable** for making a tent? **Rather,** this is **not difficult.** The reason the hat is prohibited is not due to making a tent, but due to concern that the wind might blow the cap off one's head and he will come to carry it by hand. The conflicting statements can be resolved as follows: **This** statement of Rav Sheshet, which permits wearing the hat, is referring to a case **where it is** fitted **firmly** on his head. **That** statement, which prohibits wearing the hat, is referring to a case **where it is not** fitted **firmly.**[NH]

שְׁלַח לֵיהּ רָמִי בַּר יְחֶזְקֵאל לְרַב הוּנָא: אֵימָא לָן אִיזִי הָנָךְ מִילֵּי מְעַלְּיָיתָא דְּאָמְרַתְּ לָן מִשְּׁמֵיהּ דְּרַב, תַּרְתֵּי בְּשַׁבָּת וַחֲדָא בַּתּוֹרָה.

Rami bar Yeḥezkel sent to Rav Huna: Say to us, please, those excellent statements that you said to us in the name of Rav, two with regard to the *halakhot* **of Shabbat, and one with regard to the Torah.**

שְׁלַח לֵיהּ: הָא דְּתַנְיָא ״גּוֹד בְּכִיסְנָא מוּתָּר לִנְטוֹתָהּ בְּשַׁבָּת״ אָמַר רַב: לֹא שָׁנוּ אֶלָּא בִּשְׁנֵי בְּנֵי אָדָם, אֲבָל בְּאָדָם אֶחָד – אָסוּר.

Rav Huna **sent to him** in response: With regard to **that which was taught** in a *baraita*: **It is permitted to spread a large wineskin** and suspend it **by its straps on Shabbat, Rav said: They only taught** that it is permitted if it is performed **by two people**[N] together. They do not stretch the wineskin like a tent; rather, they place it without stretching it. **However, it is prohibited for one person** to do so by himself, due to the concern that he may establish a tent of sorts.

אָמַר אַבָּיֵי: וְכִילָּה, אֲפִילּוּ בַּעֲשָׂרָה בְּנֵי אָדָם – אָסוּר, אִי אֶפְשָׁר דְּלָא מִימַּתְחָא פּוּרְתָּא.

Abaye said: And it is prohibited to spread **a canopy**[H] on Shabbat **even with ten people.** The reason for this is that **it is impossible that it will not be stretched a bit** for a certain period of time, which would establish a temporary tent.

אִידָּךְ מַאי הִיא – דְּתַנְיָא ״כִּירָה שֶׁנִּשְׁמְטָה אַחַת מִיַּרְכוֹתֶיהָ – מוּתָּר לְטַלְטְלָהּ, שְׁתַּיִם – אָסוּר״. רַב אָמַר: אֲפִילּוּ חַד נַמִי אָסוּר, גְּזֵירָה שֶׁמָּא יִתְקַע.

And the other *halakha* with regard to Shabbat, **what is it? As it was taught** in a *baraita*: In the case of **a stove, one of whose legs fell,**[H] **it is permitted to move it** on Shabbat. Since it remains a vessel, it may be moved if it is taking up a space that is needed. However, if **two** of its legs fell, **it is prohibited,** since it is then a broken vessel. **Rav said: Even** if only **one** leg fell, **it is also prohibited** to handle it, due to **a decree lest one fasten** the leg in place forcefully and be liable for preparing a vessel for use.

תּוֹרָה, דְּאָמַר רַב: עֲתִידָה תּוֹרָה שֶׁתִּשְׁתַּכַּח מִיִּשְׂרָאֵל, שֶׁנֶּאֱמַר ״וְהִפְלָא ה׳ אֶת מַכֹּתְךָ״, הַפְלָאָה זוֹ אֵינִי יוֹדֵעַ מַהוּ, כְּשֶׁהוּא אוֹמֵר ״לָכֵן הִנְנִי יוֹסִיף לְהַפְלִיא אֶת הָעָם הַזֶּה הַפְלֵא וָפֶלֶא״ הֱוֵי אוֹמֵר: הַפְלָאָה זוֹ תּוֹרָה.

With regard to **Torah,** Rav Huna related **that Rav said: The Torah is destined to be forgotten from the Jewish people.**[N] **It is stated** at the conclusion of the curses in the Torah's reproof: **"And the Lord will make your plagues astonishing,** and the plagues of your seed, great plagues of long continuance, and evil diseases of long continuance" (Deuteronomy 28:59). **This** term of **astonishment,** mentioned in the verse in addition to the explicit punishments, **I do not know what it is.** But **when** the verse **states** elsewhere: **"Therefore, behold, I will continue to astonish this people with wondrous astonishment,** and the wisdom of its wise will be lost, and the understanding of its men of understanding shall be hidden" (Isaiah 29:14), you must **say: This astonishment** is referring to forgetting the **Torah.**

תָּנוּ רַבָּנַן: כְּשֶׁנִּכְנְסוּ רַבּוֹתֵינוּ לַכֶּרֶם בְּיַבְנֶה אָמְרוּ: עֲתִידָה תּוֹרָה שֶׁתִּשְׁתַּכַּח מִיִּשְׂרָאֵל, שֶׁנֶּאֱמַר ״הִנֵּה יָמִים בָּאִים נְאֻם ה׳ אֱלֹהִים וְהִשְׁלַחְתִּי רָעָב בָּאָרֶץ לֹא רָעָב לַלֶּחֶם וְלֹא צָמָא לַמַּיִם כִּי אִם לִשְׁמוֹעַ אֵת דִּבְרֵי ה׳״ וּכְתִיב ״וְנָעוּ מִיָּם עַד יָם וּמִצָּפוֹן וְעַד מִזְרָח יְשׁוֹטְטוּ לְבַקֵּשׁ אֶת דְּבַר ה׳ וְלֹא יִמְצָאוּ״.

The Sages taught a similar idea in the *Tosefta*: **When our Sages entered the vineyard in Yavne, they said: The Torah is destined to be forgotten from the Jewish people,** as **it is stated: "Behold, days are approaching, says the Lord God, and I will send forth a hunger in the land, not a hunger for bread and not a thirst for water, but for hearing the words of the Lord"** (Amos 8:11). **And it states: "And they will drift from sea to sea, and from north to east they will roam to find the word of the Lord, but they will not find it"** (Amos 8:12).

״דְּבַר ה׳״ – זוֹ הֲלָכָה, ״דְּבַר ה׳״ – זֶה הַקֵּץ, ״דְּבַר ה׳״ – זוֹ נְבוּאָה.

"The word of the Lord" in this context bears many meanings. **"The word of the Lord"; that is** *halakha*. **"The word of the Lord"; that is the end** of days.[N] **"The word of the Lord"; that is prophecy.** All these will be lost from the Jewish people.

NOTES

Fitted firmly…not fitted firmly – מִיהֲדַק...דְּלָא מִיהֲדַק: Rashi adds that fitted firmly means tied with a strap underneath one's chin. The opinion of Rabbeinu Ḥananel is cited in *Tosafot*. He explains this differently. In his opinion, the first opinion is not rejected, and the felt hat is prohibited because of establishing a tent. There is a distinction between a hat that is firm, and is therefore, contrary to Rashi's interpretation, prohibited because the brim does not bend and appears to be a tent, and a hat that is not firm. The Rashba asserts that the phrase: Rather, it is not difficult, is problematic according to this approach. However, from Rabbeinu Tam's explanation, it is apparent that, according to this approach, the word rather does not appear in the talmudic text.

By two people – בִּשְׁנֵי בְּנֵי אָדָם: Rabbeinu Yona explains that tying a wineskin is prohibited when it is performed by one person because he ties it very slowly, in a manner similar to building. On the other hand, when two people tie the wineskin in place together, the act is accomplished immediately. This is permitted because it is not similar to building, which is generally not accomplished all at once. Therefore, a canopy, which cannot be immediately set in place even with the aid of several people, may not be spread even by ten people.

The Torah is destined to be forgotten from the Jewish people – עֲתִידָה תּוֹרָה שֶׁתִּשְׁתַּכַּח מִיִּשְׂרָאֵל: Some commentaries explain Rav's statement as follows: The Torah is destined to be forgotten if the Oral Law is transmitted by word of mouth, rather than being written down. Therefore, it is imperative to commit the Oral Law to writing to prevent it from being forgotten (*Korban Netanel*).

The word of the Lord; that is the end of days – דְּבַר ה׳ זֶה הַקֵּץ: See Rashi and *Tosafot*. Since "It is the honor of God to conceal a matter [*haster davar*]" (Proverbs 25:2), and the end of days is known to God alone and no one else, this statement should be interpreted to mean that the word of God [*devar Hashem*], i.e., that which is uniquely His, is referring to the end of days (*Iyyei HaYam*; *Ein Ya'akov*).

HALAKHA

Fitted firmly…not fitted firmly – מִיהֲדַק...דְּלָא מִיהֲדַק: It is inappropriate to leave one's home on Shabbat wearing a hat for protection against the sun, due to the concern lest the wind lift it off his head and he come to carry it in the public domain. If the hat is firmly fitted on his head, it is permitted (*Shulḥan Arukh, Oraḥ Ḥayyim* 301:41).

A large wineskin by its straps…a canopy, etc. – גּוֹד בְּכִיסְנָא...וְכִילָּה וכו׳: When opening a curtain, one must make certain not to spread it like a tent. A large drapery must be opened by at least two people. A canopy with a roof may not be stretched on Shabbat, even by several people working together, because it will inevitably become a temporary tent for at least a brief period, as per the opinion of Rav and Abaye as explained by the Rambam (Rambam *Sefer Zemanim, Hilkhot Shabbat* 22:32; *Shulḥan Arukh, Oraḥ Ḥayyim* 315:12).

A stove, one of whose legs fell – כִּירָה שֶׁנִּשְׁמְטָה אַחַת מִיַּרְכוֹתֶיהָ: It is prohibited to carry a stove, a stool, or the like if one of its legs has fallen off, due to the concern lest one reattach the missing leg and thereby transgress the prohibition against building or completing a vessel. This ruling is in accordance with the opinion of Rav (Rambam *Sefer Zemanim, Hilkhot Shabbat* 26:6; *Shulḥan Arukh, Oraḥ Ḥayyim* 308:16).

וּמַאי "יְשׁוֹטְטוּ לְבַקֵּשׁ אֶת דְּבַר ה'" – אָמְרוּ: עֲתִידָה אִשָּׁה שֶׁתִּטּוֹל כִּכָּר שֶׁל תְּרוּמָה וְתַחֲזוֹר בְּבָתֵּי כְנֵסִיּוֹת וּבְבָתֵּי מִדְרָשׁוֹת, לֵידַע אִם טְמֵאָה הִיא וְאִם טְהוֹרָה הִיא, וְאֵין מֵבִין.

And what is the meaning of: "**They will roam to find the word of the Lord,** but they will not find it"? **They said: It is destined that a woman will take a loaf of *teruma*** bread **and circulate among the synagogues and study halls to ascertain whether it is ritually impure or whether it is ritually pure, and there** will be **none** who **understands.**

אִם טְהוֹרָה הִיא וְאִם טְמֵאָה הִיא?! בְּהֶדְיָא כְּתִיב בֵּיהּ: "מִכָּל הָאוֹכֶל אֲשֶׁר יֵאָכֵל"! אֶלָּא: לֵידַע אִם רִאשׁוֹנָה הִיא וְאִם שְׁנִיָּה הִיא. וְאֵין מֵבִין.

The Gemara asks: How is it possible that they will be unable to understand **whether** the loaf **is impure or whether it is ritually impure? It is explicitly written** in the Torah **with regard to this: "All food that is eaten** upon which water falls shall contract impurity, and all liquid drunk in any vessel shall contract impurity" (Leviticus 11:34). There can be no doubt as to the question of whether or not the loaf can become impure. **Rather,** the Gemara explains: The woman seeks **to ascertain whether it** assumes **first**-degree ritual impurity status **or whether it** assumes second-degree ritual impurity status; **and there** will be **none** who **understands.**

הָא נַמִי מַתְנִיתִין הִיא, כִּדְתְנַן: הַשֶּׁרֶץ שֶׁנִּמְצָא בַּתַּנּוּר – הַפַּת שֶׁבְּתוֹכוֹ שְׁנִיָּה, שֶׁהַתַּנּוּר תְּחִילָּה.

The Gemara asks: **That too is an** explicit **mishna,** and how is it that none will know an explicit mishna? **As we learned** in a mishna: If **the** carcass of a **creeping animal was found in** the airspace of **an oven, the bread inside it** assumes **second**-degree ritual impurity status, **as the** creeping animal, which is a primary source of impurity, renders the **oven** impure with **first**-degree ritual impurity. The oven then renders the bread impure with second-degree ritual impurity.[H]

מִסְתַּפְּקָא לְהוּ הָא דַּאֲמַר לֵיהּ רַב אַדָּא בַּר אַהֲבָה לְרָבָא: לִיתַחְזְיֵיהּ הַאי תַּנּוּרָא כְּמַאן דְּמָלֵי טוּמְאָה, וְתֶיהֱוֵי פַּת רִאשׁוֹנָה!

The Gemara responds: **They are uncertain** with regard to **that which Rav Adda bar Ahava said to Rava: Let us view this oven as one filled with impurity, and** the **bread will** then assume **first**-degree ritual impurity status. In other words, the legal status of food in the airspace of an earthenware vessel that also has the carcass of a creeping animal in its airspace is that of food that came into contact with the creeping animal, even if the food does not come into contact with the carcass of a creeping animal.

אֲמַר לֵיהּ: לָא אָמְרִינַן לִיתַחְזְיֵיהּ הַאי תַּנּוּרָא כְּמַאן דְּמָלֵי טוּמְאָה. דְּתַנְיָא: יָכוֹל יְהוּ כָּל הַכֵּלִים מִיטַּמְּאִין בַּאֲוִיר כְּלִי חֶרֶס – תַּלְמוּד לוֹמַר "כָּל אֲשֶׁר בְּתוֹכוֹ יִטְמָא מִכָּל הָאוֹכֶל אֲשֶׁר יֵאָכֵל", אוֹכָלִין – מִטַּמְּאִין בַּאֲוִיר כְּלִי חֶרֶס, וְאֵין כֵּלִים מִטַּמְּאִין בַּאֲוִיר כְּלִי חֶרֶס.

He said to him that **we do not say: Let us view the oven as one filled** with **ritual impurity, as it was taught** in a *baraita*: One **might** think that **all vessels should become ritually impure in the airspace of an earthenware vessel** that has the carcass of a creeping animal in its airspace; therefore, **the verse states:** "And any earthenware vessel in which any of them falls, **all that is in it shall be impure,** and you shall break it. **All food that is eaten,** upon which water comes, shall be impure; and all drink that may be drunk, in any vessel, shall be impure" (Leviticus 11:33–34). The *baraita* learns from the juxtaposition of these verses that **foods become ritually impure in the airspace of earthenware vessels, but vessels do not become ritually impure in the airspace of earthenware vessels.**[H] Apparently, the airspace of an oven is not considered filled with the impurity of the carcass of a creeping animal. If that were the case, even vessels would become ritually impure.

תַּנְיָא, רַבִּי שִׁמְעוֹן בֶּן יוֹחַי אוֹמֵר: חַס וְשָׁלוֹם שֶׁתִּשְׁתַּכַּח תּוֹרָה מִיִּשְׂרָאֵל, שֶׁנֶּאֱמַר "כִּי לֹא תִשָּׁכַח מִפִּי זַרְעוֹ". אֶלָּא מָה אֲנִי מְקַיֵּים "יְשׁוֹטְטוּ לְבַקֵּשׁ אֶת דְּבַר ה' וְלֹא יִמְצָאוּ" – שֶׁלֹּא יִמְצְאוּ

An opposing view **was taught** in another *baraita*. **Rabbi Shimon ben Yoḥai says: Heaven forfend that the Torah should be forgotten from the Jewish people, as it is stated:** "And this song shall answer to him as a witness, **for it shall not be forgotten from his seed**" (Deuteronomy 31:21). **Rather, how do I explain: "They will roam to find the word of God, but they will not find it"?** It means **that they will not find**

HALAKHA

Bread in a ritually impure stove – פַּת בְּתַנּוּר טָמֵא: If the carcass of a creeping animal fell into the airspace of an oven, the bread inside the oven assumes second-degree ritual impurity status from the oven, which assumed first-degree ritual impurity status from the creeping animal in its airspace (Rambam *Sefer Tahara, Hilkhot She'ar Avot HaTumot* 11:2).

Foods become ritually impure in the airspace of earthenware vessels, but vessels do not become ritually impure in the airspace of earthenware vessels – אוֹכָלִין מִטַּמְּאִין בַּאֲוִיר כְּלִי חֶרֶס וְאֵין כֵּלִים מִטַּמְּאִין בַּאֲוִיר כְּלִי חֶרֶס: Food and drink in the airspace of an earthenware vessel become ritually impure if the earthenware vessel becomes impure, even if the food and drink did not come into contact with it. However, vessels in the airspace of an earthenware vessel do not become ritually impure (Rambam *Sefer Tahara, Hilkhot Kelim* 13:2–3).

הֲלָכָה בְּרוּרָה וּמִשְׁנָה בְּרוּרָה בְּמָקוֹם אֶחָד.

clear *halakha*[N] and clear teaching together, but rather there will be disputes among the Sages.

תַּנְיָא, רַבִּי יוֹסֵי בֶּן אֱלִישָׁע אוֹמֵר: אִם רָאִיתָ דּוֹר שֶׁצָּרוֹת רַבּוֹת בָּאוֹת עָלָיו – צֵא וּבְדוֹק בְּדַיָּינֵי יִשְׂרָאֵל. שֶׁכָּל פּוּרְעָנוּת שֶׁבָּאָה לָעוֹלָם לֹא בָּאָה אֶלָּא בִּשְׁבִיל דַּיָּינֵי יִשְׂרָאֵל, שֶׁנֶּאֱמַר ״שִׁמְעוּ נָא זֹאת רָאשֵׁי בֵּית יַעֲקֹב וּקְצִינֵי בֵּית יִשְׂרָאֵל הַמְתַעֲבִים מִשְׁפָּט וְאֵת כָּל הַיְשָׁרָה יְעַקֵּשׁוּ בּוֹנֶה צִיּוֹן בְּדָמִים וִירוּשָׁלַיִם בְּעַוְלָה רָאשֶׁיהָ בְּשֹׁחַד יִשְׁפֹּטוּ וְכֹהֲנֶיהָ בִּמְחִיר יוֹרוּ וּנְבִיאֶיהָ בְּכֶסֶף יִקְסֹמוּ וְעַל ה׳ יִשָּׁעֵנוּ וגו׳״.

It was taught in a *baraita* that **Rabbi Yosei ben Elisha says: If you see a generation that many troubles are befalling it, go and examine the judges of Israel.** Perhaps their sins are the cause, as **any calamity that comes to the world comes due to the judges of Israel** acting corruptly, **as it is stated: "Please hear this, heads of the house of Jacob, and officers of the house of Israel, who abhor justice and pervert all equity, who build up Zion with blood, and Jerusalem with iniquity. Their heads they judge for bribes, and their priests teach for hire, and their prophets divine for money; yet they lean upon the Lord,** saying: Is not the Lord in our midst? No evil shall befall us" (Micah 3:9–11).

רְשָׁעִים הֵן, אֶלָּא שֶׁתָּלוּ בִּטְחוֹנָם בְּמִי שֶׁאָמַר וְהָיָה הָעוֹלָם. לְפִיכָךְ מֵבִיא הַקָּדוֹשׁ בָּרוּךְ הוּא עֲלֵיהֶן שָׁלֹשׁ פּוּרְעָנִיּוֹת כְּנֶגֶד שָׁלֹשׁ עֲבֵירוֹת שֶׁבְּיָדָם. שֶׁנֶּאֱמַר ״לָכֵן בִּגְלַלְכֶם צִיּוֹן שָׂדֶה תֵחָרֵשׁ וִירוּשָׁלַיִם עִיִּין תִּהְיֶה וְהַר הַבַּיִת לְבָמוֹת יָעַר״.

The Gemara comments: **They are wicked, but they placed their trust in the One Who spoke and the world came into being,**[N] the Almighty. **Therefore, the Holy One, Blessed be He, brings upon them three calamities corresponding to the three transgressions** for which **they are responsible,** as **it is stated** in the following verse: **"Therefore, because of you, Zion shall be plowed as a field, and Jerusalem shall become heaps, and the Temple Mount as the high places of a forest"** (Micah 3:12).

וְאֵין הַקָּדוֹשׁ בָּרוּךְ הוּא מַשְׁרֶה שְׁכִינָתוֹ עַל יִשְׂרָאֵל עַד שֶׁיִּכְלוּ שׁוֹפְטִים וְשׁוֹטְרִים רָעִים מִיִּשְׂרָאֵל, שֶׁנֶּאֱמַר ״וְאָשִׁיבָה יָדִי עָלַיִךְ וְאֶצְרֹף כַּבֹּר סִגָּיִךְ, וְאָסִירָה כָּל בְּדִילָיִךְ וְאָשִׁיבָה שֹׁפְטַיִךְ כְּבָרִאשֹׁנָה וְיֹעֲצַיִךְ כְּבַתְּחִלָּה וגו׳״.

And the Holy One, Blessed be He, will not rest His Divine Presence on the Jewish people until evil judges and officers shall be eliminated from the Jewish people, as it is stated: "And I will turn My hand upon you, and I will purge away your dross as with lye, and I will remove all your alloy. And I will restore your judges as at first, and your counselors as at the beginning; afterward you shall be called the city of righteousness, a faithful city" (Isaiah 1:25–26).

אָמַר עוּלָּא: אֵין יְרוּשָׁלַיִם נִפְדֵּית אֶלָּא בִּצְדָקָה, שֶׁנֶּאֱמַר ״צִיּוֹן בְּמִשְׁפָּט תִּפָּדֶה וְשָׁבֶיהָ בִּצְדָקָה״.

Ulla said: Jerusalem will be redeemed only through righteousness, as it is stated: "Zion will be redeemed with justice and those who return to her with righteousness" (Isaiah 1:27).

אָמַר רַב פָּפָּא: אִי בָּטְלִי יְהִירֵי – בָּטְלִי אַמְגּוּשֵׁי, אִי בָּטְלִי דַּיָּינֵי – בָּטְלִי גְּזִירְפָּטֵי.

Rav Pappa said: If the arrogant will cease to exist, **the** Persian **fire priests will cease** to exist as well. **If the** deceitful **judges** will cease to exist, **the royal officers** [*gazirpatei*][L] and taskmasters **will** cease to exist.

אִי בָּטְלִי יְהִירֵי – בָּטְלִי אַמְגּוּשֵׁי, דִּכְתִיב ״וְאֶצְרֹף כַּבֹּר סִגָּיִךְ״.

He explains: **If the arrogant will cease, the** Persian **fire priests will cease, as it is written: "And I will purge away your dross** [***sigayikh***] **as with lye,** and I will remove all your alloy [*bedilayikh*]." This teaches that when the conceited and haughty [*sigim*] are purged, the priests of fire, who are separated [*muvdalim*] from the fear of God, will also cease.

אִי בָּטְלִי דַּיָּינֵי בָּטְלִי גְּזִירְפָּטֵי – דִּכְתִיב ״הֵסִיר ה׳ מִשְׁפָּטַיִךְ פִּנָּה אֹיְבֵךְ״.

He said: **If the** deceitful **judges cease, the royal officers** and taskmasters will **cease, as it is written: "The Lord has removed your judgment, cast out your enemy"** (Zephaniah 3:15).

אָמַר רַבִּי מַלַּאי מִשּׁוּם רַבִּי אֶלְעָזָר בְּרַבִּי שִׁמְעוֹן: מַאי דִּכְתִיב ״שָׁבַר ה׳ מַטֵּה רְשָׁעִים שֵׁבֶט מוֹשְׁלִים״ – ״שָׁבַר ה׳ מַטֵּה רְשָׁעִים״ – אֵלּוּ הַדַּיָּינִין שֶׁנַּעֲשׂוּ מַקֵּל לְחַזָּנֵיהֶם. ״שֵׁבֶט מוֹשְׁלִים״ – אֵלּוּ תַּלְמִידֵי חֲכָמִים שֶׁבְּמִשְׁפְּחוֹת הַדַּיָּינִין. מָר זוּטְרָא אָמַר: אֵלּוּ תַּלְמִידֵי חֲכָמִים שֶׁמְּלַמְּדִים הִלְכוֹת צִיבּוּר לְדַיָּינֵי בּוּר.

Rabbi Mallai said in the name of Rabbi Elazar, son of Rabbi Shimon: What is the meaning of **that which is written: "The Lord has broken the staff of the wicked, the rod of the rulers"** (Isaiah 14:5)? He explains: **"The Lord has broken the staff of the wicked"; these are the judges who have become staffs for their attendants.** The attendants abuse people, and the judges provide the attendants with legal backing and moral support. **"The rod of the rulers"; these are the Torah scholars** who are members of **the families of the judges.** These Torah scholars assist their relatives, the judges, conceal their faults. **Mar Zutra said: These are the Torah scholars who teach communal *halakhot* to ignorant judges.** They teach ignorant judges just enough Torah and modes of conduct to prevent the people from realizing how ignorant they are, enabling them to maintain their positions.

NOTES

Clear *halakha* – הֲלָכָה בְּרוּרָה: This statement is to be understood as follows: As long as the Great Sanhedrin met in the Chamber of the Hewn Stone in the Temple, every legal discussion concluded with a vote that determined the *halakha*. After the destruction of the Temple, the number of disputes increased (*Tosefot Rid*). Some commentaries emphasize the problem to be that clear *halakha* cannot be found in one place; rather, people will be forced to seek answers in many places, as in each place they will know only a bit.

They placed their trust in the One Who spoke and the world came into being – שֶׁתָּלוּ בִּטְחוֹנָם בְּמִי שֶׁאָמַר וְהָיָה הָעוֹלָם: One explanation of the fact that these people are called wicked is because they believed that since God determines the world order and planted the evil inclination within each person, individuals do not bear responsibility for their actions (*Ahavat Eitan*).

LANGUAGE

Royal officers [*gazirpatei*] – גְּזִירְפָּטֵי: From the Aramaic *gauzir*, meaning official, and the Iranian suffix pati, meaning lord. This was the title of a Sasanian functionary.

אָמַר רַבִּי אֱלִיעֶזֶר בֶּן מַלַּאי מִשּׁוּם רֵישׁ לָקִישׁ: מַאי דִּכְתִיב "כִּי כַפֵּיכֶם נְגֹאֲלוּ בַדָּם וְאֶצְבְּעוֹתֵיכֶם בֶּעָוֺן שִׂפְתוֹתֵיכֶם דִּבְּרוּ שֶׁקֶר לְשׁוֹנְכֶם עַוְלָה תֶהְגֶּה".

Rabbi Eliezer ben Mallai said in the name of Reish Lakish: What is the meaning of **that which is written: "For your hands are defiled with blood, and your fingers with iniquity; your lips have spoken lies, your tongue utters wickedness"** (Isaiah 59:3)?

"כִּי כַפֵּיכֶם נְגוֹאֲלוּ בַדָּם" – אֵלּוּ הַדַּיָּינִין, "וְאֶצְבְּעוֹתֵיכֶם בֶּעָוֺן" – אֵלּוּ סוֹפְרֵי הַדַּיָּינִין, "שִׂפְתוֹתֵיכֶם דִּבְּרוּ שֶׁקֶר" – אֵלּוּ עוֹרְכֵי הַדַּיָּינִין, "לְשׁוֹנְכֶם עַוְלָה תֶהְגֶּה" – אֵלּוּ בַּעֲלֵי דִּינִין.

He explains: **"For your hands are defiled with blood";**[N] **these are the judges** who take bribes in their hands. **"And your fingers with iniquity"; these are the scribes of the judges,** who write falsehood with their fingers. **"Your lips have spoken lies"; these are the legal advisors.**[N] **"Your tongue utters wickedness"; these are the litigants** themselves.

וְאָמַר רַבִּי מַלַּאי מִשּׁוּם רַבִּי יִצְחָק מִגְּדָלָאָה: מִיּוֹם שֶׁפֵּירֵשׁ יוֹסֵף מֵאֶחָיו לֹא טָעַם טַעַם יַיִן, דִּכְתִיב "וּלְקָדְקֹד נְזִיר אֶחָיו".

And Rabbi Mallai said in the name of Rabbi Yitzḥak from Migdal: From the day that Joseph took leave from his brothers, he did not sample a taste of wine, as it is written: "They shall be on the head of Joseph, **and on the crown of the head of he who was separated** [*nezir*] **from his brothers"** (Genesis 49:26). The language of the verse alludes to the fact that Joseph conducted himself like a nazirite and abstained from wine.

רַבִּי יוֹסֵי בְּרַבִּי חֲנִינָא אָמַר: אַף הֵן לֹא טָעֲמוּ טַעַם יַיִן, דִּכְתִיב "וַיִּשְׁתּוּ וַיִּשְׁכְּרוּ עִמּוֹ" מִכְּלָל דְּעַד הָאִידָּנָא לָא (הֲוָה שִׁיכְרוּת). וְאִידָךְ – שִׁיכְרוּת הוּא דְּלָא הֲוָה, שְׁתִיָּה מִיהָא הֲוָה.

Rabbi Yosei, son of Rabbi Ḥanina, said: Joseph's brothers **too did not sample the taste of wine** during the intervening period, due to their remorse, **as it is written: "And they drank and became drunk with him"** (Genesis 43:34). **By inference: Until now there was no drunkenness,** as they abstained from drinking. **And the other** Sage, Rabbi Mallai, holds: **It was drunkenness** of which **there was none; however, there was drinking** on the part of the brothers during the intervening years.

וְאָמַר רַבִּי מַלַּאי: בִּשְׂכַר "וְרָאֲךָ וְשָׂמַח בְּלִבּוֹ" זָכָה לְחֹשֶׁן הַמִּשְׁפָּט עַל לִבּוֹ.

And Rabbi Mallai said: It is stated in the verse: "And the anger of the Lord was kindled against Moses, and He said: Is there not Aaron your brother the Levite, I know that he can surely speak, and also behold, he is coming out to greet you, and he will see you and be glad in his heart" (Exodus 4:14). Rabbi Mallai taught that **as reward for** Aaron's lack of jealousy at seeing his brother Moses rise to greatness, as it is stated: **"And he will see you and be glad in his heart," he merited** to become the High Priest, and **for the breastplate of judgment** to rest **on his heart.**

שָׁלְחוּ לֵיהּ בְּנֵי בַּשְׂכַּר לְלֵוִי: כִּילָּה מַהוּ? כְּשׁוּתָא בְּכַרְמָא מַהוּ? מֵת בְּיוֹם טוֹב מַהוּ?

The Gemara returns to the laws of a canopy. **The inhabitants of** the town of **Bashkar sent to Levi: What is** the *halakha* with regard to spreading **a canopy** on Shabbat? Additionally, **what is** the *halakha* with regard to **hops in a vineyard?** Do they constitute a prohibited mixture of diverse kinds? Finally, **what is** the *halakha* with regard to one who **died on a Festival?** How can the people attend to his burial?

אַדְּאָזֵיל, נָח נַפְשֵׁיהּ דְּלֵוִי. אֲמַר שְׁמוּאֵל לְרַב מְנַשְּׁיָא: אִי חַכִּימַתְּ – שְׁלַח לְהוּ. שְׁלַח לְהוּ: "כִּילָּה" – חָזַרְנוּ עַל כָּל צִידֵּי כִּילָּה וְלֹא מָצִינוּ לָהּ צַד הֶיתֵּר.

As the messenger **was going** with the question, **Levi died. Shmuel said to Rav Menashya: If you are wise** and able to respond, **send them** answers to their questions. **He sent them:** With regard to **a canopy, we reviewed all aspects of** the matter of the **canopy, and we did not find any permissible aspect.**

וְלִישְׁלַח לְהוּ כִּדְרָמִי בַּר יְחֶזְקֵאל? לְפִי שֶׁאֵינָן בְּנֵי תוֹרָה.

The Gemara asks: **And let him send them** that it can be permitted **in accordance with** the opinion of **Rami bar Yeḥezkel.** The Gemara answers: He did not want to reveal that leniency to them, **because they are not** well versed **in Torah,**[N] and they would not distinguish between permitted and prohibited methods of spreading the canopy.

NOTES

Your hands are defiled with blood – כַּפֵּיכֶם נְגֹאֲלוּ בַדָּם: Some explain that the word blood [*dam*] is referring here to money [*damim*], implying that the judges' hands were filled with bribes (Maharsha).

The legal advisors – עוֹרְכֵי הַדַּיָּינִין: In ancient times, there were no attorneys to prosecute or defend a litigant in rabbinical courts. Rather, each party stated his own case. The legal advisors referred to here were people who acted improperly by teaching litigants to present advantageous claims. This compromised the legal system, because the parties were supposed to present the facts. The interpretation of these facts and the halakhic conclusions were to be left to the judges. Consequently, these legal advisors were viewed unfavorably.

Because they were not well versed in Torah – שֶׁאֵינָן בְּנֵי תוֹרָה: This explanation appears in several places in the Talmud. Essentially, it means that anywhere in which there are no people learned in the Torah, the ruling is stringent with regard to practices that require nuanced understanding of the *halakha* and the ability to distinguish between permitted practices and similar prohibited ones. Still, the Sages were lenient with regard to those practices in places in which Torah scholars lived, based on the assumption that they would know how to maintain the appropriate *halakhic* distinctions.

״כְּשׁוּתָא בְּכַרְמָא – עִירְבּוּבָא״. וְלִישְׁלַח לְהוּ כְּדְרַבִּי טַרְפוֹן? דְּתַנְיָא: כְּשׁוּת, רַבִּי טַרְפוֹן אוֹמֵר: אֵין כִּלְאַיִם בַּכֶּרֶם, וַחֲכָמִים אוֹמְרִים: כִּלְאַיִם בַּכֶּרֶם. וְקַיְימָא לַן: כׇּל הַמֵּיקֵל בָּאָרֶץ – הֲלָכָה כְּמוֹתוֹ בְּחוּץ לָאָרֶץ! לְפִי שֶׁאֵינָן בְּנֵי תוֹרָה.

He also told them: **Hops in a vineyard are** a forbidden **mixture** of diverse kinds. The Gemara asks: **And let him send them** the message that it is permitted **in accordance with** the opinion of **Rabbi Tarfon, as it was taught** in the *Tosefta*: With regard to **hops, Rabbi Tarfon says:** They do **not** constitute a prohibited mixture of **food crops in a vineyard, and the Rabbis say:** They constitute a forbidden mixture of **food crops in a vineyard.**[H] **And we maintain** that **anyone who is lenient** with regard to the *halakhot* of diverse kinds **in Eretz** Yisrael, even if the *halakha* is not ruled in accordance with his opinion, **the *halakha* is** ruled **in accordance with his** opinion **outside** of **Eretz** Yisrael, where the *halakhot* of diverse kinds apply only by rabbinic law. The Gemara explains: He did not reveal this leniency to them, **because they were not** well versed in **Torah.**

מַכְרִיז רַב: הַאי מַאן דְּבָעֵי לְמִיזְרַע כְּשׁוּתָא בְּכַרְמָא – לִיזְרַע. רַב עַמְרָם חֲסִידָא מְנַגֵּיד עִילָוֵיהּ.

With regard to the matter of hops in a vineyard, the Gemara relates that **Rav would announce: One who seeks to sow hops in a vineyard, let him sow.** In contrast, **Rav Amram Ḥasida** would **administer lashes for** sowing hops in a vineyard.

רַב מְשַׁרְשְׁיָא יָהֵיב לֵיהּ פְּרוּטָה לְתִינוֹק גּוֹי וְזָרַע לֵיהּ. וְלִיתֵּן לֵיהּ לְתִינוֹק יִשְׂרָאֵל! אָתֵי לְמִיסְרַךְ. וְלִיתֵּן לֵיהּ לְגָדוֹל גּוֹי! אָתֵי לְאִיחְלוּפֵי בְּיִשְׂרָאֵל.

The Gemara relates that **Rav Mesharshiya would give a *peruta* to a gentile child, and** the child **would sow** hops **for him.**[H] The Gemara asks: **And let him give** the *peruta* **to a Jewish child,** who is also not obligated in mitzva observance. The Gemara answers: **He may come to continue**[N] this habit and violate the prohibition as an adult. The Gemara asks: **And let him give** the *peruta* **to an adult gentile.** The Gemara answers: **He may come to confuse** him **with a Jew.**

״מֵת״. שְׁלַח לְהוּ: מֵת לֹא יִתְעַסְּקוּ בֵּיהּ לֹא יְהוּדָאִין וְלֹא אַרְמָאִין, לֹא בְּיוֹם טוֹב רִאשׁוֹן וְלֹא בְּיוֹם טוֹב שֵׁנִי.

With regard to a person who **died** on a Festival, **he sent them** in response: If a person **died** on a Festival, **neither Jews nor Arameans,** i.e., gentiles, **should attend to his** burial, **neither on the first day of a Festival, nor on the second day of a Festival** observed in the Diaspora.

אִינִי?! וְהָאָמַר רַבִּי יְהוּדָה בַּר שֵׁילַת אָמַר רַבִּי אַסִּי: עוּבְדָּא הֲוָה בְּבֵי כְּנִישְׁתָּא דְּמָעוֹן בְּיוֹם טוֹב הַסָּמוּךְ לְשַׁבָּת,

The Gemara asks: **Is that so? Didn't Rabbi Yehuda bar Sheilat say** that **Rabbi Asi said: There was an incident in the synagogue** of the settlement **of Maon**[B] **on a Festival adjacent to Shabbat.** A person died,

HALAKHA

Hops in a vineyard – כְּשׁוּת בַּכֶּרֶם: Outside Eretz Yisrael, it is permitted to sow hops in a vineyard as per the custom of the three elders (see *Berakhot* 22a, p. 144). It is prohibited to sow wheat, barley, and grape seed or two species of vegetable and grape seed together on the same plot of land. The *halakha* is not in accordance with the stringent position of the Rabbis (Rambam *Sefer Zera'im*, *Hilkhot Kilayim* 8:13).

He would give a *peruta* to a gentile child, and the child would sow hops for him – יָהֵיב לֵיהּ פְּרוּטָה לְתִינוֹק גּוֹי וְזָרַע לֵיהּ: Outside of Eretz Yisrael, the laws of diverse kinds only apply by rabbinic law. Indeed, one may even have a gentile child sow prohibited mixtures of diverse kinds, e.g., wheat, barley, and grape seed, on his behalf (*Kesef Mishne*; Rambam *Sefer Zera'im*, *Hilkhot Kilayim* 8:13).

NOTES

He may come to continue – אָתֵי לְמִיסְרַךְ: This issue is discussed by the early commentaries (see *Tosafot*). The Rashba explains that a child may come to continue a practice that he performed as a child on behalf of adults. However, there is no concern that he will continue to perform activities he performs on his own behalf, as he understands that certain activities are permitted to him because he is a minor.

BACKGROUND

The synagogue of the settlement of Maon – בֵּי כְּנִישְׁתָּא דְּמָעוֹן: This is referring to the synagogue of the town of Beit Maon, which was situated very close to Tiberias. Consequently, the heads of its synagogue were able to approach Rabbi Yoḥanan, who lived in Tiberias, and ask him about the *halakha* of burying the dead.

Perek **XX**
Daf **139** Amud **b**

וְלָא יָדַעְנָא אִי מִלְּפָנֶיהָ אִי מִלְּאַחֲרֶיהָ, וְאָתוּ לְקַמֵּיהּ דְּרַבִּי יוֹחָנָן. וַאֲמַר לְהוּ: יִתְעַסְּקוּ בֵּיהּ עֲמָמִין.

and I do not know whether the Festival occurred **before** Shabbat **or after** Shabbat. **And they came before Rabbi Yoḥanan, and he said to them: Let gentiles attend to his** burial.

וְאָמַר רָבָא: מֵת בְּיוֹם טוֹב רִאשׁוֹן – יִתְעַסְּקוּ בּוֹ עֲמָמִין, בְּיוֹם טוֹב שֵׁנִי – יִתְעַסְּקוּ בּוֹ יִשְׂרָאֵל, וַאֲפִילּוּ בְּיוֹם טוֹב שֵׁנִי שֶׁל רֹאשׁ הַשָּׁנָה, מַה שֶּׁאֵין כֵּן בְּבֵיצָה. לְפִי שֶׁאֵינָן בְּנֵי תוֹרָה.

And likewise, **Rava said:** If a person **died on the first day of a Festival,**[NH] **gentiles may attend to his** burial; **on the second day of a Festival**[H] observed in the Diaspora, **Jews may attend to his** burial. **And** this is the *halakha* **even on the second day of the festival of Rosh HaShana, which is not so with regard to an egg.** With regard to an egg laid on the Festival, the two days of Rosh HaShana are considered one long day that cannot be disconnected. Therefore, in contrast to other two-day Festivals in the Diaspora, use of an egg laid on the first day of Rosh HaShana is prohibited on the second day. However, in deference to the dead, the Sages were lenient with regard to burial on the second day of Rosh HaShana. Why then did Rav Menashya prohibit the inhabitants of Bashkar from attending to the burial on a Festival? The Gemara answers: **Because they were not** well versed in **Torah.**

NOTES

If a person died on…a Festival – מֵת בְּיוֹם טוֹב: Rashi explains that this is referring only to one who died before the Festival and whose body was awaiting burial when the Festival commenced. The *ge'onim* and the Rambam explain that it is referring even to one who died on the Festival itself, because it is improper to delay burying the dead any more than necessary.

HALAKHA

If a person died on the first day of a Festival – מֵת בְּיוֹם טוֹב רִאשׁוֹן: If one dies and must be buried on the first day of a Festival, gentiles should engage in the preparation of the grave, the coffin, and the shrouds. If there are no gentiles available, burial is postponed. However, clothing the deceased, warming water for the purification, and removing and placing the deceased in the grave may be performed by Jews on the Festival (Rambam *Sefer Zemanim*, *Hilkhot Yom Tov* 1:23; *Shulḥan Arukh*, *Oraḥ Ḥayyim* 526:1).

If a person died on the second day of a Festival – מֵת בְּיוֹם טוֹב שֵׁנִי: If a person died on the second day of a Festival in the Diaspora, Jews attend to his burial, performing even those preparations prohibited on the first day of the Festival (see previous note). This applies to the second day of Rosh HaShana, in accordance with the opinion of Rava (Rambam *Sefer Zemanim*, *Hilkhot Yom Tov* 1:23; *Shulḥan Arukh*, *Oraḥ Ḥayyim* 526:4).

אָמַר רַבִּי אָבִין בַּר רַב הוּנָא אָמַר רַב חָמָא בַּר גּוּרְיָא: מִתְעַטֵּף אָדָם בְּכִילָּה וּבְכַסְכַּסֶּיהָ וְיוֹצֵא לִרְשׁוּת הָרַבִּים בְּשַׁבָּת, וְאֵינוֹ חוֹשֵׁשׁ.

Rabbi Avin bar Rav Huna said that **Rav Ḥama bar Gureya said: A person may wrap himself in a canopy**[H] **and in its straps and go out to the public domain on Shabbat, and he need not be concerned** about violating the prohibited act of carrying out a burden.

מַאי שְׁנָא מִדְּרַב הוּנָא, דַּאֲמַר רַב הוּנָא אָמַר רַב: הַיּוֹצֵא בְּטַלִּית שֶׁאֵינָהּ מְצוּיֶּיצֶת כְּהִילְכָתָהּ בְּשַׁבָּת – חַיָּיב חַטָּאת. צִיצִית לְגַבֵּי טַלִּית – חֲשִׁיבִי, וְלָא בָּטְלִי. הָנֵי לָא חֲשִׁיבִי – וּבָטְלִי.

The Gemara asks: In **what** way is the *halakha* with regard to the straps **different from that** which **Rav Huna** said? **As Rav Huna said** that **Rav said: One who goes out** unwittingly to the public domain **on Shabbat with a** four-cornered **garment that does not have the requisite ritual fringes attached**[H] **is liable** to bring **a sin-offering,** because the remaining fringes are not an integral part of the garment. Since they do not fulfill the mitzva, they are considered a burden that may not be carried into the public domain on Shabbat. The Gemara answers: There is a distinction between the cases. **Ritual fringes are significant relative to a garment and are not negated.** They are considered an independent entity that may not be carried out into the public domain. **These** straps of a canopy **are not significant and are negated.**

אָמַר רַבָּה בַּר רַב הוּנָא: מַעֲרִים אָדָם עַל הַמְשַׁמֶּרֶת בְּיוֹם טוֹב לִתְלוֹת בָּהּ רִמּוֹנִים, וְתוֹלֶה בָּהּ שְׁמָרִים. אָמַר רַב אַשִׁי: וְהוּא דְּתָלָה בָּהּ רִמּוֹנִים.

Rabba bar Rav Huna said: According to the Rabbis, who prohibit suspending a strainer on a Festival, **a person** may nevertheless **employ artifice** and circumvent the prohibition against suspending a **strainer** by taking it **on a Festival** and **suspending it**[H] for the purpose of **pomegranates in it,** which is permitted. Once the strainer is suspended, he may **suspend it** in order to filter **sediment** from the wine, as even the Rabbis hold that on a Festival it is permitted to do this straining through a strainer that is already suspended. **Rav Ashi said: And this** is only permitted provided **that he** actually **suspended pomegranates in it** before using it to strain wine. It must be obvious to all that he used the strainer in a permitted manner.

מַאי שְׁנָא מֵהָא, דְּתַנְיָא: מַטִּילִין שֵׁכָר בַּמּוֹעֵד לְצוֹרֶךְ הַמּוֹעֵד, שֶׁלֹּא לְצוֹרֶךְ הַמּוֹעֵד – אָסוּר. אֶחָד שֵׁכַר תְּמָרִים וְאֶחָד שֵׁכַר שְׂעוֹרִים. אַף עַל פִּי שֶׁיֵּשׁ לָהֶן יָשָׁן – מַעֲרִים וְשׁוֹתֶה מִן הֶחָדָשׁ.

The Gemara asks: In **what** way **is** that *halakha* **different from that which was taught** in a *baraita*: **One may begin brewing beer during** the intermediate days of **a Festival for the purpose of** using it on **the Festival.**[H] If it is **not for the purpose of the Festival, it is prohibited.** This is the *halakha* **both** with regard to **date beer and** with regard to **barley beer.** And **even though they have old** beer, **one may employ artifice and** say that he wishes to **drink from the new,** and that he is making beer on the intermediate days of the Festival for that purpose. Apparently, it is permitted to employ artifice even without actively demonstrating that one is performing the action for a permitted purpose. This contradicts the opinion of Rav Ashi.

הָתָם לָא מוֹכְחָא מִילְּתָא, הָכָא – מוֹכְחָא מִילְּתָא.

The Gemara answers: **There,** with regard to beer, **the matter is not evident.** When people see someone starting to brew beer, they have no way of knowing whether or not he has beer at home, and consequently, whether or not the action itself is prohibited in that case. However, **here,** with regard to a strainer, **the matter is evident,** as people see him suspending a strainer for wine, which is prohibited.

אָמְרוּ לֵיהּ רַבָּנַן לְרַב אַשִׁי: חֲזִי מָר הַאי צוּרְבָא מֵרַבָּנַן, וְרַב הוּנָא בֶּן רַבִּי חִיּוֹן שְׁמֵיהּ, וְאָמְרִי לַהּ רַב הוּנָא בְּרַבִּי חַלְוָון שְׁמֵיהּ, דִּשְׁקַל בְּרָא דְּתוּמָא וּמַנַּח בִּבְרָזָא דְּדַנָּא, וַאֲמַר: לְאַצְנוֹעֵיהּ קָמִיכַּוֵּינָא. וַאֲזִיל וְנָאֵים בְּמִבְרָא, וְעָבַר לְהַךְ גִּיסָא וְסָיֵיר פֵּירֵי, וַאֲמַר: אֲנָא לְמֵינַם קָמִיכַּוֵּינָא.

On the topic of artifice, the Gemara relates that **the Rabbis said to Rav Ashi: Master, observe this Torah scholar, and Rav Huna ben Rabbi Ḥayon is his name, and some say** that **his name is Rav Huna, son of Rabbi Ḥalvan, who took a slice of garlic and placed it in the spout of a barrel, and said: I intend to store it.** He thereby stopped the spout on Shabbat.[H] **And** similarly, **he went and slept in a ferry** on the river, and the ferryman sailed the ferry across the river, **and he** thereby **crossed to the other side**[HN] **and inspected the fruit** of his vineyard. He said: **I intend to sleep.** In this way, he crosses the river by boat on Shabbat, which is a prohibited activity.

HALAKHA

A person may wrap himself in a canopy – מִתְעַטֵּף אָדָם בְּכִילָּה: One is permitted to wrap himself in a canopy that has straps attached to it and wear it in the public domain on Shabbat. The straps are insignificant relative to the canopy and are not considered a burden (Rambam *Sefer Zemanim*, *Hilkhot Shabbat* 19:20; *Shulḥan Arukh*, *Oraḥ Ḥayyim* 301:39).

One who goes out on Shabbat with a garment that does not have the requisite ritual fringes attached – הַיּוֹצֵא בְּטַלִּית שֶׁאֵינָהּ מְצוּיֶּיצֶת כְּהִילְכָתָהּ בְּשַׁבָּת: On Shabbat, one who wears a garment into the public domain with ritual fringes that have not been attached properly is liable to bring a sin-offering for carrying a burden. The reason for this ruling is that the fringes are not considered part of the garment because they were not affixed in accordance with *halakha* (Rambam *Sefer Zemanim*, *Hilkhot Shabbat* 19:20; *Shulḥan Arukh*, *Oraḥ Ḥayyim* 13:1, 301:38).

A person may employ artifice…by taking a strainer on a Festival and suspending it, etc. – מַעֲרִים אָדָם עַל הַמְשַׁמֶּרֶת בְּיוֹם טוֹב וכו׳: One may employ artifice and suspend a strainer on a Festival in order to place pomegranates on it and then place wine sediment on it afterward (Rambam *Sefer Zemanim*, *Hilkhot Yom Tov* 3:17; *Shulḥan Arukh*, *Oraḥ Ḥayyim* 510:4).

One may begin brewing beer on the intermediate days of a Festival for the purpose of using it on the Festival – מַטִּילִין שֵׁכָר בַּמּוֹעֵד לְצוֹרֶךְ הַמּוֹעֵד: Although certain labors are prohibited on the intermediate days of a Festival, it is nonetheless permitted to start brewing beer for the purpose of using it on the Festival. If one brews beer for use on the Festival, one need not limit production to the precise amount needed. However, one should employ artifice *ab initio*. If the newly brewed beer is higher quality than one's old beer, one may employ artifice *ab initio*, as per the conclusion of the Gemara in *Moed Katan* and here (Rambam *Sefer Zemanim*, *Hilkhot Yom Tov* 7:8; *Shulḥan Arukh*, *Oraḥ Ḥayyim* 533:1).

Stopping the spout of a barrel – סְתִימַת בְּרֵז חָבִית: If wine was seeping out of a barrel through a hole, it is prohibited to close the hole on Shabbat in any manner. However, a Torah scholar may employ artifice and say that he intends to store garlic in the hole (Rambam *Sefer Zemanim*, *Hilkhot Shabbat* 23:3; *Shulḥan Arukh*, *Oraḥ Ḥayyim* 314:11).

And slept in a ferry and…crossed to the other side – וְנָאֵים בְּמִבְרָא, וְעָבַר לְהַךְ גִּיסָא: It is prohibited to board a ship or a boat on Shabbat knowing that a gentile will sail it. However, a Torah scholar may employ artifice and say that he is boarding the ship just to sleep or stroll on it, even though he knows that the gentile will cause the ship to sail. Nowadays, employing artifice is prohibited because Torah scholars are not considered to be of high enough caliber (*Tur*, *Oraḥ Ḥayyim* 339).

NOTES

And slept in the ferry and crossed to the other side – וְנָאֵים בְּמִבְרָא וְעָבַר לְהַךְ גִּיסָא: Most authorities explain that the prohibition violated by this trip is the general prohibition to travel through water, lest one come to fix or fashion a boat. Other commentaries explain that it is prohibited due to carrying an object four cubits in a *karmelit* (*Tosefot Rid*).

אֲמַר לְהוּ: הַעֲרָמָה קָאָמְרַתְּ? הַעֲרָמָה בִּדְרַבָּנַן הִיא, וְצוּרְבָא מֵרַבָּנַן לָא אָתֵי לְמֶיעֱבַד לְכַתְּחִילָּה.

Rav Ashi **said to them: Are you speaking of artifice?**[N] **This is artifice** employed to circumvent **a rabbinic** prohibition, **and a Torah scholar will not come to perform** the action *ab initio* without artifice. Therefore, there is no reason to prohibit him from doing so.

מתני׳ נוֹתְנִין מַיִם עַל גַּבֵּי הַשְּׁמָרִים בִּשְׁבִיל שֶׁיִּצּוֹלוּ. וּמְסַנְּנִין אֶת הַיַּיִן בְּסוּדָרִין, וּבִכְפִיפָה מִצְרִית.

MISHNA **One may pour water over sediment**[H] that is in a strainer on Shabbat **so that it will become clear** and clean. **And** similarly, **one may filter wine**[H] **through cloths and through an Egyptian basket** made from palm leaves. Since these liquids are drinkable even without filtering, doing so does not violate the prohibition of selecting.

וְנוֹתְנִין בֵּיצָה בְּמְסַנֶּנֶת שֶׁל חַרְדָּל, וְעוֹשִׂין אָנוּמְלִין בְּשַׁבָּת. רַבִּי יְהוּדָה אוֹמֵר: בְּשַׁבָּת – בְּכוֹס, בְּיוֹם טוֹב – בְּלָגִין, וּבְמוֹעֵד – בֶּחָבִית. רַבִּי צָדוֹק אוֹמֵר: הַכֹּל לְפִי הָאוֹרְחִין.

And likewise, **one may place an egg in a mustard strainer**[BH] in order to separate the yolk from the egg-white, **and one may prepare** ***anumlin*****,**[L] a wine-based drink, **on Shabbat. Rabbi Yehuda says: On Shabbat** one may only make *anumlin* in a small **cup; on a Festival, in a** larger **vessel; and on the intermediate days of a Festival,** one may even prepare it **in a barrel. Rabbi Tzadok says:** There is no objective principle; rather, **it is all according to the** number of **guests;** if they are numerous, one may prepare a larger quantity of *anumlin*.

גמ׳ אָמַר זְעִירִי: נוֹתֵן אָדָם יַיִן צָלוּל וּמַיִם צְלוּלִין לְתוֹךְ הַמְּשַׁמֶּרֶת בְּשַׁבָּת וְאֵינוֹ חוֹשֵׁשׁ. אֲבָל עֲכוּרִין – לֹא.

GEMARA **Ze'iri said: A person may place clear wine and clear water into a strainer on Shabbat,**[H] **and he need not be concerned** over the prohibition of selecting, as the wine is drinkable even without this filtering. **However,** doing so with **murky** liquids, **no,** one may not strain them.

מֵיתִיבִי, רַבָּן שִׁמְעוֹן בֶּן גַּמְלִיאֵל אוֹמֵר: טוֹרֵד אָדָם חָבִית שֶׁל יַיִן, יֵינָהּ וּשְׁמָרֶיהָ, וְנוֹתֵן לְתוֹךְ הַמְּשַׁמֶּרֶת בְּשַׁבָּת וְאֵינוֹ חוֹשֵׁשׁ! תַּרְגְּמָהּ זְעֵירִי: בֵּין הַגִּיתּוֹת שָׁנוּ.

The Gemara **raises an objection** from a *baraita*: **Rabban Shimon ben Gamliel says: A person may stir a barrel of wine,** mixing **its wine and its sediment, and place it in a strainer on Shabbat, and he need not be concerned.** Apparently, it is permitted to place even murky wine in a strainer. **Ze'iri explained that** *baraita* and resolved the difficulty: **That was taught** with regard to wine **between the presses,** when the wine has yet to ferment and will remain murky even after filtering.

״מְסַנְּנִין אֶת הַיַּיִן בְּסוּדָרִין״. אָמַר רַב שִׁימִי בַּר חִיָּיא: וּבִלְבַד שֶׁלֹּא יַעֲשֶׂה גּוּמָּא.

We learned in the mishna: **One may filter wine through cloths** on Shabbat. **Rav Shimi bar Ḥiyya said:** This is permitted **provided one does not make a hole**[H] in the cloth through which to pour the wine, as one must diverge from the usual, weekday manner of performing this activity.

NOTES

Artifice – **הַעֲרָמָה:** Artifice is permitted in cases that are not fundamentally prohibited, but involve activity that is prohibited either by rabbinic decree or due to concern that one might come to transgress a Torah prohibition. Consequently, when a Torah scholar, who is aware of the severity of the Torah prohibition and the parameters of the rabbinic decree, acts in a manner that is not clearly perceived as a transgression, artifice is permitted.

BACKGROUND

Strainer – **מְסַנֶּנֶת:**

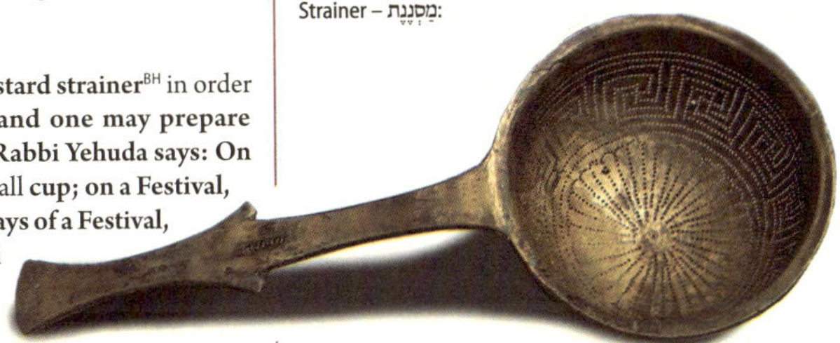

Roman strainer from the talmudic period

LANGUAGE

Anumlin – **אָנוּמְלִין:** From the Greek **οἰνόμελι**, *oinomeli*, meaning wine mixed with honey.

HALAKHA

One may pour water over sediment – **נוֹתְנִין מַיִם עַל גַּבֵּי הַשְּׁמָרִים:** It is permitted on Shabbat to pour water onto wine sediment that was suspended in a strainer before Shabbat, as stated in the mishna according to Rashi's explanation (Rambam *Sefer Zemanim*, *Hilkhot Shabbat* 8:14; *Shulḥan Arukh*, *Oraḥ Ḥayyim* 319:9).

And one may filter wine, etc. – **וּמְסַנְּנִין אֶת הַיַּיִן וכו׳:** One is permitted to filter wine on Shabbat in an atypical manner, e.g., through cloths or utilizing an Egyptian basket. However, in deference to Shabbat, one must make certain to avoid lifting the basket from the base of the vessel and clearly demonstrating that he is making a change (Rambam *Sefer Zemanim*, *Hilkhot Shabbat* 22:33; *Shulḥan Arukh*, *Oraḥ Ḥayyim* 319:12).

An egg in a mustard strainer – **בֵּיצָה בְּמְסַנֶּנֶת חַרְדָּל:** On Shabbat, it is permitted to crack an egg into a strainer in which mustard is being strained, so long as the mustard was placed in the strainer before Shabbat (*Mishna Berura*). This is the ruling even though this will cause the egg yolk and white to separate (Rambam *Sefer Zemanim*, *Hilkhot Shabbat* 8:14; *Shulḥan Arukh*, *Oraḥ Ḥayyim* 319:15).

A person may place clear wine and clear water into a strainer on Shabbat – **נוֹתֵן אָדָם יַיִן צָלוּל וּמַיִם צְלוּלִין לְתוֹךְ הַמְּשַׁמֶּרֶת בְּשַׁבָּת:** Clear water and clear wine may be placed in a strainer on Shabbat, because these liquids are drinkable even without straining, and the straining does not effect a positive change in the liquid. If one has used a cloth to strain clear liquid, it is then prohibited to strain water through that cloth, because doing so might whiten and launder the cloth. Nevertheless, it is permitted to use a cloth to strain wine or other liquids. It is forbidden to strain murky water or wine. However, wine straight from the press, which is still fermenting, may be stirred together with the sediment and strained. According to the Rambam, it is prohibited to strain even clear water or wine with a strainer. The use of a cloth is permitted only for clear liquids but not for murky ones. The *halakha* is in accordance with the first opinion (*Mishna Berura*, quoting the *Or Zarua*), and in accordance with the ruling of Rabban Shimon ben Gamliel, as explained by Ze'iri (Rambam *Sefer Zemanim*, *Hilkhot Shabbat* 8:14; *Shulḥan Arukh*, *Oraḥ Ḥayyim* 319:10).

Provided one does not make a hole – **וּבִלְבַד שֶׁלֹּא יַעֲשֶׂה גּוּמָּא:** When straining murky (*Mishna Berura*) wine on Shabbat through a cloth, one should not make a hole in the cloth, to diverge from the method of straining on weekdays, as per the opinion of Rav Shimi bar Ḥiyya (Rambam *Sefer Zemanim*, *Hilkhot Shabbat* 21:17; *Shulḥan Arukh*, *Oraḥ Ḥayyim* 319:11).

HALAKHA

The cover of a barrel – כִּיסּוּי חָבִית: It is prohibited to cover the entire mouth of a barrel with a cloth on Shabbat, due to the concern that this may constitute constructing a tent. Rather, one should leave part of the mouth of the barrel uncovered. If the barrel is so full that there is less than a handbreadth between the liquid and the cover, it is permitted to cover the entire opening (Ran; Rosh; see *Mishna Berura*; Rambam *Sefer Zemanim, Hilkhot Shabbat* 21:17; *Shulḥan Arukh, Oraḥ Ḥayyim* 315:13).

Twigs in the mouth of a barrel – קִיסְמִין בְּפִי חָבִית: On Shabbat, one may not fill the mouth of a vessel with straw and twigs before pouring murky (*Mishna Berura*) wine into it, because the straw and twigs strain the wine (*Shulḥan Arukh, Oraḥ Ḥayyim* 319:13).

Pouring liquid from one vessel to another – עֵירוּי מַשְׁקֶה מִכְּלִי לִכְלִי: It is permitted to pour liquid from one vessel to another on Shabbat, even if one prevents the dregs from entering the second vessel. However, one must make certain to leave drops of the liquid in the dregs so that this act will not appear to be actual selecting (*Shulḥan Arukh, Oraḥ Ḥayyim* 319:14).

״וּבִכְפִיפָה מִצְרִית״. אָמַר רַב חִיָּיא בַּר אַשִׁי אָמַר רַב: וּבִלְבַד שֶׁלֹּא יַגְבִּיהַּ מִקַּרְקָעִיתוֹ שֶׁל כְּלִי טֶפַח.

We also learned in the mishna: **And** it is permitted to filter wine on Shabbat **through an Egyptian basket. Rav Ḥiyya bar Ashi said** that **Rav said** the following caveat to that statement: It is permitted **provided one does not lift** the basket **a handbreadth from the bottom of the** lower **vessel.** This ensures that one performs the activity in an atypical manner (Rabbeinu Yona).

אָמַר רַב: הַאי פְּרוּנְקָא, אַפַּלְגֵיהּ דְּכוּבָא – שָׁרֵי, אַכּוּלֵּיהּ כּוּבָא – אָסוּר.

Rav said: It is permitted to place **this cover** that has holes for filtering **over half a barrel,**[H] but **it is prohibited** to spread it **over the entire barrel,** in order that it not appear as though one is using it as a filter (Rabbeinu Ḥananel).

אָמַר רַב פָּפָּא: לָא נִיהֲדַק אִינִישׁ צִינִּיתָא בְּפוּמֵּיהּ דְּכוּזָנֵי דְּחָבִיתָא, מִשּׁוּם דְּמִיחֲזֵי כִּמְשַׁמֶּרֶת.

Rav Pappa said: A person may not attach a bundle of straw to the mouth of a barrel's spigot,[H] **because it appears like a strainer.**

דְּבֵי רַב פָּפָּא שָׁאפוּ שִׁיכְרָא מִמָּנָא לְמָנָא. אֲמַר לֵיהּ רַב אַחָא מִדִּיפְתִּי לְרָבִינָא: הָאִיכָּא נִיצוֹצוֹת! נִיצוֹצוֹת לְבֵי רַב פָּפָּא לָא חֲשִׁיבִי.

The Gemara relates: The members **of Rav Pappa's household would carefully pour beer from one vessel to another**[H] so that the dregs from one vessel would not pass to the other. **Rav Aḥa from Difti said to Ravina: But there are the** final **drops,** which remain when one pours the beer into another vessel. When pouring the final drops from the dregs left in the vessel, one is in violation of the prohibition of selecting. He replied: In Rav Pappa's house they would leave the final drops in the first vessel together with the dregs. They would not attempt to separate them, as **the last drops were not significant to the household of Rav Pappa,** because beer was always readily available in his house.

״וְנוֹתְנִין בֵּיצָה בִּמְסַנֶּנֶת״. תָּנֵי יַעֲקֹב קַרְחָה:

And we further learned in the mishna: **One may place an egg in a** mustard **strainer** on Shabbat in order to separate the yolk from the egg-white. The Sage, **Ya'akov Korḥa, taught** a reason for this:

Perek **XX**
Daf **140** Amud **a**

לְפִי שֶׁאֵין עוֹשִׂין אוֹתָהּ אֶלָּא לְגָוֶון.

Because it is only made to enhance the **color** of the food. That does not negate the egg-white as significant food in the sense that it would be considered waste, and therefore, no actual selection is performed.

אִיתְּמַר, חַרְדָּל שֶׁלְּשׁוֹ מֵעֶרֶב שַׁבָּת, לְמָחָר, אָמַר רַב: מְמַחוֹ בִּכְלִי, אֲבָל לֹא בְּיָד.

It is stated: With regard to **mustard that one kneaded on Shabbat eve, on the following day,** Shabbat, **Rav said: One may dissolve it** in wine or water **with a vessel, but not with** his **hand,** as using a vessel diverges from the normal method of preparation.

אֲמַר לֵיהּ שְׁמוּאֵל: בְּיָד, אַטּוּ כָּל יוֹמָא מְמַחוּ לֵיהּ בְּיָד?! מַאֲכַל חֲמוֹרִים הוּא! אֶלָּא אָמַר שְׁמוּאֵל: מְמַחוֹ בְּיָד, וְאֵינוֹ מְמַחוֹ בִּכְלִי.

Shmuel said to him: Why may he not dissolve it **with** his **hand? Is that to say that he dissolves it with** his **hand every day?** If it is prepared in that manner, **it is donkey food.** Certainly dissolving by hand is not the manner in which mustard is prepared during the week. Therefore, dissolving mustard with a vessel should not be permitted on Shabbat. **Rather, Shmuel said** the opposite: **He may dissolve it with** his **hand** as a divergence from the typical method of preparation, **but he may not dissolve it** in the usual manner, **with a vessel.**

אִתְּמַר, רַבִּי אֶלְעָזָר אָמַר: אֶחָד זֶה וְאֶחָד זֶה – אָסוּר, וְרַבִּי יוֹחָנָן אָמַר: אֶחָד זֶה וְאֶחָד זֶה – מוּתָּר. אַבָּיֵי וְרָבָא דְּאָמְרִי תַּרְוַיְיהוּ: אֵין הֲלָכָה כְּרַבִּי יוֹחָנָן.

It is stated that *amora'im* from Eretz Yisrael also disputed this issue, as **Rabbi Elazar said: Both this and that,** dissolving by hand and with a vessel, **are prohibited;** while **Rabbi Yoḥanan said: Both this and that are permitted. Abaye and Rava both said:** The *halakha* **is not in accordance with** the lenient opinion of **Rabbi Yoḥanan.**

קָם רַבִּי יוֹחָנָן בְּשִׁיטָתֵיהּ דְּרַבִּי אֶלְעָזָר, קָם רַבִּי אֶלְעָזָר בְּשִׁיטָתֵיהּ דִּשְׁמוּאֵל. אַבַּיֵּי וְרָבָא דְּאָמְרִי תַּרְוַיְיהוּ: הֲלָכָה כְּרַבִּי יוֹחָנָן.

Subsequently, **Rabbi Yoḥanan stood** and adopted **the opinion of Rabbi Elazar** and prohibited both methods of dissolving. **Rabbi Elazar stood** and adopted **the opinion of Shmuel,** who prohibited using a vessel but permitted it by hand. Given these stances, **Abaye and Rava both said:** The ***halakha* is in accordance with** the opinion of **Rabbi Yoḥanan,** who prohibited both methods.

אִימֵּיהּ דְּאַבַּיֵּי עֲבַדָא לֵיהּ וְלָא אֲכַל, דְּבֵיתְהוּ דִּזְעֵירָא עֲבַדָא לֵיהּ לְרַב חִיָּיא בַּר אַשִׁי וְלָא אֲכֵיל, אֲמַרָה לֵיהּ: לְרַבָּךְ עֲבִידִי לֵיהּ וַאֲכַל, וְאַתְּ לָא אָכְלַתְּ?! אָמַר רָבָא בַּר שַׁבָּא: הֲוָה קָאֵימְנָא קַמֵּיהּ דְּרָבִינָא וּבַחְשִׁי לֵיהּ בְּשׁוּפְתָּא דְּתוּמָא, וַאֲכַל.

The Gemara relates: **Abaye's mother,** actually his foster mother, **prepared** mustard **for him, and he did not eat it. Ze'eira's wife prepared** mustard **for Rav Ḥiyya bar Ashi,** her husband's student, **and he did not eat** it. **She said to him: I made this for your rabbi and he ate** it, **and you do not eat it? Rava bar Shabba said: I was standing before Ravina, and they stirred** mustard **for him with the inner part of the garlic, and he ate** it.

אָמַר מָר זוּטְרָא: לֵית הִלְכְתָא כְּכָל הָנֵי שְׁמַעֲתָתָא, אֶלָּא כִּי הָא דְּאִתְּמַר: חַרְדָּל שֶׁלָּשׁוֹ מֵעֶרֶב שַׁבָּת, לְמָחָר מְמַחוֹ בֵּין בַּיָּד בֵּין בִּכְלִי, וְנוֹתֵן לְתוֹכוֹ דְּבַשׁ. וְלֹא יִטְרוֹף אֶלָּא מְעָרֵב.

Mar Zutra said: The ***halakha* is not in accordance with any of these statements.**[N] **Rather, it is in accordance with this** one, **as it was stated: Mustard that one kneaded on Shabbat eve,**[H] **on the following day he may dissolve it either by hand or with a vessel, and he may place honey in it. And** when he dissolves it **he may not beat** it forcefully as would a craftsman, **but** he may **mix** it gently.

שַׁחֲלַיִים שֶׁשְּׁחָקָן מֵעֶרֶב שַׁבָּת, לְמָחָר – נוֹתֵן לְתוֹכָן שֶׁמֶן וָחוֹמֶץ, וּמַמְשִׁיךְ לְתוֹכָן אַמִיתָא, וְלֹא יִטְרוֹף אֶלָּא מְעָרֵב. שׁוּם שֶׁרִיסְּקוֹ מֵעֶרֶב שַׁבָּת, לְמָחָר – נוֹתֵן לְתוֹכוֹ פּוֹל וּגְרִיסִין, וְלֹא יִשְׁחוֹק אֶלָּא מְעָרֵב, וּמַמְשִׁיךְ אֶת אַמִיתָא לְתוֹכָן. מַאי אַמִיתָא? נִינְיָיא. אָמַר אַבַּיֵּי: שְׁמַע מִינָּהּ – הַאי נִינְיָיא מַעַלְיָא לְתַחְלֵי.

Cress that one ground on Shabbat eve, on the following day he may place oil and vinegar in it, and add *amita* into the mixture, **and he may not beat** it, **but** he may **mix** it. Similarly, **garlic that one crushed on Shabbat eve,**[H] **on the following day, he may place beans and grits in it, and he may not pound, but mix, and he may add *amita*** into the mixture. The Gemara asks: **What is *amita*?** The Gemara answers: It is **mint. Abaye said: Learn from this** that adding **mint is beneficial for cress.**

״וְעוֹשִׂין אָנוּמְלִין בְּשַׁבָּת״. תָּנוּ רַבָּנַן: עוֹשִׂין אָנוּמְלִין בְּשַׁבָּת, וְאֵין עוֹשִׂין אָלוּנְטִית. וְאֵיזוֹ הִיא אָנוּמְלִין וְאֵיזוֹ הִיא אָלוּנְטִית? אָנוּמְלִין – יַיִן וּדְבַשׁ וּפִלְפְּלִין, אָלוּנְטִית – יַיִן יָשָׁן וּמַיִם צְלוּלִין וַאֲפַרְסְמוֹן, דְּעָבְדִי לְבֵי מַסּוּתָא לְמֵיקַר.

We also learned in the mishna: **One may prepare *anumlin* on Shabbat. The Sages taught** in a *baraita*: **One may prepare *anumlin* on Shabbat. However, one may not prepare *aluntit*.**[HL] The *baraita* explains: **And what is *anumlin* and what is *aluntit*? *Anumlin*** is a drink, which is a mixture of **wine, honey, and pepper. *Aluntit*** is a mixture of **aged wine and clear water and balsam, which they prepare** for use after bathing in **a bathhouse to cool down** from the heat of the bathhouse. It is prohibited to prepare it on Shabbat because it is a form of remedy.

אָמַר רַב יוֹסֵף: זִימְנָא חֲדָא עַלִּית בָּתַר מָר עוּקְבָא לְבֵי בָאנֵי, כִּי נְפַקִי אֲתַאי אַשְׁקְיַין חַמְרָא חַד כָּסָא – וְחַשִׁי מִבִּינְתָא דְּרֵאשִׁי וְעַד טוּפְרָא דְּכַרְעִי. וְאִי אַשְׁקְיַין כָּסָא אַחֲרִינָא – הֲוַאי מִסְתַּפֵינָא דִּלְמָא מְנַכּוּ לִי מִזְּכוּתָא דְּעָלְמָא דְּאָתֵי. וְהָא מָר עוּקְבָא דְּשָׁתֵי כָּל יוֹמָא! שָׁאנֵי מָר עוּקְבָא דְּדָשׁ בֵּיהּ.

Rav Yosef said: On **one occasion, I followed Mar Ukva into a bathhouse. When I exited, he came** and **gave me one cup** of this **wine to drink, and I felt** its chill **from the hairs on my head** down **to the toenails on my feet. And if he had given me another cup to drink,** and if I would have survived it, **I would have feared a reduction of my merit in the World-to-Come.** The Gemara asks: **Didn't Mar Ukva drink** this wine **every day?** How was he not harmed? The Gemara answers: **Mar Ukva was different, as** he **grew accustomed to it.**

NOTES

The *halakha* is not in accordance with any of these statements – לֵית הִלְכְתָא כְּכָל הָנֵי שְׁמַעֲתָתָא: This expression should not necessarily be taken as a total rejection of all the preceding statements. Rather, it means that most of the statements are rejected. Indeed, according to one view, Rabbi Yoḥanan had permitted dissolving mustard both by hand and with a vessel (see *Tosafot, Ketubot* 54a).

LANGUAGE

***Aluntit* – אָלוּנְטִית:** The etymology of this word is uncertain. It is probably from the Greek **οἰνάνθη**, *oinanathe*, a wine-based ointment.

HALAKHA

Mustard that one kneaded on Shabbat eve – חַרְדָּל שֶׁלָּשׁוֹ מֵעֶרֶב שַׁבָּת: Mustard that was kneaded before Shabbat may be mixed on Shabbat with wine or water (*Mishna Berura*), even with a ladle. One may also mix honey into it but may not beat it (*Mishna Berura*) in the usual manner. Rather, one may mix in the honey a little at a time, in accordance with the conclusion of Mar Zutra, who was a later authority (Rambam *Sefer Zemanim, Hilkhot Shabbat* 8:14, 22:12; *Shulḥan Arukh, Oraḥ Ḥayyim* 321:15).

Cress that one ground on Shabbat eve…garlic that one crushed on Shabbat eve – שַׁחֲלַיִים שֶׁשְּׁחָקָן מֵעֶרֶב שַׁבָּת...שׁוּם שֶׁרִיסְּקוֹ מֵעֶרֶב שַׁבָּת: On Shabbat, it is permitted to add food and liquid to cress and garlic that were mixed on Shabbat eve. One may not beat them, but may mix them gently. Some authorities rule that one must change the usual, weekday method of preparation and mix them by hand rather than with a vessel, or first place the food in a bowl and then add the liquid (Rambam *Sefer Zemanim, Hilkhot Shabbat* 22:12; *Shulḥan Arukh, Oraḥ Ḥayyim* 321:16).

One may prepare *anumlin* on Shabbat. However, one may not prepare *aluntit* – עוֹשִׂין אָנוּמְלִין בְּשַׁבָּת, וְאֵין עוֹשִׂין אָלוּנְטִית: It is permitted to blend a mixture of wine, honey, and pepper, because it is a beverage. However, one may not blend a mixture of old wine, water, and balsam oil, because it is a medicine (Rambam *Sefer Zemanim, Hilkhot Shabbat* 22:11; *Shulḥan Arukh, Oraḥ Ḥayyim* 321:17).

מתני׳ אֵין שׁוֹרִין אֶת הַחִילְתִּית בְּפוֹשְׁרִין, אֲבָל נוֹתֵן לְתוֹךְ הַחוֹמֶץ. וְאֵין שׁוֹלִין אֶת הַכַּרְשִׁינִין, וְלֹא שָׁפִין אוֹתָן, אֲבָל נוֹתֵן לְתוֹךְ הַכְּבָרָה אוֹ לְתוֹךְ הַכַּלְכָּלָה.

MISHNA **One may not soak asafoetida**[BH] **in lukewarm water** to prepare a medicinal drink from it; **however, one may place** it **into vinegar** like a standard spice. **And one may not soak vetches**[N] in water in order to separate them from their chaff, **nor rub them** by hand so as to remove their chaff. **However, one may place** them **into a sieve or into a basket,** and if the chaff gets removed, so be it.[H]

אֵין כּוֹבְרִין אֶת הַתֶּבֶן בִּכְבָרָה וְלֹא יִתְּנֶנּוּ עַל גַּבֵּי מָקוֹם גָּבוֹהַּ בִּשְׁבִיל שֶׁיֵּרֵד הַמּוֹץ, אֲבָל נוֹטֵל הוּא בִּכְבָרָה וְנוֹתֵן לְתוֹךְ הָאֵיבוּס.

One may not sift straw in a sieve, and similarly, **one may not place it on a high place so that that the chaff** blows away in the wind; **however, one may take** the straw **in a sieve and place it into the trough** of an animal, and one need not be concerned if the chaff is removed in the process.[H]

גמ׳ אִיבַּעְיָא לְהוּ: שָׁרָה מַאי? תַּרְגְּמָא רַב אַדָּא נַרְשָׁאָה קַמֵּיהּ דְּרַב יוֹסֵף: שָׁרָה – חַיָּיב חַטָּאת.

GEMARA **A dilemma was raised before** the Sages: If one unwittingly **soaked** asafoetida on Shabbat, **what** is the *halakha*? **Rav Adda from** the city of **Naresh interpreted it before Rav Yosef: If one soaked** it, **he is liable** to bring **a sin-offering.**

אֲמַר לֵיהּ אַבַּיֵי: אֶלָּא מֵעַתָּה שָׁרָה אוּמְצָא בְּמַיָּא, הָכִי נַמִי דְּמִיחַיַּיב?! אֶלָּא אָמַר אַבַּיֵי: מִדְּרַבָּנַן, שֶׁלֹּא יַעֲשֶׂה כְּדֶרֶךְ שֶׁהוּא עוֹשֶׂה בַּחוֹל.

Abaye said to him: But if that is so, if **one soaked a piece of meat in water,** would you **also** say **that he is liable?** No cooking was performed at all. **Rather, Abaye said:** It is prohibited **by rabbinic decree,** so **that one will not conduct** himself on Shabbat **in the manner in which he conducts** himself **during the week.**

בְּעָא מִינֵּיהּ רַבִּי יוֹחָנָן מֵרַבִּי יַנַּאי: מַהוּ לִשְׁרוֹת אֶת הַחִלְתִּית בַּצּוֹנֵן? אֲמַר לֵיהּ: אָסוּר. וְהָא אֲנַן תְּנַן: ״אֵין שׁוֹרִין אֶת הַחִלְתִּית בַּפּוֹשְׁרִין״ הָא בַּצּוֹנֵן – מוּתָּר!

Rabbi Yoḥanan raised a dilemma before Rabbi Yannai: What is the *halakha* with regard **to soaking asafoetida in cold water** on Shabbat? Rabbi Yannai **said to him: It is prohibited.** Rabbi Yoḥanan asked: **Didn't we learn** in the mishna: **One may not soak asafoetida in lukewarm** water, indicating that **it is permitted** to soak it **in cold** water?

אֲמַר לֵיהּ: אִם כֵּן, מַה בֵּין לִי וְלָךְ? מַתְנִיתִין יְחִידָאָה הִיא, דְּתַנְיָא: אֵין שׁוֹרִין אֶת הַחִלְתִּית לֹא בַּחַמִּין וְלֹא בַּצּוֹנֵן, רַבִּי יוֹסֵי אוֹמֵר: בַּחַמִּין – אָסוּר, בַּצּוֹנֵן – מוּתָּר.

Rabbi Yannai **said to him: If so, that** is the difference **between my** knowledge **and yours,** as I am able to analyze the *halakha* more profoundly. In this case, the mishna is not a reliable source, as **the mishna** expresses **an individual** opinion.[N] **As it was taught** in the *Tosefta*: **One may neither soak asafoetida in hot** water **nor in cold** water. **Rabbi Yosei says: In hot** water it is **prohibited; in cold** water it is **permitted.** The mishna that does not prohibit cold water is in accordance with the individual opinion of Rabbi Yosei, but the *halakha* is not ruled based on that opinion.

לְמַאי עָבְדִי לֵיהּ – לְיוּקְרָא דְּלִיבָּא. רַב אַחָא בַּר יוֹסֵף חָשׁ בְּיוּקְרָא דְּלִיבָּא, אֲתָא לְקַמֵּיהּ דְּמָר עוּקְבָא. אֲמַר לֵיהּ: זִיל שְׁתִי תְּלָתָא תִּיקְלֵי חִילְתְּתָא בִּתְלָתָא יוֹמֵי. אֲזַל אִישְׁתִּי חַמְשָׁא בְּשַׁבָּת, וּמַעֲלֵי שַׁבָּת. לְצַפְרָא אֲזַל שְׁאַל בֵּי מִדְרְשָׁא, אֲמַרוּ לֵיהּ: תָּנָא דְּבֵי רַב אַדָּא, וְאָמְרִי לָהּ – תָּנָא דְּבֵי מָר בַּר רַב אַדָּא: שׁוֹתֶה אָדָם קַב אוֹ קַבַּיִים – וְאֵינוֹ חוֹשֵׁשׁ.

The Gemara asks: **For what** purpose **is** soaked asafoetida **prepared?** The Gemara answers: As a cure **for heaviness of the heart.** One who feels a pain in his heart drinks asafoetida. The Gemara relates: **Rav Aḥa bar Yosef felt heaviness in** his **heart. He came before Mar Ukva** to ask his advice. Mar Ukva **said to him: Go drink** the weight of **three shekels of asafoetida in three days. He went and drank on Thursday and Shabbat eve. In the morning, he went** and **asked in the study hall** if he could drink it on Shabbat. **They said to him:** The Sage **from the school of** Rav Adda **taught, and others say,** that the Sage **from the school of** Mar bar Rav Adda **taught: A person may drink** asafoetida on Shabbat, even **a** ***kav*** **or two** ***kav*****, and he need not be concerned** about the decree prohibiting medicine, because asafoetida is drunk by healthy people as well.

BACKGROUND

Asafoetida [*ḥiltit*] – **חִלְתִּית**: *Ferula assafoetida*, also known as devil's dung or giant fennel, is a perennial plant of the umbel family. It has a thick root and a stem with leafed branches. The asafoetida grows to a height of 2–3 m. It is native mainly to Afghanistan and the neighboring regions. The plant grows for several years until it blossoms and produces fruit, after which it dies.

Medicinal asafoetida is manufactured from the resin found in the root of the plant. It was used, and is still used today, as a medicine in the form of powder, creams, pills, etc., both for intestinal diseases and for strengthening the nervous system. In certain places, asafoetida is even used as a spice. Consumption of asafoetida in amounts of more than a gram is dangerous and can lead to poisoning.

Asafoetida plant

HALAKHA

Soaking asafoetida – **שְׁרִיַּית חִלְתִּית**: Asafoetida may not be soaked on Shabbat because it is primarily utilized as a medicine. It is permitted, however, to place it in vinegar, since even healthy people drink it in this manner. If it was already soaking from the day before, it is permitted to continue soaking it on Shabbat. If a person drank asafoetida on the two days prior to Shabbat for medicinal purposes, it may be soaked on Shabbat, because interrupting treatment is dangerous (Rambam *Sefer Zemanim, Hilkhot Shabbat* 22:7; *Shulḥan Arukh, Oraḥ Ḥayyim* 321:18).

Handling vetches – **טִיפּוּל בְּכַרְשִׁינִין**: It is prohibited to soak vetches on Shabbat. In addition, one may not rub them by hand to remove the chaff. However, one may place them in a sieve so that the waste falls off on its own (*Shulḥan Arukh, Oraḥ Ḥayyim* 319:8).

Handling straw – **טִיפּוּל בְּתֶבֶן**: One may not sift straw on Shabbat or place it in a high place so that the chaff will separate and blow away. However, it is permitted to lift it with a sieve and place it in a trough, even though the chaff will thereby separate on its own (Rambam *Sefer Zemanim, Hilkhot Shabbat* 21:32; *Shulḥan Arukh, Oraḥ Ḥayyim* 324:1).

NOTES

And one may not soak [*sholin*] vetches – **וְאֵין שׁוֹלִין אֶת הַכַּרְשִׁינִין**: According to the version of the mishna that includes the word *sholin*, the verb means pouring water over vetches to separate them from their waste (Rashi). An alternate version is *shorin*, soaking, which would be prohibited because the vetches thereby become fit for eating.

The mishna expresses an individual opinion – **מַתְנִיתִין יְחִידָאָה הִיא**: If it can be demonstrated that the mishna is in accordance with the opinion of an individual Sage's opinion, the *halakha* is ruled in accordance with the unattributed mishna. It would be in accordance with the majority opinion found in the more detailed source. This concept appears, in a very different form, in the Jerusalem Talmud, which cited Rabbi Yoḥanan as saying: For naught we have toiled, meaning, all the toil in studying and analyzing this mishna has been for naught, and he must accept the *halakha* from his teacher.

אָמַר לְהוּ: לְשְׁתּוֹת – לָא קָמִיבַּעְיָא לִי, כִּי קָא מִיבַּעְיָא לִי – לִשְׁרוֹת, מַאי? אֲמַר לְהוּ רַב חִיָּיא בַּר אָבִין: בְּדִידִי הֲוָה עוּבְדָּא, וַאֲתַאי שְׁאֵילְתֵּיהּ לְרַב אַדָּא בַּר אַהֲבָה, וְלָא הֲוָה בִּידֵיהּ. אֲתַאי שְׁאֵילְתֵּיהּ לְרַב הוּנָא, וַאֲמַר: הָכִי קָאָמַר רַב ״שׁוֹרֶה בְּצוֹנֵן וּמַנִּיחַ בַּחַמָּה״.

Rav Aḥa bar Yosef **said to them:** With regard **to drinking, I have no dilemma. When I raised a dilemma,** it is with regard **to soaking** asafoetida; what is the *halakha*? **Rav Ḥiyya bar Avin said to them:** There was an **incident** that happened **with me, and I came** and **asked** that question **to Rav Adda bar Ahava, and he did not have** an answer for it. **I came** and **asked Rav Huna, and he said** that **this is what Rav is saying: One may soak** asafoetida **in cold water and place** it **in the sun** to warm it so it will be fit to drink.

כְּמַאן דְּשָׁרֵי? אֲפִילּוּ לְמַאן דְּאָסַר, הָנֵי מִילֵּי – הֵיכָא דְּלָא אִישְׁתִּי כְּלָל, אֲבָל הָכָא כֵּיוָן דְּאִישְׁתִּי חַמְשָׁא וּמַעֲלֵי שַׁבְּתָא, אִי לָא שָׁתֵי בְּשַׁבָּת – מִיסְתַּכֵּן.

The Gemara asks: Was Rav's ruling **according to** the opinion of **the one who permitted** soaking asafoetida in cold water? The Gemara answers: His ruling could be **even according to** the opinion of **the one who prohibited** doing so; **this** prohibition **applies only when he had not drunk** asafoetida **at all; however, here, since he drank** it **on Thursday and on Shabbat eve, if he does not drink on Shabbat he** would thereby be **endangered.** Therefore, he is permitted even to soak the asafoetida.

מִיסְתַּמֵּיךְ וְאָזֵיל רַב אַחָא בַּר יוֹסֵף אַכַּתְפֵּיהּ דְּרַב נַחְמָן בַּר יִצְחָק בַּר אַחְתֵּיהּ, אֲמַר לֵיהּ: כִּי מָטֵינַן לְבֵי רַב סַפְרָא – עַיְּילִינָא, כִּי מָטוּ – עַיְּילֵיהּ. בְּעָא מִינֵּיהּ: מַהוּ לְכַסְכּוּסֵי כִּיתָּנִיתָא בְּשַׁבְּתָא? לְרַכּוֹכֵי כִּיתָּנִיתָא קָא מִיכַּוֵּין – וְשַׁפִּיר דָּמֵי, אוֹ דִילְמָא: לְאוֹלוּדֵי חִיוָּרָא קָמִיכַּוֵּין, וַאֲסִיר? אֲמַר לֵיהּ: לְרַכּוֹכֵי קָא מִיכַּוֵּין, וְשַׁפִּיר דָּמֵי.

The Gemara relates another incident involving Rav Aḥa bar Yosef: **Rav Aḥa bar Yosef was walking** and **leaning on the shoulder of Rav Naḥman bar Yitzḥak, his sister's son.** Rav Aḥa **said to him: When we arrive at Rav Safra's house, bring me in. When they arrived,** Rav Naḥman **brought him in.** Rav Aḥa then **raised a dilemma before** Rav Safra: **What is the** *halakha* pertaining **to rubbing** and thereby softening **a linen shirt** that is hard after being laundered **on Shabbat?** Does **one intend to soften the shirt, and one may well** do so**? Or perhaps he intends to generate whiteness** in the shirt, **and it is prohibited?** Rav Safra **said to him: He intends to soften, and one may well** do so.

כִּי נְפַק אֲתָא, אֲמַר לֵיהּ: מַאי בְּעָא מָר מִינֵּיהּ? אֲמַר לֵיהּ: בָּעֵי מִינֵּיהּ: מַהוּ לְכַסְכּוּסֵי כִּיתָּנִיתָא בְּשַׁבְּתָא, וַאֲמַר לִי: שַׁפִּיר דָּמֵי.

When Rav Aḥa **emerged** and **came** from Rav Safra's house, Rav Naḥman **said to him: What dilemma did the Master raise before** Rav Safra? Rav Aḥa **said to him: I raised** the following **dilemma before him: What is** the *halakha* pertaining **to rubbing** and thereby softening **a linen shirt on Shabbat, and he said to me: One may well** do so.

וְתִבָּעֵי לֵיהּ לְמָר סוּדָרָא? סוּדָרָא לָא קָא מִיבַּעְיָא לִי, דִּבְעֵי מֵרַב הוּנָא וּפָשֵׁיט לִי.

Rav Naḥman bar Yitzḥak asked: **And let the Master raise** the same **dilemma** with regard to rubbing **a scarf.** He replied: **I did not raise the dilemma** with regard to a **scarf, as I raised it before Rav Huna. And he resolved it for me** and said that it is permitted (Rif).

וְתִיפְשׁוֹט לֵיהּ לְמָר מִסּוּדָרָא! אֲמַר לֵיהּ: הָתָם – מֶיחֱזֵי כִּי אוֹלוּדֵי חִיוָּרָא, הָכָא – לָא מֶיחֱזֵי כְּאוֹלוּדֵי חִיוָּרָא.

Rav Naḥman asked him: **And let the Master resolve** the dilemma with regard to a shirt **from** Rav Huna's ruling with regard to **a scarf.** Rav Aḥa **said to him:** There is a difference between the cases: **There,** in the case of a shirt, **it appears that one is generating whiteness,** whereas **here,** in the case of a scarf, **it does not appear that one is generating whiteness,** as people are not so particular with the whiteness of a scarf, and one's intention is undoubtedly to soften it.[H]

אֲמַר רַב חִסְדָּא: הַאי כִּיתָּנִיתָא,

Rav Ḥisda said: With regard to **this linen shirt,**

Perek **XX**
Daf **140** Amud **b**

מִשְׁלְפוּ לְדִידָהּ מִקַּנְיָא – שָׁרֵי, קַנְיָא מִמֶּנָּה – אָסוּר. אָמַר רָבָא: וְאִם כְּלִי קֵיוָאֵי הוּא – מוּתָּר.

to remove it from the reed upon which it is hanging **is permitted;** however, to remove **the reed from it is prohibited.** Since the reed is not a vessel, it is set-aside. **Rava said: And if it is** hung on **a weaver's vessel,**[H] **it is permitted** to remove the vessel as well. Although its primary function is for a prohibited labor, since it is a vessel, it may be moved.

אֲמַר רַב חִסְדָּא: הַאי כִּישְׁתָּא דְּיַרְקָא, אִי חֲזְיָא לְמַאֲכַל בְּהֵמָה – שָׁרֵי לְטַלְטוּלֵי, וְאִי לָא – אֲסִיר.

Rav Ḥisda said: This bundle of vegetables, if it is suitable for animal food, it is permitted to move it on Shabbat, **but if not, it is prohibited** to move it.[H]

HALAKHA

Softening clothes – רִיכּוּךְ בְּגָדִים: On Shabbat, one is permitted to rub clothes that have hardened after washing and drying in order to soften them. However, according to the version of the Gemara cited in the *Beit Yosef*, it is prohibited to rub a scarf and other linen garments, because the brushing of the garment constitutes the prohibited act of whitening (Rambam *Sefer Zemanim, Hilkhot Shabbat* 22:17; *Shulḥan Arukh, Oraḥ Ḥayyim* 302:5).

HALAKHA

Removing a shirt from a reed…and if it is a weaver's vessel, etc. – ...הוֹצָאַת כְּתוֹנֶת מִקָּנֶה וְאִם כְּלִי קֵיוָאֵי הוּא וכו׳: If garment was hung to dry on a reed that was not designated as a vessel, the garment may be removed. However, the reed may not be moved, as it is set-aside. If, however, one hung the garment on a vessel, even a vessel whose primary function is for prohibited labor, it is permitted even to move the vessel (Rambam *Sefer Zemanim, Hilkhot Shabbat* 25:18; *Shulḥan Arukh, Oraḥ Ḥayyim* 308:16).

Moving bundles of vegetables – טִלְטוּל חֲבִילוֹת יָרָק: Bundles of vegetables or soft hay (*Mishna Berura*) that were prepared as animal food may be moved on Shabbat, even if they are large (Rambam *Sefer Zemanim, Hilkhot Shabbat* 26:16; *Shulḥan Arukh, Oraḥ Ḥayyim* 308:28).

BACKGROUND

Meat hook – תליא דבישרא:

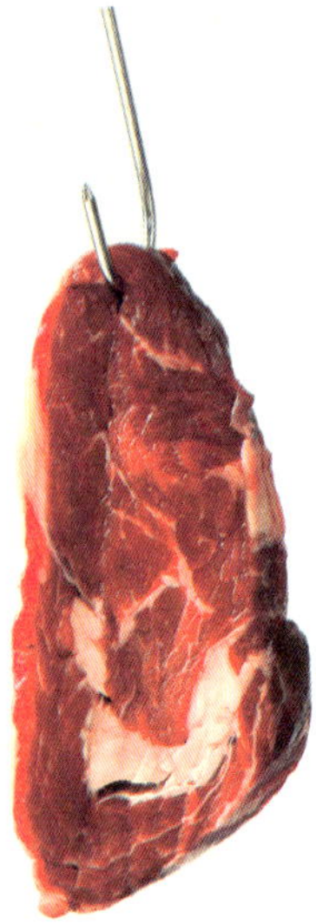

Hook used for meat

HALAKHA

The proper manner of breaking bread – דרך בציעה: One should not cut a small slice of bread because it appears miserly, and one should not cut a slice larger than the volume of an egg because it appears gluttonous (Rambam *Sefer Ahava*, *Hilkhot Berakhot* 7:3).

LANGUAGE

Neck [*unka*] – אונקא: From the Arabic عنق, *'unq*, meaning neck.

אמר רב חייא בר אשי אמר רב: האי תליא, דבשרא – שרי לטלטולי, דכוורי – אסיר.

Rav Ḥiyya bar Ashi said that **Rav said** as follows: In the case of **this hook,** if it is used for hanging **meat,**[B] **it is permitted to move it,** as it is also suitable for other uses. However, if it is a hook for hanging **fish, it is prohibited** to move it, because it smells bad (Rabbeinu Ḥananel) and is used exclusively for fish.

אמר רב קטינא: העומד באמצע המטה – כאילו עומד בכריסה של אשה. ולאו מילתא היא.

Rav Ketina said: One who stands on a board **in the middle of a bed,** it is **as though he were standing on the stomach of a woman.** Just as he would certainly injure the woman, he will certainly break the bed (*ge'onim*). The Gemara comments: **And it is not** a correct **matter,** and it is not accepted as *halakha*.

ואמר רב חסדא: בר בי רב דזבין ירקא – ליזבין אריכא, כישא כי כישא, ואורכא ממילא.

On the topic of the bundle of vegetables, the Gemara cites additional advice on similar issues that **Rav Ḥisda said** to poor scholars experiencing difficulty earning a livelihood: **A student of a Torah academy who buys vegetables should buy long ones. A bundle is a bundle,** and they have a standard thickness at a standard price. **However, the** addition of **length** comes **on its own** for free.

ואמר רב חסדא: בר בי רב דזבין קניא – ליזבין אריכא, טונא כי טונא, ואורכא ממילא.

And Rav Ḥisda also **said: A student of a Torah academy who buys reeds should buy long ones,** since **a bundle is a bundle.** Bundles of reeds have a standard thickness, **but the length** comes **on its own** for free.

ואמר רב חסדא: בר בי רב [דלא נפישא ליה ריפתא] – לא ליכול ירקא, משום דגריר. ואמר רב חסדא: אנא לא בעניותי אכלי ירקא, ולא בעתירותי אכלי ירקא. בעניותי – משום דגריר, בעתירותי – דאמינא: היכא דעייל ירקא ליעול בשרא וכוורי.

And Rav Ḥisda further **said: A student of a Torah academy who does not have much bread should not eat a vegetable, because it whets** the appetite. **And Rav Ḥisda said: I** neither **ate a vegetable in my** state of **poverty, nor did I eat a vegetable in my** state of **wealth. In my poverty,** I did not eat a vegetable **because it whets** the appetite. **In my wealth,** I did not eat a vegetable **because I said: Where a vegetable enters, let meat and fish enter** instead.

ואמר רב חסדא: בר בי רב דלא נפישא ליה ריפתא – לא ליבצע בצועי. ואמר רב חסדא: בר בי רב דלא נפישא ליה ריפתא – לא ליבצע, מאי טעמא – דלא עביד בעין יפה. ואמר רב חסדא: אנא מעיקרא לא הואי בצענא עד דשדאי ידי בכולי מנא ואשכחי [ביה כל צרכי].

And Rav Ḥisda said: A student of a Torah academy who does not have much bread should not cut it into thin slices; rather, he should eat what he has in one helping. **And Rav Ḥisda said: A student of a Torah academy who does not have much bread should not break it**[H] for guests. **What is the reason? As he will not do so in a generous manner. And Rav Ḥisda said: Originally, I would not break** bread **until I placed my hand in the entire dish** to assure **that I found** that there was enough bread **to meet my needs.**

ואמר רב חסדא: האי מאן דאפשר ליה למיכל נהמא דשערי ואכל דחיטי – קעבר משום "בל תשחית". ואמר רב פפא: האי מאן דאפשר למישתי שיכרא ושתי חמרא – עובר משום "בל תשחית". ולאו מילתא היא, בל תשחית דגופא עדיף.

And Rav Ḥisda also **said: One who is able to eat barley bread and** nevertheless **eats wheat** bread **violates the prohibition against** wanton **destruction.** One who wastes resources is comparable to one who destroys items of value. **And Rav Pappa said: One who is able to drink beer and** nevertheless **drinks wine violates the prohibition against** wanton **destruction.** The Gemara comments: **And this is not** a correct **matter,** as **the prohibition against destruction of one's body takes precedence.** It is preferable for one to care for his body by eating higher quality food than to conserve his money.

ואמר רב חסדא: בר בי רב דלית ליה משחא – נימשי במיא דחריצי.

And Rav Ḥisda said: A student of a Torah academy who has no oil should wash, i.e., smear himself, **with ditch water,** as the scum that accumulates in it is as useful as oil.

ואמר רב חסדא: בר בי רב דזבין אומצא – ליזבין אונקא, דאית ביה תלתא מיני בישרא.

And Rav Ḥisda said: A student of a Torah academy who buys meat should buy from the neck [*unka*],[L] **as there are three types of meat** there.

ואמר רב חסדא: בר בי רב דזבין כיתוניתא – ליזבן מדנהר אבא, וניחוורה כל תלתין יומין, דמפטיא ליה תריסר ירחי שתא, ואנא ערבא. מאי כיתוניתא – כיתא נאה.

And Rav Ḥisda said: A student of a Torah academy who buys a linen shirt [*kitonita*] **should buy** it **from** those who work by **the river Abba, and should wash it every thirty days, so that it will last him for the twelve months of the year. And I guarantee** that the shirt will remain in good shape. The Gemara comments: **What is** the meaning of ***kitonita*? A fine class** [***kita***], as fine clothing provide one entry into a well-dressed class of people.

וַאֲמַר רַב חִסְדָּא: בַּר בֵּי רַב לָא לֵיתִיב אַצִּיפְתָּא חַדְתָּא, דִּמְכַלְיָא מָאנֵיהּ.

And Rav Ḥisda said: A student of a Torah academy should not sit on a new mat, as its dampness **ruins his garments.**

וַאֲמַר רַב חִסְדָּא: בַּר בֵּי רַב לָא לִישְׁדַּר מָאנֵיהּ לְאוּשְׁפִּיזֵיהּ לְחַוּוֹרֵיהּ לֵיהּ, דְּלָאו אוֹרַח אַרְעָא, דִּילְמָא חָזֵי בֵּיהּ מִידֵּי וְאָתֵי לְמִגְנְיָא.

And Rav Ḥisda said: A student of a Torah academy should not give his clothes to his host to wash for him, as that is **not proper behavior,** for the host **might see something on it,** such as signs of a seminal emission, **and he will be demeaned** in the eyes of his host.

אֲמַר לְהוּ רַב חִסְדָּא לִבְנָתֵיהּ: תֶּיהֱווּ צְנִיעָתָן בְּאַפֵּי גַּבְרַיְיכוּ, לָא תֵּיכְלוּן נַהֲמָא בְּאַפֵּי גַּבְרַיְיכוּ.

After citing Rav Ḥisda's recommendations to students, the Gemara cites his advice to his daughters. **Rav Ḥisda said to his daughters: Be modest before your husbands; do not eat bread before your husbands,**[N] lest you eat too much and be demeaned in their eyes.

לָא תֵּיכְלוּן יַרְקָא בְּלֵילְיָא, לָא תֵּיכְלוּן תַּמְרֵי בְּלֵילְיָא, וְלָא תִּשְׁתּוּן שִׁיכְרָא בְּלֵילְיָא, וְלָא תֵּיפְנוּן הֵיכָא דְּמִפְּנֵי גַּבְרַיְיכוּ.

Similarly, he advised: **Do not eat vegetables at night,** as vegetables cause bad breath. **Do not eat dates at night and do not drink beer at night,** as these loosen the bowels. **And do not relieve** yourself **in the place where your husbands relieve** themselves, so that they will not be revolted by you.

וְכִי קָא קָארֵי אַבָּבָא אִינִישׁ לָא תֵּימְרוּן "מַנּוּ" אֶלָּא "מַנִּי".

And when a person calls at the door seeking to enter, **do not say: Who is it,** in the masculine form, **but** rather: **Who is it,** in the feminine form. Avoid creating the impression that you have dealings with other men.

נָקֵיט מַרְגָּנִיתָא בַּחֲדָא יְדֵיהּ, וְכוֹרָא בַּחֲדָא יְדֵיהּ. מַרְגָּנִיתָא – אַחֲוֵי לְהוּ, וְכוֹרָא לָא אַחֲוֵי לְהוּ, עַד דְּמִיצְטַעֲרָן, וַהֲדַר אַחֲוֵי לְהוּ.

In order to demonstrate the value of modesty to his daughters, Rav Ḥisda **held a pearl in one hand and a clod of earth in the other. The pearl he showed them** immediately, **and the clod of earth, he did not show them until they were upset** due to their curiosity, **and then he showed it to them.** This taught them that a concealed object is more attractive than one on display, even if it is less valuable.

"אֵין שׁוֹלִין אֶת הַכַּרְשִׁינִין". מַתְנִיתִין דְּלָא כִּי הַאי תַּנָּא; דְּתַנְיָא, רַבִּי אֱלִיעֶזֶר בֶּן יַעֲקֹב אוֹמֵר: אֵין מַשְׁגִּיחִין בִּכְבָרָה כָּל עִיקָּר.

We learned in the mishna: **One may not soak vetches** in water in order to separate them from their chaff. However, one may take the straw in a sieve and place it into the trough of an animal. The Gemara comments: **The mishna is not in accordance with** the opinion of **this *tanna*, as it was taught** in a *baraita*: **Rabbi Eliezer ben Ya'akov says: One may not look at a sieve at all** on Shabbat, lest one come to violate the prohibited labor of selecting.

מתני׳ גּוֹרְפִין מִלִּפְנֵי הַפְּטָם, וּמְסַלְּקִין לַצְּדָדִין מִפְּנֵי הָרְעִי, דִּבְרֵי רַבִּי דּוֹסָא. וַחֲכָמִים אוֹסְרִין. נוֹטְלִין מִלִּפְנֵי בְּהֵמָה זוֹ וְנוֹתְנִין לִפְנֵי בְּהֵמָה זוֹ בְּשַׁבָּת.

MISHNA One may sweep hay **from before an animal that is being fattened, and one may move** hay **to the sides for an animal that grazes** on its own in the field (Rabbeinu Ḥananel);[N] this is **the statement of Rabbi Dosa. And the Rabbis prohibit** doing so. **One may take** hay **from before this animal and place it before that animal on Shabbat.**

גמ׳ אִיבַּעְיָא לְהוּ: רַבָּנַן אַרֵישָׁא פְּלִיגִי, אוֹ אַסֵּיפָא פְּלִיגִי, אוֹ אַתַּרְוַיְיהוּ פְּלִיגִי?

GEMARA A dilemma was raised before the Sages: Do **the Rabbis,** who are stringent, **disagree with the first clause** of Rabbi Dosa's statement, **or** do **they disagree with the latter** clause of the mishna, **or** do **they disagree with both** clauses?

תָּא שְׁמַע: דְּתַנְיָא, וַחֲכָמִים אוֹמְרִים: אֶחָד זֶה וְאֶחָד זֶה – לֹא יְסַלְּקֶנּוּ לַצְּדָדִין.

Come and **hear** a resolution from that which **was taught** in a *baraita*. **And the Rabbis say:** With regard to **both this,** hay placed before an animal set aside for fattening, **and that,** hay placed before an animal that grazes on its own, **one may not move** it **to the sides.** Apparently, the Rabbis rule stringently in both cases.

NOTES

Do not eat bread before your husbands – לָא תֵּיכְלוּן נַהֲמָא בְּאַפֵּי גַּבְרַיְיכוּ: Some commentaries explain that this prohibition is referring to a case where the husband has already eaten his fill. If his wife continues eating, she will appear gluttonous in his eyes (*Me'iri*). Alternately, Rav Ḥisda is not referring to eating at mealtimes; rather, he is advising that a wife should not eat between meals (Rabbi Ya'akov Emden).

An animal that is being fattened…an animal that grazes on its own in the field – הַפְּטָם...הָרְעִי: In the Jerusalem Talmud, it is explained that an animal that is being fattened will not eat certain foods, since it is accustomed to eating quality food. An animal grazing on its own will eat these lesser-quality foods, since food is less readily available to it.

אָמַר רַב חִסְדָּא: מַחֲלוֹקֶת בְּאֵיבוּס שֶׁל קַרְקַע, אֲבָל בְּאֵיבוּס שֶׁל כְּלִי – דִּבְרֵי הַכֹּל מוּתָּר. וְאֵיבוּס שֶׁל קַרְקַע מִי אִיכָּא לְמַאן דְּשָׁרֵי? הָא קָא מְשַׁוֵּי גּוּמוֹת! אֶלָּא, אִי אִיתְּמַר הָכִי אִיתְּמַר: אָמַר רַב חִסְדָּא מַחֲלוֹקֶת בְּאֵיבוּס שֶׁל כְּלִי, אֲבָל בְּאֵיבוּס שֶׁל קַרְקַע – דִּבְרֵי הַכֹּל אָסוּר.

Rav Ḥisda said: This **dispute is with regard to a trough**[H] formed **in the ground; however, with regard to a trough which is a vessel, everyone agrees that it is permitted.** The Gemara expresses surprise: **Is there anyone who permits** doing so in a **trough** formed in **the ground? Isn't one leveling holes** and thereby performing the prohibited labors of building or plowing? **Rather, if it was stated, it was stated as follows: Rav Ḥisda said:** This **dispute** applies only **to a trough that is a vessel; however, with regard to a trough** formed in **the ground, everyone agrees that it is prohibited,** due to the concern lest one level holes.

״וְנוֹטְלִין מִלִּפְנֵי בְהֵמָה״. תָּנָא חֲדָא: נוֹטְלִין מִלִּפְנֵי בְהֵמָה שֶׁפִּיהָ יָפֶה, וְנוֹתְנִין לִפְנֵי בְהֵמָה שֶׁפִּיהָ רַע. וְתַנְיָא אִידַּךְ: נוֹטְלִין מִלִּפְנֵי בְהֵמָה שֶׁפִּיהָ רַע וְנוֹתְנִין לִפְנֵי בְהֵמָה שֶׁפִּיהָ יָפֶה!

We also learned in the mishna: **One may take** hay **from before** this **animal** and place it before that animal. **It was taught in one** *baraita*: **One may take** hay **from before an animal whose mouth is fine and place it before an animal whose mouth is foul. And it was taught in another** *baraita*: **One may take** hay **from before an animal whose mouth is foul and place it in front of an animal whose mouth is fine.** There is an apparent contradiction between the two *baraitot*.

אָמַר אַבָּיֵי: אִידִי וְאִידִי מִקַּמֵּי חֲמָרָא לְקַמֵּי תּוֹרָא – שָׁקְלִינַן, מִקַּמֵּי תּוֹרָא לְקַמֵּי חֲמָרָא – לָא שָׁקְלִינַן. וְהָא דְּקָתָנֵי ״נוֹטֵל מִלִּפְנֵי בְהֵמָה שֶׁפִּיהָ יָפֶה״ – בַּחֲמוֹר, דְּלֵית לֵיהּ רִירֵי. ״וְנוֹתְנִין לִפְנֵי בְהֵמָה שֶׁפִּיהָ רַע״ – בְּפָרָה,

Abaye said: Both **this** *baraita* **and that** *baraita* hold that **one may take** hay **from before a donkey** and place it **before an ox.** However, **one may not take** hay **from before an ox** and place it **before a donkey.** The formulation of the *baraitot* can be explained as follows: **That which was taught: One may take** hay **from before an animal whose mouth is fine,**[H] is referring to a **donkey,** and the reason the *baraita* says its mouth is fine is **because it has no spittle.** Therefore, the donkey does not dampen the remaining hay with its saliva. **And** the statement: **And one may place it before an animal whose mouth is foul,** is referring to **a cow,**

HALAKHA

Sweeping a trough – גְּרִיפַת אֵיבוּס: On Shabbat, one may not sweep the bottom of a trough used by an ox that is being fattened, even if the trough is an actual vessel and not a trough formed in the ground. This is a rabbinic decree due to the concern lest one level holes in the ground when using a trough formed in the ground. This ruling is in accordance with the opinion of the Rabbis (Rambam *Sefer Zemanim*, *Hilkhot Shabbat* 26:19; *Shulḥan Arukh*, *Oraḥ Ḥayyim* 324:15).

An animal whose mouth is fine – בְּהֵמָה שֶׁפִּיהָ יָפֶה: On Shabbat, one may move food that was placed before a donkey and place it before an ox, but not the opposite, because the food will be spoiled by the ox's saliva and the donkey will not eat it. Therefore, the ox's food is set-aside (Rambam *Sefer Zemanim*, *Hilkhot Shabbat* 26:19; *Shulḥan Arukh*, *Oraḥ Ḥayyim* 324:14).

Perek **XX**
Daf **141** Amud **a**

דְּאִית לַהּ רִירֵי.

which has spittle.

וְהָא דְּקָתָנֵי ״נוֹטְלִין מִלִּפְנֵי בְהֵמָה שֶׁפִּיהָ רַע״ – בַּחֲמוֹר דְּלָא דָּיֵיק וְאָכֵיל, ״וְנוֹתְנִין לִפְנֵי בְהֵמָה שֶׁפִּיהָ יָפֶה״ – בְּפָרָה דְּדָיְיקָא וְאָכְלָה.

And that which was taught in the other *baraita*: **One may take** hay **from before an animal whose mouth is foul,** is referring to **a donkey.** Its mouth is foul **because it does not discern** between different foods **and** it **eats** everything. **And** the statement: **One may place it before an animal whose mouth is fine,** is referring **to a cow, which discerns** between different foods **and** only then **it eats.**

מַתְנִי׳ הַקַּשׁ שֶׁעַל גַּבֵּי הַמִּטָּה – לֹא יְנַעַנְעֶנּוּ בְּיָדוֹ, אֶלָּא מְנַעַנְעוֹ בְּגוּפוֹ. וְאִם הָיָה מַאֲכַל בְּהֵמָה, אוֹ שֶׁהָיָה עָלָיו כַּר אוֹ סָדִין – מְנַעַנְעוֹ בְּיָדוֹ.

MISHNA With regard to **straw that is on top of a bed,**[H] if a person wishes to lie on it, **he may not move it with his hand** to smooth it, as the straw is set aside for kindling; **rather, he may move it with his body.** Since moving straw with one's body is not the usual manner, it is permitted. **And if** the straw **was** designated as **animal food, or a pillow or sheet was on it,** which would clearly indicate that the straw was placed on the bed so one could sleep on it, the straw is not considered set-aside, and **one may move it** even **with his hand.**

מַכְבֵּשׁ שֶׁל בַּעֲלֵי בָתִּים – מַתִּירִין, אֲבָל לֹא כּוֹבְשִׁין. וְשֶׁל כּוֹבְסִין – לֹא יִגַּע בּוֹ. רַבִּי יְהוּדָה אוֹמֵר: אִם הָיָה מוּתָּר מֵעֶרֶב שַׁבָּת – מַתִּיר אֶת כּוּלּוֹ וְשׁוֹמְטוֹ.

A press which belongs to a homeowner, one may loosen it on Shabbat. This press is used to dry and press clothing after laundering. One loosens it to remove clothing from it. **However, one may not press** clothing with it on Shabbat.[N] **And** in the case of a press that **belongs to a launderer,**[H] which is made specifically for pressing and requires professional expertise for its operation, **one may not touch it. Rabbi Yehuda says: If** the launderer's press **was loosened** somewhat **on Shabbat eve, he may loosen it completely**[N] on Shabbat **and remove** the garment.

HALAKHA

Straw that is on top of a bed – הַקַּשׁ שֶׁעַל גַּבֵּי הַמִּטָּה: If there is straw on a bed, which is presumably set-aside because it might be used for kindling, it is prohibited to move it on Shabbat with one's hands. However, one may move the straw with one's body in an atypical manner. If the straw was prepared as animal food, or if one placed a pillow or a sheet on it before Shabbat, it is not set-aside and one is allowed to shake it off with one's hands (Rambam *Sefer Zemanim*, *Hilkhot Shabbat* 25:22; *Shulḥan Arukh*, *Oraḥ Ḥayyim* 311:8).

Laundry press – מַכְבֵּשׁ כְּבִיסָה: If one's garments were placed in a professional launderer's press after they were washed, it is prohibited to remove them on Shabbat, even for Shabbat use. The press is tightly sealed, and loosening it is similar to disassembling a building. However, if the garments are in a homeowner's press, which is more loosely sealed, it is permissible to loosen the press and remove the clothing on Shabbat (Rambam *Sefer Zemanim*, *Hilkhot Shabbat* 26:12; *Shulḥan Arukh*, *Oraḥ Ḥayyim* 302:4).

NOTES

However, one may not press clothing with it on Shabbat – אֲבָל לֹא כּוֹבְשִׁין: Rashi explains that pressing garments on Shabbat is prohibited because it is considered a weekday activity and it is inappropriate to perform actions of that sort on Shabbat. Other commentaries state that there is a concern that one may forcefully wedge together the components of the press, thereby performing the prohibited labor of building (Rashash).

He may loosen it completely – מַתִּיר אֶת כּוּלּוֹ: A variant reading of the mishna states: He identifies his garments and removes them. In other words, if the launderer's press was already loosened, one who recognizes his articles of clothing may remove them from among the others (see *Melekhet Shlomo*).

גמ׳ אָמַר רַב נַחְמָן: הַאי פּוּגְלָא, מִלְמַעְלָה לְמַטָּה – שָׁרֵי, מִלְּמַטָּה לְמַעְלָה – אֲסִיר.

GEMARA With regard to moving items that are set aside, the Gemara cites that which **Rav Naḥman said: This radish,** which was buried in the earth, if it was buried **from top to bottom,** with its wide end at the top and its narrow end at the bottom, **it is permitted** to remove it on Shabbat. When the radish is buried in that manner, one does not move the earth when he removes the radish. However, if the radish was buried in the earth **from bottom to top,** with the wide end at the bottom, **it is prohibited.**

אָמַר רַב אַדָּא בַּר אַבָּא, אָמְרִי בֵּי רַב: תָּנֵינָא דְּלָא כְּרַב נַחְמָן ״הַקַּשׁ שֶׁעַל גַּבֵּי הַמִּטָּה – לֹא יְנַעְנְעֶנּוּ בְּיָדוֹ, אֲבָל מְנַעְנְעוֹ בְּגוּפוֹ. וְאִם הָיָה מַאֲכַל בְּהֵמָה, אוֹ שֶׁהָיָה עָלָיו כַּר אוֹ סָדִין – מְנַעְנְעוֹ בְּיָדוֹ״. שְׁמַע מִינַּהּ: טִלְטוּל מִן הַצַּד – לָא שְׁמֵיהּ טִלְטוּל, שְׁמַע מִינַּהּ.

Rav Adda bar Abba said: They say in **the school of Rav: We already learned** in the mishna that the *halakha* is **not** in accordance with the opinion of **Rav Naḥman:** With regard to **straw on top of a bed, one may not move it with his hand, but he may move it with his body. And if it is animal food, or a pillow or sheet is on it, he may move** it even **with his hand. Conclude from here** that **moving** an item **in an atypical manner**[H] **is not considered moving.** The Gemara concludes: Indeed, **conclude from here** that this is indeed the case.

אָמַר רַב יְהוּדָה: הָנֵי פִּלְפְּלֵי מֵידַק חֲדָא חֲדָא בְּקַתָּא דְּסַכִּינָא – שָׁרֵי, תַּרְתֵּי – אֲסִיר. רָבָא אָמַר: כֵּיוָן דִּמְשַׁנֵּי – אֲפִילּוּ טוּבָא נָמֵי.

The Gemara cites a somewhat similar case.[N] **Rav Yehuda said:** In the case of **these peppers, crushing them**[H] **one by one with the handle of a knife is permitted.** However, crushing **two** at a time **is prohibited,** because it appears to be a prohibited labor. **Rava said: Since he alters** the manner in which he performs this activity, **even** crushing **many** at a time **is also** permitted.

אָמַר רַב יְהוּדָה: מַאן דְּסָחֵי בְּמַיָּא – לִינַגֵּיב נַפְשֵׁיהּ בְּרֵישָׁא, וַהֲדַר לִיסְלִיק, דִּילְמָא אָתֵי לְאַתּוֹיֵי אַרְבַּע אַמּוֹת בְּכַרְמְלִית.

Rav Yehuda also **said: One who bathes in water should first dry himself** immediately upon exiting,[H] **and then ascend** to the coast, **lest he come to carry** the remaining drops of water on his body **four cubits in a** ***karmelit.***

אִי הָכִי, כִּי קָא נָחֵית נָמֵי, קָא דָּחֵי כֹּחוֹ אַרְבַּע אַמּוֹת, וְאָסִיר! כֹּחוֹ בְּכַרְמְלִית לָא גָּזְרוּ.

The Gemara asks: **If so,** if there is a concern about carrying water, there should be concern **when one descends** into the water **as well.** In that case, **his force propels** water **four cubits** into the river, **and** it should be **prohibited.** The Gemara answers: With regard to movement that results from **his force in a** ***karmelit,*** the Sages **did not** issue a **decree.** Since one does not directly propel the water, but the water moves only as an extension of his motion, and since the river is a *karmelit,* and the prohibition to carry there is only a rabbinic law, the Sages did not issue a decree for one who descends into the water.

אָמַר אַבָּיֵי וְאִיתֵּימָא רַב יְהוּדָה: טִיט שֶׁעַל גַּבֵּי רַגְלוֹ מְקַנְּחוֹ בַּקַּרְקַע, וְאֵין מְקַנְּחוֹ בַּכּוֹתֶל.

In a similar decree, **Abaye said, and some say** that it was stated by **Rav Yehuda:** If one has **mud on his foot, he may wipe it**[H] **on the ground** on Shabbat, **but he may not wipe it on a wall.**

אָמַר רָבָא: מַאי טַעְמָא בַּכּוֹתֶל לֹא מִשּׁוּם דְּמִיחְזֵי כְּבוֹנֶה, הָא בִּנְיָן חַקְלָאָה הוּא!

Rava said: What is the reason that he may **not** wipe it off **on a wall?** Is it **because it appears like building,** as he is adding plaster to the wall? **That is the building of a field laborer,** which is not an actual building. There is no concern in that case because in adding plaster to that building, one does not perform the prohibited labor of building.

אֶלָּא אָמַר רָבָא: מְקַנְּחוֹ בַּכּוֹתֶל, וְאֵין מְקַנְּחוֹ בַּקַּרְקַע, דִּילְמָא אָתֵי לְאַשְׁוֹויֵי גּוּמּוֹת.

Rather, Rava said: On the contrary, **He may wipe it on a wall, but he may not wipe it on the ground.** This is due to the concern **lest one come to level holes** in the ground while wiping his foot.

אִיתְּמַר, מָר בְּרֵיהּ דְּרָבִינָא אָמַר: אֶחָד זֶה וְאֶחָד זֶה אָסוּר, רַב פָּפָּא אָמַר: אֶחָד זֶה וְאֶחָד זֶה – מוּתָּר.

It is stated that other *amora'im* disputed this issue. **Mar, son of Ravina, said: Both this,** wiping the mud on a wall, **and that,** wiping the mud on the ground, **are prohibited. Rav Pappa said: Both this and that are permitted.**

לְמָר בְּרֵיהּ דְּרָבִינָא בְּמַאי מְקַנַּחְ לֵיהּ? מְקַנַּחְ לֵיהּ בְּקוֹרָה.

The Gemara asks: **According to** the opinion of **Mar, son of Ravina, with what may he wipe** his foot? The Gemara answers: Even according to his opinion, there is a permitted manner to clean his foot; **he wipes it on a beam** on the ground.

אָמַר רָבָא: לָא לֵיתִיב אִינִישׁ אַפּוּמֵּיהּ דְּלֶחְיָיא, דִּילְמָא מִיגַּנְדְּרָא לֵיהּ חֵפֶץ וְאָתֵי לְאַתּוֹיֵי.

Rava said: A person should not sit on Shabbat right **at the entrance** to a closed alleyway[H] where **a side post** is placed as a symbolic partition enabling one to carry inside the alleyway. The reason for this is that **perhaps an object will roll** into the public domain **and one will come to get it,** as there is no conspicuous demarcation between inside and outside the alleyway.

HALAKHA

Moving an item in an atypical manner – טִלְטוּל מִן הַצַּד: Objects that one is prohibited to move on Shabbat are prohibited only if they are moved in their typical manner. Moving these items in an indirect manner is permitted (Rambam *Sefer Zemanim, Hilkhot Shabbat* 25:14–15; *Shulḥan Arukh, Oraḥ Ḥayyim* 311:8).

Crushing peppers – דִּיכַת פִּלְפְּלִים: One is permitted to crush peppers on Shabbat if they are to be eaten on Shabbat (*Mishna Berura*) and if they are crushed in an unusual manner, even if one crushes a large amount at one time. For instance, one may crush them with the handle of a knife and in a bowl, as opposed to utilizing a mortar and pestle. This ruling is in accordance with the view of Rava (Rambam *Sefer Zemanim, Hilkhot Shabbat* 25:14–15; *Shulḥan Arukh, Oraḥ Ḥayyim* 321:7).

Emerging from a river – יְצִיאָה מִן הַנָּהָר: One who bathes in a river on Shabbat (see *Mishna Berura*) must dry off thoroughly when emerging from the water so that no water will remain on his body and be carried four cubits in a *karmelit*. This ruling is in accordance with Rav Yehuda (Rambam *Sefer Zemanim, Hilkhot Shabbat* 15:22; *Shulḥan Arukh, Oraḥ Ḥayyim* 326:7).

If one has mud on his foot, he may wipe it, etc. – טִיט שֶׁעַל גַּבֵּי רַגְלוֹ מְקַנְּחוֹ וכו׳: One who has mud on his shoe or on his foot may wipe it off on a wall but not on the ground, due to concern that one might level holes, as stated by Rava. Some authorities prohibit wiping the mud off on a wall and permit only the use of a beam, in accordance with the opinion of Mar, son of Ravina (Rif). Other commentaries even permit the use of the ground, in accordance with Rav Pappa's opinion (Rosh). The later commentaries did not reach a consensus on this issue, although most of them agreed that only a wall should be used. This is the ruling of the *Beit Yosef*, in accordance with the decision of the majority of early commentaries. The *Baḥ*, however, favored the more stringent approach (Rambam *Sefer Zemanim, Hilkhot Shabbat* 21:2; *Shulḥan Arukh, Oraḥ Ḥayyim* 302:6).

Sitting at the entrance to an alleyway – יְשִׁיבָה בְּפֶתַח הַמָּבוֹי: Although the law permits one to utilize and carry under the beam marking the entrance to an alleyway, a person should nonetheless not sit by the edge of the alleyway or by the side post (*Mishna Berura*), lest an object roll out of his hand and he come to retrieve it from the public domain, as stated by Rava (Rambam *Sefer Zemanim, Hilkhot Shabbat* 17:17; *Shulḥan Arukh, Oraḥ Ḥayyim* 365:5).

NOTES

The succession of topics in the Gemara – מַהֲלַךְ סוּגְיַית הַגְּמָרָא: The Gemara seems to be presenting a series of unrelated *halakhot*. Nevertheless, the items share several common features. In particular, all the cases involve rabbinic decrees that prohibit actions that could lead to performance of a prohibited labor, although each action in and of itself lacks even the appearance of a prohibition. Some commentaries state that most of these decrees are in accordance with the opinion of Rabbi Yehuda, who holds that an unintentional act is prohibited (*Tosefot Rid*).

וַאֲמַר רָבָא: לָא לִיצַדַּד אִינִישׁ כּוּבָא, דִּילְמָא אָתֵי לְאַשְׁוֹויֵי גּוּמוֹת.

And Rava also **said** a similar decree: **A person may not position a barrel**[HN] on a dirt floor, **lest he come to level holes** in the ground while smoothing the surface upon which he is positioning the barrel.

וַאֲמַר רָבָא: לָא לִיהַדּוּק אִינִישׁ אוּדְרָא בְּפוּמָא דְּשִׁישָׁא, דִּילְמָא אָתֵי לִידֵי סְחִיטָה.

And furthermore, **Rava said: A person may not stuff a rag into the mouth of a jug** [*shisha*][HL] on Shabbat, **lest he come to** violate the prohibition of **squeezing** liquid from the cloth.

אָמַר רַב כָּהֲנָא: טִיט שֶׁעַל גַּבֵּי בִּגְדוֹ מְכַסְכְּסוֹ מִבִּפְנִים וְאֵין מְכַסְכְּסוֹ מִבַּחוּץ.

Rav Kahana said: With regard to **mortar that is on one's garment**[H] on Shabbat, **one may rub it off from the inside, but one may not rub it off from the outside,** because that is comparable to the prohibited labor of laundering.

מֵיתִיבִי: טִיט שֶׁעַל גַּבֵּי מִנְעָלוֹ – מְגָרְרוֹ בְּגַב סַכִּין, וְשֶׁעַל בִּגְדוֹ – מְגָרְרוֹ בַּצִּפּוֹרֶן, וּבִלְבַד שֶׁלֹּא יְכַסְכֵּס. מַאי לָאו – שֶׁלֹּא יְכַסְכֵּס כְּלָל! לֹא, שֶׁלֹּא יְכַסְכֵּס מִבַּחוּץ, אֶלָּא מִבִּפְנִים.

The Gemara **raises an objection** from that which we learned: With regard to **mortar that is on one's shoe, he may scrape it off with the back of a knife** as a departure from the typical manner of scraping. **And** mortar **which is on one's clothes, he may scrape off with his fingernail, as long as he does not rub it.** The Gemara asks: **What, is it not** saying **that he may not rub** it at **all?** The Gemara rejects that premise: **No,** it is saying **that he may not rub** it **from the outside, rather from the inside.**

אָמַר רַבִּי אַבָּהוּ אָמַר רַבִּי אֶלְעָזָר אָמַר רַבִּי יַנַּאי: מְגָרְרִין מִנְעָל חָדָשׁ, אֲבָל לֹא יָשָׁן.

Rabbi Abbahu said that **Rabbi Elazar said** that **Rabbi Yannai said: One may scrape** mud off of **a new shoe** on Shabbat, **but not** off of **an old** shoe, because a layer of the shoe will be removed, which constitutes the prohibited labor of smoothing.

HALAKHA

A person may not position a barrel – לָא לִיצַדַּד אִינִישׁ כּוּבָא: It is prohibited to straighten or tilt a full (*Mishna Berura*) barrel on the ground on Shabbat. Since it is heavy, one will inevitably even out holes in the ground (*Shulḥan Arukh, Oraḥ Ḥayyim* 337:4).

Rags in the mouth of a jug – מוֹכִין בְּפִי כַד: It is prohibited to stuff wet (*Mishna Berura*) rags into the mouth of a jug on Shabbat, because one will inevitably squeeze the liquid out of them (Rambam *Sefer Zemanim, Hilkhot Shabbat* 22:15; *Shulḥan Arukh, Oraḥ Ḥayyim* 320:16).

Mortar that is on one's garment – טִיט שֶׁעַל גַּבֵּי בִּגְדוֹ: If one has mortar on his clothing, he may rub it off from the inside, since it does not have the appearance of laundering. He may not rub it off from the outside. It is also permitted to scrape it off with a fingernail, as that is considered atypical, as per the opinion of Rav Huna. Some authorities explain that this *halakha* applies only to wet mud. However, it is prohibited to rub off dry mud, because that constitutes the prohibited labor of grinding (Rambam *Sefer Zemanim, Hilkhot Shabbat* 22:17; *Shulḥan Arukh, Oraḥ Ḥayyim* 302:7).

NOTES

A person may not position a barrel – לָא לִיצַדַּד אִינִישׁ כּוּבָא: Some commentaries explain that this means that one should not tip a barrel on its side to pour from it, due to the possibility that the edge of the barrel will dig a hole in the ground. Instead, one should lift the barrel off of the ground and then pour from it (*ge'onim*).

LANGUAGE

Jug [*shisha*] – שִׁישָׁא: From the Middle Persian *šīšag*, meaning bottle or jug.

Perek XX
Daf 141 Amud b

בַּמֶּה מְגָרְרוֹ? אָמַר רַבִּי אַבָּהוּ: בְּגַב סַכִּין.

With what does one scrape it off? Rabbi Abahu said: With the back of a knife, which is a departure from the typical manner of doing so.

אָמַר לֵיהּ הַהוּא סָבָא: סַמֵּי דִּידָךְ מִקַּמֵּי הָא דְּתָנֵי רַבִּי חִיָּיא: אֵין מְגָרְרִין לֹא מִנְעָל חָדָשׁ וְלֹא מִנְעָל יָשָׁן, וְלֹא יָסוּךְ אֶת רַגְלוֹ שֶׁמֶן וְהוּא בְּתוֹךְ הַמִּנְעָל אוֹ בְּתוֹךְ הַסַּנְדָּל, אֲבָל סָךְ אֶת רַגְלוֹ שֶׁמֶן וּמַנִּיחַ בְּתוֹךְ הַמִּנְעָל אוֹ בְּתוֹךְ הַסַּנְדָּל. וְסָךְ כׇּל גּוּפוֹ שֶׁמֶן וּמִתְעַגֵּל עַל גַּבֵּי קָטַבְלִיָא וְאֵינוֹ חוֹשֵׁשׁ.

A certain Elder said to Rabbi Abbahu: **Delete your** teaching **before this** statement **taught by Rabbi Ḥiyya: One may not scrape** at all; **neither a new shoe nor an old shoe,**[H] **and one may not smear oil on one's foot**[H] **while it is inside the shoe or inside the sandal,** as the oil is absorbed by the leather of the shoe and strengthens it, which constitutes performance of the prohibited labor of tanning. **However, one may smear oil on his foot** in the typical manner **and place** it afterward **in a shoe or in a sandal,** and he need not be concerned that this oil will enhance the shoe leather. **And he may** likewise **smear oil on his entire body with oil and roll on a leather carpet, and** he need **not be concerned.**

אָמַר רַב חִסְדָּא: לֹא שָׁנוּ אֶלָּא לְצַחְצְחוֹ, אֲבָל לְעַבְּדוֹ – אָסוּר.

Rav Ḥisda said: They only taught this in a case where he does so in order **to polish** the sandal or carpet. **But** if he does so **to tan** the sandal or carpet, **it is prohibited.**

״לְעַבְּדוֹ״ פְּשִׁיטָא! וְתוּ: לְצַחְצְחוֹ, מִי אִיכָּא מַאן דְּשָׁרֵי?

The Gemara raises a difficulty: If he does so **to tan** the leather, it is **obvious** that it is prohibited, as tanning is a labor prohibited by Torah law. **And furthermore:** If he does so in order **to polish it, is there an opinion that permits** one to perform this act intentionally on Shabbat *ab initio*?

אֶלָּא, אִי אִיתְּמַר הָכִי אִיתְּמַר, אָמַר רַב חִסְדָּא: לֹא שָׁנוּ אֶלָּא שִׁיעוּר לְצַחְצְחוֹ, אֲבָל שִׁיעוּר לְעַבְּדוֹ – אָסוּר.

Rather, if it was stated, it was stated as follows: Rav Ḥisda said: They only taught that it is permitted to do so on Shabbat in a case where one smears **a measure** sufficient only **to polish it; however,** if one smears **a measure** sufficient **to tan it, it is prohibited,** even if he did not intend to tan the leather.

HALAKHA

Scraping off a shoe – גֵּירוּד מִנְעָל: It is prohibited to scrape dirt off both a new and an old shoe on Shabbat, with a knife or with a fingernail. Scraping is tantamount to the labor of smoothing the leather, in accordance with the *baraita* taught by Rabbi Ḥiyya. However, one may scrape the dirt off a shoe against a wall (*Magen Avraham*; Rambam *Sefer Zemanim, Hilkhot Shabbat* 22:18; *Shulḥan Arukh, Oraḥ Ḥayyim* 302:8).

One may not smear oil on one's foot, etc. – וְלֹא יָסוּךְ אֶת רַגְלוֹ שֶׁמֶן וכו׳: It is prohibited to smear oil on one's foot on Shabbat while wearing a new (Rambam) shoe or sandal because that approximates tanning. However, it is permitted to smear oil on one's foot and then put on a shoe or smear oil on one's entire body in order to rest on a leather carpet, as long as there is not enough oil to tan the leather and the intention is not to process the leather (Rambam *Sefer Zemanim, Hilkhot Shabbat* 23:10; *Shulḥan Arukh, Oraḥ Ḥayyim* 327:4).

תָּנוּ רַבָּנַן: לֹא יֵצֵא קָטָן בְּמִנְעָל גָּדוֹל, אֲבָל יוֹצֵא הוּא בְּחָלוּק גָּדוֹל.

The Sages taught in a *baraita*: **A small** person **may not go out in** a too **large shoe,** due to concern lest the shoe fall off and he will come to carry it in the public domain; **but he may go out in** a too **large cloak.**[H] Even if it does not fit him properly, it will certainly not fall off.

וְלֹא תֵּצֵא אִשָּׁה בְּמִנְעָל מְרוּפָּט, וְלֹא תַּחֲלוֹץ בּוֹ. וְאִם חָלְצָה – חֲלִיצָתָהּ כְּשֵׁרָה.

And a woman may not go out on Shabbat **in a shoe that is torn on top,**[N] lest she be mocked, remove it, and carry it on Shabbat. **And** a shoe of that kind **may not be used to perform *ḥalitza*,** as it is not a suitable shoe. *Ḥalitza* is performed by a widow bound in a levirate bond with her brother-in-law. **However, if she performed *ḥalitza*** with it, **her *ḥalitza* is valid,** since ultimately it is a shoe.[HN]

וְאֵין יוֹצְאִין בְּמִנְעָל חָדָשׁ. בְּאֵיזֶה מִנְעָל אָמְרוּ – בְּמִנְעָל שֶׁל אִשָּׁה.

And one may not go out on Shabbat wearing **a new shoe,**[H] due to the concern that it will not fit properly, and then one will remove it and carry it. The Gemara comments: In **what case** did **they say** that one may not wear a new **shoe?** They said this **with regard to a woman's shoe,** as women are very particular about having their shoes fit properly.

תָּנֵי בַּר קַפָּרָא: לֹא שָׁנוּ אֶלָּא שֶׁלֹּא יָצְאָה בּוֹ שָׁעָה אַחַת מִבְּעוֹד יוֹם, אֲבָל יָצְאָה בּוֹ מֵעֶרֶב שַׁבָּת – מוּתָּר.

Bar Kappara taught: They only taught that she may not go out wearing a new shoe on Shabbat **if she did not** yet **go out** wearing **it for any** length of **time while** it was still **day. However, if she went out** wearing **it on Shabbat eve,** at which point she would have ascertained if it fits her, she is **permitted** to go out wearing it on Shabbat.

תָּנֵי חֲדָא: שׁוֹמְטִין מִנְעָל מֵעַל גַּבֵּי אִימוּס, וְתַנְיָא אִידָךְ: אֵין שׁוֹמְטִין! לָא קַשְׁיָא; הָא – רַבִּי אֱלִיעֶזֶר, הָא – רַבָּנַן.

One *baraita* taught: One may remove a shoe from the shoemaker's **last,** the frame on which a shoe is shaped, on Shabbat. **And another *baraita* taught** the opposite: **One may not remove it.** The Gemara explains that this is **not difficult: This *baraita*,** which prohibits doing so, is in accordance with the opinion of **Rabbi Eliezer,** and **that *baraita*,** which permits doing so, is in accordance with the opinion of **the Rabbis.** Rabbi Eliezer and the Rabbis dispute the applicability of the *halakhot* of ritual purity and impurity in a similar case.

דִּתְנַן: מִנְעָל שֶׁעַל גַּבֵּי אִימוּס, רַבִּי אֱלִיעֶזֶר מְטַהֵר, וַחֲכָמִים מְטַמְּאִים.

As we learned in a mishna: **A shoe that** remains **on a last,**[N] **Rabbi Eliezer deems it pure,** i.e., unable to become impure, as in his opinion the shoe is not yet complete, and therefore it is not yet a vessel and cannot become impure. **And the Rabbis deem it** capable of becoming **impure,** as in their opinion, the shoe is completed, and any vessel whose work is complete can become ritually impure.[H] Correspondingly, the Rabbis, who hold that a shoe on a last is a completed vessel, hold that it may be moved on Shabbat.[H] Rabbi Eliezer, who holds that it is an incomplete vessel, holds that it may not be moved.

הָנִיחָא לְרָבָא, דְּאָמַר: דָּבָר שֶׁמְּלַאכְתּוֹ לְאִיסּוּר, בֵּין לְצוֹרֶךְ גּוּפוֹ בֵּין לְצוֹרֶךְ מְקוֹמוֹ – מוּתָּר, שַׁפִּיר.

The Gemara poses a question: **It works out well according to** the opinion of **Rava, who said:** Moving **an object whose** primary **function is for a prohibited** use, **whether for the purpose** of utilizing the object **itself** to perform a permitted action **or for the purpose of** utilizing **its place, is permitted. It is well** understood that one may move the last slightly while removing the shoe, since removing the shoe is considered utilizing the last's place.

אֶלָּא לְאַבַּיֵי, דְּאָמַר: לְצוֹרֶךְ גּוּפוֹ – מוּתָּר, לְצוֹרֶךְ מְקוֹמוֹ – אָסוּר, מַאי אִיכָּא לְמֵימַר?

However, according to Abaye, who **said** that **for the purpose** of utilizing the object **itself** to perform a permitted action, **it is permitted;** however, **for the purpose of utilizing its place, it is prohibited, what can be said?** It is prohibited to move the last, which is clearly a utensil whose primary function is for a prohibited use. How is it possible to remove the shoe without moving the last?

הָכָא בְּמַאי עָסְקִינַן – בְּרָפוּי. דְּתַנְיָא, רַבִּי יְהוּדָה אוֹמֵר: אִם הָיָה רָפוּי – מוּתָּר.

The Gemara answers: **With what are we dealing here?** It is **with** a shoe placed **loosely** on the last, so the shoe can be removed without moving the last. **As it was taught** in a *baraita*: **Rabbi Yehuda says: If it was loose, it is permitted.**

HALAKHA

A small person may not go out in a too large shoe…in a too large cloak – לֹא יֵצֵא קָטָן בְּמִנְעָל גָּדוֹל...בְּחָלוּק גָּדוֹל: It is prohibited to go out on Shabbat wearing a shoe that is too large, because it might fall off and one might come to carry it. However, it is permitted to wear a large cloak, in which case no such concern exists (Rambam *Sefer Zemanim, Hilkhot Shabbat* 19:15; *Shulḥan Arukh, Oraḥ Ḥayyim* 301:7).

Ḥalitza with a torn shoe – מִנְעָל מְרוּפָּט בַּחֲלִיצָה: *Ab initio, Ḥalitza* must be performed with a shoe that is whole. Nevertheless, if *ḥalitza* is performed with a torn shoe that is not entirely shredded (*Tosafot*), the *ḥalitza* is valid after the fact. If the shoe is so torn that it cannot be worn, the *ḥalitza* is invalid (Rambam *Sefer Nashim, Hilkhot Yibbum VaḤalitza* 4:19; *Shulḥan Arukh, Even HaEzer* 169:21).

And a woman may not go out in a shoe that is torn on top…wearing a new shoe – וְלֹא תֵּצֵא אִשָּׁה בְּמִנְעָל מְרוּפָּט...בְּמִנְעָל חָדָשׁ: A woman may not wear a shoe on Shabbat that is torn at the top because she might be mocked, causing her to remove the shoe and carry it. Likewise, she may not go out wearing a new shoe that she has never worn before, because if it does not fit her she might remove it. However, the *halakha* with regard to new shoes does not apply to men, since they are not as particular about those matters (Rambam *Sefer Zemanim, Hilkhot Shabbat* 19:15; *Shulḥan Arukh, Oraḥ Ḥayyim* 303:13).

The purity of a new shoe – טָהֳרַת מִנְעָל חָדָשׁ: A shoe on a last, although it has never been worn, can contract ritual impurity imparted by treading because it is a completed vessel. This ruling is in accordance with the opinion of the Rabbis (Rambam *Sefer Tahara, Hilkhot Kelim* 24:5).

Removing a shoe from a last – מִנְעָל מֵעַל אִימוּס: It is permitted to remove a new shoe or an old one (*Mishna Berura*) from a last on Shabbat, since the last is considered a utensil, albeit one whose primary function is prohibited. This ruling is in accordance with the opinion of the Rabbis. One may likewise cause the last to fall away from the shoe (*Mishna Berura*; Rambam *Sefer Zemanim, Hilkhot Shabbat* 26:12; *Shulḥan Arukh, Oraḥ Ḥayyim* 308:14).

NOTES

A shoe that is torn on top [*meruppat*] – מִנְעָל מְרוּפָּט: Some commentaries explain that *meruppat* means that the shoe is too large, so the foot does not fit snugly in the shoe.

***Ḥalitza* with a shoe – חֲלִיצָה בְּמִנְעָל:** The tradition observed by the Sages is that the shoe with which *ḥalitza* is performed must be suitable to be worn by the brother-in-law. If the shoe is torn on top, the concern is that it might not be suitable for wearing. Some explain that a shoe which is completely torn is invalid for *ḥalitza*, even after the fact (*Tosafot*).

A shoe that remains on a last – מִנְעָל שֶׁעַל גַּבֵּי אִימוּס: According to the *Tosefta* in tractate *Teharot*, Rabbi Eliezer and the Rabbis disagree whether or not a shoe, which is a cover that protects the last, is considered a vessel.

טַעְמָא – דְּרָפוּי, הָא לָא רָפוּי – לָא. הָנִיחָא לְאַבָּיֵי, דְּאָמַר: דָּבָר שֶׁמְּלַאכְתּוֹ לְאִיסּוּר, לְצוֹרֶךְ גּוּפוֹ – מוּתָּר, לְצוֹרֶךְ מְקוֹמוֹ – אָסוּר, שַׁפִּיר.

The Gemara infers: **The reason** it is permitted is only **because it is loose; however,** if it is **not loose, no,** it is prohibited. **It works out well according to** the opinion of **Abaye,** who **said** that moving **an object** whose primary **function** is **for** a **prohibited** use **for the purpose** of utilizing the object **itself** to perform a permitted action **it is permitted;** however, **for the purpose of utilizing its place, it is prohibited** to move it. **It is well** understood that it is prohibited to move the last if the shoe is tightly attached to it.

אֶלָּא לְרָבָא, דְּאָמַר: בֵּין לְצוֹרֶךְ גּוּפוֹ בֵּין לְצוֹרֶךְ מְקוֹמוֹ – מוּתָּר, מַאי אִירְיָא רָפוּי? אֲפִילּוּ לָא רָפוּי נַמִי!

However, according to Rava, who said that moving **an object whose** primary **function** is **for a prohibited** use, **whether for the purpose** of utilizing the object **itself** to perform a permitted action **or for the purpose of** utilizing **its place, is permitted, why** discuss **specifically** a case where it is **loose? Even if it were not loose,** it should **also** be permitted to move it.

דְּרַבִּי יְהוּדָה מִשּׁוּם דְּרַבִּי אֱלִיעֶזֶר הוּא; דְּתַנְיָא, רַבִּי יְהוּדָה אוֹמֵר מִשּׁוּם רַבִּי אֱלִיעֶזֶר: אִם הָיָה רָפוּי – מוּתָּר.

The Gemara answers: **That** *baraita* **is** the opinion of **Rabbi Yehuda in the name of Rabbi Eliezer,** and it is not a clarification of the opinion of the Rabbis. Although Rabbi Eliezer holds that the shoe is not yet completed, nevertheless, Rabbi Yehuda says in the name of Rabbi Eliezer that it is permitted to carry it. **As it was taught** in a *baraita*: **Rabbi Yehuda says in the name of Rabbi Eliezer: If it was** already **loose** and no longer requires a last, **it is permitted** to move it, since it is a completed vessel and no longer needs the last to shape it.

הדרן עלך תולין

Summary of **Perek XX**

This chapter did not come to final halakhic conclusions about the topics it addressed, each of which will be discussed further in the tractate. The discussion regarding building on Shabbat clarified that there is a distinction between building a permanent structure, which constitutes the prohibited labor of building, and building a temporary structure, which is not prohibited by Torah law. However, the Sages issued several decrees regarding the construction of temporary structures and created many distinctions regarding what is permitted or prohibited in the construction of these structures. There are no absolute guidelines, and each case must be analyzed separately.

The discussion regarding food preparation on Shabbat also did not arrive at firm conclusions with regard to the full range of relevant topics. The general principle of food preparation on Shabbat is that an item that is already edible may be added to and improved for human consumption, provided one does not violate any full-fledged prohibited labor. Although the chapter also discussed guidelines for preparing animal feed, this topic will be fully explained only in Chapter Twenty-four.

Introduction to **Perek XXI**

This chapter, too, deals with the laws of set-aside [*muktze*], items that are set aside and may not be handled on Shabbat, though from a fresh perspective. Here, too, the discussion is not about different items that are set aside, but about particular categories of items that all agree may not be moved on Shabbat because they are not utensils and are not fit to be handled. It was clear to the Sages that such items may not be handled directly; the discussion in this chapter primarily addresses the question of whether it is permitted to move these types of set-aside items, and set-aside items generally, through another object or for the sake of something else. In order to do this, it is necessary to clarify somewhat the scope of the concept of a base for a forbidden article. This refers to a utensil upon which a set-aside item rests; the utensil which serves as the base may not be handled, just as though it itself were set-aside. It is necessary to explain the circumstances in which it is permitted to remove the set-aside object in order to use the items that lie underneath or which are connected to it in some other way. The details of this *halakha* form the content of this chapter.

מתני׳ נוֹטֵל אָדָם אֶת בְּנוֹ וְהָאֶבֶן בְּיָדוֹ, וְכַלְכָּלָה וְהָאֶבֶן בְּתוֹכָהּ. וּמְטַלְטְלִין תְּרוּמָה טְמֵאָה עִם הַטְּהוֹרָה וְעִם הַחוּלִּין.

MISHNA **A person may take his son** in his hands on Shabbat, **and** even though there **is a stone,** which is a set-aside item, **in** the child's **hand,**[H] it is not prohibited to pick up the child. **And** it is permissible to take **a basket with a stone inside it** on Shabbat. **And one may move ritually impure *teruma,*** which may not be eaten and is set-aside, **with ritually pure *teruma,* as well as with non-sacred** produce.

רַבִּי יְהוּדָה אוֹמֵר: אַף מַעֲלִין אֶת הַמְּדוּמָּע בְּאֶחָד וּמֵאָה.

Rabbi Yehuda says: One may even lift a measure of *teruma* that was nullified from **a mixture**[N] **of one hundred** measures of non-sacred produce **and one** measure of *teruma.* When a measure of *teruma* is mixed with non-sacred produce, if the non-sacred produce is one hundred times the measure of *teruma,* the *teruma* is nullified. However, the Sages instituted that one must remove an amount equivalent to that measure of *teruma* and give it to a priest. The remainder is considered non-sacred produce. Rabbi Yehuda permits removing that measure on Shabbat to render the mixture permitted to eat.

גמ׳ אָמַר רָבָא: הוֹצִיא תִּינוֹק חַי וְכִיס תָּלוּי בְּצַוָּארוֹ – חַיָּיב מִשּׁוּם כִּיס. תִּינוֹק מֵת וְכִיס תָּלוּי לוֹ בְּצַוָּארוֹ – פָּטוּר.

GEMARA **Rava said:** If one **carried out a living baby** to the public domain on Shabbat, **and** the baby had **a purse** that **was hanging** around **his neck,**[H] **he is liable for** carrying out **the purse.** However, one who carried out **a dead baby, with a purse hanging** around **his neck, is exempt.**

״תִּינוֹק חַי וְכִיס תָּלוּי לוֹ בְּצַוָּארוֹ – חַיָּיב מִשּׁוּם כִּיס״ וְלִיחַיַּיב נַמִּי מִשּׁוּם תִּינוֹק!

Rava said: If one **carried out a living baby** to the public domain on Shabbat, **and a purse was hanging** around the baby's **neck, he is liable for** carrying out **the purse.** The Gemara asks: **And let him be liable for** carrying out the **baby as well.**

רָבָא כְּרַבִּי נָתָן סְבִירָא לֵיהּ, דַּאֲמַר: חַי נוֹשֵׂא אֶת עַצְמוֹ.

The Gemara responds: **Rava holds in accordance with** the opinion of **Rabbi Natan,**[N] **who said: A living being carries itself.** Therefore, one who carries a living being from one domain to another is not liable.

וְלִיבַּטֵל כִּיס לְגַבֵּי תִּינוֹק, מִי לָא תְּנַן: אֶת הַחַי בְּמִטָּה פָּטוּר אַף עַל הַמִּטָּה, שֶׁהַמִּטָּה טְפֵילָה לוֹ!

The Gemara asks: **And let** the **purse be negated relative to** the **baby;** and he should be exempt for carrying out the purse as well. **Didn't we learn in a mishna:** One who carries out a **living** person **on a bed is exempt even for** carrying out **the bed, because the bed is secondary to** the person? The same should be said with regard to the purse, relative to the baby.

מִטָּה לְגַבֵּי חַי – מְבַטְּלִי לֵיהּ, כִּיס לְגַבֵּי תִּינוֹק – לָא מְבַטְּלִי לֵיהּ.

The Gemara answers: In a case where **a bed** is **relative to a living being,** the living being **negates it,** as the bed is needed to carry the person and is secondary to him. However, in a case where **a purse** is **relative to a baby,** the baby does **not negate it,** since it is independently significant.

״תִּינוֹק מֵת וְכִיס תָּלוּי לוֹ בְּצַוָּארוֹ – פָּטוּר״ וְלִיחַיַּיב מִשּׁוּם תִּינוֹק! רָבָא כְּרַבִּי שִׁמְעוֹן סְבִירָא לֵיהּ, דְּאָמַר: כׇּל מְלָאכָה שֶׁאֵין צָרִיךְ לְגוּפָהּ – פָּטוּר עָלֶיהָ.

And Rava said: One who carried out **a dead baby with a purse hanging** around the baby's **neck is exempt.** The Gemara asks: **And let him be liable** for carrying out the **baby.** The Gemara answers: **Rava holds in accordance with** the opinion of **Rabbi Shimon, who said:** With regard to **any labor that is not needed for its own sake, one is exempt for** performing **it** on Shabbat. One who carries out a corpse does not do so because he needs it; rather, he does so for the sake of the corpse, i.e., to bury it or to move it from a degrading place. Therefore, he has not performed a labor prohibited by Torah law. Similarly, he is also exempt for carrying out the purse because due to his distress and mourning he negates the purse, as it is insignificant relative to the baby.

HALAKHA

A child holding a set-aside item in his hand – תִּינוֹק הַמַּחֲזִיק מוּקְצֶה בְּיָדוֹ: On Shabbat, if a child longs for his father to lift him, it is permitted for the father to lift the child even if he is holding a stone in his hand (Rambam *Sefer Zemanim, Hilkhot Shabbat* 25:16; *Shulḥan Arukh, Oraḥ Ḥayyim* 309:1).

A baby with a purse hanging around his neck – תִּינוֹק וְכִיס תָּלוּי בְּצַוָּארוֹ: One who carries a living baby with a purse hanging around his neck on Shabbat is liable for carrying the purse, since the purse is not secondary to the baby (Rambam *Sefer Zemanim, Hilkhot Shabbat* 18:17).

NOTES

One may lift from a mixture – מַעֲלִין אֶת הַמְּדוּמָּע: Nullification is an important concept in the *halakhot* governing mixtures of prohibited and permitted foods. In principle, when a portion of prohibited food is mixed together with a larger amount of permitted food, the prohibited food is nullified by the permitted food. The proportion of permitted food to prohibited food necessary for nullification varies based on the nature of the mixture and the prohibition.

For example, one hundred units of permitted grain are required to nullify one unit of teruma. If the ratio in the mixture is less than that, the entire mixture assumes the legal status of teruma and may be eaten only by a priest. In either case, the Sages require that one unit be removed from the mixture and given to a priest as *teruma.* That is done in order to prevent the priests from incurring financial loss; otherwise, they would lose the rights to the teruma in the mixture.

Rava holds in accordance with the opinion of Rabbi Natan – רָבָא כְּרַבִּי נָתָן סְבִירָא לֵיהּ: Rava himself is of the opinion that everyone agrees with Rabbi Natan that a living being carries itself. However, since this is not explicitly stated, the Gemara presents Rava's opinion simply as being in accordance with the opinion of Rabbi Natan (Rabbeinu Aharon HaLevi). Alternatively, the Rabbis only concede to Rabbi Natan with regard to a baby able to walk. Here, the Gemara is also referring to an infant who cannot yet walk (Rashba).

NOTES

Who has longings – **שֶׁיֵּשׁ לוֹ גִּיעְגּוּעִין**: Some commentaries explain that the baby longs for the stone and would cry if his father would take it from him. Therefore, the Sages permit the father to carry both of them (*Tosefot Rid*).

תְּנַן: נוֹטֵל אָדָם אֶת בְּנוֹ וְהָאֶבֶן בְּיָדוֹ. אָמְרִי דְּבֵי רַבִּי יַנַּאי: בְּתִינוֹק שֶׁיֵּשׁ לוֹ גִּיעְגּוּעִין עַל אָבִיו.

We learned in the mishna: **A person may take his son** in his hands on Shabbat; **and** this is permitted even though there **is a stone in** the child's **hand.** As it can be inferred from this mishna that the stone is negated relative to the child, why, then, is he liable in the case of a purse hanging around a live baby's neck? Let the purse be negated relative to the baby. The Sages **of the school of Rabbi Yannai say:** You cannot infer from this mishna that the stone is negated and therefore it is permitted to move it. Rather, the mishna is referring **to a baby who has longings**[N] **for his father.** It is permitted for the father to move the stone because if the father does not lift him, the baby might take ill.

אִי הָכִי,

The Gemara asks: **If so,**

Perek **XXI**
Daf **142** Amud **a**

NOTES

Even a dinar as well – **אֲפִילּוּ דִּינָר נַמִּי**: Rashi ruled stringently that one may not even hold the hand of a baby who is carrying money. The Ramban explains that the Sages issued a decree prohibiting only lifting the baby, lest he come to lift the dinar with his own hands.

The basket should be a base for a prohibited object – **תֶּיהֱוֵי כַּלְכָּלָה בָּסִיס לְדָבָר הָאָסוּר**: Some commentaries explained that this *halakha* is not based on the *halakhot* of a base for a prohibited object because those do not apply in a case where one forgets and misplaces the prohibited object on the base. Therefore, it is a misnomer to use the term: A base for a prohibited object. Rather, the Gemara asks why one needs to move the stone at all (*Tosefot Rid*). Others explained that the Gemara is referring to all cases involving baskets, including one where a stone is purposely placed in the basket. Furthermore, even in a case where one forgot the stone in the basket, the Sages only permitted carrying the basket in an unusual manner (*Me'iri*).

HALAKHA

A basket of fruit with a stone inside it – **כַּלְכָּלַת פֵּירוֹת וְאֶבֶן בָּהּ**: On Shabbat, if a basket full of fruit has a stone inside it, and the fruit will be ruined if spilled on the ground, as is the case with figs or grapes, one may lift and carry the basket with the fruit and the stone in it. However, if the fruit will not be ruined if spilled on the ground, one spills the fruit and the stone out of the basket, replaces the fruit and carries the basket (Rambam *Sefer Zemanim, Hilkhot Shabbat* 25:16; *Shulḥan Arukh, Oraḥ Ḥayyim* 309:3).

And let him…take the fruits in his hands – **וְנִינְקְטִינְהוּ בְּיָדַיִם**: On Shabbat, when fruits lie scattered in a courtyard, one may not gather them into a basket as one would do during the week. Rather, one should lift a few at a time and eat them (*Shulḥan Arukh, Oraḥ Ḥayyim* 335:5).

A broken basket – **כַּלְכָּלָה פְּחוּתָה**: A basket with a hole sealed by a stone may be carried on Shabbat, because the stone is part of the side of the basket (Rambam *Sefer Zemanim, Hilkhot Shabbat* 25:16; *Shulḥan Arukh, Oraḥ Ḥayyim* 335:2).

מַאי אִירְיָא אֶבֶן, אֲפִילּוּ דִּינָר נַמִּי! אַלְמָה אָמַר רָבָא: לֹא שָׁנוּ אֶלָּא אֶבֶן, אֲבָל דִּינָר – אָסוּר! אֶבֶן, אִי נָפְלָה לָהּ – לָא אָתֵי אֲבוּהּ לְאִיתוּיֵי דִּינָר, אִי נָפֵיל – אָתֵי אֲבוּהּ לְאַתוּיֵי.

why does the mishna refer **specifically** to moving **a stone?** The same should hold true **even** for **a dinar, as well.**[N] **Why,** then, **did Rava say: They only taught** this in a case where the child has **a stone** in his hand; **however,** if the child has **a dinar** in his hand, it is **prohibited** to lift the child? The Gemara answers: Actually, lifting the child with a dinar should also be permitted. However, the Sages issued a decree prohibiting lifting the child with a dinar because with regard to a **stone, if it falls, his father will not come to bring** it. However, with regard to **a dinar, if it falls, his father will come to bring it.**

תַּנְיָא כְּווֹתֵיהּ דְּרָבָא: הַמּוֹצִיא כֵּלָיו מְקוּפָּלִים וּמוּנָּחִים עַל כְּתֵפוֹ, וְסַנְדָּלָיו וְטַבְּעוֹתָיו בְּיָדוֹ – חַיָּיב. וְאִם הָיָה מְלוּבָּשׁ בָּהֶן פָּטוּר.

It was taught in a *baraita* **in accordance with** the opinion of **Rava: On** Shabbat, **one who carries out his clothes** to the public domain while they are **folded and placed on his shoulder, and his sandals** on his feet **and his rings in his hand,** not on his fingers, **is liable. And if he was wearing them, he is exempt** for all of them, as they are negated relative to him.

הַמּוֹצִיא אָדָם וְכֵלָיו עָלָיו, וְסַנְדָּלָיו בְּרַגְלָיו, וְטַבְּעוֹתָיו בְּיָדָיו – פָּטוּר. וְאִילּוּ הוֹצִיאָן כְּמוֹת שֶׁהֵן – חַיָּיב.

One who carries out a person with his garments on him, and his sandals on his feet, and his rings on the fingers of **his hands,** i.e., wearing all of his clothes and jewelry in the typical manner, **is exempt, whereas if he carried them out as they are,** i.e., the person was holding his clothes in his hands, **he is liable** for carrying out the clothes, just as Rava said.

״כַּלְכָּלָה וְהָאֶבֶן בְּתוֹכָהּ״. וְאַמַּאי?! תֶּיהֱוֵי כַּלְכָּלָה בָּסִיס לְדָבָר הָאָסוּר! אָמַר רַבָּה בַּר בַּר חָנָה אָמַר רַבִּי יוֹחָנָן: הָכָא בְּכַלְכָּלָה מְלֵאָה פֵּירוֹת עָסְקִינַן. וְלִישְׁדִינְהוּ לְפֵירֵי, וְנִישְׁדֵי לְאֶבֶן, וְנִינְקְטִינְהוּ בְּיָדַיִם! כִּדְרַבִּי אֶלְעַי אָמַר רַב: בְּפֵירוֹת הַמִּיטַּנְּפִין, הָכָא נַמִּי – בְּפֵירוֹת הַמִּיטַּנְּפִין –

We learned in the mishna: **And** it is permissible to take **a basket with a stone inside it** on Shabbat. The Gemara asks: **And why** may he do so? The **basket should be a base for a prohibited object,**[N] and a base for a prohibited object is set-aside and may not be moved on Shabbat. **Rabba bar bar Ḥana said** that **Rabbi Yoḥanan said: Here, we are dealing with a basket full of fruit.**[H] The basket is a base for permitted items as well, not only a base for the stone. The Gemara asks: Why may he move the basket and the stone? There is an alternative. **And let him throw the fruit and throw** the **stone** out of the basket, **and take** the fruit **in his hands,**[H] and there will be no need to move the stone. The Gemara answers: **As Rabbi Elai** said that **Rav said** in a different context: It is referring **to fruits that become soiled** and ruined. **Here, too,** it is referring **to fruits that become soiled** and ruined if he throws them down.

וְלִינַעֲרִינְהוּ נְעוֹרֵי! אָמַר רַב חִיָּיא בַּר אַשִׁי אָמַר רָבָא: הָכָא בְּכַלְכָּלָה פְּחוּתָה עָסְקִינַן, דְּאֶבֶן גּוּפָהּ נַעֲשֵׂית דּוֹפֶן לַכַּלְכָּלָה.

The Gemara asks a question: **And let him shake them** until the stone is on one side of the basket, enabling him to throw the stone out of the basket. **Rav Hiyya bar Ashi said** that **Rava said: Here, we are dealing with a broken basket**[H] with a hole, in which the **stone serves as a side of the basket** by sealing the hole. Therefore, he cannot throw it out of the basket.

"מְטַלְטְלִין תְּרוּמָה וכו׳". אָמַר רַב חִסְדָּא: לֹא שָׁנוּ אֶלָּא שֶׁטְּהוֹרָה לְמַטָּה וּטְמֵאָה לְמַעְלָה, אֲבָל טְהוֹרָה לְמַעְלָה וּטְמֵאָה לְמַטָּה – שָׁקֵיל לֵיהּ לַטְּהוֹרָה וְשָׁבֵיק לֵיהּ לַטְּמֵאָה.

We learned in the mishna: **And one may move** ritually impure *teruma*[H] with ritually pure *teruma*. **Rav Ḥisda said: They only taught** this in a case **where** the **pure** *teruma* **is on the bottom and the impure** *teruma* **is on the top.** In that case, if one wants to reach the pure *teruma*, there is no alternative to taking the impure *teruma* as well. **However,** if the **pure** *teruma* **is on the top and the impure** *teruma is* **on the bottom, he takes the pure** *teruma* **and leaves the impure** *teruma.*

וְכִי טְהוֹרָה לְמַטָּה נַמִי, לִישְׁדִינְהוּ וְלִינְקְטִינְהוּ! אָמַר רַבִּי אֶלְעַאי אָמַר רַב: בְּפֵירוֹת הַמִּיטַּנְּפִין עֲסָקִינַן.

The Gemara asks a question: **And when the pure** *teruma* **is on the bottom too, let him throw** the impure fruit, **and take** the pure fruit. **Rabbi Elai said** that **Rav said:** It is referring **to fruits that become soiled** and ruined, which cannot be thrown from the basket.

מֵיתִיבִי: "מְטַלְטְלִין תְּרוּמָה טְמֵאָה עִם הַטְּהוֹרָה וְעִם הַחוּלִּין, בֵּין שֶׁטְּהוֹרָה לְמַעְלָה וּטְמֵאָה לְמַטָּה, בֵּין שֶׁטְּמֵאָה לְמַעְלָה וּטְהוֹרָה לְמַטָּה" תְּיוּבְתָּא דְּרַב חִסְדָּא!

The Gemara **raises an objection** to the statement of Rav Ḥisda: **One may move impure** *teruma* **with the pure** *teruma* **and with the non-sacred produce, whether the pure is on the top and the impure is on the bottom, or whether the impure is on the top and the pure is on the bottom.** This is **a conclusive refutation of** the statement of **Rav Hisda.**

אָמַר לָךְ רַב חִסְדָּא: מַתְנִיתִין – לְצוֹרֶךְ גּוּפוֹ, בָּרַיְיתָא – לְצוֹרֶךְ מְקוֹמוֹ.

The Gemara answers that **Rav Ḥisda** could have **said to you: The mishna,** which, according to Rav Ḥisda, permits moving the impure *teruma* with the pure *teruma* only when the pure *teruma* is on top, is referring to a case where he needs the basket **for the purpose of** utilizing the object **itself,** i.e., he wants to eat the fruit. The *baraita* is referring to a case where he needs the basket **for the purpose of** utilizing **its place,** i.e., he wants to move the basket in order to vacate its place, in which case he may move it even if it contains impure *teruma* exclusively.

מַאי דּוֹחְקֵיהּ דְּרַב חִסְדָּא לְאוֹקְמֵי מַתְנִיתִין לְצוֹרֶךְ גּוּפוֹ?

The Gemara asks: **What impelled Rav Ḥisda to establish the mishna** as referring specifically to a case where he needs the basket **for the purpose of** utilizing the object **itself?** Why can't he explain the mishna as referring to any case?

אָמַר רָבָא: מַתְנִיתִין כְּוָותֵיהּ דַּיְיקָא, דְּקָתָנֵי סֵיפָא: מָעוֹת שֶׁעַל הַכַּר – מְנַעֵר אֶת הַכַּר וְהֵן נוֹפְלוֹת. וְאָמַר רַבָּה בַּר בַּר חָנָה אָמַר רַבִּי יוֹחָנָן: לֹא שָׁנוּ אֶלָּא לְצוֹרֶךְ גּוּפוֹ, אֲבָל לְצוֹרֶךְ מְקוֹמוֹ – מְטַלְטְלוֹ וְעוֹדָן עָלָיו. וּמִדְּסֵיפָא לְצוֹרֶךְ גּוּפוֹ – רֵישָׁא נַמִי לְצוֹרֶךְ גּוּפוֹ.

Rava said: The mishna is **precise in accordance with** the opinion of Rav Ḥisda, **as it is taught in the latter clause,** the next mishna: With regard to **coins that are on a cushion, he shakes the cushion and** the coins **fall. And Rabba bar bar Ḥana said** that **Rabbi Yoḥanan said:** They **only taught** that he may shake the cushion in a case where it is **for the purpose of** utilizing the cushion **itself. However,** if he needs it **for the purpose of** utilizing **its place, he may move it,** even though the coins **are still on it. And from** the fact **that the latter clause** of the mishna is referring to a case where he needs the cushion **for the purpose of** utilizing the cushion **itself, the first clause, too,** is referring to a case where he needs the basket **for the purpose of** utilizing the basket **itself.**

"רַבִּי יְהוּדָה אוֹמֵר אַף מַעֲלִין וכו׳". וְאַמַּאי?! הָא קָא מְתַקֵּן!

We learned in the mishna that **Rabbi Yehuda says. One may even lift** a measure of *teruma* that was nullified from a mixture of one hundred measures of non-sacred produce and one measure of *teruma.* The Gemara asks: **And why** is it permitted? **Isn't he rendering** the produce **fit** for consumption? The Sages issued a decree prohibiting the performance of any action that renders an item fit for use on Shabbat.

רַבִּי יְהוּדָה כְּרַבִּי אֱלִיעֶזֶר סְבִירָא לֵיהּ, דְּאָמַר: תְּרוּמָה בְּעֵינָא מֻחְתָּא.

The Gemara answers: **Rabbi Yehuda holds in accordance with** the opinion of **Rabbi Eliezer, who said:** *Teruma* is considered as if it is **placed in its pure** unadulterated **state.** By lifting the measure of *teruma,* one does not render the rest of the mixture fit for consumption. It is considered as if the measure of *teruma* never intermingled with the rest of the produce and the measure that he lifted from the produce is the measure that fell into the produce.

דִּתְנַן: סְאָה תְּרוּמָה שֶׁנָּפְלָה לְפָחוֹת מִמֵּאָה נִדְמְעוּ, וְנָפַל מִן הַמְדוּמָּע לְמָקוֹם אַחֵר. רַבִּי אֱלִיעֶזֶר אוֹמֵר: מְדַמַּעַת כִּתְרוּמַת וַדַּאי.

As we learned in a mishna: A *se'a* of *teruma* **that fell into less than one hundred** *se'a* of non-sacred produce causes it to become a prohibited **mixture.** The *teruma* is not nullified by the non-sacred produce. **And** then, if a *se'a* **from the mixture fell into a different place** with non-sacred produce, **Rabbi Eliezer says:** The *se'a* from the original mixture **renders it a** prohibited **mixture** in the same way that **definite** *teruma* would. This is due to the concern that the same *se'a* of *teruma* that fell into the first mixture never intermingled with the produce and subsequently fell into the second mixture. Therefore, it requires nullification like unadulterated *teruma.*

HALAKHA

Moving ***teruma*** **– טִלְטוּל תְּרוּמָה:** It is permitted for an Israelite to carry *teruma* on Shabbat, even though it is prohibited for him to eat it. In addition, ritually impure *teruma,* which may not be eaten, may be carried together with pure *teruma* if the following conditions are met: (1) Both the impure and the pure *teruma* are in the same vessel; (2) the pure produce is beneath the impure produce; (3) the fruit will be ruined when spilled on the ground, as is the case with figs or grapes, rendering moot the option of spilling the contents of the vessel and replacing only the pure *teruma.* However, in a situation where the produce will not be ruined when spilled on the ground, one empties the vessel and replaces the permitted produce, in accordance with the opinions of Rav Ḥisda and Rabbi Elai (Rambam *Sefer Zemanim, Hilkhot Shabbat* 25:20).

וַחֲכָמִים אוֹמְרִים: אֵין הַמְדוּמָּע מְדַמֵּעַ אֶלָּא לְפִי חֶשְׁבּוֹן.

And the Rabbis say: The *se'a* from the original prohibited **mixture only renders** the second one a prohibited **mixture according to** the **proportion** of *teruma* in the entire mixture. In other words, the percentage of *teruma* in each *se'a* of the original mixture is representative of the percentage of *teruma* in the entire mixture. Only that measure of *teruma* need be nullified. Rabbi Eliezer's opinion that the *teruma* in the mixture is not considered mixed, and it is considered as if it was placed in its pure unadulterated state, corresponds to Rabbi Yehuda's opinion that by lifting the measure of *teruma,* one does not render the rest of the mixture fit for consumption.

אֵימַר דִּשְׁמַעְתְּ לֵיהּ לְחוּמְרָא, לְקוּלָּא מִי שְׁמַעְתְּ לֵיהּ?!

The Gemara rejects this: **Say that you heard** that Rabbi Eliezer expresses his opinion in this matter **to rule stringently. Did you hear** him express his opinion **to rule leniently?** He expressed concern lest the fallen *teruma* might not have intermingled with the non-sacred produce in the first mixture, and therefore, the second mixture is prohibited. However, he does not consider this a certainty.

אֶלָּא הוּא דְּאָמַר כְּרַבִּי שִׁמְעוֹן, כִּדְתְנַן: סְאָה תְּרוּמָה שֶׁנָּפְלָה לְמֵאָה, וְלֹא הִסְפִּיק לַהֲגְבִּיהָּ עַד שֶׁנָּפְלָה אַחֶרֶת – הֲרֵי זוֹ אֲסוּרָה. וְרַבִּי שִׁמְעוֹן מַתִּיר.

Rather, Rabbi Yehuda **stated his** *halakha* **in accordance with** the opinion of **Rabbi Shimon, as we learned** in a mishna: If a ***se'a*** of ***teruma*** **fell into one hundred** *se'a* of non-sacred produce, **and he did not manage to lift** that *se'a* from the mixture **until another** *se'a* of *teruma* **fell** into the mixture, **this** entire mixture **is prohibited.** This is because two *se'a* of *teruma* are mixed with one hundred *se'a* of non-sacred produce. **And Rabbi Shimon permits** the mixture. Rabbi Shimon holds that the first *se'a* that fell into the produce is not mixed with it; it is placed in its unadulterated state. When the second *se'a* falls, it is also placed in its unadulterated state, and the two *se'a* do not join together.

וּמִמַּאי? דִּילְמָא הָתָם בְּהָא קָמִיפַּלְגִי; דְּתַנָּא קַמָּא סָבַר: אַף עַל גַּב דְּנָפְלוּ בְּזֶה אַחַר זֶה – כְּמַאן דְּנָפַל בְּבַת אַחַת דָּמֵי, וְהָא לַחֲמִשִּׁין נָפְלָה, וְהָא לַחֲמִשִּׁין נָפְלָה. וְרַבִּי שִׁמְעוֹן סָבַר: קַמַּיְיתָא בְּטֵיל בְּמֵאָה, וְהָא תִּיבְטִיל בְּמֵאָה וְחַד!

The Gemara rejects this comparison: **And from what** does that conclusion ensue? **Perhaps there, they are disagreeing with regard to this: That the first *tanna* holds: Even though** two *se'a* of *teruma* **fell one after another, it is as** though **they fell at once, and this** *se'a* of *teruma* **fell into fifty** *se'a* of non-sacred produce, **and this** *se'a* of *teruma* **fell into fifty** *se'a* of non-sacred produce, which are insufficient to nullify *teruma.* **And Rabbi Shimon holds: The first** *se'a* **was nullified** immediately when it fell **into one hundred** *se'a,* **and this** *se'a* **will be nullified in one hundred and one** *se'a.* There is no connection between this dispute and the opinion that by lifting the measure of *teruma,* one does not render the rest of the mixture fit for consumption.

אֶלָּא, הוּא דְּאָמַר כְּרַבִּי שִׁמְעוֹן בֶּן אֶלְעָזָר. דְּתַנְיָא, רַבִּי שִׁמְעוֹן בֶּן אֶלְעָזָר אוֹמֵר: נוֹתֵן עֵינָיו בְּצַד זֶה וְאוֹכֵל מִצַּד אַחֵר.

Rather, Rabbi Yehuda **stated his** *halakha* **in accordance with** the opinion of **Rabbi Shimon ben Elazar. As it was taught** in a *baraita* that **Rabbi Shimon ben Elazar says:** One need not lift a *se'a* from the mixture in order to render it permitted to eat. It is sufficient if **he casts his eyes on this side** of the mixture and decides to separate a *se'a* from the produce on that side, **and he eats from a different side** of the mixture and physically separates the *se'a* later. Lifting a *se'a* from the mixture does not render the mixture fit for consumption, as it is permitted to partake from the mixture even without removing a *se'a*. That is the rationale for Rabbi Yehuda's opinion.

וּמִי סָבַר לֵיהּ כְּוָותֵיהּ?

The Gemara asks: **And does** Rabbi Yehuda **hold in accordance with** the opinion of Rabbi Shimon ben Elazar?

Perek **XXI**
Daf **142** Amud **b**

וְהָא מִיפְלַג פָּלֵיג עִילָּוֵיהּ; דְּתַנְיָא, רַבִּי יְהוּדָה אוֹמֵר: מַעֲלִין אֶת הַמְדוּמָּע בְּאֶחָד וּמֵאָה, רַבִּי שִׁמְעוֹן בֶּן אֶלְעָזָר אוֹמֵר: נוֹתֵן עֵינָיו בְּצַד זֶה וְאוֹכֵל מִצַּד אַחֵר!

Doesn't he disagree with him? As it was taught in a *baraita* that **Rabbi Yehuda says: One may lift** a measure of *teruma* that was nullified from **a mixture of one hundred** measures of non-sacred produce **and one** measure of *teruma.*[N] **Rabbi Shimon ben Elazar says: One casts his eyes on this side** of the mixture and decides to separate a *se'a* from the produce on that side, **and he eats from a different side** of the mixture.

NOTES

Opinions with regard to lifting from a mixture of *teruma* – שִׁיטוֹת בְּהַעֲלָאַת הַמְדוּמָּע: The Gemara concludes that both Rabbi Yehuda and Rabbi Shimon ben Elazar agree that there is no need to actually remove a portion from the mixture. The question is: With regard to what do they disagree? According to some commentaries, Rabbi Shimon ben Elazar permits looking to one side and eating from the other. However, he believes that one may not take remedial action and separate part of the produce. Rabbi Yehuda, however, holds that removing part of the produce is not a remedial action, as eating the mixture is permitted without it. Therefore, removing part of the produce is permitted on Shabbat (*Tosefot Rid*).

דְּרַבִּי יְהוּדָה עֲדִיפָא מִדְּרַבִּי שִׁמְעוֹן בֶּן אֶלְעָזָר.

The Gemara rejects this: Fundamentally, the two *tanna'im* agree, but the opinion of **Rabbi Yehuda is more far-reaching than** the opinion of **Rabbi Shimon ben Elazar.** Rabbi Yehuda says that since thought is sufficient, lifting the *se'a* does not render the produce fit for consumption, and it is preferable if he lifts the *se'a* even on Shabbat.

מתני׳ הָאֶבֶן שֶׁעַל פִּי הֶחָבִית – מַטָּה עַל צִדָּהּ וְהִיא נוֹפֶלֶת. הָיְתָה בֵּין הֶחָבִיּוֹת – מַגְבִּיהַּ, וּמַטָּה עַל צִדָּהּ וְהִיא נוֹפֶלֶת.

MISHNA With regard to **a stone,** which is set-aside on Shabbat and may not be moved, that was placed **on the mouth of a barrel, one tilts** the barrel **on its side, and** the stone **falls. If** the barrel **was among** other **barrels,** and the other barrels might break if the stone falls on them, **he lifts** the barrel to distance it from the other barrels, **and** then **tilts it on its side, and** the stone **falls.**

מָעוֹת שֶׁעַל הַכַּר – מְנַעֵר אֶת הַכַּר וְהֵן נוֹפְלוֹת. הָיְתָה עָלָיו לִשְׁלֶשֶׁת – מְקַנְּחָהּ בִּסְמַרְטוּט, הָיְתָה שֶׁל עוֹר – נוֹתְנִין עָלֶיהָ מַיִם עַד שֶׁתִּכְלֶה.

With regard to **coins that are on a cushion,**[H] **he shakes the cushion and** the coins **fall. If there was bird dung** (*Arukh*) **on** the cushion,[H] **he wipes it with a rag,** but he may not wash it with water due to the prohibition against laundering. If the cushion **was** made **of leather,** and laundering is not a concern, **he places water on it until** the bird dung **ceases.**

גמ׳ אָמַר רַב הוּנָא אָמַר רַב: לֹא שָׁנוּ אֶלָּא בְּשׁוֹכֵחַ, אֲבָל בְּמַנִּיחַ – נַעֲשָׂה בָּסִיס לְדָבָר הָאָסוּר.

GEMARA **Rav Huna said** that **Rav said: They only taught** this *halakha* with regard to a stone in a case **where one forgets** the stone on the barrel. **However, if he places** the stone on the barrel, the barrel **becomes a base for a prohibited object,** which itself may not be moved throughout Shabbat.

[״הָיְתָה בֵּין הֶחָבִיּוֹת כו׳״]. מַאן תַּנָּא דְּכָל הֵיכָא דְּאִיכָּא אִיסּוּרָא וְהֶיתֵּרָא – בְּהֶיתֵּרָא טָרְחִינַן, בְּאִיסּוּרָא לָא טָרְחִינַן?

We learned in the mishna: **If** the barrel **was among** other **barrels,** he lifts the barrel and then tilts it on its side, and the stone falls. The Gemara asks: **Who is** the ***tanna*** who holds **that any place that there is a prohibited** item **and a permitted** item, **we** may **exert** ourselves **for the permitted** item,[N] but **we** may **not exert** ourselves **for the prohibited** item? One must exert himself to lift the barrel, and he may not remove the stone, although doing so would minimize his exertion.

אָמַר רַבָּה בַּר בַּר חָנָה אָמַר רַבִּי יוֹחָנָן: רַבָּן שִׁמְעוֹן בֶּן גַּמְלִיאֵל הִיא, דִּתְנַן: הַבּוֹרֵר קִטְנִית בְּיוֹם טוֹב, בֵּית שַׁמַּאי אוֹמְרִים בּוֹרֵר אוֹכֶל וְאוֹכֵל, וּבֵית הִלֵּל אוֹמְרִים: בּוֹרֵר כְּדַרְכּוֹ בְּחֵיקוֹ וּבְתַמְחוּי.

Rabba bar bar Ḥana said that **Rabbi Yoḥanan said: It is Rabban Shimon ben Gamliel. As we learned** in a mishna: With regard to **one who selects legumes on a Festival,**[H] separating edible and inedible, **Beit Shammai say: He selects food and eats** it immediately and leaves the waste. **And Beit Hillel say: He selects in his usual manner,** and may even remove the waste and leave the food, **in his lap or in a large vessel.**

וְתַנְיָא, אָמַר רַבָּן שִׁמְעוֹן בֶּן גַּמְלִיאֵל: בַּמֶּה דְּבָרִים אֲמוּרִים – שֶׁהָאוֹכֶל מְרוּבֶּה עַל הַפְּסוֹלֶת, אֲבָל פְּסוֹלֶת מְרוּבָּה עַל הָאוֹכֶל – דִּבְרֵי הַכֹּל בּוֹרֵר אוֹכֶל

And it was taught in a *baraita* that **Rabban Shimon ben Gamliel said: In what** case **are these matters,** the dispute between Beit Shammai and Beit Hillel, **stated:** In a case **where the** quantity of the **food is greater than the** quantity of **the waste. However, if** the quantity of **the waste is greater than the** quantity of the **food, everyone agrees** that **one selects** the **food** to avoid the exertion involved in removing the waste, which itself may not be moved. The same is true here. He moves the barrel and not the stone, which is like waste.[N]

וְהָא הָכָא, דְּכִי אוֹכֶל מְרוּבֶּה עַל הַפְּסוֹלֶת דָּמֵי!

The Gemara asks: **And here,** in the case of the barrel, **isn't it comparable to** a case where **the food** is **greater than the waste,** as the barrel, which is food, is bigger and heavier than the stone. In addition, it is easier to move the stone. Nevertheless, he is not permitted to do so, in accordance with the opinion of Beit Hillel.

הָכָא נַמִי, כֵּיוָן דְּאִי בָּעֵי לְמִישְׁקַל לָא מִשְׁתַּקֵיל לֵיהּ יַיִן עַד דְּשָׁקֵיל לָהּ לְאֶבֶן – כִּפְסוֹלֶת מְרוּבָּה עַל הָאוֹכֶל דָּמֵי.

The Gemara answers: **Here, too, since if he wants to take** the wine, the **wine cannot be taken until he removes the stone,** the legal status of the stone is **like** that of **waste** which is **greater** in quantity **than the food,** and it cannot be likened to the case of selecting. In this case, he is unable to move the barrel without moving the stone.

הָיְתָה בֵּין הֶחָבִיּוֹת מַגְבִּיהַּ. תַּנְיָא, רַבִּי יוֹסֵי אוֹמֵר: הָיְתָה הֶחָבִית מוּנַּחַת בָּאוֹצָר, אוֹ שֶׁהָיוּ כְּלֵי זְכוּכִית מוּנָּחִין תַּחְתֶּיהָ – מַגְבִּיהַּ לְמָקוֹם אַחֵר, וּמַטָּה עַל צִדָּהּ וְהִיא נוֹפֶלֶת. וְנוֹטֵל הֵימֶנָּה מַה שֶּׁצָּרִיךְ לוֹ, וּמַחֲזִירָהּ לִמְקוֹמָהּ.

We learned in the mishna: **If** the barrel **was among** other **barrels, he lifts** the barrel. **It was taught** in a *baraita*: **Rabbi Yosei says: If the barrel was placed in a storeroom** amongst other barrels, or if **glass vessels were placed beneath it,** preventing him from tilting the barrel and letting the stone fall, **he lifts** the barrel and moves it **to a different place, and he tilts it on its side, and** the stone **falls. And** then **he takes from** the barrel **what he needs, and restores** the barrel **to its place.**

HALAKHA

A stone on the mouth of a barrel…coins that are on a cushion – הָאֶבֶן שֶׁעַל פִּי הֶחָבִית...מָעוֹת שֶׁעַל הַכַּר: On Shabbat, in a case where there is a stone on top of a barrel or coins on top of a cushion, one tilts the barrel and lets the stone fall, and similarly, one tilts the cushion and lets the coins fall. However, if the barrel was situated among other barrels and tilting the barrel where it stands is impossible, one may move the barrel with the stone and tilt it elsewhere. This applies only if one forgot the stone on the barrel on Shabbat eve. If one left it there intentionally, it is prohibited, in accordance with Rav's explanation of the mishna (Rambam *Sefer Zemanim, Hilkhot Shabbat* 25:17; *Shulḥan Arukh, Oraḥ Ḥayyim* 309:4).

If there was bird dung on it – הָיְתָה עָלָיו לִשְׁלֶשֶׁת: It is prohibited to clean a dirty garment with water on Shabbat due to the prohibition of laundering. Rather, one may gently wipe it with a rag, making certain not to squeeze liquid from the rag. If the garment was made of leather, it is permitted to rub it clean with water (Rambam *Sefer Zemanim, Hilkhot Shabbat* 22:18; *Shulḥan Arukh, Oraḥ Ḥayyim* 302:9).

One who selects legumes on a festival – הַבּוֹרֵר קִטְנִיּוֹת בְּיוֹם טוֹב: One may select legumes in the typical manner on a Festival, by selecting the waste from the food. However, one may not do so with a vessel designated for this purpose. If the quantity of the waste is greater than the quantity of the food, one selects the food from the waste, unless doing so requires extra exertion. The *halakha* is in accordance with the opinions of Beit Hillel and Rabban Shimon ben Gamliel (Rambam *Sefer Zemanim, Hilkhot Yom Tov* 3:15; *Shulḥan Arukh, Oraḥ Ḥayyim* 510:2).

NOTES

We may exert ourselves for the permitted item – בְּהֶיתֵּרָא טָרְחִינַן: This statement, by Rabban Shimon ben Gamliel, can be understood to mean that when the effort required to select the food and the waste is equal, it is preferable to select the food rather than the waste.

A barrel, waste, and food – חָבִית פְּסוֹלֶת וְאוֹכֶל: According to Rashi, who has a variant reading of the Gemara, the explanation is simple. Since in any case one must lift the entire barrel to access the wine, there is no reason to permit first removing the stone alone. With regard to the standard version of the Gemara, there are a number of interpretations suggested by the different commentaries. The essence of these interpretations is that if one would like to access the barrel, he has no choice but to move the stone. Therefore, the stone has the status of waste, as in a case where the quantity of waste is greater than the quantity of food. Consequently, one may not exert himself to move the stone alone (see Ramban and Rashba).

HALAKHA

Moving for the purpose of utilizing its place – **טִלְטוּל לְצוֹרֶךְ מְקוֹמוֹ**: Tilting a barrel to remove a stone or shaking a cushion to remove coins is permitted only in cases where one seeks to utilize the barrel or the cushion itself. However, if he seeks to utilize its place, one may move the barrel with the stone, or the cushion with the coins (Rambam *Sefer Zemanim, Hilkhot Shabbat* 25:17; *Shulḥan Arukh, Oraḥ Ḥayyim* 309:5).

Moving by means of a loaf or a baby – **טִלְטוּל עַל יְדֵי כִּכָּר אוֹ תִּינוֹק**: If one must move a corpse to maintain its dignity, or if one seeks to utilize the place that the corpse is lying, he may place a loaf of bread or a baby on the corpse and move it. This applies only to moving a corpse, but not to other set-aside objects that may not be moved (Rambam *Sefer Zemanim, Hilkhot Shabbat* 26:21; *Shulḥan Arukh, Oraḥ Ḥayyim* 311:5).

NOTES

For the purpose of utilizing its place – **לְצוֹרֶךְ מְקוֹמוֹ**: This does not mean that utilizing its place is more significant than utilizing itself. Rather, if one seeks to utilize the cushion itself, he can shake off coins without moving them. If one seeks to utilize its place, however, he must move the coins as well (*Tiferet Shmuel*).

Holds in accordance with the opinion of Rabbi Yehuda – **כְּרַבִּי יְהוּדָה סְבִירָא לֵיהּ**: The dispute between Rabbi Yehuda and Rabbi Shimon is with regard to food that was originally designated for consumption by people, but that became spoiled. Rabbi Yehuda deems the food set-aside because it is no longer fit for consumption by people. Therefore, it is prohibited to move it, even for animals. In contrast, Rabbi Shimon holds that there is no prohibition of set-aside, and therefore, it is permitted to move food that is unfit for consumption by people.

LANGUAGE

Saddlebag [*diskaya*] – **דִּסְקַיָּא**: From the Greek δισάκκιον, *disakyon*, which means a double-bag or two bags tied together loaded onto an animal.

"מָעוֹת שֶׁעַל הַכַּר". אָמַר רַב חִיָּיא בַּר אַשִׁי אָמַר רַב: לֹא שָׁנוּ אֶלָּא בְּשׁוֹכֵחַ, אֲבָל בְּמַנִּיחַ – נַעֲשָׂה בָּסִיס לְדָבָר הָאָסוּר.

We learned in the mishna: With regard to **coins that are on a cushion,** he shakes the cushion and the coins fall. **Rav Ḥiyya bar Ashi said** that **Rav said: They only taught** this *halakha* with regard to a case **where one forgets** the coins on the cushion; **however, if he places** the coins on the cushion, the cushion **becomes a base for a prohibited object** and may not be moved at all.

אָמַר רַבָּה בַּר בַּר חָנָה אָמַר רַבִּי יוֹחָנָן: לֹא שָׁנוּ אֶלָּא לְצוֹרֶךְ גּוּפוֹ, אֲבָל לְצוֹרֶךְ מְקוֹמוֹ – מְטַלְטְלוֹ וְעוֹדָן עָלָיו. וְכֵן תָּנֵי חִיָּיא בַּר רַב מִדִּיפְתִּי: לֹא שָׁנוּ אֶלָּא לְצוֹרֶךְ גּוּפוֹ, אֲבָל לְצוֹרֶךְ מְקוֹמוֹ – מְטַלְטְלוֹ וְעוֹדָן עָלָיו.

Rabba bar bar Ḥana said that **Rabbi Yoḥanan said: They only taught** the *halakha* that one shakes the cushion and the coins fall, when he needs the cushion **for the purpose of** utilizing the cushion **itself; but** if he needs it **for the purpose of** utilizing **its place,**[HN] **he moves** the cushion **with** the coins **still on it. And likewise, Hiyya bar Rav from Difti taught** in a *baraita:* **They only taught** the *halakha* that one shakes the cushion and the coins fall, when he needs the cushion **for the purpose of** utilizing the cushion **itself, but** if he needs it **for the purpose of** utilizing **its place, he moves** the cushion **with** the coins **still on it.**

"מָעוֹת שֶׁעַל הַכַּר מְנַעֵר וכו׳". אָמַר רַבִּי אוֹשַׁעְיָא: שָׁכַח אַרְנְקִי בֶּחָצֵר – מַנִּיחַ עָלֶיהָ כִּכָּר אוֹ תִּינוֹק, וּמְטַלְטְלָהּ. אָמַר רַב יִצְחָק: שָׁכַח לְבֵינָה בֶּחָצֵר – מַנִּיחַ עָלֶיהָ כִּכָּר אוֹ תִּינוֹק, וּמְטַלְטְלָהּ. אָמַר רַבִּי יְהוּדָה בַּר שֵׁילָא אָמַר רַבִּי אַסִי: פַּעַם אַחַת שָׁכְחוּ דִּסְקַיָּא מְלֵאָה מָעוֹת בִּסְרַטְיָא, וּבָאוּ וְשָׁאֲלוּ אֶת רַבִּי יוֹחָנָן, וְאָמַר לָהֶן: הַנִּיחוּ עָלֶיהָ כִּכָּר אוֹ תִּינוֹק וְטַלְטְלוּהָ.

We learned in the mishna: With regard to **coins that are on a cushion, he shakes** the cushion and the coins fall.

Rabbi Oshaya said: If **one forgot a purse** of money **in the courtyard** on Shabbat eve, and he remembers it on Shabbat and wants to bring it into the house, **he places a loaf** of bread **or a baby on it and moves it.**[H] The purse becomes a base for a permitted object and may be moved.

Rav Yitzhak said: If **one forgot a brick in the courtyard, he places a loaf** of bread **or a baby on it and moves it.**

Rabbi Yehuda bar Sheila said that **Rabbi Asi said: Once, they forgot a saddlebag** [*diskaya*][L] **full of coins in a main street, and they came and asked Rabbi Yoḥanan, and he said to them: Place a loaf or a baby on it, and move it.**

אָמַר מָר זוּטְרָא: הִלְכְתָא כְּכׇל הָנֵי שְׁמַעְתָּתָא בְּשׁוֹכֵחַ. רַב אַשִׁי אָמַר: אֲפִילּוּ שָׁכַח נָמֵי [לֹא], וְלֹא אָמְרוּ כִּכָּר אוֹ תִּינוֹק אֶלָּא לְמֵת בִּלְבַד.

Mar Zutra said: The *halakha* **is in accordance with all these statements in** the case of one who **forgets.** However, if one intentionally left an object, even a valuable object, on Shabbat eve, he may not employ artifice and move it the following day. **Rav Ashi said:** If **one forgot,** he may **also not** employ artifice, **and they only stated** that movement by means of **a loaf or a baby for** the purposes of moving **a corpse alone.**

אַבָּיֵי מַנַּח כַּפָּא אַכִּיפֵי. רָבָא מַנַּח סַכִּינָא אַבַּר יוֹנָה וּמְטַלְטְלָהּ. אָמַר רַב יוֹסֵף: כַּמָּה חֲרִיפָא שְׁמַעְתָּתָא דְּדַרְדְּקֵי! אֵימַר דְּאָמוּר רַבָּנַן בְּשׁוֹכֵחַ, לְכַתְּחִילָּה מִי אָמוּר?!

The Gemara relates: **Abaye** would **place a spoon on bundles** of produce, so that he would be able to move the bundles because of the spoon. **Rava** would **place a knife on a** slaughtered **young dove and move it. Rav Yosef said** mockingly: **How sharp is the** *halakha* **of children? Say** that **the Sages stated** this *halakha* only in a case **where one forgets,** but **did they say** that one may do so ***ab initio***?

אָמַר אַבָּיֵי: אִי לָאו דְּאָדָם חָשׁוּב אֲנָא, כַּפָּא אַכִּיפֵי לָמָּה לִי? הָא חֲזוּ לְמִיזְגָּא עֲלַיְיהוּ!

Abaye explained his actions and **said: If not** for the fact that **I am an important person, why** would **I** need to place **a spoon on the bundles? Aren't** the bundles themselves **suited to lean upon?** I could have carried the bundles without the spoon.

אָמַר רָבָא: אֲנָא, אִי לָאו דְּאָדָם חָשׁוּב אֲנָא – סַכִּינָא אַבַּר יוֹנָה לָמָּה לִי? הָא חֲזֵי לִי לְאוּמְצָא!

Similarly, **Rava said: If not** for the fact that **I am an important person, why** would **I** need to place **a knife on a young dove? Isn't** the young dove itself **suited** to be eaten as **raw meat?**

טַעְמָא – דַּחֲזֵי לְאוּמְצָא, הָא לָא חֲזֵי לְאוּמְצָא – לָא. לְמֵימְרָא דְּרָבָא כְּרַבִּי יְהוּדָה סְבִירָא לֵיהּ?

The Gemara asks: **The reason** that it is permitted to move the slaughtered dove **is** because **it is suited** to be eaten by a person as **raw meat;** but if **it is not suited** to be eaten by a person as **raw meat, no,** it may not be moved. **Is that to say** that **Rava holds in accordance with the** opinion of **Rabbi Yehuda,**[N] that on Shabbat it is prohibited to move food that was originally designated for human consumption and is now only suited for animal consumption?

וְהָאָמַר רָבָא לְשַׁמָּעֵיהּ: טְווֹי לִי בַּר אַוְוזָא, וּשְׁדִי מֵיעֵיהּ לְשׁוּנְרָא!

Didn't Rava say to his attendant on a Festival: **Roast a duck for me, and throw its intestines to the cat.** Moving the duck's intestines was permitted in order to feed the cat. Similarly, moving the dove should have been permitted not because it is raw meat fit for consumption by a person, but because it is suited for consumption by a dog.

הָתָם כֵּיוָן דְּמַסְרַח – דַּעְתֵּיהּ עִילָּוֵיהּ מֵאֶתְמוֹל.

The Gemara answers: **There, since** the intestines **will putrefy** as time passes, they are **on his mind from yesterday.** Since Shabbat eve, he has had in mind to feed them to the cat.

הָכִי נַמִי מִסְתַּבְּרָא, דְּרָבָא כְּרַבִּי יְהוּדָה סְבִירָא לֵיהּ. דְּדָרֵשׁ רָבָא: אִשָּׁה לֹא תִּכָּנֵס לְבֵית הָעֵצִים לִיטּוֹל מֵהֶן אוּד, וְאוּד שֶׁנִּשְׁבַּר – אָסוּר לְהַסִּיקוֹ בְּיוֹם טוֹב, לְפִי שֶׁמַּסִּיקִין בְּכֵלִים וְאֵין מַסִּיקִין בְּשִׁבְרֵי כֵלִים. שְׁמַע מִינַּהּ.

The Gemara adds: **So too, it is reasonable** to say **that Rava holds in accordance with** the opinion of **Rabbi Yehuda, as Rava taught: A woman may not enter the wood storehouse to take a** wooden **poker** to stoke a fire on a Festival.[H] **And** with regard to **a poker that broke, it is prohibited to kindle** a fire with **it on a Festival, as one may kindle** a fire on a Festival **with vessels** that may be moved, **but one may not kindle** a fire **with broken vessels** that broke during the Festival. They are set-aside and prohibited. **Conclude from it** that Rava ruled in accordance with the opinion of Rabbi Yehuda with regard to the *halakhot* of set-aside.

מתני׳ בֵּית שַׁמַּאי אוֹמְרִים: מַעֲבִירִין מֵעַל הַשֻּׁלְחָן עֲצָמוֹת וּקְלִיפִּין, וּבֵית הִלֵּל אוֹמְרִים: מְסַלֵּק אֶת הַטַּבְלָא כּוּלָּהּ וּמְנַעֲרָהּ.

MISHNA **Beit Shammai say: One** may **clear bones and shells** left from the Shabbat meal **from the table**[H] with his hand. **And Beit Hillel say: One** may **remove the entire board** [*tavla*][L] that is the table surface **and shake** the bones and shells **off of it,** but he may not lift them with his hand because they are set-aside and may not be moved.

מַעֲבִירִין מִלִּפְנֵי הַשֻּׁלְחָן פֵּירוּרִין פָּחוֹת מִכַּזַּיִת, וְשַׂעַר שֶׁל אֲפוּנִין, וּשְׂעַר עֲדָשִׁים – מִפְּנֵי שֶׁהוּא מַאֲכַל בְּהֵמָה.

One may **clear** bread **crumbs from the table,** even if they are **less than an olive-bulk, and pea and lentil pods.** Even though it is not fit for human consumption, it may be moved **because it is animal fodder.**

סְפוֹג, אִם יֵשׁ לוֹ עוֹר בֵּית אֲחִיזָה – מְקַנְּחִין בּוֹ, וְאִם לָאו – אֵין מְקַנְּחִין בּוֹ. (וַחֲכָמִים אוֹמְרִים): בֵּין כָּךְ וּבֵין כָּךְ נִיטָּל בְּשַׁבָּת, וְאֵינוֹ מְקַבֵּל טוּמְאָה.

With regard to **a sponge, if it has leather** as **a handle, one may wipe** the table **with it, and if not, one may not wipe** the table **with it**[H] lest he come to squeeze liquid from it. **And the Rabbis say: Both this,** a dry sponge with a handle, **and that,** one without a handle, **may be moved on Shabbat and it does not become ritually impure.** A sponge is not among the substances that can become ritually impure,[N] neither by Torah law nor by rabbinic decree.

גמ׳ אָמַר רַב נַחְמָן: אָנוּ אֵין לָנוּ אֶלָּא בֵּית שַׁמַּאי כְּרַבִּי יְהוּדָה, וּבֵית הִלֵּל כְּרַבִּי שִׁמְעוֹן.

GEMARA **Rav Naḥman said:** Reverse the two opinions, as **we have only Beit Shammai in accordance with** the opinion of **Rabbi Yehuda,** who prohibits moving set-aside items, **and Beit Hillel in accordance with** the opinion of **Rabbi Shimon,** who permits doing so.

״מַעֲבִירִין מִלִּפְנֵי הַשֻּׁלְחָן פֵּירוּרִין״. מְסַיַּיע לֵיהּ לְרַבִּי יוֹחָנָן, דְּאָמַר רַבִּי יוֹחָנָן: פֵּירוּרִין שֶׁאֵין בָּהֶן כַּזַּיִת – אָסוּר לְאַבְּדָן בַּיָּד.

We learned in the mishna: **One** may **clear** bread **crumbs from the table.** The Gemara comments: This **supports** the opinion of **Rabbi Yoḥanan, as Rabbi Yoḥanan said:** With regard to **crumbs that are less than an olive-bulk,**[H] **it is prohibited to destroy them by hand**[N] in deference to the food.

״שְׂעַר שֶׁל אֲפוּנִין״. מַנִּי? רַבִּי שִׁמְעוֹן הִיא, דְּלֵית לֵיהּ מוּקְצֶה.

We learned in the mishna: One may clear **pea** and lentil **pods** from the table on Shabbat. The Gemara asks: **Whose** opinion **is it** in the mishna? It is the opinion of **Rabbi Shimon, who is not** of the opinion that there is a prohibition of **set-aside.**

אֵימָא סֵיפָא: סְפוֹג, אִם יֵשׁ לוֹ בֵּית אֲחִיזָה – מְקַנְּחִין בּוֹ, וְאִם לָאו – אֵין מְקַנְּחִין בּוֹ. אֲתָאן לְרַבִּי יְהוּדָה, דְּאָמַר ״דָּבָר שֶׁאֵין מִתְכַּוֵּין – אָסוּר״!

Say the latter clause of the mishna: With regard to **a sponge, if it has leather** as **a handle, one may wipe** the table **with it, and if not, one may not wipe** the table **with it. We have arrived at** the opinion **of Rabbi Yehuda, who said: An unintentional act is prohibited,** as he certainly does not intend to squeeze liquid from the sponge.

בְּהָא אֲפִילּוּ רַבִּי שִׁמְעוֹן מוֹדֶה, דְּאַבָּיֵי וְרָבָא דְּאָמְרִי תַּרְוַיְיהוּ: מוֹדֶה רַבִּי שִׁמְעוֹן בִּפְסִיק רֵישֵׁיהּ וְלֹא יָמוּת.

The Gemara answers: **In that** case, **even Rabbi Shimon agrees** that it is prohibited, **as it is Abaye and Rava who both say: Rabbi Shimon agrees in** a case of: **Cut off its head will it not die,** i.e., inevitable consequences. When the prohibited outcome that ensues from the unintentional action is inevitable, Rabbi Shimon agrees that it is prohibited. Squeezing liquid from a sponge is an inevitable consequence.

HALAKHA

A wooden poker to stoke the fire on a Festival – אוּד בְּיוֹם טוֹב: On a Festival, it is prohibited to take a piece of wood, whether damp or dry (*Mishna Berura*), from a pile of wood and utilize it as a poker to stoke a fire in an oven. This is because it is considered as if one was completing the production process of a vessel (Rambam *Sefer Zemanim, Hilkhot Yom Tov* 4:11; *Shulḥan Arukh, Oraḥ Ḥayyim* 507:3).

One may clear bones and shells from the table – מַעֲבִירִין מֵעַל הַשֻּׁלְחָן קְלִיפּוֹת וַעֲצָמוֹת: On Shabbat, it is permitted to move bones fit for dogs and shells fit for use as animal fodder from the table. However, if they are not even suitable for use as animal fodder, one may only shake the table so they fall off, as per the opinion of Beit Hillel, according to *Tosafot* (Rambam *Sefer Zemanim, Hilkhot Shabbat* 26:16; *Shulḥan Arukh, Oraḥ Ḥayyim* 308:27).

Wiping the table with a sponge – קִינּוּחַ בִּסְפוֹג: One may not wipe a surface with a sponge on Shabbat unless the sponge has a handle. If it does not, the concern is that one might squeeze liquid from the sponge (Rambam *Sefer Zemanim, Hilkhot Shabbat* 22:15; *Shulḥan Arukh, Oraḥ Ḥayyim* 320:17).

Crumbs that are less than an olive-bulk – פֵּירוּרִין שֶׁאֵין בָּהֶן כַּזַּיִת: It is permitted to destroy crumbs that are less than an olive-bulk, in accordance with the version of this *halakha* in tractate *Berakhot*. Nevertheless, it is customary to do so in a respectful manner. Failure to do so leads to poverty (see *Magen Avraham*; Rambam *Sefer Ahava, Hilkhot Berakhot* 7:11; *Shulḥan Arukh, Oraḥ Ḥayyim* 180:4).

LANGUAGE

Board [*tavla*] – טַבְלָה: From the Latin word tabula, meaning a board, especially a wooden board that serves as a cover for a table and a writing tablet.

NOTES

A sponge with regard to ritual impurity – סְפוֹג לְעִנְיַן קַבָּלַת טוּמְאָה: Although the Torah lists materials and vessels that can become ritually impure, the list is not comprehensive. The Sages decreed that certain items that do not appear on the Torah's list, e.g., glass vessels, can also become ritually impure. One of their guiding principles is that materials coming from the sea, e.g., fish skin and bones, cannot become impure. Therefore, a sponge, which is from the sea and is not a vessel, cannot become impure.

Crumbs that are less than an olive-bulk, it is prohibited to destroy them by hand – פֵּירוּרִין שֶׁאֵין בָּהֶן כַּזַּיִת – אָסוּר לְאַבְּדָן בַּיָּדַיִם: The version of this passage that appears in Rabbeinu Ḥananel is the version that appears in *Tosafot*: Crumbs that are less than an olive-bulk may be destroyed by hand. That is the reading in tractate *Berakhot* as well. According to that reading, in this context the phrase one may clear means that one may throw away the small crumbs, and one need not make certain to keep them on the table. According to *Tosafot* in tractate *Berakhot*, even if it is permitted to throw away small crumbs, it is customary to do so in a respectful manner.

הָנֵי גַּרְעִינִין דְּתַמְרֵי אַרְמָיָיתָא שְׁרוּ לְטַלְטוּלִינְהוּ, הוֹאִיל וַחֲזָיִין אַגַּב אִמָּן. וּדְפַרְסָיָיתָא – אָסוּר.

With regard to **those pits of Aramean dates,**[H] which are low quality and occasionally fed to animals, **it is permitted to move** the pits **since** they **are fit** for use **due to their origin,** i.e., the dates that were prepared as animal feed beforehand. **And** moving pits **of Persian**[N] dates **is prohibited.** Since those dates are high quality and are not prepared for animals, their pits, too, are not prepared for that use.

שְׁמוּאֵל מְטַלְטֵל לְהוּ אַגַּב רִיפְתָּא. (שרנ״ם שפ״ז סִימָן). שְׁמוּאֵל לְטַעְמֵיהּ, דְּאָמַר שְׁמוּאֵל: עוֹשֶׂה אָדָם כׇּל צְרָכָיו בַּפַּת.

The Gemara relates that **Shmuel** would **carry them along with bread.**[N] The letters *shin, resh, nun, mem, shin, peh, zayin* are a **mnemonic** of the Sages whose opinions are cited below: Shmuel, Rabba, Huna, Ameimar, Sheshet, Pappa, Zekharya. The Gemara comments: **Shmuel's** statement is consistent **with his reasoning, as Shmuel said: A man may perform all his needs with bread.**[H] As long as the bread remains edible, he need not be concerned that he is treating the bread contemptuously.

רַבָּה מְטַלְטֵל לְהוּ אַגַּב לָקְנָא דְּמַיָּא. רַב הוּנָא בְּרֵיהּ דְּרַב יְהוֹשֻׁעַ עָבֵיד לְהוּ כִּגְרָף שֶׁל רְעִי. אֲמַר לֵיהּ רַב אַשִׁי לְאָמֵימַר: וְכִי עוֹשִׂין גְּרָף שֶׁל רְעִי לְכַתְּחִילָּה?

Rabba would move them along with a pitcher of water. Rav Huna, son of Rav Yehoshua, would render them a chamber pot with excrement. The Sages permitted moving repulsive vessels. Here, too, he would collect all the date pits and then move them out because they were disgusting. **Rav Ashi said to Ameimar: And may one create a chamber pot with excrement *ab initio*?**[H] Although the Sages permitted moving a container of excrement, they did not permit creating one *ab initio* so that it would be permitted to move it.

רַב שֵׁשֶׁת זָרֵיק לְהוּ בְּלִישָּׁנֵיהּ. רַב פַּפָּא זָרֵיק לְהוּ אֲחוֹרֵי הַמִּטָּה. אָמְרוּ עָלָיו עַל רַבִּי זְכַרְיָה בֶּן אַבְקוּלָס שֶׁהָיָה מַחֲזִיר פָּנָיו אֲחוֹרֵי הַמִּטָּה וְזוֹרְקָן.

Rav Sheshet would dispose of the pits **with his tongue. Rav Pappa would dispose of them behind the divan** on which he sat while eating because he did not want to move them in another manner. **They said about Rabbi Zekharya ben Avkolas that he would turn his face** toward the **back of the divan and dispose of them.**

הדרן עלך נוטל אדם את בנו

HALAKHA

Pits of Aramean dates – גַּרְעִינֵי תְּמָרִים אֲרַמִּיּוֹת: It is permitted to move date pits in a place where they are fed to animals. A prominent person should be stringent and move them only in an unusual manner, as per the custom of Rabbi Zekharya ben Avkolas (Rambam *Sefer Zemanim, Hilkhot Shabbat* 26:16; *Shulḥan Arukh, Oraḥ Ḥayyim* 308:30).

A man may perform all his needs with bread – עוֹשֶׂה אָדָם כׇּל צְרָכוֹ בַּפַּת: Bread may be used for all of a person's needs provided that the bread is not ruined, as per the opinion of Shmuel and the Gemara in tractate *Berakhot* (Rambam *Sefer Ahava, Hilkhot Berakhot* 7:9; *Shulḥan Arukh, Oraḥ Ḥayyim* 171:1).

And may one create a chamber pot of excrement *ab initio* – וְכִי עוֹשִׂין גְּרָף שֶׁל רִיעִי לְכַתְּחִילָּה: One may not cause a container to assume the legal status of a chamber pot of excrement *ab initio*, so that it will become so repulsive that it will be permitted to move it (see *Magen Avraham* and *Mishna Berura*), as per the opinion of Rav Ashi (Rambam *Sefer Zemanim, Hilkhot Shabbat* 25:24; *Shulḥan Arukh, Oraḥ Ḥayyim* 308:36).

NOTES

Aramean…and Persian – אַרְמָיָיתָא...וּדְפַרְסָיָיתָא: Some explain that Aramean date pits are soft and can be eaten by people, whereas Persian date pits are entirely unfit to be eaten by people (Rabbeinu Ḥananel). In addition, vestiges of the fruit remain attached to Aramean date pits, and therefore, they may be moved on Shabbat. That is not the case with the pits of Persian dates (*Me'iri*). Others explain that Persian date pits are typically used for burning and therefore may not be moved, as opposed to Aramean date pits, which are softer and fit for use as animal feed (Rashba).

Carrying along with bread – טִלְטוּל אַגַּב לֶחֶם: The question arises with regard to this statement and with regard to the mishna as well: According to the opinion that permits the carrying of crumbs along with a board, why don't the bread and the board become a base for a prohibited object? *Tosafot* answer that an object only becomes a base for a prohibited object if the prohibited object was placed on it with the intention of leaving it there throughout Shabbat. However, if the intention was to leave it there only for part of the day, the base does not assume the status of the base for a prohibited object. Others explain that since the bread crumbs or the date pits are insignificant, they are negated relative to the board or the slice of bread on which they are placed. Therefore, they do not become a base for a prohibited object (Ra'avad).

Summary of **Perek XXI**

Most of the Sages accepted the *halakha* that one is forbidden on Shabbat to handle a base of a forbidden article. However, this chapter clarified that the rule applies only to moving the item in a normal fashion; when necessary, there is room for leniency with regard to moving such items in an unusual or indirect fashion. Similarly, when there is a need to move something connected to a set-aside item, such as a child who is holding a set-aside item, or a barrel upon which a set-aside item is resting, the Sages allowed it and did not apply the prohibition of a base for a forbidden article. It was also explained in this chapter that the *halakha* is generally not highly stringent with regard to the laws of set-aside on Shabbat, and it is permitted to move something in order to protect the honor of Shabbat or to remove an item that people find repulsive. This is especially true according to the view of Rabbi Shimon, which was accepted as normative.

Introduction to **Perek XXII**

This chapter also deals with different types of prohibitions subsumed under the category of *shevut*. Here, too, there is no single theme that unites all the topics addressed, although most of them deal with food preparation on Shabbat. Arranging the chapter's contents in a different order than is presented in the Mishna would allow us to identify several general questions that serve as the basis for the details that are discussed in this chapter.

One of these issues relates to the laws of squeezing on Shabbat. Squeezing is not listed as a primary category of prohibited labor. Its prohibition is not based on the act of squeezing alone; indeed, squeezing can be a subcategory of at least two primary categories of labor, depending on the circumstances: It can be a subcategory of the labor of threshing, which is defined abstractly as removing the desired contents from within an unwanted wrapping or shell, and it can be a subcategory of the labor of whitening, when the squeezing is performed in the process of washing.

However, the relationship between squeezing and threshing is not completely clear and uniform. For example, in the practical discussions regarding milking animals on Shabbat, the question arises as to the extent to which one should understand milking as a form or subcategory of squeezing or threshing. This leads to the question of whether milking should be viewed as a Torah prohibition or a rabbinic decree. Similarly, it is necessary to delineate the fine differences between types of squeezing that can be viewed as a subcategory of threshing and other types of squeezing that are externally similar to the first type but differ with regard to the intent of the person squeezing or the purpose of the act itself.

Also discussed in this chapter is breaking a barrel in order to remove food from inside it. The chapter likewise deals with various kinds of food preparation. These forms of food preparation all involve actions that are similar to squeezing and require one to identify the fine line separating a prohibited labor from actions that are externally similar to it but are different because of the intent of the person performing the action. Examples of this include heating up, soaking, and cooling foods on Shabbat: Are these acts forbidden because of their similarity to cooking, or are they perhaps totally permitted and not prohibited even by rabbinic decree? This chapter also comes to conclusions regarding some issues that the Gemara began to address in previous chapters but had not yet resolved.

מתני׳ חָבִית שֶׁנִּשְׁבְּרָה מַצִּילִין הֵימֶנָּה מְזוֹן שָׁלֹשׁ סְעוּדוֹת, וְאוֹמֵר לַאֲחֵרִים: בֹּאוּ וְהַצִּילוּ לָכֶם, וּבִלְבַד שֶׁלֹּא יִסְפּוֹג. אֵין סוֹחֲטִין אֶת הַפֵּירוֹת לְהוֹצִיא מֵהֶן מַשְׁקִין, וְאִם יָצְאוּ מֵעַצְמָן – אֲסוּרִין. רַבִּי יְהוּדָה אוֹמֵר: אִם לָאוֹכָלִין – הַיּוֹצֵא מֵהֶן מוּתָּר, וְאִם לְמַשְׁקִין – הַיּוֹצֵא מֵהֶן אָסוּר. חַלּוֹת דְּבַשׁ שֶׁרִיסְּקָן מֵעֶרֶב שַׁבָּת וְיָצְאוּ מֵעַצְמָן – אֲסוּרִין, וְרַבִּי אֱלִיעֶזֶר מַתִּיר.

MISHNA From **a barrel** of wine or oil **that broke** on Shabbat, **one may rescue from it**[H] **food** sufficient **for three meals,** and one may also **say to others: Come and rescue** food **for yourselves.** This applies **provided that one does not soak up** the wine or oil with a sponge or rag, due to the prohibition of squeezing. **One may not squeeze fruits** on Shabbat in order **to extract liquids from them. And if** liquids **seeped out on their own, it is prohibited** to use them on Shabbat. **Rabbi Yehuda says: If** the fruits were designated **for eating,** the liquid **that seeps from them** on Shabbat **is permitted.** There is no concern lest one purposely squeeze liquids from fruit that is designated for eating. **And if** the fruits were originally designated **for liquids,**[N] the liquids **that seep from them** on Shabbat **are prohibited.** In the case of **honeycombs that one crushed on Shabbat eve, and** honey and wax **seeped** from them **on their own** on Shabbat, **they are prohibited, and Rabbi Eliezer permits** using them.

גמ׳ תָּנָא: לֹא יִסְפּוֹג בְּיַיִן, וְלֹא יְטַפֵּחַ בְּשֶׁמֶן, שֶׁלֹּא יַעֲשֶׂה כְּדֶרֶךְ שֶׁהוּא עוֹשֶׂה בְּחוֹל. תָּנוּ רַבָּנַן: נִתְפַּזְּרוּ לוֹ פֵּירוֹת בֶּחָצֵר – מְלַקֵּט עַל יָד עַל יָד וְאוֹכֵל. אֲבָל לֹא לְתוֹךְ הַסַּל וְלֹא לְתוֹךְ הַקּוּפָּה, שֶׁלֹּא יַעֲשֶׂה כְּדֶרֶךְ שֶׁהוּא עוֹשֶׂה בְּחוֹל.

GEMARA It was taught in the *Tosefta*: **One may not soak up wine and** one **may not collect oil** in his hand, so **that one will not conduct** himself on Shabbat **in the manner that he conducts** himself **during the week. The Sages taught** in a *baraita*: **If one's fruit was scattered in a courtyard**[NH] on Shabbat, **one may collect them from hand to hand,** a little at a time, **and eat** them immediately. **However,** one may **not** collect them **into a basket or into a box,** so **that one will not conduct** himself on Shabbat **in the manner that he conducts** himself **during the week.**

״אֵין סוֹחֲטִין אֶת הַפֵּירוֹת״. אָמַר רַב יְהוּדָה אָמַר שְׁמוּאֵל: מוֹדֶה הָיָה רַבִּי יְהוּדָה לַחֲכָמִים בְּזֵיתִים וַעֲנָבִים. מַאי טַעְמָא – כֵּיוָן דִּלְסְחִיטָה נִינְהוּ יָהֵיב דַּעְתֵּיהּ. וְעוּלָּא אָמַר רַב: חָלוּק הָיָה רַבִּי יְהוּדָה אַף בְּזֵיתִים וַעֲנָבִים. וְרַבִּי יוֹחָנָן אָמַר: הֲלָכָה כְּרַבִּי יְהוּדָה בִּשְׁאָר פֵּירוֹת, וְאֵין הֲלָכָה כְּרַבִּי יְהוּדָה בְּזֵיתִים וַעֲנָבִים.

We learned in the mishna: **One may not squeeze fruit** on Shabbat, and the liquid that seeps from fruit on its own is prohibited. Rabbi Yehuda, however, distinguishes between fruit that is designated for eating, in which case the liquid that seeps out on its own is permitted, and fruit that is designated for juicing, in which case the liquid that seeps out on its own on Shabbat is prohibited. **Rav Yehuda said** that **Shmuel said: Rabbi Yehuda concedes to the Rabbis with regard to olives and grapes.** Even if they were designated for eating, the liquid that seeps from them on its own on Shabbat is prohibited. **What is the reason** for this? **Since they are** generally used **for squeezing, one had in mind** from the outset that these would serve that purpose as well, even if he designated them for eating. **And Ulla** said that **Rav said: Rabbi Yehuda was in disagreement even with regard to olives and grapes. And Rabbi Yoḥanan said: The *halakha* is** in accordance with the opinion of **Rabbi Yehuda with regard to other fruits, and the *halakha* is not in accordance with** the opinion of **Rabbi Yehuda with regard to olives and grapes.**

אָמַר רַבָּה אָמַר רַב יְהוּדָה אָמַר שְׁמוּאֵל: מוֹדֶה הָיָה רַבִּי יְהוּדָה לַחֲכָמִים בְּזֵיתִים וַעֲנָבִים, וּמוֹדִים חֲכָמִים לְרַבִּי יְהוּדָה בִּשְׁאָר פֵּירוֹת.

Rabba said that **Rav Yehuda said** that **Shmuel said** as follows: **Rabbi Yehuda would concede to the Rabbis with regard to olives and grapes, and the Rabbis would concede to Rabbi Yehuda with regard to other fruit.**

אָמַר לֵיהּ רַבִּי יִרְמְיָה לְרַבִּי אַבָּא: אֶלָּא בְּמַאי פְּלִיגִי? אָמַר לֵיהּ: לְכִי תִשְׁכַּח. אָמַר רַב נַחְמָן בַּר יִצְחָק: מִסְתַּבְּרָא, בְּתוּתִים וְרִמּוֹנִים פְּלִיגִי.

Rabbi Yirmeya said to Rabbi Abba: If it is true that they agree with each other, **with regard to what do they disagree? He said to him: When you find** it, i.e., examine this matter and you will find areas in which they disagree. **Rav Naḥman bar Yitzḥak said: It stands to reason that they disagree with regard to mulberries and pomegranates,** which have intermediate status, between olives and grapes, which are always considered designated for juicing, and other fruits, which are not.

NOTES

For eating…for liquids – לָאוֹכָלִין...לְמַשְׁקִין: The prohibition against squeezing is a subcategory of the prohibited labor of threshing, which entails removing the edible, inside part from the insignificant outer shell. Therefore, liquid that seeps from fruit designated for consumption cannot be considered threshing, since the fruit itself is significant. The liquid is considered food that separated from other food, which is permitted like any other food item that was divided into smaller parts.

If one's fruit was scattered in a courtyard – נִתְפַּזְּרוּ לוֹ פֵּירוֹת בֶּחָצֵר: Some commentaries explain that the discussion is limited to a case where the fruit was scattered throughout the courtyard. However, if the fruit fell in one place, it is permitted to gather it into a basket in the standard manner (Rabbeinu Yona). An alternate interpretation is that the fruit is mixed with pebbles and dirt, and therefore there is concern that one may perform the prohibited labor of selecting the waste from the edible (Ramban). The Rambam states that the concern is that one will press the fruit together in the basket and thereby violate the prohibited labor of gathering sheaves into a pile.

HALAKHA

Rescuing from a broken barrel – הַצָּלָה מֵחָבִית שְׁבוּרָה: If a barrel breaks on Shabbat, one may rescue the measure of wine or oil that one requires for three meals. If one uses a single utensil, he may collect even more. It is also permitted to tell others to rescue wine or oil for themselves. However, it is prohibited to soak up wine or oil with an absorbent material, because one might come to squeeze it (Rambam *Sefer Zemanim*, *Hilkhot Shabbat* 22:16; *Shulḥan Arukh*, *Oraḥ Ḥayyim* 335:1).

If one's fruit was scattered in a courtyard – נִתְפַּזְּרוּ לוֹ פֵּירוֹת בֶּחָצֵר: If one's fruit was scattered in a courtyard on Shabbat, he may pick up a small amount at a time and eat it. However, one may not collect large quantities of fruit in a basket, because that is conduct identical to the manner that he conducts himself during the week (Rambam *Sefer Zemanim*, *Hilkhot Shabbat* 21:11; *Shulḥan Arukh*, *Oraḥ Ḥayyim* 335:5).

דְּתַנְיָא: זֵיתִים שֶׁמָּשַׁךְ מֵהֶן שֶׁמֶן, וַעֲנָבִים שֶׁמָּשַׁךְ מֵהֶן יַיִן, וְהִכְנִיסָן בֵּין לֶאֱוֹכֶל בֵּין לְמַשְׁקִין – הַיּוֹצֵא מֵהֶן אָסוּר. תּוּתִים שֶׁמָּשַׁךְ מֵהֶן מַיִם, וְרִמּוֹנִים שֶׁמָּשַׁךְ מֵהֶן יַיִן, וְהִכְנִיסָן לָאֳכָלִין – הַיּוֹצֵא מֵהֶן מוּתָּר, לְמַשְׁקִין וְלִסְתָם – הַיּוֹצֵא מֵהֶן אָסוּר, דִּבְרֵי רַבִּי יְהוּדָה. וַחֲכָמִים אוֹמְרִים: בֵּין לָאֳכָלִין בֵּין לְמַשְׁקִין – הַיּוֹצֵא מֵהֶן אָסוּר.

As it was taught in a *baraita*: With regard to **olives from which one squeezed oil**[H] **and grapes from which one squeezed wine** before Shabbat (*Tosafot*), and **he** subsequently **brought them into** his house, **whether** he brought them in **for** use as **food or whether** he brought them in **for** use of their **liquids, that which seeps from them** on its own on Shabbat **is prohibited.** However, with regard to **mulberries from which one squeezed water,** i.e., juice, **and pomegranates from which one squeezed wine,** i.e., pomegranate juice, **and he brought them into** the house, if he originally **brought them in for** use as **food, what seeps from them is permitted. And** if he brought them in **for** use of their **liquids, and** similarly, if he brought them in **without specifying** his intention, **what seeps from them is prohibited.** This is **the statement of Rabbi Yehuda. And the Rabbis say: Whether** he brought them into the house **for** use as **food or whether** he brought them in **for** use of their **liquids, what seeps from them is prohibited.**

וְסָבַר רַבִּי יְהוּדָה סְתָם אָסוּר?! וְהָתְנַן: חֲלֵב הָאִשָּׁה מְטַמֵּא לְרָצוֹן וְשֶׁלֹּא לְרָצוֹן, חֲלֵב בְּהֵמָה אֵינוֹ מְטַמֵּא אֶלָּא לְרָצוֹן.

The Gemara questions this *baraita*: **And does Rabbi Yehuda maintain that** in the case of **undesignated** fruit that was not designated for a specific purpose, the liquid that seeps on its own **is prohibited? Didn't we learn** in a mishna: **A woman's milk** is considered a liquid and therefore **renders** food susceptible to **ritual impurity,**[HN] whether the milk was expressed **volitionally and** whether it was expressed **unvolitionally?** On the other hand, **milk of an animal only renders** food susceptible to **ritual impurity** if it was milked **volitionally** but not if it drips out on its own.

אָמַר רַבִּי עֲקִיבָא: קַל וָחוֹמֶר הוּא, וּמָה חֲלֵב הָאִשָּׁה שֶׁאֵינוֹ מְיוּחָד אֶלָּא לִקְטַנִּים – מְטַמֵּא לְרָצוֹן וְשֶׁלֹּא לְרָצוֹן, חֲלֵב הַבְּהֵמָה שֶׁמְּיוּחָד בֵּין לִקְטַנִּים בֵּין לִגְדוֹלִים – אֵינוֹ דִּין שֶׁיְּטַמֵּא בֵּין לְרָצוֹן וּבֵין שֶׁלֹּא לְרָצוֹן? אָמְרוּ לוֹ: אִם טִמֵּא חֲלֵב הָאִשָּׁה שֶׁלֹּא לְרָצוֹן – שֶׁדַּם מַגֵּפָתָהּ טָמֵא, יְטַמֵּא חֲלֵב הַבְּהֵמָה

Rabbi Akiva said: It is an *a fortiori* inference that this is incorrect: **Just as a woman's milk, which is intended only for young** children, is considered a liquid and **renders** food susceptible to **ritual impurity** both if the milk is expressed **volitionally and** if it is expressed **unvolitionally, the milk of an animal, which is intended for both young and old, is it not logical that it should render** food susceptible to **ritual impurity, both** if it was expressed **volitionally and** if it was expressed **unvolitionally? They said to him** that this *a fortiori* inference can be refuted in the following way: **If a woman's milk** renders food susceptible to **ritual impurity** even when the milk was expressed **unvolitionally, as** the status of **the blood of her wound is** also that of a liquid that renders food susceptible to **ritual impurity,**[HN] that does not mean that **the milk of an animal** renders food susceptible to **ritual impurity**

HALAKHA

Squeezing fruit – סְחִיטַת פֵּירוֹת: It is prohibited to squeeze liquid from olives and grapes on Shabbat. If juice seeps from them on its own, it is prohibited to drink or use the juice on Shabbat. It is also prohibited to squeeze mulberries and pomegranates on Shabbat. If juice seeps from them, it is prohibited to drink the juice if the fruit was designated for juicing. However, if the fruit was designated for eating the juice is permitted. The *halakha* is in accordance with the mishna according to the explanation of Shmuel (Rambam *Sefer Zemanim, Hilkhot Shabbat* 21:12; *Shulḥan Arukh, Oraḥ Ḥayyim* 320:1).

Ritual impurity of a woman's milk – טוּמְאַת חֲלֵב אִשָּׁה: Mother's milk is always considered a liquid and renders food susceptible to ritual impurity, whether or not the milk was expressed intentionally (Rambam *Sefer Tahara, Hilkhot Tumat Okhalin* 10:4).

As the blood of her wound renders food susceptible to ritual impurity – שֶׁדַּם מַגֵּפָתָהּ טָמֵא: Blood from a wound in a person with a severe form of ritual impurity renders food susceptible to ritual impurity and renders it ritually impure simultaneously (Rambam *Sefer Tahara, Hilkhot Tumat Okhalin* 10:5).

NOTES

Renders food susceptible to ritual impurity – מְטַמֵּא: Food can become ritually impure only if it was rendered susceptible to impurity through contact with liquid (see Leviticus 11:38). Although the only liquid mentioned in the Torah in this regard is water, the Sages debate whether other liquids are also capable of rendering fruit susceptible to impurity. Inclusion in the group of liquids that confer susceptibility to ritual impurity depends on the particular liquid's similarity to water based on derivations from the verses. Therefore, only a derivation like an *a fortiori* inference or a verbal analogy can determine a liquid's status in this regard.

As the blood of her wound renders food susceptible to ritual impurity – שֶׁדַּם מַגֵּפָתָהּ טָמֵא: There is a special derivation cited by Rashi that teaches that human blood is considered a liquid. Therefore, if it comes into contact with food, it renders the food susceptible to ritual impurity. There is no distinction in this regard between different kinds of human blood; any kind of human blood renders food susceptible to ritual impurity. Animal blood that flows when the animal is slaughtered is also considered a liquid and renders food susceptible to ritual impurity; however, other kinds of animal blood are not considered to be liquids.

שֶׁלֹּא לְרָצוֹן – שֶׁדַּם מַגֵּפָתָהּ טָהוֹר! אָמַר לָהֶן: מַחְמִיר אֲנִי בְּחָלָב מִבְּדָם, שֶׁהַחוֹלֵב לִרְפוּאָה – טָמֵא, וְהַמַּקִּיז לִרְפוּאָה – טָהוֹר. אָמְרוּ לוֹ: סַלֵּי זֵיתִים וַעֲנָבִים יוֹכִיחוּ, שֶׁהַמַּשְׁקִין הַיּוֹצְאִין מֵהֶן לְרָצוֹן – טְמֵאִין, שֶׁלֹּא לְרָצוֹן – טְהוֹרִים.

if it was expressed **unintentionally, as the blood of its wound is ritually pure,**[H] meaning that it does not render food susceptible to ritual impurity. Rabbi Akiva **said to them: I am** more **stringent with regard to milk than with regard to blood,**[N] **as** if **one milks** an animal **for medicinal purposes,** the milk renders food susceptible to **ritual impurity, and** if **one lets** blood **for medicinal purposes,**[H] the status of the blood is not that of a liquid and is **ritually pure,**[N] in the sense that it does not render food susceptible to ritual impurity. **They said to him:** The case of **baskets of olives and grapes will prove** that there is a difference between liquids that emerge of his own volition and those that do not, **as liquid that seeps from them**[H] **volitionally** renders food susceptible to **ritual impurity.**[N] However, liquid that seeps from them **unvolitionally**[N] **is ritually pure,** i.e., it does not render food susceptible to ritual impurity. Apparently, liquid renders food susceptible to ritual impurity only if it emerged of its own volition.

מַאי לָאו "לְרָצוֹן" – דְּנִיחָא לֵיהּ, "שֶׁלֹּא לְרָצוֹן", בִּסְתָמָא. וּמַה זֵיתִים וַעֲנָבִים דִּבְנֵי סְחִיטָה נִינְהוּ – שֶׁלֹּא לְרָצוֹן וְלֹא כְּלוּם, תּוּתִים וְרִמּוֹנִים דְּלָאו בְּנֵי סְחִיטָה נִינְהוּ לֹא כָּל שֶׁכֵּן?

The Gemara analyzes the terms of that mishna: **What, is it not** true that the term **volitionally** is referring to a situation where one **is pleased** with the emergence of liquids, **and** the term **unvolitionally** is referring **to** an **indeterminate** situation, where he expressed no preference? This leads to a conclusion with regard to our original topic of discussion. **Just as** in the case of **olives and grapes, which are** primarily **designated for squeezing** in order to extract oil and wine respectively, if liquid leaked from them **unvolitionally,** in the sense that one did not intend for the liquid to emerge, **it has no** significance and does not render food susceptible to ritual impurity; in the case of **mulberries and pomegranates, which are not** typically **designated for squeezing, is it not all the more so** that liquid that seeps from them unvolitionally does not render food susceptible to ritual impurity?

לֹא, "לְרָצוֹן" – בִּסְתָמָא, "שֶׁלֹּא לְרָצוֹן" – דְּגַלֵּי אַדַּעְתֵּיהּ, דַּאֲמַר "לֹא נִיחָא לִי". וְאִיבָּעֵית אֵימָא: שָׁאנֵי סַלֵּי זֵיתִים וַעֲנָבִים, כֵּיוָן דִּלְאִיבּוּד קָיְימִי – מֵעִיקָּרָא אַפְקוֹרֵי מַפְקְרֵי לְהוּ.

The Gemara refutes this argument: **No,** the term **volitionally** is referring even to a situation where one's preference **is indeterminate,** and the term **unvolitionally** is referring to a situation where **one revealed his mind-set** explicitly and **said: I am not pleased** if liquid emerges. **And if you wish, say** instead that **baskets of olives and grapes are different; since** the liquid that leaks from them **stands to be lost, one renounces it from the outset.** No proof can be cited from this mishna. Generally speaking, however, the legal status of liquids that are not designated to be lost from the outset is that of liquids, even if one did not express pleasure with their emergence.

אַשְׁכַּחַן רַבִּי יְהוּדָה דְּמוֹדֵי לְרַבָּנַן בְּזֵיתִים וּבַעֲנָבִים. רַבָּנַן דְּמוֹדוּ לֵיהּ לְרַבִּי יְהוּדָה בִּשְׁאָר פֵּירוֹת מְנָלַן? – דְּתַנְיָא: סוֹחֲטִין

We have found in the *baraita* cited above that **Rabbi Yehuda conceded to the Rabbis with regard to olives and grapes,** that liquid that seeps from them on its own on Shabbat, both volitionally and unvolitionally, is prohibited during Shabbat. **From where do we** conclude that **the Rabbis concede to Rabbi Yehuda with regard to other fruits** and distinguish between fruits designated for eating and those designated for juicing? **As it was taught** in a *baraita*: **One may squeeze**

NOTES

Blood and milk – דָּם וְחָלָב: The Sages listed seven liquids that render susceptible to ritual impurity foods with which they come into contact: Water, dew, wine, blood, oil, honey, and milk. The inclusion of each liquid on this list is derived either from explicit verses or by means of the hermeneutic principles. The Sages included milk because it is similar to blood in that both emerge from people. Indeed, the Sages taught that in certain cases blood becomes turbid and becomes milk. However, Rabbi Akiva stated that there is a specific verse that proves milk is a liquid in this regard and that there is no connection between the *halakhot* of milk and blood. His proof is that there are cases where milk is treated more stringently than blood. Therefore, milk is not considered a type of blood.

If one lets blood for medicinal purposes, the blood is ritually pure – הַמַּקִּיז לִרְפוּאָה טָהוֹר: The *Me'iri* explains that these *halakhot* apply to human blood as well. According to this opinion, not all blood renders food susceptible to ritual impurity. Only blood from a corpse renders food susceptible to ritual impurity.

Baskets of olives and grapes…liquid that seeps from them volitionally renders food susceptible to ritual impurity – סַלֵּי זֵיתִים וַעֲנָבִים...שֶׁהַמַּשְׁקִין הַיּוֹצְאִין מֵהֶן לְרָצוֹן טְמֵאִין: Although the Sages taught that liquid that seeps from baskets of grapes renders food susceptible to ritual impurity, this was an additional rabbinic decree dealing with situations where one harvests grapes in baskets lined with tar, from which the liquid does not escape. It is only due to this consideration that the decree was issued (Rashba).

Volitionally and unvolitionally – לְרָצוֹן וְשֶׁלֹּא לְרָצוֹן: There are two aspects to the concept of volition with regard to rendering food susceptible to ritual impurity. The first aspect is the owner's approval at the time that the liquid renders the food susceptible to ritual impurity. The liquid has this effect only if it makes contact with the food with the owner's knowledge and approval. If it fell on the food accidentally, without the owner's knowledge, it does not render food ritually impure. The second aspect concerns liquids other than water. The Torah only mentions water, and all other liquids render food susceptible to ritual impurity due to their similarity to water based on derivations from verses. Therefore, all other liquids have the legal status of water only if they became liquids through the owner's volition. If that is not the case, their legal status is not that of water and they do not render food susceptible to ritual impurity. The dispute between Rabbi Akiva and the Rabbis relates to this second requirement.

HALAKHA

As the blood of its wound is ritually pure – שֶׁדַּם מַגֵּפָתָהּ טָהוֹר: Blood from an animal's wound does not render food susceptible to ritual impurity when it comes into contact with food (Rambam *Sefer Tahara, Hilkhot Tumat Okhalin* 10:3).

If one lets blood for medicinal purposes – הַמַּקִּיז לִרְפוּאָה: Blood that was drawn from a person for medicinal purposes is not considered a liquid and does not render food susceptible to ritual impurity (Rambam *Sefer Tahara, Hilkhot Tumat Okhalin* 10:3).

Liquid from olives and grapes – מַשְׁקֵי זֵיתִים וַעֲנָבִים: Olive oil and grape juice render food susceptible to ritual impurity if the owner of the fruit desires that they emerge from the fruit (Rambam *Sefer Tahara, Hilkhot Tumat Okhalin* 1:2).

בִּפְגָעִין וּבִפְרִישִׁין וּבְעוּזְרָדִין, אֲבָל לֹא בְּרִמּוֹנִים. וְשֶׁל בֵּית מְנַשְּׁיָא בַּר מְנַחֵם הָיוּ סוֹחֲטִין בְּרִמּוֹנִים.

plums and quinces and crab apples. However, one may **not** squeeze **pomegranates,** because they are typically squeezed for their juice, as people **from the house of Menashya bar Menaḥem would squeeze pomegranates** during the week. Apparently, the Rabbis concede to Rabbi Yehuda with regard to fruits other than pomegranates and mulberries.

וּמִמַּאי דְּרַבָּנַן הִיא, דִּילְמָא רַבִּי יְהוּדָה הִיא? וְתֶהֱוֵי נַמִּי רַבִּי יְהוּדָה, אֵימַר דְּשָׁמְעַתְּ לֵיהּ לְרַבִּי יְהוּדָה יָצְאוּ מֵעַצְמָן, סוֹחֲטִין לְכַתְּחִילָּה מִי שָׁמְעַתְּ לֵיהּ? אֶלָּא מַאי אִית לָךְ לְמֵימַר – כֵּיוָן דְּלָאו בְּנֵי סְחִיטָה נִינְהוּ – אֲפִילּוּ לְכַתְּחִילָּה; אֲפִילּוּ תֵּימָא רַבָּנַן, כֵּיוָן דְּלָאו בְּנֵי סְחִיטָה נִינְהוּ – אֲפִילּוּ לְכַתְּחִילָּה. שְׁמַע מִינָּהּ: רַבָּנַן הִיא, שְׁמַע מִינָּהּ.

The Gemara objects: **And from where** is it ascertained that this *baraita* **is** in accordance with the opinion **of the Rabbis? Perhaps it is** in accordance with the opinion of **Rabbi Yehuda.** The Gemara answers: **And let** this *baraita* **also be** the opinion of **Rabbi Yehuda: Say that you heard** that according to **Rabbi Yehuda,** juice that **seeped out on its own** is permitted; **did you hear** that **squeezing** it is permitted *ab initio*? **Rather, what have you to say? Since they are not** fruits that are generally **designated for squeezing,** it is permitted to squeeze them **even *ab initio*.** That being the case, **even if you say** the *baraita* is in accordance with the opinion of **the Rabbis,** the same reasoning applies: **Since they are not** generally **designated for squeezing,** it is permitted to squeeze them **even *ab initio*.** Even the Rabbis would permit squeezing fruits such as plums, quinces, and crab apples. Since the *baraita* does not permit squeezing pomegranates, **learn from it** that the *baraita* **is** in accordance with the opinion of **the Rabbis.** The Gemara concludes: Indeed, **learn from it.**

״שֶׁל בֵּית מְנַשְּׁיָא בַּר מְנַחֵם הָיוּ סוֹחֲטִין בְּרִמּוֹנִים״. אָמַר רַב נַחְמָן: הֲלָכָה כְּשֶׁל בֵּית מְנַשְּׁיָא בַּר מְנַחֵם.

It was taught in the *baraita* cited above that people **from the house of Menashya bar Menaḥem would squeeze pomegranates** on weekdays. This indicates that it is typical for people to squeeze pomegranates, and therefore it is prohibited to do so on Shabbat. **Rav Naḥman said:** The ***halakha* is in accordance with** the practice of the people **from the house of Menashya bar Menaḥem.** In other words, squeezing pomegranates is considered typical, and therefore it is prohibited on Shabbat.

אָמַר לֵיהּ רָבָא לְרַב נַחְמָן: מְנַשְּׁיָא בֶּן מְנַחֵם תַּנָּא הוּא?! וְכִי תֵּימָא ״הֲלָכָה כִּי הַאי תַּנָּא דְּסָבַר לָהּ כְּשֶׁל מְנַשְּׁיָא בֶּן מְנַחֵם״, וּמִשּׁוּם דְּסָבַר כִּמְנַשְּׁיָא בֶּן מְנַחֵם הֲלָכָה כְּמוֹתוֹ? מְנַשְּׁיָא בֶּן מְנַחֵם הָוֵי רוּבָּא דְּעָלְמָא?!

Rava said to Rav Naḥman: Is **Menashya ben Menaḥem a *tanna*** that you say the *halakha* is in accordance with his opinion? **And if you say** that Rav Naḥman meant that the ***halakha* is in accordance with this *tanna*, who held in accordance with** the practice of the people **from** the house of **Menashya ben Menaḥem,** there is still room to ask: Does it make sense that **because he held in accordance with** the practice of the people from the house of **Menashya ben Menaḥem, the *halakha* is in accordance with his opinion?** Does **Menashya ben Menaḥem** constitute **the majority of the world?**[N] Since most people do not squeeze pomegranates, the practice of the people from the house of Menashya ben Menaḥem should be irrelevant relative to the typical practice of others.

אִין, דִּתְנַן: הַמְקַיֵּים קוֹצִים בַּכֶּרֶם, רַבִּי אֱלִיעֶזֶר אוֹמֵר: קִדֵּשׁ, וַחֲכָמִים אוֹמְרִים: אֵינוֹ מְקַדֵּשׁ אֶלָּא דָּבָר שֶׁכָּמוֹהוּ מְקַיְּימִין. וְאָמַר רַבִּי חֲנִינָא: מַאי טַעְמָא דְּרַבִּי אֱלִיעֶזֶר – שֶׁכֵּן בַּעֲרַבְיָא מְקַיְּימִין קוֹצֵי שָׂדוֹת לִגְמַלֵּיהֶם.

Rav Naḥman answered: **Yes,** in cases of this kind, halakhic rulings are based even on practices that are not universal, **as we learned** in a mishna that addresses the prohibition of diverse kinds, particularly forbidden food crops in a vineyard. With regard to one who **maintains thorns in a vineyard,**[H] **Rabbi Eliezer says: He rendered** the crops a **forbidden** mixture of food crops in a vineyard.[N] **And the Rabbis say: Only** a crop **that** people typically **maintain renders** a vineyard **forbidden. And Rabbi Ḥanina said: What is the reason for** the opinion of **Rabbi Eliezer? Because in Arabia they maintain the thorns of the fields** to feed them **to their camels.** There, thorns are treated as a bona fide crop. According to this opinion, since thorns are maintained in one place, they are considered to be significant everywhere. The same reasoning applies to the issue of juicing pomegranates.

מִידֵּי אִירְיָא; דַּעֲרַבְיָא – אַתְרָא, הָכָא – בְּטֵלָה דַּעְתּוֹ אֵצֶל כׇּל אָדָם!

The Gemara rejects this answer: **Is this comparable? Arabia** is **a place,**[N] and a custom practiced in an entire country is significant. **Here,** with regard to the practice of the house of Menashya bar Menaḥem, who was an individual, **his opinion** is rendered **irrelevant by** the opinions of **all other men.**

NOTES

Does Menashya ben Menaḥem constitute the majority of the world – מְנַשְּׁיָא בֶּן מְנַחֵם הָוֵי רוּבָּא דְּעָלְמָא: The discussion concerns the following question: Is the behavior of individuals, e.g., those who squeeze pomegranates, irrelevant in determining *halakha* for the general population? Or is the fact that some individuals act in a certain way enough of a factor to determine that that conduct or practice is normative?

Food crops in a vineyard – כִּלְאֵי הַכֶּרֶם: The Torah states: "Do not sow your vineyard with two kinds of seed, lest the fullness of the seed which you have sown be rendered forbidden together with the yield of the vineyard" (Deuteronomy 22:9). The Sages derived from this verse that crops planted in a vineyard are forbidden and render the yield of the vineyard itself forbidden. The application of this *halakha* depends on the question of which plants constitute a forbidden food crop in a vineyard.

Arabia is a place – דַּעֲרַבְיָא אַתְרָא: Rashba adds that Arabia is a place where people commonly raise camels, and their custom is to cultivate thorns as camel fodder. Consequently, the custom in Arabia should impact the assessment of normative behavior in places where people raise camels. On the other hand, there was no particular reason for the custom of the people of the house of Menashya bar Menaḥem, and therefore their personal preferences are irrelevant in determining general halakhic norms.

HALAKHA

Thorns in a vineyard – קוֹצִים בַּכֶּרֶם: If plants that are not generally cultivated grow on their own in a vineyard, and most people in that area do not sustain those plants, they do not constitute a forbidden food crop in a vineyard. This is so even if the owner of the vineyard wants to use them to feed his animals and the like, in accordance with the opinion of the Rabbis (Rambam *Sefer Zera'im, Hilkhot Kilayim* 5:18; *Shulḥan Arukh, Yoreh De'a* 296:14).

אֶלָּא, הַיְינוּ טַעְמָא כִּדְרַב חִסְדָּא; דְּאָמַר רַב חִסְדָּא: תְּרָדִין שֶׁסְּחָטָן וּנְתָנָן בְּמִקְוֶה – פּוֹסְלִין אֶת הַמִּקְוֶה בְּשִׁינּוּי מַרְאֶה. וְהָא לָאו בְּנֵי סְחִיטָה נִינְהוּ! אֶלָּא מַאי אִית לָךְ לְמֵימַר – כֵּיוָן דְּאַחְשְׁבִינְהוּ – הֲוָה לְהוּ מַשְׁקֶה. הָכָא נַמִי כֵּיוָן דְּאַחְשְׁבִינְהוּ הֲוָה לְהוּ מַשְׁקֶה.

Rather, this is the reason for Rav Naḥman's statement: It is **in accordance with** the opinion of **Rav Ḥisda, as Rav Ḥisda said:** In the case of **beets that one squeezed** and then **placed** their juice **in a ritual bath,** the juice **invalidates the ritual bath**[N] if it causes a **change of appearance.** Any liquid that causes the water of a ritual bath to change color invalidates the ritual bath. Rav Ḥisda elaborated: **Aren't** beets typically **not designated for squeezing? Rather, what have you to say? Since he ascribed it significance, it is** considered **a liquid. Here, too,** with regard to pomegranates, **since he ascribed it significance, it is** considered **a liquid.** Even if one person ascribes significance to a liquid, it assumes for him the status of a liquid and is prohibited on Shabbat.

רַב פַּפָּא אָמַר: מִשּׁוּם דַּהֲוֵי דָּבָר שֶׁאֵין עוֹשִׂין מִמֶּנּוּ מִקְוֶה לְכַתְּחִילָּה, וְכָל דָּבָר שֶׁאֵין עוֹשִׂין מִמֶּנּוּ מִקְוֶה לְכַתְּחִילָּה – פּוֹסֵל אֶת הַמִּקְוֶה בְּשִׁינּוּי מַרְאֶה.

Rav Pappa said that the reason Rav Ḥisda ruled that beet juice invalidates the ritual bath is **because it is something with which one may not make a ritual bath *ab initio*,** and there is a principle: **Anything with which one may not make a ritual bath *ab initio*,** i.e., anything other than water, snow, or ice, **invalidates the ritual bath**[H] if it causes a **change of appearance,** even if it does not have the legal status of a liquid.

תְּנַן הָתָם: נָפַל לְתוֹכוֹ יַיִן אוֹ חוֹמֶץ וּמוֹחַל וְשִׁינָּה מַרְאָיו – פָּסוּל. מַאן תַּנָּא דְּמוֹחַל מַשְׁקֶה הוּא? אָמַר אַבַּיֵּי: רַבִּי יַעֲקֹב הִיא. דְּתַנְיָא, רַבִּי יַעֲקֹב אוֹמֵר: מוֹחַל הֲרֵי הוּא כְּמַשְׁקֶה. וּמַה טַּעַם אָמְרוּ ״מוֹחַל הַיּוֹצֵא בַּתְּחִלָּה טָהוֹר״ – לְפִי שֶׁאֵינוֹ רוֹצֶה בְּקִיּוּמוֹ.

We learned in a mishna **there,** in tractate *Mikvaot*: **If wine or vinegar or** olive **discharge,** i.e., the liquid that comes from olives but is not oil, **fell into** a ritual bath **and changed its appearance,** the ritual bath **is invalid.**[H] The Gemara asks: **Who is the *tanna*** who holds **that** olive **discharge is** considered **liquid? Abaye said: It is Rabbi Ya'akov, as it was taught** in a *baraita* that **Rabbi Ya'akov says:** The legal status of olive **discharge is like** that of **a liquid.**[H] **And what** is the **reason** the Sages **said that** olive **discharge that emerges at the outset,** before one begins to press the olives for their oil, **is ritually pure,** meaning that it does not render food susceptible to ritual impurity? It is not because the olive discharge is not considered a liquid but **because he does not want its existence;** the owner would prefer that the olive discharge not yet emerge and instead emerge together with and mix with the oil.

רַבִּי שִׁמְעוֹן אוֹמֵר: מוֹחַל אֵינוֹ כְּמַשְׁקֶה, וּמַה טַּעַם אָמְרוּ ״מוֹחַל הַיּוֹצֵא מֵעִיקּוּל בֵּית הַבַּד טָמֵא״ – לְפִי שֶׁאִי אֶפְשָׁר לוֹ בְּלֹא צִיחְצוּחֵי שֶׁמֶן.

Rabbi Shimon says: The legal status of olive **discharge is not like** that of **a liquid. And what** is the **reason** the Sages **said that the** olive **sap that emerges from the bale of the olive press** after the olives were pressed **is** capable of rendering foods susceptible to become **ritually impure? Because it is impossible** that **it** will **not** contain **drops of oil** that come with it from the olives.

מַאי בֵּינַיְיהוּ? אִיכָּא בֵּינַיְיהוּ דְּאָתֵי בָּתַר אִיצַּצְתָּא. רָבָא אָמַר: מִשּׁוּם דַּהֲוֵי דָּבָר שֶׁאֵין עוֹשִׂין הֵימֶנּוּ מִקְוֶה, וּפוֹסֵל אֶת הַמִּקְוֶה בְּשִׁינּוּי מַרְאֶה.

The Gemara asks: **What is** the practical difference **between them?** They both agree that olive discharge that emerges at the outset is incapable of rendering food susceptible to ritual impurity and that olive discharge that emerges from the bale of the olive press is capable of rendering food susceptible to ritual impurity. The Gemara answers: **There is** a practical difference **between them** with regard to olive discharge **that comes after extensive pressing;** according to Rabbi Ya'akov, it is considered a liquid and renders food susceptible to ritual impurity, and according to Rabbi Shimon, it is not a liquid and does not render food susceptible to ritual impurity. **Rava said:** The reason that olive discharge invalidates a ritual bath is not because it is a liquid, but rather, **because it is something with which one may not make a ritual bath** *ab initio,* **and it** therefore **invalidates a ritual bath** if it causes a **change of appearance.**

אָמַר רַב יְהוּדָה אָמַר שְׁמוּאֵל: סוֹחֵט אָדָם אֶשְׁכּוֹל שֶׁל עֲנָבִים לְתוֹךְ הַקְּדֵרָה, אֲבָל לֹא לְתוֹךְ הַקְּעָרָה. אָמַר רַב חִסְדָּא, מִדִּבְרֵי רַבֵּינוּ נִלְמַד: חוֹלֵב אָדָם עֵז לְתוֹךְ הַקְּדֵרָה, אֲבָל לֹא לְתוֹךְ הַקְּעָרָה. אַלְמָא קָסָבַר: מַשְׁקֶה הַבָּא לָאוֹכֶל – אוֹכֶל הוּא.

Rav Yehuda said that **Shmuel said: A person may squeeze a cluster of grapes** on Shabbat **into a pot** with food in it,[H] and it is not considered squeezing a liquid but rather adding one food to another; **however,** he may **not** squeeze the liquid **into an** empty **bowl.**[N] **Rav Ḥisda said: From the statement of our Rabbi,** Shmuel, **we learn** that **one may milk a goat into a pot** of food[H] on Shabbat, because it is not considered to be the manner of squeezing that is prohibited as a subcategory of the labor of threshing; **however,** one may **not** do so **into an** empty **bowl.** The Gemara deduces: **Apparently, he holds** that **liquid that comes into food** is not considered liquid, but rather, **it is food.**

NOTES

Invalidating a ritual bath – פְּסִילַת הַמִּקְוֶה: There are two ways that liquids that fall into a ritual bath can invalidate it. The first way is if the ritual bath does not contain its requisite volume of forty *se'a*, and three *log* or more of drawn water, or any other liquid like water, falls into it. The second way is if a liquid that cannot be used in a ritual bath is poured into a ritual bath that contains the requisite forty *se'a* and alters the color of the water.

A person may squeeze a cluster of grapes into a pot; however, he may not squeeze the liquid into an empty bowl – סוֹחֵט אָדָם אֶשְׁכּוֹל שֶׁל עֲנָבִים לְתוֹךְ הַקְּדֵרָה, אֲבָל לֹא לְתוֹךְ הַקְּעָרָה: The commentaries explain that the prohibition against squeezing juice, which is a subcategory of the labor of threshing, primarily involves separating food from waste. However, the parts of the grapes that remain after juicing are considered waste only if the intent was to use the grapes exclusively for their juice. Therefore, if one squeezes juice from grapes into another food, it is merely considered a form of food preparation in which one transfers food, i.e., the grapes, into another dish. The difference between squeezing juice into a pot or into a bowl is that there is food in the pot. When the juice is squeezed into a pot of food, the juice becomes part of that food. It is considered food that was merely separated from its original source. On the other hand, if one squeezes the juice into an empty bowl, it is clear that the purpose is to remove the liquid from the fruit, which is prohibited (see Rav Hai Gaon).

HALAKHA

Anything with which one may not make a ritual bath *ab initio* invalidates the ritual bath – וְכָל דָּבָר שֶׁאֵין עוֹשִׂין מִמֶּנּוּ מִקְוֶה לְכַתְּחִילָּה פּוֹסֵל אֶת הַמִּקְוֶה: If a substance that cannot be used to make a ritual bath, such as wine, falls into a ritual bath and alters the appearance of the water, the ritual bath is invalid (Rambam *Sefer Tahara, Hilkhot Mikvaot* 7:1).

Liquids that invalidate a ritual bath – מַשְׁקִים הַפּוֹסְלִים מִקְוֶה: Wine, vinegar, and olive discharge that fall into a ritual bath and alter its appearance invalidate it (Rambam *Sefer Tahara, Hilkhot Mikvaot* 7:9; *Shulḥan Arukh, Yoreh De'a* 201:25).

The legal status of olive discharge is like that of a liquid – מוֹחַל הֲרֵי הוּא כְּמַשְׁקֶה: Olive discharge that emerges from olives after they are pressed has the legal status of oil and is considered a liquid. It can become ritually impure and can render food susceptible to ritual impurity like other liquids. The *halakha* is in accordance with the opinion of Rabbi Ya'akov (Rambam *Sefer Tahara, Hilkhot Tumat Okhalin* 10:13).

A person may squeeze a cluster of grapes into a pot with food in it – סוֹחֵט אָדָם אֶשְׁכּוֹל שֶׁל עֲנָבִים לְתוֹךְ הַקְּדֵרָה: It is permitted to squeeze juice from grapes into a pot of food on Shabbat in order to improve the flavor of the food, as liquid that is squeezed from fruit directly into food is considered food. However, it is prohibited to squeeze grapes into a bowl without food, or into a vessel that contains only liquids (*Hashlama*; *Me'iri*; Rambam *Sefer Zemanim, Hilkhot Shabbat* 8:10; *Shulḥan Arukh, Oraḥ Ḥayyim* 320:4).

One may milk a goat into a pot of food – חוֹלֵב אָדָם עֵז לְתוֹךְ הַקְּדֵרָה: It is prohibited to milk an animal into an empty bowl on Shabbat and on a Festival. However, on a Festival, it is permitted to milk an animal designated for eating, provided the milk goes directly into a bowl of food to improve the food, or into a bowl with breadcrumbs that will absorb the milk. However, one may not milk all one's animals into a bowl with just one piece of bread in it. Nowadays, several authorities take into consideration the discomfort animals experience when they are not milked and allow milking into utensils containing just one piece of bread (Rambam *Sefer Zemanim, Hilkhot Shabbat* 8:10; *Shulḥan Arukh, Oraḥ Ḥayyim* 505).

HALAKHA

A *zav* who milks a goat, the milk is ritually impure – הֶחָלָב טָמֵא זָב שֶׁחוֹלֵב אֶת הָעֵז: If a *zav* milks a goat, the milk is ritually impure from the very first drop (Rambam *Sefer Tahara, Hilkhot Tumat Okhalin* 9:2).

מְתִיב רָמִי בַּר חָמָא: זָב שֶׁחוֹלֵב אֶת הָעֵז – הֶחָלָב טָמֵא וְאִי אָמְרַתְּ ״מַשְׁקֶה הַבָּא לָאוֹכָלִין אוֹכֶל הוּא״ – בְּמַאי אִיתְכַּשַּׁר?

Rami bar Ḥama raised an objection from the following mishna: In the case of **a *zav* who milks a goat, the milk is ritually impure**[H] whether or not the *zav* actually touched it, as a *zav* renders items ritually impure simply by moving them, or being moved by them, even without direct contact. **And if you say** that **liquid that comes** directly **into food is food** and not liquid, in the case of one who milked directly into a pot of food, the milk should be considered food. The *halakha* is that food cannot become ritually impure unless it is rendered susceptible to ritual impurity through contact with a liquid. **With what** liquid was this milk **rendered susceptible** to ritual impurity?

כִּדְאָמַר רַבִּי יוֹחָנָן: בְּטִיפָּה הַמְלוּכְלֶכֶת עַל פִּי הַדַּד. הָכָא נַמִי: בְּטִיפָּה הַמְלוּכְלֶכֶת עַל פִּי הַדַּד.

The Gemara answers: **As Rabbi Yoḥanan said** in a different context, that a particular statement is referring to **the** first **drop, which is smeared on the top of the teat** in order to moisten it and facilitate nursing or milking, **here too,** it is rendered susceptible to ritual impurity by means **of the drop which is smeared on the top of the teat.** This drop was not intended to fall into the pot of food and is therefore considered a liquid and renders the food susceptible to ritual impurity.

מְתִיב רָבִינָא: טְמֵא מֵת שֶׁסָּחַט זֵיתִים וַעֲנָבִים,

Ravina raised an objection based on what we learned in another mishna: In the case of **one who is ritually impure** with impurity imparted by **a corpse who squeezed olives or grapes**

Perek **XXII**
Daf **145** Amud **a**

NOTES

One who smooths by squeezing grapes – הַמַּחֲלִיק בַּעֲנָבִים: Most of the commentaries on the Mishna explain the case differently, and a similar approach appears in the Jerusalem Talmud: The mishna is not discussing loaves of bread but cakes of pressed figs onto which one would pour grape juice. Some commentaries state that most of this liquid is lost, since it is not absorbed by the figs. Other authorities explain that the juice is intended to provide the figs with a polished sheen rather than to be consumed (see Rambam's Commentary on the Mishna, and other commentaries).

Everyone agrees…is not food – דְּכוּלֵּי עָלְמָא...לָאו אוֹכֶל: The *ge'onim* had a variant text with an opposite formulation: Everyone agrees that…is food. Most commentaries agree that the Gemara reads better according to Rashi's version. However, the *halakha* is in accordance with the text of the *ge'onim* (Rashba).

HALAKHA

One who cuts olives – הַמְפַצֵּעַ בְּזֵיתִים: If one cuts olives with ritually impure hands, the olives are rendered susceptible to ritual impurity by the liquid that seeps out. They also become ritually impure, because cutting them completes their processing and they are then considered food, which can become ritually impure. However, if one cut them to salt them or to check if they have oil, they are not rendered susceptible to ritual impurity (Rambam *Sefer Tahara, Hilkhot Tumat Okhalin* 11:14).

כְּבֵיצָה מְכוּוֶּנֶת – טָהוֹר. הָא יוֹתֵר מִכְּבֵיצָה – טָמֵא. וְאִי אָמְרַתְּ ״מַשְׁקֶה הַבָּא לָאוֹכֶל אוֹכֶל הוּא״ בְּמַאי אִיתְכַּשַּׁר? הוּא מוֹתִיב לָהּ וְהוּא מְפָרֵק לָהּ: בְּסוֹחֵט לְתוֹךְ הַקְּעָרָה.

in the **exact** amount of **an egg-bulk,** the liquid **is ritually pure.** Even though the person touched the food, less than an egg-bulk of food cannot become ritually impure. Once the first drop of liquid is squeezed out, less than an egg-bulk of food remains, and it cannot render the liquid impure. By inference, if he squeezed **more than an egg-bulk,** the liquid **is ritually impure. And if you say** that **liquid that comes into food is** considered **food, in what** manner was this liquid **rendered susceptible** to ritual impurity? **He raised the objection and he resolved it:** It is referring to a case **where** one **squeezes into an** empty **bowl,** in which case the juice is considered a liquid.

אָמַר רַבִּי יִרְמְיָה: כְּתַנָּאֵי; הַמַּחֲלִיק בַּעֲנָבִים – לֹא הוּכְשַׁר, רַבִּי יְהוּדָה אוֹמֵר: הוּכְשַׁר. מַאי לָאו בְּהָא קָמִיפַּלְגִי; מָר סָבַר: מַשְׁקֶה הַבָּא לָאוֹכֶל – אוֹכֶל הוּא, וּמָר סָבַר: לָאו אוֹכֶל הוּא.

Rabbi Yirmeya said: The question of whether liquid squeezed directly from one food into another is considered liquid or food is **parallel to** the following dispute between ***tanna'im***. We learned in a mishna: In the case of **one who smooths** bread before baking it **by** squeezing **grapes**[N] onto it, the bread **was not rendered susceptible** to ritual impurity. **Rabbi Yehuda says: It was rendered susceptible** to ritual impurity. **What, do they not disagree about this?** One **Sage held that liquid that comes into food is food,** and therefore it cannot render bread susceptible to ritual impurity, **and** one **Sage held** that **it is not food** but rather a liquid, and therefore it renders the bread susceptible to ritual impurity.

אָמַר רַב פָּפָּא: דְּכוּלֵּי עָלְמָא – מַשְׁקֶה הַבָּא לָאוֹכֶל – לָאו אוֹכֶל הוּא, וְהָכָא – בְּמַשְׁקֶה הַבָּא לְאִיבּוּד קָמִיפַּלְגִי. מָר סָבַר: מַשְׁקֶה הוּא, וּמָר סָבַר: לָאו מַשְׁקֶה הוּא. וּבִפְלוּגְתָּא דְּהָנֵי תַּנָּאֵי, דְּתַנְיָא: הַמְפַצֵּעַ בְּזֵיתִים בְּיָדַיִם מְסוֹאָבוֹת – הוּכְשַׁר, לְסוֹפְתָן בַּמֶּלַח – לֹא הוּכְשַׁר.

Rav Pappa said that the disputes are not necessarily parallel; it can be explained that **everyone agrees that liquid that comes into food is not food,**[N] **and here they disagree with regard to liquid that goes to waste,** as the liquid that dripped onto the bread eventually evaporates due to the heat of the oven. One **Sage,** Rabbi Yehuda, **held** that **it is** nonetheless **a liquid** and therefore can render the bread susceptible to ritual impurity, **and** one **Sage held that it is not a liquid. And** they disagree in **the dispute between these *tanna'im*, as it was taught** in a *baraita*: In the case of **one who cuts olives**[H] **with soiled,** i.e., ritually impure, **hands,** the olives **are rendered susceptible** to ritual impurity through the liquid that comes from them, and his hands render the olives ritually impure. If he cut them in order **to dip them in salt,** the olives **are not rendered susceptible** to ritual impurity, because if that liquid emerged from the olives against the owner's will, the liquid cannot render food susceptible to ritual impurity.

לֵידַע אִם הִגִּיעוּ זֵיתָיו לְמִסּוֹק אִם לָאו – לֹא הוּכְשַׁר, רַבִּי יְהוּדָה אוֹמֵר: הוּכְשַׁר. מַאי לָאו בְּהָא קָמִיפַּלְגִי, דְּמָר סָבַר: מַשְׁקֶה הָעוֹמֵד לְאִיבּוּד – מַשְׁקֶה הוּא, וּמָר סָבַר: לָאו מַשְׁקֶה הוּא.

If he was cutting in order **to ascertain whether his olives have reached** the stage of ripeness at which they are fit **to be harvested or not, they are not rendered susceptible** to ritual impurity. **Rabbi Yehuda said: They are rendered susceptible** to ritual impurity. **What, do they not disagree with regard to this?** One **Sage,** Rabbi Yehuda, **held** that **liquid** that emerges when one tests the olives but **which stands to** go to waste, **is liquid** and renders food susceptible to ritual impurity; **and** one **Sage held that it is not liquid** and does not render food susceptible to ritual impurity.

אָמַר רַב הוּנָא בְּרֵיהּ דְּרַב יְהוֹשֻׁעַ: הָנֵי תַּנָּאֵי – בְּמַשְׁקֶה הָעוֹמֵד לְאִיבּוּד פְּלִיגִי, וְהָנָךְ תַּנָּאֵי – בְּמַשְׁקֶה הָעוֹמֵד לְצַחְצְחוֹ קָמִיפַּלְגִי.

Rav Huna, son of Rav Yehoshua, said: The last two disputes are not necessarily parallel. **These** *tanna'im*, who disagreed with regard to olives, **disagreed with regard to liquid that stands** to go **to waste, and those** *tanna'im*, who disagreed with regard to the liquid on the bread, **disagreed with regard to liquid that stands** to be used **to shine it.**

אָמַר רַבִּי זֵירָא אָמַר רַב חִיָּיא בַּר אַשִׁי אָמַר רַב: סוֹחֵט אָדָם אֶשְׁכּוֹל שֶׁל עֲנָבִים לְתוֹךְ הַקְּדֵרָה, אֲבָל לֹא לְתוֹךְ הַקְּעָרָה. וְדָג לְצִירוֹ – אֲפִילּוּ לְתוֹךְ הַקְּעָרָה.

Rabbi Zeira said that **Rav Ḥiyya bar Ashi said** that **Rav said: A person may squeeze a cluster of grapes into a pot** with food in it on Shabbat, because liquid that is squeezed directly into food is considered food rather than liquid; **however,** one may **not** do so **into a bowl** that is empty or that contains liquid. **And** squeezing a **fish for its brine** is permitted **even into a bowl.**

יָתֵיב רַב דִּימִי וְקָאָמַר לַהּ לְהָא שְׁמַעְתָּא. אָמַר לֵיהּ אַבָּיֵי לְרַב דִּימִי: אַתּוּן מִשְּׁמֵיהּ דְּרַב מַתְנִיתוּן וְלָא קַשְׁיָא לְכוּ, אֲנַן מִשְּׁמֵיהּ דִּשְׁמוּאֵל מַתְנִינַן לַהּ – וְקַשְׁיָא לַן: מִי אָמַר שְׁמוּאֵל ״דָּג לְצִירוֹ אֲפִילּוּ לְתוֹךְ הַקְּעָרָה״ וְהָאִיתְּמַר: כְּבָשִׁים שֶׁסְּחָטָן, אָמַר רַב: לְגוּפָן – מוּתָּר, לְמֵימֵיהֶן – פָּטוּר, אֲבָל אָסוּר.

Rav Dimi sat and stated this ***halakha*****. Abaye said to Rav Dimi: You teach** this *halakha* **in the name of Rav and it is not difficult for you; we teach it in the name of Shmuel and it is difficult for us** for the following reason: **Did Shmuel say** that it is permitted to squeeze **a fish for its brine even into a bowl? Wasn't it stated** that there was a dispute with regard to **pickled vegetables that one squeezed?**[H] **Rav said:** If he wants to squeeze them because he needs the vegetables **themselves** without the liquid, **it is permitted** to do so even *ab initio* on Shabbat. And if he squeezes them because he needs **their liquid, he is exempt** from bringing a sin-offering, **but it is prohibited** to do so *ab initio*.

וּשְׁלָקוֹת – בֵּין לְגוּפָן בֵּין לְמֵימֵיהֶן – מוּתָּר. וּשְׁמוּאֵל אָמַר: אֶחָד כְּבָשִׁים וְאֶחָד שְׁלָקוֹת, לְגוּפָן – מוּתָּר, לְמֵימֵיהֶן – פָּטוּר אֲבָל אָסוּר.

And with regard to **boiled vegetables, whether** he needs the vegetables **themselves** without their liquid **or whether** he wants to squeeze the vegetables **for their liquids, it is permitted** to squeeze them on Shabbat. **And Shmuel said:** With regard to **both pickled vegetables and boiled vegetables,** if he squeezes them **for** the vegetables **themselves, it is permitted, and** if he squeezes them **for their liquids, he is exempt** from bringing a sin-offering, **but it is prohibited** to do so *ab initio*. Apparently, squeezing fish for its brine[H] falls into the category of squeezing boiled items for their liquid, which according to Shmuel is prohibited. As such, Shmuel's two statements appear contradictory.

אָמַר לֵיהּ: הָאֱלֹהִים, ״עֵינַי רָאוּ וְלֹא זָר (כָּלוּ כִלְיוֹתַי בְּחֵקִי וגו׳״). מִפּוּמֵּיהּ דְּרַבִּי יִרְמְיָה שְׁמִיעַ לִי, וְרַבִּי יִרְמְיָה מֵרַבִּי זֵירָא, וְרַבִּי זֵירָא מֵרַב חִיָּיא בַּר אַשִׁי, וְרַב חִיָּיא בַּר אַשִׁי מֵרַב.

He said to him: You can certainly rely on my version of this statement. To underscore his point, he uttered the oath-like expression: **By God!** and applied the verse: "Whom I shall see for myself; **my eyes have seen it, and not another's**" (Job 19:27).[N] **I heard** this tradition **from the mouth of Rabbi Yirmeya, and Rabbi Yirmeya** heard it **from Rabbi Zeira, and Rabbi Zeira** heard it **from Rav Ḥiyya bar Ashi, and Rav Ḥiyya bar Ashi** heard it **from Rav,** and each transmitter of this tradition is a reliable source.

NOTES

My eyes have seen it, and not another's – עֵינַי רָאוּ וְלֹא זָר: Abaye asked whether or not this statement was attributed to Rav in order to resolve the difficulty with regard to Shmuel, whose two statements are contradictory. Therefore, Rav Dimi told him exactly who transmitted this *halakha*, declaring that each is a reliable source. The attribution to Rav could therefore be relied upon as though they had heard the *halakha* directly from Rav himself.

HALAKHA

Pickled vegetables that one squeezed, etc. – כְּבָשִׁים שֶׁסְּחָטָן וכו׳: It is permitted to squeeze pickled vegetables or boiled vegetables into an empty bowl if one's intention is to improve the taste of the vegetables and not to utilize their liquid. If one is squeezing them in order to utilize the liquid, it is permitted to squeeze the vegetables into a pot of food. Rabbeinu Ḥananel rules stringently and prohibits doing so even in that case. All the commentaries agree that it is prohibited to squeeze the vegetables for their liquid into an empty bowl. The ruling is based on the shared opinion of Shmuel and Rabbi Yoḥanan, who disagree with Rav's opinion that it is permitted to squeeze boiled vegetables even for their liquid. However, the combined position of Rav and Shmuel, which is also confirmed by the Sage from the school of Menashe, overrules Rabbi Yoḥanan's view that one is liable to bring a sin-offering for that transgression (*Maggid Mishne*; Rambam *Sefer Zemanim, Hilkhot Shabbat* 21:13; *Shulḥan Arukh, Oraḥ Ḥayyim* 320:7).

Fish for its brine – דָּג לְצִירוֹ: It is prohibited to squeeze fish to extract its brine, in accordance with the conclusion of the Gemara and the opinion of Shmuel and Rabbi Yoḥanan (*Shulḥan Arukh, Oraḥ Ḥayyim*, 32:7–8).

גּוּפָא: כְּבָשִׁים שֶׁסְּחָטָן, אָמַר רַב: לְגוּפָן – מוּתָּר, לְמֵימֵיהֶן – פָּטוּר אֲבָל אָסוּר. וּשְׁלָקוֹת, בֵּין לְגוּפָן בֵּין לְמֵימֵיהֶן – מוּתָּר. וּשְׁמוּאֵל אָמַר: אֶחָד זֶה וְאֶחָד זֶה, לְגוּפָן – מוּתָּר, לְמֵימֵיהֶן – פָּטוּר אֲבָל אָסוּר. רַבִּי יוֹחָנָן אָמַר: אֶחָד כְּבָשִׁים וְאֶחָד שְׁלָקוֹת, לְגוּפָן – מוּתָּר, לְמֵימֵיהֶן – חַיָּיב חַטָּאת.

Apropos the topic of squeezing pickled vegetables, the Gemara addresses **the matter itself.** We learned that with regard to **pickled vegetables that one squeezed, Rav said** that if he squeezes them **for themselves, it is permitted,** and if he squeezes them **for their liquids he is exempt** from bringing a sin-offering, **but it is prohibited** to do so *ab initio*; **and** with regard to **boiled vegetables,** if he squeezes them **both for themselves and for their liquids it is permitted. And Shmuel said:** With regard to **both this,** pickled vegetables, **and that,** boiled vegetables, squeezing **for** the vegetables **themselves** without liquid **is permitted;** squeezing them **for their liquids, one is exempt, but it is prohibited** to do so *ab initio*. **Rabbi Yoḥanan said:** With regard to **both pickled vegetables and boiled vegetables,** if one squeezes them for the vegetables **themselves it is permitted;** if one squeezes them **for their liquids, he is liable to** bring **a sin-offering** for having performed a labor prohibited by Torah law.

מֵיתִיבִי: סוֹחֲטִין כְּבָשִׁים בַּשַּׁבָּת לְצוֹרֶךְ הַשַּׁבָּת, אֲבָל לֹא לְמוֹצָאֵי שַׁבָּת. וְזֵיתִים וַעֲנָבִים לֹא יִסְחוֹט, וְאִם סָחַט – חַיָּיב חַטָּאת. קַשְׁיָא לְרַב, קַשְׁיָא לִשְׁמוּאֵל, קַשְׁיָא לְרַבִּי יוֹחָנָן. רַב מְתָרֵץ לְטַעְמֵיהּ, שְׁמוּאֵל מְתָרֵץ לְטַעְמֵיהּ, רַבִּי יוֹחָנָן מְתָרֵץ לְטַעְמֵיהּ.

The Gemara **raises an objection** based on that which was taught in a *baraita*: **One may squeeze pickled vegetables on Shabbat for the purpose of** using them on **Shabbat but not for the conclusion of Shabbat. And one may not squeeze olives and grapes** at all on Shabbat, **and if one squeezed** them unwittingly, he is **liable to** bring **a sin-offering.** Apparently, it is permitted to squeeze pickled vegetables *ab initio* on Shabbat for any purpose, even for their juice, and if so, it is **difficult** according **to** the opinion of **Rav,** it is **difficult** according **to** the opinion of **Shmuel,** and it is **difficult** according **to** the opinion of **Rabbi Yoḥanan,** which all assert that squeezing pickled vegetables for their juice is prohibited on some level. The Gemara responds that **Rav interprets** the *baraita* **according to his** line of **reasoning, Shmuel interprets** the *baraita* **according to his** line of **reasoning,** and **Rabbi Yoḥanan interprets** the *baraita* **according to his** line of **reasoning.** The Gemara proceeds to elucidate how the *baraita* is explained according to each opinion.

רַב מְתָרֵץ לְטַעְמֵיהּ: סוֹחֲטִין כְּבָשִׁים בַּשַּׁבָּת לְצוֹרֶךְ הַשַּׁבָּת, אֲבָל לֹא לְמוֹצָאֵי שַׁבָּת. בַּמֶּה דְּבָרִים אֲמוּרִים – לְגוּפָן, אֲבָל לְמֵימֵיהֶן – פָּטוּר אֲבָל אָסוּר. וּשְׁלָקוֹת, בֵּין לְגוּפָן בֵּין לְמֵימֵיהֶן – מוּתָּר. וְזֵיתִים וַעֲנָבִים – לֹא יִסְחוֹט, וְאִם סְחָטָן – חַיָּיב חַטָּאת.

Rav interprets the *baraita* **according to his** line of **reasoning** by emending the *baraita* and adding to it:[N] **One may squeeze pickled vegetables on Shabbat for the purpose of Shabbat, but not for the conclusion of Shabbat. In what** case **is this statement said?** When one squeezes the vegetables **for themselves; however,** if one squeezes them **for their liquid,** he is **exempt** from bringing a sin-offering, **but it is prohibited** to do so. **And** with regard to **boiled vegetables, whether** one squeezes them **for themselves or** whether he does so **for their liquid, it is permitted. And** with regard to **olives and grapes, one may not squeeze** them at all, **and if one squeezed them** unwittingly **he is liable to** bring **a sin-offering.**

שְׁמוּאֵל מְתָרֵץ לְטַעְמֵיהּ: סוֹחֲטִין כְּבָשִׁים בַּשַּׁבָּת לְצוֹרֶךְ הַשַּׁבָּת, הוּא הַדִּין לִשְׁלָקוֹת. בַּמֶּה דְּבָרִים אֲמוּרִים – לְגוּפָן, אֲבָל לְמֵימֵיהֶן – פָּטוּר אֲבָל אָסוּר. וְזֵיתִים וַעֲנָבִים – לֹא יִסְחוֹט, וְאִם סָחַט – חַיָּיב חַטָּאת.

Shmuel interprets the *baraita* **according to his** line of **reasoning** by emending the *baraita* and adding to it: **One may squeeze pickled vegetables on Shabbat for the purpose of Shabbat,** and **the same is true for boiled vegetables. In what** case **is this statement said?** When one squeezes them **for themselves; however,** if he squeezes them **for their liquids,** he is **not liable** to bring a sin-offering, **but it is prohibited** to do so. **And** with regard to **olives and grapes, one may not squeeze** them at all, **and if one squeezed** them unwittingly, he is **liable to** bring **a sin-offering.**

רַבִּי יוֹחָנָן מְתָרֵץ לְטַעְמֵיהּ: סוֹחֲטִין כְּבָשִׁים לְצוֹרֶךְ הַשַּׁבָּת, אֲבָל לֹא לְמוֹצָאֵי שַׁבָּת. אֶחָד כְּבָשִׁים וְאֶחָד שְׁלָקוֹת, בַּמֶּה דְּבָרִים אֲמוּרִים – לְגוּפָן, אֲבָל לְמֵימֵיהֶן – לֹא יִסְחוֹט, וְאִם סָחַט – נַעֲשָׂה כְּמִי שֶׁסָּחַט זֵיתִים וַעֲנָבִים, וְחַיָּיב חַטָּאת.

And **Rabbi Yoḥanan** also **interprets** the *baraita* **according to his** line of **reasoning** by emending the *baraita* and adding to it: **One may squeeze pickled vegetables for the purpose of Shabbat but not for the conclusion of Shabbat,** and that ruling applies **both to pickled vegetables and to boiled vegetables. In what** case **is this statement said?** When one squeezes them **for themselves, but** if he does so **for their liquids, one may not squeeze** them, **and if one squeezed** them unwittingly, **he becomes like one who squeezed olives or grapes, and he is liable to** bring **a sin-offering.**

אָמַר רַב חִיָּיא בַּר אַשִׁי אָמַר רַב: דְּבַר תּוֹרָה – אֵינוֹ חַיָּיב אֶלָּא עַל דְּרִיסַת זֵיתִים וַעֲנָבִים בִּלְבַד. וְכֵן תָּנֵי דְּבֵי מְנַשֶּׁה: דְּבַר תּוֹרָה – אֵינוֹ חַיָּיב אֶלָּא עַל דְּרִיסַת זֵיתִים וַעֲנָבִים בִּלְבַד. וְאֵין עֵד מִפִּי עֵד כָּשֵׁר

Rav Ḥiyya bar Ashi said that **Rav said: By Torah law,**[H] **one is only liable for stomping** on **olives and grapes,** and all other prohibitions related to squeezing or juicing are rabbinic decrees and protective measures. **And similarly, it was taught in** the **school of Menashe: By Torah law, one is only liable for stomping on olives and grapes.** And it was taught in the school of Menashe: **And** testimony of one **witness** based solely on what he learned **from the mouth of** another **witness,** i.e., hearsay testimony, **is valid**

NOTES

Interprets the *baraita* according to his line of reasoning by emending the *baraita* and adding to it – מְתָרֵץ לְטַעְמֵיהּ: In general, emendations of tannaitic texts are only made when it can be proven that the current text is unreliable or has internal contradictions. In this context, since the issue is a *baraita*, which is always considered less authoritative than a mishna, and the text that appears in the *baraita* is difficult according to all known opinions on the matter, the Sages resolved the textual difficulty by adding a significant amount of text to the *baraita*.

HALAKHA

The prohibition of squeezing by Torah law – אִיסּוּר סְחִיטָה מִן הַתּוֹרָה: By Torah law, one is liable for squeezing only if one crushes grapes or olives to use the liquid. The prohibition to squeeze other types of fruit is by rabbinic law, in accordance with the Sage of the school of Menashe (Rambam *Sefer Zemanim*, *Hilkhot Shabbat* 8:10).

אֶלָּא לְעֵדוּת אִשָּׁה בִּלְבַד.

only for testimony that **a woman's** husband died, enabling her to remarry.[N][H] Only in that case can a ruling rely on hearsay testimony, and that is specifically so the woman will be allowed to remarry.

אִיבַּעְיָא לְהוּ עֵד מִפִּי עֵד לְעֵדוּת בְּכוֹר מַהוּ? רַב אַמִי אָסֵיר וְרַב אַסִי שָׁרֵי.

A dilemma was raised before the Sages about a related matter: With regard to **hearsay testimony in testimony** permitting a priest to eat **a firstborn** animal,[N] **what is** the *halakha*? After the destruction of the Temple, the Sages decreed that if a priest has the firstborn offspring of a kosher animal and it becomes blemished, he must bring witnesses to testify that he did not cause the blemish. Priests were suspected of violating the prohibition against inflicting a wound on firstborn animals to enable them to eat the animals. The question here pertains to a case in which there is no one available who can testify that he saw firsthand how the animal was blemished, but there is someone who heard from an eyewitness how the blemish was caused. **Rav Ami prohibited** accepting hearsay testimony in this case, **and Rav Asi permitted** doing so.

אֲמַר לֵיהּ רַב אַמִי לְרַב אַסִי: וְהָא תָּנָא דְּבֵי מְנַשְּׁיָא: אֵין עֵד מִפִּי עֵד כָּשֵׁר אֶלָּא לְעֵדוּת אִשָּׁה בִּלְבַד! אֵימָא: לְעֵדוּת שֶׁהָאִשָּׁה כְּשֵׁרָה לָהּ בִּלְבַד. רַב יֵימַר אַכְשַׁר עֵד מִפִּי עֵד לִבְכוֹר. קָרֵי עֲלֵיהּ מָרֵימָר: יֵימָר שָׁרֵי בּוּכְרָא. וְהִלְכְתָא: עֵד מִפִּי עֵד כָּשֵׁר לִבְכוֹר.

Rav Ami said to Rav Asi: Didn't the school of Menashya teach that **hearsay testimony is only valid in testimony** enabling **a woman** to remarry, indicating that it is not accepted in the case of a firstborn animal? Rav Asi answered: Emend the previously cited ruling and **say:** Hearsay testimony is **only** valid **in testimony for which** the testimony of **a woman is valid.** A woman's testimony is accepted with regard to the death of a man, enabling his wife to remarry, and it is also accepted with regard to a firstborn animal. **Rav Yeimar deemed hearsay testimony** valid in permitting the slaughter of a firstborn animal that developed a blemish. **Mareimar called him: Yeimar who permits the firstborn;** Mareimar was of the opinion that testimony of that kind is invalid and cannot provide the basis to allow the animal to be slaughtered. The Gemara concludes: **And the *halakha* is** that **hearsay testimony is valid with regard to a firstborn** animal.[H]

"חַלּוֹת דְּבַשׁ". כִּי אֲתָא רַב הוֹשַׁעְיָא מִנְּהַרְדְּעָא, אֲתָא וְאַיְיתֵי מַתְנִיתָא בִּידֵיהּ: זֵיתִים וַעֲנָבִים שֶׁרִיסְּקָן מֵעֶרֶב שַׁבָּת, וְיָצְאוּ מֵעַצְמָן – אֲסוּרִין, וְרַבִּי אֶלְעָזָר וְרַבִּי שִׁמְעוֹן מַתִּירִין.

We learned in the mishna that according to Rabbi Eliezer, honey that flows on its own from **honeycombs** is permitted on Shabbat. **When Rav Hoshaya came from Neharde'a, he came and brought a *baraita* with him:** With regard to **olives and grapes that one crushed before Shabbat and** their juices **seeped out on their own**[H] on Shabbat, the juices **are prohibited** for use on Shabbat; **and Rabbi Elazar and Rabbi Shimon permit** using them.

אֲמַר רַב יוֹסֵף: גַּבְרָא יְתֵירָא אֲתָא לְאַשְׁמְעִינַן?! אֲמַר לֵיהּ אַבַּיֵי: טוּבָא קָא מַשְׁמַע לָן, דְּאִי מִמַּתְנִיתִין – הֲוָה אָמִינָא: הָתָם הוּא – דְּמֵעִיקָּרָא אוּכְלָא וּלְבַסּוֹף אוּכְלָא, אֲבָל הָכָא – דְּמֵעִיקָּרָא אוּכְלָא וּלְבַסּוֹף מַשְׁקֶה – אֵימָא לָא, קָא מַשְׁמַע לָן.

Rav Yosef said rhetorically: **Did he** merely **come to teach us an additional person?** This opinion already appears in the mishna in the name of Rabbi Elazar. Did Rav Hoshaya cite the *baraita* merely to add the name of Rabbi Shimon? **Abaye said to him: He is teaching us a great deal, as if** we learned this matter **from the mishna** alone, **I would have said: It is there that it is** permitted, because **initially** it was **food and ultimately** it remained **food,** since it is possible to assert that the honey that seeped is a food rather than a liquid. **However, here,** with regard to olives and grapes, **which initially** were **food and ultimately** became **liquid, say** that it is **not** permitted even according to Rabbi Elazar. Therefore, **he is teaching us** that Rabbi Elazar rules leniently even in the case of olives and grapes.

NOTES

Testimony enabling a woman to remarry – עֵדוּת אִשָּׁה: This is referring to testimony that a woman's husband has died, which permits her to remarry. Testimony from people whose testimony is not accepted in other circumstances is accepted for this purpose, including a single witness, a witness providing secondhand testimony, certain relatives, women, slaves, a non-Jew who mentions it incidentally, and others. With regard to the reason for this leniency, see Rashi's commentary on the Gemara here. The Rambam explains that since testimony enabling a woman to remarry establishes a fact rather than attests to an action, and since if the testimony is false, the lie is likely to be exposed, it is not considered testimony in the formal, legal sense of the term.

Testimony permitting a priest to eat a firstborn animal – עֵדוּת בְּכוֹר: The Torah commands one to give the firstborn offspring of kosher animals to a priest. During the Temple period, unblemished firstborn animals were offered as sacrifices, and their meat would be eaten by the priests. Blemished firstborn animals also belonged to the priests, and the priests could eat them as non-sacred meat once experts determined that the blemish is permanent. Priests were suspected of purposely causing blemishes to firstborn animals so that they would be allowed to eat them. Consequently, the Sages decreed that priests could not eat the meat of a firstborn animal without testimony to the cause of the blemish. Since this testimony was required only to alleviate suspicion, the Sages were lenient with regard to its requirements.

HALAKHA

Those who are valid for testimony enabling a woman to remarry – הַכְּשֵׁרִים לְעֵדוּת אִשָּׁה: Hearsay testimony is admissible to ascertain that a man died overseas, to enable his wife to remarry. Similarly, testimony is accepted for this purpose from a single witness, a woman, a slave, and a relative (Rambam *Sefer Nashim, Hilkhot Geirushin* 12:15; *Shulḥan Arukh, Even HaEzer* 17:3).

Testimony with regard to a firstborn animal – עֵדוּת בְּכוֹר: Hearsay testimony is admissible to ascertain that a firstborn animal's blemish was not purposely inflicted by a priest (Rambam *Sefer Korbanot, Hilkhot Bekhorot* 2:15; *Shulḥan Arukh, Yoreh De'a* 314:5).

Olives and grapes that one crushed before Shabbat and their juices seeped out on their own – זֵיתִים וַעֲנָבִים שֶׁרִיסְּקָן מֵעֶרֶב שַׁבָּת, וְיָצְאוּ מֵעַצְמָן: On Shabbat it is permitted to use liquid that seeps from olives and grapes that were crushed before Shabbat (Rambam *Sefer Zemanim, Hilkhot Shabbat* 21:15; *Shulḥan Arukh, Oraḥ Ḥayyim* 252:5, 320:2).

מתני׳ כֹּל שֶׁבָּא בַּחַמִּין מֵעֶרֶב שַׁבָּת – שׁוֹרִין אוֹתוֹ בַּחַמִּין בַּשַּׁבָּת. וְכֹל שֶׁלֹּא בָּא בַּחַמִּין מֵעֶרֶב שַׁבָּת – מְדִיחִין אוֹתוֹ בַּחַמִּין בַּשַּׁבָּת. חוּץ מִן הַמָּלִיחַ הַיָּשָׁן (וְדָגִים מְלוּחִין קְטַנִּים) וְקוֹלְיַיס הָאִיסְפָּנִין, שֶׁהֲדָחָתָן זוֹ הִיא גְּמַר מְלַאכְתָּן.

MISHNA Any salted food item **that was** already **placed in hot water,**[H] i.e., cooked, **before Shabbat, one may soak it in hot water** even **on Shabbat. And anything that was not placed in hot water before Shabbat, one may rinse it in hot water on Shabbat** but may not soak it, **with the exception of old salted fish and small salted fish and** the ***kolyas ha'ispanin***[B] fish, **for which rinsing** with hot water **itself is completion of the prohibited labor** of cooking.

גמ׳ כְּגוֹן מַאי? אֲמַר רַב סָפְרָא: כְּגוֹן תַּרְנְגוֹלְתָּא דְּרַבִּי אַבָּא. וַאֲמַר רַב סָפְרָא: זִימְנָא חֲדָא אִיקְלָעִית לְהָתָם, וְאוֹכְלַן מִינֵּיהּ, וְאִי לָא רַבִּי אַבָּא דְּאַשְׁקְיַין חַמְרָא בַּר תְּלָתָא טַרְפֵּי – אִיתְנַסִּי.

GEMARA We learned in the mishna that an item that was cooked before Shabbat may be soaked in hot water on Shabbat. The Gemara asks: **In what case** would soaking in hot water be required after the item was already cooked? **Rav Safra said: In the case of the chicken of Rabbi Abba,**[N] which for medical reasons was cooked so thoroughly that it completely dissolved. **And Rav Safra said: One time I happened to come there and he fed me** chicken prepared that way, **and if not** for the fact that **Rabbi Abba gave me three-leaf-,** i.e., year, **old wine to drink, I would have been forced** to vomit.

רַבִּי יוֹחָנָן רָייק מִכּוּתָּח דְּבַבְלָאֵי. אֲמַר רַב יוֹסֵף: וְלִירוֹק אֲנַן מִתַּרְנְגוֹלְתָּא דְּרַבִּי אַבָּא. וְעוֹד, אֲמַר רַב גָּזָא: זִימְנָא חֲדָא אִיקְלָעִית לְהָתָם, וַעֲבְדִית כּוּתָּח דְּבַבְלָאֵי, שְׁאִילוּ מִינֵּיהּ כָּל בְּרִיחֵי מַעַרְבָא.

The Gemara relates that Rabbi Yoḥanan would spit from the thought of Babylonian *kutaḥ*,[L] because he found it so disgusting. **Rav Yosef said: Then we should spit from** the thought of **Rabbi Abba's chicken,** which is even more disgusting to people from Babylonia. **And furthermore, Rav Gaza said:** On **one occasion I happened to come there,** to Eretz Yisrael, **and I prepared Babylonian *kutaḥ*,** and **all of the sick people of the West,** Eretz Yisrael, **asked me for it.** Apparently, not everyone in Eretz Yisrael found it disgusting.

״כֹּל שֶׁלֹּא בָּא בַּחַמִּין וכו׳״. הֵדִיחַ מַאי? אָמַר רַב יוֹסֵף: הֵדִיחַ – חַיָּיב חַטָּאת. אֲמַר מָר בְּרֵיהּ דְּרָבִינָא: אַף אֲנַן נַמִי תְּנֵינָא ״חוּץ מִמָּלִיחַ יָשָׁן וְקוֹלְיַיס הָאִיסְפָּנִין שֶׁהֲדָחָתָן זוֹ הִיא גְּמָר מְלַאכְתָּן״ שְׁמַע מִינָּהּ.

We learned in the mishna: **Anything that was not** cooked **in hot water** before Shabbat, one may rinse it in hot water on Shabbat except for salted fish and *kolyas ha'ispanin*. The Gemara asks: If **one** unwittingly **rinsed** it, **what is** the *halakha*? **Rav Yosef said:** If **one rinsed** these foods, he is **liable to** bring **a sin-offering** for having performed the prohibited labor of cooking. **Mar, son of Ravina, said: We, too, have** also **learned** this ruling in the mishna, which states: **Except for old salted fish and *kolyas ha'ispanin*, rinsing itself is completion of their prohibited labor** of cooking. One who rinses these items is considered to have performed a prohibited labor. The Gemara concludes: Indeed, **learn from this** that this is the ruling.

יְתֵיב רַבִּי חִיָּיא בַּר אַבָּא וְרַבִּי אַסִּי קַמֵּיהּ דְּרַבִּי יוֹחָנָן, וִיתֵיב רַבִּי יוֹחָנָן וְקָא מְנַמְנֵם. אֲמַר לֵיהּ רַבִּי חִיָּיא בַּר אַבָּא לְרַבִּי אַסִּי: מִפְּנֵי מָה עוֹפוֹת שֶׁבְּבָבֶל שְׁמֵנִים? אֲמַר לֵיהּ: כַּלֵּךְ לְמִדְבַּר עַזָּה וְאַרְאֲךָ שְׁמֵנִים מֵהֶן. מִפְּנֵי מָה מוֹעֲדִים שֶׁבְּבָבֶל שְׂמֵחִים? מִפְּנֵי שֶׁהֵן עֲנִיִּים. מִפְּנֵי מָה תַּלְמִידֵי חֲכָמִים שֶׁבְּבָבֶל מְצוּיָּינִין? לְפִי שֶׁאֵינָן בְּנֵי תוֹרָה. מִפְּנֵי מָה גּוֹיִם מְזוֹהָמִים? מִפְּנֵי שֶׁאוֹכְלִין שְׁקָצִים וּרְמָשִׂים.

Apropos relations between the Jews of Eretz Yisrael and Babylonia, the Gemara relates: **Rabbi Ḥiyya bar Abba and Rabbi Asi were sitting before Rabbi Yoḥanan, and Rabbi Yoḥanan was sitting and dozing.** In the meantime the two of them conversed. **Rabbi Ḥiyya bar Abba said to Rabbi Asi: For what** reason **are the fowl in Babylonia fatter** than those in Eretz Yisrael? **He said to him:** This is not at all the case; **go to the desert of Gaza** in Eretz Yisrael, **and I will show you** fowl that are **fatter than them.** Rabbi Ḥiyya bar Abba then asked: **For what** reason are **Festivals in Babylonia more joyous** than those in Eretz Yisrael? Rabbi Asi answered him: **Because** in Babylonia **they are poor,** and it is only on Festivals that they have a lot to eat, which causes them to rejoice. Rabbi Ḥiyya then asked: **For what** reason **are Torah scholars in Babylonia distinguished** by their special rabbinic garb? Rabbi Asi answered: **Because they are not well-versed in Torah.**[N] If they would not distinguish themselves by dressing differently, they would not be respected for their Torah knowledge. He then asked: **For what** reason **are gentiles** ethically **contaminated?** He answered: **Because they eat abominable creatures and crawling things,** and that causes bad character traits.

HALAKHA

Any salted food item that was already placed in hot water, etc. – כֹּל שֶׁבָּא בַּחַמִּין וכו׳: One is permitted to soak food that was cooked before Shabbat and is dry, e.g., whose sauce was poured off (*Mishna Berura*), in hot water on Shabbat, even in a primary vessel, i.e., one that was heated directly on the fire (*Magen Avraham*). If the food was not yet cooked, it is permitted to rinse it with hot water from a secondary vessel, i.e., a vessel into which hot water was poured (*Magen Avraham*). However, it is prohibited to rinse old salted fish or other types of fish whose cooking process is completed in this manner (Rambam *Sefer Zemanim, Hilkhot Shabbat* 22:8; *Shulḥan Arukh, Oraḥ Ḥayyim* 318:4).

BACKGROUND

***Kolyas ha'ispanin* – קוֹלְיַיס הָאִיסְפָּנִין:** A kind of mackerel, also known as *Scomber colias*, which can be found in several bodies of water, none in the vicinity of Eretz Yisrael. Its skin is soft and thin, and it is not eaten cooked, but rather smoked or salted. According to the *ge'onim*, the Hebrew name for this fish is *shavut*.

Kolyas ha'ispanin

NOTES

The chicken of Rabbi Abba – תַּרְנְגוֹלְתָּא דְּרַבִּי אַבָּא: Some commentaries explain that this chicken was heavily salted. Therefore, it was necessary to soak it after cooking it to temper the saltiness (Rabbeinu Ḥananel).

Because they are not well-versed in Torah – לְפִי שֶׁאֵינָן בְּנֵי תוֹרָה: Rabbi Elazar Moshe Horowitz explains that the general population of Babylonia was not well-versed in Torah. Therefore, they would not have respected their Sages if they did not dress in special garments.

LANGUAGE

***Kutaḥ* – כּוּתָּח:** From the Persian katax, meaning milk or buttermilk.

אִיתְּעַר בְּהוּ רַבִּי יוֹחָנָן, אֲמַר לְהוּ: דַּרְדְּקֵי! לֹא כָּךְ אָמַרְתִּי לָכֶם "אֱמוֹר לַחָכְמָה אֲחוֹתִי אָתְּ" אִם בָּרוּר לְךָ הַדָּבָר כַּאֲחוֹתְךָ שֶׁהִיא אֲסוּרָה לְךָ – אוֹמְרֵהוּ, וְאִם לָאו – לֹא תֹּאמְרֵהוּ! אָמְרוּ לֵיהּ: וְלֵימָא לָן מָר אֵיזֶה מֵהֶן. מִפְּנֵי מָה עוֹפוֹת שֶׁבְּבָבֶל שְׁמֵנִים? מִפְּנֵי שֶׁלֹּא גָּלוּ, שֶׁנֶּאֱמַר "שַׁאֲנַן מוֹאָב מִנְּעוּרָיו וְשֹׁקֵט הוּא אֶל שְׁמָרָיו וּבַגּוֹלָה לֹא הָלָךְ".

Rabbi Yoḥanan woke up due to their discussion **and said to them:** You **children, did I not tell you this,** that the verse **"Say to wisdom: You are my sister,** and call understanding your kin" (Proverbs 7:4) means that **if the matter is as clear to you as the fact that your sister is forbidden to you,**[H] **say it, and if not, do not say it;** and these explanations that you offered are unfounded. **They said to him: Then will the Master tell us** the answers to **some of them?** He said to them: **Why are the fowl in Babylonia fatter** than those in Eretz Yisrael? **Because they were not exiled, as it says: "Moab has been at ease since his youth and he has settled on his lees,** and he was not emptied from vessel to vessel **and did not go into captivity;** therefore his taste remained in him and his scent did not change" (Jeremiah 48:11). Apparently, one who is not exiled retains his strength.

וְהָכָא מְנָלַן דְּגָלוּ – דְּתַנְיָא, רַבִּי יְהוּדָה אוֹמֵר: חֲמִשִּׁים וּשְׁתַּיִם שָׁנָה לֹא עָבַר אִישׁ בִּיהוּדָה, שֶׁנֶּאֱמַר "עַל הֶהָרִים אֶשָּׂא בְכִי וָנֶהִי וגו׳ מֵעוֹף הַשָּׁמַיִם וְעַד בְּהֵמָה נָדְדוּ הָלָכוּ". בְּהֵמָ"ה בְּגִימַטְרִיָּא חַמְשִׁין וְתַרְתֵּין הָווּ.

And here in Eretz Yisrael, **from where do we** derive **that** even the animals and birds **were exiled? As it was taught** in a *baraita*: **Rabbi Yehuda says** that **no person passed through** the land of **Judea** for **fifty-two years, as it is stated: "I will raise crying and wailing for the mountains** and a lamentation for the pastures of the wilderness, for they have been burned, with no person passing through, and they do not hear the voice of the cattle, **from the bird of the heavens to the beast** [*behema*, spelled *beit, heh, mem, heh*], **all have fled and gone"** (Jeremiah 9:9). ***Behema*** **has a numerical value of fifty-two,** alluding to the fact that no one passed through for fifty-two years. From the verse cited in this *baraita*, it is clear that even the animals and birds were exiled, as it states: "All have fled and gone."

אָמַר רַבִּי יַעֲקֹב אָמַר רַבִּי יוֹחָנָן: כּוּלָּן חָזְרוּ, חוּץ מִקּוֹלְיָיס הָאִיסְפָּנִין. דַּאֲמַר רַב: הָנֵי מַדְרֵי דְּבָבֶל מְהַדְרִי מַיָּא לְעֵין עֵיטָם, וְהַאי כֵּיוָן דְּלָא שָׁרֵיר שִׁדְרֵיהּ לָא מָצֵי סָלֵיק.

Rabbi Ya'akov said that **Rabbi Yoḥanan said: They all returned except for the** ***kolyas ha'ispanin*****, as Rav said: Those inclines of Babylonia return the water** through underground watercourses **to the spring of Eitam** in Eretz Yisrael, and the fish also returned through these watercourses. **And this** fish, the *kolyas*, **because its spine is not strong, it could not ascend** these watercourses and did not return to Eretz Yisrael.

מִפְּנֵי מָה מוֹעֲדִים שֶׁבְּבָבֶל שְׂמֵחִים? מִפְּנֵי שֶׁלֹּא הָיוּ בְּאוֹתָהּ קְלָלָה, דִּכְתִיב "וְהִשְׁבַּתִּי כָּל מְשׂוֹשָׂהּ חַגָּהּ חָדְשָׁהּ וְשַׁבַּתָּהּ וְכֹל מוֹעֲדָהּ". וּכְתִיב "חָדְשֵׁיכֶם וּמוֹעֲדֵיכֶם שָׂנְאָה נַפְשִׁי הָיוּ עָלַי לָטֹרַח". מַאי "הָיוּ עָלַי לָטֹרַח"? – אָמַר רַבִּי אֶלְעָזָר: אָמַר הַקָּדוֹשׁ בָּרוּךְ הוּא: לֹא דַּיָּין לְיִשְׂרָאֵל שֶׁחוֹטְאִין לְפָנַי, אֶלָּא שֶׁמַּטְרִיחִין אוֹתִי לֵידַע אֵיזוֹ גְּזֵירָה קָשָׁה אָבִיא עֲלֵיהֶן! אָמַר רַבִּי יִצְחָק: אֵין לְךָ כָּל רֶגֶל וָרֶגֶל שֶׁלֹּא בָּאֲתָה בּוֹלֶשֶׁת לְצִיפּוֹרִי. וְאָמַר רַבִּי חֲנִינָא: אֵין לְךָ כָּל רֶגֶל וָרֶגֶל שֶׁלֹּא בָּא לִטְבֶרְיָה אֶגְמוֹן וְקַמְטוֹן וּבַעַל זְמוֹרָה.

Rabbi Yoḥanan continued to answer the questions of Rabbi Ḥiyya bar Abba and Rabbi Asi: **For what** reason are the **Festivals in Babylonia more joyous** than those in Eretz Yisrael? **Because they were not** included **in that curse** with which Eretz Yisrael was cursed, **as it is written: "And I will cause all of her happiness to cease, her Festival, her New Moon, and her Shabbat and all her Festivals"** (Hosea 2:13). **And it is** also **written: "My soul hates your New Moons and your Festivals; they are a burden to Me;** I am weary to bear them" (Isaiah 1:14). **What is** the meaning of the phrase: **"They are a burden to me"? Rabbi Elazar said** that **the Holy One, Blessed be He, said: Is it not enough for the Jewish people that they sin before Me, that they** also **burden Me to know which harsh decree I will bring upon them? Rabbi Yitzḥak said:** Because of this curse, **there is not a single Festival on which troops did not come to Tzippori** to conduct searches or to collect taxes. **And Rabbi Ḥanina said: There is not a single Festival on which an** ***egmon***[L] **and a** ***kamton***[L] **and a branch bearer,**[B] Roman officials, **did not come to Tiberias** to collect taxes, thereby disrupting the festive celebrations.

מִפְּנֵי מָה תַּלְמִידֵי חֲכָמִים שֶׁבְּבָבֶל מְצוּיָּינִין? לְפִי שֶׁאֵינָן בְּנֵי מְקוֹמָן. דְּאָמְרִי אֱינָשֵׁי: בְּמָתָא – שְׁמַאי, בְּלָא מָתָא – תּוֹתְבַאי. "הַבָּאִים יַשְׁרֵשׁ יַעֲקֹב יָצִיץ וּפָרַח יִשְׂרָאֵל", תָּנֵי רַב יוֹסֵף: אֵלּוּ תַּלְמִידֵי חֲכָמִים שֶׁבְּבָבֶל, שֶׁעוֹשִׂין צִיצִין וּפְרָחִים לַתּוֹרָה.

For what reason are **the Torah scholars in Babylonia distinguished** by special garb? **Because they are not native to that place** and therefore require special dress to distinguish themselves, **as people say** in the folk expression: **In my own city,** I am honored for **my name; in a place that is not my own city,** I am honored for **my clothing.** The Gemara then praised the Sages of Babylonia by interpreting the verse "In days **to come Jacob will take root, Israel will bud and blossom"** (Isaiah 27:6). **Rav Yosef taught: These are the Torah scholars in Babylonia, who add buds and blossoms to the Torah.**

מִפְּנֵי מָה גּוֹיִם מְזוֹהָמִין? שֶׁלֹּא עָמְדוּ עַל הַר סִינַי. שֶׁבְּשָׁעָה

Rabbi Yoḥanan then explained to them: **Why are gentiles** ethically **contaminated?** It is because **they did not stand on Mount Sinai. As when**

HALAKHA

As clear to you as the fact that your sister is forbidden to you – בָּרוּר לְךָ הַדָּבָר כַּאֲחוֹתְךָ שֶׁהִיא אֲסוּרָה לְךָ: A judge must investigate each case extensively and should not issue a ruling until the *halakha* is absolutely clear to him beyond a shadow of a doubt (Rambam *Sefer Shofetim, Hilkhot Sanhedrin* 20:7; *Shulḥan Arukh, Ḥoshen Mishpat* 10:1).

BACKGROUND

Branch bearer – בַּעַל זְמוֹרָה: Apparently, this title referred to a Roman official, since it was common for officials, called *licotor*, carrying a bundle of branches or staffs used to give lashes, to march before high-ranking officers as a sign of governmental authority.

Roman officials carrying bundles of staffs as a sign of authority

LANGUAGE

Egmon **– אֶגְמוֹן:** From the Greek ἡγεμών, *egemon*, meaning general or ruler. It is usually written *hegmon*, with a *heh* instead of an *alef*.

Kamton **– קַמְטוֹן:** From the Latin comito, meaning accompany or follow. Comito originated from the Latin comes, meaning companion, which refers to the escorts of important people. The Latin word comes in the sense of government or a nobleman is derived from the same root (see Rashi).

שֶׁבָּא נָחָשׁ עַל חַוָּה הִטִּיל בָּהּ זוּהֲמָא. יִשְׂרָאֵל שֶׁעָמְדוּ עַל הַר סִינַי – פָּסְקָה זוּהֲמָתָן, גּוֹיִם שֶׁלֹּא עָמְדוּ עַל הַר סִינַי – לֹא פָּסְקָה זוּהֲמָתָן. אֲמַר לֵיהּ רַב אַחָא בְּרֵיהּ דְּרָבָא לְרַב אַשִׁי: גֵּרִים מַאי? אֲמַר לֵיהּ: אַף עַל גַּב דְּאִינְהוּ לָא הָווּ, מַזָּלַיְיהוּ הָווּ, דִּכְתִיב ״אֶת אֲשֶׁר יֶשְׁנוֹ פֹּה עִמָּנוּ עוֹמֵד הַיּוֹם לִפְנֵי ה׳ אֱלֹהֵינוּ וְאֵת אֲשֶׁר אֵינֶנּוּ פֹּה וגו׳״.

the snake came upon Eve,[N] i.e., when it seduced her to eat from the Tree of Knowledge, **it infected her with** moral **contamination,** and this contamination remained in all human beings. When the **Jewish people stood at Mount Sinai, their contamination ceased,** whereas **gentiles did not stand at Mount Sinai,** and **their contamination never ceased. Rav Aḥa, the son of Rava, said to Rav Ashi: What** about **converts?** How do you explain the cessation of their moral contamination? Rav Ashi **said to him: Even though they** themselves **were not** at Mount Sinai, **their guardian angels were** present, **as it is written:** "It is not with you alone that I make this covenant and this oath, but **with he that stands here with us today before the Lord our God, and with he that is not here** with us today" (Deuteronomy 29:13–14), and this includes converts.

וּפְלִיגָא דְּרַבִּי אַבָּא בַּר כָּהֲנָא, דְּאָמַר רַבִּי אַבָּא בַּר כָּהֲנָא: עַד שְׁלֹשָׁה דּוֹרוֹת לֹא פָּסְקָה זוּהֲמָא מֵאֲבוֹתֵינוּ; אַבְרָהָם הוֹלִיד אֶת יִשְׁמָעֵאל, יִצְחָק הוֹלִיד אֶת עֵשָׂו, יַעֲקֹב הוֹלִיד שְׁנֵים עָשָׂר שְׁבָטִים שֶׁלֹּא הָיָה בָּהֶן שׁוּם דּוֹפִי.

The Gemara points out that this opinion **disagrees with Rabbi Abba bar Kahana, as Rabbi Abba bar Kahana said: Until three generations** passed, the moral **contamination did not cease from our forefathers: Abraham fathered Ishmael,** who was of lowly moral stature; **Isaac fathered Esau;** finally, **Jacob fathered twelve tribes in whom there was no flaw.** Rabbi Abba bar Kahana holds that the moral contamination ceased in the Patriarchs long before the Revelation at Sinai.

מתני׳ שׁוֹבֵר אָדָם אֶת הֶחָבִית לֶאֱכוֹל הֵימֶנָּה גְּרוֹגְרוֹת, וּבִלְבַד שֶׁלֹּא יִתְכַּוֵּין לַעֲשׂוֹת כְּלִי. וְאֵין נוֹקְבִין מְגוּפָה שֶׁל חָבִית – דִּבְרֵי רַבִּי יְהוּדָה, וַחֲכָמִים מַתִּירִין. וְלֹא יִקְבֶנָּה מִצִּדָּהּ, וְאִם הָיְתָה נְקוּבָה – לֹא יִתֵּן עָלֶיהָ שַׁעֲוָה, מִפְּנֵי שֶׁהוּא מְמָרֵחַ. אָמַר רַבִּי יְהוּדָה: מַעֲשֶׂה בָּא לִפְנֵי רַבָּן יוֹחָנָן בֶּן זַכַּאי בַּעֲרָב, וְאָמַר: חוֹשְׁשַׁנִי לוֹ מֵחַטָּאת.

MISHNA **A person may break a barrel**[NH] on Shabbat in order **to eat dried figs from it,**[N] **provided he does not intend to make a vessel. And one may not perforate the plug of a barrel**[HB] to extract wine from it; rather, one must remove the plug entirely to avoid creating a new opening for the barrel. This is **the statement of Rabbi Yehuda. And the Rabbis permit** puncturing the plug, but they too restrict this leniency and say that **one may not perforate** the plug of the barrel **on its side. And if it was** already **perforated, one may not apply wax to it**[H] to seal the hole, **because** in doing so **he spreads** the wax evenly on the barrel and thereby violates the prohibited labor of smoothing. **Rabbi Yehuda said: An incident** of that kind **came before Rabban Yoḥanan ben Zakkai in** the city of **Arav, and he said: I am concerned for him,** because he may be liable **to** bring **a sin-offering** as a result of this.

גמ׳ אָמַר רַבִּי אוֹשַׁעְיָא: לֹא שָׁנוּ אֶלָּא דְּרוּסוֹת, אֲבָל מְפוֹרָדוֹת – לֹא. וּמְפוֹרָדוֹת לֹא?

GEMARA **Rabbi Oshaya said: They only taught** that it is permitted to break open a barrel when the figs were **pressed** together. This is because in that case it is permissible to use a utensil to separate the figs, that utensil may also be utilized to break open the barrel. **However,** if the figs were already **separated,** it is **not** permitted to handle a utensil for the sole purpose of breaking the barrel. The Gemara asks: **And** is it **not** permitted to break the barrel for **separated** figs?

NOTES

The snake came upon Eve – שֶׁבָּא נָחָשׁ עַל חַוָּה: See Rashi for the source of this homiletic interpretation. The majority of commentaries understood this phrase, the plain sense of which would refer to sexual intercourse, as a metaphor. As a consequence of Eve's accepting the snake's advice, humanity became morally corrupt, unable to become completely purified until the Torah was given to the Jewish people, or until the period of the Patriarchs, depending on the two views cited in the Gemara.

A person may break a barrel – שׁוֹבֵר אָדָם אֶת הֶחָבִית: There is a dispute with regard to the rationale for this leniency. Rashi explained that it is based on the fact that breaking a barrel is a destructive act that does not constitute a violation of Torah law. The Ran and other commentaries add that destructive acts are only permitted *ab initio* in cases of this kind, where one performs the act to fulfill a Shabbat need.

To eat dried figs from it – לֶאֱכוֹל הֵימֶנָּה גְּרוֹגְרוֹת: The Hebrew term usually used for dried figs that were pressed together is *deveilim*. By using the term *gerogerot*, the mishna teaches that even if the figs were only somewhat attached due to their having been packed tightly together, it is permitted to bring a utensil to cut them apart and to open the barrel, even according to Rabbi Neḥemya (*Adderet Eliyahu*).

BACKGROUND

Barrel and plug – חָבִית וּמְגוּפָה: During the week, people would either remove the plug from a barrel or make a hole in it to pour out wine. Afterward they would seal it with wax to preserve the flavor of the wine.

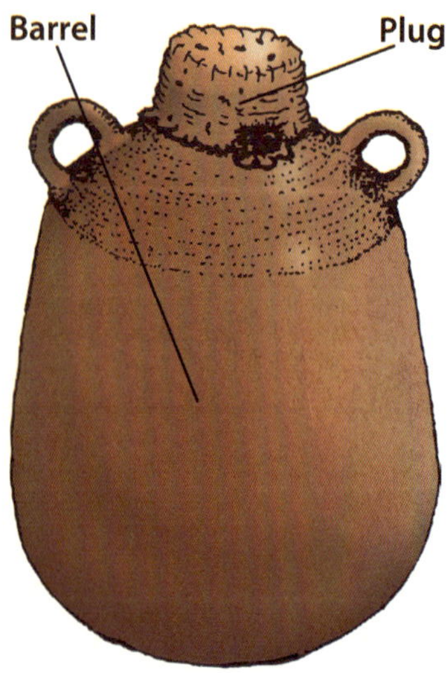

Earthenware barrel with a plug or cover on top

HALAKHA

Breaking a barrel – שְׁבִירַת חָבִית: On Shabbat, it is prohibited to break a barrel that was whole. However, if it was broken previously and its pieces were reattached with pitch or the like, it is permitted to break the barrel on Shabbat, provided that one does not intend to create a utensil. The *halakha* is in accordance with our mishna and the Gemara in tractate *Beitza* (*Tosafot*; Rambam *Sefer Zemanim, Hilkhot Shabbat* 23:2; *Shulḥan Arukh, Oraḥ Ḥayyim* 314:1).

Perforating the plug of a barrel – נְקִיבַת מְגוּפָה: It is permitted to perforate the top of a barrel plug, because it is not similar to creating an opening in the barrel. The *halakha* is in accordance with the opinion of the Rabbis (Rambam *Sefer Zemanim, Hilkhot Shabbat* 23:2; *Shulḥan Arukh, Oraḥ Ḥayyim* 314:6)

If it was already perforated, one may not apply wax to it – הָיְתָה נְקוּבָה לֹא יִתֵּן עָלֶיהָ שַׁעֲוָה: On Shabbat, one may not spread wax over a hole on a barrel to seal it, because this is a violation of the labor of smoothing (Rambam *Sefer Zemanim, Hilkhot Shabbat* 23:11; *Shulḥan Arukh, Oraḥ Ḥayyim* 314:11).

מֵיתִיבִי, רַבִּי שִׁמְעוֹן בֶּן גַּמְלִיאֵל אוֹמֵר: מֵבִיא אָדָם אֶת הֶחָבִית שֶׁל יַיִן וּמַתִּיז רֹאשָׁהּ בַּסַּיִיף, וּמַנִּיחָהּ לִפְנֵי הָאוֹרְחִים בַּשַּׁבָּת וְאֵינוֹ חוֹשֵׁשׁ! הַהִיא רַבָּנַן, מַתְנִיתִין – רַבִּי נְחֶמְיָה הִיא.

The Gemara **raises an objection** based on a *baraita*: **Rabban Shimon ben Gamliel says: A person may bring a barrel of wine and cut off** the **top** of the barrel **with a sword**[H] **and place it before the guests on Shabbat without concern** that it is prohibited to move the sword or that doing so constitutes the creation of a new vessel, which is prohibited. Apparently, it is permitted to move a sword in order to open a barrel on Shabbat even if it is not needed to cut the contents of the barrel. The Gemara answers for Rabbi Oshaya: **That** *baraita*, which cites the opinion of Rabban Shimon ben Gamliel, is in accordance with the opinion of **the Rabbis,** whereas **our mishna is** in accordance with the opinion of **Rabbi Neḥemya,** who said that it is prohibited to move any utensil on Shabbat for any purpose other than that for which the utensil is designated.

וּמַאי דּוֹחֲקֵיהּ דְּרַבִּי אוֹשַׁעְיָא לְאוֹקְמֵי מַתְנִיתִין כְּרַבִּי נְחֶמְיָה וּבִדְרוּסוֹת, לוֹקְמָהּ בִּמְפוֹרָדוֹת וְרַבָּנַן! אֲמַר רָבָא: מַתְנִיתִין קַשִּׁיתֵיהּ, מַאי אִירְיָא דְּתָנֵי ״גְּרוֹגְרוֹת״ לִיתְנֵי ״פֵּירוֹת״! אֶלָּא שְׁמַע מִינָּהּ – בִּדְרוּסוֹת.

The Gemara asks: **And what forced Rabbi Oshaya to establish the mishna in accordance with** the minority opinion of **Rabbi Neḥemya** and to say that it is referring only **to** the case of a **pressed** dried figs? **Let him establish** that the mishna is referring even **to separated** figs **and** is in accordance with the opinion of **the Rabbis. Rava said: The mishna** posed **a difficulty for him; why did** the *tanna* **teach particularly** about **dried figs? Let him teach** a more general *halakha* with regard to **fruit. Rather, learn from here that** the mishna is referring specifically to **pressed** dried figs, and it is because one requires a utensil to separate them that he may use it to open the barrel as well.

תַּנְיָא חֲדָא: חוּתָלוֹת שֶׁל גְּרוֹגְרוֹת וְשֶׁל תְּמָרִים – מַתִּיר וּמַפְקִיעַ וְחוֹתֵךְ. וְתַנְיָא אִידָךְ: מַתִּיר, אֲבָל לֹא מַפְקִיעַ וְלֹא חוֹתֵךְ! לָא קַשְׁיָא; הָא – רַבָּנַן הָא – רַבִּי נְחֶמְיָה. דְּתַנְיָא, רַבִּי נְחֶמְיָה אוֹמֵר: אֲפִילּוּ תַּרְוָוד, וַאֲפִילּוּ טַלִּית, וַאֲפִילּוּ סַכִּין אֵין נִיטָּלִין אֶלָּא לְצוֹרֶךְ תַּשְׁמִישָׁן.

It was taught in one *baraita*: If one has sealed, wicker **baskets of dried figs or of dates,**[H] **one may untie** the basket's knot on Shabbat, and **unbraid** the basket **and cut** it open. **And it was taught in another** *baraita*: **One may untie** the knot, **but one may not unbraid or cut** the basket. There is a contradiction between these two *baraitot*. The Gemara resolves this contradiction: This is **not difficult. This** *baraita*, which permits all of these actions, is in accordance with the opinion of **the Rabbis. That** *baraita*, which prohibits unbraiding and cutting, is in accordance with the opinion of **Rabbi Neḥemya. As it was taught** in a *baraita* that **Rabbi Neḥemya says: Even a large spoon and even a cloak and even a knife may only be taken** on Shabbat **for their** designated **use,** and it is therefore prohibited to take a knife to cut open baskets of fruit.

בָּעוּ מִינֵּיהּ מֵרַב שֵׁשֶׁת: מַהוּ לְמִיבְרַז חָבִיתָא בְּבוּרְטְיָא בְּשַׁבְּתָא? לְפִיתְחָא קָמִיכַּוֵּין – וַאֲסִיר, אוֹ דִּילְמָא: לְעַיִן יָפָה קָמִיכַּוֵּין, וְשָׁרֵי! אֲמַר לֵיהּ: לְפִיתְחָא קָא מִכַּוֵּין – וַאֲסִיר.

The students **raised a dilemma before Rav Sheshet: What is** the *halakha* with regard to whether or not it is permitted **to perforate a barrel with a spear** [*burtiya*][NL] **on Shabbat?** Is the assumption that **one intends to** make **an opening** in the barrel **and** it is therefore **prohibited, or perhaps** is the assumption that **one** merely **intends to** display **generosity and it is permitted?** Rav Sheshet **said to them: He intends to** make **an opening** in the barrel **and it is prohibited.**

מֵיתִיבִי, רַבָּן שִׁמְעוֹן בֶּן גַּמְלִיאֵל אוֹמֵר: מֵבִיא אָדָם חָבִית שֶׁל יַיִן וּמַתִּיז רֹאשָׁהּ בַּסַּיִיף! הָתָם וַדַּאי לְעַיִן יָפָה קָמִיכַּוֵּין. הָכָא אִם אִיתָא דִּלְעַיִן יָפָה קָמִיכַּוֵּין – לְפַתּוֹחֵי מִיפְתַּח.

The Gemara **raises an objection** based on that which was taught in the *baraita* that **Rabban Shimon ben Gamliel says: One may bring a barrel of wine** on Shabbat **and cut off its top with a sword.** This contradicts Rav Sheshet's opinion that opening a barrel with a spear is prohibited? He answered them: **There,** in the case of the sword, since one essentially destroys the barrel by cutting off its top, **he certainly intends to** display **generosity** by breaking the barrel open in his guests' honor. However, **here,** in the case of spearing a hole in the barrel, **if it were** true that **he intends** to display **generosity, let him open** the top of the barrel by removing its plug. By perforating the barrel, he indicates that he specifically wants there to be a small hole.

״אֵין נוֹקְבִין מְגוּפָה וכו׳״. אָמַר רַב הוּנָא: מַחֲלוֹקֶת לְמַעְלָה, אֲבָל מִן הַצַּד – דִּבְרֵי הַכֹּל אָסוּר. וְהַיְינוּ דְּקָתָנֵי ״לֹא יִקְּבֶנָּה מִצִּדָּהּ״. וְרַב חִסְדָּא אָמַר: מַחֲלוֹקֶת מִן הַצַּד, אֲבָל עַל גַּבָּהּ – דִּבְרֵי הַכֹּל מוּתָּר. וְהָא דְּקָתָנֵי ״לֹא יִקְּבֶנָּה מִצִּדָּהּ״ הָתָם בְּגוּפָהּ דְּחָבִית.

We learned in the mishna: **And one may not perforate the plug** of a barrel; this is the statement of Rabbi Yehuda, and the Rabbis permit it. **Rav Huna said:** This **dispute** is only with regard to a case where one seeks to make a perforation **on top** of the plug; **however,** if he seeks to perforate it **from the side, everyone agrees that it is prohibited,** because people sometimes puncture a barrel beneath the plug in this way. **And that is** what the mishna **is teaching: One may not perforate it on its side.** Whereas **Rav Ḥisda said:** This **dispute** is with regard to a case where one seeks to perforate it **from the side; however,** if one seeks to perforate it **on top, everyone agrees that it is permitted, and** with regard to **that which** the mishna **is teaching: One may not perforate it on its side, there** it is referring to perforating **the barrel itself,** not the plug.

HALAKHA

A person may bring a barrel of wine and cut off the top with a sword – מֵבִיא אָדָם אֶת הֶחָבִית שֶׁל יַיִן וּמַתִּיז רֹאשָׁהּ בַּסַּיִיף: One is permitted to remove the top of a barrel with a sword, because one is not creating an opening and one's intention is merely to display his generosity. However, making a hole in any other way is prohibited, in accordance with the opinion of Rav Sheshet (Rambam *Sefer Zemanim, Hilkhot Shabbat* 23:2; *Shulḥan Arukh, Oraḥ Ḥayyim* 314:6).

Wicker baskets of dried figs or of dates – חוּתָלוֹת שֶׁל גְּרוֹגְרוֹת וְשֶׁל תְּמָרִים: If one has tightly woven baskets containing dried fruits, it is permitted to untie or cut the rope that keeps them closed, or even to cut the baskets themselves on Shabbat, in accordance with the opinion of the Rabbis in the *baraita* (*Shulḥan Arukh, Oraḥ Ḥayyim* 314:8).

NOTES

With a spear – בְּבוּרְטְיָא: Some commentaries explain that the term *burtiya* refers to a special type of drill used to make holes in the plugs of barrels. According to this explanation, it is easy to understand why Rav Sheshet would prohibit using this tool, because one would create a real opening in the same manner as he would during the week (see Rabbeinu Ḥananel and *Me'iri*).

LANGUAGE

Spear [*burtiya*] – בּוּרְטְיָא: Either from the Greek **βέλος**, *belos*, meaning missile and **ῥυτήρ**, *rutèr*, meaning one who draws a missile, or from the Latin verutum, meaning spear.

HALAKHA

Any opening that is not made to insert and to remove is not an opening – **כָּל פֶּתַח שֶׁאֵינוֹ עָשׂוּי לְהַכְנִיס וּלְהוֹצִיא – אֵינוֹ פֶּתַח**: According to Torah law, only a hole that is used both to insert something into an area and to remove something from it is considered an opening. However, the Sages prohibited fashioning openings that serve only one of these purposes, as stated by Rabba. Included in this decree is the prohibition against creating a new hole in a barrel or adding to a preexisting hole on Shabbat. However, one may reopen an old hole that was sealed (Rambam *Sefer Zemanim, Hilkhot Shabbat* 23:1, 10:16).

תָּנוּ רַבָּנַן: אֵין נוֹקְבִין נֶקֶב חָדָשׁ בַּשַּׁבָּת, וְאִם בָּא לְהוֹסִיף – מוֹסִיף. וְיֵשׁ אוֹמְרִים: אֵין מוֹסִיפִין. וְשָׁוִין שֶׁנּוֹקְבִין נֶקֶב יָשָׁן לְכַתְּחִילָּה. וְתַנָּא קַמָּא, מַאי שְׁנָא מִנֶּקֶב חָדָשׁ דְּלָא – דְּקָא מְתַקֵּן פִּיתְחָא, אוֹסוֹפֵי נַמִי – קָא מְתַקֵּן פִּיתְחָא!

The Sages taught in a *baraita*: **One may not create a new hole** in a vessel **on Shabbat. And if one seeks to add** to and widen an already existing hole, **one may add** to it; **and some say** that **one may not** even **add** to an already existing hole. **And** all opinions, even those who generally prohibit creating new holes, agree **that one may perforate** the seal over **an old hole,** even ***ab initio*****. And** with regard to the opinion of **the first** ***tanna*****,** the Gemara asks: **What is different** about perforating the seal over an old hole that makes it permitted, whereas **creating a new hole is not** permitted? Is it because in creating the new hole **he is creating an opening?** If so, by **adding** to an already existing hole **he is also creating an opening.**

אָמַר רַבָּה: דְּבַר תּוֹרָה – כָּל פֶּתַח שֶׁאֵינוֹ עָשׂוּי לְהַכְנִיס וּלְהוֹצִיא – אֵינוֹ פֶּתַח, וְרַבָּנַן הוּא דְּגָזוּר מִשּׁוּם לוּל שֶׁל תַּרְנְגוֹלִין, דְּעָבִיד לְעַיּוֹלֵי אֲוֵירָא וּלְאַפּוֹקֵי הַבְלָא. "וְאִם בָּא לְהוֹסִיף מוֹסִיף" אוֹסוֹפֵי וַדַּאי בְּלוּל שֶׁל תַּרְנְגוֹלִים – לָא אָתֵי לְאוֹסוֹפֵי,

Rabba said: Actually, even creating a new hole is not prohibited, because **by Torah law, any opening that is not made to** both **insert and to remove is not** considered **an opening,**[H] and a hole that one perforates in a barrel is intended exclusively to remove the contents of the barrel. **And it was the Sages who issued a decree** that one may not perforate a vessel **because** it is similar to perforating **a chicken coop,** which is designated for use in both directions, e.g., **to let in air and to let out heat,** and it is therefore prohibited by Torah law. **And** therefore we learned that **if one seeks to add** to an existing hole **one may add** to it. There is no reason to prohibit this due to concern that one may do so in a chicken coop, because **one will certainly not come to add to** an already existing hole **in a chicken coop,**

Perek **XXII**
Daf **146** Amud **b**

HALAKHA

Perforating an old hole – **לִנְקוֹב נֶקֶב יָשָׁן**: With regard to a barrel with a hole that was sealed, if the hole was below the level of the sediment in the barrel, it is prohibited to open it on Shabbat. If the hole was above the level of the sediment, it is permitted, even if it is a large hole (*Mishna Berura*), in accordance with the *baraita* as explained by Rava (Rambam *Sefer Zemanim, Hilkhot Shabbat* 23:1; *Shulḥan Arukh, Oraḥ Ḥayyim* 314:2).

מִשּׁוּם רִיחֲשָׁא. "וְיֵשׁ אוֹמְרִים: אֵין מוֹסִיפִים" – זִימְנִין דְּלָא תַּקְנֵיהּ מֵעִיקָּרָא, וְאָתֵי לְאַרְוֹחֵי בֵּיהּ. דָּרַשׁ רַב נַחְמָן מִשּׁוּם רַבִּי יוֹחָנָן: הֲלָכָה כְּיֵשׁ אוֹמְרִים.

because one does not want **vermin** to enter the coop. **And** when we learned that **some say** that **one may not add** to a preexisting hole, that ruling is also due to a decree lest one come to do so in a chicken coop, as **sometimes one does not properly** create the opening **initially, and comes to expand it** so that it will be fit for use. In that case, widening the opening is considered its completion. **Rav Naḥman taught in the name of Rabbi Yoḥanan:** The ***halakha*** **is in accordance with** the statement cited as: **Some say.**

"וְשָׁוִין שֶׁנּוֹקְבִין נֶקֶב יָשָׁן לְכַתְּחִלָּה". אָמַר רַב יְהוּדָה אָמַר שְׁמוּאֵל: לֹא שָׁנוּ אֶלָּא בְּמָקוֹם הֶעָשׂוּי לְשַׁמֵּר, אֲבָל לְחַזֵּק – אָסוּר. הֵיכִי דָּמֵי לְשַׁמֵּר, הֵיכִי דָּמֵי לְחַזֵּק? אָמַר רַב חִסְדָּא: לְמַעְלָה מִן הַיַּיִן – זֶהוּ לְשַׁמֵּר, לְמַטָּה מִן הַיַּיִן – זֶהוּ לְחַזֵּק. רָבָא אָמַר: לְמַטָּה מִן הַיַּיִן נַמִי זֶהוּ לְשַׁמֵּר. וְהֵיכִי דָּמֵי לְחַזֵּק – כְּגוֹן שֶׁנִּיקְבָהּ לְמַטָּה מִן הַשְּׁמָרִים.

We learned in the *baraita*: **And** everyone **agrees that one may perforate an old hole**[H] that was sealed ***ab initio*****. Rav Yehuda said** that **Shmuel said: They only taught** this **in a place where** the hole **is made to strain** the wine from the sediment; **however,** if it was made **to reinforce** the barrel, it is **prohibited** (*ge'onim*). The Gemara asks: **What are the circumstances** in which a hole is considered to have been made **to strain** and **what are the circumstances** in which a hole is meant **to reinforce** the barrel? **Rav Ḥisda said:** If one perforates the barrel **above** the level of **the wine, that is** a hole designated **to strain** the wine, and if one perforates the barrel **below** the level of **the wine, that is** a hole designated **to reinforce** the barrel. **Rava said:** A hole made **below** the level of **the wine is also** designated **to strain** the wine, **and what are the circumstances** in which a hole is meant **to reinforce** the barrel? It is in a case **where one perforated it below the sediment.**

אָמַר לֵיהּ אַבַּיֵי לְרָבָא: תַּנְיָא דִּמְסַיַּיע לָךְ; "בַּיִת סָתוּם – יֵשׁ לוֹ אַרְבַּע אַמּוֹת, פָּרַץ אֶת פַּצִּימָיו – אֵין לוֹ אַרְבַּע אַמּוֹת. בַּיִת סָתוּם אֵינוֹ מְטַמֵּא כָּל סְבִיבָיו, פָּרַץ אֶת פַּצִּימָיו – מְטַמֵּא כָּל סְבִיבָיו".

Abaye said to Rava: A *baraita* **was taught that supports your** opinion[N] that any opening retains its status unless it is absolutely clear that it is no longer used for that purpose. When dividing a courtyard between the owners of the houses in it, in addition to an equal share of the courtyard, each receives the four cubits adjoining each entrance leading from his house to the courtyard. **A house** with a **sealed** entrance still **has the four cubits** adjoining that entrance,[NH] because the entrance can be reopened. It is only if **one broke its doorposts** and sealed the entrance that the entrance has been completely negated and **it does not have** the **four cubits** adjoining it. This applies similarly to the *halakhot* of ritual impurity: A house in which there is a corpse transmits ritual impurity only through its doorways. **A house** with **sealed** entrances **does not render all of its surroundings ritually impure;**[NH] the ritual impurity only extends opposite the entrances. However, if **one broke its doorposts,** it is no longer considered an entrance, and **it renders all of its surroundings ritually impure.**

גּוּבְתָּא, רַב אָסַר, וּשְׁמוּאֵל שָׁרֵי. מְחַתֵּךְ לְכַתְּחִלָּה – דְּכוּלֵּי עָלְמָא לָא פְּלִיגִי דְּאָסוּר. אַהֲדוּרֵי – דְּכוּלֵּי עָלְמָא לָא פְּלִיגִי דְּשָׁרֵי. כִּי פְּלִיגִי – דַּחֲתִיכָה וְלָא מִתַּקְנָא. מַאן דְּאָסַר – גָּזְרִינַן דִּילְמָא אָתֵי לְמִיחְתַּךְ לְכַתְּחִלָּה, וּמַאן דְּשָׁרֵי – לָא גָּזְרִינַן.

With regard to inserting a **reed** through a hole in a barrel[H] in order to draw wine through it, **Rav prohibited** doing so on Shabbat, **and Shmuel permitted** doing so. The Gemara elaborates: With regard to **cutting** and inserting the reed ***ab initio*, everyone agrees** that **it is prohibited,** because this is considered fashioning a utensil. With regard to **restoring** a prepared reed to its place, **everyone agrees that it is permitted. When they disagree is** in a case where the reed **has been cut but not** yet **inserted** into the barrel. **The one who prohibits** doing so, Rav, holds that **we issue a decree** that prohibits inserting the reed due to the concern that **perhaps one will come to cut** the reed ***ab initio*** for this purpose; **and the one who permits** doing so, Shmuel, holds that **we do not issue a decree** in that situation.

כְּתַנָּאֵי: אֵין חוֹתְכִין שְׁפוֹפֶרֶת בְּיוֹם טוֹב וְאֵין צָרִיךְ לוֹמַר בְּשַׁבָּת. נָפְלָה – (אֵין) מַחֲזִירִין אוֹתָהּ בְּשַׁבָּת, וְאֵין צָרִיךְ לוֹמַר בְּיוֹם טוֹב, וְרַבִּי יֹאשִׁיָּה מֵיקֵל.

The Gemara notes that Rav and Shmuel's dispute is **parallel to** a dispute between *tanna'im*: **One may not cut** a reed **tube on a Festival, and needless to say,** it is prohibited **on Shabbat.** And if it was already cut but **fell, one may restore it** to its place **on Shabbat, and needless to say,** it is permitted to do so **on a Festival. And Rabbi Yoshiya is lenient** in this matter.

רַבִּי יֹאשִׁיָּה אַהַיָּיא? אִילֵימָא אַרֵישָׁא – הָא קָמְתַקֵּן מָנָא! אֶלָּא אַסֵּיפָא – תַּנָּא קַמָּא נַמִּי מִישְׁרָא קָשָׁרֵי! אֶלָּא: דַּחֲתִיכָה וְלָא מִתַּקְנָא אִיכָּא בֵּינַיְיהוּ, מָר סָבַר: גָּזְרִינַן, וּמָר סָבַר: לָא גָּזְרִינַן. דְּרַשׁ רַב שֵׁישָׁא בְּרֵיהּ דְּרַב אִידִי מִשְּׁמֵיהּ דְּרַבִּי יוֹחָנָן: הֲלָכָה כְּרַבִּי יֹאשִׁיָּה.

The Gemara asks with regard to the statement of **Rabbi Yoshiya: On which** section of the *baraita* is he commenting? **If you say** that he is referring to **the first clause** of the *baraita*, which discusses cutting a tube, **isn't he creating a vessel,** which is a prohibited labor? How could Rabbi Yoshiya permit doing so? **Rather,** say that he is referring **to the latter clause** of the *baraita*, which discusses restoring a fallen tube to its place; **the first *tanna* also permits** doing so, leaving no room for further leniency by Rabbi Yoshiya. **Rather,** it is with regard to a case in which **it was cut but not inserted** into the barrel that **there is** a practical difference **between them: One Sage,** the first *tanna*, **held that we issue a decree** that prohibits doing so, **and one Sage held that we do not issue a decree.** The Gemara concludes: **Rav Sheisha, son of Rav Idi, taught** publicly **in the name of Rabbi Yoḥanan:** The ***halakha* is in accordance with** the opinion of **Rabbi Yoshiya.**

"וְאִם הָיְתָה נְקוּבָה וכו'". מִשְׁחָא; רַב אָסַר, וּשְׁמוּאֵל שָׁרֵי. מַאן דְּאָסַר – גָּזְרִינַן מִשּׁוּם שַׁעֲוָה, וּמַאן דְּשָׁרֵי – לָא גָּזְרִינַן. אֲמַר לֵיהּ רַב שְׁמוּאֵל בַּר בַּר חָנָה לְרַב יוֹסֵף: בְּפֵירוּשׁ אָמְרַתְּ לָן מִשְּׁמֵיהּ דְּרַב "מִשְׁחָא שָׁרֵי".

And we also learned in the mishna: **And if** the barrel **was** already **perforated,** one may not seal the hole with wax. There is a dispute among the *amora'im* whether or not it is permitted to seal that hole with **oil: Rav prohibited** doing so, **and Shmuel permitted** doing so. The Gemara explains: **The one who prohibits** doing so, Rav, holds that **we issue a decree** prohibiting oil **due to** concern lest one come to seal the hole with **wax. And the one who permits** doing so, Shmuel, holds that **we do not issue a decree** prohibiting oil due to concern lest one come to use wax to seal the hole. **Rav Shmuel bar bar Ḥana said to Rav Yosef:** How is Rav cited as prohibiting the sealing of the hole in a barrel with oil on Shabbat? **You told us explicitly in Rav's name: Oil is permitted** for use in sealing a hole.

NOTES

A *baraita* was taught that supports your opinion – תַּנְיָא דִּמְסַיַּיע לָךְ: Rabbi Akiva Eiger in *Derush VeḤiddush* explains that the proof that Abaye cites from the *baraita* should not be understood as support for the opinion of Rava in his dispute with Rav Ḥisda. Rather, it is proof that when an opening has been sealed in the most effective manner possible, the original opening is completely negated and it is as though there had never been a hole.

Four cubits for each entrance to a house – אַרְבַּע אַמּוֹת לְבַיִת: In tractate *Bava Batra*, where the primary discussion of this *halakha* appears, the Gemara describes precisely how a courtyard that belongs to partners is divided. When heirs or partners split a courtyard, each receives a portion of the property, and additionally, each receives four cubits adjacent to every doorway to the courtyard that can be utilized as an entrance. In deciding these *halakhot*, it is crucial to know exactly what is defined as the house and what is considered the entrance.

Ritual impurity in a sealed house – טוּמְאַת בַּיִת סָתוּם: Rashi and *Tosafot* disagree whether a sealed house transmits ritual impurity in a circumference of four cubits all around it like a grave, or whether it transmits ritual impurity only under ledges adjacent to the house, which would constitute a tent over a corpse were the corpse to be removed from the house at that location.

HALAKHA

Four cubits for each entrance to a house – אַרְבַּע אַמּוֹת לְבַיִת: When partners divide a courtyard, each is granted four cubits adjacent to each doorway to the courtyard, even if the entrance to the house was sealed. However, if the door frame was destroyed and the doorway sealed, then the entrance is totally negated and the owner does not receive the four cubits adjacent to it (Rambam *Sefer Kinyan, Hilkhot Shekhenim* 2:7; *Shulḥan Arukh, Ḥoshen Mishpat* 172:1, 7).

Ritual impurity of a sealed house – טוּמְאַת בַּיִת סָתוּם: A house in which there is a corpse transmits ritual impurity to the outside only through an opening through which the dead body could exit, even if the opening was sealed. However, if the house has no openings at all, or its doorposts have been destroyed and its entrances sealed, the house assumes the legal status of a grave and transmits ritual impurity to the entire surrounding area (Rambam *Sefer Tahara, Hilkhot Tumat Met* 7:1).

A reed in a barrel – קָנֶה בְּחָבִית: It is permitted to insert a hollow reed into the hole in a barrel on Shabbat, even if there had never been a reed there previously, in accordance with Rabbi Yoshiya, whose statement supports the ruling of Shmuel (Rambam *Sefer Zemanim, Hilkhot Shabbat* 23:6; *Shulḥan Arukh, Oraḥ Ḥayyim* 314:5).

אֲמַר טָבוּת רִישְׁבָּא אֲמַר שְׁמוּאֵל: הַאי טַרְפָּא דְּאָסָא – אָסוּר. מַאי טַעְמָא? רַב יֵימָר מִדִּפְתִּי אָמַר: גְּזֵירָה מִשּׁוּם מַרְזֵב, רַב אַשִׁי אָמַר: גְּזֵירָה שֶׁמָּא יִקְטוֹם. מַאי בֵּינַיְיהוּ? אִיכָּא בֵּינַיְיהוּ: דִּקְטִים וּמַנְחִי.

The Gemara cites a statement that **Tavut the hunter said** that **Shmuel said:** With regard to **this myrtle leaf, it is prohibited** to insert it into a hole in a barrel[H] to be used as a spout. The Gemara asks: **What is the reason** for this? **Rav Yeimar of Difti said:** It is **a decree** issued **due to** the concern lest one come to make **an** actual **spout** on Shabbat. **Rav Ashi said:** It is **a decree** issued **lest one cut** a myrtle leaf from its branch on Shabbat for this purpose. The Gemara asks: **What is** the practical difference **between them?** The Gemara answers: **There is** a practical difference **between them** in a case in which the leaves **were** already **cut and placed,**[N] as in that case, Rav Ashi's concern would not apply, but Rav Yeimar would still rule stringently.

בֵּי סַדְיָא, רַב אָסַר וּשְׁמוּאֵל שָׁרֵי. בְּרַכִּין – דְּכוּלֵּי עָלְמָא לָא פְּלִיגִי דְּשָׁרֵי, בְּקָשִׁין – דְּכוּלֵּי עָלְמָא לָא פְּלִיגִי דְּאָסוּר, כִּי פְּלִיגִי – בְּמִיצְעֵי. מַאן דַּאֲסַר – מֶיחֱזֵי כְּמַשּׂוֹי. וּמַאן דְּשָׁרֵי – לָא מֶיחֱזֵי כְּמַשּׂוֹי.

The Gemara cites another dispute between Rav and Shmuel: With regard to **felt cloths** upon which people typically sit but that may also be worn as cloaks, the Sages disagreed whether or not one may wrap himself in them on Shabbat and transfer them from one place to another through a public domain. **Rav prohibited** doing so, **and Shmuel permitted** doing so. The Gemara elaborates: **With regard to** articles made of **soft** felt,[H] **everyone agrees** that **it is permitted,** as their legal status is that of other garments. **With regard to** articles made of **hard** felt, **everyone agrees** that **it is prohibited. When they disagree,** it is **with regard to** felt articles that have an **intermediate** level of softness. **The one who prohibits** wearing them, Rav, holds that one who wears these as a garment **appears as** one carrying **a burden, and the one who permits** wearing them, Shmuel, holds that **it does not appear as** one carrying **a burden,** because the material appears to be a garment.

וְהָא דְּרַב לָאו בְּפֵירוּשׁ אִיתְּמַר, אֶלָּא מִכְּלָלָא אִיתְּמַר. דְּרַב אִיקְּלַע לְהַהוּא אַתְרָא דְּלָא הֲוָה לֵיהּ רַוְוחָא, נְפַק יְתֵיב בְּכַרְמְלִית. אַיְיתוּ לֵיהּ בֵּי סַדְיָא – לָא יְתֵיב. מַאן דַּחֲזָא סָבַר – מִשּׁוּם דְּבֵי סַדְיָא אָסוּר. וְלֹא הִיא, דְּרַב אַכְרוֹזֵי מַכְרִיז: בֵּי סַדְיָא שָׁרֵי. וּמִשּׁוּם כְּבוֹד רַבּוֹתֵינוּ לֹא יָשַׁב עָלָיו. וּמַאן נִינְהוּ – רַב כָּהֲנָא וְרַב אַסִי.

The Gemara points out that **this** opinion attributed **to Rav was not stated explicitly** by him; **rather, it was stated by inference,** i.e., based on Rav's conduct, it was concluded that this is his opinion. **As Rav happened** to come **to a certain place** where **there was not** enough **room** for him and his students inside the house, and therefore, **he went** out **and sat in a** ***karmelit.*** **They brought him felt** cloths by wearing them outside, and **he did not sit** on them. **One who saw** this incident **assumed** that he refused to sit on them **because it is prohibited** to move **cloths** in this manner; **however, that is not so,** as **Rav** used to **proclaim** that **it is permitted** to move articles made of **felt** in this manner. **And it was in deference to our Rabbis**[P] who were there that **he did not sit on it,** as he did not want to sit on a higher and more distinguished surface than they did. The Gemara adds: **And who were** these Rabbis? **Rav Kahana and Rav Asi,** who were Rav's disciples and colleagues.

מתני׳ נוֹתְנִין תַּבְשִׁיל לְתוֹךְ הַבּוֹר בִּשְׁבִיל שֶׁיְּהֵא שָׁמוּר, וְאֶת הַמַּיִם הַיָּפִים בָּרָעִים בִּשְׁבִיל שֶׁיִּצַּנְּנוּ, וְאֶת הַצּוֹנֵן בְּחַמָּה בִּשְׁבִיל שֶׁיֵּחַמּוּ. מִי שֶׁנָּשְׁרוּ כֵּלָיו בַּדֶּרֶךְ בַּמַּיִם – מְהַלֵּךְ בָּהֶן וְאֵינוֹ חוֹשֵׁשׁ. הִגִּיעַ לֶחָצֵר הַחִיצוֹנָה – שׁוֹטְחָן בַּחַמָּה, אֲבָל לֹא כְּנֶגֶד הָעָם.

MISHNA **One may place** a cooked **dish into an** empty **pit**[H] on Shabbat **so that it will be protected** from the heat, **and** similarly, one may place **good** potable **water** into a vessel and place the vessel **into bad,** non-potable water **so that** the potable water **will cool off. And** one may also place **cold water** out **in the sun so that** it **will be heated.** They also taught: **Someone whose garments fell into water** while walking **on the road**[H] **may** replace them and continue to **walk** wearing **them and need not be concerned** about violating the prohibitions against wringing or laundering. When he **reaches the outer courtyard** of a place where he can leave his clothes, **he spreads them in the sun** to dry, **but not opposite the masses,** as they will suspect him of laundering on Shabbat.

HALAKHA

A myrtle leaf in a barrel – עָלֶה הֲדַס בֶּחָבִית: One is prohibited to insert a myrtle leaf into the hole of a barrel to be used as a spout on Shabbat. The Sages prohibited this because one might come to fashion an actual spout. However, some authorities permit using a myrtle leaf when there are several cut leaves ready (Rosh and *Tur*), in accordance with the Gemara's explanation of Rav Ashi's ruling (*Shulḥan Arukh, Oraḥ Ḥayyim* 314:5 and in the comment of the Rema).

Types of felt – מִינֵי לֶבֶד: It is prohibited to wrap oneself in hard felt in the manner in which one wears a garment and bring the cloth into a public domain or a *karmelit* on Shabbat. If the felt is not so hard and is thin, similar to regular garments (*Magen Avraham*, based on Rambam), it is permitted, in accordance with the Gemara's conclusion that even Rav is not strict in that case (Rambam *Sefer Zemanim, Hilkhot Shabbat*, 19:17; *Shulḥan Arukh, Oraḥ Ḥayyim* 301:35).

One may place a cooked dish into an empty pit – נוֹתְנִין תַּבְשִׁיל לְתוֹךְ הַבּוֹר: One may place a pot of food into a pit on Shabbat to preserve it. In addition, one may place a vessel of potable water into non-potable water without being concerned that he appears to be insulating food in a prohibited manner (Rambam *Sefer Zemanim, Hilkhot Shabbat* 22:9; *Tur, Oraḥ Ḥayyim* 318).

Someone whose garments fell into water on the road, etc. – מִי שֶׁנָּשְׁרוּ כֵּלָיו בַּדֶּרֶךְ וכו׳: In the case of one whose garments became wet on Shabbat, it is permitted to continue walking in them, and he need not be concerned that water will be squeezed from them. However, one may not lay them out to dry, because it creates the impression that one laundered the clothing on Shabbat. Once the Sages prohibited this, it was prohibited to do so even in the innermost chambers, where no one will see it (Rambam *Sefer Zemanim, Hilkhot Shabbat*, 22:20; *Shulḥan Arukh, Oraḥ Ḥayyim* 301:45).

NOTES

Cut and placed – דִּקְטִים וּמַנְחִי: Some commentaries explain that this means that the leaf was already cut and inserted into the hole in the barrel before Shabbat (Rabbeinu Ḥananel, *Me'iri*, and others).

PERSONALITIES

Deference to our Rabbis – כְּבוֹד רַבּוֹתֵינוּ: Rav Kahana and Rav Asi were among the first *amora'im* in Babylonia. When Rav arrived from Eretz Yisrael, they were already exceptionally learned. Nevertheless, they deferred to Rav and became his disciple-colleagues, accepting the halakhic traditions that he brought from Eretz Yisrael. Apparently, Rav Asi was the head of the yeshiva in the city of Hutzal and was considered to be the equal of Shmuel, Rav's colleague.

Rav Kahana was among the greatest Sages of the generation despite his young age. The Talmud recounts the powerful impression he eventually made on the leading Sages of Eretz Yisrael. Because of their greatness in Torah and their prominence, Rav showed tremendous deference to both Rav Kahana and Rav Asi. He even refused to sit on a raised surface so that he would not seem to be demeaning his respected colleagues relative to himself.

גמ׳ פְּשִׁיטָא! מַהוּ דְּתֵימָא: נִיגְזַר מִשּׁוּם אַשְׁוּוֹיֵי גּוּמוֹת – קָא מַשְׁמַע לַן.

GEMARA The Gemara is puzzled by the *halakha* that was taught about placing food in a pit: It is **obvious** that it is permitted. The Gemara answers: **Lest you say: Let us issue a decree** prohibiting this **due to** concern lest one perform the prohibited labor of **leveling holes** in the pit when he places the pot in it, **it teaches us** that no decree was issued due to this concern.

״וְאֶת הַמַּיִם הַיָּפִים בְּרָעִים״. פְּשִׁיטָא! סֵיפָא אִיצְטְרִיכָא לֵיהּ ״וְאֶת הַצּוֹנֵן בַּחַמָּה״. הָא נַמִי פְּשִׁיטָא! מַהוּ דְּתֵימָא: נִיגְזוֹר דִּילְמָא אָתֵי לְאַטְמוֹנֵי בְּרֶמֶץ, קָא מַשְׁמַע לַן.

We also learned in the mishna: One may place **good water into bad water** on Shabbat in order to cool it off. The Gemara says: It is **obvious** that it is permitted. The Gemara explains: It is **necessary** to mention **the latter clause** of the mishna, which states that it is permitted to place **cold water** out **in the sun.** The Gemara expresses surprise: **This, too, is obvious.** The Gemara answers: **Lest you say that we should issue a decree** prohibiting this action, because **perhaps one will come to insulate it in hot ashes** to warm it up, which also heats the water without actually placing it on the fire, **it teaches us** that we do issue a decree in that case.

״מִי שֶׁנָּשְׁרוּ וכו׳״. אָמַר רַב יְהוּדָה אָמַר רַב: מִכָּל מָקוֹם שֶׁאָסְרוּ חֲכָמִים מִפְּנֵי מַרְאִית הָעַיִן – אֲפִילּוּ בְּחַדְרֵי חֲדָרִים אָסוּר. תְּנַן: שׁוֹטְחָן בַּחַמָּה אֲבָל לֹא כְּנֶגֶד הָעָם! תַּנָּאֵי הִיא; דְּתַנְיָא: שׁוֹטְחָן בַּחַמָּה אֲבָל לֹא כְּנֶגֶד הָעָם, רַבִּי אֶלְעָזָר וְרַבִּי שִׁמְעוֹן אוֹסְרִין.

We learned in the mishna that **one whose** garments **fell** into water need not be concerned about wringing or laundering the clothing and may replace them and continue walking, and then place them to dry in the sun, but not before the masses. This is so that they will not suspect him of laundering on Shabbat. In this regard, the Gemara cites that which **Rav Yehuda said** that **Rav said: Wherever the Sages prohibited** an action **due to** the **appearance** of prohibition,[N] **even in the innermost chambers** where no one will see it, **it is prohibited,** as the Sages did not distinguish between different circumstances. The Gemara says: **We learned** in the mishna that **one may spread them in the sun but not opposite the masses,** which contradicts that principle. The Gemara explains: **It is** a dispute between ***tanna'im*****, as it was taught** in a *baraita*: **One may spread them out in the sun but not opposite the masses. Rabbi Elazar and Rabbi Shimon prohibit** doing so, which is a precedent for the opinion that Rav Yehuda stated in the name of Rav.

אָמַר רַב הוּנָא

Rav Huna said:

NOTES

Due to the appearance of prohibition – **מִפְּנֵי מַרְאִית הָעַיִן**: The *halakha* is in accordance with the opinion of Rav: Any action that is prohibited in public because it creates the appearance of wrongdoing is also prohibited in private. That is because the Sages do not make distinctions in their decrees, because if the decree is in effect only when the reason applies, it will not be observed. Nevertheless, there are authorities who are lenient in cases in which the decree was issued to prevent violation of rabbinic law. These authorities reason that in those cases, the Sages did not prohibit actions performed in private in their decree (*Tiferet Yisrael*).

Perek **XXII**
Daf **147** Amud **a**

הַמְנַעֵר טַלִּיתוֹ בְּשַׁבָּת – חַיָּיב חַטָּאת. וְלָא אֲמַרַן אֶלָּא בַּחֲדַתֵּי, אֲבָל בְּעַתִּיקֵי – לֵית לַן בַּהּ. וְלָא אֲמַרַן אֶלָּא בְּאוּכָמֵי, אֲבָל בְּחִיוָּרֵי וְסוּמָּקֵי – לֵית לַן בַּהּ. וְהוּא דְּקָפִיד עֲלַיְיהוּ.

One who shakes his cloak on Shabbat[NH] to remove dust that collected on it **is liable to** bring **a sin-offering** for violating the prohibition of laundering. The Gemara qualifies this ruling: **We only stated** this *halakha* **with regard to new** garments, **but with regard to old** garments, **we have no** problem **with** this behavior. **And we only stated** this **with regard to black** garments, **but with regard to white or red** garments, **we have no** problem, as shaking off the dust would not be prohibited. **And this** prohibition applies only **when one is particular about** keeping **them** clean, but if one does not insist on wearing clean garments, **we have no** problem **with it,** i.e., it is not prohibited to shake off the dust.

עוּלָּא אִיקְּלַע לְפוּמְבְּדִיתָא, חֲזָא רַבָּנַן דְּקָא מְנַפְּצִי גְּלִימַיְיהוּ. אֲמַר: קָמְחַלְּלִין רַבָּנַן שַׁבְּתָא! אֲמַר לְהוּ רַב יְהוּדָה: נְפוּצֵי לֵיהּ בְּאַפֵּיהּ, אֲנַן לָא קָפְדִינַן מִידֵּי.

The Gemara relates that **Ulla happened to** come to **Pumbedita,** and while there **he saw rabbis shaking their cloaks** to remove dust. **He said: The Rabbis are desecrating Shabbat. Rav Yehuda said to** the Rabbis whom Ulla criticized: You may continue to **shake** your cloaks **in his presence. We are not at all particular about this,** and it is therefore permitted for us to shake the dust from our cloaks.

אַבָּיֵי הֲוָה קָאֵי קַמֵּיהּ דְּרַב יוֹסֵף, אֲמַר לֵיהּ: הַב לִי כּוּמְתַאי. [חֲזָא דְּאִיכָּא טַלָּא עֲלֵיהּ, הֲוָה קָמְחַסֵּם לְמִיתְּבָה לֵיהּ. אָמַר לֵיהּ: נְפוֹץ שְׁדֵי, אֲנַן לָא קָפְדִינַן מִידֵּי.

The Gemara also relates that **Abaye was standing before Rav Yosef.** Rav Yosef **said to him: Give me my hat.** Abaye **saw that there was dew on it,** and **he hesitated to give** it **to him,** because he feared violating a prohibition by shaking off the dew. Rav Yosef **said to him: Shake** off the dew and **throw** me the hat; **we are not at all particular** about the cleanliness of the hat, and it is therefore permitted to shake off the dew.

NOTES

One who shakes his cloak on Shabbat – **הַמְנַעֵר טַלִּיתוֹ בְּשַׁבָּת**: See the commentaries of Rashi and *Tosafot.* Others explain that this prohibition refers specifically to shaking actual dirt off one's garments. According to this explanation, the discussion with regard to dew on Rav Yosef's hat is not referring to dew but to dirt of some sort (Rabbeinu Ḥananel; Rabbeinu Yehonatan).

HALAKHA

One who shakes his cloak on Shabbat – **הַמְנַעֵר טַלִּיתוֹ בְּשַׁבָּת**: One may not shake dew or water off his new black cloak on Shabbat if he would not wear it otherwise. One who does so is liable to bring a sin-offering for violating the prohibited labor of laundering. One is not liable for shaking dirt off a white or red garment on Shabbat (*Mishna Berura*). This is in accordance with the ruling of the Gemara as explained in *Tosafot* (Rambam *Sefer Zemanim, Hilkhot Shabbat* 10:18; *Shulḥan Arukh, Oraḥ Ḥayyim* 302:1).

אָמַר רַב יִצְחָק בַּר יוֹסֵף אָמַר רַבִּי יוֹחָנָן: הַיּוֹצֵא בְּטַלִּית מְקוּפֶּלֶת מוּנַּחַת לוֹ עַל כְּתֵיפוֹ בַּשַּׁבָּת – חַיָּיב חַטָּאת. תַּנְיָא נַמִּי הָכִי סוֹחֲרֵי כְּסוּת הַיּוֹצְאִים בְּטַלִּיתוֹת מְקוּפָּלוֹת וּמוּנָּחוֹת עַל כְּתֵיפָן בַּשַּׁבָּת – חַיָּיבִין חַטָּאת. וְלֹא סוֹחֲרֵי כְּסוּת בִּלְבַד אָמְרוּ, אֶלָּא כׇּל אָדָם, אֶלָּא שֶׁדַּרְכָּן שֶׁל מוֹכְרִין לָצֵאת כָּךְ.

Rav Yitzḥak bar Yosef said that **Rabbi Yoḥanan said: One who goes out with a cloak folded**[NH] **and resting on his shoulder on Shabbat is liable to** bring **a sin-offering** for carrying in the public domain. **This** ruling **was also taught** in a *baraita*: **Clothing merchants who go outs with cloaks folded and resting on their shoulders on Shabbat are liable to** bring **a sin-offering. And they did not say** this **only with regard to clothing merchants; rather, any person** is liable for this transgression, **and** they **only stated** the *halakha* in these terms **because it is the** usual **manner for merchants to go out this way.**

וְחֶנְוָנִי הַיּוֹצֵא בְּמָעוֹת הַצְּרוּרִין לוֹ בִּסְדִינוֹ – חַיָּיב חַטָּאת. וְלֹא חֶנְוָנִי בִּלְבַד אָמְרוּ, אֶלָּא כׇּל אָדָם, אֶלָּא שֶׁדַּרְכּוֹ שֶׁל חֶנְוָנִי לָצֵאת כָּךְ. וְהָרַטָּנִין יוֹצְאִין בְּסוּדָרִין שֶׁעַל כְּתֵיפָן. וְלֹא רַטָּנִין בִּלְבַד אָמְרוּ, אֶלָּא כׇּל אָדָם, אֶלָּא שֶׁדַּרְכָּן שֶׁל רַטָּנִין לָצֵאת בְּכָךְ.

And likewise, **a shopkeeper who goes out with coins bound in his cloak is liable to** bring **a sin-offering.**[H] **And they did not say** this **only with regard to a shopkeeper; rather, any person** is liable for this, **and** they **only stated** the *halakha* in these terms because **it is the** usual **manner of a shopkeeper to go out this way. And runners,** i.e., foot messengers, **may go out** on Shabbat **with scarves on their shoulders,** because this is how they typically wear them. **And they did not say** this **only with regard to runners; rather, any person** is permitted to do this, **but it is** simply **the** usual **manner of runners to go out this way.**

אָמַר רַבִּי יְהוּדָה: מַעֲשֶׂה בְּהוּרְקָנוֹס בְּנוֹ שֶׁל רַבִּי אֱלִיעֶזֶר בֶּן הוּרְקָנוֹס שֶׁיָּצָא בְּסוּדָר שֶׁעַל כְּתֵיפוֹ בַּשַּׁבָּת, אֶלָּא שֶׁנִּימָא כְּרוּכָה לוֹ בְּאֶצְבָּעוֹ. וּכְשֶׁבָּא הַדָּבָר לִפְנֵי חֲכָמִים אָמְרוּ: אֲפִילּוּ אֵין נִימָא כְּרוּכָה לוֹ בְּאֶצְבָּעוֹ. דָּרַשׁ רַב נַחְמָן בַּר רַב חִסְדָּא מִשְּׁמֵיהּ דְּרַב חִסְדָּא: הֲלָכָה – אַף עַל פִּי שֶׁאֵין נִימָא כְּרוּכָה לוֹ בְּאֶצְבְּעוֹתָיו.

Rabbi Yehuda said: There was an incident involving Hyrcanus, son of Rabbi Eliezer ben Hyrcanus, who went outside with a scarf on his shoulder[H] **on Shabbat. However, a thread** from the garment **was tied around his finger** so that the garment would not fall. **When this matter came before the Sages, they said:** It is permitted to go out in that manner **even if a thread is not tied around one's finger.** And likewise, **Rav Naḥman bar Rav Ḥisda taught in the name of Rav Ḥisda:** The *halakha* is that one may go outside with a garment around one's shoulders **even if a thread** from the garment **is not tied around one's finger.**

עוּלָּא אִיקְּלַע לְבֵי אַסִּי בַּר הִינִי, בָּעוּ מִינֵּיהּ: מַהוּ לַעֲשׂוֹת מַרְזֵב בַּשַּׁבָּת? אֲמַר לְהוּ, הָכִי אֲמַר רַבִּי אֶלְעַי: אָסוּר לַעֲשׂוֹת מַרְזֵב בַּשַּׁבָּת. מַאי מַרְזֵב? אָמַר רַבִּי זֵירָא: כִּיסֵי בַּבְלָייתָא.

Ulla happened to come **to the house of Asi bar Hini.** The members of the household **asked him: What is** the *halakha*: Is it permitted **to make a spout** of one's garment **on Shabbat?** Ulla **said to them** that **this is what Rabbi Elai said: It is prohibited to make a spout on Shabbat.** The Gemara asks: **What is** the **spout** referred to here? **Rabbi Zeira said:** It is referring to **Babylonian pockets,** which were formed by lifting up the bottom of the cloaks and tying them to their shoulders to make pocket-like folds in their garments.

רַבִּי יִרְמְיָה הֲוָה יָתֵיב קַמֵּיהּ דְּרַבִּי זֵירָא. אָמַר לֵיהּ: הָכִי מַאי? אָמַר לֵיהּ: אָסוּר. וְהָכִי מַאי? אָמַר לֵיהּ: אָסוּר. אֲמַר רַב פַּפָּא: נְקוֹט הַאי כְּלָלָא בִּידָךְ: כֹּל אַדַּעְתָּא דְּלִכְנוּפֵי – אָסוּר, כֹּל דְּלְהִתְנָאוֹת – שָׁרֵי. כִּי הָא דְּרַב שֵׁישָׁא בְּרֵיהּ דְּרַב אִידִי מִתְנָאֶה בִּסְדִינוֹ הֲוָה.

The Gemara relates that **Rabbi Yirmeya was sitting before Rabbi Zeira** and showed him a certain fold and **said to him: What is** the *halakha* with regard to **this** kind of fold on Shabbat? **He said to him:** It is **prohibited** to make it on Shabbat. He then showed him another fold and asked: **And what is** the *halakha* with regard to **this? He said to him:** It is **prohibited. Rav Pappa said: Grasp this principle: Any** fold made **to gather** one's clothing from the ground **is prohibited,** and **any** fold **that is** merely **to beautify oneself** is **permitted,** as the precedent of **Rav Sheisha, son of Rav Idi, who was beautifying himself with his garment** by folding it on his shoulders.

כִּי אֲתָא רַב דִּימִי אֲמַר: פַּעַם אַחַת יָצָא רַבִּי לַשָּׂדֶה, וְהָיוּ שְׁנֵי צִידֵּי טַלִּיתוֹ מוּנָּחִין עַל כְּתֵיפוֹ. אָמַר לְפָנָיו יְהוֹשֻׁעַ בֶּן זֵירוּז בֶּן חָמִיו שֶׁל רַבִּי מֵאִיר: בָּזוֹ לֹא חִיֵּיב רַבִּי מֵאִיר חַטָּאת. אָמַר לֵיהּ: דִּקְדֵּק רַבִּי מֵאִיר עַד כָּאן? שִׁלְשֵׁל רַבִּי טַלִּיתוֹ.

When Rav Dimi came from Eretz Yisrael to Babylonia, **he said:** On **one occasion, Rabbi** Yehuda HaNasi **went out into a field, and the two sides of his cloak were resting on his shoulders.**[H] **Yehoshua ben Zeiruz, son of the father-in-law of Rabbi Meir, said before** Rabbi Yehuda HaNasi: **In** a case like **this, didn't Rabbi Meir hold one liable to** bring **a sin-offering? Rabbi said to him: Was Rabbi Meir exacting to that** extent, i.e., he considered wearing a garment in this fashion to be carrying on Shabbat? If so, it is preferable to avoid questionable practices; immediately **Rabbi** Yehuda HaNasi **lowered his cloak** from his shoulders.

NOTES

A cloak folded – טַלִּית מְקוּפֶּלֶת: Many commentaries disagree over the precise definition of the Gemara's references to folding a cloak like a spout and forming Babylonian pockets (see Rashi and *Tosafot*), since the Gemara itself does not provide a precise description of the different methods of folding. Some authorities state that Babylonian pockets refer to folding the cloak on all sides into a cylindrical shape that appears like a bundle of vegetables. Some of the *ge'onim* have a variant reading of the text, *kushei baklayta*, meaning bundles of vegetables (*ge'onim*; *Me'iri*).

HALAKHA

One who goes out with a cloak folded – הַיּוֹצֵא בְּטַלִּית מְקוּפֶּלֶת: It is prohibited to go out on Shabbat wearing a cloak if the top is covering one's head and the bottom is resting on his shoulders. However, if it covers one's body like a regular garment, it is permitted, in accordance with the explanation of Rabbeinu Ḥananel and the *Roke'aḥ* (Rambam *Sefer Zemanim*, *Hilkhot Shabbat* 19:19; *Shulḥan Arukh*, *Oraḥ Ḥayyim* 301:29).

A shopkeeper who goes out with coins bound in his cloak is liable to bring a sin-offering – הַיּוֹצֵא בְּמָעוֹת הַצְּרוּרִין לוֹ בִּסְדִינוֹ חַיָּיב חַטָּאת: One who walks from a private domain into a public domain on Shabbat with coins bound in his garments is liable because that is the standard way of carrying them. However, there is no prohibition to wear that garment in the home (Rema; Rambam *Sefer Zemanim*, *Hilkhot Shabbat* 12:12; *Shulḥan Arukh*, *Oraḥ Ḥayyim* 301:32).

Going out with a scarf on one's shoulder – יוֹצְאִין בְּסוּדָר שֶׁעַל כְּתֵיפוֹ: One may go out on Shabbat with a scarf folded over his shoulder, even without tying a thread to his finger (Rambam *Sefer Zemanim*, *Hilkhot Shabbat* 19:19; *Shulḥan Arukh*, *Oraḥ Ḥayyim* 301:34).

Folding a cloak over one's body – קִיפּוּל טַלִּית עַל גּוּפוֹ: If one goes out wrapped in a cloak on Shabbat, it is prohibited to fold it over on both sides or over his shoulders to prevent it from tearing or getting dirty. However, it is permitted to fold it in a manner that enhances one's appearance, according to local fashion (according to the Rambam's interpretation; *Shulḥan Arukh*, *Oraḥ Ḥayyim* 301:31).

כִּי אֲתָא רָבִין אֲמַר: לֹא יְהוֹשֻׁעַ בֶּן זֵירוּז הֲוָה – אֶלָּא יְהוֹשֻׁעַ בֶּן כְּפוּסָאֵי הָיָה, חֲתָנוֹ שֶׁל רַבִּי עֲקִיבָא. אָמַר: בָּזוֹ לֹא חִיֵּיב רַבִּי עֲקִיבָא חַטָּאת. אָמַר לוֹ: דִּקְדֵּק רַבִּי עֲקִיבָא עַד כָּאן? שִׁלְשֵׁל רַבִּי טַלִּיתוֹ. כִּי אֲתָא רַב שְׁמוּאֵל בַּר רַב יְהוּדָה אָמַר: נִשְׁאַל אִיתְּמַר.

When Ravin came from Eretz Yisrael to Babylonia **he said: It was not Yehoshua ben Zeiruz; rather, it was Yehoshua ben Kefusai, Rabbi Akiva's son-in-law,** and **he said: In** a case like **this, didn't Rabbi Akiva hold one liable to** bring **a sin-offering?** Rabbi Yehuda HaNasi **said to him: Was Rabbi Akiva exacting to that** extent? If so, it is preferable to avoid questionable practices. Immediately, **Rabbi** Yehuda HaNasi **lowered his cloak** from his shoulders. **When Rav Shmuel bar Rav Yehuda came, he said:** This is not what happened, as Rabbi Yehuda HaNasi himself did not wear his cloak folded up on his shoulders on Shabbat. Rather **it was stated** that Rabbi **was asked,** meaning that this question came before him, and he wanted to rule leniently, until he was informed that some of the greatest Sages of the generation ruled stringently.

מתני׳ הָרוֹחֵץ בְּמֵי מְעָרָה וּבְמֵי טְבֶרְיָא וְנִסְתַּפֵּג אֲפִילּוּ בְּעֶשֶׂר אֲלוּנְטִיאוֹת – לֹא יְבִיאֵם בְּיָדוֹ. אֲבָל עֲשָׂרָה בְּנֵי אָדָם מִסְתַּפְּגִין בַּאֲלוּנְטִית אַחַת פְּנֵיהֶם יְדֵיהֶם וְרַגְלֵיהֶם, וּמְבִיאִין אוֹתָן בְּיָדָן.

MISHNA **One who bathes** on Shabbat **in** a ritual bath formed by **cave water**[N] **or in the water of Tiberias and dried himself even with ten towels may not carry them in his hand,** lest he forget that it is Shabbat and wring the water from them. **However, ten people may** use **one towel** to **dry their faces, hands, and feet, and may carry them in their hands.** Even though in this case the towel would be quite wet, it is permitted to handle the towel because there are several people present, and they will remind each other that it is prohibited to wring a towel on Shabbat.

סָכִין וּמְמַשְׁמְשִׁין, אֲבָל לֹא מִתְעַמְּלִין וְלֹא מִתְגָּרְרִין. אֵין יוֹרְדִין לְקוֹרְדִּימָא, וְאֵין עוֹשִׂין אַפִּיקְטְוִיזִין, וְאֵין מְעַצְּבִין אֶת הַקָּטָן, וְאֵין מַחֲזִירִין אֶת הַשֶּׁבֶר. מִי שֶׁנִּפְרְקָה יָדוֹ וְרַגְלוֹ לֹא יִטְרְפֵם בְּצוֹנֵן, אֲבָל רוֹחֵץ הוּא כְּדַרְכּוֹ, וְאִם נִתְרַפֵּא – נִתְרַפֵּא.

Apropos the waters of Tiberias, the mishna discusses the *halakhot* of bathing and medicine on Shabbat. **One may smear oil** on his body **and** gently **rub** his body with his hand; **however, one may not exert himself** with vigorous massage or by means of exercise in order to benefit from the therapeutic effects of sweating; **and one may not scrape** the oil off with a scraper. Additionally, **one may not go into a swampy river** [***kurdima***],[L] on Shabbat. **And one may not make a drug to induce vomiting, nor may one align a young** infant's bones to straighten them, **nor may one reset a break** in a bone. **One whose hand or foot was dislocated may not move them about** vigorously **in cold** water, which is the standard method of treatment; **however, one may wash** the limb **in the typical manner, and if one is cured** through this washing, **he is cured.**

גמ׳ קָתָנֵי מֵי מְעָרָה דּוּמְיָא דְּמֵי טְבֶרְיָא, מַה מֵּי טְבֶרְיָא – חַמִּין, אַף מֵי מְעָרָה חַמִּין. ״הָרוֹחֵץ״ – דִּיעֲבַד אִין, לְכַתְּחִילָּה – לָא. מִכְּלָל

GEMARA The *tanna* of the mishna **teaches** the case **of cave water** that is **similar to the** case **of water of Tiberias; just as the water of Tiberias is hot, so too the cave water is hot.**[H] The Gemara also infers from the formulation of the mishna: With regard to **one who bathes, after the fact,**[N] **yes,** one may dry himself; however, **one may not** bathe ***ab initio***, as had the mishna intended to permit bathing *ab initio* it would have said: One may bathe in cave water. This proves **by inference**

Perek **XXII**
Daf **147** Amud **b**

דִּלְהִשְׁתַּטֵּף כָּל גּוּפוֹ, אֲפִילּוּ לְכַתְּחִילָּה – שַׁפִּיר דָּמֵי. מַנִּי? רַבִּי שִׁמְעוֹן הִיא, דְּתַנְיָא: לֹא יִשְׁתַּטֵּף אָדָם בֵּין בְּחַמִּין בֵּין בְּצוֹנֵן, דִּבְרֵי רַבִּי מֵאִיר. רַבִּי שִׁמְעוֹן מַתִּיר. רַבִּי יְהוּדָה אוֹמֵר: בְּחַמִּין – אָסוּר, בְּצוֹנֵן – מוּתָּר.

that **rinsing one's entire body** by pouring water on it rather than bathing in the standard fashion may **well** be done **even *ab initio*.** The Gemara asks: According to **whose** opinion is our mishna? The Gemara answers: **It is** in accordance with the opinion of **Rabbi Shimon, as it was taught** in a *baraita*: **One may not rinse himself** on Shabbat, **neither with hot** water **nor with cold** water; this is **the statement of Rabbi Meir. Rabbi Shimon permits** rinsing one's body even with hot water. **Rabbi Yehuda says** that there is a distinction: **With hot** water **it is prohibited** and **with cold** water **it is permitted.**

NOTES

One who bathes in cave water – הָרוֹחֵץ בְּמֵי מְעָרָה: In the period of the Mishna, ritual baths were not in buildings. Consequently, people would immerse themselves in natural bodies of water, often found in caves. Cave water in the Gemara seems to refer to hot water used as a ritual bath. The Rif and the Rambam explain that the water in these ritual baths was naturally hot, like the hot springs of Tiberias. On the other hand, the Ramban and Rabbeinu Yona explain that the cave water was heated by fire before Shabbat.

One who bathes, after the fact – הָרוֹחֵץ דִּיעֲבַד: *Tosafot* in tractate *Sota* (2a) discuss certain aspects of talmudic grammar, including the question of whether a phrase beginning with the definite article ⊠h, meaning: One who…, expresses approval of an action after the fact, but does not allow it *ab initio*. *Tosafot* prove that this cannot be assumed in every instance where the definite article is employed. The style and context of the entire sentence must be examined to determine whether that conclusion is appropriate in each particular case.

LANGUAGE

A swampy river [*kurdima*] – קוֹרְדִּימָא: This term seems to be an Aramaic synonym of *piluma*, which is the version found in some texts. The Greek form πήλωμα, *pèleuma*, is derived from πηλός, *pelos*, meaning cement or thick mud. Some think that *kurdima*, or its alternate version, *kurima*, is the name of a specific river that is very muddy.

HALAKHA

Bathing in hot water on Shabbat – רְחִיצָה בְּחַמִּין בַּשַּׁבָּת: It is prohibited to bathe one's entire body in hot water on Shabbat, even if the water was heated the day before. This prohibition applies even if one does not bathe one's entire body at once, but washes his limbs incrementally. However, it is permitted to wash part of one's body on Shabbat. It is also permitted to wash one's entire body in the hot springs of Tiberias. This applies only to bathing in the springs themselves but not in water drawn from the springs (Rambam *Sefer Zemanim, Hilkhot Shabbat* 22:20; *Shulḥan Arukh, Oraḥ Ḥayyim* 326:1).

״וְנִסְתַּפֵּג אֲפִילּוּ בְּעֶשֶׂר אֲלוּנְטִיּוֹת״. רֵישָׁא רְבוּתָא קָא מַשְׁמַע לָן, וְסֵיפָא רְבוּתָא קָא מַשְׁמַע לָן. רֵישָׁא רְבוּתָא קָא מַשְׁמַע לָן – דַּאֲפִילּוּ הָנֵי דְּלָא נְפִישִׁי בְּהוּ מַיָּא, כֵּיוָן דְּחַד הוּא – אָתֵי לִידֵי סְחִיטָה. וְסֵיפָא רְבוּתָא קָא מַשְׁמַע לָן, אֲפִילּוּ הָנֵי דִּנְפִישִׁי בְּהוּ מַיָּא, כֵּיוָן דְּרַבִּים נִינְהוּ – מַדְכְּרִי אַהֲדָדֵי.

The mishna addressed the permissibility of drying oneself with a towel after bathing on Shabbat, and added the phrase: **And dried himself off even with ten towels.** The Gemara comments on the formulation of the mishna: **The first clause teaches us a novel** concept, **and the latter clause teaches us a novel** concept. The Gemara explains: **The first clause:** One who…dried himself even with ten towels may not carry them, **teaches us a novel** concept, **that** the prohibition applies **even** to **these** towels, **which do not have much water** absorbed **in them.** The reason for this is that **since he is one** person, **he** may **come to squeeze** them. **And the latter clause teaches us a novel** concept, that **even these** ten people may carry the towel that they have all used, despite the fact **that they have** absorbed **much water** and the towel is very wet. The reason for this is that **since they are many** people, **they remind each other** not to wring the towel.

תָּנוּ רַבָּנַן: מִסְתַּפֵּג אָדָם בַּאֲלוּנְטִית, וּמַנִּיחָהּ בַּחַלּוֹן. וְלֹא יִמְסְרֶנָּה לְאוֹלְיָירִין, מִפְּנֵי שֶׁחֲשׁוּדִים עַל אוֹתוֹ דָּבָר. רַבִּי שִׁמְעוֹן אוֹמֵר: מִסְתַּפֵּג בַּאֲלוּנְטִית אַחַת, וּמְבִיאָהּ בְּיָדוֹ לְתוֹךְ בֵּיתוֹ.

The Sages taught in a *baraita*: **One may dry himself with a towel** on Shabbat **and leave it in the window** of the bathhouse; **and one may not give it to the bath attendants, because they are suspect in this matter**[N] of wringing out towels. **Rabbi Shimon says: One may dry himself with a single towel**[H] **and carry it in his hand into his home,** and there is no concern lest he wring out the water.

אֲמַר לֵיהּ אַבַּיֵי לְרַב יוֹסֵף: הִלְכְתָא מַאי? אֲמַר לֵיהּ: הָא רַבִּי שִׁמְעוֹן, הָא רַבִּי, הָא שְׁמוּאֵל, הָא רַבִּי יוֹחָנָן.

Abaye said to Rav Yosef: What is the *halakha* with regard to carrying a towel home after using it to dry himself? Rav Yosef **said to him: There is Rabbi Shimon, there is Rabbi** Yehuda HaNasi, **there is Shmuel,** and **there is Rabbi Yoḥanan,** all of whom permit it.

רַבִּי שִׁמְעוֹן – הָא דַּאֲמַרַן. רַבִּי – דְּתַנְיָא, אָמַר רַבִּי: כְּשֶׁהָיִינוּ לְמֵדִין תּוֹרָה אֵצֶל רַבִּי שִׁמְעוֹן בִּתְקוֹעַ הָיִינוּ מַעֲלִין שֶׁמֶן וַאֲלוּנְטִית מֵחָצֵר לַגַּג, וּמִגַּג לַקַּרְפֵּף, עַד שֶׁהָיִינוּ מַגִּיעִין אֵצֶל מַעְיָן שֶׁהָיִינוּ רוֹחֲצִין בּוֹ. שְׁמוּאֵל – דְּאָמַר רַב יְהוּדָה אָמַר שְׁמוּאֵל: מִסְתַּפֵּג אָדָם בַּאֲלוּנְטִית, וּמְבִיאָהּ בְּיָדוֹ לְתוֹךְ בֵּיתוֹ. רַבִּי יוֹחָנָן – דְּאָמַר רַבִּי חִיָּיא בַּר אַבָּא אָמַר רַבִּי יוֹחָנָן: הֲלָכָה, מִסְתַּפֵּג אָדָם בַּאֲלוּנְטִית וּמְבִיאָהּ בְּיָדוֹ לְתוֹךְ בֵּיתוֹ.

The Gemara elaborates: **Rabbi Shimon** rules leniently, **as we have** already **stated** that he permits bathing and drying oneself with a towel and then bringing it home. **Rabbi** Yehuda HaNasi agrees, **as it was taught** in a *baraita* that **Rabbi** Yehuda HaNasi **said: When we would study Torah**[N] **with Rabbi Shimon in Tekoa, we would carry oil and towels from the courtyard to the roof and from the roof into an enclosure** similar to a courtyard **until we reached the spring in which we would bathe,** without passing through a public domain. In Rabbi Yehuda HaNasi's opinion, it is permitted to carry a towel both before and after using it to dry oneself. **Shmuel** is also lenient, as **Rav Yehuda said** that **Shmuel said** explicitly: **One may dry himself with a towel and carry it in his hand into his home. Rabbi Yoḥanan** is also lenient, as **Rabbi Ḥiyya bar Abba said** that **Rabbi Yoḥanan said:** The ***halakha*** is that **one may dry himself with a towel and carry it in his hand into his house.**

וּמִי אָמַר רַבִּי יוֹחָנָן הָכִי?! וְהָאָמַר רַבִּי יוֹחָנָן: הֲלָכָה כִּסְתָם מִשְׁנָה. וּתְנַן: וְנִסְתַּפֵּג אֲפִילּוּ בְּעֶשֶׂר אֲלוּנְטִיּוֹת – לֹא יְבִיאֵם בְּיָדוֹ! הַהוּא כְּבֶן חֲכִינַאי מַתְנֵי לָהּ.

The Gemara challenges this last point: **And did Rabbi Yoḥanan** really **say that? Didn't Rabbi Yoḥanan state** a principle that **the *halakha* is in accordance with an unattributed mishna,** in which the name of the *tanna* who issued the rulings does not appear? **And we learned** explicitly in our mishna, which is unattributed, that if one bathed **and dried himself even with ten towels, he may not carry them in his hand.** The Gemara answers: Rabbi Yoḥanan's version of the mishna does not teach this *halakha* unattributed; rather, it **teaches it in accordance with** the opinion of **ben Ḥakhinai,** which is the opinion of an individual Sage that is not the accepted *halakha*.

אָמַר רַבִּי חִיָּיא בַּר אַבָּא אָמַר רַבִּי יוֹחָנָן: הָאוֹלְיָירִין מְבִיאִין בַּלְּרֵי נָשִׁים לְבֵי בָּנֵי, וּבִלְבַד שֶׁיִּתְכַּסֶּה בָּהֶן רֹאשָׁן וְרוּבָּן. סַכְּנִיתָא – צָרִיךְ לְקַשֵּׁר שְׁנֵי רָאשֶׁיהָ לְמַטָּה. אָמַר רַבִּי חִיָּיא בַּר אַבָּא אָמַר רַבִּי יוֹחָנָן: לְמַטָּה מִכְּתֵפַיִים. אֲמַר לְהוּ רָבָא לִבְנֵי מְחוֹזָא: כִּי מַעַבְרִיתוּ מָאנֵי לִבְנֵי חֵילָא – שַׁרְבִּיבוּ בְּהוּ לְמַטָּה מִכְּתֵפִים.

Rabbi Ḥiyya bar Abba said that **Rabbi Yoḥanan said: Bath attendants may bring women's bathing garments** [*balarei*][L] **to the bathhouse** on Shabbat **as long as they cover their heads and the majority of their bodies with them,** so that they are being worn rather than carried. With regard to the **large scarf**[N] that is worn draped over one's shoulders, **one must tie its two ends** together **below** so that it will not fall. **Rabbi Ḥiyya bar Abba said** that **Rabbi Yoḥanan said:** This means that one must tie it **below the shoulders.** In a similar vein, **Rava said to the inhabitants of** his city, **Meḥoza: When you transport clothing for the soldiers** who are staying in the city, **extend them beneath your shoulders** so that you will wear them like a garment and not simply carry them.[H]

NOTES

They are suspect in this matter – שֶׁחֲשׁוּדִים עַל אוֹתוֹ דָּבָר: The bath attendants are suspect of wringing a towel used by one person in order to give it to another to use (*Arukh*).

When we would study Torah, etc. – כְּשֶׁהָיִינוּ לְמֵדִין תּוֹרָה וכו׳: While it appears that Rabbi Yehuda HaNasi is simply relating the custom of the students of Rabbi Shimon, who certainly acted in accordance with his opinion when they were in his presence (Rashba), nevertheless, since Rabbi Yehuda HaNasi relates that they followed this practice without qualification, apparently he agrees with this ruling.

Scarf – סַכְּנִיתָא: The Rambam explained that this refers to a small scarf that does not cover one's head and most of his body, and that is why it must be tied.

HALAKHA

One may dry himself with a single towel – מִסְתַּפֵּג אָדָם בַּאֲלוּנְטִית: It is permitted to dry oneself with a towel on Shabbat and carry it home where a joining of courtyards [*eiruv*] has been established (*Mishna Berura*). There is no concern that he will wring the towel. However, he may not hand the towel to a bath attendant, due to the concern that he wring it (Rambam *Sefer Zemanim, Hilkhot Shabbat* 22:20; *Shulḥan Arukh, Oraḥ Ḥayyim* 301:48).

Ways to wear various garments in order to transfer them on Shabbat – דֶּרֶךְ לְבִישַׁת בְּגָדִים שׁוֹנִים לְצוֹרֶךְ הֲבָאָתָם בְּשַׁבָּת: It is permitted to carry articles of clothing on Shabbat provided that one wears them as a garment. Scarves that do not cover one's head and the majority of one's body must be tied so they do not fall, in accordance with the opinion of Rabbi Yoḥanan (Rambam *Sefer Zemanim, Hilkhot Shabbat* 19:19; *Shulḥan Arukh, Oraḥ Ḥayyim* 301:34).

LANGUAGE

Bathing garments [*balarei*] – בַּלְּרֵי נָשִׁים: From the Latin balnearia, meaning bathing garments.

״סָכִין וּמְמַשְׁמְשִׁין״. תָּנוּ רַבָּנַן: סָכִין וּמְמַשְׁמְשִׁין בִּבְנֵי מֵעַיִם בְּשַׁבָּת, וּבִלְבַד שֶׁלֹּא יַעֲשֶׂה כְּדֶרֶךְ שֶׁהוּא עוֹשֶׂה בַּחוֹל. הֵיכִי עָבֵיד? רַבִּי חָמָא בַּר חֲנִינָא אָמַר: סָךְ וְאַחַר כָּךְ מְמַשְׁמֵשׁ, רַבִּי יוֹחָנָן אָמַר: סָךְ וּמְמַשְׁמֵשׁ בְּבַת אַחַת.

We learned in the mishna: **One may smear oil and rub** a person's body by hand on Shabbat. **The Sages taught** in a *baraita*: **One may smear oil** on **and rub** his **intestinal** area **on Shabbat,**[H] and it is not a prohibited form of healing, **provided he does not do so in the manner in which he does during the week.** The Gemara asks: **How** then **does one do** this on Shabbat? **Rabbi Ḥama bar Ḥanina said: One** first **smears oil and afterward rubs**[N] the body. And **Rabbi Yoḥanan said: One smears oil and rubs simultaneously.**

״אֲבָל לֹא מִתְעַמְּלִין״. אָמַר רַבִּי חִיָּיא בַּר אַבָּא אָמַר רַבִּי יוֹחָנָן: אָסוּר לַעֲמוֹד בְּקַרְקָעִיתָהּ שֶׁל דְּיוֹמְסֶת, מִפְּנֵי שֶׁמְּעַמֶּלֶת וּמְרַפֵּא. אָמַר רַבִּי יְהוּדָה אָמַר רַב: כָּל יָמֶיהָ שֶׁל דְּיוֹמְסֶת עֶשְׂרִים וְאֶחָד יוֹם, וַעֲצֶרֶת מִן הַמִּנְיָן. אִיבַּעְיָא לְהוּ: עֲצֶרֶת (בַּתְּחִלָּה) לְהַאי גִּיסָא, אוֹ לְהַאי גִּיסָא? תָּא שְׁמַע, דַּאֲמַר שְׁמוּאֵל: כּוּלְּהוּ שַׁקְיָינֵי מִדִּיבְחָא וְעַד עַצַרְתָּא מָעַלּוּ. דִּילְמָא, הָתָם הוּא – דִּכְמָה דְּקָרִיר עָלְמָא מָעַלִּי, אֲבָל הָכָא – מִשּׁוּם הַבְלָא הוּא, כֵּיוָן דְּחָמֵים עָלְמָא – טְפֵי מַעֲלֵי.

The mishna taught: **However, one may not exert himself**[H] on Shabbat. **Rabbi Ḥiyya bar Abba said** that **Rabbi Yoḥanan said: It is prohibited to stand on the floor of** the therapeutic bathhouse of **Deyomset**[HL] on Shabbat, **because it warms and heals** even if one is not bathing or exerting himself. **Rav Yehuda said** that **Rav said: The entire period** that bathing in **Deyomset** is therapeutic **is twenty-one days; and *Shavuot* is included.** The Gemara **raises a dilemma: Is *Shavuot* on this side,** at the beginning, of the twenty-one-day period, **or on this side,** at the end, of the twenty-one days? **Come** and **hear** a resolution to this dilemma from that which **Shmuel said: All** medicinal **drinks are effective from Passover to *Shavuot***; apparently, the waters of the Deyomset are therapeutic in the time period leading up to *Shavuot*. The Gemara rejects this proof: **Perhaps there,** with regard to medicinal drinks, **it is** so, because **the cooler the world, the better** these drinks heal; **however, here,** with regard to bathing, the therapeutic effect is **due to the heat,** and therefore **the warmer the world, the better.** The time period during which bathing is effective would only begin with *Shavuot*.

אֲמַר רַבִּי חֶלְבּוֹ: חַמְרָא דִּפְרוּגַיְיתָא וּמַיָּא דִּדְיוֹמְסֶת קִיפְּחוּ עֲשֶׂרֶת הַשְּׁבָטִים מִיִּשְׂרָאֵל.

Apropos Deyomset, the Gemara cites that **Rabbi Ḥelbo said: The wine of Phrygia** [*Perugaita*][L] **and the water** of **the Deyomset deprived Israel** of the **ten** lost **tribes.** Because the members of these tribes were attracted to the pleasures of wine and bathing and did not occupy themselves with Torah, they were lost to the Jewish people.

רַבִּי אֶלְעָזָר בֶּן עֲרָךְ אִיקְּלַע לְהָתָם, אִימְּשִׁיךְ בָּתְרַיְיהוּ אִיעֲקַר תַּלְמוּדֵיהּ. כִּי הֲדַר אֲתָא, קָם לְמִיקְרֵי בְּסִפְרָא, בְּעָא לְמִיקְרָא ״הַחֹדֶשׁ הַזֶּה לָכֶם״ אֲמַר: הַחֵרֵשׁ הָיָה לִבָּם. בָּעוּ רַבָּנַן רַחֲמֵי עֲלֵיהּ, וַהֲדַר תַּלְמוּדֵיהּ.

The Gemara relates that once **Rabbi Elazar ben Arakh**[P] **happened** to come **there,** to Phrygia and Deyomset, and **he was drawn after them,** and his **Torah learning was forgotten. When he returned, he stood to read from a** Torah **scroll** and **was supposed to read** the verse: **"This month shall be for you** [*haḥodesh hazeh lakhem*]**"** (Exodus 12:2),[N] but he had forgotten so much that he could barely remember how to read the Hebrew letters, and instead he read: **Have their hearts become deaf** [*haḥeresh haya libbam*], interchanging the similar letters *reish* for *dalet*, *yod* for *zayin*, and *beit* for *khaf*. **The Sages** prayed and **asked** for God to have **mercy on him, and his learning was restored.**

וְהַיְינוּ דִּתְנַן, רַבִּי נְהוֹרַאי אוֹמֵר: הֱוֵי גּוֹלֶה לִמְקוֹם תּוֹרָה, וְאַל תֹּאמַר שֶׁהִיא תָּבֹא אַחֲרֶיךָ, שֶׁחֲבֵרֶיךָ יְקַיְּימוּהָ בְּיָדֶךָ, וְאֶל בִּינָתְךָ אַל תִּשָּׁעֵן. תָּנָא: לֹא רַבִּי נְהוֹרַאי שְׁמוֹ אֶלָּא רַבִּי נְחֶמְיָה שְׁמוֹ, וְאָמְרִי לָהּ רַבִּי אֶלְעָזָר בֶּן עֲרָךְ שְׁמוֹ, וְלָמָּה נִקְרָא שְׁמוֹ רַבִּי נְהוֹרַאי – שֶׁמַּנְהִיר עֵינֵי חֲכָמִים בַּהֲלָכָה.

And that is what **we learned** in a mishna that **Rabbi Nehorai says: Exile yourself to a place of Torah and do not say that it will follow you,** as if you are in a place of Torah, **your colleagues will establish it in your hands, and do not rely on your understanding** alone. **It was taught: Rabbi Nehorai was not his name, but rather Rabbi Neḥemya was his name; and some say** that **Rabbi Elazar ben Arakh was his name** and his statement was based on the personal experience of forgetting his Torah due to his failure to exile himself to a place of Torah. **And why was he called Rabbi Nehorai?** It was **because he would illuminate** [*manhir*] **the eyes of the Sages in *halakha*.**

HALAKHA

One may smear oil on and rub his intestinal area on Shabbat – סָכִין וּמְמַשְׁמְשִׁין בִּבְנֵי מֵעַיִם בְּשַׁבָּת: One may smear oil on and massage the intestinal area on Shabbat, but it must be performed in a manner different from the manner it is performed during the week. Therefore, one applies the oil and rubs immediately, and he does so gently and not vigorously, as per the opinion of Rabbi Yoḥanan (Rambam *Sefer Zemanim, Hilkhot Shabbat* 21:28; *Shulḥan Arukh, Oraḥ Ḥayyim* 327:2).

One may not exert himself – לֹא מִתְעַמְּלִין: Exertion is prohibited on Shabbat. For example, it is prohibited to step on someone's body to cause him to sweat. It is similarly prohibited to walk or exercise in order to sweat. This is included in the decree prohibiting medical treatments on Shabbat (Rambam *Sefer Zemanim, Hilkhot Shabbat* 21:28; *Shulḥan Arukh, Oraḥ Ḥayyim* 328:42).

It is prohibited to stand on the floor of Deyomset – אָסוּר לַעֲמוֹד בְּקַרְקָעִיתָהּ שֶׁל דְּיוֹמְסֶת: It is prohibited to stand on the floor of the Deyomset bathhouse on Shabbat, because the water warms and heals, and healing is prohibited on Shabbat (Rambam *Sefer Zemanim, Hilkhot Shabbat* 21:28).

NOTES

One first smears oil and afterward rubs – סָךְ וְאַחַר כָּךְ מְמַשְׁמֵשׁ: This means that one smears oil on a specific part of his body and immediately rubs it, which differs from the standard method during the week, which involved smearing oil on his entire body and only then rubbing in the oil (*Me'iri*).

This month shall be for you [*haḥodesh hazeh lakhem*], etc. – הַחֹדֶשׁ הַזֶּה לָכֶם וכו׳: Rabbi Elazar's error resulted from the similarity between the letters *reish* and *dalet*, *yod* and *zayin*, and *beit* and *khaf*. The Gemara relates the details of the error to underscore that even Rabbi Elazar ben Arakh, who was likened to an ever-flowing spring, reached so lowly a state when he left the company of the Sages (Maharsha).

LANGUAGE

Deyomset – דְּיוֹמְסֶת: The origin of this word is unclear. Some authorities suggest that it refers to the bathhouses of the ancient city Emmaus, and Deyomset is a corrupted version of the name of that city. Other commentaries suggest that the word derives from the Greek **δημόσιος**, *dèmosios*, an adjective that refers to a public area, especially a bathhouse.

Phrygia [*Perugaita*] – פְּרוּגַיְיתָא: This is a reference to the small kingdom of Phrygia, **Φρυγία**, in Asia Minor.

PERSONALITIES

Rabbi Elazar ben Arakh – רַבִּי אֶלְעָזָר בֶּן עֲרָךְ: A preeminent disciple of Rabban Yoḥanan ben Zakkai, at the time of the destruction of the Second Temple. Rabban Yoḥanan ben Zakkai perceived Rabbi Elazar ben Arakh as his most outstanding disciple, surpassing both Rabbi Yehoshua and Rabbi Eliezer HaGadol, and praised him greatly, both in his presence and in his absence. He was a great scholar of *aggada* and of the esoterica of the Torah. However, as the midrash relates, he did not wish to settle with his colleagues in Yavne. Rather, following his wife's advice, he settled elsewhere, abandoning his Torah study, as the Gemara here relates. Apparently, he died young, long before his contemporaries. As such, Rabbi Elazar ben Arakh left a limited imprint in talmudic literature. The stamp of his genius is apparent despite its absence from so many other realms.

״אֲבָל לֹא מִתְגָּרְרִין״. תָּנוּ רַבָּנַן: אֵין גּוֹרְרִין בְּמַגְרֶרֶת בַּשַּׁבָּת. רַבָּן שִׁמְעוֹן בֶּן גַּמְלִיאֵל אוֹמֵר: אִם הָיוּ רַגְלָיו מְלוּכְלָכוֹת בְּטִיט וּבְצוֹאָה – גּוֹרֵר כְּדַרְכּוֹ וְאֵינוֹ חוֹשֵׁשׁ. רַב שְׁמוּאֵל בַּר יְהוּדָה עָבְדָא לֵיהּ אִימֵּיהּ מַגְרַרְתָּא דְּכַסְפָּא.

The mishna taught: **However, one may not scrape** off the oil on Shabbat. **The Sages taught** in a *baraita*: **One may not scrape** his body **with a scraper on Shabbat. Rabban Shimon ben Gamliel says: If one's feet were dirty with mortar and excrement he** may scrape them **in the usual manner** with a scraper[H] **and need not be concerned** about violating a prohibition. **Rav Shmuel bar Yehuda's mother made him a silver scraper**[B] to use on Shabbat to distinguish it from a weekday.

״אֵין יוֹרְדִין לְקוּרְדִּימָא וכו׳״. מַאי טַעְמָא? מִשּׁוּם פִּיקָא.

The mishna also taught that **one may not enter a swampy river**[H] full of mud on Shabbat. The Gemara explains: **What is the reason** for this? **Due to the mud,**[N] as it is likely that one will slip and fall and come to violate the prohibitions of bathing and wringing out his clothes.

״וְאֵין עוֹשִׂין אַפִּיקְטוִיזִין בַּשַּׁבָּת״. אָמַר רַבָּה בַּר בַּר חָנָה אָמַר רַבִּי יוֹחָנָן: לֹא שָׁנוּ אֶלָּא בְּסַם, אֲבָל בְּיָד – מוּתָּר. תַּנְיָא, רַבִּי נְחֶמְיָה אוֹמֵר: אַף בַּחוֹל אָסוּר, מִפְּנֵי הֶפְסֵד אוֹכָלִין.

We also learned in the mishna that **one may not make a drug to induce vomiting** on Shabbat.[H] **Rabba bar bar Ḥana said** that **Rabbi Yoḥanan said: They only taught** that this is prohibited **with a drug,** which is considered a medicine; **however,** inducing vomiting **by hand is permitted. It was taught** in a *baraita* that **Rabbi Neḥemya says: Even during the week,** if one need not vomit for medical reasons, **it is prohibited** to induce vomiting **because** it causes **loss of food.**

״וְאֵין מְעַצְּבִין אֶת הַקָּטָן״. אָמַר רַבָּה בַּר בַּר חָנָה אָמַר רַבִּי יוֹחָנָן: לְפוּפֵי יְנוּקָא בַּשַּׁבָּת – שַׁפִּיר דָּמֵי. וְהָאֲנַן תְּנַן: אֵין מְעַצְּבִין! הָתָם בְּחוּמְרֵי שִׁדְרָה, דְּמֵיחֲזֵי כְּבוֹנֶה.

And we learned in the mishna that **one may not align a young** infant's bones[B] in order to straighten them on Shabbat. **Rabba bar bar Ḥana said** that **Rabbi Yoḥanan said:** With regard to **swaddling an infant**[H] on Shabbat, one may **well** do so. The Gemara challenges this statement: **Didn't we learn** in the mishna that **one may not align** an infant's bones? The Gemara answers: **There,** the mishna is referring to **the bones,** vertebrae, **of the spine, because** straightening them **appears like** the prohibited labor of **building.**

״וְאֵין מַחֲזִירִין אֶת הַשֶּׁבֶר״. אָמַר רַבִּי חָנָא בַּגְדָּתָאָה אָמַר שְׁמוּאֵל:

We also learned in the mishna that **one may not reset a break** in a bone on Shabbat. **Rav Ḥana of Baghdad said** that **Shmuel said:**

BACKGROUND

Scraper – מַגְרֶרֶת: Scrapers were used to clean oil off the body after lubrication.

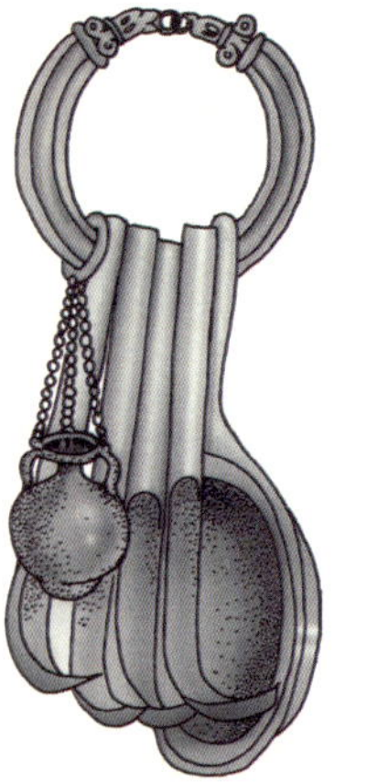

Illustration of a ring containing silver scrapers and an oil dispenser from the mishnaic period. The scraper belonging to Rav Shmuel bar Yehuda was apparently similar to these.

Aligning a young infant's bones – מְעַצְּבִין אֶת הַקָּטָן: Cases of limbs being malformed in childbirth are common, such as thigh sprains from birth, and it is often necessary to straighten various limbs in order to bring them to their proper location. These acts of orthopedic alignment are known in Hebrew as *itzuv*.

HALAKHA

Scraping with a scraper – גְּרִירָה בְּמַגְרֶרֶת: It is prohibited to use a scraper to scrape dirt off one's body on Shabbat. However, if one's hands or feet are dirty with mud, it is permitted, as the *halakha* is in accordance with the view of Rabban Shimon ben Gamliel (Rambam *Sefer Zemanim, Hilkhot Shabbat* 21:30; *Shulḥan Arukh, Oraḥ Ḥayyim* 327:3).

One may not enter a swampy river – אֵין יוֹרְדִין לְקוּרְדִּימָא: It is prohibited to walk in a slippery, wet place on Shabbat, lest one fall into the water and come to wring his garments. This ruling is based on one of the interpretations of the word *kurdima*, swampy river (Rambam *Sefer Zemanim, Hilkhot Shabbat* 21:29; *Shulḥan Arukh, Oraḥ Ḥayyim* 301:46 in the comment of the Rema).

Vomiting on Shabbat – הֲקָאָה בְּשַׁבָּת: One may not induce vomiting on Shabbat unless he is in pain from overeating or the like. Since it is also prohibited to take medicine on Shabbat, it is permitted to induce vomiting only with one's hand, but not through use of a drug (Rambam *Sefer Zemanim, Hilkhot Shabbat* 21:31; *Shulḥan Arukh, Oraḥ Ḥayyim* 328:39).

Swaddling an infant – לְפוּפֵי יְנוּקָא: It is permitted to tightly swaddle an infant on Shabbat, even if it is done to prevent his bones from becoming misaligned. This is not considered a prohibited medicinal practice. However, one may not manually correct a child's vertebrae unless he is in danger, because it is comparable to building (Rambam *Sefer Zemanim, Hilkhot Shabbat* 21:31, 22:26).

NOTES

One may not enter a swampy river [*kurdima*]…due to the mud – אֵין יוֹרְדִין לְקוּרְדִּימָא...מִשּׁוּם פִּיקָא: There are several explanations for this prohibition. Some commentaries explain that *kurdima* is the name of a place where there is healing water and mud. Therefore, it is prohibited to go there on Shabbat, just as there is a prohibition against entering the Deyomset (Rambam; see also Rabbeinu Ḥananel). Other authorities explain that since there is a great deal of mud in the *kurdima*, there is a concern that one who bathes there may sink in the deep swamp. This would require others to come and save him, which would place their lives at risk and necessitate the desecration of Shabbat (*ge'onim*).

הֲלָכָה מַחֲזִירִין אֶת הַשֶּׁבֶר. רַבָּה בַּר בַּר חָנָה אִיקְּלַע לְפוּמְבְּדִיתָא, לָא עַל לְפִירְקֵיהּ דְּרַב יְהוּדָה. שַׁדְרֵיהּ לְאַדָּא דַּיָּילָא, אֲמַר לֵיהּ: זִיל גַּרְבֵּיהּ. אֲזַיל גַּרְבֵּיהּ, אֲתָא, אַשְׁכְּחֵיהּ דְּקָא דָּרֵישׁ: אֵין מַחֲזִירִין אֶת הַשֶּׁבֶר. אֲמַר לֵיהּ: הָכִי אָמַר רַב חָנָא בַּגְדָּתָאָה אָמַר שְׁמוּאֵל: הֲלָכָה, מַחֲזִירִין אֶת הַשֶּׁבֶר. אֲמַר לֵיהּ: הָא חָנָא דִּידַן, וְהָא שְׁמוּאֵל דִּידַן – וְלָא שְׁמִיעַ לִי, וְלָאו בְּדִינָא גַּרְבְּתִיךְ?!

The ***halakha*** is that **one may reset a break**[H] on Shabbat, which was the ruling in Shmuel's version of the mishna. The Gemara relates that **Rabba bar bar Ḥana happened** to come **to Pumbedita** and **he did not enter Rav Yehuda's lecture.** Rav Yehuda **sent for Adda, his attendant,** and **said to him: Go drag him** to the lecture. **He went and dragged him** forcibly to the lecture (Rabbeinu Ḥananel). Rabba bar bar Ḥana **came and found** Rav Yehuda **teaching** that **one may not reset a break** on Shabbat. **He said to him: This is what Rav Ḥana of Baghdad said** that **Shmuel said:** The ***halakha*** is that **one may reset a break** on Shabbat. Rav Yehuda **said to him: Ḥana is ours,**[N] a Babylonian scholar, **and Shmuel is ours, and** nevertheless, **I did not** yet **hear** this *halakha*; **did I not rightfully drag you** to the lecture?

"מִי שֶׁנִּפְרְקָה יָדוֹ כו'". רַב אַוְיָא הֲוָה יָתֵיב קַמֵּיהּ דְּרַב יוֹסֵף, שְׁנָיא לֵיהּ יְדֵיהּ. אֲמַר לֵיהּ: הָכִי מַאי? אָסוּר. וְהָכִי מַאי? אֲמַר לֵיהּ: אָסוּר. אַדְּהָכִי אִיתְפַּח יְדֵיהּ.

We learned in the mishna that **one whose hand was dislocated** may not treat it by vigorously moving it about in water.[H] The Gemara relates that **Rav Avya was** once **sitting before Rav Yosef and his hand became dislocated.** Rav Avya then displayed a variety of hand positions and **he said to him: What** is the ruling with regard to **this?** Am I permitted to place my hand in this way, or is it a violation of the prohibition against healing on Shabbat? Rav Yosef said to him: **It is prohibited.** Rav Avya again asked: **And what** is the ruling if I position my hand in **this** way? Rav Yosef **said to him: It is prohibited. In the meantime, his hand** was restored to its proper location and **was healed.**

אֲמַר לֵיהּ: מַאי תִּיבָּעֵי לָךְ, הָא תְּנַן "מִי שֶׁנִּפְרְקָה יָדוֹ אוֹ רַגְלוֹ – לֹא יְטָרְפֵם בְּצוֹנֵן, אֲבָל רוֹחֵץ כְּדַרְכּוֹ. וְאִם נִתְרַפֵּא – נִתְרַפֵּא". אֲמַר לֵיהּ: וְלָא תְּנַן "אֵין מַחֲזִירִין אֶת הַשֶּׁבֶר" וְאָמַר רַב חָנָא בַּגְדָּתָאָה אָמַר שְׁמוּאֵל: הֲלָכָה מַחֲזִירִין אֶת הַשֶּׁבֶר? אֲמַר לֵיהּ: כּוּלְּהוּ בַּחֲדָא מְחִיתָא מְחִיתִנְהוּ?! הֵיכָא דְּאִיתְּמַר – אִיתְּמַר, הֵיכָא דְּלָא אִיתְּמַר – לָא אִיתְּמַר.

Rav Yosef **said to him: What is your dilemma? We learned** in our mishna that **one whose hand or foot was dislocated** on Shabbat **may not** vigorously **move it about in cold water; however, he may rinse it in the usual manner, and if it is healed, it is healed.** Rav Avya **said to him:** That is no proof, **as didn't we learn** in our mishna that **one may not reset a break, and Rav Ḥana of Baghdad said** that **Shmuel said** that **the *halakha*** is that **one may** indeed **reset a broken bone.** Therefore, perhaps a dislocated limb may also be treated on Shabbat. Rav Yosef **said to him: Were all these woven together in a single weave? Where it was stated** that an alternative version of the mishna exists, **it was stated;**[N] **where it was not stated, it was not stated.** Therefore, the ruling of the mishna with regard to a dislocated limb must be observed.

הדרן עלך חבית

HALAKHA

One may reset a break – מַחֲזִירִין אֶת הַשֶּׁבֶר: A broken or fully dislocated bone may be reset on Shabbat, in accordance with the ruling of Shmuel and his version of the mishna, as per Rashi's explanation (*Shulḥan Arukh, Oraḥ Ḥayyim* 328:47).

Resetting a dislocated limb – הַחֲזָרַת נֶקַע: If one's hand or foot was completely dislocated from its joint, it may be reset on Shabbat (*Shulḥan Arukh, Oraḥ Ḥayyim* 328:47; see *Magen Avraham* and *Mishna Berura*). However, if it is not completely dislocated and does not pose a danger to the limb, one may only wash it in the usual manner. If it is healed in this manner, so be it (*Shulḥan Arukh, Oraḥ Ḥayyim* 328:30).

NOTES

Ḥana is ours – הָא חָנָא דִּידַן: Everything that was taught publicly in lectures and in the study hall was known to the local Sages. Nevertheless, the possibility existed that a Sage would teach a halakhic ruling to one of his students, who would in turn transmit this teaching to only a few others, resulting in a situation where other students of that Sage were unfamiliar with that ruling. In this context, Rabba bar bar Ḥana, who came from Eretz Yisrael, was the only one familiar with this halakhic tradition from Rav Ḥana and Shmuel, both of whom were Babylonian, while Rav Yehuda, who was the preeminent disciple of Shmuel, was unfamiliar with it.

Where it was stated, it was stated – הֵיכָא דְּאִיתְּמַר אִיתְּמַר: The rationale behind the distinction between a broken bone and a dislocated limb is that a broken bone is a more serious condition, and if it is not immediately reset the entire limb may be in jeopardy. That is not true of a dislocation (*Tosefot Rid*).

Summary of **Perek XXII**

In this chapter, the Gemara attempted to clarify the rules of squeezing on Shabbat. Its main conclusions were as follows: It is prohibited to squeeze an item if one's main intent in doing so is to make use of the liquid that emerges. At times this may constitute a Torah prohibition, while at other times it constitutes a rabbinic one. On the other hand, if one's intent is to improve the food item by squeezing liquid from it, even though the action is the same as in the case outlined previously, the act is not defined as a prohibited labor and is permitted according to Torah law. Nonetheless, in certain cases the Sages prohibited squeezing as a precautionary measure in order to ensure that one not perform a prohibited labor.

In the continuation of the chapter, the Gemara came to the following conclusions regarding food preparation: If a food can be eaten in its current state, it is permitted to enhance its taste. Thus, one may add hot water to improve a food unless it is otherwise inedible or the hot water changes the food into a completely different item.

The Gemara arrived at similar conclusions regarding breaking a barrel in order to eat the food that is inside: It all depends upon the extent to which the action improves the barrel. If the act improves the barrel, then breaking it is prohibited, whereas if it causes significant damage to the barrel and only slight improvement, it is permitted even *ab initio*. Additionally, if one's primary intent is to remove the food rather than to improve the receptacle, breaking the barrel is permitted.

The Gemara also arrived at some lenient conclusions regarding squeezing as a function of the labor of laundering, based on the view that this constitutes an unintentional act and a labor not necessary for its own sake, and that the Rabbis did not prohibit it.

Introduction to **Perek XXIII**

There dwelt men of Tyre also therein, who brought in fish and all manner of ware, and sold on the Shabbat to the children of Judah and in Jerusalem. Then I contended with the nobles of Judah and said to them: What evil thing is this that you do and profane the Shabbat day?

(Nehemiah 13:16–17)

The prohibition of commercial activity on Shabbat is one of the earliest known decrees enacted by the Sages to protect Torah law. This decree is generally explained as a protective measure to prevent writing on Shabbat, as commercial activity generally requires writing in order to record and approve legally binding transactions. Although Torah law does not prohibit commercial activity itself on Shabbat, commercial transactions often entail numerous activities that are prohibited on Shabbat, such as carrying objects from one domain to another, fixing utensils or completing their production, and handling objects that may not be handled on Shabbat.

As the decree prohibiting commercial activity was already widely known and accepted in talmudic times, this chapter examines the scope of the prohibition and seeks to determine precisely which activities fall under the decree. In addition to prohibiting direct and explicitly formulated business transactions, the decree also encompasses related activities, such as hiring workers and granting or receiving a loan. However, since the source of this prohibition is rabbinic, there are instances where there is room for leniency, such as when the commercial activity is for the sake of a mitzva or when there is no concern for possible violation of Shabbat.

Respect for the dead is another factor that allows for the relaxation of some of the stringencies of Shabbat, as respect for the dead honors both the living and the deceased. However, the details of what exactly may be done for this purpose need to be spelled out, especially because a corpse is a severe form of a set-aside entity that may not be moved directly. This chapter also considers which activities may not be done even out of respect for the dead.

מתני׳ שׁוֹאֵל אָדָם מֵחֲבֵירוֹ כַּדֵּי יַיִן וְכַדֵּי שֶׁמֶן וּבִלְבַד שֶׁלֹּא יֹאמַר לוֹ ״הַלְוֵינִי״. וְכֵן הָאִשָּׁה מֵחֲבֶירְתָּהּ כִּכָּרוֹת. וְאִם אֵינוֹ מַאֲמִינוֹ – מַנִּיחַ טַלִּיתוֹ אֶצְלוֹ, וְעוֹשֶׂה עִמּוֹ חֶשְׁבּוֹן לְאַחַר שַׁבָּת. וְכֵן עֶרֶב פֶּסַח בִּירוּשָׁלַיִם שֶׁחָל לִהְיוֹת בְּשַׁבָּת, מַנִּיחַ טַלִּיתוֹ אֶצְלוֹ וְנוֹטֵל אֶת פִּסְחוֹ, וְעוֹשֶׂה עִמּוֹ חֶשְׁבּוֹן לְאַחַר יוֹם טוֹב.

MISHNA **One may borrow**[H] **jugs of wine and jugs of oil from another** on Shabbat, **as long as one does not say** the following **to him: Loan me. And similarly, a woman** may borrow **from another loaves** of bread on Shabbat. **And if** the lender **does not trust him** that he will return them, the borrower **may leave his cloak**[N] **with him** as collateral **and make** the proper **calculation with him after Shabbat. And similarly,** on **the eve of Passover in Jerusalem, when** it **occurs on Shabbat,** one who is procuring a Paschal lamb **may leave his cloak with him,** i.e., the person from whom he is purchasing it, **and take** the lamb to bring as **his Paschal lamb, and** then **make** the proper **calculation with him after the Festival.**

גמ׳ אֲמַר לֵיהּ רָבָא בַּר רַב חָנָן לְאַבָּיֵי: מַאי שְׁנָא ״הַשְׁאִילֵנִי״ וּמַאי שְׁנָא ״הַלְוֵינִי״? אֲמַר לֵיהּ: ״הַשְׁאִילֵנִי״ – לָא אָתֵי לְמִיכְתַּב, ״הַלְוֵינִי״ – אָתֵי לְמִיכְתַּב.

GEMARA It was taught in the mishna that one is permitted to borrow jugs from another on Shabbat, but one may not use the phrase loan me. **Rava bar Rav Ḥanan said to Abaye: What is different** about the expression **let me borrow,** that makes it permitted? **And what is different** about the expression **loan me**[N] that makes it prohibited? **He said to him:** If someone says **let me borrow,** the lender **will not come to write** down the loan because the expression indicates that the borrower intends to return the object in its current state within a short amount of time. On the other hand, the expression **loan me** indicates a more extended loan in which the object is not necessarily returned in exactly the same manner in which it was taken. Therefore, the lender **will come to write** down the terms of the loan.

וְהָא כֵּיוָן דְּבַחוֹל, זִימְנִין דְּבָעֵי לְמֵימַר לֵיהּ ״הַלְוֵינִי״ וְאָמַר לֵיהּ ״הַשְׁאִילֵנִי״ וְלָא קָפֵיד עִילָּוֵיהּ, וְאָתֵי לְמִיכְתַּב, בְּשַׁבָּת נַמִי אָתֵי לְמִיכְתַּב. אֲמַר לֵיהּ: (בַּחוֹל דְּלָא שְׁנָא כִּי אֲמַר לֵיהּ ״הַלְוֵינִי״ לָא שְׁנָא כִּי אֲמַר לֵיהּ ״הַשְׁאִילֵנִי״, לָא קָפְדִינַן עִילָּוֵיהּ – אָתֵי לְמִיכְתַּב), בְּשַׁבָּת כֵּיוָן דְּ״הַשְׁאִילֵנִי״ הוּא דְּשָׁרוּ לֵיהּ רַבָּנַן ״הַלְוֵינִי״ לָא שָׁרוּ לֵיהּ – מִינְכְּרָא מִילְּתָא, וְלָא אָתֵי לְמִיכְתַּב.

Rava bar Rav Ḥanan challenged Abaye's answer: **But since on weekdays there are times one intends to say loan me and** instead **says let me borrow, and** the lender **is not particular about his** imprecise terminology and **he comes to write** down the terms of the loan, **on Shabbat he will also come to write.** Abaye **said to him: On a weekday, when there is no difference if one says loan me or let me borrow,** lenders **are not particular about his** terminology, and the lender will therefore **come to write** down the terms of the loan. **On Shabbat, since** only the expression **let me borrow was allowed by the Sages,** while the expression **loan me was not permitted, the matter is recognizable.** Both of the parties must bear in mind which terminology is acceptable, **and** the lender **will not come to write.**

אמר ליה רבא בר רב חנן לאביי: מִכְּדִי אָמְרוּ רַבָּנַן ״כָּל מִילֵּי דְּיוֹם טוֹב כַּמָּה דְּאֶפְשָׁר לְשַׁנּוֹיֵי – מְשַׁנֵּינַן״, הָנֵי נָשֵׁי דְּמַלְיָין חַצְבַּיְיהוּ מַיָּא, מַאי טַעְמָא לָא מְשַׁנִּין? מִשּׁוּם דְּלָא אֶפְשָׁר. הֵיכִי לֶעְבְּדִי – דְּמַלְיָין בְּחַצְבָּא רַבָּא לִימְלוּ בְּחַצְבָּא זוּטָא – הָא קָא מַפְשׁוּ בְּהִילּוּכָא, דְּמַלְיָין בְּחַצְבָּא זוּטָא לִימְלוּ בְּחַצְבָּא רַבָּא – קָא מַפְשׁוּ בְּמַשּׂוֹי.

Rava bar Rav Ḥanan said to Abaye: Now, since the Sages said that with regard to **all matters of a Festival, as much as we can change** the way we do things from the manner in which we do them on weekdays, **we change,**[H] **these women who fill their pitchers with water,**[H] **what is the reason they do not change** the way they draw water from their normal weekday procedure? Abaye answers: **Because it is not possible** to change the procedure. **How would they do it** differently? If you say that **those who** normally **fill a large pitcher should fill a small pitcher** on a Festival, **they would** thereby **add** to their **walking** and expend extra effort. Conversely, if **those who** normally **fill a small pitcher would fill a large pitcher** on a Festival, **they would** thereby **add** to the weight of their **load.** Even though these methods are different from the norm, they would cause added exertion. Therefore, the Sages did not require that one draw water in an unusual fashion.

NOTES

The borrower may leave his cloak with him – מַנִּיחַ טַלִּיתוֹ אֶצְלוֹ: The borrower may not say that the cloak is collateral. Rather, the lender will understand the borrower's intention in leaving the cloak (Rashba). Although this resembles a business transaction, the Sages did not prohibit it (*Tosefot Rid*), because the very prohibition of conducting business on Shabbat is itself a rabbinic decree.

Let me borrow and loan me – הַשְׁאִילֵנִי וְהַלְוֵינִי: See Rashi and *Tosafot*, who both attempt to clarify the distinction between these two phrases. From the conclusion of the Gemara, it is apparent that the very fact that a person must be careful to use a particular expression reminds the individual that it is Shabbat, which is the purpose of the decree. An opinion cited by *Tosafot* notes that in some languages there is no difference between these expressions. In these languages, the borrower should simply say: Give me, which does not have any connotations of a loan (Rashba).

HALAKHA

Borrowing on Shabbat – שְׁאִילָה בְּשַׁבָּת: It is permitted to borrow objects or food and drink on Shabbat. However, as the mishna teaches, the borrower must be careful not to speak of it as a loan. If the lender does not trust him, the borrower may leave something as collateral but may not explicitly say: Here is the collateral (Rambam *Sefer Zemanim*, *Hilkhot Shabbat* 23:12; *Shulḥan Arukh*, *Oraḥ Ḥayyim* 307:11 and in the comment of the Rema).

Changing one's habits on Festivals – שִׁינּוּי בְּיוֹם טוֹב: Even though carrying an object from one domain to another is permitted on a Festival, one may not carry a large load in the usual weekday manner. Rather, one should carry the object differently (Rambam *Sefer Zemanim*, *Hilkhot Yom Tov* 5:1; *Shulḥan Arukh*, *Oraḥ Ḥayyim* 510:8).

Drawing water on a Festival – מִילּוּי מַיִם בְּיוֹם טוֹב: Even though one must carry a heavy object in an atypical manner on a Festival, if it is impossible to change the way the object is handled, or if doing so would require more effort, one does not need to carry it differently. This is in accordance with Abaye's ruling (Rambam *Sefer Zemanim*, *Hilkhot Yom Tov* 5:1; *Shulḥan Arukh*, *Oraḥ Ḥayyim* 510:10).

ניפרוס סודרא – אתי לידי סחיטה. נכסייה בנכתמא – זימנין דמיפסק, ואתי למקטריה. הלכך: לא אפשר.

If you say that, in order to draw water in an unusual manner, **we should** require a woman to **spread a cloth** over the vessel, she **may come to** violate the prohibition of **squeezing** water from the cloth. And if **we would cover it with a lid, sometimes it is severed** from the pitcher, **and one will** then **come to tie it. Therefore,** since **it is impossible** to require women to draw water any other way, women draw water on a Festival in the usual manner.

ואמר ליה רבא בר רב חנן לאביי: תנן, לא מספקין ולא מטפחין ולא מרקדין ביום טוב. וקא חזינן דעבדין, ולא אמרינן להו ולא מידי. ולטעמיך, הא דאמר רבא: לא ליתיב איניש אפומא דלחייא, דילמא מיגנדר ליה חפץ ואתי לאיתויי, והא קא חזינן נמי דמותבי חצבי, ויתבן אפומא דמבואה, ולא אמרינן להו ולא מידי. אלא: הנח לישראל, מוטב שיהו שוגגין ואל יהו מזידין.

And Rava bar Rav Ḥanan said to Abaye: Did we not **learn** in a mishna that **one may not clap** hands, **or clap one's hand against one's body,**[N] **or dance on a Festival?**[H] **And we see,** however, **that people do** these things, **and we do not say anything** to stop **them.**[H] Abaye responded: **And according to your reasoning,** what about **this** *halakha* that **Rava said: One may not sit** on Shabbat **at the entrance** of a private alleyway next to **the post,** which delineates its boundaries, **lest an object roll away** into the public domain **and he come to bring it** back? **And yet we see that** women **put down their jugs and sit at the entrance of the alleyway, and we do not say anything to stop them. Rather,** in these matters we rely on a different principle: **Leave the Jewish people** alone, and do not rebuke them. **It is better that they be unwitting** in their halakhic violations **and** that **they not be intentional** sinners, for if they are told about these prohibitions they may not listen anyway.

סבור מינה הני מילי בדרבנן, אבל בדאורייתא – לא. ולא היא, לא שנא בדרבנן ולא שנא בדאורייתא. דהא תוספת דיום הכפורים דאורייתא היא, וקא חזינן להו דקאכלי ושתו עד שתחשך, ולא אמרינן להו ולא מידי.

There were those who **understood from this** statement that **this** *halakha* **applies only to rabbinic** prohibitions **but not to Torah** prohibitions, with regard to which we must certainly reprimand transgressors. However, **that is not so. There is no difference** between **rabbinic** prohibitions **and Torah** prohibitions. In both cases one does not reprimand those who violate unwittingly and would not listen to the reprimand. **For** the requirement of **adding to Yom Kippur** by beginning the fast while it is still day **is from the Torah, and we see** women **who eat and drink** on the eve of Yom Kippur **up until nightfall, and we do not say anything to them.** Thus, this rule, which applies to rabbinic prohibitions, applies to Torah prohibitions as well.

"וכן אשה מחבירתה ככרות". בשבת הוא דאסיר, אבל בחול – שפיר דמי. לימא מתניתין דלא כהלל; דתנן, וכן היה הלל אומר: לא תלוה אשה ככר לחבירתה עד שתעשינה דמים, שמא יוקרו חטין ונמצאו באות לידי רבית.

We learned in the mishna: **And similarly, a woman** may borrow **loaves** of bread **from another** on Shabbat. However, as in the previous *halakha*, she may not ask for them using the word loan. The Gemara asks: Is it only **on Shabbat that it is prohibited, but on a weekday it seems well.** Is it permitted to borrow bread as a loan on a weekday? If so, **let us say that the mishna is not in accordance with** the opinion of **Hillel, for we learned** in a mishna: **And thus Hillel would say: A woman may not loan a loaf**[H] of bread **to another**[N] **until she calculates** its **monetary** value, **lest wheat become more valuable and they come to** violate the prohibition against lending with **interest.** If the price of wheat rises and the borrower returns the same sized loaf of bread, she will have returned something of greater value than what she borrowed, and therefore she will have paid interest on her loan. From here we see that even on weekdays it is prohibited to borrow a loaf of bread from another person.

אפילו תימא הלל, הא – באתרא דקייץ דמיה, הא – באתרא דלא קייץ דמיה.

The Gemara answers: **Even if you say** that the mishna is in accordance with the opinion of **Hillel,** we may distinguish between the cases such that there is no contradiction: **This** case, in which the mishna permits borrowing a loaf of bread as a loan, is applicable **in a place** where **the price** of the loaf **is set,**[H] while **this** statement, which was said by Hillel, is applicable **in a place** where **its price is not set.**

NOTES

Clapping [*mesappekin*]...clapping against one's body [*metappeḥin*] – מספקין...מטפחין: Elsewhere, Rashi reverses the definitions of these terms and explains that *metappeḥin* means clapping and *mesappekin* is tapping one's hand against one's leg.

And thus Hillel would say: A woman may not loan a loaf of bread to another, etc. – וכן היה הלל אומר לא תלוה אשה ככר לחבירתה וכו׳: Hillel used the example of loaves of bread because, generally speaking, no two people make exactly the same sized loaf of bread (Rashba). The possibility of incurring interest exists in this case. Since the woman borrowed such a small amount, i.e., a loaf or two of bread, she is likely to return an actual loaf, even if the price of wheat has risen, because she does not want to appear miserly (Ramban).

HALAKHA

One may not clap hands, or clap one's hand against one's body, or dance on a Festival – לא מספקין ולא מטפחין ולא מרקדין: It is prohibited to dance, clap, or make other noises that accompany or stimulate song and dance on Shabbat or on a Festival. This is a rabbinic decree, lest one come to fashion or repair a musical instrument. However, if one performs one of these actions in an unusual manner, it is permitted (Rambam). Nowadays, people are permitted do these things because it is better that they do so unwittingly without knowingly violating the *halakha*. Some authorities rule that nowadays, since people do not generally have expertise in fixing or constructing musical instruments, all of these actions are permitted (Rema, based on *Tosafot*; Rambam *Sefer Zemanim*, *Hilkhot Shabbat* 23:5; *Shulḥan Arukh*, *Oraḥ Ḥayyim* 339:3, 524:1).

Rebuking violators – מחאה לעבריינים: If people commonly violate a prohibition unwittingly, we do not rebuke them for doing so, for they might continue to violate it intentionally. This even applies to Torah prohibitions, provided they are not explicitly stated in the Torah (Ran; Rosh, based on other sources elsewhere in the Talmud). Later authorities say that this *halakha* applies only to prohibitions that are not punishable by excision [*karet*]. However, we do rebuke those who unwittingly violate transgressions that carry a punishment of excision (*Mishna Berura*; Rambam *Sefer Zemanim*, *Hilkhot Shevitat Asor* 1:7; *Shulḥan Arukh*, *Oraḥ Ḥayyim* 608:2).

Loaning food or objects – הלוואת מאכלים וחפצים: It is prohibited to loan anything that cannot be returned in its original form, except for money. The rationale is that the price of the object might increase and the parties involved would then violate the prohibition of charging and paying interest. If someone did borrow such an object, he should calculate its value immediately upon borrowing it and repay the loan based upon that price. Some authorities rule that when it comes to bread and other common household items, people are not particular about the slight differences in value, and it is therefore permitted to give them as a loan even without calculating their precise monetary value (*Tur*; Rambam *Sefer Mishpatim*, *Hilkhot Malve VeLoveh* 10:2; *Shulḥan Arukh*, *Yoreh De'a* 162:1 and in the comment of the Rema).

This is in a place where the price of the loaf is set – הא באתרא דקייץ דמיה: If a commodity has a set market price, it is permitted to loan it, and the borrower is permitted to return the same amount of that commodity. This ruling is in accordance with the answer of the Gemara (*Shulḥan Arukh*, *Yoreh De'a* 162:3).

״וְאִם אֵינוֹ מַאֲמִינוֹ״. אִיתְּמַר: הַלְוָואַת יוֹם טוֹב, רַב יוֹסֵף אָמַר: לֹא נִיתְּנָה לִיתָּבַע, וְרַבָּה אָמַר: נִיתְּנָה לִיתָּבַע. רַב יוֹסֵף אָמַר: ״לֹא נִיתְּנָה לִיתָּבַע״. דְּאִי אָמְרַתְּ ״נִיתְּנָה לִיתָּבַע״ – אָתֵי לְמִיכְתַּב. רַבָּה אָמַר: נִיתְּנָה לִיתָּבַע, דְּאִי אָמְרַתְּ ״לֹא נִיתְּנָה״ – לָא יָהֵיב לֵיהּ, וְאָתֵי לְאִימָּנוּעֵי מִשִּׂמְחַת יוֹם טוֹב.

The mishna taught further that **if** the lender **does not trust** the one who borrows from him on Shabbat or a Festival, the borrower may leave his cloak as collateral. On this topic, the Gemara cites that which **was said** in an amoraic dispute with regard to **loans on a Festival: Rav Yosef said** that such a loan **cannot be claimed** in court. Although the borrower is obligated to return the object or reimburse the lender, the lender cannot force him to do so by taking legal action. **And Rabba said** that such a loan is like any other type of loan and **can be claimed** in court.[H] The Gemara explains these two positions: **Rav Yosef said** that a loan made on a Festival **cannot be claimed** in court, **for if you say** that **it can be claimed,** there is a concern that the lender may **come to write** the details of the loan on the Festival so that he can claim it later. **Rabba said** that it **can be claimed, for if you say** that **it cannot** be claimed, the lender **will not give him** anything to borrow, **and** the potential borrower **will refrain from rejoicing on the Festival.**

תְּנַן: אִם אֵינוֹ מַאֲמִינוֹ – מַנִּיחַ טַלִּיתוֹ אֶצְלוֹ. אִי אָמְרַתְּ בִּשְׁלָמָא לֹא נִיתְּנָה לִיתָּבַע – מִשּׁוּם הָכִי מַנִּיחַ טַלִּיתוֹ אֶצְלוֹ, וְעוֹשֶׂה עִמּוֹ חֶשְׁבּוֹן לְאַחַר שַׁבָּת. אֶלָּא אִי אָמְרַתְּ ״נִיתְּנָה לִיתָּבַע״ אַמַּאי מַנִּיחַ טַלִּיתוֹ אֶצְלוֹ? לִיתֵּן לֵיהּ וְלִתְבְּעֵיהּ. אָמַר: לָא בָּעֵינָא דְּלִיקוּם בְּדִינָא וְדַיָּינָא.

We learned in the mishna that **if he does not trust him, he may leave his cloak with him** as collateral. The Gemara attempts to show that this *halakha* supports Rav Yosef's position: **Granted,** this *halakha* makes sense **if you say** that loans given on a Festival **cannot be claimed,** in accordance with Rav Yosef's position. **Due to this, he leaves his cloak with him and makes a calculation with him after Shabbat. However, if you say** that loans given on a Festival **can** indeed **be claimed** in court, **why** then **would he leave his cloak with him? Let him give him** the item on loan **and bring him to court** if he does not return it. The Gemara rejects this argument because the lender can **say: I do not want to stand in judgment** before **judges;** he may prefer taking collateral so that he will not need to go to court at a later time.

מְתִיב רַב אִידִי בַּר אָבִין: הַשּׁוֹחֵט אֶת הַפָּרָה וְחִילְּקָהּ בְּרֹאשׁ הַשָּׁנָה, אִם הָיָה חֹדֶשׁ מְעוּבָּר – מְשַׁמֵּט, וְאִם לָאו – אֵינוֹ מְשַׁמֵּט.

Rav Idi bar Avin raised an objection to the view of Rav Yosef, based on a mishna pertaining to **one who slaughters a cow and divides it** among purchasers **on Rosh HaShana**[H] of a year that follows the Sabbatical Year [*shemitta*]. Even during the times of the Temple, they were already celebrating two days of Rosh HaShana. The first day was possibly the last day of the month of Elul and possibly the first day of the month of Tishrei, which is the actual date of Rosh Hashana.[N] The question therefore arises as to whether those who bought the meat of the cow initiated their debt on the final day of the Sabbatical Year, in which case the debts would be canceled, or whether the transactions took place on the first day of the following year, in which case the debts may still be collected. The mishna said that **if** it becomes clear that Elul of the previous year **was a full** thirty-day **month,** the Sabbatical Year[N] **cancels** the debts because the very end of the Sabbatical Year cancels the ability to collect all previous debts. **And if** this was **not** the case, and the first day of Rosh HaShana was actually the first day of the new year, the Sabbatical Year **does not cancel** the loan.

וְאִי לֹא נִיתְּנָה לִיתָּבַע – מַאי מְשַׁמֵּט? שָׁאנֵי הָתָם, דְּאִיגַּלַּאי מִילְּתָא דְּחוֹל הוּא.

Based on that mishna, Rav Idi bar Avin makes the following argument: **If** a loan given on a Festival **cannot be claimed** in court, **what is** the meaning of the word **cancels?** In any event, the lender could not have presented his claim against the borrower in court. The Gemara rejects this argument: **It is different there,** in an instance in which the month of Elul has thirty days, **for it has become clear that** the first day of Rosh HaShana **was a regular weekday.** The loan could therefore be claimed in court, if not for the fact that it was canceled by the Sabbatical Year.

תָּא שְׁמַע מִסֵּיפָא: אִם לָאו – אֵינוֹ מְשַׁמֵּט. אִי אָמְרַתְּ בִּשְׁלָמָא נִיתְּנָה לִיתָּבַע – הַיְינוּ דְּקָתָנֵי ״אֵינוֹ מְשַׁמֵּט״. אֶלָּא אִי אָמְרַתְּ ״לֹא נִיתְּנָה לִיתָּבַע״ – אַמַּאי אֵינוֹ מְשַׁמֵּט? דְּאִי יָהֵיב לֵיהּ – שָׁקֵיל.

The Gemara attempts to bring a different proof: **Come** and **hear** a proof for this **from** what we learned in **the latter clause** of that mishna: **If** the month of Elul did **not** turn out to be a full month, such that the first day of Rosh HaShana was actually the first day of the new year, the Sabbatical Year **does not cancel** the loan. **Granted, if you say** that a loan given on a Festival **can be claimed, that which was taught that it does not cancel** the loan is understandable. **But if you say** that **it cannot be claimed, why** does it teach that **it does not cancel** the loan? In any event, the lender cannot make a claim on it in court. The Gemara explains: A loan given on a Festival cannot be claimed in court, but since it has not been canceled, **if** the borrower **gives him** the money **he may take it.**

HALAKHA

Claiming a loan that was made on a Festival – תְּבִיעַת הַלְוָואַת יוֹם טוֹב: Loans made on a Festival, including food and drinks (*Magen Avraham*), are like all other loans and can be claimed in court. This ruling follows the opinion of Rabba, whose opinions are generally accepted in his disputes with Rav Yosef, and whose opinion is supported by the Gemara's discussion (Rambam *Sefer Zemanim, Hilkhot Yom Tov* 4:25; *Shulḥan Arukh, Oraḥ Ḥayyim* 525:1).

One who slaughters a cow and divides it on Rosh HaShana – הַשּׁוֹחֵט אֶת הַפָּרָה וְחִילְּקָהּ בְּרֹאשׁ הַשָּׁנָה: If a butcher slaughtered a cow on Rosh HaShana immediately following the Sabbatical Year, and people bought the meat on credit, and it turned out that the first day of Rosh HaShana was really the thirtieth day of Elul, the butcher cannot demand payment of their debts. This is because the debts were canceled by the conclusion of the Sabbatical Year. However, several authorities rule that debts owed to a storekeeper are not canceled by the Sabbatical Year. The butcher can indeed demand payment of the debts (Ra'avad, based on the Jerusalem Talmud; Rambam *Sefer Zera'im, Hilkhot Shemitta VeYovel* 9:5).

NOTES

Two days of Rosh HaShana – שְׁנֵי יְמֵי רֹאשׁ הַשָּׁנָה: During the Temple period, and even later, the beginning of the new month was determined by the testimony of eyewitnesses who saw the new moon. Consequently, the thirtieth day of the month of Elul was observed as Rosh HaShana, due to the possibility that witnesses would come and testify that they saw the new moon. However, if witnesses would not come on that day, it would be understood retroactively that it had not been Rosh HaShana, but rather the thirtieth day of Elul. Thus, Rosh HaShana would actually be the following day.

The Sabbatical Year – שְׁנַת הַשְּׁבִיעִית: The Torah states that debts are canceled during the seventh, Sabbatical Year . From the verse: "At the end of seven years you shall make a release" (Deuteronomy 15:1), the Sages derived that the cancelation of loans takes place at the very end of the Sabbatical Year. After the last moment of the Sabbatical Year, all previous outstanding debts are annulled. Nevertheless, even when the Sabbatical Year is observed according to Torah law, it is still considered to be an act of piety to repay debt after it has been canceled. However, the lender should initially refuse to accept payment by verbally renouncing the claim.

HALAKHA

One repays a debt during the Sabbatical Year – הַמַּחֲזִיר חוֹב בַּשְּׁבִיעִית: If one is repaid a loan that was canceled by the Sabbatical Year, he must say: I relinquish my claim. If the borrower says: Nevertheless, I want you to accept my payment, the lender may accept it. It is commendable for the lender and borrower to follow this course of action (Rambam *Sefer Zera'im, Hilkhot Shemitta VeYovel* 9:28; *Shulḥan Arukh, Ḥoshen Mishpat* 67:36).

Consecrating offerings on Shabbat or on a Festival – הַקְדָּשַׁת קׇרְבָּנוֹת בַּשַּׁבָּת וּבְחַג: It is prohibited by rabbinic decree to consecrate animals or objects on Shabbat or on a Festival. However, it is permitted to consecrate a Paschal lamb on Shabbat or to consecrate a Festival peace-offering on the Festival. These are Torah obligations that have a set time; therefore, the Sages were lenient (Rambam *Sefer Zemanim, Hilkhot Shabbat* 23:14 and *Sefer Korbanot, Hilkhot Korban Pesaḥ* 1:19).

מִכְּלָל דְּרֵישָׁא, אִי יָהֵיב לֵיהּ – לָא שָׁקֵיל? רֵישָׁא צָרִיךְ לְמֵימַר לֵיהּ "מְשַׁמֵּט אֲנִי", סֵיפָא – לָא צָרִיךְ לְמֵימַר לֵיהּ "מְשַׁמֵּט אֲנִי". כִּדְתְנַן: הַמַּחֲזִיר חוֹב בַּשְּׁבִיעִית, יֹאמַר לוֹ "מְשַׁמֵּט אֲנִי".

The Gemara is surprised at this statement: Does this prove **by inference that, in the first clause** of the mishna, **if** the borrower **gives him** the money, **he may not take it?** One does not have to refuse repayment of a loan that the Sabbatical Year has canceled. One is simply not allowed to demand repayment from the borrower. The Gemara explains the difference between the two clauses of the mishna: In the **first clause** of the mishna, in which the first day of Rosh HaShana turned out to be the last day of Elul, the lender **must say to him: I relinquish** my claim against you. However, in **the latter clause** of the mishna, in which the first day of Rosh HaShana is the first day of the new year, **he does not need to say to him: I relinquish** my claim. This is **as we learned** in a mishna: When **one repays a debt during the Sabbatical Year,**[H] the lender **should say to him: I relinquish** my claim.

וְאִם אָמַר לוֹ "אַף עַל פִּי כֵן" – יְקַבֵּל מִמֶּנּוּ, מִשּׁוּם שֶׁנֶּאֱמַר "וְזֶה דְּבַר הַשְּׁמִטָּה".

And if the borrower **says to him: Nonetheless,** I want to repay you, **he may accept it due to that which is stated: "And this is the manner of the release** [*devar hashemitta*], every creditor shall release that which he has lent to his neighbor; he shall not exact it of his neighbor or brother because the Lord's Sabbatical Year has been proclaimed" (Deuteronomy 15:2). The manner of the release, *devar hashemitta*, can be rendered: The statement of release. The Sages derived that, although the creditor must verbally release the debtor from obligation, if the debtor persists in his desire to repay the debt, the creditor may accept payment. If, however, the loan was made after the Sabbatical Year, as is the case in the latter clause of the mishna, the creditor need not verbally release the debtor from obligation.

רַב אָוְיָא שָׁקֵיל מַשְׁכּוֹנָא, רַבָּה בַּר עוּלָּא מַעֲרִים אִיעֲרוּמֵי.

The Gemara relates that **Rav Avya would take collateral** for loans that he gave on a Festivals. **Rabba bar Ulla would circumvent** the issue by taking something from the borrower after the conclusion of the Festival and holding onto it until the repayment of the loan.

"וְכֵן עֶרֶב פֶּסַח". אָמַר רַבִּי יוֹחָנָן: מַקְדִּישׁ אָדָם פִּסְחוֹ בַּשַּׁבָּת, וַחֲגִיגָתוֹ בְּיוֹם טוֹב. נֵימָא מְסַיַּיע לֵיהּ "וְכֵן עֶרֶב פֶּסַח בִּירוּשָׁלַיִם שֶׁחָל לִהְיוֹת בַּשַּׁבָּת מַנִּיחַ טַלִּיתוֹ אֶצְלוֹ וְנוֹטֵל אֶת פִּסְחוֹ וְעוֹשֶׂה עִמּוֹ חֶשְׁבּוֹן לְאַחַר יוֹם טוֹב".

We learned in the mishna: **And similarly, on the eve of Passover** in Jerusalem, when it occurs on Shabbat, one who needs to obtain an animal for the Paschal lamb may leave his cloak with the owner of the lamb as collateral and then make the appropriate calculations with him after the Festival. **Rabbi Yoḥanan said: A person may consecrate his Paschal lamb on Shabbat and his Festival** peace-**offering on the Festival.**[H] The Gemara suggests: **Shall we say** that the mishna **supports him?** It states: **And similarly,** on **the eve of Passover in Jerusalem which occurred on Shabbat, one may leave one's cloak with him and take his Paschal lamb and make** the appropriate **calculation with him after the Festival.** Here, we see that the lamb itself is consecrated on Shabbat, which follows the opinion of Rabbi Yoḥanan.

הָכָא בְּמַאי עָסְקִינַן – בְּמַמְנֶה אֲחֵרִים עִמּוֹ עַל פִּסְחוֹ, דְּמֵעִיקָּרָא מִיקְדַּשׁ וְקָאֵי.

The Gemara rejects this suggestion: This is not necessarily the case, for **with what are we dealing here? With** a case **in which one registers others** to participate **with him in** bringing **his Paschal lamb.**[N] In other words, the case is not one in which a person consecrates a previously unconsecrated animal but rather a case in which one allows others to join with him in registering for an animal **that was** already **consecrated from the outset.**

וְהָא אֲנַן תְּנַן "אֵין נִמְנִין עַל הַבְּהֵמָה בַּתְּחִילָּה בְּיוֹם טוֹב". שָׁאנֵי הָכָא, כֵּיוָן דְּרָגִיל אֶצְלוֹ – כְּמַאן דְּאִימְּנֵי בֵּיהּ מֵעִיקָּרָא דָּמֵי.

The Gemara challenges this: **But we learned** in a mishna: **One may not initially register for an animal on the Festival.** Therefore, even if the animal has been consecrated in advance, it is prohibited to register for it on the Festival, and it should certainly be prohibited to do so on Shabbat. The Gemara answers: The case **here is different. Since** each person who joins **regularly** registers together **with him,** the legal status of that person **is like** that of **one who registered for it from the outset.**

NOTES

A case in which one registers others to participate with him in bringing his Paschal lamb – בְּמַמְנֶה אֲחֵרִים עִמּוֹ עַל פִּסְחוֹ: The Paschal lamb is not eaten by one individual. Rather, it is shared by a group of people, each of whom must join the group in advance. Sometimes one person would purchase the animal, a lamb or a kid, and then others would pay him for their share and join in the offering.

וְהָא תָּנֵי רַבִּי הוֹשַׁעְיָא: הוֹלֵךְ אָדָם אֵצֶל רוֹעֶה הָרָגִיל אֶצְלוֹ וְנוֹתֵן לוֹ טָלֶה לְפִסְחוֹ וּמַקְדִּישׁוֹ, וְיוֹצֵא בּוֹ. הָתָם נַמִי, כֵּיוָן דְּרָגִיל אֶצְלוֹ – אַקְדּוֹשֵׁי לֵיהּ מֵעִיקָּרָא, וְהָא ״מַקְדִּישׁ״ קָתָנֵי. הֶקְדֵּשׁ עִילּוּי, מִדְּרַבָּנַן.

The Gemara raises another proof to the view of Rabbi Yoḥanan: **But Rabbi Hoshaya taught: One** who wants to bring a Paschal lamb and does not have his own lamb **may go to a shepherd to whom he normally goes, and** the shepherd **may give him a lamb** to be used **for his Paschal lamb, and he may consecrate it and fulfill his obligation with it.** This indicates that one may consecrate an animal on Shabbat. The Gemara answers: **There, too,** it is referring to a special case. **Since he normally goes to him** every year, the shepherd has already **consecrated it beforehand,** prior to Shabbat. The Gemara challenges this explanation: **But it taught that one may consecrate it,** indicating that the animal is only now being consecrated. The Gemara answers: This is not an actual sanctification in the normal sense, but rather **consecration by valuation.** By consecrating their animals on their own, the owners add further sanctity to the offering. This process is merely **rabbinic,** and it may be performed on Shabbat according to all opinions.

וּמִי אָמַר רַבִּי יוֹחָנָן הָכִי? וְהָא אָמַר רַבִּי יוֹחָנָן: הֲלָכָה כִּסְתָם מִשְׁנָה, וּתְנַן: לֹא מַקְדִּישִׁין וְלֹא מַעֲרִיכִין וְלֹא מַחֲרִימִין וְלֹא מַגְבִּיהִין תְּרוּמוֹת וּמַעַשְׂרוֹת, כׇּל אֵלּוּ – בְּיוֹם טוֹב אָמְרוּ, קַל וָחוֹמֶר בַּשַּׁבָּת. לָא קַשְׁיָא; כָּאן – בְּחוֹבוֹת שֶׁקָּבוּעַ לָהֶן זְמַן, כָּאן – בְּחוֹבוֹת שֶׁאֵין קָבוּעַ לָהֶן זְמַן.

The Gemara questions the very basis of this discussion: **Did Rabbi Yoḥanan** really **say this? But Rabbi Yoḥanan stated** as a general principle that the ***halakha*** is always **in accordance with an unattributed mishna,** i.e., a mishna that does not mention the name of the Sage whose ruling is quoted in the mishna. **And we learned** in an unattributed mishna: **One may not consecrate, or take a valuation vow, or consecrate** objects for use by the priests or the Temple, **or separate** ***terumot*** **or tithes;**[H] **they said** all of these prohibitions with regard to **a Festival,** and it is **an** ***a fortiori*** **inference** that these activities are prohibited **on Shabbat** as well. How, then, would Rabbi Yoḥanan have permitted sanctifying an animal on Shabbat or on a Festival? The Gemara answers: This is **not difficult. Here,** in the case in which Rabbi Yoḥanan deems it permitted, it is referring **to obligations that have a set time,** such that if the person does not consecrate the animal right now he will no longer be able to fulfill the mitzva. **There,** in the mishna that prohibits these activities, the prohibition is referring to **obligations that do not have a set time,** and one can therefore consecrate the animal after Shabbat.

מתני׳ מוֹנֶה אָדָם אֶת אוֹרְחָיו וְאֶת פַּרְפְּרוֹתָיו מִפִּיו, אֲבָל לֹא מִן הַכְּתָב. מֵפִיס אָדָם עִם בָּנָיו וְעִם בְּנֵי בֵּיתוֹ עַל הַשּׁוּלְחָן, וּבִלְבַד שֶׁלֹּא יִתְכַּוֵּין לַעֲשׂוֹת מָנָה גְּדוֹלָה כְּנֶגֶד מָנָה קְטַנָּה. וּמַטִּילִין חֲלָשִׁין עַל הַקָּדָשִׁים בְּיוֹם טוֹב, אֲבָל לֹא עַל הַמָּנוֹת.

MISHNA **One may count his guests** who are coming to his meal **and his appetizers,** as long as he does so **from memory; but** one may **not** read them **from a written** list, the reason for which will be explained in the Gemara. **A person may draw lots with his children and family members at the table** on Shabbat, in order to determine who will receive which portion, **as long as he does not intend to set a large portion against a small portion** in such a lottery. Rather, the portions must be of equal size. **And one may cast lots**[N] among the priests **for sanctified foods on a Festival, but not for the** specific **portions.**

Perek **XXIII**
Daf **149** Amud **a**

גמ׳ מַאי טַעְמָא? רַב בֵּיבָי אָמַר: גְּזֵירָה שֶׁמָּא יִמְחוֹק. אַבָּיֵי אָמַר: גְּזֵירָה שֶׁמָּא יִקְרָא בִּשְׁטָרֵי הֶדְיוֹטוֹת.

GEMARA We learned in the mishna that one may not read the names of his guests or the appetizers served in his meal from a written list. The Gemara asks: **What is the reason** for this prohibition? **Rav Beivai said:** It is **a decree lest one erase** something that is written on the list if he regrets inviting a particular guest or changes his mind about a particular dish. **Abaye said:** It is **a decree lest one read regular** business **documents.**

מַאי בֵּינַיְיהוּ? אִיכָּא בֵּינַיְיהוּ: דִּכְתַב אַכּוֹתֶל, וּמִידְלֵי. לְמַאן דַּאֲמַר שֶׁמָּא יִמְחוֹק – לָא חָיְישִׁינַן, וּלְמַאן דַּאֲמַר שֶׁמָּא יִקְרָא – חָיְישִׁינַן.

The Gemara asks: **What is** the practical difference **between them?** The Gemara answers: **There is** a difference **between them** in a case in which the **writing is on a wall and** it is **raised** higher than a person can reach. **According to the one who says** that the decree was made **lest one erase** something from the list, in a case such as this **we are not concerned** about erasure because one cannot even reach the writing. **But according to the one who says** that the decree was made **lest one read** business documents, **we are** still **concerned** in this case.

HALAKHA

One may not consecrate, or take a valuation vow, or consecrate objects for use by the priests or the Temple, or separate *terumot* or tithes – לֹא מַקְדִּישִׁין וְלֹא מַעֲרִיכִין וְלֹא מַחֲרִימִין וְלֹא מַגְבִּיהִין תְּרוּמוֹת וּמַעְשְׂרוֹת: One may not consecrate animals or objects, take a valuation vow, or separate *terumot* or tithes on Shabbat or on a Festival because these resemble commercial activities (Rambam *Sefer Zemanim*, *Hilkhot Shabbat* 23:14 and *Sefer Korbanot*, *Hilkhot Korban Pesaḥ* 1:19; *Shulḥan Arukh*, *Oraḥ Ḥayyim* 339:4, 524:1).

NOTES

One may cast lots – וּמַטִּילִין חֲלָשִׁין: The rationale for this ruling is that by casting lots, the priests display affection for the mitzva of eating the sacrifices (Rambam).

וּלְמַאן דְּאָמַר ״שֶׁמָּא יִמְחוֹק״ נֵיחוּשׁ שֶׁמָּא יִקְרָא. וְתוּ: לְשֶׁמָּא יִמְחוֹק לָא חָיְישִׁינַן? וְהָתַנְיָא: לֹא יִקְרָא לְאוֹר הַנֵּר, וְאָמַר רַבָּה: אֲפִילּוּ גָּבוֹהַּ שְׁתֵּי קוֹמוֹת, אֲפִילּוּ גָּבוֹהַּ שְׁתֵּי מַרְדְּעוֹת, אֲפִילּוּ עֲשָׂרָה בָּתִּים זֶה עַל גַּבֵּי זֶה – לֹא יִקְרָא.

The Gemara asks: **And according to the one who says** that the decree was made **lest one erase, we should** also **be concerned lest one read**[N] business documents. **And furthermore, are we** really **not concerned lest one erase** when the writing is high up? **But wasn't it taught** in a *baraita* that **one may not read by the light of a lamp** on Shabbat lest one adjust the lamp toward oneself; **and Rabba said: Even even** if the lamp was **two statures** of a person **high, and even** as high as **two plow handles, and even** if it was as high as **ten houses one atop the other, one may not read** by its light. This clearly demonstrates that when we are concerned that one may violate *halakha*, we do not distinguish between situations in which such a violation is more or less likely.

אֶלָּא, אִיכָּא בֵּינַיְיהוּ: דִּכְתַב אַכּוֹתֶל וּמִיתַּתִּי, לְמַאן דְּאָמַר שֶׁמָּא יִמְחוֹק – חָיְישִׁינַן, לְמַאן דְּאָמַר שֶׁמָּא יִקְרָא – לָא חָיְישִׁינַן, גּוּדָא בִּשְׁטָרָא לָא מִיחְלַף.

Rather, there is a difference **between them** in a case in which the **writing** is **on a wall and it is low down. According to the one who says** that the reason for the decree is **lest one erase,** in a case such as this **we are concerned** because one can easily reach the writing and erase it. However, **according to the one who says** that the decree was made **lest one read** business documents, **we are not concerned** because **a wall will not be confused with a document,** and reading from the wall will not cause one to then read business documents.

וּלְמַאן דְּאָמַר ״שֶׁמָּא יִקְרָא״ לֵיחוּשׁ שֶׁמָּא יִמְחוֹק. אֶלָּא, אִיכָּא בֵּינַיְיהוּ: דְּחַיְּיק אַטַּבְלָא וְאַפִּינְקָס. לְמַאן דְּאָמַר שֶׁמָּא יִמְחוֹק – לָא חָיְישִׁינַן. לְמַאן דְּאָמַר שֶׁמָּא יִקְרָא – חָיְישִׁינַן.

The Gemara asks further: **And according to the one who says** that the concern is **lest one read, we should** also **be concerned lest one erase. Rather, there is** a practical difference **between them** in a case where the writing is **engraved on a tablet or on a board. According to the one who says** that the concern is **lest one erase,** in a case such as this **we are not concerned.** Since the writing is not in ink, there is no concern that he will erase it. **According to the one who says** that the concern is **lest one read** business documents, **we are concerned.** The style of writing is irrelevant in terms of the likelihood that one will end up reading business documents.

וּלְמַאן דְּאָמַר ״שֶׁמָּא יִמְחוֹק״ לֵיחוּשׁ שֶׁמָּא יִקְרָא. וְכִי תֵּימָא: טַבְלָא וּפִינְקָס בִּשְׁטָרָא לָא מִיחְלַף – וְהָתַנְיָא: מוֹנֶה אָדָם כַּמָּה מִבִּפְנִים וְכַמָּה מִבַּחוּץ, וְכַמָּה מָנוֹת עָתִיד לְהַנִּיחַ לִפְנֵיהֶם מִכְּתָב שֶׁעַל גַּבֵּי הַכּוֹתֶל, אֲבָל לֹא מִכְּתָב שֶׁעַל גַּבֵּי טַבְלָא וּפִינְקָס.

The Gemara asks further: **According to the one who says** that the concern is **lest one erase, we should** also **be concerned lest one read** business documents. **And if you say: A tablet or a board will not be confused with a document, but wasn't it taught** explicitly in a *baraita*: **One may count how many** guests will sit **inside, and how many** guests will sit **outside, and how many portions he will place before them**[H] **from writing that is on the wall, but not from writing that is on a tablet or a board?**

הֵיכִי דָּמֵי? אִילֵּימָא דִּכְתִיב מִיכְתַּב – מַאי שְׁנָא הָכָא וּמַאי שְׁנָא הָכָא? אֶלָּא לָאו – דְּחַיְּיק, וְקָתָנֵי: מִכְּתָב שֶׁעַל גַּבֵּי הַכּוֹתֶל, אֲבָל לֹא מִכְּתָב שֶׁעַל גַּבֵּי טַבְלָא וּפִינְקָס.

The Gemara attempts to clarify this: **What are the circumstances** of the case described in this statement? **If you say that it was written** in ink, **what is the difference here,** when the writing is on a wall, **and what is the difference here,** when the writing is on a tablet? **Rather, is it not** a case of a list **that has been engraved, and** nonetheless **it teaches** that one may read **from writing that is on the wall but not from writing that is on a tablet or a board?**

אֶלָּא לְעוֹלָם דִּכְתַב אַכּוֹתֶל וּמִידְלִי. וּדְקָא קַשְׁיָא לָךְ דְּרַבָּה – דְּרַבָּה תַּנָּאֵי הִיא. דְּתַנְיָא: מוֹנֶה אָדָם אֶת אוֹרְחָיו וְאֶת פַּרְפְּרוֹתָיו מִפִּיו, אֲבָל לֹא מִן הַכְּתָב. רַבִּי אַחָא מַתִּיר מִכְּתָב שֶׁעַל גַּבֵּי הַכּוֹתֶל.

Rather, we should **actually** explain **that the writing was on a wall and was raised.**[N] **And** with regard to **what was difficult for you,** based on **Rabba's** statement that prohibited reading by candlelight on Shabbat regardless of the height of the candle, which presumably means that in our case, too, we should be stringent regardless of the height of the writing, that statement of **Rabba** is the subject of dispute between ***tanna'im*, as it was taught** in a *baraita*: **One may count one's guests and one's appetizers from memory, but not from a written** list. **Rabbi Aḥa permits** reading **from a written** list **that is on a wall.**

הֵיכִי דָּמֵי? אִילֵּימָא דִּכְתִיב מִתַּתָּא – לֵיחוּשׁ שֶׁמָּא יִמְחוֹק. אֶלָּא לָאו – דִּכְתַב וּמִידְלִי. וּשְׁמַע מִינָּהּ: דְּרַבָּה תַּנָּאֵי הִיא, שְׁמַע מִינָּהּ.

The Gemara attempts to clarify this: **What are the circumstances** in which Rabbi Aḥa permits this? **If you say that it is written below,** low down on the wall, **we should be concerned** that **perhaps one will erase** it. **Rather, is it not** referring to a case **in which it is written and** the location of the writing **is raised** such that it is high up on the wall, **and conclude from this that** the statement **of Rabba is** the subject of dispute among the ***tanna'im***? The Gemara concludes: Indeed, **conclude from this** that it is so.

NOTES

Lest one erase…lest one read – שֶׁמָּא יִמְחוֹק...שֶׁמָּא יִקְרָא: Since these two concerns are so similar to one another, and it is impossible to rule out the possibility that a person might erase or read a business document on Shabbat, we accept both concerns expressed by Rav Beivai and Abaye. Therefore, they only disagree about cases where only one concern is applicable.

Rather, we should actually explain that the writing was on a wall and was raised – אֶלָּא לְעוֹלָם דִּכְתַב אַכּוֹתֶל וּמִידְלִי: The commentaries dispute the meaning of this part of the discussion. The Rif and others explain that it is a continuation of the previous discussion with regard to the distinction between the positions of Rav Beivai and Abaye. Other commentaries say that this statement introduces a new discussion, which attempts to resolve the differences between the mishna and the *baraita* with regard to reading a list on a wall.

HALAKHA

Reading lists of guests or food – קְרִיאַת רְשִׁימַת הָאוֹרְחִים וְהַמַּאֲכָלִים: It is prohibited to read lists of guests or food that one has prepared for a meal on Shabbat, even if they are written high up on a wall. The rationale is the concern that one might read business documents on Shabbat. Even if the list is engraved, rather than written, on a tablet or a board, it is still prohibited to read the list. However, if the list is engraved on a wall, it is permitted to read it. This ruling is in accordance with the opinion of Abaye (Rambam *Sefer Zemanim*, *Hilkhot Shabbat* 23:19; *Shulḥan Arukh*, *Oraḥ Ḥayyim* 307:12).

וְהָנֵי תַּנָּאֵי כְּהָנֵי תַּנָּאֵי; דְּתַנְיָא: אֵין רוֹאִין בַּמַּרְאָה בְּשַׁבָּת, רַבִּי מֵאִיר מַתִּיר בְּמַרְאָה הַקָּבוּעַ בַּכּוֹתֶל.

The Gemara comments that in this matter, **these *tanna'im* are like those *tanna'im*,** who also argued over the same principle, **as it was taught** in a *baraita*: **One may not look in a mirror on Shabbat**[NH] lest one see a hair hanging and pluck it. **Rabbi Meir permits** looking **in a mirror that is fixed on a wall.**

מַאי שְׁנָא הַקָּבוּעַ בַּכּוֹתֶל – דְּאַדְּהָכִי וְהָכִי מִדְּכַר, שֶׁאֵינוֹ קָבוּעַ נַמִּי – אַדְּהָכִי וְהָכִי מִדְּכַר.

The Gemara questions Rabbi Meir's leniency: **What is different** about a mirror that is **fixed on a wall?** In that situation we say **that, in the meantime,** while one goes to bring scissors or another appliance to cut one's hair, **one will remember** that it is Shabbat and that it is prohibited to cut hair. If so, with regard to a mirror **that is not fixed** on a wall, we can **also** say that **in the meantime one will remember.**

הָכָא בְּמַרְאָה שֶׁל מַתֶּכֶת עָסְקִינַן, וְכִדְרַב נַחְמָן אָמַר רַבָּה בַּר אֲבוּהּ. דְּאָמַר רַב נַחְמָן אָמַר רַבָּה בַּר אֲבוּהּ: מִפְּנֵי מָה אָמְרוּ ״מַרְאָה שֶׁל מַתֶּכֶת – אֲסוּרָה״ – מִפְּנֵי שֶׁאָדָם עָשׂוּי לְהַשִּׁיר בָּהּ נִימִין הַמְדוּלְדָּלִין.

Rather, **here we are dealing with a metal mirror, and** it is **as Rav Naḥman** said that **Rabba bar Avuh said, for Rav Naḥman said** that **Rabba bar Avuh said: For what** reason **did** the Sages **say** that **a metal mirror is prohibited** for use on Shabbat? **Because a person may remove hanging hairs with it,** meaning that one may use the sharp edge of the mirror itself to cut the hairs. If the mirror is permanently set on the wall, we are not concerned that one will do this. This is similar to the view that one may read writing that is high up on a wall because it is impractical to erase the writing.

תָּנוּ רַבָּנַן: כְּתָב הַמְהַלֵּךְ תַּחַת הַצּוּרָה וְתַחַת הַדְּיוֹקְנָאוֹת – אָסוּר לִקְרוֹתוֹ בְּשַׁבָּת. וּדְיוֹקְנָא עַצְמָהּ – אַף בְּחוֹל אָסוּר לְהִסְתַּכֵּל בָּהּ, מִשּׁוּם שֶׁנֶּאֱמַר ״אַל תִּפְנוּ אֶל הָאֱלִילִים״. מַאי תַּלְמוּדָא? אָמַר רַבִּי חָנִין: אַל תִּפְנוּ אֶל מִדַּעְתְּכֶם.

The Sages taught in a *baraita*: With regard to **writing that is under a picture**[H] **or under graven images** [*deyokenaot*],[L] **it is prohibited to read it on Shabbat** lest one end up reading business documents. **And** with regard to an idolatrous **image**[H] **itself, even on a weekday it is prohibited to look at it, because it says: "Do not turn toward idols** [*al tifnu el ha'elilim*]**"**[N] or make yourselves molten gods, I am the Lord your God" (Leviticus 19:4). The Gemara asks for clarification: **What is the** biblical **derivation?** How does this verse indicate that one may not look at an idolatrous image? **Rabbi Ḥanin said: Do not push God** [*al tefannu El*] **out of your mind** by looking at these images (*Arukh*).

״מֵפִיס אָדָם עִם בָּנָיו וכו׳״. עִם בָּנָיו וְעִם בְּנֵי בֵּיתוֹ – אִין, וְעִם אַחֵר – לָא. מַאי טַעְמָא? כִּדְרַב יְהוּדָה אָמַר שְׁמוּאֵל. דְּאָמַר רַב יְהוּדָה אָמַר שְׁמוּאֵל: בְּנֵי חֲבוּרָה הַמַּקְפִּידִין זֶה עַל זֶה – עוֹבְרִין מִשּׁוּם מִדָּה וּמִשּׁוּם מִשְׁקָל, וּמִשּׁוּם מִנְיָן, וּמִשּׁוּם לוֹוִין וּפוֹרְעִין בְּיוֹם טוֹב.

We learned in the mishna that **a person may draw lots with one's children** and family members at the table on Shabbat to see who will receive which meal portion. The Gemara infers: **With one's children and family members, yes,** it is permitted, **but with another** person it is **not. What is the reason** for this? The Gemara explains that it is **as Rav Yehuda** said that **Shmuel said,** for **Rav Yehuda said** that **Shmuel said: Members of a group** who are eating together on Shabbat or on a Festival and **who are particular with each other**[H] that no one receive a larger portion than anyone else **are in violation of** the prohibitions of **measuring, and weighing, and counting** merchandise on Shabbat or a Festival, **and** they are also in violation **of** the prohibition against **lending and repaying on a Festival.**

NOTES

One may not look in a mirror on Shabbat – אֵין רוֹאִין בַּמַּרְאָה בְּשַׁבָּת: Rabbeinu Ḥananel teaches that this prohibition is not based on the possibility of accidentally removing hairs. Rather, the law pertains to the mirror itself: Perhaps one will find dirt or rust on the mirror and polish it, thus violating of the prohibition of repairing on Shabbat. Rabbeinu Zeraḥya HaLevi explains that, according to the Gemara's conclusion, all mirrors are prohibited due to the concern that one may use a metal one.

Do not turn toward idols [*al tifnu el ha'elilim*] – אַל תִּפְנוּ אֶל הָאֱלִילִים: Most of the commentaries understand that the word idols [*elilim*] is referring to anything that lacks true value, as well as to idols. Rashi and other commentaries do not explain the Gemara's teaching: Do not push God out of your mind [*al tefannu El mida'atkhem*], as cited above. Rather, they translate the phrase as follows: Do not turn toward your opinions [*al tifnu el da'atkhem*]. The Gemara warns people not to turn to things that human beings imagine on their own and which lack real significance.

LANGUAGE

Graven images [*deyokenaot*] – דְּיוֹקְנָאוֹת: The origin of this word is not entirely clear. Some authorities state that it is derived from the Greek **δείκανον**, *deikanon*, which refers to a picture, especially an embroidered one. Others think that it is related to the word **εἰκών**, *eikon*, which means statue or picture, with the added Hebrew or Greek prefix *d* or *diyu*.

HALAKHA

One may not look into a mirror on Shabbat – אֵין רוֹאִין בַּמַּרְאָה בְּשַׁבָּת: One may not look into a metal mirror on Shabbat, since it generally has a sharp edge that can be used to trim hairs. Even if the mirror is attached permanently to a wall, it is still prohibited to use it. However, it is permitted to look into any other type of mirror, with regard to which there is no concern that one will use it to trim one's hair. This ruling is in accordance with the *Tosefta* (Rambam *Sefer Zemanim*, *Hilkhot Shabbat* 22:14; *Shulḥan Arukh*, *Oraḥ Ḥayyim* 302:13).

Writing that is under a picture – כְּתָב הַמְהַלֵּךְ תַּחַת הַצּוּרָה: It is prohibited to read the writing underneath pictures and graven images on Shabbat, lest one read business documents (Rashi; Rambam *Sefer Zemanim*, *Hilkhot Shabbat* 23:19; *Shulḥan Arukh*, *Oraḥ Ḥayyim* 307:15).

An idolatrous image – דְּיוֹקָן אֱלִילִי: It is prohibited to look at an idolatrous image because one may derive pleasure from looking at it (*Tosafot*; *Shakh*; Rambam *Sefer HaMadda*, *Hilkhot Avoda Zara* 2:2; *Shulḥan Arukh*, *Yoreh De'a* 142:15).

Members of a group who are particular with each other – בְּנֵי חֲבוּרָה הַמַּקְפִּידִין זֶה עַל זֶה: If members of a formal group eat together on Shabbat or a Festival, and they are particular with one another, insisting on fair compensation for each item, they are prohibited to exchange portions with one another or return a portion that one has previously borrowed from another. This constitutes a violation of conducting business on Shabbat or a Festival (Rambam *Sefer Nezikin*, *Hilkhot Geneiva* 7:10). The *Shulḥan Arukh* and other authorities do not mention this *halakha* because, according to the interpretation of *Tosafot*, the law with regard to such a group is no different than the law with regard to any informal group of people (*Beit Yosef*).

וּכְדִבְרֵי (בֵּית הִלֵּל) אַף מִשּׁוּם רִבִּית.

And according to Beit Hillel, they **even** violate the prohibition of **interest.** In Beit Hillel's view, it is prohibited to loan or return objects without determining their monetary value, lest the object rise in value and the borrower end up returning an item that is more expensive than the one he borrowed.

אִי הָכִי – בָּנָיו וּבְנֵי בֵּיתוֹ נַמִי. בָּנָיו וּבְנֵי בֵּיתוֹ הַיְינוּ טַעְמָא – כִּדְרַב יְהוּדָה אָמַר רַב. דְּאָמַר רַב יְהוּדָה אָמַר רַב: מוּתָּר לְהַלְווֹת בָּנָיו וּבְנֵי בֵּיתוֹ בְּרִבִּית, כְּדֵי לְהַטְעִימָן טַעַם רִבִּית.

The Gemara asks: **If** this is **so,** and one violates so many prohibitions when drawing lots, it should be prohibited to do so with **one's children and family members also.** The Gemara answers: With regard to **one's children and family members, this is the reason** that it is permitted: **It is like** the ruling that **Rav Yehuda** said that **Rav said, for Rav Yehuda said** that **Rav said: It is permitted to loan to one's children and family members with interest, in order to let them experience a taste of** how difficult it is to repay a loan taken with **interest.** Also, in the case of family members, all the money, including the money used to repay the loan, belongs to the same person. Therefore, there is no real prohibition of interest.

אִי הָכִי – מָנָה גְּדוֹלָה כְּנֶגֶד מָנָה קְטַנָּה נַמִי.

The Gemara asks: **If** this is **so,** and everything in this case actually belongs to the father, and he uses a lottery system in order to educate his family, it should be permitted to cast lots for **a big portion against a small portion also.**

אִין הָכִי נַמִי, וְחַסּוֹרֵי מִיחַסְּרָא וְהָכִי קָתָנֵי: מֵפִיס אָדָם עִם בָּנָיו וְעִם בְּנֵי בֵּיתוֹ עַל הַשֻּׁלְחָן, אֲפִילּוּ מָנָה גְּדוֹלָה כְּנֶגֶד מָנָה קְטַנָּה. מַאי טַעְמָא – כִּדְרַב יְהוּדָה אָמַר רַב. עִם בָּנָיו וְעִם בְּנֵי בֵּיתוֹ – אִין, עִם אֲחֵרִים – לָא. מַאי טַעְמָא – כִּדְרַב יְהוּדָה אָמַר שְׁמוּאֵל. מָנָה גְּדוֹלָה כְּנֶגֶד מָנָה קְטַנָּה – אַף בַּחוֹל לַאֲחֵרִים אָסוּר. מַאי טַעְמָא – מִשּׁוּם קוּבְיָא.

The Gemara answers: **Yes, it is indeed so, and** the mishna **is incomplete and it teaches the following: A person may draw lots with his children**[H] **and his family members at the table,** and he may **even** do so with **a large portion against a small portion. What is the reason** for this? It is **in accordance with** the ruling that **Rav Yehuda** said that **Rav said.** Although **with one's children and family members, yes,** this is permitted, **with others it is not. What is the reason** for this? It is **in accordance with** the ruling that **Rav Yehuda** said that **Shmuel said:** Raffling **a large portion against a small portion is prohibited** to do **for other people, even on a weekday. What is the reason? Due to** the prohibition against gambling with **dice,**[HN] which is prohibited by rabbinic law as a form of theft.

״מַטִּילִין חֲלָשִׁין עַל וכו׳״. מַאי ״אֲבָל לֹא עַל הַמָּנוֹת״? אָמַר רַבִּי יַעֲקֹב בְּרֵיהּ דְּבַת יַעֲקֹב: אֲבָל לֹא עַל הַמָּנוֹת שֶׁל חוֹל בְּיוֹם טוֹב. פְּשִׁיטָא. מַהוּ דְּתֵימָא: הוֹאִיל וּכְתִיב ״וְעַמְּךָ כִּמְרִיבֵי כֹהֵן״ – אֲפִילּוּ מָנוֹת דְּחוֹל נַמִי – קָא מַשְׁמַע לַן.

The mishna taught that **one may draw lots for** the sacrifices[H] but not for the specific portions. This statement is not entirely clear, and the Gemara asks: **What** is the meaning of the phrase: **But not for the** specific **portions? Rabbi Ya'akov, son of the daughter of Ya'akov, said** that it means: **But** one may **not** draw lots **for the weekday** [*ḥol*] **portions**[N] **on a Festival.** The Gemara challenges: This is **obvious.** The Gemara answers: **Lest you say** that **since** the priests are naturally quarrelsome, which the Sages derive from that which **is written:** "Yet let no man strive, neither let any man reprove, **for your people are like those that strive with the priest**" (Hosea 4:4), and in order to maintain peace between them **even** lotteries for **weekday portions** were **also** permitted, therefore, the mishna **teaches us** that this is not the case.

וְאָמַר רַבִּי יַעֲקֹב בְּרֵיהּ דְּבַת יַעֲקֹב: כֹּל שֶׁחֲבֵירוֹ נֶעֱנָשׁ עַל יָדוֹ – אֵין מַכְנִיסִין אוֹתוֹ בִּמְחִיצָתוֹ שֶׁל הַקָּדוֹשׁ בָּרוּךְ הוּא. מְנָלַן. אִילֵימָא מִשּׁוּם דִּכְתִיב ״וַיֹּאמֶר ה׳ מִי יְפַתֶּה אֶת אַחְאָב וְיַעַל וְיִפּוֹל בְּרָמוֹת גִּלְעָד וַיֹּאמֶר זֶה בְּכֹה וְזֶה אֹמֵר בְּכֹה וַיֵּצֵא הָרוּחַ וַיַּעֲמוֹד לִפְנֵי ה׳ וַיֹּאמֶר אֲנִי אֲפַתֶּנּוּ וגו׳ וַיֹּאמֶר אֵצֵא וְהָיִיתִי רוּחַ שֶׁקֶר בְּפִי כׇּל נְבִיאָיו וַיֹּאמֶר תְּפַתֶּה וְגַם תּוּכָל צֵא וַעֲשֵׂה כֵן״.

Having quoted Rabbi Ya'akov, son of the daughter of Ya'akov, the Gemara brings another teaching of this *amora.* **And Rabbi Ya'akov, son of the daughter of Ya'akov, said: Anyone** who causes **another to be punished on his account,** they **do not bring him within the partition of the Holy One, Blessed be He,** even if he is right. The Gemara asks: **From where do we** know this? **If you say** it is **because** of what is written in the prophecy of Micaiah, that proof can be disputed. **It is written: "And the Lord said: Who will entice Ahab to go up and fall at Ramot Gilad? And one said: In this manner, and another said: In that manner. And the spirit came out and stood before the Lord and said: I will entice him.** And the Lord said to it: With what? **And it said: I will go out and will be a lying spirit in the mouth of all of his prophets. And He said: You shall entice him and will prevail. Go out and do this"** (1 Kings 22:20–22).

HALAKHA

A person may draw lots with his children – מֵפִיס אָדָם עִם בָּנָיו: It is permitted to distribute food portions to one's family members based on a lottery, provided that the portions are of equal size. However, it is prohibited to do so with other people. If the portions are of unequal size, even family members may not draw lots for them because this violates the prohibition of gambling, as the opinion of Rav, which permits this, is rejected in tractate *Bava Metzia* (Rif; Rosh). The Rambam permits drawing lots for unequal portions with one's family members (Rambam *Sefer Zemanim, Hilkhot Shabbat* 23:17; *Shulḥan Arukh, Oraḥ Ḥayyim* 322:6).

Due to the prohibition against gambling with dice – מִשּׁוּם קוּבְיָא: It is prohibited to play dice or any other game in which the winner takes more than the loser. This is considered a form of stealing by rabbinic decree (Rambam *Sefer Nezikin, Hilkhot Gezeila VaAveida* 6:7; *Shulḥan Arukh, Ḥoshen Mishpat* 370:2).

One may draw lots for sacrifices – וּמַטִּילִין חֲלָשִׁין עַל הַקׇּרְבָּנוֹת: The priests are permitted to draw lots for portions of the Festival sacrifices on the Festival (see Ra'avad) because it is an act that demonstrates love for the mitzva. However, it is prohibited for them do so for non-sacred food (Rambam *Sefer Zemanim, Hilkhot Yom Tov* 4:20).

NOTES

Due to the prohibition against gambling with dice – מִשּׁוּם קוּבְיָא: Dice players, who are professional gamblers, are among the people that the Sages disqualified as witnesses. The Sages disagreed with regard to the rationale for this *halakha.* According to some, the winnings from playing dice are not acquired in a legal manner because the other players do not expect to lose when they place their bets. Therefore, one who takes money in this fashion is considered a robber by rabbinic decree. *Tosafot* offer a somewhat similar explanation. Even according to those who say that money won through gambling is not considered stolen, gambling is nonetheless considered despicable behavior.

Weekday [*ḥol*] portions – מָנוֹת דְּחוֹל: In his Commentary on the Mishna, the Rambam interpreted the phrase: Portions of *ḥol*, to mean: Portions that are non-sacred food [*ḥullin*]. Therefore, the priests may not draw lots for non-sacred food.

וְאָמְרִינַן מַאי רוּחַ? אָמַר רַבִּי יוֹחָנָן: זֶה רוּחוֹ שֶׁל נָבוֹת. וּמַאי "צֵא"? אָמַר רַב: צֵא מִמְּחִיצָתִי. וְדִילְמָא הָתָם הַיְינוּ טַעְמָא, דִּכְתִיב "דּוֹבֵר שְׁקָרִים לֹא יִכּוֹן".

And we said: What is this **spirit? Rabbi Yoḥanan said: This is the spirit of Naboth** the Jezreelite, who asked to avenge his death at the hands of Ahab. **And what is** the meaning of the words: **Go out,** which God commanded him? **Rav said:** It means that he was given permission to entice Ahab, but God said: **Leave from within My partition.** Therefore, it seems that the spirit of Naboth was told to leave God's area because it caused Ahab to be punished. The Gemara rejects this proof: **But perhaps there, the reason is as it is written: "One who speaks lies shall not dwell** before My eyes" (Psalms 101:7), and this is the only reason that the spirit of Naboth was removed from within God's partition.

אֶלָּא מֵהָכָא "שָׂבַעְתָּ קָלוֹן מִכָּבוֹד שְׁתֵה גַּם אַתָּה וְהֵעָרֵל וגו׳". "שָׂבַעְתָּ קָלוֹן מִכָּבוֹד" – זֶה נְבוּכַדְנֶצַּר, "שְׁתֵה גַּם אַתָּה וְהֵעָרֵל" – זֶה צִדְקִיָּה. חֲדָא: דְּכוּלֵּיהּ קְרָא בִּנְבוּכַדְנֶצַּר כְּתִיב, וְעוֹד: צִדְקִיָּה צַדִּיקָא, מַאי הֲוָה לֵיהּ לְמֶיעֱבַד לֵיהּ? דְּאָמַר רַבִּי יְהוּדָה אָמַר רַב: בְּשָׁעָה שֶׁבִּקֵּשׁ אוֹתוֹ רָשָׁע לַעֲשׂוֹת לְאוֹתוֹ צַדִּיק כָּךְ וכו׳.

Rather, it is derived **from here: "You are filled with shame instead of honor. Drink, you, and be like one who is uncircumcised,** the cup of the Lord's right hand will turn to you and filthiness shall be upon your glory" (Habakkuk 2:16). The verse is expounded: **"You are filled with shame instead of honor"; this** is referring to **Nebuchadnezzar. "Drink, you, and be like one who is uncircumcised"; this is** referring to **Zedekiah,** who was also punished for being the cause of Nebuchadnezzar's punishment, as will be explained. The Gemara rejects this proof: **One** objection to this is **that the entire verse is written about Nebuchadnezzar. And furthermore,** with regard to **Zedekiah, the righteous one, what could he have done to him?** For **Rav Yehuda said** that **Rav said** about this matter: **When that wicked man wanted to do this to that righteous man,** his foreskin was stretched, as will be explained.

אֶלָּא מֵהָכָא "גַּם עֲנוֹשׁ לַצַּדִּיק לֹא טוֹב" – אֵין "לֹא טוֹב" אֶלָּא רַע. וּכְתִיב "כִּי לֹא אֵל חָפֵץ רֶשַׁע אַתָּה לֹא יְגֻרְךָ רָע". צַדִּיק אַתָּה ה׳, וְלֹא יָגוּר בִּמְגוּרְךָ רָע.

Rather, the basis for this idea is **from here: "Punishment is also not good for the righteous"** (Proverbs 17:26), meaning that it is not good for a righteous person to issue punishment. **There is no** meaning of **not good other than evil. And it says: "For You are not a God that desires wickedness, evil will not dwell with You"** (Psalms 5:5), meaning that **You,** God, **are righteous and evil shall not dwell** with You **in Your place of dwelling.** Even a righteous person who punishes someone and is called evil and cannot dwell within God's partition.

מַאי מַשְׁמַע דְּהַאי חֲלָשִׁים לִישָּׁנָא דְּפוּרָא הוּא – דִּכְתִיב "אֵיךְ נָפַלְתָּ מִשָּׁמַיִם הֵילֵל בֶּן שָׁחַר נִגְדַּעְתָּ לָאָרֶץ חוֹלֵשׁ עַל גּוֹיִם וגו׳". אָמַר רַבָּה בַּר רַב הוּנָא: מְלַמֵּד שֶׁהָיָה מַטִּיל פּוּר עַל גְּדוֹלֵי מַלְכוּת, לֵידַע אֵיזֶה בֶּן יוֹמוֹ שֶׁל מִשְׁכַּב זָכוּר. וּכְתִיב "כָּל מַלְכֵי גוֹיִם כּוּלָּם וגו׳", אָמַר רַבִּי יוֹחָנָן: שֶׁנָּחוּ מִמִּשְׁכַּב זָכוּר.

The Gemara asks: **From where** may it be **inferred that this** term used in the mishna, ***ḥalashim*****, is a word for lots? As it is written: "How have you fallen from heaven, O day-star, son of the morning! How have you been cut down to the ground, casting lots [*ḥolesh*] over the nations!"** (Isaiah 14:12), and **Rabba bar Rav Huna said:** This verse **teaches us that he,** Nebuchadnezzar, **would cast lots [*ḥolesh*] for the royal leaders** of the nations he had captured, **in order to know whose day** it was to service him with **homosexual relations. And it is written: "All the kings of the nations, all of them**[N] sleep in glory, every one in his own house" (Isaiah 14:18). **And Rabbi Yoḥanan said:** The meaning of this verse is **that they rested from homosexual relations.**

וְאָמַר רַבִּי יוֹחָנָן: כָּל יָמָיו שֶׁל אוֹתוֹ רָשָׁע לֹא נִמְצָא שְׂחוֹק בְּפֶה כָּל בְּרִיָּה, שֶׁנֶּאֱמַר "נָחָה שָׁקְטָה כָּל הָאָרֶץ פָּצְחוּ רִנָּה" – מִכְּלָל דְּעַד הַשְׁתָּא לֹא הֲוָה רִנָּה.

And Rabbi Yoḥanan said: All of the days of the life **of that wicked man, laughter could not be found in the mouth of any creature, as it is stated: "The whole earth is at rest and is quiet; they break forth into singing"** (Isaiah 14:7). This proves **by inference** that **until now there was not any song.**

וְאָמַר רַבִּי יִצְחָק אָמַר רַבִּי יוֹחָנָן: אָסוּר לַעֲמוֹד בְּבֵיתוֹ שֶׁל אוֹתוֹ רָשָׁע, שֶׁנֶּאֱמַר "וּשְׂעִירִים יְרַקְּדוּ שָׁם".

And Rabbi Yitzḥak said that **Rabbi Yoḥanan said: It is prohibited** even nowadays **to stand in** the ruins of **the house of that wicked man,** Nebuchadnezzar, in Babylonia, for **it is stated** about that place: **"And demons shall dance there"** (Isaiah 13:21). There is concern that one may be injured by the harmful forces there (Maharsha).

וְאָמַר רַב יְהוּדָה אָמַר רַב: בְּשָׁעָה שֶׁבִּיקֵּשׁ אוֹתוֹ רָשָׁע לַעֲשׂוֹת לְאוֹתוֹ צַדִּיק כָּךְ, נִמְשְׁכָה עָרְלָתוֹ שְׁלֹשׁ מֵאוֹת אַמָּה, וְהָיְתָה מְחַזֶּרֶת עַל כָּל הַמְּסִיבָּה כּוּלָּהּ, שֶׁנֶּאֱמַר "שָׂבַעְתָּ קָלוֹן מִכָּבוֹד שְׁתֵה גַּם אַתָּה וְהֵעָרֵל". עָרֵל בְּגִימַטְרִיָּא שְׁלֹשׁ מֵאוֹת הָוֵי.

And Rav Yehuda said that **Rav said: At the time** when **that wicked man,** Nebuchadnezzar, **wanted to do to that righteous man,** Zedekiah,[N] **this** act of sodomy, **his foreskin was stretched three hundred cubits, and it surrounded the entire** company at Nebuchadnezzar's **feast, as it is stated:** "Woe to one who gives his neighbor drink, who puts your venom in and also makes him drunk so that you may look upon their nakedness. **You are filled with shame instead of honor. Drink, you, and be like one who is uncircumcised [*vehe'arel*]"** (Habakkuk 2:15–16). The word ***arel*****,** which refers here to one who is uncircumcised and also connotes the foreskin, **has a numerical value of three hundred.**

NOTES

All of the kings of the nations, all of them, etc. – **כָּל מַלְכֵי גוֹיִם כּוּלָּם וכו׳**: In other words, after Nebuchadnezzar's death, all of the kings he had captured slept honorably in their own homes. While he was alive, they slept in shame in his palace (Maharsha).

Nebuchadnezzar and Zedekiah – **נְבוּכַדְנֶצַּר וְצִדְקִיָּה**: The exposition about Nebuchadnezzar's homosexual activity is based on the following verse, which is not quoted in the Gemara: "Woe to one who gives his neighbor drink, who puts your venom in and also makes him drunk so that you may look upon their nakedness" (Habakkuk 2:15). This is interpreted as an allusion to Nebuchadnezzar's practice of intoxicating his male guests so he could engage in homosexual relations with them (Maharsha). This basic storyline is one that was familiar in talmudic times, due to current events. The memoirs of the early Roman emperors are replete with stories similar to these about Nebuchadnezzar.

ואמר רב יהודה אמר רב: בשעה שירד אותו רשע לגיהנם רעשו כל יורדי גיהנם, אמרו: שמא למשול עליהם הוא בא, או ליחלות כמותם הוא בא? שנאמר "גם אתה חולית כמונו אלינו נמשלת". יצאתה בת קול ואמרה "ממי נעמת רדה והשכבה את ערלים".

And Rav Yehuda also **said** that **Rav said: When that wicked man descended into Gehenna, everyone who had** already **descended to Gehenna trembled,** and **they said,** referring to themselves in third person: **Perhaps he is coming to rule over them; or is he coming to be weakened like them? As it is stated:** "They all answer and say to you: **Have you also become weak like us? Have you become like us [*eleinu nimshalta*]?"** (Isaiah 14:10). The Hebrew phrase: *Eleinu nimshalta,* can mean: Have you become like us, or alternatively: Have you come to rule over us. **A Divine Voice emerged and said: "Whom do you pass in beauty? Go down and be laid with the uncircumcised"** (Ezekiel 32:19). This confirmed that Nebuchadnezzar has the same status in Gehenna as everyone else.

"איך שבת נוגש שבתה מדהבה" אמר רבי יהודה אמר רב: שבתה אומה זו שאמרה

On a related note, the verse states: "And you shall take up this parable against the king of Babylonia and you shall say: **How has the oppressor ceased. The exactor of gold has ceased"** (Isaiah 14:4). **Rav Yehuda said** that **Rav said:** The meaning of this verse is that **this nation that said:**

Perek **XXIII**
Daf **150** Amud **a**

HALAKHA

A person may not hire workers on Shabbat – לא ישכור אדם פועלים בשבת: It is prohibited to hire workers on Shabbat (Rambam *Sefer Zemanim, Hilkhot Shabbat* 23:12; *Shulḥan Arukh, Oraḥ Ḥayyim* 307:2).

One may not wait for nightfall at the edge of the Shabbat boundary – אין מחשיכין על התחום וכו׳: It is prohibited to walk to the edge of the Shabbat boundary toward the end of Shabbat in order to hire workers or perform an activity prohibited on Shabbat immediately after Shabbat ends. However, one may walk to the edge of the boundary to retrieve one's animal or to perform any activity that is permitted on Shabbat. Some authorities rule that it is only permitted to retrieve one's animal if the animal can walk on its own (Rambam *Sefer Zemanim, Hilkhot Shabbat* 24:3; *Shulḥan Arukh, Oraḥ Ḥayyim* 306:1).

Telling a gentile on Shabbat – אמירה לגוי: The Sages prohibited asking a gentile to perform a prohibited labor on Shabbat (Rambam *Sefer Zemanim, Hilkhot Shabbat* 6:1).

NOTES

Telling a gentile to do something that is prohibited for a Jew on Shabbat violates a rabbinic prohibition – אמירה לגוי שבות: Some commentaries interpret this question as a statement of surprise: If the statement is referring to another who is a gentile, one should be permitted to ask the gentile to hire workers because asking a gentile to perform a prohibited labor on Shabbat is only prohibited by rabbinic law. According to this interpretation, prohibiting to ask a gentile to hire laborers on Shabbat, which is also only prohibited by rabbinic law, involves issuing a decree to prevent violation of another decree, which is contrary to a halakhic principle adopted by the Sages (*Me'iri*).

מדוד והבא. ואיכא דאמרי: שאמרה "מאד מאד הביא בלא מדה".

Measure and bring a lot of money, **has ceased. And some say** that the meaning of the statement is that this nation **said: Bring very, very much, without measure.**

"ורבו יתירה הוספת לי". אמר רב יהודה אמר רב ירמיה בר אבא: מלמד שרכב על ארי זכר, וקשר תנין בראשו, לקיים מה שנאמר "וגם את חית השדה נתתי לו לעבדו".

The Gemara cites another verse pertaining to Nebuchadnezzar: **"And surpassing greatness was added unto me"** (Daniel 4:33), about which **Rav Yehuda said** that **Rav Yirmeya bar Abba said: This teaches that** Nebuchadnezzar **rode atop a male lion and tied a serpent to its head, fulfilling what was said** of him: **"And the beasts of the field I have also given him to serve him"** (Jeremiah 27:6).

מתני׳ לא ישכור אדם פועלים בשבת, ולא יאמר אדם לחבירו לשכור לו פועלים. אין מחשיכין על התחום לשכור לו פועלים ולהביא פירות, אבל מחשיך הוא לשמור, ומביא פירות בידו. כלל אמר אבא שאול: כל שאני זכאי באמירתו – רשאי אני להחשיך עליו.

MISHNA A person may not hire workers on Shabbat[H] to work for him after Shabbat because even speaking about weekday matters is prohibited on Shabbat. Similarly, **a person may not tell another** on Shabbat **to hire workers for him. One may not** even **wait for nightfall at** the edge of **the Shabbat boundary**[H] in order to leave the boundary immediately after Shabbat **to hire workers for himself or to bring produce** from his field. **But he may wait for nightfall** at the edge of the Shabbat boundary in order **to guard** his produce that is outside the Shabbat boundary, **and** he may then **bring produce** back **in his hand,** since he did not initially intend to wait at the edge of the boundary for this purpose. **Abba Shaul stated a** general **principle:** With regard to **anything that I am permitted to discuss** on Shabbat, **I am permitted to wait for nightfall** at the edge of the Shabbat boundary **for its sake.**

גמ׳ (פשיטא) מאי שנא הוא ומאי שנא חבירו? אמר רב פפא: חבר גוי. מתקיף לה רב אשי: אמירה לגוי שבות.

GEMARA The beginning of the mishna taught that one may not hire workers on Shabbat, and one may not tell another to hire workers for him. The Gemara finds this puzzling and states: This is **obvious. What is the difference between him and another?** Just as he is prohibited from hiring workers on Shabbat, others are also prohibited from doing so. **Rav Pappa said: Another** is referring to **a gentile. Rav Ashi strongly objects to this:** This is itself a prohibition, for **telling a gentile** to do something that is prohibited for a Jew on Shabbat[H] violates a **rabbinic prohibition.**[N]

אֶלָּא אָמַר רַב אַשִׁי: אֲפִילּוּ תֵּימָא חֲבֵירוֹ יִשְׂרָאֵל, הָא קָא מַשְׁמַע לַן: לֹא יֹאמַר אָדָם לַחֲבֵירוֹ ״שְׂכוֹר לִי פּוֹעֲלִים״, אֲבָל אוֹמֵר אָדָם לַחֲבֵירוֹ ״הֲנִרְאֶה שֶׁתַּעֲמוֹד עִמִּי לָעֶרֶב״? וּמַתְנִיתִין מַנִּי – כְּרַבִּי יְהוֹשֻׁעַ בֶּן קָרְחָה. דְּתַנְיָא: לֹא יֹאמַר אָדָם לַחֲבֵירוֹ ״הֲנִרְאֶה שֶׁתַּעֲמוֹד עִמִּי לָעֶרֶב״? רַבִּי יְהוֹשֻׁעַ בֶּן קָרְחָה אוֹמֵר: אוֹמֵר אָדָם לַחֲבֵירוֹ ״הֲנִרְאֶה שֶׁתַּעֲמוֹד עִמִּי לָעֶרֶב״?

Rather, Rav Ashi said: Even if you say that it is referring to **another Jew,** it can be said that the novel element of this ruling is not the statement itself but what can be derived from it. **This is what it is teaching us: One may not say to another** explicitly on Shabbat: **Hire workers for me, but one may say to another: Does it seem that you will join me this evening?**[N] This is permitted even though both of them understand that the questioner intends to hire the other person to work for him. **And** in accordance with **whose** opinion is **the mishna? It is in accordance with** the opinion of **Rabbi Yehoshua ben Korḥa; as it was taught** in a *baraita*: **A person may not say to another** on Shabbat: **Does it seem that you will join me this evening? Rabbi Yehoshua ben Korḥa says: A person may say to another** on Shabbat: **Does it seem that you will join me this evening?**[H]

אָמַר רַבָּה בַּר בַּר חָנָה אָמַר רַבִּי יוֹחָנָן: הֲלָכָה כְּרַבִּי יְהוֹשֻׁעַ בֶּן קָרְחָה. וְאָמַר רַבָּה בַּר בַּר חָנָה אָמַר רַבִּי יוֹחָנָן: מַאי טַעְמָא דְּרַבִּי יְהוֹשֻׁעַ בֶּן קָרְחָה – דִּכְתִיב ״מִמְּצוֹא חֶפְצְךָ וְדַבֵּר דָּבָר״; דִּיבּוּר – אָסוּר, הִרְהוּר – מוּתָּר.

Rabba bar bar Ḥana said that **Rabbi Yoḥanan said:** The *halakha* **is in accordance with** the opinion of **Rabbi Yehoshua ben Korḥa. And Rabba bar bar Ḥana said** that **Rabbi Yoḥanan said: What is the reason for Rabbi Yehoshua ben Korḥa's** ruling? **As it is written** in the verse from which we derive the prohibition to speak on Shabbat about activities that one may not perform on that day: "And you shall honor it by not doing your ways, **nor pursuing your business, nor speaking of it**" (Isaiah 58:13). We derive from this verse that **speaking is prohibited,** but merely **contemplating** these matters **is permitted.**

רָמֵי לֵיהּ רַב אַחָא בַּר רַב הוּנָא לְרָבָא: מִי אָמַר רַבִּי יוֹחָנָן דִּיבּוּר אָסוּר הִרְהוּר מוּתָּר, אַלְמָא: הִרְהוּר לָאו כְּדִיבּוּר דָּמֵי. וְהָאָמַר רַבָּה בַּר בַּר חָנָה אָמַר רַבִּי יוֹחָנָן: בְּכׇל מָקוֹם מוּתָּר לְהַרְהֵר – חוּץ מִבֵּית הַמֶּרְחָץ וּמִבֵּית הַכִּסֵּא. שָׁאנֵי הָתָם, דְּבָעֵינַן ״וְהָיָה מַחֲנֶיךָ קָדוֹשׁ״, וְלֵיכָּא.

Rav Aḥa bar Rav Huna raised a contradiction to Rava: Did Rabbi Yoḥanan really **state** as a general principle that **speaking is prohibited,** but **contemplating is permitted? Consequently,** we can derive from here that **contemplation is not tantamount to speech. But Rabba bar bar Ḥana said** that **Rabbi Yoḥanan said: It is permitted to think** about Torah **in any place except for a bathhouse and a bathroom.** This statement indicates that contemplation is tantamount to speech, as even thought is prohibited in these locations. The Gemara answers: **It is different there, for** with regard to Torah **we need** to fulfill the verse: "For the Lord your God walks in the midst of your camp to deliver you and to give your enemies before you; **therefore, your camp shall be sacred** so that He see no unseemly thing in you and turn away from you" (Deuteronomy 23:15); **and** the requirement to be sacred is **not** fulfilled if one thinks about Torah while in the bathhouse or bathroom.

הָכָא נַמִּי כְּתִיב ״וְלֹא יִרְאֶה בְךָ עֶרְוַת דָּבָר״. הַהוּא מִיבְּעֵי לֵיהּ לִכְדְרַב יְהוּדָה, דְּאָמַר רַב יְהוּדָה: גּוֹי עָרוֹם אָסוּר לִקְרוֹת קְרִיַּת שְׁמַע כְּנֶגְדּוֹ.

The Gemara challenges this: But **here, too,** with regard to a bathhouse and a bathroom, **it is written: "So that He see no unseemly thing** [*davar*] **in you"** (Deuteronomy 23:15). We can infer that this prohibits speech [*dibbur*] but not contemplation. The Gemara answers: **That** verse is not referring to speech. **It is needed for** the ruling of **Rav Yehuda, for Rav Yehuda said: Opposite a naked gentile,**[N] **it is prohibited to recite *Shema*,** as this is included in the prohibition of unseemly things mentioned above.[H]

מַאי אִירְיָא גּוֹי, אֲפִילּוּ יִשְׂרָאֵל נַמִּי? לָא מִיבַּעְיָא קָאָמַר; לָא מִיבַּעְיָא יִשְׂרָאֵל דְּאָסוּר; אֲבָל גּוֹי כֵּיוָן דִּכְתִיב בֵּיהּ ״אֲשֶׁר בְּשַׂר חֲמוֹרִים בְּשָׂרָם״ – אֵימָא שַׁפִּיר דָּמֵי, קָא מַשְׁמַע לַן.

The Gemara asks: **Why did** Rav Yehuda **teach** this prohibition **particularly** with regard to **a gentile? Even** in the presence of a naked **Jew,** reciting *Shema* is **also** prohibited. The Gemara answers: That ruling **is stated** employing the style of: **There is no need.** The Gemara explains: **There is no need** to state this *halakha* with regard to **a Jew,** as it is certainly **prohibited** to recite *Shema* in the presence of a naked Jew. **However,** with regard to **a gentile, since it is written about him: "Whose flesh is as the flesh of donkeys"** (Ezekiel 23:20), perhaps his flesh is not considered nakedness, and one may **say that it seems well** and permitted. Therefore, Rav Yehuda **teaches us** that it is also prohibited to recite *Shema* before a naked gentile.

HALAKHA

Does it seem that you will join me this evening – הֲנִרְאֶה שֶׁתַּעֲמוֹד עִמִּי לָעֶרֶב: One is permitted to ask another person: Does it seem that you will join me this evening, even if it is understood that the speaker wants to hire the listener to work for him after Shabbat (Rambam *Sefer Zemanim, Hilkhot Shabbat* 24:4; *Shulḥan Arukh, Oraḥ Ḥayyim* 307:7).

Sacred matters in the presence of nudity – דִּבְרֵי קְדוּשָּׁה כְּנֶגֶד הָעֶרְוָה: It is prohibited to recite *Shema* or other prayers in the presence of nakedness, including that of a gentile (Rambam *Sefer Ahava, Hilkhot Keriat Shema* 3:16; *Shulḥan Arukh, Oraḥ Ḥayyim* 75:4).

NOTES

Does it seem that you will join me this evening – הֲנִרְאֶה שֶׁתַּעֲמוֹד עִמִּי לָעֶרֶב: Some authorities explain that the person speaking is not hinting that he wants to hire the listener. Rather, the speaker is asking to meet that evening so that the listener can hire workers for him (*Tosefot Rid*).

A naked gentile – גּוֹי עָרוֹם: The question with regard to the status of a naked gentile depends on the nature of the prohibition of reciting *Shema* in the presence of one who is unclothed. Is the rationale a matter of the sexual arousal that might result, or is it simply a Torah decree and the rationale is irrelevant? If it is a Torah decree, there is reason to assume that the prohibition only applies to a Jew, in the same way that the *halakhot* of ritual impurity apply only to Jews. Therefore, the nakedness of a gentile would not be considered prohibited nakedness.

אֵימָא הָכִי נַמִי. אָמַר קְרָא "וְעֶרְוַת אֲבִיהֶם לֹא רָאוּ".

The Gemara asks: Why not **say** that **it is indeed so,** that gentile flesh is not considered nakedness? The Gemara rejects this idea: **The verse** already **said** with regard to the sons of Noah: "And they walked backward and covered their father's nakedness, and their faces were turned backward, **and they did not see their father's nakedness**" (Genesis 9:23). The verse uses the term nakedness with regard to Noah, who was a gentile.

וְדִיבּוּר מִי אֲסִיר? וְהָא רַב חִסְדָּא וְרַב הַמְנוּנָא דְּאָמְרִי תַּרְוַיְיהוּ: חֶשְׁבּוֹנוֹת שֶׁל מִצְוָה – מוּתָּר לְחַשְׁבָן בְּשַׁבָּת. וְאָמַר רַבִּי אֶלְעָזָר: פּוֹסְקִים צְדָקָה לַעֲנִיִּים בְּשַׁבָּת. וְאָמַר רַבִּי יַעֲקֹב בַּר אִידִי אָמַר רַבִּי יוֹחָנָן: מְפַקְּחִין פִּיקּוּחַ נֶפֶשׁ וּפִיקּוּחַ רַבִּים בְּשַׁבָּת, וְהוֹלְכִין לְבָתֵּי כְנֵסִיּוֹת לְפַקֵּחַ עַל עִסְקֵי רַבִּים בְּשַׁבָּת.

The Gemara addresses the basis of the *halakha* mentioned above: **And is it speaking** about proscribed activities **prohibited** on Shabbat? **But Rav Ḥisda and Rav Hamnuna both said: It is permitted to make calculations pertaining to a mitzva**[H] **on Shabbat, and Rabbi Elazar said** that this means that **one may apportion charity for the poor on Shabbat. And Rabbi Ya'akov bar Idi said** that **Rabbi Yoḥanan said: One may attend to** activities necessary for **saving a life or for communal needs on Shabbat, and one may go to a synagogue to attend to communal affairs on Shabbat.**

וְאָמַר רַבִּי שְׁמוּאֵל בַּר נַחְמָנִי אָמַר רַבִּי יוֹחָנָן: הוֹלְכִין לְטַרְטֵיאוֹת וּלְקִרְקְסָאוֹת וּלְבַסִּילְקָאוֹת לְפַקֵּחַ עַל עִסְקֵי רַבִּים בְּשַׁבָּת. וְתָנָא דְּבֵי מְנַשֶּׁה: מְשַׁדְּכִין עַל הַתִּינוֹקוֹת לֵיאָרֵס בְּשַׁבָּת, וְעַל הַתִּינוֹק לְלַמְּדוֹ סֵפֶר וּלְלַמְּדוֹ אוּמָּנוּת. אָמַר קְרָא "מִמְּצוֹא חֶפְצְךָ וְדַבֵּר דָּבָר", חֲפָצֶיךָ – אֲסוּרִים, חֶפְצֵי שָׁמַיִם – מוּתָּרִין.

And Rabbi Shmuel bar Naḥmani said that **Rabbi Yoḥanan said: One may go to theaters** [*tarteiot*],[L] **and circus performances** [*kirkesaot*],[LB] **and courthouses** [*basilkaot*][L] **to attend to communal affairs on Shabbat. And** one of the Sages in **the school of Menashe taught: One may** make the necessary arrangements to **pair off children** so that they will **be betrothed on Shabbat, and** one may likewise make arrangements **for a child** by finding someone **to teach him** how to read **books and to teach him a craft.** If speaking about monetary matters is prohibited on Shabbat, how is it possible to participate in all these activities? The Gemara answers that although speaking about similar things is generally prohibited on Shabbat, it is permitted in these cases because **the verse said: "Nor pursuing your business, nor speaking of it"** (Isaiah 58:13), which indicates that **your business** matters **are prohibited** to speak of on Shabbat, but **the business of Heaven,** matters which have religious significance, **is permitted** to speak of.

אָמַר רַב יְהוּדָה אָמַר שְׁמוּאֵל: חֶשְׁבּוֹנוֹת שֶׁל [מַלָּךְ] וְשֶׁל מַה בְּכָךְ – מוּתָּר לְחַשְׁבָן בְּשַׁבָּת. תַּנְיָא נַמִי הָכִי: חֶשְׁבּוֹנוֹת שֶׁעָבְרוּ וְשֶׁעֲתִידִין לִהְיוֹת – אָסוּר לְחַשְׁבָן, שֶׁל מַלָּךְ

Rav Yehuda said that **Shmuel said:** With regard to **calculations of: What is it to you,** [*mallakh*],[N] calculations that are in no way relevant to the person making them, **and of: What** significance **does it have** [*ma bekhakh*], calculations that do not have any practical significance, it is **permitted to make them on Shabbat.** This **was also taught** in the *Tosefta*: **Calculations** with regard to matters **that have passed** or **that will be in the future may not be calculated**[H] on Shabbat. However, with regard to calculations of: **What is it to you,**

HALAKHA

Calculations pertaining to a mitzva – חֶשְׁבּוֹנוֹת שֶׁל מִצְוָה: It is permitted to speak about matters pertaining to a mitzva on Shabbat, such as calculating amounts to be apportioned as charity or issues relating to the needs of the community (Rambam *Sefer Zemanim, Hilkhot Shabbat* 24:5; *Shulḥan Arukh, Oraḥ Ḥayyim* 306:6).

Prohibited calculations – חֶשְׁבּוֹנוֹת אֲסוּרִים: It is prohibited to make calculations pertaining to weekday matters on Shabbat, even if the matter has passed, such as calculating one's previous expenses. However, this rule applies only when one still owes money. If one has already paid all of these debts, then the calculation is of no practical relevance [*ma bekhakh*] and is permitted (Rambam *Sefer Zemanim, Hilkhot Shabbat* 23:18; *Shulḥan Arukh, Oraḥ Ḥayyim* 307:6).

LANGUAGE

Theaters [*tarteiot*] – טַרְטֵיאוֹת: From the Greek θέατρον, *theatron*, meaning a place where performances are staged or a place of public gathering.

Circus performances [*kirkesaot*] – קִרְקְסָאוֹת: From the Latin circus, meaning an arena where fights between animals or between animals and humans are staged for the public.

Courthouses [*basilkaot*] – בַּסִּילְקָאוֹת: From the Greek βασιλική, *basilikè*, or the Latin basilica, which refer to a large hall or palace that is divided into several parts by rows of columns.

BACKGROUND

Theaters and circuses – תֵּיאַטְרוֹת וְקִרְקְסָאוֹת: Permission to enter theaters and circuses on Shabbat was not limited to public gatherings at which important decisions were made relating to the city, but also applied to entrance during performances. At times, Jews were brought out before the audience either as a form of public disgrace or to participate in matches with gladiators or with animals. Oftentimes, it was possible for the crowd to save the lives of the fighters, and for this reason attending these events was considered a matter of saving Jewish lives and protecting the community.

NOTES

What is it to you [*mallakh*] – חֶשְׁבּוֹנוֹת שֶׁל מַלָּךְ: Many interpretations have been offered for the term *mallakh*. Some commentaries explain that it is related to the words *meyalekh* and *mehalekh*, referring to calculations of guests who come and go. This is similar to the statement that permits determining which guests will come eat at one's home (Rabbeinu Ḥananel; *Arukh*). Other authorities suggest that the word is related to advice [*nimlakh*] and is referring to words of advice that one gives to others that are not directly pertinent to oneself (Rashi). An alternative explanation cited in the *Arukh* maintains that the word is king [*melekh*] and is referring to calculating the cost of various projects that the government is interested in implementing.

וְשֶׁל מָה בְּכָךְ – מוּתָּר לְחוֹשְׁבָן.

and of: What significance **does it have,** it **is permitted to calculate them.**

וּרְמִינְהוּ: חוֹשְׁבִין חֶשְׁבּוֹנוֹת שֶׁאֵינָן צְרִיכִין, וְאֵין מְחַשְּׁבִין חֶשְׁבּוֹנוֹת שֶׁצְּרִיכִין בְּשַׁבָּת. כֵּיצַד, אוֹמֵר אָדָם לַחֲבֵירוֹ: כָּךְ וְכָךְ פּוֹעֲלִים הוֹצֵאתִי עַל שָׂדֶה זוֹ, כָּךְ וְכָךְ דִּינָרִין הוֹצֵאתִי עַל דִּירָה זוֹ. אֲבָל לֹא יֹאמַר לוֹ: כָּךְ וְכָךְ הוֹצֵאתִי, וְכָךְ וְכָךְ אֲנִי עָתִיד לְהוֹצִיא.

The Gemara **raises a contradiction** based on what was taught in another *baraita*: **One may make calculations that are unnecessary, but one may not make calculations that are necessary on Shabbat. How so? One may say to another: I sent out such and such** number of **workers to this field, and I spent such and such** number of *dinar* **for this home. But he may not say to him: I spent such and such** amount of money, **and I am going to spend such and such** amount **in the future.** Apparently, one is permitted to calculate one's previous expenditures on Shabbat.

וּלְטַעְמִיךְ, קַשְׁיָא לָךְ הִיא גּוּפָא. אֶלָּא, הָא דְּאִיכָּא אַגְרָא דַּאֲגִירָא גַּבֵּיהּ, הָא – דְּלֵיכָּא אַגְרָא דַּאֲגִירָא גַּבֵּיהּ.

The Gemara responds: **And according to your reasoning, it itself,** the *Tosefta* quoted previously, **is difficult for you,** for it prohibits calculating past expenditures while allowing one to make calculations that do not have practical significance. **Rather,** it must be explained in the following manner: **This** *Tosefta*, which taught that it is prohibited to calculate past expenses, is referring to a case in which **he has payment with him** that he still owes his workers. Therefore, although his calculation pertains to projects that have already been completed, it is still relevant in a practical manner. And **this** *baraita*, which taught that it is permitted to calculate past expenses, is referring to a case **in which he does not have payment with him** that he must still pay his workers, and therefore his calculation does not have practical significance.

״אֵין מַחְשִׁיכִין״. תָּנוּ רַבָּנַן: מַעֲשֶׂה בְּחָסִיד אֶחָד שֶׁנִּפְרְצָה לוֹ פֶּרֶץ בְּתוֹךְ שָׂדֵהוּ, וְנִמְלַךְ עָלֶיהָ לְגוֹדְרָהּ, וְנִזְכַּר שֶׁשַּׁבָּת הוּא, וְנִמְנַע אוֹתוֹ חָסִיד וְלֹא גְּדָרָהּ. וְנַעֲשָׂה לוֹ נֵס, וְעָלְתָה בּוֹ צְלָף וּמִמֶּנָּה הָיְתָה פַּרְנָסָתוֹ וּפַרְנָסַת אַנְשֵׁי בֵּיתוֹ.

We learned in the mishna that **one may not wait for nightfall** at the edge of the Shabbat boundary in order to hire workers or bring produce from outside of the boundary immediately after Shabbat. **The Sages taught: There was an incident with a pious man**[N] **in** which **a breach was made in** the fence around **his field, and** when he saw it **he decided to fence it in. And** then **he remembered that it was Shabbat. And that pious man refrained from fixing the fence** forever because he had thought about fixing it on Shabbat. **And a miracle was done for him, and a caper bush grew in** the breach, thereby closing it up. **And from it** and its produce he then **received his livelihood and the livelihood of the members of his household.**

אָמַר רַב יְהוּדָה אָמַר שְׁמוּאֵל: מוּתָּר לְאָדָם לוֹמַר לַחֲבֵירוֹ ״לִכְרַךְ פְּלוֹנִי אֲנִי הוֹלֵךְ לְמָחָר״, שֶׁאִם יֵשׁ בּוּרְגָּנִין – הוֹלֵךְ.

Rav Yehuda said that **Shmuel said: A person is permitted to say to another** on Shabbat: **I am going to such and such city tomorrow,**[H] **for if there were small guardhouses** [*burganin*][LBN] **one would be permitted to walk.** If small guardhouses, from which the surrounding area and fields could be watched, were located along the way one needs to travel, the entire area would attain the status of a single city, and walking from one part to the other on Shabbat would be permitted *ab initio*. Since it would be permitted to traverse this area on Shabbat with *burganin* present, it is permitted to talk about such a journey on Shabbat, even when these guardhouses are not present. This is because it is permitted to speak about or prepare for something that can be done in a permitted fashion on Shabbat, even in the absence of the conditions that make it permitted.

HALAKHA

I am going to such and such city tomorrow – לִכְרַךְ פְּלוֹנִי אֲנִי הוֹלֵךְ לְמָחָר: It is permitted to say to another person: I am going to such and such city tomorrow. It is even permitted to say: Come with me, as it would be permitted to walk there on Shabbat if there were continuous housing. In addition, one may speak with others about doing something after Shabbat that is permissible to do on Shabbat (Rambam *Sefer Zemanim*, *Hilkhot Shabbat* 24:3; *Shulḥan Arukh*, *Oraḥ Ḥayyim* 307:8).

LANGUAGE

Guardhouses [*burganin*] – בּוּרְגָּנִין: The origin of this word is unclear. Some think that it is a derivative of Greek or Latin. Others say that it comes from the German word *burg*, which refers to a fortress or settled area. The word may have been picked up by Roman soldiers and eventually spread to the rest of the Roman Empire.

BACKGROUND

Guardhouses [*burganin*] – בּוּרְגָּנִין: *Burganin* were small fortified houses where an appointed official, or a *burgani*, would sit. He was charged with military responsibility over the area surrounding the *burgan*.

Burgan

NOTES

There was an incident with the pious man – מַעֲשֶׂה בְּחָסִיד: The pious man did not actually violate a prohibition by thinking about repairing his fence on Shabbat, as it was already established that it is permitted to think about one's affairs. Still, he refrained from actualizing this unintentional thought. He was rewarded with a miracle due to his exceptional display of scrupulousness (Maharsha; *Taz*).

For if there were small guardhouses [*burganin*] – שֶׁאִם יֵשׁ בּוּרְגָּנִין: The Gemara in tractate *Eiruvin* teaches the details of the various *halakhot* with regard to Shabbat boundaries. In general terms, one may not walk past the boundaries of the location in which one establishes his presence at the beginning of Shabbat. The Shabbat boundary is defined as a distance of two thousand cubits beyond the settled area in which one is spending Shabbat. At times, however, there are houses, guard booths, and the like between two different towns. If there is contiguous housing in which the buildings are no more than seventy cubits apart, the entire expanse is considered one continuous area of settlement, and it is permitted to walk from one town to another even over great distances.

HALAKHA

One may wait for nightfall at the edge of the Shabbat boundary in order to attend to the needs of a bride or the needs of a corpse – מַחְשִׁיכִין עַל הַתְּחוּם לְפַקֵּחַ עַל עִסְקֵי כַּלָּה וְעַל עִסְקֵי הַמֵּת: It is permitted to wait for nightfall at the edge of the Shabbat boundary for the sake of a bride or a corpse (Rambam *Sefer Zemanim*, *Hilkhot Shabbat* 24:5; *Shulḥan Arukh*, *Oraḥ Ḥayyim* 306:3).

It is prohibited for a person to attend to his weekday affairs before he recites *havdala* – אָסוּר לוֹ לְאָדָם שֶׁיַּעֲשֶׂה חֲפָצָיו קוֹדֶם שֶׁיַּבְדִּיל: When Shabbat ends, one may neither perform prohibited labor nor eat before reciting *havdala*. However, if one recited *havdala* during the evening prayer, one is permitted to perform labor before reciting *havdala* over wine. Reciting: The One who distinguishes between the sacred and the profane, without reciting a blessing and without a cup of wine, permits one to engage in labor but not to eat (Rambam *Sefer Zemanim*, *Hilkhot Shabbat*, 29:5; *Shulḥan Arukh*, *Oraḥ Ḥayyim* 299:10).

NOTES

To cut him a myrtle branch – לְמִיגְזָא לֵיהּ אָסָא: It was customary to make a wedding canopy from myrtle branches, and people would assume this responsibility on behalf of the bride.

תְּנַן: אֵין מַחְשִׁיכִין עַל הַתְּחוּם לִשְׂכּוֹר פּוֹעֲלִים וּלְהָבִיא פֵּירוֹת. בִּשְׁלָמָא לִשְׂכּוֹר פּוֹעֲלִים – דִּבְשַׁבָּת לָא מָצֵי אָגַר, אֶלָּא לְהָבִיא פֵּירוֹת – לֵימָא: שֶׁאִם יֵשׁ שָׁם מְחִיצּוֹת – מֵבִיא. מַשְׁכַּחַת לָהּ בְּפֵירוֹת הַמְחוּבָּרִים.

We learned in the mishna: **One may not wait for nightfall at** the edge of **the Shabbat boundary** in order **to hire workers or bring produce** after Shabbat from the other side of the boundary. **Granted,** it makes sense that it is prohibited to wait at the Shabbat boundary **in order to hire workers,** as **one may not hire** workers under any circumstances on Shabbat. **But** if one waits there in order **to bring produce,** why is it prohibited? **Let us say that** since one would be permitted to bring produce at the edge of the boundary on Shabbat *ab initio* **if there were partitions there, one may** wait for nightfall at the border to **bring** produce even when there are not partitions present, in accordance with Rav Yehuda's ruling mentioned above. The Gemara answers: **You find** a case where bringing **produce** is not permitted under any circumstances; **that is** when the produce is still **attached** to the ground, as there is no permitted way to pick produce on Shabbat.

וְהָתָנֵי רַבִּי אוֹשַׁעְיָא: אֵין מַחְשִׁיכִין עַל הַתְּחוּם לְהָבִיא תֶּבֶן וָקַשׁ; בִּשְׁלָמָא קַשׁ – מַשְׁכַּחַת לָהּ בִּמְחוּבָּר. אֶלָּא תֶּבֶן, הֵיכִי מַשְׁכַּחַת לָהּ? בְּתִיבְנָא סַרְיָא.

The Gemara again questions Rav Yehuda's ruling: **But Rabbi Oshaya taught: One may not wait for nightfall at the** edge of **the Shabbat boundary in order to bring in hay and straw** after Shabbat. **Granted,** Rabbi Oshaya taught that it is prohibited in the case of **straw; you find** the case of straw that is still **attached** to the ground, which it is clearly prohibited to pick under any circumstances. **But hay,** which has already been detached from the ground, **how do you find** a case in which it would be prohibited to carry it on Shabbat, even with partitions present? The Gemara answers: Rabbi Oshaya's ruling referred **to rotten straw,** which may not be carried on Shabbat because it is considered set-aside [*muktze*].

תָּא שְׁמַע: מַחְשִׁיכִין עַל הַתְּחוּם לְפַקֵּחַ עַל עִסְקֵי כַּלָּה וְעַל עִסְקֵי הַמֵּת. עַל עִסְקֵי כַּלָּה וּמֵת – אִין, עַל עִסְקֵי אַחֵר – לָא.

Come and **hear** a proof with regard to this matter based on what was taught elsewhere: **One may wait for nightfall at the** edge of the Shabbat boundary in order **to attend to the needs of a bride or the needs of a corpse.**[H] The Gemara infers from this that **for the needs of a bride or a corpse, yes,** one is permitted to wait for nightfall at the edge of the Shabbat boundary, but **for the needs of another person, no,** it is not permitted.

בִּשְׁלָמָא אַחֵר דּוּמְיָא דְּכַלָּה מַשְׁכַּחַת לָהּ: לְמִיגְזָא לֵיהּ אָסָא. אֶלָּא מֵת מַאי נִיהוּ? לְהָבִיא לוֹ אָרוֹן וְתַכְרִיכִין – וְקָתָנֵי: מֵת – אִין, אֲבָל אַחֵר – לָא.

Granted, with regard to attending to the needs of **another** in a manner **similar to attending to** the needs of **a bride, you find** a case where it is prohibited **to cut him a myrtle** branch[N] as was customarily done for brides because this is absolutely prohibited on Shabbat. **But** with regard to **a corpse, what is it** that one might do which would be prohibited to do for others? **To bring for it a coffin and shrouds. And it teaches** that for **a corpse, yes,** it is permitted, **but** for **another** it is **not.**

וְאַמַּאי? לֵימָא: שֶׁאִם יֵשׁ שָׁם מְחִיצּוֹת – מֵבִיא. מֵת נַמִי מַשְׁכַּחַת לָהּ – לְמִיגְזָא לֵיהּ גְּלִימָא.

And why is it prohibited to do so for others? **Let us say that** since one would be permitted to bring these items on Shabbat **if there were partitions there, one may** wait for nightfall at the edge of the border to **bring** these items after Shabbat, in accordance with the ruling of Rav Yehuda. The Gemara answers: In the case of **a corpse, you also find** a case where bringing an item is prohibited under any circumstance, e.g., if one is waiting **to cut a garment for** the corpse to use as shrouds. There is no permissible way to do that on Shabbat. In that case, it would be prohibited to wait at the edge of the Shabbat boundary for this purpose if not for the fact that it is for the sake of a corpse, as it is a mitzva to attend to the needs of a corpse.

״אֲבָל מַחְשִׁיכִין״. וְאַף עַל גַּב דְּלָא אַבְדִּיל? וְהָאָמַר רַבִּי אֶלְעָזָר בֶּן אַנְטִיגְנוֹס מִשּׁוּם רַבִּי אֱלִיעֶזֶר בֶּן יַעֲקֹב: אָסוּר לוֹ לְאָדָם שֶׁיַּעֲשֶׂה חֲפָצָיו קוֹדֶם שֶׁיַּבְדִּיל. וְכִי תֵּימָא – דְּאַבְדִּיל בִּתְפִלָּה, וְהָאָמַר רַב יְהוּדָה אָמַר שְׁמוּאֵל: הַמַּבְדִּיל בִּתְפִלָּה – צָרִיךְ שֶׁיַּבְדִּיל עַל הַכּוֹס. וְכִי תֵּימָא – דְּאַבְדִּיל עַל הַכּוֹס, כּוֹס בַּשָּׂדֶה מִי אִיכָּא? תַּרְגְּמָא רַבִּי נָתָן בַּר אַמִּי קַמֵּיהּ דְּרָבָא: בֵּין הַגִּיתּוֹת שָׁנוּ.

We learned in the mishna: **But one may wait for nightfall** at the Shabbat boundary in order to guard one's produce. The Gemara asks: **And** is this the case **even if he has not** recited **the blessing of distinction** [*havdala*] marking the end of Shabbat? **But didn't Rabbi Elazar ben Antigonos say in the name of Rabbi Eliezer ben Ya'akov** that **it is prohibited for a person to tend to his** weekday **affairs** after Shabbat **before he recites *havdala*?**[H] **And if you say** that this is referring to a case **in which one** already **recited *havdala* during prayer,** as formulated by the Sages in the blessing of: Who graciously grants knowledge, **didn't Rav Yehuda say** that **Shmuel said** that **one who recites *havdala* in prayer must** still **recite *havdala* over a cup** of wine? **And if you say** that this is an instance **in which one** already **recited *havdala* over a cup** of wine, **does one have a cup** of wine **in the field? Rabbi Natan bar Ami explained** this **before Rava: They taught** this *halakha* with regard to a unique case in which the edge of the Shabbat boundary was situated **among wine presses,** and one took wine from the wine press and recited *havdala* over it.

אָמַר לֵיהּ רַבִּי אַבָּא לְרַב אַשִׁי: בְּמַעְרְבָא אָמְרִינַן הָכִי: ״הַמַּבְדִּיל בֵּין קוֹדֶשׁ לְחוֹל״, וְעָבְדִינַן צוֹרְכִין. אָמַר רַב אַשִׁי: כִּי הֲוֵינָא בֵּי רַב כָּהֲנָא הֲוָה אָמַר ״הַמַּבְדִּיל בֵּין קוֹדֶשׁ לְחוֹל״ וּמְסַלְּתִינַן סִילְתֵי.

Rabbi Abba said another explanation **to Rav Ashi: In the West,** in Eretz Yisrael, **we say this** at the end of Shabbat: **The One who distinguishes between the sacred and the mundane, and** then **we attend to our needs,** as reciting *havdala* over a cup is unnecessary in order to begin doing labor after Shabbat. It is therefore possible that the mishna addressed a similar case. Similarly, **Rav Ashi said: When I was in the house of Rav Kahana, he would say: The One who distinguishes between the sacred and the mundane,** at the end of Shabbat, and **we would cut wood**[N] to burn for light and heat.

כְּלָל אָמַר אַבָּא שָׁאוּל כֹּל שֶׁאֲנִי וכו׳. (אִיבַּעְיָא לְהוּ): אַבָּא שָׁאוּל אַהַיָּיא? אִילֵימָא אַרֵישָׁא קָאֵי ״אֵין מַחְשִׁיכִין עַל הַתְּחוּם לִשְׂכּוֹר פּוֹעֲלִים לְהָבִיא פֵּירוֹת״,

We learned in the mishna: **Abba Shaul stated a** general **principle:** With regard to **anything that I am** permitted to discuss on Shabbat, I am permitted to wait for nightfall at the edge of the Shabbat boundary for its sake. The Gemara raises a **dilemma: To which** part of the mishna did **Abba Shaul's** statement **refer? If you say** that it **relates to the first clause** of the mishna, which taught: **One may not wait for nightfall at the** edge of the Shabbat boundary in order **to hire workers or to bring produce,**

NOTES

And we would cut wood – וּמְסַלְּתִינַן סִילְתֵי: Some commentaries state that this phrase actually means that they arranged piles of wood (*ge'onim*).

Perek **XXIII**
Daf **151** Amud **a**

הַאי ״כֹּל שֶׁאֲנִי זַכַּאי בַּאֲמִירָתוֹ רַשַּׁאי אֲנִי בַּחֲשִׁיכָתוֹ״? ״כֹּל שֶׁאֵינִי זַכַּאי בַּאֲמִירָתוֹ אֵינִי רַשַּׁאי בַּחֲשִׁיכָתוֹ״ מִיבָּעֵי לֵיהּ. אֶלָּא אַסֵּיפָא קָאֵי: ״אֲבָל מַחְשִׁיךְ הוּא לִשְׁמוֹר וּמֵבִיא פֵּירוֹת בְּיָדוֹ״, הַאי ״כֹּל שֶׁאֲנִי זַכַּאי בַּחֲשִׁיכָתוֹ רַשַּׁאי אֲנִי בַּאֲמִירָתוֹ״ מִיבָּעֵי לֵיהּ.

this phrase: **Anything that I am permitted to discuss** on Shabbat **I am permitted to wait for nightfall for its sake,** is not appropriate. Rather, the mishna **should have** formulated the principle in the negative: With regard to **anything that I am not permitted to discuss** on Shabbat, **I am not permitted to wait for nightfall for its sake,** similar to the phraseology at the beginning of the mishna. **Rather, it is referring to the latter clause** of the mishna, which taught: **But he may wait for nightfall** in order **to guard** his produce, **and he may bring produce in his hand.** But even if this is correct, the phraseology does not fit. **It should have** said the opposite: **Anything for which I am permitted to wait for nightfall I am permitted to discuss.**

לְעוֹלָם אַסֵּיפָא קָאֵי, וְאַבָּא שָׁאוּל אַהָא קָאֵי; דְּאָמַר רַב יְהוּדָה אָמַר שְׁמוּאֵל: מוּתָּר לְאָדָם לוֹמַר לַחֲבֵירוֹ: שְׁמוֹר לִי פֵּירוֹת שֶׁבִּתְחוּמְךָ, וַאֲנִי אֶשְׁמוֹר לְךָ פֵּירוֹת שֶׁבִּתְחוּמִי. וְקָאָמַר אַבָּא שָׁאוּל לְתַנָּא קַמָּא: מִי לֹא מוֹדֵית דְּמוּתָּר אָדָם לוֹמַר לַחֲבֵירוֹ ״שְׁמוֹר לִי פֵּירוֹת שֶׁבִּתְחוּמְךָ וַאֲנִי אֶשְׁמוֹר לְךָ פֵּירוֹת שֶׁבִּתְחוּמִי״?

The Gemara explains: **Actually, it is referring to the latter clause** of the mishna, **and Abba Shaul relates to this** statement that **Rav Yehuda said** that **Shmuel said: It is permitted for a person to say to another** on Shabbat: **Guard** my **produce that is in your boundary**[H] **for me, and I will guard** your **produce in my boundary for you. And** this is what **Abba Shaul said to the first *tanna*: Do you not agree** that **it is permitted for a person to say to another: Guard** my **produce that is in your boundary for me, and I will guard** your **produce that is in my boundary for you?** It is in such a case that Abba Shaul permitted waiting for nightfall at the edge of the Shabbat boundary in order to guard produce.

וְאֵימָא: כֹּל שֶׁאֲנִי זַכַּאי בַּאֲמִירָתוֹ – רַשַּׁאי אֲנִי לְהַחְשִׁיךְ עָלָיו, כְּלָל לְאַתּוֹיֵי מַאי? לְאַתּוֹיֵי הָא, דְּתָנוּ רַבָּנַן: אֵין מַחְשִׁיכִין עַל הַתְּחוּם לְהָבִיא בְּהֵמָה. הָיְתָה עוֹמֶדֶת חוּץ לַתְּחוּם – קוֹרֵא לָהּ וְהִיא בָּאָה. כְּלָל אָמַר אַבָּא שָׁאוּל: כֹּל שֶׁאֲנִי זַכַּאי בַּאֲמִירָתוֹ – רַשַּׁאי אֲנִי לְהַחְשִׁיךְ עָלָיו.

The Gemara still finds this difficult: **And say** simply: With regard to **anything that I am permitted to discuss, I am permitted to wait for nightfall for its sake.** When Abba Shaul stated that his ruling was a general **principle, what** did that come **to include?** The Gemara answers: It comes **to include that which the Sages taught** in the *Tosefta*: **One may not wait for nightfall at the Shabbat boundary** in order **to bring an animal**[H] immediately after Shabbat. If the animal **is standing** right **outside of the boundary,**[H] **one may call it** so that it will **come** to him. **Abba Shaul said a** general **principle:** With regard to **anything that I am permitted to discuss**[H] on Shabbat, **I am permitted to wait for nightfall for its sake.** Here, since it is permitted to call to the animal, it is also permitted to wait for nightfall in order to retrieve it.

HALAKHA

Guard my produce that is in your boundary – שְׁמוֹר לִי פֵּירוֹת שֶׁבִּתְחוּמְךָ: One is permitted to say to another person on Shabbat: Guard my produce that is in your boundary, and I will guard your produce that is in my boundary. This ruling is in accordance with the ruling of the Gemara (*Shulḥan Arukh*, *Oraḥ Ḥayyim* 307:10).

One may not wait for nightfall at the Shabbat boundary to bring in an animal, etc. – אֵין מַחְשִׁיכִין עַל הַתְּחוּם לְהָבִיא בְּהֵמָה וכו׳: See the *Halakha* note on 150a, p. 386.

If the animal is standing outside of the boundary – הָיְתָה עוֹמֶדֶת חוּץ לַתְּחוּם: If one's animal is standing outside of the Shabbat boundary, he may call it so it will return within the Shabbat boundary, in accordance with the ruling of the *baraita* (Rambam *Sefer Zemanim*, *Hilkhot Shabbat* 24:3; *Shulḥan Arukh*, *Oraḥ Ḥayyim* 306:2).

Anything that I am permitted to discuss – כֹּל שֶׁאֲנִי זַכַּאי בַּאֲמִירָתוֹ: One is permitted to wait for nightfall at the Shabbat boundary in order to attend to anything that one is permitted to speak about or ask for on Shabbat, in accordance with the ruling of Abba Shaul (Rambam *Sefer Zemanim*, *Hilkhot Shabbat* 24:5; *Shulḥan Arukh*, *Oraḥ Ḥayyim* 306:3, 307:8).

וּמַחְשִׁיכִין לְפַקֵּחַ עַל עִסְקֵי כַּלָּה וְעַל עִסְקֵי הַמֵּת לְהָבִיא לוֹ אָרוֹן וְתַכְרִיכִין. וְאוֹמְרִים לוֹ: לֵךְ לְמָקוֹם פְּלוֹנִי, וְאִם לֹא מָצָאתָ בְּמָקוֹם פְּלוֹנִי – הָבֵא מִמָּקוֹם פְּלוֹנִי. לֹא מָצָאתָ בְּמָנֶה – הָבֵא בְּמָאתַיִם. רַבִּי יוֹסֵי בְּרַבִּי יְהוּדָה אוֹמֵר: וּבִלְבַד שֶׁלֹּא יַזְכִּיר לוֹ סְכוּם מֶקַח.

The Sages also said: **And** all agree that **one may wait for nightfall to attend to the needs of a bride and the needs of a corpse,** such as **to bring it a coffin and shrouds. And one may say to him,** to one's messenger, on Shabbat: **Go to such and such place** to buy them, **and if you do not find them in that place, bring** them **from such and such a place.** Similarly, one may instruct one's messenger: **If you do not find** them **for one hundred** dinar, **buy them for two hundred.** However, **Rabbi Yosei, son of Rabbi Yehuda, says:** One is permitted to give instructions to a messenger on Shabbat, **provided one does not mention to him** a specific monetary **amount**[N] to spend on **the transaction.**

מתני׳ מַחְשִׁיכִין עַל הַתְּחוּם לְפַקֵּחַ עַל עִסְקֵי כַּלָּה וְעַל עִסְקֵי הַמֵּת לְהָבִיא לוֹ אָרוֹן וְתַכְרִיכִים. גּוֹי שֶׁהֵבִיא חֲלִילִין בַּשַּׁבָּת – לֹא יִסְפּוֹד בָּהֶן יִשְׂרָאֵל, אֶלָּא אִם כֵּן בָּאוּ מִמָּקוֹם קָרוֹב. עָשׂוּ לוֹ אָרוֹן וְחָפְרוּ לוֹ קֶבֶר – יִקָּבֵר בּוֹ יִשְׂרָאֵל. וְאִם בִּשְׁבִיל יִשְׂרָאֵל – לֹא יִקָּבֵר בּוֹ עוֹלָמִית.

MISHNA One may wait for nightfall at the Shabbat boundary to attend to the needs of a bride and the needs of a corpse, such as **to bring him a coffin and shrouds.** If **a gentile brought flutes**[HB] **on Shabbat** in order to play music during the eulogy and funeral procession, **a Jew may not eulogize with them** as accompaniment, **unless they were brought from a nearby location** within the Shabbat boundary and transporting them did not include any violation of *halakha*. If gentiles **made someone a coffin and dug him a grave**[H] on Shabbat, and they then changed their minds and decided to give it to someone else, **a Jew may be buried in it. However, if it was** initially intended **for a Jew,** a Jew **may never be buried in it.**

גמ׳ מַאי מִמָּקוֹם קָרוֹב? רַב אָמַר: מִמָּקוֹם קָרוֹב מַמָּשׁ, וּשְׁמוּאֵל אָמַר: חָיְישִׁינַן שֶׁמָּא חוּץ לַחוֹמָה לָנוּ.

GEMARA The mishna taught that if a gentile brought something from a nearby location on Shabbat, a Jew is permitted to make use of it. The Gemara asks: **What** exactly is considered to be **from a nearby location? Rav said:** Something that is **from a location that is actually nearby,** meaning that we know with certainty where the object was brought from. **And Shmuel said:** Even if we do not know exactly where it was brought from, **we are concerned that it may have stayed overnight** just **outside the** city **wall,**[H] which is still within the Shabbat boundary, and no prohibition was violated for the sake of the object. Therefore, it would only be prohibited to use such an object if it was known with certainty that it had been brought from outside the Shabbat boundary. Thus, Rav and Shmuel disagree[N] with regard to a situation in which we do not know where the object was brought from on Shabbat.

דַּיְקָא מַתְנִיתִין כְּוָותֵיהּ דִּשְׁמוּאֵל, דְּקָתָנֵי ״עָשָׂה לוֹ אָרוֹן וְחָפַר לוֹ קֶבֶר יִקָּבֵר בּוֹ יִשְׂרָאֵל״ אַלְמָא: מִסְּפֵיקָא שָׁרֵי, הָכָא נַמִי – מִסְּפֵיקָא שָׁרֵי,

The language of the mishna is precise according to Shmuel's opinion, **as it teaches:** If a gentile **made someone a coffin and dug him a grave** on Shabbat and then changed his mind and decided to give it to someone else, **a Jew may be buried in it. Consequently,** we can derive that if **it is uncertain** whether the coffin and grave were made for a Jew, **it is permitted. Here, too,** in a case in which a gentile brings flutes, if **it is uncertain** whether their transportation was in violation of *halakha*, **it is permitted.**

NOTES

A specific monetary amount – סְכוּם מֶקַח: Some commentaries explain this to mean that one may not calculate the cost of this mitzva and then add the amount to previous debts that the person owes (*Ba'al Halakhot Gedolot*).

The dispute between Rav and Shmuel – מַחְלוֹקֶת רַב וּשְׁמוּאֵל: The *ge'onim* explain this dispute in an entirely different manner and their version of the text of this dispute was also different from the one cited here. In their view, it is Rav who is lenient and permits the use of flutes if they were brought from a nearby location on Shabbat. Shmuel, on the other hand, is concerned that even if they appear to have been brought from a nearby location, it is possible that they were transported overnight from a more distant location and arrived right outside the city walls during the night. Therefore, one must confirm that the flutes were not brought from a distant location. According to this interpretation, the text as it appears in the Gemara, which is based on Rashi's version of the text, must be emended. In addition, the proof for Shmuel's opinion cited in the Gemara must be understood as being based on the opinion of the Rabbis, who dispute the view of Rabbi Yehuda and rule that even if there is an important person in the city, the *halakha* is stringent, and one may not bathe in the heated water immediately after Shabbat (see Ramban, Rashba, and Ran).

BACKGROUND

Flutes – חֲלִילִין: In talmudic times, it was customary for Jews and gentiles to play musical instruments during a funeral procession to intensify the feeling of mourning. It is apparent from the discussion in the Gemara that flutes were an essential component in preparing to bury the dead in an honorable fashion.

Ancient relief of a flute player at a funeral

HALAKHA

If a gentile brought flutes – גּוֹי שֶׁהֵבִיא חֲלִילִין: If a gentile brought flutes or anything else to be used for a Jewish burial on Shabbat, one must wait the amount of time that it takes to bring these objects from a nearby location before using them after Shabbat. If the location from which the objects were brought is known, one must wait the amount of time it takes to bring them from that specific place (Rambam *Sefer Zemanim, Hilkhot Shabbat* 6:5; *Shulḥan Arukh, Oraḥ Ḥayyim* 325:15).

Gentiles made someone a coffin and dug him a grave – עָשׂוּ לוֹ אָרוֹן וְחָפְרוּ לוֹ קֶבֶר: If a gentile dug a grave or made a coffin for another gentile on Shabbat, the coffin and grave may be used for a Jewish burial. However, if they were made for a Jew, that Jew may never be buried in them. Nevertheless, they may be used for burying another Jew. This law applies only when Shabbat was publicly desecrated to make the coffin and dig the grave. However, if they were made in private, they may be used for the Jew. In this case, it is necessary to wait after Shabbat the amount of time it would take to make them (Rambam *Sefer Zemanim, Hilkhot Shabbat* 24:5; *Shulḥan Arukh, Oraḥ Ḥayyim* 325:14).

We are concerned that it may have stayed overnight outside the wall – חָיְישִׁינַן שֶׁמָּא חוּץ לַחוֹמָה לָנוּ: If it was uncertain from where a gentile brought flutes or other objects for the burial, it is assumed that they were brought from outside of the Shabbat boundary. Therefore, before using them after Shabbat, a Jew must wait the amount of time it would take to bring them from outside of the boundary (Rambam *Sefer Zemanim, Hilkhot Shabbat* 24:6; *Shulḥan Arukh, Oraḥ Ḥayyim* 325:16).

וְתַנְיָא כְּוָותֵיהּ דְּרַב: עִיר שֶׁיִּשְׂרָאֵל וְגוֹיִם דָּרִים בָּהּ, וְהָיְתָה בָּהּ מֶרְחָץ הַמַּרְחֶצֶת בַּשַּׁבָּת. אִם רוֹב גּוֹיִם – לָעֶרֶב רוֹחֵץ בָּהּ מִיָּד, אִם רוֹב יִשְׂרָאֵל – יַמְתִּין עַד כְּדֵי שֶׁיֵּחַמּוּ חַמִּין. מֶחֱצָה עַל מֶחֱצָה – (אָסוּר, וְיַמְתִּין) עַד כְּדֵי שֶׁיֵּחַמּוּ חַמִּין. רַבִּי יְהוּדָה אוֹמֵר: בְּאַמְבַּטֵי קְטַנָּה, אִם יֵשׁ בָּהּ רָשׁוּת – רוֹחֵץ בָּהּ מִיָּד.

And a *baraita* **was taught in accordance with** the opinion of **Rav:** In the case of **a city in which** both **Jews and gentiles live and in which there is a bathhouse that functions on Shabbat, if there is a majority of gentiles** in the city, the *halakha* is that **in the evening,** after Shabbat, a Jew **may bathe in it immediately. If there is a majority of Jews** in the city, a Jew **must wait until** the amount of time necessary **to heat up water** after Shabbat has passed, so that one will not benefit from the fact that the water was heated on Shabbat. If the population of the city is **half** Jewish **and half** gentile, **it is prohibited** to bathe there immediately after Shabbat, **and** one **must wait until** the amount of time necessary **to heat up water** after Shabbat has passed. **Rabbi Yehuda says:** In the case of **a small bath, if there is a ruling power** in the city, a Jew **may bathe in it immediately** after Shabbat.

מַאי "רָשׁוּת"? אָמַר רַב יְהוּדָה אָמַר רַב יִצְחָק בְּרֵיהּ דְּרַב יְהוּדָה: אִם יֵשׁ בָּהּ אָדָם חָשׁוּב, שֶׁיֵּשׁ לוֹ עֲשָׂרָה עֲבָדִים שֶׁמְּחַמְּמִין לוֹ עֲשָׂרָה קוּמְקוּמִין בְּבַת אַחַת בְּאַמְבַּטֵי קְטַנָּה – מוּתָּר לִרְחוֹץ בָּהּ מִיָּד.

The Gemara asks: **What is** the meaning the phrase: **A ruling power? Rav Yehuda said** that **Rav Yitzḥak, son of Rav Yehuda, said:** It means that **if there is an important person in** the city **who has ten slaves who heat ten water jugs** [*kumkumin*][L] **for him at once in a small bath, it is permitted** for a Jew **to bathe in it immediately** after Shabbat. This is because this bath may have been heated immediately after Shabbat for the use of this important person, rather than on Shabbat itself.

"עָשׂוּ לוֹ אָרוֹן וְחָפְרוּ לוֹ קֶבֶר וכו'". אַמַּאי? הָכָא נַמִּי יַמְתִּין בִּכְדֵי שֶׁיֵּעָשׂוּ. אָמַר עוּלָּא: בְּעוֹמֵד בְּאִסְרַטְיָא. תֵּינַח קֶבֶר, אָרוֹן מַאי אִיכָּא לְמֵימַר? אָמַר רַבִּי אַבָּהוּ: בְּמוּטָּל עַל קִבְרוֹ.

The mishna taught that if gentiles **made someone a coffin and dug him a grave** and then changed their minds and decided to make it available to someone else, it is permitted for a Jew to be buried in it. The Gemara asks: **Why? Here, too, one should** at the very least have to **wait** after Shabbat the amount of time necessary **for them to do** the work after Shabbat. The Gemara answers: **Ulla said:** The mishna is addressing a case **in which** the grave **is located in** a public **street.**[N] This indicates that it was intended for a gentile because Jews are not usually buried there. The Gemara asks further: **Granted,** in the case of a **grave,** the *halakha* is understandable. However, in the case of a **coffin, what is there to say?** Why isn't a Jew required to wait after Shabbat for the amount of time it would take to make the coffin? **Rabbi Abbahu said:** The mishna addresses a case **in which** the coffin was already **placed over the grave** of a gentile, which proves that it was intended for him.

מתני׳ עוֹשִׂין כׇּל צׇרְכֵי הַמֵּת: סָכִין וּמְדִיחִין אוֹתוֹ, וּבִלְבַד שֶׁלֹּא יָזִיז בּוֹ אֵבֶר. שׁוֹמְטִין אֶת הַכַּר מִתַּחְתָּיו, וּמַטִּילִין אוֹתוֹ עַל הַחוֹל בִּשְׁבִיל

MISHNA **One may perform all of the needs of the dead** on Shabbat.[H] **One may smear** oil on the body **and rinse it** with water, **and** all of this is permitted **provided that one does not move any of its limbs,** which would constitute a violation of the laws of set-aside objects. When necessary, **one may** also **remove a pillow from beneath it** and thereby **place it on** cold **sand in order**

Perek **XXIII**
Daf **151** Amud **b**

שֶׁיַּמְתִּין. קוֹשְׁרִין אֶת הַלֶּחִי, לֹא שֶׁיַּעֲלֶה – אֶלָּא שֶׁלֹּא יוֹסִיף. וְכֵן קוֹרָה שֶׁנִּשְׁבְּרָה – סוֹמְכִין אוֹתָהּ בְּסַפְסָל אוֹ בַּאֲרוּכוֹת הַמִּטָּה, לֹא שֶׁתַּעֲלֶה אֶלָּא שֶׁלֹּא תוֹסִיף.

to delay its decomposition. Similarly, **one may tie the jaw** of a corpse that is in the process of opening. One may **not** move it directly so **that it will rise** back to its original position, **but** so **that it will not continue** to open. **And similarly,** if one has **a** roof **beam that has broken** on Shabbat, **one may support it with a bench or with long** poles from **a bed.** One may **not** move it so **that the beam will rise** back to its original place, **but** so **that it will not continue** to fall.

LANGUAGE

Water jug [*kumkum*] – **קוּמְקוּם:** From the Greek **κουκκούμιον**, *kukumion*, and the Latin cucuma, which refer to a vessel similar to an earthenware jug that is used primarily to hold water.

NOTES

A grave located in a public street – **בְּעוֹמֵד בְּאִסְרַטְיָא:** The *ge'onim* explain that the issue being discussed is not the permissibility of burying a Jew in the grave. Rather, the issue pertains to the case mentioned at the end of the mishna: If the grave was dug for a Jew, it may never be used. Why is it not possible to wait after Shabbat for the amount of time it would take to dig the grave? The Gemara answers that it is speaking about a grave located on a public street. Therefore, it is obvious for whom it was intended. The Gemara then asks about the case of the coffin: When is it ever obvious for whom a coffin is intended? The answer is that the coffin was placed upon the grave so that everyone knew that it was not intended for the burial of a Jew.

HALAKHA

One may perform all of the needs of the dead on Shabbat – **עוֹשִׂין כׇּל צׇרְכֵי הַמֵּת:** One may attend to a corpse and do whatever is necessary for its honor on Shabbat, such as smearing it with oil or rinsing it. Similarly, one may secure its jaw so that its mouth will not open further, but one may not move it back to its original position. It is prohibited to move any of the corpse's limbs due to the prohibition of set-aside objects, as explained in the mishna (Rambam *Sefer Zemanim, Hilkhot Shabbat* 26:20; *Shulḥan Arukh, Oraḥ Ḥayyim* 311:7).

גמ׳ וְהָאָמַר רַב יְהוּדָה אָמַר שְׁמוּאֵל: מַעֲשֶׂה בְּתַלְמִידוֹ שֶׁל רַבִּי מֵאִיר שֶׁנִּכְנַס אַחֲרָיו לְבֵית הַמֶּרְחָץ, בִּיקֵּשׁ לְהָדִיחַ קַרְקַע, אָמַר לוֹ: אֵין מְדִיחִין. לָסוּךְ קַרְקַע – אָמַר לוֹ: אֵין סָכִין. קַרְקַע בְּקַרְקַע – מַחְלְפָא, מֵת בְּקַרְקַע לָא מִיחֲלַף.

GEMARA The Gemara questions the mishna's lenient ruling with regard to smearing oil on a corpse: **But didn't Rav Yehuda say** that **Shmuel said: There was an incident with a student of Rabbi Meir who followed him into the bathhouse** on Shabbat. The student **wanted to rinse the ground.** Rabbi Meir **said to him: One may not rinse** on Shabbat. The student wanted to **smear the ground** with oil. Rabbi Meir **said to him: One may not smear** on Shabbat. This indicates that it is prohibited to rinse or smear anything that may not be moved on Shabbat. The Gemara responds: **The ground** in one place **can be confused with the ground** in another place, and the Sages therefore prohibited these activities even on a tiled floor, such as that of a bathhouse, due to a concern that one may come to do so on a dirt floor and smooth it out. However, **a corpse cannot be confused with the ground,** and it is therefore permitted to rinse a corpse and smear it with oil.

"כָּל" לְאַתּוֹיֵי מַאי? לְאַתּוֹיֵי הָא דְּתָנוּ רַבָּנַן: מְבִיאִין כְּלֵי מֵיקַר וּכְלֵי מַתָּכוֹת וּמַנִּיחִין עַל כְּרֵיסוֹ, כְּדֵי שֶׁלֹּא תִּפּוֹחַ. וּפוֹקְקִין אֶת נְקָבָיו כְּדֵי שֶׁלֹּא תִּיכָּנֵס בָּהֶן הָרוּחַ.

We learned in the mishna that one may attend to all the needs of the dead on Shabbat. The Gemara asks: **What does** the word **all include** in the mishna's ruling that one may have thought is not included? The Gemara answers: It is meant **to include that which the Sages taught: One may bring cold vessels and metal vessels and place them on** the corpse's **stomach so that it does not swell. And one may seal up its orifices so that air will not enter them** and cause swelling.

וְאַף שְׁלֹמֹה אָמַר בְּחָכְמָתוֹ "עַד שֶׁלֹּא יֵרָתֵק חֶבֶל הַכֶּסֶף" – זֶה חוּט הַשִּׁדְרָה, "וְתָרוּץ גּוּלַּת הַזָּהָב" – זֶה אַמָּה, "וְתִשָּׁבֶר כַּד עַל הַמַּבּוּעַ" – זֶה הַכֶּרֶס, "וְנָרוֹץ הַגַּלְגַּל אֶל הַבּוֹר" – זֶה פֶּרֶשׁ.

And King **Solomon also said in his wisdom** with regard to old age and death: "Before the silver cord is snapped asunder, and the golden bowl is shattered, and the pitcher is broken at the fountain, and the wheel falls, shattered, into the pit" (Ecclesiastes 12:6), which the Gemara explains as follows: **"Before the silver cord is snapped asunder"; this is** a reference to **the spinal cord. "And the golden bowl [*gullat*] is shattered"; this is** a reference to **the member,** which is like a spring of water [*gulla*]. **"And the pitcher is broken at the fountain"; this is** a reference to **the stomach,** which looks like a pitcher that swells and ruptures. **"And the wheel [*galgal*] falls, shattered, into the pit"; this is** a reference to **excrement** [*gelalim*].

וְכֵן הוּא אוֹמֵר "וְזֵרִיתִי פֶרֶשׁ עַל פְּנֵיכֶם פֶּרֶשׁ חַגֵּיכֶם". אָמַר רַב הוּנָא וְאָמְרִי לָהּ אָמַר רַב חַגָּא: אֵלּוּ בְּנֵי אָדָם שֶׁמַּנִּיחִין דִּבְרֵי תוֹרָה, וְעוֹשִׂין כָּל יְמֵיהֶם כְּחַגִּים. אָמַר רַבִּי לֵוִי אָמַר רַב פַּפִּי אָמַר רַבִּי יְהוֹשֻׁעַ: לְאַחַר שְׁלֹשָׁה יָמִים כְּרֵיסוֹ נִבְקַעַת וְנוֹפֶלֶת לוֹ עַל פָּנָיו, וְאוֹמֶרֶת לוֹ "טוֹל מַה שֶּׁנָּתַתָּ בִּי".

And similarly, it says in the verse: **"And I will spread dung upon your faces, even the dung of your Festival offerings"** (Malachi 2:3). **Rav Huna said, and some say** that it was **Rav Ḥagga** who **said:** This verse is referring to **those people who neglect the words of the Torah and turn all of their days into Festivals. Rabbi Levi said** that **Rav Pappi said** that **Rabbi Yehoshua said: Three days after** death, **the stomach** of the dead[B] **bursts and falls onto his face and says to him: Take what you have put inside me.**

מתני׳ אֵין מְעַצְּמִין אֶת הַמֵּת בַּשַּׁבָּת, וְלֹא בַּחוֹל עִם יְצִיאַת נֶפֶשׁ. וְהַמְעַצֵּים עִם יְצִיאַת הַנֶּפֶשׁ – הֲרֵי זֶה שׁוֹפֵךְ דָּמִים.

MISHNA **One may not shut** the eyes **of the dead**[B] **on Shabbat** because the body is set-aside. **And one may not** shut the eyes even **on a weekday while the soul departs.** One must wait until the person has died. **And one who shuts** the eyes **while the soul departs is a murderer** because he has hastened the person's death.[H]

BACKGROUND

The stomach of the dead – כְּרֵיסוֹ שֶׁל אָדָם: After a person dies, the body begins to decompose, which generates a large amount of gas that causes the stomach to swell and eventually to burst from the pressure.

The eyes of the dead – עֵינֵי הַמֵּת: If the eyes of a dead person are not closed immediately after death, it will be very difficult to close them due to rigor mortis, the bodily stiffness that follows death.

HALAKHA

One who shuts the eyes while the soul departs – וְהַמְעַצֵּים עִם יְצִיאַת הַנֶּפֶשׁ: One may not shut the eyes of a person who is dying, nor may one perform any action that will hasten a person's death by even a moment (Rambam *Sefer Shofetim*, *Hilkhot Evel* 4:5; *Shulḥan Arukh*, *Yoreh De'a* 339:1).

גמ׳ תָּנוּ רַבָּנַן: הַמְעַצְּמוֹ עִם יְצִיאַת הַנֶּפֶשׁ – הֲרֵי זֶה שׁוֹפֵךְ דָּמִים. מָשָׁל לְנֵר שֶׁכָּבָה וְהוֹלֶכֶת, אָדָם מַנִּיחַ אֶצְבָּעוֹ עָלֶיהָ – מִיָּד כָּבְתָה. תַּנְיָא, רַבָּן שִׁמְעוֹן בֶּן גַּמְלִיאֵל אוֹמֵר: הָרוֹצֶה שֶׁיִּתְעַצְּמוּ עֵינָיו שֶׁל מֵת – נוֹפֵחַ לוֹ יַיִן בְּחוֹטְמוֹ, וְנוֹתֵן שֶׁמֶן בֵּין רִיסֵי עֵינָיו, וְאוֹחֵז בִּשְׁנֵי גּוּדָלֵי רַגְלָיו – וְהֵן מִתְעַצְּמִין מֵאֲלֵיהֶן.

GEMARA **The Sages taught: One who shuts** a person's **eyes while the soul departs is a murderer.** This is **analogous to a lamp that is gradually becoming extinguished** but could continue to burn a little longer. **If a person places his finger on it, it is immediately extinguished. It was taught** in a *baraita* that **Rabban Shimon ben Gamliel says: One who wants the eyes of a corpse to close should blow wine up its nose, and place oil between its eyelids, and grab hold of its two big toes, and** its eyes **will shut by themselves.**

תַּנְיָא, רַבָּן שִׁמְעוֹן בֶּן גַּמְלִיאֵל אוֹמֵר: תִּינוֹק בֶּן יוֹמוֹ חַי – מְחַלְּלִין עָלָיו אֶת הַשַּׁבָּת, דָּוִד מֶלֶךְ יִשְׂרָאֵל מֵת – אֵין מְחַלְּלִין עָלָיו אֶת הַשַּׁבָּת. תִּינוֹק בֶּן יוֹמוֹ חַי מְחַלְּלִין עָלָיו אֶת הַשַּׁבָּת, אָמְרָה תוֹרָה: חַלֵּל עָלָיו שַׁבָּת אֶחָד, כְּדֵי שֶׁיִּשְׁמוֹר שַׁבָּתוֹת הַרְבֵּה. דָּוִד מֶלֶךְ יִשְׂרָאֵל מֵת – אֵין מְחַלְּלִין עָלָיו – כֵּיוָן שֶׁמֵּת אָדָם, בָּטֵל מִן הַמִּצְוֹת. וְהַיְינוּ דְּאָמַר רַבִּי יוֹחָנָן: ״בַּמֵּתִים חָפְשִׁי״ כֵּיוָן שֶׁמֵּת אָדָם – נַעֲשָׂה חָפְשִׁי מִן הַמִּצְוֹת.

Incidental to the Gemara's discussion of corpses, it cites that which **was taught** in a *baraita*: **Rabban Shimon ben Gamliel says:** For **a living day-old baby, one desecrates Shabbat** to save his life. Yet for the **deceased David, king of Israel, one does not desecrate Shabbat. For a day-old baby we desecrate Shabbat** because **the Torah says: Desecrate one Shabbat for him so that he can observe many** ***Shabbatot.*** But for the **deceased David, king of Israel, one does not desecrate** Shabbat, as **once a person dies he is idle from mitzvot. And this is what Rabbi Yoḥanan said** with regard to the verse: **"Set apart among the dead** [***bametim ḥofshi***]**,** like the slain that lie in the grave, whom You remember no more" (Psalms 88:6). **Once a person dies, he becomes free** [***ḥofshi***] **from the mitzvot.**

וְתַנְיָא, רַבִּי שִׁמְעוֹן בֶּן אֶלְעָזָר אוֹמֵר: תִּינוֹק בֶּן יוֹמוֹ חַי – אֵין צָרִיךְ לְשׁוֹמְרוֹ מִן הַחוּלְדָּה וּמִן הָעַכְבָּרִים, אֲבָל עוֹג מֶלֶךְ הַבָּשָׁן מֵת – צָרִיךְ לְשׁוֹמְרוֹ מִן הַחוּלְדָּה וּמִן הָעַכְבָּרִים, שֶׁנֶּאֱמַר ״וּמוֹרַאֲכֶם וְחִתְּכֶם יִהְיֶה״, כָּל זְמַן שֶׁאָדָם חַי – אֵימָתוֹ מוּטֶּלֶת עַל הַבְּרִיּוֹת, כֵּיוָן שֶׁמֵּת – בָּטְלָה אֵימָתוֹ.

And it was also **taught** in a *baraita* that **Rabbi Shimon ben Elazar said: It is not necessary to protect a live day-old baby from a weasel or from mice,** for they run away from the baby. **But if Og, the king of Bashan, is dead, it is necessary to protect** even **him from a weasel or from mice, as it is stated: "And the fear of you and the dread of you** [***ḥittekhem***] **shall be** upon every beast of the earth, and upon every bird of the heavens" (Genesis 9:2). The Gemara explains: **As long as a person is alive** [***ḥai***]**, he is feared by the animals. Once he dies, he is no longer feared.**

אָמַר רַב פַּפָּא: נְקִיטִינַן, אַרְיֵה אַבֵּי תְּרֵי – לָא נָפֵיל. הָא קָא חָזֵינַן דְּנָפֵיל. הַהוּא כִּדְרָמִי בַּר אַבָּא, דְּאָמַר רָמִי בַּר אַבָּא: אֵין חַיָּה שׁוֹלֶטֶת בָּאָדָם עַד שֶׁנִּדְמֶה לוֹ כִּבְהֵמָה; שֶׁנֶּאֱמַר ״אָדָם בִּיקָר בַּל יָלִין נִמְשַׁל כַּבְּהֵמוֹת נִדְמוּ״. אָמַר רַבִּי חֲנִינָא: אָסוּר לִישַׁן בְּבַיִת יְחִידִי, וְכָל הַיָּשֵׁן בְּבַיִת יְחִידִי אֲחָזַתּוּ לִילִית.

Rav Pappa said: We hold[N] that **a lion does not pounce upon two** people. The Gemara challenges this: **But** how can that be? **We see that it does pounce** upon two people. The Gemara answers: **That** statement of Rav Pappa must be **in accordance with** that which **Rami bar Abba said: An animal does not overpower a person until he appears to it as an animal, as it is stated: "But man does not abide in honor, he is like the beasts that perish"** (Psalms 49:13). However, animals do not attack people who are human in their spiritual character. In a similar vein, **Rabbi Ḥanina said: It is prohibited to sleep alone in a house,**[NH] **and anyone who sleeps alone in a house will be seized by** the evil spirit **Lilith.**

וְתַנְיָא, רַבִּי שִׁמְעוֹן בֶּן אֶלְעָזָר אוֹמֵר: עֲשֵׂה עַד שֶׁאַתָּה מוֹצֵא וּמָצוּי לְךָ וְעוֹדְךָ בְּיָדְךָ, וְאַף שְׁלֹמֹה אָמַר בְּחָכְמָתוֹ ״וּזְכוֹר אֶת בּוֹרְאֶיךָ בִּימֵי בְּחוּרוֹתֶיךָ עַד [אֲשֶׁר] (שֶׁ) לֹא יָבֹאוּ יְמֵי הָרָעָה״ – אֵלּוּ יְמֵי הַזִּקְנָה ״וְהִגִּיעוּ שָׁנִים אֲשֶׁר תֹּאמַר אֵין לִי בָּהֶם חֵפֶץ״ – אֵלּוּ יְמֵי הַמָּשִׁיחַ, שֶׁאֵין בָּהֶם לֹא זְכוּת וְלֹא חוֹבָה.

It was also **taught** in a *baraita* with regard to the appreciation of life: **Rabbi Shimon ben Elazar says: Perform** mitzvot **while you** still **find** opportunities, **and you have** the financial means, **and you are still under your** own **control.**[N] **And** King **Solomon also said, in his wisdom: "And remember your Creator in the days of your youth, before the evil days come** and the years arrive when you will say: I have no desire for them" (Ecclesiastes 12:1). Rabbi Shimon ben Elazar explains: "The evil days"; **these are the days of old age. "And the years arrive when you will say: I have no desire for them"; these are the days of Messiah, in which there is neither merit nor liability.**

וּפְלִיגָא דִּשְׁמוּאֵל, דְּאָמַר שְׁמוּאֵל: אֵין בֵּין הָעוֹלָם הַזֶּה לִימוֹת הַמָּשִׁיחַ אֶלָּא שִׁיעְבּוּד מַלְכִיּוֹת בִּלְבַד, שֶׁנֶּאֱמַר ״כִּי לֹא יֶחְדַּל אֶבְיוֹן מִקֶּרֶב הָאָרֶץ״.

The Gemara comments that this explanation **disagrees with** the view of **Shmuel, for Shmuel said: There is no** difference **between this world and the days of Messiah except for subjugation** to foreign **kingdoms alone,** from which we will be released in the Messianic era, **as it is stated: "For the poor will never cease from the land,** therefore I command you, saying: You shall surely open your hand to your brother, to your poor and your needy in your land." (Deuteronomy 15:11). This indicates that the ways of the world, including the existence of wealthy and poor socioeconomic strata, will continue forever.

NOTES

We hold – נְקִיטִינַן: Rashi explains that this term refers to an oral tradition passed down from previous generations. The expression means that the tradition received from our forefathers is cherished and accepted.

It is prohibited to sleep alone in a house – אָסוּר לִישַׁן בְּבַיִת יְחִידִי: Some commentaries explain that this prohibition is based on the principle that one may not place oneself in a dangerous situation. Perhaps one who is alone will be gripped with fear and will be traumatized (*Me'iri*).

And you are still under your own control – וְעוֹדְךָ בְּיָדְךָ: The commentaries state that this is referring to the period in one's life prior to old age, when one still exercises control over all of his belongings and assets (Maharsha, Rabbi Yoshiya Pinto).

HALAKHA

It is prohibited to sleep alone in a house – אָסוּר לִישַׁן בְּבַיִת יְחִידִי: One should not sleep alone in a house (*Sefer Mitzvot Gedolot*, positive mitzvot 79).

תניא, רבי אלעזר הקפר אומר: לעולם יבקש אדם רחמים על מדה זו, שאם הוא לא בא – בא בנו, ואם בנו לא בא – בן בנו בא, שנאמר "כי בגלל הדבר הזה", תנא דבי רבי ישמעאל: גלגל הוא שחוזר בעולם. אמר רב יוסף: נקיטינן, האי צורבא מרבנן לא מיעני – והא קא חזינן דמיעני. אם איתא דמיעני, אהדורי אפתחא לא מיהדר.

It was taught in a *baraita* that **Rabbi Elazar HaKappar says: A person should always request** divine **mercy with regard to this condition** of poverty, **for if he does not come** to a state of poverty, **his son will, and if his son does not come** to such a state **his grandson will, as it is stated:** "You shall surely give him and your heart shall not be grieved when you give to him, **for due to this thing** [*biglal hadavar hazeh*] the Lord your God will bless you in all your work and in all that you put your hand toward" (Deuteronomy 15:10). With regard to this verse, the ***tanna* from the school of Rabbi Yishmael taught:** Due to [*biglal*] this thing means that **it is a wheel** [*galgal*] **that turns in the world,** upon which people continuously rise and fall. **Rav Yosef said: We hold** that **a Torah scholar will not become poor.** The Gemara challenges this statement: **But we see that they do become poor.** The Gemara answers: Even so, **if there is** a Torah scholar **who becomes poor, he will** still **never** have to **go around** asking for charity **at** people's **doors.**[N]

אמר לה רבי חייא לדביתהו: כי אתי עניא – אקדימי ליה ריפתא, כי היכי דלקדמו לבניך. אמרה ליה: מילט קא לייטת להו? אמר לה: קרא קא כתיב "כי בגלל הדבר הזה", ותנא דבי רבי ישמעאל: גלגל הוא שחוזר בעולם, תניא רבי גמליאל ברבי אומר: "ונתן לך רחמים ורחמך והרבך" כל המרחם על הבריות – מרחמין עליו מן השמים, וכל שאינו מרחם על הבריות – אין מרחמין עליו מן השמים.

In a similar vein, the Gemara relates that **Rabbi Ḥiyya said to his wife: When a poor person comes** to the house, **be quick to give him bread so that they will be quick** to give bread **to your children. She said to him:** Are **you cursing them,** your children? **He said to her: It is a verse that is written,** as it says: **"Due to this thing,"** and the Sages expounded that **it is a wheel that** continuously **turns in the world.** Similarly, **it was taught** in a *baraita* that **Rabbi Gamliel, son of Rabbi** Yehuda HaNasi, **says:** The verse that states: **"And He will show you mercy and have compassion on you and multiply you"** (Deuteronomy 13:18) teaches us that **anyone who has compassion for** God's **creatures**[H] **will receive compassion from Heaven, and anyone who does not have compassion for** God's **creatures will not receive compassion from Heaven.**

"עד אשר לא תחשך השמש והאור" – זו פדחת והחוטם, "והירח" – זו נשמה, "והכוכבים" – אלו הלסתות, "ושבו העבים אחר הגשם" – זו מאור עיניו של אדם, שהולך אחר הבכי. אמר שמואל: האי דמעתא, עד ארבעין שנין – הדרא, מכאן ואילך – לא הדרא.

The Gemara returns to verses from Ecclesiastes that relate to death and old age. It is written: **"Before the sun and the light** and the moon and the stars **are darkened,** and the clouds return after the rain" (Ecclesiastes 12:2). The Sages taught: "The sun and the light"; **this** is referring to **the forehead**[N] **and the nose** which stick out from a person's face. **"And the moon"; this** is referring to **the soul,** which shines within a person. **"And the stars"; these are the cheeks.**[N] **"And the clouds return after the rain"; this is the light of a person's eyes, which goes** and dwindles **after one cries** as if it were covered by clouds. **Shmuel said:** With regard to **the tear** that a person cries, **until** one reaches the age of **forty years, one's vision returns** and is not harmed. **From here on,** once a person reaches the age of forty, **it does not return,** and every time a person cries his vision is weakened.

ואמר רב נחמן: האי כוחלא, עד ארבעין שנין – מרווח, מכאן ואילך – אפילו מליא כאביסנא דגירדאי – אוקומי מוקים, ארווחי לא מרווח. מאי קא משמע לן – דכמה דאלים מכוחלא טפי מעלי.

And similarly, **Rav Naḥman said:** With regard to medicinal **eye shadow, until** one reaches the age of **forty years, it enhances** his eyesight. **From here and on, even if one fills it** as thick **as a weaver's pin** [*avisana degirda'ei*],[L] **it will maintain** his eyesight but **it will not enhance** it. The Gemara asks about this: **What is he teaching us** with the example of a weaver's pin? The Gemara answers: Generally speaking, **the more eye shadow** one applies, **the more beneficial** it is.

רבי חנינא שכיבא ליה ברתיה, לא הוה קא בכי עלה. אמרה ליה דביתהו: תרנגולתא אפיקת מביתך? אמר לה: תרתי, תכלא ועיורא? סבר לה כי הא דאמר רבי יוחנן משום רבי יוסי בן קצרתה: שש דמעות הן, שלש יפות ושלש רעות. של עשן ושל בכי

The Gemara relates a story: When **Rabbi Ḥanina's daughter died, he did not cry over her. His wife said to him:** Have you merely **let a chicken out of your house,** that you do not show any signs of sorrow? **He said to her:** If I cry, I will suffer **twice,** from **bereavement and** from **blindness.** The Gemara explains: **He held in accordance with** the statement that **Rabbi Yoḥanan said in the name of Rabbi Yosei ben Ketzarta: There are six** types of **tears, three** of which **are good** for the eyes **and three** of which **are bad.** Tears that come **from smoke, and from crying** out of sorrow,

NOTES

He will never go around asking for charity at people's doors – אהדורי אפתחא לא מיהדר: The rationale for this statement is that people will take special care of a Torah scholar and make sure that he is not disgraced in this way. An alternative explanation is that a scholar will conduct himself in a frugal and self-disciplined manner and will not allow himself to reach a situation that would necessitate going door-to-door asking for charity (Maharsha).

The sun…the forehead – השמש...פדחת: In his commentary to Ecclesiastes, Rashi explains that the forehead is compared to the sun because in youth one's forehead is smooth and shiny, and its light is later dimmed by the wrinkles of old age.

The stars, these are the cheeks – והכוכבים אלו הלסתות: In his commentary on Ecclesiastes, Rashi explains that this refers to the jawbone, which protrudes and is visible from under the hair of one's beard that covers his cheeks.

LANGUAGE

Weaver's pin [*avisana degirda'ei*] – אביסנא דגירדאי: It seems that the correct version of this phrase is that of the *Arukh*, *akhsena degarda'ei*. Its origin is the Greek ἄξων, *axon*, which refers to a weaver's needle.

HALAKHA

Anyone who has compassion for God's creatures – המרחם על הבריות: God acts with compassion toward one who has compassion on the poor. One should constantly be aware that he is seeking sustenance from God, and just as he hopes that God will answer his own prayers, he should be receptive to the requests of the poor (*Tur*). It is therefore customary to give charity before prayer (Rambam *Sefer Zera'im*, *Hilkhot Mattenot Aniyyim* 10:2; *Shulḥan Arukh*, *Yoreh De'a* 247:3)

וְשֶׁל בֵּית הַכִּסֵּא – רָעוֹת, שֶׁל סַם וְשֶׁל שְׂחוֹק וְשֶׁל פֵּירוֹת – יָפוֹת.

and from pain in **the bathroom are bad** for the eyes. Tears that come **from** medicinal **drugs, and from laughter, and from** sharp **produce are good** for the eyes.

״בַּיּוֹם שֶׁיָּזוּעוּ שׁוֹמְרֵי הַבַּיִת וְהִתְעַוְּתוּ וגו׳״. ״בַּיּוֹם שֶׁיָּזוּעוּ שׁוֹמְרֵי הַבַּיִת״ – אֵלּוּ הַכְּסָלִים וְהַצְּלָעוֹת, ״וְהִתְעַוְּתוּ אַנְשֵׁי הֶחָיִל״ – אֵלּוּ שׁוֹקַיִם, ״וּבָטְלוּ הַטּוֹחֲנוֹת״ – אֵלּוּ שִׁינַּיִם, ״וְחָשְׁכוּ הָרוֹאוֹת בָּאֲרוּבּוֹת״ – אֵלּוּ עֵינַיִם.

The Gemara continues to interpret verses from the Book of Ecclesiastes. The verse states: **"On the day when the keepers of the house shall tremble,** and the strong men **shall bow themselves,** and the grinders cease because they are few, and those that look out the windows shall be dimmed" (Ecclesiastes 12:3). **"On the day when the keepers of the house shall tremble"; this** is referring to **the flanks and ribs** that surround and protect a person's internal organs. **"And the strong men shall bow themselves"; these are the thighs,** which support a person's strength. **"And the grinders cease"; these are the teeth,** which decay and fall out. **"And those that look out the windows shall be dimmed"; these are the eyes,** which become dimmer.

אֲמַר לֵיהּ קֵיסָר לְרַבִּי יְהוֹשֻׁעַ בֶּן חֲנַנְיָה: מַאי טַעְמָא לָא אָתֵית לְבֵי אֲבִידָן? אֲמַר לֵיהּ: טוּר תַּלְג סַחֲרוּנִי גְּלִידִין, כַּלְבּוֹהִי לָא נָבְחִין, טַחֲנוֹהִי לָא טוֹחֲנִין. בֵּי רַב אָמְרִי: אַדְּלָא אֲבֵידְנָא בָּחֵישְׁנָא.

The Gemara relates: The Roman **emperor said to Rabbi Yehoshua ben Ḥananya: What is the reason you did not come to the House of Avidan?** This was a place in which dialogues and debates were conducted. Rabbi Yehoshua ben Ḥananya **said to him** enigmatically: **The snowy mountain is surrounded with ice,** meaning that his hair had turned white; **his dogs do not bark,** meaning that his voice could no longer be heard; **his grinders have ceased grinding,** meaning that his teeth had fallen out. In **the school of Rav they say** that he added: **I am searching for that which I have not lost,** because an old man walks bent over and appears to be searching for something.

תַּנְיָא, רַבִּי יוֹסֵי בַּר קִיסְמָא אוֹמֵר: טָבָא תְּרֵי מִתְּלָת, וַוי לָהּ לַחֲדָא דְּאָזְלָא וְלָא אָתְיָא. מַאי הִיא? אֲמַר רַב חִסְדָּא: יַנְקוּתָא. כִּי אֲתָא רַב דִּימִי אֲמַר: יַנְקוּתָא – כְּלִילָא דְוַורְדָּא, סָבוּתָא – כְּלִילָא דְחִילְפָא. תָּנָא מִשְּׁמֵיהּ דְּרַבִּי מֵאִיר: דּוֹק בְּכַכֵּי וְתִשְׁכַּח בְּנִיגְרֵי, שֶׁנֶּאֱמַר ״וַנִּשְׂבַּע לֶחֶם וַנִּהְיֶה טוֹבִים וְרָעָה לֹא רָאִינוּ״. אֲמַר לֵיהּ שְׁמוּאֵל לְרַב יְהוּדָה: שִׁינָּנָא, שְׁרֵי שַׂקָּיךְ וְעַיֵּיל לַחְמָךְ. עַד אַרְבְּעִין שְׁנִין – מֵיכְלָא מְעַלֵּי, מִכָּאן וְאֵילָךְ – מִשְׁתֵּי מְעַלֵּי.

It was taught in a *baraita* that **Rabbi Yosei bar Kisma says:** The **two** feet of one's youth **are better than the three** of old age, when one walks with a cane. **Woe to the one who goes and does not come back. What is this** referring to? **Rav Ḥisda said: Youth.** Similarly, **when Rav Dimi came** from Eretz Yisrael to Babylonia **he said: Youth is a crown of roses; old age is a crown of thorns.** The Sage **taught in the name of Rabbi Meir: Grind** food **with your teeth** and you will **find in your feet**[N] the strength to carry your body, **as it is stated: "For we were sated with our bread and were well, and saw no evil"** (Jeremiah 44:17). **Shmuel said to Rav Yehuda: Large-toothed one; untie your sack,** that is, your mouth, **and insert your food. Until** the age of **forty years, food is beneficial; from here and on, drinking is beneficial.**

אֲמַר לֵיהּ הַהוּא גּוֹזָאָה לְרַבִּי יְהוֹשֻׁעַ בֶּן קָרְחָה: מֵהָכָא לְקָרְחִינָא כַּמָּה הָוֵי? אֲמַר לֵיהּ: כְּמֵהָכָא לְגוֹזַנְיָא. אֲמַר לֵיהּ צְדוֹקִי: בַּרְחָא קַרְחָא בְּאַרְבְּעָה. אֲמַר לֵיהּ: עִיקָּרָא שְׁלִיפָא בִּתְמָנְיָא.

Having quoted some aphorisms of the Sages, the Gemara relates the following conversation: **A certain eunuch** who was an apostate **said** the following **to Rabbi Yehoshua ben Korḥa** as a provocation: **How far is it from here to Karḥina?** The provocateur's intention was to hint to the fact that Rabbi Yehoshua ben Korḥa was bald [*kere'aḥ*]. **He said to him: It is the same as** the distance **from here to** the mountains of **Gozen,** hinting at the eunuch's castration, which in Aramaic is *goza* (Rav Ya'akov Emden). The apostate **said to him: A bald buck**[N] is sold **for four** *dinar*. **He said to him: A castrated goat** [*ikkara shelifa*][L] is sold **for eight.**

חַזְיֵיהּ דְּלָא סָיֵים מְסָאנֵיהּ, אֲמַר לֵיהּ: דְּעַל סוּס – מֶלֶךְ, דְּעַל חֲמוֹר – בֶּן חוֹרִין, וּדְמַנְעֲלֵי בְּרִיגְלוֹהִי – בַּר אִינִישׁ, דְּלָא הָא וְלָא הָא – דַּחֲפִיר וּקְבִיר טָב מִינֵּיהּ. אֲמַר לֵיהּ: גּוֹזָא גּוֹזָא, תְּלָת אֲמַרְתְּ לִי תְּלָת שְׁמַעַתְּ; הַדְרַת פָּנִים – זָקָן, שִׂמְחַת לֵב – אִשָּׁה, ״נַחֲלַת ה׳ – בָּנִים״ – בָּרוּךְ הַמָּקוֹם שֶׁמְּנָעָךְ מִכּוּלָּם. אֲמַר לֵיהּ: קַרְחָא מְצוֹיְינָא. אֲמַר לֵיהּ: עִיקָּרָא שְׁלִיפָא תּוֹכֵחָה.

The apostate **saw that** Rabbi Yehoshua ben Korḥa **was not wearing shoes.** He **said to him:** One who rides **on a horse** is **a king.** One who rides **on a donkey** is **a free man. And one who wears shoes is** at least **a human being.** One who does **neither this nor that,** someone **who is buried** in the earth **is better than him. He said to him: Eunuch, eunuch, you said to me three things,** and now **hear three** things: **The glory of a face is the beard, the joy of the heart is a wife,** and **"the portion of the Lord is children"** (Psalms 127:3); **blessed is the Omnipresent who has denied you all of them,** for a eunuch does not have a beard, a wife or children. **He said to him:** Does **a bald man quarrel? He said to him:** Does **a castrated male goat** speak words of **rebuke?**

NOTES

Grind food with your teeth and you will find in your feet – דּוֹק בְּכַכֵּי וְתִשְׁכַּח בְּנִיגְרֵי: Rabbi Meir's advice is meant as preparation for old age. If a person eats well during the younger years, his strength will be preserved even in old age (Maharsha).

Bald buck – בַּרְחָא קַרְחָא: Rabbeinu Ḥananel explained that after the eunuch degraded Rabbi Yehoshua ben Korḥa, calling him a "bald buck," Rabbi Yehoshua responded by saying that the eunuch was just goading him to admit to the superiority of a eunuch over a bald person. His statement: Does a castrated male goat speak words of rebuke, means: You are not quarreling with me, you are just scolding me.

LANGUAGE

Castrated goat [*ikkara shelifa*] **– עִיקָּרָא שְׁלִיפָא:** The version in the *Arukh* is *ika shelifa*. The word *ika* is from the Greek **αἴξ**, *aix*, or **αἰγός**, *aigos*, meaning goat.

אמר ליה רבי לרבי שמעון בן חלפתא: מפני מה לא הקבלנו פניך ברגל, כדרך שהקבילו אבותי לאבותיך? אמר ליה: סלעים נעשו גבוהים, קרובים נעשו רחוקים, משתים נעשו שלש, משים שלום בבית בטל.

The Gemara again addresses old age: **Rabbi** Yehuda HaNasi **said to Rabbi Shimon ben Ḥalafta: For what** reason **did we not greet you during the Festival the way that my fathers greeted your fathers?** This was a polite way of asking Rabbi Shimon ben Ḥalafta why he had not come to visit Rabbi Yehuda HaNasi. He **said to him:** Because I have grown old,[B] and **the rocks** on the road **have become tall,** and destinations that are **near have become far away,**[N] and my **two** feet **have been made into three** with the addition of a cane, and **that which brings peace to the house,**[N] namely, the sexual drive which motivates a couple to make peace, **is no more.**

"וסגרו דלתים בשוק וגו'" – אלו נקביו של אדם, "בשפל קול הטחנה" – בשביל קורקבן שאינו טוחן, "ויקום לקול הצפור" – שאפילו צפור מנערתו משנתו, "וישחו כל בנות השיר" – שאפילו (קול שירים ושירות) דומות עליו כשוחה.

The Gemara continues to expound the verses of the final chapter of Ecclesiastes. The verse states: "And the doors shall be shut in the marketplace when the sound of the grinding is low, and one shall start up at the voice of a bird, and all the daughters of music shall be brought low" (Ecclesiastes 12:4). The Sages expounded: **"And the doors shall be shut in the marketplace"; these are a person's orifices,** which cease to function normally. The interpretation continues: **"When the sound of the grinding is low"; because the stomach is not grinding** and digesting one's food. **"And one shall start up at the voice of a bird";** because one is unable to sleep deeply such **that even a bird will wake him from his sleep. "And all the daughters of music shall be brought low";** this means **that even the voices of male and female singers will seem to him like** mere **conversation,** and he will no longer derive pleasure from song.

ואף ברזילי הגלעדי אמר לדוד: "בן שמנים שנה אנכי היום האדע בין טוב לרע" – מכאן שדעותן של זקנים משתנות, "אם יטעם עבדך את אשר אוכל ואת אשר אשתה" – מכאן ששפתותיהן של זקנים מתרפטות, "אם אשמע עוד בקול שרים ושרות" – מכאן שאזניהם של זקנים מתכבדות.

And even Barzilai the Gileadite said to David: "Today I am eighty years old, can I discern between good and bad? Can your servant taste what I eat or what I drink? Can I hear any more the voice of singing men and singing women?" (II Samuel 19:36). The Gemara explains: "Can I discern between good and bad"; **from here** we derive **that the minds of the elderly change** and they no longer discern properly. **"Can your servant taste what I eat or what I drink"; from here** we derive **that the lips of the elderly crack and wither. "Can I hear any more the voice of singing men and singing women"; from here** we derive **that the ears of the elderly become heavy.**

אמר רב: ברזילי הגלעדי שקרא הוה, דההיא אמתא דהויא בי רבי בת תשעין ותרתין שנין, והות טעמא קידרא. רבא אמר: ברזילי הגלעדי שטוף בזמה הוה, וכל השטוף בזמה – זקנה קופצת עליו. תניא, רבי ישמעאל ברבי יוסי אומר: תלמידי חכמים, כל זמן שמזקינין – חכמה נתוספת בהם, שנאמר: "בישישים חכמה ואורך ימים תבונה". ועמי הארץ, כל זמן שמזקינין – טפשות נתוספת בהן, שנאמר "מסיר שפה לנאמנים וטעם זקנים יקח.

Rav said: Barzilai the Gileadite was a liar and he merely wanted to avoid joining David upon his return to Jerusalem, for an eighty year old man is not usually this debilitated. **For there was a particular maidservant in the house of Rabbi** Yehuda HaNasi **who was ninety-two years old, and she would taste** the food that was cooking **in the pots. Rava said:** Barzilai was speaking the truth, but **Barzilai the Gileadite was steeped in promiscuity, and anyone who is steeped in promiscuity is overtaken by old age** before his time. **It was taught** in a *baraita* that **Rabbi Yishmael, son of Rabbi Yosei, says: As Torah scholars grow older, wisdom is increased in them, as it is stated: "With aged men is wisdom; and length of days brings understanding"** (Job 12:12). **And as ignoramuses grow older, foolishness is increased in them, as it is stated: "He removes the speech of men of trust and takes away the understanding of the aged"** (Job 12:20).

"גם מגבוה יראו" שאפילו גבשושית קטנה דומה עליו כהרי הרים, "וחתחתים בדרך" בשעה שמהלך בדרך נעשו לו תוהים. "וינאץ השקד" – זו קליבוסת, "ויסתבל החגב" – אלו עגבות, "ותפר האביונה" – זו חמדה.

The Gemara continues interpreting verses from Ecclesiastes. The verse states: "Also when they shall be afraid of that which is high and terrors shall be on the road, and the almond tree shall blossom, and the grasshopper shall drag itself along, and the caper berry shall fail, for a person goes to his eternal home, and the mourners circle the marketplace" (Ecclesiastes 12:5). The Gemara explains: **"Also when they shall be afraid of that which is high";** this means **that even a small knoll** on the road **seems to him,** the elderly, **like the highest of mountains. "And terrors shall be on the road";**[N] this means **that while he is walking on the road he will have terrors,** i.e., he will fear falling or otherwise suffering injury. **"And the almond tree shall blossom"; this is the hip bone** that protrudes from the skin of an elderly person. **"And the grasshopper [*ḥagav*] shall drag itself along [*yistabbel*]";** by replacing the letter *ḥet* of *ḥagav* with an *ayin*, **this** can be understood as referring to the **buttocks [*agavot*]** which become heavy [*sevel*]. **"And the caper berry shall fail"; this is** sexual **desire** that ceases.

BACKGROUND

Old age and weakness – זקנה ותשישות: The Gemara describes examples of the weakness and illness that accompany old age. The protrusion of the hip bone is particularly noticeable when an elderly person suffers from weight loss as a result of the weakness of old age, known as senile marasmus.

NOTES

Destinations that are near have become far away – קרובים נעשו רחוקים: In a midrash in *Vayikra Rabba* it is explained that this means that the ears that could once hear well, can now only hear with difficulty and from close by.

That which brings peace to the house – משים שלום בבית: In *Anaf Yosef* it is explained that this phrase is referring to digestion, which makes peace within one's body. If one cannot properly digest his food, he suffers significant discomfort and a lack of internal peace.

And terrors shall be on the road – וחתחתים בדרך: In his commentary to Ecclesiastes, Rashi explains that the word terrors [*ḥatḥatim*] stems from the word *ḥita*, meaning fear. This phrase means that one will be afraid while traveling.

רַב כָּהֲנָא הֲוָה פָּסֵיק סִידְרָא קַמֵּיהּ דְּרַב, כִּי מַטָא לְהַאי קְרָא נָגֵיד וְאִתְנַח. אֲמַר: שְׁמַע מִינָּהּ בְּטַל לֵיהּ חֶמְדֵּיהּ דְּרַב. אָמַר רַב כָּהֲנָא: מַאי דִּכְתִיב ״כִּי הוּא אָמַר וַיֶּהִי״ – זוֹ אִשָּׁה, ״הוּא צִוָּה וַיַּעֲמוֹד״ – אֵלּוּ בָּנִים. תָּנָא: אִשָּׁה חֵמֶת מָלֵא צוֹאָה, וּפִיהָ מָלֵא דָּם – וְהַכֹּל רָצִין אַחֲרֶיהָ.

The Gemara relates that **Rav Kahana was reading** biblical **verses before Rav. When he got to this verse,** Rav **sighed.** Rav Kahana **said:** We can **derive from this that Rav's desire has ceased. Rav Kahana** also **said: What is** the meaning of **that which is written:** "For He spoke and it was, He commanded and it stood" (Psalms 33:9)? He understands this to mean that God created man with desires that push him to do things he would not do if he acted purely on the judgment of his intellect, and Rav Kahana therefore interprets the verse in the following manner: **"For He spoke and it was"; this is a woman** that a man marries. **"He commanded and it stood"; these are the children** who one works hard to raise. A *tanna* **taught** in a *baraita*: **A woman is** essentially **a flask full of feces,** a reference to the digestive system, **and her mouth is full of blood,** a euphemistic reference to menstruation, yet men are not deterred **and they all run after her** with desire.

״כִּי הוֹלֵךְ הָאָדָם אֶל בֵּית עוֹלָמוֹ״ אֲמַר רַבִּי יִצְחָק: מְלַמֵּד שֶׁכָּל צַדִּיק וְצַדִּיק נוֹתְנִין לוֹ מָדוֹר לְפִי כְּבוֹדוֹ. מָשָׁל לְמֶלֶךְ שֶׁנִּכְנַס הוּא וַעֲבָדָיו לְעִיר, כְּשֶׁהֵן נִכְנָסִין – כּוּלָּן בְּשַׁעַר אֶחָד נִכְנָסִין, כְּשֶׁהֵן לָנִין – כָּל אֶחָד וְאֶחָד נוֹתְנִין לוֹ מָדוֹר לְפִי כְּבוֹדוֹ.

The Gemara interprets the continuation of the verse cited above: **"For a person goes to his eternal home"** (Ecclesiastes 12:5). **Rabbi Yitzḥak said: This teaches that each and every righteous person is given a dwelling place** in the World-to-Come **in accordance with his honor.** The Gemara offers **a parable** in which **a king enters a city along with his servants. When they enter, they all enter through a single gate;** however, **when they sleep, each one is given a dwelling place in accordance with his honor.** So too, although everyone dies, not everyone receives the same reward in the World-to-Come.

וְאָמַר רַבִּי יִצְחָק: מַאי דִּכְתִיב ״כִּי הַיַּלְדוּת וְהַשַּׁחֲרוּת הָבֶל״ דְּבָרִים שֶׁאָדָם עוֹשֶׂה בְּיַלְדוּתוֹ – מַשְׁחִירִים פָּנָיו לְעֵת זִקְנָתוֹ.

And Rabbi Yitzḥak said: What is the meaning of **that which is written: "For childhood and youth** [*shaḥarut*] **are vanity"** (Ecclesiastes 11:10)? Sinful **things that a person does in his youth darken** [***mashḥirin***] **his face** with shame **as he grows old** (Rabbi Yoshiya Pinto).

וְאָמַר רַבִּי יִצְחָק: קָשָׁה רִימָּה לַמֵּת כְּמַחַט בִּבְשַׂר הַחַי, שֶׁנֶּאֱמַר ״אַךְ בְּשָׂרוֹ עָלָיו יִכְאָב״. אָמַר רַב חִסְדָּא: נַפְשׁוֹ שֶׁל אָדָם מִתְאַבֶּלֶת עָלָיו כָּל שִׁבְעָה, שֶׁנֶּאֱמַר ״וְנַפְשׁוֹ עָלָיו תֶּאֱבָל״. וּכְתִיב ״וַיַּעַשׂ לְאָבִיו אֵבֶל שִׁבְעַת יָמִים״.

And Rabbi Yitzḥak said: The maggots that eat the flesh of the deceased **are as painful to the dead as a needle in the flesh of the living, as it says** with regard to the dead: **"But his flesh is in pain for him,** and his soul mourns over him" (Job 14:22). **Rav Ḥisda said: A person's soul mourns for him** during **all seven days** of mourning following his death, **as it is stated: And his soul mourns over him," and it is** also **written: "And he mourned his father seven days"** (Genesis 50:10).

אָמַר רַב יְהוּדָה: מֵת שֶׁאֵין לוֹ מְנַחֲמִין הוֹלְכִין עֲשָׂרָה בְּנֵי אָדָם וְיוֹשְׁבִין בִּמְקוֹמוֹ. הַהוּא דִּשְׁכִיב בְּשַׁבְבוּתֵיהּ דְּרַב יְהוּדָה לָא הָיוּ לוֹ מְנַחֲמִין,

Rav Yehuda said: In the case of **a deceased person who has no comforters,**[NH] i.e., he has nobody to mourn for him, **ten people should go and sit in his place** and accept condolences. The Gemara relates the story of **a certain person who died in Rav Yehuda's neighborhood** and **who did not have** any **comforters,** i.e., mourners;

NOTES

A deceased person who has no comforters – מֵת שֶׁאֵין לוֹ מְנַחֲמִין: Maharsha explains that since the soul mourns for the person, the people who come to offer comfort are in fact coming to comfort the deceased himself. This explains why the Gemara uses the expression: A deceased person who has no comforters.

HALAKHA

A deceased person who has no comforters – מֵת שֶׁאֵין לוֹ מְנַחֲמִין: If a person passes away and has no relatives to mourn for him, ten people come and sit in the person's home for a full seven days while others come and comfort them, in accordance with the example of Rav Yehuda. However, the Rema writes: I have not seen people do this. Even so, if the deceased has no mourners, ten people gather and pray in the place where the person died for all seven days of mourning, in accordance with Rav Yehuda's actions as related in the Gemara (Rambam *Sefer Shofetim*, *Hilkhot Evel* 13:4; *Shulḥan Arukh*, *Yoreh De'a* 376:3).

Perek **XXIII**
Daf **152** Amud **b**

כָּל יוֹמָא הֲוָה דָּבַר רַב יְהוּדָה בֵּי עֲשָׂרָה, וְיָתְבִי בְּדוּכְתֵּיהּ. לְאַחַר שִׁבְעָה יָמִים אִיתְחֲזֵי לֵיהּ בְּחֶילְמֵיהּ דְּרַב יְהוּדָה, וְאָמַר לֵיהּ: תָּנוּחַ דַּעְתְּךָ שֶׁהִנַּחְתָּ אֶת דַּעְתִּי.

every day of the seven day mourning period, **Rav Yehuda would take ten** people **and** they would **sit in his place,** in the house of the deceased. **After seven days** had passed the deceased **appeared** to **Rav Yehuda in his dream and said to him: Put your mind to rest, for you have put my mind to rest.**

אֲמַר רַבִּי אַבָּהוּ: כֹּל שֶׁאוֹמְרִים בִּפְנֵי הַמֵּת יוֹדֵעַ, עַד שֶׁיִּסָּתֵם הַגּוֹלֵל. פְּלִיגִי בָּהּ רַבִּי חִיָּיא וְרַבִּי שִׁמְעוֹן בְּרַבִּי; חַד אָמַר: עַד שֶׁיִּסָּתֵם הַגּוֹלֵל, וְחַד אָמַר: עַד שֶׁיִּתְעַכֵּל הַבָּשָׂר.

Rabbi Abbahu said: Everything people say before the deceased,[N] **he knows, until** the tomb **is sealed** with **the top-stone. Rabbi Ḥiyya and Rabbi Shimon, son of Rabbi** Yehuda HaNasi, **disagreed with regard to** the meaning of **this** statement. **One** of them **said** that the deceased is aware **until** the tomb **is sealed** with **the top-stone,** which is referring to the covering of the grave (*Tosafot*). **And one** of them **said** that it is **until the flesh decomposes.**

NOTES

Everything people say before the deceased – כֹּל שֶׁאוֹמְרִים בִּפְנֵי הַמֵּת: This statement is a continuation of the previous discussion about a person's soul remaining with his body for a period of time after death. The Sages disagree about the duration of this time period.

NOTES

Royal garments – **בִּגְדֵי מַלְכוּת**: The Maharsha explains that the wise servants wear the royal garments that have been lent to them only when they perform honorable and clean activities. When they are engaged in other types of activities, they leave the garments in their boxes. On the other hand, the foolish servants do not pay attention to the fact that the clothes are not their own, and wear them even when engaged in ignoble and dirty activities.

LANGUAGE

Box [*kufsa*] – **קוּפְסָא**: From the Latin word *capsa*, meaning a container, especially one used for books.

מַאן דַּאֲמַר עַד שֶׁיִּתְעַכֵּל הַבָּשָׂר – דִּכְתִיב ״אַךְ בְּשָׂרוֹ עָלָיו יִכְאָב וְנַפְשׁוֹ עָלָיו תֶּאֱבָל״. מַאן דַּאֲמַר עַד שֶׁיִּסָּתֵם הַגּוֹלֵל – דִּכְתִיב ״וְיָשׁוֹב הֶעָפָר עַל הָאָרֶץ כְּשֶׁהָיָה וגו׳״.

The one who said that it is **until the flesh decomposes** can support his position based on that **which is written** in the following verse: **"But his flesh grieves for him, and his soul mourns over him"** (Job 14:22). This indicates that the deceased is aware of the pain of his flesh in the grave. **The one who said** that the deceased is aware only **until** the tomb **is sealed** with **the top-stone** can support his view based on that **which is written** in a different verse: **"And the dust returns to the earth as it was,** and the spirit returns to God who gave it" (Ecclesiastes 12:7). This indicates that when the body returns to the earth, the spirit also returns to its place and is no longer aware of what is happening to the body.

תָּנוּ רַבָּנַן: ״וְהָרוּחַ תָּשׁוּב אֶל הָאֱלֹהִים אֲשֶׁר נְתָנָהּ״ – תְּנֵהָ לוֹ כְּמוֹ שֶׁנְּתָנָהּ לְךָ בְּטָהֳרָה – אַף אַתָּה בְּטָהֳרָה. מָשָׁל לְמֶלֶךְ בָּשָׂר וָדָם שֶׁחִילֵּק בִּגְדֵי מַלְכוּת לַעֲבָדָיו. פִּקְחִין שֶׁבָּהֶן קִיפְּלוּם וְהִנִּיחוּם בְּקוּפְסָא, טִפְּשִׁים שֶׁבָּהֶן הָלְכוּ וְעָשׂוּ בָּהֶן מְלָאכָה. לְיָמִים בִּיקֵּשׁ הַמֶּלֶךְ אֶת כֵּלָיו, פִּקְחִין שֶׁבָּהֶן הֶחֱזִירוּם לוֹ כְּשֶׁהֵן מְגוֹהָצִין, טִפְּשִׁין שֶׁבָּהֶן הֶחֱזִירוּם לוֹ כְּשֶׁהֵן מְלוּכְלָכִין. שָׂמַח הַמֶּלֶךְ לִקְרַאת פִּקְחִין, וְכָעַס לִקְרַאת טִפְּשִׁין.

The Sages taught with regard to the verse: **"And the spirit returns to God who gave it"** (Ecclesiastes 12:7) that the words: Who gave it, mean: As it was given. In other words, **give it to Him as He gave it to you;** just as He gave it to you **in purity, you too** should return it to God **in purity.** The Gemara cites **a parable of a king of flesh and blood who distributed royal garments**[N] **to his servants. The wise ones folded them and placed them in a box [*kufsa*]**[L] to protect them, whereas **the foolish ones went and worked in them.** After **a period of time the king requested** that **his garments** be returned to him. The **wise ones returned them to him pressed,** as they were when the servants received them, and **the foolish ones returned them dirty. The king was happy to greet the wise ones and angry to greet the foolish ones.**

עַל פִּקְחִין אָמַר: יִנָּתְנוּ כֵּלַי לָאוֹצָר, וְהֵם יֵלְכוּ לְבָתֵּיהֶם לְשָׁלוֹם. וְעַל טִפְּשִׁין אָמַר: כֵּלַי יִנָּתְנוּ לַכּוֹבֵס, וְהֵן יִתְחַבְּשׁוּ בְּבֵית הָאֲסוּרִים.

With regard to the wise ones he said: My garments shall be given back **to the storehouse, and let them go to their homes in peace. And with regard to the foolish ones he said: My garments shall be given to the launderer, and they,** the fools, **will be locked up in prison** as a punishment for degrading the king's garments for their own purposes.

אַף הַקָּדוֹשׁ בָּרוּךְ הוּא, עַל גּוּפָן שֶׁל צַדִּיקִים אוֹמֵר ״יָבֹא שָׁלוֹם יָנוּחוּ עַל מִשְׁכְּבוֹתָם״ וְעַל נִשְׁמָתָן הוּא אוֹמֵר ״וְהָיְתָה נֶפֶשׁ אֲדוֹנִי צְרוּרָה בִּצְרוֹר הַחַיִּים״. עַל גּוּפָן שֶׁל רְשָׁעִים הוּא אוֹמֵר ״אֵין שָׁלוֹם אָמַר ה׳ לָרְשָׁעִים״ וְעַל נִשְׁמָתָן הוּא אוֹמֵר ״וְאֵת נֶפֶשׁ אוֹיְבֶיךָ יְקַלְּעֶנָּה בְּתוֹךְ כַּף הַקָּלַע״.

The Holy One, Blessed be He, also acts in this way. **With regard to the bodies of the righteous,** which are likened to the royal garments that are well kept, **it states: "He enters into peace, they rest on their beds** each one that walks in his uprightness" (Isaiah 57:2). **And with regard to their souls, it states: "And the soul of my lord shall be bound in the bundle of life** with the Lord your God" (I Samuel 25:29). And conversely, **with regard to the bodies of the wicked, it states: "There is no peace, says the Lord, for the wicked"** (Isaiah 57:21), **and with regard to their souls, it states: "And the souls of your enemies He shall sling out in the hollow of a sling"** (I Samuel 25:29).

תַּנְיָא, רַבִּי אֱלִיעֶזֶר אוֹמֵר: נִשְׁמָתָן שֶׁל צַדִּיקִים גְּנוּזוֹת תַּחַת כִּסֵּא הַכָּבוֹד, שֶׁנֶּאֱמַר ״וְהָיְתָה נֶפֶשׁ אֲדֹנִי צְרוּרָה בִּצְרוֹר הַחַיִּים״, וְשֶׁל רְשָׁעִים זוֹמְמוֹת וְהוֹלְכוֹת, [וּמַלְאָךְ אֶחָד עוֹמֵד בְּסוֹף הָעוֹלָם וּמַלְאָךְ אַחֵר עוֹמֵד בְּסוֹף הָעוֹלָם, וּמְקַלְּעִין נִשְׁמָתָן זֶה לָזֶה], שֶׁנֶּאֱמַר ״וְאֵת נֶפֶשׁ אוֹיְבֶיךָ יְקַלְּעֶנָּה בְּתוֹךְ כַּף הַקָּלַע״.

It was taught in a *baraita* that **Rabbi Eliezer says: The souls of the righteous are stored beneath the Throne of Glory, as it is stated: "And the soul of my lord shall be bound in the bundle of life"** (I Samuel 25:29). **And** the souls **of the wicked are continuously tied up, and one angel stands at** one **end of the world and another angel stands at** the other **end of the world and they sling the souls** of the wicked back and forth **to one another, as it is stated: "And the souls of your enemies He shall sling out in the hollow of a sling"** (I Samuel 25:29).

אָמַר לֵיהּ רַבָּה לְרַב נַחְמָן: שֶׁל בֵּינוֹנִים מַאי? אָמַר לֵיהּ: אִיכָּא שְׁכִיבְנָא לָא אָמְרִי לְכוּ הַאי מִילְּתָא. הָכִי אָמַר שְׁמוּאֵל: אֵלּוּ וָאֵלּוּ לְדוּמָה נִמְסָרִין, הַלָּלוּ – יֵשׁ לָהֶן מָנוֹחַ, הַלָּלוּ – אֵין לָהֶן מָנוֹחַ. אָמַר (לֵיהּ) רַב מָרִי: עֲתִידִים צַדִּיקִים דְּהָווּ עַפְרָא, דִּכְתִיב ״וְיָשׁוֹב הֶעָפָר עַל הָאָרֶץ כְּשֶׁהָיָה״.

Rabba said to Rav Naḥman: What happens to the souls **of middling people,** who are neither righteous nor wicked? Rav Naḥman **said to him:** It is good that you asked me this question, for even **if I were dead I would not** have been able **to tell you** that. As **Shmuel said as follows: These and those,** the souls of the wicked and of the middling people, **are handed over to Duma,** the angel in charge of spirits. But **these,** the souls of the middling people, **have rest, and these,** the souls of the wicked, **do not have rest. Rav Mari said:** Even the bodies of **the righteous will** not be preserved and will **become dust, as it is written: "And the dust returns to the earth as it was"** (Ecclesiastes 12:7).

הַנְהוּ קָפוּלָאֵי דַּהֲווּ קָפְלֵי בְּאַרְעָא דְּרַב נַחְמָן, נְחַר בְּהוּ רַב אַחַאי בַּר יֹאשִׁיָּה. אֲתוּ וְאָמְרוּ לֵיהּ לְרַב נַחְמָן: נְחַר בָּן גַּבְרָא. אֲתָא וַאֲמַר לֵיהּ: מַאן נִיהוּ מָר? אֲמַר לֵיהּ: אֲנָא אַחַאי בַּר יֹאשִׁיָּה. אָמַר לֵיהּ: וְלָאו אָמַר רַב מָרִי: עֲתִידִי צַדִּיקֵי דְּהָווּ עַפְרָא? אֲמַר לֵיהּ: וּמַנִּי מָרִי, דְּלָא יָדַעְנָא לֵיהּ. אֲמַר לֵיהּ: וְהָא קְרָא כְּתִיב ״וְיָשֹׁב הֶעָפָר עַל הָאָרֶץ כְּשֶׁהָיָה״?

The Gemara cites a related story: **The diggers who were digging in Rav Naḥman's land** came upon a grave, and **Rav Aḥai bar Yoshiya,**[NP] who was buried there, **rebuked them. They came and said to Rav Naḥman:** A deceased **person** just **rebuked us.** Rav Naḥman **came and said to** the person buried there: **Who is the Master,** i.e., who are you? He **said to him: I am Aḥai bar Yoshiya.** Rav Naḥman **said to him:** How has your body been preserved? **Didn't Rav Mari say** that **the righteous will turn to dust?** Rav Aḥai **said to him: And who is Mari, whom I do not know?** Why should I be concerned about what he says? Rav Naḥman **said to him:** Even without Rav Mari's statement, **there is an** explicit **verse which is written: "And the dust will return to the earth as it was"** (Ecclesiastes 12:7).

אֲמַר לֵיהּ: דְּאַקְרְיָיךְ קֹהֶלֶת לָא אַקְרְיָיךְ מִשְׁלֵי, דִּכְתִיב ״וּרְקַב עֲצָמוֹת קִנְאָה״ כָּל מִי שֶׁיֵּשׁ לוֹ קִנְאָה בְּלִבּוֹ – עַצְמוֹתָיו מַרְקִיבִים, כָּל שֶׁאֵין לוֹ קִנְאָה בְּלִבּוֹ – אֵין עַצְמוֹתָיו מַרְקִיבִים.

Rav Aḥai **said to him: Whoever taught you** the book of **Ecclesiastes did not teach you** the book of **Proverbs, for it is written** in Proverbs: "A tranquil heart is the life of the flesh, **but envy is the rotting of the bones"** (Proverbs 14:30). This means that **anyone who has envy in his heart** during his lifetime, **his bones rot** in the grave, and **anyone who does not have envy in his heart, his bones do not rot.**

גַּשְׁשֵׁיהּ, חַזְיֵיהּ דְּאִית בֵּיהּ מְשָׁשָׁא. אֲמַר לֵיהּ: לֵיקוּם מָר לְגַוֵּיהּ דְּבֵיתָא. אֲמַר לֵיהּ: גָּלֵית אַדַּעְתָּךְ דַּאֲפִילּוּ נְבִיאֵי לָא קָרֵית, דִּכְתִיב ״וִידַעְתֶּם כִּי אֲנִי ה׳ בְּפִתְחִי אֶת קִבְרוֹתֵיכֶם״.

Rav Naḥman **touched him** and **saw that he had substance.** Rav Naḥman **said to him: Let the Master arise** and come **into my house.** Rav Aḥai **said to him: You have revealed** that **you have not even studied Prophets,**[N] and it is not just the Writings of which you are ignorant, **for it is written: "And you shall know that I am the Lord when I open up your graves** and lift you up from your graves, My nation" (Ezekiel 37:13). As long as the dead have not been instructed to leave their graves, leaving of their own accord is prohibited.

אֲמַר לֵיהּ: וְהָכְתִיב ״כִּי עָפָר אַתָּה וְאֶל עָפָר תָּשׁוּב״. אֲמַר לֵיהּ: הַהוּא – שָׁעָה אַחַת קוֹדֶם תְּחִיַּית הַמֵּתִים.

Rav Naḥman once again asked Rav Aḥai about the preservation of the flesh, and **he said: But it is written: "For you are dust and you shall return to dust"** (Genesis 3:19), so why has your body not turned into dust? He **said to him: That** verse applies to the righteous only **one hour before the resurrection of the dead,** so that they, too, may be created anew (Maharsha).

אֲמַר לֵיהּ הַהוּא מִינָא לְרַבִּי אַבָּהוּ: אָמְרִיתוּ ״נִשְׁמָתָן שֶׁל צַדִּיקִים גְּנוּזוֹת תַּחַת כִּסֵּא הַכָּבוֹד״. אוֹבָא טַמְיָא הֵיכָא אַסְקֵיהּ לִשְׁמוּאֵל בִּנְגִידָא? אֲמַר לֵיהּ: הָתָם בְּתוֹךְ שְׁנֵים עָשָׂר חֹדֶשׁ הֲוָה. דְּתַנְיָא: כָּל שְׁנֵים עָשָׂר חֹדֶשׁ גּוּפוֹ קַיָּים, וְנִשְׁמָתוֹ עוֹלָה וְיוֹרֶדֶת. לְאַחַר שְׁנֵים עָשָׂר חֹדֶשׁ הַגּוּף בָּטֵל.

A certain apostate once **said to Rabbi Abbahu: You say** that **the souls of the righteous are stored beneath the Throne of Glory,** but if so, **how did the oracle woman raise up Samuel using necromancy** if his soul was no longer in this world? Rabbi Abbahu **said to him: There, it was within twelve months** of his death, **as it was taught** in a *baraita*: For **a full twelve months** a deceased person's **body remains and his soul ascends and descends,** such that it is sometimes in this world with its body. **After twelve months, the body ceases** to exist

Notes

Rav Aḥai bar Yoshiya – רַב אַחַאי בַּר יֹאשִׁיָּה: Some explain that the people digging in Rav Naḥman's land were actually plowing his field and came across the grave. They did not know what to do with the body and went to ask Rav Naḥman. Rav Aḥai bar Yoshiya appeared to Rav Naḥman in a dream and their entire conversation took place in that dream (*Pardes Rimonim*).

Ecclesiastes, Proverbs, Prophets – קֹהֶלֶת, מִשְׁלֵי, נְבִיאִים: During the talmudic period, the common educational curriculum began with studying Torah and continued with the Prophets. Then the longer works of the Writings: Job, Proverbs and Psalms, were studied, followed by the shorter Writings: the five Scrolls [*Megillot*], including Ecclesiastes. Thus, Rav Aḥai bar Yoshiya said that Rav Naḥman was even not an expert in the subjects taught to children, including Proverbs and the Prophets.

Personalities

Rav Aḥai bar Yoshiya – רַב אַחַאי בַּר יֹאשִׁיָּה: Rav Aḥai was one of the later *tanna'im* who lived during the time of Rabbi Yehuda HaNasi. Apparently, he was the son of the *tanna*, Rabbi Yoshiya, who was a student of Rabbi Yishmael. Rav Aḥai lived in the Babylonian city of Hutzal, although he conducted business in Neharde'a and was buried there. From the few sources that provide background about his life, it appears that he earned a living as a businessman, but was also the leader of the city of Hutzal and the surrounding villages. His teachings are quoted several times in the Talmud and the halakhic midrash. Rav Naḥman lived and was active in Nehardа'a a few generations after Rav Aḥai bar Yoshiya.

Perek **XXIII**
Daf **153** Amud **a**

וְנִשְׁמָתוֹ עוֹלָה וְשׁוּב אֵינָהּ יוֹרֶדֶת.

and his soul ascends to its place beneath the Throne of Glory, **and does not descend anymore.**

אָמַר רַב יְהוּדָה בְּרֵיהּ דְּרַב שְׁמוּאֵל בַּר שֵׁילַת מִשְּׁמֵיהּ דְּרַב: מֵהֶסְפֵּדוֹ שֶׁל אָדָם נִיכָּר אִם בֶּן הָעוֹלָם הַבָּא הוּא אִם לָאו. אִינִי, וְהָאֲמַר לֵיהּ רַב לְרַב שְׁמוּאֵל בַּר שֵׁילַת: אַחֵים בְּהֶסְפֵּידָא, דְּהָתָם קָאֵימְנָא. לָא קַשְׁיָא, הָא – דְּמַחְמוּ לֵיהּ וְאַחֵים, הָא – דְּמַחְמוּ לֵיהּ וְלָא אַחֵים.

Rav Yehuda, son of Rav Shmuel bar Sheilat, said in the name of Rav: From a person's eulogy it is apparent whether or not he has a share in the World-to-Come. If the listeners are pained and brought to tears during the eulogy, it is clear that the person was righteous. The Gemara asks: **Is that so? Didn't Rav say to Rav Shmuel bar Sheilat: Stir** the hearts of those gathered **during** my **eulogy, for I will be standing there** and listening to your words? Even a person as great as Rav needed to give instructions about his eulogy. The Gemara answers: This is **not difficult,** for **this** statement, which maintains that those who merit a share in the World-to-Come can be identified by their eulogies, is referring to a situation in which **they** attempt to **stir** the listener **and he is stirred;**[N] while **that** statement is referring to a situation in which **they** attempt to **stir** the listener **and he is not stirred.** That is an indication that the deceased person was not righteous.

Notes

They attempt to stir the listener and he is stirred – דְּמַחְמוּ לֵיהּ וְאַחֵים: If a eulogy is an indication that the deceased has earned a share in the World-to-Come, it is unnecessary to attempt to stir the hearts of the listeners, as it serves no purpose. If a speaker stirs the emotions of the crowd, an outpouring of emotion would not indicate the deceased's greatness. Nevertheless, even when the eulogizer attempts to deliver a moving eulogy, the listeners are not necessarily moved by every eulogy and thus the fact that they are stirred reflects well on the deceased.

אמר ליה אביי לרבה: כגון מר, דסנו ליה כולהו פומבדיתאי, מאן אחים הספידא? אמר ליה: מיסתיא את ורבה בר רב חנן.

Abaye said to Rabba: In the case of the Master, i.e., Rabba, **whom all of the inhabitants of** his city, **Pumbedita,**[P] **hate, who will be stirred during his eulogy? He said to him: It is sufficient for me** if **you and Rabba bar Rav Ḥanan** are stirred.

בעא מיניה רבי אלעזר מרב: איזהו בן העולם הבא? אמר ליה: ״ואזניך תשמענה דבר מאחריך לאמר זה הדרך לכו בו כי תאמינו וכי תשמאילו״. רבי [illegible]א אמר: כל שדעת רבותינו נוחה הימנו. ״ו[illegible] בשוק הסופדים״. בני גלילא אמרי: עשה [illegible]ים לפני מטתך, בני יהודה אמרי: עשה דברים לאחר מטתך. ולא פליגי, מר כי אתריה ומר כי אתריה.

Rabbi Elazar raised a dilemma before **Rav: Which** type of person **has a share in the World-to-Come?** He **said to him:** We can derive this from the verse: **"And your ears shall hear a word behind you, saying: This is the path, walk on it, when you turn to the right or to the left"** (Isaiah 30:21). In other words, if people eulogize one by saying that others should follow in his path, he must have a share in the World-to-Come. **Rabbi Ḥanina said: Anyone with whom our Rabbis are pleased** has a share in the World-to-Come. In interpreting the verse: **"And the eulogizers walk about the marketplace"** (Ecclesiastes 12:5), **the people of the Galilee say: Do things** that you will want people to say at your eulogy **in front of your bier. The people of Judea say: Do things** that you want people to say at your eulogy **behind your bier.** The Gemara remarks: **And they do not disagree;** this **Sage** expressed it according to the norm **in his place, and** this **Sage** expressed it differently according to the norm **in his place.** The custom in the Galilee was that the eulogizers would stand before the bier and the custom in Judea was that eulogizers would stand behind the bier.

תנן התם, רבי אליעזר אומר: שוב יום אחד לפני מיתתך. שאלו תלמידיו את רבי אליעזר: וכי אדם יודע איזהו יום ימות? אמר להן: וכל שכן, ישוב היום שמא ימות למחר, ונמצא כל ימיו בתשובה. ואף שלמה אמר בחכמתו: ״בכל עת יהיו בגדיך לבנים ושמן על ראשך אל יחסר״.

We learned there in a mishna that **Rabbi Eliezer says: Repent one day before your death.**[H] **Rabbi Eliezer's students asked him: But does a person know the day** on which **he will die? He said to them: All the more so** this is a good piece of advice, and **one should repent today lest he die tomorrow; and** by following this advice **one will spend his entire life in** a state of **repentance. And** King **Solomon also said in his wisdom: "At all times your clothes should be white, and oil shall not be absent from upon your head"** (Ecclesiastes 9:8), meaning that a person always needs to be prepared.

אמר רבי יוחנן בן זכאי: משל למלך שזימן את עבדיו לסעודה, ולא קבע להם זמן. פיקחין שבהן קישטו את עצמן וישבו על פתח בית המלך, אמרו: כלום חסר לבית המלך? טיפשין שבהן הלכו למלאכתן, אמרו: כלום יש סעודה בלא טורח?

Similarly, **Rabban Yoḥanan ben Zakkai said** the following story as **a parable** to this lesson: The situation is comparable **to a king who invited his servants to a feast and did not set a time for them** to come. **The wise among them adorned themselves and sat at the entrance to the king's house. They said: Is the king's house missing anything** necessary for the feast? Certainly the king could invite them at any moment. **The fools among them went to** attend to **their work and said: Is there such thing as a feast without** the **toil** of preparing for it? While the feast is being prepared, we will attend to other matters.

בפתאום ביקש המלך את עבדיו. פיקחין שבהן נכנסו לפניו כשהן מקושטין, והטיפשים נכנסו לפניו כשהן מלוכלכין. שמח המלך לקראת פיקחים, וכעס לקראת טיפשים. אמר: הללו שקישטו את עצמן לסעודה – ישבו ויאכלו וישתו, הללו שלא קישטו עצמן לסעודה – יעמדו ויראו.

Suddenly, the king requested that **his servants** come to the feast. **The wise among them entered before him adorned** in their finest clothes, **and the fools entered before him dirty. The king was happy to greet** the **wise ones and angry to greet** the **fools.** The king **said: These** wise servants **who adorned themselves for the feast shall sit and eat and drink,** but **these** fools **who did not adorn themselves for the feast shall stand and watch.** There is a similar outcome for people who think that their day of death and judgment is far away and do not prepare themselves for it.

חתנו של רבי מאיר משום רבי מאיר אמר: אף הן נראין כמשמשין. אלא, אלו ואלו יושבין, הללו – אוכלין, והללו – רעבין, הללו שותין והללו צמאים, שנאמר ״כה אמר ה׳ הנה עבדי יאכלו ואתם תרעבו הנה עבדי ישתו ואתם תצמאו הנה עבדי ירנו מטוב לב ואתם תצעקו מכאב לב״.

Rabbi Meir's son-in-law said in the name of Rabbi Meir: If the punishment for those who did not prepare themselves in advance was merely to stand and watch, it would not be severe enough because **they also look like servants** at the feast, which is not such a disgraceful punishment. **Rather, these and these,** both groups of people, **sit** at the feast.[N] **These** wise and righteous people **eat, and these** wicked fools **are hungry; these** righteous people **drink, and these** wicked people **are thirsty, as it is stated:** "Therefore, **thus said the Lord,** God: **Behold, My servants shall eat and you shall be hungry; behold, My servants shall drink and you shall be thirsty;** behold, My servants shall rejoice and you shall be ashamed. **Behold, My servants shall sing from a joyous heart and you shall scream from a pained heart"** (Isaiah 65:13–14).

דבר אחר: ״בכל עת יהיו בגדיך לבנים״ – אלו ציצית, ״ושמן על ראשך אל יחסר״ – אלו תפילין.

Alternatively, the verse quoted above can be interpreted in the following way: **"At all times let your clothes be white";**[N] **this** is clothing that contains **ritual fringes** [*tzitzit*], which are white. **"And oil shall not be absent from upon your head"; these** words hint to **phylacteries,** which are worn on the head.

הדרן עלך שואל

PERSONALITIES

Rabba in Pumbedita – רבה בפומבדיתא: Rabba was the head of the yeshiva in Pumbedita for many years and was a fearless leader. Since he would not refrain from strongly reprimanding the leaders of the city for their negative character traits, he was not well loved by the local people. However, neither he nor his student Abaye saw fault in this, for Abaye said: If a Sage is beloved by the inhabitants of his city it is not because he is such a great leader, but because he does not rebuke them in matters related to fear of Heaven (*Ketubot* 105b).

HALAKHA

Repent one day before your death – שוב יום אחד לפני מיתתך: A person should always view himself as if death is at hand, and that he may die at any moment in his current sinful state. These thoughts will cause a person to repent immediately. One should not say: When I grow old I will return to God, lest one die before reaching old age. This is the meaning of that which King Solomon said: "At all times your clothes should be white" (Rambam *Sefer HaMadda*, *Hilkhot Teshuva* 7:2).

NOTES

These and these sit at the feast – אלו ואלו יושבין: The midrash similarly states that one who sits at a meal and does not eat suffers more than if he were merely hungry. This is the punishment of the wicked.

Let your clothes be white – בגדיך לבנים: This statement refers to ritual fringes because they are white. Although in past generations the fringes included threads which were dyed sky blue [*tekhelet*], one can fulfill the mitzva with white threads alone when the special sky blue dye is unavailable. The phrase: At all times, is used because the mitzva applies at all times. Similarly, the phrase: Shall not be absent, is the source for the law that one must wear phylacteries on his head even if those which are worn on the arm are unavailable (Maharsha).

Summary of **Perek XXIII**

The discussion in this chapter of the *halakhot* relating to business activity on Shabbat can be summarized as follows: Not only is it forbidden to engage actively in any business activity or transaction on Shabbat, it is prohibited even to speak about such activities, even if they are for the purpose of Shabbat itself. Nonetheless, when necessary for the purpose of Shabbat, the Sages did permit conducting certain business activities in a roundabout fashion, by hinting or by avoiding common business expressions. This leniency stems from the fact that business activity is not inherently prohibited on Shabbat, but rather is forbidden by rabbinic decree. We do not add to rabbinic decrees with additional layers of safeguards meant to distance people from violation. Therefore, in these situations the Sages were satisfied with the requirement that people use particular formulations that would remind them of the sanctity of Shabbat and that would thereby ensure they not violate actual prohibited labors.

This decree against the discussion of monetary matters on Shabbat applies to mundane causes and personal needs. However, it is permissible and even fitting to discuss mitzva causes on Shabbat, even when they include preparation for the performance of prohibited labors after Shabbat; this does not demonstrate disregard for the honor of Shabbat.

Attending to the needs of the deceased is a mitzva and an important way of upholding human dignity. Consequently, the Sages permitted certain activities in order to ensure that the deceased not suffer unnecessary degradation when located in an undignified place, as it is forbidden to move a corpse on Shabbat. Yet, they did not allow burying or even moving a corpse on Shabbat. Although *halakha* is greatly concerned for of the dignity of the deceased, the wellbeing of the living is even more important, as the living are still obligated to fulfill mitzvot. Even the preservation of the dignity of the deceased does not override outright Shabbat prohibitions.

Introduction to **Perek XXIV**

But the seventh day is Shabbat to the Lord your God; you shall not do any manner of work, you, your son, your daughter, your man-servant, your maid-servant, your ox, your donkey, nor any of your cattle, nor your stranger that is within your gates; that your man-servant and your maid-servant may rest as well as you.

(Deuteronomy 5:13)

The *halakhot* discussed in this chapter relate primarily to what may and may not be done for animals on Shabbat. Some of these issues have already been addressed in earlier chapters, and Chapter Five was devoted to clarifying the laws of transporting items that are on an animal from one domain to another on Shabbat. This chapter addresses a more limited and specific issue, namely, the details of the prohibition of driving a laden animal on Shabbat. For example, what is the source of the prohibition? The Gemara considers whether the Torah expressly forbids driving a laden animal, whether the prohibition stems from a rabbinic decree not to make use of animals, or whether it is derived from the positive command to allow animals to rest. Similarly, the chapter examines the severity and scope of this prohibition.

This chapter also explores issues related to the preparation of food for animals on Shabbat. There are several considerations in this regard: One may not perform a labor prohibited by Torah law for the purposes of an animal, just as one may not do so for human beings. However, since it is necessary to care for one's animals, the Gemara clarifies which activities may be performed in order to provide food for them. The chapter seeks to establish the fundamental basis for determining the *halakha* in these cases. It also addresses whether the prohibition of set-aside objects is suspended for the purpose of attending to the needs of animals.

מתני׳ מִי שֶׁהֶחְשִׁיךְ בַּדֶּרֶךְ – נוֹתֵן כִּיסוֹ לַגּוֹי, וְאִם אֵין עִמּוֹ גּוֹי – מַנִּיחוֹ עַל הַחֲמוֹר. הִגִּיעַ לֶחָצֵר הַחִיצוֹנָה – נוֹטֵל אֶת הַכֵּלִים הַנִּיטָּלִין בַּשַּׁבָּת, וְשֶׁאֵינָן נִיטָּלִין בַּשַּׁבָּת – מַתִּיר הַחֲבָלִים, וְהַשַּׂקִּין נוֹפְלִין מֵאֵילֵיהֶם.

MISHNA **One** who was traveling on Shabbat eve and **night fell,** and Shabbat began while he was still **en route,**[H] **gives his** money **pouch to a gentile** traveling with him. **And if there is no gentile with him he places it on the donkey.** Once **he reached the outer courtyard**[H] of the city, where belongings can be securely placed, **he takes the vessels that may be moved on Shabbat** off the donkey. With regard to the vessels **that may not be moved on Shabbat, he unties the ropes** that attach his bags to the donkey, **and the bags** of vessels **fall on their own.**

גמ׳ מַאי טַעְמָא שָׁרוּ לֵיהּ רַבָּנַן לְמֵיתַב כִּיסֵיהּ לַגּוֹי? קִים לְהוּ לְרַבָּנַן דְּאֵין אָדָם מַעֲמִיד עַצְמוֹ עַל מָמוֹנוֹ, אִי לָא שָׁרֵית לֵיהּ – אָתֵי לְאֵיתוּיֵי אַרְבַּע אַמּוֹת בִּרְשׁוּת הָרַבִּים.

GEMARA We learned in the mishna: One who was traveling on Shabbat eve and night fell, and Shabbat began while he was still en route, gives his money pouch to a gentile. The Gemara asks: **What is the reason** that **the Sages permitted him to give his pouch to a gentile?** Is it not prohibited for a Jew to ask a gentile to perform a prohibited labor on Shabbat? The Gemara answers: **The Sages maintain** that **a person does not restrain himself** when faced with losing **his money.**[N] **If you do not permit him** to give his pouch to a gentile, **he will come to carry four cubits in a public domain,** thereby violating a Torah prohibition.

אָמַר רָבָא: דַּוְקָא כִּיסוֹ, אֲבָל מְצִיאָה – לֹא. פְּשִׁיטָא, ״כִּיסוֹ״ תְּנַן! מַהוּ דְּתֵימָא: הוּא הַדִּין אֲפִילּוּ מְצִיאָה, וְהַאי דְּקָתָנֵי כִּיסוֹ – אוֹרְחָא דְּמִילְּתָא קָתָנֵי, קָא מַשְׁמַע לָן. וְלָא אֲמַרַן אֶלָּא דְּלָא אָתֵי לִידֵיהּ, אֲבָל אָתֵי לִידֵיהּ – כְּכִיסֵיהּ דָּמֵי.

Rava said: This allowance to give the pouch to a gentile is **specifically** with regard to **his** own **pouch, but** in the case of **a lost object** that he found, **no,** it was not permitted.[H] The Gemara asks: That is **obvious,** as **we learned** in the mishna: **His pouch,** and nothing else. The Gemara answers: Rava specified this **lest you say** that **the same is true even** with regard to **a lost object,** that one may give it to a gentile on Shabbat, and **the** mishna **taught** the case of **his pouch** merely because it is the **manner** in **which the matter** typically occurs. Therefore, Rava **teaches us** that the mishna is in fact establishing a *halakha* restricted to his pouch. The Gemara comments: **And we only said** that this allowance does not apply to a lost object when **it did not come into his possession** before Shabbat. **However,** if the object already **came into his possession** before Shabbat, **its** legal status is **like** that of **his pouch.**

אִיכָּא דְּאָמְרִי; בָּעֵי רָבָא: מְצִיאָה הַבָּאָה לְיָדוֹ מַהוּ? כֵּיוָן דַּאֲתָא לִידֵיהּ – כְּכִיסֵיהּ דָּמֵי, אוֹ דִּילְמָא: כֵּיוָן דְּלָא טָרַח בַּהּ – לָאו כְּכִיסֵיהּ דָּמֵי? תֵּיקוּ.

Some state this dilemma in a different manner. **Rava raised a dilemma:** With regard to **a lost object that came into his possession** before Shabbat, **what is** the ruling? Is the *halakha* that **since it** already **came into his possession, its** legal status is **like** that of **his pouch? Or perhaps, since he did not exert** himself to acquire **it, its** legal status is **not like** that of **his pouch.** Since he expended no effort, he would be capable of restraining himself even when faced with losing it. Therefore, there is no need for the Sages to permit him to give it to a gentile. The Gemara concludes: **Let** this dilemma **stand** unresolved.

״אֵין עִמּוֹ גּוֹי״. טַעְמָא, דְּאֵין עִמּוֹ גּוֹי, הָא יֵשׁ עִמּוֹ גּוֹי – לַגּוֹי יָהֵיב לֵיהּ. מַאי טַעְמָא? חֲמוֹר אַתָּה מְצוּוֶּה עַל שְׁבִיתָתוֹ, גּוֹי – אִי אַתָּה מְצוּוֶּה עַל שְׁבִיתָתוֹ.

We learned in the mishna: **And if there is no gentile with him** he places it on the donkey. The Gemara infers: **The reason** is specifically because **there is no gentile with him;** if **there is a gentile with him, he gives it to the gentile** and does not place it on a donkey. The Gemara asks: **What is the reason** for this *halakha*? The Gemara answers: With regard to **a donkey** belonging to a Jew, **you are commanded with regard to its rest** on Shabbat. With regard to **a gentile, you are not commanded with regard to his rest** and no Torah prohibition is being violated.

HALAKHA

One who was traveling and night fell while he was en route – מִי שֶׁהֶחְשִׁיךְ בַּדֶּרֶךְ: One who is traveling and Shabbat begins while he is still on the road may give his money to a gentile to carry it for him if there is a gentile traveling with him. If there is no gentile with him, he may place his pouch on the donkey (Rambam *Sefer Zemanim, Hilkhot Shabbat* 6:22; *Shulḥan Arukh, Oraḥ Ḥayyim* 266:1).

Once he reached the outer courtyard – הִגִּיעַ לֶחָצֵר הַחִיצוֹנָה: One who is traveling on Shabbat eve and arrives after nightfall at a location where he can securely leave his belongings, may take the vessels that may be moved on Shabbat from his donkey. With regard to the rest of the vessels, i.e., the vessels that may not be moved on Shabbat, he may untie the ropes that attach his bags to the donkey and let the bags of vessels fall on their own (Rambam *Sefer Zemanim, Hilkhot Shabbat* 21:10; *Shulḥan Arukh, Oraḥ Ḥayyim* 266:9).

Specifically with regard to his own pouch, but in the case of a lost object, no – דַּוְקָא כִּיסוֹ, אֲבָל מְצִיאָה לֹא: One may give a gentile an object that he is carrying on Shabbat if it is one's own property. However, it is prohibited to give a gentile someone else's lost object that one found after Shabbat began (Rambam *Sefer Zemanim, Hilkhot Shabbat* 6:22; *Shulḥan Arukh, Oraḥ Ḥayyim* 266:1).

NOTES

A person does not restrain himself when faced with losing his money – אֵין אָדָם מַעֲמִיד עַצְמוֹ עַל מָמוֹנוֹ: The early commentaries pointed out that the Gemara applied this same principle to prohibit taking objects out of a burning house on Shabbat, and asked why it is cited here as a reason for leniency. They answered that in the case of a house fire, panic reigns and if certain allowances were made, people would allow themselves to remove even prohibited items from the house. In this case, there is no sense of panic, and therefore there is no concern that one will extend the leniency to prohibited items (*Tosefot Rid*).

חמור וחרש שוטה וקטן – אחמור מנח ליה, לחרש שוטה וקטן לא יהיב ליה. מאי טעמא – הני אדם, האי – לאו אדם. חרש ושוטה – לשוטה, שוטה וקטן – לשוטה.

The Gemara teaches an additional *halakha*: If there was no gentile with him but there was **a donkey, a deaf-mute, an imbecile, and a minor,**[H] meaning someone under thirteen years old, **one places it on the donkey,** but **one neither gives it to the deaf-mute, nor the imbecile, nor the minor. What is the reason** for this? Although they are not obligated to fulfill mitzvot, **these** are **people,** but **this** donkey **is not a person.** It is preferable to place it on the donkey rather than give it to a person. And if **a deaf-mute and an imbecile**[HN] were with him, he gives it to **the imbecile.** If **an imbecile and a minor**[H] were with him, he gives it to **the imbecile.**

איבעיא להו: חרש וקטן מאי? אליבא דרבי אליעזר לא תיבעי לך, דתניא, רבי יצחק אומר משום רבי אליעזר: תרומת חרש

A dilemma was raised before the Sages: If **a deaf-mute and a minor**[H] were with him, **what** is the ruling? To whom does he give his pouch? The Gemara answers: **According to** the opinion **of Rabbi Eliezer you have no dilemma.** Rabbi Eliezer holds that a deaf-mute has a greater degree of halakhic intelligence than does a minor, **as it was taught** in a *baraita*: **Rabbi Yitzḥak says in the name of Rabbi Eliezer: The *teruma* of a deaf-mute** that he separated from his produce

HALAKHA

A donkey, a deaf-mute, an imbecile, and a minor – חמור וחרש שוטה וקטן: One who was traveling and Shabbat began, and a donkey, a deaf-mute, an imbecile, and a minor were alongside him, should place his pouch on the donkey rather than hand it to the deaf-mute, the imbecile, or the minor, because it is preferable to place it on an animal rather than give it to a person (Rambam *Sefer Zemanim, Hilkhot Shabbat* 20:7; *Shulḥan Arukh, Oraḥ Ḥayyim* 266:3).

A deaf-mute and an imbecile – חרש ושוטה: One who was traveling with a deaf-mute and an imbecile should give his pouch to the imbecile, who is completely lacking in halakhic intelligence (Rambam *Sefer Zemanim, Hilkhot Shabbat* 20:6; *Shulḥan Arukh, Oraḥ Ḥayyim* 266:4).

An imbecile and a minor – שוטה וקטן: A minor will possess halakhic intelligence and be obligated to observe mitzvot when he reaches majority. Therefore, one who is traveling with an imbecile and a minor should give his pouch to the imbecile, even though the minor is not currently obligated to observe mitzvot (Rambam *Sefer Zemanim, Hilkhot Shabbat* 20:6; *Shulḥan Arukh, Oraḥ Ḥayyim* 266:5).

A deaf-mute and a minor – חרש וקטן: One who is traveling with a deaf-mute and a minor may give his pouch to whomever he prefers. As the dilemma in the Gemara was not resolved, both the Rif and the Rosh ruled that one may act in accordance with either possibility (Rambam *Sefer Zemanim, Hilkhot Shabbat* 20:6; *Shulḥan Arukh, Oraḥ Ḥayyim* 266:5).

NOTES

A deaf-mute and an imbecile – חרש ושוטה: When the Sages refer to an imbecile they mean someone who has no halakhic intelligence at all, and is therefore exempt from all mitzvot and liabilities and has the halakhic status of an animal (Rabbeinu Ḥananel). However, since he is a human being, one may not place an object on him as one may on an animal. When they refer to a deaf-mute they mean someone whose halakhic intelligence is limited. This was a consequence of the deaf-mute's inability to communicate with his surroundings in ancient times. Although he is not obligated in mitzvot, the Sages imposed certain strictures with regard to him, and there are circumstances in which he can even facilitate the fulfillment of mitzvot by others.

Perek **XXIV**
Daf **153** Amud **b**

לא תצא לחולין, מפני שהוא ספק.

does not vacate its sanctified status and assume **non-sacred** status **because his** status with regard to halakhic intelligence **is uncertain.** According to Rabbi Eliezer, a deaf-mute apparently has a degree of halakhic intelligence, and therefore has a greater obligation in mitzvot than a minor.

כי תיבעי לך – אליבא דרבנן, דתנן: חמשה לא יתרומו, ואם תרמו אין תרומתן תרומה. אלו הן: חרש שוטה וקטן, והתורם את שאינו שלו, וגוי שתרם את של ישראל אפילו ברשותו – אין תרומתו תרומה.

When you raise this dilemma, the issue **is in accordance with** the opinion of **the Rabbis, as we learned** in a mishna: There are **five** categories of people who **may not separate *teruma***[NH] *ab initio*, **and if they separated *teruma*, their *teruma* is not** considered ***teruma*. They are: A deaf-mute, an imbecile, and a minor, and one who separates *teruma*** from produce **that is not his; and a gentile who separated *teruma*** from the produce **of a Jew, even with his permission, his *teruma* is not** considered ***teruma*** because a gentile cannot be appointed as an agent to separate *teruma*, and all the more so he cannot separate *teruma* on his own. The deaf-mute and the minor have the same legal status according to the Rabbis; therefore, a dilemma arises as to which of them should receive the pouch on Shabbat.

מאי, לחרש יהיב ליה – דקטן אתי לכלל דעת, או דילמא: לקטן יהיב ליה, דחרש אתי לאחלופי בגדול פיקח? איכא דאמרי: לחרש יהיב ליה, איכא דאמרי: לקטן יהיב ליה.

What should one do? Should **he give it to the deaf-mute** because **the minor** will eventually **reach the stage of** halakhic **intelligence,** when he will be obligated to observe the mitzvot, and it is preferable that he not become accustomed to desecrating Shabbat? **Or perhaps** he should **give it to the minor,** because if he is allowed to give it to the **deaf-mute,** onlookers **will mistake him for an adult with** halakhic **intelligence** and conclude that it is permitted to give his pouch to an adult? In that case it would be preferable to give the pouch to a minor, as it is clear that he is not obligated in mitzvot. Regarding this *halakha*, **some say** that **he gives it to the deaf-mute** and **some say** that **he gives it to the minor,** and no definitive conclusion was reached.

NOTES

Five categories of people who may not separate *teruma* – חמשה לא יתרומו: It is explained in the Jerusalem Talmud in tractate *Terumot* that these categories are derived from the verse: "Speak to the children of Israel, that they take for Me an offering [*teruma*]; of every man whose heart makes him willing you shall take My offering. And this is the offering which you shall take of them" (Exodus 25:2–3). The phrase "the children of Israel" excludes gentiles; the phrase "from every man" excludes minors; the phrase "whose heart makes him willing" excludes imbeciles and deaf-mutes who lack the heart, i.e., the halakhic intelligence, to volunteer; and the phrase "that you shall take from them" excludes one who separates *teruma* from property that does not belong to him.

HALAKHA

Five categories of people who may not separate *teruma* – חמשה לא יתרומו: There are five categories of people whose separation of *teruma* is not considered *teruma*. They are: A deaf-mute, an imbecile, a minor, a gentile who separated *teruma* on behalf of a Jew, and a Jew who separated *teruma* from someone else's produce without the owner's consent (Rambam *Sefer Zera'im, Hilkhot Terumot* 4:2; *Shulḥan Arukh, Yoreh De'a* 331:30).

אֵין שָׁם לֹא גּוֹי וְלֹא חֲמוֹר וְלֹא חֵרֵשׁ וְלֹא שׁוֹטֶה וְלֹא קָטָן, מַאי? אָמַר רַבִּי יִצְחָק: עוֹד אַחֶרֶת הָיְתָה, וְלֹא רָצוּ חֲכָמִים לְגַלּוֹתָהּ. מַאי ״עוֹד אַחֶרֶת הָיְתָה״ – מוֹלִיכוֹ פָּחוֹת פָּחוֹת מֵאַרְבַּע אַמּוֹת. אַמַּאי לֹא רָצוּ חֲכָמִים לְגַלּוֹתָהּ – מִשּׁוּם ״כְּבוֹד אֱלֹהִים הַסְתֵּר דָּבָר וּכְבוֹד מְלָכִים חֲקוֹר דָּבָר״. וְהָכָא, מַאי ״כְּבוֹד אֱלֹהִים״ אִיכָּא? דִּילְמָא אָתֵי לְאַתּוֹיֵי אַרְבַּע אַמּוֹת בִּרְשׁוּת הָרַבִּים.

The Gemara asks: If **there is neither a gentile nor a donkey nor a deaf-mute nor an imbecile nor a minor there, what** should one do? **Rabbi Yitzḥak said: There was another manner** of dealing with this situation, **and the Sages did not want to reveal it.** The Gemara asks: To **what** was Rabbi Yitzḥak referring when he said: **There was another manner?** The Gemara answers: The alternative is to **move** the pouch in increments, **each less than four cubits,**[H] and thereby carry the object in the public domain without violating a Torah prohibition. The Gemara asks: **Why didn't the Sages want to reveal this** alternative? The Gemara answers that it is **due to** the verse: **"It is the glory of God to conceal a thing; but the glory of kings is to search out a matter"** (Proverbs 25:2). **And here, what glory of God is there** in concealing this option? The Gemara answers: If one were to move the pouch in this manner, there is concern **lest** he **come to carry** the object **four cubits in the public domain.**

תַּנְיָא, רַבִּי אֱלִיעֶזֶר אוֹמֵר: בּוֹ בַּיּוֹם גָּדְשׁוּ סְאָה. רַבִּי יְהוֹשֻׁעַ אוֹמֵר: בּוֹ בַּיּוֹם מָחֲקוּ סְאָה.

The ruling that one should give his pouch to a gentile rather than carry in increments each less than four cubits was among the eighteen decrees issued in accordance with the position of Beit Shammai, enumerated in the first chapter of tractate *Shabbat*. Sages of later generations disagreed with regard to these eighteen decrees: **It was taught** in a *baraita* that **Rabbi Eliezer says: On that day they** measured with **a large *se'a***[N] measurement, i.e., they did well to issue these decrees, which construct a fence around the Torah to prevent its violation. **Rabbi Yehoshua said: On that very day they** measured with a **minimal *se'a*,** i.e., because these decrees are difficult to observe, they not only will lead people to violate the decrees, but to violate Torah prohibitions as well.

תַּנְיָא, מָשָׁל דְּרַבִּי אֱלִיעֶזֶר, לְמָה הַדָּבָר דּוֹמֶה – לְקוּפָּה מְלֵאָה קִישּׁוּאִין וּדְלוּעִין, אָדָם נוֹתֵן לְתוֹכָהּ חַרְדָּל – וְהִיא מַחֲזֶקֶת. מָשָׁל דְּרַבִּי יְהוֹשֻׁעַ, לְמָה הַדָּבָר דּוֹמֶה – לַעֲרֵיבָה מְלֵאָה דְּבַשׁ, נוֹתֵן לְתוֹכָהּ רִימּוֹנִים וֶאֱגוֹזִים – וְהִיא מְקִיאָה.

It was taught in another *baraita*: The Sages articulated **a parable** to illustrate the opinion of **Rabbi Eliezer. To what is this matter similar?** It is similar **to a basket full of squash and gourds into which a person places mustard seeds.** Just as the basket also **holds** the mustard, the decree will also endure. They also articulated **a parable** to illustrate the opinion of **Rabbi Yehoshua: To what is this matter similar?** It is similar **to a large bowl full of honey into which** one **places pomegranates and walnuts.** Just as the bowl **expels** the honey from inside it, so too, the decree will cause Torah prohibitions to be violated.

אָמַר מָר: אֵין עִמּוֹ גּוֹי – מַנִּיחוֹ עַל הַחֲמוֹר. וְהָא מְחַמֵּר, וְרַחֲמָנָא אָמַר ״לֹא תַעֲשֶׂה כׇל מְלָאכָה״!

We learned in the mishna that **the Master said:** When **there is no gentile with him, one places** the pouch **on the donkey.** The Gemara asks: **Isn't he** thereby **driving** a laden **animal? And the Torah stated:** "And the seventh day is Shabbat for the Lord your God, **you shall not perform any manner of labor,** neither you, nor your son, nor your daughter, nor your slave, nor your maidservant, nor your animal, nor your stranger that is within your gates" (Exodus 20:10). He is causing the prohibited labors of carrying from domain to domain and of carrying in the public domain by placing the pouch on his donkey on Shabbat.

אָמַר רַב אַדָּא בַּר אַהֲבָה: מַנִּיחוֹ עָלֶיהָ כְּשֶׁהִיא מְהַלֶּכֶת. וְהָא אִי אֶפְשָׁר דְּלָא קָיְימָא לְהַשְׁתִּין מַיִם וּלְהָטִיל גְּלָלִים, וְאִיכָּא עֲקִירָה וְהַנָּחָה! כְּשֶׁהִיא מְהַלֶּכֶת – מַנִּיחוֹ עָלֶיהָ, כְּשֶׁהִיא עוֹמֶדֶת – נוֹטְלוֹ הֵימֶנָּה. אִי הָכִי, אֲפִילּוּ חֲבֵרוֹ נָמֵי!

Rav Adda bar Ahava said: One places the pouch **on** the donkey **as it is walking,**[H] because in doing so he does not commit a full-fledged violation of the Torah prohibition against carrying out from domain to domain on Shabbat. A full-fledged violation consists of lifting and placing the object. Because the animal was already walking when the pouch was placed on it, the animal performed no lifting. The Gemara asks: **Isn't it impossible** that the animal **will not stand** in its place at some point after it begins walking, either in order **to urinate or to defecate, and** when it begins walking again **there is** both an act of **lifting and** an act of **placing** performed by the donkey. The Gemara answers: There is a solution to that problem. **When** the donkey **is walking, one places** the pouch **on it,** and **when it stands, he removes it.** The Gemara asks: **If so,** one could **even** place the pouch **on another** Jew **as well,** as there would be neither lifting nor placing.

אָמַר רַב פָּפָּא: כֹּל שֶׁבְּגוּפוֹ חַיָּיב חַטָּאת – בַּחֲבֵרוֹ פָּטוּר אֲבָל אָסוּר, כֹּל שֶׁחֲבֵרוֹ פָּטוּר אֲבָל אָסוּר – בַּחֲמוֹרוֹ מוּתָּר לְכַתְּחִלָּה.

Rav Pappa said: Any action **that** if one performs it **by himself, he is liable**[H] to bring **a sin-offering** for it, if he performed it **by means of another,** he is **exempt but** it is still **prohibited** for him to do so. And **any** action **that** if performed by means of **another,** he is **exempt** from bringing a sin-offering **but** it is still **prohibited** for him to do so, performing the action **by means of his donkey is permitted *ab initio*.**

HALAKHA

Move the pouch in increments, each less than four cubits – מוֹלִיכוֹ פָּחוֹת פָּחוֹת מֵאַרְבַּע אַמּוֹת: One who is traveling with money on Shabbat eve, and has neither a gentile, nor a donkey, nor a deaf-mute, nor an imbecile, nor a minor with him at nightfall, may carry it in increments smaller than four cubits until he reaches his destination (Rambam *Sefer Zemanim, Hilkhot Shabbat* 20:7; *Shulḥan Arukh, Oraḥ Ḥayyim* 266:7).

One places the pouch on the donkey as it is walking – מַנִּיחוֹ עָלֶיהָ כְּשֶׁהִיא מְהַלֶּכֶת: When placing his pouch atop an animal on Shabbat, one must place it while the animal is walking and remove it when the animal stops. When the animal starts moving again he places it again. He does so to avoid performing a full-fledged act of carrying, which would consist of lifting and placing (Rambam *Sefer Zemanim, Hilkhot Shabbat* 20:6; *Shulḥan Arukh, Oraḥ Ḥayyim* 266:2).

Any action that if one performs it by himself he is liable – כֹּל שֶׁבְּגוּפוֹ חַיָּיב: If one lifts an object on Shabbat and places it on another person while that person is walking, and then takes it from him before that person stops, neither person is liable, even if they were walking from one domain to another. This is because there was no full-fledged act of carrying, which would consist of lifting and placing (Rambam *Sefer Zemanim, Hilkhot Shabbat* 13:12).

NOTES

On that day they measured with a large *se'a* – בּוֹ בַּיּוֹם גָּדְשׁוּ סְאָה: *Tosafot* understand the dispute between Rabbi Eliezer and Rabbi Yehoshua to be limited to the decree requiring one to give his pouch to a gentile on Shabbat. Others explain that the rest of the eighteen decrees were motivated by concern for ritual impurity or for violation of a prohibition. However, in this case it is possible to avoid carrying in the public domain by carrying the pouch in increments of less than four cubits. Therefore, the decree requiring one to give his pouch to a gentile can be considered an added stricture that people will not be able to fulfill and that will cause them to carry the pouch four cubits, thereby violating a Torah prohibition (Maharsha).

אָמַר רַב אַדָּא בַּר אַהֲבָה: הָיְתָה חֲבִילָתוֹ מוּנַּחַת לוֹ עַל כְּתֵיפוֹ – רָץ תַּחְתֶּיהָ עַד שֶׁמַּגִּיעַ לְבֵיתוֹ. דַּוְקָא רָץ, אֲבָל קַלֵּי קַלֵּי – לָא.

Rav Adda bar Ahava said: One who was traveling on Shabbat eve and **his package was resting on his shoulder**[NH] as night fell, **he runs beneath it,** i.e., with his package on his shoulder, **until he reaches his home.** The Gemara infers: **Specifically** one **runs** until he reaches home; **however,** walking **a little bit** at a time, **no,** he may not do so.

מַאי טַעְמָא? כֵּיוָן דְּלֵית לֵיהּ הֶיכֵּירָא – אָתֵי לְמֵיעֲבַד עֲקִירָה וְהַנָּחָה. סוֹף סוֹף, כִּי מָטֵא לְבֵיתֵיהּ אִי אֶפְשָׁר דְּלָא קָאֵי פּוּרְתָּא, וְקָמְעַיֵּיל מֵרְשׁוּת הָרַבִּים לִרְשׁוּת הַיָּחִיד! דְּזָרֵיק לֵיהּ כִּלְאַחַר יָד.

The Gemara asks: **What is the reason** for this? **Since,** when walking in the usual manner, **he has no conspicuous** reminder that it is Shabbat, there is concern lest **he come to** perform the acts of **lifting and placing** by stopping to rest on his way home. The Gemara asks: **Ultimately, when he reaches his home, it is impossible that** he will **not** stop and **stand a bit, and** at that point, **he** will have performed the prohibited labor of **carrying** the package **from the public domain into the private domain** of his house. The Gemara answers: This is referring to a case in which he does not place the package in the typical manner when he reaches his home. Rather, **he throws it** down **in an unusual manner.** Since he did not perform the action in the typical manner, it is not prohibited by Torah law.

אָמַר רָמִי בַּר חָמָא: הַמְחַמֵּר אַחַר בְּהֶמְתּוֹ בְּשַׁבָּת, בְּשׁוֹגֵג – חַיָּיב חַטָּאת, בְּמֵזִיד – חַיָּיב סְקִילָה. מַאי טַעְמָא? אָמַר רָבָא: דְּאָמַר קְרָא ״לֹא תַעֲשֶׂה כׇל מְלָאכָה אַתָּה וּבְהֶמְתֶּךָ״ בְּהֶמְתּוֹ דּוּמְיָא דִּידֵיהּ, מָה הוּא – בְּשׁוֹגֵג חַיָּיב חַטָּאת, בְּמֵזִיד חַיָּיב סְקִילָה, אַף בְּהֶמְתּוֹ נַמִי, בְּשׁוֹגֵג – חַיָּיב חַטָּאת, בְּמֵזִיד – חַיָּיב סְקִילָה.

With regard to the topic of driving a donkey on Shabbat, the Gemara cites that which **Rami bar Ḥama said:** With regard to **one who drives his** laden **animal on Shabbat,** if he does so **unwittingly, he is liable** to bring a **sin-offering,** and if he does so **intentionally, he is liable** to be executed by **stoning.** The Gemara asks: **What is the reason** for this ruling? **Rava said that the verse states: "You shall not perform any manner of labor, neither you…nor your animal"** (Exodus 20:10). From this he derived: **His animal** is **similar to himself; just as he,** if he performed a prohibited labor on Shabbat **unwittingly, he is liable** to bring a **sin-offering,** and if he did so **intentionally, he is liable** to be executed by **stoning, so too,** if he performed a prohibited labor by means of **his animal,** if he did so **unwittingly, he is liable** to bring a **sin-offering,** and if he did so **intentionally, he is liable** to be executed by **stoning.**

אָמַר רָבָא: שְׁתֵּי תְשׁוּבוֹת בַּדָּבָר; חֲדָא: דִּכְתִיב ״תּוֹרָה אַחַת יִהְיֶה לָכֶם לָעוֹשֶׂה בִּשְׁגָגָה וְהַנֶּפֶשׁ אֲשֶׁר תַּעֲשֶׂה בְּיָד רָמָה״ הוּקְּשָׁה כׇּל הַתּוֹרָה כּוּלָּהּ לַעֲבוֹדָה זָרָה, מָה עֲבוֹדָה זָרָה – דְּעָבֵיד מַעֲשֶׂה בְּגוּפֵיהּ, הָכָא נַמִי – עַד דְּעָבֵיד מַעֲשֶׂה בְּגוּפֵיהּ.

Rava said: There are **two** possible **responses** with which this **statement** can be rejected. **One** is, **as it is written: "You shall have one law** [*Torah*] **for him that does unwittingly…** and for the proselyte who resides among them. **But the soul that does with a high hand,** whether he be home-born or a stranger, he blasphemes the Lord; and that soul shall be cut off from among his people" (Numbers 15:29–30). This verse is referring to one who worships idolatry unwittingly. **The entire Torah is juxtaposed to idolatry,** and from that juxtaposition it is derived: **Just as** in the case of **idolatry** one is liable only **when he performs an action with his body,**[N] i.e., himself, **here too,** in the case of Shabbat, he is liable **only if he performs an action with his body,** i.e., himself. He is not liable for an action performed by his animal.

וְעוֹד, תְּנַן: הַמְחַלֵּל אֶת הַשַּׁבָּת בְּדָבָר שֶׁחַיָּיבִין עַל שִׁגְגָתוֹ חַטָּאת וְעַל זְדוֹנוֹ סְקִילָה, מִכְּלָל דְּאִיכָּא מִידֵּי דְּאֵין חַיָּיבִין עַל שִׁגְגָתוֹ חַטָּאת וְלֹא עַל זְדוֹנוֹ סְקִילָה.

And furthermore, with regard to the statement that if he drove the laden donkey he is liable to be executed by stoning, **we learned** in a mishna that enumerates those who are executed by stoning: **One who desecrates Shabbat**[H] **by** performing **a matter that for its unwitting** performance one is **liable** to bring **a sin-offering, and for its intentional** performance one is **liable** to be executed by **stoning. By inference, there is** another **matter,** another prohibition, **that for which its unwitting** performance one is **not liable** to bring **a sin-offering, and for which its intentional** performance one is **not liable to be executed by stoning.**

וּמַאי נִיהוּ, לָאו דִּמְחַמֵּר? לָא, תְּחוּמִין וְאַלִּיבָּא דְּרַבִּי עֲקִיבָא, וְהַבְעָרָה אַלִּיבָּא דְּרַבִּי יוֹסֵי.

And what is that Torah prohibition? Is it not the **prohibition** of **driving** a laden **animal?**[N] Apparently, driving a laden animal and other labors performed by means of animals on Shabbat are not punishable by stoning, even though they are prohibited by Torah law. The Gemara rejects this second proof. **No,** this is not necessarily so. It is possible that the mishna is referring to the prohibition of Shabbat **limits, and** it is **in accordance with** the opinion **of Rabbi Akiva,** who holds that it is a Torah prohibition but that one is neither liable to bring a sin-offering for violating it unwittingly, nor is he liable to be executed by stoning for violating it intentionally. **And** likewise, it may refer to the prohibition of **kindling** a fire on Shabbat **in accordance with** the opinion of **Rabbi Yosei,** who holds that it is not punishable by stoning but by lashes, like other prohibitions.

NOTES

His package was resting on his shoulder – הָיְתָה חֲבִילָתוֹ מוּנַּחַת לוֹ עַל כְּתֵיפוֹ: Here the Gemara does not suggest the solution of carrying the package in increments of less than four cubits, because the Gemara is discussing a large package, which would make it difficult for the person carrying it to stop so frequently (*Me'iri*). The Sages did not permit running with one's pouch as they did with a package, because the weight of the package would serve as a conspicuous reminder to continue running. Since a pouch is small, there is concern that even if he ran with it he might forget and end up carrying it in the usual manner (Rambam).

When he performs an action with his body – דְּעָבֵיד מַעֲשֶׂה בְּגוּפֵיהּ: There is a fundamental rule throughout the Torah that one is liable to be punished only for violating prohibitions that he himself performed. Although in monetary matters one is liable for damage caused by his animal, that liability does not extend to corporal or capital punishment.

The prohibition of driving a laden animal – לָאו דִּמְחַמֵּר: The essence of the Gemara's question here is based on the assumption that a Shabbat prohibition for which one does not incur severe punishment is certainly not one of the standard prohibited labors, but rather one that is independent of the standard prohibited labors. Therefore, it is reasonable to posit that that this exceptional prohibition is the prohibition of performing labor by means of an animal on Shabbat. Even in rejecting the difficulty raised, the Gemara identifies other anomalous Shabbat prohibitions, e.g., going beyond the Shabbat limits, or kindling a fire according to the opinion of Rabbi Yosei.

HALAKHA

His package was resting on his shoulder – הָיְתָה חֲבִילָתוֹ מוּנַּחַת לוֹ עַל כְּתֵיפוֹ: One who is carrying a package on his shoulder when Shabbat begins should run home with the package. This is permitted only if he runs; walking with the package in his usual manner is prohibited, lest he forget that it is Shabbat and perform the prohibited labor of carrying by lifting and placing. When he reaches his home, he throws the package down in an unusual manner, by dropping it behind him off his shoulder, because in that way he does not perform an act of placing prohibited by Torah law (Rambam *Sefer Zemanim, Hilkhot Shabbat* 13:9; *Shulḥan Arukh, Oraḥ Ḥayyim* 266:11).

One who desecrates Shabbat – הַמְחַלֵּל אֶת הַשַּׁבָּת: One who desecrates Shabbat unwittingly is liable to bring a sin-offering. If he did so intentionally he is punishable by *karet*, and if there are witnesses and forewarning, he is liable to be executed by stoning (Rambam *Sefer Zemanim, Hilkhot Shabbat* 1:1).

רַב זְבִיד מַתְנֵי הָכִי, אָמַר רָמִי בַּר חָמָא: הַמְחַמֵּר אַחַר בְּהֵמָה בְּשַׁבָּת, בְּשׁוֹגֵג – אֵינוֹ חַיָּיב חַטָּאת, בְּמֵזִיד – חַיָּיב סְקִילָה.

Rav Zevid taught this **as follows. Rami bar Ḥama said:** With regard to **one who drives his** laden **animal on Shabbat,**[H] if he does so **unwittingly, he is liable** to bring **a sin-offering,** and if he does so **intentionally, he is liable** to be executed by **stoning.**

מְתִיב רָבָא: הַמְחַלֵּל אֶת הַשַּׁבָּת בְּדָבָר שֶׁחַיָּיבִין עַל שִׁגְגָתוֹ חַטָּאת – חַיָּיבִין עַל זְדוֹנוֹ סְקִילָה. הָא אֵין חַיָּיבִין עַל שִׁגְגָתוֹ חַטָּאת – אֵין חַיָּיבִין עַל זְדוֹנוֹ סְקִילָה!

Rava raised an objection based on that which was taught in a *baraita*: **One who desecrates Shabbat by** performing **a matter that for its unwitting** performance one is **liable** to bring **a sin-offering,** then **for its intentional** performance one is **liable** to be executed by **stoning.** The Gemara explains: By inference, for **a matter that for its unwitting** performance one is **not liable** to bring **a sin-offering, for its intentional** performance one is **not liable** to be executed by **stoning.** This contradicts Rami bar Ḥama's statement.

מִי קָתָנֵי "הָא אֵין חַיָּיבִין כו׳"? הָכִי קָאָמַר: דָּבָר שֶׁחַיָּיבִין עַל שִׁגְגָתוֹ חַטָּאת – חַיָּיבִין עַל זְדוֹנוֹ סְקִילָה, וְיֵשׁ דָּבָר שֶׁאֵין חַיָּיבִין עַל שִׁגְגָתוֹ חַטָּאת – וְחַיָּיבִין עַל זְדוֹנוֹ סְקִילָה, וּמַאי נִיהוּ – מְחַמֵּר.

The Gemara answers: **Was it taught** in the *baraita*: By inference, for a matter that for its unwitting performance one is **not liable** to bring a sin-offering, for its intentional performance one is not liable to be executed by stoning? The *baraita* can be understood differently, **and this is what it is saying:** With regard to **a matter that for its unwitting** performance one is **liable** to bring **a sin-offering, for its intentional** performance one is always **liable** to be executed by **stoning.** However, **there is** also **a matter that for its unwitting** performance one is **not liable** to bring **a sin-offering,** and nevertheless, **for its intentional** performance one is **liable to be executed by stoning. And what is that** case? It is the case of **driving** a laden **animal.**

רָבָא אֲחוּהּ דְּרַב מָרִי בַּר רָחֵל, וְאָמְרִי לַהּ אֲבוּהּ דְּרַב מָרִי בַּר רָחֵל. לְלִישָּׁנָא בָּתְרָא קַשְׁיָא, הָא דְּרַב אַכְשְׁרֵיהּ לְרַב מָרִי בַּר רָחֵל וּמַנְּיֵיהּ בְּפוּרְסֵיהּ דְּבָבֶל. דִּילְמָא תְּרֵי מָרִי בַּר רָחֵל הֲווּ.

Rava, the brother of Rav Mari bar Raḥel,[P] cites a different opinion with regard to the *halakha* of driving a laden animal on Shabbat, **and some say** that he was **the father of Rav Mari bar Raḥel** and stated this *halakha*. As an aside, the Gemara comments: **According to the latter version** above, that Rava was the father of Rav Mari bar Raḥel, the fact **that Rav** needed to **validate** the status of **Rav Mari bar Raḥel**[N] **and** only then **appoint him as an official [*pursei*]**[L] **of Babylonia is difficult.** This incident teaches that Rav Mari bar Raḥel's father was not Jewish, and before he could be appointed his status required validation through the fact that his mother was Jewish. If Rav Mari bar Raḥel's father was a sage named Rava, why was it necessary to validate his status by means of his mother's lineage? The Gemara answers: **Perhaps there were two** people named **Mari bar Raḥel.** One was the son of a convert and a Jewish mother, and the other was the son of a Sage named Rava.

הֲוָה מַתְנֵי לַהּ לְהָא שְׁמַעְתֵּיהּ מִשְּׁמֵיהּ דְּרַבִּי יוֹחָנָן לִפְטוֹר; אָמַר רַבִּי יוֹחָנָן: הַמְחַמֵּר אַחַר בְּהֶמְתּוֹ בַּשַּׁבָּת – פָּטוּר מִכְּלוּם.

In any event, that Sage **taught his *halakha* in the name of Rabbi Yoḥanan to exempt** one who drives a laden animal, as **Rabbi Yoḥanan said: One who drives a** laden **animal on Shabbat is exempt from any** punishment.

HALAKHA

Working with one's animal on Shabbat – עֲבוֹדָה בִּבְהֶמְתּוֹ בְּשַׁבָּת: It is prohibited to have an animal carry out a burden on Shabbat, as it is stated: "That your ox and your donkey may rest" (Exodus 23:12). One who has his animal carry out a burden on Shabbat does not receive lashes, because it is a prohibition that stems from a positive commandment and he is only liable to receive lashes for violating a negative commandment. One who drives a laden animal on Shabbat is exempt, because he did not perform the prohibited labor himself. However, it is still prohibited to do so (Rambam *Sefer Zemanim, Hilkhot Shabbat* 20:1).

NOTES

Rav needed to validate the status of Rav Mari – אַכְשְׁרֵיהּ לְרַב מָרִי דְּרַב: The Sages interpreted the verse: "From among your brethren you shall set yourself a king" (Deuteronomy 17:15), to mean that only one born Jewish can be crowned king or appointed to any other position of authority. Even a convert, who is a full-fledged Jew and obligated in all of the mitzvot, cannot be appointed to those positions. Rav ruled that one born to a Jewish mother and a non-Jewish father can be appointed to positions of authority other than king.

LANGUAGE

Official [*pursei*] – פּוּרְסֵיהּ: From the Greek ἔφορος, *eforos*, meaning supervisor, official, or clerk.

PERSONALITIES

Rav Mari bar Raḥel – רַב מָרִי בַּר רָחֵל: He is also called Rav Mari, son of Shmuel's daughter, and was a Babylonian *amora* in the generation of Rava. Rav Mari's unusual appellation can be understood in the context of Shmuel's family history. Shmuel's daughters were abducted and two of them were brought to Eretz Yisrael, where one was taken by a gentile who later converted. He was known as Issur the convert and was a confidant of the prominent Jewish leaders of the generation in Babylonia. His son Rav Mari is attributed genealogically to his mother, rather than to his father, since Issur converted after Rav Mari was conceived. Other Sages born to well-known mothers from prominent families were also known by their mothers' names, unrelated to problematic lineage. Since Rava is a combination of the title, Rav, and the name, Abba, Rav Mari could not have been both the son of the Sage Rava and the son of Issur the convert. The version that identifies his father as Rava is referring to a different Rav Mari bar Raḥel, who was known by the name of his mother for a different reason.

Rav Mari the son of Shmuel's daughter was apparently a wealthy merchant, in addition to being a prominent Sage worthy of being appointed as an official in Babylonia. Rav Mari had three sons who were Sages: Rav Aḥa Sabba, Mar Zutra, and Rava bar Rav Mari.

בְּשׁוֹגֵג לָא מִחַיַּיב חַטָּאת – דְּהוּקְשָׁה כָּל הַתּוֹרָה כּוּלָּהּ לַעֲבוֹדָה זָרָה. בְּמֵזִיד נַמִי לָא מִיחַיַּיב – דִּתְנַן: הַמְחַלֵּל אֶת הַשַּׁבָּת בְּדָבָר שֶׁחַיָּיבִין עַל שִׁגְגָתוֹ חַטָּאת וְעַל זְדוֹנוֹ סְקִילָה. הָא אֵין חַיָּיבִין עַל שִׁגְגָתוֹ חַטָּאת – אֵין חַיָּיבִין עַל זְדוֹנוֹ סְקִילָה.

The Gemara explains: For driving the animal **unwittingly, he is not liable** to bring **a sin-offering** because **all of** the prohibitions in **the Torah were juxtaposed to** the prohibition of **idolatry,** from which the principle is derived that one is liable only for actions that he himself performed. And for driving the animal **intentionally, he is also not liable** to be executed by stoning, **as we learned** in the mishna: **One who desecrates Shabbat by** performing **a matter that for its unwitting** performance one is **liable** to bring **a sin-offering, and for its intentional** performance one is **liable to be executed by stoning.** By inference, for **a matter that for its unwitting** performance one is **not liable** to bring **a sin-offering, for its intentional** performance one is **not liable** to be executed by **stoning.**

בְּלָאו נַמִי לָא מִיחַיַּיב, דַּהֲוָה לֵיהּ לָאו שֶׁנִּיתַּן לְאַזְהָרַת מִיתַת בֵּית דִּין, וְכָל לָאו שֶׁנִּיתַּן לְאַזְהָרַת מִיתַת בֵּית דִּין – אֵין לוֹקִין עָלָיו.

And similarly, **he is not** even **liable** to be flogged **for** violating a Torah **prohibition** for which the punishment is lashes. Even though the Torah explicitly warns against performing labor on Shabbat, **it is a prohibition that was** fundamentally **given,** not as a standard prohibition punishable by lashes, but rather **as a warning of court-imposed capital punishment, and** for **any prohibition that was given as a warning of court-imposed capital punishment,**[N] if the death penalty is not imposed for any reason, **one is not flogged for its** violation.

NOTES

A prohibition that was given as a warning of court-imposed capital punishment – לָאו שֶׁנִּיתַּן לְאַזְהָרַת מִיתַת בֵּית דִּין: In principle, one who violates a Torah prohibition after being forewarned by witnesses is flogged with forty lashes. However, there are certain categories of prohibitions for which one is not punished with lashes. One such type is called a prohibition that was given as a warning of court-imposed capital punishment. In other words, a prohibition whose punishment is explicitly articulated in the Torah as court-imposed capital punishment is excluded from the punishment of lashes. This is patently clear in a case where one is actually sentenced to death. Based on the principle that two punishments are not imposed for one transgression, the one being punished receives the more severe punishment, i.e., execution. The same principle applies to a case where the death sentence cannot be administered for some reason, e.g., where there was no forewarning. Since this prohibition possesses an element of the death penalty, it is classified as a prohibition that was given as a warning of court-imposed capital punishment, and there is no possibility of punishment by lashes.

Perek **XXIV**
Daf **154** Amud **b**

וַאֲפִילּוּ לְמַאן דַּאֲמַר לוֹקִין לִיכְתּוֹב רַחֲמָנָא ״לֹא תַעֲשֶׂה כָּל מְלָאכָה וּבְהֶמְתֶּךָ״, ״אַתָּה״ לָמָּה לִי? הוּא נִיהוּ דְּמִיחַיַּיב, בְּהֶמְתּוֹ – לָא מִיחַיַּיב.

And even according to the one who said that **one is flogged** for violating a prohibition that was given as a warning of court-imposed capital punishment, the *halakha* with regard to driving a laden animal can be derived by means of an inference from the language of the verse. **Let the Torah write: "You shall not perform any manner of labor… and** neither shall **your animal." Why do I need** the superfluous word **you** in the phrase: You and your animal? Rather it is to teach that **it is he** himself **who is liable** for performing a prohibited labor on Shabbat; however, for a prohibited labor performed by **his animal, he is not liable.**

״הִגִּיעַ לֶחָצֵר הַחִיצוֹנָה״. אָמַר רַב הוּנָא: הָיְתָה בְּהֶמְתּוֹ טְעוּנָה כְּלֵי זְכוּכִית – מֵבִיא כָּרִים וּכְסָתוֹת וּמַנִּיחַ תַּחְתֶּיהָ, וּמַתִּיר הַחֲבָלִים וְהַשַּׂקִּין נוֹפְלִים.

We learned in the mishna: Once **he reached the outer courtyard,** he may untie the ropes that attach his bags to the donkey, **and the bags** of vessels that may not be moved on Shabbat fall on their own. **Rav Huna said:** If **one's animal was laden with glass vessels,**[H] which would break if he let them fall to the ground, **he may bring cushions and blankets and place** them **beneath** the animal **and untie the ropes and** let **the bags fall** onto the cushions.

וְהָאֲנַן תְּנַן: נוֹטֵל אֶת הַכֵּלִים הַנִּיטָּלִין בְּשַׁבָּת!

The Gemara asks: Why is it necessary to unload glass vessels in so complicated a manner? **Didn't we learn** in the mishna: **He takes the vessels that may be moved on Shabbat** off the donkey? As glass vessels fall into that category, why not simply remove the glass vessels and then untie the bags?

כִּי קָאָמַר רַב הוּנָא – בְּקַרְנֵי דְּאוּמָּנָא, דְּלָא חֲזְיָא לֵיהּ. וְהָא קָא מְבַטֵּל כְּלִי מֵהֵיכָנוֹ! בִּשְׁלִיפֵי זוּטְרֵי.

The Gemara answers: **When Rav Huna stated** this *halakha*, he was referring **to the horns of a blood letter,**[N] **which are not suitable** for any other purpose and are therefore set-aside on Shabbat due to prohibition and repulsiveness. The Gemara asks: **Isn't he** thereby **negating a vessel's preparedness?** Initially, the cushion was available for any use. Since it now has the set-aside vessels on it, the cushion, too, may no longer be moved. The Sages ruled that one may not place a vessel in a circumstance that will render it prohibited to move. The Gemara answers: This mishna is referring **to small bundles** of glass vessels that will not break if the cushions are subsequently removed from beneath them.

HALAKHA

If one's animal was laden with glass vessels – הָיְתָה בְּהֶמְתּוֹ טְעוּנָה כְּלֵי זְכוּכִית: If one's animal is laden with glass vessels that are set-aside on Shabbat, e.g., a blood letter's horns, it is permitted to place cushions and blankets beneath the animal and allow the bags containing the vessels to fall on their own. However, he may do so only in a case where the glass vessels are small, enabling him to remove the cushions and blankets, so that the preparedness of the cushions and the blankets is not negated by the set-aside objects. If there are large chunks of glass on the animal, one allows them to fall on the ground and break, because the Sages are not concerned about the minimal loss incurred (Rambam *Sefer Zemanim, Hilkhot Shabbat* 21:10; *Shulḥan Arukh, Oraḥ Ḥayyim* 266:9).

NOTES

Horns of a blood letter – קַרְנֵי דְּאוּמָּנָא: According to most commentaries, this is referring to vessels already used for bloodletting that are therefore repulsive and not suitable for any use, not even to cover another vessel (Rashba). In that case, even Rabbi Shimon would agree that they are set-aside. Others explain that these vessels are set-aside due to monetary loss. Since they are designated for bloodletting, their owner treats them with extreme care and does not use them for any other purpose (*Tosefot Rid*).

מֵיתִיבִי: הָיְתָה בְּהֶמְתּוֹ טְעוּנָה טֶבֶל וְעַשָׁשִׁיּוֹת – מַתִּיר אֶת הַחֲבָלִים וְהַשַּׂקִּין נוֹפְלִין, וְאַף עַל פִּי שֶׁמִּשְׁתַּבְּרִין. הָתָם בְּכוּלְסָא. דַּיְקָא נַמִי, דְּקָתָנֵי דּוּמְיָא דְּטֶבֶל. מָה טֶבֶל – דְּלָא חֲזֵי לֵיהּ, אַף הָכָא נַמִי – לָא חֲזֵי לֵיהּ.

The Gemara **raises an objection** based on that which was taught in a *baraita*: If **one's animal was laden with untithed produce**[N] **and chunks of** glass [*ashashiot*],[N] **one unties the ropes and the bags fall** on their own, **even though they break.** Apparently, placing cushions beneath the animal is prohibited. The Gemara answers: **There,** the *baraita* is not referring to vessels but rather **to chunks** [*kulsa*][L] **of glass** that are designated to be broken so that they can be melted and crafted into vessels. The Gemara adds: The language of the *baraita* is **also precise, as it teaches** that chunks are **similar** to **untithed produce: Just as untithed produce is not fit for his** use, **here too,** the chunks **are also not fit for his** use.

וּמַאי אַף עַל פִּי שֶׁמִּשְׁתַּבְּרִין – מַהוּ דְּתֵימָא: לְהֶפְסֵד מוּעָט נַמִי חָשְׁשׁוּ, קָא מַשְׁמַע לַן.

The Gemara explains: **And what** is the meaning of the phrase: **Even though they break?** If the mishna is indeed referring to chunks of glass, they are designated to be broken. Rather, **lest you say** that the Sages **were also concerned** about a **minimal loss,** as certainly some small slivers of glass will be lost when the chunks fall and break, the *tanna* in the *baraita* **teaches us** that the Sages did not consider minimal loss a reason significant enough to permit carrying the prohibited glass.

תַּנְיָא, רַבִּי שִׁמְעוֹן בֶּן יוֹחַי אוֹמֵר: הָיְתָה בְּהֶמְתּוֹ טְעוּנָה שְׁלִיף שֶׁל תְּבוּאָה – מַנִּיחַ רֹאשׁוֹ תַּחְתֶּיהָ, וּמְסַלְּקוֹ לְצַד אַחֵר, וְהוּא נוֹפֵל מֵאֵלָיו.

It was taught in a *baraita* that **Rabbi Shimon ben Yoḥai says:** If **one's animal was loaded with a burden of** untithed **grain, he may place his head beneath** the pile **and move it**[N] **to a different side** of the animal, **and it falls by itself.** The Sages prohibited moving set-aside objects in the typical manner, but there is no concern about doing so in an unusual manner.

חֲמוֹרוֹ שֶׁל רַבָּן גַּמְלִיאֵל הָיְתָה טְעוּנָה דְּבַשׁ וְלֹא רָצָה לְפוֹרְקָהּ עַד מוֹצָאֵי שַׁבָּת, לְמוֹצָאֵי שַׁבָּת מֵתָה. וְהָאֲנַן תְּנַן: נוֹטֵל כֵּלִים הַנִּיטָּלִין! כְּשֶׁהִדְבִּישׁ. הִדְבִּישׁ לְמַאי חֲזֵי? לְכִתִּיתָא דְּגַמְלֵי.

The Gemara relates: **Rabban Gamliel's donkey was laden with honey**[H] **and he did not want to unload** the donkey **until the conclusion of Shabbat. At the conclusion of Shabbat,** the donkey **died** of fatigue. The Gemara asks: **Didn't we learn** in the mishna: **He takes the vessels that may be moved** on Shabbat off the donkey? Why, then, did Rabban Gamliel not unload the honey? The Gemara answers: This is a case **where the honey had spoiled.** The Gemara asks: **For what** use **is spoiled honey suited?** Why did Rabban Gamliel bring it? The Gemara answers: It can be used **to** rub on **the wounds of camels.**

וְלִישְׁרֵי חֲבָלִים וְיִפְּלוּ שַׂקִּין! מִיצְטְרוּ זִיקֵי. וְיָבִיא כָּרִים וּכְסָתוֹת וְיַנִּיחַ תַּחְתֵּיהֶן! מִטַּנְּפִי, וְקָמְבַטֵּל כְּלִי מֵהֵיכָנוֹ. וְהָאִיכָּא צַעַר בַּעֲלֵי חַיִּים! קָסָבַר: צַעַר בַּעֲלֵי חַיִּים דְּרַבָּנַן.

The Gemara asks: **And let** Rabban Gamliel **untie** the **ropes and** the **bags will fall** on their own. The Gemara answers: It was due to the concern that **the jugs** containing the honey would **crack.** The Gemara asks: **And let him bring cushions and blankets and place them beneath the jugs.** The Gemara answers: He was concerned lest **they become soiled and he** would thereby **negate the vessel's preparedness,** i.e., the cushions and blankets would be rendered unusable. The Gemara asks: **Isn't there** the matter **of the suffering of a living creature?**[H] He should suffer monetary loss rather than cause the animal to suffer. The Gemara answers: Rabban Gamliel **holds** that causing **a living creature to suffer** is prohibited not by Torah law but rather **by rabbinic law.** Therefore, he need not suffer monetary loss due to the rabbinic prohibition (Ramban).

אַבָּיֵי אַשְׁכְּחֵיהּ לְרַבָּה דְּקָא מְשַׁפְשֵׁף לֵיהּ לִבְרֵיהּ אַגַּבָּא דַּחֲמָרָא. אָמַר לֵיהּ: קָא מִשְׁתַּמֵּשׁ מָר בְּבַעֲלֵי חַיִּים! אָמַר לֵיהּ: צְדָדִין הֵן, וּצְדָדִין לָא גְּזַרוּ בְּהוּ רַבָּנַן. מְנָא תֵּימְרָא – דִּתְנַן: מַתִּיר חֲבָלִים וְהַשַּׂקִּין נוֹפְלִין. מַאי לָאו בְּחִבּוּר גּוּוַלְקֵי, דַּהֲווֹ לְהוּ צְדָדִין, וּצְדָדִין לָא גְּזַרוּ בְּהוּ רַבָּנַן.

The Gemara relates: **Abaye found Rabba sliding his son on the back of a donkey** on Shabbat to entertain him. **He said to him: The Master is making use of living creatures** on Shabbat,[N] and the Sages prohibited doing so. Rabba **said to him:** I placed my son on the side of the donkey, and as **they are sides, the Sages did not issue a decree** prohibiting making use of **them. From where do you say** that this is so? **As we learned** in the mishna: **One may untie** the **ropes and the bags fall** on their own. What, **is it not** referring to a case **where one attached** the bags by means of *guvalaki*,[LB] where the bags are strapped to the animal and the only way to loosen them involves leaning against the sides of animal in order to unstrap them? **That is** because it is a case of making use of the **sides, and the Sages did not issue a decree prohibiting making use** of an animal's **sides.**

NOTES

Untithed produce – טֶבֶל: The parallel between untithed produce and chunks of glass is clear. Just as untithed produce requires an additional step in order to render it usable, so too, the glass has no function in its present state and one must melt and blow it in order to render it usable (Ramban).

Chunks of glass [*ashashiot*] – עֲשָׁשִׁיּוֹת: The Hebrew word *ashashit* has two meanings. One meaning is a translucent glass lantern. The other meaning is a large chunk of raw material, not necessarily glass. It was necessary for the Gemara to explain that in this context the reference is to the second meaning.

He may place his head beneath the pile and move it – מַנִּיחַ רֹאשׁוֹ תַּחְתֶּיהָ, וּמְסַלְּקוֹ: Even though moving set-aside items is prohibited in any manner, it is permitted in this case because it involves moving the items in an unusual manner, and failure to move them would cause suffering to a living creature (Rashba).

Making use of living creatures on Shabbat – שִׁימּוּשׁ בְּבַעֲלֵי חַיִּים: It is prohibited to make use of animals on Shabbat, even when it involves neither a Torah prohibition nor a violation of the mitzva to rest one's animal. Due to a decree of the Sages, it is also prohibited to make use of trees on Shabbat, lest one break off a branch either for the benefit of tree itself or for use as an animal prod. The Sages disputed the scope of this decree. Does it extend to the sides of the tree or the animal, i.e., using the tree or animal in an unconventional way, or is it limited to using them in the conventional manner?

LANGUAGE

Chunks [*kulsa*] – כּוּלְסָא: The correct version of this word is *bulsa* (*Arukh*), from the Greek βῶλος, *bolos*, meaning a chunk, a clod of earth, or a metal bar.

Guvalaki – גּוּוַלְקֵי: From the Iranian jūwalak, meaning sack or knapsack.

HALAKHA

An animal laden with a heavy load – בְּהֵמָה הַטְּעוּנָה מַשּׂאוֹי כָּבֵד: One whose animal is laden with a heavy burden on Shabbat may unload it by shifting the items to the other side of the animal and allowing them to fall on their own. This ruling is in accordance with the opinion of Rabbi Shimon ben Yoḥai, as the *halakha* with regard to the suffering of living creatures is not in accordance with the opinion of Rabban Gamliel (Rambam *Sefer Zemanim*, *Hilkhot Shabbat* 21:10; *Shulḥan Arukh*, *Oraḥ Ḥayyim* 266:9).

Suffering of a living creature – צַעַר בַּעֲלֵי חַיִּים: It is prohibited by Torah law to cause a living creature to suffer. This is a factor that must be always taken into consideration (Rambam *Sefer Zemanim*, *Hilkhot Shabbat* 21:10; *Shulḥan Arukh*, *Oraḥ Ḥayyim* 266:9).

BACKGROUND

One attached by means of *guvalaki* – חִבּוּר גּוּוַלְקֵי: In this method, the bags are attached and it is impossible to remove the bags merely by untying the ropes. One must lean on the donkey in order to lift up the bags.

Guvalaki method of attaching bags

לָא, בְּחִבֵּר אַגַּלְוָוקִי, דְּלָא הָוֵו צְדָדִין. אִי נַמִי, בְּלֶכְּתָא.

Abaye answered: **No,** this is a case **where one attached** the bags by means of ***agalavki***,[B] i.e., where the bags were not tightly strapped to the animal, but rather attached by means of a hook. In such a case, **there is** no need to make use of **the sides** of the animal in order to unhook the strap. **Alternatively,** the bags were tied to the sides of the animal **with a rope,** which could likewise be untied with ease and without leaning against the animal.

אֵיתִיבֵיהּ: שְׁתַּיִם בִּידֵי אָדָם וְאַחַת בָּאִילָן – כְּשֵׁרָה, וְאֵין עוֹלִין לָהּ בְּיוֹם טוֹב. מַאי לָאו – דְּחָק בֵּיהּ בָּאִילָן, דְּהָווּ לְהוּ צְדָדִין וּצְדָדִין אֲסוּרִין!

Abaye **raised an objection to** Rabba's opinion based on that which was taught in a mishna: A *sukka* that had **two** of its walls on the ground, built **by a person, and one** wall **on a tree**[H] is **valid** and can be used to fulfill the mitzva of *sukka*. **However, one may not enter it on the festival** day of *Sukkot* because it is prohibited to use trees rooted in the ground on Shabbat or a Festival. **What,** is this **not** referring to a case **where one carved** a hole **in the tree** and inserted a beam into the hole for support, in which case **these are sides** of the tree that are being used, and apparently, using the **sides** of the tree is **prohibited?**

לָא, דְּכַפְיֵיהּ לָאִילָן וְאַנַּח סִיכּוּךְ עִילָּוֵיהּ, דְּקָמִשְׁתַּמֵּשׁ בָּאִילָן. אִי הָכִי, אֵימָא סֵיפָא: שָׁלֹשׁ בִּידֵי אָדָם וְאַחַת בָּאִילָן – כְּשֵׁרָה, וְעוֹלִין לָהּ בְּיוֹם טוֹב. וְאִי דְּכַפְיֵיהּ לָאִילָן – אַמַּאי עוֹלִין לָהּ בְּיוֹם טוֹב?

Rabba rejected this: **No,** it is referring to a case **where one bent the tree** over **and placed the roofing atop it,** as in that case, **he is making use of the tree** itself and not its sides. Abaye asked: **If so, say the latter clause** of the mishna: If there are **three** walls built **by a person and one on a tree,**[N] it is a **valid** *sukka* **and one may enter it on a Festival. And if one bent a tree** and placed the roofing atop it, **why may one enter it on a Festival?**

וְאֶלָּא מַאי – צְדָדִין אֲסוּרִין? סוֹף סוֹף, אַמַּאי עוֹלִין לָהּ בְּיוֹם טוֹב? אֶלָּא: הָתָם בְּגַוְאזָא פְּרַסְכַּנָא, דְּאִילָן גּוּפֵיהּ דּוֹפֶן בְּעָלְמָא הוּא דְּשַׁוְויֵהּ. דַּיְקָא נַמִי, דְּקָתָנֵי, זֶה הַכְּלָל: כָּל אִילּוּ שֶׁיִּנָּטֵל הָאִילָן וִיכוֹלָה לַעֲמוֹד – עוֹלִין לָהּ בְּיוֹם טוֹב, שְׁמַע מִינָּהּ.

Rabba rejected this question: **Rather, what** would you say? Making use of **sides is prohibited.** If so, the same problem still exists, why is the *sukka* fit for use in the latter case? **Ultimately, why may one enter it on a Festival? Rather, there** it is referring to a case **where the branches** [*gavaza*][L] **are spread out and where one made the tree itself into a wall,** not where he leaned a wall against it. The language of the mishna **is also precise.** The wall may not be used if it is an integral part of the *sukka*, meaning that it is one of the three required walls. However, if it serves as a fourth wall, one may use the *sukka* on a Festival **as it is taught** that **this is the principle:** In **any** case where **if the tree was taken** the *sukka* would still **be able to stand, one may enter it on a Festival.** Then it is clear that the walls are not leaning against the tree; rather, the tree itself serves as a wall. The Gemara says in summary: **Learn from here** that this is so.

לֵימָא כְּתַנָּאֵי אֵין עוֹלִין לָהּ בְּיוֹם טוֹב רַבִּי שִׁמְעוֹן בֶּן אֶלְעָזָר אוֹמֵר מִשּׁוּם רַבִּי מֵאִיר: עוֹלִין לָהּ בְּיוֹם טוֹב. מַאי לָאו, בְּהָא קָמִיפַּלְגִי; דְּמָר סָבַר: צְדָדִין אֲסוּרִין, וּמָר סָבַר: מוּתָּרִין?

The Gemara suggests: **Let us say** that these *amora'im* disagree in a dispute **parallel** to a dispute between ***tanna'im*** with regard to making use of the sides of a tree, as it was taught in the *Tosefta*: **One may not enter** a *sukka* whose walls are leaning against a tree **on a Festival. Rabbi Shimon ben Elazar says in the name of Rabbi Meir: One may enter it on a Festival. What, is it not that they are disagreeing about this** issue, **as this Master,** meaning the Rabbis, **holds** that making use of the **sides is prohibited, and this Master,** Rabbi Meir, **holds** that **they are permitted?**

אָמַר אַבַּיֵי: לָא, דְּכוּלֵּי עָלְמָא צְדָדִין אֲסוּרִין, וְהָכָא בְּצִדֵּי צְדָדִין קָמִיפַּלְגִי; מָר סָבַר: צִדֵּי צְדָדִין אֲסוּרִין, וּמָר סָבַר: צִדֵּי צְדָדִין מוּתָּרִין.

Abaye said: No. Everyone agrees that the **sides are prohibited, and it is** with regard to the **sides of the sides,** i.e., not a wall leaning against the tree itself, but a wall that is supported by a beam that is placed in the hole carved in the tree, that **they disagree. This Master,** meaning the Rabbis, **holds** that the **sides of the sides are prohibited, and this Master,** Rabbi Meir, **holds** that the **sides of the sides are permitted.**

רָבָא אָמַר: מַאן דְּאָסַר בִּצְדָדִין – אָסַר נַמִי בְּצִדֵּי צְדָדִין, מַאן דְּשָׁרֵי בְּצִדֵּי צְדָדִין – שָׁרֵי נַמִי בִּצְדָדִין. אֵיתִיבֵיהּ רַב מְשַׁרְשִׁיָּא לְרָבָא: נָעַץ

Rava said: The one who prohibited making use of the **sides also prohibited** making use of the **sides of the sides,** and **the one who permitted** making use of the **sides also permitted** making use of the **sides of the sides. Rav Mesharshiyya raised an objection** to the opinion of Rava: If one **drove**

BACKGROUND

One who attached by means of *agalavki* – חִבֵּר אַגַּלְוָוקִי: In this method, the bags are attached by means of a strap. Each bag can be removed individually by detaching it from its strap and it is not necessary to lean against the donkey.

Agalavki method of attaching bags

HALAKHA

A *sukka* that is attached to a tree – סוּכָּה הַמְחוּבֶּרֶת בְּאִילָן: A *sukka* whose walls are made in trees is valid. However, if it is constructed so that the *sukka* could not stand were the tree not there, one may not enter it on the first day of the *Sukkot* festival due to the prohibition against making use of trees on a Festival. However, he may enter the *sukka* during the intermediate days of the Festival, except on Shabbat (Rambam *Sefer Zemanim, Hilkhot Shofar VeSukka VeLulav* 4:6; *Shulḥan Arukh, Oraḥ Ḥayyim* 628:3).

NOTES

Three walls built by a person and one on a tree – שָׁלֹשׁ בִּידֵי אָדָם וְאַחַת בָּאִילָן: The precise meaning of this case is subject to dispute. Some hold that it refers to roofing resting partially atop the tree (Rashi, *Tosafot*, and others), and this was prohibited because it was common to place objects atop the roofing. Another opinion states that this is referring to a case where one elevated the walls of the *sukka*, and the floor of the *sukka* is resting partially on the tree and partially on the ground (Rashi in tractate *Sukka*; *Tosefot Rid*).

LANGUAGE

Branches [*gavaza*] – גַּוְאזָא: From the early Iranian language Avestan, in which this word appears as gawāza and means a shepherd's staff.

יתד באילן ותלה בה כלכלה, למעלה מעשרה טפחים – אין עירובו עירוב, למטה מי׳ טפחים – עירובו עירוב.

a stake in a tree and hung a four-by-four handbreadth **basket from it** into which he placed the food for his joining of the Shabbat boundaries, if the basket was **above ten handbreadths** from the ground, **his *eiruv* is not** a valid ***eiruv***. It is prohibited for him to take the bread from the basket on Shabbat, because the basket's area and height render it a private domain, and he is standing in a different domain. If the basket was **below ten handbreadths** from the ground, **his *eiruv* is** a valid ***eiruv***.[N]

טעמא – דנעץ יתד באילן, הא לא נעץ – אפילו למטה מי׳ טפחים אין עירובו עירוב. והא האי תנא, דקאסר בצדדין וקשרי בצדי צדדין!

The Gemara examines this statement: **The reason** for this distinction between above and below ten handbreadths is specifically because **he drove a stake into a tree** and hung the basket from it. **However, if he did not drive** a stake into a tree, but tied the basket to the tree itself, **even** if it was **below ten handbreadths** from the ground **his *eiruv* is not** a valid ***eiruv***. If he were to take the bread from the basket he would be making use of the sides of the tree, which is prohibited on Shabbat. **And isn't** it the case that **this** is the ***tanna*** who **prohibits using** the **sides** of the tree, **and** nevertheless, **he permits using** the **sides of the sides,**[H] contrary to Rava's opinion?

אמר רב פפא: הכא בכלכלה דחוקה עסקינן, דבהדי דשקיל ליה לעירוב – קמניד ליה לאילן, וקמשתמש באילן גופיה. והלכתא: צדדין – אסורין, צדי צדדין – מותרין.

Rav Pappa said: Here, we are dealing with a narrow-mouthed **basket** that is tightly tied to the tree. Since it is difficult to remove anything from it, **when he takes the** bread for the ***eiruv*** **he moves the tree, and he is** thereby **using the** sides of the **tree itself** and not the sides of the sides of the tree. The Gemara concludes: **And the *halakha*** is that use of the **sides** of a tree or an animal **is prohibited** on Shabbat, but use of the **sides of the sides is permitted.**[N]

אמר רב אשי: השתא דאמרת ״צדדין אסורין״, האי דרגא דמדלא – לא לינחיה איניש אדיקלא, דהוו להו צדדין. אלא לינחיה אגוואזי לבר מדיקלא, וכי סליק – לא לינח כרעיה אגוואזי, אלא ליתנח אקנין.

Rav Ashi said: Now that you said that the *halakha* is that use of the **sides is prohibited,** with regard to **this ladder** that one climbs to an **elevated** area, **a person may not lean it against the palm tree** itself **because it is** considered use of the **sides** of the tree on Shabbat. **Rather, he should lean it on stakes** that are **external** to the trunk of **the palm tree. And when** one **climbs** the ladder, **he should not place his foot on the stakes. Rather, he should place it on the rungs** of the ladder because it is prohibited to use the sides of the tree.

מתני׳ מתירין פקיעי עמיר לפני בהמה, ומפספסין את הכיפין, אבל לא את(א) הזירין. אין מרסקין לא את השחת ולא את החרובין לפני בהמה, בין דקה ובין גסה. רבי יהודה מתיר בחרובין לדקה.

MISHNA **One may untie *peki'in* of grain before an animal** on Shabbat, **and one may spread the *kifin***[H] **but not the *zirin*.** These terms will be explained in the Gemara. **One may not crush hay or carobs**[H] **before an animal** on Shabbat in order to facilitate its eating. He may do so **neither** for a **small** animal [***daka***] **nor** for a **large** one. **Rabbi Yehuda permits** to do so **with carobs for a small** animal, because it can swallow the hard carobs only with difficulty.

גמ׳ אמר רב הונא: הן הן פקיעין, הן הן כיפין. פקיעין – תרי, כיפין – תלתא(ב), זירין – דארזי. והכי קאמר: מתירין פקיעי עמיר לפני בהמה ומפספסין, והוא הדין לכיפין. אבל לא את הזירין – לא לפספס ולא להתיר. אמר רב חסדא: מאי טעמא דרב הונא – קא סבר: למטרח באוכלא – טרחינן, לשויי אוכלא – לא משוינן.

GEMARA **Rav Huna said: They are** called ***peki'in*** and **they are** also called ***kifin***. The difference between them is that ***peki'in*** are tied with **two** knots, whereas ***kifin*** are tied with **three.**[N] ***Zirin***, which may not be moved on Shabbat, are bundles **of cedar** branches[N] eaten by animals when the branches are small and moist. **And this is what** the mishna **is saying: One may untie *peki'in* of grain before an animal and spread** them, **and the same is true for *kifin***, **but not** for ***zirin***, which **one** may **neither spread nor untie. Rav Ḥisda said: What is the reason** for the opinion of **Rav Huna? He holds** that with regard **to exerting** oneself **with food** on Shabbat, **one may exert** himself; however, with regard **to rendering food** edible, **one** may **not render** it so. Bundles of crops which are fit for animal consumption in their present state may be further prepared on Shabbat. Cedar branches cannot be eaten when bound together; therefore, one may not exert himself to untie them and render them edible on Shabbat.

NOTES

His *eiruv* is a valid *eiruv* – עירובו עירוב: This is referring to a joining of Shabbat boundaries. When one wants to travel beyond the Shabbat limits, he must designate a place for himself near the boundary and place some food there. He thereby establishes his Shabbat resting place there, allowing him to extend his Shabbat limit by an additional two thousand cubits beyond that point. In order to establish a proper *eiruv* it must already be present at dusk on Friday. Although one is not required to eat the food, it must be accessible for him to eat it at that time. Therefore, an *eiruv* placed somewhere inaccessible on Shabbat is not a valid *eiruv*.

And the *halakha* is that use of the sides is prohibited, but use of the sides of the sides is permitted – והלכתא: צדדין אסורין, צדי צדדין מותרין: Some commentaries explain that the fact that it is necessary to establish the *halakha* both for sides and for sides of sides indicates that the Gemara accepts the basis of Rava's assertion that there is a connection between the two disputes. Even so, the Gemara concludes that the *halakha* is in accordance with the third opinion, which states that use of sides is prohibited and use of sides of sides is permitted (*Adderet Eliyahu*; see *Tosafot*).

Two…three – תרי...תלתא: Some explain instead that two is referring to two bundles tied together as one, and three is referring to three tied together (Rabbeinu Ḥananel).

Cedar branches – דארזי: The *ge'onim* explain that this term can also refer to bundles of straw and the like, and specifically to stalks or branches that are rigid like wood.

HALAKHA

Sides…sides of the sides – צדדין...צדי צדדין: It is prohibited to make use of the sides of an animal on Shabbat; therefore, one may neither ride an animal nor hang on the sides of an animal. However, making use of the sides of the sides, i.e., using something resting on the side of an animal, is permitted (Rambam *Sefer Zemanim, Hilkhot Shabbat* 21:9; *Shulḥan Arukh, Oraḥ Ḥayyim* 305:18).

One may untie *peki'in* of grain before an animal…*kifin* – מתירין פקיעי עמיר לפני בהמה...וכיפין: One may untie bundles of grain on Shabbat but may not spread them out for an animal. The principle is: One may render edible something that is not edible; however, he may not exert himself to further prepare food that is already edible. Others say that the Sages permitted untying a bundle of straw only when it is tied with a temporary knot (Rambam *Sefer Zemanim, Hilkhot Shabbat* 21:18; *Shulḥan Arukh, Oraḥ Ḥayyim* 324:4 and in the comment of the Rema).

Crushing hay and carobs – ריסוק שחת וחרובין: One may not crush hay or carobs for either large or small animals on Shabbat, because they are already soft and edible. However, it is permitted to crush hard carobs (*Mishna Berura*; Rambam *Sefer Zemanim, Hilkhot Shabbat* 21:18; *Shulḥan Arukh, Oraḥ Ḥayyim* 324:8).

רַב יְהוּדָה אָמַר: הֵן הֵן פְּקִיעִין, הֵן הֵן זִירִין. פְּקִיעִין – תְּרֵי, זִירִין – תְּלָתָא. כִּיפִּין – דְּאַרְזֵי. וְהָכִי קָאָמַר: מַתִּירִין פְּקִיעֵי עָמִיר לִפְנֵי בְּהֵמָה, אֲבָל פַּסְפּוּסֵי – לֹא. וְכִיפִּין – פַּסְפּוּסֵי נַמִי מְפַסְפְּסִינַן, אֲבָל לֹא הַזִּירִין לְפַסְפֵּס[א] אֶלָּא לְהַתִּיר. אָמַר רָבָא: מַאי טַעְמָא דְּרַב יְהוּדָה – קָסָבַר: שָׁוֵי אוּכְלָא – מְשַׁוֵּינַן, מִטְרַח בְּאוּכְלָא – לָא טָרְחִינַן.

Rav Yehuda understood the mishna differently and **said: They are** called ***peki'in* and they are** also called ***zirin*.** The difference between them is that *peki'in* are tied with **two** knots, whereas *zirin* are tied with **three.** ***Kifin*** are bundles **of cedar** branches. **And this is what** the mishna **is saying: One may untie *peki'in* of grain before an animal; however,** with regard to **spreading them, no,** he may not spread them. **And** with regard to ***kifin*, one** may **also spread them. However,** that is **not** the case with regard to ***zirin*,** as it is prohibited to **spread** them, and it is **only** permitted **to untie** them. **Rava said: What is the reason** for **Rav Yehuda's** opinion? **He holds** the opposite of Rav Huna's opinion. He holds that with regard to **rendering food** edible, **one** may **render** it so; however, with regard to **exerting** oneself on Shabbat **with food** that is already in an edible state, **one** may **not exert** himself.

תְּנַן: דְּאֵין מְרַסְּקִין אֶת הַשַּׁחַת וְאֶת הֶחָרוּבִין לִפְנֵי בְּהֵמָה, בֵּין דַּקָּה וּבֵין גַּסָּה. מַאי לָאו – חָרוּבִין דּוּמְיָא דְּשַׁחַת, מַה שַּׁחַת – דְּרַכִּיכֵי, אַף חָרוּבִין – דְּרַכִּיכֵי, אַלְמָא: לָא טָרְחִינַן בְּאוּכְלָא, וּתְיוּבְתֵּיהּ דְּרַב הוּנָא!

We learned in the mishna: **One may not crush hay or carobs before an animal** on Shabbat in order to facilitate its eating. He may do so **neither** for a **small** animal **nor** for a **large** one. **Is this not** referring to **carobs** that are **similar to hay? Just as** it is referring to **hay that is soft, so too,** it is referring to **carobs that are soft. Apparently, we do not exert** ourselves **with food.** Since the carobs are suitable for animal consumption without being crushed, it is prohibited to exert oneself and crush them. **And** this is **a conclusive refutation** of the opinion of **Rav Huna.**

אָמַר לָךְ רַב הוּנָא: לָא, שַׁחַת דּוּמְיָא דְּחָרוּבִין; מָה חָרוּבִין – דְּאַקּוּשֵׁי, אַף שַׁחַת – דְּאַקּוּשֵׁי. הֵיכִי מַשְׁכַּחַתְּ לָהּ – בְּעִילֵי זוּטְרֵי.

The Gemara answers that **Rav Huna** could have **said to you: No,** the mishna is referring to **hay** that is **similar to carobs. Just as** it is referring to **carobs that are hard, so too,** it is referring to **hay that is hard** and crushing it renders it edible. The Gemara asks: **How is it** possible **to find** hay that is so hard that an animal cannot eat it? The Gemara answers: It is referring **to young donkeys,** that can only eat hay that is crushed well.

תָּא שְׁמַע: רַבִּי יְהוּדָה מַתִּיר בֶּחָרוּבִין לַדַּקָּה. לַדַּקָּה – אִין, לַגַּסָּה – לָא. אִי אָמְרַתְּ בִּשְׁלָמָא תַּנָּא קַמָּא סָבַר: מִיטְרַח בְּאוּכְלָא לָא טָרְחִינַן, שַׁוּוֹיֵ מְשַׁוֵּינַן. הַיְינוּ דְּקָא אָמַר ר׳ יְהוּדָה: הֶחָרוּבִין לַדַּקָּה נַמִי שַׁוּוֹיֵ אוּכְלָא הוּא. אֶלָּא אִי אָמְרַתְּ תַּנָּא קַמָּא סָבַר: שַׁוּוֹיֵ אוּכְלָא לָא מְשַׁוֵּינַן, מִיטְרַח בְּאוּכְלָא מִטָּרְחִינַן, רַבִּי יְהוּדָה דְּמַתִּיר בֶּחָרוּבִין לַדַּקָּה, כׇּל שֶׁכֵּן לַגַּסָּה!

Come and **hear** a proof from that which we learned in the continuation of the mishna: **Rabbi Yehuda permits** crushing **carobs for a small** animal. The Gemara infers: **For a small** animal, **yes,** it is permitted; **for a large one, no,** it is not permitted. **Granted, if you say** that the **first *tanna* holds:** One may **not exert** himself **with food** on Shabbat, but with regard to **rendering** food edible, **one** may **render** food edible, **that** explains **that which Rabbi Yehuda** said in response: Feeding **carobs to a small animal is also** a case of **rendering food** edible because the animal cannot eat hard carobs. **However, if you say** that the **first *tanna* holds** that with regard to **rendering** food edible, **one** may **not render** food edible on Shabbat, but with regard to **exerting** oneself **with food, one** may **exert** himself, then **Rabbi Yehuda, who permits** crushing **carobs for a small** animal, **all the more so** he should permit crushing carobs **for a large** one. If carobs are suitable for consumption by a small animal, all the more so are they suitable for consumption by a large animal.

מִי סָבְרַתְּ ״דַּקָּה״ דַּקָּה מַמָּשׁ? מַאי דַּקָּה – גַּסָּה, וּמַאי קָרֵי לָהּ דַּקָּה – דְּדַיְיקָא בְּאוּכְלָא.

The Gemara rejects this: **Do you hold that** the small animal [*daka*] mentioned here is referring to **an actual small** animal? No; rather, **what** is the meaning of ***daka*** here? It is referring to a **large** animal. **And what** is the reason that the mishna **calls it *daka*? Because it is particular** [***dayka***] **about** its **food.**[N] Since this animal can eat uncrushed carobs when there is no alternative, one may exert himself and crush them for it.

הָא מִדְּקָתָנֵי רֵישָׁא ״בֵּין דַּקָּה וּבֵין גַּסָּה״ – מִכְּלָל דְּרַבִּי יְהוּדָה ״דַּקָּה״ דַּקָּה מַמָּשׁ קָאָמַר! קַשְׁיָא.

The Gemara asks: From the fact **that it is taught in the first clause** of the mishna: **Neither** for a **small** animal **nor** for a **large** animal, **it can be inferred** that when **Rabbi Yehuda** said ***daka*,** **he meant an actual small** animal. The Gemara was unable to answer to find an answer to this question and it remains **difficult.** Nonetheless, Rav Huna's opinion was not refuted.

תָּא שְׁמַע: מְחַתְּכִין

Therefore, **come** and **hear** a proof from that which we learned in another mishna: **One may chop**

NOTES

An animal that is particular about its food – דְּדַיְיקָא בְּאוּכְלָא: Some explain that this means the animal chews its food well with its teeth and eats both hard and soft foods. In that case, the Gemara would permit preparing the food, because it involves exerting oneself with food rather than rendering food edible (Ramban).

את הדלועין לפני הבהמה, ואת הנבלה לפני הכלבים. מאי לאו, דלועין דומיא דנבלה; מה נבלה – דרכיכא, אף דלועין – דרכיכי, אלמא: טרחינן באוכלא, ותיובתא דרב יהודה! אמר לך רב יהודה: לא, נבלה דומיא דדלועין; מה דלועין – דאשוני, אף נבלה – דאשונא. והיכי משכחת לה – בבשר פילי. אי נמי: בגורייאתא זוטרי.

pumpkins before an animal[H] and an animal **carcass before dogs.**[H] **Is this not** referring to **pumpkins** that are **similar to an** animal **carcass? Just as an** animal **carcass is soft, so too,** the **pumpkins** referred to here **are soft. Apparently, one** may **exert** himself **with food, and this is a conclusive refutation of** the opinion of **Rav Yehuda.** The Gemara answers that **Rav Yehuda** could have **said to you: No,** the mishna is referring to an animal **carcass** that is **similar to pumpkins. Just as** the reference is to **pumpkins that are hard, so too,** the reference is to an animal **carcass that is hard,** and chopping it renders it edible. The Gemara asks: **And how is it** possible **to find** an animal carcass that is so hard that another animal cannot eat it? The Gemara answers: The mishna is referring to **elephant flesh. Alternatively,** it can be explained that the mishna is referring to more common animal meat placed **before puppies** that can eat only chopped meat.

תא שמע, דתני רב חנן מנהרדעא: מפרכינן תבן ואספסתא ומערבין. אלמא: טרחינן באוכלא! תבן – בתיבנא סריא, אספסתא – בעילי זוטרי.

Come and hear a proof from **that which Rav Ḥanan of Neharde'a taught: One** may **crumble straw and alfalfa** on Shabbat **and mix** the two together, and the animal then eats the straw because it is mixed with the alfalfa. **Apparently,** one may **exert** himself **with food** on Shabbat. The Gemara rejects this proof: No, the **straw** mentioned here is **rotten straw** that requires special preparation to render it suitable for animal consumption, and **alfalfa** is taught with regard to **young donkeys** who can only eat it in small pieces.

מתני׳ אין אובסין את הגמל, ולא דורסין, אבל מלעיטין. ואין מאמירין את העגלים, אבל מלעיטין. ומהלקטין לתרנגולין, ונותנין מים למורסן, אבל לא גובלין, ואין נותנין מים לפני דבורים ולפני יונים שבשובך, אבל נותנין לפני אווזין ותרנגולין, ולפני יוני הרדיסיות.

MISHNA **One may not forcibly overfeed a camel** on Shabbat[H] **and one may not force-feed** it, even if in doing so he does not overfeed the camel. **However, one may place food into its mouth. And** the mishna makes a distinction, which will be explained in the Gemara, between two manners of placing food in the mouths of cattle. **One may not** place food in **the mouths of calves** on Shabbat in the manner of ***hamra'a*****, but one may** do so in the manner of ***halata*****. And one may force-feed chickens. And one may add water to bran** used as animal feed, **but one may not knead** the mixture. **And one may not place water before bees or before doves in a dove-cote,** because they are capable of finding their own food; **however, one may place** water **before geese and chickens and before hardisian** [***hardeisiyyot***][L] **doves.**

גמ׳ מאי "אין אובסין"? אמר רב יהודה: אין עושין לה אבוס בתוך מעיה. מי איכא כי האי גוונא? אין, וכדאמר רב ירמיה מדיפתי: לדידי חזי לי ההוא טייעא דאכלא כורא, ואטעינא כורא.

GEMARA We learned in the mishna that one may not forcibly overfeed a camel on Shabbat. The Gemara asks. **What is** meaning of: **One may not forcibly overfeed? Rav Yehuda said: One may not** feed a camel to the point that **it creates a trough inside of its stomach.** The Gemara asks: **Is there** the possibility of feeding a camel **in that manner?** The Gemara answers: **Yes; and as Rav Yirmeya of Difti said: I saw** an **Arab who fed** his camel **a** ***kor*** of food **and loaded it** with another ***kor*** on its back.

LANGUAGE

Hardisian [*hardeisiyyot*] doves – יוני הרדיסיות: There are two distinct versions of the word *hardeisiyyot* explained in the Talmud. One is *herodesiyyot*, named for King Herod, who introduced this species of dove to Israel and raised them. The other is *rodosiyyot*, named for the doves' place of origin, the island of Rhodes in the Mediterranean Sea. Hardisian doves were domesticated and their owners were responsible for their sustenance, unlike earlier species of doves whose owners would merely provide them with a dove-cote and extra food.

HALAKHA

Pumpkins before an animal – את הדלועין לפני הבהמה: On Shabbat, one may cut hard pumpkins for an animal, provided that the pumpkins were picked before Shabbat (*Magen Avraham*; Rambam *Sefer Zemanim, Hilkhot Shabbat* 21:18; *Shulḥan Arukh, Oraḥ Ḥayyim* 324:6).

An animal carcass before dogs – ואת הנבלה לפני הכלבים: On Shabbat it is permitted to cut an animal carcass for dogs, even if the animal died on Shabbat itself, provided the carcass is too hard for the dogs to chew. However, if the dogs could eat it uncut, one may not exert himself and cut it (Rambam *Sefer Zemanim, Hilkhot Shabbat* 21:18; *Shulḥan Arukh, Oraḥ Ḥayyim* 324:7).

One may not forcibly overfeed…on Shabbat – אין אובסין בשבת: One may not forcibly overfeed an animal on Shabbat, nor may one cram food into a place in its throat where the animal cannot expel it. However, it is permitted to place food into a place in the animal's mouth where the animal can expel it (Rambam *Sefer Zemanim, Hilkhot Shabbat* 21:35; *Shulḥan Arukh, Oraḥ Ḥayyim* 324:9).

״אֵין מַאֲמִירִין״. אֵיזוֹ הִיא הַמְרָאָה וְאֵיזוֹ הִיא הַלְעָטָה? אָמַר רַב יְהוּדָה: הַמְרָאָה – לְמָקוֹם שֶׁאֵינָהּ יְכוֹלָה לְהַחֲזִיר, הַלְעָטָה – לְמָקוֹם שֶׁיְּכוֹלָה לְהַחֲזִיר. רַב חִסְדָּא אָמַר: אִידִי וְאִידִי לְמָקוֹם שֶׁאֵינָהּ יְכוֹלָה לְהַחֲזִיר, וְהַמְרָאָה – בִּכְלִי, הַלְעָטָה – בְּיָד.

We learned in the mishna: **One may not** place food in the mouths of calves on Shabbat in the manner of ***hamra'a***, but one may do so in the manner of *halata*. The Gemara asks: **Which is *hamra'a* and which is *halata*? Rav Yehuda said: *Hamra'a*** is positioning food **into a place** in the animal's throat **from which it cannot return** and expel the food. ***Halata*** is positioning food **into a place** in the animal's mouth **from which it can return** and expel the food. **Rav Ḥisda said: Both this and that** refer to positioning food **into a place from which** the animal **cannot return** and expel the food; **however,** the difference between them is that in ***hamra'a*** the food is placed **with a vessel,** whereas **in *halata*** the food is placed **by hand.**

מְתִיב רַב יוֹסֵף: מְהַלְקְטִין לְתַרְנְגוֹלִין, וְאֵין צָרִיךְ לוֹמַר שֶׁמַּלְקִיטִין. וְאֵין מַלְקִיטִין לְיוֹנֵי שׁוֹבָךְ וּלְיוֹנֵי עֲלִיָּיה, וְאֵין צָרִיךְ לוֹמַר שֶׁאֵין מְהַלְקְטִין. מַאי ״מְהַלְקְטִין״ וּמַאי ״מַלְקִיטִין״? אִילֵימָא ״מְהַלְקְטִין״ – דְּסָפֵי לֵיהּ בְּיָדַיִם, ״מַלְקִיטִין״ – דְּשָׁדֵי לֵיהּ קַמַּיְיהוּ, מִכְּלָל דְּיוֹנֵי שׁוֹבָךְ וְיוֹנֵי עֲלִיָּיה מִישְׁדָּא קַמַּיְיהוּ נַמִי לָא?!

Rav Yosef raised an objection from that which was taught in the *Tosefta*: **One may force-feed [*mehalketin*] chickens, and needless to say, one may *malkitin*. And one may not *malkitin* doves in a dove-cote or doves in an attic, and needless to say, one may not force-feed.** The Gemara asks: **What is *mehalketin* and what is *malkitin*? If you say** that ***mehalketin*** means **that one feeds** the bird **by hand** and ***malkitin*** means **that one throws** the food **before them, by inference, throwing food before doves in a dove-cote or** before **doves in an attic is also not** permitted. But why would that be prohibited?

אֶלָּא לָאו: ״מְהַלְקְטִין״ – לְמָקוֹם שֶׁאֵינָהּ יְכוֹלָה לְהַחֲזִיר, ״מַלְקִיטִין״ – לְמָקוֹם שֶׁיְּכוֹלָה לְהַחֲזִיר, מִכְּלָל – דְּהַמְרָאָה בִּכְלִי, וּתְיוּבְתָּא דְּרַב יְהוּדָה!

Rather, is it not that ***mehalketin*** means positioning food **into a place from which** the bird **cannot return** and expel the food, and ***malkitin*** means positioning food **into a place from which it can return** and expel the food? Therefore, *mehalketin* in the case of birds is similar to *halata* into a camel's mouth, which the mishna permitted. **By inference,** the ***hamra'a*** prohibited in the mishna is performed **with a vessel, and** this poses **a conclusive refutation** to the opinion **of Rav Yehuda.**

אָמַר לָךְ רַב יְהוּדָה: לְעוֹלָם ״מְהַלְקְטִין״ – דְּסָפֵי לֵיהּ בְּיָדַיִם, ״מַלְקִיטִין״ – דְּשָׁדֵי לֵיהּ קַמַּיְיהוּ. וּדְקָא קַשְׁיָא לָךְ: יוֹנֵי שׁוֹבָךְ וְיוֹנֵי עֲלִיָּיה לְמִישְׁדָּא קַמַּיְיהוּ נַמִי לָא?! הָנֵי מְזוֹנוֹתָן עָלֶיךָ, וְהָנֵי – אֵין מְזוֹנוֹתָן עָלֶיךָ. כִּדְתַנְיָא: נוֹתְנִין מְזוֹנוֹת לִפְנֵי כֶּלֶב, וְאֵין נוֹתְנִין מְזוֹנוֹת לִפְנֵי חֲזִיר. וּמָה הֶפְרֵשׁ בֵּין זֶה לָזֶה, זֶה – מְזוֹנוֹתָיו עָלֶיךָ וְזֶה – אֵין מְזוֹנוֹתָיו עָלֶיךָ.

Rav Yehuda could have **said to you: Actually, *mehalketin*** means **that one feeds** the bird **by hand,** and ***malkitin*** mean **that one throws** the food **before them. And that which was difficult for you: Is throwing** food **before doves in a dove-cote or doves in an attic also not** permitted on Shabbat? This is not difficult because with regard to **these** chickens and geese that were mentioned, sole responsibility for **their sustenance** is incumbent **upon you** as they are incapable of providing for themselves. **However,** in the case of **these** doves, responsibility for **their sustenance** is **not** incumbent **upon you,** and therefore, it is prohibited to place food before them,[H] **as it was taught** in a *baraita*: **One may place sustenance before a dog**[N] on Shabbat, **but one may not place sustenance before a pig.**[N] **And what** is the **difference between this and that?** In **this** case of the dog, responsibility **for its sustenance is** incumbent **upon you, and in that** case of the pig, responsibility **for its sustenance is not** incumbent **upon you,** as no Jew raises pigs.

אָמַר רַב אַשִׁי: מַתְנִיתִין נַמִי דַּיְקָא ״אֵין נוֹתְנִין מַיִם לִפְנֵי דְּבוֹרִים וְלִפְנֵי יוֹנִים שֶׁבַּשּׁוֹבָךְ אֲבָל נוֹתְנִין לִפְנֵי אַוָּזִין וְלִפְנֵי תַּרְנְגוֹלִין וְלִפְנֵי יוֹנֵי הַרְדֵּיסִיּוֹת״ מַאי טַעְמָא? לָאו מִשּׁוּם דְּהָנֵי מְזוֹנוֹתָן עָלֶיךָ וְהָנֵי אֵין מְזוֹנוֹתָן עָלֶיךָ?

Rav Ashi said: The language of **the mishna is also precise** in support of this explanation, as we learn: **And one may not place water before bees or before doves in a dove-cote** because they are capable of finding their own food; **however, one may place** water **before geese and chickens and before hardisian doves. What is the reason** for this distinction? **Is it not because** for **these,** geese and chickens, responsibility for **their sustenance** is incumbent **upon you, and** for **those,** bees and doves, responsibility for **their sustenance** is **not** incumbent **upon you?**

וְלִיטַעְמִיךְ, מַאי אִירְיָא מַיָּא, אֲפִילּוּ חִיטֵּי וְשַׂעֲרֵי נַמִי לָא! אֶלָּא שָׁאנֵי מַיָּא דִּשְׁכִיחִי בְּאַגְמָא.

The Gemara rejects this proof: **And according to your reasoning,** why did the mishna cite a case **specifically** involving **water? Even wheat and barley** should **also not** be permitted. **Rather,** the reason for the distinction between the *halakhot* is that **water is different because it is found in a lake** or in other reservoirs, and therefore one need not exert himself to provide water for bees and doves. That is not the case with the rest of their food.

HALAKHA

Placing sustenance before animals on Shabbat – **נְתִינַת מְזוֹנוֹת לְבַעֲלֵי חַיִּים בְּשַׁבָּת**: One may not place water or food before animals capable of finding their own food on Shabbat, but one may do so before animals for which the responsibility for their sustenance is incumbent upon people (Rambam *Sefer Zemanim, Hilkhot Shabbat* 21:36; *Shulḥan Arukh, Oraḥ Ḥayyim* 324:11).

NOTES

Feeding a dog – **הַאֲכָלַת כֶּלֶב**: Apparently, although the Gemara is referring here to a dog that one does not own, nevertheless, he is permitted to feed it. Some explain this based on the verse concerning the *halakhot* of an animal with a condition that will cause it to die within twelve months [*tereifa*]: "You shall cast it to a dog" (Exodus 22:30). These commentaries teach that the dogs were rewarded for their behavior during the Exodus: "Against any of the children of Israel shall not a dog whet his tongue," (Exodus 11:7; *Me'iri*).

Feeding a pig – **הַאֲכָלַת חֲזִיר**: Although it is prohibited to feed an animal on Shabbat if one is not responsible for its sustenance, it is permitted to give a gentile food in one's courtyard despite the fact that responsibility for his sustenance is not incumbent upon a Jew. The Sages draw a distinction between the cases. A Jew is required to treat gentiles well in order to encourage good relations, much as he gives charity to both gentiles and Jews. Furthermore, since people are considered more important than other beings, the Sages permit giving food to a gentile on Shabbat in order to preserve human dignity (*Me'iri*).

דָּרַשׁ רַבִּי יוֹנָה אַפִּיתְחָא דְּבֵי נְשִׂיאָה: מַאי דִּכְתִיב (״יוֹדֵעַ) צַדִּיק דִּין דַּלִּים״ יוֹדֵעַ הַקָּדוֹשׁ בָּרוּךְ הוּא בְּכֶלֶב שֶׁמְּזוֹנוֹתָיו מוּעָטִין, לְפִיכָךְ שׁוֹהָה אֲכִילָתוֹ בְּמֵעָיו שְׁלֹשָׁה יָמִים. כִּדְתְנַן: כַּמָּה תִּשְׁהֶה אֲכִילָתוֹ בְּמֵעָיו וִיהֵא טָמֵא – בְּכֶלֶב – שְׁלֹשָׁה יָמִים מֵעֵת לְעֵת, וּבְעוֹפוֹת וּבְדָגִים – כְּדֵי שֶׁתִּפּוֹל לָאוּר וְתִשָּׂרֵף.

Returning to the discussion of feeding dogs, the Gemara cites additional statements on the topic. **Rabbi Yona taught at the entrance to the house of the *Nasi*: What is** the meaning of **that which is written: "The righteous man takes knowledge of the cause of the poor"** (Proverbs 29:7)?[N] **The Holy One, Blessed be He, knows that for a dog, its sustenance is scarce** and they are not fed sufficiently. **Therefore, its food remains in its intestines for three days** so that the dog will be sustained by that food, **as we learned** in a mishna dealing with the *halakhot* of ritual impurity: After an animal eats flesh from a corpse, **how long does its food remain in its intestines** undigested **and** therefore **ritually impure?**[H] **In** the case of **a dog** it is for **three twenty-four hour periods, and for fowl and fish,** who digest their food quickly, it is **the equivalent** of **the** time it takes **for** the flesh **to fall into the fire and be consumed** by the fire.

אָמַר רַב הַמְנוּנָא, שְׁמַע מִינַּהּ: אוֹרַח אַרְעָא לְמִשְׁדָּא אוּמְצָא לְכַלְבָּא. וְכַמָּה? אָמַר רַב מָרִי: מְשַׁח אוּדְנֵיהּ, וְחוּטְרָא אֲבַתְרֵיהּ. הָנֵי מִילֵּי – בְּדַבְרָא, אֲבָל בְּמָתָא – לָא, דְּאָתֵא לְמִסְרַךְ. אָמַר רַב פַּפָּא: לֵית דְּעַנְיָא מִכַּלְבָּא, וְלֵית דְּעָתִיר מֵחֲזִירָא.

Rav Hamnuna said: Learn from it: It is **the way of the world,** i.e., proper conduct, **to throw a piece of meat before a dog,** as even the Holy One, Blessed be He, concerns Himself with the dog's sustenance. The Gemara asks: **And how much food** should one give to a dog? **Rav Mari said:** Give it the equivalent of **the measure of its ear and** strike it immediately **thereafter with a staff** so that the dog will not grow attached to the one who fed it. **This applies** specifically when one is **in the field, but in the city,** one should **not** give anything to a dog because the dog **will be drawn** to follow him and remain with him. **Rav Pappa said: There is no** creature **poorer than a dog, and no** creature **richer than a pig,** as pigs will eat anything, and people provide them with plentiful amounts of food.

תַּנְיָא כְּוָותֵיהּ דְּרַב יְהוּדָה: אֵיזוֹ הִיא הַמְרָאָה וְאֵיזוֹ הִיא הַלְעָטָה? הַמְרָאָה – מַרְבִּיצָהּ וּפוֹקֵס אֶת פִּיהָ וּמַאֲכִילָהּ כַּרְשִׁינִין וּמַיִם בְּבַת אַחַת, הַלְעָטָה – מַאֲכִילָהּ מְעוּמָּד וּמַשְׁקָהּ מְעוּמָּד, וְנוֹתְנִין כַּרְשִׁינִין בִּפְנֵי עַצְמָן וּמַיִם בִּפְנֵי עַצְמָן.

With regard to the halakhic ruling, a *baraita* **was taught in accordance with** the opinion of **Rav Yehuda: What is *hamra'a* and what is *halata*?**[H] ***Hamra'a*** is when a person forcibly **lays** the animal on the ground **and forces its mouth open and feeds it vetch and water simultaneously** so that the animal will be unable to expel it. ***Halata*** is when **one feeds** the animal while it is **standing and gives it to drink** while it is **standing,** i.e., gives it food and drink in the usual manner, **and one gives it vetch separately and water separately,** to augment what the animal eats on its own.

״מְהַלְקְטִין לְתַרְנְגוֹלִין כו׳״. אָמַר אַבָּיֵי: אֲמַרִיתָהּ קַמֵּיהּ דְּמָר, מַתְנִיתִין מַנִּי? וַאֲמַר לִי: רַבִּי יוֹסֵי בַּר יְהוּדָה הִיא, דְּתַנְיָא: אֶחָד נוֹתֵן אֶת הַקֶּמַח וְאֶחָד נוֹתֵן לְתוֹכוֹ מַיִם – הָאַחֲרוֹן חַיָּיב, דִּבְרֵי רַבִּי. רַבִּי יוֹסֵי בַּר יְהוּדָה אוֹמֵר: אֵינוֹ חַיָּיב עַד שֶׁיְּגַבֵּל.

We learned in the mishna: **And one may force-feed chickens,** and one may add water to bran, but one may not knead the mixture. **Abaye said: I said this before my Master,** Rabba: **Whose** opinion is it in **the mishna? And he said to me: It is** the opinion of **Rabbi Yosei bar Yehuda, as it was taught** in a *baraita*: If **one person places flour and** another **one places water into it, the latter is liable** to bring a sin-offering for performing the prohibited labor of kneading. This is **the statement of Rabbi** Yehuda HaNasi. **Rabbi Yosei bar Yehuda says: One is only liable** when he actually **kneads** the flour and water together. He is not liable for merely adding water to the flour. This is similar to the ruling of the mishna that one may pour water into the bran but may not knead the mixture.

דִּילְמָא עַד כָּאן לָא קָאָמַר רַבִּי יוֹסֵי בַּר יְהוּדָה הָתָם – אֶלָּא קֶמַח דְּבַר גִּיבּוּל הוּא, אֲבָל מוּרְסָן דְּלָאו בַּר גִּיבּוּל הוּא – אֲפִילּוּ רַבִּי יוֹסֵי בַּר יְהוּדָה מוֹדֶה? לָא סָלְקָא דַּעְתָּךְ, דְּתַנְיָא בְּהֶדְיָא: אֵין נוֹתְנִין מַיִם לַמּוּרְסָן, דִּבְרֵי רַבִּי. רַבִּי יוֹסֵי בַּר יְהוּדָה אוֹמֵר: נוֹתְנִין מַיִם לַמּוּרְסָן.

The Gemara rejects this: **Perhaps Rabbi Yosei bar Yehuda only stated** that actual kneading is required to be liable for performing the prohibited labor of kneading **in** the case of **flour, which can be kneaded; however,** in the case of **bran, which cannot be kneaded** into a dough, **even Rabbi Yosei bar Yehuda** would **concede** that it is prohibited, even if one does not actually knead the mixture. The Gemara rejects this statement: It should **not enter your mind** to explain it that way, **as it was taught explicitly** in a *baraita*: **One may not place water into bran** on Shabbat; this is **the statement of Rabbi** Yehuda HaNasi. **Rabbi Yosei bar Yehuda says: One may place water into bran.**[H]

תָּנוּ רַבָּנַן: אֵין גּוֹבְלִין אֶת הַקָּלִי וְיֵשׁ אוֹמְרִים גּוֹבְלִין. מַאן וְיֵשׁ אוֹמְרִים? אָמַר רַב חִסְדָּא:

The Sages taught: On Shabbat, **one may not knead** sweet **flour** made from unripe grain that was dried in an oven, **and some say: One may knead** it. The Gemara asks: **Whose is** the opinion introduced as: **And some say?**[N] **Rav Ḥisda said:**

NOTES

The righteous man takes knowledge of the cause of the poor – יוֹדֵעַ צַדִּיק דִּין דַּלִּים: The simple understanding of this verse refers to the ideal manner in which a righteous person should treat the poor. Rabbi Yona taught that it refers to the Holy One, Blessed be He, Who sees to the needs of all living creatures (Maharsha).

Whose is the opinion introduced as: And some say – מַאן וְיֵשׁ אוֹמְרִים: Although the Gemara states that opinions introduced as: And some say, are attributed to Rabbi Natan, the Sages were aware that there are exceptions. There are even some disputes where Rabbi Natan disagrees with the opinion of: And some say (*Tosafot*).

HALAKHA

A ritually impure object that was eaten – דָּבָר טָמֵא שֶׁנֶּאֱכַל: Flesh of a corpse eaten by an animal does not transmit ritual impurity while still in the animal's stomach. If the animal died and the flesh remained in its stomach for three full days in the case of a dog, or for one full day in the case of other animals, the flesh is considered to have been digested and is ritually pure, in accordance with the ruling of Rabbi Yehuda ben Beteira in a mishna in tractate *Oholot* (Rambam *Sefer Tahara, Hilkhot Tumat Met* 20:4).

***Hamra'a* and *halata* – הַמְרָאָה וְהַלְעָטָה:** On Shabbat, one may not force an animal to the ground and forcibly feed it water and vetch simultaneously. However, if an animal is standing, one may feed it water and vetch separately as per the *Tosefta* (Rambam *Sefer Zemanim, Hilkhot Shabbat* 21:35).

Placing water into bran – נְתִינַת מַיִם לַמּוּרְסָן: One may not knead bran and water together for animals on Shabbat, but it is permitted to pour water into the bran and to pass a spoon through it, or pour it from one vessel into another so that they will mix together. That is the ruling of most halakhic authorities, because the unattributed mishna is in accordance with the opinion of Rabbi Yosei bar Yehuda (Rambam *Sefer Zemanim, Hilkhot Shabbat* 21:34; *Shulḥan Arukh, Oraḥ Ḥayyim* 324:3). However, others prohibit even pouring water into the bran, in accordance with the opinion of Rabbi Yehuda HaNasi (*Sefer Mitzvot Gadol*; *Tosafot*).

NOTES

***Shatit* – שַׁתִית:** *Shatit* is a dish made with flour and honey. The flour is prepared from roasted barley dried in an oven while the sheaves are still moist (Rashi).

Emptying – לְפָרֵק: Some explain that this means unloading a burden from an animal on Shabbat. Others explain that this refers to unpacking bundles of a crop (*Arukh*).

HALAKHA

Mixing *shatit* on Shabbat – גִּיבּוּל שַׁתִית בְּשַׁבָּת: One may not stir a large amount of flour made from roasted barley into liquid all at once. It is permitted to mix flour made from unripe roasted wheat with vinegar, provided the mixture is watery. However, this is prohibited if the mixture is thick, because it looks like kneading. On Shabbat one alters the manner in which he prepares the *shatit* by adding the vinegar to the flour instead of the weekday method of adding the flour to the vinegar (Rambam *Sefer Zemanim, Hilkhot Shabbat* 21:33; *Shulḥan Arukh, Oraḥ Ḥayyim* 321:14 and see the *Mishna Berura*).

רַבִּי יוֹסֵי בְּרַבִּי יְהוּדָה הִיא. וְהָנֵי מִילֵּי – הוּא דִּמְשַׁנֵּי. הֵיכִי מְשַׁנֵּי? אָמַר רַב חִסְדָּא: עַל יָד עַל יָד. וְשָׁוִין שֶׁבּוֹחֲשִׁין אֶת הַשָּׁתִית בְּשַׁבָּת וְשׁוֹתִים זִיתוֹם הַמִּצְרִי.

It is the opinion of **Rabbi Yosei, son of Rabbi Yehuda. And this** leniency **applies only** in a case **where one alters** the way that he kneads. The Gemara asks: **How does one alter** the manner in which he kneads? **Rav Ḥisda said:** One does not knead the dough all at once but rather **a little bit at a time.** It was also taught: **And they agree that one may mix the *shatit*,**[N] roasted barley to which honey is added, **on Shabbat,**[H] **and drink Egyptian beer,** as it is not considered to be for medicinal purposes.

וְהָאָמַרְתְּ ״אֵין גּוֹבְלִין״! לָא קַשְׁיָא, הָא – בְּעָבָה, הָא – בְּרַכָּה. וְהָנֵי מִילֵּי – הוּא דִּמְשַׁנֵּי.

The Gemara asks: **Didn't you say: One may not knead?** That contradicts the statement that they agree that it is permitted to stir the *shatit*. The Gemara answers: This is **not difficult,** as there is a distinction between the cases. **This** dispute with regard to *shatit* is referring **to** mixing a **thick** mixture, which is similar to kneading. However, **that** statement where they agree that mixing is permitted is referring **to a soft,** thin mixture that cannot be kneaded. **And** all of **these** statements are referring to a case **where one alters** the way he kneads or stirs.

הֵיכִי מְשַׁנֵּי? אָמַר רַב יוֹסֵף: בַּחוֹל נוֹתֵן אֶת הַחוֹמֶץ וְאַחַר כָּךְ נוֹתֵן אֶת הַשָּׁתִית, בְּשַׁבָּת – נוֹתֵן אֶת הַשָּׁתִית וְאַחַר כָּךְ נוֹתֵן אֶת הַחוֹמֶץ. לֵוִי בְּרֵיהּ דְּרַב הוּנָא בַּר חִיָּיא אַשְׁכְּחֵיהּ לְגַבָּלָא דְּבֵי נָשֵׁיהּ דְּקָא גָבֵיל וְסָפֵי לֵיהּ לְתוֹרֵיהּ, בְּטַשׁ בֵּיהּ. אֲתָא אֲבוּהּ אַשְׁכְּחֵיהּ, אָמַר לֵיהּ: הָכִי אֲמַר אֲבוּהָ דְּאִמָּךְ מִשְּׁמֵיהּ דְּרַב, וּמַנּוּ – רַבִּי יִרְמְיָה בַּר אַבָּא: גּוֹבְלִין וְלֹא מַסְפִּין. וּדְלָא לָקֵיט בְּלִישָּׁנֵיהּ – מְהַלְקִיטִין לֵיהּ. וְהָנֵי מִילֵּי – הוּא דִּמְשַׁנֵּי.

The Gemara asks: **How does one alter** the manner in which he performs these actions? **Rav Yosef said:** On a **weekday one** first **places the vinegar** in a vessel **and then places the *shatit*. On Shabbat one** first **places the *shatit* and then places the vinegar.** The Gemara relates that **Levi, son of Rav Huna bar Ḥiyya, found the one who kneads in his parents' home kneading** bran on Shabbat **and feeding it to his ox. He kicked him** so that he would stop. When **his father came** and **found him,** he **said to him: This** is what **your mother's father said in the name of Rav.** The Gemara interjects: **And who** is his mother's father? It is **Rabbi Yirmeya bar Abba,** who said: **One may knead but not feed** animals, **and** a calf **that does not take** the food **with its tongue may be fed** on Shabbat. **And this applies** only **when one alters** the manner in which he does so.

הֵיכִי מְשַׁנֵּי? אָמַר רַב יֵימָר בַּר שְׁלַמְיָא מִשְּׁמֵיהּ דְּאַבַּיֵי: שְׁתִי וָעֵרֶב. וְהָא לָא מְעָרֵב שַׁפִּיר! אָמַר רַב יְהוּדָה: מְנַעֲרוֹ לַכְּלִי.

The Gemara asks: **How does one alter** the manner in which he does so? **Rav Yeimar bar Shelamya said in the name of Abaye:** One moves the ladle or stirring utensil in the directions of **warp and woof.** The Gemara asks: **Isn't** it the case that **it will not mix well,** so what is the point of stirring it that way? **Rav Yehuda said:** It means that **one pours it into** another **vessel** and in the process it is mixed.

כְּתִיב אַפִּינְקְסֵיהּ דִּזְעֵירִי: אֲמָרִית קֳדָם רַבִּי, וּמַנּוּ – רַבִּי חִיָּיא, מַהוּ לְגַבֵּל? אֲמַר: אָסוּר. מַהוּ לְפָרֵק? אֲמַר: מוּתָּר. אֲמַר רַב [מְנַשְּׁיָא]: חַד קַמֵּי חַד, תְּרֵי קַמֵּי תְּרֵי – שַׁפִּיר דָּמֵי, תְּלָתָא קַמֵּי תְּרֵי – אָסוּר. רַב יוֹסֵף אָמַר: קַב וַאֲפִילּוּ קַבַּיִים. עוּלָּא אָמַר: כּוֹר וַאֲפִילּוּ כּוֹרַיִים.

It was written in Ze'eiri's notebook: I said before my rabbi, and the Gemara asks: **And who is** his rabbi? It is **Rabbi Ḥiyya.** And Ze'eiri said before him: **What is** the ruling? Is it permitted **to knead** on Shabbat? **He said:** It is **prohibited. What is** the ruling with regard to **emptying**[N] food from a vessel before one animal to place it before another animal? **He said:** It is **permitted. Rav Menashya said:** Placing **one** trough **before one** animal or **two** troughs **before two** animals, one may **well** do so. Placing **three** troughs **before two** animals **is prohibited,** because it is considered to be superfluous labor as he is bringing the animals more food than they need. **Rav Yosef said:** It is permitted to add **a *kav*** of additional food **or even two *kav*. Ulla said:** One may add **a *kor* or even two *kor*** and there is no need for concern.

כְּתִיב אַפִּינְקְסֵיהּ דְּלֵוִי: אֲמָרִית קֳדָם רַבִּי, וּמַנּוּ – רַבֵּינוּ הַקָּדוֹשׁ, עַל דַּהֲווּ גָּבְלִין שְׁתִיתָא בְּבָבֶל, וַהֲוָה צָוַח רַבִּי, וּמַנּוּ – רַבֵּינוּ הַקָּדוֹשׁ, עַל דַּהֲווּ גָּבְלִין שְׁתִיתָא, וְלֵית דְּשָׁמֵיעַ לֵיהּ, וְלֵית חֵילָא בִּידֵיהּ לְמֵיסַר – מִדְּרַבִּי יוֹסֵי בְּרַבִּי יְהוּדָה.

It was written in Levi's notebook: I said before my rabbi, and the Gemara asks: **And who is** his rabbi? It is **our holy Rabbi,** Rabbi Yehuda HaNasi. Levi spoke **about** the fact that **people would knead *shatit* in Babylonia, and my rabbi, and who is it, our holy Rabbi, cried** in protest over the fact that **people would knead *shatit*. And** there was **no one who listened to him, and he did not have the power to prohibit** it **due to** the people's reliance on the opinion of **Rabbi Yosei, son of Rabbi Yehuda,** who permitted doing so.

כְּתִיב אַפִּינְקְסֵיהּ דְּרַבִּי יְהוֹשֻׁעַ בֶּן לֵוִי: הַאי מַאן דְּבְחַד בְּשַׁבָּא – יְהֵי גְּבַר וְלָא חֲדָא בֵּיהּ.

After citing relevant *halakhot* written in the notebooks of various Sages, the Gemara relates that **it was written in Rabbi Yehoshua ben Levi's notebook: One who** was born **on the first day of the week,** Sunday, **will be a person and there will not be one in him.**

מַאי "[וְלָא חֲדָא בֵּיהּ]"? אִילֵימָא וְלָא חַד לְטִיבוּ – וְהָאָמַר רַב אָשֵׁי: אֲנָא בְּחַד בְּשַׁבָּא הֲוַאי! אֶלָּא – לָאו חֲדָא לְבִישׁוּ, וְהָאָמַר רַב אָשֵׁי: אֲנָא וְדִימִי בַּר קָקוּזְתָּא הֲוֵוין בְּחַד בְּשַׁבָּא, אֲנָא – מֶלֶךְ, וְהוּא – הֲוָה רֵישׁ גַּנָּבֵי! אֶלָּא: אִי כּוּלֵּי לְטִיבוּ, אִי כּוּלֵּי לְבִישׁוּ. מַאי טַעְמָא – דְּאִיבְּרוּ בֵּיהּ אוֹר וְחוֹשֶׁךְ?

The Gemara asks: **What is** the meaning of the phrase: **There will not be one in him? If you say** that **there is not one** quality **for the best,** that cannot be, **as Rav Ashi said: I was born on the first day of the week,** and one cannot say that there was nothing good about him. **Rather,** it must mean that **there is not one** quality **for the worst. Didn't Rav Ashi say: I and Dimi bar Kakuzta were** both born **on the first day of the week. I** became **a king,** the head of a yeshiva, **and he became the head of** a gang of **thieves,** clearly a negative quality. **Rather,** one born on a Sunday **is either completely for the best or completely for the worst. What is the reason** for this? It is **because** both **light and darkness were created** on the first day of Creation.[N]

הַאי מַאן דְּבִתְרֵי בְּשַׁבָּא – יְהֵי גְּבַר רַגְזָן. מַאי טַעְמָא – מִשּׁוּם דְּאִיפְּלִיגוּ בֵּיהּ מַיָּא. הַאי מַאן דִּבְתְלָתָא בְּשַׁבָּא – יְהֵי גְּבַר עֲתִיר, וְזַנַּאי יְהֵא. מַאי טַעְמָא – מִשּׁוּם דְּאִיבְּרוּ בֵּיהּ עֲשָׂבִים. הַאי מַאן דְּבְאַרְבְּעָה בְּשַׁבָּא – יְהֵי גְּבַר חַכִּים וְנָהִיר, מַאי טַעְמָא – מִשּׁוּם דְּאִיתְּלוּ בֵּיהּ מְאוֹרוֹת.

One who was born **on the second day of the week,** Monday, **will be a short-tempered person. What is the reason** for this? It is **because on that day,** the second day of Creation, **the** upper and lower **waters were divided.** Therefore, it is a day of contentiousness.

One who was born **on the third day of the week will be a rich man and a promiscuous** person. **What is the reason** for this? It is **because on that day,** the third day, **vegetation was created.** It grows abundantly but is also mixed together without boundaries between the grass and the plants.

One who was born **on the fourth day of the week will be a wise and enlightened person. What is the reason** for this? It is **because the** heavenly **lights were hung** in the heavens **on that day,** and wisdom is likened to light.

הַאי מַאן דְּבְחַמְשָׁה בְּשַׁבָּא – יְהֵי גְּבַר גּוֹמֵל חֲסָדִים. מַאי טַעְמָא – מִשּׁוּם דְּאִיבְּרוּ בֵּיהּ דָּגִים וְעוֹפוֹת. הַאי מַאן דְּבְמַעֲלֵי שַׁבְּתָא – יְהֵי גְּבַר חָזְרָן, אָמַר רַב נַחְמָן בַּר יִצְחָק: חָזְרָן בְּמִצְוֹת. הַאי מַאן דְּבְשַׁבְּתָא יְהֵי – בְּשַׁבְּתָא יָמוּת, עַל דְּאַחִילּוּ עֲלוֹהִי יוֹמָא רַבָּא דְּשַׁבְּתָא. אָמַר רָבָא בַּר רַב שֵׁילָא: וְקַדִּישָׁא רַבָּא יִתְקְרֵי.

One who was born **on the fifth day of the week will be a person who performs acts of kindness. What is the reason** for this? It is **because on that day the fish and fowl were created,** and they do not receive their sustenance by performing work for people. They are sustained by the kindness of God alone.

One who was born **on the sixth day of the week will be a seeker. Rav Naḥman bar Yitzḥak said** that this means that he will be **one who seeks out mitzvot,** as most of the activity on Friday involves preparation for Shabbat.

One who was born **on Shabbat will die on Shabbat, because they desecrated the great day of Shabbat on his** behalf. **Rava bar Rav Sheila said: And he will be called a** person of **great sanctity** because he was born on the sacred day of Shabbat.

NOTES

Because both light and darkness were created on the first day of Creation – דְּאִיבְּרוּ בֵּיהּ אוֹר וְחוֹשֶׁךְ: Those whose version of the Gemara includes this phrase explain: Just as light and darkness were created on the first day of Creation and separated from each another, so too, those born on the first day of the week will be either completely good, like light, or completely wicked, like darkness (*Ḥokhmat Manoaḥ*).

אֲמַר לְהוּ רַבִּי חֲנִינָא: פּוּקוּ אֱמַרוּ לֵיהּ לְבַר לֵיוָאִי: לֹא מַזַּל יוֹם גּוֹרֵם, אֶלָּא מַזַּל שָׁעָה גּוֹרֵם. הַאי מַאן דִּבְחַמָּה יְהֵי גְּבַר זִיוְתָן, יְהֵי אָכֵיל מִדִּילֵיהּ וְשָׁתֵי מִדִּילֵיהּ, וְרָזוֹהִי גַּלְיָין. אִם גָּנֵיב – לָא מַצְלַח. הַאי מַאן דִּבְכוֹכָב נוֹגַהּ יְהֵי גְּבַר עַתִּיר וְזַנַּאי יְהֵי, מַאי טַעְמָא – מִשּׁוּם דְּאִיתְיְלִיד בֵּיהּ נוּרָא. הַאי מַאן דִּבְכוֹכָב יְהֵי גְּבַר נָהִיר וְחַכִּים, מִשּׁוּם דְּסָפְרָא דְּחַמָּה הוּא. הַאי מַאן דִּבְלְבָנָה יְהֵי גְּבַר סָבֵיל מַרְעִין, בָּנֵאי וְסָתֵיר, סָתֵיר וּבָנֵאי, אָכֵיל דְּלָא דִּילֵיהּ וְשָׁתֵי דְּלָא דִּילֵיהּ, וְרָזוֹהִי כַּסְיָין, אִם גָּנַב – מַצְלַח. הַאי מַאן דִּבְשַׁבְּתַאי יְהֵי גְּבַר מַחְשְׁבָתֵיהּ בָּטְלִין, וְאִית דְּאָמְרִי: כׇּל דְּמַחְשְׁבִין עֲלֵיהּ בָּטְלִין. הַאי מַאן דִּבְצֶדֶק יְהֵי גְּבַר צַדְקָן, אָמַר רַב נַחְמָן בַּר יִצְחָק: וְצַדְקָן בְּמִצְוֹת. הַאי מַאן דִּבְמַאְדִּים יְהֵי גְּבַר אָשֵׁיד דְּמָא. אָמַר רַב אַשִׁי: אִי אוּמָּנָא, אִי גַּנָּבָא, אִי טַבָּחָא, אִי מוֹהֲלָא. אֲמַר רַבָּה: אֲנָא בְּמַאְדִּים הֲוַאי! אֲמַר אַבַּיֵי: מָר נַמִי עָנֵישׁ וְקָטֵיל.

Rabbi Ḥanina said to his students who heard all this: **Go and tell the son of Leiva'i,** Rabbi Yehoshua ben Levi: **It is not the constellation of the day** of the week **that determines** a person's nature; **rather,** it is **the constellation of the hour**[B] that **determines** his nature.[B]

One who was born **under** the influence of **the sun will be a radiant person; he will eat from his own** resources **and drink from his own** resources, **and his secrets will be exposed. If he steals he will not succeed,** because he will be like the sun that shines and is revealed to all.

One who was born **under** the influence of **Venus will be a rich and promiscuous person. What is the reason** for this? **Because fire was born** during the hour of Venus, he will be subject the fire of the evil inclination, which burns perpetually.

One who was born **under** the influence of **Mercury will be an enlightened and expert man, because** Mercury **is the sun's scribe,** as it is closest to the sun.

One who was born **under** the influence of **the moon will be a man who suffers pains, who builds and destroys, and destroys and builds.** He will be a man **who eats not from his own** resources **and drinks not from his own** resources, **and whose secrets are hidden. If he steals he will succeed,** as he is like the moon that constantly changes form, whose light is not its own, and who is at times exposed and at times hidden.

One who was born **under** the influence of **Saturn will be a man whose thoughts are for naught. And some say** that **everything that** others **think about him** and plan to do to him **is for naught.**

One who was born **under** the influence of **Jupiter** [*tzedek*] **will be a just** person [*tzadkan*]. **Rav Naḥman bar Yitzḥak said: And just** in this context means just **in** the performance of **mitzvot.**

One who was born **under** the influence of **Mars will be one who spills blood. Rav Ashi said:** He will be **either a blood letter, or a thief, or a slaughterer** of animals, **or a circumciser. Rabba said: I was** born **under** the influence of **Mars** and I do not perform any of those activities. **Abaye said: My Master also punishes and kills** as a judge.

BACKGROUND

The constellation of the hour – מַזַּל שָׁעָה: The seven planetary bodies mentioned here: The sun, Venus, Mercury, the moon, Saturn, Jupiter, and Mars influence different hours of the day and night on different days of the week. See the table below for their influence beginning with the first hour of the night.

Hours	Sunday	Monday	Tuesday	Wednesday	Thursday	Friday	Shabbat
1	Mercury	Jupiter	Venus	Saturn	Sun	Moon	Mars
2	Moon	Mars	Mercury	Jupiter	Venus	Saturn	Sun
3	Saturn	Sun	Moon	Mars	Mercury	Jupiter	Venus
4	Jupiter	Venus	Saturn	Sun	Moon	Mars	Mercury
5	Mars	Mercury	Jupiter	Venus	Saturn	Sun	Moon
6	Sun	Moon	Mars	Mercury	Jupiter	Venus	Saturn
7	Venus	Saturn	Sun	Moon	Mars	Mercury	Jupiter
8	Mercury	Jupiter	Venus	Saturn	Sun	Moon	Mars
9	Moon	Mars	Mercury	Jupiter	Venus	Saturn	Sun
10	Saturn	Sun	Moon	Mars	Mercury	Jupiter	Venus
11	Jupiter	Venus	Saturn	Sun	Moon	Mars	Mercury
12	Mars	Mercury	Jupiter	Venus	Saturn	Sun	Moon
13	Sun	Moon	Mars	Mercury	Jupiter	Venus	Saturn
14	Venus	Saturn	Sun	Moon	Mars	Mercury	Jupiter
15	Mercury	Jupiter	Venus	Saturn	Sun	Moon	Mars
16	Moon	Mars	Mercury	Jupiter	Venus	Saturn	Sun
17	Saturn	Sun	Moon	Mars	Mercury	Jupiter	Venus
18	Jupiter	Venus	Saturn	Sun	Moon	Mars	Mercury
19	Mars	Mercury	Jupiter	Venus	Saturn	Sun	Moon
20	Sun	Moon	Mars	Mercury	Jupiter	Venus	Saturn
21	Venus	Saturn	Sun	Moon	Mars	Mercury	Jupiter
22	Mercury	Jupiter	Venus	Saturn	Sun	Moon	Mars
23	Moon	Mars	Mercury	Jupiter	Venus	Saturn	Sun
24	Saturn	Sun	Moon	Mars	Mercury	Jupiter	Venus

The stars and their qualities – הַכּוֹכָבִים וּתְכוּנוֹתֵיהֶם: Astrology, which was considered to be a serious science over the course of many generations, was highly developed in Babylonia. Nevertheless, the Talmud discusses astrology relatively infrequently and when it does, the discussion is on the level of folklore, lacking development or complexity. This is apparently because most of the Sages maintained that the constellations do not control the Jewish people.

Some of the qualities ascribed here to various astrological signs are related to the visible qualities of the stars themselves, like the qualities attributed to the sun and the moon. Those born under the sign of Venus are ascribed certain qualities because the luminaries were hung on that day. This may be explained because the conclusion of Shabbat is the time associated with Venus, and it is also the time when, according to the Rabbis, fire was discovered by people. Mercury is described as the sun's scribe because even the early astrologers were aware that it was the closest planet to the sun. Saturn is generally regarded as a sign related to misfortune, even though it is ascribed a different meaning here. Jupiter is considered a sign of fortune and righteousness. Mars was considered to be a sign of war and murder, because of its red color and because of its association with the Roman god Mars.

אִיתְּמַר, רַבִּי חֲנִינָא אוֹמֵר: מַזָּל מַחְכִּים, מַזָּל מַעֲשִׁיר, וְיֵשׁ מַזָּל לְיִשְׂרָאֵל. רַבִּי יוֹחָנָן אָמַר: אֵין מַזָּל לְיִשְׂרָאֵל. וְאָזְדָא רַבִּי יוֹחָנָן לְטַעְמֵיהּ, דְּאָמַר רַבִּי יוֹחָנָן: מִנַּיִן שֶׁאֵין מַזָּל לְיִשְׂרָאֵל – שֶׁנֶּאֱמַר "כֹּה אָמַר ה׳ אֶל דֶּרֶךְ הַגּוֹיִם אַל תִּלְמָדוּ וּמֵאוֹתוֹת הַשָּׁמַיִם אַל תֵּחָתּוּ כִּי יֵחַתּוּ הַגּוֹיִם מֵהֵמָּה", הֵם יֵחַתּוּ, וְלֹא יִשְׂרָאֵל.

It was stated that Rabbi Ḥanina says: A constellation makes one wise and a constellation makes one wealthy,[N] and there is a constellation for the Jewish people that influences them. Rabbi Yoḥanan said: There is no constellation for the Jewish people that influences them. The Jewish people are not subject to the influence of astrology. And Rabbi Yoḥanan follows his own reasoning, as Rabbi Yoḥanan said: From where is it derived that there is no constellation for the Jewish people? As it is stated: "Thus said the Lord: Learn not the way of the nations, and be not dismayed at the signs of heaven; for the nations are dismayed at them" (Jeremiah 10:2). The nations will be dismayed by them, but not the Jewish people.

וְאַף רַב סָבַר אֵין מַזָּל לְיִשְׂרָאֵל, דְּאָמַר רַב יְהוּדָה אָמַר רַב: מִנַּיִן שֶׁאֵין מַזָּל לְיִשְׂרָאֵל – שֶׁנֶּאֱמַר "וַיּוֹצֵא אוֹתוֹ הַחוּצָה". אָמַר אַבְרָהָם לִפְנֵי הַקָּדוֹשׁ בָּרוּךְ הוּא: רִבּוֹנוֹ שֶׁל עוֹלָם "בֶּן בֵּיתִי יוֹרֵשׁ אוֹתִי". אָמַר לוֹ: לָאו, "כִּי אִם אֲשֶׁר יֵצֵא מִמֵּעֶיךָ".

And Rav also holds that there is no constellation for the Jewish people, as Rav Yehuda said that Rav said: From where is it derived that there is no constellation for the Jewish people? As it is stated with regard to Abraham: "And He brought him outside, and said: Look now toward heaven, and count the stars, if you are able to count them; and He said unto him: So shall your offspring be" (Genesis 15:5). The Sages derived from this that Abraham said before the Holy One, Blessed be He: Master of the Universe, "Behold, You have given me no offspring, and one born in my house is to be my heir" (Genesis 15:3). The Holy One, Blessed be He, said to him: No. "And, behold, the word of the Lord came to him, saying: This man shall not be your heir; rather, one that will come forth from your own innards shall be your heir" (Genesis 15:4).

אָמַר לְפָנָיו: רִבּוֹנוֹ שֶׁל עוֹלָם, נִסְתַּכַּלְתִּי בְּאִיצְטַגְנִינוּת שֶׁלִּי וְאֵינִי רָאוּי לְהוֹלִיד בֵּן. אָמַר לֵיהּ: צֵא מֵאִיצְטַגְנִינוּת שֶׁלְּךָ, שֶׁאֵין מַזָּל לְיִשְׂרָאֵל. מַאי דַּעְתִּיךְ –

Abraham said before Him: Master of the Universe, I looked at my astrological map, and according to the configuration of my constellations I am not fit to have a son. The Holy One, Blessed be He, said to him: Emerge from your astrology, as the verse states: "And He brought him outside," as there is no constellation for Israel. What is your thinking?

Perek **XXIV**
Daf **156** Amud **b**

דְּקָאֵי צֶדֶק בְּמַעֲרָב, מְהַדְרָנָא וּמוֹקְמִינָא לֵיהּ בְּמִזְרָח. וְהַיְינוּ דִּכְתִיב "מִי הֵעִיר מִמִּזְרָח צֶדֶק יִקְרָאֵהוּ לְרַגְלוֹ".

Is it because Jupiter is situated in the west that you cannot have children? I will restore it and establish it in the east. And that is the meaning of that which is written with regard to Abraham: "Who has raised up one from the east, he will call justice [*tzedek*] to his steps [*leraglo*]. He gives nations before him, and makes him rule over kings; his sword makes them as the dust, his bow as the driven stubble" (Isaiah 41:2). God established Jupiter [*tzedek*] in the east on behalf of [*leraglo*] Abraham.

וּמִדִּשְׁמוּאֵל נַמִי, אֵין מַזָּל לְיִשְׂרָאֵל. דִּשְׁמוּאֵל וְאַבְלֵט הֲווּ יָתְבִי, וַהֲווּ קָאָזְלִי הָנָךְ אֱינָשֵׁי לְאַגְמָא. אֲמַר לֵיהּ אַבְלֵט לִשְׁמוּאֵל: הַאי גַּבְרָא אָזֵיל וְלָא אָתֵי, טָרֵיק לֵיהּ חִיוְיָא וּמָיֵית. אֲמַר לֵיהּ שְׁמוּאֵל: אִי בַּר יִשְׂרָאֵל הוּא – אָזֵיל וְאָתֵי. אַדְּיָתְבִי אָזֵיל וְאָתֵי.

And from that which transpired to Shmuel, one can also conclude that there is no constellation for the Jewish people. The Gemara relates that Shmuel and the gentile sage Ablet[P] were sitting, and they saw these people were going to the lake. Ablet said to Shmuel: This person will go and he will not return, because a snake will bite him and he will die. Shmuel said to him: If he is a Jew, he will go and come back. As they were sitting for a while, the person they discussed went away and then returned.

קָם אַבְלֵט, שַׁדְיֵהּ לְטוּנֵיהּ אַשְׁכַּח בֵּיהּ חִיוְיָא דִּפְסִיק וּשְׁדִי בְּתַרְתֵּי גּוּבֵי. אֲמַר לֵיהּ שְׁמוּאֵל: מַאי עֲבַדְתְּ? אֲמַר לֵיהּ: כָּל יוֹמָא הֲוָה מְרַמֵינַן רִיפְתָּא בַּהֲדֵי הֲדָדֵי וְאָכְלִינַן. הָאִידָּנָא הֲוָה אִיכָּא חַד מִינַּן דְּלָא הֲוָה לֵיהּ רִיפְתָּא, הֲוָה קָא מִיכְסַף. אֲמִינָא לְהוּ: אֲנָא קָאֵימְנָא וְאָרְמֵינָא. כִּי מְטַאי לְגַבֵּיהּ שְׁוַאי נַפְשַׁאי כְּמַאן דִּשְׁקִילִי מִינֵּיהּ, כִּי הֵיכִי דְּלָא לִיכְסִיף. אֲמַר לֵיהּ: מִצְוָה עֲבַדְתְּ! נְפַק שְׁמוּאֵל וְדָרַשׁ: "וּצְדָקָה תַּצִּיל מִמָּוֶת" וְלֹא מִמִּיתָה מְשׁוּנָּה, אֶלָּא מִמִּיתָה עַצְמָהּ.

Ablet stood up, threw down the person's burden, and inside he found a snake cut and cast in two pieces. Shmuel said to him: What did you do to merit being saved from death? The person said to him: Every day we all take bread together and eat from the bread. Today, there was one of us who did not have bread, and when it came time to gather the bread, he was embarrassed because he did not have any to give. I said to the others: I will go and take the bread. When I came to the person who did not have bread, I rendered myself as one who was taking from him so that he would not be embarrassed. Shmuel said to him: You performed a mitzva. Shmuel went out and taught based on this incident that even though it is written: "And charity will save from death" (Proverbs 10:2), it does not only mean that it will save a person from an unusual death[N] but even from death itself.

NOTES

A constellation makes one wise and… makes one wealthy – מַזָּל מַחְכִּים, מַזָּל מַעֲשִׁיר: Many commentaries discussed this opinion and concluded that Rabbi Ḥanina does not mean to say that everything is determined by one's constellation. He himself stated: Everything is in the hands of Heaven, except for fear of Heaven; the choice between good and evil remains in the purview of human beings. Similarly, those who deny the influence of one's constellation do not completely deny it; rather, they hold that the constellation does not dictate everything but it exerts an influence in a certain direction. However, a person has the power to free himself from the limitations of his fundamental nature and to forge his own path in life (*ge'onim*; *HaKotev*; *Pardes Rimonim*).

PERSONALITIES

Ablet – אַבְלֵט: This gentile sage was very close with Shmuel, and the Talmud relates several encounters and discussions between them. Ablet was also quite familiar with Jewish customs. The Jerusalem Talmud also records conversations between him and Jewish Sages. Although Ablet's origins are not clear, his name indicates that he was probably Babylonian. Obalit is phonetically similar to the Babylonian name Sanbalat.

NOTES

Not only from an unusual death – וְלֹא מִמִּיתָה מְשׁוּנָּה: This must be understood in light of the Gemara in tractate *Bava Batra* which explains that the verse: "And charity will save from death," refers to an unusual form of death, since even people who give charity eventually die. Here, the Gemara adds that it also means that one who gives charity will merit living a long life (Maharsha).

ומדרבי עקיבא נמי, אין מזל לישראל. דרבי עקיבא הויא ליה ברתא, אמרי ליה כלדאי: ההוא יומא דעיילה לבי גננא – טריק לה חיויא ומיתא. הוה דאיגא אמילתא טובא. ההוא יומא שקלתה למכבנתא, דצתא בגודא, איתרמי איתיב בעיניה דחיויא. לצפרא כי קא שקלה לה – הוה קא סריך ואתי חיויא בתרה.

And from that which transpired to **Rabbi Akiva as well** it can be derived that **there is no constellation for the Jewish people, as Rabbi Akiva had a daughter, and Chaldean**[B] astrologers **told him** that **on the same day that she enters the wedding canopy, a snake will bite her and she will die. She was very worried about this. On that day,** her wedding day, **she took** the ornamental **pin** from her hair **and stuck it** into a hole **in the wall** for safekeeping, and **it happened** that it **entered** directly **into the eye of the snake. In the morning, when she took** the pin, **the snake was pulled and came out with it.**

אמר לה אבוה: מאי עבדת? אמרה ליה: בפניא אתא עניא, קרא אבבא, והוו טרידי כולי עלמא בסעודתא, וליכא דשמעיה. קאימנא, שקלתי לריסתנאי דיהבית לי, יהבתיה ניהליה. אמר לה: מצוה עבדת! נפק רבי עקיבא ודרש: "וצדקה תציל ממות" ולא ממיתה משונה, אלא ממיתה עצמה.

Her father Rabbi Akiva **said to her: What did you do** to merit being saved from the snake? She told him: **In the evening a poor person came and knocked on the door, and everyone was preoccupied with the feast and nobody heard him. I stood** and **took the portion that you had given me** and **gave it to him.** Rabbi Akiva **said to her: You performed a mitzva,** and you were saved in its merit. **Rabbi Akiva went out and taught** based on this incident that even though it is written: **"And charity will save from death"** (Proverbs 10:2), it does **not** mean that it will save a person only **from an unusual death, but** even **from death itself.**

ומדרב נחמן בר יצחק נמי, אין מזל לישראל. דאימיה דרב נחמן בר יצחק אמרי לה כלדאי: בריך גנבא הוה. לא שבקתיה גלויי רישיה. אמרה ליה: כסי רישיך, כי היכי דתיהוו עלך אימתא דשמיא, ובעי רחמי. לא הוה ידע אמאי קאמרה ליה. יומא חד יתיב קא גריס תותי דיקלא, נפל גלימא מעילויה רישיה דלי עיניה חזא לדיקלא, אלמיה יצריה, סליק פסקיה לקיבורא בשיניה.

And from that which transpired to **Rav Naḥman bar Yitzḥak as well** it can be derived that **there is no constellation for the Jewish people, As Chaldean** astrologers **told Rav Naḥman bar Yitzḥak's mother: Your son will be a thief. She did not allow him** to **uncover his head. She said to** her son: **Cover your head**[NH] **so that the fear of Heaven will be upon you, and pray for** Divine **mercy. He did not know why she said** this **to him. One day he was sitting and studying beneath a palm tree** that did not belong to him, and **the cloak fell off of his head. He lifted his eyes** and **saw the palm tree. He was overcome by impulse** and **he climbed up and detached a bunch of dates with his teeth.** Apparently, he had an inborn inclination to steal, but was able to overcome that inclination with proper education and prayer.

מתני׳ מחתכין את הדלועין לפני הבהמה, ואת הנבלה לפני הכלבים, רבי יהודה אומר: אם לא היתה נבלה מערב שבת – אסורה, לפי שאינה מן המוכן.

MISHNA **One may cut the pumpkins before an animal** on Shabbat, as long as they were picked prior to Shabbat. **And** likewise one may cut **an** animal **carcass before the dogs** on Shabbat. **Rabbi Yehuda says: If it was not** already **a carcass,** i.e., it was not dead, **prior to Shabbat, it is prohibited** to cut it or even move it on Shabbat **because it is not prepared** for use on Shabbat.

גמ׳ איתמר (ער״ל שח״ז סימן) אמר עולא: הלכה כרבי יהודה. (ושמואל אמר: הלכה כרבי שמעון).

GEMARA A dispute between the *amora'im* with regard to the prohibition of set-aside on Shabbat **was stated.** ***Ayin, reish, lamed, shin, ḥet, zayin*** **is a mnemonic** for the names of the *amora'im* who stated the following *halakhot*. **Ulla said:** The ***halakha*** **is in accordance with** the opinion **of Rabbi Yehuda,** who holds that there is a prohibition of set-aside on Shabbat. **And Shmuel said:** The ***halakha*** **is in accordance with** the opinion **of Rabbi Shimon.**

ואף רב סבר הלכה כרבי יהודה מדכרכי דזוזי דרב אסר ושמואל שרי ואף לוי סבר הלכה כרבי יהודה. כי הא דלוי כי הוו מייתי טריפתא לקמיה ביומא טבא לא הוה חזי לה אלא כי יתיב אקילקליתא. דאמר: דילמא לא מתכשרא, ואפילו לכלבים לא חזיא.

And Rav also holds that the ***halakha*** **is in accordance with** the opinion **of Rabbi Yehuda.** From where is it ascertained that this is Rav's opinion? **From that which** was taught with regard to **the mats that are** on **ships; Rav prohibited** moving them on Shabbat due to the prohibition of set-aside, **and Shmuel permitted** moving them. **And Levi also holds** that the ***halakha*** **is in accordance with** the opinion **of Rabbi Yehuda, as** can be seen from his practice when **they would bring a** slaughtered animal with regard to which there was concern that it was **an animal with a condition that will cause it to die within twelve months** [*tereifa*], **before Levi on a Festival. He would** examine it **only when he was sitting** near **a garbage** dump, **as he said: Perhaps it would not be** determined to be **kosher and** it would **not be suited even for dogs,** and then it would be prohibited to move the carcass. Apparently, he holds that it is prohibited to move a carcass that was not prepared for use before Shabbat.

BACKGROUND

Chaldeans – כלדאי: As indicated in a number of Talmudic sources, the Chaldeans, or *Kasdim* as they are referred to in the book of Daniel (2:4), were apparently neither magicians nor sorcerers, from whom it would have been prohibited by Torah law to receive counsel. Rather, it seems they were the leading scientists of the time. They specialized in astrology, in predicting a person's fate based on the stars. Although Jewish men and women consulted the Chaldeans regularly and this was not considered to be a violation of a prohibition, not everyone permitted it (see *Tosafot*).

NOTES

Covering the head – כיסוי הראש: From several Talmudic sources it is apparent that not all men covered their heads. Prominent Torah scholars covered their heads with a scarf. Since children never covered their heads, Rav Naḥman bar Yitzḥak was exceptional in this regard. In subsequent generations covering one's head became standard practice.

HALAKHA

Covering the head – כיסוי הראש: A man may not walk four cubits with his head uncovered even under a roof (*Mishna Berura*), as covering one's head is a custom of piety and leads to fear of God. The story of Rav Naḥman bar Yitzḥak is one of many sources that mention this custom. Although there are halakhic authorities who explicitly characterized covering one's head as merely a custom of piety (Maharshal; Vilna Gaon), the majority of Jewish men are especially vigilant when it comes to covering their heads (*Shulḥan Arukh, Oraḥ Ḥayyim* 2:6).

וּשְׁמוּאֵל אָמַר: הֲלָכָה כְּרַבִּי שִׁמְעוֹן. וְאַף זְעֵירִי סָבַר הֲלָכָה כְּרַבִּי שִׁמְעוֹן דִּתְנַן: בְּהֵמָה שֶׁמֵּתָה – לֹא יְזִיזֶנָּה מִמְּקוֹמָהּ, וְתַרְגְּמָא זְעֵירִי: בְּבֶהֱמַת קָדָשִׁים, אֲבָל בְּחוּלִּין – שַׁפִּיר דָּמֵי. וְאַף רַבִּי יוֹחָנָן אָמַר: הֲלָכָה כְּרַבִּי שִׁמְעוֹן. וּמִי אָמַר רַבִּי יוֹחָנָן הָכִי? וְהָא אָמַר רַבִּי יוֹחָנָן: הֲלָכָה כִּסְתָם מִשְׁנָה, וּתְנַן:

And Shmuel said: The ***halakha* is in accordance with** the opinion of **Rabbi Shimon,** who holds that the prohibition of set-aside does not apply on Shabbat. **And Ze'eiri also holds** that the ***halakha* is in accordance with** the opinion of **Rabbi Shimon, as we learned** in a mishna: With regard to **an animal that died** on Shabbat, **one may not move it from its place** on Shabbat. **And Ze'eiri explained:** This prohibition only applies **to a consecrated animal,**[N] as consecrated items may not be fed to dogs in deference to their sanctity; therefore, it is set-aside and may not be moved on Shabbat. **However, in** the case of **a non-sacred** animal, one may **well** move it and use it because it does not have set-aside status. **And Rabbi Yoḥanan also said** that the ***halakha* is in accordance with** the opinion of **Rabbi Shimon.** The Gemara asks: **And did Rabbi Yoḥanan** really **say that? Didn't Rabbi Yoḥanan say:** The ***halakha* is in accordance with an unattributed mishna, and we learned** in a mishna:

NOTES

A consecrated animal – **בְּהֵמַת קָדָשִׁים**: An consecrated animal that died without being redeemed can no longer be redeemed or regain non-sacred status. Therefore, it is prohibited to derive benefit from it. On Shabbat and Festivals it is set-aside according to all opinions, similar to a clump of dirt or raw materials, whose set-aside status is even more stringent than that of prohibited vessels.

Perek **XXIV**
Daf **157** Amud **a**

אֵין מְבַקְּעִין עֵצִים מִן הַקּוֹרוֹת, וְלֹא מִן הַקּוֹרָה שֶׁנִּשְׁבְּרָה בְּיוֹם טוֹב! רַבִּי יוֹחָנָן, הַהוּא – כְּרַבִּי יוֹסֵי בַּר יְהוּדָה מַתְנֵי לָהּ. תָּא שְׁמַע: מַתְחִילִין בַּעֲרֵימַת הַתֶּבֶן, אֲבָל לֹא בְּעֵצִים שֶׁבַּמּוּקְצֶה! הָתָם בְּאַרְזֵי וְאַשּׁוּחֵי, דְּמוּקְצֶה מֵחֲמַת חֶסְרוֹן כִּיס אֲפִילּוּ רַבִּי שִׁמְעוֹן מוֹדֶה.

One may chop wood neither from beams set aside for building **nor from a beam that broke on a Festival.**[H] Apparently, this unattributed mishna is in accordance with the opinion of Rabbi Yehuda. The Gemara answers that **Rabbi Yoḥanan** answered: **That** mishna **is** actually **in accordance with** the opinion of **Rabbi Yosei bar Yehuda,** which is an individual opinion. **Come** and **hear: One may start** a fire on a Festival **with a pile of straw**[H] **but not with wood that is from the** wood **storage** behind one's house, because that wood is set aside for other uses. Apparently, this is an unattributed mishna in accordance with the opinion of Rabbi Yehuda with regard to the prohibition of set-aside. The Gemara answers: **There,** the mishna is **referring to** wood from **cedar and fir** trees that are **set aside due to monetary loss. Even Rabbi Shimon concedes** that the prohibition of set-aside is in effect in that case.

תָּא שְׁמַע: אֵין מַשְׁקִין וְשׁוֹחֲטִין אֶת הַמִּדְבָּרִיּוֹת, אֲבָל מַשְׁקִין וְשׁוֹחֲטִין אֶת הַבַּיָּיתוֹת!

Come and **hear** a proof from another mishna: **One may neither give water to nor slaughter** non-domesticated **desert** animals, animals that are always grazing in the fields. Since people do not generally tend to them, they are considered set-aside and may not be used. Giving them water would ease removal of their hides. **However, one may give water to and slaughter domesticated animals.**[H] This is apparently an unattributed mishna in accordance with the opinion of Rabbi Yehuda.

רַבִּי יוֹחָנָן סְתָמָא אַחֲרִינָא אַשְׁכַּח, "בֵּית שַׁמַּאי אוֹמְרִים: מַגְבִּיהִין מֵעַל הַשֻּׁלְחָן עֲצָמוֹת וּקְלִיפִּין, וּבֵית הִלֵּל אוֹמְרִים: מְסַלֵּק אֶת הַטַּבְלָה כּוּלָּהּ וּמְנַעֲרָהּ". וְאָמַר רַב נַחְמָן: אָנוּ אֵין לָנוּ אֶלָּא בֵּית שַׁמַּאי כְּרַבִּי יְהוּדָה, וּבֵית הִלֵּל כְּרַבִּי שִׁמְעוֹן.

The Gemara answers: **Rabbi Yoḥanan found a different unattributed** mishna in accordance with the opinion of Rabbi Shimon. **Beit Shammai say: One may lift bones and peels** and shells, which are set-aside, **from the table** on Shabbat. **And Beit Hillel say: One** must **remove the entire board** from atop the table **and shake it;** however, he may not lift the set-aside objects. **And Rav Naḥman said** to reverse the two opinions, and **we have only Beit Shammai in accordance with** the opinion of **Rabbi Yehuda, and Beit Hillel in accordance with** the opinion of **Rabbi Shimon.** As the *halakha* is always ruled in accordance with the opinion of Beit Hillel, this mishna has the authority of an unattributed mishna.

HALAKHA

One may chop wood neither from beams set aside for building nor from a beam that broke on a Festival – **אֵין מְבַקְּעִין עֵצִים מִן הַקּוֹרוֹת, וְלֹא מִן הַקּוֹרָה שֶׁנִּשְׁבְּרָה בְּיוֹם טוֹב**: One may not chop wood on a Festival from beams that were set aside for building, or from a beam that broke on the Festival (Rambam *Sefer Zemanim, Hilkhot Yom Tov* 2:12; *Shulḥan Arukh, Oraḥ Ḥayyim* 501:1).

One may start a fire with a pile of straw – **מַתְחִילִין בַּעֲרֵימַת הַתֶּבֶן**: One may take kindling from piles of straw on a Festival *ab initio*, if the straw was designated exclusively for that purpose (Rambam *Sefer Zemanim, Hilkhot Yom Tov* 2:11; *Shulḥan Arukh, Oraḥ Ḥayyim* 518:7).

Giving water to and slaughtering animals – **הַשְׁקָאַת וּשְׁחִיטַת בְּהֵמוֹת**: On a Festival, one may not give water or food to fish and birds that are set-aside, lest one come to take one for slaughter. However, one may slaughter or give water to animals that graze outside of the boundaries of the city and come back at night to sleep within it, because they are considered to be designated for eating from before the Festival (Rambam *Sefer Zemanim, Hilkhot Yom Tov* 2:2, 17; *Shulḥan Arukh, Oraḥ Ḥayyim* 496:2, 498:3).

פְּלִיגִי בָּהּ רַב אַחָא וְרָבִינָא, חַד אָמַר: בְּכָל הַשַּׁבָּת כּוּלָּהּ הֲלָכָה כְּרַבִּי שִׁמְעוֹן, לְבַר מִמּוּקְצֶה מֵחֲמַת מִיאוּס, וּמַאי נִיהוּ – נֵר יָשָׁן. וְחַד אָמַר: בְּמוּקְצֶה מֵחֲמַת מִיאוּס נַמִּי הֲלָכָה כְּרַבִּי שִׁמְעוֹן, לְבַר מִמּוּקְצֶה מֵחֲמַת אִיסּוּר וּמַאי נִיהוּ – נֵר שֶׁהִדְלִיקוּ בָּהּ בְּאוֹתָהּ שַׁבָּת. אֲבָל מוּקְצֶה מֵחֲמַת חֶסְרוֹן כִּיס – אֲפִילּוּ רַבִּי שִׁמְעוֹן מוֹדֶה, דִּתְנַן: כָּל הַכֵּלִים נִיטָּלִין בַּשַּׁבָּת, חוּץ מִמַּסָּר הַגָּדוֹל וְיָתֵד שֶׁל מַחֲרֵישָׁה.

Rav Aḥa and Ravina disputed this matter. **One said: In all of** the *halakhot* **of Shabbat**[N] in which there is a tannaitic dispute involving Rabbi Shimon, the ***halakha* is in accordance with** the opinion of **Rabbi Shimon, except for** the case of an item **set aside due to repulsiveness. And what is that** case? It is the case of **an old** oil **lamp,** which may not be moved on Shabbat, contrary to Rabbi Shimon's opinion. **And one said: In** the case of an item **set aside due to repulsiveness,** the ***halakha* is also in accordance with** the opinion of **Rabbi Shimon.** The *halakha* is in accordance with the opinion of Rabbi Shimon **except for** the case of **set aside due to prohibition. And what is that** case? It is the case of moving **an** oil **lamp that one kindled** for **that** very **Shabbat. However,** with regard to an item **set aside due to monetary loss, even Rabbi Shimon concedes** that it is prohibited to move that item, **as we learned** in a mishna according to his position: **All vessels may be moved on Shabbat except for a large saw and the blade of a plow,** both of which are prohibited. Due to their significance, their owners make certain that they will not be damaged.

מתני׳ מְפִירִין נְדָרִים בַּשַּׁבָּת, וְנִשְׁאָלִין לִנְדָרִים שֶׁהֵן לְצוֹרֶךְ הַשַּׁבָּת. וּפוֹקְקִין אֶת הַמָּאוֹר, וּמוֹדְדִין אֶת הַמַּטְלִית, וּמוֹדְדִין אֶת הַמִּקְוֶה. וּמַעֲשֶׂה בִּימֵי אָבִיו שֶׁל רַבִּי צָדוֹק וּבִימֵי אַבָּא שָׁאוּל בֶּן בָּטְנִית, שֶׁפָּקְקוּ אֶת הַמָּאוֹר בְּטָפִיחַ, וְקָשְׁרוּ אֶת הַמְּקֵידָה בִּגְמִי לֵידַע אִם יֵשׁ בַּגִּיגִית פּוֹתֵחַ טֶפַח אִם לָאו. וּמִדִּבְרֵיהֶם לָמַדְנוּ, שֶׁפּוֹקְקִין וּמוֹדְדִין וְקוֹשְׁרִין בַּשַּׁבָּת.

MISHNA A father or husband **may nullify** his daughter's or his wife's **vows on Shabbat,**[H] **and one may request** from a Sage **to dissolve vows**[H] **that are for the purpose of Shabbat.** Failure to dissolve the vow will compromise one's fulfillment of the mitzva to delight in Shabbat. **And one may seal a window** on Shabbat to prevent light from entering, **and one may measure a rag** to determine whether or not it is large enough to contract ritual impurity, **and one may measure a ritual bath** to determine if it contains enough water for immersion. The mishna relates that there was **an incident in the time of Rabbi Tzadok's father and the time of Abba Shaul ben Botnit,** in which they **sealed a window using an earthenware vessel**[N] **and tied an earthenware shard with** a long **reed-grass** with a temporary knot, in order **to ascertain whether or not the roofing had an opening** the size of **a handbreadth. And from their statements** and their actions, **we derived that one may seal** a window, **and measure, and tie** a knot **on Shabbat.**

גמ׳ אִיבַּעְיָא לְהוּ: הֲפָרָה – בֵּין לְצוֹרֶךְ וּבֵין שֶׁלֹּא לְצוֹרֶךְ; וּשְׁאֵלָה – לְצוֹרֶךְ – אִין, שֶׁלֹּא לְצוֹרֶךְ – לָא. וּמִשּׁוּם הָכִי קָפַלְגִינְהוּ מֵהֲדָדֵי.

GEMARA We learned in the mishna that it is permitted to nullify vows and to request that Sages dissolve vows[N] for the purpose of Shabbat. In an attempt to understand the mishna, **a dilemma was raised** before the Sages: Is **nullification** of vows on Shabbat permitted **both for the purpose** of Shabbat **and** when it is **not for the purpose** of Shabbat? **And the request** to dissolve vows, when it is **for the purpose** of Shabbat, **yes,** it is permitted, but when it is **not for the purpose** of Shabbat, **no,** it is prohibited? **And** is it **due to that** distinction that the *tanna* of the mishna **separated** the cases **from each other** and listed them separately?

אוֹ דִּילְמָא: הֲפָרָה נַמִּי, לְצוֹרֶךְ – אִין, שֶׁלֹּא לְצוֹרֶךְ – לָא. וְהָא דְּקָא פָּלֵיג לְהוּ מֵהֲדָדֵי – מִשּׁוּם דַּהֲפָרָה אֵין צָרִיךְ בֵּית דִּין, וּשְׁאֵלָה צְרִיכָה בֵּית דִּין?

Or perhaps with regard to **nullification** of vows on Shabbat **as well,** when it is **for the purpose** of Shabbat, **yes,** it is permitted, but when they are **not for the purpose** of Shabbat, **no,** it is prohibited; **and** the fact **that** the *tanna* of the mishna **separated** the cases **from each other** and listed them separately is **due to** the fact **that** for **nullification one does not require a court,** and a husband or father can nullify a woman's vows on his own, **but** for **the request** to dissolve vows **one requires a court.**

תָּא שְׁמַע, דִּתְנֵי זוּטֵי דְּבֵי רַב פַּפָּא: מְפִירִין נְדָרִים בַּשַּׁבָּת לְצוֹרֶךְ הַשַּׁבָּת. לְצוֹרֶךְ הַשַּׁבָּת – אִין, שֶׁלֹּא לְצוֹרֶךְ הַשַּׁבָּת – לָא.

Come and **hear** a resolution to the dilemma from **that which** the Sage, **Zutei, of the school of Rav Pappa taught: One may nullify vows on Shabbat for the purpose of Shabbat.** Apparently, when the nullification is **for the purpose of Shabbat, yes,** it is permitted to nullify vows, but when it is **not for the purpose of Shabbat, no,** it is prohibited.

NOTES

In all of the *halakhot* of Shabbat – בְּכָל הַשַּׁבָּת כּוּלָּהּ: The Gemara here is referring not only to the prohibition of set-aside, but also to Rabbi Shimon's opinion with regard to all *halakhot* of Shabbat, including his rulings concerning unintended actions and prohibited labor not necessary for its own sake (Rashba).

Earthenware vessel [*tafiaḥ*] – טָפִיחַ: The *ge'onim* explained that *tafiaḥ* refers to a type of plant used to fill a window or to a type of wicker basket.

Nullification of vows and dissolution of vows – הֲפָרַת נְדָרִים וְהַתָּרַת נְדָרִים: The *halakhot* of vows and their nullification are stated in the Torah (Numbers 30) and explained in an entire tractate, tractate *Nedarim*. In essence, when either a young woman still under her father's auspices or a married woman takes a vow, her father or her husband respectively can nullify the vow on the day that he hears it if he does not approve of it. The Sages explained based on the verses that this is permitted only in certain situations. Only vows taken with regard to matters between the woman and her husband or between the young woman and her father can be nullified. Vows that do not affect the woman's relationship with her husband or father cannot be nullified. Vows may not only be nullified; one may also request that a sage dissolve his vow. Although this does not appear explicitly in the Torah, the Sages found allusions to it in the same portion. One who took a vow can request that a single Sage or a court of three dissolve it. Tractate *Nedarim* deals extensively with the problems that arise in this process. The standard scenario involves the person who took the vow declaring that he did not initially anticipate that it would be so difficult to fulfill the vow, and had he known, he would not have taken the vow in the first place. There is no designated time frame for dissolving one's vows and one can request that his vows be dissolved at any time. There are also some vows that a Sage cannot dissolve, e.g., a vow made to another person, which would require that person's agreement to dissolve it. In addition, a vow cannot be dissolved if it was taken before a large group and was contingent on their agreement.

HALAKHA

Nullification of vows on Shabbat – הֲפָרַת נְדָרִים בְּשַׁבָּת: A husband may nullify his wife's vows on Shabbat even if it has no impact on Shabbat itself, as if he fails to do so, he will not have another chance. However, he may not say to her: It is nullified. He nullifies it in his heart and says to her: Take it and eat, or: Take it and drink (Rambam *Sefer Hafla'a*, *Hilkhot Nedarim* 13:8; *Shulḥan Arukh*, *Yoreh De'a* 234:24).

Dissolution of vows on Shabbat – הַתָּרַת נְדָרִים בְּשַׁבָּת: It is permitted to request that a Sage dissolve one's vows on Shabbat for the purpose of Shabbat, even if he could have requested before Shabbat that they be dissolved (Rambam *Sefer Hafla'a*, *Hilkhot Shevuot* 6:6 and *Sefer Zemanim*, *Hilkhot Shabbat* 24:6; *Shulḥan Arukh*, *Yoreh De'a* 228:3).

לִישָּׁנָא אַחֲרִינָא, אִיבַּעְיָא לְהוּ: "לְצוֹרֶךְ" אַתַּרְוַיְיהוּ קָתָנֵי, וְשֶׁלֹּא לְצוֹרֶךְ – לָא, אַלְמָא: הֲפָרַת נְדָרִים מֵעֵת לְעֵת. אוֹ דִּילְמָא: כִּי קָתָנֵי לְצוֹרֶךְ – אַשְּׁאֵלָה הוּא דְּקָתָנֵי, אֲבָל הֲפָרַת נְדָרִים – אֲפִילּוּ שֶׁלֹּא לְצוֹרֶךְ. אַלְמָא: הֲפָרַת נְדָרִים כׇּל הַיּוֹם.

The Gemara cites **another version** of the **dilemma** that **was raised** before the Sages. Was the phrase: When they are **for the purpose** of Shabbat, **taught about both of them,** and nullification is only permitted for the purpose of Shabbat, **but** when it is **not for the purpose** of Shabbat, **no,** it is prohibited? If so, **apparently, nullification of vows** may be performed **for an entire twenty-four hour** period[H] after hearing the vow, and the father or husband can wait until after Shabbat to nullify the vow if he does not need to do so for the purpose of Shabbat. **Or perhaps when** the mishna **taught** that it is permitted when the nullification is **for the purpose** of Shabbat, **that** was **taught** only with regard to the **request** to dissolve that which was prohibited by the vow, **but nullification of vows** may be performed on Shabbat **even** when it is **not for the purpose** of Shabbat. If so, **apparently nullification of vows** may be performed only **for the entire day** that the husband or father heard the vow. Once Shabbat concludes, the vow may longer be nullified. Therefore, even vows whose nullification is not for the purpose of Shabbat may be nullified on Shabbat.

תָּא שְׁמַע; דְּתָנֵי רַב זוּטֵי דְּבֵי רַב פַּפֵּי: מְפִירִין נְדָרִים בְּשַׁבָּת לְצוֹרֶךְ הַשַּׁבָּת. לְצוֹרֶךְ הַשַּׁבָּת – אִין, שֶׁלֹּא לְצוֹרֶךְ הַשַּׁבָּת – לָא. אַלְמָא: הֲפָרַת נְדָרִים מֵעֵת לְעֵת.

Come and **hear** a resolution to the dilemma from **that which** the Sage, **Zutei, of the school of Rav Pappa taught: One may nullify vows on Shabbat for the purpose of Shabbat.** Apparently, when the nullification is **for the purpose of Shabbat, yes,** it is permitted to nullify vows, but when it is **not for the purpose of Shabbat, no,** it is prohibited. If so, **apparently nullification of vows** may be performed **for the entire twenty-four hour** period after hearing the vow.

אָמַר רַב אַשִׁי, וְהָאֲנַן תְּנַן: הֲפָרַת נְדָרִים כׇּל הַיּוֹם, וְיֵשׁ בַּדָּבָר לְהָקֵל וּלְהַחְמִיר. כֵּיצַד? נָדְרָה לֵילֵי שַׁבָּת – מֵיפֵר לֵילֵי שַׁבָּת וְיוֹם הַשַּׁבָּת עַד שֶׁתֶּחְשַׁךְ, נָדְרָה עִם חֲשֵׁכָה – מֵיפֵר עַד שֶׁלֹּא תֶּחְשַׁךְ, שֶׁאִם לֹא הֵפֵר מִשֶּׁחֲשֵׁכָה – אֵינוֹ יָכוֹל לְהָפֵר. תַּנָּאֵי הִיא, דְּתַנְיָא: הֲפָרַת נְדָרִים כׇּל הַיּוֹם, רַבִּי יוֹסֵי בַּר יְהוּדָה וְרַבִּי אֶלְעָזָר בְּרַבִּי שִׁמְעוֹן אָמְרוּ: מֵעֵת לְעֵת.

Rav Ashi said: Didn't we learn in a mishna that **one may nullify vows for the entire day, and** there is both a **leniency and a stricture in this matter** to extend or curtail the period during which the vow may be nullified. **How so? If** the woman **vowed** on **Shabbat evening,** her father or husband **may nullify** the vow on **Shabbat evening and** on **Shabbat day until dark.** However, if she **vowed** before Shabbat **at nightfall,** her father or husband **may** only **nullify** the vow **until nightfall, as if he did not nullify** the vow **before nightfall, he can no** longer **nullify** it because the day ended. The Gemara answers that **this** issue **is** subject to **a tannaitic** dispute, **as it was taught** in a *baraita*: **One may nullify vows for the entire day. Rabbi Yosei bar Yehuda and Rabbi Elazar, son of Rabbi Shimon, said: For a twenty-four hour** period.

"וְנִשְׁאָלִים לִנְדָרִים". אִיבַּעְיָא לְהוּ: כְּשֶׁלֹּא הָיָה לוֹ פְּנַאי, אוֹ דִּלְמָא: אֲפִילּוּ הָיָה לוֹ פְּנַאי? תָּא שְׁמַע: דְּאִיזְדַּקִּיקוּ לֵיהּ רַבָּנַן לְרַב זוּטְרָא בְּרֵיהּ דְּרַב זֵירָא, וְשָׁרוּ לֵיהּ נִדְרֵיהּ וְאַף עַל גַּב דַּהֲוָה לֵיהּ פְּנַאי.

We learned in the mishna: **And one may request** from a Sage **to** dissolve **vows** on Shabbat. **A dilemma was raised** before the Sages: Is this only permitted **when one did not have time** to request to have the vow dissolved before Shabbat, **or perhaps** it is permitted **even if one had time** before Shabbat to request to have his vow dissolved? **Come** and **hear** a resolution to this dilemma from the fact **that the Sages attended to Rav Zutra, the son of Rav Zeira, and dissolved his vow even though he had time** to request its dissolution before Shabbat.

"שֶׁפָּקְקוּ אֶת הַמָּאוֹר בְּטָפִיחַ וְקָשְׁרוּ אֶת הַמְּקִידָה בְּגֶמִי". אָמַר רַב יְהוּדָה אָמַר רַב: הֵילְקְטִי קְטַנָּה הָיְתָה בֵּין שְׁנֵי בָתִּים, [וְטוּמְאָה הָיְתָה שָׁם].

The mishna related: They **sealed a window using an earthenware vessel and tied an earthenware shard with a** long **reed-grass. Rav Yehuda said** that **Rav said** in explanation: **There was a small alleyway** [*heilketei*][L] **between two houses, and there was ritual impurity** imparted by a corpse **there** in the alleyway,[NB]

HALAKHA

The time for nullification of vows – זְמַן הֲפָרַת נְדָרִים: A father or husband can nullify his daughter's or wife's vows for the entire day on which he hears about the vow. The day is defined not as a twenty-four hour period, but rather from nightfall to nightfall. As soon as night falls after the vow was taken, it can no longer be nullified (Rambam *Sefer Hafla'a, Hilkhot Nedarim* 12:15; *Shulḥan Arukh, Yoreh De'a* 234:21).

LANGUAGE

Small alleyway [*heilketei*] – הֵילְקְטִי: From the Greek **εἱρκτή**, *eirktè*, meaning a closed place, the inside of a house, and the like. The letters r and l are commonly interchanged.

BACKGROUND

Ritual impurity between houses – הַטּוּמְאָה בֵּין הַבָּתִּים: The impurity is imparted by a corpse beneath the cracked roofing between the houses. In the image below, the window facing the alleyway was sealed with an earthenware vessel to prevent the ritual impurity from entering the house.

Ritual impurity between houses

NOTES

There was ritual impurity imparted by a corpse there – וְטוּמְאָה הָיְתָה שָׁם: The Rambam explains that the corpse was in one of the houses and there was a window with a glass windowpane between the two houses. The glass broke and they were uncertain whether or not there was an opening of a handbreadth through which the ritual impurity could spread. Therefore, they sealed the broken windowpane with a small piece of earthenware and then measured it to see if the opening was the size of a handbreadth (Rambam's Commentary on the Mishna).

וְגִיגִית סְדוּקָה מוּנַּחַת עַל גַּבָּן. וּפָקְקוּ אֶת הַמָּאוֹר בְּטָפִיחַ וְקָשְׁרוּ אֶת הַמְּקֵידָה בְּגֶמִי, לֵידַע אִם יֵשׁ שָׁם בַּגִּיגִית פּוֹתֵחַ טֶפַח אִם לָאו.

and there was **a cracked roofing placed atop** the two houses. If the roofing was intact it would have the legal status of a tent over a corpse, rendering everything in the alleyway, and, through the windows, everything in the houses, ritually impure. However, since the roofing was cracked and the corpse was directly beneath the opening, if the opening was the size of a handbreadth or more, the entire alleyway and the houses would not become impure. Only the area directly over the corpse extending through the opening is impure. **And** that is the reason that **they sealed the window** of the house **with an earthenware vessel,** so that the ritual impurity would not enter the houses, **and they tied an earthenware shard**[H] **with a** long **reed-grass** inserted into the opening in the roofing in order **to ascertain whether or not there is an opening there in the roofing the size of a handbreadth.**[N]

״וּמִדִּבְרֵיהֶם לָמַדְנוּ שֶׁפּוֹקְקִין וּמוֹדְדִין וְקוֹשְׁרִין בְּשַׁבָּת״. עוּלָּא אִיקְּלַע לְבֵי רֵישׁ גָּלוּתָא. חַזְיֵיהּ לְרַבָּה בַּר רַב הוּנָא דְּיָתֵיב בְּאַוְונָא דְּמַיָּא, וְקָא מָשַׁח לֵיהּ. אֲמַר לֵיהּ: אֵימַר דְּאָמְרִי רַבָּנַן מְדִידָה דְּמִצְוָה, דְּלָאו מִצְוָה מִי אֲמוּר? אֲמַר לֵיהּ: מִתְעַסֵּק בְּעָלְמָא אֲנָא.

The mishna concludes: **And from their statements** and their actions, **we derived that one may seal** a window, **and measure, and tie** a knot **on Shabbat.** The Gemara relates: **Ulla happened** to come **to the house of the Exilarch. He saw Rabba bar Rav Huna sitting in a tub** [*avna*][L] **of water**[B] **and measuring it.** He **said to** Rabba bar Rav Huna: **Say that the Sages said** that it is permitted to measure on Shabbat only **a measurement for a mitzva.**[H] However, with regard to a measurement like this one, **which is not** for **a mitzva, did they say** that it is permitted? Rabba bar Rav Huna **said to him: I am merely acting unawares**[N] and am not at all interested in the measurements. Therefore, it is not prohibited.

הדרן עלך מי שהחשיך
וסליקא לה מסכת שבת

HALAKHA

They tied an earthenware shard – וְקָשְׁרוּ אֶת הַמְּקֵידָה: For the sake of a mitzva, such as taking measurements that are required by the Torah, it is permitted to tie a non-permanent knot on Shabbat, even one that requires professional skill (*Magen Avraham*; Rambam *Sefer Zemanim, Hilkhot Shabbat* 10:6; *Shulḥan Arukh, Oraḥ Ḥayyim* 317:1).

Measurement for a mitzva – מְדִידָה דְּמִצְוָה: It is permitted to think about, speak about, or measure things that pertain to religious matters and the fulfillment of mitzvot (Rambam *Sefer Zemanim, Hilkhot Shabbat* 24:5; *Shulḥan Arukh, Oraḥ Ḥayyim* 306:7).

NOTES

Whether or not there is an opening there in the roofing the size of a handbreadth – אִם יֵשׁ שָׁם בַּגִּיגִית פּוֹתֵחַ טֶפַח: Some explain this to mean that there was not an entire corpse in either of the houses. Rather, there was an olive-bulk of a corpse directly beneath the opening in the roofing. If the hole in the roofing was the size of a handbreadth, the ritual impurity would not spread to the entire area beneath the roofing. Some explained that the earthenware shard was not permanently affixed to the opening, and therefore it is not considered to have sealed it (*Me'iri*). Others explain that they measured the roofing that remained surrounding the opening. If its area was a handbreadth, then it would assume the legal status of a tent and would transmit ritual impurity to objects beneath it (Rabbi Elazar Moshe Horowitz).

Merely acting unawares – מִתְעַסֵּק בְּעָלְמָא: The Sages ruled that one who had no intention whatsoever to perform a given action is liable only for violations involving forbidden animal fats or forbidden sexual relations, due to the pleasure derived from them. However, with regard to the *halakhot* of Shabbat, one has no liability in that situation due to the principle that one is liable on Shabbat only for planned, thoughtful, creative labor.

LANGUAGE

Tub [*avna*] – אַוְונָא: Apparently, this should be read as *avazana*, from the Middle Persian ābzan, meaning bathtub.

BACKGROUND

Tub of water – אַוְונָא דְּמַיָּא:

Bathtub for a single person found in Masada, from the end of the second Temple period

Summary of **Perek XXIV**

Although driving a laden animal on Shabbat is prohibited by Torah law, the Sages concluded that this activity is not one of the thirty-nine prohibited labors for which one is liable to be punished with stoning. Rather, it is an independent prohibition with its own source, and it is not as severe as the thirty-nine prohibited labors. Therefore, the Sages permitted making use of animals in cases of significant need, such as in order to avoid a financial loss, provided one does so differently than usual. With regard to the parameters concerning food preparation for animals on Shabbat, it appears that anything which is absolutely necessary for the animal may be done on Shabbat as long as it does not involve a full-fledged prohibited labor. This includes handling set-aside items and preparing food. However, even rabbinic prohibitions may not be violated for anything non-essential or in order to provide an animal a higher level of comfort.

Image **Credits**

p323 © Bullenwächter; **p326** © Patrice78500; **p389** © Longbow4u; **p392** © Jastrow; **p411** © Crni Bombarder; **p426** © sailko.

Page numbers refer to the original Koren Talmud edition.

The following קדיש *requires the presence of a* מנין.

יִתְגַּדַּל וְיִתְקַדַּשׁ שְׁמֵהּ רַבָּא
בְּעָלְמָא דְּהוּא עָתִיד לְאִתְחַדָּתָא
וּלְאַחֲיָאָה מֵתַיָּא, וּלְאַסָּקָא יָתְהוֹן לְחַיֵּי עָלְמָא
וּלְמִבְנֵא קַרְתָּא דִירוּשְׁלֵם, וּלְשַׁכְלָלָא הֵיכְלֵהּ בְּגַוַּהּ
וּלְמֶעְקַר פָּלְחָנָא נֻכְרָאָה מֵאַרְעָא
וְלַאֲתָבָא פָּלְחָנָא דִשְׁמַיָּא לְאַתְרֵהּ
וְיַמְלִיךְ קֻדְשָׁא בְּרִיךְ הוּא בְּמַלְכוּתֵהּ וִיקָרֵהּ
(נוסח ספרד: וְיַצְמַח פּוּרְקָנֵהּ וִיקָרֵב מְשִׁיחֵהּ)
בְּחַיֵּיכוֹן וּבְיוֹמֵיכוֹן וּבְחַיֵּי דְכָל בֵּית יִשְׂרָאֵל
בַּעֲגָלָא וּבִזְמַן קָרִיב, וְאִמְרוּ אָמֵן.

יְהֵא שְׁמֵהּ רַבָּא מְבָרַךְ לְעָלַם וּלְעָלְמֵי עָלְמַיָּא.

יִתְבָּרַךְ וְיִשְׁתַּבַּח וְיִתְפָּאַר וְיִתְרוֹמַם וְיִתְנַשֵּׂא
וְיִתְהַדָּר וְיִתְעַלֶּה וְיִתְהַלָּל
שְׁמֵהּ דְּקֻדְשָׁא בְּרִיךְ הוּא
לְעֵלָּא מִן כָּל בִּרְכָתָא
/בעשרת ימי תשובה: לְעֵלָּא לְעֵלָּא מִכָּל בִּרְכָתָא/
וְשִׁירָתָא, תֻּשְׁבְּחָתָא וְנֶחֱמָתָא, דַּאֲמִירָן בְּעָלְמָא
וְאִמְרוּ אָמֵן. (קהל: אָמֵן)

עַל יִשְׂרָאֵל וְעַל רַבָּנָן
וְעַל תַּלְמִידֵיהוֹן וְעַל כָּל תַּלְמִידֵי תַלְמִידֵיהוֹן
וְעַל כָּל מָאן דְּעָסְקִין בְּאוֹרַיְתָא
דִּי בְּאַתְרָא (בארץ ישראל: קַדִּישָׁא) הָדֵין, וְדִי בְּכָל אֲתַר וַאֲתַר
יְהֵא לְהוֹן וּלְכוֹן שְׁלָמָא רַבָּא
חִנָּא וְחִסְדָּא, וְרַחֲמֵי, וְחַיֵּי אֲרִיכֵי, וּמְזוֹנֵי רְוִיחֵי
וּפֻרְקָנָא מִן קֳדָם אֲבוּהוֹן דִּי בִשְׁמַיָּא
וְאִמְרוּ אָמֵן.

יְהֵא שְׁלָמָא רַבָּא מִן שְׁמַיָּא
וְחַיִּים (טוֹבִים) עָלֵינוּ וְעַל כָּל יִשְׂרָאֵל
וְאִמְרוּ אָמֵן.

Bow, take three steps back, as if taking leave of the Divine Presence, then bow, first left, then right, then center, while saying:

עֹשֶׂה שָׁלוֹם/ בעשרת ימי תשובה: הַשָּׁלוֹם/ בִּמְרוֹמָיו
הוּא יַעֲשֶׂה בְרַחֲמָיו שָׁלוֹם, עָלֵינוּ וְעַל כָּל יִשְׂרָאֵל
וְאִמְרוּ אָמֵן.

The following Kaddish requires the presence of a minyan.

Magnified and sanctified may His great name be,
in the world that will in future be renewed,
reviving the dead and raising them up to eternal life.
He will rebuild the city of Jerusalem
and in it re-establish His Temple.
He will remove alien worship from the earth
and restore to its place the worship of Heaven.
Then the Holy One, blessed be He,
will reign in His sovereignty and splendor.
May it be in your lifetime and in your days,
(*Nusaḥ Sepharad:* make His salvation flourish,
and hasten His messiah,)
and in the lifetime of all the House of Israel,
swiftly and soon – and say: Amen.

May His great name be blessed for ever and all time.

Blessed and praised,
glorified and exalted,
raised and honored,
uplifted and lauded
be the name of the Holy One,
blessed be He,
beyond any blessing,
song, praise and consolation uttered in the world –
and say: Amen.

To Israel, to the teachers,
their disciples and their disciples' disciples,
and to all who engage in the study of Torah,
in this (*in Israel add:* holy) place or elsewhere,
may there come to them and you great peace,
grace, kindness and compassion,
long life, ample sustenance and deliverance,
from their Father in Heaven –
and say: Amen.

May there be great peace from heaven,
and (good) life for us and all Israel –
and say: Amen.

Bow, take three steps back, as if taking leave of the Divine Presence, then bow, first left, then right, then center, while saying:

May He who makes peace in His high places,
in His compassion make peace for us and all Israel –
and say: Amen.

The following paragraph is recited three times:

הַדְרָן עֲלָךְ מַסֶּכֶת שַׁבָּת וְהַדְרָךְ עֲלָן, דַּעְתָּן עֲלָךְ מַסֶּכֶת שַׁבָּת וְדַעְתָּךְ עֲלָן, לָא נִתְנְשֵׁי מִנָּךְ מַסֶּכֶת שַׁבָּת וְלָא תִתְנְשֵׁי מִנָּן, לָא בְּעָלְמָא הָדֵין וְלָא בְּעָלְמָא דְאָתֵי.

יְהִי רָצוֹן מִלְּפָנֶיךָ יהוה אֱלֹהֵינוּ וֵאלֹהֵי אֲבוֹתֵינוּ, שֶׁתְּהֵא תוֹרָתְךָ אֻמָּנוּתֵנוּ בָּעוֹלָם הַזֶּה, וּתְהֵא עִמָּנוּ לָעוֹלָם הַבָּא. חֲנִינָא בַּר פַּפָּא, רָמֵי בַּר פַּפָּא, נַחְמָן בַּר פַּפָּא, אֲחַאי בַּר פַּפָּא, אַבָּא מָרִי בַּר פַּפָּא, רַפְרָם בַּר פַּפָּא, רָכִישׁ בַּר פַּפָּא, סוּרְחַב בַּר פַּפָּא, אַדָּא בַּר פַּפָּא, דָּרוּ בַּר פַּפָּא.

הַעֲרֶב נָא יהוה אֱלֹהֵינוּ אֶת דִּבְרֵי תוֹרָתְךָ בְּפִינוּ וּבְפִי עַמְּךָ בֵּית יִשְׂרָאֵל, וְנִהְיֶה אֲנַחְנוּ וְצֶאֱצָאֵינוּ (וְצֶאֱצָאֵי צֶאֱצָאֵינוּ) וְצֶאֱצָאֵי עַמְּךָ בֵּית יִשְׂרָאֵל, כֻּלָּנוּ יוֹדְעֵי
שְׁמֶךָ וְלוֹמְדֵי תוֹרָתְךָ לִשְׁמָהּ. מֵאֹיְבַי תְּחַכְּמֵנִי מִצְוֺתֶךָ תהלים קיט
כִּי לְעוֹלָם הִיא־לִי: יְהִי־לִבִּי תָמִים בְּחֻקֶּיךָ לְמַעַן לֹא אֵבוֹשׁ: לְעוֹלָם לֹא־אֶשְׁכַּח פִּקּוּדֶיךָ כִּי־בָם חִיִּיתָנִי: בָּרוּךְ אַתָּה יהוה לַמְּדֵנִי חֻקֶּיךָ: אָמֵן אָמֵן אָמֵן סֶלָה וָעֶד.

מוֹדִים אֲנַחְנוּ לְפָנֶיךָ יהוה אֱלֹהֵינוּ וֵאלֹהֵי אֲבוֹתֵינוּ שֶׁשַּׂמְתָּ חֶלְקֵנוּ מִיּוֹשְׁבֵי בֵּית הַמִּדְרָשׁ, וְלֹא שַׂמְתָּ חֶלְקֵנוּ מִיּוֹשְׁבֵי קְרָנוֹת. שֶׁאָנוּ מַשְׁכִּימִים וְהֵם מַשְׁכִּימִים, אָנוּ מַשְׁכִּימִים לְדִבְרֵי תוֹרָה, וְהֵם מַשְׁכִּימִים לִדְבָרִים בְּטֵלִים. אָנוּ עֲמֵלִים וְהֵם עֲמֵלִים, אָנוּ עֲמֵלִים וּמְקַבְּלִים שָׂכָר, וְהֵם עֲמֵלִים וְאֵינָם מְקַבְּלִים שָׂכָר. אָנוּ רָצִים וְהֵם רָצִים, אָנוּ רָצִים לְחַיֵּי הָעוֹלָם הַבָּא, וְהֵם רָצִים לִבְאֵר
שַׁחַת, שֶׁנֶּאֱמַר: וְאַתָּה אֱלֹהִים תּוֹרִדֵם לִבְאֵר שַׁחַת תהלים נה
אַנְשֵׁי דָמִים וּמִרְמָה לֹא־יֶחֱצוּ יְמֵיהֶם וַאֲנִי אֶבְטַח־בָּךְ:

יְהִי רָצוֹן מִלְּפָנֶיךָ יהוה אֱלֹהַי, כְּשֵׁם שֶׁעֲזַרְתַּנִי לְסַיֵּם מַסֶּכֶת שַׁבָּת כֵּן תְּעַזְּרֵנִי לְהַתְחִיל מַסֶּכְתּוֹת וּסְפָרִים אֲחֵרִים וּלְסַיְּמָם, לִלְמֹד וּלְלַמֵּד לִשְׁמֹר וְלַעֲשׂוֹת וּלְקַיֵּם אֶת כָּל דִּבְרֵי תַלְמוּד תּוֹרָתְךָ בְּאַהֲבָה, וּזְכוּת כָּל הַתַּנָּאִים וְאָמוֹרָאִים וְתַלְמִידֵי חֲכָמִים יַעֲמֹד לִי וּלְזַרְעִי שֶׁלֹּא תָמוּשׁ הַתּוֹרָה מִפִּי וּמִפִּי זַרְעִי וְזֶרַע זַרְעִי
עַד עוֹלָם, וְיִתְקַיֵּם בִּי: בְּהִתְהַלֶּכְךָ תַּנְחֶה אֹתָךְ בְּשָׁכְבְּךָ משלי ו
תִּשְׁמֹר עָלֶיךָ וַהֲקִיצוֹתָ הִיא תְשִׂיחֶךָ: כִּי־בִי יִרְבּוּ יָמֶיךָ משלי ט
וְיוֹסִיפוּ לְךָ שְׁנוֹת חַיִּים: אֹרֶךְ יָמִים בִּימִינָהּ בִּשְׂמֹאולָהּ משלי ג
עֹשֶׁר וְכָבוֹד: יהוה עֹז לְעַמּוֹ יִתֵּן יהוה יְבָרֵךְ אֶת־עַמּוֹ תהלים כט
בַשָּׁלוֹם:

The following paragraph is recited three times:

הַדְרָן We shall return to you, tractate *Shabbat,* and your glory is upon us. Our thoughts are upon you, tractate *Shabbat,* and your thoughts are upon us. We will not be forgotten from you, tractate *Shabbat,* and you will not be forgotten from us; neither in this world nor in the World-to-Come.

יְהִי רָצוֹן May it be Your will, Lord our God and God of our ancestors, that Your Torah will be our avocation in this world and will accompany us to the World-to-Come. Ḥanina bar Pappa, Ramei bar Pappa, Naḥman bar Pappa, Aḥai bar Pappa, Abba Mari bar Pappa, Rafram bar Pappa, Rakhish bar Pappa, Surḥav bar Pappa, Adda bar Pappa, Daru bar Pappa.

הַעֲרֶב נָא Please, Lord our God, make the words of Your Torah sweet in our mouths and in the mouths of Your people, the house of Israel, so that we, our descendants (and their descendants), and the descendants of Your people, the house of Israel, may all know Your name and
study Your Torah for its own sake. Your commandments *Psalms 119*
make me wiser than my enemies, for they are ever with me. Let my heart be undivided in Your statutes, in order that I may not be put to shame. I will never forget Your precepts, for with them You have quickened me. Blessed are You, O Lord; teach me Your statutes. Amen, Amen, Amen, Selah, Forever.

מוֹדִים We give thanks before You, Lord Our God and God of our ancestors, that You have placed our lot among those who sit in the study hall and that you have not given us our portion among those who sit idly on street corners. We rise early and they rise early. We rise early to pursue matters of Torah and they rise early to pursue frivolous matters. We toil and they toil. We toil and receive a reward and they toil and do not receive a reward. We run and they run. We run to the life of the World-to-Come and they run to the pit of destruction,
as it is stated: But You, God, will bring them down into *Psalms 55*
the pit of destruction; men of blood and deceit shall not live out half their days; but as for me, I will trust in You.

יְהִי רָצוֹן May it be Your will, Lord my God, just as you have assisted me in completing tractate *Shabbat* so assist me to begin other tractates and books and conclude them to learn and to teach, to observe and to perform, and to fulfill all the teachings of Your Torah with love. And may the merit of all the *tanna'im* and *amora'im* and Torah scholars stand for me and my descendants so that the Torah will not move from my mouth and from the mouths of my descendants and the descendants of my
descendants forever. And may the verse: When you *Proverbs 6*
walk, it shall lead you, when you lie down, it shall watch over you; and when you awaken, it shall talk with you
be fulfilled in me. For in the Torah your days shall be *Proverbs 9*
multiplied, and the years of your life shall be increased.
Length of days is in her right hand; in her left hand are *Proverbs 3*
riches and honor. May the Lord give strength to His *Psalms 29*
people; the Lord will bless His people with peace.

וְגִיגִית סְדוּקָה מוּנַּחַת עַל גַּבָּן. וּפָקְקוּ אֶת הַמָּאוֹר בְּטָפִיחַ [א]וְקָשְׁרוּ אֶת הַמְּקֵידָה בְּגֶמִי, לֵידַע אִם יֵשׁ שָׁם בַּגִּיגִית פּוֹתֵחַ טֶפַח אִם לָאו.§ "וּמִדִּבְרֵיהֶם לָמַדְנוּ שֶׁפּוֹקְקִין וּמוֹדְדִין וְקוֹשְׁרִין בְּשַׁבָּת".§ עוּלָּא אִיקְלַע לְבֵי רֵישׁ גָּלוּתָא. חַזְיֵיהּ לְרַבָּה בַּר רַב הוּנָא דְּיָתֵיב *בְּאַוּוֹנָא דְמַיָּא, וְקָא מָשַׁח לֵיהּ. אֲמַר לֵיהּ: [ב]אֵימַר דְּאָמְרִי רַבָּנַן מְדִידָה דְּמִצְוָה, דְּלָאו מִצְוָה מִי אָמוּר? אֲמַר לֵיהּ: מִתְעַסֵּק בְּעָלְמָא אֲנָא.§

וְגִיגִית סְדוּקָה מוּנַּחַת עַל גַּבָּיו. וְהַמֵּת מוּטָל בַּהֵילְקֵטִי תַּחַת הַגִּיגִית [כְּנֶגֶד] הַסֶּדֶק וְלִפְנֵי מוֹת הַמֵּת פָּקְקוּ בַּשַּׁבָּת הַמָּאוֹר בְּטָפִיחַ שֶׁמָּא אֵין בְּסֶדֶק הַגִּיגִית פּוֹתֵחַ טֶפַח וְנִמְנָא הַמֵּת מוּטָל בְּאֹהֶל שֶׁאֵין לוֹ מָקוֹם לָצֵאת דֶּרֶךְ מַעְלָה וְחוֹר שֶׁבֵּין שְׁנֵי בָּתִּים מַכְנִיס אֶת הַטּוּמְאָה לְצַד שְׁנֵי בַּמְּלָא אֲגָרוּף לְפִיכָךְ סְתָמוּהוּ בִּכְלִי חֶרֶס וְגַבּוֹ כְּנֶגֶד הַהֵילְקֵט וּכְלִי חֶרֶס אֵינוֹ מְטַמֵּא מִגַּבּוֹ וְחוֹצֵץ: וְקָשְׁרוּ מְקֵידָה. שֶׁהִיא רְחָבָה טֶפַח: בְּגֶמִי לֵידַע. אִם תִּכָּנֵס בְּסֶדֶק הַגִּיגִית וּבְמַסֶּכֶת אֳהָלוֹת (פ"י) שָׁנִינוּ (דְּאֵין) חִילּוּק בָּאֲרוּבָּה שֶׁבְּתוֹךְ הַבַּיִת וְטוּמְאָה מִקְצָתָהּ כְּנֶגֶד אֲרוּבָּה וּמִקְצָתָהּ בְּתוֹךְ הַבַּיִת בֵּין יֵשׁ בָּאֲרוּבָּה פּוֹתֵחַ טֶפַח לְאֵין בָּאֲרוּבָּה פּוֹתֵחַ טֶפַח וַאֲנִי לֹא יָכוֹלְתִּי לְהָבִין בּוֹ וּלְהָכִי נָקַט גֶּמִי שֶׁרָאוּי לְמַאֲכַל בְּהֵמָה וְלָא מִיבַּטֵּל לֵיהּ לִהְיוֹת קֶשֶׁר שֶׁל קַיָּימָא דְּמִינְתַּק כְּשֶׁיָּבֵשׁ: בְּאַוּוֹנָא. בְּגִיגִית מְלֵאָה מַיִם: מִתְעַסֵּק. שֶׁלֹּא לְצוֹרֶךְ אֶלָּא לְאִיעַסּוּקֵי בְּעָלְמָא:

הדרן עלך מי שהחשיך וסליקא לה מסכת שבת

באוונא דמיא. אמבטי של מים, וכך פירש בערוך: מדידה דמצוה דלאו דמצוה מי אמור כו'. בפקיקה לא בעינן של מצוה, כדפירש' לעיל בשילהי "כל הכלים" (דף קכו:). אלא דווקא במדידה בעינן של מצוה:

הדרן עלך מי שהחשיך וסליקא לה מסכת שבת

מד א מיי' פ"י מהל' שבת הלכה ו סמג לאוין סה טוש"ע א"ח סימן שיז סעיף א:

מה ב מיי' פכ"ד מהל' שבת הלכה ה סמג שם טוש"ע א"ח סימן שו סעיף ו:

[ברי"ף וברא"ש איתא באגנא וכן הוא ברש"י שם וע' בערוך ערך אודנא וכן בברכות כב. ר' זירא הוה יתיב באגנא דמיא פרש"י באגנא גיגית]

הדרן עלך מי שהחשיך וסליקא לה מסכת שבת

רבינו חננאל

אבל מוקצה [מחמת] חסרון כים אפילו ר"ש מודה דתנן כל הכלים ניטלין בשבת חוץ ממסר הגדול ויתד של מחרישה וקיי"ל דכל היכא דפליגי רב אחא ורבינא הלכתא כדברי המיקל ואסקינן בה הלכה למעשה. שהלכה כרבי שמעון בהלכות שבת כולן ואין הלכה כרבי יהודה אלא במוקצה מחמת איסורו ואשכחנן ר' יוחנן דאמר מודה ר' שמעון בזה. דגרסינן בפרק כירה א"ר חייא בר אבא א"ר יוחנן אין מוקצה לר' שמעון אלא כעין שמן שבנר בשעה שדולק הואיל והוקצה לאיסורו והוקצה למצוותו ומוקצה מחמת חסרון כיס דברי הכל מוקצה הוא ואסור וקשיא לן הדא הלכתא דאמרינן בפ' כירה [ד' מ"ה] כי אתא ר' יצחק בר יוסף אמר הלכה כר' יהודה. וריב"ל אמר הלכה כר"ש וכו' וצריכא עיונא. (ואם) [ואכן] יש לומר הא ר' יצחק בר יוסף א"ר יוחנן הלכה כר' יהודה. הא ריב"ל פליג עליה ואמר הלכתא כר"ש ואע"ג [דאמר] רב יוסף [התם] היינו דאמר רבה בר בר חנה א"ר יוחנן אמרו הלכה כר' שמעון וליה לא ס"ל (דא"ל) [וא"ל] אביי לרב יוסף ואת לא תסברא דר' יוחנן כר' יהודה סבירא ליה הני כולהו שמעתתא לא דייקינן: מתני' מפירין נדרים בשבת ונשאלין לנדרים שהן לצורך השבת ומבעיא לן האי דקתני מפירין נדרים בשבת לצורך הוא אבל שלא לצורך השבת לא אלמא הפרת נדרים מעת לעת או דלמא כי קתני לצורך אשאלה בלבד. אבל הפרת נדרים אפילו שלא לצורך השבת מפירין. אלמא הפרת נדרים כל אותו היום בלבד וסלקא כתנאי דתניא הפרת נדרים כל אותו היום. ר' יוסי בר יהודה ור' אלעזר בר שמעון אומר מעת לעת והלכתא הפרת נדרים כל היום בלבד וגרסינן בפ' נערה המאורסה אביה ובעלה מפירין נדריה פי' שמועה זו והכי פסקה לה [התם] ר"ש בן פזי אריב"ל אין הלכה כאותו הזוג. ונשאלין לנדרים לצורך השבת. ומיבעיא לן בשלא היה לו פנאי ופשטנא אפילו היה לו פנאי מערב (יום) [שבת] והוה אפשר להו לשאל נשאלין בשבת ושפיר דמי. מפירין נדרים שמפר הבעל לאשתו ונשאלין לנדרים שאילה לחכמים ומפרשינן בפרק נערה המאורסה סבר רב יוסף למימר נשאלין נדרים ביחיד מומחה בשבת ביחיד מומחה אין [בשלשה הדיוטות] לא דמורה בי דינא א"ל אביי כיון דסבירא לן אפילו מעומד ואפילו בקרובין ואפילו בלילה לא מחזי בי דינא. אמר רבא אמר רב נחמן הלכתא נשאלין נדרים מעומד יחידי ובלילה ובשבת ובקרובין ואפילו אפשר להן מבע"י: פוקקין את המאור. פירוש מניחין בגג מקום פתוח כגון זרת הן חסר הן יתיר ליכנס ממנו אור ונקרא מאור ותנן [פרק י"ג] העושה לו מאור בתחלה שיעורו מלא מקדח גדול של לשכה שירי המאור רום אצבעיים על רוחב גודל. ואם רוצה בשבת לסותמו מותר ועל זה שנינו פוקקין את המאור ופירושו סותמין את המאור כאשר פירשנו ומודדין את המטלית ואת המקוה אם הוא אמה על אמה ברום שלש ראוי לטבול בו: פקקו את המאור בטפיח. פי' טפיח כלי חרס קטן והוא כגון פתיא [וברבים] נקראין פתוותא כדגרסינן בע"ז בגמרא אלו דברים של נכרים אוסרין ואיסורן איסור הנאה [ד' ל"ג ע"ב] וכדתנן זמורה שהיא קשורה בטפיח ממלאין בה בשבת וקושרין את המקידה בגמי פי' מקידה כלי חרס כגון זה ששנינו בפ' היה מביא את מנחתה היה מביא את מנחתה פיילי של (חדשה) [חרס] ונותן בתוכה חצי לוג מים מן הכיור*). וזו שאמר רב יהודה אמר רב הילקטי קטנה היתה בין ב' בתים וגיגית סדוקה מונחת על גבן ופקקו את המאור בטפיח וקשרו את המקידה בגמי לידע אם יש בגיגית פותח טפח אם לאו מדבריהם למדנו שפוקקין ומודדין וקושרין בשבת וכך פירושו היה שם ב' בתים. והילקטי מלשון תל המתלקט והוא כמין קיר חוצצין ביניהן: וגיגית כלי כמין פתיא סדוק או כמין כפושא מפולשת והיה קבוע בכותל (חלול) [חלון] פתוח ובאותה שבת היה המת מוטל בבית אחד ובבית האחר היו רוצים להכנס בו כהנים ולא היו יודעים בבירור אם יש בגיגית פותח טפח ומביא את הטומאה אם לאו שכך שנו במשנתנו. טפח על טפח על רום טפח מביא את הטומאה. ועוד שנינו פרק העושה מאור [פי"ג משנה ד'] לזון את עיניו ולדבר עם חבירו ולתשמיש בפותח טפח וסתמו את המאור בטפיח הוא כמין כלי לכסות את המאור הפתוח שלא יאהילו העומדים על הגג באותו המאור ויטמאו מן הטומאה המוטלת בתוך הבית כנגד המאור שהיה נפתח המאור יתר ממלא מקדח גדול של לשכה שזה שיעורו ומפורש במשנתנו פרק [הנזכר] לפיכך הוצרכו לסותמו. ואותה הגיגית היתה בכותל גבוהה מקומת אדם ופישוט זרועותיו ולמטה מן הגג מכדי תליית אדם ופישוט זרועותיו ולקחו מקידה שהיא כלי חרס ויש בה בכולה טפח וקשרוה בגמי ושלשלוה והעמידה כנגד פי הגיגית לראות אם פי הגיגית נתמלאה הנה יש בה טפח ומביאה הטומאה מבית לבית ואם היא פחותה ממלא הגיגית נתברר שאין בגיגית פותח טפח ואינה מביאה הטומאה. ויש אומרים קשרו המקידה בגמי בראש הקנה ושיעור פתחה של גיגית אם יש בה פותח טפח ואם לאו. עולא איקלע לבי ריש גלותא חזייה לרבה בר רב הונא דיתיב באדנא דמיא והיה מודד המים גובה במים ורוחבו. אמר לו אימר דאמרינן שהתירו חכמים מדידה דמצוה כגון מדידה של מקוה שצריך לטבילת מקוה מדידה דלאו מצוה מי אמור א"ל מתעסק בעלמא אנא כלומר אני מודד ולא מתכוון למדידה אני:

הדרן עלך מי שהחשיך בדרך. תהלה לעל במתי עב דורך:

גירסא ירושלמי בר"ה פרק אם אין מכירין בתחלתו. אמר עד אחד נולד לאיש פלוני בשבת מלין אותו על פיו חששה מוצאי שבת מטלטלין אותו על פיו. ר' חייא אמר מטלטלין אפומא (דימלותא) [דמלייתא]. רבי מתניאה מטלטל על אברתיה דזיהרא. ר' (ממל) [אמי מל] על פי נשים דאמרי שמשא הות בסוסיתא:

סליקא לה מסכת שבת. משירי אהודנו צח דודי. כי כביר מצאה ידי.

מי שזיכני להתחיל והוא יזכני לסיים. חזק ונתחזק הכותב לעד לא יוזק.

רב נסים גאון

אם יש בגיגית. עיקר דיליה במס' אהלות (פרק ג משנה ו) כזית מן המת פתחו בטפח והמת פתחו בד' טפחים להציל את הטומאה על הפתחים אבל להוציא את הטומאה בפותח טפח. אמר ליה אנא מתעסק בעלמא אנא. עיקר שלו כבר פירשנו בפרק כלל גדול שהמתעסק פטור לענין שבת כמו שאמרו בכריתות בפרק אכל חלב (דף יט) אמר רב נחמן אמר שמואל מתעסק בחלבים ובעריות חייב שכבר נהנה מתעסק בשבת פטור מלאכת מחשבת אסרה תורה ובגמרא דהזורק דבני מערבא (סוף פירקא) גרסי המתעסק בשבת פטור היך עבידה אמר הריני קוצר חצי גרוגרת וקצר כגרוגרת פטור:

סליק מי שהחשיך וסליקא לה מסכתא דשבת בסייעתא דשמיא

אחר השלמת המסכת יאמר זה ויועיל לזכרון בעזרת השם יתברך:

א) **הדרן** עלך מסכת שבת והדרך עלן דעתן עלך מסכת שבת ודעתך עלן לא נתנשי מינך מסכת שבת ולא תתנשי מינן לא בעלמא הדין ולא בעלמא דאתי:

יאמר כן שלש פעמים ואחר כך יאמר

יהי רצון מלפניך יי אלהינו ואלהי אבותינו שתהא תורתך אומנותנו בעולם הזה ותהא עמנו לעולם הבא ב) חנינא בר פפא רמי בר פפא נחמן בר פפא אחאי בר פפא אבא מרי בר פפא רפרם בר פפא רכיש בר פפא סורחב בר פפא אדא בר פפא דרו בר פפא:

הערב נא יי אלהינו את דברי תורתך בפינו ובפיפיות עמך בית ישראל ונהיה כולנו אנחנו וצאצאינו וצאצאי עמך בית ישראל כולנו יודעי שמך ולומדי תורתך: מאויבי תחכמני מצותיך כי לעולם היא לי: יהי לבי תמים בחקיך למען לא אבוש: לעולם לא אשכח פקודיך כי בם חייתני: ברוך אתה יי למדני חקיך: אמן אמן אמן סלה ועד:

מודים אנחנו לפניך יי אלהינו ואלהי אבותינו ששמת חלקנו מיושבי בית המדרש ולא שמת חלקנו מיושבי קרנות שאנו משכימים והם משכימים אנו משכימים לדברי תורה והם משכימים לדברים בטלים אנו עמלים והם עמלים אנו עמלים ומקבלים שכר והם עמלים ואינם מקבלים שכר אנו רצים והם רצים אנו רצים לחיי העולם הבא והם רצים לבאר שחת שנאמר ואתה אלהים תורידם לבאר שחת אנשי דמים ומרמה לא יחצו ימיהם ואני אבטח בך:

יהי רצון מלפניך יי אלהי כשם שעזרתני לסיים מסכת שבת כן תעזרני להתחיל מסכתות וספרים אחרים ולסיימם ללמוד וללמד לשמור ולעשות ולקיים את כל דברי תלמוד תורתך באהבה וזכות כל התנאים ואמוראים ותלמידי חכמים יעמוד לי ולזרעי שלא תמוש התורה מפי ומפי זרעי וזרע זרעי עד עולם. ויתקיים בי בהתהלכך תנחה אותך בשכבך תשמור עליך והקיצות היא תשיחך: כי בי ירבו ימיך ויוסיפו לך שנות חיים: אורך ימים בימינה בשמאלה עושר וכבוד: ה' עוז לעמו יתן ה' יברך את עמו בשלום:

יִתְגַּדַּל וְיִתְקַדַּשׁ שְׁמֵהּ רַבָּא. בְּעָלְמָא דְּהוּא עָתִיד לְאִתְחַדָּתָא וּלְאַחֲיָא מֵתַיָּא. וּלְאַסָּקָא לְחַיֵּי עָלְמָא. וּלְמִבְנֵי קַרְתָּא דִירוּשְׁלֵם. וּלְשַׁכְלֵל הֵיכְלֵהּ בְּגַוַּהּ. וּלְמֶעֱקַר פּוּלְחָנָא נֻכְרָאָה מֵאַרְעָא. וְלַאֲתָבָא פּוּלְחָנָא דִשְׁמַיָּא לְאַתְרֵיהּ. וְיַמְלִיךְ קוּדְשָׁא בְּרִיךְ הוּא בְּמַלְכוּתֵהּ וִיקָרֵיהּ. [וְיַצְמַח פּוּרְקָנֵהּ וִיקָרֵב מְשִׁיחֵהּ.] בְּחַיֵּיכוֹן וּבְיוֹמֵיכוֹן וּבְחַיֵּי דְכָל בֵּית יִשְׂרָאֵל בַּעֲגָלָא וּבִזְמַן קָרִיב. וְאִמְרוּ אָמֵן: יְהֵא שְׁמֵהּ רַבָּא מְבָרַךְ לְעָלַם וּלְעָלְמֵי עָלְמַיָּא. יִתְבָּרַךְ וְיִשְׁתַּבַּח וְיִתְפָּאַר וְיִתְרוֹמַם וְיִתְנַשֵּׂא וְיִתְהַדָּר וְיִתְעַלֶּה וְיִתְהַלָּל שְׁמֵהּ דְּקוּדְשָׁא בְּרִיךְ הוּא. לְעֵלָּא מִן כָּל (בעשי"ת וּלְעֵלָּא מִכָּל) בִּרְכָתָא וְשִׁירָתָא תֻּשְׁבְּחָתָא וְנֶחֱמָתָא דַּאֲמִירָן בְּעָלְמָא וְאִמְרוּ אָמֵן: עַל יִשְׂרָאֵל וְעַל רַבָּנָן וְעַל תַּלְמִידֵיהוֹן וְעַל כָּל תַּלְמִידֵי תַלְמִידֵיהוֹן וְעַל כָּל מָאן דְּעָסְקִין בְּאוֹרַיְתָא דִּי בְאַתְרָא (בא"י קַדִּישָׁא) הָדֵין וְדִי בְכָל אֲתַר וַאֲתַר. יְהֵא לְהוֹן וּלְכוֹן שְׁלָמָא רַבָּא חִנָּא וְחִסְדָּא וְרַחֲמִין וְחַיִּין אֲרִיכִין וּמְזוֹנֵי רְוִיחֵי וּפוּרְקָנָא מִן קֳדָם אֲבוּהוֹן דְּבִשְׁמַיָּא וְאַרְעָא וְאִמְרוּ אָמֵן: יְהֵא שְׁלָמָא רַבָּא מִן שְׁמַיָּא וְחַיִּים טוֹבִים עָלֵינוּ וְעַל כָּל יִשְׂרָאֵל וְאִמְרוּ אָמֵן: עֹשֶׂה שָׁלוֹם (בעשי"ת הַשָּׁלוֹם) בִּמְרוֹמָיו הוּא בְּרַחֲמָיו יַעֲשֶׂה שָׁלוֹם עָלֵינוּ וְעַל כָּל יִשְׂרָאֵל וְאִמְרוּ אָמֵן:

א) פי' הגון על זה תמצא בספר החיים שחיבר אחי הגאון מהר"ל מפראג בספר זכיות ח"א פ"ג. ב) בסיומא וסוף תשובת הרמ"א ז"ל וכן בסוף יש"ש בב"ק כתוב רמזים על הזכרת שמות הללו.

תלמוד בבלי

— מהדורת נאה —

שבת · חלק ז

Steinsaltz Center

ירושלים

KOREN

Please note that the number ranges that appear at the bottom of each daf of the Vilna pages indicate the corresponding pages of the Koren Talmud Bavli translation and commentary.

תלמוד בבלי

הוצאת קורן ירושלים

מהדורת נאה

מסכת שבת

דף קלז: עד דף קנז:

COMMENTARY BY

Rabbi Adin Even-Israel Steinsaltz

EDITOR-IN-CHIEF

Rabbi Dr Tzvi Hersh Weinreb

EXECUTIVE EDITOR

Rabbi Joshua Schreier

•

STEINSALTZ CENTER
KOREN PUBLISHERS JERUSALEM

נד א מיי' פ"ב מהל' מילה הלכה ד סמג עשין כח טוש"ע י"ד סי' רסד סעיף ד:

נה ב מיי' שם הלכה ג טוש"ע שם סעי' ה:

נו ג מיי' שם הלכה ה טור וש"ע שם סעיף ו:

נז ד מיי' פ"ג מהל' מילה הלכה א סמג שם טוש"ע י"ד סי' רסה סעיף א:

נח ה מיי' שם הלכה ד סמג שם טוש"ע י"ד סי' רסח סעיף ה:

נט ו מיי' שם הלכה ה סמג שם טוש"ע י"ד סי' רסז סעיף יב:

א ז מיי' פכ"א מהל' שבת הלכה יז ופ"ג מהל' י"ט הלכה יז סמג לאוין סה עה טוש"ע א"ח סי' שטו סעי' ט וסי' שיט סעיף ט וסי' תקי סעיף ד:

תורה אור

מל ולא פרע את המילה – כאילו לא מל.§

גמ' אמר רבי אבינא א"ר ירמיה בר אבא אמר רב: בשר החופה את רוב גובהה של עטרה.§ "ואם היה בעל בשר וכו'".§ אמר שמואל: קטן המסורבל בבשר, רואין אותו, כ"ז שמתקשה ונראה מהול – אינו צריך למול, ואם לאו – צריך למול. במתניתא תנא, רשב"ג אומר: קטן המסורבל בבשר רואין אותו, כל זמן שמתקשה ואינו נראה מהול – צריך למולו, ואם לאו – אינו צריך למולו. מאי בינייהו? איכא בינייהו: נראה ואינו נראה.§ "מל ולא פרע".§ ת"ר: המל אומר: "אקב"ו על המילה". אבי הבן אומר: "אקב"ו להכניסו בבריתו של אברהם אבינו". העומדים (א) אומרים: כשם שנכנס לברית כך יכנס לתורה לחופה ולמע"ט. והמברך אומר: "אשר קידש ידיד מבטן, חוק בשארו שם, וצאצאיו חתם באות ברית קדש. על כן בשכר זאת, אל חי חלקנו, (ב) צוה* להציל ידידות שארינו משחת, למען בריתו אשר שם בבשרנו בא"י כורת הברית". המל את הגרים אומר: "ברוך אתה ה' אלהינו מלך העולם אקב"ו על המילה". והמברך אומר: "אקב"ו למול את הגרים ולהטיף מהם דם ברית, שאילמלא דם ברית לא נתקיימו שמים וארץ שנאמר: 'אם לא בריתי יומם ולילה חוקות שמים וארץ לא שמתי' (ירמיהו לג) בא"י כורת הברית". המל את העבדים אומר: "אקב"ו על המילה", והמברך אומר: "אקב"ו למול את העבדים ולהטיף מהם דם ברית *שאילמלא דם ברית חוקות שמים וארץ לא נתקיימו, שנאמ': 'אם לא בריתי יומם ולילה חוקות שמים וארץ לא שמתי' [נדרים לב.] בא"י כורת הברית".§

הדרן עלך רבי אליעזר דמילה

רבי אליעזר אומר: תולין את המשמרת בי"ט, ונותנין לתלויה בשבת. וחכ"א: אין תולין את המשמרת בי"ט, ואין נותנין לתלויה בשבת, אבל נותנין לתלויה ביו"ט.§

גמ' השתא ר"א, אוסופי אהל עראי לא מוספינן, למיעבד לכתחלה שרי?! מאי היא – דתנן, *פקק החלון, ר"א אומר: בזמן שקשור ותלוי – פוקקין בו, ואם לאו – אין פוקקין בו. וחכ"א: בין כך ובין כך – פוקקין בו. ואמר רבה בר בר חנה א"ר יוחנן: *הכל מודים שאין עושין אהל עראי בתחלה בי"ט, ואין צ"ל בשבת. לא נחלקו אלא להוסיף, שר"א אומר: אין מוסיפין בי"ט, ואין צ"ל בשבת. וחכ"א: מוסיפין בשבת, ואין צ"ל ביום טוב. ר"א סבר לה כרבי יהודה, דתניא: *אין בין יום טוב לשבת אלא אוכל נפש בלבד, רבי יהודה מתיר אף מכשירי אוכל נפש. אימר דשמעינן ליה לר' יהודה – במכשירין שאי אפשר לעשותם מערב יום טוב, במכשירין שאפשר לעשותם מעיו"ט מי שמעת ליה?! דר"א עדיפא מדרבי יהודה.§ "וחכ"א".§ איבעיא להו: תלה מאי? אמר רב יוסף: תלה – חייב חטאת. א"ל אביי: אלא מעתה, תלא כוזא בסיכתא הכי נמי דמיחייב?! אלא

פרע. גילה: גמ' רוב גובהה. לא תימא רוב העטרה דקתני מתני' רוב היקפה, אלא אפילו רוב גובהה במקום אחד: קטן המסורבל בבשר. פלטר"י בלע"ז, שהשמן ועב, ולאחר שנימול נראה כמכוסהו: כל זמן שמתקשה. ומתוך הקישוי מתפשט בשרו. בדשמואל גרסינן: ונראה מהול. במתניתא גרסינן: ואינו נראה מהול: איכא בינייהו נראה ואינו נראה. לשמואל, נראה מהול – הוא דאין צריך למולו; הא נראה ואינו נראה – צריך. למתניתא, אינו נראה – הוא דצריך; הא נראה ואינו נראה – אינו צריך: אשר קידש ידיד מבטן. יצחק קרי ידיד, על שם "אשר אהבת" (בראשית כב): מבטן. דקודם שנולד נתקדש למצוה זו, דכתיב (שם יז): "אבל שרה אשתך וגו' והקימותי את בריתי אתו", היינו מילה: בשארו. בבשרו: שם. חק של מילה: וצאצאיו. אחריו: חתם באות. זו של ברית קדש: צוה להציל ידידות שארינו משחת. מגיהנם, דכתיב: "גם את בדם בריתך שלחתי אסיריך מבור אין מים בו" (זכריה ט):

הדרן עלך ר' אליעזר דמילה

תולין את המשמרת. שמסננין בה שמרי יין, ומותח פיה לכל צד בעגול, ונעשה כאהל על חלל הכלי שקורין אשטנד"א. ואע"ג דעביד אהל, שרי בי"ט, כדמפרש בגמרא. אבל בשבת – מיתלא לכתחילה לא, אבל אם תלויה היא – נותנין לתוכה שמרים ומסנן, דאין דרך בורר בכך: גמ' פקק החלון. כגון ארובת הגג: אלא להוסיף. כגון פקק זה שאינו אלא תוספת עראי על האהל: סבר ליה כרבי יהודה. הלכך הכא שרי, דמכשירי אוכל נפש הוא: שאי אפשר לעשותן מעי"ט. כגון שפוד שנרצם בי"ט: עדיפא. חזקה, דהוא שרי אפילו מכשירין שאפשר מעיו"ט: תלה כוזא בסיכתא. תלה כלי קטן במגוד: ה"נ דמיחייב. והכא מאי חיובא איכא באהל עראי? בנין גמור לא הוי, ומדרבנן הוא דמיתסר:

אלא

מל ולא פרע את המילה כאילו לא מל. תימה: אמאי איצטריך למיתני הא? כיון דכבר תנא דבשר החופה את רוב העטרה מעכב המילה, וכי לא פרע – עדיין רוב עטרה מכוסה: אבי הבן אומר כו'. רבינו שמואל גריס אבי הבן ברישא, והדר המל אומר. וכבר הנהיג לעשות כן לברך אבי הבן קודם המילה, משום ד"להכניסו" – להבא משמע, כדאמרינן בפ"ק דפסחים (ד' ז. ושם): ב"לבער" – כ"ע לא פליגי דלהבא משמע. ועוד: *דכל המצות מברך [שם] עליהן עובר לעשייתן. ור"ת החזיר המנהג לקדמותו, וגרס המל ברישא, והדר אבי הבן, כמו שכתוב בכל הספרים. וכן מוכח כולה סוגיא מדקאמר; העומדים שם אומרים: כשם שהכניסו לברית. מכלל שכבר הכניסו. ועוד: דגבי גר דבסמוך גרס ברישא המל כו', והדר המברך אומר: אקב"ו למול את הגרים. ונראה הוא שזהו כנגד ברכת אבי הבן, והתם א"א לשנות הגירסא. שיש באותה ברכה "להטיף מהן דם ברית כו' ברוך כורת הברית" – משמע דכל זה הוא אחר המילה. ועוד: דהמברך מברך לעולם אחר המילה, כמו במילת קטן. והיא דפסחים ה"פ: ב"לבער" כ"ע לא פליגי דלהבא משמע טפי מלשעבר, ומיהו: לשעבר נמי משמע. כי פליגי ב"על ביעור", מר סבר: דמשמע מעיקרא טפי מלהבא, ומר סבר: להבא נמי משמע כמו מעיקרא. והא דאמרינן דכל המצות מברך עובר לעשייתן – ה"מ כשהמברך עצמו עושה המצוה: ידיד מבטן. אומר ר"ת שהוא אברהם אבינו, שנקרא "ידיד", שנאמר (ירמיה יא): "מה לידידי בביתי" כדדרשינן במנחות בפרק "כל המנחות" (ד' נג: ושם). ושלשת האבות נזכרים: "חוק בשארו שם" – הוא יצחק, ו"צאצאיו חתם באות ברית קדש" – הוא יעקב וצאצאיו הוא ובניו, כמו שתרגם יונתן "הצאצאים והצפיעות" – בניא ובני בניא, (ישעיה כב) כלומר: יוצאי חלציו*: במצותיו וצונו למול את העבדים. שנאמר: "יליד בית ומקנת כסף" (בראשית יז):

הדרן עלך ר' אליעזר דמילה

תולין. אבל נותנין לתלויה ביום טוב. וצריך לפרש ולומר שאם היה עושהו מאתמול – לא היה טוב כל כך וחזק. והא דתניא בפרקין דלעיל (ד' קלד. ושם) דאין מסננין את החרדל במסננת שלו בי"ט – אם היה עושהו מאתמול לא היה מתקלקל: דרבי אליעזר עדיפא מדר"י. תימה: ולר"א תיקשה ליה הנהו קראי דדריש בפ"ק דמגילה (ד' ז:) דקאמר: ורבי יהודה, כתיב "הוא" וכתיב "לכם", ולא קשיא; כאן – במכשירין שאפשר וכו'. וכ"ת: ר"א הוה דריש "הוא" לדרשה אחרינא – א"כ מנ"ל התם דרבי יהודה הוה מפליג? לימא דרבי יהודה הוה דריש ליה לדרשה אחריתי כר' אליעזר! ונראה דבדאורייתא מודה ר' אליעזר דמכשירין דאפשר אסורים, *וכי שרי להו הכא – ה"מ באהל עראי, דאינו אלא מדרבנן, גזירה אטו אהל קבע, כדאמרינן בביצה בפרק "המביא" (ד' לג:). מיהו קשה: מנ"ל דעדיפא? דילמא בהא מודה אפילו רבי יהודה!

*) [ועי' תוס' מנחות נג. ד"ה בן]

אלא

רבינו חננאל

מעת לעת להבראותו. וזה מפורש ביבמות בפר' הערל וכל הטמאים: מתני' ואלו הן ציצין המעכבין את המילה. א"ר אבינא א"ר ירמיה בר אבא אמר רב בשר החופה את רוב גובהה של עטרה וכו' וכן הלכתא. ואם הוא בעל בשר מתקנו מפני מראית העין כלומר אע"פ שהציצין הללו אינן חופין רוב גובהה של עטרה מתקנו מפני שלא יהא נראה כערלה: אמר שמואל קטן המסורבל בבשר רואין אותו כל זמן שמתקשה [ונראה מהול אין צריך למול במתניתא תנא רשבג"א קטן המסורבל בבשר רואין אותו כ"ז שמתקשה] שאינו נראה מהול צריך למול ואמרי' מאי ביניהם איכא ביניהם [נראה] ואינו נראה צריך למול לרשב"ג דאמר ואינו נראה מהול כלל צריך למול אבל אם נראה ואינו נראה אינו צריך למול הו' מסורבל מסובב בבשר כדכתי' כפיתו סרבלתהון וכו'. מל ולא פרע את המילה וכו'. פי' מי שמל ולא פרע את המילה כלומר לא קרע את העור וגילה את העטרה כאלו לא מל:

הדרן עלך ר' אלעזר אם לא הביא. עז ותהלה לאל אבי. שית עזר גלילין. חלץ באזר וההלין. בפ' ר' אליעזר תולין:

ר' אליעזר אומר תולין את המשמרת ביו"ט וכו' ואקשי' עלה השתא ר' אליעזר להוסיף באהל עראי מחמיר ואמר אין מוסיפין לכתחלה (שאי) [מאי היא]. דתנן פקק החלון ר' אליעזר אומר בזמן שקשור ותלוי פוקקין בו כו' ופקק זה כגון מסך לסתום בו חללו של חלון ואמר רבה בר בר חנה א"ר יוחנן הכל מודים שאין עושין אהלי עראי בתחלה ביו"ט ואין צריך לומר בשבת לא נחלקו אלא להוסיף שר' אליעזר אומר אין מוסיפין ביו"ט ואין צ"ל בשבת וחכ"א מוסיפין בשבת ואין צ"ל ביו"ט ומפרקינן ר' אליעזר סבר לה כר' יהודה דתניא אין בין יו"ט לשבת אלא אוכל נפש בלבד. ר' יהודה אומר אף מכשירי אוכל נפש וזה שמתיר ר' אליעזר לעשות אהל לכתחלה ביו"ט לתלות המשמרת מפני שהוא מכשירי אוכל נפש כדי לשמר היין לשתות בשמחת יו"ט ונמצא ר' אליעזר מיקל מר' יהודה שר' יהודה אינו מתיר אלא במכשירין שאי אפשר לעשותן מעיו"ט אבל במכשירין שאפשר לעשותן מעיו"ט כגון שימור היין וכדומה לו אוסר ור' אליעזר מתיר אפילו בזה. ואין הלכה

יבמות מז: עה.

[תוספ' פט"ז]

[מנחות מב. תוספ' ברכות פ"ו כל הענין עד סופו]

הג"מ יעב"ץ ז"ל ניקד לזה בחירי"ק

הגהות הב"ח

(א) גמ' העומדין שם אומרים כשם שהכנסתו לברית כך תכניסהו לתור' כצ"ל וכן בסמוך: (ב) שם חלקנו צורנו צוה:

לעיל קכה: עירובין מד. סוכה כז:

[תוספ' סוכה פ"א לעיל קכה: וש"נ]

[תוספ' מגילה פ"א ביצה כח. לו: מגילה ז: לעיל קכד.]

[ועי' תוס' לפסחים סח: ד"ה מה רחיה רשות]

אלא אמר אביי: א*מדרבנן היא, שלא יעשה כדרך שהוא עושה בחול. מנקיט אביי חומרי מתניתא, ותני: בהגוד והמשמרת כילה וכסא גלין – לא יעשה, ואם עשה – פטור אבל אסור. גאהלי קבע – לא יעשה, ואם עשה – חייב חטאת. דאבל מטה וכסא טרסקל ואסלא – מותר לנטותן לכתחילה.§ "ואין נותנין לתלויה בשבת".§ איבעיא להו: שימר מאי? אמר רב כהנא: השימר – חייב חטאת. מתקיף לה רב ששת: מי איכא מידי דרבנן מחייבי חטאת, ורבי אליעזר שרי לכתחילה?! מתקיף לה רב יוסף: אלמה לא?! הרי עיר של זהב, דר"מ מחייב חטאת ורבי אליעזר שרי לכתחילה! מאי היא – דתניא: *לא תצא אשה בעיר של זהב, ואם יצאה – חייבת חטאת, דברי ר"מ. וחכמים אומרים: לא תצא, ואם יצאה – פטורה. *ר"א אומר: יוצאה אשה בעיר של זהב לכתחילה. א"ל אביי: מי סברת ר"א אדר"מ קאי, דאמר "חייבת חטאת"? אדרבנן קאי? דאמרי "פטור אבל אסור", ואמר להו איהו: מותר לכתחילה. *ומשום מאי מתרינן ביה? רבה אמר: משום בורר, רבי זירא אמר: משום מרקד. אמר רבה: כוותי דידי מסתברא, מה דרכו של בורר – נוטל אוכל ומניח הפסולת, אף הכא נמי – נוטל את האוכל ומניח את הפסולת. אמר ר' זירא: כוותי דידי מסתברא, מה דרכו של מרקד – פסולת מלמעלה ואוכל מלמטה, אף הכא נמי – פסולת מלמעלה ואוכל מלמטה. תני רמי בר יחזקאל: זטלית כפולה – לא יעשה, ואם עשה – פטור אבל אסור. היה כרוך עליה חוט או משיחה – מותר לנטותה לכתחילה. בעא מיניה רב כהנא מרב: כילה מהו? א"ל: אף מטה אסורה. מטה מהו? א"ל: אף כילה מותרת. כילה ומטה מהו? א"ל: כילה אסורה, ומטה מותרת. ולא קשיא; הא – דקאמר "אף מטה אסורה" – כדקרמנאי, הא דקאמר ליה "אף כילה מותרת" – כדרמי בר יחזקאל. "כילה אסורה ומטה מותרת" – כדידן. אמר רב יוסף: חזינא להו לכילי דבי רב הונא דמאורתא נגידו, ומצפרא חביטא רמיא. *אמר רב משום רבי חייא: חוילון, מותר לנטותו ומותר לפורקו. ואמר שמואל משום רבי חייא: כילת

עירובין קב.

רש"י

אלא אמר אביי מדרבנן. קא קשרי לה חכמים דמתניתין, דלא שבקינן ליה למיתליה, למיעבד עובדא דחול: מנקיט. מלקיט: חומרי מתנייתא. כללות של ברייתות: חומר = קשר. כלומר: כללות שמלא בברייתות, בגוד לבדה, ובמשמרת לבדה, ובכילה לבדה, ובכסא גלין לבדה – ושנאן כולן: הפטורין אבל אסורין בחומר אחד, והמותרים לכתחילה בחומר אחד: הגוד. הוא עור של בהמה תפור, ופיו רחב מאד ויש לו שנצים, ועוברי דרכים ממלאין אותו יין או חלב במקום שתוקעין שם אהליהם ללון, ושוטחין אותו ופיו מתוח ע"ג יתידות, והרוח עוברת מתחתיו ומצננו שלא יתקלקל היין. והוי דומה לאהל לאחר שנמתח: כילה. שיש[א] בגגה טפח: וכסא גלין. כמו מטה גללניתא ד"כירה" (לעיל דף מז:), והוא שם מקום. ומפרקין מטותיהן וכסאותן וטוענין אותן עמהן, וחוזרין ומחזירין אותן: לא יעשה. דאהל עראי נינהו. וכסא גלין נמי, גזרה שמא יתקע בחוזק: אבל מטה. שלנו, המחוברת ועומדת, אם היתה זקופה או מוטה על לדיה – מותר לנטותה לישבה על רגליה. ואע"ג דהשתא עביד אהל – שרי, דלא מידי עביד אלא ליתובה בעלמא: כסא טרסקל. כך שמו, ובלע"ז פלודסטויי"ל. ועליונו של עור, ומקפלין אותו. וכשמסלקין אותו סומכין אותו לכותל, וכשרוצה לישב עליו נוטהו ויושב על ד' רגלים: ואסלא. עשוי כעין כסא טרסקל, אבל עור הפרוש עליו נקוב לבית הכסא – מותר לנטותו לכתחילה, דהא עביד וקאי: שימר. נתן שמרים לתלויה, וסינן: חייבת חטאת. דלאו תכשיט הוא, אלא משוי: פטור. דתכשיט הוא, ולכתחילה אסור דילמא שלפא ומחויא: יוצאה אשה. דמאן דרכה למיפק בעיר של זהב – אשה חשובה, ואשה חשובה לא שלפא ומחויא: משום מאי מתרינן ביה. למשמר: משום בורר. דהאי נמי בורר הוא: כוותי דידי מסתברא. דאי אתרו ביה משום בורר, התראה היא: דנוטל אוכל ומניח פסולת. *ולרבא ה"ה נמי דאי אתרו ביה משום מרקד הויא התראה. אבל לרבי זירא, אי אתרו ביה משום בורר – לאו התראה היא, דלא דמי לבורר, שהאוכל למטה ופסולת למעלה, מה שאין כן בבורר קטנית, שהפסולת למטה: טלית כפולה לא יעשה. לשטוח טליתו על גבי ארבע יתידות לישן תחתיה, וראשיו מתכפלין לכאן ולכאן לצד הארץ, והויא ליה לכתלים להגן מן החמה, דהוי אהלא: כרך עליה. מבעוד יום: חוט או משיחה. ונתנה על הגם שעל הקנוף כשהיא מכופלת, וכרך עליה חוט למשכה בו לפורסה לכאן ולכאן – מותר למושכה בו בשבת, דמוסיף על אהל עראי הוא, ואינו כעושה לכתחילה: כדקרמנאי. היינו גללניתא*, שפורקה ומחזירה, והוא שם מקום. לשון אחר: קרמנאי – מוכרי בגדי פשתן מוכרין עליהן: כדרמי. כרך עליה חוט: כדידן. מטה שהיתה זקופה, והוא מושיבה על רגליה: דמאורתא נגידו ומצפרא חביטא. בלילי שבת ראיתים פרושות, ולבקר ראיתים מושלכים לארץ. אלמא: מותר לפורקה, וה"נ מותר לנטותה: וילון. מסך שכנגד הפתח: מותר לנטותו. שאין אהל אלא מי שעשוי כעין גג: כילת

תוספות

אלא אמר אביי מדרבנן. ואף על גב דתלא כוזא בסיכתא אפילו איסור דרבנן ליכא – במילי דרבנן שייך שפיר לחלק. אבל אי במשמרת מדאורייתא אסור – אין שייך לחלק. מ"ר: כסא גלין. לא כפי' הקונטרס מטה גללניתא דשלהי כירה, ואסור משום שמא יתקע. דכולה שמעתא איירי באיסור אהל. אלא היינו [כעין] מטה שפורסין עליה עור, ואסור משום אהל כשמושיב תחילה המטה ואחר כך פורס העור, דהוי ממטה למעלה ואסור. כדאיתא בכילה בפ' "המביא כדי יין" (ד' לג.) דפוריא אסור מלמטה למעלה. מ"ר: כסא טרסקל. יש בהן עור. וכשרוצה לישב עליו נוטה העור ויושב על ד' רגלים, כדפירש בקונטר'. וכגון שהוא קבוע בכסא, דאם לא כן היה אסור לנטותו, כדאמר בפ' "המביא" (שם דף לג:): אמר רב יהודה, האי מדורתא, מלמעלה למטה – שרי. פירוש: כשנותנין עצים מכאן ומכאן, ונותנין עליהם עצים ארוכים ארכן לרחב של אלו, ובמביא תחילה עצים שנותן למעלה ואחרי כן עצים שמכאן ומכאן – אינו כן דרך עשיית אהל לעשות הגג תחילה ואחריו הדפנות, ושרי, וכה"ג קרי מלמעלה למטה. מלמטה למעלה – אסור, וכן ביעתא. פירוש: כשנותנין בילים ע"ג האסכלא שקורין גרדיי"ל, וכשנותנין הבילים תחילה, ואוחז בהן בידו עד שמביא הכלי תחתיהן – שרי, דהיינו מלמעלה למטה. וכן קידרא שמושיבה על שתי חביות, שצריך לאוחזה בידו ואחר כך לסדר תחתיה החביות. וכן חביתא – חביות שמסדרין באוצר, ומושיבין אחת על גבי שתים. וכן פוריא – לפרוס העור תחילה באויר, ואח"כ להביא המטה תחתיו. ומיהו, יש לפרש הך דשמעתא באינו קשור, ומיירי כגון שעושה מלמעלה למטה, אבל משמע דבכל ענין מיירי. מ"ר. וכל הנהו דאסרינן בכילה, אומר ר"ת: דדווקא דברים שיש להם מחיצה עד לארץ, אבל להושיב הקדרה על טרפיד בי"ט – שרי אפילו מלמטה למעלה, להביא הטרפיד תחילה ואחר כך להושיב הקדרה. וכן להושיב השולחן על גבי ספסלין. וביעתא וקידרא וחביתא ופוריא – י"ל שיש להם מחיצה. מ"ר: מי סברת דר' אליעזר קאי אדר"מ כו'. לא ידע רבי מאי קמשני*): מה דרכו של בורר. לא תקשה אההיא דשלהי "כלל גדול" (לעיל דף עד.), כמו שפי' שם (בד"ה בורר ואוכל): כרך עליה חוט או משיחה מותר לנטותה. כגון ששייר בה טפח, דבענין אחר לא הוה שרי, כדאשכחן בפרק בתרא דעירובין (דף קב.): כרוך בודיא ושייר בה טפח למחר פושטת, דמוסיף על אהל עראי הוא. אי נמי: כריכת חוט או משיחה מועלת בלא שייר בה טפח: בעא מיניה רב כהנא מרב כו'. ונראה לר"י: ששאלו לו סתם בכל כילות אם הם מותרות, אמר ליה: אפילו מטה יש מהן שאסורות. הדר בעא: אם כל מטות אסורות. אמר ליה: אף כילות מותרות. אמר ליה: כיון שאין אתה מחלק בשניהם, מהו להשוותן כילה ומטה, ובמקום שאסור זה כנגדו אסור זה? א"ל: כילה אסורה ומטה מותרת. וכן יש לפרש ההיא דפרק "אלו טרפות" (חולין דף נג.): יש דרוסה לחתול? א"ל: אף לחולדה יש דרוסה. יש דרוסה לחולדה? א"ל: אף לחתול אין דרוסה. לחתול ולחולדה יש דרוסה או אין להם דרוסה? א"ל: לחתול יש דרוסה ולחולדה אין דרוסה. ומפרש התם דבגדיים וטלאים יש דרוסה לחתול ולא לחולדה, ובאימרי רברבי אין דרוסה אפילו לחתול, ובעופות יש דרוסה אפילו לחולדה. יש ליישב כעין שפירש הר"ר יצחק בן ר"מ (פי') התם, שכשהיה עוסק באימרי שאלו אם יש דרוסה לחולדה, וכן כולם. מ"ר: אף כילה מותרת כדרמי בר יחזקאל. הוה מצי למימר כי ההיא דשנינו בסמוך לכילי דבי רב הונא, וי"ל: כדרמי בר יחזקאל הוו: שאין

*) [נ"ל פירוש דאף אם לא קאי אר"מ מ"מ הדבר תמוה איך יחלקו בסברות רחוקות כ"כ אם לא שלא ידע ר"א מסברת ר"מ כלום וזהו כוונת התוס'].

מסורת הש"ס

[לקמן קמ.]

לעיל נט: תוספ' פ"ה

עדיות פ"ב מ"ז

[עי' תוס' לעיל נג: ד"ה משום ותוס' ב"ק כ. ד"ה ורבי אליעזר]

[נ"ל ולרבה]

[עי' לעיל מז:]

הגהות הגר"א

[א] רש"י ד"ה כילה שיש בגגה טפח. נ"ב אבל הרי"ף והרמב"ם כתבו דוקא שאין בגגה וג' סמוך לגגה טפח:

גליון הש"ס

גמ' דתניא לא תצא אשה. ע"ל סב ע"א: תוס' ד"ה מי סברת וכו' לא ידע. כעין זה לעיל קיח ע"ב תוד"ה אלו היה וש"נ:

עין משפט נר מצוה

ב א ב מיי' פכ"א מהל' שבת הלכה יז ופכ"ב שם הלכה כח סמג לאוין סה טוש"ע א"ח סימן שטו סעיף ג ד ו ט:

ג ג מיי' פכ"ב שם הלכה כז:

ד ד מיי' שם הלכה כח סמג שם טוש"ע שם סעיף ה:

ה ה מיי' פ"א מהל' שבת הלכה יד סמג שם:

ו ו מיי' שם הלכה יא ופכ"א הלכה יז סמג שם:

ז ז ח מיי' פכ"ב מהל' שבת הלכה כט סמג שם טוש"ע א"ח סי' שטו סעיף י:

רבינו חננאל

הלכה כר' אליעזר: מתני' וחכ"א אין תולין את המשמרת ביו"ט. איבעיא לן תלא מאי וסליקא חיובא מדרבנן (ובלבד) שלא יעש' כדרך שהוא עושה בחול. מנקיט אביי חומרי מתנייתא ותני הגוד והמשמרת כילה וכסא [גלין] לא יעשה ואם עשה פטור אבל אסור כלומר איסורא דרבנן. אהל קבוע לא יעשה ואם עשה חייב חטאת אבל המטה והכסא והטרסקל והאסלא מותר לנטותו בתחלה. פי' משמרת הא דאמרן והיא מסננת של יין. גוד הוא חמת מים. בלולב [וערבה] (הגזול) (דף מח) משכיה דההוא גברא דעבדינן ליה גודא. ומלינן ביה מיא והולכי דרכים נועצים יתידות בארץ וקושרין (אחת) [אותו] זה בחוטין עבין ותולין אותו באלו היתידות להצטנן מימיו. כילה שיש בגגה טפח כסא גלין הוא של חוליות. טוענין עליו קרשים ויושבין עליו וכשעומדין פורקין אותו מטה כגון הא דידן ולא בריוא לן מלאכתה אלא דברים מוכיחין שהיא מטה (גיליתא) [גללניתא]. והכרעים שמחזיר רפויין הן ולפיכך היא מותרת כדאמרינן (לעיל מז ע"ב) אם היה רפוי מותר. ולגבה היא עשויה במסמרים והיא זקופה ומרביצה לישן עליה הואיל ולגבה עשויה אינה חשובה באהל וכן כסא לשבת בו וזה שאמר גורר אדם מטה וכסא וספסל שלשתן טעם אחד הן. טרסקל הוא קערה פשוטה כגון שלחן קטן וכדתניא ר' יוסי בר' יהודה נעץ קנה ברה"ר והניח בראשו טרסקל וזרק ונח על גביו גם זה לגביו עשוי לאכול בו. או לתת בו חפצים. אסלא הוא ספסל של ברזל. דתנן האסלא טמא המדרס וטמא מת (פרשה) [ופירושו] היא טמאה מדרס. והברזל טמא טמא מת. וספסל זה של ברזל. ועליו עור נטוי לישב עליו. ותנן עור האסלא וחלל שלו מצטרפין לטפח ואמרינן בתחלת עירובין מאי עור אסלא אמר רבה בר בר חנה א"ר יוחנן עור אסלא עור כסא של בית הכסא והוא שאמרנו ספסל של ברזל נטוי עליו עור נקוב באמצע כשיעור שיט הן חסר הן יתר ויושב עליו אדם ותחתיו גרף כדי לקבל בו הרעי לפיכך נקרא עור כסא של בית הכסא אלו כולן מותר לנטותן בתחלה. ואין נותנין לתלויה בשבת ר' אליעזר דתני ונותנין לתלויה בשבת סבר מותר לשמר בתחלה בשבת וחכמים אוסרין ואיבעיא לן אליבא דרבנן שימר מאי ואמר רב כהנא חייב חטאת ופי' שימור בשוגג חייב חטאת דלא אשכחן במזיד בשבת חייב חטאת. אלא כל שהוא בשבת בשוגג חייב חטאת במזיד חייב מיתה ועל זה הטעם אמרו משום מאי מתרינן ביה רבה אמר משום בורר ר' זירא אמר משום מרקד. סבר בורר ומרקד שניהן אבות מלאכות הן ובורר ומרקד כעין דבר אחד הן ולא נחלקו בשמותן אלא מפני שהיה במקדש ולמה (רבא) [רבה] ור' זירא אלא להודיעך שאם התרו בו משום מרקד אליבא דרבה אינו חייב וכן אליבא דר' זירא אם התרו בו משום בורר. והלכתא כר' זירא: תאני רמי בר יחזקאל טלית כפול לא יעשה ואם עשה פטור אבל אסור. פי' אדם שקפל טלית וקשרה בין ב' כתלים והדביק קצוות הטלית בארץ ונכנס לישן תחתיה בגגה כאמצע ושופעת ויורדת למטה בארץ כמלוא קומת אדם ברוחב אהל עראי הוא. ומפני שאין בגגה טפח ולא בפחות משלשה לפיכך פטור אבל אסור. ואם היו עליה חוטין מאתמול ונטה אותה מותר. והא דבעי רב כהנא מרב כילה מהו א"ל אף מטה אסורה מכלל שגם כילה אסורה פי' מטה דקרמינא. היא מטה של פרסיים. ורב לטעמיה דאשכחינן בסוף כירה רב ושמואל דאמרי תרוייהו המחזיר מטה של פרסיים בשבת חייב חטאת ומסתברא דהאי מטה של פרסיים לא יתכן לו להחזירה אלא אם יתקע לפי שמלבנותיה וכרעיה דחוקין ואינן נשלבין אלא אם יתקע בהן וכיון שתקע בהן חייב כולה היא כילה שיש בגגה טפח או בפחות משלשה סמוך לגגה טפח. שמצינו באהלי טומאה טפח והנה נטה אהל קבוע

רב נסים גאון

פרק ר' אליעזר אומר תולין: אבל מטה כסא טרסקל ואסלא מותר לנטותן לכתחילה. משכחת לה בעירובין בפרק מבוי (דף י) מאי עור אסלא אמר רבה בר בר חנה אמר ר' יוחנן עור כסא של בית הכסא:

עין משפט נר מצוה

ח א מיי' פכ"ב מהל' שבת הלכה ל טוש"ע א"ח סי' שטו סעיף יא:

ט ב ג מיי' פכ"ב מהל' שבת הלכה לא סמג שם טוש"ע א"ח סי' שא סעיף מ:

י ד מיי' שם טוש"ע שם סעיף מא:

יא ה ו מיי' שם הלכה לב סמג שם טוש"ע א"ח סי' שטו סעיף יב:

יב ז מיי' פכ"ו שם הלכה ו סמג שם טוש"ע שם סי' שח סעיף טז:

יג ח מיי' פי"א מהל' שאר אבות הטומאות הלכה ב:

יד ט מיי' פ"ה מהל' טומאת מת הלכה ו ופי"ג מהל' כלים הלכה א ב:

*כִּילַּת חֲתָנִים מוּתָּר לִנְטוֹתָהּ וּמוּתָּר לְפוֹרְקָהּ. אֲמַר רַב שֵׁשֶׁת בְּרֵיהּ דְּרַב אִידִי: [א]לָא אֲמַרַן אֶלָּא שֶׁאֵין בְּגַגָּהּ טֶפַח, אֲבָל יֵשׁ בְּגַגָּהּ טֶפַח – אֲסוּרָה. וְכִי אֵין בְּגַגָּהּ טֶפַח נַמִי לָא אֲמַרַן אֶלָּא שֶׁאֵין בְּפָחוֹת מִשְּׁלֹשָׁה סָמוּךְ לְגַגָּהּ טֶפַח, אֲבָל יֵשׁ בְּפָחוֹת מִשְּׁלֹשָׁה סָמוּךְ לְגַגָּהּ טֶפַח – אָסוּר[א]. וְלָא אֲמַרַן אֶלָּא שֶׁאֵין בְּשִׁיפּוּעָהּ טֶפַח, אֲבָל יֵשׁ בְּשִׁיפּוּעָהּ טֶפַח – *שִׁפּוּעֵי אֹהָלִים כְּאֹהָלִים דָּמוּ. וְלָא אֲמַרַן אֶלָּא דְּלָא נָחִית מִפּוּרְיָא טֶפַח, אֲבָל נָחִית מִפּוּרְיָא טֶפַח – אָסוּר.§ *וְאָמַר רַב שֵׁשֶׁת בְּרֵיהּ דְּרַב אִידִי: הַאי [ב]סִיאָנָא שָׁרֵי. וְהָאִיתְּמַר: סִיאָנָא אָסוּר! לָא קַשְׁיָא, [ג]הָא – דְּאִית בֵּיהּ טֶפַח, הָא – דְּלֵית בֵּיהּ טֶפַח. אֶלָּא מֵעַתָּה, שַׁרְבֵּיב בִּגְלִימָא טֶפַח ה"נ *דְּמִיחַיַּיב?! *אֶלָּא לָא קַשְׁיָא, [ד]הָא – דְּמִיהֲדַק, הָא – דְּלָא מִיהֲדַק. שְׁלַח לֵיהּ רָמִי בַּר יְחֶזְקֵאל לְרַב הוּנָא: אֵימָא לָן אִיזִי הָנָךְ מִילֵּי מְעַלְּיָיתָא דְּאָמַרְתְּ לָן מִשְּׁמֵיהּ דְּרַב, תַּרְתֵּי בְּשַׁבָּת וַחֲדָא בַּתּוֹרָה. שְׁלַח לֵיהּ: הָא דְּתַנְיָא "גּוֹד בְּכִיסְנָא מוּתָּר לִנְטוֹתָהּ בְּשַׁבָּת" אָמַר רַב: לֹא שָׁנוּ אֶלָּא [ה]בְּב' בְּנֵי אָדָם, אֲבָל בְּאָדָם אֶחָד – אָסוּר. אָמַר אַבַּיֵי: [ו]וְכִילָּה, אֲפִילּוּ בִּי' בְּנֵי אָדָם – אָסוּר, אִי אֶפְשָׁר דְּלָא מִימַּתְחָא פּוּרְתָּא. אִידָךְ מַאי הִיא – דְּתַנְיָא: *)"כִּירָה שֶׁנִּשְׁמְטָה אַחַת מִיַּרְכוֹתֶיהָ – מוּתָּר לְטַלְטְלָהּ, שְׁתַּיִם – אָסוּר". רַב אָמַר: אֲפִילּוּ [ז]חַד נַמִי אָסוּר, גְּזֵירָה שֶׁמָּא יִתְקַע. תּוֹרָה, דְּאָמַר רַב: עֲתִידָה תּוֹרָה שֶׁתִּשְׁתַּכַּח מִיִּשְׂרָאֵל, שֶׁנֶּאֱמַר: °"וְהִפְלָא ה' אֶת מַכֹּתְךָ", *הַפְלָאָה זוֹ אֵינִי יוֹדֵעַ מַהוּ, כְּשֶׁהוּא אוֹמֵר °"לָכֵן הִנְנִי יוֹסִף לְהַפְלִיא אֶת הָעָם הַזֶּה הַפְלֵא וָפֶלֶא" הֱוֵי אוֹמֵר: הַפְלָאָה זוֹ תּוֹרָה. ת"ר: *כְּשֶׁנִּכְנְסוּ רַבּוֹתֵינוּ לַכֶּרֶם בְּיַבְנֶה אָמְרוּ: עֲתִידָה תּוֹרָה שֶׁתִּשְׁתַּכַּח מִיִּשְׂרָאֵל, שֶׁנֶּאֱמַר °"הִנֵּה יָמִים בָּאִים נְאֻם ה' אֱלֹהִים וְהִשְׁלַחְתִּי רָעָב בָּאָרֶץ לֹא רָעָב לַלֶּחֶם וְלֹא צָמָא לַמַּיִם כִּי אִם לִשְׁמֹעַ אֵת דִּבְרֵי ה'", וּכְתִיב: °"וְנָעוּ מִיָּם עַד יָם וּמִצָּפוֹן וְעַד מִזְרָח יְשׁוֹטְטוּ לְבַקֵּשׁ אֶת דְּבַר ה' וְלֹא יִמְצָאוּ". "דְּבַר ה'" – זוֹ הֲלָכָה, "דְּבַר ה'" – זֶה הַקֵּץ, "דְּבַר ה'" – זוֹ נְבוּאָה. וּמַאי "יְשׁוֹטְטוּ לְבַקֵּשׁ אֶת דְּבַר ה'" – אָמְרוּ: עֲתִידָה אִשָּׁה שֶׁתִּטּוֹל כִּכָּר שֶׁל תְּרוּמָה וְתַחֲזוֹר בְּבָתֵּי כְנֵסִיּוֹת וּבְבָתֵּי מִדְרָשׁוֹת, לֵידַע אִם טְמֵאָה הִיא וְאִם טְהוֹרָה הִיא, וְאֵין מֵבִין. אִם טְהוֹרָה הִיא וְאִם טְמֵאָה הִיא?! בְּהֶדְיָא כְּתִיב בֵּיהּ: °"מִכָּל הָאֹכֶל אֲשֶׁר יֵאָכֵל"! אֶלָּא: לֵידַע אִם רִאשׁוֹנָה הִיא וְאִם שְׁנִיָּה הִיא, וְאֵין מֵבִין. הָא נַמִי מַתְנִיתִין הִיא, כִּדְתְנַן: *[ח]הַשֶּׁרֶץ שֶׁנִּמְצָא בַּתַּנּוּר – הַפַּת שֶׁבְּתוֹכוֹ שְׁנִיָּה, שֶׁהַתַּנּוּר תְּחִילָּה. מִסְתַּפְּקָא לְהוּ הָא דַּאֲמַר לֵיהּ רַב אַדָּא בַּר אַהֲבָה לְרָבָא: לִיחֲזְיֵיהּ הַאי תַּנּוּרָא כְּמַאן דְּמָלֵי טוּמְאָה, וְתֶיהֱוֵי פַּת רִאשׁוֹנָה! א"ל: לָא אָמְרִינַן לִיחֲזְיֵיהּ הַאי תַּנּוּרָא כְּמַאן דְּמָלֵי טוּמְאָה. *דְּתַנְיָא: יָכוֹל יְהוּ כָּל הַכֵּלִים מִיטַּמְּאִין בַּאֲוִיר כְּלִי חֶרֶס – ת"ל: "כֹּל אֲשֶׁר בְּתוֹכוֹ יִטְמָא מִכָּל הָאֹכֶל אֲשֶׁר יֵאָכֵל", [ט]אוֹכָלִין(א) – מִטַּמְּאִין בַּאֲוִיר כְּלִי חֶרֶס, וְאֵין כֵּלִים מִטַּמְּאִין בַּאֲוִיר כְּלִי חֶרֶס. תַּנְיָא, רַבִּי שִׁמְעוֹן בֶּן יוֹחַי אוֹמֵר: חַס וְשָׁלוֹם שֶׁתִּשְׁתַּכַּח תּוֹרָה מִיִּשְׂרָאֵל, שֶׁנֶּאֱמַר: °"כִּי לֹא תִשָּׁכַח מִפִּי זַרְעוֹ". אֶלָּא מָה אֲנִי מְקַיֵּים "יְשׁוֹטְטוּ לְבַקֵּשׁ אֶת דְּבַר ה' וְלֹא יִמְצָאוּ" – שֶׁלֹּא יִמְצְאוּ הֲלָכָה

(ר"ת ל"ג אלא) (דברים כח) (ישעיהו כט) (עמוס ח) (שם) (ויקרא יא) (דברים לא)

*) [ערוך פי' כירה זו כלי מתכת הוא וכל זמן שתורת כלי עליה מותר לטלטלה לצורך מקומה לפיכך אם אחת מירכותיה נשמטה עדיין היא כלי שיכולה לעמוד בשלש אבל אם נטלו שתים בטלה מתורת כלי שאינה יכולה לעמוד בשתים.]

רש"י

כִּילַּת חֲתָנִים. לָא דָּמְיָא לִשְׁאָר כִּילּוֹת. שֶׁשְּׁאָר כִּילּוֹת פְּרוּסוֹת עַל גַּבֵּי קִינוּף, שֶׁהִיא לְד' רַגְלַיִם וְיֵשׁ לָהּ גַּג, דְּהָוֵי אֹהֶל. וְשֶׁל חֲתָנִים – עַל גַּבֵּי נַקְלִיטִין, שֶׁאֵינָם אֶלָּא שְׁנַיִם בְּאֶמְצָעִית הַמִּטָּה, וְקָנֶה נָתוּן עֲלֵיהֶם וְהַבֶּגֶד נָתוּן עָלָיו, וְנוֹפֵל לְכָאן וּלְכָאן, וְאֵין לָהּ גַּג טֶפַח – הִלְכָּךְ לָאו אֹהֶל הוּא: בְּפָחוֹת מִג'. שֶׁהִיא הוֹלֶכֶת וּמִתְפַּשֶּׁטֶת לְמַטָּה: וְלָא אֲמַרַן אֶלָּא שֶׁאֵין בְּשִׁיפּוּעָהּ טֶפַח. שֶׁאֵין כָּל צַד וָצַד(ב) נִפְשָׁט לְמַטָּה לְהִתְרַחֵק טֶפַח מִכְּנֶגֶד אֶמְצָעִיתוֹ, דְּהַיְינוּ שֶׁאֵין בְּרָחְבּוֹ לְמַטָּה טְפָחַיִים. וְכִילַּת חֲתָנִים אֵינָהּ עֲשׂוּיָה לִישַׁן תַּחְתֶּיהָ: אֲבָל נָחְתָא מִפּוּרְיָא טֶפַח. הַהוּא טֶפַח הָוֵה קִיר לָאֹהֶל, וְהַמִּטָּה נַעֲשֵׂית לוֹ גַּג: סִיָּאנָא. כּוֹבַע שֶׁל לֶבֶד פלטר"ך: אָסוּר. לָצֵאת בּוֹ בְּשַׁבָּת, וּלְקַמֵּיהּ מְפָרֵשׁ וְאָזֵיל: הָא דְּאִית בֵּיהּ טֶפַח. שֶׁהוּא מִתְפַּשֵּׁט לְהַלָּן מֵרֹאשׁוֹ טֶפַח – אָסוּר מִשּׁוּם אֹהֶלָא: אֶלָּא מֵעַתָּה שַׁרְבֵּיב בִּגְלִימֵיהּ טֶפַח. הִנִּיחַ טַלִּיתוֹ עַל רֹאשׁוֹ כְּדֶרֶךְ שֶׁהוּא מִתְעַטֵּף(ג), וְהִרְחִיקָהּ לְהַלָּן מֵרֹאשׁוֹ טֶפַח: אֶלָּא. טַעְמָא לָאו מִשּׁוּם אֹהֶל הוּא, אֶלָּא מִשּׁוּם שֶׁלֹּא יַגְבִּיהֶנּוּ הָרוּחַ מֵרֹאשׁוֹ, וְאָתֵי לְאַתּוּיֵי אַרְבַּע אַמּוֹת. הִלְכָּךְ: מִיהֲדַק בְּרֹאשׁוֹ שַׁפִּיר – שָׁרֵי, לָא מִיהֲדַק – אָסוּר: תַּרְתֵּי בְּשַׁבָּת וַחֲדָא בַּתּוֹרָה. שֶׁהָיִיתָ רָגִיל לוֹמַר שְׁנֵי דְּבָרִים מִשְּׁמוֹ בְּהִלְכוֹת שַׁבָּת, וְאַחַת בַּתּוֹרָה כִּדְלְקַמָּן: גּוֹד בְּכִיסְנָא. גּוֹד בִּרְלוּוֹעוֹתָיו, וּמוּנָּח עַל מָקוֹם קָבוּעַ שֶׁלּוֹ: מוּתָּר לִנְטוֹתוֹ בְּשַׁבָּת. וְהָא דַּאֲמַרַן לְעֵיל פָּטוּר אֲבָל אָסוּר – הֵיכָא דְּלָא הָוֵי מְתוּקָּן בְּכִיסְנִין: בְּב' בְּנֵי אָדָם. לָא מִימְתַּח לֵיהּ שַׁפִּיר: בְּאָדָם אֶחָד. מִמְתַּח לֵיהּ שַׁפִּיר, שֶׁמּוֹתְחוֹ עַל יָתֵד זוֹ וְקוֹשְׁרוֹ בָּהּ, וְחוֹזֵר וּמוֹתְחוֹ עַל זוֹ וְקוֹשְׁרוֹ בָּהּ. כָּךְ פֵּירְשׁוּ רַבּוֹתַי, וְכֵן מָצָאתִי בִּתְשׁוּבַת הַגְּאוֹנִים, וַאֲנִי יוֹדֵעַ מַהוּ: אִידָךְ. דְּשַׁבָּת מַאי הִיא: מִיַּרְכוֹתֶיהָ. פִּטְפּוּטִים שֶׁלָּהּ, כְּעֵין רַגְלַיִם: שֶׁמָּא יִתְקַע. כְּשֶׁמְּחַבֵּר לָהּ הָרֶגֶל יִתְקָעֶנָּה בְּחוֹזֶק וְהָוֵי בּוֹנֶה. אֲבָל *(ת"ק) הֵיכָא דְּלֹא נִשְׁמְטָה אֶלָּא אַחַת – לָא חָיֵישׁ לְמִתְקַע כּוּלֵּי הַאי: הַפְלֵא וָפֶלֶא. סֵיפָא דִּקְרָא – "וְאָבְדָה חָכְמַת חֲכָמָיו": בְּכֶרֶם. עַל שֵׁם שֶׁהָיוּ יוֹשְׁבִין שׁוּרוֹת שׁוּרוֹת כְּכֶרֶם: זוֹ הֲלָכָה. כִּדְכְתִיב (דברים ה): "[לְהַגִּיד לָכֶם] אֶת דְּבַר ה'", דְּהַיְינוּ תּוֹרָה: זוֹ נְבוּאָה. כִּדְכְתִיב (הושע א): "דְּבַר ה' אֲשֶׁר הָיָה אֶל הוֹשֵׁעַ" וגו': זֶה הַקֵּץ. לֹא יָדְעָנָא מְהֵיכָא: בְּהֶדְיָא כְּתִיב. וְתוֹרָה שֶׁבִּכְתָב הֲרֵי כְּתוּבָה וּמוּנַּחַת, יִקְרְאוּ וְיִרְאוּ: שֶׁהַתַּנּוּר תְּחִלָּה. שֶׁנִּטְמָא מִן הָאֲוִיר, כִּדְכְתִיב (ויקרא יא): "אֶל תּוֹכוֹ", וְהוּא חוֹזֵר וּמְטַמֵּא אוֹכָלִין שֶׁבְּתוֹכוֹ מִן הָאֲוִיר: כְּמַאן דְּמָלֵי טוּמְאָה. כְּשֶׁנָּפַל הַשֶּׁרֶץ בַּאֲוִירוֹ, דְּהָא בְּלָא נְגִיעָה מְטַמֵּא. וְהִלְכָּךְ, כְּמַאן דְּמָלֵי טוּמְאָה הוּא, וְתֶהֱוֵי פַּת רִאשׁוֹנָה: לָא ס"ד. לְמֶיהֱוֵי כְּמַאן דְּמָלֵי טוּמְאָה: דְּתַנְיָא יָכוֹל יְהוּ כָּל הַכֵּלִים טְמֵאִים מֵאֲוִיר כְּלִי חֶרֶס. שֶׁאִם הָיָה כְּלִי אַחֵר בְּתוֹכוֹ שֶׁיִּטַּמָּא מֵחֲמַת הַשֶּׁרֶץ שֶׁבַּאֲוִיר הַחִיצוֹן, אוֹ מֵחֲמַת שֶׁיְּטַמְּאֶנּוּ אֲוִיר כְּלִי הַחִיצוֹן שֶׁהוּא טָמֵא: תַּלְמוּד לוֹמַר כֹּל אֲשֶׁר בְּתוֹכוֹ יִטְמָא. וּסְמִיךְ לֵיהּ "מִכָּל הָאוֹכֶל אֲשֶׁר יֵאָכֵל": אוֹכָלִין. וּמַשְׁקִין שֶׁבְּתוֹכוֹ טְמֵאִים, וְלֹא כֵּלִים. שְׁמַע מִינָּהּ תַּרְתֵּי: חֲדָא, דְּלָא אָמְרִינַן חָזְיֵיהּ כְּמַאן דְּמָלֵי טוּמְאָה. דְּאִם כֵּן, אִם כְּלִי שֶׁטֵּף הוּא הַפְּנִימִי, שֶׁמִּתְטַמֵּא מִגַּבּוֹ, יְהֵא טָמֵא, דְּהָא נָגַע בְּטוּמְאָה. אֶלָּא לָא אָמְרִינַן: "חָזְיֵיהּ כְּמַאן דְּמָלֵי טוּמְאָה", וְאוֹכָלִין וּמַשְׁקִין שֶׁבַּחִיצוֹן הוּא דְּמִטַּמְּאֵי מֵחֲמַת הַכְּלִי, שֶׁהַכְּלִי רִאשׁוֹן וְהֵם שְׁנִיִּים. אֲבָל כֵּלִים – לָא, דְּהוֹאִיל דְּאֵין טוּמְאָה זוֹ בָּאָה אֶלָּא מֵחֲמַת הַכְּלִי, אַשְׁמְעִינַן הַאי קְרָא שֶׁאֵין כְּלִי שֶׁאֵינוֹ אַב הַטּוּמְאָה מְטַמֵּא כְּלִי:

תוספות

שאין בשיפועה טפח. הרבה יש תימה(ד) איך יתכן זה; דא"כ, למה הוא ראוי אם לכל השיפוע אין טפח? ויש לפרש: כגון שהסדין שפרוס על הכילה מונח על גבי קנים מרודים, ולא פשטו הסדין היטב, ומונח ונופל בין קנה לקנה כעין שורות, דיש עכשיו בין כל קנה שיפוע ואין באותו שיפוע טפח, ודוחק. וי"מ: שאין בשיפוע טפח בגובה י', דכשילא השיפוע טפח אין מגס עד למטה גובה י', דלא חשיב אהל. כדאשכחן בפ"ק דסוכה (דף י.) דבכילה כי הך מותר לישן בסוכה, דאמר רב יהודה אמר שמואל: מותר לישן בכילת חתנים אע"פ שיש לה גג, והוא שאינה י' טפחים. ואין נראה לר"י, דודאי נהי דגבי סוכה לא חשיב אהל, וכן לגבי ק"ש כדאיתא התם (דף י:), מיהו לגבי שבת חשיב, ואסירי. שהרי משמרת וביעתא וקידרא וחביתא אסירי משום אהל, ולא משמע שיש בגובהן י' טפחים. מ"ר. ועוד קשה מדלקמן גבי כפיפה מצרית. ובשם רבינו שמואל פי': דל"ג להאי לישנא כלל שיפועי אהלים כאהלים דמו, דבסוף פ"ק דסוכה (דף יט:) מסקינן דשיפוע אהלים לאו כאהלים דמו. ואי משום הא – לא איריא, דיש לפרש דהתם באין בשיפועו טפח, והכא – כשיש בשיפועו טפח:

הא דמהדק. פירש ר"ח: שאינו נכפף, דאז נראה כעין אהל. דלא מהדק – שהוא נכפף, ואז אין נראה כעין אהל:

דבר ה' זה הקץ. דכתיב גבי גלות שבעים: "לכלות דבר ה' מפי ירמיה" (עזרא א). מ"ר: ולישלח

רבינו חננאל

קבוע וחייב חטאת במטה של פרסיים כדאמרן תוב בעא מיניה כילה מהו וא"ל אף מטה מותרת מכלל ששתיהן מותרות כילה שאין בגגה טפח ויש עליה חוטין קשורין מאתמול והוא כגון הטלית שאמר רמי בר יחזקאל ומטה היא גליתא מטה שהמחזירה אין צריך לתקע שמלבנותיה וכרעיה אינן דוחקות וברפיון נכנסין ויוצאין. תוב בעא מיניה כילה ומטה מהו. א"ל כילה אסורה ומטה מותרת. פי' כילה אסורה שיש בגגה טפח. ומטה מותרת כדין. והיא מטה גליתא שהיו מחזירין אותה בשבת בבית רב חמא ומפורש בסוף פרק כירה. והני כילי דבי רב הונא ודבי רב פפא ורב הונא בריה דרב יהושע דהוו מאורתא נגידין ובצפרא חביטא רמיין. יש מי שאומרים משלבות היו בארץ שאסור לטלטלן בשבת ואנו קבלנו מרבותינו כי נטויות היו מע"ש ומשוכות למעלה כמין כפולות ובבקר הי' משפיען ומשרבבין אותן למטה ונמצאו מוסיפין כחכמים שחולקין על ר' אליעזר ואומרים מוסיפין באהלי עראי בשבת ואין צ"ל ביו"ט וכדאמרינן בהמוצא תפילין הנהו דיכרי דהוו בי רב הונא דבימָמא בעי טולא ובליליא בעו אוירא אתו לקמיה דרב א"ל זיל כרוך (פוריא) [בודיא] ושייר בה טפח ולמחר פושטה דמוסיף על אהל עראי הוא ושפיר דמי. ובתרה א' הא שמעתא דשמואל כילת חתנים וכו' שמעינן מינה דכולהו חד טעמא אינון אמר רב משום ר' חייא וילון פי' פרוכת מותר לנטותו ומותר לפרקו וזה בזמן שכרוכין עליו ב' חוטין או משיחות דלא גרע מטלית כפולה כילת חתנים כדאמרן שאין בגגה טפח ולא בפחות מג' סמוך לגגה טפח וגם אינה יורדת למטה מן המטה טפח. צ"ע שכעין שמועה זו בפרק מי שהוציאוהו גוים: גמ' פעם אחת לא נכנסו לנמל עד שחשכה ונתקשה בעינינו הדבר מכמה פנים וכולן נכוחים למבין. ועוד מפני מה כשנתפרקו אפי' על הארץ למה מניחין אותן ובין לצורך גופן ובין לצורך מקומן שרי. ואנו פירשנו מה שקבלנו. ולפי שהוא מלאכת שמים הזכרנו דברים ודברי זולתנו שאמרו מוטלות ומושלכות לארץ היו לא כתבנו הפירכא שעל הדברים הללו. וראינו סיוע על הטעם שהזכרנו כי קבלנוהו וסוגיין של דברים הללו בפרק המוצא תפילין שגזרום רבותינו בענין תוספת אהלים. כלומר טעם אחד הן. ולולי כן הקושיא היה מקשה מהן: סיינא. כובע שמשימין בני אדם בראשיהן יוצא כמין פסל מן הראש כשיעור טפח הן יתר. ואנן ראינוהו פעמים רבות ועושין אותו להאהל על הפנים שלא יכם השמש. וכשהוא מהודק ביותר ואינו נכפף כבגד חשוב כאהל ואסור: הא דתנן גוד בכיסנא מותר פי' חמת שיש עליה חוטין או משיחות קשורין מצדדיה מותר לנטותה בשבת באותן היתידות המוכנין לה. אמר רב בשני בני אדם מותר אבל באדם אחד אסור. כי צריך לתת חוטי הצד האחד ולפיכך אסור שנמצא נוטה אהל. וזה שאמר אביי בכילה שיש בגגה טפח שאסור לנטותה בשבת אפילו בעשרה בני אדם אי אפשר דלא מימתחא ביה פורתא פשוטה היא. והא דתניא כירה שנשמטה אחת מירכותיה מותר לטלטלה ב' אסור לטלטלה. כירה זו כלי מתכות היא וכל זמן שתורת כלי עליה מותר לטלטלה לצורך מקומה. לפיכך אם נטלה אחת מירכותיה עדיין כלי היא שיכולה לעמוד בג' אבל אם ניטלו ב' בטלה מתורת כלי שאינה יכולה לעמוד בשתים. רב אמר אפילו אחת אם ניטלה אסור לטלטלה גזירה שמא יתקע והלכתא כרב: **אמר** רב עתידה תורה שתשתכח מישראל שנאמר והפלא ה' את מכותך וגו' ושאר השמועה פשוטה היא. והא דרב אדא בר אהבה דאמר ליה לרבא ליחזייה לתנור כמאן דמלי טומאה

מסורת הש"ס

עירובין קב. ע"ש לעיל מה: ע"ש

[סוכה יט:]

עירובין קב: ושם

[תמורה ג: מכות יג: ע"ש]

[תוספ' עדיות פ"א]

עיין רש"ל

פסחים כ.

הגהות הב"ח

(א) גמ' אוכלין ומשקין מטמאין באויר: (ב) רש"י ד"ה ולא אמרן כו' צד וצד נתפשט למטה: (ג) ד"ה אלא מעתה וכו' מתעטף בה על ראשו והרחיקה: (ד) תום' ד"ה שאין וכו' תימה. נ"ב ובעירובין דף קב תירץ רש"י על זה כעין תירוץ שכתבו התוס' כאן:

הגהות הגר"א

[א] גמ' (ולא אמרן אלא שאין בש"ט אבל יש בש"ט שפועי אהלים כאהלים דמו) תא"מ ונ"ב הרמב"ם ל"ג לה (ועמ"ש רבינו בא"ח סי' שטו ס"ק כא):

גליון הש"ס

גמ' הא נמי מתני' היא עי' חולין קי ע"א תוד"ה דתנן הככר: רש"י ד"ה זה כו' לא ידענא. עי' ברכות נה ע"ב רש"י ד"ה מאן שמעת ליה וש"נ:

רב נסים גאון

כשנכנסו רבותינו לכרם ביבנה. כבר פירשו בברכות בגמ' דבני מערבא וכי כרם שם אלא אלו תלמידי חכמים שהם עשוים שורות שורות ככרם.

אין

הֲלָכָה בְּרוּרָה וּמִשְׁנָה בְּרוּרָה בְּמָקוֹם אֶחָד.§ תַּנְיָא, רַבִּי יוֹסֵי בֶּן אֱלִישָׁע אוֹמֵר: אִם רָאִיתָ דּוֹר שֶׁצָּרוֹת רַבּוֹת בָּאוֹת עָלָיו – צֵא וּבְדוֹק בְּדַיָּינֵי יִשְׂרָאֵל. *שֶׁכָּל פּוּרְעָנוּת שֶׁבָּאָה לָעוֹלָם לֹא בָּאָה אֶלָּא בִּשְׁבִיל דַּיָּינֵי יִשְׂרָאֵל, שֶׁנֶּאֱמַר: (מיכה ג) °"שִׁמְעוּ נָא זֹאת רָאשֵׁי בֵּית יַעֲקֹב וּקְצִינֵי בֵּית יִשְׂרָאֵל הַמְתַעֲבִים מִשְׁפָּט וְאֵת כָּל הַיְשָׁרָה יְעַקֵּשׁוּ בּוֹנֶה צִיּוֹן בְּדָמִים וִירוּשָׁלַיִם בְּעַוְלָה רָאשֶׁיהָ בְּשׁוֹחַד יִשְׁפּוֹטוּ וְכֹהֲנֶיהָ בִּמְחִיר יוֹרוּ וּנְבִיאֶיהָ בְּכֶסֶף יִקְסוֹמוּ וְעַל ה' יִשָּׁעֵנוּ וגו'" *רְשָׁעִים הֵן, אֶלָּא שֶׁתָּלוּ בִּטְחוֹנָם בְּמִי שֶׁאָמַר וְהָיָה הָעוֹלָם. לְפִיכָךְ מֵבִיא הקב"ה עֲלֵיהֶן ג' פּוּרְעָנִיּוֹת כְּנֶגֶד ג' עֲבֵירוֹת שֶׁבְּיָדָם. שֶׁנֶּאֱמַר: (שם) °"לָכֵן בִּגְלַלְכֶם צִיּוֹן שָׂדֶה תֵחָרֵשׁ וִירוּשָׁלַיִם עִיִּין תִּהְיֶה וְהַר הַבַּיִת לְבָמוֹת יָעַר". [א]וְאֵין הקב"ה מַשְׁרֶה שְׁכִינָתוֹ עַל יִשְׂרָאֵל עַד שֶׁיִּכְלוּ שׁוֹפְטִים וְשׁוֹטְרִים רָעִים מִיִּשְׂרָאֵל, שֶׁנֶּאֱמַר: (ישעיהו א) °"וְאָשִׁיבָה יָדִי עָלַיִךְ וְאֶצְרוֹף כַּבּוֹר סִגָיִךְ, וְאָסִירָה כָּל בְּדִילָיִךְ וְאָשִׁיבָה שׁוֹפְטַיִךְ כְּבָרִאשׁוֹנָה וְיוֹעֲצַיִךְ כְּבַתְּחִלָּה וגו'". *אָמַר עוּלָּא: [ב]אֵין *יְרוּשָׁלַיִם נִפְדֵּית אֶלָּא בִּצְדָקָה, שֶׁנֶּאֱמַר: (שם) °"צִיּוֹן בְּמִשְׁפָּט תִּפָּדֶה וְשָׁבֶיהָ בִּצְדָקָה". אָמַר רַב פָּפָּא: אִי בָּטְלִי יְהִירֵי – בָּטְלִי אַמְגּוּשֵׁי, אִי בָּטְלִי דַּיָּינֵי – בָּטְלִי *גַּזִירְפַּטֵי. אִי בָּטְלִי יְהִירֵי – בָּטְלִי אַמְגּוּשֵׁי, דִּכְתִיב: "וְאֶצְרוֹף כַּבּוֹר סִגָיִךְ". אִי בָּטְלִי דַּיָּינֵי בָּטְלִי גַּזִירְפַּטֵי – דִּכְתִיב: (צפניה ג) °"הֵסִיר ה' מִשְׁפָּטַיִךְ פִּנָּה אֹיְבֵךְ". אָמַר רַבִּי מְלַאי מִשּׁוּם ר"א בְּר' שִׁמְעוֹן: מ"ד (ישעיהו יד) °"שָׁבַר ה' מַטֵּה רְשָׁעִים שֵׁבֶט מוֹשְׁלִים" – "שָׁבַר ה' מַטֵּה רְשָׁעִים" – אֵלּוּ הַדַּיָּינִין שֶׁנַּעֲשׂוּ מַקֵּל לְחַזָּנֵיהֶם. "שֵׁבֶט מוֹשְׁלִים" – אֵלּוּ ת"ח שֶׁבְּמִשְׁפְּחוֹת הַדַּיָּינִין. מָר זוּטְרָא אָמַר: אֵלּוּ תַּלְמִידֵי חֲכָמִים שֶׁמְּלַמְּדִים הִלְכוֹת צִיבּוּר לְדַיָּינֵי בּוּר. אָמַר ר"א בֶּן מְלַאי מִשּׁוּם ר"ל: מַאי דִּכְתִיב (שם כט) °"כִּי כַפֵּיכֶם נְגֹאֲלוּ בַדָּם וְאֶצְבְּעוֹתֵיכֶם בֶּעָוֹן שִׂפְתוֹתֵיכֶם דִּבְּרוּ שֶׁקֶר לְשׁוֹנְכֶם עַוְלָה תֶהְגֶּה". "כִּי כַפֵּיכֶם נְגֹאֲלוּ בַדָּם" – אֵלּוּ הַדַּיָּינִין, "וְאֶצְבְּעוֹתֵיכֶם בֶּעָוֹן" – אֵלּוּ סוֹפְרֵי הַדַּיָּינִין, "שִׂפְתוֹתֵיכֶם דִּבְּרוּ שֶׁקֶר" – אֵלּוּ עוֹרְכֵי הַדַּיָּינִין, "לְשׁוֹנְכֶם עַוְלָה תֶהְגֶּה" – אֵלּוּ בַּעֲלֵי דִינִין. וְאָמַר רַב מְלַאי מִשּׁוּם ר' יִצְחָק מִגְדְּלָאָה: מִיּוֹם שֶׁפֵּירַשׁ יוֹסֵף מֵאֶחָיו לֹא טָעַם טַעַם יַיִן, דִּכְתִיב: (בראשית מט) °"וּלְקָדְקֹד נְזִיר אֶחָיו". ר' יוֹסֵי בְּר' חֲנִינָא אָמַר: אַף הֵן לֹא טָעֲמוּ טַעַם יַיִן, דִּכְתִיב: (שם מג) °"וַיִּשְׁתּוּ וַיִּשְׁכְּרוּ עִמּוֹ" מִכְּלָל דְּעַד הָאִידָּנָא לָא (הֲוָה שִׁיכְרוּת). וְאִידָךְ – שִׁיכְרוּת הוּא דְּלָא הֲוָה, שְׁתִיָּה מִיהָא הֲוָה. וְאָמַר רַבִּי מְלַאי: בִּשְׂכַר (שמות ד) °"וְרָאֲךָ וְשָׂמַח בְּלִבּוֹ" זָכָה לְחֹשֶׁן הַמִּשְׁפָּט עַל לִבּוֹ.§ שָׁלְחוּ לֵיהּ בְּנֵי בִּשְׂכַּר לְלֵוִי: כִּילָה מַהוּ? כְּשׁוּתָא בְּכַרְמָא מַהוּ? מֵת בְּיו"ט מַהוּ? אַדְּאָזֵיל, נָח נַפְשֵׁיהּ דְּלֵוִי. אָמַר שְׁמוּאֵל לְרַב מְנַשְּׁיָא: אִי חַכִּימַת – שְׁלַח לְהוּ. שְׁלַח לְהוּ: "כִּילָה" – חָזַרְנוּ עַל כָּל צִידֵּי כִּילָה וְלֹא מָצִינוּ לָהּ צַד הֶיתֵּר. וְלִישְׁלַח לְהוּ כִּדְרָמֵי בַּר יְחֶזְקֵאל? לְפִי שֶׁאֵינָן בְּנֵי תוֹרָה. "כְּשׁוּתָא בְּכַרְמָא – עִירְבוּבָא". וְלִישְׁלַח לְהוּ כְּדר"ט? דְּתַנְיָא: *כִּישׁוּת, ר' טַרְפוֹן אוֹמֵר: אֵין כִּלְאַיִם בַּכֶּרֶם, וַחֲכָמִים אוֹמְרִים: כִּלְאַיִם בַּכֶּרֶם. וְקִי"ל: *כָּל הַמֵּיקֵל בָּאָרֶץ – הֲלָכָה כְּמוֹתוֹ בְּחו"ל! לְפִי שֶׁאֵינָן בְּנֵי תוֹרָה. מַכְרִיז רַב: הַאי מַאן דְּבָעֵי לְמִיזְרַע כְּשׁוּתָא בְּכַרְמָא – לִיזְרַע. רַב עַמְרָם חֲסִידָא מְנַגֵּיד עִילָּוֵיהּ, רַב מְשַׁרְשְׁיָא יָהֵיב לֵיהּ פְּרוּטָה לְתִינוֹק גּוֹי וְזָרַע לֵיהּ. וְלִיתֵּן לֵיהּ לְתִינוֹק יִשְׂרָאֵל! אָתֵי לְמִיסְרַךְ. וְלִיתֵּן לֵיהּ לְגָדוֹל גּוֹי! אָתֵי לְאִיחְלוּפֵי בְּיִשְׂרָאֵל. "מֵת". שְׁלַח לְהוּ: מֵת לֹא יִתְעַסְּקוּ בֵּיהּ לֹא יְהוּדָאִין וְלֹא אַרְמָאִין, לֹא בְּיוֹם טוֹב רִאשׁוֹן וְלֹא בְּיוֹם טוֹב שֵׁנִי. אִינִי?! וְהָאָמַר רַבִּי יְהוּדָה בַּר שֵׁילַת אָמַר רַבִּי אַסִּי: עוּבְדָא הֲוָה בְּבֵי כְּנִישְׁתָּא דְּמָעוֹן בְּיוֹם טוֹב הַסָּמוּךְ לַשַּׁבָּת, וְלֹא

רש"י

הֲלָכָה בְּרוּרָה. בִּטְעָמִים שֶׁלֹּא יְהֵא בָּהּ מַחֲלוֹקֶת: ג' עֲבֵירוֹת. "בְּשֹׁחַד יִשְׁפּוֹטוּ", "בִּמְחִיר יוֹרוּ", וּ"נְבִיאֶיהָ בְּכֶסֶף יִקְסֹמוּ": ג' פּוּרְעָנִיּוֹת. שָׂדֶה תֵחָרֵשׁ, עִיִּין תִּהְיֶה וּלְבָמוֹת יָעַר: וְיוֹעֲצַיִךְ כְּבַתְּחִלָּה. וְאַחַר כָּךְ יִקָּרֵא לָךְ עִיר הַצֶּדֶק לְשָׁרוֹת בָּהּ שְׁכִינָה: אִי בָּטְלִי יְהִירֵי. יִשְׂרָאֵל מִתְיַהֲרִים בִּבְלוֹרִית וּבְמַלְבּוּשֵׁי יְהִירוּת כְּפָרְסִים הַלָּלוּ: בַּטּוּלֵי אַמְגּוּשֵׁי. יִבָּטְלוּ מְסִיתִים וּמַדִּיחִים הַמְשַׂנְּאִים אוֹתָנוּ: סִגָיִךְ. הֵם גַּסֵּי הָרוּחַ שֶׁמְּגַדְּלִין עַצְמָן, לְשׁוֹן "יִשְׂגֶּה מְאֹד" (איוב ח). וְאַח"כ "וְאָסִירָה כָּל בְּדִילָיִךְ" – אֵלּוּ אוֹתָם הַמַּבְדִּילִים שׂוֹנְאֵי יִשְׂרָאֵל מִן הקב"ה בִּשְׁקָרֵיהֶם וּבְפַחֲזוּתָם: בָּטְלִי דַּיָּינֵי. רְשָׁעִים מִיִּשְׂרָאֵל שֶׁמַּטִּין דִּין: בָּטְלִי. מֵעַל יִשְׂרָאֵל: גַּזִירְפַּטֵי. נוֹגְשֵׂי שׁוֹטְרֵי גוֹיִם: שֶׁנַּעֲשׂוּ מַקֵּל לְחַזָּנֵיהֶם. לְשַׁמָּשֵׁיהֶן נוֹתְנִין יָד, וְהָוְיָין לָהֶן לְחוֹזֶק, לוֹמַר: לֵךְ הֱיֵה שָׁלִיחַ וְהַזְמֵן אֶת פְּלוֹנִי לְבֵ"ד אִם לֹא תַּרְבֶּה שָׂכָר, וְאַחַר פְּסַק דִּין לֵךְ הָרְדֵהוּ לִיכָּנֵס לְמַשְׁכְּנוֹ: שֵׁבֶט מוֹשְׁלִים. מַקֵּל אֶגְרוֹפִין שֶׁל מוֹשְׁלִים, הַיְינוּ דַּיָּינִים רְשָׁעִים שֶׁת"ח שֶׁבְּמִשְׁפְּחוֹתָם לָהֶם לְמַקֵּל וּלְאֶגְרוֹף, שֶׁעַל יְדֵיהֶם הָיוּ מַעֲמִידִין אוֹתָן, וּמְחַפִּין עֲלֵיהֶם, וְעוֹשִׂין סַנֵּיגְרוֹן לְדִבְרֵיהֶם: לְדַיָּינֵי בּוּר. שֶׁבְּהַבְטָחַת אוֹתָן ת"ח מַעֲמִידִין דַּיָּינֵי בוּר לָדוּן אֶת כָּל הַבָּא, וְהַרְבֵּה דִינִין שֶׁאֵין נִמְלָכִים בָּהֶן וּמַטִּין אוֹתָן: כַּפֵּיכֶם נְגוֹאֲלוּ בַדָּם אֵלּוּ הַדַּיָּינִין. שֶׁכַּפֵּיהֶן פְּשׁוּטִין לְקַבֵּל שׁוֹחַד, וּמַטִּין אֶת הַדִּין, וְנוֹטְלִין מָמוֹן מִן הַבְּעָלִים שֶׁלֹּא כַּדִּין וְנוֹתְנוּ לְשֶׁכְּנֶגְדוֹ, וַהֲרֵי הוּא כְּנוֹטֵל נִשְׁמָתוֹ: סוֹפְרֵי הַדַּיָּינִין. שֶׁכּוֹתְבִין שְׁטָרוֹת שֶׁל רְמִיָּה: עוֹרְכֵי הַדַּיָּינִין. מְלַמְּדִין אֶת בַּעֲלֵי דִינִין לִטְעוֹן: עִמּוֹ. מִכְּלָל דְּעַד הַשְׁתָּא לֹא: זָכָה לְחֹשֶׁן הַמִּשְׁפָּט. שֶׁכְּנֶגֶד הַלֵּב. שֶׁהָיָה גָּדוֹל מִמֶּנּוּ, וְקוֹדֶם לְמֹשֶׁה נִגְלֵית שְׁכִינָה עַל אַהֲרֹן, כְּדִכְתִיב (שמואל א ב): "הֲנִגְלֹה נִגְלֵיתִי אֶל בֵּית אָבִיךָ". וְנֶאֶמְרָה לוֹ נְבוּאָה שֶׁל מִצְרַיִם הַכְּתוּבָה (יחזקאל כ) עַד "וַיַּמְרוּ בִי", וְאעפ"כ לֹא נִתְקַנֵּא בּוֹ בְּזֹאת: בְּנֵי בִשְׂכַר. שֵׁם מָקוֹם: כִּילָה מַהוּ. לִנְטוֹתָהּ בְּשַׁבָּת: כְּשׁוּתָא. הִימְלוֹן שֶׁגָּדֵל עַל הַהִגָּא, מַהוּ בְּכַרְמָא? יָרָק הוּא – וְכִלְאַיִם בְּכֶרֶם, אוֹ אִילָן הוּא – וְאֵינוֹ כִּלְאַיִם בְּכֶרֶם: וְלִישְׁלַח לְהוּ. צַד הֶיתֵּר בָּהּ: כִּדְרָמֵי בַּר יְחֶזְקֵאל. כָּרַךְ עָלֶיהָ חוּט אוֹ מְשִׁיחָה: וּמְשַׁנֵּי לְפִי שֶׁאֵינָן בְּנֵי תוֹרָה. וּמְקִילֵּי טְפֵי: עִירְבוּבָא. כִּלְאַיִם: וְקִי"ל. בִּבְרָכוֹת, בְּפֶרֶק "כֵּיצַד" גַּבֵּי עָרְלָה. וְה"ה לְכִלְאַיִם, שֶׁאַף הִיא מִצְוָה הַתְּלוּיָה בָּאָרֶץ, וְאֵינָהּ נוֹהֶגֶת מִן הַתּוֹרָה אֶלָּא בָּאָרֶץ: יָהֵיב פְּרוּטָה לְתִינוֹק גּוֹי. קָסָבַר בְּחוּץ לָאָרֶץ שָׁרֵי. וּמִיהוּ, כָּל כַּמָּה דְּאֶפְשָׁר – מְשַׁנֵּי, שֶׁלֹּא יִלְמְדוּ לְהָקֵל:

תוספות

ולישלח להו כר"ט. הא לא פריך לישלח להו כר' יאשיה – דאמר: אינו חייב עד שיזרע חטה ושעורה וחרצן במפולת יד, דשמא הם לא שאלו כשותא בכרמא מהו, אלא היכא שעשה כדין איסור כלאים ג' מינים כאחד. ועוד: שמא לא ס"ל כר' יאשיה. ואע"ג דקי"ל כר' יאשיה בספ"ק דקדושין (דף לט.), ה"ל: לא נהריתו – [לא] קי"ל כר' יאשיה. ואמר נמי בברכות פרק "מי שמתו" (דף כב.): נהוג עלמא כתלת סבי, כר' אילעי בראשית הגז, כרבי יאשיה בכלאים, כר' יהודה בן בתירא בדברי תורה. מיהו, י"ל: שלא היו סבורין כן, דהא קאמר נמי נהוג כרבי יהודה בדברי תורה, ואפ"ה פליגי עליה אמוראי טובא בשמעתא דהתם. וקאמר נמי כרבי אילעי בראשית הגז, דאמר אינו נוהג אלא בארץ – ואפ"ה אמרינן בחולין, בשילהי פ' "הזרוע" (דף קלו.), אמר רב חסדא: האי טבחא דלא מפריש מתנתא – ליהוי בשמתא דה' אלהי ישראל. ואמר נמי דרבא קניס אטמא. ואפילו רב נחמן גופיה דאמר נהוג עלמא כתלת סבי – אמר התם דקניס גלימא. וא"ת: נהי דלא ס"ל כר' יאשיה, מ"מ לישלח להו כרבי יאשיה, דכל המיקל בארץ הלכה כמותו בחו"ל! וי"ל: דלא שייך למימר הכי אלא במין של איסור, דהמתירו חושבו מין היתר בארץ – הלכה כמותו בחו"ל. אבל בדבר שאינו תלוי אלא בזריעה – חטה ושעורה וחרצן במפולת יד, בהא לא אמר הלכה כמותו בחו"ל. מ"ר:

רב עמרם חסידא מנגיד עלה רב משרשיא יהיב ליה פרוטה לגוי כו'. קשיא לי: אמאי? הא אמרינן לעיל דהלכה כר"ט דמיקל בחו"ל! וצריך לומר: דבמקומם לא היו בני תורה:

וליתן ליה לתינוק ישראל. אומר רבי: שקבלה הוא בידינו שזה המקשה רב אחא בר יעקב. והיינו הא דאמר בעירובין בשילהי "בכל מערבין" (דף מ: ושם) גבי ברכת זמן על הכוס ביוה"כ, דמפרש התם דלא אפשר, דהיכי ליעביד כו' ליתביה לתינוק – לית הלכתא כרב אחא בר יעקב, דילמא אתי למיסרך. ולא מצינו במקום אחר דאית ליה לרב אחא האי סברא. וי"מ: דהוא ההוא דפ' בתרא דנדה (דף סז:) דאתקין ביממא דתמניא משום גנבי, ולא חיישינן לסרך בתה במקום צורך. ולא נהירא: דמאי שנא דנקיט טפי רב אחא בר יעקב מכל שאר אמוראי דהתם? ועל ההיא דהתם אומר ר"ת שמותר ליתן לתינוק לשתות כוס של ברכה כי מיקלע מילה ביוה"כ, ולא חיישינן דילמא אתי למיסרך – כיון שאין זה מנהג [בקבוע] ולא דמי לכוס דיוה"כ דאי הוו יהבי ליה אתי למיסרך אף כשיהיה גדול – כיון שעושין מנהג לשתות בכל שנה ושנה ביוה"כ:

י"ט

עין משפט נר מצוה

טו א מיי' פכ"ג מהל' סנהדרין הלכה ט סמג לאוין רו טוש"ע ח"מ סי' ח סעיף ב:

כ"ג הרש"ל והריעב"ן מחקו

טז ב מיי' פ"י מהל' מתנות עניים הלכה א סמג עשין קסב טוש"ע י"ד סי' רמז:

[גיר' הערוך ערך גז ז' גאזי דפאטי פי' סריסי וקוטרי הקרים ובערך יהיר גרס גזירפטי פי' רשעים]

רבינו חננאל

ותהוי פת ראשונה הכא הוא מפורש בפסחים בסוף פ"א: וזה שהשיב רב מנשיא לבני בי בשכר על הכילה ועל הכשות בכרם ועל המת ביו"ט כולן לאיסור לפי שאינן בני תורה. מהא שמעינן שאפילו דברים המותרים כגון אלו וכדומה להן המסורין לעם הארץ אין אדם רשאי להורות להן להיתר אלא יחמיר עליהן

מסורת הש"ס

[יבמות סג. ע"ש ב"ב ח. ע"ש]

[יומא ע:]

סנהדרין לח.

[נ"ל ישראל וכ"א ברמב"ם ובטור וע"ע מ"ש על הגליון סנהדרין לח.]

[תוספ' סוף פרק ג דכלאים]

ברכות לו.

יום טוב שני יתעסקו בו ישראל. ובביצה (ד' ו.) מסקינן בתר הך מילתא, אמר רבינא: האידנא דאיכא חברי – חיישינן. פירוש: ולא יתעסקו בו ישראל פן ילוו עליהם חברי לעשות מלאכה ביו"ט, כיון שרואין שעושין בשביל מת. ומעשה היה והוליכו מת חוץ לתחום ביו"ט, והלכו אחריו בסוסים להתעסק במת, וכעס ר"ת אף על ההולכים ברגל בלא סוסים. ושמע רבי דטעמו משום דמסיק רבינא האידנא דאיכא חברי. ולדידן אע"ג דליכא למיחש – יש לאסור כיון דמסיק הכי. גם יש ליראה פן ילוו השרים להתעסק במלאכתן ולכתוב מה שהם רוצים. ושלח להם ר"ת: בני בשכר אינם בני תורה, בני מליאון (ז)(אותה העיר) בני תורה*:

ציצית חשיבי ולא בטלי. שאינם מבוטלין לפי שחשובים הם בעיניו, שדעתו ליתן בטלית ציצית רביעית, כך פי' ר"ת: הא לא חשיבי ובטלי. על זה סמך רבי להניח באבנטו רצועות התלויות בו. ויש שקושרים בהם בתי שוקים דבטלי, דלא חשיבי כולי האי: מאי שנא מהא דתניא כו'. פי': [וס"ל כרבי יוסי בר' יהודה דאמר מערימין], לעיל בפ' "כל כתבי" (דף קיז:):

*תלא דבישרא כו'. לא כפירוש הקונטרס דפי' בשר מליח שתלו ליבשו, דהל"ל הא בפרק "מפנין" דמה שייך הכא? ועוד: למה מזכיר תלא? ועוד: מוכח לעיל בפרק "מפנין" (דף קכח.) דדג מליח נמי חזי לאומצא. ועוד: דהכא בטלטול איירי, ואמרינן לעיל דרב במוקצה לטלטל סבר לה כר"ש! ונראה כפי' הערוך: דמשום תלא נקטיה, ובלא בשר. אלא תלא דבשרא לא ממאיס, ושרי לטלטולי, ושל דגים – מאיס, והוי מוקצה מחמת מיאוס. והשתא אתי שפיר באיסור דתלא כעין כישא דירקא. ור' פי' לנו: דלתלא דבשרא רגיל להיות בו תורת כלי, אבל של דגים לא, ולא משום מוקצה מחמת מיאוס, דלא איירי שמעתין במוקצה מחמת מיאוס. מ"ר:

אבל

וְלָא יָדְעֲנָא אִי מִלְּפָנֶיהָ אִי מִלְּאַחֲרֶיהָ, וְאָתוּ לְקַמֵּיהּ דְּרַבִּי יוֹחָנָן. וַאֲמַר לְהוּ: יִתְעַסְּקוּ בֵּיהּ עֲמָמִין. *וְאָמַר רָבָא: מֵת בְּיו"ט רִאשׁוֹן – יִתְעַסְּקוּ בּוֹ עֲמָמִין, בְּיוֹם טוֹב שֵׁנִי – יִתְעַסְּקוּ בּוֹ יִשְׂרָאֵל, וַאֲפִילּוּ בְּיו"ט שֵׁנִי שֶׁל רֹאשׁ הַשָּׁנָה, מַה שֶּׁאֵין כֵּן בְּבֵיצָה. לְפִי שֶׁאֵינָן בְּנֵי תוֹרָה.§ א"ר אָבִין בַּר רַב הוּנָא אָמַר רַב חָמָא בַּר גּוּרְיָא: מִתְעַטֵּף אָדָם בְּכִילָּה וּבְכַסְכַּסֶּיהָ וְיוֹצֵא לרה"ר בַּשַּׁבָּת, וְאֵינוֹ חוֹשֵׁשׁ. מ"ש מִדְּרַב הוּנָא, *דְּאָמַר רַב הוּנָא אָמַר רַב: הַיּוֹצֵא בְּטַלִּית שֶׁאֵינָהּ מְצוּיֶּיצֶת כְּהִילְכָתָהּ בַּשַּׁבָּת – חַיָּיב חַטָּאת. צִיצִית לְגַבֵּי טַלִּית – חֲשִׁיבִי, וְלָא בָּטְלִי. הָנֵי לָא חֲשִׁיבִי – וּבָטְלִי. אָמַר(א) רַבָּה בַּר רַב הוּנָא: מַעֲרִים אָדָם עַל הַמְשַׁמֶּרֶת בְּיו"ט לִתְלוֹת בָּהּ רִמּוֹנִים, וְתוֹלֶה בָּהּ שְׁמָרִים. אָמַר רַב אַשִׁי: וְהוּא דְּתָלָה בָּהּ רִמּוֹנִים. מַאי שְׁנָא מֵהָא, דְּתַנְיָא: *מַטִּילִין שֵׁכָר בַּמּוֹעֵד לְצוֹרֶךְ הַמּוֹעֵד, שֶׁלֹּא לְצוֹרֶךְ הַמּוֹעֵד – אָסוּר. אֶחָד שֵׁכַר תְּמָרִים וְאֶחָד שֵׁכַר שְׂעוֹרִים. אע"פ שֶׁיֵּשׁ לָהֶן יָשָׁן – מַעֲרִים וְשׁוֹתֶה מִן הֶחָדָשׁ. הָתָם לָא מוֹכְחָא מִילְּתָא, הָכָא – מוֹכְחָא מִילְּתָא. אֲמַרוּ לֵיהּ רַבָּנַן לְרַב אַשִׁי: חֲזִי מָר הַאי צוּרְבָא מֵרַבָּנַן, וְרַב הוּנָא ב"ר חַיּוֹן שְׁמֵיהּ, וְאָמְרִי לַהּ רַב הוּנָא בַּר חַלָּוֹן שְׁמֵיהּ, דְּשָׁקֵל בְּרָא דְּתוּמָא וּמַנַּח בְּבִרְזָא דְּדַנָּא, וַאֲמַר: לְאַצְנוּעֵיהּ קָמִיכַּוֵּינָא. וְאָזֵיל וְנָאֵים בְּמַבְרָא, וְעָבַר לְהָךְ גִּיסָא וְסָיֵיר פֵּירֵי, וַאֲמַר: אֲנָא לְמֵינַם קָמִיכַּוֵּינָא. אֲמַר לְהוּ: הַעֲרָמָה קָאָמְרַתְּ? הַעֲרָמָה בִּדְרַבָּנַן הִיא, וְצוּרְבָא מֵרַבָּנַן לָא אָתֵי לְמֶיעֱבַד לְכַתְּחִילָּה.§

מתני' נוֹתְנִין מַיִם ע"ג הַשְּׁמָרִים בִּשְׁבִיל שֶׁיִּצּוֹלוּ. וּמְסַנְּנִין אֶת הַיַּיִן[א] בְּסוּדָרִין, *וּבִכְפִיפָה מִצְרִית. *וְנוֹתְנִין בֵּיצָה בִּמְסַנֶּנֶת שֶׁל חַרְדָּל, וְעוֹשִׂין אֲנוּמְלִין בַּשַּׁבָּת. ר' יְהוּדָה אוֹמֵר: בַּשַּׁבָּת – בַּכּוֹס, בְּיו"ט – בַּלָּגִין, וּבַמּוֹעֵד – בֶּחָבִית. רַבִּי צָדוֹק אוֹמֵר: הַכֹּל לְפִי הָאוֹרְחִין.§

גמ' *אָמַר זְעֵירִי: נוֹתֵן אָדָם יַיִן צָלוּל וּמַיִם צְלוּלִין לְתוֹךְ הַמְשַׁמֶּרֶת בַּשַּׁבָּת וְאֵינוֹ חוֹשֵׁשׁ. אֲבָל עֲכוּרִין – לָא. מֵיתִיבִי, רַבָּן שִׁמְעוֹן בֶּן גַּמְלִיאֵל אוֹמֵר: טוֹרֵד אָדָם חָבִית שֶׁל יַיִן, יֵינָהּ וּשְׁמָרֶיהָ, וְנוֹתֵן לְתוֹךְ הַמְשַׁמֶּרֶת בַּשַּׁבָּת וְאֵינוֹ חוֹשֵׁשׁ! תַּרְגְּמָהּ זְעֵירִי: בֵּין הַגִּיתּוֹת שָׁנוּ.§ "מְסַנְּנִין אֶת הַיַּיִן בְּסוּדָרִין".§ אָמַר רַב שִׁימִי בַּר חִיָּיא: וּבִלְבַד שֶׁלֹּא יַעֲשֶׂה גּוּמָא.§ "וּבִכְפִיפָה מִצְרִית".§ אָמַר רַב חִיָּיא בַּר אַשִׁי אָמַר רַב: וּבִלְבַד שֶׁלֹּא יַגְבִּיהַּ מִקַּרְקָעִיתוֹ שֶׁל כְּלִי טֶפַח. אָמַר *רַב: הַאי *)פְּרוֹנְקָא, אַפַּלְגֵיהּ דְּכוּבָא – שָׁרֵי, אַכּוּלֵּיהּ כּוּבָא – אָסוּר. אָמַר רַב פַּפָּא: לָא נִיהֲדַק אִינִישׁ(ג) **)צִינְיָיתָא בְּפוּמֵיהּ דְּכוּזָנֵי דְּחָבִיתָא, מִשּׁוּם דְּמֵיחֱזֵי כִּמְשַׁמֶּרֶת. דְּבֵי רַב פַּפָּא שָׁאפוּ שִׁיכְרָא מִמָּנָא לְמָנָא(ג). אֲמַר לֵיהּ רַב אַחָא מִדִּיפְתִּי לְרָבִינָא: הָאִיכָּא נִיצוֹצוֹת! נִיצוֹצוֹת לְבֵי רַב פַּפָּא לָא חֲשִׁיבִי.§ "וְנוֹתְנִין בֵּיצָה בִּמְסַנֶּנֶת".§ תָּנֵי יַעֲקֹב קָרְחָה:

לפי

*) [עי' תוס' ביצה לב: ד"ה מלמטה למעלה]. **) גי' הערוך בערך צבת א' לא נהדק אינש צבתא אפומא דכוזינתא.

ולא ידענא אי מלפניה. אם חל י"ט בע"ש ומת בו ביום, ומפני שלא יוכלו להתעסק בו למחר התירו לקוברו ע"י עממים: אי מלאחריה. והוא מת בשבת, ומפני שנשתהא כבר והיה מסריח, התירו: מת ביו"ט ראשון כו'. מת שנשתהא, כגון שמת בשבת ולמחר היה יו"ט: מה שאין כן בביצה. דאין ר"ה שוה לימים טובים של גליות. דאילו ר"ה אמיר יו"ט שני דיליה, וולדה בזה אסורה בזה: מתעטף אדם בכילה. שהוא כסדין, ומתעטף בה דרך מלבוש: וכסכסיה. רצועות התלויות בה, ולא אמרינן הך רצועות לאו לצורך עיטוף נינהו והוה משאוי ההוא שעתא, שאין כיסכסין עשויין אלא לנטותה באהל: חייב חטאת. ואילו לא היתה מצוייצת כלל לא מיחייב, דהא לבושיה הוא. אלמא הציציות הוויין לו משאוי, הואיל ואינן כמצותו אינן צריכין לה. ומן הבגד ממש אינן דליחשבינן כוותיה: חשיבי. משום דשל תכלת הן, ולא בטלי, והוו בה משוי: מערים אדם על המשמרת ביו"ט. לרבנן, דאמרי: "אין תולין את המשמרת ביום טוב", ואוקימנא דטעמא לאו משום אהל אלא משום עובדא דחול – מערים ותולה אותה לצורך רמונים דלאו עובדין דחול נינהו, ומסנן בה שמרים הואיל ונתלית. דהא אמרינן: נותנין לתלויה ביו"ט: והוא דתלי בה רמונים. ברישא, דמוכח מילתא דמעיקרא לאו לשמרים תלייה: מטילין. ברסיי"ר בלע"ז: במועד. בחולו של מועד: מערים ושותה מן החדש. אלמא בלא שום הוכחה מותר להערים: התם לאו מוכחא מילתא. דמילתא דאיסורא הוא, דהרואה אומר לצורך המועד הוא, שאין הכל יודעין שיש לו מן הישן. הכא מוכחא מילתא לאיסור – דסתם תולה משמרת לשמרים הוא תולה, ואי לא יהיב בה רימונים ברישא להצניע בעלמא, כי יהיב בה שמרים – מוכח דלהכי תלייה: ברא דתומא. גלע של שום: ומנח בברזא דדנא. מקום שיש בו נקב בחבית והיין יוצא[ב], נותנו שם בשבת לסתום. והוי כמתקן, ומערים לכתחלה: ואומר לאצנועיה. להאי ברא דתומא מיכוינא. ועוד עביד אחריתי: אזל נאים במברא – בספינה רחבה העשויה לעבור המים, והיא של גוי, ויודע הוא שיעבירנה הגוי לצד האחר: וסייר פירי. ומשמר שם פירות כרמו. ונמצא שהגוי מעבירו במים בשבת: הערמה בדרבנן היא. ה"ג: הך הערמה לאו באיסורא דאורייתא הוא, אלא באיסורא דרבנן. דא"נ עביד ממש בלא הערמה – אדרבנן הוא דעבר. הלכך, כיון דצורבא מרבנן הוא – לא אחמירו עליה, דהוא לא אתי למעבד לכתחילה להדיא בלא הערמה, לעבור שם לפני הכל: **מתני'** נותנין מים. בשבת ע"ג שמרים הנתונים במשמרת מבעוד יום: כדי שיצולו. שיהו צלולין לזוב*) את היין מפני הקמחים שקורים ייר"ש: בסודרין ובכפיפה מצרית. העשויה מנצרי דקל: כפיפה. סל: ונותנין ביצה במסננת. שהחרדל נתון בה להסתנן, וקולטת את הפסולת. ואף הביצה החלמון שלה נוטף ומסתנן עמו, והוה ליה לחרדל למראה, והחלבון שהוא קשור נשאר למעלה. ורבינו הלוי פירש: סינונה של ביצה לתוך תבשיל היא, ולא לתוך חרדל. ובמסננת של חרדל הוא דשרי משום שינוי, ויורד לתוך הקערה שהוא כלי שני, ומתלבן התבשיל: אינומלין. פוסו"ן: לגין. גדול מכוס וקטן מחבית: **גמ'** טורד. מערבב: בין הגתות שנו. שכל היינות עכורין, ושותין אותן בשמריהם. הלכך: אין כאן תיקון, דבלאו הכי משתתי: שלא יעשה גומא. מן הסודר בפי הכלי כי עובדא דחול. אי נמי, אתי לידי סחיטה: שלא יגביה. הכפיפה מקרקעית(ד) כלי התחתון טפח, כמדת אהל: פרונקא. בגד ששוטחין על גיגית יין לכסותה: אפלגא דכובא שרי. דלאו אוהלא הוי: לא ניהדק איניש ציניתא בפומא דכוזני דחביתא. כלי חרס קטן שמערין בו יין מחבית, לא יתן בפיו קשין וקסמים בחוזקה, לפי שאין לך מסננת גדולה מזו: שפו שיכרא. כל היכא דתני לשון שפוי – בנחת הוא, והפסולת נשאר בשולי הכלי: והאיכא ניצוצות. קטנות הנישופות באחרונה מתוך הפסולת, שקורין ברייש"ש, והנהו מוכחן דבורר הוא: ניצוצות בי רב פפא לא חשיבי.(ה) שחנוני מטיל שכר היה, כדאמרינן בבבא מציעא (דף סה:) ובפסחים (דף קיג.). הלכך אינו מקפיד לניצוצות כל כך, וכשמגיע לניצוצות – משליך הן ופסולתן לחוץ. ותחלת שפייתן(ו) מן הפסולת ניכר דלאו בורר הוא:

לפי

*) כאן יש ערבוב דברים ע"י חסרון נקודות המבדילות ונ"ל כדי שיצולו. שיהיו צלולין לזוב: את היין. מפני הקמחים וכו'. ועי' פירש"י להרי"ף.

עין משפט נר מצוה

יז א מיי' פ"א מהל' י"ט הלכה כג סמג לאוין עה טוש"ע א"ח סי' תקנו סעיף א:

יח ב מיי' שם טוש"ע שם סעיף ד:

יט ג מיי' פי"ט מהל' שבת הלכה כ סמג לאוין סה טוש"ע א"ח סי' שא סעיף לט:

כ ד מיי' שם טוש"ע שם סעיף לח וסי' יג סעיף א:

כא ה מיי' פ"ג מהל' י"ט הלכה יז סמג לאוין עה טוש"ע א"ח סי' תקי סעיף ד:

[וע"ע תוס' ביצה ו. ד"ה והאידנא]

כב ו מיי' פ"ז שם הלכה ח סמג שם טוש"ע שם סי' תקלג סעיף א:

כג ז מיי' פכ"ג מהל' שבת הלכה ג טוש"ע שם סי' שיד סעיף יא:

כד ח טור א"ח סימן שלט:

כה ט מיי' פ"ח מהל' שבת הלכה יד ופכ"א הלכה יז סמג שם טוש"ע א"ח סי' שיט סעיף ט:

כו י מיי' פ"ח שם ופ"ג מהלכות י"ט הלכה יז סמג שם טוש"ע שם סעיף טו:

כז כ ל מ נ מיי' פ"ח מהל' שבת הלכה יא ופכ"א הלכה יז סמג שם טוש"ע שם סעיף ...

כח ס ע מיי' פכ"ב שם הלכה לג טוש"ע שם סעיף יג:

כט פ מיי' שם סמג שם טוש"ע א"ח סי' שטו סעיף ...

ל צ טוש"ע שם סימן שיט סעיף יג:

לא ק שם סעיף יד:

הגהות הב"ח

(א) גמ' לא חשיבי ובטלי אמר (רבה) תז"מ ונ"ב ס"א ר' אבין: (ב) שם לא ניהדק אינש (ציניתא) תז"מ ונ"ב ס"א צבתא: (ג) שם ממנא למנא בנבאתא א"ל ר' אחא: (ד) רש"י ד"ה שלא יגביה וכו' מקרקעיתו של כלי: (ה) ד"ה ניצוצות וכו' לא חשיבי שסודני ומטיל לשכר היה: כדאמרי' בב"מ. נ"ב ע"ש דף סה דקאמר רב פפא טרשא דידי שרי מ"ט שכראי לא פסיד ובפסחי' דף קיג קאמרי' תמרי בחלוזך לבי סודנא רהוט וכו' אמר רב פפא אי לאו דרמאי שכרא לא איעתרי מאי סודנא אמר רב חסדא סוד נאה וכו' ובספ"ק דנדה קא"ל רבא לרב פפא סודני ופירש"י שתי לשונות: (ו) בא"ד ותחלת שפייתן שאין הפסולת ניכר לאו בורר הוא: (ז) תוס' ד"ה יו"ט שני כו' בני מליאון (אותה העיר) תא"מ ונ"ב הגה"ה היא:

גליון הש"ס

מתני' ומסננין את היין בסודרין. עי"ל קיא ע"א תוד"ה האי מסוכרייתא: תוס' ד"ה תלא כו' ושל דגים מאיס. עי"ל יט ע"ב תוד"ה הני כרכי.

הגהות הגר"א

[א] במשנה ומסננין את היין. נ"ב [illegible]

רבינו חננאל

לאיסור. וזה שאמר מתעטף אדם בכילה וכוסכיא ויוצא בה לרה"ר פי' כוסכיא חוטין ומשיחות שעליה. הלכה היא דקא מקשינן עלה מדרב הונא דאמר היוצא בטלית שאינה מצויצת כהלכתה כגון שתלה ציצית בג' כנפי הטלית והניח הרביעית אותן חוטי הציצית כיון שאינה מצוייצת בד' כנפות שלה אינה חשובה ציצית דמצוה. וכחוטין דעלמא הן חשובין והוצא בה חייב חטאת ופרקינן ציצית לגבי טלית חשיבי ולא בטלי שלב האדם רוצה בקיומן כי בדעתו שיתלה הרביעית וילבשנה. אבל כוסכיא לגבי כילה אינו צריך להן ובטלי: והא דאמר רבה בר בר חנה מערים אדם על המשמרת ביו"ט לתלות בה רמונים ותולה בה שמרים אליבא דרבנן שאסורים לתלות ולשמר לכתחלה ואע"פ שהיא אסורה והוא דתלה לה רמונים כרב אשי ואע"ג דאמרינן מ"ש מהא דתניא מטילין שכר במועד וכו' התם בשכר במועד לא מוכחא מלתא הכא במשמרת מוכחא מילתא ולשמר הוא תולה ואם תלה בה רמונים אין ואי לא לא. והא דאמרו ליה לרב אשי על רב הונא בר חיון. ואמרי לה בר חילון דהוה שקיל ברא דתומיא ומנח בבירזא דדנא פי' שהיה נוטל ראש שום ונותנן בנקב של חבית שיוצא ממנו היין ולא היה מסתפק מאותה חבית אלא חבית שבאוצר והיה מערים וסותם הנקב בראש השום והיה אומר להצניע ראש השום אני צריך ועוד היה הולך וישן במעברא וכו' אמר להו רב אשי הערמה מדרבנן היא והערמה לכתחלה ת"ח לא עבדי: ונותנין המים על השמרים בשביל שיצלו אמר זעירי נותן אדם יין צלול ומים צלולין לתוך המשמרת בשבת ואינו חושש אבל עכורין לא. ואם בין הגתות הוא שעדיין היין תוסס ואינו צלול טורד אדם חבית יינה ושמריה בשבת ואינו חושש ואפילו אליבא דרבנן וליכא דפליג בהא ומסננן את היין בסודרין אמר רב שימי בר חייא ובלבד שלא יעשה גומא. פי' שלא ימשוך קצות הסודר למעלה וישאר כמו גומא באמצעיתו. ובקפיפה מצרית. ואמרינן משמיה דרב שלא יגביה מקרקעיתו של כלי טפח. שכן מצינו באהלי טומאה טפח: וכל מקום שיש בו חלל טפח כאהל חשוב ואין עושין אהלי עראי לכתחלה בשבת: פראנקא. פי' כסוי בפי הקנקן ויש בו נקבים כדי לסנן בו היין כאשר יציקוהו בקנקן. אם יהיה זה הכיסוי בחצי פי הכלי אינו מסנן. ואם הוא בכל הפה של כלי הרי הוא כמסננת ונראה כמשמר היין במשמרת: וי"א פרונקא מטלית של בגד שעשאו לכסוי כלי בתחלת במה טומנין ומ"ש מפרונקא דמר ואומר עוד בע"ז פרק אין מעמידין בהמה בפונדקאות פש ליה חמרא בכובה ציירה בפרונקיא פי' נשאר לו יין בכלי קשר פי הכלי בסמרטוטין: לא ניהדוק צבתא בפומא דכוזא משום דמחזי כמשמרת. פי' צבתא בפומא דכוזא מוך חדש וכדומה לו והוא מלשון מצאי צבתים או כרוכות וי"א לוף של דקל וכדומה לו: ונותנין ביצה במסננת של חרדל תני יעקב קרחה

לפי

לפי שאין עושין אותה אלא לגוון. איתמר, חרדל שלשו מע"ש, למחר, אמר רב: ממחו בכלי, אבל לא ביד. א"ל שמואל: ביד, אטו כל יומא ממחו ליה ביד?! מאכל חמורים הוא! אלא אמר שמואל: ממחו ביד, ואינו ממחו בכלי. איתמר, ר"א אמר: אחד זה ואחד זה – אסור, ורבי יוחנן אמר: אחד זה ואחד זה – מותר. אביי ורבא דאמרי תרוייהו: אין הלכה כרבי יוחנן. קם רבי יוחנן בשיטתיה דר"א, קם רבי אלעזר בשיטתיה דשמואל. אביי ורבא דאמרי תרווייהו: הלכה כרבי יוחנן. *אימיה דאביי עבדא ליה ולא אכל, דביתהו דזעירא עבדא ליה לרב חייא בר אשי ולא אכיל, א"ל: לרבך עבידי ליה ואכל, ואת לא אכלת?! אמר רבא בר שבא: הוה קאימנא קמיה דרבינא ובחשי ליה בשופתא דתומא, ואכל. אמר מר זוטרא: *לית הלכתא ככל הני שמעתתא, אלא כי הא דאתמר: אחרדל שלשו מע"ש, למחר ממחו בין ביד בין בכלי, ונותן לתוכו דבש. ולא יטרוף אלא מערב. בשחליים ששחקן מע"ש, למחר – נותן לתוכן שמן וחומץ, וממשיך לתוכן אמיתא, ולא יטרוף אלא מערב. גשום שריסקו מע"ש, למחר – נותן לתוכו פול וגריסין, ולא ישחוק אלא מערב, וממשיך את אמיתא לתוכן. *מאי אמיתא? נינייא. אמר אביי: ש"מ – האי נינייא מעליא לתחלי.§ "ועושין אנומלין בשבת".§ *ת"ר: דעושין אנומלין בשבת, ואין עושין *אלונטית. ואיזו היא אנומלין ואיזו היא אלונטית? אנומלין – יין ודבש ופלפלין, אלונטית – יין ישן ומים צלולין ואפרסמון, דעבדי לבי מסותא למיקר. אמר רב יוסף: זימנא חדא עלית בתר מר עוקבא לבי באני, כי נפקי אתאי אשקיין החמרא חד כסא – וחשי מבינתא דראשי ועד טופרא דכרעי. ואי אשקיין כסא אחרינא – הואי מסתפינא דלמא מנכו לי מזכותא דעלמא דאתי. והא מר עוקבא דשתי כל יומא! שאני מר עוקבא דדש ביה.§ **מתני'** אין שורין את החילתית בפושרין, יאבל נותן לתוך החומץ. זואין שולין את הכרשינין, ולא שפין אותן, אבל נותן לתוך הכברה או לתוך הכלכלה. חאין כוברין את התבן בכברה ולא יתננו על גבי מקום גבוה בשביל שירד המוץ, אבל נוטל הוא בכברה ונותן לתוך האיבוס.§ **גמ'** איבעיא להו: שרה מאי? תרגמא רב אדא נרשאה קמיה דרב יוסף: שרה – חייב חטאת. א"ל אביי: אלא מעתה שרה אומצא במיא, הכי נמי דמיחייב?! אלא אמר אביי: *מדרבנן, שלא יעשה כדרך שהוא עושה בחול. בעא מיניה רבי יוחנן מר' ינאי: מהו לשרות את החלתית בצונן? א"ל: אסור. והא אנן תנן: "אין שורין את החלתית בפושרין", הא בצונן – מותר! א"ל: *א"כ, מה בין לי ולך? מתניתין יחידאה היא, דתניא: *טאין שורין את החלתית לא בחמין ולא בצונן, רבי יוסי אומר: בחמין – אסור, בצונן – מותר. למאי עבדי ליה – ליוקרא דליבא. רב אחא בר יוסף חש ביוקרא דליבא, אתא לקמיה דמר עוקבא. א"ל: זיל שתי תלתא תיקלי חילתתא בתלתא יומי. אזל אישתי חמשא בשבת, ומעלי שבת. לצפרא אזל שאל בי מדרשא, אמרו ליה: תנא דבי רב אדא, ואמרי לה – תנא דבי מר בר רב אדא: ישותה אדם קב או קביים – ואינו חושש. אמר להו: לשתות – לא קמיבעיא לי, כי קא מיבעיא לי – לשרות, מאי? אמר להו רב חייא בר אבין: בדידי הוה עובדא, ואתאי שאילתיה לרב אדא בר אהבה, ולא הוה בידיה. אתאי שאילתיה לרב הונא, ואמר: הכי קאמר רב "שורה בצונן ומניח בחמה". כמאן דשרי? כאפילו למאן דאסר, ה"מ – היכא דלא אישתי כלל, אבל הכא כיון דאישתי חמשא ומעלי שבתא, אי לא שתי בשבת – מיסתכן. מיסתמיך ואזיל רב אחא בר יוסף אכתפיה דרב נחמן בר יצחק בר אחתיה, א"ל: כי מטינן לבי רב ספרא – עיילינא, כי מטו – עייליה. בעא מיניה: מהו לכסכוסי כיתניתא בשבתא? לרכוכי כיתניתא קא מיכוין – ושפיר דמי, או דילמא: לאולודי חיורא קמיכוין, ואסיר? א"ל: ללרכוכי קא מיכוין, ושפיר דמי, כי נפק אתא, א"ל: מאי בעא מר מיניה? א"ל: בעי מיניה: מהו לכסכוסי כיתניתא בשבתא, ואמר לי: שפיר דמי. ותבעי ליה למר סודרא? סודרא לא קא מיבעיא לי, דבעי מרב הונא ופשיט לי. *ותיפשיט ליה למר מסודרא! א"ל: מהתם – מיחזי כי אולודי חיורא, הכא – לא מיחזי כאולודי חיורא. אמר רב חסדא: האי כיתניתא, משלפו

לפי שאין עושין(א) אלא לגוון. למראה, שהחלמון יפה לגוון ולא החלבון, הלכך אידי ואידי אוכל הוא, ואין כאן ברירת פסולת מאוכל: ממחו. דיסטיפדי"ר בלע"ז, במים או ביין: ממחו בכלי. משמע: זהו שינוי שלו: ואינו ממחו ביד. דממחו ליה שפיר טפי: אלא אמר שמואל ממחו ביד. שאין זה דרכו בחול: קם ר' יוחנן בשיטתיה דר"א. חזר בו ואסר: אביי ורבא דאמרי תרוייהו הלכה כר' יוחנן. דאסר: לרבך. לזעירי: בשופתא דתומא. אמלעי של שום: ולא יטרוף. כדרך שטורפין ביצים בקערה בכף, דרך טריפה שמכה בכח: שחליים. כרישין, והיו שוחקין אותם במים: ממשיך. נותן: אמיתא. מינט"א בלע"ז: מעליא לתחלי. לערב עם שחליים: ואין עושין אלונטית. שאינה למשקה נאה, אלא לצנן לאחר המרחץ, ודוגמת רפואה: וחשי מבינתא דרישא. הרגשתי בלינתו מעברת ראשי עד לפרני רגלי: מנכו לי מזכיותי. אם הייתי ניאול ממנו שלא אמות: שתי כל יומא. ולא היה מזיקו: דדש ביה. רגיל בו: **מתני'** חילתית. חלטי"ת בלשון ישמעאל, ובלע"ז לזרי"א. ושורין אותו בפושרין, ושותין אותן המים לרפואה: אבל נותן. החלתית: בתוך החומץ. ומטבל בו מאכלו. ולקמיה מפרש אמאי אין שורין: ואין שולין את הכרשינין. מליף עליהם מים בכלי לברור פסולתן, כדתנן במסכת ביצה (דף יד:): אף מדיח ושולה: ולא שפין אותן. ביד להסיר פסולת, דהוה ליה בורר: אבל נותן לתוך הכברה. ואע"פ דפעמים שהפסולת נופל דרך נקבי הכברה, ונמצא נתברר מאליו: תבן. הוא שעושין מן הקש, מחתכין אותו במוריגין ועושה כל זנב(ב) השבולת תבן: מוץ. הוא מוקן השבולת העליון, ואינו ראוי למאכל, וכוברין אותו(ג) בכברין שיפול המוץ: אבל נוטל(ד) בכברה. ליתן בתוך האבוס, ואע"פ שהמוץ נופל מאליו – כר"ש, דאמר: דבר שאין מתכוין מותר: **גמ'** שרה. חילתית בפושרין, מאי? אומצא. בשר חי: שלא יעשה כו'. לא שבקוה רבנן למעבד עובדי דחול: אם כן. דלא ידענא לפרושי מתני' טפי מינך, מה בין לי ולך? מתניתין יחידאה היא. ור' יוסי אמרה, אבל לרבנן – אף בצונן אסור: ליוקרא דליבא. שלבו כבד עליו: תלתא תיקלי חילתתא. משקל ג' זהובים: שאיל בי מדרשא. מה יעשה בשבת: לשתות לא קמיבעיא לי. דבלאו רפואה משקה הוא, ותנן: כל המשקין שותה (לעיל דף קט:): לשרות. דתנן מתניתין: אין שורין: כמאן דשרי. בעיא הוא, הך דרב לימא כרבי יוסי דשרי בצונן, אבל לרבנן – אסור: עיילינא. הכניסני. ואיש זקן היה: לכסכוסי כיתניתא. חלוק כתונת של פשתן שנתכבסה, והרי היא קשה, ומשפשפה בין שתי ידיו והיא מתרככה, ואף הליבון שלה מאהיל על ידי השפשוף: אולודי חיורא. הליבון מאהיל: התם מיחזי כאולודי חיורא. שמקפיד על ליבונו וזוהרו של סודר יותר מכיתניתא:
משלפה

עין משפט נר מצוה

לב א מיי' פ"ח מהל' שבת הל' יד ופכ"ב הלכה יב סמג לאוין סה טוש"ע א"ח סי' שכא סעיף טו:
לג ב ג מיי' פכ"ב שם טוש"ע שם סעיף טז:
לד ד מיי' שם טוש"ע שם סעיף יז:
לה ה מיי' פ"ד מהל' דעות הלכה יז:
לו ו מיי' פכ"ב מהל' שבת הלכה ז סמג לאוין סה טוש"ע א"ח סי' שכא סעיף יח:
לז ז (מיי' פ"ח מהל' שבת) סמג לאוין סה טוש"ע א"ח סי' שיט סעיף ח:
לח ח מיי' פכ"א שם הלכה לב סמג שם טוש"ע א"ח סי' שכל סעיף א:
לט ט י כ מיי' פכ"א שם הלכה כב ופכ"ב שם הל' ז סמג שם טוש"ע א"ח סי' שכא סעיף יח:
[ע' תוס' כתובות נד. ד"ה לית]
מ ל מ מיי' פכ"ב שם הלכה יז סמג שם טוש"ע א"ח סי' שב סעיף ה:

רבינו חננאל

לפי שאין עושין אותה אלא לגוון. פי' לצבעו להתראות בו גוונא של ביצה מאכל המרם. פי' זה המאכל ממורם הוא כדתנן (נתן) [נטל] את הדם ונתנו לממרס בו על הרובד הרביעי וי"א מאכל חמורים הוא כלומר אינו מאכל ב"א אלא מאכל חמורים הוא: חרדל שלשו מע"ש חלקו עליו רב ושמואל ור' יוחנן ור' אלעזר ודבריהן פשוטין הן ומר זוטרא דהוא בתרא אמר לית הלכתא ככל הני שמעתתא אלא כי הא דתניא חרדל שלשו מע"ש למחר מניחו בין ביד בין בכלי ונותן לתוכו דבש ולא יטרוף אלא מערב. שום שריסקו מע"ש למחר נותן לתוכו פול או גריסין ולא ישחוק אלא מערב. וממשיך את האמיתה לתוכה מאי אמיתה נגחה. אנומלין יין ושמן ודבש ופלפלין אלונתית יין ישן ומים צלולין ואפרסמון: אין שורין את החלתית בפושרין אבל נותן לתוך החומץ ומיבעיא לן שרה מאי. ומסקנא שרה אמר אביי איסורא מדרבנן וא"ר יוחנן מתניתין יחידאה היא והוא ר' יוסי אבל חכ"א בין בחמין בין בצונן אסור וסוגיא דשמעתא אם שרה מאתמול לשתות חלתית בשבת מותר. אבל לשרותו אסור אפילו בצונן. ואם שרה קודם השבת ועכשיו בשבת חושש אם לא ישתה מסתכן מותר לו לשרות בתוכו ולהניחה בחמה: לכסכוסי כיתונתא. פי' לרכוכי קא מיכוון ושרי או דלמא לאולודי וכו'. פי' לקבץ מקצת הבגד של פשתים לתוך ידו לשופו מפני שרוחצין הבגד ומתייבש בשמש או ברוח עומד אנסו פי' קשה ורוצה לרככו נותן הבגד לתוך ידיו ומוליך ומביא ידיו עד שיעשה הבגד ההוא כמו קפולין קטנים כמין קמטין כי הא דא"ר זירא בפ' חבית (דף קמז) מאי מרוב כגון*) כסכוסי מאני דמתחזי כמרוב וכי הא דתנן בפ' האשה שהיא עושה צרכיה: צריכה לכסכס ג' פעמים על כל דבר ודבר ואמרי' בגמ' בעי ר' ירמיה אמטויי חד ואיתויי [חד] או דלמא אמטויי [חד] ואיתויי [תרתי] תיקו: וכן עוד מפורש בתלמוד א"י בענין מוליך ומביא שבלולב. מהא שמעינן דכיסכוס בעין שפשוף הוא ומתקבץ הבגד פי' יתכמש ונראה קמטין קמטין וכשלובשו מתפשט וכדאמרינן אמר רב כהנא ואיתמא רב יהודה טיט שעל בגדו מכסכסו מבפנים. ומרקדי להאי כיתונתא. שמעינן מנה דסודרא ליתיה כתינתא ולא יתכן לומר שהוא צמר שאם הוא צמר איך אומר לו היה לך ללמוד פשתים מצמר. והדבר רחוק ביניהם ואינה אלא צמר גפן שזה קרוב לזה ופשט

*) לפנינו בגמ' איתא שם כיסו בכליתא.

מסורת הש"ס

[ע' קדושין לח:]
[לעיל קכח.]
ע"ז ל.
[שם איתא אלונתית אבל בערוך גרס כגי' שלפנינו]
[לעיל קלח.]
[חולי' קלד:]
[תוספ' פי"ז]
ס"א לאיסורא

רב נסים גאון

אין שורין את הכרשינין. גרסי' בגמ' דבני מערבא תני אין שורין את הכרשינים משום בורר ולא שפין אותן משום דש אין כוברין את התבן משום מרקד. גורפין מלפני הפטם ומסלקין לצדדין מפני הרעי בגמ' דבני מערבא גרסי מה שהפטם אוכל ומותיר הרעי אוכל:
הרעי

הגהות הב"ח

(א) רש"י ד"ה לפי שאין עושין אותה אלא: (ב) ד"ה תבן וכו' כל זנב השבלים תבן: (ג) ד"ה מוץ וכו' בכברה כדי שיפול: (ד) ד"ה אבל נוטל הוא בכברה ונותן לתוך האבוס:

גליון הש"ס

גמ' אמר מר זוטרא לית הלכתא ככל הני שמעתתא. עיין כתובות דף נ"ד ע"א תוס' ד"ה לית הלכתא: רש"י ד"ה אבל נוטל וכו' נופל מאליו כר"ש. עיין לעיל דף נ"ד ע"א ברש"י ד"ה כלאים לחבלים:

עין משפט נר מצוה

מא א ב מיי' פכ"ה מהל' שבת הל' יח סמג לאוין סה טוש"ע א"ח סי' שח סעיף טז:
מב ג מיי' פכ"ו מהל' שבת הל' טז סמג שם טוש"ע שם סעיף כז וכח:
מג ד מיי' פ"ז מהל' ברכות הלכה ג:
מד ה ו מיי' פכ"ו מהל' שבת הלכה יט סמג לאוין סה טוש"ע א"ח סי' שכד סעיף טו:
מה ז מיי' שם טוש"ע שם סעיף יד:

אבל באיבום של קרקע דברי הכל אסור. אע"ג דמרבן שרינן לרבי שמעון (לעיל דף נה.), הכא רגילות הוא להתכוין לאשווי גומות, ואיישינן טפי שמא יתכוין:

הקש

ᵃמשלפו לדידה מקניא – שרי, קניא ממנה – אסור. אמר רבא: *ᵇואם כלי קיואי הוא – מותר. אמר רב חסדא: ᵍהאי *כישתא דירקא, אי חזיא למאכל בהמה – שרי לטלטולי, ואי לא – אסיר. אמר רב חייא בר אשי אמר רב: האי *תליא, דבשרא – שרי לטלטולי, דכוורי – אסיר.

אמר רב קטינא: העומד באמצע המטה – כאילו עומד בכריסה של אשה. ולאו מילתא היא. ואמר רב חסדא: בר בי רב דזבין ירקא – ליזבין אריכא, כישא כי כישא, ואורכא ממילא. ואמר רב חסדא: בר בי רב דזבין קניא – ליזבין אריכא, טונא כי טונא, ואורכא ממילא. ואמר רב חסדא: בר בי רב [*דלא נפישא ליה ריפתא] – לא ליכול ירקא, משום דגריר. ואמר רב חסדא: אנא לא בעניותי אכלי ירקא, ולא בעתירותי אכלי ירקא. בעניותי – משום דגריר, בעתירותי – דאמינא: היכא דעייל ירקא ליעול בשרא וכוורי(א). ואמר רב חסדא: בר בי רב דלא נפישא ליה ריפתא – לא ליבצע בצועי. ואמר רב חסדא: בר בי רב דלא נפישא ליה ריפתא – *לא ליבצע, מ"ט – ᵈדלא עביד בעין יפה. ואמר רב חסדא: אנא מעיקרא לא הואי בצענא עד דשדאי ידי בכולי מנא ואשכחי [ביה כל צרכי]. ואמר רב חסדא: האי מאן דאפשר ליה למיכל נהמא דשערי ואכל דחיטי – קעבר משום "בל תשחית". ואמר רב פפא: האי מאן דאפשר למישתי שיכרא ושתי חמרא – עובר משום "בל תשחית". ולאו מילתא היא, *בל תשחית דגופא עדיף. ואמר רב חסדא: בר בי רב דלית ליה משחא – נימשי במיא דחריצי. ואמר רב חסדא: בר בי רב דזבין אומצא – ליזבין אונקא, דאית ביה תלתא מיני בישרא. וא"ר חסדא: בר בי רב דזבין כיתוניתא – ליזבן מדנהר אבא, וניחוורה כל תלתין יומין, דמפטיא ליה תריסר ירחי שתא, ואנא ערבא. מאי כיתוניתא – כיתא נאה. וא"ר חסדא: בר בי רב לא ליתיב אציפתא חדתא, דמכליא מאניה. וא"ר חסדא: בר בי רב לא לישדר מאניה לאושפיזיה לחוורינהו ליה, דלאו אורח ארעא, דילמא חזי ביה מידי ואתי למגנייא. אמר להו רב חסדא לבנתיה: תיהוי צניעתן באפי גברייכו, לא תיכלון נהמא באפי גברייכו, לא תיכלון ירקא בליליא, לא תיכלון תמרי בליליא, ולא תשתון שיכרא בליליא, ולא תיפנון היכא דמפני גברייכו. וכי קא קארי אבבא איניש לא תימרון "מנו" אלא "מני". נקיט *מרגניתא בחדא ידיה, וכורא בחדא ידיה. מרגניתא – אחוי להו, וכורא לא אחוי להו, עד דמיצטערן, והדר אחוי להו.§ "אין שולין את הכרשינין"*.§ מתני' דלא כי האי תנא; דתניא, ר"א בן יעקב אומר: אין משגיחין בכברה כל עיקר.§ **מתני'** גורפין מלפני הפטם, ומסלקין לצדדין מפני הרעי, דברי רבי דוסא. וחכמים אוסרין. נוטלין מלפני בהמה זו ונותנין לפני בהמה זו בשבת.§ **גמ'** איבעיא להו: רבנןארישא פליגי, או אסיפא פליגי, או אתרווייהו פליגי? ת"ש: דתניא, וחכמים אומרים: ᵉאחד זה ואחד זה – לא יסלקנו לצדדין. אמר רב חסדא: מחלוקת באיבום של קרקע, אבל באיבום של כלי – דברי הכל מותר. ואיבום של קרקע מי איכא למאן דשרי? הא קא משוי גומות! אלא, אי איתמר הכי איתמר: א"ר חסדא ᵛמחלוקת באיבום של כלי, אבל באיבום של קרקע – דברי הכל אסור.§ "ונוטלין מלפני בהמה".§ תנא חדא: נוטלין מלפני בהמה שפיה יפה, ונותנין לפני בהמה שפיה רע. ותניא אידך: נוטלין מלפני בהמה שפיה רע ונותנין לפני בהמה שפיה יפה! אמר אביי: ᶻאידי ואידי מקמי חמרא לקמי תורא – שקלינן, מקמי תורא לקמי חמרא – לא שקלינן. והא דקתני "נוטל מלפני בהמה שפיה יפה" – בחמור, דלית ליה רירי. "ונותנין לפני בהמה שפיה רע" – בפרה, דאית

רש"י

משלפא לדידה מקניא. כששוטחין אותה לנגבה תוחבים קנה מבית יד לבית יד, וכשנוטלה בשבת ישלפנה מן הקנה ולא הקנה ממנה, דלא חזי לטלטולי, דלהספקה קאי: ואם כלי קיואי היא. קנה של אורגים, דתורת כלי עליו שרי: תליא דבשרא. בשר מליח התלוי לייבשו, ומלא החבל קרי תליא: שרי. דנאכל חי באומצא: דכוורי. אין נאכלין חיין: באמצע מטה. שאיש ואשתו רגילין בה לישן: כאילו עומד כו'. דמהרהר: ליזבין אריכא. אגודה ארוכה של כרוב ארוך ושל כרישין ארוכים: כישא כי כישא. שכל אגודות הגנין שוות בעוביין, שלכולן מדה אחת לחבל שהוא אגוד בו: ואורכא ממילא. כלומר ארכו של זה שהוא ארוך מחבירו, הוא משתכר בו: קניא. חבילי קנים לעצים: לא ליכול ירקא. ירק חי(ב), כרישין ניריפו"ל ושחלייס: משום דגריר ליבא. ומאכילו לחם הרבה ואין לו: לא ליבצע בצועי. מורשיליונ"ט בלע"ז. לא יאכל עכשיו מעט פת שימלא לו, ולאחר שעה מעט – מפני שאין לו דרך שביעה, אלא יצרף ויאכל יחד: מעיקרא. קודם שנתעשרתי: עד דשדאי ידי בכולא מנא. כשהייתי ממשמש בסל ומוצא בו פת הרבה, הייתי מברך המוציא: דלית ליה משחא. שהיו סכין ידיהן שמן קודם מים אחרונים, להעביר את הזוהמא: במיא דחריצי. הנקוים יחד, וגדל עליהם ירקרוקית עבה ונוחה כשמן: אונקא. צואר: תלתא מיני בשרא. יטעום בו ג' מיני מטעמים, שמן וכחוש וגיד הצואר: מדנהר אבא. מאותו מקום שפשתנו יפה: דמפטיא ליה תריסר ירחי שתא ואנא ערבא. אני ערב בדבר שמתקיים לו שנה שלימה, ותפטיהו, שלא יצטרך לקנות חלוק: כיתא נאה. כת נאה, ראויה להושיב בעליה בכת נאה: אציפתא חדתא. מחצלת חדשה של גמי לח, ולחלוחית הגמי מבלה הבגדים: לאושפיזא. לפונדקית שלא ישלח חלוקו ללבן: דילמא חזיא בהו. קרי ומגניא עליה: לא תיכלון נהמא באפי גברייכו. פעמים תאכל הרבה ותתגנה עליו: לא תיכלון ירקא בלילה. מפני ריח הפה: שיכרא ותמרי. משלשלין ומביאין לידי הפחה: היכא דמפני גברייכו. בגילוי בפניהם בשדות, ואפילו שלא בפניהם. שמכיר מקומו ומקומכם, ונמאסת' לו בזוכרו: לא תימרון מנו. חי הוא, ואין זכר לא תרגילו לשונכם לדבר עם זכרים: אלא מני. מי היא: נקיט מרגניתא בחדא ידיה וכורא בחדא ידיה. כשבעליך ממשמש בך להתאוות ליך לתשמיש, ואוחז הדדים בידו אחת והאחרת על אותו מקום: מרגניתא אחוין ליה. הדדין המגילהו לו, שתתרבה תאותו. ומקום תשמיש אל תמציאהו לו מהר, כדי שיתרבה תאותו ותחבתו ויצטער, הדר אחוי ליה: כורא. לשון כור נורפין (לעיל דף עח.). לשון אחר: בור, לשון בור שוחה: מתניתין. דקתני: אבל נותנין לתוך הכברה: **מתני'** גורפין מלפני הפטם. שור שמפטמין אותו גורפין אבוס שלפניו בשבת לתת לתוכו התבן והשעורין, ולא יתערב בהן עפרורית ויקוץ במאכלו: ומסלקין. תבן(ג) שלפניו לצדדין כשהוא רב, כדי שלא ידרסנו ברעי: וחכמים אוסרים. מפ' בגמ' אהייא: ונוטלין מלפני בהמה זו. שעורין ותבן, ונותנין לפני זו, ולא אמרינן טלטול דלא חזי הוא, אלא ודאי חזי הוא, דאין בהמה קצה במאכל הניטל מלפני חבירתה: **גמ'** ארישא פליגי. אגורפין, ואסרי לגרוף, משום דפעמים שהאבוס של קרקע וקא מכוין לאשווי גומות שלא יפלו השעורים לתוכו: או אסיפא פליגי. ומשום דלא חזי שיש בו(ד) שנמאס במדרס רגליו: תא שמע. דאתרווייהו פליגי: אחד זה ואחד זה. אחד גריפת האבוס ואחד תבן שלפניו, לא יסלקנו לצדדין: של קרקע. כעין שעושין גדר קטן לפני בהמה ונותנין מאכל לפנים ממנו, דאיכא למיחש לאשווי גומות: מחלוקת באבוס של כלי. וגזרו רבנן גזרה אטו של קרקע: אידי ואידי. לקמיה מפרש: שפיה יפה. שתיהן המשניות סבירא להו: מקמי חמרא לקמי תורא שקלינן. שאינו מטיל רירין, ואין מה שלפניו נמאס, וראוי לתתו לפני שור: מקמי תורא לקמי חמרא לא שקלינן:

רבינו חננאל

רב חסדא דלרכוכי מיכוון ושרי. אמר רב חסדא הא כיתניתא משלפה לדילא מקניא: פי' למשוך הבגד ששוטחו בקנה להנגב ונעשה נגוב וישאר הקנה במקומו. ולא מטלטלין מותר אבל למשוך הקנה מן הבגד ולטלטלו בשבת אסור שהקנה אינו כלי להטלטל בחצר. אמר רבא ואם כלי קיואי מותר. פי' אם הוא הבגד שטוח בכלי האורג וכלי האורג נקראין כלי קיואי כדאמרינן בפרק ואלו קשרים שחייבין עליהן. אתמר אמר רב נחמן אמר שמואל כלי קיואי מותר לטלטלו בשבת ואפי' כובד העליון וכובד התחתון אבל לא את העמודים ותוב בעא מיניה ר' יוחנן מרבי יהודה בר ליואי כלי קיואי כגון כובד העליון וכובד התחתון כו'. האי תלא דבשרא פי' יתד של עץ עשוי לתלות בו בשר ופעמים שתולין בו זולתו [שרי לטלטולי] אבל העץ שתולין בו דגים. כיון שהדגים ריחם רע וקשה אין תולין בו דבר אחר ומסיחין דעתן ממנו ומוקצה מחמת מיאום הוא ואסור: **מדנהר** אבא. שם מקום הוא: **ציפיתא** חדתא. פי' מחצלת חדשה בזרא בחרא ידא. כגון אבן שאין לה דמים ולא צורך. ומפני שהסתירה מהן נתייקרה בעיניהם ופייסוהו להראותה להן: **מתני'** אין שולין את הכרשינין ולא שפין כו' גורפין מלפני הפטם ומסלקין לצדדים כו'. פי' גורפין המאכל של בהמה מלפני הפטם ומאכל שאר בהמות מסלקין לצדדין דברי ר' דוסא חכמים אוסרין ואיבעיא לן רבנן ארישא פליגי והיא גורפין [או] אסיפא פליגי והוא שמסלקין לצדדין ואמרינן ת"ש וחכ"א אחד זה ואחד זה לא יסלקנו לצדדין. ש"מ רבנן אתרווייהו פליגי. אמר רב חסדא מחלוקת באבום של כלי ואפי' בזה חכמים אוסרין אבל באבום של קרקע דברי הכל אסור לגרוף

הגהות הב"ח

(א) דלא נפישא ליה ריפתא (לא ליבלע וכו' יפה) תא"מ ונ"ב ס"א לא ליבלע בלועי והשאר נמחק והכי משמע מפירש"י: (ב) רש"י ד"ה לא ליכול ירקא ירק חי. נ"ב עיין פרק כילד מעברין בדף נה במ"ש התוס' בד"ה כל עיר: (ג) ד"ה ויסלק תבן מלפניו לצדדין: (ד) ד"ה או אסיפא וכו' שיש בו מה שנמאס:

מסורת הש"ס

[לעיל קיג.] [בערוך איתא הורצא] [ע' תוס' לעיל קלט: ד"ה תלא] [עי' תוס' עירובין נה: ד"ה כל עיר וכו' נראה דלא גרסי להגך ד' מילות] ברכות מו: [לעיל קכט.] [גירס' אחרינא ופירושו עי' בערוך ערך כזר א'] נ"ל וכו'

דְּאִית לָהּ רִירֵי. וְהָא דְּקָתָנֵי "נוֹטְלִין מִלִּפְנֵי בְהֵמָה שֶׁפִּיהָ רַע" – בַּחֲמוֹר דְּלָא דָּיֵיק וְאָכֵיל, "וְנוֹתְנִין לִפְנֵי בְהֵמָה שֶׁפִּיהָ יָפֶה" – בְּפָרָה דְּדָיְיקָא וְאָכְלָה.§ **מתני'** *[א]הַקַּשׁ שֶׁעַל גַּבֵּי הַמִּטָּה – לֹא יְנַעַנְעֶנּוּ בְּיָדוֹ, אֶלָּא מְנַעְנְעוֹ בְּגוּפוֹ. וְאִם הָיָה מַאֲכַל בְּהֵמָה, אוֹ שֶׁהָיָה עָלָיו כַּר אוֹ סָדִין – מְנַעְנְעוֹ בְּיָדוֹ. [ב]מַכְבֵּשׁ שֶׁל בַּעֲלֵי בָתִּים – מַתִּירִין, אֲבָל לֹא כּוֹבְשִׁין. וְשֶׁל כּוֹבְסִין – לֹא יִגַּע בּוֹ. ר' יְהוּדָה אוֹמֵר: אִם הָיָה מוּתָּר מֵעֶ"שׁ – מַתִּיר אֶת כּוּלּוֹ וְשׁוֹמְטוֹ.§ **גמ'** *אָמַר רַב נַחְמָן: הַאי פּוּגְלָא, מִלְּמַעְלָה לְמַטָּה – שָׁרֵי, מִלְּמַטָּה לְמַעְלָה – אָסִיר. אָמַר רַב אַדָּא בַּר אַבָּא, אָמְרִי בֵּי רַב: תָּנֵינָא דְּלָא כְּרַב נַחְמָן "הַקַּשׁ שֶׁעַ"ג הַמִּטָּה – לֹא יְנַעְנְעוֹ בְּיָדוֹ, אֲבָל מְנַעְנְעוֹ בְּגוּפוֹ. וְאִם הָיָה מַאֲכַל בְּהֵמָה, אוֹ שֶׁהָיָה עָלָיו כַּר אוֹ סָדִין – מְנַעְנְעוֹ בְּיָדוֹ". ש"מ: *[ג]טִלְטוּל מִן הַצַּד – לָא שְׁמֵיהּ טִלְטוּל, ש"מ. אָמַר רַב *יְהוּדָה: הָנֵי פִּלְפְּלֵי מֵידָק חֲדָא חֲדָא בְּקַתָּא דְּסַכִּינָא – שָׁרֵי, תַּרְתֵּי – אָסִיר. רָבָא אָמַר: [ד]כֵּיוָן דִּמְשַׁנֵּי – אֲפִילּוּ טוּבָא נַמִי. *אָמַר רַב יְהוּדָה: [ה]מַאן דְּסָחֵי בְּמַיָּא – לִינְגִּיב נַפְשֵׁיהּ בְּרֵישָׁא, וַהֲדַר לִיסְלִיק, דִּילְמָא אָתֵי לְאַתּוּיֵי ד' אַמּוֹת בְּכַרְמְלִית. אִי הָכִי, כִּי קָא נָחֵית נַמִי, קָא דָּחֵי כֹּחוֹ ד' אַמּוֹת, וְאָסִיר! *כֹּחוֹ בְּכַרְמְלִית לָא גָּזְרוּ. אָמַר אַבָּיֵי וְאִיתֵּימָא רַב יְהוּדָה: טִיט שֶׁעַ"ג רַגְלוֹ מְקַנְּחוֹ בַּקַּרְקַע, וְאֵין מְקַנְּחוֹ בַּכּוֹתֶל. אָמַר רָבָא: מ"ט בַּכּוֹתֶל לָא – מִשּׁוּם דְּמֶיחֱזֵי כְּבוֹנֶה, הָא בִּנְיָן חַקְלָאָה הוּא! אֶלָּא אָמַר רָבָא: [ו]מְקַנְּחוֹ בַּכּוֹתֶל, וְאֵין מְקַנְּחוֹ בַּקַּרְקַע, דִּילְמָא אָתֵי לְאַשְׁוּוּיֵי גּוּמוֹת. אִיתְּמַר, מָר בְּרֵיהּ דְּרָבִינָא אָמַר: אֶחָד זֶה וְאֶחָד זֶה אָסוּר, רַב פַּפָּא אָמַר: אֶחָד זֶה וְאֶחָד זֶה – מוּתָּר. לְמָר בְּרֵיהּ דְּרָבִינָא בְּמַאי מְקַנְּחִי לֵיהּ? מְקַנְּחִי לֵיהּ בַּקּוֹרָה. *אָמַר רָבָא: (א)[ז]לָא לֵיתִיב אִינִישׁ אַפּוּמֵּיהּ דְּלֶיחְיָא, דִּילְמָא מִיגַּנְדְּרָא לֵיהּ חֵפֶץ וְאָתֵי לְאַתּוּיֵי. וְאָמַר רָבָא: [ח]לָא לִיצַדֵּד אִינִישׁ כּוּבָא(ב), דִּילְמָא אָתֵי לְאַשְׁוּוּיֵי גּוּמוֹת. וְאָמַר רָבָא: [ט]לָא לִיהַדּוֹק אִינִישׁ אוּדְרָא בְּפוּמָּא דְשִׁישָׁא, דִּילְמָא אָתֵי לִידֵי סְחִיטָה. אָמַר רַב כָּהֲנָא: [י]טִיט שֶׁעַ"ג בִּגְדוֹ מְכַסְכְּסוֹ מִבִּפְנִים וְאֵין מְכַסְכְּסוֹ מִבַּחוּץ. מֵיתִיבִי: טִיט שֶׁעַ"ג מִנְעָלוֹ – מְגָרְרוֹ בְּגַב סַכִּין[א], וְשֶׁעַל בִּגְדוֹ – מְגָרְרוֹ בַּצִּפּוֹרֶן, וּבִלְבַד שֶׁלֹּא יְכַסְכֵּם. מַאי לָאו – שֶׁלֹּא יְכַסְכֵּם כְּלָל! לֹא, שֶׁלֹּא יְכַסְכֵּם מִבַּחוּץ, אֶלָּא מִבִּפְנִים. א"ר אַבָּהוּ א"ר אֶלְעָזָר אָמַר ר' יַנַּאי: מְגָרְרִין מִנְעָל חָדָשׁ, אֲבָל לֹא יָשָׁן.

בַּמֶּה

רש"י

דְּאִית לָהּ רִירֵי. וְאִימְאִיס, וְהָא דְּקָרֵי לָהּ הָכָא פִּיהָ יָפֶה וְהָכָא פִּיהָ רַע – כִּדְמְפָרֵשׁ וְאָזֵיל: פִּיהָ יָפֶה – דְּלֵית לֵיהּ רִירֵי; פִּיהָ רַע – דְּלָא דָּיֵיק וְאָכֵיל, שֶׁאוֹכֵל קוֹצִים וְדַרְדָּרִים: **מתני'** הַקַּשׁ שֶׁעַל הַמִּטָּה. וּסְתָמָא לְהַסָּקָה, וּמוּקְצֶה הוּא. וּבָא לִשְׁכַּב עָלָיו, וּמְנַעְנְעוֹ כְּדֵי שֶׁיְּהֵא נָח וְרַךְ לִשְׁכַּב: לֹא יְנַעְנְעֶנּוּ בְּיָדוֹ. דְּמוּקְצֶה הוּא: אֲבָל מְנַעְנְעוֹ בְּגוּפוֹ. בִּכְתֵפָיו, וְטִלְטוּל מִן הַצַּד הוּא, דְּלָא שְׁמֵיהּ טִלְטוּל: אוֹ שֶׁהָיָה עָלָיו כַּר אוֹ סָדִין. דְּגַלֵּי דַּעְתֵּיהּ דְּאַקְצְיֵיהּ לִשְׁכִיבָה, מֵעַתָּה תּוֹרַת כְּלִי עָלָיו: מַכְבֵּשׁ. פרש"א, שְׁנֵי לְוָחִים חֲרוּכִים וּכְבֵדִים, וְסוֹדְרִין בְּגָדִים עַל הַתַּחְתּוֹן, וּמוֹרִידִין הָעֶלְיוֹן עָלָיו. וְכוֹבְשִׁים אֶת הַבְּגָדִים עַל יְדֵי יְתֵדוֹת. שֵׁשׁ עַמּוּדִים קְבוּעִין מְנוּקָבִין בְּאַרְבַּע הַפֵּיאוֹת שֶׁל הַתַּחְתּוֹנוֹת, וְהָעֶלְיוֹנָה מְנוּקֶּבֶת בְּאַרְבַּע זָוִיּוֹתֶיהָ, וְעוֹלָה וְיוֹרֶדֶת בָּעַמּוּדִים. וּכְפִי מַה שֶּׁהוּא רוֹצֶה לִכְבּוֹשׁ מוֹרִידָהּ, וְתוֹחֵב יָתֵד בְּנֶקֶב הָעַמּוּד, וְאֵינָהּ יְכוֹלָה לַעֲלוֹת: מַתִּירִין. אֶת הַמַּכְבֵּשׁ, שֶׁנּוֹטֵל אֶת הַיָּתֵד וְהוּא נִיתָּר, דְּהַיְינוּ לוֹרֶךְ שַׁבָּת, שֶׁנּוֹטֵל אֶת הַכֵּלִים: אֲבָל לֹא כּוֹבְשִׁין. דְּהַיְינוּ לוֹרֶךְ חוֹל: וְשֶׁל כּוֹבְסִין לֹא יִגַּע בּוֹ. מִפְּנֵי שֶׁהוּא עָשׂוּי לְתַקֵּן הַבְּגָדִים, וְתוֹחֲבוֹ בַּחֲזָקָה וּמִיהַדַּק, וְהַתָּרָה שֶׁלּוֹ דּוֹמָה לִסְתִירָה: **גמ'** הַאי פּוּגְלָא. לְנוֹן שֶׁטּוֹמְנִין בַּקַּרְקַע לְהִתְקַיֵּים, כְּשֶׁבָּא לְתָלְשׁוֹ מִלְמַעְלָה לְמַטָּה – שָׁרֵי אִם הָיָה רֹאשָׁהּ מִלְמַעְלָה וְעוּקְצָהּ מִלְּמַטָּה, וְתוֹלְשָׁהּ מֵרֹאשָׁהּ הֶעָבֶה תְּחִילָּה וְעוּקְצָהּ נִמְשָׁךְ אַחֲרֶיהָ – מוּתָּר לְפִי שֶׁהַגּוּמָא רְחָבָה מִלְמַעְלָה וְאֵין מְזִיזִין הַקַּרְקַע כְּשֶׁהוּא שׁוֹמְטָהּ. אֲבָל אִם תּוֹלְשָׁהּ מִלְּמַטָּה לְמַעְלָה, שֶׁתַּחְתּוֹנָהּ נָתוּן לְמַעְלָה וְרֹאשׁ עֶלְיוֹנָהּ שֶׁהוּא עָב נָתוּן לְמַטָּה, וְהוּא שׁוֹמְטָהּ מִסּוֹפָהּ לְרֹאשָׁהּ – אָסוּר. לְפִי שֶׁהַגּוּמָא קְצָרָה מִלְמַעְלָה, וּכְשֶׁהוּא תּוֹלְשָׁהּ מֵזִיז הֶעָפָר וּמְטַלְטְלוֹ. וְאַע"ג דְּטִלְטוּל מִן הַצַּד הוּא – שְׁמֵיהּ טִלְטוּל, וְאָסוּר: תָּנֵינָא דְּלָא כְּר"נ. דַּאֲפִילּוּ מִמַּתְנִיתִין שָׁמְעִינַן דְּלָא שְׁמֵיהּ טִלְטוּל, דְּקָתָנֵי: מְנַעְנְעוֹ בְּגוּפוֹ: מֵידָק. דָּיֵיק: חֲדָא חֲדָא. לָאו טוֹחֵן הוּא, אֶלָּא כִּלְאַחַר יָד: דְּקָמְשַׁנֵּי. שֶׁלֹּא בְּרֵחַיִם וְשֶׁלֹּא בִּמְדוֹכָה: לְאַתּוּיֵי ד' אַמּוֹת. מַיִם שֶׁעָלָיו: קָא דָּחֵי כֹּחוֹ. אֶת הַמַּיִם ד' אַמּוֹת: אֶחָד זֶה וְאֶחָד זֶה אָסוּר. זֶה מִשּׁוּם בּוֹנֶה, וְזֶה מִשּׁוּם אַשְׁוּוּיֵי גּוּמוֹת: אֶחָד זֶה וְאֶחָד זֶה מוּתָּר. אֵין דֶּרֶךְ מִתְכַּוֵּין בְּכָךְ, וְקַיְ"ל כְּר"ש: בַּקּוֹרָה. בְּעֵץ הַמּוּטָּל עַל הַקַּרְקַע(ג): אַפּוּמָּא דְּלֶחְיָיא. שֶׁל מָבוֹי, דְּלֵיכָּא הֶכֵּירָא: אוּדְרָא. מוֹכִין שֶׁסּוֹתְמִין בָּהֶן פִּי הַפַּךְ: שִׁישָׁא. פַּךְ: מְכַסְכְּסוֹ. מְשַׁפְשְׁפוֹ: מִבִּפְנִים. דְּלָא מוֹכְחָא מִילְּתָא לְאִיתְחֲזוּיֵי כִּמְלַבֵּן, וּמְלַבֵּן מַמָּשׁ לָא הָוֵי, דְּאֵין נוֹתֵן שָׁם מַיִם: כִּסְכּוּם. דָּמֵי לִמְכַבֵּס: אֲבָל לֹא יָשָׁן. שֶׁקּוֹלְפוֹ, וְהָוֵי מְמַחֵק:

תוספות

הקש שע"ג המטה. בריש פרק "כירה" (דף לו:) פי' מה הוא קש: **הני** פלפלי מידק חדא כו'. פירש ר"ת *בשאלתות דרב אחאי, בפרשת "אמור אל הכהנים" מפרש: דבי"ט מיירי. וקשה לר': דהוה ליה לפרש בהדיא, כיון דבמכילתין לא מיירי אלא בשבת! ועוד: היכי אסר רב יהודה כולי האי בפלפלין? הא אפילו מלח שרינא בפ"ק דביצה (ד' יד.) במדוך של עץ! אלא נראה לרבי דהכא בשבת איירי, ואגב דאיירי בטלטול ע"י שינוי – מייתי ליה הכא. ובכולה שמעתא נמי מייתי מילי דשבת טובא, אע"ג דלא שייכן הכא כולי האי. אבל בי"ט נראה לר"י דשרי בלא שינוי, אפי' במדוך של אבן כשאר תבלין. דתנן בפ"ק דביצה (שם), ב"ה אומר: תבלין נדוכין במדוך של אבן, והמלח במדוך של עץ. ואמרי' בגמרא: דכ"ע מלח בעי שינוי. מ"ט? רב הונא ורב חסדא, חד אמר: כל הקדרות כולן צריכות מלח, ואין כל הקדרות צריכות תבלין. וחד אמר: כולן מפיגין טעמן, ומלח אין מפיגה טעמא. מאי בינייהו? איכא בינייהו דידע מאי בעי בשולי(ד) אי נמי: מוריקא. פירוש: מוריקא אינה מפיגה טעמא. למ"ד משום הפגת טעם – אסור. ולמ"ד משום כל הקדרות כו' – שרי. א"כ פלפלין דהכא – נמי שרי, דאין כל הקדרות צריכות פלפלין. וא"כ (ס"א ואי נמי) למ"ד נמי משום הפגת טעם – פלפלין שרו, דצריך לומר נמי שמפיגים טעמם, מדלא קאמר איכא בינייהו פלפלין. ומיהו, אומר רבי: דאין זה דקדוק, שצריך לפרש שם בע"א דקשיא למ"ד דשרי מוריקא משום דאין כל הקדרות צריכות מוריקא, א"כ יהא מותר לקוצרו ולטוחנו מן המחובר? אע"כ צריך לפרש: יש בו הפגת טעם, ולא כשאר תבלין – להכי שרי, למ"ד אין כל הקדרות כו' כיון דאיכא נמי קצת הפגת טעמא. והשתא אתי שפיר דלקצור אסור. ומהשתא אין ראיה להתיר פלפלין, דשמא אין בהם הפגת טעם כלל. ומיהו, אומר ר"י: דע"כ הם מפיגין טעמם, דתנן בפ"ב דביצה (ד' כג.): ג' דברים רבי אלעזר בן עזריה מתיר וחכמים אוסרין: שוחקין את הפלפלין ברחים שלהן. והיכי הוה שרי רבי אלעזר בן עזריה אי לא מפיגין טעמא? ואין סברא לומר דבהא פליגי רבי אלעזר בן עזריה ורבנן, דמר סבר דמפיגין טעמא ומר סבר אין מפיגין טעמא. אלא, מדשרי ר' אלעזר בן עזריה – ש"מ דמפיגין טעמא. ורבנן דאסרי – משום דברחים שלהם מיחזי טפי כי עובדא דחול. ועוד: תניא בהדיא בתוספתא דביצה, בתר פלוגתא דבית שמאי ובית הלל: הפלפלין כתבלין. על כן נראה לר"י דמותר לכתוש פלפלין ביום טוב, אפילו במדוך של אבן. ומיהו, היכא דידע מאי קדרה בעי בשולי – אסור במדוך של אבן, דלא ידענא כמאן הלכתא, ואזלינן לחומרא. ולא שייך למימר: "בשל סופרים הלך אחר המיקל" היכא דאם הוא קולא בדבר אחד חומרא הוא בדבר אחר. מיהו, במדוך של עץ ממ"נ שרי, אפי' במדוכה של אבן כעין שלנו שקורין מורטיי"ר. כיון שהמדוך של עץ דלא אסרינן התם היכא דידע מאי קדרה בעי בשולי אלא בלא שינוי. ושומין הנדוכים בי"ט – נראה לר"י דשרי, אפי' ידע מאי קדרה בעי בשולי, לפי שמפיגין טעמן יותר מדאי ושרי. מידי דהוי אשוטט ומבשל, דשרי לכ"ע אפילו יודע מאי קדרה בעי בשולי, דנראה הוא דהפגת טעם היינו שתש כח התבלין, ואינם חדין כל כך ויכול לתקן הדבר כשמרבה התבלין. אבל הפגת טעם שומין – אין יכול לתקן, מידי דהוה אשוטט ואופה ומבשל. וגם רוח רעה שורה עליהן [נדה יז.] אם דכן מערב י"ט(ה), אפילו במדוך של אבן או של ברזל שרי. ועוד: דאין נראה שיהו בכלל תבלין, דלא מיקרי תבלין אלא ירקות כעין כמון, אבל שומין ובצלים – אינם בכלל תבלין*): **דילמא** אתי לאשוויי גומות. אע"ג דרבא ס"ל בסוף פ"ב דביצה (ד' כג.) בדבר שאין מתכוין כר"ש – גזרינן, הכא כשיהא עסוק לקנח רגלו ישכח שבת, ויתכוין לאשווי גומות. כעין שמצינו בפ' בתרא דעירובין (ד' קד.): דנשים המשחקות באגוזים ובתפוחים – אסור, דילמא אתי לאשווי גומות. **אודרא** אפומא דשישא. פי' בפ' "מ' שרלים" (לעיל ד' קיא:) [בד"ה האי מסוכרייתא שם ע"א]: כלומר: במתכוין, שמשכחת שבת מחמת שחוק שלהן:

*) [וע"ע תוס' ביצה יד. ד"ה בית הלל]

עין משפט נר מצוה

[נ"ל וכן בשאלתות]

מו א מיי' פכ"ה מהל' שבת הלכה כב סמג לאוין סה טוש"ע או"ח סי' שיא סעיף ח:

מז ב מיי' פכ"ו שם הל' יב סמג שם טוש"ע או"ח סי' שב סעיף ד:

מח ג מיי' פכ"ה שם הל' יד טו סמג שם טוש"ע או"ח סי' שיא סעיף ח:

מט ד מיי' פכ"א שם הלכה כ סמג שם טוש"ע או"ח סי' שכא סעיף ז:

נ ה מיי' פט"ו שם הל' כב סמג שם טוש"ע או"ח סימן שכו סעיף ז:

נא ו מיי' פכ"א שם הל' ב סמג שם טוש"ע או"ח סימן שב סעיף ו:

נב ז מיי' פי"ז שם הל' יז טוש"ע או"ח סי' שסה סעיף ה:

נג ח טוש"ע או"ח סי' של סעיף ד:

[ברא"ש ביצה פ"א סי' כא איתא רב הונא]

נד ט מיי' פכ"ב שם הלכה טו סמג שם טוש"ע שם סי' שב סעיף טז:

נה י מיי' פכ"ב שם הלכה יז סמג שם טוש"ע או"ח סי' שב סעיף ז:

רב נסים גאון

טיט שעל גבי מנעל איכא חספא דרבא משכחת לה בפרק כל הכלים ניטלין בשבת (דף קכד) רבא הוה קאזיל בריסתקא דמחוזא איתוס מסאניה בטינא אתא שמעיה שקל חספא וקא מכפר ליה:

לקמן קמח: ביצה ל.

רבינו חננאל

הקש שע"ג המטה לא ינענעו בידו אבל מנענעו בגופו: אמר רב נחמן האי פוגלא מלמעלה למטה שרי ממטה למעלה אסור. יש מי שאומרים לא יגררה ויש מי שאומרים מותר לגררה ממעלה וכבר פירשנו דברי רב נחמן בפרק כל הכלים. אמר רב יהודה [הני] פלפלי [מידק] חדא חדא בקתא דסכינא שרי למידק. פי' ביו"ט אבל בלדכן אסור דהא אין מפיגין טעמן והוה ליה למידק מעיו"ט. רבא אמר כיון דמשני אפי' טובא והלכתא כרבא ביו"ט ויש מי שמתיר כי האי גוונא אפי' בשבת: טיט שע"ג רגליו הלכתא כמר בריה דרבנא דאסר בין בקרקע ובין בכותל ולא שרי אלא בקורה בלבד. ואמר רבא לא לצדד איניש כובא בארעא דלא אתו לאשויי גומות ואמר רבא לא ליהדוק איניש אודרא בפומיה דשישא דלמא אתו לידי סחיטה. פי' לא ידחוק אדם מוכין שרויין בפי אשישא שמא יבא לידי סחיטה טיט שעל בגדו מכסכסו מבפנים ואין מכסכסו מבחוץ או מגררו בצפורן כסכסו כבר פירשנוהו למעלה. וכל אלו שאמר רבא אסור אחד בשבת ואחד ביו"ט לא שנא וגירור במנעל

מסורת הש"ס

לעיל נ.

לעיל קכג.

[לעיל מג: קכג.]

[נ"ל ואמר]

[לעיל ק: קח.]

הגהות הב"ח

(א) גמ' אמר רבא (לא ליתיב איניש) תא"מ ונ"ב גי' אלפסי לא ליקתמן איניש וע"ל בדף קמח: (ב) שם כובא בארעא דילמא: (ג) רש"י ד"ה בקורה וכו' הקרקע הס"ד ואח"כ מ"ה לא ליצדד לא ילדנו להשוות הס"ד: (ד) תוס' ד"ה הני וכו' מאי בעי בשולי למ"ד משום הפגת טעם שרי אי נמי מוריקא וכו' דשרי ה"ל נמי שרי דהכא נמי אין כל הקדרות: (ה) בא"ד מערב י"ט הלכך אפי' במדוך:

הגהות הגר"א

[א] גמ' ושעל בגדו מגררו בצפורן. נ"ב וכ"ש בגב סכין:

גליון הש"ס

גמ' דילמא אתי לידי סחיטה. עיין לקמן קמח ע"א תוס' ד"ה כבכוס: רש"י ד"ה מבפנים וכו' ומלבן ממש לא הוי דאין נותן שם מים. עיין לקמן דף קמב ריש ע"ב ברש"י ד"ה חייב חטאת וצ"ע:

בַּמֶּה מְגָרְרוֹ? א"ר אַבָּהוּ: בְּגַב סַכִּין. א"ל הַהוּא סָבָא: סַמֵּי דִּידָךְ מִקַּמֵּי הָא דְּתָנֵי רַבִּי חִיָּיא: *[א]אֵין מְגָרְרִין לֹא מִנְעָל חָדָשׁ וְלֹא מִנְעָל יָשָׁן, [ב]וְלֹא יָסוּךְ אֶת רַגְלוֹ שֶׁמֶן וְהוּא בְּתוֹךְ הַמִּנְעָל אוֹ בְּתוֹךְ הַסַּנְדָּל, אֲבָל סָךְ אֶת רַגְלוֹ שֶׁמֶן וּמַנִּיחַ בְּתוֹךְ הַמִּנְעָל אוֹ בְּתוֹךְ הַסַּנְדָּל. וְסָךְ כָּל גּוּפוֹ שֶׁמֶן וּמִתְעַגֵּל ע"ג קָטַבְלְיָא וְאֵינוֹ חוֹשֵׁשׁ. אָמַר רַב חִסְדָּא: לֹא שָׁנוּ אֶלָּא לְצַחְצְחוֹ, אֲבָל לְעַבְּדוֹ – אָסוּר. "לְעַבְּדוֹ" פְּשִׁיטָא! [ג]וְתוּ: לְצַחְצְחוֹ, מִי אִיכָּא מַאן דְּשָׁרֵי? אֶלָּא, אִי אִיתְּמַר הָכִי אִיתְּמַר, אָמַר רַב חִסְדָּא: [ד]לֹא שָׁנוּ אֶלָּא שִׁיעוּר לְצַחְצְחוֹ, אֲבָל שִׁיעוּר לְעַבְּדוֹ – אָסוּר. ת"ר: [ה]לֹא יֵצֵא קָטָן בְּמִנְעָל גָּדוֹל, אֲבָל יוֹצֵא הוּא בְּחָלוּק גָּדוֹל. [ו]וְלֹא תֵּצֵא אִשָּׁה בְּמִנְעָל מְרוּפָּט, וְלֹא תַּחֲלוֹץ בּוֹ. [ז]וְאִם חָלְצָה – חֲלִיצָתָהּ כְּשֵׁרָה. וְאֵין יוֹצְאִין בְּמִנְעָל חָדָשׁ. בְּאֵיזֶה מִנְעָל אָמְרוּ – בְּמִנְעָל שֶׁל אִשָּׁה. תָּנֵי בַּר קַפָּרָא: ל"ש אֶלָּא [ח]שֶׁלֹּא יָצְאָה בּוֹ שָׁעָה אַחַת מִבְּעוֹד יוֹם, אֲבָל יָצְאָה בּוֹ מֵעֶ"שׁ – מוּתָּר. תָּנֵי חֲדָא: [ט]שׁוֹמְטִין מִנְעָל מֵעַל גַּבֵּי אִימּוּס, וְתַנְיָא אִידָךְ: אֵין שׁוֹמְטִין! לָא קַשְׁיָא; הָא – ר' אֱלִיעֶזֶר, הָא – רַבָּנַן. *דִּתְנַן: מִנְעָל שֶׁעַל גַּבֵּי *אִימּוּס, רַבִּי אֱלִיעֶזֶר מְטַהֵר, [י]וַחֲכָמִים מְטַמְּאִים. הָנִיחָא לְרָבָא, *דְּאָמַר: דָּבָר שֶׁמְּלַאכְתּוֹ לְאִיסּוּר, בֵּין לְצוֹרֶךְ גּוּפוֹ בֵּין לְצוֹרֶךְ מְקוֹמוֹ – מוּתָּר, שַׁפִּיר. אֶלָּא לְאַבַּיֵי, דְּאָמַר: *לְצוֹרֶךְ גּוּפוֹ – מוּתָּר, לְצוֹרֶךְ מְקוֹמוֹ – אָסוּר, מַאי אִיכָּא לְמֵימַר? הָכָא בְּמַאי עָסְקִינַן – בְּרָפוּי. דְּתַנְיָא, רַבִּי יְהוּדָה אוֹמֵר: אִם הָיָה רָפוּי – מוּתָּר. טַעְמָא – דְּרָפוּי, הָא לֹא רָפוּי – לֹא. הָנִיחָא לְאַבַּיֵי, דְּאָמַר: דָּבָר שֶׁמְּלַאכְתּוֹ לְאִיסּוּר, לְצוֹרֶךְ גּוּפוֹ – מוּתָּר, לְצוֹרֶךְ מְקוֹמוֹ – אָסוּר, שַׁפִּיר. אֶלָּא לְרָבָא, דְּאָמַר: בֵּין לְצוֹרֶךְ גּוּפוֹ בֵּין לְצוֹרֶךְ מְקוֹמוֹ – מוּתָּר, מַאי אִירְיָא רָפוּי? אֲפִי' לֹא רָפוּי נַמִי! הַהִיא – דְּרַבִּי יְהוּדָה מִשּׁוּם דְּרַבִּי אֱלִיעֶזֶר הוּא; דְּתַנְיָא, ר' יְהוּדָה אוֹמֵר מִשּׁוּם רַבִּי אֱלִיעֶזֶר: אִם הָיָה רָפוּי – מוּתָּר.§

הדרן עלך תולין

נוטל *[כ]אָדָם אֶת בְּנוֹ וְהָאֶבֶן בְּיָדוֹ, וְכַלְכָּלָה וְהָאֶבֶן בְּתוֹכָהּ. וּמְטַלְטְלִין תְּרוּמָה טְמֵאָה עִם הַטְּהוֹרָה וְעִם הַחוּלִּין. רַבִּי יְהוּדָה אוֹמֵר: אַף מַעֲלִין אֶת הַמְדוּמָּע בְּאֶחָד וּמֵאָה.§ **גמ'** אָמַר רָבָא: [ל]הוֹצִיא תִּינוֹק חַי וְכִיס תָּלוּי בְּצַוָּארוֹ – חַיָּיב מִשּׁוּם כִּיס. תִּינוֹק מֵת וְכִיס תָּלוּי לוֹ בְּצַוָּארוֹ – פָּטוּר. "תִּינוֹק חַי וְכִיס תָּלוּי לוֹ בְּצַוָּארוֹ – חַיָּיב מִשּׁוּם כִּיס" וְלִיחַיַּיב נַמִי מִשּׁוּם תִּינוֹק! רָבָא כְּרַבִּי נָתָן סְבִירָא לֵיהּ, *דְּאָמַר: חַי נוֹשֵׂא אֶת עַצְמוֹ. וְלִיבַטֵּל כִּיס לְגַבֵּי תִּינוֹק, מִי לָא תְּנַן: *אֶת הַחַי בְּמִטָּה פָּטוּר אַף עַל הַמִּטָּה, שֶׁהַמִּטָּה טְפֵלָה לוֹ! מִטָּה לְגַבֵּי חַי – מְבַטְּלֵי לֵיהּ, כִּיס לְגַבֵּי תִּינוֹק – לָא מְבַטְּלֵי לֵיהּ. "תִּינוֹק מֵת וְכִיס תָּלוּי לוֹ בְּצַוָּארוֹ – פָּטוּר" וְלִיחַיַּיב מִשּׁוּם תִּינוֹק! רָבָא כְּר"שׁ ס"ל, דְּאָמַר: *כָּל מְלָאכָה שֶׁא"צ לְגוּפָהּ – פָּטוּר עָלֶיהָ. תְּנַן: נוֹטֵל אָדָם אֶת בְּנוֹ וְהָאֶבֶן בְּיָדוֹ. אָמְרִי דְּבֵי רַבִּי יַנַּאי: [מ]בְּתִינוֹק שֶׁיֵּשׁ לוֹ גַּעְגּוּעִין עַל אָבִיו. אִי הָכִי, מַאי

(סנהדרין לה: לעיל צג:)

רש"י

בַּמֶּה מְגָרְרוֹ. לְחָדָשׁ: וְהוּא בְּתוֹךְ הַמִּנְעָל. מִפְּנֵי שֶׁהַמִּנְעָל נֶהֱנֶה מִמֶּנּוּ וְנִמְלָא מְעַבְּדוֹ: מִתְגַּלְגֵּל: מִתְעַגֵּל. קָטַבְלְיָא. עוֹר שָׁלוּק שֶׁעוֹשִׂין מִמֶּנּוּ מִשְׁטָחוֹת לְשֻׁלְחָן וּלְמִטָּה: אֶלָּא לְצַחְצְחוֹ. לֹא שָׁנוּ דְּמוּתָּר לָסוּךְ שֶׁמֶן לְרַגְלוֹ וְנוֹתְנוֹ בְּתוֹךְ הַמִּנְעָל, אֶלָּא שֶׁמִּתְכַּוֵּין לְצַחְצְחוֹ לַמִּנְעָל: וּלְצַחְצְחוֹ מִי שָׁרֵי. בְּמִתְכַּוֵּין, הָא אִיכָּא לְמִיגְזַר אַטּוּ לְעַבְּדוֹ: שִׁיעוּר לְצַחְצְחוֹ. שֶׁלֹּא הָיָה כ"כ שֶׁמֶן הַנִּישּׁוֹף לָעוֹר מִגּוּפוֹ, כְּדֵי לְעַבֵּד לָעוֹר, אֶלָּא לְצַחְצְחוֹ. וּמִיהוּ, אִיהוּ אֲפִי' לְצַחְצֵחַ לֹא מִתְכַּוֵּין: לֹא יֵצֵא. אָדָם קָטָן בְּמִנְעָל שֶׁהוּא גָּדוֹל לוֹ, מִשּׁוּם דְּנוֹפֵל מֵרַגְלוֹ וְאָתֵי לְאַתּוּיֵי: אֲבָל יוֹצֵא בְּחָלוּק גָּדוֹל. דְּלָא נָפֵיל מִינֵּיהּ. וּלְמִישְׁלַף וְאַתּוּיֵי לָא חָיְישִׁינַן, דְּלָא קָאֵי עָרוֹם בַּשּׁוּק: מְרוּפָּט. קָרוּעַ מִלְמַעְלָה, דִּגְנַאי הוּא לָהּ, וְכִי חָיְיכִי עֲלָהּ – שָׁלְפָה וּמַיְיתֵי לָהּ: וְלֹא תַּחֲלוֹץ בּוֹ. לְכַתְּחִלָּה, דְּלָאו נַעַל מְעַלְּיָא הוּא: בְּמִנְעָל חָדָשׁ. כִּדְמְפָרֵשׁ וְאָזֵיל, שֶׁלֹּא יָצְאָה בּוֹ מִבְּעוֹד יוֹם. וּבְאִשָּׁה קָיְימִינַן, דְּאִשָּׁה מַקְפֶּדֶת אִם אֵינוֹ מְכוּוָּן לְמִדַּת רַגְלָהּ. אֲבָל יָצְאָה בּוֹ כְּבָר – הִכִּירָה בּוֹ דִּמְכוּוָּן הוּא לָהּ, אָז אֵינָהּ מַקְפֶּדֶת: אִימּוּס. פורמ"ה: ר' אֱלִיעֶזֶר מְטַהֵר. אַלְמָא לָאו כְּלִי הוּא, וּבְשַׁבָּת נַמִי אָסוּר לְטַלְטְלוֹ: הָנִיחָא לְרָבָא דְּאָמַר. בְּפֶ' "כָּל הַכֵּלִים": דָּבָר שֶׁמְּלַאכְתּוֹ לְאִיסּוּר, בֵּין שֶׁהוּא צָרִיךְ לְהִשְׁתַּמֵּשׁ בְּגוּפוֹ שֶׁל כְּלִי, בֵּין שֶׁאֵינוֹ צָרִיךְ אֶלָּא לִמְקוֹמוֹ – מוּתָּר לְטַלְטְלוֹ, מֵאַחַר שֶׁתּוֹרַת כְּלִי עָלָיו. שַׁפִּיר אִיכָּא לְאוֹקוּמֵי לְהָא דְּתָנֵי "שׁוֹמְטִין" כְּרַבָּנַן; דְּכֵיוָן דִּכְלִי הוּא, וְאִימּוּס נַמִי כְּלִי הוּא, וְאַף עַל גַּב דִּמְלַאכְתּוֹ דְּאִימּוּס לְאִיסּוּר, לְתַקֵּן מִנְעָלִין – מְטַלְטְלִין לְהַאי אִימּוּס מִשּׁוּם צוֹרֶךְ מְקוֹמוֹ, דְּהַיְינוּ מִנְעָל שֶׁהָאִימּוּס נָתוּן לְתוֹכוֹ: אֶלָּא לְאַבַּיֵי. נְהִי נַמִי דְּמִנְעָל שֶׁעַל הָאִימּוּס לְרַבָּנַן כְּלִי הוּא – אִימּוּס מִיהָא מְלַאכְתּוֹ לְאִיסּוּר הוּא, וְזֶה שֶׁשּׁוֹמֵט מִמֶּנּוּ אֶת הַמִּנְעָל – אֵינוֹ צָרִיךְ לְגוּפוֹ שֶׁל אִימּוּס, וְהֵיכִי מְטַלְטֵל לֵיהּ? בְּרָפוּי. שֶׁהַמִּנְעָל נִשְׁמָט מֵאֵלָיו, וְא"צ לְטַלְטֵל הָאִימּוּס: הָא לָאו רָפוּי לֹא. וְע"כ טַעְמָא מִשּׁוּם דְּאִימּוּס אָסוּר לְטַלְטֵל לְצוֹרֶךְ מְקוֹמוֹ: ה"ג: הַהִיא רַבִּי יְהוּדָה מִשּׁוּם רַבִּי אֱלִיעֶזֶר הוּא. כִּי אֲמָרָהּ לֵיהּ ר' יְהוּדָה לְהַהוּא דְּמַפְלִיג בֵּין רָפוּי לְשֶׁאֵינוֹ רָפוּי – אַלִּיבָּא דְּרַבִּי אֱלִיעֶזֶר אֲמַר, דְּאָמַר: מִנְעָל שֶׁעַל הָאִימּוּס לָאו גְּמַר כְּלִי הוּא כָּל זְמַן שֶׁמְּחוּסָּר הוֹצָאָה. וּלְעִנְיַן שַׁבָּת נַמִי, אָסוּר לְטַלְטְלוֹ מִשּׁוּם דְּלָאו כְּלִי הוּא. וְאַשְׁמְעִינַן דְּרָפוּי לָאו מְחוּסָּר הוֹצָאָה הוּא, וּמוּתָּר לְטַלְטְלוֹ. דְּאִילּוּ לְרַבָּנַן, אַף עַל גַּב דְּאֵין רָפוּי – מוּתָּר. דְּטַעְמָא דְּשֶׁאֵין רָפוּי אָסוּר לְרַבִּי יְהוּדָה – לָאו מִשּׁוּם אִימּוּס הוּא, אֶלָּא מִשּׁוּם מִנְעָל גּוּפֵיהּ:

הדרן עלך תולין

נוטל. וְהָאֶבֶן בְּיָדוֹ. בְּחָצֵר, וְלָא אָמְרִי' דִּמְטַלְטֵל לָאֶבֶן: עִם הַטְּהוֹרָה. אַגַּב הַטְּהוֹרָה, וְאַגַּב חוּלִּין. אֲבָל טְמֵאָה בְּאַפֵּי נַפְשָׁהּ – לָאו בַּת טִלְטוּל הוּא: אַף מַעֲלִין אֶת הַמְדוּמָּע. סְאָה תְּרוּמָה שֶׁנָּפְלָה לְק' שֶׁל חוּלִּין, דְּקַיְ"ל דְּעוֹלָה – מוּתָּר לְהַעֲלוֹתוֹ לִסְאָה תְּרוּמָה מֵהֶן בְּשַׁבָּת, וְיִהְיוּ הַחוּלִּין מוּתָּרִין, וְלָא אָמְרִינַן מְתַקֵּן הוּא. וּבִגְמָרָא מְפָרֵשׁ טַעְמָא: **גמ'** חַיָּיב מִשּׁוּם כִּיס. וְלָא מִשּׁוּם תִּינוֹק, כִּדְמְפָרֵשׁ וְאָזֵיל. מִשּׁוּם כִּיס מִיהוּ חַיָּיב, וְלָא אָמְרִינַן אִיהוּ לָא מַפֵּיק לֵיהּ אֶלָּא תִּינוֹק קָא מַפֵּיק לֵיהּ. וּלְקַמֵּיהּ פָּרֵיךְ לָהּ מִמַּתְנִיתִין: פָּטוּר. לְגַמְרֵי, כִּדְמְפָרֵשׁ וְאָזֵיל: מִטָּה לְגַבֵּי חַי מְבַטֵּל לָהּ. לִהְיוֹת טְפֵילָה לוֹ, שֶׁהֲרֵי צָרִיךְ לָהּ: מְלָאכָה שֶׁאֵינָהּ צְרִיכָה לְגוּפָהּ. וּמוֹצִיא מֵת לְקוֹבְרוֹ – מְלָאכָה שֶׁא"צ לְגוּפָהּ הִיא, כִּדְאָמַר בְּ"הַמַּצְנִיעַ"*. וְכִיס שֶׁהָיָה תָּלוּי בְּצַוָּארוֹ לְשַׂחֵק בּוֹ – אַגַּב מְרָרֵיהּ מְבַטֵּל לֵיהּ לְגַבֵּי תִּינוֹק שֶׁמֵּת, וְלָא חָשֵׁיב לֵיהּ הַהִיא שַׁעְתָּא: וְהָאֶבֶן בְּיָדוֹ. מִדְּשָׁרֵי לֵיהּ בְּטִלְטוּל בֶּחָצֵר – ש"מ לָאו כְּמַאן דְּנָקֵיט לָהּ אִיהוּ לָאֶבֶן דָּמֵי, וּלְגַבֵּי כִּיס הֵיכִי מְחַיְּיבַתְּ לֵיהּ? בְּתִינוֹק שֶׁיֵּשׁ לוֹ גַּעְגּוּעִין עַל אָבִיו. שֶׁאִם לֹא יִטְּלֶנּוּ יֶחֱלֶה. וְלָא הֶעֱמִידוּ טִלְטוּל שֶׁלֹּא בְּיָדַיִם בִּמְקוֹם סַכָּנָה, וְאַע"ג דְּלָאו סַכָּנַת נֶפֶשׁ גְּמוּרָה אֶלָּא סַכָּנַת חוֹלִי: אָתֵי

[דף לז:]

תוספות

במנעל מרופט כו' ואם חלצה חליצתה כשרה. וא"ת: אמאי גזרינן בפרק "מצות חליצה" (יבמות דף קב.) מנעל אטו מנעל מרופט כיון דליעבד חליצתה כשרה? ואומר ר"י: דגזרינן אטו מרופט יותר מדאי, שאינו חופה רוב רגלו, דאם חלצה בו – אין חליצתה כשרה.

מ"ר: **ההיא** דרבי יהודה משום דרבי אליעזר היא. מכאן ראיה דרבי יהודה שרי דבר שמלאכתו לאיסור לצורך גופו ולצורך מקומו, כמו שפירשתי בסוף פרק "במה מדליקין" (דף לו:) ד"ה הא ר"י:

הדרן עלך תולין

נוטל. רבא כרבי נתן ס"ל. פירש' בפ' "המצניע"[א] (לעיל ד' לג.):

תינוק מת וכיס תלוי בצוארו פטור. דאגב מרריה מבטיל ליה לכיס. א"נ: תינוק חי הוא צריך לכיס לטייל בו התינוק, אבל תינוק מת – מה צריך לכיס? והוי מלאכה שאינה צריכה לגופה[ב], ופטור, שלא הוציא כדרך המוציאין: **אי** הכי מאי איריא אבן אפי' דינר נמי. אי אמרת בשלמא דתרווייהו מבטל להו, בין אבן ובין דינר, ואין כאן טלטול מוקצה כלל – היינו דנקט אבן. משום דאי נפיל – לא אתי אבוה לאתויי. אבל דינר, אי נפיל אתי אבוה לאתויי – לא. אלא אי אמרינן דתרווייהו לא בטלי, ואפ"ה שרינן איסור מוקצה כשמטלטל התינוק עם האבן משום גיעגועין – בדינר נמי לישתרי. דלא שייך למימר דילמא אתי אבוה לאתויי, דמאי נפקא לן מינה דהשתא נמי דאיכא איסור מוקצה שרינן ליה משום גיעגועין! ומשני: דאע"פ שיש איסור מוקצה כשמטלטל התינוק עם האבן, ושרינן ליה משום גיעגועין – מיהו יש לנו להחמיר במוקצה יותר כשמטלטלו בידים משמטלטלו אגב תינוק. אף על גב דההיא שעתא נמי איכא מוקצה – הלכך גזרינן דילמא נפיל בדינר, ואתי אבוה לאתויי. כך פירש רבינו שמואל:

ונשדינהו

עין משפט נר מצוה

נו א מיי' פכ"ב מהלכות שבת הלכה יח סמג שם טוש"ע או"ח סי' שב סעיף ח:

נז ב ג ד מיי' (שם הל' יח) ופכ"ג הלכה י סמג שם טוש"ע או"ח סי' שכז סעיף ד:

נח ה מיי' פי"ט שם הל' טו סמג שם טוש"ע או"ח סי' שא סעיף ז:

נט ו מיי' וסמג שם טוש"ע או"ח סי' שג סעיף יג:

ס ז מיי' פ"ד מהל' יבום הלכה יט סמג עשין כב טוש"ע אה"ע סימן קסט סעיף כא כב:

סא ח מיי' פי"ט מהל' שבת הלכה טו סמג לאוין סה טוש"ע או"ח סי' שג סעיף יג:

סב ט מיי' פכ"ו מהל' שבת הלכה יב סמג שם טוש"ע א"ח סי' שח סעיף יד:

סג י מיי' פכ"ד מהלכות כלים הלכה ה:

א כ מיי' פכ"ה מהלכות שבת הלכה טז סמג לאוין סה טוש"ע או"ח ס' שט סעיף א:

ב ל מיי' פי"ח מהלכות שבת הלכה יז:

ג מ מיי' פכ"ה שם הל' טז סמג שם טוש"ע א"ח סי' שט סעיף א:

רבינו חננאל

וגירור מנעל הלכה כדתני ר' חייא אין מגררין לא מנעל חדש ולא מנעל ישן. ולא יסוך רגלו שמן והוא בתוך המנעל או בתוך הסנדל. אבל סך את רגלו בשמן ומניחה בתוך המנעל או בתוך הסנדל וסך כל גופו שמן ומתעגל ע"ג קטבליא. פי' ספרה. ואינו חושש ואמר רב חסדא לא שנו אלא אם נתן שמן מעט שיעור לצחצחו אבל שיעור לעבדו אסור. [אבל] לצחצחו אסור וכ"ש לעבדו. וכן הלכה: ת"ר לא יצא קטן במנעל גדול אבל יוצא הוא בחלוק גדול. פי' של אדם גדול ולא תצא אשה במנעל מרופט רפוי שמשתרבב מן הרגל כמו שאמור אם יטעום עבדך את אשר אכל ואת אשר אשתה מיכן [ואמר לקמן] (קלג) ששפתותיהן של זקנים מתרפטות ואין יכול לקפוץ שפתותיו לטעום החך המאכל וכן עוד לא תצא אשה במנעל חדש בשבת אא"כ יצאה בו שעה אחת מבע"י: תני חדא שומטין מנעל מע"ג האימום בשבת. אימום זה דפוס של מנעל ואליבא דרבנן שאומרין מנעל שע"ג אימום כלי הוא ומקבל טומאה. ותניא אידך אין שומטין הא לרבי אליעזר דאמר מנעל ע"ג אימום אינו כלי ואינו מקבל טומאה דתנן בסדר טהרות בבא בתרא פ' סנדל עמקי וכים של שנצות מנעל על האמום ר' אליעזר מטהר וחכמים מטמאין. פי' ר' אליעזר מטהר סבר מנעל על האמום אינו כלי לפיכך אינו מטמא ובשבת אסור לשומטו וחכמים שמטמאין סברי מנעל על האמום כבר נגמרה מלאכתו וכלי הוא לקבל טומאה. וכיון שהוא כלי מותר לשומטו בשבת והלכה כחכמים ואקשינן עלה הניחא לרבא דאמר דבר שמלאכתו לאיסור כגון האימום וכיוצא בו מכלי אומנות מלאכה בין לצורך מקומו מותר לטלטלו שפיר לטעמייהו דרבנן דסברי שומטין מנעל מעל אמום בשבת אלא (לאבין) [לרבא] דאמר לצורך גופו בלבד שרי אמום מאי לצורך גופו איכא דשומטין ומפרקינן הכא במאי עסקינן ברפוי כלומר מנעל זה רפוי הוא על האמום ואינו צריך להגביהו אלא מושך המנעל מעליו ונשאר האמום במקומו דתניא ר' יהודה אומר אם היה רפוי מותר וחזרנו להקשות על זה הפירוק לרבא ופשוטה היא ופריק רבא הא ר' יהודה משום ר' אליעזר היא כלומר אפילו ר' אליעזר שאמר אין שומטין סבר הני מילי כשהוא מהודק דצריך לטלטוליה ולאשמוטיה אבל אם היה רפוי שמושך המנעל והאמום נשאר במקומו מותר לשומטו אבל חכמים סבירא להו אע"פ שאינו רפוי אלא מהודק אם אינו לצורך גופו מותר לטלטלו לצורך מקומו:

הדרן עלך רבי אליעזר אומר תולין

פרק כא נוטל אדם את בנו והאבן בידו כו'. אמר רבא הוציא תינוק חי וכיס תלוי לו בצוארו חייב משום כיס תינוק מת וכיס תלוי לו בצוארו פטור. פי' תינוק מת לקברו והכים עמו כדאמר ריש לקיש

רב נסים גאון

תני בר קפרא לא שנו אלא שלא יצאת בו שעה אחת מבעוד יום. בגמ' דבני מערבא בפרק במה אשה יוצאת (הלכה ג) ובפרק כל ישראל יש להם חלק (הלכה א) גרסי כמה שיעורו והכין גרסי לא ילבש אדם מנעלים וסנדלים

מסורת הש"ס

[תוספ' פ"ד]

כלים פכ"ו מ"ד [סנהדרין סח.]

לעיל קכד.

[נ"ל אימום וכן הוא בערוך ובמשנה דכלים ובמפרשים שעליו]

[לעיל קכג:]

לעיל מז.

לעיל לג. [עירובין קג. יומא סו.]

[לעיל קה. וש"נ]

הגהות הב"ח

(א) תוס' ד"ה נוטל וכו' בפ' המצניע. נ"ב ד' לג בד"ה אבל אדם: (ב) ד"ה תינוק וכו' שאינה צריכה לגופה אי נמי אפי' צריך לו פטור שלא הוציא:

גליון הש"ס

גמ' ולא יסוך את רגלו שמן. וכן איתא בירושלמי ספ"ח דשביעי' לענין שמן שביעית:

אתי לאתויי. וטעמא לאו משום טלטול הוא, דאפילו לאוחזו בידו והתינוק מהלך ברגליו אסר ליה רבא, דילמא נפיל ואתי לאתויי. וכיון דלאו סכנת נפש היא לא שרו ביה טלטול: תניא כוותיה דרבא. דכי נקט לה עליון, כמאן דאפקא תחתון גופיה דמי, ומיחייב: וסנדליו וטבעותיו בידו. בקומצו, שלא כדרך מלבוש: המוציא אדם וכליו עליו. מלובש בהן: וטבעותיו בידיו. באצבעותיו. מדלא תנא בידו, כדנקט רישא: פטור. דבגדיו בטלי לגביה, ועליו הוא פטור כרבי נתן: ואילו הוציאן כמות שהן. שהיה אותו עליון אחוז בהן ולא מלובש – חייב הנושא, והיינו כרבא: תיהוי כלכלה בסים. והיא עצמה תיאסר: מליאה פירות. דעיקר נעשית בסיס לפירות, הלכך אבן מיטלטלת אגב כלי ופירות, שהוא מותר: ונינקטינהו בידים. ילקטם מעל הארץ בידיו, ויחזירם לכלכלה ויטלטלם, ולמה התירו אבן לטלטל אגב כלי ופירות? בפירות המיטנפין. בפירות מבושלין ורכין מאד, כגון תאנים ותותים וענבים, שאם ישליכם לארץ יטנפו: ולנערינהו נעורי. עד שיסתלקו הפירות מן האבן לתוך הכלכלה לבדן, וישליך האבן לבדה בנעורתה: פחותה. שנפחת דופנה או שוליה: וטמאה למעלה. והוא צריך לטהורה, ואינו יכול ליטול הטמאה בידים לפי שהיא מוקצה. לפיכך יטלטל הכל עד השלחן וישליך הכל עליו, ויטול הטהורה: לישדינהו. לארץ כולן: ולינקטינהו. לטהורה ביד, ויחזירה לכלכלה: מתני' לצורך גופו. שצריך לטהורה לגופה לאוכלה. הלכך, אי לאו דטהורה למטה – לא שרו ליה לטלטולי לטמאה, אלא שקיל לטהורה ומנחי לה לשלחן: ברייתא לצורך מקומו. שצריך למקום הכלי, וע"כ כולו הוא צריך לסלקו משם, ושרו ליה רבנן לטלטל האי אטו האי: ומאי דוחקיה כו'. דאיצטריך למימר לא שנו אלא שהטמאה למעלה, לשבקי כדקס"ד, בין שטמאה למעלה בין שטמאה למטה, ולוקמי בצריך למקומו: אלא לצורך גופו. שצריך לכר לשכב עליו שם ולא לסלקו, לפיכך לא התירו לו ליטלו עם המעות, אלא מנערו במקומו. אבל צריך למקום הכר – מטלטל הכל ביחד: ומדסיפא כו' רישא נמי לצורך גופו. הלכך, אי הוה טהורה למעלה – לא הוי שרי ליה לטלטולי טמאה, כדקתני גבי מעות: מנערו ונופלות, ומטלטל היתרא לחודיה: הא קמתקן. שמביאה לידי היתר, וניגזר ביה אטו תיקון שע"י מלאכה: כר"א דאמר תרומה. הואיל וניתנה להעלות אחת שירצה, בעינא מחתא – כאילו מונחת לבדה ואינה מעורבת, הלכך לא קמתקן מידי: מדמעת. זה שנפרד משם, ואוסר ל"ט של חולין כאילו היא תרומה ודאי: וחכ"א אין המדומע מדמע. חולין אחרים אלא לפי חשבון התרומה שבמדומע, כגון: אם תחילתו נדמע ס' של חולין ע"י סאה תרומה, וחזרה סאה ממנו ונפלה לתוך אחרים – לא חשבינן תרומה אלא ס' שבסאה זו, ומדמע עד ל"ט שכנגדו. ואם יש חולין יותר מק' כנגדו – עולה: אימר דשמעת ליה. לר"א דאמר תרומה כמאן דמחתא בעינא: לחומרא. לדמעה כתרומה ודאי: לקולא. דלא ליהוי המעלה אותה בשבת כמתקן: מי אמר. הא ודאי מתקן הוא ע"כ: הוא דאמר. רבי יהודה דמתני' כרבי שמעון, דאמר: לקולא נמי כמאן דמחתא בעינא דמיא: למאה. וראויה להעלותה, ויתכשרו החולין: עד שנפלה אחרת. ועכשיו אין בה חולין כדי להעלותה באחד וק': ר"ש מתיר. קס"ד משום דס"ל קמייתא כמאן דמחתא בעינא דמיא, ונמצאת אחרונה זו נופלת בתוך ק' של חולין: בטל בק'. והוו להו ככולהו חולין. ומיהו, כיון דצריך להעלותה – ע"כ המעלה מתקנו: נותן עיניו. במדומע בצד זה, להעלותו לתרומה, ואוכל בצד אחר. הלכך, הואיל ובלא העלאה מתחיל ואוכל – אין תיקון בהעלאתו:

ס"א אלא

תרומות פ"ה מ"ו תמורה יב. ע"ש

תרומות פ"ה מ"ח

בכורות נט. [ע"ש תוס' ד"ה במחשבה ותוס' מנחות נה. ד"ה במחשבה]

*) [ועי' תוס' חולין נט: ד"ה לא]

מאי איריא אבן, אפילו דינר נמי! אלמה אמר רבא: [א]לא שנו אלא אבן, אבל דינר – אסור! אבן, אי נפלה לה – לא אתי אבוה לאיתויי, דינר, אי נפיל – אתי אבוה לאתויי. תניא כוותיה דרבא: [ב]המוציא כליו מקופלים ומונחים על כתפו, וסנדליו וטבעותיו בידו – חייב. ואם היה מלובש בהן פטור. [ג]המוציא אדם וכליו עליו, וסנדליו ברגליו, וטבעותיו בידיו – פטור. ואילו הוציאן כמות שהן – חייב.§ "כלכלה והאבן בתוכה".§ ואמאי?! תיהוי כלכלה בסים לדבר האסור! אמר רבה בר בר חנה אמר ר' יוחנן: הכא בכלכלה מלאה פירות עסקינן. ולישדינהו לפירי, ונישדי לאבן, [ד]ונינקטינהו בידים! כדרבי אלעי אמר רב: בפירות המיטנפין, [ה]ה"נ – בפירות המיטנפין. ולינערינהו נעורי! *אמר רב חייא בר אשי אמר רבא: [ו]הכא בכלכלה פחותה עסקינן, דאבן גופה נעשית דופן לכלכלה.§ [ז]"מטלטלין תרומה וכו'".§ אמר רב חסדא: לא שנו [ח]אלא שטהורה למטה וטמאה למעלה, אבל טהורה למעלה וטמאה למטה – שקיל ליה לטהורה ושביק ליה לטמאה. וכי טהורה למטה נמי, לישדינהו ולינקטינהו! אמר רבי אלעי אמר רב: [ט]בפירות המיטנפין עסקינן. מיתיבי: "מטלטלין תרומה טמאה עם הטהורה ועם החולין, בין שטהורה למעלה וטמאה למטה, בין שטמאה למעלה וטהורה למטה" תיובתא דרב חסדא! אמר לך רב חסדא: [י]מתניתין – לצורך גופו, ברייתא – לצורך מקומו. מאי דוחקיה דרב חסדא לאוקמי מתניתין לצורך גופו? אמר רבא: מתני' כוותיה דייקא, דקתני סיפא: מעות שעל הכר – מנער את הכר והן נופלות. ואמר רבה בר בר חנה אמר רבי יוחנן: לא שנו אלא לצורך גופו, אבל לצורך מקומו – מטלטלו ועודן עליו. ומדסיפא לצורך גופו – רישא נמי לצורך גופו.§ "רבי יהודה אומר אף מעלין וכו'".§ ואמאי?! [כ]הא קא מתקן! רבי יהודה כר' אליעזר סבירא ליה, דאמר: תרומה בעינא מחתא. *דתנן: סאה תרומה שנפלה לפחות ממאה ונדמעו, ונפל מן המדומע למקום אחר. רבי אליעזר אומר: מדמעת כתרומת ודאי. וחכמים אומרים: [ל]אין המדומע מדמע אלא לפי חשבון. אימר דשמעת ליה לחומרא, לקולא מי שמעת ליה?! אלא הוא דאמר כר"ש, כדתנן: *[מ]סאה תרומה שנפלה למאה, ולא הספיק להגביה עד שנפלה אחרת – הרי זו אסורה. ור"ש מתיר. וממאי? דילמא התם בהא קמיפלגי; דתנא קמא סבר: אע"ג דנפלו בזה אחר זה – כמאן דנפל בבת אחת דמי, והא לחמשין נפלה, והא לחמשין נפלה. ור"ש סבר: קמייתא בטיל במאה, והא תיבטיל במאה וחד! אלא, הוא דאמר כרבי שמעון בן אלעזר. דתניא, ר' שמעון בן אלעזר אומר: *נותן עיניו בצד זה ואוכל מצד אחר. ומי סבר ליה כוותיה? והא

והא

ונשדינהו לפירי ונשדייה לאבן. ואם תאמר: גבי קטן נמי, נשדייה לאבן מידו, ואמאי שרי לטלטולי עם האבן? וי"ל: אם ישליכו מידו – יצעק התינוק ויבכה. וא"ת: מ"מ דלא שרינן לטלטל תינוק אלא כשיש לו גיעגועין, תיבטל אבן אגב תינוק כמו שהיא בטלה אגב כלכלה מלאה פירות! וי"ל: דאינו צריך כל כך טלטול התינוק. וא"ת: אפילו אין הכלכלה מלאה פירות תיבטל האבן אגבה, כי היכי דבטלי בפ"ב דביצה (דף כא:) שיורי הכוס אגב הכוס, אי לאו דאיסורי הנאה נינהו! וי"ל: שאני שיורי, דגריעי יותר מדאי, ובטלו טפי. וכן צ"ל מתוך שמעתא גופה דביצה, כמו שפירשתי לעיל בסוף "כירה" (דף מז. בד"ה הוה):

ונשדינהו לפירי ונשדייה לאבן כו'. וא"ת: מכל מקום נינקטינהו לפירי בידים, ויניח האבן בכלכלה. והא אמרינן לקמן: לא שנו אלא שטהורה למטה וטמאה למעלה, אבל טהורה למעלה וטמאה למטה – שקיל לה לטהורה ושביק לה לטמאה. והיינו על כרחך בידיו, דאי זריק לה בכלי – א"כ גם בטמאה למעלה יכול לזורקה בכלי. אלא שמע מינה דשקיל לה בידיו, וא"כ הכי נמי לישקלינהו לפירי בידיו! וי"ל: דמיירי שפי הכלכלה צר הוא, ואינו יכול להכניס שם ידיו. אי נמי, י"ל: דההיא דלקמן מיירי בתרומה שהיא בכלים קטנים בתוך הקופה, שאין דרך להניח טמאה וטהורה ביחד, אלא בכלים זה בפני עצמו וזה בפ"ע. ולהכי מצי שקיל לטהורה שהיא למעלה בידיו. אבל כלכלה דהכא – אין כאן כלים, ולא מצי נקיט להו בידיו פן יפול לארץ. והשתא לא צריכנא לשינויא קמא דפירות המיטנפין, דהא כיון דאבן עצמה הוי דופן לכלכלה, אפי' הוי שדי לפירות ולאבן, והדר שקיל לפירי ושבק לאבן – לא הוי ליה במאי לאנחינהו, כיון שהכלכלה פחותה*) שהאבן נעשה לה דופן. והא דלא קאמר "אלא" – לפי שלא הוזכר אמורא לעיל. א"נ: השתא יש להעמיד נמי בפירות המיטנפין, דאל"כ נוכל להשליך הסל בקרקע ולהוליך בכלכלה מעט מעט כמה שתוכל להחזיק עד מקום הפחת. מ"ר:

הכא נמי בפירות המיטנפין. וא"ת: אכתי יטלם בידו ויניחם בתוך כלי אחר, או על גבי טבלא או ע"ג סודר כדמוכח בסמוך גבי תרומה. דאמר רב חסדא: לא שנו אלא שטהורה למטה וטמאה למעלה, אבל טהורה למעלה וטמאה למטה – שקיל לטהורה ושביק הטמאה. ואע"ג דמוקמינן נמי בפירות המיטנפין! וי"ל: דהתם מיירי כגון שטהורה מונחת בסלים קטנים בפני עצמה, וכן הטמאה, ואותם סלים מונחים בתוך כלי אחד גדול. והיו סלים של טהורה למעלה מסלים של טמאה, דיכול ליקח סלי טהורה ולהניחם ע"ג קרקע. אבל אם מונחת זו על גב זו בלא שום כלי, כי הכא, שהפירות מונחים ביחד – בהא ודאי לא אמר שביק לה לטמאה ושקיל לה לטהורה. מ"ר:

שנפלה לפחות מק' חולין. מכאן משמע דתרומה עולה באחד ומאה עם האיסור, ורש"י לא פירש כן בפרק "גיד הנשה" (חולין דף צט:) גבי כל איסורין שבתורה במאה, דלפירו' שיטתו לא אתי' מסקנא הכי*):

ד א מיי' וסמג שם וטוש"ע שם:
ה ב ג מיי' פי"ח מהל' שבת הלכה יז ופי"ט הלכה יט:
ו ד טוש"ע א"ח סי' שלה סעיף ה:
ז ה מיי' פכ"ה שם הל' טז טוש"ע א"ח סי' שט סעיף ג:
ח ו מיי' שם טוש"ע שם סעיף ב:
ט ז ח ט י מיי' שם הלכה כ:
י כ (מיי' פכ"ג שם הלכה ט והלכה טו):
יא ל מיי' פי"ג מהל' תרומות הל' ג:
יב מ שם הלכה י:

רבינו חננאל

פוטר היה ר' שמעון במוציא את המת לקברו והלכתא כרבא דקאי כר' שמעון דסבר כל מלאכה שאינה צריכה לגופה פטור עליה. ובפרק יציאות השבת אוקימנא להא דתני זב שיצא בכיס שלו בשבת פטור כר' שמעון דסבר מלאכה שאינה צריכה לגופה פטור ולא תימא מלאכה צריכה לגופה כגון מר לעשות טס וס"ת להגיהו אלא אפי' מר לחפור בו וס"ת לקרות בו מלאכה צריכה לגופה היא וכי לא פטר ר' שמעון אלא מלאכה שאינה צריכה לגופה אבל מלאכה שצריכה לגופה אפי' ר' שמעון מחייב ותניא כרבא המוציא כלים מקופלין ומונחין לו על כתפו וסנדליו וטבעתו בידו חייב. ואם היה מלובש בהן פטור. המוציא אדם וכליו וסנדליו ברגליו וטבעתו בידו פטור. שאלו הוציא כמות שהן חייב והלכתא כוותיה: **מתני'** מטלטלין תרומה טמאה עם הטהור' אוקמה רב חסדא למתניתין הא בשטהורה למטה וטמאה למעלה ואותבוה הא מטלטלין תרומה טמאה עם הטהורה ועם החולין בין טהורה למטה וטמאה למעלה ובין טהורה למעלה וטמאה למטה. ופרקה רב חסדא מתני' לצורך גופו כדי לאכלו. שאינו מותר לו לטלטלו אלא הראוי לו לאכילה. וברייתא לצורך מקומו שצריך לפנות המקום לבית המדרש או לאורחים שמותר לו לטלטל לצורך מקומו. אפילו מה שאינו ראוי לאכילה. ואמרינן מאי דוחקיה דרב חסדא לאוקימנא למתני' לצורך גופו אמר רבא מתניתא קשיתיה דקתני סיפא מעות שעל הכר נוער את הכר והן נופלות ואוקימנא ר' יוחנן לצורך גופו דאי לצורך מקומו אפי' עודן עליו מטלטלן ואמר רב חסדא לא מוקמינן מתניתין בתרי טעמי ומדסיפא לצורך גופו רישא נמי לצורך גופו: **פיסקא** דמתני' ר' יהודה אומר אף מעלין את המדומע באחד ומאה. פי' מדומע תרומה שנפלה בחולין ודימעה מעלין אותה אם יש שם מאה ואחד.

רב נסים גאון

וסנדלים חדשים אלא אם כן הילך בהן מבעוד יום כמה יהא הילוכן בני ביתיה דבר קפרא אמרין (מן דבית רבא דבר קפרא אמרין) מן דבית רבה דבר קפרא עד בית רבה דר' הושעיא צפראי אמרין מכניסתא דבבלאי עד דרתיה דר' חמא בר חנינא טבראי אמרין מן סדרא רבה עד חנותיה דר' הושעיא: **הניחא** לרבא דאמר דבר שמלאכתו לאיסור בין לצורך גופו בין לצורך מקומו מותר שפיר אלא לאביי דאמר דבר שמלאכתו לאיסור לצורך גופו מותר לצורך מקומו אסור מאי איכא למימר. ומשכחת עיקר דיליה בפרק כל הכלים ניטלין בשבת (דף קכג:): **פרק כא נוטל** אדם את בנו ר' יהושע אומר אף מעלין את המדומע באחד ומאה. פירושו שבעת שיפול חלק אחד תרומה בצ"ט חלקים חולין כולן אסורין לישראל וימכרו לכהן ואם יפול חלק במאה חלקים מוציאין

יג א מיי' פכ"ה מהל' שבת הל' יז טוש"ע א"ח סי' שט סעיף ד:
יד ב מיי' פכ"ה שם הל' יח טוש"ע א"ח סי' שב סעיף ט:
טו ג מיי' פ"ב שם הלכה יז טוש"ע א"ח סי' שט סעיף ד:
טז ד ה מיי' פ"ב מהל' י"ט הל' ה ועי' סמג לאוין סה טוש"ע א"ח סי' תקי סעיף ב:
יז ו מיי' פכ"ה מהל' שבת הלכה יז טוש"ע א"ח סי' שט סעיף ה:
יח ז מיי' פ"ה שם הלכה כד סמג שם טוש"ע א"ח סי' שיא סעיף ה:

שאוכל מרובה על הפסולת. פי' בקונטרס: משום דהשתא הוי טרחא יתירא למישקליה לאוכל. ואינו נראה לר"י: דאי משום טרחא הוי – מאי קאמרי בסמוך הכא נמי כיון דאי בעי למישקל לא מישתקיל ליה עד דשקיל ליה לאבן, כפסולת מרובה על האוכל דמי. היכי הוי משום האי טעמא כפסולת מרובה על האוכל? ולכך הוצרך רש"י לפרש דל"ג עד דשקיל ליה לאבן. על כן נראה לר"ת: דטעמא משום דכי אוכל מרובה על הפסולת, הוה פסולת כבטל לגבי רובו, ומותר ליטלו מן האוכל ולזורקו. אבל פסולת מרובה על האוכל – לא בטיל ליה פסולת *לגבי אוכל. והשתא אתי שפיר גירסת הספרים. דגבי חבית נמי, כיון דאי בעי למישקל לא משתקיל ליה(ה) עד דשקיל ליה לאבן – כפסולת מרובה על האוכל דמי. דכיון שאין יכול כלל ליטול מן היין בלא נטילת האבן – לא חשיב כבטיל לגבי האוכל, כיון שהאוכל אינו ניכר כלל, ואינו יכול ליטול הימנו כשהאבן על פי החבית. מ"ר. והא דמוקי לה בספ"ק דבילה (ד' יד: ושם) כגון דנפיש בטרחא וזוטר בשיעורא – *אאוכל קאי, ולא אפסולת. ולפירש"י, קאי אפסולת ולא אאוכל [וע"כ לא יברור הפסולת דנפיש בטירחא]:

לא שנו אלא בשבת. וא"ת: תרתי דרב למה ליה? וי"ל: חדא מכלל חבירתה איתמר. והא לא תקשה: תרתי מתני' למה לי – דהוה אמינא אבן ודאי שרי בשכח שנראה טפי ככיסוי החבית אבל מעות שעל גבי הכר אפילו בשכח ה"א דאסיר:

נ"ל אאוכל קאי שהאוכל נפיש בטרחא ואפ"ה בורר אוכל הואיל וזוטר בשיעורא ולא בטל ליה פסולת

וְהָא מִיפְלִיג פָּלֵיג עִילָּוֵיהּ; דְּתַנְיָא, *רַבִּי יְהוּדָה אוֹמֵר: מַעֲלִין אֶת הַמְדוּמָּע בְּאֶחָד וּמֵאָה, רַבִּי שִׁמְעוֹן בֶּן אֶלְעָזָר אוֹמֵר: נוֹתֵן עֵינָיו בְּצַד זֶה וְאוֹכֵל מִצַּד אַחֵר! דְּרַבִּי יְהוּדָה עֲדִיפָא מִדְּר"ש בֶּן אֶלְעָזָר.§ **מתני'** *א הָאֶבֶן שֶׁעַ"פ הֶחָבִית – מַטָּהּ עַל צִדָּהּ וְהִיא נוֹפֶלֶת. הָיְתָה בֵּין הֶחָבִיּוֹת – מַגְבִּיהַּ, וּמַטָּהּ עַל צִדָּהּ וְהִיא נוֹפֶלֶת. מָעוֹת שֶׁעַל הַכַּר – מְנַעֵר אֶת הַכַּר וְהֵן נוֹפְלוֹת. *ב הָיְתָה עָלָיו *לִשְׁלֶשֶׁת – מְקַנְּחָהּ בִּסְמַרְטוּט, הָיְתָה שֶׁל עוֹר – נוֹתְנִין עָלֶיהָ מַיִם עַד שֶׁתִּכְלֶה.§ **גמ'** אָמַר רַב הוּנָא אָמַר רַב: *ג לֹא שָׁנוּ אֶלָּא בְּשׁוֹכֵחַ, אֲבָל בְּמַנִּיחַ – נַעֲשָׂה בָּסִיס לְדָבָר הָאָסוּר.§ ["הָיְתָה בֵּין הֶחָבִיּוֹת כו'"].§ מַאן תַּנָּא דְּכָל הֵיכָא דְּאִיכָּא אִיסּוּרָא וְהֶיתֵּרָא – בְּהֶיתֵּרָא טָרְחִינַן, בְּאִיסּוּרָא לָא טָרְחִינַן? אָמַר רַבָּה בַּר בַּר חָנָה אָמַר רַבִּי יוֹחָנָן: רשב"ג הִיא, דִּתְנַן: *הַבּוֹרֵר קִטְנִית בְּיו"ט, ב"ש אוֹמְרִים בּוֹרֵר אוֹכֶל וְאוֹכֵל, וּב"ה אוֹמְרִים: ד בּוֹרֵר כְּדַרְכּוֹ בְּחֵיקוֹ וּבְתַמְחוּי. *וְתַנְיָא, אָמַר רשב"ג: ה בַּמֶּה דְּבָרִים אֲמוּרִים – שֶׁהָאוֹכֶל מְרוּבֶּה עַל הַפְּסוֹלֶת, אֲבָל פְּסוֹלֶת מְרוּבָּה עַל הָאוֹכֶל – דִּבְרֵי הַכֹּל בּוֹרֵר אוֹכֶל. וְהָא הָכָא, דְּכִי אוֹכֶל מְרוּבֶּה עַל הַפְּסוֹלֶת דָּמֵי! הָכָא נַמִי, כֵּיוָן דְּאִי בָּעֵי לְמִישְׁקַל לָא מִשְׁתַּקֵּיל לֵיהּ יַיִן עַד דְּשָׁקֵיל לָהּ(א) לָאֶבֶן – כִּפְסוֹלֶת מְרוּבָּה עַל הָאוֹכֶל דָּמֵי.§ הָיְתָה בֵּין הֶחָבִיּוֹת מַגְבִּיהַּ.§ תַּנְיָא, רַבִּי יוֹסֵי אוֹמֵר: הָיְתָה הֶחָבִית מוּנַּחַת בָּאוֹצָר, אוֹ שֶׁהָיוּ כְּלֵי זְכוּכִית מוּנָּחִין תַּחְתֶּיהָ – מַגְבִּיהַּ לְמָקוֹם אַחֵר, וּמַטָּהּ עַל צִדָּהּ וְהִיא נוֹפֶלֶת. וְנוֹטֵל הֵימֶנָּה מַה שֶּׁצָּרִיךְ לוֹ, וּמַחֲזִירָהּ לִמְקוֹמָהּ.§ "מָעוֹת שֶׁעַל הַכַּר".§ אָמַר רַב חִיָּיא בַּר אַשִׁי אָמַר רַב: לֹא שָׁנוּ אֶלָּא בְּשׁוֹכֵחַ, אֲבָל בְּמַנִּיחַ – נַעֲשָׂה בָּסִיס לְדָבָר הָאָסוּר. אָמַר רַבָּה בַּר בַּר חָנָה אָמַר ר' יוֹחָנָן: ו לֹא שָׁנוּ אֶלָּא לְצוֹרֶךְ גּוּפוֹ, אֲבָל לְצוֹרֶךְ מְקוֹמוֹ – מְטַלְטְלוֹ וְעוֹדָן עָלָיו. וְכֵן תָּנֵי חִיָּיא בַּר רַב מִדִּיפְתִּי: לֹא שָׁנוּ אֶלָּא לְצוֹרֶךְ גּוּפוֹ, אֲבָל לְצוֹרֶךְ מְקוֹמוֹ – מְטַלְטְלוֹ וְעוֹדָן עָלָיו.§ "מָעוֹת שֶׁעַל הַכַּר מְנַעֵר וכו'".§ א"ר אוֹשַׁעְיָא: שָׁכַח אַרְנָקִי בֶּחָצֵר – מַנִּיחַ עָלֶיהָ כִּכָּר אוֹ תִּינוֹק, וּמְטַלְטְלָהּ. אָמַר רַב יִצְחָק: שָׁכַח לְבֵינָה בֶּחָצֵר – מַנִּיחַ עָלֶיהָ כִּכָּר אוֹ תִּינוֹק, וּמְטַלְטְלָהּ. אָמַר רַבִּי יְהוּדָה בַּר שֵׁילָא אָמַר ר' אַסִּי: פַּעַם אַחַת שָׁכְחוּ דִּסְקַיָּא מְלֵאָה מָעוֹת בְּסִרְטְיָא, וּבָאוּ וְשָׁאֲלוּ אֶת ר' יוֹחָנָן, וְאָמַר לָהֶן: הַנִּיחוּ עָלֶיהָ כִּכָּר אוֹ תִּינוֹק וְטַלְטְלוּהָ. אָמַר מָר זוּטְרָא: הִלְכְתָא כְּכָל הָנֵי שְׁמַעְתָּתָא בְּשׁוֹכֵחַ. רַב אַשִׁי אָמַר: אֲפִילּוּ שָׁכַח נַמִי [לֹא], ז וְלֹא אָמְרוּ *כִּכָּר אוֹ תִּינוֹק אֶלָּא לְמֵת בִּלְבַד. אַבָּיֵי מַנַּח כַּפָּא אַכֵּיפֵי. רָבָא מַנַּח סַכִּינָא אַבַּר יוֹנָה וּמְטַלְטְלָהּ. אָמַר רַב יוֹסֵף: כַּמָּה חֲרִיפָא שְׁמַעְתָּתָא דְּדַרְדְּקֵי! אֵימַר דְּאָמוּר רַבָּנַן בְּשׁוֹכֵחַ, לְכַתְּחִילָּה מִי אָמוּר?! אָמַר אַבָּיֵי: אִי לָאו *דְּאָדָם חָשׁוּב אֲנָא, כַּפָּא אַכֵּיפֵי לָמָּה לִי? הָא חֲזוּ לְמִיזְגָּא עֲלַיְיהוּ! אָמַר רָבָא: אֲנָא, אִי לָאו דְּאָדָם חָשׁוּב אֲנָא – סַכִּינָא אַבַּר יוֹנָה לָמָּה לִי? הָא חֲזִי לִי לְאוּמְצָא! טַעְמָא – דַּחֲזִי לְאוּמְצָא, הָא לָא חֲזֵי לְאוּמְצָא – לָא. *לֵימָא מְסַיַּיע לֵיהּ לְרַבָּה, דְּרָבָא כְּרַבִּי יְהוּדָה סְבִירָא לֵיהּ? וְהָאָמַר רָבָא לְשַׁמָּעֵיהּ: טְוֵי לִי בַּר אַוְוזָא, וּשְׁדֵי מֵעֵיהּ לְשׁוּנְרָא! הָתָם

ה. וְאָמַר: כֵּיוָן דְּאֶפְשָׁר לֵיהּ לְמֵיעֲבַד עוֹנֶג שַׁבָּת בכה"ג, לִיתֵּן עֵינָיו בְּצַד זֶה וְלֶאֱכוֹל בְּצַד אַחֵר – אֵין מַעֲלִין: דְּרַבִּי יְהוּדָה עֲדִיפָא. מֵיקַל טְפֵי פּוּרְתָּא, וְאָמַר: כֵּיוָן דְּיָכוֹל לִיתֵּן (עָלָיו) עֵינָיו בְּצַד זֶה וְלֶאֱכוֹל בְּצַד זֶה – לָא הָוֵי מְתַקֵּן בְּהַעֲלָאָתוֹ, וּמַעֲלִין: **מתני'** מַטָּהּ עַל צִדָּהּ. מַטֶּה חָבִית עַל לִדָּהּ אִם צָרִיךְ לִיטּוֹל מִן הַיַּיִן, וְהָאֶבֶן נוֹפֶלֶת. וְלֹא יְטַלְטְלֶנָּה בְּיָדַיִם: הָיְתָה בֵּין הֶחָבִיּוֹת. וְיָרֵא שֶׁלֹּא תִּפּוֹל הָאֶבֶן עַל הֶחָבִיּוֹת וְיִשָּׁבְרוּ: מַגְבִּיהַּ. לֶחָבִית כּוּלָּהּ, וּמְסַלְּקָהּ מִבֵּין הֶחָבִיּוֹת, וְשָׁם מַטָּהּ עַל לִדָּהּ: לִשְׁלֶשֶׁת. שׁוּם דָּבָר מִיאוּס, כְּגוֹן רוֹק אוֹ צוֹאָה: מְקַנְּחָהּ בִּסְמַרְטוּט. וְלֹא יִתֵּן עָלֶיהָ מַיִם. דִּסְתָם כַּר שֶׁל בֶּגֶד הוּא, וּבֶגֶד – שְׁרִיָּיתוֹ בְּמַיִם הוּא כִּבּוּסוֹ: הָיְתָה. לִשְׁלֶשֶׁת זוֹ עַל כַּר שֶׁל עוֹר, דְּלָאו בַּר כִּיבּוּס הוּא: נוֹתֵן עָלֶיהָ מַיִם עַד שֶׁתִּכְלֶה. וּמִיהוּ, כִּיבּוּס מַמָּשׁ לֹא(ב). וְהוֹאִיל וּסְתָם כָּרִים וּכְסָתוֹת רַכִּים נִינְהוּ, שַׁיָּיךְ לְמֵימַר בְּהוּ כִּיבּוּס בְּעוֹרוֹת רַכִּין. וּמִיהוּ, שְׁרִיָּיתָן לֹא זֶהוּ כִּבּוּסָן. וְכֵן מְפוֹרָשׁ בִּזְבָחִים בְּפֶרֶק "דַּם חַטָּאת": **גמ'** לֹא שָׁנוּ. מַטָּהּ עַל לִדָּהּ דְּחָבִית: אֶלָּא בְּשׁוֹכֵחַ. שֶׁשָּׁכַח הָאֶבֶן עָלֶיהָ בֵּין הַשְּׁמָשׁוֹת, וְלֹא מִדַּעַת: נַעֲשָׂה חָבִית בָּסִיס לְדָבָר הָאָסוּר. וְאָסוּר לְהַטּוֹתָהּ, שֶׁאַף הֶחָבִית מוּקְצָה: מַאן תַּנָּא. דְּמַתְנִיתִין, דְּקָתָנֵי: מַגְבִּיהַּ וּמַטָּהּ עַל לִדָּהּ. דְּאִית לֵיהּ, דְּכִי טָרַח – מִטְרַח בֶּחָבִית דְּהָוֵי הֶיתֵּרָא, וְלֹא יִטּוֹל הָאֶבֶן מַמָּשׁ דְּהָוֵי אִיסּוּרָא. וְאַע"ג דְּהַשְׁתָּא נַמִי אֶבֶן מִטַּלְטֵל בַּהֲדֵי חָבִית: רַבָּן שִׁמְעוֹן. אַלִּיבָּא דְּבֵית הִלֵּל: בּוֹרֵר אוֹכֶל וְאוֹכֵל. הַמַּאֲכָל יִטּוֹל, וְהַפְּסוֹלֶת יִשָּׁאֵר בַּכְּלִי: בּוֹרֵר כְּדַרְכּוֹ. נוֹטֵל פְּסוֹלֶת וּמַנִּיחַ אוֹכֶל, אִם יִרְצֶה: כְּשֶׁהָאוֹכֶל מְרוּבֶּה עַל הַפְּסוֹלֶת. דְּאִי שָׁקֵיל אוֹכֶל מַפֵּישׁ בְּטִרְחָא: דִּבְרֵי הַכֹּל בּוֹרֵר אוֹכֶל. דִּבְהֶיתֵּירָא טָרַח וְלֹא בְּאִיסּוּרָא. וּפָרְכִינַן, וְהָא הָכָא דְּמַתְנִיתִין, דְּאוֹכֶל מְרוּבֶּה עַל הַפְּסוֹלֶת, וְכִי מַגְבִּיהַּ הָאֶבֶן עִם הֶחָבִית טָרַח טְפֵי, וַהֲוָה(ג) לְמִשְׁקַל פְּסוֹלֶת כְּר"ש: כֵּיוָן דְּאִי בָּעֵי לְמִשְׁקַל. לְכוּלֵּי יַיִן מִן הֶחָבִית לָא מִשְׁתַּקֵּיל לֵיהּ יַיִן שֶׁבְּשׁוּלֶיהָ עַד דְּשָׁקֵיל וּמַגְבַּהּ לָהּ לֶחָבִית – כִּפְסוֹלֶת מְרוּבָּה דָּמֵי. דְּאִי בִּתְחִלָּתוֹ לָא מַגְבַּהּ לָהּ לֶחָבִית – סוֹף סוֹף מִיבָּעֵי לֵיהּ לְאַגְבּוּהָהּ תּוּ לֶחָבִית. הִלְכָּךְ הָוֵה לֵיהּ מַפֵּישׁ בְּטִרְחָא: ה"ג: לָא מִשְׁתַּקֵּל לֵיהּ(ד) עַד דְּשָׁקֵיל לָהּ. וְל"ג: עַד דְּשָׁקֵיל לָהּ לָאֶבֶן: הָיְתָה הֶחָבִית מוּנַּחַת בָּאוֹצָר. כְּלוֹמַר: בְּמָקוֹם מְכוּנָּס, שֶׁאוֹצְרִין שָׁם חָבִיּוֹת הַרְבֵּה, וְדוֹאֵג שֶׁמָּא יְטַלֶּנָּה וְתִפּוֹל הָאֶבֶן עַל הֶחָבִית שֶׁאֶצְלָהּ: לֹא שָׁנוּ. דִּמְנַעֵר: נַעֲשָׂה. הַכַּר בָּסִיס לַמָּעוֹת, וְאַף הַכַּר אָסוּר בְּטִלְטוּל: לֹא שָׁנוּ. דִּמְנַעֲרָהּ וְאֵינוֹ מְטַלְטְלָהּ בְּעוֹדָן עָלֶיהָ: אֶלָּא שֶׁצָּרִיךְ לְגוּפוֹ. שֶׁל כַּר, לִשְׁכַּב עָלָיו. הִלְכָּךְ בְּנִיעוּר סַגְיָא, וְשָׁדֵי לְהוּ בְּאַתְרַיְיהוּ: אֲבָל צָרִיךְ לִמְקוֹמוֹ. שֶׁל כַּר – מְטַלְטְלוֹ עִם הַמָּעוֹת לְמָקוֹם אַחֵר: דִּסְקַיָּא מְלֵאָה מָעוֹת. גָּרְסִינַן: בְּסִרְטְיָא. רה"ר: הַנִּיחוּ עָלֶיהָ כִּכָּר אוֹ תִּינוֹק. דְּלִישְׁתְּרֵי לְטַלְטְלָהּ אַגַּבַּיְיהוּ תּוֹךְ ד' אַמּוֹת, וְטַלְטְלוּהָ פָּחוֹת פָּחוֹת מִד' אַמּוֹת, אוֹ בִּמְחִיצָּה שֶׁל בְּנֵי אָדָם, כִּדְאָמְרִי' בְּעֵירוּבִין (דף מג:): בְּשׁוֹכֵחַ. אֲבָל בְּמַנִּיחַ מִדַּעַת מֵעֶרֶב (יוֹם) שַׁבָּת – לֹא הִתִּירוּ לוֹ לְטַלְטְלָהּ ע"י כִּכָּר אוֹ תִּינוֹק: אֶלָּא לְמֵת. מִשּׁוּם כְּבוֹד הַבְּרִיּוֹת, כְּשֶׁמּוּטָּל בַּחַמָּה: אַבָּיֵי מַנַּח כַּפָּא אַכֵּיפֵי. מַנִּיחַ תַּרְוָוד עַל הָעוֹמָרִים, לְטַלְטְלָן אַגַּב תַּרְוָוד: אַבַּר יוֹנָה. חַי [בְּלֹא] מְלִיחַ: חֲרִיפָא שְׁמַעְתָּתָא דְּדַרְדְּקֵי. סְבוּרִים הֵם שֶׁהֵם חֲרִיפִים: אֵימַר דְּאָמוּר רַבָּנַן. בְּאַרְנָקִי וְדִסְקַיָּא מַנִּיחַ עָלֶיהָ כִּכָּר אוֹ תִּינוֹק – בִּשְׁכָחָה, וּבִמְקוֹם הַפּוּרְפָּה, וּמִשּׁוּם הֶפְסֵד מָמוֹן: אָמַר אַבָּיֵי. אֲנָא שַׁפִּיר מְטַלְטַלְנָא כֵּיפֵי, וַאֲפִילּוּ בְּלֹא תַּרְוָוד: אִי לָאו דְּאָדָם חָשׁוּב אֲנָא. וַאֲנָא מַחְמִיר עַל עַצְמִי שֶׁלֹּא יִלְמְדוּ מִמֶּנִּי לְהָקֵל בָּאִסּוּרִין: כַּפָּא אַכֵּיפֵי לָמָּה לִי. בְּלָאו כַּפָּא נַמִי שָׁרֵי לְטַלְטְלִינְהוּ, דְּהָא חֲזוּ לְמִיזְגָּא עֲלַיְיהוּ: לְאוּמְצָא. לְאוֹכְלוֹ חַי בְּשַׁבָּת. שֶׁיֵּשׁ בְּנֵי אָדָם שֶׁדַּעְתָּן יָפֶה וְאוֹכְלִים בָּשָׂר חַי, וְקָרוּ לָהּ אוּמְצָא: הָא לָא חֲזֵי לְאוּמְצָא לָא. וְאַע"ג דַּחֲזוּ לְשׁוּנְרָא, דְּאָמְרִינַן: מוּכָן לְאָדָם לָא הָוֵי מוּכָן לִכְלָבִים: כְּר' יְהוּדָה. בְּמַסֶּכֶת בֵּיצָה (דף ו:): טְוֵי לִי בַּר אַוְוזָא. בְּיוֹם טוֹב: וּשְׁדֵי מֵעֵיהּ לְשׁוּנְרָא. אַלְמָא: מְטַלְטֵל לְהוּ מִשּׁוּם שׁוּנְרָא. וְאַע"ג דְּהָאִידָנָא לָא חֲזֵי לְאָדָם, דְּלָאו אוֹרַח אַרְעָא לְמֵיכְלָא בְּיוֹם טוֹב. וּמִיהוּ, מֵאֶתְמוֹל לְאָדָם הֲווּ קָיְימִי: הָתָם

[תוספ' פט"ו] [לעיל קכה:] זבחים צג: [פי' צואת תרנגולים. ערוך] [לעיל קכה: ע"ש] ביצה יד: ג"ז שם ע"ש [לעיל ל: מג:] [לעיל נא. וש"נ] ב"ק נ:

רבינו חננאל

ואקשינן אמאי והא קא מתקן טיבלא תמצא עושה מעשה בשבת ופרקי' ר' יהודה דאמר כי מעלין את המדומע כר' אליעזר סבירא ליה דאמר תרומה בעינא מחתא. פי' תרומה שנפלה בחולין אין מחשבין אותה שנתערבה בכל החולין אלא כאילו נתונה במקום אחד היא וכשנוטל ממאה ואחד סאין סאה אנן אומרין כי היא היא התרומה. אבל שאר החולין מתוקנין היו מקודם. ולא היה אסור אלא זו הסאה שנוטלה במקום התרומה שנפלה בלבד. דתנן סאה של תרומה שנפלה לפחות ממאה ונדמעו ונפל מן המדומע למקום אחד. ר' אליעזר אומר מדומע כתרומה ודאי. פי' סאה תרומה שנפלה לתוך חמשים סאין חולין ועוד נפלה מאלו החמשים ואחד סאין סאה אחת לששים סאה חולין ר' אליעזר סבר הכל אסור [illegible] וששים האחרונים שאני אומר הסאה של תרומה עצמה היא שנפלה בששים האחרונים לפי שאין המדומע עולה אלא בא' ומאה ואין באחד מהן מאה בעת נפילתה בהן וחכ"א אין המדומע מדמע אלא לפי חשבון פי' סאה שנפלה לחמשים סאין ונפלה מאלו החמשים סאין לפחות מחמשים מדמעת אבל אם נפלה סאה לששים סאין עולה לפי שאילו היתה סאה במאה סאין ואחת היתה עולה וחזרנו עוד להקשות אימור דשמעת ליה לר' אליעזר שמחשב מכלל נ"א סאין הללו הסאה האחת שנפלה לס' סאין אחרות תרומה כולה. ומדמעת עד מאה ואחת לחומרא לקולא לתקן בשבת מי שמעת ליה ולא עמדה ופירקנן פירוק אחר והוא ר' יהודה סבר לה כר' שמעון דתנן סאה של תרומה שנפלה למאה חולין ונדמעו ולא הספיק להגביהה עד שנפלה האחרת הרי זו אסורה ור' שמעון מתיר ת"ק סבר כיון שלא הגביהה נמצא שנפלו ב' סאין למאה סאין ואין עולין כי פחות ממאה הן. ור' שמעון סבר מאותה העת שנפלה סאה תרומה למאה חולין הותרו המאה. ונשארו חולין בהכשרן. וסאה אחת בתוכן תרומה התרומה היא אסורה בלבד וכשנפלה אחר כן עוד סאה אחרת תרומה עליהן על מאה חולין נפלה ועולה כו' ופרקי' לה ודברים פשוטין הן. והדרנן ומוקמינן ר' יהודה דמתני' כר' שמעון בן אלעזר דאמר נותן עיניו בצד זה כלומר מחשב להוציא התרומה מצד זה ואוכל מצד אחר ש"מ כי התרומה מחתא במקום אחד. ואקשינן וכי ר' יהודה בר' שמעון בן אלעזר סבירא ליה והא מפלג פליג עליה דתניא ר' יהודה אומר מעלין את המדומע באחד ומאה ר' שמעון אומר נותן עיניו בצד זה ואוכל מצד זה ומפרקי' דר' יהודה עדיפא שר' יהודה מתיר אפי' להעלותה ור' שמעון אינו מתיר להעלותה אלא לתת עיניו בצד זה ולאכול מצד זה. ותרווייהו סבירא להו סאה תרומה שנפלה למאה חולין בעת שנפלה מותרין הן ובתקונן הן ואין צריכין תיקון אלא סילוק סאה אחת מהן בלבד במקום התרומה: **פיסקא** האבן שעל

הגהות הב"ח

(א) גמ' עד דשקיל לה כפסולת כצ"ל ותיבת לאבן נמחק: (ב) רש"י ד"ה נותן וכו' כיבוס ממש לא להכי: (ג) ד"ה דברי הכל וכו' והוה ליה למשקל: (ד) ד"ה ה"ג לא משתקיל ליה יין עד: (ה) תוס' ד"ה שאוכל וכו' לא משתקיל ליה יין עד:

גליון הש"ס

גמ' מאן תנא דכל היכא דאיכא איסורא והיתרא. עיין לעיל דף נא ע"ב תוס' ד"ה אינו נוטל:

רב נסים גאון

מוציאין חלק אחד והשאר מותר לישראל ותמצא עיקר דבר זה בסיפרי מכל חלבו את מקדשו ממנו שאם נפל לתוכו הרי זה מקדשו מיכן אמרו תרומה עולה באחד ומאה אין לי אלא תרומה טהורה ותמצא במשנת תרומות ותוספות תרומות מזה הענין הרבה ועיקרו מה שהזכרנו' ובגמ' דערלה בפרק ב' (ירושלמי שם הלכה א) מניין שהן עולין אמר ר' יונה כתיב (במדבר יח) מכל חלבו את מקדשו ממנו דבר שאתה מרים ממנו שאם יפול לתוכו הרי זה מקדשו וכמה הוא אחד ממאה ואיתא נמי בפרק ד' דתרומות התרומה צריך להרים כמה שהוא במשנה במסכת ערלה בראש פרק ב' התרומה ותרומת מעשר של דמאי מצטרפין זה עם זה ואינו צריך להרים וכו' וטעמו של דבר לפי שהתרומות והחלה והביכורים הם נכסי כהן וצריך להרים תרומה ויתנה ואם לא ירים ויתן לו הרי זה גוזל ממנו ואין להם בעלים שראויין להם לפיכך אינו צריך להרים

הָתָם כֵּיוָן דְּמַסְרַח – דַּעֲתֵיהּ עִילָּוֵיהּ מֵאֶתְמוֹל. הָכִי נַמִי מִסְתַּבְּרָא, דְּרָבָא כְּר' יְהוּדָה סְבִירָא לֵיהּ. *דְּדָרַשׁ רָבָא: אִשָּׁה לֹא תִּכָּנֵס לְבֵית הָעֵצִים לִיטּוֹל מֵהֶן אוּד, וְאוּד שֶׁנִּשְׁבַּר – אָסוּר לְהַסִּיקוֹ בְּיוֹם טוֹב, לְפִי *שֶׁמַּסִּיקִין בְּכֵלִים וְאֵין מַסִּיקִין בְּשִׁבְרֵי כֵלִים. שְׁמַע מִינָּהּ.§

מתני' *ב"ש אוֹמְרִים: *מַעֲבִירִין מֵעַל הַשֻּׁלְחָן עֲצָמוֹת וּקְלִיפִּין, וּב"ה אוֹמְרִים: *מְסַלֵּק אֶת הַטַּבְלָא כּוּלָּהּ וּמְנַעֲרָהּ. מַעֲבִירִין(א) מִלִּפְנֵי הַשֻּׁלְחָן פֵּירוּרִין פָּחוֹת מִכַּזַּיִת, וְשֵׂעָר שֶׁל אֲפוּנִין, וְשֵׂעָר עֲדָשִׁים – מִפְּנֵי שֶׁהוּא מַאֲכַל בְּהֵמָה. סְפוֹג, אִם יֵשׁ לוֹ עוֹר בֵּית אֲחִיזָה – מְקַנְּחִין בּוֹ, וְאִם לָאו – אֵין מְקַנְּחִין בּוֹ(ב). *(וַחֲכָמִים אוֹמְרִים): בֵּין כָּךְ וּבֵין כָּךְ *נִיטָּל בְּשַׁבָּת, וְאֵינוֹ מְקַבֵּל טוּמְאָה.§ **גמ'** *אָמַר רַב נַחְמָן: אָנוּ אֵין לָנוּ אֶלָּא ב"ש כְּרַבִּי יְהוּדָה, וּב"ה כְּרַבִּי שִׁמְעוֹן.§ "מַעֲבִירִין(ג) מִלִּפְנֵי הַשֻּׁלְחָן פֵּירוּרִין".§ מְסַיֵּיעַ לֵיהּ לְר' יוֹחָנָן, *דְּאָמַר רַבִּי יוֹחָנָן: פֵּירוּרִין שֶׁאֵין בָּהֶן כַּזַּיִת – אָסוּר לְאַבְּדָן בַּיָּד.§ "שֵׂעָר שֶׁל אֲפוּנִין".§ מַנִּי? ר"ש הִיא, דְּלֵית לֵיהּ מוּקְצֶה. אֵימָא סֵיפָא: סְפוֹג, אִם יֵשׁ לוֹ בֵּית אֲחִיזָה – מְקַנְּחִין בּוֹ, וְאִם לָאו – אֵין מְקַנְּחִין בּוֹ. אֲתָאן לְר' יְהוּדָה, דְּאָמַר "דָּבָר שֶׁאֵין מִתְכַּוֵּין – אָסוּר"! בְּהָא אֲפִילּוּ ר"ש מוֹדֶה, *דְּאַבַּיֵי וְרָבָא דְּאָמְרִי תַּרְוַיְיהוּ: מוֹדֶה ר"ש בִּפְסִיק רֵישֵׁיהּ וְלֹא יָמוּת. הָנֵי גַּרְעִינִין דְּתַמְרֵי אַרְמָיָיתָא שְׁרוּ לְטַלְטוֹלִינְהוּ, הוֹאִיל וְחַזְיָין אַגַּב אִמָּן. וּדְפַרְסָיָיתָא – אָסוּר. שְׁמוּאֵל מְטַלְטֵל לְהוּ אַגַּב רִיפְתָּא.§ (שרנ"ם שפ"ז סִימָן).§ שְׁמוּאֵל לְטַעְמֵיהּ, *דְּאָמַר שְׁמוּאֵל: עוֹשֶׂה אָדָם כָּל צְרָכוֹ בְּפַת. *רַבָּה מְטַלְטֵל לְהוּ אַגַּב לֶקְנָא דְּמַיָּא. רַב הוּנָא בְּרֵיהּ דְּרַב יְהוֹשֻׁעַ עָבֵיד לְהוּ כִּגְרָף שֶׁל רְעִי. א"ל רַב אַשִׁי לְאַמֵּימָר: *וְכִי עוֹשִׂין גְּרָף שֶׁל רְעִי לְכַתְּחִילָּה? רַב שֵׁשֶׁת זָרֵיק לְהוּ בְּלִישָּׁנֵיהּ. רַב פַּפָּא זָרֵיק לְהוּ אֲחוֹרֵי הַמִּטָּה. *אָמְרוּ עָלָיו עַל רַבִּי זְכַרְיָה בֶּן אַבְקוּלָס שֶׁהָיָה מַחֲזִיר פָּנָיו אֲחוֹרֵי הַמִּטָּה וְזוֹרְקָן.§

הדרן עלך נוטל אדם את בנו

רש"י

הָתָם כֵּיוָן דְּמַסְרַח. מֵעַיָּיא, אִי מַמְנַע לֵיהּ עַד אוּרְתָּא: מֵאֶתְמוֹל דַּעְתֵּיהּ עֲלֵיהּ. לְשׁוּנְרָא, וּבֵין הַשְּׁמָשׁוֹת נַמִי מוּכָן לַבְּהֵמָה הֲוָה: אוּד. פורגו"ן דִּסְתָם עֵצִים לְהַסָּקָה נִיתְּנוּ, וְלֹא לְטִלְטוּל כְּלִי: וְאוּד שֶׁנִּשְׁבַּר. בְּיו"ט: בְּשִׁבְרֵי כֵלִים. שֶׁנִּשְׁבְּרוּ הַיּוֹם, דְּהָווּ לְהוּ נוֹלָד: ש"מ. דִּכְרַבִּי יְהוּדָה סְבִירָא לֵיהּ, דְּאִית לֵיהּ מוּקְצֶה:

מתני' מַעֲבִירִין. בְּיָדַיִם מֵעַל הַשֻּׁלְחָן: עֲצָמוֹת. קָשִׁין, שֶׁאֵינָן רְאוּיִין לְכֶלֶב: וּקְלִיפִּין. שֶׁל אֱגוֹזִים, דְּלֵית לְהוּ לְב"ש מוּקְצֶה: וּב"ה אוֹמְרִים מְסַלֵּק אֶת הַטַּבְלָא. שֶׁיֵּשׁ תּוֹרַת כְּלִי עָלֶיהָ, אֲבָל לֹא יְטַלְטֵל הַקְּלִיפִּין בְּיָדַיִם, כְּרַבִּי יְהוּדָה: מַעֲבִירִין מֵעַל הַשֻּׁלְחָן. סְתָמָא הִיא: פֵּירוּרִין פָּחוֹת מִכַּזַּיִת. וְכ"שׁ כַּזַּיִת, כִּדְמְפָרֵשׁ טַעְמָא שֶׁהֵם מַאֲכַל בְּהֵמָה: וְשֵׂעָר שֶׁל אֲפוּנִין. שַׂרְבִּיטִין שֶׁל קִטְנִית שֶׁהַקִּטְנִית גָּדֵל בָּהֶם: אֲפוּנִין. יי"ש: עוֹר בֵּית אֲחִיזָה. [בֵּית אֲחִיזָה] שֶׁל עוֹר שֶׁאוֹחֲזוּ בּוֹ: מְקַנְּחִין בּוֹ. טַבְלָא: אֵין מְקַנְּחִין בּוֹ. שֶׁכְּשֶׁאוֹחֲזוֹ נִסְחָט בֵּין אֶצְבְּעוֹתָיו: נִיטָּל בְּשַׁבָּת. כְּשֶׁהוּא נָגוּב: וְאֵינוֹ מְקַבֵּל טוּמְאָה. דְּאֵינוֹ לֹא כְּלִי עֵץ וְלֹא בֶּגֶד וְלֹא שַׂק וְלֹא מַתֶּכֶת: **גמ'** אָנוּ אֵין לָנוּ. אֵין אָנוּ סוֹמְכִין עַל מִשְׁנָתֵינוּ כְּמוֹת שֶׁהִיא שְׁנוּיָה, אֶלָּא מוּחְלֶפֶת שִׁיטָתָהּ, וּב"ש כְּרַבִּי יְהוּדָה כו': אָסוּר לְאַבְּדָן בַּיָּד. מִדְּקָתָנֵי "מַעֲבִירִין" בְּיָדַיִם, וְלָא זָרֵיק לְהוּ: דְּלֵית לֵיהּ מוּקְצֶה. דְּאִי ר' יְהוּדָה מֵאֶתְמוֹל לָאו לִבְהֵמָה קָיְימִי, שֶׁהֲרֵי הָאוֹכֵל הָיָה עִמָּהֶן, וְהַיּוֹם לוֹקֵחַ מֵהֶם: שֶׁאֵין מִתְכַּוֵּין. שֶׁאֵין מִתְכַּוֵּין לִסְחוֹט: גַּרְעִינִין. שֶׁל תְּמָרִים וְהֵם לִבְהֵמָה: אַרְמָיָיתָא. תְּמָרִים רָעִים הֵם, וּמַאֲכִילִין הַתְּמָרִים עַצְמָן לִבְהֵמָה, הִלְכָּךְ אַגַּב אִימַּיְיהוּ לִבְהֵמָה נַמִי קָיְימִי: פַּרְסָיָיתָא. תְּמָרִים טוֹבִים הֵם, וְאֵין מַאֲכִילִין אוֹתָן לִבְהֵמָה: כָּל צוֹרְכוֹ. מִשְׁתַּמֵּשׁ בּוֹ, וְאֵין כָּאן מִשּׁוּם בִּזָּיוֹן, וּמְמַחֵהוּ בְּתַבְשִׁיל: לֶקְנָא דְּמַיָּא. סֵפֶל שֶׁל מַיִם: גְּרָף שֶׁל רְעִי. לוֹקְטָן לְפָנָיו כְּשֶׁאוֹכֵל הַתְּמָרִים עַד שֶׁנִּמְאָסוֹת בְּעֵינָיו, וְנוֹטְלָן אוֹתָן מִפָּנָיו כִּגְרָף שֶׁל רְעִי, וְנוֹתְנָן לִבְהֵמָה: זָרֵיק לְהוּ בְּלִישָּׁנֵי'. אֶל עֵבֶר הַשֻּׁלְחָן: אֲחוֹרֵי הַמִּטָּה. שֶׁהוּא מֵיסֵב עָלֶיהָ:

הדרן עלך נוטל

תוספות

התם כיון דמסרח. ומתקלקל, ואין ראוי למאכל אדם – מאתמול דעתיה עילויה ליתנו לבהמה. אע"ג דבשער של אפונין ושל עדשים אסרינן לרבי יהודה, אע"ג דחזו למאכל בהמה. וכן גרעינין דלעיל, בפרק "במה מדליקין" (דף כט.), דאמרינן לרבי יהודה, אכלן – אין מסיקין בגרעינין, מ"מ הכא שרי, כדפי' התם: **ליטול** מהן אוד. נראה לר"ת כפירוש ה"ג: דאסירי משום תיקוני מנא. דלפירו' זה(ד) דאע"ג דלא מתקלא ליה – גזרינן שלא יבא לידי תיקון כלי: **עצמות** וקליפין. לא כפירוש הקונטרס דפירש: אפילו קשין ואין ראויין לאכילת כלבים. *דהאי תנא אמרינן בגמרא דכרבי שמעון סבירא ליה, ור"ש בעי לכל הפחות ראויות למאכל בהמה. דקתני: מעבירין מעל השלחן פירורין כו' מפני שהוא מאכל בהמה, ומוקמינן בגמרא כוותיה:

אנו אין לנו אלא ב"ש כר"י כו'. במסכת עדיות לא מיתניא בהדי קולי ב"ש וחומרי ב"ה, והיינו כרב נחמן. והא דלא מייתי סייעתא מהתם – משום דמאי אולמא דהא מהא:

פירורין שאין בהן כזית אסור לאבדן ביד. פי' בקונט': מדקתני "מעבירין" ולא קתני "זורקין". וקשה לרבי: דברישא נמי קתני "מגביהין מעל השלחן עצמות וקליפין" ולא קתני "זורקין" אע"פ שמותר לאבדן ביד. ועוד, דאמרינן בברכות, בריש "אלו דברים" (דף נב:): וב"ה אומרים, אם שמש ת"ח הוא נוטל פירורין שיש בהן כזית. ומניח פירורין שאין בהן כזית. ומסייע ליה לר' יוחנן, דאמר: פירורין שאין בהן כזית מותר לאבדן ביד. ואי אפשר ליגרס התם אסור. *ונראה לר' דהכא גרסי' מותר, ודייק מדאצטריך למיתני "מפני שהוא מאכל בהמה" דהיינו משמע דלא חזי לאדם, והוו כשאר מאכל בהמה ומותר לאבדן. מ"ר:

ואם לאו אין מקנחין בו. אית ספרים דגרסי: וחכ"א בין כך ובין כך מקנחין בו. ולא יתכן, דאמר בגמרא דבאין לו עור בית אחיזה – אפילו ר"ש מודה דאסור, משום דפסיק רישיה הוא. וה"ר יצחק מדלפירא גרס: בין כך ובין כך אין מקנחין בו, כרבי יהודה דאמר דבר שאין מתכוין אסור. ואין נראה לר"י, דהא בגמרא משמע דברישא מודה ר' יהודה(ה), דאמר: אימא סיפא, ספוג אם יש לו עור בית אחיזה מקנחין בו, ואם לאו – אין מקנחין בו. אתאן לרבי יהודה. אם כן, בין כך ובין כך אין מקנחין בו – לא רבי יהודה ולא ר' שמעון, אלא ודאי לא גרסינן ליה כלל. מ"ר:

שמואל מטלטל להו אגב ריפתא. אף על גב דכר"ש סבירא ליה, דשרי לקמן בפרק בתרא (דף קנו:) נבלה שנתנבלה בשבת – מיהו מחמיר היה, משום דהוה אדם חשוב, כאביי ורבא דלעיל. ר"ת: **רבא** מטלטל להו אגב לקנא דמיא. והא רבא סבר לעיל כר"י דאית ליה מוקצה, ואנוחי לקנא דמיא היכי שרי לכתחילה? ויש לומר: דשני לן בין היכא דאפשר למיעבד האי טלטול מאתמול, להיכא דלא אפשר. דכיפין ובר יונה היו מאתמול בידו, והיה יכול לטלטלם. אבל הני גרעיני תמרה – לא אפשר. ושרי אפילו לרבי יהודה, ואף לאדם חשוב. דאמר בביצה פרק "יו"ט" (דף כא:) דאמר ליה אביי לרב יוסף: הני סופלי לחיותא היכי שדינן ביומא טבא? לרבי יוסי דאמר לכם ולא לכלבים חזיין להסקה, כו' בשבת מאי איכא למימר? מטלטלין להו אגב ריפתא כדשמואל. אלמא דאפילו רב יוסף דלא בעי למישרי לעיל אגב כפא וסכינא אפילו דבר הראוי לאדם – שרי התם גרעיני תמרה אגב ריפתא:

הדרן עלך נוטל האדם את בנו

עין משפט נר מצוה

יט א מיי' פ"ד מהל' י"ט הלכה יא סמג לאוין עה טוש"ע א"ח סי' תקז סעיף ג:
כ ב מיי' פכ"ה מהלכות שבת הלכה טז סמג לאוין סה טוש"ע א"ח סי' שח סעיף כז:
כא ג מיי' פכ"ב שם הלכה טז סמג שם טוש"ע א"ח סי' שכ סעיף יז:
כב ד מיי' פ"ז מהל' ברכות הלכה יא טוש"ע א"ח סי' קפ סעיף ד:
(ועי' תוס' ביצה ב. ד"ה מגביהין) (ועי' תוס' ביצה ב. ד"ה וב"ה)
כג ה מיי' פכ"ו מהל' שבת הלכה טז סמג לאוין סה טוש"ע א"ח סי' שח סעיף ל:
כד ו מיי' פ"ז מהלכות ברכות הל' ט טוש"ע א"ח סי' קפ סעיף א:
כה ז מיי' פכ"ו מהל' שבת הלכה כד וכ"ה הלכה יג סמג לאוין סה טוש"ע א"ח סי' שח סעיף לו:
כו ח מיי' פכ"ו שם הל' טז טוש"ע שם סעיף ל:
(ועי' תוס' מנחות נח: ד"ה והיכא דאמרי דזהו מסוגיות הפוכות)

מסורת הש"ס

ביצה לג. וש[ם] | (שם לב.) לעיל כח: כט. וקכב: | לקמן קנז. [ביצה ב. תוספ' פי"ז מתני' איפכא ע"ש] | נ"א מקנחין בו וניטל | [לקמן קמז. ע"ש ביצה ב.] | ברכות נב: ע"ש | לעיל עה. קג. קיא: קיז. קכ: וקלג: סוכה לג: כתובות ו. בכורות כה. [ביצה לו.] | ברכות נ: לעיל כח: | [נ"ל רבא עי' תוס' ד"ה רבה] | [ביצה שם. לו:] | [תוספ' פי"ז]

רבינו חננאל

פי החבית מטה על צדה והיא נופלת. אמר רב הונא אמר רב לא שנו אלא בשוכח אבל במניח נעשה בסים לדבר האסור. פי' נעשת החבית כֵּן לאבן ואסור להטות החבית כלל. והלכתא כוותיה דרבא דר' אמי אמר ר' יוחנן קאי כוותיה. בפרק כל הכלים: **היתה** בין החביות מגביהה מטה על צדה כו'. תניא (א') ר' יוסי אומר היתה החבית מונחת באוצר או שהיו כלי זכוכית מונחין תחתיה מגביהה למקום אחד ומטה על צדה ונוטל מה שצריך לו ומחזירה למקומה. מעות שעל הכר נמי אוקמוה משמ' דרב בשוכח אבל במניח נעשת הכר בסים למעות ואסור אפילו לנערן ואמר רבה משמיה דר' יוחנן לא שנו אלא לצורך גופו כגון שצריך (סבר) לישב עליו אבל אם הוא צריך למקומו מטלטלין ועודן עליו. וכן תני חייא בר רב מדפתי והא דא"ר הושעיא שכח ארנקי בחצר ור' יצחק דאמר שכח לבינה בחצר ויהודה בר שילא דאמר שכחו דסקיא מלאה מעות בסטין ואמרו שמניח עליה ככר או תינוק ומטלטלו ואמר מר זוטרא הלכתא ככל הני שמעתתא בשכח ולית הלכתא כוותייהו אלא הלכתא כרב אשי דהוא בתראה דאמר לא אמרו ככר או תינוק אלא למת בלבד. אביי מנח כפא פי' תרווד אכיפי הן כגון כיפה של צמר ורבא מנח סכינא אבר יונה והוא מליח אבל היה מבושל והיה מטלטל בן יונה אגב סכינא אמר שאלו מותרין לטלטלן בשבת דתניא בראשונה היו אומרים ג' כלים מותרין בשבת מקצוע של דבילה וזומלוסטרין וסכין קטנה שע"ג השולחן וכפה היא זומליסטרון כדתנן ניטלה כיפה טמאה משום מזלג. ואקשינן על רבה טעמא דחזי לאומצא הא לא חזי לאומצא לא דהא מוקצה הוא כלומר כר' יהודה סבירא ליה ולא כר' שמעון דאי ר' שמעון לית ליה מוקצה אלא אפילו בשר תפוח שרי לטלטוליה וכל בשר אחר בין חי בין מליח. ותוב אקשינן עליה ומי סבר לה רבא כר' יהודה והא א"ל רבא לשמעיה טוי לי בר אווזא ביו"ט ושדי מיעיא לשונרא כר' שמעון דאי כר' יהודה הא אמר כל דבר שאינו מוכן לאכילה אסור לטלטלו ואפילו בהמה לא היה מתיר לבודקה אלא באשפה שאם תמצא טריפה יניחנה באשפה. ומסקנא דשמעתא דרבה כר' יהודה ס"ל ופשוטה היא: **מתני'** בה"א מגביהין מעל השולחן עצמות וקליפין וכו'. אמר רב נחמן אנו אין לנו אלא ב"ש כר' יהודה וב"ה כר' שמעון מעבירין מעל גבי השלחן פירורין פחות מכזית מסייע ליה לר' יוחנן דאמר פירורין שאין בהן כזית מותר לאבדן ביד. ספוג אם יש לו עור בית אחיזה מקנחין בו ואם לאו אין מקנחין בו אפילו לר' שמעון דהא אי אפשר שלא לסחוט באחוז בספוג אלא אם יש לו עור בית אחיזה. גרעינין דתמרי. ארמי ארמייתא שרי לטלטולי הואיל וחזיין על גב אימן. פי' רכים הן ונאכלין עם התמרים עצמן. דפרסייתא שמואל מטלטלינהו ואגב ריפתא וכו' שמעתא: **הדרן עלך נוטל אדם**

הגהות הב"ח

(א) במשנה מעבירין מעל השלחן פירורין: (ב) שם מקנחין בו (וחכ"א) תא"מ ונ"ב רש"י ותוספות ואלפסי לא גרסי וחכ"א אבל מפי' המשניות להרמב"ם משמע דגרס לה: (ג) גמ' מעבירין מעל השלחן פירורין: (ד) תוס' ד"ה ליטול וכו' דלפירוש זה אע"ג: (ה) ד"ה ואם לאו וכו' מודה ר' יהודה דאמרינן אימא:

רב נסים גאון

להרים: **רבא** כר' נתן סבירא ליה דאמר חי נושא את עצמו. עיקר דבריו של ר' נתן בפרק המצניע (דף לד) ר' נתן אומר על השחוטין חייב על החיים פטור מפני שהחי נושא את עצמו. רבא כר' שמעון סבירא ליה דאמר מלאכה שאינה צריכה לגופה פטור עליה ועיקר דבריו של ר' שמעון גם בפרק המצניע (דף לג) דתנן וכן כזית מן המת וכעדשה מן השרץ חייב ור' שמעון פוטר וגרסי' בגמ' אמר רבה אמר ר' יוחנן ורב יוסף אמר ריש לקיש פוטר היה ר' שמעון אף במוציא את המת לקוברו וכבר פירשנו זה בפרק יציאות השבת: **הכי** נמי מסתברא דרבא כר' יהודה סבירא ליה דדרש רבא אשה לא תכנס לבין העצים ליטול מהן אוד אוד שנשבר ביום טוב אסור להסיקו לפי שמסיקים בכלים ואין מסיקין בשברי כלים וזה שוה לדברי ר' יהודה שאמר במשנה בפ' במה מדליקין (ד' כט) ואין מסיקין בשברי כלים דברי ר' יהודה הואיל וסברא ליה כוותיה בנולד במוקצה נמי דתנן בסוף מסכתא (לקמן דף קנו) ר' יהודה אומר אם לא היתה נבילה מערב שבת אסורה לפי שאינה מן המוכן כר' יהודה סבירא ליה ולכך אמר סכינא אבר יונה למה לי הא חזי לאומצא דדייקת מינה הא לא חזי לאומצא לא וכמו שאמר בתחילת מסכת יום טוב (דף ב) דאית ליה מוקצה אית ליה נולד ודלית ליה מוקצה לית ליה נולד כי הכלל עיקר אחד חוזר והיא ההכנה: **אמר** רב נחמן אנו אין לנו אלא בית שמאי כרבי יהודה ובית הלל כרבי שמעון וכן אמרו עוד מני ר' שמעון היא דלית ליה מוקצה ועיקר דברי רבי יהודה ור' שמעון בפרק כירה (דף מד) וכבר פירשנוה למעלה. אתאן לרבי יהודה דאמר דבר שאין מתכוין אסור עיקר דבריו של ר' יהודה במשנה במסכת בכורות (דף לג) ובמס' יום טוב (דף כג) וכבר פירשנו דבריו גם במס' זו בפ' כירה:

סליק פרק נוטל

רבא

א א ב מיי' פכ"ב מהל' שבת הלכה טז סמג לאוין סה טוש"ע א"ח סי' שלה סעיף א:
ב ג מיי' שם פכ"א הל' יא טוש"ע שם סעיף ה:

[בפסקי תוספות איתא כסותו]

ג ד ה ו מיי' פכ"א מהל' שבת הלכה יב סמג שם טוש"ע א"ח סי' שכ סעיף א:
ד ז מיי' פ"י מהלכות טומאת אוכלין הל' ד:
ה ח שם הל' ה ופ"א מהל' משכב ומושב הלכה טז:

[עיין תוס' ביצה ג. ד"ה ר"י אמר]

חבית. ובלבד שלא יספוג. אפילו יש לו עור בית אחיזה, דליכא חשש סחיטה – אסור, כדמפרש בגמרא: שלא יעשה כדרך שעושה בחול: **מלקט** על יד ואוכל. נראה דל"ג "ואוכל", מדקתני סיפא: אבל לא לתוך הסל ולא לתוך הקופה. משמע, הנך דווקא אסירי משום עובדא דחול, אבל לתוך *כפו שרי: **ורבי** יוחנן אמר הלכה כרבי יהודה בשאר פירות. בריש מסכת ביצה (דף ג. ושם): רבי יוחנן רמי דר' יהודה אדרבי יהודה, תנן: ר"י אומר אם לאוכלין היוצא מהן מותר, אם למשקין כו'. אלמא: כל לאוכלין אוכלא דאיפרת הוא. ורמינהו: ועוד אמר ר"י, מתנה אדם על הכלכלה של פירות ביו"ט ראשון ואוכלה בשני, וכן ביצה שנולדה בראשון אוכלה בשני. בשני אין, בראשון לא. ואמר רבי יוחנן: מוחלפת השיטה. וצריך לומר דהיא דמתנה אדם מחליף, דאי מתני' מחליף – אם כן במאי דנקט הכא ר' יהודה הוה ליה למינקט רבנן, וה"ל למימר הלכה כרבנן בשאר פירות. מ"ר. *ולי נראה דאפילו אפיך מתני' אתי שפיר, כעין שמצינו בב"ק בפרק "הגוזל" קמא (דף צו:) דתנן: גזל בהמה והוכחשה, עבדים והזקינו – משלם כשעת הגזלה, ר"מ אומר: בעבדים אומר לו הרי שלך לפניך. ואמר בגמרא, אמר רבי חנינא בר אבדימי אמר רב: הלכה כר"מ. ופריך: ורב שביק רבנן ועביד כר"מ כו'. עד דמסיק: דרב מתניתין איפכא אתנא'. אלמא, אע"פ שהיה שונה במתניתין: "וחכ"א בעבדים אומר לו הרי שלך לפניך", וה"ל למימר השתא הלכה כחכמים – אפ"ה נקט ר"מ – לפי מה שהאחרים שונין המשנה. ה"נ נקט רבי יוחנן "רבי יהודה" בשמעתין. וכן נמי מצינו בשילהי פ"ק דסוכה (דף יט:) דתנן: העושה סוכתו כמין צריף, ר"א פוסל וחכמים מכשירין. ואמרינן בגמרא, אביי אשכחיה לרב יוסף דגני בכילת חתנים בסוכה. א"ל: כמאן, כר"א? א"ל: שבקת רבנן ועבדת כר"א? אמר ליה: ברייתא איפכא תניא. השתא היה לו להשיב רב יוסף כרבנן, ולא כר"א. כיון דאיהו איפכא תני, אלא כן דרך התלמוד בכל מקום. נראה לי: **הלכה** כר' יהודה בשאר פירות. אע"ג דבריש ביצה (ד' ג.) גזר ר' יוחנן ביצה שנולדה ביו"ט משום משקין שזבו, והכא לא גזר בשאר פירות – י"ל דשייך טפי לגזור בביצה, לפי שהיא עומדת ליסחט מן התרנגולת *ודרך לגומעה חיה. אבל שאר פירות אין עומדים ליסחט כלל. מ"ר: **שמשך** מהן שמן כו'. פי' בקונט': שמשך – זב מאליהן, כמו נהרות המושכין. ולפירושו צריך לומר: הכניסן בין לאוכלין כו' היינו: הכניסן מתחילתן. ואין הלשון משמע כן. ועוד קשה לר"י: דאי משך מאליו קאמר, גבי תותים שמשך מהם מים – ה"ל למימר "שמשכו" או "שנמשכו". דמים בכל מקום לשון רבים! ועוד קשה לר"י: אם כן, הך ברייתא הוה תיובתא דרב ורבי יוחנן, דאמרי לעיל: חלוק היה רבי יהודה בזיתים וענבים. דהכא משמע דבזיתים וענבים מודה! אלא נראה לר"י: דמשך – אאדם קאי, וסחטן תחילה ושוב הכניסן. דהשתא לרב ורבי יוחנן דסברי: חלוק היה רבי יהודה בזיתים וענבים – נקט דוקא משך, דאיכא למיחש טפי דילמא יהיב דעתיה לסחוט משקה אחר שהכניסו נמי לאכילה, מאחר שסחטן תחילה להוציא מהן משקה. הא לא משך – לא. ולשמואל דאמר: מודה רבי יהודה בזיתים וענבים – נקט משך משום רבותא דתותים ורמונים; דאפילו משך, הכניסן לאוכלין – היוצא מהן מותר. מ"ר: **חלב** האשה מטמא לרצון ושלא לרצון. והא דתנן במסכת מכשירין (פ"א): כל משקה שתחילתו לרצון, אף על פי שאין סופו לרצון, או שסופו לרצון, אף על פי שאין תחלתו לרצון – מכשיר. לא דמי רצון דהתם לרצון דהכא; דהתם מיירי בשעת נפילתן על הזרעים שיהא לרצון, דבעינן "יותן" דומיא "דכי יתן", מה יתן דניחא ליה, אף יותן דניחא ליה. אבל הכא מיירי בשעת פרישה מן האשה או מן הבהמה: **לרצון** ושלא לרצון. כדמפרש בסמוך טעמא, משום דדם מגפתה טמא וחלב ודם חד הוא, דדם נעכר ונעשה חלב. ולא צריכין למה שפי' בקונט' משום דאיקרי משקה, שנאמר: "ותפתח את נאד החלב ותשקהו". ונראה לר"י: דהא דאיצטריך לפרש האי טעמא בפ' "דם נדה" (נדה דף נה:) גבי חלב האשה – הנ"מ לרבי עקיבא דשמעתין, דלית ליה טעמא (*) דפרישה. או למאן דלית ליה דם נעכר ונעשה חלב. אבל לרבנן דשמעתין – לא צריך[ז], כדפרישית לחלב האשה, אלא דוקא לטמא חלב בהמה לרצון. *מ"ר: מחמיר

חבית [א]שֶׁנִּשְׁבְּרָה מַצִּילִין הֵימֶנָּה מְזוֹן שָׁלֹשׁ סְעוּדוֹת, וְאוֹמֵר לַאֲחֵרִים: בֹּאוּ וְהַצִּילוּ לָכֶם, וּבִלְבַד שֶׁלֹּא יִסְפּוֹג. *אֵין סוֹחֲטִין אֶת הַפֵּירוֹת לְהוֹצִיא מֵהֶן מַשְׁקִין, וְאִם יָצְאוּ מֵעַצְמָן – אֲסוּרִין. ר' יְהוּדָה אוֹמֵר: אִם לָאוֹכָלִין – הַיּוֹצֵא מֵהֶן מוּתָּר, וְאִם לְמַשְׁקִין – הַיּוֹצֵא מֵהֶן אָסוּר. *חַלּוֹת דְּבַשׁ שֶׁרִיסְּקָן מֵעֶ"שׁ וְיָצְאוּ מֵעַצְמָן – אֲסוּרִין(א), וְרַבִּי אֱלִיעֶזֶר מַתִּיר.§ **גמ'** תָּנָא: לֹא [ב]יִסְפּוֹג בְּיַיִן, וְלֹא יְטַפֵּחַ בְּשֶׁמֶן, שֶׁלֹּא יַעֲשֶׂה כְּדֶרֶךְ שֶׁהוּא עוֹשֶׂה בַּחוֹל. ת"ר: [ג]נִתְפַּזְּרוּ לוֹ פֵּירוֹת בֶּחָצֵר – מְלַקֵּט עַל יָד וְאוֹכֵל. אֲבָל לֹא לְתוֹךְ הַסַּל וְלֹא לְתוֹךְ הַקּוּפָּה, שֶׁלֹּא יַעֲשֶׂה כְּדֶרֶךְ שֶׁהוּא עוֹשֶׂה בַּחוֹל.§ "אֵין סוֹחֲטִין אֶת הַפֵּירוֹת".§ *אָמַר רַב יְהוּדָה אָמַר שְׁמוּאֵל: מוֹדֶה הָיָה רַבִּי יְהוּדָה לַחֲכָמִים בְּזֵיתִים וַעֲנָבִים. מ"ט – כֵּיוָן דִּלְסְחִיטָה נִינְהוּ יָהֵיב דַּעְתֵּיהּ. וְעוּלָּא אָמַר רַב: חָלוּק הָיָה ר' יְהוּדָה אַף בְּזֵיתִים וַעֲנָבִים. וְרַבִּי יוֹחָנָן אָמַר: הֲלָכָה כְּרַבִּי יְהוּדָה בִּשְׁאָר פֵּירוֹת, וְאֵין הֲלָכָה כְּרַבִּי יְהוּדָה בְּזֵיתִים וַעֲנָבִים. אָמַר רַבָּה אָמַר רַב יְהוּדָה אָמַר שְׁמוּאֵל: מוֹדֶה הָיָה רַבִּי יְהוּדָה לַחֲכָמִים בְּזֵיתִים וַעֲנָבִים, [ד]וּמוֹדִים חֲכָמִים לְרַבִּי יְהוּדָה בִּשְׁאָר פֵּירוֹת. א"ל רַבִּי יִרְמְיָה לְרַבִּי אַבָּא: אֶלָּא בְּמַאי פְּלִיגִי? א"ל: לְכִי תִּשְׁכַּח. אָמַר רַב נַחְמָן בַּר יִצְחָק: מִסְתַּבְּרָא, בְּתוּתִים וְרִמּוֹנִים פְּלִיגִי. דְּתַנְיָא: [ה]זֵיתִים שֶׁמָּשַׁךְ מֵהֶן שֶׁמֶן, וַעֲנָבִים שֶׁמָּשַׁךְ מֵהֶן יַיִן, וְהִכְנִיסָן בֵּין לָאוֹכֶל בֵּין לְמַשְׁקִין – הַיּוֹצֵא מֵהֶן אָסוּר. [ו]תּוּתִים שֶׁמָּשַׁךְ מֵהֶן מַיִם, וְרִמּוֹנִים שֶׁמָּשַׁךְ מֵהֶן יַיִן, וְהִכְנִיסָן לָאוֹכָלִין – הַיּוֹצֵא מֵהֶן מוּתָּר, לְמַשְׁקִין וְלִסְתָם – הַיּוֹצֵא מֵהֶן אָסוּר, דִּבְרֵי רַבִּי יְהוּדָה. וַחֲכָמִים אוֹמְרִים: בֵּין לָאוֹכָלִין בֵּין לְמַשְׁקִין – הַיּוֹצֵא מֵהֶן אָסוּר. וְסָבַר רַבִּי יְהוּדָה סְתָם אָסוּר?! *וְהָתְנַן: [ז]חֲלֵב הָאִשָּׁה מְטַמֵּא לְרָצוֹן, וְשֶׁלֹּא לְרָצוֹן חֲלֵב בְּהֵמָה אֵינוֹ מְטַמֵּא אֶלָּא לְרָצוֹן. אָמַר ר' עֲקִיבָא: קַל וָחוֹמֶר הוּא, וּמָה חֲלֵב הָאִשָּׁה שֶׁאֵינוֹ מְיוּחָד אֶלָּא לִקְטַנִּים – מְטַמֵּא לְרָצוֹן וְשֶׁלֹּא לְרָצוֹן, חֲלֵב הַבְּהֵמָה שֶׁמְּיוּחָד בֵּין לִקְטַנִּים בֵּין לִגְדוֹלִים – אֵינוֹ דִּין שֶׁיְּטַמֵּא בֵּין לְרָצוֹן וּבֵין שֶׁלֹּא לְרָצוֹן? אָמְרוּ לוֹ: אִם טָמֵא חֲלֵב הָאִשָּׁה שֶׁלֹּא לְרָצוֹן – [ח]שֶׁדַּם מַגֵּפָתָהּ טָמֵא, יְטַמֵּא חֲלֵב הַבְּהֵמָה שֶׁלֹּא

חָבִית. מַצִּילִין הֵימֶנָּה מְזוֹן ג' סְעוּדוֹת. וַאֲפִילּוּ בְּכֵלִים הַרְבֵּה, דְּאִילּוּ בְּחַד מָנָא – אָמְרִי' בְּ"כָל כִּתְבֵי הַקֹּדֶשׁ" (לעיל דף קכ.) דְּכַמָּה דְּבָעֵי מַצִּיל: לָכֶם. כָּל אֶחָד מְזוֹן ג' סְעוּדוֹת: וּבִלְבַד שֶׁלֹּא יִסְפּוֹג. שֶׁלֹּא יָשִׂים סְפוֹג בִּמְקוֹם הַיַּיִן לַחֲזוֹר וּלְהַטִּיפוֹ בִּכְלִי, גְּזֵירָה שֶׁמָּא יִסְחוֹט: אֵין סוֹחֲטִין אֶת הַפֵּירוֹת. דַּהֲוָה לֵיהּ מְפָרֵק(ב), תּוֹלָדָה דְּדִישָׁה: אֲסוּרִין. גְּזֵירָה שֶׁמָּא יִסְחוֹט לְכַתְּחִילָּה: רַבִּי יְהוּדָה אוֹמֵר אִם לָאוֹכָלִין. הֵם מְכוּוָּנִין אוֹתָם פֵּירוֹת – הַיּוֹצֵא מֵהֶן מוּתָּר, דְּלָא נִיחָא לֵיהּ בְּמַה שֶּׁזָּבוּ, וְלֵיכָּא לְמִגְזַר בְּהֵן שֶׁמָּא יִסְחוֹט: וְאִם לְמַשְׁקִין. מְכוּוָּנִין – אֲסוּרִין, דְּנִיחָא לֵיהּ בְּמַאי דְּנָפְקָא מִינַּיְיהוּ, וְנִתְקַיְּימָה מַחֲשַׁבְתּוֹ, וְאִיכָּא לְמִיגְזַר שֶׁמָּא יִסְחוֹט. וְהָכִי אָמְרִי' בְּבֵיצָה, דְּטַעְמָא דְּמַשְׁקִין שֶׁזָּבוּ מִשּׁוּם שֶׁמָּא יִסְחוֹט הוּא: חַלּוֹת דְּבַשׁ. מֵאַחַר שֶׁמְּרוּסָּקִין, הַדְּבַשׁ זָב מֵאֵלָיו מִתּוֹךְ הַשַּׁעֲוָה, וְאֵין דֶּרֶךְ לְסוֹחֲטוֹ. הִלְכָּךְ, רַבִּי אֱלִיעֶזֶר מַתִּיר, וַחֲכָמִים אוֹסְרִין – גְּזֵירָה אַטּוּ שֶׁאֵינָן מְרוּסָּקִין, דִּילְמָא מְרַסֵּק לְהוּ(ג): **גמ'** וִיטַפַּח. מַכְנִיס בּוֹ כַּפּוֹ וְהַשֶּׁמֶן נִדְבָּק בָּהּ, וּמְקַנְּחוֹ בִּשְׂפַת הַכְּלִי. וַאֲסָרוּהָ מִשּׁוּם עוּבְדִּין דְּחוֹל: מוֹדֶה ר' יְהוּדָה בְּזֵיתִים. דְּאַע"ג דְּהִכְנִיסָן לָאוֹכָלִין, הַיּוֹצֵא מֵהֶן אָסוּר. דְּכֵיוָן דְּרוּבָּן לִסְחִיטָה קָיְימִי, כִּי אָתוּ לִידֵי מַשְׁקֶה – יָהֵיב דַּעְתֵּיהּ לְמֶיהֱוֵי נִיחָא לֵיהּ בְּהָכִי: אֲפִי' בְּזֵיתִים וַעֲנָבִים. הוֹאִיל וְהָנֵי לָאוֹכָלִין נִכְנְסוּ: מִסְתַּבְּרָא בְּתוּתִים וְרִמּוֹנִים פְּלִיגִי. דְּאִיכָּא דְּבָעוּ לְהוּ לְמַשְׁקִין, הִלְכָּךְ מַשְׁווּ לְהוּ רַבָּנַן כְּזֵיתִים וַעֲנָבִים, וְר' יְהוּדָה פָּלֵיג עֲלַיְיהוּ. אֲבָל שְׁאָר פֵּירוֹת – לֵיכָּא דְּבָעֵי לְהוּ לְמַשְׁקִין, הִלְכָּךְ מוֹדוּ רַבָּנַן בָּהֶם: שֶׁמָּשַׁךְ. זָב מֵאֲלֵיהֶן, כְּמוֹ "נְהָרוֹת הַמּוֹשְׁכִין" (לעיל דף קלא.): וְהִכְנִיסָן. מִתְּחִילָּתָן, בֵּין לָאוֹכָלִין בֵּין לְמַשְׁקִין כו'. דְּרִמּוֹנִים קָרֵי יַיִן מִשּׁוּם דְּאִית לְהוּ קִיוּהָא: וַחכ"א כו'. וְהָא דְּנָקַט רַב נַחְמָן לִישָּׁנָא דְּמִסְתַּבְּרָא, וְלָא אָמַר בְּהֶדְיָא דִּבְתוּתִים וְרִמּוֹנִים פְּלִיגִי – מִשּׁוּם דְּאִיכָּא לְמֵימַר פְּלִיגֵי בְּתוּתִים וְרִמּוֹנִים, וְה"ה לִשְׁאָר פֵּירוֹת, וּלְהוֹדִיעֲךָ כֹּחוֹ דְּרַבִּי יְהוּדָה נָקַט לְהוּ. וְאִי מִשּׁוּם בָּרַיְיתָא דִּלְקַמָּן, דְּשָׁמְעִינַן מִינָּהּ דְּמוֹדִים חֲכָמִים לְרַבִּי יְהוּדָה בִּשְׁאָר פֵּירוֹת – לָאו בְּהֶדְיָא שָׁמְעִינַן לָהּ, דְּאִיכָּא לְמֵימַר רַבִּי יְהוּדָה הִיא, כִּדְפָרְכִינַן עֲלָהּ: וְסָבַר רַבִּי יְהוּדָה סְתָם. שֶׁלֹּא פֵּירֵשׁ לְאוֹכֶל וְלֹא לְמַשְׁקֶה, הָוֵי הַמַּשְׁקֶה הַזָּב מֵהֶן אָסוּר: וְהָתְנַן חֲלֵב הָאִשָּׁה מְטַמֵּא. מַכְשִׁיר: לְרָצוֹן וְשֶׁלֹּא לְרָצוֹן. בֵּין שֶׁיָּצָא מִמֶּנָּה לְרָצוֹן, בֵּין שֶׁיָּצָא שֶׁלֹּא לְרָצוֹן, שֶׁהֶחָלָב קָרוּי מַשְׁקֶה, שֶׁנֶּאֱמַר: "וַתִּפְתַּח אֶת נֹאד הֶחָלָב וַתַּשְׁקֵהוּ" (שופטים ד): חֲלֵב הַבְּהֵמָה אֵינוֹ מְטַמֵּא אֶלָּא אִם כֵּן יָצָא לְרָצוֹן. וְאִי לָא – לָא חָשֵׁיב מַשְׁקֶה, וְאִם נָגַע בּוֹ שֶׁרֶץ – אֵינוֹ מְקַבֵּל טוּמְאָה. וְטַעְמָא מְפָרֵשׁ לְקַמֵּיהּ: שֶׁדַּם

בילה ג. חולין יד:
לעיל יט:
חולין יד:
מכשירין פ"ו מ"ח כריתות יג.
י"ג דפריסות
[ועי' תוס' נדה יט: ד"ה כתיב הכא]

רבינו חננאל

חבית שנשברה מצילין הימנה מזון ג' סעודות וכו' תנא לא יספוג ביין רדפיו ולא יזוחח ראשון ביד כדרך שהוא עושה בחול. לא יטפח כדאמרינן בכל מקום טופח ע"מ להטפיח ורדחון רפרק החורל בחבירו וכו'. מעשה באחר שפרע ראשה של אשה כו' עד שמרה עומדת על פתח חצירה ושיבר הפך בפניה. ובה כאיסר שמן. גילתה ראשה והיתה מטפחת ומנחת על ראשה וכו': **ת"ר** נתפזרו לו פירות בחצירו מלקט על יד על יד ואוכל. אבל לא לתוך הסל ולא לתוך הקופה שלא יעשה כדרך שהוא עושה בחול וכו' וחלקו רב יהודה אמר שמואל ורב ועולא כל חד וחד מעמיד חלוקת ר' יהודה וחכמים ור' יוחנן אמר הלכה כר' יהודה בשאר פירות ואין הלכה כמותו בזיתים וענבים. א"ר אבא אמר רב יהודה אמר שמואל מודה היה רבי יהודה לחכמים בזיתים וענבים ומודים חכמים לרבי יהודה בשאר פירות. ובמאי פליגי בתותים ורמונים דתניא זיתים שמשך מהן שמן וענבים שמשך מהן יין והכניסן בין לאוכלין בין למשקין היוצא מהן אסור. תותים שמשך מהן מים ורמונים שמשך מהן יין והכניסן לאוכלין היוצא מהן מותר למשקין ולסתם היוצא מהן אסור דברי ר' יהודה וחכ"א בין לאוכלין בין למשקין היוצא מהן אסור. נמצאת חלוקת ר' יהודה וחכמים בתותים ורמונים ובה א"ר יוחנן הלכה כר' יהודה בשאר פירות וכיון שפסק ר' יוחנן הלכה כר' יהודה הוצרכנו לברר דבריו ולפיכך אמרינן וסבר ר' יהודה סתם אסור והתנן

הגהות הב"ח

(א) במשנה ור"א מתיר. נ"ב ר' אלעזר גרסי' עי' בפירש"י בפ"ק דשבת דף יט ריש ע"ב: (ב) רש"י ד"ה אין סוחטין וכו' מפרק דהוא תולדה: (ג) ד"ה חלות וכו' להו הס"ד ואח"כ מ"ה ולא יטפח: (ד) תוס' ד"ה לרצון וכו' לא צריך לחלב האשה כדפי' אלא:

*) נ"א ועוד ור"י לא איירי רק משאר פירות גם מזיתים וענבים אבל מתותים ורמונים אינו מזכיר כלום דעתו מש"כ ר' יהודה דאמר בפי' תותים ורמונים אם הכניסן לאוכלין היוצא מהן מותר והן דומין לביצה ואפ"ה ס"ל דבראשון אסור בביצה וע"כ רמי ליה אהדדי במסכת עירובין לט. ובמס' ביצה והיותר פשוט שאין להגיה כלום וצ"ל ודרך לגומעה ור"ל לייכא דאף אם עומדת לסחיטה ומ"מ צריך עוד תיקון ואינו ראוי למות למשקין שזבו שא"צ שום תקון ע"ז ודרך כו':

שֶׁלֹּא לְרָצוֹן – אשְׁדַם מַגֵּפָתָהּ טָהוֹר! אָמַר לָהֶן: מַחְמִיר אֲנִי בְּחָלָב מִבְּדָם, שֶׁהַחוֹלֵב לִרְפוּאָה – טָמֵא, בוְהַמַּקִּיז לִרְפוּאָה – טָהוֹר. אָמְרוּ לוֹ: סַלֵּי זֵיתִים וַעֲנָבִים יוֹכִיחוּ, גשֶׁהַמַּשְׁקִין הַיּוֹצְאִין מֵהֶן לְרָצוֹן – טְמֵאִין, שֶׁלֹּא לְרָצוֹן – טְהוֹרִים. מַאי לָאו "לְרָצוֹן" – דְּנִיחָא לֵיהּ, "שֶׁלֹּא לְרָצוֹן", בִּסְתָמָא. וּמַה זֵיתִים וַעֲנָבִים דִּבְנֵי סְחִיטָה נִינְהוּ – שֶׁלֹּא לְרָצוֹן וְלֹא כְּלוּם, תּוּתִים וְרִמּוֹנִים דְּלָאו בְּנֵי סְחִיטָה נִינְהוּ לֹא כ"ש? לֹא, "לְרָצוֹן" – בִּסְתָמָא, "שֶׁלֹּא לְרָצוֹן" – דְּגַלֵּי אַדַּעְתֵּיהּ, דַּאֲמַר "לֹא נִיחָא לִי". וְאִיבָּעֵית אֵימָא: שָׁאנֵי סַלֵּי זֵיתִים וַעֲנָבִים, כֵּיוָן דִּלְאִיבּוּד קָיְימִי – מֵעִיקָּרָא אַפְקוֹרֵי מַפְקַרֵי לְהוּ. אַשְׁכַּחַן ר' יְהוּדָה דְּמוֹדֵי לְרַבָּנַן בְּזֵיתִים וּבַעֲנָבִים. רַבָּנַן דְּמוֹדוּ לֵיהּ לְרַבִּי יְהוּדָה בִּשְׁאָר פֵּירוֹת מְנָלַן? – דְּתַנְיָא: סוֹחֲטִין בְּפַגְעִין

שֶׁדַם מַגֵּפָתָהּ. שֶׁל אִשָּׁה, אִם נִגַּף רַגְלָהּ אוֹ יָדָהּ, וְכָל חַבּוּרָה שֶׁיָּצָא מִמֶּנָּה דָּם, כִּדְאָמַר בְּפֶרֶק דַּם הַנִּדָּה (נדה דף נה:): דַּם חֲלָלִים, דְּהַיְינוּ דַּם הָרוּג, קָרוּי מַשְׁקֶה, שֶׁנֶּאֱמַר: "וְדַם חֲלָלִים יִשְׁתֶּה". וְ"דַם מַגֵּפָתוֹ" מְפָרֵשׁ הָתָם דְּדַם חֲלָלִים הָוֵי, דְּמַה לִּי קַטְלֵיהּ כּוּלֵּיהּ מַה לִּי קַטְלֵיהּ פַּלְגָא. וְחָלָב כְּדַם מַגֵּפָתוֹ, דְּדָם נֶעְכָּר וְנַעֲשֶׂה חָלָב. וְדַם מַגֵּפָתָהּ סְתָמֵיהּ שֶׁלֹּא לְרָצוֹן הוּא, וְטָמֵא: יִטַּמֵּא חֲלֵב הַבְּהֵמָה שֶׁלֹּא לְרָצוֹן. בִּתְמִיָּה: שֶׁהֲרֵי דַּם מַגֵּפָתָהּ טָהוֹר, דִּבְהֵמָה לָאו בִּכְלַל חָלָל הוּא. וּמִיהוּ, דַּם שְׁחִיטָה מַכְשִׁר, מִשּׁוּם דְּאִיתְקַשׁ לְמַיִם, דִּכְתִיב (דברים יב): "עַל הָאָרֶץ תִּשְׁפְּכֶנּוּ כַּמָּיִם": מַחְמִיר ע"כ אֲנִי בְּחָלָב. לְטַמְּאוֹ אַף שֶׁלֹּא לְרָצוֹן, מִבְּדָם: שֶׁהַחוֹלֵב. לִרְפוּאַת הַבְּהֵמָה, שֶׁלֹּא יַזִּיקֶנָּה חֲלָבָהּ – טָמֵא, דְּהָא לְרָצוֹן הוּא. וְהַמַּקִּיז דָּם לִבְהֶמְתּוֹ לִרְפוּאָה – טָהוֹר, דְּדַם מַגֵּפָתָהּ הִיא. וְהוֹאִיל וְהַחוֹלֵב לִרְפוּאָה טָמֵא – אַף הַנּוֹטֵף שֶׁלֹּא לְרָצוֹן טָמֵא: אָמְרוּ לוֹ. אֵינוֹ דּוֹמֶה שֶׁלֹּא לְרָצוֹן לַיּוֹצֵא לְרָצוֹן, שֶׁהֲרֵי סַלֵּי זֵיתִים וַעֲנָבִים יוֹכִיחוּ, שֶׁהַמַּשְׁקֶה כו': שֶׁלֹּא לְרָצוֹן בִּסְתָמָא. וְקָתָנֵי טְהוֹרִין – דְּלָא חֲשִׁיב מַשְׁקֶה. אִי רַבִּי יְהוּדָה קָאָמַר לָהּ – קַשְׁיָא, וְאִי רַבָּנַן קָאָמְרִי – כָּל שֶׁכֵּן טְהוֹרִין לְרַבִּי יְהוּדָה. דְּהָא מִידֵי דְּלְרַבָּנַן מַשְׁקֶה הוּא – לְרַבִּי יְהוּדָה לָאו מַשְׁקֶה הוּא, וְכ"ש מִידֵי דְּלְרַבָּנַן לָאו מַשְׁקֶה. וְהַשְׁתָּא וּמַה זֵיתִים וַעֲנָבִים כו'. וְהוּא הַדִּין מָצֵי לְמִירְמֵי נַמִי זֵיתִים וַעֲנָבִים אַזֵּיתִים וַעֲנָבִים, דְּקָתָנֵי לְעֵיל דְּמוֹדֶה בְּהוּ רַבִּי יְהוּדָה דְּאַף לְאוֹכָלִין הַיּוֹצֵא מֵהֶן אָסוּר. אֶלָּא הָא אַלִּימָא לֵיהּ לְאַקְשׁוּיֵי, דְּתוּתִים וְרִמּוֹנִים דְּלָאו בְּנֵי סְחִיטָה נִינְהוּ קָתָנֵי לְעֵיל דִּסְתָם אָסוּר, וְהָכָא קָתָנֵי דַּאֲפִי' זֵיתִים וַעֲנָבִים סְתָמָא לָאו לְמַשְׁקֶה: דְּגַלֵּי דַּעְתֵּיהּ. בְּהֶדְיָא, וַאֲמַר לָא נִיחָא לִי, וְהָוֵי גִּילּוּי דַּעְתָּא טְפֵי מֵהִכְנִיסוֹ לְאוֹכָלִין: וְאִיבָּעֵית אֵימָא שָׁאנֵי סַלֵּי זֵיתִים וַעֲנָבִים וכו'. וְדַוְוקָא נָקַט סַלִּין, שֶׁהַמַּשְׁקֶה הַנּוֹטֵף מֵהֶן נוֹפֵל לָאָרֶץ וְהוֹלֵךְ לְאִיבּוּד, הִלְכָּךְ סְתָמָא לָא נִיחָא לֵיהּ: אַפְקוּרֵי מַפְקִיר. לְהַהוּא מַשְׁקֶה. אֲבָל שְׁאָר כֵּלִים, אֲפִילּוּ תּוּתִים וְרִמּוֹנִים – אֵימָא לָךְ סְתָמָא לְמַשְׁקֶה: בְּפַגְעִין

מחמיר אני בחלב מבדם שהחולב לרפואה טמא והמקיז לרפואה טהור. א"כ מאי דמטמינן חלב האשה – לא מחמת דם הוא, דדם נעכר ונעשה חלב. דא"כ חולב לרפואה טהור כמו דם, אלא ודאי משום דכתיב: "ותפתח את נאד החלב". ואומר רבי: דבחנם נקט חולב לרפואה, דהכי נמי הו"מ להשיב לרבנן מחלב בהמה גופה שדמה טהור(א) וחלבה טמא. א"כ, החלב אינו טמא מחמת דם אלא משום דכתיב: "ותפתח את נאד החלב", וא"כ שלא לרצון נמי, מהאי טעמא יהא טמא. מ"ר: **סלי** זיתים וענבים יוכיחו שמשקה היוצא מהן לרצון טמא שלא לרצון טהור. בשילהי מסכת מכשירין מסיים: לא אם אמרת בסלי זיתים וענבים – שהרי תחילתו אוכל וסופו משקה, תאמרו בחלב שתחילתו וסופו משקה: **מאי** לאו לרצון דניחא ליה ושלא לרצון בסתמא. ולרצון ושלא לרצון דגבי חלב אשה – ליכא למימר דמיירי בשלא לרצון בסתמא, ודווקא בסתמא. אבל אמר לא ניחא לי – אינו מטמא. דהא לפי מה שפירשתי הטעם משום דם מגפתה, אפי' אמר לא ניחא לי – נמי מטמא. אלא משמע דשלא לרצון דקתני בכולהו, באשה ובהמה וזיתים וענבים – מיירי בכל ענין, בין מסתמא, בין אמר לא ניחא לי: **תותים** ורימונים דלאו בני סחיטה נינהו. תימה לי: מאי קשה? דילמא הא דתניא לעיל גבי תותים ורמונים למשקין, ולסתם היוצא מהן אסור – הנ"מ במשך דוקא, והכא בלא משך איירי, הלכך: שלא לרצון, דהיינו בסתמא – לא חשיב משקה: **לא** לרצון בסתמא ושלא לרצון דגלי דעתיה דאמר לא ניחא לי. (ב)דתניא התם בכריתות פרק "אמרו לו" (דף יג.): התירו(ג) לו למגע טמא מת להניק את בנה ובנה טהור. ופריך: בנה אמאי טהור? כיון דינק חלב איטמי ליה מחלב! וכי תימא לא איתכשר – איתכשר בטיפה המלוכלכת ע"פ הדד. ואע"ג דחלב אשה משקה הוא, ואין צריך הכשר – [משמע ליה] דמה שהוא בפי התינוק שהתינוק יונק – חשיב כאוכל, וצריך הכשר, לפי שזהו מאכלו של תינוק. וקאמר דאיתכשר בטיפה המלוכלכת בפי הדד, דהוי משקה כסתם חלב דלאו לאוכל בעי ליה. ומשני רב נחמן אמר רבה בר אבוה(ד): בתקיפה אחת, שלא הניח טיפה המלוכלכת ע"פ הדד. אמר רבא: שתי תשובות בדבר, חדא: דקא חזינן ליה לפומיה דינוקא דמלא חלבא, ועוד: מקום חלב מעין הוא, דהא תנן: חלב האשה מטמא לרצון ושלא לרצון. מאי היא – דלא ניחא ליה, וקתני מטמא. פי': אלמא חשיבא כמעין, מדמטמא שלא לרצון. וכיון דחשוב כמעין – גם בפי התינוק נמי יהא חשוב כמשקה, כמו שאם היה מעין, ואין צריך הכשר. כך צריך לפרש, דאת"ל דאינו מזכיר מעין, אלא כלומר דכמשקה חשיב – א"כ מאי צריך למימר שלא לרצון מאי היא כו'? דמדקתני "לרצון מטמא" הו"מ למיפרך: אלמא לרצון חשיב כי משקה, ואשה דמניקה את בנה לרצון הוא. אלא אמר רבא כו' עד ולרבא מקום חלב מעין הוא ולא צריך הכשר. והתנן: האשה שנטף חלב מדדיה ונפל לאויר התנור, התנור טמא. וקשיא לן: במאי איתכשר! ואמר ר' יוחנן: בטיפה המלוכלכת ע"פ הדד. והשתא קשה לר"י: מאי קאמר "במאי איתכשר", דמדבעי הכשר – אלמא אוכל חשיב ליה, וא"כ איך יטמא אוכל את התנור, והא אין אוכל מטמא כלי? ואומר ר"י, דה"פ: וקשיא לן במאי איתכשר, כלומר: לא מבעיא שאין התנור טמא, אלא חלב הנוטף מדדיה גופה, אמאי יהא טמא הא לא איתכשר? ומשני: בטיפה המלוכלכת ע"פ הדד, ואותה טיפה עצמה המלוכלכת ע"פ הדד תטמא התנור, שהיא חשובה משקה ומשקה מטמא כלי, כדאמרינן בפ' קמא דמכילתין (דף יג:). והשתא פריך שפיר לרבא, דאמר דאפילו אמר לא ניחא לי מטמא חלב האשה, דחשיב משקה – והכא חשיב ליה אוכל. אבל לר"נ אמר רבה בר אבוה – אתי שפיר, דהכא דאמר לא ניחא לי – ודאי חשיב ליה אוכל. ונטף חלב מדדיה חשיב לא ניחא ליה, כיון שהוא נופל לאויר תנור ואזיל לאיבוד, דודאי לא ניחא ליה. ועוד פריך התם לרבא: מדתניא ט' משקין בזב הזיעה וליחה סרוחה והריעי טהורים מכלום, דמעת עינו ודם מגפתו וחלב האשה מטמא טומאת משקין ברביעית, רוקו וזובו ומימי רגליו מטמא טומאה חמורה בכל שהוא. ואי אמרת מקום חלב מעין הוא – חלב באשה נמי יטמא טומאה חמורה בכל שהוא, כזובו ורוקו. וקשה לרבי: מאי קפריך? לעולם מעין הוא, ואפ"ה לא יטמא טומאה חמורה – משום דבעינן דומיא דרוק, כדאיתא בנדה (ד' נו.): מה רוק שמתגלגל ויוצא וחוזר ונבלע, אף כל שמתגלגל ויוצא וחוזר ונבלע. יצא חלב שבאשה שמתגלגל ויוצא, ואינו חוזר ונבלע. ותימה הוא לומר דמה שהוא חוזר ונבלע גרם לו ליחשב כמעין. ומכל מקום, ודאי כן הוא! וצריך לומר: דמה שהיה חושבו רבא כמעין להיות חשיב משקה בפי התינוק – היינו משום דסלקא דעתיה שחוזר ונבלע. ומייתי ראיה מן המשנה דחוזר ונבלע הוא, מדקתני מטמא שלא לרצון. דהיינו אמר לא ניחא לי, א"כ חוזר ונבלע הוא. דאי לאו הכי – אם אמר לא ניחא ליה לא יהיה מטמא. והשתא פריך ליה מהכא דאינו חוזר ונבלע, אלמא מקום חלב האשה לאו מעין הוא! ופריך: אי הכי, קשה הא דקתני "מטמא שלא לרצון". ומשני: מי סברת שלא לרצון דלא ניחא ליה – לא, שלא לרצון בסתמא, דדעתיה דתינוק קרובה גבי חלב. אבל אמר לא ניחא ליה – טהור. והיא דנטף חלב מדדיה ונפל לתוך התנור – כאומר לא ניחא ליה חשיב, דודאי לא ניחא ליה כיון שהלך לאיבוד. והא דקאמר: שלא לרצון בסתמא – היינו כשנופל בקערה, שאינו הולך לאיבוד. דמהני טעמא דדעתיה דתינוק קרובה גבי חלב לאחשוביה או כמשקה. ובפי התינוק לעולם כאוכל חשיב. והשתא קשה לר"י: חדא, דבשמעתא מסקינן איפכא: לרצון – בסתמא, ושלא לרצון – דאמר לא ניחא ליה. ודומיא דהך דזיתים וענבים הוי ההוא דחלב האשה, דאי לאו הכי – לא שייך למימר יוכיחו. וכ"ת: ס"ל כאיבעית אימא, דאמר שאני סלי זיתים וענבים כיון דלאיבוד קיימא אפקורי מפקר להו – אכתי קשה: דדומיא דהכי אית לן למימר בחלב האשה דאזיל לאיבוד, וא"כ היינו באומר לא ניחא ליה. והתם מטמא דוקא סתמא, אבל לא ניחא ליה – טהור! ועוד קשה לרבי: מאי קאמר התם: אלא קשה הא מתני', וקאמר נמי: מי סברת שלא לרצון לא ניחא ליה, וקאמר דלא ניחא(ה) טהור. ואמאי? והא טעמא שלא לרצון טמא – היינו משום דחשיב דם מגפתו, דדם נעכר ונעשה חלב כדפי' לעיל, וא"כ גם אמר לא ניחא ליה נמי יהא טמא. מ"ר מי

ו א ב מיי' פ"י מהלכות טומאות אוכלין הל"ג:

ז ג מיי' פ"א שם הלכה ב ופ"י הלכה יב:

רבינו חננאל

והתנן במס' מכשירין אמרו לו זיתים וענבים יוכיחו שהמשקין היוצא מהן לרצון טמאין פי' מקבלין טומאה. מפני שהן משקין והמשקין אין צריכין הכשר ושלא לרצון טהורין כלומר אוכלין הן. וכיון שלא הוכשרו אינן מטמאין. ובאנו להעמיד משנה זו לרצון דניחא ליה. שלא לרצון בסתמא להודיע כי אפילו זיתים וענבים דבני סחיט' נינהו סתמא אוכל הן. וכ"ש תותים ורמונים. ואמרינן לא. פי' לרצון דמתניתין בסתמא. וכל סתם משקה הוא חשוב. ופי' שלא לרצון דגלי אדעתא בפי' שאין רצונו להוציא מהן משקין. (איכא) [איבעיא] תימא שאני סלי זיתים וענבים כיון שהסלין לאו בני קיבול משקה הן דבר ידוע הוא שכל משקה השותת מהן לעפר והולך וזהו לאיבוד כאילו מעיקרא הפקירן וכשאינן חשובין ולפיכך הן טהורין. תוב אתינן לפרושי דרבנן מודו לי' לר' יהודה בשאר פירות מהא דתניא סוחטין בפגעים. יש מי שאומר ספיגיל ובפרישין ובעוזרדין אבל לא ברמונים. ואוקימנא אפילו תימא רבנן כיון דלא בני סחיטה נינהו אפילו לכתחלה. ושל בית מנשיא היו סוחטין בחול ברמונים ועושין ממנו יין של רמונים כלומר שהרמונים בני סחיטה נינהו כזיתים וענבים ואסור לסוחטן בשבת. אמר רב נחמן הלכה כשל בית מנשיא בן מנחם. ואמרינן וכי מנשיא תנא הוא. ואוקימנא האי תנא

שייך לעמוד הקודם

הגהות הב"ח

(א) תום' ד"ה מחמיר וכו' שדמה טהור. נ"ב ובתוספות יו"ט סוף מס' מכשירין מתרץ קושיא זו דבאמת דם בהמה לשתיה מכשיר כמו חלב שהוא לשתיה ע"כ מוכרח לומר מדם הקזה והחולב לרפוא' ע"ש: (ב) ד"ה לא לרצון וכו' לא ניחא לי תניא כצ"ל ואות ד' נמחק: (ג) בא"ד התירו לה למגע טמא מת: (ד) בא"ד אמר רבה בר אבוה שינק בתקיפה: (ה) בא"ד וקאמר דלא ניחא ליה טהור:

עין משפט נר מצוה

ח א מיי' פ"ה מהלכות כלאים הל"ח טוש"ע יו"ד סימן רצו סעיף יד:

ט ב מיי' פ"ז מהלכות מקוואות הלכה א סמג עשין רמח:

י ג מיי' שם והלכה ט סמג שם טוש"ע יו"ד סימן רא סעיף כה:

יא ד מיי' פ"י מהלכות טומאת אוכלין הלכה יג ופי"א הלכה ו:

יב ה מיי' פ"ח מהלכות שבת הל"י סמג לאוין סה טור שו"ע או"ח סימן שכ סעיף ד:

יג ו ז מיי' שם וסמג שם טור שו"ע או"ח סימן תקה:

יד ח ט מיי' פ"ט מהל' טומאת אוכלין הל"ב:

גמרא

בפגעין ובפרישין ובעוזרדין, אבל לא ברמונים. ושל בית מנשיא בר מנחם היו סוחטין ברמונים. וממאי דרבנן היא, דילמא ר' יהודה היא? ותהוי נמי ר' יהודה, אימר דשמעת ליה לר' יהודה יצאו מעצמן, סוחטין לכתחילה מי שמעת ליה? אלא מאי אית לך למימר – כיון דלאו בני סחיטה נינהו – אפילו לכתחילה; אפילו תימא רבנן, כיון דלאו בני סחיטה נינהו – אפילו לכתחילה. ש"מ: רבנן היא, ש"מ. "של בית מנשיא בר מנחם היו סוחטין ברמונים". אמר רב נחמן: הלכה כשל בית מנשיא בר מנחם. א"ל רבא לרב נחמן: מנשיא בן מנחם תנא הוא?! וכי תימא "הלכה כי האי תנא דסבר לה כשל מנשיא בן מנחם", ומשום דסבר כמנשיא בן מנחם הלכה כמותו? מנשיא בן מנחם הוי *רובא דעלמא?! אין, דתנן: *המקיים קוצים בכרם, ר"א אומר: קידש, וחכ"א: [א]אינו מקדש אלא דבר שכמוהו מקיימין. וא"ר חנינא: מ"ט דרבי *אליעזר – שכן בערביא מקיימין קוצי שדות לגמליהם. מידי איריא; דערביא – אתרא, הכא – בטלה דעתו אצל כל אדם! אלא, היינו טעמא כדרב חסדא; דאמר רב חסדא: תרדין שסחטן ונתנן במקוה – פוסלין את המקוה בשינוי מראה. והא לאו בני סחיטה נינהו! אלא מאי אית לך למימר – כיון דאחשבינהו – הוה להו משקה. ה"נ כיון דאחשבינהו הוה להו משקה. רב פפא אמר: משום דהוי דבר שאין עושין ממנו מקוה לכתחילה, [ב]וכל דבר שאין עושין ממנו מקוה לכתחילה – פוסל את המקוה בשינוי מראה. *תנן התם: [ג]נפל לתוכו יין או חומץ ומוחל ושינה מראיו – פסול. מאן תנא דמוחל משקה הוא? אמר אביי: רבי יעקב היא. *דתניא, ר' יעקב אומר: [ד]מוחל הרי הוא כמשקה. ומה טעם אמרו "מוחל היוצא בתחלה טהור" – לפי שאינו רוצה בקיומו. ר"ש אומר: מוחל אינו כמשקה, ומה טעם אמרו "מוחל היוצא מעיקול בית הבד טמא" – לפי שאי אפשר לו בלא ציחצוחי שמן. מאי בינייהו? איכא בינייהו דאתי בתר איצצתא. רבא אמר: משום דהוי דבר שאין עושין הימנו מקוה, ופוסל את המקוה בשינוי מראה. אמר רב יהודה אמר שמואל: [ה]סוחט אדם אשכול של ענבים לתוך הקדרה, אבל לא לתוך הקערה. אמר רב חסדא, מדברי רבינו נלמד: *[ו]חולב אדם עז לתוך הקדרה, אבל לא לתוך הקערה. [ז]אלמא קסבר: משקה הבא לאוכל – אוכל הוא. מתיב רמי בר חמא: *[ח]זב שחולב את העז – החלב טמא, ואי אמרת: "משקה הבא לאוכלין אוכל הוא", במאי איתכשר? *כדאמר ר' יוחנן: בטיפה המלוכלכת ע"פ הדד. הכא נמי: בטיפה המלוכלכת ע"פ הדד. מתיב רבינא: *[ט]טמא מת שסחט זיתים וענבים, כביצה

תוספות

מי דמי ערביא אתרא הוא. הו"מ למיפרך: הניחא לרבי אליעזר, לרבנן מאי איכא למימר? אלא פריך דאפילו לרבי אליעזר לא ניחא. ומה שקשה מאנשי הוצל דפרק "המצניע" (לעיל דף צב:) פירשתי שם (ד"ה ואת"ל): **ה"נ** כיון דאחשביה הוו להו משקה. תחלה ס"ד דסוחטין בפגעין כו' – היינו סחיטה ממש. אבל השתא – אי אפשר לומר. דהא פשיטא דאסור, דכיון דאחשביה הוה להו משקה. אלא סוחטין דקתני – היינו בליי"ר בלע"ז, למתק הפרי כדפי' בקונטרס: **אמר** אביי ר' יעקב היא. קשה לי: לימא דהאי מוחל דקתני – היינו במוחל היוצא מעקול בית הבד, ודברי הכל. וכי תימא מדקתני מוחל סתמא – משמע דבכל מוחל איירי, לא היא. דע"כ אפי' לרבי יעקב לא איירי בכל מוחל, דהא מודה דמוחל היוצא בתחילה טהור! י"ל דמוחל היוצא מעקול בית הבד לא הוה קרינן ליה מוחל סתם, כיון דאי אפשר לו בלא לאלוחי שמן: **חולב** אדם עז כו'. נראה לר"ת: דהיינו דווקא בי"ט, דחזיא בהמה לאכילה הוי כמו אוכלא דאיפרת. אבל בשבת לא חזיא לשחיטה – כמו דש תשיבא, שהבהמה היא כפסולת וכשחולב הוי כנוטל אוכל מתוך פסולת. וכן משמע בבה"ג, דבי"ט איירי. ומיהו, סחיטת זיתים וענבים דשרי לעיל לתוך הקדירה היינו אפי' בשבת, כיון דאשכול חזיא לאכילה:

כבילה

רש"י

בפגעין. פרונ"ש בלע"ז, ולהוציא מימיהן לשתות: ובפרישין. קויידונ"ץ: ובעוזרדין. קורמ"ש. דלאו אורחייהו בהכי, ואין כאן משום דש: אבל לא ברמונים. דאורחייהו בהכי: ושל בית מנשיא. היו רגילין לסחוט רמונים בחול, אלמא איכא דסחיט להו, הלכך בשבת אסור: אלא מאי אית לך למימר. לר' יהודה, כיון דלאו בני סחיטה כו'. וכי היכי דלרבי יהודה שרי לכתחילה מהאי טעמא, מהשתא אפי' תימא רבנן, ושרו ליה מהאי טעמא: מנשיא תנא הוא. בתמיה: וכי איהו פליג למימר דבשבת אסור, דתימא הלכתא כוותיה? והא לא הוזכר אלא לדברי התנא לראיה דהאי תנא הוא סבר כוותיה: וכ"ת. הא דאמר הלכה כשל בית מנשיא, ה"ק: הלכה כהאי תנא דאסר ברימונים, הואיל וקאי מנשיא כוותיה, דסוחטין רימונים בחול. אלמא: בני סחיטה נינהו: הוי רובא דעלמא. דמשום איהו לחודיה נשווי דרך רמונים לסחיטה: קוצים. קרדונ"ש: מקדש. את התבואה משום כלאים, דזריעה הוא: ואמר רבי חנינא כו'. אלמא: משום חד מקום דאחשבינהו, משוינן להו דבר חשוב: אתרא. הוא, וחשיבות דרבים הוי חשיבותא: הכא. חד גברא לחודיה הוא, נימא בטלה דעתו: אלא היינו טעמא. דרב נחמן, דאמר הלכה: אין סוחטין: כרב חסדא. אע"ג דלעלמא לא חשיב, כיון דאחשיב איהו – הוי לדידיה משקה. והכי מפרש רב נחמן לברייתא דלעיל: סוחטין בפגעין ובפרישין למתק הפרי, ולא לצורך המשקה. אבל לא ברימונים ואפילו למתקן(א), דשל בית מנשיא היו סוחטין בחול לצורך משקה, הלכך בשבת אסור אפי' למתק, הואיל ואיכא חד דעביד לשם משקה. ולא משום דמנשיא רובא דעלמא, אלא קיישינן, אי שרית ליה למתק – אתי למעבד לשום משקה, וכיון דאיהו מחשב ליה הוי משקה ומיחייב. אבל בפגעין ליכא(ב) למיחש, דאין אדם עושה אותו למשקה: בשינוי מראה. לא בשלשת לוגין, דלא הוזכרו שלש לוגין אלא במים שאובין, אבל שאר משקין לא פסלי אא"כ נשתנה מראה המקוה על ידיהן: רב פפא אמר. טעמא דתרדין לאו משום חשיבותא דאחשבינהו הוא, ולעולם לאו משקה נינהו. והא דמפסיל – משום דכל דבר שאין עושין ממנו מקוה שאינו מים או שלג או ברד – פוסל את המקוה בשינוי מראה: נפל לתוכו. של מקוה יין או חומץ או מוחל. והוא כמין מים, וזב מן הזיתים, וג' מינים יש בו: כשטוענן מתחילה במעטן להתחמם ולהתבשל מאליהן מוחל זב מהן, והוא צלול כמים. ולאחר שעמדו ימים ודחקו זה את זה חוזר מוחל לזוב מהן, והוא קרוב להיות כשמן. ולאחר שעגלן להוציא שמנן בבית הבד ומשתהה התפוח של גפת בעקלים שהוא אגוד בהן בבית הבד, חוזר מוחל וזב מהן: מאן תנא דמוחל משקה הוא. קס"ד דאין מקוה נפסל אלא על ידי משקה, ואפילו בשינוי מראה: בתחילה. בתחילת טעינתן של זיתים: מעקול בית הבד. לאחר שנסחט שמנו, או לפני סחיטתו: מאי בינייהו. במאי פליגי. הואיל ותרווייהו מודו דמוחל היוצא בתחילה טהור, והיוצא מעקל בית הבד טמא, באיזה מוחל נחלקו, דלמר הוי משקה וטמא, ולמר לא הוי משקה וטהור? דאתי בתר איצצתא. לאחר שהתחילו להתחמם ודחקו זה את זה ונשתהה הכומר ימים: רבא אמר. קמייתא דקתני: מוחל פוסל מקוה – דברי הכל הוא, ומשום דהוי כו': לתוך הקדרה. של תבשיל לתקנו. דמוכחא מילתא דלאו למשקה בעי ליה, אלא לאוכל, ואין זה דרך פריקתו, והוי כמפריד אוכל מאוכל: אבל לא לתוך הקערה. דזימנין דלמשקה קאי, ואף על גב דבקערה לא שתי איניש – לא מוכחא מילתא, ואיכא איסור: אלמא. מדקאמר: סוחט לתוך הקדרה, קסבר כו': החלב טמא. שהזב מטמא כל דבר במשא, והרי היסט הקילוח. ולא קמפליג בין לתוך הקדרה בין לתוך הכוס: ואי אמרת אוכל הוא. הא אין אוכל מקבל טומאה שלא בהכשר, והאי במאי איתכשר: כדאמר רבי יוחנן. במסכת כריתות, גבי האשה שנטף חלב מדדיה: בטיפה המלוכלכת על פי הדד. טיפה ראשונה מלכלכת בה פי הדד בדעת, ונוחה ליחלב, והיא הוי משקה כשתסס חלב, דלא לאוכל בעי ליה: טמא מת שסחט זיתים וענבים

כבילה

רבינו חננאל

דאמר סוחטין בפגעין ובפרישין ובעוזרדין אבל לא ברמונים וסבר לה כמנשיא בן מנחם שסוחט בחול ברמונים להוציא מהן מים וכן כמו זיתים וענבי' וקיי"ל כוותיה ואקשינן וכי מנשיא הוה רובא לעלמא. ומהדרינן אין. כי הא דתנן המקיים קוצים בכרם וכו' ואוקימנא אע"פ שאין דרך בני אדם לקיים קוצים בכרם כיון שבערביא מקיימין קידש הכא נמי אע"פ שאין דרך בני אדם לסחוט רמונים בחול כיון שסוחטין של בית מנשיא בחול בשבת אסור לסחוט ודחינן ערביא מקום בני אדם רבים ומנשיא אדם אחד הוא ובטלה דעתו אצל [כל] בני אדם ואתינן לטעמא אחריתי אלא האי תנא כטעמיה דרב חסדא דאמר תרדין שסחטן ונתנן למקוה פסלו המקוה בשנוי מראה וכיון שהזכרנו פסולות המקוה אמרינן. תנן התם [נפל] לתוכו יין ומוהל כו' פי' מוהל המים היוצאים מעוקל בית הבד עת שטוען קורות בית הבד על הזיתים הטחונין והוא מי הזיתים ויש בהן צחצוחי שמן: איצצאי דוחק. כדגרסינן בפרק המפקיד (דף מ ע"א)

אמר ר' יהודה אמר שמואל סוחט אדם אשכול של ענבים בתוך הקדירה אבל לא לתוך הקערה. אמר רב חסדא מדברי רבינו נלמד חולב אדם עז לתוך הקדירה אבל לא לתוך הקערה אלמא קא סבר משקה הבא לאוכל אוכל הוא. ואותביה רמי [בר חמא] זב שחלב עז החלב טמא. כלומר (טמא) [שטימא אותה] הזב בנגיעתו. וא"ת אוכל הוא במאי אתכשר ופרקינן כר' יוחנן דאמר איתכשר בטפה המלוכלכת על

מסורת הש"ס

[לעיל נב. וכם נסמן]

כלאים פ"ה מ"ח ב"ב קנו:

[נ"ל אלעזר]

מקוואות פ"ז מ"ד

תוספ' דטהרות פרק י

[ע"ל תוס' עג: ד"ה מפרק וכו']

טהרות פ"ג מ"ג

כריתות יג. פסחים לג:

טהרות פ"ג מ"ג

הגהות הב"ח

(א) רש"י ד"ה כרב חסדא וכו' ואפילו למתקן הואיל דשל בית וכו': (ב) בא"ד למיחש להכי דאין אדם:

גליון הש"ס

רש"י ד"ה לתוך הקדירה ואין זה דרך פריקתו. עיין לעיל דף עג ע"ב תוספות ד"ה מפרק:

רב נסים גאון

פכ"ב רבא אמר משום דהוה דבר שאין עושין ממנו מקוה לכתחילה וכל דבר שאין עושין ממנו מקוה לכתחילה פוסל את המקוה בשינוי מראה. עיקר דיליה בתורת כהנים מקוה מים לא מקוה כל המשקין כולן פרט לשנפל בתוכו מי כבשין ומי צבעין ושינו את מראיו ובתוספתא טבול יום (פרק א) חומר במשקין שאין להן טהרת הגוף ואין להן טהרה מטומאתן ואינן טהורין בגוף ופוסלין את המקוה בשינוי מראה מה שאין כן במים: **כדאמר** ר' יוחנן בטיפה על פי הדד. משכחת לה במס' כריתות בפרק אמרו לו אכלת חלב (דף יג) ולרבא מקום חלב מעין הוא ולא צריך הכשר והתנן האשה שחלב מדדיה ונפל לאויר תנור תנור טמא וקשיא לן במאי איתכשר ואמר ר' יוחנן בטיפה מלוכלכת ע"פ הדד ואין

כביצה מכוונת טהור. מִשְׁנָה הִיא בְּמַסֶּכֶת טָהֳרוֹת, וּמְפָרֵשׁ בָּהּ בְּהֶדְיָא: וּבִלְבַד שֶׁלֹּא יִגַּע בַּמַּשְׁקֶה, שֶׁאֵינוֹ נוֹגֵעַ אֶלָּא בָּאוֹכֶל. וְכֵיוָן דִּכְבֵיצָה מְכוּוֶּנֶת הוּא, לְכִי סָחֵיט טִיפָּה קַמַּיְיתָא – חָסֵר לֵיהּ מִכְּבֵיצָה. וְאֵין הָאוֹכֶל, אַע"פ שֶׁהוּא טָמֵא, מְטַמֵּא הַמַּשְׁקֶה – שֶׁאֵין אוֹכֶל מְטַמֵּא אֲחֵרִים בְּפָחוֹת מִכְּבֵיצָה. אֲבָל אִם הָיָה נוֹגֵעַ בְּמַשְׁקֶה – אִיטַּמֵּי לֵיהּ מַשְׁקֶה מִטִּיפָּה רִאשׁוֹנָה, שֶׁהַמַּשְׁקֶה מְקַבֵּל טוּמְאָה בְּכָל שֶׁהוּא. וְה"נ תָּנֵי בָּהּ בְּהֶדְיָא יוֹתֵר מִכְּבֵיצָה – טָמֵא. שֶׁכֵּיוָן שֶׁיָּצְאָה טִיפָּה רִאשׁוֹנָה – נִטְמְאָה בִּכְבֵיצָה. וּטְמֵא מֵת דְּנָקַט, שֶׁאֵינוֹ מְטַמֵּא בְּהֶיסֵּט. וְה"ה לִטְמֵא שֶׁרֶץ וְכָל טְמֵאֵי מַגָּע. וּטְמֵא מֵת לְרַבּוּתָא נָקַט, דְּהָוֵי אַב הַטּוּמְאָה, מִשּׁוּם דְּקָתָנֵי סֵיפָא: אֲבָל זָב שֶׁסּוֹחֵט זֵיתִים וַעֲנָבִים אֲפִי' גַּרְגִּיר יְחִידִי טָמֵא, שֶׁכֵּיוָן שֶׁיָּצְאָה טִיפָּה רִאשׁוֹנָה נִטְמָא הַמַּשְׁקֶה בְּמַשָּׂא הַזָּב: וְאִי אָמְרַתְּ כו'. דְּקס"ד אֲפִי' סוֹחֵט לְתוֹךְ הַקְּדֵירָה: כְּתַנָּאֵי. מַשְׁקֶה הַבָּא לָאוֹכֶל, אוֹכֶל הוּא אוֹ מַשְׁקֶה הוּא: הַמַּחֲלִיק בָּעֲנָבִים. נַחְתּוֹם הַמַּחֲלִיק פְּנֵי כִּכָּרוֹתָיו בַּעֲנָבִים, שֶׁסּוֹחֵט הַמַּשְׁקֶה עַל הַכִּכָּר: הוּכְשַׁר. הָאוֹכֶל *הָעֲנָבִים הוּכְשְׁרוּ: הַבָּא. לְצוֹרֶךְ אוֹכֶל, כְּגוֹן שֶׁסְּחָטָן לְשֵׁם הַפַּת: ה"ג: דְּכ"ע מַשְׁקֶה הַבָּא לָאוֹכֶל לָאו אוֹכֶל הוּא. אֶלָּא מַשְׁקֶה הוּא. וְהַיְינוּ טַעְמָא דְּמ"ד לֹא הוּכְשַׁר – שֶׁמִּתְּחִילָּה נִסְחַט אַדַּעְתָּא דְּאָזֵיל לְאִיבּוּד, שֶׁהָאוּר שׁוֹאֲבוֹ וְשׂוֹרְפוֹ: הַמְפַצֵּעַ בַּזֵּיתִים. בלעי"ר, כְּדֵי שֶׁיִּהְיוּ רַכִּין: הוּכְשַׁר. דְּנִיחָא לֵיהּ בְּמַשְׁקֶה דְּטָיֵיף עֲלַיְיהוּ, שֶׁמִּתּוֹךְ כָּךְ הֵם מַרְבִּים טַעַם: לְסוֹפְתָן בְּמֶלַח. שֶׁמִּתּוֹךְ שֶׁהֵן קָשִׁין אֵין הַמֶּלַח נִדְבָּק בָּהֶן, וּמְפַצְּעָם לְרַכְּכָן מִבַּחוּץ מְעַט: לֹא הוּכְשַׁר. דְּלָא מְכַוֵּין לְמַשְׁקֶה דִּידְהוּ דְּלִיעֲבַר: לֵידַע אִם הִגִּיעוּ זֵיתָיו לְמְסוֹק. צָרִיךְ הוּא לִרְאוֹת אִם שׁוּמְנוֹ נוֹחַ לָצֵאת. מִיהוּ, הַמַּשְׁקֶה אָזֵיל לְאִיבּוּד: הָנֵי תַּנָּאֵי. דִּמְפַצֵּעַ, וַדַּאי בְּמַשְׁקֶה הָעוֹמֵד לְאִיבּוּד פְּלִיגֵי, כִּדְאָמְרִי'. אֲבָל תַּנָּאֵי דְּמַחֲלִיק – לָאו בְּעוֹמֵד לְאִיבּוּד פְּלִיגֵי, דְּלָאו לְאִיבּוּד אָזֵיל – שֶׁהֲרֵי לְצַחְצֵחַ הָאוֹכֶל נְתָנוֹ, וַהֲרֵי מְצַחְצְחוֹ. אֶלָּא בְּמַשְׁקֶה הָעוֹמֵד לְצַחְצְחוֹ לְאוֹכֶל קָא מִיפַּלְגֵי, דְּא"נ מַשְׁקֶה הַבָּא לָאוֹכֶל מַשְׁקֶה הוּא – ה"מ הֵיכָא דְּקָא שָׁרֵיף לֵיהּ. א"נ שָׁטַר בֵּיהּ רִיפְתָּא דְּתוֹרַת מַשְׁקֶה עָבֵיד, אֲבָל לְצַחְצְחוֹ פְּלִיגֵי: וְדָג לְצִירוֹ. סְחִיטַת דָּג לְהוֹצִיא צִירוֹ – לָאו מַשְׁקֶה הוּא, אֶלָּא אוֹכָלִין: כְּבָשִׁין. יָרָק חַי כָּבוּשׁ בְּיַיִן וְחוֹמֶץ: לְגוּפוֹ. אִם לֶאֱכוֹל הַכְּבָשִׁים סוֹחֲטָן מִמַּשְׁקֶה הַצָּף עֲלֵיהֶן וְהַנִּבְלָע בָּהֶן – מוּתָּר לְכַתְּחִילָּה, דְּלָא מְפָרֵק הוּא, הוֹאִיל וְלָאו לְמַשְׁקֶה הוּא צָרִיךְ: פָּטוּר. שֶׁאֵין זֶה מְפָרֵק, שֶׁאֵין הַמַּשְׁקֶה הַזֶּה יוֹצֵא מִן הַכְּבָשִׁים, שֶׁלֹּא גָּדַל בְּתוֹכָן. אֲבָל אָסוּר, אַטּוּ זֵיתִים וַעֲנָבִים: שְׁלָקוֹת. אֲפִילּוּ לְמֵימֵיהֶן, לָאו מַשְׁקֶה נִינְהוּ אֶלָּא אוֹכֶל: לְמֵימֵיהֶן פָּטוּר אֲבָל אָסוּר. וְהָא שְׁלָקוֹת דּוּמְיָא דְּדָג לְצִירָן הוּא, וְלָא שָׁרֵי לֵיהּ שְׁמוּאֵל לְכַתְּחִילָּה: עֵינַי רָאוּ וְלֹא זָר. הָא דְּבָעֵינָא לְמֵימַר לָךְ דְּמִשְּׁמֵיהּ דְּרַב אִיתְּמַר: סוֹחֲטִין כְּבָשִׁין. וְלָא מַפְלִיג בֵּין לְגוּפָן בֵּין לְמֵימֵיהֶן, וְשָׁרֵי לְכַתְּחִילָּה. וְקַשְׁיָא לְכוּלְּהוּ, דְּלֵיכָּא בְּהוּ דְּשָׁרֵי כְּבָשִׁין לְמֵימֵיהֶן לְכַתְּחִילָּה: דְּבַר תּוֹרָה. כְּלוֹמַר: אָסְרָה תּוֹרָה מְלָאכָה. וּדְרִיכַת זֵיתִים וַעֲנָבִים הוּא דַּהֲוְיָא מְלָאכָה, אֲבָל שְׁאָר דְּרִיכוֹת – לָאו אוֹרְחַיְיהוּ בְּהָכִי וְלָאו מְלָאכָה נִינְהוּ:

תורה אור

כְּבֵיצָה מְכוּוֶּנֶת – טָהוֹר. הָא יוֹתֵר מִכְּבֵיצָה – טָמֵא. וְאִי אָמְרַתְּ "מַשְׁקֶה הַבָּא לָאוֹכֶל אוֹכֶל הוּא" בְּמַאי אִיתַּכְשַׁר? הוּא מוֹתִיב לַהּ וְהוּא מְפָרֵק לַהּ: בְּסוֹחֵט לְתוֹךְ הַקְּעָרָה. א"ר יִרְמְיָה: כְּתַנָּאֵי; *הַמַּחֲלִיק בָּעֲנָבִים – לֹא הוּכְשַׁר, רַבִּי יְהוּדָה אוֹמֵר: הוּכְשַׁר. מַאי לָאו בְּהָא קָמִיפַּלְגִי; מ"ס: מַשְׁקֶה הַבָּא לָאוֹכֶל – אוֹכֶל הוּא, וּמ"ס: לָאו אוֹכֶל הוּא. אָמַר רַב פַּפָּא: דְּכוּלֵּי עָלְמָא[א] – מַשְׁקֶה הַבָּא לָאוֹכֶל – לָאו אוֹכֶל הוּא, וְהָכָא – בְּמַשְׁקֶה הַבָּא לְאִיבּוּד קָמִיפַּלְגִי. מָר סָבַר: מַשְׁקֶה הוּא, וּמ"ס: לָאו מַשְׁקֶה הוּא. וּבִפְלוּגְתָּא דְּהָנֵי תַּנָּאֵי, דְּתַנְיָא: אהַמְפַצֵּעַ בְּזֵיתִים בְּיָדַיִם מְסוֹאָבוֹת – הוּכְשַׁר, לְסוֹפְתָן בְּמֶלַח – לֹא הוּכְשַׁר. לֵידַע אִם הִגִּיעוּ זֵיתָיו לְמִסּוֹק אִם לָאו – לֹא הוּכְשַׁר, רַבִּי יְהוּדָה אוֹמֵר: הוּכְשַׁר. מַאי לָאו בְּהָא קָמִיפַּלְגִי, דְּמ"ס: מַשְׁקֶה הָעוֹמֵד לְאִיבּוּד – מַשְׁקֶה הוּא, וּמ"ס: לָאו מַשְׁקֶה הוּא. אָמַר רַב הוּנָא בְּרֵיהּ דְּרַב יְהוֹשֻׁעַ: הָנֵי תַּנָּאֵי – בְּמַשְׁקֶה הָעוֹמֵד לְאִיבּוּד פְּלִיגִי, וְהָנָךְ תַּנָּאֵי – בְּמַשְׁקֶה הָעוֹמֵד לְצַחְצְחוֹ קָמִיפַּלְגִי. א"ר זֵירָא אָמַר רַב חִיָּיא בַּר אַשִׁי אָמַר רַב: סוֹחֵט אָדָם אֶשְׁכּוֹל שֶׁל עֲנָבִים לְתוֹךְ הַקְּדֵרָה, אֲבָל לֹא לְתוֹךְ הַקְּעָרָה. בוְדָג לְצִירוֹ – אֲפִילּוּ לְתוֹךְ הַקְּעָרָה. יְתֵיב רַב דִּימִי וְקָאָמַר לַהּ לְהָא שְׁמַעְתָּא. א"ל אַבַּיֵי לְרַב דִּימִי: אַתּוּן מִשְּׁמֵיהּ דְּרַב מַתְנִיתוּן וְלָא קַשְׁיָא לְכוּ, אֲנַן מִשְּׁמֵיהּ דִּשְׁמוּאֵל מַתְנִינַן לַהּ – וְקַשְׁיָא לָן: מִי אֲמַר שְׁמוּאֵל "דָּג לְצִירוֹ אֲפִי' לְתוֹךְ הַקְּעָרָה" וְהָאִיתְּמַר: כְּבָשִׁים שֶׁסְּחָטָן, אָמַר רַב: לְגוּפָן – מוּתָּר, לְמֵימֵיהֶן – פָּטוּר, אֲבָל אָסוּר. וּשְׁלָקוֹת – בֵּין לְגוּפָן בֵּין לְמֵימֵיהֶן – מוּתָּר. וּשְׁמוּאֵל אָמַר: אֶחָד כְּבָשִׁים וְאֶחָד °שְׁלָקוֹת, לְגוּפָן – מוּתָּר, לְמֵימֵיהֶן – פָּטוּר אֲבָל אָסוּר. א"ל: הָאֱלֹהִים, °"עֵינַי רָאוּ וְלֹא זָר (כָּלוּ כִלְיוֹתַי בְּחֵקִי וגו')". מִפּוּמֵּיהּ דְּר' יִרְמְיָה שְׁמִיעַ לִי, וְר' יִרְמְיָה מֵר' זֵירָא, וְר' זֵירָא מֵרַב חִיָּיא בַּר אַשִׁי, וְרַב חִיָּיא בַּר אַשִׁי מֵרַב. § גּוּפָא: כְּבָשִׁים שֶׁסְּחָטָן, אָמַר רַב: לְגוּפָן – מוּתָּר, לְמֵימֵיהֶן – פָּטוּר אֲבָל אָסוּר. וּשְׁלָקוֹת, בֵּין לְגוּפָן בֵּין לְמֵימֵיהֶן – מוּתָּר. וּשְׁמוּאֵל אָמַר: גאֶחָד זֶה וְאֶחָד זֶה, לְגוּפָן – מוּתָּר, לְמֵימֵיהֶן – פָּטוּר אֲבָל אָסוּר. רַבִּי יוֹחָנָן אָמַר: אֶחָד כְּבָשִׁים וְאֶחָד שְׁלָקוֹת, לְגוּפָן – מוּתָּר, לְמֵימֵיהֶן – חַיָּיב חַטָּאת. מֵיתִיבִי: סוֹחֲטִין כְּבָשִׁים בְּשַׁבָּת לְצוֹרֶךְ הַשַּׁבָּת, אֲבָל לֹא לְמוֹצ"ש. וְזֵיתִים וַעֲנָבִים לֹא יִסְחוֹט, וְאִם סָחַט – חַיָּיב חַטָּאת. קַשְׁיָא לְרַב, קַשְׁיָא לִשְׁמוּאֵל, קַשְׁיָא לְר' יוֹחָנָן. רַב מְתָרֵץ לְטַעְמֵיהּ, שְׁמוּאֵל מְתָרֵץ לְטַעְמֵיהּ, ר' יוֹחָנָן מְתָרֵץ לְטַעְמֵיהּ, רַב מְתָרֵץ לְטַעְמֵיהּ: סוֹחֲטִין כְּבָשִׁים בְּשַׁבָּת לְצוֹרֶךְ הַשַּׁבָּת, אֲבָל לֹא לְמוֹצ"ש. בד"א – לְגוּפָן, אֲבָל לְמֵימֵיהֶן – פָּטוּר אֲבָל אָסוּר. וּשְׁלָקוֹת, בֵּין לְגוּפָן בֵּין לְמֵימֵיהֶן – מוּתָּר. וְזֵיתִים וַעֲנָבִים – לֹא יִסְחוֹט, וְאִם סְחָטָן – חַיָּיב חַטָּאת. שְׁמוּאֵל מְתָרֵץ לְטַעְמֵיהּ: סוֹחֲטִין כְּבָשִׁים בְּשַׁבָּת לְצוֹרֶךְ הַשַּׁבָּת, הוּא הַדִּין לִשְׁלָקוֹת. בד"א – לְגוּפָן, אֲבָל לְמֵימֵיהֶן – פָּטוּר אֲבָל אָסוּר. וְזֵיתִים וַעֲנָבִים – לֹא יִסְחוֹט, וְאִם סָחַט – חַיָּיב חַטָּאת. ר' יוֹחָנָן מְתָרֵץ לְטַעְמֵיהּ: סוֹחֲטִין כְּבָשִׁים לְצוֹרֶךְ הַשַּׁבָּת, אֲבָל לֹא לְמוֹצ"ש. אֶחָד כְּבָשִׁים וְאֶחָד שְׁלָקוֹת, בד"א – לְגוּפָן, אֲבָל לְמֵימֵיהֶן – לֹא יִסְחוֹט, וְאִם סָחַט – נַעֲשָׂה כְּמִי שֶׁסָּחַט זֵיתִים וַעֲנָבִים, וְחַיָּיב חַטָּאת. אָמַר רַב חִיָּיא בַּר אַשִׁי אָמַר רַב: דדְּבַר תּוֹרָה – אֵינוֹ חַיָּיב אֶלָּא עַל דְּרִיסַת זֵיתִים וַעֲנָבִים בִּלְבַד. וְכֵן תָּנֵי דְּבֵי מְנַשֶּׁה: דְּבַר תּוֹרָה – אֵינוֹ חַיָּיב אֶלָּא עַל דְּרִיסַת זֵיתִים וַעֲנָבִים בִּלְבַד. *הוְאֵין עֵד מִפִּי עֵד כָּשֵׁר

אלא

לעדות

כביצה מכוונת טהור. פי' בקונטרס: שאע"פ שהאוכל טמא אינו מטמא את המשקה, שאין אוכל מטמא בפחות מכביצה. והאי טעמא לא ניחא אלא למ"ד בפרק "כל שעה" (פסחים דף לג: ושם): משקים מיפקד פקידי, אבל למ"ד התם מיבלע בליעי – טמאים המשקין מאליהן כיון שנגע באוכל. [ומשני התם: דבמתני' מיירי בענבים שלא הוכשרו. לאימת מתכשרי – לכי סחיט להו, וכי סחיט להו בליר שעוריה. והשתא לפי' רש"י מה בכך]? מיד כשיצאה הטיפה ראשונה(א) נטמאה, הואיל ואוכל מקבל טומאה בכל שהוא. ומה שהקשה ר"ת לפירו', פי' לעיל בריש "המצניע" (דף צא.):

דכ"ע משקה הבא לאוכל לאו אוכל הוא. לא מצינן למימר דכ"ע אוכל הוא(ב) א"כ מ"ט דמ"ד הוכשר?:

אם הגיעו זיתיו למסוק כו'. מה שקשה ליה לרב נחמן דמפרש בפ"ק (דף יז.) דגזרו לבצור בטהרה, משום דפעמים שאדם הולך כו'. שם פירשתי בד"ה "גוזרני":

כבשים שסחטן לגופן מותר למימיהן פטור אבל אסור. רב לטעמיה. דאמר לקמן: דבר תורה אינו חייב אלא על דריכת זיתים וענבים. ולפירוש הקונטרס, דפי' משום דאתי המשקה מעלמא – קשה לרבי: אמאי גזרו להדוקי אודרא אפומא דשישא בשלהי "תולין" (לעיל דף קמא.) שמא יסחוט? הא אפילו סחיט ליכא איסור דאורייתא! מיהו, י"ל: דהתם רבא דקאמר לה, וס"ל כר' יוחנן דמחייב חטאת:

ורבי יוחנן אמר אחד כבשין ואחד שלקות לגופן מותר למימיהן חייב חטאת. ובדג לצירו נמי הוה מחייב ר' יוחנן חטאת, לתוך הקערה, דדג לצירו מדמינן לשלקות בכולה שמעתיה, דפריך מדשמואל דשלקות אההיא דדג לצירו. ופי' ר"ת: דהלכה כר' יוחנן, דקי"ל כוותיה לגבי רב ושמואל. ושמעינן ממילתא דר"י שאסור לסחוט כבשים ושלקות למימיהן, ואם סחט – חייב חטאת. ולא הפריש בסחיטה בין קדירה לקער', אלא הכל אסור. מתוך אלו דברים מתברר שאין הלכה לא כשמואל ולא כרב, שאמרו: סוחט אדם אשכול של ענבים לתוך הקדירה. ויש שמעמידין דברי רב ושמואל ביו"ט, מדדייק רב חסדא מדברי שמואל כן. ואין לנו להדורי אפירכי ולאפוקי שמעתא מדוכתיה, אלא ודאי בשבת קאמרי רב ושמואל ואין הלכה כמותן לא בשבת ולא ביו"ט, ע"כ פי' ר"ת. ומה שדקדק מדלא מפליג ר' יוחנן, משמע דמיירי אפילו לתוך הקדירה – אין זה דיוק, דהא רב ושמואל נמי אסרי סתמא בכבשים(ג) למימיהן. ואע"ג דשרו לסחוט בהדיא אשכול של ענבים לתוך הקדירה. ומה שדחה דברי המעמידין דברי רב ושמואל ביו"ט – אומר ר"ת שהדין עמו, אבל דברי רב חסדא ביום טוב, כדפירשתי לעיל:

בהמה

רבינו חננאל

פי הדף שנפסלה מאוכל והיא מכשרת במשקה ואותיב רבינא טמא מת שסחט זיתים וענבי' וכו' ופרקינן בסוחט לתוך הקערה שהוא ודאי משקה. ומפני מה לא פירק פירוק זה לגבי חולב עז חדא מתרי תלתא טעמא קאמר. א"ר ירמיה כתנאי. המחלק בענבים לא הוכשר. פי' מחלק משפשף פעמים שמתמצה בהן משקין. ומחליקן בו. ולפיכך אמר ר' יהודה הוכשר שכך משקה גמור הוא. ות"ק אמר משקה הבא לאוכל הוא וכאוכל הוא חשוב ואינו מכשיר ובא רב הונא ופירש כי התנאין החולקין במחלק במחליק בענבים פליגי במשקה העומד לצחצחו ואלו החולקין במפצע זיתים בידים מסואבות פליגי. במשקה העומד לאיבוד. א"ר זירא א"ר חייא בר אשי אמר רב סוחט אדם אשכול של ענבים לתוך הקדרה אבל לא לתוך הקערה וכן פירושו כל דבר הנסחט בקדירה הוא אוכל ומותר ולתוך הקערה משקה הוא ואסור. זולתי הדג שאפילו סחיטתו בקערה שרי. והא דאתמר כבשים שסחטן אמר רב לגופן מותר וכו'. דברים פשוטין הן. ואין צריכין לפנים ולא לפני פנים. אמנם צריכין אנו לברר כמי ההלכה. לפיכך אנו מזכירין דברי כולן: **גופא** כבשים שסחטן כגון ירקות וראשי לפתות וכרוב וכל הדומה להן. אמר רב לגופן מותר כלומר סחטן להסיר מימיהן ולאכלן מותר. אבל אם כוונתו למימיהן והוא צירן פטור אבל אסור. ושלקות כגון ירקות וכדומה להן שלקן מקודם השבת ונשארו מימיהן בהן וכן דגים מלוחין בין לגופו בין למימיהן מותר. ושמואל אמר אחד כבשים ואחד שלקות לגופן מותר למימיהן פטור אבל אסור ור' יוחנן אמר אחד כבשים וא' שלקות לגופן מותר למימיהן חייב חטאת ומותבינן עלייהו סוחטין כבשים בשבת לצורך השבת אבל לא למוצ"ש. זיתים וענבים לא יסחוט ואם סחט חייב חטאת קשיא לרב וקשיא לשמואל וקשיא לר' יוחנן וכל אחד מהן מתרץ מתניתא כו' לטעמיה ודבריהן פשוטין הן אבל אנחנו כותבין תירוץ. טעמא דר' יוחנן דהלכתא כוותיה דקי"ל כל היכא דפליגי רב ושמואל ור' יוחנן הלכה כר' יוחנן. ולפיכך מדקדקינן בדבריו להעמיד הלכה כר' [illegible]. ר' יוחנן מתרץ לטעמיה סוחטין כבשים בשבת לצורך השבת. אבל לא למוצ"ש ואחד כבשים ואחד שלקות לגופן אבל למימיהן לא יסחוט ואם סחט נעשה כמי שסחט זיתים וענבים וחייב חטאת. ולא הפריש בסחיטתן בין קדירה לקערה אלא הכל אסור. ומתוך אלו הדברים מתברר שאין הלכה לא כשמואל ולא כרב שאומר סוחט אדם אשכול של ענבים לתוך הקדירה אבל לא לתוך הקערה. ויש שמעמידין דברי רב ושמואל ביו"ט. מדדייק רב חסדא מדברי שמואל. [illegible] חולב אדם עז לתוך הקדירה אבל לא לתוך הקערה כדי לקיים דבריהם להיות הלכה ואינן דבריהם נכונים שאפילו ביו"ט כל אלו אסורין ולינק בפיו מן הבהמה ביו"ט אסור וכ"ש לחלוב כדגרסינן בסוף פרק חרש (שנשא) פקחת. אבא שאול אומר גונקין היינו שיונקין מן בהמה טהורה ביו"ט ואקשינן עליה היכי דמי אי דאיכא סכנה אפילו בשבת שרי אי דליכא סכנה אפילו ביו"ט אסור. ומפרקי' לא צריכא דאית צערא (וסכנא) [illegible] כלאחר יד הוא [illegible] בשבת דאיסור סקילה הוא גזור רבנן. יו"ט דאיסור לאו הוא לא גזור רבנן. הנה אפי' לינק בפיו ביו"ט לא התירו אלא במקום שיש צער כ"ש לחלוב במקום שאין צער שודאי אסור. ואין לנו להדורי אפירכי ולאפוקי שמעתא מדוכתא אלא ודאי בשבת קאמר. ושאמר רב חסדא אחר כך ביו"ט הוא ואין הלכה כמותם לא בשבת ולא ביו"ט וכך קיבלנו מרבותינו והא דתנא דבי מנשה דבר תורה אינו חייב אלא על דריכת זיתים וענבים בלבד. לא קשיא הא דר' יוחנן(*) ושאר פירות זולתי זיתים וענבים סלקא שמעתא כר' יהודה דאמר לאוכלין היוצא מהן מותר למשקין

*) ונראה דר"ל דהנא דבי מנשה [illegible]

עין משפט נר מצוה

טו א מיי' פ"ח מהלכות טומאת אוכלין הל"ו:
טז ב טוש"ע או"ח סימן שכ סעיף ח:
יז ג מיי' פ"ח מהלכות שבת הל"י ופכ"א הל' יג סמג לאוין סה טוש"ע או"ח שם סעיף ז:
יח ד מיי' פ"ח שם הל"י ופכ"א הלכה יב:
יט ה מיי' פי"ז מהלכות עדות הלכה א סמג עשין קט טור שו"ע חו"מ סימן כח סעיף א:

רש"ל ועי' מהרש"ל

הגהות הב"ח

(א) תוס' ד"ה כביצה וכו' הטיפה ראשונה וכו' [illegible]

הגהות הגר"א

(א) גמ' [illegible] משקה הבא לאוכל לאו אוכל הוא [illegible]

גליון הש"ס

גמ' שלקות לגופן מותר למימיהן [illegible]

מעשרות פ"א מ"ח

יבמות פז: וקף קכב. בכורות לו. מו:

עין משפט נר מצוה

[ועי' שבות יעקב חלק ב' סימן קטז]

כ א מיי' פ"ב מהלכות בכורות הלכה טו סמג עשין ריא טוש"ע יו"ד סימן שיד סעיף ה:

כא ב מיי' פכ"א מהל' שבת הלכה טז טור שו"ע או"ח סימן רנב סעיף ה וסי' שכ סעיף ב:

כב ג מיי' פכ"ב שם הלכה ח סמג לאוין סה טוש"ע או"ח סימן שיח סעיף ד:

כג ד מיי' פ"כ מהלכות סנהדרין הלכה ז סמג עשין כז טור שו"ע חו"מ סימן י סעיף א:

מסורת הש"ס

לְעֵדוּת אִשָּׁה. לוֹמַר לְאִשָּׁה מֵת בַּעְלֵיךְ, דְּאַקִּילוּ בָּהּ רַבָּנַן מִשּׁוּם עִיגּוּנָא. וְכָל דִּמְקַדֵּשׁ אַדַּעְתָּא דְּרַבָּנַן *מְקַדֵּשׁ, *וְאַפְקוּעֵי רַבָּנַן לְקִדּוּשִׁין מִינֵּיהּ: לְעֵדוּת בְּכוֹר. בְּכוֹר בְּיַד כֹּהֵן, כְּשֶׁנְּתָנוֹ יִשְׂרָאֵל לוֹ שָׁלֵם וְאֵירַע לוֹ בּוֹ מוּם, קי"ל בִּבְכוֹרוֹת (דף לה.): נֶחְשְׁדוּ כֹּהֲנִים לְהַטִּיל מוּם בִּבְכוֹר, וְאֵין נֶאֱמָן לוֹמַר מוּם זֶה נָפַל בּוֹ מֵאֵילָיו. וְצָרִיךְ לְהָבִיא עֵדִים, וְאָמְרִינַן הָתָם דְּאִשָּׁה כְּשֵׁרָה לְעֵדוּת זוֹ: אֵימָא לְעֵדוּת שֶׁהָאִשָּׁה כְּשֵׁרָה לָהּ. וְהַאי נַמִי כְּשֵׁרָה לָהּ: גַּבְרָא יַתִּירָא. ר"ש, דְּמַתְנִי' ר"א תְּנַן בָּהּ: אֲתָא לְאַשְׁמְעִינַן. בִּתְמִיָּה. כְּלוֹמַר: מַה בָּא לְלַמְּדֵנוּ אִם לֹא זֹאת? מתני' כֹּל שֶׁבָּא בַּחַמִּין. כְּלוֹמַר שֶׁנִּתְבַּשֵּׁל: שׁוֹרִין אוֹתוֹ בַּחַמִּין. כְּדֵי שֶׁיְּהֵא נִמּוֹחַ: וְכֹל שֶׁלֹּא בָּא בַּחַמִּין. כְּגוֹן בָּשָׂר יָבֵשׁ, שֶׁאוֹכְלִין אוֹתוֹ חַי ע"י הַדְּחָק: מְדִיחִין אוֹתוֹ. וְלָא אָמְרִי' זֶהוּ בִּישּׁוּלֵיהּ, אֲבָל לֹא שׁוֹרִין: חוּץ מִן הַמָּלִיחַ יָשָׁן. דָּג מָלִיחַ שֶׁל שָׁנָה שֶׁעָבְרָה: וְקוּלְיָיס הָאִיסְפָּנִין. שֵׁם דָּג שֶׁאוֹכְלִין אוֹתוֹ מֵחֲמַת מִלְחוֹ ע"י הֲדָחָה בַּחַמִּין, וְהָנָךְ אֲפִילּוּ הֲדָחָה נַמִי לֹא, שֶׁזֶּהוּ גְּמַר מְלַאכְתָּן וַהֲוֵי בִּשּׁוּל: גמ' כְּגוֹן מַאי. הָוֵי בָּא בַּחַמִּין, שֶׁאוֹזְרִין וְשׁוֹרִין אוֹתוֹ בַּחַמִּין: תַּרְנְגוֹלְתֵּיהּ דר' אַבָּא. מְבַשְּׁלָהּ וְשׁוֹרֶה אוֹתָהּ יָמִים רַבִּים בַּחַמִּין לְמָחוֹת מֵאֵלֶיהָ, וְאוֹכְלָהּ לִרְפוּאָה: בַּר תְּלָתָא טַרְפֵי. בֶּן ג' שָׁנִים: אִתְנוּסֵי. הָיִיתִי נֶאֱנָס לְהָקִיא מֵחֲמַת מִיאוּס: רָיֵיק. רוֹקֵק מִכּוּתָּחָא דְּבַבְלָאֵי כְּשֶׁזּוֹכְרוֹ, שֶׁהָיָה מָאוּס בְּעֵינָיו: אָמַר רַב יוֹסֵף כו'. קָשֶׁה הָיָה בְּעֵינָיו שֶׁנִּמְאָסִין בְּנֵי בָּבֶל עַל בְּנֵי אֶרֶץ יִשְׂרָאֵל. אָמַר: אָנוּ נַמִי יֵשׁ לָנוּ לָרוֹק מִתַּרְנְגוֹלְתֵּיהּ דר' אַבָּא שֶׁהֵם אוֹכְלִים: וְעוֹד כּוּתָּח. אֵינוֹ מָאוּס כָּל כָּךְ בְּעֵינֵי שְׁאָר בְּנֵי מַעֲרָבָא: דְּהָא אָמַר רַב גָּזָא כו'. וְשָׁאֲלוּ מִינֵּיהּ אוֹתוֹ כּוּתָּח: בְּרִיחֵי. חוֹלִים: הֵדִיחַ. קוּלְיָיס, מַאי? חַיָּיב חַטָּאת. דַּהֲוֵי בִּישּׁוּל: מִפְּנֵי מָה עוֹפוֹת שֶׁבְּבָבֶל שְׁמֵנִים. מְשַׁל א"י: כַּלֵּךְ. לְכָה לָךְ, אֶלָּא שֶׁקִּיצֵּר הַלָּשׁוֹן: לְמִדְבַּר עַזָּה. וְהִיא מֵא"י: מוֹעֲדִים שֶׁבְּבָבֶל שְׂמֵחִים. רְגִילִים לִשְׂמוֹחַ בַּמּוֹעֲדִים יוֹתֵר מֵא"י: מִפְּנֵי שֶׁהֵם עֲנִיִּים. וְכָל הַשָּׁנָה אֵין לָהֶם שִׂמְחָה בְּמַאֲכָל וּמִשְׁתֶּה, וְאֵין לָהֶם מַרְגּוֹעַ מִמְּלָאכָה, לְפִיכָךְ בַּמּוֹעֲדִים כָּל שִׂמְחָתָם: מְצוּיָּינִין. מְצַיְּינִין עַצְמָן בִּלְבוּשִׁים נָאִים: מְצוּיָּינִין. מְקוּשָּׁטִין: שֶׁאֵינָן בְּנֵי תוֹרָה. כָּל כָּךְ, לְכַבְּדָם כִּבְנֵי אֶרֶץ יִשְׂרָאֵל מֵחֲמַת תּוֹרָתָם — מְכַבְּדִים אוֹתָם מֵחֲמַת לְבוּשֵׁיהֶן, שֶׁנִּרְאִין חֲשׁוּבִים: דַּרְדְּקֵי. בַּחוּרִים שֶׁלֹּא הִגִּיעוּ לִסְבָרָא: מִפְּנֵי שֶׁלֹּא גָּלוּ. הָעוֹפוֹת, כְּמוֹ אוֹתָן שֶׁל א"י כִּדְאָמְרִינַן לְקַמָּן: שַׁאֲנַן מוֹאָב מִנְּעוּרָיו וגו'. סֵיפֵיהּ דִּקְרָא "עַל כֵּן עָמַד טַעְמוֹ בּוֹ". אַלְמָא: הַגּוֹלִין מְפִיגִין טַעְמָן וְשַׁמְנָן: נ"ב שָׁנָה. מִשֶּׁגָּלוּ בִּימֵי צִדְקִיָּה בְּחָרְבוֹת יְרוּשָׁלַיִם עַד שֶׁנִּפְקְדוּ בִּימֵי כּוֹרֶשׁ, וְאָז עָלוּ מֵהֶם לְיַיסֵּד אֶת הַבַּיִת י"ח שָׁנִים קוֹדֶם גְּמַר הַבִּנְיָן שֶׁהָיָה לְסוֹף ע' שָׁנָה, בִּשְׁנַת שְׁתַּיִם לְדָרְיָוֶשׁ כִּדְאָמְרִי' בִּמְגִילָּה (דף יא:): וְכוּלָּן חָזְרוּ. הַבְּהֵמוֹת וְעוֹפוֹת וְאַף הַדָּגִים, חוּץ מִן קוּלְיָיס הָאִסְפָּנִין. וְכוּלָּן חָזְרוּ — דְּהָא "עַד בְּהֵמָה" כְּתִיב, וּמִכְּלָל דְּמִכָּאן וְאֵילָךְ הָדוּר חוּץ מִקּוּלְיָיס כִּדְמְפָרֵשׁ: הָנֵי מַדְרֵי דְּבָבֶל מְהַדְּרִי מַיָּא לְעֵין עֵיטָם. מַדְרוֹנוֹת שֶׁבְּבָבֶל מַחֲזִירִין מַיִם הַנִּשְׁפָּכִים בָּהֶן לְעֵין עֵיטָם, שֶׁהוּא מָקוֹם גָּבוֹהַּ שֶׁבְּא"י. שֶׁאוֹתוֹ מַעְיָין מֵבִיא מַיִם לְבֵית טְבִילַת כֹּה"ג בְּיוֹה"כ דְּמְתוּקָּן בְּחוֹמַת עֲזָרָה עַל גַּבֵּי שַׁעַר הַמַּיִם, כִּדְאָמְרִינַן בְּסֵדֶר יוֹמָא (דף לא.): עֵין עֵיטָם גָּבוֹהַּ מִקַּרְקַע הָעֲזָרָה כ"ג אַמּוֹת. וְהֵיאָךְ מַחֲזִירִין — שֶׁיֵּשׁ בְּפְרָת סִילוֹנוֹת וְסוּלָּמוֹת לְמַטָּה מִן הַקַּרְקַע (הַיָּם), וְדֶרֶךְ אוֹתָן סוּלָּמוֹת חוֹזְרִין הַמַּיִם לְא"י, וְחוֹזְרִין וְנוֹבְעִין בְּמַעְיָינוֹת. וְהַדָּגִים חָזְרוּ דֶּרֶךְ אוֹתָן סוּלָּמוֹת, שֶׁנּוֹחִים לְהַעֲלוֹתָן יוֹתֵר מִדֶּרֶךְ פְּרָת עַצְמוֹ: וְהַאי. קוּלְיָיס הָאִסְפָּנִין: כֵּיוָן דְּלָא שָׁרֵיר שִׁדְרֵיהּ. אֵין קָשֶׁה שִׁדְרָה שֶׁלּוֹ: לְטַבֶּרְיָה. לָבוֹז וּלְהַטִּיל עֲלֵיהֶם עוֹל. וְלֹא שֶׁמִּתְכַּוְּונִין לְבַטְּלָן מִשִּׂמְחַת הָרֶגֶל, אֲבָל הַקְּלָלָה גָּרְמָה לְכָךְ: קוּמְטִין. *לָשׁוֹן לַעַז הוּא שִׁלְטוֹן: בּוֹלֶשֶׁת. חֵיל הַמֶּלֶךְ: צִיפּוֹרִי וְטַבֶּרְיָא מֵא"י: שֶׁאֵינָן בִּמְקוֹמָם. שֶׁמֵּא"י גָּלוּ לְשָׁם, וְהַגּוֹלֶה לְמָקוֹם נָכְרִי מְצַיֵּין עַצְמוֹ בְּמַלְבּוּשִׁים שֶׁיְּהֵא חָשׁוּב: בְּמָתָא שְׁמַאי. בְּעִירִי אֵינִי צָרִיךְ לְהִתְכַּבֵּד אֶלָּא בִּשְׁמִי שֶׁאֲנִי נִיכָּר בּוֹ: בְּלָא מָתָא. בְּמָקוֹם שֶׁאֵינָהּ עִירִי: תּוֹתְבַאי. כְּבוֹדִי תָּלוּי בְּשַׂלְמָתִי. "שַׂלְמָתוֹ" מְתַרְגְּמִינַן תּוֹתְבֵיהּ (שמות כב): צִיצִין. לְמָחִין: הַבָּאִים. אוֹתָן שֶׁל יַעֲקֹב שֶׁיָּבֹאוּ לְבָבֶל — יַשְׁרִשׁוּ וְיַעֲשׂוּ נִיצָּן וּפְרָחִים לַתּוֹרָה. וְסַיְיעְתָּא אַתְיָא לְר' יוֹחָנָן, דְּטַעְמָא דְּמְצַוְּיינִין לָאו לְפִי שֶׁאֵינָן בְּנֵי תוֹרָה כִּדְרַבִּי אַסִּי, אֶלָּא לְפִי שֶׁאֵינָן בִּמְקוֹמָן: כְּשֶׁבָּא

תורה אור

בְּהֵמָה בְּגִימַטְרִיָּא. אַסְמַכְתָּא בְּעָלְמָא הִיא, דנ"ב נָפְקָא לָן בְּלָאו גִּימַטְרִיָּא, כְּדְפִי' בְּקוּנְטְרֵס: שׂוֹבֵר

אֶלָּא לְעֵדוּת אִשָּׁה בִּלְבַד. *אִיבַּעְיָא לְהוּ: עֵד מִפִּי עֵד לְעֵדוּת בְּכוֹר מַהוּ? רַב אַמֵּי אָסֵיר וְרַב אַסִּי שָׁרֵי. א"ל רַב אַמֵּי לְרַב אַסִּי: וְהָא תָּנָא דְּבֵי מְנַשְּׁיָא: אֵין עֵד מִפִּי עֵד כָּשֵׁר אֶלָּא לְעֵדוּת אִשָּׁה בִּלְבַד! אֵימָא: לְעֵדוּת שֶׁהָאִשָּׁה כְּשֵׁרָה לָהּ בִּלְבַד. רַב יֵימָר אַכְשַׁר עֵד מִפִּי עֵד לִבְכוֹר. קְרֵי עֲלֵיהּ מָרֵימָר: יֵימָר שָׁרֵי בּוּכְרָא. [א]וְהִלְכְתָא: עֵד מִפִּי עֵד כָּשֵׁר לִבְכוֹר.§ "חֲלוֹת דְּבַשׁ".§ כִּי אֲתָא רַב הוֹשַׁעְיָא מִנְּהַרְדְּעָא, *אֲתָא וְאַיְיתִי מַתְנִיתָא בִּידֵיהּ: זֵיתִים וַעֲנָבִים שֶׁרִיסְּקָן מֵעֶ"שׁ, וְיָצְאוּ מֵעַצְמָן — אֲסוּרִין, [ב]וְר"א וְר"ש מַתִּירִין. אֲמַר רַב יוֹסֵף: גַּבְרָא יַתִּירָא אֲתָא לְאַשְׁמְעִינַן?! א"ל אַבַּיֵי: טוּבָא קמ"ל, דְּאִי מִמַּתְנִיתִין — הֲוָה אָמִינָא: הָתָם הוּא — דְּמֵעִיקָּרָא אוּכְלָא וּלְבַסּוֹף אוּכְלָא, אֲבָל הָכָא דְּמֵעִיקָּרָא אוּכְלָא וּלְבַסּוֹף מַשְׁקֶה — אֵימָא לָא, קמ"ל.§

מתני' *[ג]כֹּל שֶׁבָּא בַּחַמִּין מֵעֶרֶב שַׁבָּת — שׁוֹרִין אוֹתוֹ בַּחַמִּין בַּשַּׁבָּת. וְכֹל שֶׁלֹּא בָּא בַּחַמִּין מֵעֶרֶב שַׁבָּת — מְדִיחִין אוֹתוֹ בַּחַמִּין בַּשַּׁבָּת. חוּץ מִן הַמָּלִיחַ הַיָּשָׁן (וְדָגִים מְלוּחִין קְטַנִּים) *וְקוּלְיָיס הָאִיסְפָּנִין, שֶׁהֲדָחָתָן זוֹ הִיא גְּמַר מְלַאכְתָּן.§

גמ' כְּגוֹן מַאי? אָמַר רַב סָפְרָא: כְּגוֹן תַּרְנְגוֹלְתָּא דר' אַבָּא. וְאָמַר רַב סָפְרָא: זִימְנָא חֲדָא אִיקְלַעִית לְהָתָם, וְאוֹכְלַן מִינֵּיהּ, וְאִי לָא רַבִּי אַבָּא דְּאַשְׁקְיַין חַמְרָא בַּר תְּלָתָא טַרְפֵי — אִיתְנְסִי. רַבִּי יוֹחָנָן רָיֵיק מִכּוּתָּח דְּבַבְלָאֵי. אֲמַר רַב יוֹסֵף: וְלִירוֹק אֲנַן מִתַּרְנְגוֹלְתָּא דְּרַבִּי אַבָּא. וְעוֹד, אֲמַר רַב גָּזָא: זִימְנָא חֲדָא אִיקְלָעִית לְהָתָם, וַעֲבַדִית כּוּתָּח דְּבַבְלָאֵי, שְׁאִילוּ מִינֵּיהּ *כָּל בְּרִיחֵי מַעֲרָבָא.§ "כֹּל שֶׁלֹּא בָּא בַּחַמִּין וכו'".§ הֵדִיחַ מַאי? אָמַר רַב יוֹסֵף: הֵדִיחַ — חַיָּיב חַטָּאת. אָמַר מָר בְּרֵיהּ דְּרָבִינָא: אַף אֲנַן נַמִי תְּנֵינָא "חוּץ מִמָּלִיחַ יָשָׁן וְקוּלְיָיס הָאִיסְפָּנִין שֶׁהֲדָחָתָן זוֹ הִיא גְּמַר מְלַאכְתָּן" שְׁמַע מִינַּהּ. יְתִיב רַבִּי חִיָּיא בַּר אַבָּא וְרַבִּי אַסִּי קַמֵּיהּ דְּרַבִּי יוֹחָנָן, וִיתֵיב רַבִּי יוֹחָנָן וְקָא מְנַמְנֵם. אֲמַר לֵיהּ רַבִּי חִיָּיא בַּר אַבָּא לְרַבִּי אַסִּי: מִפְּנֵי מָה עוֹפוֹת שֶׁבְּבָבֶל שְׁמֵנִים? א"ל: כַּלֵּךְ לְמִדְבַּר עַזָּה וְאַרְאֲךָ שְׁמֵנִים מֵהֶן. מִפְּנֵי מָה מוֹעֲדִים שֶׁבְּבָבֶל שְׂמֵחִים? מִפְּנֵי שֶׁהֵן עֲנִיִּים. מִפְּנֵי מָה ת"ח שֶׁבְּבָבֶל מְצוּיָּינִין? לְפִי שֶׁאֵינָן בְּנֵי תוֹרָה. מִפְּנֵי מָה גּוֹיִם מְזוֹהָמִי'? מִפְּנֵי שֶׁאוֹכְלִין שְׁקָצִי' וּרְמָשִׂי'*. אִיתְּעַר בְּהוּ רַבִּי יוֹחָנָן, אֲמַר לְהוּ: דַּרְדְּקֵי! לֹא כָּךְ אָמַרְתִּי לָכֶם °"אֱמֹר לַחָכְמָה אֲחֹתִי אָתְּ" *[ד]אִם בָּרוּר לְךָ הַדָּבָר כַּאֲחוֹתְךָ שֶׁהִיא אֲסוּרָה לְךָ — אוֹמְרֵהוּ, וְאִם לָאו — לֹא תֹּאמְרֵהוּ! אָמְרוּ לֵיהּ: וְלֵימָא לָן מָר אֵיזֶה מֵהֶן. מִפְּנֵי מָה עוֹפוֹת שֶׁבְּבָבֶל שְׁמֵנִים? מִפְּנֵי שֶׁלֹּא גָּלוּ, שֶׁנֶּאֱמַר: °"שַׁאֲנַן מוֹאָב מִנְּעוּרָיו וְשֹׁקֵט הוּא אֶל שְׁמָרָיו וּבַגּוֹלָה לֹא הָלָךְ". וְהָכָא מְנָלַן דְּגָלוּ — דְּתַנְיָא, *"רַבִּי יְהוּדָה אוֹמֵר: נ"ב שָׁנָה לֹא עָבַר אִישׁ בִּיהוּדָה, שֶׁנֶּאֱמַר: °"עַל הֶהָרִים אֶשָּׂא בְכִי וָנֶהִי וגו' מֵעוֹף הַשָּׁמַיִם וְעַד בְּהֵמָה נָדְדוּ הָלָכוּ". בְּהֵמ"ה בְּגִימַטְרִיָּא חַמְשִׁין וְתַרְתֵּין הָווּ. א"ר יַעֲקֹב א"ר יוֹחָנָן: כּוּלָּן חָזְרוּ, חוּץ מִקּוּלְיָיס הָאִיסְפָּנִין. *דְּאָמַר רַב: הָנֵי מַדְרֵי דְּבָבֶל מְהַדְּרִי מַיָּא לְעֵין עֵיטָם, וְהַאי כֵּיוָן דְּלָא שָׁרֵיר שִׁדְרֵיהּ לָא מָצֵי סָלֵיק. מִפְּנֵי מָה מוֹעֲדִים שֶׁבְּבָבֶל שְׂמֵחִים? מִפְּנֵי שֶׁלֹּא הָיוּ בְּאוֹתָהּ קְלָלָה, דִּכְתִיב: °"וְהִשְׁבַּתִּי כָּל מְשׂוֹשָׂהּ חַגָּהּ חָדְשָׁהּ וְשַׁבַּתָּהּ וְכֹל מוֹעֲדָהּ", וּכְתִיב: °"חָדְשֵׁיכֶם וּמוֹעֲדֵיכֶם שָׂנְאָה נַפְשִׁי הָיוּ עָלַי לָטֹרַח". *מַאי "הָיוּ עָלַי לָטֹרַח"? א"ר אֶלְעָזָר: אָמַר הקב"ה: לֹא דַּיָּין לְיִשְׂרָאֵל שֶׁחוֹטְאִין לְפָנַי, אֶלָּא שֶׁמַּטְרִיחִין אוֹתִי לֵידַע אֵיזוֹ גְּזֵירָה קָשָׁה אָבִיא עֲלֵיהֶן! א"ר יִצְחָק: אֵין לְךָ כָּל רֶגֶל וָרֶגֶל שֶׁלֹּא בָּאתָה בּוֹלֶשֶׁת לְצִיפּוֹרִי. וְאָמַר רַבִּי חֲנִינָא: אֵין לְךָ כָּל רֶגֶל וָרֶגֶל שֶׁלֹּא בָּא לְטַבֶּרְיָה אֶגְמוֹן וְקָמְטוֹן וּבַעַל זְמוֹרָה. מִפְּנֵי מָה ת"ח שֶׁבְּבָבֶל מְצוּיָּינִין? לְפִי שֶׁאֵינָן(א) בְּנֵי מְקוֹמָן. דְּאָמְרֵי אִינָשֵׁי: בְּמָתָא — שְׁמַאי, בְּלָא מָתָא — תּוֹתְבַאי. °"הַבָּאִים יַשְׁרֵשׁ יַעֲקֹב יָצִיץ וּפָרַח יִשְׂרָאֵל", תָּנֵי רַב יוֹסֵף: אֵלּוּ תַּלְמִידֵי חֲכָמִים שֶׁבְּבָבֶל, שֶׁעוֹשִׂין צִיצִין וּפְרָחִים לַתּוֹרָה. מִפְּנֵי מָה גּוֹיִם מְזוֹהָמִין? שֶׁלֹּא עָמְדוּ עַל הַר סִינַי. שֶׁבְּשָׁעָה שֶׁבָּא

כ"א ל"ג

משלי ז | ירמיהו מח | שם ט | הושע ב | ישעיהו א | שם כז

[יבמות נ:] | בכורות לו. ע"ש | לעיל יט: | לעיל לט. | [דג שבמקומות האספניא ושמו בלשון הקודש שיבוטא ערוך ערך אספנן] | [עי' לעיל כח.] | ב"ב טז: | סנהדרין ז: | [יומא נד.] | בכורות מז. | [מגילה לא:]

לשון קומטוס כמו קומוס ולשון רומי הוא עי' רש"י סוטה יד ד"ה גסטרא

הגהות הב"ח

(א) גמ' לפי שאינן במקומן כצ"ל ותיבת בני נמחק:

רבינו חננאל

למשקין היוצא מהן אסור. והא דתניא סוחטין בפגעים ובפרישין ובעוזרדין אבל לא ברמונים דשל בית מנשיא בן מנחם היו סוחטין ברמונים אמר רב נחמן הלכה כשל בית מנשיא בן מנחם וסלקא שמעתא דאסור לסחוט ברמונים בשבת והא דתני אין עד מפי עד כשר אלא לעדות אשה בלבד. אוקימנא לעדות שהאשה כשרה לה והלכתא עד מפי עד כשר לבכור. פי' עד מפי עד נאמן להעיד על בכור בהמה טהורה שזה המום שיש בו אפי' שראוי לבוא בידי אדם הוא לא נפל בו מידי אדם ובזו העדות החכם מתירו להאכל במומו וכ"ש בעדות גדולה מזו. ומפורש כך בבכורות פ' כל פסולי המוקדשי'. וסלקא שמעתא התם דהלכתא כרשב"ג דאמר אפילו בנו ובתו נאמנים ויש מי שאומר כי עד מפי עד נאמן בבכור אדם וטעות הוא בידו: **חלות** דבש שריסקן מע"ש ויצאו מעצמן אסורין ור' אלעזר מתיר. כי אתא רב הושעיא מנהרדעא אתא ואייתי מתניתא בידיה זיתים וענבים שריסקן מע"ש ויצאו מעצמן אסורים. ור' אלעזר ור"ש מתירין. והא מתניתא מסייעא נמי לר' יוחנן: **מתני'** כל שבאו בחמין מלפני השבת וכו'. ומיבעיא לן כגון מאי. ואמר רב ספרא כגון תרנגולתא דר' אסא שהיתה מלוחה ביותר וכשמבקשין לאוכלה שורין אותה במים חמין. אמר רב ספרא כגון זו התרנגולת אם הובאה בחמין מלפני השבת מותר לשרותה בחמין בשבת ולאוכלה. ואם לאו אסור לשרותה ומותר להדיחה והמליח הישן וקוליים האיספנין

רב נסים גאון

ואין עד מפי עד כשר אלא לעדות אשה בלבד כשאמר כי מת בעלה התירוה בית דין לינשא ואע"פ שהמועט העתיק דבר זה מזולתו וכמו שביארו דבר זה בפרק אשה שהלך בעלה וצרתה (דף קכב) והוחזקו להיות משיאין עד מפי עד וכו': **עד** מפי עד בבכור מהו. עיקר דיליה במסכת בכורות בפרק כל פסולי המוקדשין (דף לה) דתניא ר' יהושע בן קפוסאי אומר בכור בי כהן צריך ב' מן השוק להעיד עליו רבן שמעון בן גמליאל אומר אפילו בנו ובתו ואמרו הלכתא כרבן שמעון ודוקא בנו ובתו אבל אשתו לא מאי טעמא אשתו כגופו דמיא ועוד אמרו איבעיא להו עד מפי עד מהו לעדות בכור אמר ליה תני אלא לעדות אשה כשירה לו וכבר נתברר לנו שבתו כשירה והואיל ואשה כשירה לעדות בכור עד מפי עד נמי כשר לעדות בכור וכן פסקה ההלכה וזה שאמרו בבכור בהמה אבל בבכור אדם לא. גרסינן בפרק י' יוחסין (דף עד) ג' נאמנין על הבכור חיה ואמו ואביו חיה לאלתר אמו כל ז' אביו לעולם: **כגון** תרנגלתיה דר' אבא. כך פירשה אדוננו האיי גאון ז"ל תרנגולת שמבשלין אותה ומוציאין אותה מהמרק וממלאין אותה בתבלין וכשרוצה לאכול ממנה שורין אותה במים חמים ואוכלים אותה כאילו היא חמה: סליק פרק חבית

תורה אור

*שֶׁבָּא נָחָשׁ עַל חַוָּה הִטִּיל בָּהּ זוּהֲמָא. יִשְׂרָאֵל שֶׁעָמְדוּ עַל הַר סִינַי – פָּסְקָה זוּהֲמָתָן, גּוֹיִם שֶׁלֹּא עָמְדוּ עַל הַר סִינַי – לֹא פָּסְקָה זוּהֲמָתָן. א"ל רַב אַחָא בְּרֵיהּ דְּרָבָא לְרַב אַשִׁי: גֵּרִים מַאי? א"ל: אע"ג דְּאִינְהוּ לָא הָווּ, מַזָּלַיְיהוּ הָווּ, דִּכְתִיב: °"אֶת אֲשֶׁר יֶשְׁנוֹ פֹּה עִמָּנוּ עוֹמֵד הַיּוֹם לִפְנֵי ה' אֱלֹהֵינוּ וְאֵת אֲשֶׁר אֵינֶנּוּ פֹּה וגו'". (דברים כט) וּפְלִיגָא דְּר' אַבָּא בַּר כָּהֲנָא, דְּא"ר אַבָּא בַּר כָּהֲנָא: עַד שְׁלֹשָׁה דּוֹרוֹת לֹא פָּסְקָה זוּהֲמָא מֵאֲבוֹתֵינוּ; אַבְרָהָם הוֹלִיד אֶת יִשְׁמָעֵאל, יִצְחָק הוֹלִיד אֶת עֵשָׂו, יַעֲקֹב הוֹלִיד י"ב שְׁבָטִים שֶׁלֹּא הָיָה בָּהֶן שׁוּם דּוֹפִי.§

מתני' *[א]שׁוֹבֵר אָדָם אֶת הֶחָבִית לֶאֱכוֹל הֵימֶנָּה גְּרוֹגְרוֹת, וּבִלְבַד שֶׁלֹּא יִתְכַּוֵּין לַעֲשׂוֹת כְּלִי. וְאֵין נוֹקְבִין מְגוּפָה שֶׁל חָבִית – דִּבְרֵי ר' יְהוּדָה, *וַחֲכָמִים [ב]מַתִּירִין. וְלֹא יִקְּבֶנָּה מִצִּדָּהּ, וְאִם [ג]הָיְתָה נְקוּבָה – לֹא יִתֵּן עָלֶיהָ שַׁעֲוָה, מִפְּנֵי שֶׁהוּא מְמָרֵחַ. אָמַר ר' יְהוּדָה: *מַעֲשֶׂה בָּא לִפְנֵי רַבָּן יוֹחָנָן בֶּן זַכַּאי בַּעֲרָב, וְאָמַר: חוֹשְׁשַׁנִי לוֹ מֵחַטָּאת.§

גמ' א"ר אוֹשַׁעְיָא: ל"ש אֶלָּא דְּרוּסוֹת, אֲבָל מְפוֹרָדוֹת – לֹא. וּמְפוֹרָדוֹת לֹא? מֵיתִיבִי, ר' שִׁמְעוֹן בֶּן גַּמְלִיאֵל אוֹמֵר: מֵבִיא אָדָם אֶת הֶחָבִית שֶׁל יַיִן וּמַתִּיז רֹאשָׁהּ בַּסַּיִיף, וּמַנִּיחָהּ לִפְנֵי הָאוֹרְחִים בַּשַּׁבָּת וְאֵינוֹ חוֹשֵׁשׁ! הַהִיא רַבָּנַן[א], מַתְנִי' – רַבִּי נְחֶמְיָה הִיא. וּמַאי דּוֹחֲקֵיהּ דְּרַבִּי אוֹשַׁעְיָא לְאוֹקְמֵי מַתְנִיתִין כְּרַבִּי נְחֶמְיָה וּבִדְרוּסוֹת, לוֹקְמָהּ בִּמְפוֹרָדוֹת וְרַבָּנַן! אָמַר רָבָא: מַתְנִי' קַשְׁיָתֵיהּ, מַאי אִירְיָא דְּתָנֵי "גְּרוֹגְרוֹת" לִיתְנֵי "פֵּירוֹת"! אֶלָּא ש"מ – בִּדְרוּסוֹת. תַּנְיָא חֲדָא: [ד]חוֹתָלוֹת שֶׁל גְּרוֹגְרוֹת וְשֶׁל תְּמָרִים – מַתִּיר וּמַפְקִיעַ וְחוֹתֵךְ. וְתַנְיָא אִידָךְ: מַתִּיר, אֲבָל לֹא מַפְקִיעַ וְלֹא חוֹתֵךְ! לָא קַשְׁיָא; הָא – רַבָּנַן הָא – ר' נְחֶמְיָה. *דְּתַנְיָא, ר' נְחֶמְיָה אוֹמֵר: אֲפִי' תַּרְוָוד, וַאֲפִילּוּ טַלִּית, וַאֲפִילּוּ סַכִּין אֵין נִיטָּלִין אֶלָּא לְצוֹרֶךְ תַּשְׁמִישָׁן[א]. בָּעוּ מִינֵּיהּ מֵרַב שֵׁשֶׁת: °מַהוּ לְמִיבְרַז חָבִיתָא בְּבוּרְטְיָא בְּשַׁבְּתָא? לְפִיתְחָא קָמִיכַּוֵּין – וַאֲסִיר, אוֹ דִּילְמָא: לְעַיִן יָפָה קָמִיכַּוֵּין, וְשָׁרֵי! א"ל: [ה]לְפִיתְחָא קָא מִכַּוֵּין – וַאֲסִיר. מֵיתִיבִי, רשב"ג אוֹמֵר: [ו]מֵבִיא אָדָם חָבִית שֶׁל יַיִן וּמַתִּיז רֹאשָׁהּ בַּסַּיִיף! הָתָם וַדַּאי לְעַיִן יָפָה קָמִיכַּוֵּין. הָכָא אִם אִיתָא דִּלְעַיִן יָפָה קָמִיכַּוֵּין – לְפַתּוּחֵי מִיפְתַּח.§ "אֵין נוֹקְבִין מְגוּפָה וכו'".§ אָמַר רַב הוּנָא: מַחֲלוֹקֶת לְמַעְלָה, [ז]אֲבָל מִן הַצַּד – דִּבְרֵי הַכֹּל אָסוּר. וְהַיְינוּ דְּקָתָנֵי "לֹא יִקְּבֶנָּה מִצִּדָּהּ". וְרַב חִסְדָּא אָמַר: מַחֲלוֹקֶת מִן הַצַּד, אֲבָל עַל גַּבָּהּ – דִּבְרֵי הַכֹּל מוּתָּר. וְהָא דְּקָתָנֵי "לֹא יִקְּבֶנָּה מִצִּדָּהּ" הָתָם בְּגוּפָהּ דְּחָבִית. תָּנוּ רַבָּנַן: [ח]אֵין נוֹקְבִין נֶקֶב חָדָשׁ בַּשַּׁבָּת, וְאִם בָּא לְהוֹסִיף – מוֹסִיף. וְיֵשׁ אוֹמְרִים: [ט]אֵין מוֹסִיפִין. וְשָׁוִין שֶׁנּוֹקְבִין(ז) נֶקֶב יָשָׁן לְכַתְּחִילָּה. וְתַנָּא קַמָּא, מַאי שְׁנָא מִנֶּקֶב חָדָשׁ דְּלָא – דְּקָא מְתַקֵּן פִּיתְחָא, אוֹסוּפֵי נַמִי – קָא מְתַקֵּן פִּיתְחָא! אָמַר רַבָּה: [י]דְּבַר תּוֹרָה – כָּל פֶּתַח שֶׁאֵינוֹ עָשׂוּי לְהַכְנִיס וּלְהוֹצִיא – אֵינוֹ פֶּתַח, וְרַבָּנַן הוּא דִּגְזוּר מִשּׁוּם לוּל שֶׁל תַּרְנְגוֹלִין, *דְּעָבִיד לְעַיּוּלֵי אֲוִירָא וּלְאַפּוֹקֵי הַבְלָא. [לעיל קב:] "וְאִם בָּא לְהוֹסִיף מוֹסִיף" אוֹסוּפֵי וַדַּאי בְּלוּל שֶׁל תַּרְנְגוֹלִים – לָא אָתֵי לְאוֹסוּפֵי, מִשּׁוּם

רש"י

כְּשֶׁבָּא נָחָשׁ עַל חַוָּה. כְּשֶׁנָּתַן לָהּ עֵצָה לֶאֱכוֹל מִן הָעֵץ בָּא עָלֶיהָ, דִּכְתִיב (בראשית ג): "הַנָּחָשׁ הִשִּׁיאַנִי" – לְשׁוֹן נִשּׂוּאִין: גֵּרִים מַאי. שֶׁלֹּא הָיוּ עַל הַר סִינַי, מֵהֵיכָן פָּסְקָה זוּהֲמָא? מַזָּלַיְיהוּ הָווּ. בְּסִינַי. וְכָל שֶׁעָמְדוּ עַל הַר סִינַי נִתְקַדְּשׁוּ וְנִטְהֲרוּ וְנִתְרַפְּאוּ מִכָּל מוּם, וְאַף עִוְּרִים וּפִסְחִים שֶׁהָיוּ בְּיִשְׂרָאֵל, כִּדְתַנְיָא בְּסִפְרֵי: וּפְלִיגָא. הָא דַּאֲמַרַן דְּלֹא פָּסְקָה זוּהֲמָא עַד סִינַי: **מתני'** שׁוֹבֵר אָדָם חָבִית. מְלֵיאָה גְּרוֹגְרוֹת בְּסַכִּין אוֹ בְּסַיִיף, לֶאֱכוֹל מִמֶּנָּה גְּרוֹגְרוֹת, דְּאֵין בִּמְקַלְקֵל שׁוּם אִיסּוּר בְּשַׁבָּת: וּבִלְבַד שֶׁלֹּא יִתְכַּוֵּין לַעֲשׂוֹת כְּלִי. לְנוֹקְבָהּ יָפֶה בְּפֶתַח נָאֶה: אֵין נוֹקְבִין מְגוּפָה. הַדְּבוּקָה(ג) בְּפֶה הֶחָבִית לַעֲשׂוֹת נֶקֶב, אֶלָּא נוֹטֵל אֶת כּוּלָּהּ. אֲבָל כִּי נָקֵיב לָהּ – מְתַקֵּן פִּתְחָא: וַחֲכָמִים מַתִּירִין. דְּאֵין דֶּרֶךְ פֶּתַח לְחָבִית בְּכָךְ: וְלֹא יִקְּבֶנָּה מִצִּידָהּ. בַּגְּמָרָא מְפָרֵשׁ לָהּ: שֶׁהוּא מְמָרֵחַ. וְיֵשׁ כָּאן מִשּׁוּם מְמַחֵק: בַּעֲרָב. מְדִינָה*: מֵחַטָּאת. שֶׁמָּא מֵירַח הַשַּׁעֲוָה לְדוּבְקָהּ בְּדוֹפְנֵי הַכְּלִי סָבִיב הַנֶּקֶב: **גמ'** לֹא שָׁנוּ. דְּשׁוֹבֵר הֶחָבִית וּמְטַלְטֵל הַסַּיִיף לְכָךְ: אֶלָּא בִּדְרוּסוֹת. שֶׁהַגְּרוֹגְרוֹת דְּרוּסוֹת בְּעִיגּוּל, וְחוֹתְכִין מִמֶּנּוּ בְּקוֹרְדּוֹם אוֹ בְּסַיִיף. וְאַיְּידֵי דִּמְטַלְטֵל סַיִיף לַחְתּוֹךְ גְּרוֹגְרוֹת – תָּבַר בֵּיהּ נַמִי לְחָבִית: אֲבָל מְפוֹרָדוֹת. שֶׁא"צ לְחָתְכָן – לֹא יְטַלְטֵל סַיִיף לִשְׁבּוֹר הֶחָבִית,(ד) דְּמַתְנִי' ר' נְחֶמְיָה, דְּאָמַר: אֵין כְּלִי נִיטָּל אֶלָּא לְתַשְׁמִישׁ הַמְיוּחָד לוֹ, כִּדְמוֹקֵי לְקַמָּן: וְאֵינוֹ חוֹשֵׁשׁ. וְאע"ג דְּיַיִן לָאו לְמִתְחַכֵּיהּ קָאֵי: רַבָּנַן הִיא. דִּפְלִיגֵי אַדְּר' נְחֶמְיָה, וְאָמְרִי: כָּל הַכֵּלִים נִיטָּלִין לְצוֹרֶךְ וְשֶׁלֹּא לְצוֹרֶךְ: חוֹתָלוֹת. כְּלִי שֶׁל כַּפּוֹת תְּמָרִים, וְעוֹשִׂין כְּמִין סַלִּים, וְנוֹתְנִים לְתוֹכָן תְּמָרִים רָעִים לְהִתְבַּשֵּׁל: מַתִּיר. אִם הַכִּסּוּי קָשׁוּר בְּחֶבֶל: אֲבָל לֹא מַפְקִיעַ. סוֹתֵר שַׁרְשְׁרוֹת הַחֶבֶל בִּכְלִי: וְלֹא חוֹתֵךְ. דְּאֵין כְּלִי נִיטָּל אֶלָּא לְצוֹרֶךְ תַּשְׁמִישׁוֹ, וְסַכִּין אֵינוֹ עָשׂוּי לְכָךְ: לְמִיבְרַז. לִתְחוֹב, פויינדור"א בְּלַעַ"ז: בְּבוּרְטְיָא. בְּרוֹמַח, לְתוֹחֲבוֹ בְּדוֹפְנֶיהָ לִנְקוֹב: לְעַיִן יָפָה. לְהַרְחִיב מוֹצָא הַיַּיִן בְּנֶקֶב גָּדוֹל, מִדְּלָא נָקֵיב לֵיהּ כְּדֶרֶךְ הַנּוֹקְבִין נֶקֶב עָגוֹל וְיָפֶה: הָתָם וַדַּאי לְעַיִן יָפָה קָמִיכַּוֵּין. שֶׁמַּרְחִיב פִּיהָ לְמַטָּה מִמְּגוּפָתָהּ, כִּדְקָתָנֵי: מַתִּיז אֶת רֹאשָׁהּ, שְׂפַת פִּיהָ: לְפַתּוּחֵי מִיפְתַּח. יִטּוֹל מְגוּפָתָהּ: לְמַעְלָה. בְּרֹאשׁ הַמְּגוּפָה הָתָם הוּא דְּשָׁרוּ רַבָּנַן, דְּלָאו אוֹרְחָא לְמֶיעְבַּד פִּתְחָא הָתָם, אֶלָּא נוֹטֵל כָּל הַמְּגוּפָה: אֲבָל מִצִּדָּהּ. זִמְנִין דְּעָבְדִי לָהּ מִשּׁוּם פִּתְחָא, וְאֵינוֹ רוֹצֶה לְפוֹתְחָהּ לְמַעְלָה שֶׁלֹּא יִפּוֹל עָפָר אוֹ פְּסוֹלֶת בַּיַּיִן: הַיְינוּ דְּקָתָנֵי וְלֹא יִקְּבֶנָּה מִצִּדָּהּ. וְאַמְּגוּפָה קָאֵי, וְדִבְרֵי הַכֹּל: מַחֲלוֹקֶת מִן הַצַּד. הָתָם הוּא דְּקָאָסַר רַבִּי יְהוּדָה – מִשּׁוּם דְּאִיכָּא דְּעָבְדִי לֵיהּ פִּתְחָא: אֵין נוֹקְבִין נֶקֶב חָדָשׁ. בִּכְלִי: נֶקֶב יָשָׁן. שֶׁנִּסְתַּם, דְּכִי חוֹזֵר וּפוֹתֵחַ – לָאו כְּעוֹשֶׂה פֶּתַח הוּא, שֶׁהֲרֵי עָשׂוּי וְעוֹמֵד, וּסְתִימָתוֹ לָאו כְּלוּם: אוֹסוּפֵי נַמִי קָמְתַקֵּן פִּתְחָא. שֶׁמַּרְחִיבוֹ, וְיֵשׁ כָּאן מִשּׁוּם גְּמַר מְלָאכָה: הַבְלָא. סִרְחוֹן, שֶׁלֹּא יָמוּתוּ הַתַּרְנְגוֹלִין: וְאִם בָּא לְהוֹסִיף מוֹסִיף. וְלָא גָּזְרִינַן דִּילְמָא אָתֵי לְאוֹסוּפֵי בְּלוּל שֶׁל תַּרְנְגוֹלִין, דְּלָא מוֹסִיף אִינִישׁ עֲלֵיהּ:

מִשּׁוּם

תוספות

שובר אדם את החבית לאכול הימנה גרוגרות. בגמרא מוקי לה בדרוסות לרבי נחמיה, אבל לרבנן דרבי נחמיה – שרי אפילו מפורדות. ותימה לרבי, מהא דתנן בפרק "בכל מערבין" (עירובין דף לד: ושם) גבי עירוב: נתנו במגדל ונועל בפניו, ואבד המפתח – הרי זה עירוב. ופריך בגמרא: אמאי? הוא במקום אחד ועירובו במקום אחר הוא! ומשני, רב ושמואל דאמרי תרווייהו: הכא במגדל של(ה) בנין עסקינן. ור"מ היא כו'. ואמאי מבעי ליה לאוקמא הכי? ומעיקרא נמי, מאי קאמר: והלא יכול לשבר ולפתוח את המגדל וליטול את העירוב, כי היכי דהכא שרי לשבר החבית וליטול הגרוגרות. ואם באת לחלק בין נטילת העירוב לנטילת הגרוגרות – א"כ קשה היכי מוקי לה התם כר' מאיר? ונראה דהתם אסור לשבר את המגדל, והכא דשרי לשבר את החבית – משום דמיירי במוסתקי, כדמוקי לה בביצה פרק "המביא כדי יין" (דף לג: ושם) ומפ' רש"י התם: דהיינו חבית שבורה, ומדבקין שבריה בשרף של עץ שעושה ממנו זפת, וקורין רייסנ"א. ומש"ה דוקא חבית שרי, דמחמת גריעותו לא חייש עליה, וליכא למיחש שמא יתכוין לעשות כלי. וכן כולה שמעתא דהכא במוסתקי. ואע"ג דהתם בביצה לא מוקמינן הכי אלא לר"א – דפריך: ולית ליה לר"א הא דתנן: שובר אדם את החבית כו'? ועלה משני: מתני' במוסתקי. מ"מ, אפילו לרבנן מיבעי לאוקמי הכי. דרבנן לא פליגי אדר"א דקאמר לא יקטמנו, פי': לא יקטום את ההדס להריח בו – אלא משום דאיהו סבירא ליה דבקטימת קיסם חייב חטאת כשקוטמו לחצות בו שיניו. וא"כ, אי לא מוקמינן לה במוסתקי – עלייהו איכא למיפרך: ולית להו הא דתנן כו'. הלכך מיבעי לן למימר דאליבא דכולהו מיירי מתניתין במוסתקי, והשתא אתיא שמעתא שפיר. מ"ר. ובגמ' ירושלמי בפרק "בכל מערבין" מצאתי: הדא דתימא במגדל של אבן, אבל במגדל של עץ – נעשה כשובר החבית לאכול ממנה גרוגרות:

מתיר ומפקיע וחותך. אומר רבי: מההיא דעירובין (דף לד:) יש ללמוד, דהא דאמרינן (ביצה דף לא:) חותמות שבכלים מתיר ומפקיע וחותך – היינו כגון דקטיר במיתנא. אבל פותחת של עץ ושל מתכת – אסור לשבר ולהפקיע. מדקשיא ליה התם: אמאי, הוא במקום אחד ועירובו במקום אחר, דפשיטא ליה שאינו יכול להפקיע הפותחת וליטול העירוב. אע"פ שסתם מגדל שבכל התלמוד הוא כלי, כמו: הלד צדי לבית ולפור למגדל. וכי ההיא דבריש "כל הכלים" (לעיל קכב:). ובמסקנא נמי לא בעי לאוקומי אלא בקטיר במיתנא, דהיינו דוקא חותמות שבכלים, אבל דבר שהוא חזק כעין פותחת – לא הוה שרי ת"ק. מ"ר*:

הא רבנן והא ר' נחמיה. תימה לי: אמאי לא מוקי תרווייהו כר' נחמיה? והא דקתנו מתיר מפקיע וחותך – ביו"ט, והא דקתני מתיר אבל לא מפקיע וחותך – בשבת. דאיכא תנא דס"ל הכי אליבא דר' נחמיה, בביצה בפ' "המביא כדי יין" (לג:)! י"ל: דניחא ליה למימר חדא כרבנן, מדנימא תרווייהו כר' נחמיה:

משום

עין משפט נר מצוה

כד א מיי' פכ"ג מהל' שבת הלכה ב סמג לאוין סה טוש"ע או"ח סימן שיד סעיף א:
כה ב מיי' שם טוש"ע שם סעיף ו:
כו ג מיי' שם הלכה יא טוש"ע שם סעיף יא:
כז ד שם סעיף ח:
כח ה ו ז מיי' שם הל' ב טור שו"ע שם סעיף ו:
כט ח ט מיי' שם הל"א טוש"ע שם סעיף א:
ל י מיי' שם הל"א ופ"י הלכה טז סמג שם:

ביצה לג:

עירובין לה. ביצה לב. [תוספתא פט"ו]

[וע"ע תוס' עירובין לה: ד"ה בעי סכינא]

רבינו חננאל

אם לא הביאם בחמין מלפני השבת אפילו להדיחן בשבת אסור ואם עבר והדיחן חייב חטאת שגמר מלאכה. פי' מכותא מכותתא היא. ויש מי שאומר כותא כותתא היא בדיחי במערבא חולים שבמערב: **מתני'** שובר אדם את החבית לאכול ממנה גרוגרות כו'. א"ר הושעיא לא ששובר את החבית לאכול ממנה גרוגרות אלא דרוסות אבל מפורדות אינו שובר החבית אלא מוציא גרוגרות ואוכל ואינו שובר. ואוקימנא למתניתין כר' נחמיה. מדקתני גרוגרות ולא קתני פירות. והא דתניא רשב"ג אומר מביא אדם חבית של יין ומתיז ראשה בסייף ומניחה לפני האורחים לרבנן. וכן הא דתני חותלות של תמרים ושל גרוגרות ומתיר ומפקיע וחותך לרבנן והא דתני מתיר אבל לא מפקיע ולא חותך ר' נחמיה דאמר אפילו תרווד ואפילו חולית אין נוטלין אלא לצורך תשמישן: **בעו** מיניה מרב ששת מהו למיברז חביתא בבורטיא. פי' לנקוב חבית ברומח. ויש שאומר במקדח ומסקנא לפיתחא קא מיכוין ואסירי: **פיס'** אין נוקבין מגופה של החבית. פי' מגופה כסוי החבית דברי ר' יהודה וחכמים מתירין והלכה כחכמים. והני מילי שיהא הנקב בגג הכסוי אבל לנקב נקב בצד הכסוי אסור כדתנן לא יקבנה מצדה שהוא דברי הכל. וכרב הונא דהלכתא כוותיה. דהוא לגביה דרב חסדא רבו וליתא לדרב חסדא: **ת"ר** אין נוקבין נקב חדש בשבת. ואם בא להוסיף מוסיף ואקשינן עלה למה אסור לנקוב נקב חדש שנמצא מתקן פתח גם בהוסיפו בנקב ומרחיבו נמצא מתקן פתח. ולמה מותר ופריק רבא מן התורה כל פתח שאינו עשוי להכנים ולהוציא אינו חשוב פתח. ואלו הנקבים כולן אין מכניסין בהן אלא להוציא הן עשויין בלבד ומותרין. ורבנן גזרו על כל נקב מפני שלא יפתחו נקב בבית התרנגולין והוא הנקרא לול של תרנגולים כדכתיב ובלולים יעלו. וזה לול של תרנגולים עשוי להכנים רוח ולהוציא בהמות והוא כמין פתח ואסור. ומפני שהוא פתח גמור אסור מן התורה. גזרו על כל נקב אבל ההרחבה שאין אדם מרחיב בלול של תרנגולים כי מתיירא אם מרחיב הלול יכנס ממנו הנחש ויזיק אותן. וכיון שאין דרך בני אדם להרחיב בלול של תרנגולים לא גזרו בהרחבת כל נקב וזהו טעם ת"ק. וי"א

מסורת הש"ס

ע"ז כב: יבמות קג:

[לעיל קכח. פירש"י שם מקום]

ס"א ר' יוסי מתיר

[לעיל קכח.]

הגהות הב"ח

(א) גמ' ההיא רבנן היא מתניתין: (ב) שם בנקב ישן: (ג) רש"י ד"ה אין נוקבין וכו' הדבוקה בפי החבית: (ד) ד"ה אבל מפורדות וכו' החבית הס"ד ואח"כ מ"ה ואינו חושש וכו' קאי הס"ד ואח"כ מ"ה ההיא רבנן הוא וכו' ושלא לצורך הס"ד ואח"כ מ"ה מתני' ר' נחמיה היא דאמר אין כלי וכו' לקמן הס"ד ואח"כ מ"ה חותלות וכו' תמרים ועשוין כמין סלים: (ה) תוס' ד"ה שובר וכו' במגדל של בנין עסקי':

הגהות הגר"א

[א] גמ' בעו מיני' מרב ששת מהו למיברז חביתא. נ"ב ר"ל במקום שנקב אסור אם ברומח מותר טול:

גליון הש"ס

גמרא מהו למיברז חביתא. ע"ל דף מח ע"ב תוס' ד"ה וכי מה בין:

מִשּׁוּם רִיחֲשָׁא. "וְי"א: אֵין מוֹסִיפִים" – זִימְנִין דְּלָא תַּקְנֵיהּ מֵעִיקָּרָא, וְאָתֵי לְאַרְוֹחֵי בֵּיהּ. דָּרַשׁ רַב נַחְמָן מִשּׁוּם רַבִּי יוֹחָנָן: הֲלָכָה כְּיֵשׁ אוֹמְרִים.§ א"וְשָׁוִין שֶׁנּוֹקְבִין נֶקֶב יָשָׁן לְכַתְּחִלָּה".§ אָמַר רַב יְהוּדָה אָמַר שְׁמוּאֵל: לֹא שָׁנוּ אֶלָּא בְּמָקוֹם הֶעָשׂוּי לְשַׁמֵּר, אֲבָל לְחַזֵּק – אָסוּר. הֵיכִי דָּמֵי *לְשַׁמֵּר, הֵיכִי דָּמֵי לְחַזֵּק? א"ר חִסְדָּא: לְמַעְלָה מִן הַיַּיִן – זֶהוּ לְשַׁמֵּר, לְמַטָּה מִן הַיַּיִן – זֶהוּ לְחַזֵּק. (א)רָבָא אָמַר: בלְמַטָּה מִן הַיַּיִן נַמִי זֶהוּ לְשַׁמֵּר. וְהֵיכִי דָּמֵי לְחַזֵּק – כְּגוֹן שֶׁנִּיקְּבָהּ לְמַטָּה מִן הַשְּׁמָרִים. א"ל אַבַּיֵי לְרָבָא: תַּנְיָא דִּמְסַיַּיע לָךְ; *ג"בַּיִת סָתוּם – יֵשׁ לוֹ אַרְבַּע אַמּוֹת, פָּרַץ אֶת פַּצִּימָיו – אֵין לוֹ ד' אַמּוֹת. דבַּיִת סָתוּם אֵינוֹ מְטַמֵּא כָּל סְבִיבָיו, פָּרַץ אֶת פַּצִּימָיו – מְטַמֵּא כָּל סְבִיבָיו". גּוּבְתָא, רַב אָסַר, וּשְׁמוּאֵל שָׁרֵי. המְחַתֵּךְ לְכַתְּחִלָּה – דְּכ"ע לָא פְּלִיגִי דְּאָסוּר. אַהְדּוּרֵי – דְּכ"ע לָא פְּלִיגִי דְּשָׁרֵי. כִּי פְּלִיגִי – דַּחֲתִיכָה וְלָא מִתַּקְנָא. מַאן דְּאָסַר – גָּזְרִינַן דִּילְמָא אָתֵי לְמִיחְתָּךְ לְכַתְּחִלָּה, וּמַאן דְּשָׁרֵי – ולָא גָּזְרִינַן. כְּתַנָּאֵי: אֵין חוֹתְכִין שְׁפוֹפֶרֶת בְּיו"ט וְא"צ לוֹמַר בְּשַׁבָּת. נָפְלָה – (אֵין) מַחֲזִירִין אוֹתָהּ בַּשַּׁבָּת, וְאֵין צָרִיךְ לוֹמַר בְּיו"ט, וְר' יֹאשִׁיָּה מֵיקֵל. ר' יֹאשִׁיָּה אַהַיָּיא? אִילֵימָא אַרֵישָׁא – הָא קָמְתַקֵּן מָנָא! אֶלָּא אַסֵּיפָא – ת"ק נַמִי מִישְׁרָא קָשָׁרֵי! אֶלָּא: דַּחֲתִיכָה וְלָא מִתַּקְנָא אִיכָּא בֵּינַיְיהוּ, מ"ס: גָּזְרִינַן, וּמ"ס: לָא גָּזְרִינַן. דָּרַשׁ רַב שֵׁישָׁא בְּרֵיהּ דְּרַב אִידִי מִשְּׁמֵיהּ דְּר' יוֹחָנָן: הֲלָכָה כְּר' יֹאשִׁיָּה.§ "וְאִם הָיְתָה נְקוּבָה וכו'".§ מִישְׁחָא; רַב אָסַר, וּשְׁמוּאֵל שָׁרֵי. מַאן דְּאָסַר – וגָּזְרִינַן מִשּׁוּם שַׁעֲוָה, וּמַאן דְּשָׁרֵי – לָא גָּזְרִינַן. אֲמַר לֵיהּ רַב שְׁמוּאֵל בַּר בַּר חָנָה לְרַב יוֹסֵף: בְּפֵירוּשׁ אָמְרַתְּ לָן מִשְּׁמֵיהּ דְּרַב "מִישְׁחָא שָׁרֵי". אָמַר טָבוּת רִישְׁבָּא אָמַר שְׁמוּאֵל: הַאי טַרְפָּא דְּאָסָא – אָסוּר. מ"ט? רַב יֵימָר מִדִּפְתִּי אָמַר: גְּזֵירָה מִשּׁוּם מַרְזֵב, רַב אַשִׁי אָמַר: חגְּזֵירָה שֶׁמָּא יִקְטוֹם. מַאי בֵּינַיְיהוּ[א]? אִיכָּא בֵּינַיְיהוּ: דִּקְטִים וּמַנְחִי. בֵּי סַדְיָא, רַב אָסַר וּשְׁמוּאֵל טשָׁרֵי. בְּרַכִּין – דְּכוּלֵּי עָלְמָא לָא פְּלִיגִי דְּשָׁרֵי, יבְּקָשִׁין – דְּכ"ע לָא פְּלִיגִי דְּאָסוּר, כִּי פְּלִיגִי – בְּמִיצְעֵי. מַאן דְּאָסַר – מֶיחֱזֵי כְּמַשְׁוֵי. וּמַאן דְּשָׁרֵי – לָא מֶיחֱזֵי כְּמַשְׁוֵי. וְהָא דְּרַב לָאו *בְּפֵירוּשׁ אִיתְּמַר, אֶלָּא מִכְּלָלָא אִיתְּמַר. דְּרַב אִיקְּלַע לְהַהוּא אַתְרָא דְּלָא הֲוָה לֵיהּ רְוָוחָא, נְפַק יְתֵיב בְּכַרְמְלִית. אַיְיתוּ לֵיהּ בֵּי סַדְיָא לָא יְתֵיב. מַאן דַּחֲזָא סָבַר – מִשּׁוּם דְּבֵי סַדְיָא אָסוּר. וְלָא הִיא, דְּרַב אַכְרוֹזֵי מַכְרִיז: בֵּי סַדְיָא שָׁרֵי. כוּמִשּׁוּם כְּבוֹד רַבּוֹתֵינוּ לֹא יָשַׁב עָלָיו. וּמַאן נִינְהוּ – רַב כָּהֲנָא וְרַב אַסִּי.§ **מתני'** *לנוֹתְנִין תַּבְשִׁיל לְתוֹךְ הַבּוֹר בִּשְׁבִיל שֶׁיְּהֵא שָׁמוּר, וְאֶת הַמַּיִם הַיָּפִים בָּרָעִים בִּשְׁבִיל שֶׁיִּצַּנְּנוּ, וְאֶת הַצּוֹנֵן בַּחַמָּה בִּשְׁבִיל שֶׁיַּחַמּוּ. *מִי שֶׁנָּשְׁרוּ כֵּלָיו בַּדֶּרֶךְ בַּמַּיִם – מְהַלֵּךְ בָּהֶן וְאֵינוֹ חוֹשֵׁשׁ. הִגִּיעַ לֶחָצֵר הַחִיצוֹנָה – שׁוֹטְחָן בַּחַמָּה[ב], אֲבָל לֹא כְּנֶגֶד הָעָם.§ **גמ'** פְּשִׁיטָא! מַהוּ דְּתֵימָא: נִיגְזַר מִשּׁוּם אַשְׁוּוֹיֵי גוּמּוֹת, קָא מַשְׁמַע לָן.§ "וְאֶת הַמַּיִם הַיָּפִים בָּרָעִים".§ פְּשִׁיטָא! סֵיפָא אִיצְטְרִיכָא לֵיהּ "וְאֶת הַצּוֹנֵן בַּחַמָּה". הָא נַמִי פְּשִׁיטָא! מַהוּ דְּתֵימָא: נִיגְזוֹר דִּילְמָא אָתֵי לְאַטְמוֹנֵי בְּרֶמֶץ, קמ"ל.§ ל"מִי שֶׁנָּשְׁרוּ וכו'".§ *אָמַר רַב יְהוּדָה אָמַר רַב: מכָּל מָקוֹם שֶׁאָסְרוּ חֲכָמִים מִפְּנֵי מַרְאִית הָעַיִן – אֲפִילּוּ בְּחַדְרֵי חֲדָרִים אָסוּר. תְּנַן: שׁוֹטְחָן בַּחַמָּה אֲבָל לֹא כְּנֶגֶד הָעָם! תַּנָּאֵי הִיא; דְּתַנְיָא: שׁוֹטְחָן בַּחַמָּה אֲבָל לֹא כְּנֶגֶד הָעָם, ר"א וְר"ש נאוֹסְרִין. אָמַר רַב הוּנָא

הַמְנַעֵר

רש"י

מִשּׁוּם רִיחֲשָׁא. שֶׁלֹּא יִכָּנֵס בּוֹ שֶׁרֶץ, כְּגוֹן *נְמִיָּיה וְחוּלְדָּה שֶׁמְּמִיתִים אֶת הַתַּרְנְגוֹלִים: זִימְנִין דְּלָא תַּקְנֵיהּ מֵעִיקָּרָא. שֶׁיְּהֵא כְּדֵי לְהוֹצִיא הֶבֶל וּלְהַכְנִיס אֶת הָאֲוִיר: לֹא שָׁנוּ. דְּנוֹקְבִין: אֶלָּא בְּמָקוֹם. דִּסְתִימָה זוֹ לֹא נַעֲשֵׂית אֶלָּא לִשְׁמוֹר רֵיחַ הַיַּיִן שֶׁלֹּא יֵצֵא וְיִתְקַלְקֵל, וְכֵיוָן דְּלָאו סְתִימָה מַעַלְיוּתָא עָבְדִי לַהּ – לָאו כְּלוּם הוּא: לְחַזֵּק. שֶׁיְּחַזֵּק הַכְּלִי, שֶׁלֹּא יֵצֵא יֵינוֹ. הוֹאִיל וּסְתִימָה מַעַלְיְיתָא הִיא, כִּי הָדַר נָקֵיב לַהּ – הָוֵי כְּפוֹתֵחַ לְכַתְּחִלָּה: לְמַטָּה מִן הַיַּיִן נַמִי לְשַׁמֵּר הוּא. כֵּיוָן דְּלָאו כּוֹבֶד הַיַּיִן נִשְׁעָן עָלָיו, סַגִּי לֵיהּ בִּסְתִימָה כָּל דְּהוּ: לְמַטָּה מִן הַשְּׁמָרִים. אֵצֶל שׁוּלָיו, שֶׁכָּל כּוֹבֶד הַיַּיִן נִשְׁעָן שָׁם: תַּנְיָא דִּמְסַיַּיע לָךְ. דְּלָא פָּקַע שֵׁם פֶּתַח מִינֵּיהּ אֶלָּא בִּסְתִימָה מְעַלַּיְיתָא: בַּיִת סָתוּם יֵשׁ לוֹ ד"א. קיי"ל בְּבָבָא בַּתְרָא חָצֵר מִתְחַלֶּקֶת לְפִי פְּתָחֶיהָ, לְפִי פֶּתַח הַבָּתִּים הַפְּתוּחִין לָהּ. אִם בָּאוּ לַחֲלֹק אֶת הֶחָצֵר בֵּין שְׁנַיִם, שֶׁהָיָה לָזֶה בַּיִת שֶׁפְּתוּחִין לוֹ לֶחָצֵר שְׁנֵי פְתָחִים, וְלָזֶה בַּיִת שֶׁפְּתוּחִין לוֹ לֶחָצֵר ד' פְּתָחִים – נוֹטֵל לְכָל פֶּתַח אַרְבַּע אַמּוֹת בֶּחָצֵר נֶגֶד פִּתְחוֹ לְמִדַּת רוֹחַב פִּתְחוֹ, וְהַשְּׁאָר חוֹלְקִין בְּשָׁוֶה. וְאִם נִסְתַּם אֶחָד מֵהֶם קוֹדֶם חֲלוּקַּת הֶחָצֵר, וְלֹא פֵּירֵץ אֶת פַּצִּימָיו, אֶלָּא סָתַם בֵּין שְׁנֵי הַפַּצִּימִין – אֵינוֹ מַפְסִיד [דִּין] פִּתְחוֹ בְּכָךְ. פֵּירֵץ אֶת פַּצִּימָיו, וְאַח"כ סְתָמוֹ – פָּקַע שֵׁם פֶּתַח מִינֵּיהּ: בַּיִת סָתוּם. וְהַמֵּת בְּתוֹכוֹ, אֵינוֹ מְטַמֵּא סְבִיבָיו: פָּרַץ פַּצִּימָיו. וּסְתָמוֹ – נַעֲשָׂה קֶבֶר, וּמְטַמֵּא סְבִיבָיו ד"א, כִּדְאָמַר בְּסוֹטָה (ד' מד.): מֵת תּוֹפֵס ד"א לְטוּמְאָה, וּגְזֵרָה דְּרַבָּנַן שֶׁמָּא יַאֲהִיל וְלֹא יָבִין: גּוּבְתָא. לִתְקוֹעַ קָנֶה חָלוּל בְּנֶקֶב הֶחָבִית, שֶׁיֵּצֵא הַיַּיִן דֶּרֶךְ הַקָּנֶה: מְחַתֵּךְ. רונגיי"ר, לְתַקְּנָהּ לְמִדַּת הַנֶּקֶב: אַהְדּוּרֵי. אִם נָפְלָה: וְלָא מִתַּקְנָא. לֹא נִיתְּנָה בַּנֶּקֶב לֵידַע אִם לְמִדָּתוֹ הִיא: אִי לֵימָא אַרֵישָׁא. לַחוֹתְכָהּ וּלְשַׁפּוֹתָהּ: מִשְׁחָא. שֶׁמֶן עָב: אָסוּר. לְמָרְחוֹ: טַרְפָּא דְּאָסָא. לָתֵת עָלֶה שֶׁל הֲדַס בְּנֶקֶב הֶחָבִית. שֶׁהֶעָלֶה עָשׂוּי כְּמַרְזֵב, וְהַיַּיִן זָב דֶּרֶךְ שָׁם: גְּזֵירָה מִשּׁוּם מַרְזֵב. שֶׁמָּא יָכִין מַרְזֵב: שֶׁמָּא יִקְטוֹם. הֶעָלֶה מִן הֶעָנָף. וְכֵיוָן דְּקַטְמֵיהּ הֲוָה לֵיהּ כִּמְתַקֵּן כְּלִי, כִּדְתַנְיָא בְּמַסֶּכֶת בֵּיצָה (דף לג:): לַחֲצוֹת בּוֹ שִׁינָּיו – לֹא יִקְטְמֶנּוּ, וְאִם קְטָמוֹ – חַיָּיב חַטָּאת: בֵּי סַדְיָא. לְבָדִין שֶׁקּוֹרִין פלטר"ש, וַעֲשׂוּיִין לְקַפְּלָן תַּחְתָּיו בִּמְקוֹם הַכַּר אוֹ הַכֶּסֶת: רַב אָסַר. לַהֲבִיאוֹ דֶּרֶךְ מַלְבּוּשׁ דֶּרֶךְ רְשׁוּת הָרַבִּים כְּשֶׁהוּא מְעוּטָּף בּוֹ: בְּרַכִּין. שֶׁדַּרְכָּן לְהִתְחַמֵּם בָּהֶן: דְּשָׁרוּ. דְּמַלְבּוּשׁ הֵן: וְלָא הֲוָה לֵיהּ רְווחָא. בַּבַּיִת לִמְקוֹם מוֹשָׁבָם שֶׁל תַּלְמִידִים: וּמִשּׁוּם כְּבוֹד רַבּוֹתֵינוּ. שֶׁלֹּא הָיָה לָהֶן דָּבָר לֵישֵׁב עָלָיו, וְיוֹשְׁבִין עַל גַּבֵּי קַרְקַע: רַב כָּהֲנָא וְרַב אַסִּי. תַּלְמִידֵי חֲבֵרִים הָיוּ לוֹ*: **מתני'** לְתוֹךְ הַבּוֹר. שֶׁאֵין בּוֹ מַיִם: שֶׁיְּהֵא שָׁמוּר. שֶׁלֹּא יַסְרִיחַ מֵחֲמַת הַחוֹם: וְאֶת הַמַּיִם הַיָּפִים בָּרָעִים. כְּלִי מָלֵא מַיִם יָפִים לְתוֹךְ מִקְוֵה מַיִם רָעִים, לְהִשְׁתַּמֵּר (ג)שֶׁיִּצּוֹנוּ וְלֹא יֵחַמּוּ: מִי שֶׁנָּשְׁרוּ. שֶׁנָּפְלוּ לַמַּיִם בְּשַׁבָּת: לֶחָצֵר הַחִיצוֹנָה. הַסְּמוּכָה לִמְבוֹא הָעִיר, בְּתוֹךְ הָעִיר, שֶׁהוּא מָקוֹם מִשְׁתַּמֵּר: שׁוֹטְחָן בַּחַמָּה. לְיַבְּשָׁן: אֲבָל לֹא כְּנֶגֶד הָעָם. שֶׁיַּחְשְׁדוּהוּ שֶׁכִּבְּסָן: **גמ'** פְּשִׁיטָא. דְּנוֹתְנִין תַּבְשִׁיל לְתוֹךְ הַבּוֹר: גּוּמּוֹת. שֶׁבְּקַרְקַע הַבּוֹר, שֶׁיְּהוּ שָׁוִין, לְהוֹשִׁיב הַקְּדֵרָה:

הַמְנַעֵר

תוספות

משום ריחשא. ואטו פתחא אחרינא דליכא למיחש לריחשא לא גזרינן, דדוקא אטו לול של תרנגולין גזרינן, דלא מסקי אינשי אדעתייהו שיהא עשוי להכניס ולהוציא:

פרץ פצימיו מטמא כל סביביו. פי' בקונטרס: כל סביביו – ד' אמות, כקבר. ואין נראה לזקיני הרב ר' שמשון זצ"ל: דכיון דמסיימי מחיצתא, ולית לן למיחש שמא יעלה על הבית ויאהיל עליו ולא ידע – לית לן למימר דמטמא ד' אמות כל סביביו. כדמוכח בסוטה פרק "משוח מלחמה" (ד' מד.) גבי חצר הקבר, העומד בתוכה טהור. הני מילי – חצר הקבר דמסיימא מחיצתא, אבל מת בעלמא – תפיס. ומשמע דבמת נמי, היכא דמסיימא – לא נטמא כל סביביו ד' אמות. אלא נראה לו דהכי פי': זיזין באותו בית שבולטין מחוץ לבית מכל צד, ויש בהם פותח טפח בכל אחד, אם הבית סתום, ועדיין נראית בו צורת הפתח – אינו מטמא, שסתמו של מת עומד לצאת דרך הפתח. פרץ פצימיו וחזר ובנאו כשאר כותל, ולא נותר בו כלל פתח – מטמא כל סביביו, דכל חד וחד איכא לספוקי דילמא דרך אותו מקום יצא מן הבית. מיהו, לאו פירכא היא כולי האי מה שהקשה לפירוש הקונטרס. די"ל: שלא חלקו חכמים במת. ועוד נראה: דלא קשה כלל לפי' הקונטרס, דבית נמי לא מסיימי מחיצתא שהוא מטמא הנוגע בכתלים אפילו לא יעלה על גביו, כקבר שמטמא במגע אפילו מן הצד, כדתניא בספרי בפרשת פרה אדומה: "או בקבר" – זה קבר סתום. או אינו אלא קבר פתוח, אמרת ק"ו: ומה אהל שמקבל טומאה אינו מטמא מכל צדדין כשהוא פתוח, קבר שאינו מקבל טומאה אינו דין שלא יטמא מכל צדדין כשהוא פתוח. אלמא: כשהוא סתום מטמא אף הנוגע מן הצד:

הלכה כרבי יאשיה. הלכך: מותר לתת לכתחילה גובתא שקורין רזי"ל בחבית:

משום מרזב. פי' הרב פור"ת: שלא יבוא ליתן על גגו מרזב. וקשה: דבגובתא נמי נגזר! אלא נראה לרבי כפי' הקונט': שלא יתקן מרזב ליינו, שיפול היין בתוכו וילך למרחוק. דכשלוקח עלה של הדס ומקפלו כעין מרזב נראה כעושה מרזב. אבל בגובתא, שאינו עושה בו שום מעשה – לא גזרינן. מ"ר:

אייתי ליה בי סדיא. בי מילעי הוה, דאי לאו הכי היכי איתמר מכללא:

מי שנשרו כליו במים. בדלך גרסינן[א], לשון נפילה. לא כפי' הקונטרס לעיל בפרק "במה אשה" (דף סה.) שנשרו במי גשמים. דהא אמרינן בביצה בפרק "משילין" (דף לה:): מאן דתני מנשירין לא משתבש, כדתנן "מי שנשרו כליו במים בדרך" אלמא: לשון נפילה הוא.[ב] מ"ר:

א) ר"ל דגרסי' הנו"ן דנשרו בקמץ לשון נפילה דאלו הנו"ן בחירק הוי לשון שרייה. רש"א.
ב) [ועי' תוס' ביצה לה: ד"ה מי שנשרו].

עין משפט נר מצוה

לא א ב מיי' פכ"ג מהלכות שבת הל"א סמג לאוין סה טוש"ע או"ח סימן שיד סעיף ב:
לב ג מיי' פ"ב מהלכות שכנים הל"ז טוש"ע חו"מ סימן קעב סעיף ז:
לג ד מיי' פ"ז מהלכות טומאת מת הל"א:
לד ה ו מיי' פכ"ג מהל' שבת הלכה ו סמג לאוין סה טוש"ע או"ח סימן שיד סעיף ה:
לה ז מיי' שם הלכה יא סמג שם טור שו"ע שם סעיף יא:
לו ח שם סעיף ה:
לז ט י מיי' פי"ט מהל' שבת הלכה יז סמג שם טוש"ע או"ח סימן שא סעיף לה:
לח כ מיי' פכ"ב מהל' שבת הלכה ט טור או"ח סימן שיח:
לט ל מ נ מיי' שם הל"כ סמג לאוין סה טור שו"ע או"ח סימן שא סעיף מה:

רבינו חננאל

וי"א אין מוסיפין דזמנין דלא תקניה מעיקרא ואתי לארווחי ביה הלכתא כוותיה דדרש רב נחמן בר רב חסדא משמיה דר' יוחנן הלכה כי"א. ושוין שנוקבין בנקב ישן לכתחלה ואמר רב יהודה משמיה דשמואל אינו מותר לפתוח נקב ישן אלא במקום העשוי לשמר פי' להוציא היין מן השמרים אבל לחזק אסור פי' היה נקב בחבית וסתמו שלא יהא שותת. וחלקו רב חסדא ורבה והלכתא כרבה דתניא מסייעתו ואלו דברי רבה רבה אמר למטה מן היין נמי זהו לשמר ומותר לפותחו והיכי דמי לחזק כגון שנקבה למטה מן השמרים דמוכחא מלתא שאין אדם עושה נקב בקרקעיתא של חבית להוציא יין ולא לשמר. עשאו מפני כשמפנה החבית הופכה על פיה. וזה הנקב כיון שסתמו נעשה סתום. זה בגופה של חבית ובטל מלהיות נקב בו וחשוב כפתח בית הנסתם בפירוץ פצימין שנסתלק ממנו דין פתח לגמרי. גובתא שהיא שפופרת של קנה או של עצים שנותנין בנקב החבית או ביד הנוד של יין להיות מושכין ממנו יין מן החבית או מן הנוד. רב אסר ושמואל שרי ואקימנא חלוקתן בשפופרת חתוכה ואינה מתוקנת להכניסה לנקב אבל לחתוך דברי הכל אסור. ואם היא חתוכה ומתוקנת דברי הכל מותר להחזירה בנקב החבית או בנוד למשוך ממנו יין. והעמדנו עוד חלוקת רב ושמואל כתנאי. דתניא אין חותכין שפופרת ביו"ט ואין צ"ל בשבת. נפלה מחזירין בשבת. ואין צ"ל ביו"ט. ור' יאשיה מיקל ודייקי' עלה ר' יאשיה אהייא מיקל אילימא ארישא שאמר ת"ק אין חותכין כלומר אין חותכין מקנה גדול חתיכה לעשות' שפופרת הא ר' יאשיה מיקל בהא קא מתקן כלי בשבת אלא שאמר ת"ק נפלה מחזירין אותה. בהא לימא ר' יאשיה מיקל מי החמיר שיאמר בזה מיקל הלא בזה גם ת"ק מותר קאמר. ותריצנא אלא לאו דחתיכה ולא מתקנה איכא בינייהו וכך הציעה. אין עושין שפופרת ביו"ט ואין צ"ל בשבת. ואפי' חתכה ולא מתקנה אסור אבל אם היתה כבר בחבית ונפלה מחזירין אותה בשבת ואין צ"ל ביו"ט ור' יאשיה מיקל בחתיכה ולא מתקנה נמצאו דברי רב כת"ק ודברי שמואל כר' יאשיה והלכה כר' יאשיה ודרש רב שישא בריה דרב אידי משמא דר' יוחנן הלכתא כר' יאשיה וזה שאמר חתכה ולא מתקנה לאו שצריכה תיקון כלי כגון סכין וכדומה לו אלא תיקון ביד בלבד. ואם צריכה תיקון בסכין או זולתו סכין כלי אחר אסורה. ואם היתה החבית נקובה לא יתן עליה שעוה מפני שממרח. כלומר סותם כדאמרינן התם לענין חבית שניקבה וסתמה שמרים כו' מורח מן הצדדין. וכיון דר' יהודה דמתניתין וריב"ז ורב ושמואל אמרי ש"מ שאסור לתת שעוה בחבית. וכן משחא. רב אסר גזירה במשחא אטו שעוה. והלכתא כוותיה: **טרפא** דאסא. פי' עלה הדס שנותנין על הנקב של חבית להיות מקלח בו היין ולא יהיה שותת בדופני החבית. לדברי הכל אסור ליטול עלה של הדס בשבת ולשומו בנקב של חבית כמרזב. ואפילו רב אשי לא התיר אלא שאם היה הנקב מושך ממנו*) אבל לתתו לכתחלה אוסר: **בי** סדיא רב אסר ושמואל שרי אין זה מקומו אלא בשביל שהזכיר השמועות שחלקו בהן רב אסר ושמואל שרי נסבה בגררא. ופשוטה היא. כסת זו שחלקו בה כסת בינונית לא דקה ולא קשה. ומסקינן בה אפילו זו מותר לטלטלה: **נותנין** תבשיל בתוך הבור בשביל שיהא שמור. פי' בור זה אין בו מים ונותן התבשיל בקרקעיתו מהו דתימא לגזור דלמא אתי לאשויי גומות קמ"ל דלא גזרינן. ואת המים היפים ברעים פשיטא ואת הצונן בחמין פשיטא מהו דתימא לגזור דלמא אתי לאשויי גומות**) ברמץ קמ"ל דלא גזרינן: **מתני'** מי שנשרו כליו בדרך כו'. אמר רב יהודה אמר רב כל מקום שאסרו חכמים מפני מראית העין אפילו בחדרי חדרים אסור. איני והא תנן שוטחן בחמה אבל לא כנגד העם ואוקימנא

*) נראה דל"ל מונח בנקב מותר למשוך ממנו. **) אינו מובן ואולי צ"ל דלמא אתי לאטמוני ברמץ וכדאיתא בגמ'.

מסורת הש"ס

עי' לעיל נא: רש"י ד"ה קטנה ושם משמע שנמייה

[פי' להוציא היין מן השמרי'. ערוך ערך חזק ע"ש]

ב"ב יב.

וחולדה חיות הן [כדאיתא סנהדרין לז:]

לעיל סד: ביצה ט. ע"ז יב.

הגהות הב"ח

(א) גמ' רבא אמר למטה וכו' א"ל אביי לרבה: (ב) רש"י ד"ה ואת המים וכו' להשתמר שיצוננו ולא יחמו:

הגהות הגר"א

[א] גמ' איכא בינייהו דקטים ומנח. נ"ב פי' שהוא קטום ויש עוד הרבה קטומים טור. וז"ש ומנחי אבל גירסת הרי"ף והרא"ש וש"פ ומנח: [ב] שם שוטחן בחמה. נ"ב דווקא (ועמ"ש רבינו באו"ח סימן ש"א ס"ק ק"ה):

גליון הש"ס

גמ' אמר ר"ח למעלה מן היין זהו לשמר. גי' הרי"ף למעלה מן היין זהו לחזק למטה מן היין זהו לשמר רבה אמר למעלה וכו': שם ומשום כבוד רבותינו לא ישב. עי' שבועות דף מז ע"א תוס' ד"ה הוה יתיב:

גמרא

אהַמְנַעֵר טַלִּיתוֹ בְּשַׁבָּת – חַיָּיב חַטָּאת. וְלָא אֲמַרַן אֶלָּא בַּחֲדַתֵּי, אֲבָל בְּעַתִּיקֵי – לֵית לָן בָּהּ. וְלָא אֲמַרַן אֶלָּא בְּאוּכָמֵי, אֲבָל בְּחִיוָּרֵי וְסוּמָּקֵי – לֵית לָן בָּהּ. וְהוּא דְּקָפֵיד עֲלַיְיהוּ. עוּלָּא אִיקְלַע לְפוּמְבְּדִיתָא, חֲזָא רַבָּנַן דְּקָא מְנַפְּצִי גְּלִימַיְיהוּ. אֲמַר: קָמְחַלְּלִין רַבָּנַן שַׁבְּתָא! אֲמַר לְהוּ רַב יְהוּדָה: נְפוּצֵי לֵיהּ בְּאַפֵּיהּ, אֲנַן לָא קָפְדִינַן מִידֵּי. אַבַּיֵי הֲוָה קָאֵי קַמֵּיהּ דְּרַב יוֹסֵף, א"ל: הַב לִי כּוּמְתַאי. [חֲזָא דְּאִיכָּא] טַלָּא עֲלֵיהּ, הֲוָה קָמְחַסֵּם לְמִיתְבָה לֵיהּ. א"ל: נְפוֹץ שְׁדֵי, אֲנַן לָא קָפְדִינַן מִידֵּי. *אָמַר רַב יִצְחָק בַּר יוֹסֵף א"ר יוֹחָנָן: בהַיּוֹצֵא בְּטַלִּית מְקוּפֶּלֶת מוּנַּחַת לוֹ עַל כְּתֵיפוֹ בַּשַּׁבָּת – חַיָּיב חַטָּאת. תנ"ה סוֹחֲרֵי כְּסוּת הַיּוֹצְאִים בְּטַלִּיתוֹת מְקוּפָּלוֹת וּמוּנָּחוֹת עַל כְּתֵיפָן בַּשַּׁבָּת – חַיָּיבִין חַטָּאת. וְלֹא סוֹחֲרֵי כְּסוּת בִּלְבַד אָמְרוּ, אֶלָּא כָּל אָדָם, אֶלָּא שֶׁדַּרְכָּן שֶׁל מוֹכְרִין לָצֵאת כָּךְ. וְחֶנְוָנִי גהַיּוֹצֵא בְּמָעוֹת הַצְּרוּרִין לוֹ בִּסְדִינוֹ – חַיָּיב חַטָּאת. וְלֹא חֶנְוָנִי בִּלְבַד אָמְרוּ, אֶלָּא כָּל אָדָם, אֶלָּא שֶׁדַּרְכּוֹ שֶׁל חֶנְוָנִי לָצֵאת כָּךְ. *וְהָרַטָּנִין *יוֹצְאִין בְּסוּדָרִין [א] שֶׁעַל כְּתֵיפָן. וְלֹא רַטָּנִין בִּלְבַד אָמְרוּ, אֶלָּא כָּל אָדָם, אֶלָּא שֶׁדַּרְכָּן שֶׁל רַטָּנִין לָצֵאת בְּכָךְ. א"ר יְהוּדָה: מַעֲשֶׂה בְּהוּרְקָנוֹס בְּנוֹ שֶׁל רַבִּי אֱלִיעֶזֶר בֶּן הוּרְקָנוֹס שֶׁיָּצָא בְּסוּדָר שֶׁעַל כְּתֵיפוֹ בַּשַּׁבָּת, אֶלָּא שֶׁנִּימָא כְּרוּכָה לוֹ בְּאֶצְבָּעוֹ. וּכְשֶׁבָּא הַדָּבָר לִפְנֵי חֲכָמִים אָמְרוּ: דאֲפִילּוּ אֵין נִימָא כְּרוּכָה לוֹ בְּאֶצְבָּעוֹ. דָּרַשׁ רַב נַחְמָן בַּר רַב חִסְדָּא מִשְּׁמֵיהּ דְּרַב חִסְדָּא: הֲלָכָה – אע"פ שֶׁאֵין נִימָא כְּרוּכָה לוֹ בְּאֶצְבְּעוֹתָיו. עוּלָּא אִיקְלַע לְבֵי אַסִּי בַּר הִינִי, בָּעוּ מִינֵּיהּ: מַהוּ לַעֲשׂוֹת מַרְזֵב בַּשַּׁבָּת? אֲמַר לְהוּ, הָכִי אָמַר רַבִּי אֶלְעַי: אָסוּר לַעֲשׂוֹת מַרְזֵב בַּשַּׁבָּת. מַאי מַרְזֵב? אָמַר ר' זֵירָא: כִּיסֵי בַּבְלָייתָא. ר' יִרְמְיָה הֲוָה יָתֵיב קַמֵּיהּ דְּר' זֵירָא. א"ל: הָכִי מַאי? א"ל: אָסוּר. וְהָכִי מַאי? א"ל: אָסוּר. אָמַר רַב פַּפָּא: *הנְקוֹט הַאי כְּלָלָא בִּידָךְ: כָּל אַדַּעְתָּא דְּלִכְנוּפֵי – [ב] אָסוּר, כָּל דְּלְהִתְנָאוֹת – שָׁרֵי. כִּי הָא דְּרַב שִׁישָׁא בְּרֵיהּ דְּרַב אִידִי מִתְנָאֶה בִּסְדִינוֹ הֲוָה. כִּי אֲתָא רַב דִּימִי אֲמַר: פַּעַם אַחַת יָצָא רַבִּי לַשָּׂדֶה, וְהָיוּ שְׁנֵי צִידֵּי טַלִּיתוֹ מוּנָּחִין עַל כְּתֵיפוֹ. אָמַר לְפָנָיו יְהוֹשֻׁעַ בֶּן זֵירוּז בֶּן חָמִיו שֶׁל רַבִּי מֵאִיר: בָּזוֹ לֹא חִיֵּיב ר' מֵאִיר חַטָּאת. אָמַר לֵיהּ: דִּקְדֵּק רַבִּי מֵאִיר עַד כָּאן? שִׁלְשֵׁל רַבִּי טַלִּיתוֹ. כִּי אֲתָא רָבִין אֲמַר: לֹא יְהוֹשֻׁעַ בֶּן זֵירוּז הֲוָה – אֶלָּא יְהוֹשֻׁעַ בֶּן כְּפוּסַאי הָיָה, חֲתָנוֹ שֶׁל ר' עֲקִיבָא. אָמַר: בָּזוֹ לֹא חִיֵּיב ר' עֲקִיבָא חַטָּאת. אָמַר לוֹ: דִּקְדֵּק ר"ע עַד כָּאן? שִׁלְשֵׁל רַבִּי טַלִּיתוֹ. כִּי אֲתָא רַב שְׁמוּאֵל בַּר רַב יְהוּדָה אָמַר: נִשְׁאַל אִיתְּמַר.§ **מתני'** הָרוֹחֵץ בְּמֵי מְעָרָה וּבְמֵי טְבֶרְיָא וְנִסְתַּפֵּג אֲפִילּוּ בְּעֶשֶׂר אֲלוּנְטִיאוֹת – לֹא יְבִיאֵם בְּיָדוֹ. אֲבָל עֲשָׂרָה בְּנֵי אָדָם מִסְתַּפְּגִין בַּאֲלוּנְטִית אַחַת פְּנֵיהֶם יְדֵיהֶם וְרַגְלֵיהֶם, וּמְבִיאִין אוֹתָן בְּיָדָן. סָכִין וּמְמַשְׁמְשִׁין*, אֲבָל לֹא מִתְעַמְּלִין וְלֹא מִתְגָּרְרִין. אֵין יוֹרְדִין *לְקוֹרְדִימָא, *)וְאֵין עוֹשִׂין אַפִּיקְטוֹיזִין, וְאֵין מְעַצְּבִין אֶת הַקָּטָן, וְאֵין מַחֲזִירִין אֶת הַשֶּׁבֶר. מִי שֶׁנִּפְרְקָה יָדוֹ וְרַגְלוֹ לֹא יִטְרְפֵם בְּצוֹנֵן, אֲבָל *רוֹחֵץ הוּא כְּדַרְכּוֹ, וְאִם נִתְרַפֵּא – נִתְרַפֵּא.§ **גמ'** קָתָנֵי מֵי מְעָרָה דּוּמְיָא דְּמֵי טְבֶרְיָא, מָה מֵי טְבֶרְיָא – חַמִּין, אַף מֵי מְעָרָה חַמִּין. *ו"הָרוֹחֵץ" – דִּיעֲבַד אִין, לְכַתְּחִילָּה – לָא. מִכְּלָל

דִּלְהִשְׁתַּטֵּף

*) לעיל קכג.

רש"י

הַמְנַעֵר טַלִּיתוֹ. מִן הֶעָפָר: חַיָּיב חַטָּאת. דְּזֶהוּ לִיבּוּנָהּ: אֶלָּא בְּאוּכָמֵי. שֶׁהָאָבָק מְקַלְקֵל מַרְאִיתָהּ, וְקָפֵיד עָלֶיהָ: וְהוּא דְּקָפֵיד עֲלַיְיהוּ. לְלוֹבְשָׁן עַד שֶׁיִּנָּעֵרֵס: קָמְחַלְּלִי(א) שַׁבְּתָא. וּגְלִימֵי אוּכָמֵי הֲווּ: לָא קָפְדִינַן. לֹא אִיכְפַּת לָן אִם יֵשׁ עָלֶיהָ אָבָק, הִלְכָּךְ לָאו לִיבּוּן הוּא: כּוּמְתַאי. כּוֹבָעִי: הֲוָה קָא מְחַסֵּם. לְשׁוֹן "לֹא תַחְסוֹם" (דברים כה): לְמֵיתְבָא לֵיהּ. שֶׁצָּרִיךְ לְנַעֵר הַטַּל מֵעָלֶיהָ: בְּטַלִּית מְקוּפֶּלֶת. לְאַחַר שֶׁנְּתָנָהּ עַל רֹאשׁוֹ, הִגְבִּיהַּ שִׁיפּוּלֶיהָ עַל כְּתֵפָיו: חַיָּיב חַטָּאת. שֶׁאֵין זֶה דֶּרֶךְ מַלְבּוּשׁ: וְהָרַטָּנִין. עַל שֵׁם מָקוֹם: נִימָא כְּרוּכָה עַל אֶצְבָּעוֹ. שֶׁלֹּא יִפּוֹל מִכְּתֵפָיו: בַּר הִינִי: מַרְזֵב. מְפָרֵשׁ לְקַמֵּיהּ: כִּיסוּי בַּבְלָייתָא. שֶׁמְּסַלְּקִין בִּגְדֵיהֶם מִן הָאָרֶץ כְּשֶׁהֵן אֲרוּכִין, וְכוֹפְלִין אוֹתָן כְּלַפֵּי מַעְלָה, פרונצי"ש, וּמַחֲזִיקִין אוֹתָן[ג] ע"י חוּטִין. וְהַיְינוּ כְּמִין כִּיס וּכְמוֹ מַרְזֵב: אָסוּר. מִשּׁוּם תַּקּוּנֵי מָנָא: הָכִי מַאי. קוֹלֵט חֲלוּקוֹ (בְּפָנָיו) בְּעִנְיָן אֶחָד, וְשׁוֹאֲלוֹ: כְּגוֹן זֶה מַרְזֵב, אוֹ לֹא? וְחוֹזֵר וְקוֹלְטוֹ בְּעִנְיָן אַחֵר, וְשׁוֹאֲלוֹ: לִכְנוּפֵי. שֶׁיְּהֵא מְתוּקָּן תָּמִיד לְהַעֲמִיד קִיפּוּלוֹ לְעוֹלָם: לְהִתְנָאוֹת. לְפִי שָׁעָה: מִתְנָאֶה בִּסְדִינוֹ. אַחַר שֶׁנִּתְעַטֵּף הָיָה מְתַקְּנוֹ עַל גּוּפוֹ וּמְיַישְּׁבוֹ. וּבְחוֹל קָאָמַר, כְּלוֹמַר: אַלְמָא דְּאוֹרְחֵיהּ בְּהָכִי, וְה"ה לְשַׁבָּת: שְׁנֵי צִידֵּי טַלִּיתוֹ. שֶׁבִּימִינוֹ וּבִשְׂמֹאלוֹ לְצַד הַקַּרְקַע: בֶּן זֵירוּז בָּזוֹ לֹא חִיֵּיב ר"מ חַטָּאת. בִּתְמִיָּה; דְּאֵין זֶה דֶּרֶךְ מַלְבּוּשׁ אֶלָּא דֶּרֶךְ מַשּׂוֹי: דִּקְדֵּק ר"מ ע"כ. בִּתְמִיָּה; לְחַיֵּיב חַטָּאת בְּדָבָר הַדּוֹמֶה לִהְיוֹת מוּתָּר כָּזֶה, שֶׁאֵינָהּ מְקוּפֶּלֶת וַאֲחוֹרֶיהָ נוֹפְלִין לְמַטָּה מִכְּתֵפָיו, אֶלָּא שֶׁצִּידֶּיהָ הָיוּ מוּנָּחִין עַל כְּתֵפוֹ: שִׁלְשֵׁל. הוֹרִידָהּ לְמַטָּה, שֶׁקִּבֵּל דְּבָרָיו: נִשְׁאַל אִיתְּמַר. לֹא אֵירַע מַעֲשֶׂה זֶה לְרַבִּי, אֶלָּא שֶׁאֲלוּ לְפָנָיו מַהוּ לָצֵאת בּוֹ, וּבִקֵּשׁ לְהַתִּיר עַד שֶׁאָמְרוּ לְפָנָיו מִשּׁוּם רַבִּי מֵאִיר "חַיָּיב חַטָּאת". דְּאִיהוּ סָבַר הוֹאִיל וְאֵינָהּ מְקוּפֶּלֶת, שֶׁהֲרֵי אֲחוֹרֶיהָ הָיוּ נוֹפְלִין לְמַטָּה מִן כְּתֵפָיו, אֶלָּא שֶׁצִּידֶּיהָ הָיוּ מוּנָּחִים עַל כְּתֵפָיו – הֲוָה סָבַר דֶּרֶךְ מַלְבּוּשׁ הוּא: **מתני'** מֵי מְעָרָה. מֵי מִקְוֵה מְקוֹרֶה(ב) שֶׁהוּא חַם וְאֵין חוּמּוֹ יוֹצֵא. וְדַוְקָא חַמִּין נָקַט, וּמִשּׁ"ה קָתָנֵי הָרוֹחֵץ, דִּיעֲבַד: וְנִסְתַּפֵּג. וְקִינַּח: אֲפִי' בְּעֶשֶׂר אֲלוּנְטִיּוֹת. סְדִינִין שֶׁמְּקַנְּחִין בָּהֶן, וְסִיפֵּג בָּהֶן זֶה אַחַר זֶה. וּרְבוּתָא הִיא, דְּלָא נְפִישִׁי מַיָּא בְּכָל חַד, אפ"ה לֹא יְבִיאֵם בְּיָדוֹ בְּתוֹךְ בֵּיתוֹ אֲפִי' ע"י עֵירוּב שֶׁמָּא יִשְׁכַּח וְיִסְחַט בְּבוֹאוֹ: אֲבָל עֲשָׂרָה בְּנֵי אָדָם. הוֹאִיל וּמְרוּבִּין הֵן – מַדְכְּרֵי אַהֲדָדֵי: מִסְתַּפְּגִין בַּאֲלוּנְטִית אַחַת. וְהַיְינוּ נַמִּי רְבוּתָא, דַּחֲדָא אֲלוּנְטִית לַעֲשָׂרָה(ג) נְפִישָׁא בֵּיהּ מַיָּא, אֲפִילּוּ הָכִי מְבִיאִין אוֹתָהּ בְּיָדַיִם: פְּנֵיהֶם יְדֵיהֶם וְרַגְלֵיהֶם. אוֹרְחָא דְּמִילְּתָא נָקַט, וְה"ה לְכָל גּוּפָם: סָכִין. שֶׁמֶן בְּשַׁבָּת: וּמְמַשְׁמְשִׁין. בְּיָד עַל כָּל הַגּוּף לַהֲנָאָה: אֲבָל לֹא מִתְעַמְּלִין. לְשַׁפְשֵׁף בְּכֹחַ: וְלֹא מִתְגָּרְרִין. גָּרְסִינַן. בְּמַגְרֶדֶת שֶׁקּוֹרִין אשטריי"א, דְּהָוֵי עוּבְדָּא דְּחוֹל: לְקוֹרְדִימָא. שֵׁם הַנָּהָר. וּבַגְּמָ' מְפָרֵשׁ טַעְמָא: אַפִּיקְטוֹיזִין. לְהָקִיא: וְאֵין מְעַצְּבִין אֶת הַקָּטָן. לְשׁוֹן "יָדֶיךָ עִצְּבוּנִי" (איוב י), שֶׁמְּתַקְּנִים וּמְיַישְּׁבִין עַצְמוֹתָיו וְחוּלְיוֹת שִׁדְרָתוֹ כְּמִדַּת נַלְמוֹ. וּבַגְּמָרָא אָמַר טַעְמָא: וְאֵין מַחֲזִירִין אֶת הַשֶּׁבֶר. עֶצֶם שֶׁנִּשְׁבַּר. כָּל רְפוּאָה אֲסוּרָה מִשּׁוּם שְׁחִיקַת סַמָּנִין: נִפְרְקָה. אלוייש"ר בְּלַעַ"ז, שֶׁיָּצָא הָעֶצֶם מִפֶּרֶק שֶׁלּוֹ: לֹא יִטְרְפֵם. לְשׁוֹן "בֵּיצִים טְרוּפוֹת בִּקְעָרָה" (חולין דף סד.):

תוספות

המנער טליתו. פי' ר"ח: מן הטל שעליו, דהיינו כיבוס, וליבון חייב חטאת. וכן משמע דהוי דומיא דכומתא דרב יוסף. אבל בניעור מן העפר, כדפירש בקונטרס – אין נראה שיהא שייך ליבון: **היוצא** בטלית מקופלת. איידי דאיירינן במי שנשרו כליו בדרך, שאז דרך הוא לקפל טליתו, נקטיה הכא: **הרטנין**. רטנין כמו הרהטנין *(הערוך פי' הרלים): **מהו** לעשות מרזב. נראה לרבי דלענין איסור הוצאה איירי, כמו טלית של ד' כנפו' ולוקח שני צידי רוחב טליתו של צד ימינו ונותן על כתף השמאלית ואינו פושטו על כתף, אלא מקופל ומונח על כתפו. והיינו דקאמר: מאי מרזב – כיסי בבלייתא שקורין פרונצלדר"ה. דכשהוא מונח כמו שפירשתי יש בו כיסים מרובים, וכל כיסא וכיסא נראה כמין מרזב. ומיבעיא ליה אי איכא איסור הוצאה בכך, כיון שאינה דרך מלבוש. והיינו דקאמר: כל אדעתא לכנופי – אסור. דהיינו כמו שפירשתי, ששני צידי הימין מקובצים ומונחים על כתף השמאלית, שיכול לילך במהרה ולא יכביד עליו טליתו. אדעתא דלהתנאות שפיר דמי – והיינו כשאין צידי טליתו מקובצין אלא צד אחד מונחת על כתפו אצל צוארו, וצד האחר נופל על שכמו עד הזרוע ואין בו שום כיסוי. והיינו שלשל רבי טליתו דבסמוך – שלשל אותו כמו שפירשתי, כעין להתנאות והיינו דרך מלבוש. וכן פירש בערוך ערך מרזב: אסור לעשות מרזב בשבת. פירוש: כשיעטוף אדם טליתו ויקפיל שני קצותיו כעין דרך קיפול, ויניחנה על שכמו השמאלית ויחזור ויקפל שאר הטלית שבצד הימין ויניחנה בכתפו. רק מה שפירש שקורין מרזב מה שטליתו מושפלת מהנה ומהנה וחלל כנגד השדרה דנראה כמין מרזב – אינו נראה לרבי, דא"כ מאי קאמר בתר הכי: מאי מרזב כיסי בבלייתא, הלא אינו עשוי כעין כיסא! מ"ר: **אף** מי מערה חמין.(ד) שהוחמו באור. דאי בחמי טבריא – שרי לכתחילה, כדאמר בפרק "כירה" (ד' מ. ושם): והניחו להן חמי טבריא. ובפרק "שמונה שרצים" (ד' קט. ושם:)(א): **דיעבד** אין. אמי מערה קאי, ולא תנא במתני' חמי טבריא אלא למידק אף מי מערה חמין(ב): דתניא

א) עי' רש"א ורש"ל. ב) [ועי' תוספות לעיל קט. ד"ה רוחצין ותוס' חולין טו: ד"ה אלא נור].

עין משפט נר מצוה

מ א מיי' פ"י מהלכות שבת הלכה יח סמג לאוין סה טוש"ע או"ח סימן שב סעיף א:

מא ב מיי' פי"ט שם הל' יט סמג שם טור שו"ע או"ח סימן שא סעיף כט:

[בערך רטן וסיים שם הרלים יוצאין בסודר שעל כתפיהן מקובץ ולא משולשל בשביל שלא יעכבו לרוץ]

מב ג שם סעיף לב לג:

מג ד מיי' שם טור שו"ע שם סעיף לד:

מד ה שם סעיף לא:

מה ו מיי' פכ"ב שם הלכה כ טור שו"ע או"ח סימן שכו סעיף א:

רבינו חננאל

ואוקימנא ליה דרב כתנאי: **אמר** רב הונא המנער טליתו בשבת חייב חטאת. פי' המנער כדכתיב התנערי מעפר וכדגרסינן התם ומנערה אחת לשלשים. אם יש אבק בבגד חדש שחור ומקפיד עליו. או אם יש עליו דבר טינוף אוסר רב הונא לנפצו. אבל אם הוא בגד ישן או לבן או אדום ולא קפיד עלייהו שרי וכן הלכה. וזה שראה עולא לרבנן דהוו נפצי גלימייהו ואמר הני מחללי שבתא. רבנן דפומבדיתא במלבושין דלא קפדי עלייהו הוו נפצי. (אמתא) [כומתא] הוא כמין כובע של ראש במקום סודר כדאמרינן בפרק השולח גט לאשתו האי אמתא דהוה שכיב מרה אתת בכת קמיה. ואמרה ליה עד אימת תיתעבד ותזיל ההיא אמתא שקל כומתיה ושדא בה אמר ליה קני הא וקני נפשיך. כלומר קני נפשיך בחליפין. וי"א כומתא הוא כגון כאן דומה לגביע והוה באותו הטמנ' טינוף. והוה אבי' מהסם. כלומר מתיירא כדאמרינן התם חזייה דהוה קא מהסם. א"ל רב יוסף לאביי נפוץ שדי אנן לא קפדינן מידי: היוצא בטלית מקופלת ומונחת לו על כתפו כגון אלו מוכרי כסות שמקפלין ומפשילין אותן על כתפייהו. אתמר משמיה דר' יוחנן חייב חטאת ותניא כוותיה והכי הלכתא וכן נמי היוצא וצרורין לו בסדינו מעות חייב חטאת אבל הרטנין שהם הרצים יוצאין בסודר שעל כתפיהן. ולא אלו בלבד אלא כל אדם. והנכון להיות כרוך בצוארו. או נימא כרוכה לו באצבעו. כהורקנוס בר' אליעזר. ואע"ג דאמר משמא דר' יוחנן הלכה אע"פ שאין נימא כרוכה לו על אצבעו: **עולא** איקלע לבי אסי בר (חני) [היני] בעא מיניה מהו לעשות מרזב בשבת א"ל הכי אמר ר' אלעזר אסור. כך קבלנו מרבותינו שיש בידם קבלה כי מרזב זה כשיעטוף אדם טליתו ויקפל ב' קצוותיה כמין כרך קיפול ויניחה על כתפו השמאלית ויחזור ויקפל שאר הטלית המשולשל בצידו הימין מניחה בכתפו הימין ונמצאת טליתו מקופלת מהנה ומהנה ומופשלת על כתפיו וחלל כנגד השדרה ונראה כמין מרזב. וכענין זה היה קשר (כישי) [כישא] בבלייתא שהיו קושרין ב' כריכות וקורין אותה כישא וכיסכוסי מאני*). וי"א זולתי פירוש זה. אבל חובה עלינו לומר בלשון רבותינו ומה שקיבלנוהו. וכרב פפא שהוא בתראה עבדינן ואמר כללא כל אדעתא לכנופי אסור. כל להתנאות שפיר דמי וכדרב שישא בריה דרב אידי שהיה מתנאה בסדינין כי אתא רב דימי אמר פעם אחת יצא רבי לשדה והיו ב' צידי טליתו מונחין לו על כתפו ושאר הטלית כרוכה ומופשלת לו לאחוריו. אמר לפניו יהושע בן זירוז בן חמיו של ר"מ בזו לא חייב ר"מ חטאת. כלומר זה המעשה דומה לרטנין שיוצאין בסדינין בסדינין מקובצין ולא משולשין על כתפיהן ור' מאיר לא היה בזה מחייב חטאת**) אי לא אסורה מדרבנן. א"ל ר' דקדק ר"מ עד כאן שלשל רבי טליתו: **מתני'** הרוחץ במי מערה כו'.

אוקימנא

*) עיין בערוך ערך מרזב א'. **) [אולי צ"ל אלמא דאסורה מדרבנן ואפשר דרבינו מפרש בזו לא חייב ר"מ חטאת בניחותא דחטאת לא היה מחייב רק הוי אוסר מדרבנן וצ"ע בזה.]

מסורת הש"ס

לעיל נח.

[תוספתא פ"ו]

ס"א היוצאין וכן גי' ר"ח

[יומא ג. מגילה כב:]

ס"א בבני מעיים

נ"א לפלומא

ס"א טובל

[עי' תוס' חולין ג. סד"ה המניח ועי' תוס' סוטה ב. ד"ה המקנא דיעבד]

הגהות הב"ח

(א) רש"י ד"ה קמחללי רבנן שבתא: (ב) ד"ה מי מערה וכו' מקורה שהוא חם ואין חומו: (ג) ד"ה מסתפגין וכו' אלונטית לעשר' בני אדם נפישו: (ד) תוס' ד"ה אף מי מערה חמין בחמין שהוחמו וכו' ובפ' ח' שרצים והא דקאמר דיעבד אין אמי וכו"א:

גליון הש"ס

רש"י ד"ה חייב חטאת. דזהו ליבונה. עיין לעיל דף קמא ע"א רש"י ד"ה מכפנים וצ"ע:

הגהות הגר"א

[א] גמ' יוצאין בסודרין שעל כתפן. נ"ב פי' אפילו מקופל. וז"ש רטנין ר"ל הרלים. ערוך ורמב"ם: [ב] שם כל אדעתא לכנופי. נ"ב פי' הרמב"ם שלא יקרעו או שלא יתלכלכו: [ג] רש"י ד"ה כסוי בבלייתא ומחזיקין אותן. נ"ב אבל הרמב"ם כתב אפילו בידו או על כתפו:

עין משפט
נר מצוה

מז א ב מיי' פכ"ב מהל' שבת הלכה יט טור שו"ע או"ח סימן שא סעיף מח:
מז ג ד מיי' פי"ט שם הלכה יט סמג לאוין סה טוש"ע שם סעיף לד:
מח ה ו מיי' פכ"א מהל' שבת הלכה כח סמג שם טוש"ע או"ח סימן שכו סעיף ב:
מט ז מיי' וסמג שם טוש"ע שם וסימן שכח סעיף מב:
נ ח מיי' שם:
נא ט מיי' שם הלכה ל טוש"ע או"ח סימן שכז סעיף ג:
נב י מיי' שם הלכה כט טוש"ע או"ח סי' שא סעיף מו בהג"ה:
נג כ ל מיי' שם הלכה לא סמג שם טוש"ע או"ח סי' שכח סעיף לט:
נד מ מיי' וסמג שם טור שו"ע או"ח סימן של סעיף י:
נה נ מיי' פכ"ב שם הלכה כו:

דתניא א"ר כשהיינו למדין תורה כו'. מסתמא יחידי היה, שלא היה אלא אחד מתלמידיו עמו כשהיה רוחץ. כדתניא ב"מקום שנהגו" (פסחים דף נא.) שלא ירחוץ תלמיד עם רבו, ואם היה רבו צריך לו – מותר. ומסתמא ר"ש לא היה צריך אלא לאחד כשהיה רוחץ. וכשהיו שנים לביתם היה התלמיד נושא האלונטית בפני עצמה, שר"ש לא היה נושא עמו, דהא ס"ל שיחיד מותר להביאה ולא חיישינן לסחיטה. והא דקאמר: "היינו" – ר"ל כל אחד ואחד בפני עצמו, כשהיה מגיע יומו לשמש רבו. ולעיל בפ' "כירה" (דף מ:) גרסינן: מעשה בתלמיד של ר' מאיר שנכנס אחריו לבית המרחץ. ויש ספרים דגרסי "תלמידיו" ואינו. ובכל הספרים גרסי לקמן בפרק "שואל" (דף קנא:) תלמידו. מ"ר:

צריך לקשר שני ראשיה למטה. בגיטין בפ' "הנזקין" (דף נט.) מפרש דסכניתא הוא בגד דק, דאמרינן: *סוכני וחומר כי אמגוזא ופלגא דאמגוזא. ומשום הכי צריך לקשר שני ראשיה למטה, שלא יפריחנו מעליו הרוח, ואתי לאתויי. או משום דנראה כעין משוי, לפי שהוא דק מאד ואינו נראה מלבוש, אא"כ נראה קשור:

[בגיטין אי' סוכני וחומס]

*__אין__ מעצבין את הקטן. פירשנו [בריש כל הכלים] (דקכ"ג.) ד"ה אסוי:

[שייך לעיל במשנה]

הדרן עלך חבית

גמ' דְלְהִשְׁתַּטֵּף כָּל גּוּפוֹ, אֲפִי' לְכַתְּחִילָּה – שַׁפִּיר דָּמֵי. מַנִּי? ר"ש הִיא, *דְּתַנְיָא: לֹא יִשְׁתַּטֵּף אָדָם בֵּין בְּחַמִּין בֵּין בְּצוֹנֵן, דִּבְרֵי ר"מ. ר"ש מַתִּיר. ר' יְהוּדָה אוֹמֵר: בְּחַמִּין – אָסוּר, בְּצוֹנֵן – מוּתָּר.§ "וְנִסְתַּפֵּג אֲפִילּוּ בְּעֶשֶׂר אֲלוּנְטִיּוֹת".§ רֵישָׁא רְבוּתָא קמ"ל, וְסֵיפָא רְבוּתָא קמ"ל. רֵישָׁא רְבוּתָא קמ"ל – דַּאֲפִילּוּ הָנֵי דְּלָא נְפִישֵׁי בְּהוּ מַיָּא, כֵּיוָן דְּחַד הוּא – אָתֵי לִידֵי סְחִיטָה. וְסֵיפָא רְבוּתָא קמ"ל, אֲפִילּוּ הָנֵי דִּנְפִישֵׁי בְּהוּ מַיָּא, כֵּיוָן דְּרַבִּים נִינְהוּ – מַדְכְּרֵי אַהֲדָדֵי.§ *תָּנוּ רַבָּנַן: מִסְתַּפֵּג אָדָם בַּאֲלוּנְטִית, וּמַנִּיחָהּ בַּחַלּוֹן. אוְלֹא יְמַסְּרֶנָּה לָאוֹלְיָירִין, מִפְּנֵי שֶׁחֲשׁוּדִים *עַל אוֹתוֹ דָּבָר. רַבִּי שִׁמְעוֹן אוֹמֵר: מִסְתַּפֵּג בַּאֲלוּנְטִית אַחַת, וּמְבִיאָהּ בְּיָדוֹ לְתוֹךְ בֵּיתוֹ. אֲמַר לֵיהּ אַבַּיֵּי לְרַב יוֹסֵף: הִלְכְתָא מַאי? אֲמַר לֵיהּ: הָא ר' שִׁמְעוֹן, הָא רַבִּי, הָא שְׁמוּאֵל, הָא ר' יוֹחָנָן. ר' שִׁמְעוֹן – הָא דַּאֲמַרַן. רַבִּי – *דְּתַנְיָא, אָמַר רַבִּי: כְּשֶׁהָיִינוּ לְמֵדִין תּוֹרָה אֵצֶל ר' שִׁמְעוֹן בִּתְקוֹעַ הָיִינוּ מַעֲלִין שֶׁמֶן וַאֲלוּנְטִית מֵחָצֵר לַגַּג, וּמִגַּג לְקַרְפֵּף, עַד שֶׁהָיִינוּ מַגִּיעִין אֵצֶל מַעְיָן שֶׁהָיִינוּ רוֹחֲצִין בּוֹ. שְׁמוּאֵל – דְּאָמַר רַב יְהוּדָה אָמַר שְׁמוּאֵל: מִסְתַּפֵּג אָדָם בַּאֲלוּנְטִית, וּמְבִיאָהּ בְּיָדוֹ לְתוֹךְ בֵּיתוֹ. ר' יוֹחָנָן – דְּאָמַר ר' חִיָּיא בַּר אַבָּא א"ר יוֹחָנָן: בהֲלָכָה, מִסְתַּפֵּג אָדָם בַּאֲלוּנְטִית וּמְבִיאָהּ בְּיָדוֹ לְתוֹךְ בֵּיתוֹ. וּמִי א"ר יוֹחָנָן הָכִי?! וְהָא"ר יוֹחָנָן: *הֲלָכָה כִּסְתָם מִשְׁנָה. וּתְנַן: וְנִסְתַּפֵּג אֲפִילּוּ בְּעֶשֶׂר אֲלוּנְטִיּוֹת – לֹא יְבִיאֵם בְּיָדוֹ! הַהוּא כְּבֶן חֲכִינַאי מַתְנֵי לַהּ. א"ר חִיָּיא בַּר אַבָּא אר"י: גהָאוֹלְיָירִין מְבִיאִין בַּלְּרֵי נָשִׁים לְבֵי בָנֵי, וּבִלְבַד שֶׁיִּתְכַּסֶּה בָּהֶן רֹאשָׁן וְרוּבָּן. דסְכַנִּיתָא(א) – צָרִיךְ לְקַשֵּׁר ב' רָאשֶׁיהָ לְמַטָּה. א"ר חִיָּיא בַּר אַבָּא א"ר יוֹחָנָן: לְמַטָּה מִכְּתֵפַיִים. אֲמַר לְהוּ רָבָא לִבְנֵי *מְחוֹזָא: כִּי מַעַבְרִיתוּ מָאנֵי לִבְנֵי חֵילָא – שַׁרְבִּיבוּ בְּהוּ לְמַטָּה מִכְּתֵפַיִם.§ "סָכִין וּמְמַשְׁמְשִׁין".§ *ת"ר: הסָכִין וּמְמַשְׁמְשִׁין בִּבְנֵי מֵעַיִם בְּשַׁבָּת, וּבִלְבַד שֶׁלֹּא יַעֲשֶׂה כְּדֶרֶךְ שֶׁהוּא עוֹשֶׂה בַּחוֹל. הֵיכִי עָבֵיד? ר' חָמָא בַּר חֲנִינָא אָמַר: סָךְ וְאח"כ מְמַשְׁמֵשׁ, ר' יוֹחָנָן אָמַר: וסָךְ וּמְמַשְׁמֵשׁ בְּבַת אַחַת.§ ז"אֲבָל לֹא מִתְעַמְּלִין".§ א"ר חִיָּיא בַּר אַבָּא א"ר יוֹחָנָן: חאָסוּר לַעֲמוֹד בְּקַרְקָעִיתָהּ שֶׁל דְּיוֹמֶסֶת, מִפְּנֵי שֶׁמְּעַמֶּלֶת וּמְרַפְּאָה. אָמַר ר' יְהוּדָה אָמַר רַב: כָּל יָמֶיהָ שֶׁל דְּיוֹמֶסֶת עֶשְׂרִים וְאֶחָד יוֹם, וַעֲצֶרֶת מִן הַמִּנְיָן. אִיבַּעְיָא לְהוּ: עֲצֶרֶת (בַּתְּחִלָּה) לְהַאי גִּיסָא, אוֹ לְהַאי גִּיסָא? ת"ש, דַּאֲמַר שְׁמוּאֵל: כּוּלְּהוּ שַׁקְיָינֵי *מִדִּיבְחָא וְעַד עֲצַרְתָּא מָעֲלוּ. דִּילְמָא, הָתָם הוּא – דְּכַמָּה דְּקָרִיר עָלְמָא מָעֲלֵי, אֲבָל הָכָא מִשּׁוּם הֶבְלָא הוּא, כֵּיוָן דְּחָמִים עָלְמָא – טְפֵי מָעֲלֵי. אָמַר רַבִּי חֶלְבּוֹ: חַמְרָא דִּפְרוּגַיְיתָא וּמַיָּא דִּדְיוֹמֶסֶת קִיפְּחוּ עֲשֶׂרֶת הַשְּׁבָטִים מִיִּשְׂרָאֵל. רַבִּי אֶלְעָזָר בֶּן עֲרָךְ אִיקְלַע לְהָתָם, *אִימְשִׁיךְ בָּתְרַיְיהוּ אִיעֲקַר תַּלְמוּדֵיהּ. כִּי הֲדַר אֲתָא, קָם לְמִיקְרֵי בְּסִפְרָא, בְּעָא לְמִיקְרָא °"הַחֹדֶשׁ הַזֶּה לָכֶם" אֲמַר: הַחֵרֵשׁ הָיָה לִבָּם. בָּעוּ רַבָּנַן רַחֲמֵי עֲלֵיהּ, וַהֲדַר תַּלְמוּדֵיהּ. וְהַיְינוּ דִּתְנַן, *ר' נְהוֹרָאִי אוֹמֵר: הֱוֵי גּוֹלֶה לִמְקוֹם תּוֹרָה, וְאַל תֹּאמַר שֶׁהִיא תָּבֹא אַחֲרֶיךָ, שֶׁחֲבֵרֶיךָ יְקַיְּימוּהָ בְּיָדְךָ, וְאֶל בִּינָתְךָ אַל תִּשָּׁעֵן. *תָּנָא: לֹא ר' נְהוֹרָאִי שְׁמוֹ אֶלָּא ר' נְחֶמְיָה שְׁמוֹ, וְאָמְרִי לַהּ ר' אֶלְעָזָר בֶּן עֲרָךְ שְׁמוֹ, וְלָמָּה נִקְרָא שְׁמוֹ ר' נְהוֹרָאִי – שֶׁמַּנְהִיר עֵינֵי חֲכָמִים בַּהֲלָכָה.§ "אֲבָל לֹא מִתְגָּרְרִין".§ ת"ר: *אֵין גּוֹרְרִין בְּמַגְרֶרֶת בַּשַּׁבָּת. רשב"ג אוֹמֵר: טאִם הָיוּ רַגְלָיו מְלוּכְלָכוֹת בְּטִיט וּבְצוֹאָה – גּוֹרֵר כְּדַרְכּוֹ וְאֵינוֹ חוֹשֵׁשׁ. רַב שְׁמוּאֵל בַּר יְהוּדָה עָבְדָא לֵיהּ אִימֵּיהּ מַגְרַרְתָּא דְּכַסְפָּא.§ "אֵין יוֹרְדִין לְקוֹרְדִּימָא וכו'".§ מַאי טַעְמָא? יִמִשּׁוּם פִּיקָא.§ "וְאֵין עוֹשִׂין אַפִּיקְטוִיזִין בַּשַּׁבָּת".§ אָמַר רַבָּה בַּר בַּר חָנָה אָמַר רַבִּי יוֹחָנָן: כלֹא שָׁנוּ אֶלָּא בְּסַם, אֲבָל בְּיָד – מוּתָּר. תַּנְיָא, רַבִּי נְחֶמְיָה אוֹמֵר: לאַף בַּחוֹל אָסוּר, מִפְּנֵי הֶפְסֵד אוֹכָלִין.§ "וְאֵין מְעַצְּבִין אֶת הַקָּטָן".§ אָמַר רַבָּה בַּר בַּר חָנָה אָמַר ר' יוֹחָנָן: *מלְפוּפֵי יָנוּקָא בַּשַּׁבָּת – שַׁפִּיר דָּמֵי. וְהָאֲנַן תְּנַן: אֵין מְעַצְּבִין! הָתָם נבְּחוּמְרֵי שִׁדְרָה, דְּמֶיחֱזֵי כְּבוֹנֶה.§ "וְאֵין מַחֲזִירִין אֶת הַשֶּׁבֶר".§ אָמַר רַבִּי חָנָא *)בַּגְדַתָּאָה אָמַר שְׁמוּאֵל: הֲלָכָה

*) [עמ"ש רש"י ברכות נג: וע"ע פרש"י ביבמות סז. ד"ה בגדתאה].

גמ' דְלְהִשְׁתַּטֵּף. שׁוֹפְכָן עַל גּוּפוֹ, דְּלָאו דֶּרֶךְ רְחִיצָה הִיא – שָׁרֵי לְכַתְּחִילָּה, אֲפִי' בְּחַמִּין: סֵיפָא. אֲבָל עֲשָׂרָה בְּנֵי אָדָם כו': וּמַנִּיחָהּ בַּחַלּוֹן. הַסְּמוּכָה לְכוֹתֶל הַמֶּרְחָץ: לְאוֹלְיָירִין. בַּלָּנִים: עַל אוֹתוֹ דָּבָר. סְחִיטָה: הָא רַבִּי וְהָא ר"ש כו'. הֲרֵי כָּל אֵלּוּ שֶׁמַּתִּירִין: מֵחָצֵר לַגַּג כו'. ר"ש לְטַעְמֵיהּ, דְּאָמַר בְּעֵירוּבִין (דף עד.): אֶחָד גַּגּוֹת אֶחָד חֲצֵירוֹת וְא' קַרְפֵּיפוֹת, כּוּלָּן רְשׁוּת אַחַת הֵן לְטַלְטֵל מִזֶּה לָזֶה, וַאֲפִילּוּ שֶׁל בְּעָלִים הַרְבֵּה: עַד שֶׁהָיִינוּ מַגִּיעִין כו'. וּמִסְתָמָא לֹא הָיוּ מַנִּיחִין אוֹתָהּ עַל הַמַּעְיָן בִּמְקוֹם הֶפְקֵר: כְּבֶן חֲכִינַאי מַתְנֵי לַהּ. דִּבְרֵי בֶּן חֲכִינַאי מְסַיֵּים בָּהּ, וְלָאו סְתָמָא: הָאוֹלְיָירִין. בַּלָּנִין: מְבִיאִין בַּלְּרֵי נָשִׁים. סְדִינִים שֶׁהַנָּשִׁים מִסְתַּפְּגִין בָּהֶם מוּתָּר לַהֲבִיאָן דֶּרֶךְ מַלְבּוּשׁ לְבֵית הַמֶּרְחָץ: סְכַנִּיתָא. סוּדָר גָּדוֹל [א] שֶׁתָּלוּי לוֹ בֵּין כְּתֵפָיו, וְרֹאשׁוֹ עָטוּף בּוֹ: צָרִיךְ לִקְשׁוֹר שְׁנֵי רָאשֶׁיהָ. זֶה בָּזֶה, שֶׁלֹּא תִּפּוֹל מֵרֹאשׁוֹ: כִּי מַעַבְרִיתוּ מָאנֵי לִבְנֵי חֵילָא. כְּשֶׁתָּבִיאוּ בִּגְדֵי הַגּוֹיִם, בְּנֵי הַחַיִל הַמּוּטָּלִי' עֲלֵיכֶם לְשַׁמְּשָׁן, וְאַתֶּם מְבִיאִים לָהֶם בְּשַׁבָּת דֶּרֶךְ רְשׁוּת הָרַבִּים: שַׁרְבִּיבוּ בְּהוּ לְמַטָּה מִכְּתֵפַיִים. שֶׁלֹּא יִהְיוּ שׁוּלֵיהֶם מוּנָּחִים בְּכִתְפֵיכֶם, אֶלָּא מְשׁוּכִי' לְמַטָּה, שֶׁיְּהֵא נִרְאֶה לְבוּשׁ: סָךְ וְאח"כ מְמַשְׁמֵשׁ. [דְּקָסָבַר]: בְּחוֹל מְמַשְׁמֵשׁ וְאַחַר כָּךְ סָךְ: דְּיוֹמְסִית*. שֵׁם נָהָר שֶׁמֵּימָיו מְלוּחִים: שֶׁמְּעַמֶּלֶת. מְחַמֶּמֶת: וּמְרַפֵּא. שֶׁהַטִּיט מָלוּחַ: כָּל יָמֶיהָ. יְמֵי רְפוּאָתָהּ: לְהַאי גִּיסָא כו'. מִתְּחִלַּת הַיָּמִים אוֹ בַּסּוֹף: שַׁקְיָינֵי. מַשְׁקִין לִרְפוּאָה: מִדִּבְחָא לַעֲצֶרֶת. אַלְמָא עֲצֶרֶת בַּסּוֹף: חַמְרָא דִּפְרוּגַיְתָא. שֵׁם מְדִינָה שֶׁיֵּינָהּ מְשׁוּבָּח: קִפְּחוּ עֲשֶׂרֶת הַשְּׁבָטִים. שֶׁהָיוּ בַּעֲלֵי הֲנָאָה, וַעֲסוּקִים בְּכָךְ, וְלֹא הָיוּ עוֹסְקִים בַּתּוֹרָה, וְיָצְאוּ לְתַרְבּוּת רָעָה: לְהָתָם. לְפוּרְגַּיְתָא וּדְיוֹמְסִית: אִימְשִׁיךְ בַּתְרַיְיהוּ. אַחַר הַיַּיִן וְהָרְחִיצָה: אִיעֲקַר תַּלְמוּדֵיהּ. נֶעֱקַר תַּלְמוּדוֹ וּשְׁכָחוֹ: הַחֵרֵשׁ הָיָה לִבָּם: הֱוֵי גּוֹלֶה לִמְקוֹם תּוֹרָה. אִם ת"ח אַתָּה אַל תֵּשֵׁב אֶלָּא בִּמְקוֹם ת"ח חֲבֵרְךָ, וְאַל תֹּאמַר תַּלְמִידִים הֵם יָבוֹאוּ אֵלַי וְדַי לִי בְּכָךְ, לָמָּה אֶהְיֶה גּוֹלֶה: שֶׁחֲבֵירֶיךָ יְקַיְּימוּהָ בְּיָדְךָ. שֶׁתְּהֵא רָגִיל אֶצְלָם, וּכְשֶׁתִּשְׁנֶה מַסֶּכֶת אַחַת וְהֵם אַחֶרֶת תַּשְׁמִעֶנָּה וּתְהֵא סְדוּרָה בְּפִיךָ וְאַל תִּשְׁתַּכַּח הֵימֶנָּה: וְאֶל בִּינָתְךָ אַל תִּשָּׁעֵן. לוֹמַר חָכָם גָּדוֹל אֲנִי, וְזַכְרָן, וּכְשֶׁאֶחֱזוֹר פֶּרֶק זֶה אוֹ מַסֶּכֶת זוֹ לֹא תִּשְׁתַּכַּח חֲבֶרְתָּהּ מִמֶּנִּי: מַגְרֶרֶת. אשטריי"ל, וְאָדָם מְגָרֵר בָּהּ: מַגִּירְדְתָּא דְּכַסְפָּא. לַשַּׁבָּת: מִשּׁוּם פִּיקָא. טִיט שֶׁל אוֹתוֹ נָהָר מַחֲלִיק, וּבִגְדֵי הָאָדָם נִישּׁוֹרִין בַּמַּיִם כְּשֶׁהוּא נוֹפֵל, וְאָתֵי לִידֵי סְחִיטָה: אֶלָּא בְּסַם. דְּדָמֵי לִרְפוּאָה, וּגְזֵירָה °מִשּׁוּם שְׁחִיקַת סַמָּנִין: אֲבָל בְּיָד. לְהַכְנִיס יָד לְתוֹךְ גְּרוֹנוֹ עַד שֶׁיָּקִיא – מוּתָּר: מִפְּנֵי הֶפְסֵד אוֹכָלִין. שֶׁבְּמֵעָיו, וּמִתּוֹךְ כָּךְ הוּא רָעֵב וְחוֹזֵר וְאוֹכֵל: לְפוּפֵי. אונמלוטי"א, כְּמוֹ שֶׁעוֹשִׂי' לְקָטָן שֶׁיִּתְיַישְּׁבוּ אֵבָרָיו וְלֹא יִתְעַקֵּם: בְּחוּמְרֵי שִׁדְרָה. חוּלְיוֹת שֶׁל שִׁדְרָה שֶׁנִּתְפָּרְקָה אַחַת מֵהֶן. וּלְאַחַר זְמַן קָמַיְירִי, דְּאִי בְּיוֹם לֵידָה(ב) אָמְרִי' (לעיל דף קכט:): כָּל הָאָמוּר בְּפָ' תּוֹכֵחָה דִּיחֶזְקֵאל עוֹשִׂין לְחַיָּה בַּשַּׁבָּת:

הֲלָכָה

תורה אור: שמות יב

[לעיל מו.] · [עירובין לא. [מנחות עב.] · [ובישעיה כח א גרס ומיא דדורמסקית וכן גרס רד"ק שם] · [לעיל מו. וש"נ] · [השותה לסוטה ונוחה לאחרים ביוה"כ] · סנהדרין קח. · [פסחים מב:] · אוכלסא דמחוזא] אדר"נ ספי"ד · אבות פ"ד משנה י"ד · עירובין יג: ע"ש · [תוספ' פי"ז] · [לעיל סו: פ"ב]

הגהות הב"ח

(א) גמרא סכניתא אמר ר' אבין בר רב חסדא א"ר יוחנן צריך לקשר שני וכו' ואמר ר' חייא: (ב) רש"י ד"ה בחומרי וכו' כיום לידה הא אמרינן. נ"ב סוף פ' מפנין ע"ש בכרש"י שפי' דלפופי הוא על ידי תגורות ופסיקיות:

הגהות הגר"א

[א] רש"י ד"ה סוכניתא סודר גדול. נ"ב אבל הרמב"ם פי' קטן שאין מכסה ראשו ורובו:

גליון הש"ס

גמ' אמר החרש היה לבם. עי' דבר נחמד בקרניס בליקוטים שבסוף הספר: רש"י ד"ה אלא בסם וכו' משום שחיקת סמנין. ע"ל דף קכג ע"ב ברש"י ד"ה אפיקטויזין:

רבינו חננאל

אוקימנא למתני' הרוחץ בחמין דיעבד אבל לכתחלה לרחוץ בחמין אסור. ולהשתטף בחמין נמי אפי' כל גופו מותר רר"ש דתניא לא ישתטף אדם בין בחמין בין בצונן דברי ר"מ. ור"ש מתיר. ר' יהודה אומר בחמין אסור ובצונן מותר. אע"פ דתנינן סתמא כר"ש לית הלכתא כוותיה דהא בפירוש נמי תנינן סתמא כוותיה (לעיל דף לח). מעשה שעשו אנשי טבריא כו'*) (ואע"ג דאמר עולא הלכה כאנשי טבריא הא אמר ליה רב נחמן תברינהו לסילונייהו אנשי טבריא) ואוקימנא כר"ש. ופסקי' בגמרי' אמר רבה בר בר חנה א"ר יוחנן הלכה כרבי יהודה ודקדק רב יוסף על רבה בר בר חנה וא"ל בפירוש שמיעא לך דהלכתא כר' יהודה או מכללא אמרתיה. א"ל בפירוש שמיעא ליה. וכיון דפסק ר' יוחנן בפירוש הלכה כר' יהודה כוותיה עבדינן: ומסתפג אפי' בעשר אלונטיות ולא יביאם בידו ואע"פ שאין בהם מים מרובין. דכיון דחד הוא. דלמא מינשי ועביד סחיטה. אבל אם היו ב"א הרבה אפילו אם מסתפגין כולן באלונטית אחת והיא שרוי במים כיון דרבים נינהו מדכרי אהדדי ולא אתו לידי סחיטה. ומותר להביאה בידים בחצר או מן הגג וכדומה לו מקום שמותר לו לטלטל: אוליירין הם השמשים בני אדם הנכנסין במרחץ והן חשודין בזמה שמא יטמאו לונטיות זו בשכבת זרעם. א"ל אביי לרב יוסף והלכתא מאי כו' והלכתא כי הא דא"ר חייא בר רבה א"ר יוחנן הלכה מסתפג אדם באלונטית ומביאה בידו לתוך ביתו. ומקשינן עלה הא"ר יוחנן הלכה כסתם משנה ותנן מסתפג אדם אפילו בעשר אלונטיות ולא יביאם בידו. ומפרקי' מתני' ר' יוחנן לא תאני לה סתמא. אלא כבן חכינאי מתני לה. בתלמוד א"י בפ' כירה ר' חנניה בן עקיבא התיר הבאת לונטיות: **סכינתאי** א"ר אבין בר רב חסדא א"ר יוחנן צריך לקשר ב' ראשיה למטה. א"ר חייא בר אבא א"ר יוחנן למטה מכתפים. וכן זה שאמר רבא לבני מחוזא כי מעבריתו מני דבני חילא שרביבו להו למטה מכתפים. שלא להראות משא בכתף: בלרין נשים לבי בני. פי' דהא קן של נשים כשמביאין להן האוליירין במרחץ לא התירו אלא עד שיתכסה בהן ראשו ורובו: **סכין** וממשמשין והלכתא כר' יוחנן דאמר סך וממשמש בבת אחת והוא משמוש ביד בקלות. אבל לא מתעמלין. פי' פושטין ומקפלין זרועותיהם לפניהן ולאחריהן וכן רגליהן ע"ג ירכותיהן ומתחממין ומזיעין והוא כמין מעשה רפואה ואסור. וכן אסור לעמוד בשבת בקרקעיתה של דיומסת מפני שמעמלת ומרפאה: חמרא דפרוגתא יין של פרוגיתא והוא שם מקום ומיא דרמיסת גם הוא שם מקום. כלומר יין של פרגיתא ומיא של דיומסת טובים הם וערבין ונמשך לב שותה אותן בהן ואינו רוצה להניחם ומתאחד שם ואותן מקומות אין בהן בני תורה והמתאחר שם זמן הרבה מתקפח ושכח תלמודו. אבל לא מתגרדין. גירוד זה הוא חיכוך בכלי כי הא דתנן רבנן אין גורדין במגרת בשבת רשבג"א אם היו רגליו מלוכלכות בטיט ובצואה גורד כדרכו ואינו חושש. רב ושמואל בר יהודה עבדא ליה אמיה מגרדתא דכספא להתחכך בה: **אין** יורדין לקירומא. ס"א לפילומא פי' בקעה ויש שם מים ותחתיו טיט כמו טפל. ואם יבקע ויטבע בו אינו יכול לעלות עד שמתקבצין הרבה ב"א ומעלין אותו משם. יש מי שאומרים הרוחץ באותה בקעה מצטנן ואותן המים משלשלין בני מעיו**). וזה פי' ביקא. פי' אפיקטויזין קיא. אמר רבה בר בר חנה א"ר יוחנן לא שנו אלא בסם שהוא אסור אבל ביד מותר. **ואין** מעצבין את הקטן כו'. פי' מושכין אבריו של קטן ומיישב בידו חוליות של שזירה אחת על חברתה וזהו עיצוב מלשון עצבון: **לפופי** ינוקא לחבר אברים של תינוק. וכדתרגם ויחבר ולפיף: **ואין** מחזירין את השבר אמר רב הונא בגדתאה אמר שמואל מחזירין

*) לכאורה נראה דמתיבת ואע"ג עד תברינהו לסילונייהו אנשי טבריא שייך להלן אחר תיבות כוותיה עבדינן ודו"ק. **) עיין ערוך ערך פלם א'.

^אהֲלָכָה מַחֲזִירִין אֶת הַשֶּׁבֶר. רַבָּה בַּר בַּר חָנָה אִיקְּלַע לְפוּמְבְּדִיתָא, לָא עַל לְפִירְקֵיהּ דְּרַב יְהוּדָה. שַׁדְרֵיהּ לְאַדָּא דַּיָּילָא, א"ל: זִיל גְּרַבֵיהּ. אֲזַל גְּרַבֵיהּ, אֲתָא, אַשְׁכְּחֵיהּ דְּקָא דָּרֵישׁ: אֵין מַחֲזִירִין אֶת הַשֶּׁבֶר. א"ל: הָכִי אָמַר רַב חָנָא בַּגְדָּתָאָה אָמַר שְׁמוּאֵל: הֲלָכָה, מַחֲזִירִין אֶת הַשֶּׁבֶר. א"ל: הָא חָנָא דִּידַן, וְהָא שְׁמוּאֵל דִּידַן – וְלָא שְׁמִיעַ לִי, וְלָאו בְּדִינָא גְּרַבְתִּיךְ?!§ "מִי שֶׁנִּפְרְקָה יָדוֹ כו'".§ רַב אָוְיָא הֲוָה יָתֵיב קַמֵּיהּ דְּרַב יוֹסֵף, שַׁנְיָא לֵיהּ יְדֵיהּ. א"ל: הָכִי מַאי? אָסוּר. וְהָכִי מַאי? א"ל: אָסוּר. אַדְּהָכִי אִיתְפַּח יְדֵיהּ. א"ל: מַאי תִּיבְּעֵי לָךְ, הָא תְּנַן ^ב"מִי שֶׁנִּפְרְקָה יָדוֹ אוֹ רַגְלוֹ – לֹא יִטְרְפֵם בְּצוֹנֵן, אֲבָל^(א) רוֹחֵץ כְּדַרְכּוֹ. וְאִם נִתְרַפֵּא – נִתְרַפֵּא". א"ל: וְלָא תְּנַן "אֵין מַחֲזִירִין אֶת הַשֶּׁבֶר" וְאָמַר רַב חָנָא בַּגְדָּתָאָה אָמַר שְׁמוּאֵל: הֲלָכָה מַחֲזִירִין אֶת הַשֶּׁבֶר? אֲמַר לֵיהּ: *כּוּלְּהוּ בַּחֲדָא מָחִיתָא מָחֵיתִנְהוּ?! הֵיכָא דְּאִיתְּמַר – אִיתְּמַר, הֵיכָא דְּלָא אִיתְּמַר – לָא אִיתְּמַר.§ [ביצה כח: נדה כו.]

הדרן עלך חבית

שׁוֹאֵל ^גאָדָם מֵחֲבֵירוֹ כַּדֵּי יַיִן וְכַדֵּי שֶׁמֶן וּבִלְבַד שֶׁלֹּא יֹאמַר לוֹ ^ד"הַלְוֵינִי". וְכֵן הָאִשָּׁה מֵחֲבֶירְתָּהּ כִּכָּרוֹת. וְאִם אֵינוֹ מַאֲמִינוֹ – מַנִּיחַ טַלִּיתוֹ אֶצְלוֹ, וְעוֹשֶׂה עִמּוֹ חֶשְׁבּוֹן לְאַחַר שַׁבָּת. וְכֵן עֶרֶב פֶּסַח בִּירוּשָׁלַיִם שֶׁחָל לִהְיוֹת בַּשַּׁבָּת, מַנִּיחַ טַלִּיתוֹ אֶצְלוֹ וְנוֹטֵל אֶת פִּסְחוֹ, וְעוֹשֶׂה עִמּוֹ חֶשְׁבּוֹן לְאַחַר יוֹם טוֹב.§ **גמ'** א"ל רָבָא בַּר רַב חָנָן לְאַבַּיֵי: מַאי שְׁנָא "הַשְׁאִילֵנִי" וּמַאי שְׁנָא "הַלְוֵינִי"? אֲמַר לֵיהּ: "הַשְׁאִילֵנִי" – לָא אָתֵי לְמִיכְתַּב, "הַלְוֵינִי" – אָתֵי לְמִיכְתַּב. וְהָא כֵּיוָן דְּבַחוֹל, זִימְנִין דְּבָעֵי לְמֵימַר לֵיהּ "הַלְוֵינִי" וְא"ל "הַשְׁאִילֵנִי" וְלָא קָפֵיד עִילָּוֵיהּ, וְאָתֵי לְמִיכְתַּב, בַּשַּׁבָּת נַמִּי אָתֵי לְמִיכְתַּב! א"ל: (בַּחוֹל דְּלָא שְׁנָא כִּי א"ל "הַלְוֵינִי" ל"ש כִּי א"ל "הַשְׁאִילֵנִי", לָא קָפְדִינַן עִילָּוֵיהּ – אָתֵי לְמִיכְתַּב), בַּשַּׁבָּת כֵּיוָן דְּ"הַשְׁאִילֵנִי" הוּא דְּשָׁרוּ לֵיהּ רַבָּנַן "הַלְוֵינִי" לָא שָׁרוּ לֵיהּ – מִינְכְּרָא מִילְּתָא, וְלָא אָתֵי לְמִיכְתַּב. *א"ל רָבָא בַּר רַב חָנָן לְאַבַּיֵי: מִכְּדֵי אָמְרוּ רַבָּנַן ^ה"כָּל מִילֵּי דְּיוֹם טוֹב כַּמָּה דְּאֶפְשָׁר לְשַׁנּוּיֵי – מְשַׁנֵּינַן", הָנֵי נָשֵׁי דְּמַלְיָין חַצְבַּיְיהוּ מַיָּא, מ"ט לָא מְשַׁנְּיָין? ^ומִשּׁוּם דְּלָא אֶפְשָׁר. הֵיכִי לֶעֱבְדִי – דְּמַלְיָין בְּחַצְבָּא רַבָּא לִימְלוֹ בְּחַצְבָּא זוּטָא – הָא קָא מַפְּשׁוּ בְּהִילוּכָא, דְּמַלְיָין בְּחַצְבָּא זוּטָא לִימְלוֹ בְּחַצְבָּא רַבָּא – קָא מַפְּשׁוּ בְּמַשּׂוֹי. נִיפְרוֹס

רש"י

הֲלָכָה מַחֲזִירִין אֶת הַשֶּׁבֶר. סְבִירָא לֵיהּ לִשְׁמוּאֵל מַחֲזִירִין תְּנַן: אַדָּא דַּיָּילָא. מנשטר"ל, מְמוּנֶּה: גְּרַבֵיהּ. קַח בִּגְדוֹ עַד שֶׁיָּבֹא: אֲתָא. רַבָּה, אַשְׁכְּחֵיהּ לְרַב יְהוּדָה כו': הָא חָנָא דִּידַן. מִמְּקוֹמֵנוּ הוּא, וְלֹא שָׁמַעְנוּ זֹאת מִפִּיו עַד הֵנָּה: וְלָאו בְּדִינָא גְּרַבְתִּיךְ. בִּתְמִיָּה. שֶׁאִילּוּ לֹא בָּאתָ לֹא לָמַדְנוּ: שַׁנְיָא לֵיהּ יְדֵיהּ. נִשְׁתַּנֵּית יָדוֹ מִמְּקוֹמָהּ, אשולשיי"ר בְּלַעַ"ז: הָכִי מַאי. הָיָה עוֹשֶׂה בְּעִנְיָנִים הַרְבֵּה וְשׁוֹאֵל: בַּחֲדָא מָחִיתָא מָחֵיתִנְהוּ. בַּאֲרִיגָה אַחַת אֲרַגְתּוֹ*: הֵיכָא דְּאִיתְּמַר. דְּמַתְנִיתִין לָאו דַּוְקָא תְּנַן, אִיתְּמַר:

הדרן עלך חבית

שׁוֹאֵל. שֶׁלֹּא יֹאמַר הַלְוֵינִי. מְפָרֵשׁ בַּגְּמָרָא: שֶׁחָל לִהְיוֹת בַּשַּׁבָּת. וְלֹא נִזְכַּר מֵעֶ"שׁ לִקְנוֹת: לְאַחַר יו"ט. לְיוֹם שְׁלִישִׁי: **גמ'** הַלְוֵינִי. מַשְׁמַע לִזְמַן מְרוּבֶּה, וְקיי"ל בְּמַסֶּכֶת מַכּוֹת (דף ג:): סְתָם הַלְוָאָה ל' יוֹם, וְאָתֵי מַלְוֶה זֶה לִכְתּוֹב עַל פִּנְקָסוֹ: כָּךְ וְכָךְ הִלְוֵיתִי, כְּדֵי שֶׁלֹּא יִשְׁכַּח: א"ל וְכֵיוָן דְּבַחוֹל נַמִּי זִימְנִין דְּבָעֵי לְמֵימַר הַלְוֵינִי, וְאָמַר הַשְׁאִילֵנִי וְלָא קָפֵיד עֲלֵיהּ. וְהָוְיָא הַלְוָאָה: בַּשַּׁבָּת נַמִּי. כִּי אָמַר הַשְׁאִילֵנִי – סָבַר דְּהַלְוָאָה הִיא, וְאָתֵי לְמִכְתַּב, וּמַאי הֶיכֵּר אִיכָּא? ה"ג: א"ל בַּשַּׁבָּת כֵּיוָן דְּהַשְׁאִילֵנִי שָׁרוּ לֵיהּ רַבָּנַן הַלְוֵינִי לָא שָׁרוּ לֵיהּ מִינְכְּרָא מִילְּתָא וְלָא אָתֵי לְמִכְתַּב: אָמְרוּ רַבָּנַן. בְּמַסֶּכֶת בֵּיצָה: כָּל כַּמָּה דְּאֶפְשָׁר לְשַׁנּוּיֵי מְשַׁנֵּינַן. דְּקָתָנֵינַן: הַמֵּבִיא כַּדֵּי יַיִן – לֹא יְבִיאֵם בְּסַל וּבְקוּפָּה כו': נִכְתָּמָא

תוספות

שואל אדם מחבירו כדי יין וכדי שמן ובלבד שלא יאמר לו הלויני. פירש רש"י: טעמא משום דסתם הלואה ל' יום, ולפי שהוא לזמן מרובה יותר משאלה, אתי למיכתב. וקשה לר"ת: דסתם שאלה^(ב) ל' יום, כדאמר במנחות ב"התכלת" (דף מד.*): טלית שאולה כל ל' יום פטורה מן הציצית. ואמרינן נמי התם: הדר באכסני' בא"י, והשוכר בית בחו"ל – כל ל' יום פטור מן המזוזה, מכאן ואילך – חייב במזוזה. אלמא: דסתם שאלה ל' יום איתא, ולהכי פטורה כל ל' יום דאמר שאולה היא. אבל מכאן ואילך נראה כמו שלו? ומיהו, יכול לומר לרש"י לאו משום דאי מתבע ליה לדינא בתוך ל' יום שאין צריך להחזיר, דודאי היה חייב להחזיר^(ג), דעבידי אינשי דמשאלי פחות משלשים יום, אבל טפי לא משאלי. הלכך: עד ל' יום אמרי אינשי שאולה היא. ור"י פירש לנו: דהיינו טעמא בשאלה – לפי שהיא חוזרת בעין לא אתי למיכתב. אבל לשון הלואה – אינו חוזר בעין, ואתי למיכתב. ואע"ג דכי שאיל מיניה כדי יין וכדי שמן לא הדרי בעין – מ"מ מתוך שמזכיר לו לשון שאלה – זכור הוא, ולא אתי למיכתב. מ"ר. וכן פירש ה"ר פורת:

אתקין רבא במחוזא דדרו בדוחקא כו'. ברוב ספרים אינו כתוב כאן, ולא בפירוש רש"י. וברים "המביא כדי יין" (ביצה דף ל. ושם) נראה שהוא מקומו, וזה לשון פירוש הקונטרס בביצה: דדרו בדוחקא – משוי שאדם יחיד נושא בחול על כתיפו בטורח, אם בא לשאתו לצורך יום טוב ביו"ט, כגון חבית או שק מלא פירות – ישאהו ביו"ט בדיגלא עתר שקורין פורק"א, כדרך נושאי מלא למכור, מפני שצריך לשנות. וכשמשנה ישנה להקל משאו, ולא להרבות טורח ביו"ט. ועתר זה נוח לשאת בו משא כבד, וכשנושא בו חבית הנישאת בכתף – ישנה להקל. דדרו בדיגלא, משוי חבית גדולה שרגילה לשאת בדיגלא – לידרו באגרא – ישאהו ביו"ט בב' בני אדם במוט על כתפים, דהיינו נמי שינוי להקל. דדרו באגרא, במוט על כתפים – לידרו, ביו"ט אותו משוי, באכפא – במוט, בידים משום שינוי, ואפילו אינו להקל – מ"מ שינוי הוא, ואינו מרבה טורח בשינוי. דדרו באכפא – ניפרוס סודרא, קל הוא ואינו מכביד ושינוי בעלמא הוא, ולהצנע. עד כאן לשונו. ומשמע מתוך פירושו דכל אלה משוי אחד להם בשוה, ואין זה נושא יותר אלא שנושא משאו בענין אחר ממה שהיה רגיל. וזה דתקו: שאם נפרש שכל אלו ממעטים משאם מאשר היו רגילים לשאת – קשיא הא דאמר בסמוך^(ד): מפשי בהילוכא! משמע מפירושא דאגרא נושאים שני בני אדם שפיר במוט בשנים ויש בו משוי שני בני אדם שנושאים כל מה שרגילין לשאת בדיגלא. ודיגלא היא משוי שני בני אדם, כדמשמע בבבא מציעא, בס"פ "השוכר את האומנים" (דף פג.) וקשיא לר': דהתם משמע נמי דאגרא אין בו משוי לשני בני אדם, דאמר התם: דדרו באגרא ואיתבר – משלם פלגא. מ"ט? נפיש לחד וזוטר לתרי, ודמי לפשיעה ודמי לאונס. בדיגלא – משלם כולה. משמע דלא הוי זוטר לתרי! נראה דאגרא לשום אדם אינו נראה עובדא דחול כמו דיגלא. ומשום הכי, דדרו בדיגלא לידרו באגרא ואע"פ שמפיש בהילוכא יכול לשנות כיון שאינו נראה כל כך עובדא דחול. והשתא אתי שפיר דדרו באגרא לידרו באכפא – אע"פ שבודאי מרבה במשאוי הוא בנושא בידים המוט מכשנושאו על כתיפו, מ"מ כיון שאינו נראה עובדא דחול כמו אגרא – יכול לעשות. כעין שמצינו גבי בהמה מסוכנת דתנן בביצה (דף כה.): שחטה בשדה – לא יביאנה במוט אלא מביאה בידו אברים אברים ותנן נמי (דף כט: ושם) ב"המביא כדי יין": לא יביאם בסל ובקופה, אלא מביא הוא על כתפיו, או לפניו. אלמא: הני, אע"ג דמפשי בהילוכא, כיון שאינו עושה כל כך כדרך שעושה בחול – יש לו לשנות. והכיא דבסמוך, דמליין בחצבא זוטא ודמליין בחצבא רבה – תרווייהו עובדא דחול, ובענין שנושאים זה נושאים זה. הלכך אין לו לשנות, לא להקל ולא להכביד, כדפי' טעמא. ובההיא דלעיל בריש "מפנין" (דף קכז.) – לא שייכא עובדא דחול, שאינו מטלטל אלא בבית מזוית לזוית. מ"ר. ובההיא דשחטה בשדה, פירש בריש "מפנין" (ג"ז שם) בע"א, וכמו שפירש כאן עיקר. ועוד קשה לי, לפי' הקונטרס דדרו באכפא: אמאי ניפרוס סודרא עליה? הוה ליה למימר לידרו באגרא, כיון שאינו משנה להכביד יותר מאכפא, כמו שמשמע נמי מתוך פירושו! ולפירוש רבי אתי שפיר: ניפרוס

עין משפט נר מצוה

נו א טוש"ע או"ח סימן שכח סעיף מז:
נז ב שם סעיף ל:

[ועי' תוספות שם ד"ה טלית]

א ג ד מיי' פכ"ג מהל' שבת הלכה יב סמג לאוין סה טור שו"ע או"ח סימן שז סעיף יא:
ב ה מיי' פ"ה מהלכות י"ט הלכה א ב סמג לאוין עה טוש"ע או"ח סימן תקי סעיף ח:
ג ו מיי' שם טוש"ע שם סעיף י וסימן שכג סעיף ה:

רבינו חננאל

מחזירין את השבר. רבה בר בר חנה לא על (פי') לפירקי' דרב יהודה שדריה לאדא דייאלא א"ל זיל גרד ביה אזל גרביה. פירוש*) משכיהו והביאהו מלשון פרץ נחל מעם גר כלומר הבריחהו. כדגרסינן בפרק בנות כותים נדות מעריסתן. שילא בר אבינא עבד עובדא כרב. כי קא ניחא נפשיה דרב. א"ל לרב אמי זיל צניעיה ואי לא צאית גרדיה הוא סבר גרדיה א"ל ופי' הכהו וכו': מי שנפרקה ידו או רגלו פי' שף מבוכניה לא יטרפן בצונן אבל רוחץ כדרכו ואם נתרפא נתרפא ורב אויא דשניא ליה ידיה והיה אומר לרב יוסף ומראה בידו אם יעשה בידו כך או כך מותר או אסור עד שהיה מראה לו כדי שיראהו מה שהתירו חכמים חזרה ידו למקומה ונתרפא:

הדרן עלך חבית

פרק כ"ג **שואל** אדם מחבירו כדי יין וכדי שמן ובלבד שלא יאמר לו הלויני כו'. ואוקימנא דחיישינן שמא יכתוב**) וכן שאם יאמר לו הלויני גוערין בו ואומרים לו אסור לומר כן ביום שבת לשון הלואה מינכרא מלתא ולא אתי למכתב וכיון שהזכיר א"ל רבא בר רב חנן לאביי נסיב

*) עיין בערוך השלם ערך גרב א'.
**) אינו מובן לכאורה ואולי דהיה לו גיר' הספרים בגמרא המוסגר בחצי לבנה והובא בחי' הרשב"א כאן ומפרש רבינו דהחלוק הוא דבשבת כיון שאם אומר הלוני קפדינן עלוהי יש לו היכירא ולא אתי למכתב מלשון שאלה וכו' ודו"ק:

מסורת הש"ס

[עי' פרש"י חולין נח:]

רש"ל מ"ז

[לעיל קכח: וש"נ] ביצה ל. ע"ש

הגהות הב"ח

(א) גמ' לא יטרפם בצונן (אבל רוחץ) תא"מ ונ"ב ס"א אבל טובל: (ב) תוס' ד"ה שואל וכו' דסתם שאלה נמי ל' יום: (ג) בא"ד היה חייב להחזיר אלא דעבידי: (ד) ד"ה אתקין וכו' דאמר בסמוך הא קא מפשי בהילוכא:

גליון הש"ס

מתני' שואל אדם מחבירו. עי' בירושלמי פ"ח דשביעית על מ"ד הוצא בר"ש שם:

ניפרום סודרא עליה אתי למסחטיה. מכאן מייתי ר"ת ראיה דיין ושמן לא שייכא סחיטה, לעיל בשלהי "שמונה שרצים" (דף קיא. בד"ה האי מסוכרייתא) פירשתי: **לא** מספקין ולא מטפחין. לא כפי' הקונטרס, משום דא"כ מאי איריא ביו"ט אפי' בחול המועד נמי אסור? כדתנן במועד קטן פרק בתרא (דף כח:): נשים במועד מענות, אבל לא מטפחות! אלא נראה לרבי – משום שמחה רגילין לספק ולטפח בהשמעת קול, ואסור שמא יתקן כלי שיר, כדמפרש ב"המוצא תפילין" (עירובין דף קד.): **וכן** היה הלל אומר. כרבנן דפליגי עליה ב"איזהו נשך" (ב"מ ד' עה.) וקי"ל:

רבה אמר ניתנה ליתבע. הלכה כרבה לגבי רב יוסף:

ורב אויא ורבה בר עולא מחמרי אנפשייהו כ"ה בס"א:

דאי אמרת ניתנה ליתבע אתי למיכתב. אע"פ שמזכיר לו לשון שאלה:

דאיגלאי מילתא דבחול הויא. ורב יוסף לא מיירי אלא בשבת ויו"ט ודאי:

והא אנן תנן אין נימנין כו'. פירש ה"ר פורת בשם רבינו שמואל: דל"ג ליה, חדא: דמה שייך להקשות מנמנין של רשות לנמנין של מלוה? ועוד: דמפרש התם בבילה פרק "אין צדין" (דף כז:): מאי אין נמנין – אין פוסקין דמים בתחילה לבהמה ביו"ט, הרי אני עמך בסלע הריני עמך בשתים. אבל אומר לו: הריני עמך לשליש ולרביע: ולמ"ד

תורה אור

נִיפְרוֹס סוּדָרָא – אָתֵי לִידֵי סְחִיטָה. נְכַסְיֵיהּ בִּנְכַתְמָא – זִימְנִין דְּמִיפְסַק, וְאָתֵי לְמִקְטְרֵיהּ. הִלְכָּךְ: לֹא אֶפְשָׁר. וְא"ל רָבָא בַּר רַב חָנָן לְאַבַּיֵי: תְּנַן, *לֹא [א]מְסַפְּקִין וְלֹא מְטַפְּחִין וְלֹא מְרַקְּדִין בְּיו"ט. וְקָא חָזֵינַן דְּעָבְדִין, וְלָא אָמְרִינַן לְהוּ וְלָא מִידֵּי! וּלְטַעְמִיךְ, הָא דְּאָמַר *רָבָא: *לָא לֵיתִיב אִינִישׁ אַפּוּמָּא דְּלֶחְיָיא, דִּילְמָא מִיגַּנְדַּר לֵיהּ חֵפֶץ וְאָתֵי לְאִיתוּיֵי, וְהָא קָא חָזֵינַן(א) נַמִי דְּמוֹתְבִי חַצְבֵי, וְיָתְבָן אַפּוּמָּא דִּמְבוֹאָה, וְלָא אָמְרִינַן לְהוּ וְלָא מִידֵּי! אֶלָּא: הַנַּח לְיִשְׂרָאֵל, *מוּטָב שֶׁיְּהוּ שׁוֹגְגִין וְאַל יְהוּ מְזִידִין. *סָבוּר מִינָּהּ הנ"מ בִּדְרַבָּנַן, אֲבָל בִּדְאוֹרַיְיתָא – לָא. [ב]וְלָא הִיא, ל"ש בִּדְרַבָּנַן וְל"ש בִּדְאוֹרַיְיתָא. דְּהָא תּוֹסֶפֶת דְּיוה"כ דְּאוֹרַיְיתָא הִיא, וְקָא חָזֵינַן לְהוּ דְּקָאָכְלִי וְשָׁתוּ עַד שֶׁתֶּחְשַׁךְ, וְלָא אָמְרִי' לְהוּ וְלָא מִידֵּי.§ "וְכֵן אִשָּׁה מֵחֲבֵירְתָּהּ כִּכָּרוֹת".§ בְּשַׁבָּת הוּא דַּאֲסִיר, אֲבָל בַּחוֹל – שַׁפִּיר דָּמֵי. לֵימָא מַתְנִי' דְּלָא כְּהִלֵּל; דִּתְנַן, *וְכֵן הָיָה הִלֵּל אוֹמֵר: [ג]לֹא תַּלְוֶה אִשָּׁה כִּכָּר לַחֲבֶירְתָּהּ עַד שֶׁתַּעֲשֶׂינָּה דָּמִים, שֶׁמָּא יוּקְרוּ חִטִּין וְנִמְצְאוּ בָּאוֹת לִידֵי רִבִּית! אֲפִילּוּ תֵּימָא הִלֵּל, [ד]הָא – בְּאַתְרָא דְּקַיִיץ דְּמֵיהּ, הָא – בְּאַתְרָא דְּלָא קַיִיץ דְּמֵיהּ.§ "וְאִם אֵינוֹ מַאֲמִינוֹ".§ אִיתְּמַר: הַלְוָאַת יו"ט, רַב יוֹסֵף אָמַר: לֹא נִיתְּנָה לִיתָּבַע, *וְרַבָּה אָמַר: [ה]נִיתְּנָה לִיתָּבַע. רַב יוֹסֵף אָמַר: "לֹא נִיתְּנָה לִיתָּבַע". דְּאִי אָמְרַתְּ "נִיתְּנָה לִיתָּבַע" – אָתֵי לְמִיכְתַּב. רַבָּה אָמַר: נִיתְּנָה לִיתָּבַע, דְּאִי אָמְרַתְּ "לֹא נִיתְּנָה" – לָא יָהֵיב לֵיהּ, וְאָתֵי לְאִימְּנוּעֵי מִשִּׂמְחַת יו"ט. תְּנַן: אִם אֵינוֹ מַאֲמִינוֹ – מַנִּיחַ טַלִּיתוֹ אֶצְלוֹ. אִי אָמְרַתְּ בִּשְׁלָמָא לֹא נִיתְּנָה לִיתָּבַע – מִשּׁוּם הָכִי מַנִּיחַ טַלִּיתוֹ אֶצְלוֹ, וְעוֹשֶׂה עִמּוֹ חֶשְׁבּוֹן לְאַחַר שַׁבָּת. אֶלָּא אִי אָמְרַתְּ "נִיתְּנָה לִיתָּבַע" אַמַּאי מַנִּיחַ טַלִּיתוֹ אֶצְלוֹ? לִיתֵּן לֵיהּ וְלִתְבְּעֵיהּ! אָמַר: לָא בָּעֵינָא דְּלִיקוּם בְּדִינָא וְדַיָּינָא. מְתִיב רַב אִידִי בַּר אָבִין: *[ו]הַשּׁוֹחֵט אֶת הַפָּרָה וְחִילְּקָהּ בְּרֹאשׁ הַשָּׁנָה, אִם הָיָה חֹדֶשׁ מְעוּבָּר – מְשַׁמֵּט, וְאִם לָאו – אֵינוֹ מְשַׁמֵּט. וְאִי לֹא נִיתְּנָה לִיתָּבַע – מַאי מְשַׁמֵּט? שָׁאנֵי הָתָם, דְּאִיגְּלַאי מִילְּתָא דְּחוֹל הוּא. ת"ש מִסֵּיפָא: אִם לָאו – אֵינוֹ מְשַׁמֵּט. אִי אָמְרַתְּ בִּשְׁלָמָא נִיתְּנָה לִיתָּבַע – הַיְינוּ דְּקָתָנֵי "אֵינוֹ מְשַׁמֵּט". אֶלָּא אִי אָמְרַתְּ "לֹא נִיתְּנָה לִיתָּבַע" – (ב)אַמַּאי אֵינוֹ מְשַׁמֵּט? דְּאִי יָהֵיב לֵיהּ – שָׁקֵיל. מִכְּלָל דְּרֵישָׁא, אִי יָהֵיב לֵיהּ – לָא שָׁקֵיל?! רֵישָׁא צָרִיךְ לְמֵימַר לֵיהּ "מְשַׁמֵּט אֲנִי", סֵיפָא – לֹא צָרִיךְ לְמֵימַר לֵיהּ "מְשַׁמֵּט אֲנִי". כִּדְתְנַן: *[ז]הַמַּחֲזִיר חוֹב בַּשְּׁבִיעִית, יֹאמַר לוֹ "מְשַׁמֵּט אֲנִי". וְאִם אָמַר לוֹ "אעפ"כ" – יְקַבֵּל מִמֶּנּוּ, מִשּׁוּם שֶׁנֶּאֱמַר: °"וְזֶה דְּבַר הַשְּׁמִטָּה". רַב אָוְיָא שָׁקֵיל מַשְׁכּוֹנָא, *רַבָּה בַּר עוּלָּא מַעֲרִים אִיעֲרוּמֵי.§ "וְכֵן עֶרֶב פֶּסַח".§ א"ר יוֹחָנָן: *[ח]מַקְדִּישׁ אָדָם פִּסְחוֹ בַּשַּׁבָּת, וַחֲגִיגָתוֹ בְּיו"ט. נֵימָא מְסַיַּיע לֵיהּ: "וְכֵן עֶרֶב פֶּסַח בִּירוּשָׁלַיִם שֶׁחָל לִהְיוֹת בַּשַּׁבָּת מַנִּיחַ טַלִּיתוֹ אֶצְלוֹ וְנוֹטֵל אֶת פִּסְחוֹ וְעוֹשֶׂה עִמּוֹ חֶשְׁבּוֹן לְאַחַר יו"ט". הָכָא בְּמַאי עָסְקִינַן – בְּמַמְנֶה אֲחֵרִים עִמּוֹ עַל פִּסְחוֹ, דְּמֵעִיקָּרָא מִיקְדָּשׁ וְקָאֵי. וְהָא אֲנַן תְּנַן: *[ט]"אֵין נִמְנִין עַל הַבְּהֵמָה בַּתְּחִילָּה בְּיו"ט"! שָׁאנֵי הָכָא, כֵּיוָן דְּרָגִיל אֶצְלוֹ – כְּמַאן דְּאִימְנֵי בֵּיהּ מֵעִיקָּרָא דָּמֵי. וְהָא תָּנֵי רַבִּי הוֹשַׁעְיָא: הוֹלֵךְ אָדָם אֵצֶל רוֹעֶה הָרָגִיל אֶצְלוֹ וְנוֹתֵן לוֹ טָלֶה לְפִסְחוֹ וּמַקְדִּישׁוֹ, וְיוֹצֵא בּוֹ! הָתָם נַמִי, כֵּיוָן דְּרָגִיל אֶצְלוֹ – אַקְדּוֹשֵׁי(ג) לֵיהּ מֵעִיקָּרָא, וְהָא "מַקְדִּישׁ" קָתָנֵי! הֶקְדֵּשׁ עִילּוּי, מִדְּרַבָּנַן. וּמִי אָמַר ר' יוֹחָנָן הָכִי? *וְהָא אָמַר ר' יוֹחָנָן: הֲלָכָה כִּסְתָם מִשְׁנָה, וּתְנַן: *[י]לֹא מַקְדִּישִׁין וְלֹא מַעֲרִיכִין וְלֹא מַחֲרִימִין וְלֹא מַגְבִּיהִין תְּרוּמוֹת וּמַעַשְׂרוֹת, כָּל אֵלּוּ – בְּיו"ט אָמְרוּ, ק"ו בַּשַּׁבָּת! לָא קַשְׁיָא; כָּאן – בְּחוֹבוֹת שֶׁקָּבוּעַ לָהֶן זְמַן, כָּאן – בְּחוֹבוֹת שֶׁאֵין קָבוּעַ לָהֶן זְמַן.§ **מתני'** מוֹנֶה אָדָם אֶת אוֹרְחָיו וְאֶת פַּרְפְּרוֹתָיו מִפִּיו, אֲבָל לֹא מִן הַכְּתָב. מֵפִיס אָדָם עִם בָּנָיו וְעִם בְּנֵי בֵיתוֹ עַל הַשּׁוּלְחָן, וּבִלְבַד שֶׁלֹּא יִתְכַּוֵּין לַעֲשׂוֹת מָנָה גְּדוֹלָה כְּנֶגֶד מָנָה קְטַנָּה. *וּמַטִּילִין חֲלָשִׁין עַל הַקֳּדָשִׁים בְּיו"ט, אֲבָל לֹא עַל הַמָּנוֹת.§
גמ'

[ב"מ עה.] [ביצה כז.] [גי' רב אלפס והרא"ש ורבא] [דברים טו]

בנכתמא. כיסוי: **זימנין דמיפסק כו'.** כיון דמצרכת ליה כיסוי קטר ליה בכח, וזימנין דמיפסק ואתי למקטריה, והיא קשר של קיימא דאסור מדאורייתא: **ואתי לידי סחיטה.** ודקאמר במסכת ביצה ניפרוס סודרא עלויה כו'(ד) – [התם] בדבר יבש קא מיירי: **אין מספקין.** כף אל כף משום אבל: **מטפחין.** על הלב: **מרקדין.** לשמחה, וטעמא מפרש במסכת ביצה שמא יתקן כלי שיר: **אפומא דלחייא.** לפי שאין ניכר כל כך כמו לרה"ר: **ואתי לאתויי.** חפץ המתגלגל תוך ד' אמות: **ומגנדר** חצביהן ומייתין ליה. ל"ג: **בשבת הוא דאסור.** לומר "הלויני" משום מכתב: **הא בחול שרי.** ולא חיישינן לרבית, ואף על גב דבלשון הלואה קאמר ליה: **באתרא דקייץ דמייהו.** דככרות, לא אתי לידי רבית, שאם יוקירו – יתן דמיהן: **לא ניתנה ליתבע.** בב"ד, שאין ב"ד נזקקין לה לעולם: **בדינא ודיינא.** לא לבא לדין ולא לברור דיין ולהטריח את עצמו: **השוחט את הפרה וחילקה בראש השנה.** של מוצאי שביעית ללוקחים, ובהקפה, וקיי"ל שביעית משמטת בסופה, דכתיב "מקץ": **אם היה חדש.** אלול מעובר, ועשו ראש השנה שני ימים – משמט. דיום טוב ראשון של סוף שביעית היה, ונמצאת זו הלואת שביעית. ואם לאו – הויא לה הלואת מוצאי שביעית, ואינו משמט: ל"ג: **אי אמרת בשלמא כו'.** ה"ג: **ואם לא ניתנה ליתבע מאי משמט.** הואיל ואין ב"ד נזקקין לכופו שמוטה היא ועומדת: **דחול הוא.** שהרי חדש מעובר, ולא הוי יו"ט עד למחר, הלכך: אי לאו דשביעית הוא – הוה גבי: **ואם לאו אינו משמט.** אלמא ניתנה ליתבע. ומשני: מאי אינו משמט – דאי יהיב ליה שקיל: **מכלל דרישא אי יהיב ליה לא שקיל.** בתמיה: **רישא.** דהלואת שביעית היא, אי נמי יהיב ליה לוה – צריך למימר ליה מלוה: משמט אני:(ה) **ואם אמר.** לוה: אעפ"כ איני חפץ שישמטו – יקבל ממנו: **דבר השמטה.** אפילו מקבל חובו, יזכיר לו שמיטה בדבורו: **שקיל משכונא.** בשעת הלואה מהלואת יו"ט: **מערים איערומי.** לאחר יו"ט לוקח ממנו שום חפץ ומעכבו: **פסחו בשבת.** אם חל י"ד בשבת: **וחגיגתו ביו"ט.** ביום הקרבתה מותר להקדישה. ואע"ג דתנן: ואלו אין משום שבות, אין מקדישין – הני, כיון דהקרבתן דוחה, קדושתן דוחה: **בממנה** אחרים עמו. כדכתיב (שמות יב): "במכסת נפשות": **על פסחו.** שהיה קדוש ועומד מאתמול: **אקדושי.** מקדיש ליה רועה מע"ש, שהרי יודע שזה סומך עליו: **עילוי.** מעלה בעלמא שיקדישו בעלים: **הא.** דקתני אין מקדישין – בחובות שאין קבוע להן זמן קאי, שאין הקרבתן דוחה שבת: **מתני' פרפרותיו.** מיני מעדנים: **אבל לא מן הכתב.** אם כתב מע"ש: כך וכך אורחים פלוני ופלוני זמנתי, כדי שלא ישכחם – לא יקרא באותו כתב בשבת. ובגמ' מפרש טעמא: **מפים.** לשון פיים. מטיל פיים לחלק, מי מגיע כל מנה ומנה: **ובלבד שלא יתכוין לעשות כו'.** שיהו המנות שוות, ולא תהא אחת גדולה ואחת קטנה, לזכות בגדולה הזוכה ע"פ הגורל, והמתחייב ע"פ הגורל לקטנה יתלנה. ובגמ' מפרש טעמא: **חלשים.** גורלות: **על הקדשים.** בין הכהנים: **אבל לא על המנות.** בגמרא מפרש:
גמ'

ביצה ל. וד' לו:
לעיל קמח. ביצה ל.
[ביצה ל. ע"ש]
שביעית פ"י משנה ב
ג"ז שם [מ"ח גיטין לז:]
נ"א רבון
פסחים סו: [ועי' תוספות חגיגה ח. ד"ה משום ותוס' בכורות נח. ד"ה ואי]
[לעיל מו. וש"נ]
פסחים סו: ביצה לו:
[עי' תוס' לקמן קמט:]

הגהות הב"ח

(א) גמ' והא קא חזינן נמי דמותבי אלבייהו וכו' הנח להן לישראל: (ב) שם מאי אינו משמט דאי יהיב ליה: (ג) שם אקדושי מקדיש ליה מעיקרא: (ד) רש"י ד"ה ואתא לידי סחיטה וכו' סודרא עלויה כו' ביין ושמן קמיירי: (ה) ד"ה רישא וכו' משמט אני ואם אמר לו הלוה אעפ"כ כצ"ל והד"א:

ד א מיי' פכ"ג מהלכות שבת הלכה ה סמג לאוין סה טוש"ע או"ח סימן שלט סעיף ג וסימן תקכד סעיף א:
ה ב מיי' פ"א מהלכות שביתת עשור הלכה ז סמג לאוין סה וסט טור ושו"ע או"ח סימן תרח סעיף ב:
ו ג מיי' פ"י מהלכות מלוה ולוה הלכה ב סמג לאוין קצג טוש"ע יו"ד סימן קסב סעיף א:
[נ"ל רבה]
ז ד שם סעיף ג:
[ב"ב ס: ועי' תוס' לעיל נה. ד"ה ואע"ג ותוס' ב"ב ס: ד"ה מוטב ותוס' ע"ז ז. ד"ה שהי']
ח ה מיי' פ"ד מהלכות י"ט הלכה כה טוש"ע או"ח סימן תקכה סעיף א:
ט ו מיי' פ"ט מהלכות שמיטה ויובל הלכה ה סמג עשין קמט:
י ז מיי' שם הלכה כח סמג לאוין רעה טור ושו"ע חו"מ סימן סז סעיף לו:
יא ח מיי' פכ"ג מהלכו' שבת הלכה יד ופ"א מהלכות קרבן פסח הלי"ט סמג עשין רכג:
יב ט מיי' פ"ד מהלכות י"ט הלכה יט סמג לאוין עה טוש"ע או"ח סימן תק סעיף א:
יג י מיי' פכ"ג מהלכות שבת הלכה יד סמג לאוין סה ועה טור ש"ע או"ח סימן שלט סעיף ד וסימן תקכד סעיף א:

רבינו חננאל

להא. דא"ל תנן לא מספקין ולא מרקדין ולא מטפחין. בגדרא. ופשוטה היא. ומיפרשא נמי בגמ' דהמביא כדי יין במס' יו"ט וכן שואלת אשה מחברתה ככרות. ודייקינן מינה בשבת הוא דאסור מכלל דבחול שרי מתניתין דלא כהלל כו' ומסקינן בה אפילו תימא כהלל באתרא דקייצי דמי. ואם אינו מאמינו מניח טליתו אצלו ועושה עמו חשבון לאחר שבת. אתמר הלואת יו"ט רב יוסף אמר לא נתנה ליתבע רבא אמר ניתנה ליתבע ואתינן למיגמר מן מתניתין תנן ואם אינו מאמינו מניח טליתו אצלו כו' ולא גמרינן מינה דלא מיפרשא בהדיא כחד מינייהו ומותבינן לרב יוסף מהא דתנן השוחט את הפרה וחילקה בראש השנה אם היה חדש מעובר משמט. פי' אם היה אלול מעובר נמצא יום. לקיחתו חלק מן הפרה יום חול שר"ה מחר הוא וכיון שנושה בו דמי בשר הפרה שלקח מאתמול דכיון שנכנסה שנה שביעית משמטת לדברי רבא ניחא כי נתנה ליתבע ומלוה נושה בו וכשנכנסת שביעית משמטת אלא לרב יוסף דאמר לא נתנה ליתבע אמאי צריך למיתנא משמטת בלאו הכי פטור הוא מלשלם. ואפילו בשאר שני שבוע דהא לא ניתנה ליתבע. ופריק רב יוסף שאני התם דכיון דאיגלאי מלתא דחול היא (ניתנה ליתבע דהא מלוה דחול היא) ואנן לא קאימנא אלא הלואת יו"ט ואסיקנא למשמע מסיפא ואם לאו אינו משמט לרבא דאמר ניתנה ליתבע דתובעו ונפרע ממנו [ניחא] אלא לרב יוסף דאמר לא ניתנה ליתבע קשיא כיון דתני אינו משמט הלא משמע דתובע ונפרע ממנו ואינו יכול לומר לו כי השביעית השמיטתו ופריק רב יוסף לעולם לא נתנה ליתבע והמלוה אינו יכול ליתבע אלא אם יביא הלה ויפרינו יקבל ואינו צריך לומר משמט אני. ואקשינן עליה מכלל דרישא אי יהיב ליה מעצמו לא שקיל. ופריק רב יוסף ואמר רישא אם מחזיר לו צריך שיאמר לו משמט אני. דהא נושה בו מלוה. אבל ספק שאינו נושה בו מלוה אם יבא לחשבון אינו צריך לומר לו משמט אני אלא יקבל כדתנן המחזיר חוב בשביעית צריך שיאמר משמט אני. ואם אמר לו אעפ"כ יקבל ממנו משום שנאמר וזה דבר השמטה. ומפורש ענין זה בפ' השולח גט לאשתו. וראינו רבותינו שהיו מעמידין השמועה זו כרב יוסף. חדא (דרבה) [דרבא] לגבי רב יוסף תלמיד הוא ועוד סוגיא דשמעתא רובה כרב יוסף ריהטא ועוד מדחינן רב אויא מקבל משכונא מכלל שאם אין בידו משכון אינו יכול ליתבע. ותוב רבא בר עולא מיערם איערומי כלומר לא היה תובעו בהדיא אלא היה אומר לו הלויני וכאשר יתן לו ויבאו המעות לידו אומר לו יש לי אצלך הלואת יו"ט נשתלמתי אתם מכלל כי הלואת יו"ט כי האי גוונא יתכן אבל בהדיא לא ניתנה ליתבע וראינו תשובה לגאון ופסיק כרבא. ואמר רבא בתרא הוא. וקיי"ל דהלכתא כבתראי וכן הדעת נוטה: **וכן** ערב פסחים בירושלים כו'. א"ר יוחנן מקדיש אדם פסחו בשבת וחגיגתו ביו"ט נימא מסייעא ליה וכן ערב פסח כו' ופשוטה היא. הא דתני ר' הושעיא ומקדישו אוקמינא. הקדיש עלוי מדרבנן ואקשינן עלה והא תנא דאמר הלכה כסתם משנה ותנן אין מקדשין ואין מעריכין ואין מחרימין ומפרקינן הא דא"ר יוחנן מקדיש בשבת בחובות הקבוע להן זמן. כגון פסח שאם לא יעשנו היום אינו יכול לעשותו למחר והיא מצוה עוברת והא דתנן

גמ' מ"ט? רב ביבי אמר: גזירה שמא ימחוק. אביי אמר: [א]גזירה שמא יקרא בשטרי הדיוטות. מאי בינייהו? א"ב: דכתב אכותל, ומידלי. למ"ד שמא ימחוק – לא חיישינן, ולמ"ד שמא יקרא – חיישינן. ולמ"ד "שמא ימחוק" ניחוש שמא יקרא! ותו: לשמא ימחוק לא חיישינן?! *והתניא: *לא יקרא לאור הנר, *ואמר רבה: אפי' גבוה שתי קומות, אפי' גבוה שתי מרדעות, אפי' עשרה בתים זה ע"ג זה – לא יקרא! אלא, איכא בינייהו: דכתב אכותל ומיתתי, למאן דאמר שמא ימחוק – חיישינן, למ"ד שמא יקרא – לא חיישינן, גודא בשטרא לא מיחלף. ולמ"ד "שמא יקרא" ליחוש שמא ימחוק! אלא, איכא בינייהו: דחייק אטבלא ואפינקס. למ"ד שמא ימחוק – לא חיישינן. למ"ד שמא יקרא – חיישינן. ולמ"ד "שמא ימחוק" ליחוש שמא יקרא! וכ"ת: טבלא ופינקס בשטרא לא מיחלף – והתניא: *מונה אדם כמה מבפנים וכמה מבחוץ, וכמה מנות עתיד להניח לפניהם [ב]מכתב שעל גבי הכותל, אבל לא מכתב שעל גבי טבלא ופינקס! היכי דמי? אילימא דכתיב מיכתב – מ"ש הכא ומ"ש הכא? אלא לאו – דחייק, וקתני: מכתב שעל גבי הכותל, אבל לא מכתב שע"ג טבלא ופינקס! אלא לעולם דכתב אכותל ומידלי. ודקא קשיא לך דרבה – דרבה תנאי היא. דתניא: [ג]מונה אדם את אורחיו ואת פרפרותיו מפיו, אבל לא מן הכתב. ר' אחא מתיר מכתב שעל גבי הכותל. היכי דמי? אילימא דכתיב מתתא – ליחוש שמא ימחוק. אלא לאו – דכתב ומידלי. וש"מ: דרבה תנאי היא, ש"מ. והני תנאי כהני תנאי; דתניא: [ד]*אין רואין במראה בשבת, *רבי מאיר מתיר במראה הקבוע בכותל. מ"ש הקבוע בכותל – דאדהכי והכי מדכר, שאינו קבוע נמי – אדהכי והכי מדכר! הכא במראה של מתכת עסקינן, וכדרב נחמן אמר רבה בר אבוה. דא"ר נחמן אמר רבה בר אבוה: [ה]מפני מה אמרו "מראה של מתכת – אסורה" – מפני *שאדם עשוי להשיר בה נימין המדולדלין. תנו רבנן: *[ו]כתב המהלך תחת הצורה ותחת הדיוקנאות – אסור לקרותו בשבת. [ז]ודיוקנא עצמה – אף בחול אסור להסתכל בה, משום שנאמר: °"אל תפנו אל האלילים". מאי תלמודא? אמר רבי חנין: אל תפנו אל מדעתכם. §"מפיס אדם עם בניו וכו'". § עם בניו ועם בני ביתו – אין, ועם אחר – לא. מאי טעמא? כדרב יהודה אמר שמואל. *דאמר רב יהודה אמר שמואל: [ח]בני חבורה המקפידין זה על זה – עוברין משום מדה ומשום משקל, ומשום מנין, ומשום לווין ופורעין ביו"ט.

[ויקרא יט] [תוספ' פי"ח] [ב"מ עה.]

רש"י

גמ' מ"ט. אבל לא מן הכתב: שמא ימחוק. מן האורחין, שיראה שלא הכין להם כל צרכם, ויתחרט שזימן יותר מן הראוי, וימחוק מן הכתב, כדי שלא יקראם השמש: כל הני שמא יקרא בשטרי הדיוטות של מקח וממכר קאמר[(א)]: דכתב. מניינא אכותל בדיו: ומידלי. שאינו מגיע לשם למחוק: (אפילו גבוה שאינו מגיע לשם למחוק): אפילו גבוה. שאינו מגיע שם להטות הנר – אסור. דהואיל ונמוך אסור, גבוה נמי אסור, שלא תחלוק: ומיתתי. שנמוך, ויכול להגיע שם ולמחוק: ולמ"ד שמא יקרא. היכא דליכא למיחש לשמא יקרא, ליחוש לשמא ימחוק: דחייק. בסכין בתוך העץ בטבלא שאין נוחה למחוק, ואדהכי מדכר, וליכא למיחש למחוק: גודא. כותל: פינקס. כעין לוחות של סוחרים: כמה בפנים וכמה בחוץ. את מי ומי אושיב בפנים במקום המכובד, ואת מי ומי אושיב בחוץ, שאינה כל כך ספונין: אבל לא מכתב שעל גבי טבלא ופינקס. דגודא בשטרא לא מיחלף, אבל טבלא ופינקס מיחלף: [דכתיב מיכתב. כתב של דיו]: אלא לעולם דכתב אכותל ומידלי. שאינו יכול למחוק, ולשמא יקרא לא חיישינן – דגודא בשטרא לא מיחלף. ודקשיא לך, דאע"ג דמידלי ליתסרי כדרבה, דאמר גבי נר אפילו י' בתים: דרבה תנאי היא. דאיכא דחייש לשלא תחלוק באיסור שבת דרבנן, ואיכא דמפליג: ליחוש לשמא ימחוק. דהא ר' אחא כותל דוקא נקט, ואי מתתי – מה לי כותל מה לי אגרת? אין רואין במראה. מירושלמי, לפי שהרואה במראה אינו צריך אלא לתקן שערות ראשו וזקנו, הלכך חיישי' שמא יראה נימין המדולדלות שאינן שוות עם שאר השער, *ויגלחן: דאדהכי והכי. שילך להביא תער או מספריים: מדכר. שהוא שבת: של מתכת. שאינו צריך להביא מספריים, שהיא עצמה מגלחת השער: כתב המהלך תחת הצורה ותחת הדיוקנאות. כגון בני אדם המציירים בכותל חיות משונות, או דיוקנות של בני אדם של מעשים, כגון מלחמת דוד וגלית, וכותבין תחתיה: זו צורת חיה פלונית, וזו דיוקנית פלוני ופלונית: אסור לקרותו בשבת. שמא יקרא בשטרי הדיוטות: אל מדעתכם. אל אשר אתם עושים מדעת לבבכם וחלל שלכם. אלילים לשון חללים: עם בניו ובני ביתו אין עם אחר לא. מדלא תנא "ומפיס על המנות": משום לווין ופורעין. דגזור בהו רבנן שמא יכתוב: המקפידין. שאין מוחלים ומוותרין זה לזה: וכדברי

תוספות

ולמ"ד שמא ימחוק ליחוש שמא יקרא. ולא מסיק אדעתיה גודא בשטרא לא מיחלף: בשטרי הדיוטות. פי' בקונט': של מקח וממכר. ולעיל בפרק "כל כתבי" (דף קיז: ושם) פירש: איגרות השלוחות למצוא חפץ: אלא איכא בינייהו דכתיב אכותל ומתתאי. ולא ידענא אמאי נקט מתתאי, כיון דס"ד דכ"ע אית להו דרבה: אילימא דכתיב מיכתב מ"ש הכא מ"ש הכא. פירוש: תרוייהו יהא אסור, שמא ימחוק: לעולם דכתב אכותל ומידלי ודקשיא לך דרבה דרבה תנאי היא. לפירוש הקונטרס נ"ל דהשתא דמוקי לה דכתיב אכותל ומידלי. למ"ד שמא ימחוק – איכא, דאית ליה דרבה. ולמ"ד שמא יקרא – לית ליה דרבה. והשתא מיבעיא לן למימר דבדרבה פליגי תנאי, כי היכי דפליגי אמוראי דהכא וברייתא קמייתא מיתוקמא שפיר דכתיב מכתב אכותל ומידלי, דכולהו אמוראי גודא בשטרא לא מיחלף. וקשה לפירוש זה: דהשתא לא הוה פלוגתייהו כדהוה מוקמת לה מעיקרא, למאן דאמר שמא ימחוק לא חיישינן למאן דאמר שמא יקרא חיישי'. וה"ר פורת פירש: דאביי ורב ביבי תרוייהו לית להו דרבה, דפליגי בכתב אכותל ומידלי. למאן דאמר שמא ימחוק – לא חיישינן. כיון דמידלי, ולית לן דרבה. ולשמא יקרא נמי לא חיש, קסבר: גודא בשטרא לא מיחלף. ולמ"ד שמא יקרא – חיש, דקסבר: גודא בשטרא מיחלף. ואביי לא הוה מוקי פלוגתייהו דרבי אחא ורבנן[(ב)] כרבה, דא"כ ר' אחא ע"כ לית ליה דאביי דשרי בכותל, אלמא קסבר גודא בשטרא לא מיחלף. וא"כ כמאן סבירא ליה? דאפילו רבנן לא פליגי עליה דר' אחא אלא משום דאית להו דרבה, וגזרינן שמא ימחוק. אלא הוה מפרש אביי דכ"ע לית להו דרבה, ולא חיישינן לשמא ימחוק במידלי. ובגודא בשטרא מיחלף פליגי, והא דקאמר: ש"מ דרבה תנאי היא – הו"מ למימר ודאי לכ"ע לית להו דרבה כדמפרש לאביי. אלא דלא מצי למוכח הא בהדיא, ולהכי קאמר דתנאי היא וליכא לאקשויי לרבה. והא לא מצי למימר דפליגי[(ג)] בחייק מיחק רבי אחא ורבנן, ובגודא בשטרא מיחלף פליגי. אבל כ"ע אית להו דרבה – משום דסברא הוא, כיון דחייק ואיתא נמי בכותל – פשיטא דהא לא הוי אמרי רבנן דגודא בשטרא מיחלף. וצריך לאוקמא השתא ברייתא דלעיל דחייק מיחק למאן דסבר גודא בשטרא מיחלף. וקשה קצת לפירוש זה, דה"ל למימר דכ"ע[(ד)] לית להו דרבה, ואביי ורב ביבי בגודא אי מיחלף בשטרא פליגי: ודיוקני עצמה אף בחול אסור. נראה דבשויה לשם עבודת גלולים אמר, אבל[(ה)] לנוי מותר. בני חבורה המקפידין זה על זה. כדמשמע מבנן של קדושים דלא הוו מסתכלי בצורתא דזוזא (ע"ז דף נ.), מכלל דאחריני הוו מסתכלי*: בני חבורה המקפידין זה על זה עוברין משום משקל ומשום מדה ומשום מנין. פירוש: לפי שמקפידין זה על זה עוברין אפילו על מה שאין שאר בני אדם עוברין משום מדה. כדאמרינן בבילה (דף כט.): יכול אדם לומר לחבירו מלא לי כלי זה, אבל לא במדה. פירוש: כלי שמודדין בו – אסור, דדמי למקח וממכר. והם, כיון שהם מקפידים – כל כלים הוי לגבייהו מדה, לפי שמקפידין לידע שיעורו לשלם להם הכלי. וכן משקל, ששוקלים ומכוונים זה כנגד זה ביד, ואמרינן בבילה*: אין משגיחין במאזנים ביום טוב. ומשום מנין – כדאמר בבילה (דף כט:): הולך אדם אצל חנוני הרגיל אצלו ואומר לו תן לי כו', ובלבד שלא יזכיר לו סכום מקח. שאם היו נותנים מאה אגוזים בדינר, ולקח כבר תשעים לא יאמר לו תן לי עשרים אגוזים שאתחייב לך עשרה אגוזים, שנראה שעושה להשלים הדינר. אבל יכול לומר לו: תן לי כ' אגוזים, סתם. ובבני חבורה המקפידים – אסור שיבא לידי איסור שיזכירו להשלים. וכדברי[(ו)] בית הלל – אף משום רבית, דכשהם מחזירין זה לזה הם מקפידים מה ששוות יותר. וקשה לפירוש

[וע"ע תוספות ע"ז נ. ד"ה ה"ג] [דף כח.]

רבינו חננאל

דתנן אין מקדישין בשבת ולא ביום טוב בחובות שאין קבוע להן זמן. מונה אדם את אורחיו ואת פרפריותיו מפיו אבל לא מן הכתב. ואמרינן מן הכתב מ"ט לא. רב ביבי אמר גזירה שמא ימחוק אביי אמר גזירה שמא יקרא בשטרי הדיוטות ופירושו כיון שיראה אדם קורא כמה אורחים צריך להביא כמה פרפריות אצלו אף הוא אומר מותר לקרוא בשטרי הדיוטות מאי בינייהו דכתיב אכותל במקום גבוה שאינו יכול למחוק דרב ביב בכי האי גוונא שרי. ואביי אסר. ואקשינן על רב ביבי והתנן לא יקרא לאור הנר ואמר רבה אפילו גבוה ב' קומות או ב' מרדעות ואפילו עשרה בתים זה ע"ג זה לא יקרא. והא הכא דליכא למיחש אלא שמא יטה ואפי' גבוה כמה אמר (רבא) [רבה] חיישינן ואסור. ואע"ג דסלקא כתנאי הלכתא (כרבא) [כרבה] דסתם מתניתין כוותיה ולא חיישינן אמחלוקות דברייתא וחזרנו להביא טעם אחר לומר כי אינם חלוקים אלא אם הוא הכתב בכותל נמוך שמגעת לה ויכול למחוק דלרב ביבי אסור כטעמיה ולאביי שרי דכותל בשטר לא מיחלף. ואקשינן על אביי וליחוש שמא ימחוק הואיל והכותל נמוך הוא וגם זה הטעם נדחה ואתינן לאוקמי פלוגתיה בכתב דחייק אטבלא ופנקס וגם זה נדחה. וחזרנו על הטעם הראשון דכתוב אכותל ומידלי. לרב ביבי מותר ולאביי אסור. וזה שהקשינו לרב ביבי מדברי רבה שאסר אפילו גבוה כמה. אמר לך רב ביבי דרבה תנאי היא ואנא דאמרי כתנא דשרי. דתניא מונה אדם את אורחיו ואת פרפרותיו מפיו אבל לא מן הכתב. ר' אחא מתיר מן הכתב שעל גבי הכותל ואוקימנא דכתוב אכותל ומידלי. ואמרינן הני תנאי כי הני תנאי כלומר ר' אחא ות"ק חולקין במחלוקת ר' ות"ק דיליה דלר' אחא *) צחצות הסיג מן המראה הוא מוחק לפיכך קתני אין רואין במראה ור' מתיר במראה הקבועה בכותל כת"ק דר' אחא ודמיא להא דאמרינן בכלל גדול (דף עה) דשף בין העמודים [חייב] משום **) מוחק שדומה למוחק כתב. ותלמוד א"י השף את העור ע"ג העמוד ר' אחא בשם ר' יהודה בן לוי משום מוחק ואקשינן עלה מ"ש מראה הקבועה בכותל דאדהכי והכי מדכר. ולא פירש מהו שיזכור וימנע. יש מי שאומר כי נאסר הראיה במראה בשבת שמא יראה כי עלה בו כעין חלודה (וכעין חלודה) בזה המראה ויצחצחנו בשבת ונמצא מתקן מנא. גם בהיות המראה למטה במקום נמוך עד שיתעסק להביא סכין כדי לצחצחו יזכור ששבת הוא וימנע ונדחה זה הטעם. ועמד כר"נ דאמר מפני מה מראה של מתכת אסורה מפני שאדם עשוי להשיר בה נימין המדולדלות ור' שמתיר אומר כיון שהיא גבוה לא גזרינן. ות"ק סבר גזרינן: ת"ר כתב של תחת הצורה של תחת דיוקני. פי' דיוקני צורת אדם והכתב שתחתיו אסור לקרותו בשבת ולא גרע משטרי הדיוטות דאסור בשבת. ודיוקני עצמה אסורה. אפילו בחול כטעמיה: מפים אדם עם בניו ועם כו' פי' מפים אדם מלשון פיוס כההיא דאמרי מי מפים. וכמו שאמר על השכר (פסחים קז) מיסרו ומפים. בניו ובני ביתו

*) לכאורה לפי גי' היה נ"ל להיפך דר' אחא כרבי ואולי לגירסתו היה להפך ומתחלה נעתק בטעות וצ"ע. **) לפנינו שם בגמ' איתא משום ממחק וצ"ע.

עין משפט נר מצוה

יד א ב ג מיי' פכ"ג מהלכות שבת הל' יט סמג לאוין סה טור שו"ע או"ח סימן שז סעיף יב:
טו ד ה מיי' פכ"ב מהל' שבת הלכה יד סמג שם טור שו"ע או"ח סימן שב סעיף יג:
טז ו מיי' פכ"ג שם הלכה יט סמג שם טור שו"ע או"ח סימן שז סעיף טו:
יז ז מיי' פ"ב מהלכות ע"ז הלכה ב סמג לאוין יד טוש"ע יו"ד סי' קמב סעיף טו:
יח ח מיי' פ"ז מהלכות גניבה הלכה י סמג לאוין עה [אבל הפוסקין השמיטו מטעם שכ' הב"י באו"ח סוף סי' תקי"ז]:

[תוספ' פי"ח]
[ברב אלפס איתא רבי מתיר וכו' וכ"ה בבעל המאור ובמלחמות. אבל בהרא"ש א' ר' יהודה מתיר וכו']
[עי' תוס' ע"ז כט. ד"ה המסתפר]

מסורת הש"ס

נ"ל והתנן לעיל יא.
ויגלחם במספרים כצ"ל רש"ל
[תוספ' פי"ד]

הגהות הב"ח

(א) רש"י ד"ה כל הני וכו' קאמר הס"ד ואח"כ מ"ה למ"ד שמא יקרא חיישינן ואפי' גבוה: (ב) תוס' ד"ה לעולם וכו' דר' אחא ורבנן בדרבה דא"כ: (ג) בא"ד והא לא מצי למימר דפליגי ר' אחא ורבנן בחייק מיחק ובגוד' בשטרא: (ד) בא"ד וקשה קצת לפי' זה דה"ל למימר דכ"ע אביי ורב ביבי לית להו דרבה ובגוד': (ה) ד"ה ודיוקנא וכו' אבל לשם נוי: (ו) ד"ה בני וכו' שיזכירו להשלים וכדברי הלל אף:

גליון הש"ס

גמ' אין רואין במראה בשבת. עי' ע"ז כט ע"א תוס' ד"ה המסתפר: שם כתב המהלך תחת הצורה. עי' לעיל דף קטז ע"ב תוס' ד"ה וכ"ש בשטרי:

וכדברי (*ב"ה) אף משום רבית. אי הכי – בניו ובני ביתו נמי! בניו ובני ביתו היינו טעמא – כדרב יהודה אמר רב. *דאמר רב יהודה אמר רב: מותר להלוות בניו ובני ביתו ברבית, כדי להטעימן טעם רבית. אי הכי – מנה גדולה כנגד מנה קטנה נמי! אין ה"נ, וחסורי מיחסרא והכי קתני: [א]מפים אדם עם בניו ועם בני ביתו על השלחן, אפי' מנה גדולה כנגד מנה קטנה. מ"ט – כדרב יהודה אמר רב. עם בניו ועם בני ביתו – אין, עם אחרים – לא. מ"ט – כדרב יהודה אמר שמואל. [ב]מנה גדולה כנגד מנה קטנה – אף בחול לאחרים אסור. מ"ט – משום קוביא. § [ג]"מטילין חלשין על וכו'". § מאי "אבל לא על המנות"? א"ר יעקב *בריה דבת יעקב: אבל לא [ד]על המנות של חול ביו"ט. פשיטא! מהו דתימא: הואיל וכתיב: °"ועמך כמריבי כהן" – אפי' מנות דחול נמי, קמ"ל. וא"ר יעקב *בריה דבת יעקב: כל שחבירו נענש על ידו – אין מכניסין אותו במחיצתו של הקב"ה. מנלן! אילימא משום דכתיב: °"ויאמר ה' מי יפתה את אחאב ויעל ויפול ברמות גלעד ויאמר זה בכה וזה אמר בכה ויצא הרוח ויעמוד לפני ה' ויאמר אני אפתנו וגו' ויאמר אצא והייתי רוח שקר בפי כל נביאיו ויאמר תפתה וגם תוכל צא ועשה כן". ואמרינן מאי רוח? *א"ר יוחנן: זה רוחו של נבות. ומאי "צא"? אמר רב: צא ממחיצתי. ודילמא התם היינו טעמא, דכתיב: °"דובר שקרים לא יכון". אלא מהכא: °"שבעת קלון מכבוד שתה גם אתה והערל וגו'". "שבעת קלון מכבוד" – זה נבוכדנצר, "שתה גם אתה והערל" – זה צדקיה. חדא: דכוליה קרא בנבוכדנצר כתיב, ועוד: צדקיה צדיקא, מאי הוה ליה למיעבד ליה? דא"ר יהודה אמר רב: בשעה שבקש אותו רשע לעשות לאותו צדיק כך וכו'. אלא מהכא: °"גם ענוש לצדיק לא טוב" – אין "לא טוב" אלא רע. וכתיב: °"כי לא אל חפץ רשע אתה לא יגורך רע". *צדיק אתה ה', ולא יגור במגורך רע. מאי משמע דהאי חלשיט לישנא דפורא הוא – דכתיב: °"איך נפלת משמים הילל בן שחר נגדעת לארץ חולש על גוים וגו'". אמר רבה בר רב הונא: מלמד שהיה מטיל פור על גדולי מלכות, לידע איזה בן יומו של משכב זכור. וכתיב °"כל מלכי גוים כולם וגו'", אמר רבי יוחנן: שנחו ממשכב זכור. וא"ר יוחנן: כל ימיו של אותו רשע לא נמצא שחוק בפה כל בריה, שנאמר: °"נחה שקטה כל הארץ פצחו רנה" – מכלל דעד השתא לא הוה רנה. ואמר ר' יצחק אמר ר' יוחנן: אסור לעמוד בביתו של אותו רשע, שנא': °"ושעירים ירקדו שם". ואמר רב יהודה אמר רב: בשעה שביקש אותו רשע לעשות לאותו צדיק כך, נמשכה ערלתו שלש מאות אמה, והיתה מחזרת על כל המסיבה כולה, שנאמר: "שבעת קלון מכבוד שתה גם אתה והערל". ערל בגימטריא שלש מאות הוי. ואמר רב יהודה אמר רב: בשעה שירד אותו רשע לגיהנם רעשו כל יורדי גיהנם, אמרו: שמא למשול עליהם הוא בא, או *ליחלות כמותם הוא בא? שנאמר: °"גם אתה חולית כמונו אלינו נמשלת". יצאתה ב"ק ואמרה: °"ממי נעמת רדה והשכבה את ערלים". °"איך שבת נוגש שבתה מדהבה" א"ר יהודה אמר רב: שבתה אומה זו שאמרה

מדוד

תורה אור: הושע ד · מלכים א כב · תהלים קא · חבקוק ב · משלי יז · תהלים ה · ישעיהו יד · שם · שם · שם יג · שם יד · יחזקאל לב · ישעיהו יד

רש"י

וכדברי (בית) הלל. דקיי"ש שמא יוקירו חיטי בהלואת כברות – אף משום רבית: בניו ובני ביתו נמי. ליחוש לרבית וכל הני: להלוות. משלו: בניו ובני ביתו. הסמוכים על שלחנו, דכיון דהכל משלו – אין כאן רבית: להטעימן טעם רבית. שידעו כמה קשה. אלמא: כיון דמשלו הוא – אין כאן איסור רבית. והלכך, גבי מדה ומשקל ומנין נמי, לאו קפידא הוא, אלא להשוותם בלא קנאה: אי הכי מנה גדולה כנגד מנה קטנה נמי. דמוקמינן טעמא לקמן משום קוביא, ואפי' בחול אסור. וכיון דהכל משלו, אמאי אסור להטעימן? טעמא קוביא בעלמא הוא! מאי טעמא מותר. ולא חייש לקוביא: כדרב יהודה אמר רב. דלהטעימן בעלמא הוא: עם אחר לא כדרב יהודה אמר שמואל. דכיון דמקפידין, עוברין משום מדה ומשקל ומנין: משום קוביא. דגזל הוא. דאסמכתא לא קניא, והא אסמכתא, דסמיך על הגורל, אם יפול גורל אמנה הגדולה אזכה בה, ולפיכך תלה עצמו אף לגורל הקטנה על הספק, ואילו יודע מתחלה שכן – לא היה מתרצה: של חול. של קדשים של אתמול: כמריבי כהן. ככהנים אלו, שהם בעלי מריבה: אפי' דחול נמי. לישתרי להו להפים ביו"ט, כי היכי דלא לינצו: זה בכה. אני אפתנו בכה: שבעת קלון. בנבוכדנצר משתעי, שהיה מטיל משכב זכור על המלכים. וכשהגיע יומו של צדקיהו נמשכה ערלתו ג' מאות אמה, והיינו "שבעת קלון": חדא דכוליה קרא בנבוכדנצר כתיב. שפיר מצית לאוקמי כוליה בנבוכדנצר. וה"ק: שתה גם אתה כאותם שהיית מקלה אותן, והערל – והתערל, והתגנה: בשעה שעשה לו כו'. לקמן היא, מדקאמר לאותו צדיק – ש"מ אנוס היה: ענוש לצדיק לא טוב. צדיק המעניש לא טוב, וכיון דאינו טוב – הרי הוא רע: וכתיב לא יגורך רע. אלמא אינו נכנס במחיצתו: חולש על גוים. בנבוכדנצר כתיב: ושעירים ירקדו שם. ולא אנשים, ובשביל הבריות מסתלקין המזיקין, ונמצא מבטל גזירת המלך: המסיבה מלכים שהיו מסובין ויושבין לפניו: גם אתה חולית כמונו אלינו וגו'. ביורדי גיהנם כתיב, דכתיב לעיל מיניה: "שאול מתחת רגזה לך לקראת בואך" וגו' [א]: חולית כמונו אלינו נמשלת. לשון ממשלה: נעמת. סבור אתה להיות בנועם מן האחרים:

תוספות

לפירוש זה דאס הלל לא איירי אלא במקפידין, אם כן אמאי קאמר לעיל לימא מתניתין דלא כהלל – והא הלל במקפידין איירי, ומתניתין דלעיל אתי שפיר כוותיה. דהא רישא באין מקפידין איירי, דקתני "שואל". דאילו למקפידין – אסרינן שאלה, לפי מה שפירש'. להכי נראה לפרש: עוברין משום מדה ומשום משקל – כלומר: קרובין לבא לידי כך שיעברו משום מדה – שע"י שמקפידין זה ע"ז ורגילין ליקח במדה זה מזה – גם ביו"ט יעשו כך. וגם כל בני אדם הוי אסורין בכלי של מדה, כדאמר בבילה (דף כט: ושם). אבל למקפידין נותן הוא עצה שלא ישתתפו, שקרובים הן לבא לידי איסור מדה, וכן לידי איסור משקל, מתוך שרגילים לשקול על ידי הקפדתן גם ביו"ט לא ירגישו, עד שישקלו. ולידי מנין – כשישאל אחד מהן ס' אגוזים יאמר לו: תן לי מ' להשלים ק', כמו שרגילין לעשות. ומשום לווין ופורעין ביו"ט כדאמר לעיל, דלשון הלואה אסור, והם מתוך שמקפידים יזכירו לשון הלואה. לפי שיאמר השואל אם אזכיר לו לשון שאלה משמע דהדרא בעיניה, לכך אומר לשון הלואה. וכדברי הלל אף משום רבית, דכשלוין זה מזה כבר באין לידי רבית, לפי שפעמים שזה משלם יותר, שאע"פ שמקפיד הוא – בוש הוא שלא ישלם כמו שהלוהו, בשביל שההנהו. וכיון שאינו מוחל – הוי רבית. אבל שאר בני אדם מחלי, ולא הוי רבית. והשתא מתני' איירי במקפידין, דסתם שכנים שאינם חברים – מקפידין. ומ"מ דרך שאלה מותר. ומה שדברו כאן על מקפידין – לא אמרינן אלא גבי חבורה שרגילים לישאל זה מזה תדיר, אתי לידי איסור. אבל שכנים שאינן תדירין כל כך לשאול זה מזה – מותרים, ואין לגזור בהם שמא יבאו לידי איסור. ולהכי לא משני: כי אמר מתני' דלא כהלל. דמתניתין איירי כשאין מקפידין, משום דסתמא דמתני' איירי במקפידין, כדפרישית. מ"ר: **מאי** טעמא משום קוביא. היינו כרבי יהודה בשם רבי טרפון, דאמר: אין אחד מהן נזיר, שלא נתנה נזירות אלא להפלאה. וסבירא ליה דלא מהית אינש לספיקא. ולית הלכתא הכי, אלא כאידך דר' יהודה. כדפסקינן בסנהדרין בפרק "זה בורר" (דף כה. ושם). מ"ר:

***מטילין** חלשים על הקדשים ביו"ט. תימה: דאמר בפרק ב' דקדושין (דף נג. ושם) דאין חולקין זבחים כנגד זבחים ומנחה כנגד מנחה, ומפיק לה מ"לכל בני אהרן תהיה איש כאחיו". ועוד: דפריך התם והצנועים מושכין ידיהם והגרגרנים חולקין, מאי חולקין – חוטפין כו'! ואומר רבי: דאין מועלת בהם חלוקה וגורל – שיהא ממונו לקדש בו את האשה ולהוציאו בדיינים, אבל מ"מ מטילין היו חלשין לתת לכל א' חלקו, פן יריבו ביחד. כדכתיב (הושע ד): "ועמך כמריבי כהן". והא דמשני התם: חולקין לאו דוקא אלא חוטפין. ולא משני הכי – משו' דחולקין משמע כופין לחלוק ע"כ, מחמת שחוטפין אותן שאין שלהם. מ"ר:

מה

עין משפט נר מצוה

יט א מיי' פכ"ג מהלכו' שבת הלכה יז סמג שם טוש"ע או"ח סימן שכב סעיף ו:

כ ב מיי' שם (ופ"ו מהל' גזילה ואבידה הל"ו) סמג שם ועשין ריד ולאוין עג טור שו"ע או"ח שם וטוש"ע חו"מ סימן שע סעיף ב:

כא ג ד מיי' פ"ד מהל' י"ט הלכה כ סמג לאוין עה:

[נ"ל ברה ומשום שאביו לא היה הגון לפיכך לא הזכירו. כ"כ רש"י בעירובין פ. ד"ה בריה]

[נ"ל ברה]

[שייך לעיל קמח: במשנה]

רב נסים גאון

פרק שואל. **וכדברי** הלל אף משום ריבית הוא שהוקדם זכרו בראש הפרק (דף קמח) וכן היה הלל אומר לא תלוה אשה ככר לחברתה עד שתעשנו דמים שמא יוקרו חטים או יוזלו ונמצאו באות לידי ריבית ועיקר זה במשנה בפרק אי זהו נשך (דף עה):

רבינו חננאל

ביתו אין אחרים לא. משמיה דר' יהודה אמר שמואל דאמר בני חבורה המקפידין זה על זה פי' שמדקדקין זה על זה שאומר אחד לחבירו המנה שלך שלקחתה גדולה תן לי אני כמותה והוא שוקלה בידו. ואם היה דג אומר לו לקחת דג או כדומה לו שהוא ארוך זרת צריך לתת לו (שמדתו) [תמורתו] זרת דגים או קישואין או אבטיחים וכדומה להן ואם היו אגוזים ושקדים וכדומה להן אומר לקחת עשרים או אומר לו בעת (שניטלו) [נוטלו] המתן עד שאשקול המנה ועד שאמדוד אורך הדגים והקישואים ואמנה הביצים והאגוזים והשקדים שאתה נוטל שאטול גם במשקלם וכמדתם וכמניינם. וכדברי ב"ה שאומרים לא תלוה אשה מחברתה ככרות כו': ומטילין חלשים כו'. פירוש מטילין גורלות אבל לא על המנות של חול ביו"ט: **נבוכדנאצר** אנס צדקיהו בעברה וכיון שנענש נ"נ ע"י צדקיהו נענש גם הוא שנאמר שבעת קלון מכבוד זה נבוכדנאצר שתה גם אתה והערל זה צדקיהו ואמרינן האי קרא כוליה בנ"נ כתיב ועוד צדקיהו צדיקא מאי הוה ליה למעבד. אמר רב יהודה אמר רב בשעה שעשה אותו רשע לאותו צדיק כן נמשכה

מסורת הש"ס

[נ"ל הילל]

ב"מ עה. [ושם מסיק הש"ס ולאו מילתא היא כו' ויסוב נכון על קושיא זו ביאר הט"ז באו"ח סימן שכ"ב ס"ק ד]

סנהדרין פט. קב:

[חגיגה יב: סוטה מב. סנהדרין קה.]

הגהות הב"ח

(א) רש"י ד"ה גם אתה וכו' וגו' חלית כמונו או אלינו כנ"ל והד"א:

גליון הש"ס

גמ' כל שחבירו נענש על ידו. עי' ב"ב דף כב ע"א תוס' ד"ה אנא ענשתיה:

מדוד והבא. ואיכא דאמרי: שאמרה "מאד מאד הביא בלא מדה". "ורבו יתירה הוספת לי". אמר רב יהודה אמר רב ירמיה בר אבא: מלמד שרכב על ארי זכר, וקשר תנין בראשו, לקיים מה שנאמר "וגם את חית השדה נתתי לו לעבדו".§

מתני' לא ישכור אדם פועלים בשבת, ולא יאמר אדם לחבירו לשכור לו פועלים. *אין מחשיכין על התחום לשכור לו פועלים ולהביא פירות, אבל מחשיך הוא לשמור, ומביא פירות בידו. כלל אמר אבא שאול: כל שאני זכאי באמירתו - רשאי אני להחשיך עליו.§

גמ' (פשיטא) מ"ש הוא ומ"ש חבירו? אמר רב פפא: חבר גוי. מתקיף לה רב אשי: *אמירה לגוי שבות! אלא אמר רב אשי: אפילו תימא חבירו ישראל, הא קמ"ל: לא יאמר אדם לחבירו "שכור לי פועלים", אבל אומר אדם לחבירו "הנראה שתעמוד עמי לערב"? ומתני' מני - כרבי יהושע בן קרחה. דתניא: *לא יאמר אדם לחבירו "הנראה שתעמוד עמי לערב"? רבי יהושע בן קרחה אומר: אומר אדם לחבירו "הנראה שתעמוד עמי לערב"? אמר רבה בר בר חנה אמר רבי יוחנן: הלכה כרבי יהושע בן קרחה. ואמר רבה בר בר חנה אמר רבי יוחנן: מ"ט דרבי יהושע בן קרחה - דכתיב: "ממצוא חפצך ודבר דבר", *דיבור - אסור, הרהור - מותר. רמי ליה רב אחא בר רב הונא לרבא: מי אמר ר' יוחנן דיבור אסור הרהור מותר, *אלמא: הרהור לאו כדיבור דמי. *והאמר רבה בר בר חנה אמר רבי יוחנן: בכל מקום מותר להרהר - חוץ מבית המרחץ ומבית הכסא! שאני התם, דבעינן "והיה מחניך קדוש", וליכא. הכא נמי כתיב: "ולא יראה בך ערות דבר"! ההוא מיבעי ליה לכדרב יהודה, *דאמר רב יהודה: גוי ערום אסור לקרות קריאת שמע כנגדו. מאי איריא גוי, אפי' ישראל נמי! לא מיבעיא קאמר; לא מיבעיא ישראל דאסור, אבל גוי כיון דכתיב ביה: "אשר בשר חמורים בשרם" - אימא שפיר דמי, קמ"ל. ואימא הכי נמי! אמר קרא: "וערות אביהם לא ראו". ודיבור מי אסיר?! *והא רב חסדא ורב המנונא דאמרי תרווייהו: חשבונות של מצוה - מותר לחשבן בשבת. וא"ר אלעזר: פוסקים צדקה לעניים בשבת. וא"ר יעקב בר אידי אמר רבי יוחנן: מפקחין פיקוח נפש ופיקוח רבים בשבת, והולכין לבתי כנסיות לפקח על עסקי רבים בשבת. וא"ר שמואל בר נחמני א"ר *יוחנן: הולכין לטרטיאות ולקרקסאות ולבסילקאות לפקח על עסקי רבים בשבת. ותנא דבי מנשה: משדכין על התינוקות ליארס בשבת, ועל התינוק ללמדו ספר וללמדו אומנות. *אמר קרא: "ממצוא חפצך ודבר דבר", *חפציך - אסורים, חפצי שמים - מותרין. א"ר יהודה אמר שמואל: חשבונות של [*מלך] ושל מה בכך - מותר לחשבן בשבת. תנ"ה: *חשבונות שעברו ושעתידין להיו' - אסור לחשבן, של *)מלך ושל

*) בס"י מה לך

רש"י

מדוד. מעות ודינרי זהב, והבא: ורבו יתירה הוספת לי. לאחר שהיה ז' שנים בהמה וחזר למלכותו, היה מתפאר בכך. ומהו התוספת - שקשר תנין גדול, נחש גדול, בראשו של ארי כמין אפסר: **מתני'** לא ישכור אדם פועלים. דכתיב (ישעיה נח): "ממצוא חפצך": ולא יאמר לחבירו כו'. בגמרא פריך: פשיטא, כיון דהוא אסור, חבירו נמי אסור, דהא ישראל הוא, והשולחו עובר משום "לפני עור לא תתן מכשול": אין מחשיכין על התחום. לקרב עצמו בשבת עד סוף התחום ולהחשיך שם, שיהא קרוב למקום הפועלים או לפרדס להביא פירות. דכל דבר שאסור לעשותו בשבת - אסור להחשיך עליו: אבל מחשיך הוא. להיות קרוב לבא לשמור פירותיו וזה דבר המותר בשבת לשמור פירותיו, אם היו בתוך תחומו: ומביא פירות בידו. הואיל ועיקר מחשבתו לא היה לכך: כלל אמר אבא שאול. נותן היה כלל בדבר זה להוסיף דברים אחרים כיוצא בו, ולקמיה מפרש לאתויי מאי: כל שאני זכאי באמירתו. שאני רשאי לאומרו לחבירו או לגוי בשבת לעשות למוצאי שבת - רשאי אני להחשיך עליו: **גמ'** מאי שנא כו'. ופשיטא, דכיון דאמר לא ישכור - ה"ה לא יאמר לחבירו, דהא ישראל הוא כמותו ולא מצי לאוגרינהו: אמירה לגוי שבות. וכבר סתמה רבי למתני'*: גוי שבא לכבות, אין אומרים לו כבה: הא קמ"ל. משנה יתירה, בהדיא הוא דלא לימא ליה, אבל סתמא - שרי ליה למימר: הנראה. עכשיו נראה אם תעמוד עמי לערב, אם תבא אלי לכשתחשך. ושניהן יודעין שעל מנת לשוכרו לפעולתו הוא מזהירו. וכיון דלא מפרש בהדיא - שרי, כדמפרש טעמא לקמן: דבור - אסור, הרהור - מותר: מותר להרהר. בדברי תורה: והיה מחניך קדוש. ולא כתיב ביה דבר, אלא: מקום חנייתך תהא בקדושה. וטעמא - משום דישראל מהרהרין תמיד בדברי תורה: ערות דבר. אלמא: לא אסיר ליה אלא בשעת דבור: ההיא כדרב יהודה. כלומר: לעולם "והיה מחניך קדוש" משום הרהור תורה, ואפי' אין דבור. "ולא יראה בך ערות דבר" - במילתא אחריתי מיירי, דאסור בשעת הדבור ולא בשעת הרהור, כגון להסתכל בערוה: גוי ערום. כ"ש ישראל, כדמפרש ואזיל: אימא שפיר דמי. דכבהמה בעלמא הוא: וערות אביהם. אלמא: ערוה היא דבן נח: ודבור מי אסור והא אמר רב חסדא כו'. וכל הני דבור הוא: פקוח נפש. בדבר שיש בו סכנה. פקוח = דיקומבימונ"ט: ופקוח דרבים. כגון לרשות: טרטייאות וקרקסאות ובסילקאות. מיני פלטין הן, ששם נאספו לבית הוועד: ללמדו אומנות. דהא נמי מצוה היא, דכל שאינו מלמדו אומנות מלמדו לסטות. ומצוה ילפינן מקרא בקדושין ב"האשה ניקנית" (ד' ל:): של מלך. של עצה, שאינו שלו ואין צריך בכך. כגון, הרוצה לבנות בית, כך וכך צריך להוציא בו. ול"נ: כמו מה לך. מה לך ולחשבונות הללו, הרי אין צורך בהן לא לך ולא לאחר. כגון ההיא דפרישית: ושל

תוספות

מה לי הוא ומה לי חבירו. ואם תאמר: ונימא דחבירו היינו דאמר ליה שכור לי פועלים למחר! וי"ל: דא"כ מאי איריא חבירו - אפי' הוא נמי לא מצי למימר אשכור פועלים למחר. דעד כאן לא קאמר רב יהודה אמר שמואל מותר לאדם לומר לחבירו לכרך פלוני אני הולך למחר - אלא משום דשאם יש בורגנין הולך, הא לאו הכי - לא: **ורבי** יהושע בן קרחה היא. יש מפרש דר"ע קרוי קרחה, שהיה קרח. כדתניא בפרק בתרא דבכורות (דף נח. ושם), אמר בן עזאי: כל חכמי ישראל דומין לפני כקליפת השום, חוץ מן הקרח הזה. ואומר שזה היה ר"ע, והיה לו בן ששמו יהושע, כדאמר בפרק קמא דשבועות*: א"ל ר' יהושע בנו של ר"ע לר"ע. ואין נראה לר"ת; דמה שקראו בן עזאי לר"ע קרח בבדיחותא בעלמא - אין לנו לקרותו כן כל שעה, דלשון גנות הוא. שנא': "עלה קרח עלה קרח" (מלכים ב ב). ואמרינן נמי לקמן (דף קנב.), אמר ליה ההוא צדוקי לר' יהושע בן קרחה: מהכא לקרחינאה כמה הוי? הרי שהיה מגנה אותו על שהיה קרח. ועוד, אמרי' במגילה פרק בתרא (דף כח.), שאל רבי את רבי יהושע בן קרחה: במה הארכת ימים כו'? א"ל: רבי, ברכני. א"ל: יהי רצון שתגיע לחצי ימי. ואי ר' יהושע בן קרחה בנו של ר"ע - והא קיימא לן* דלא נשא ר"ע בת כלבא שבוע עד שקיבל עליו לעסוק בתורה, ואז היה בן מ', דתניא בסוף ספרי: מ' שנה שימש ת"ח, מ' שנה פירנס את ישראל, וכל ימיו ק"כ שנים. ואמרי' בקידושין פרק בתרא (דף עב.): עד שלא מת ר"ע נולד רבי. ואפילו נולד ר' יהושע בשנה ראשונה שנשאה - לא נשאר כי אם פ' שנים מר"ע. ורבי יהושע בשעה שבירך את רבי היה בן ק"מ שנים לכל הפחות, שבפחות מע' שנה לא היה מברכו, ואז היה רבי לכל הפחות בן ס' - וא"כ לא היה מברכו רק מי' שנים! ועוד נראה שלא נשאה עד שעסק בי רב תרי סרי ותרי סרי שנין, נמצא כשהיה רבי יהושע בן קרחה בן ק"מ - היה רבי יותר מחצי ימיו! לכך נראה לר"ת דלא ר"ע היה, אלא איניש אחרינא היה ששמו קרחה. וקרחה הוא שם אדם כמו קרח, ונולד הרבה קודם ר' יהושע בנו של ר"ע*. מ"ר: **אומר** אדם לחבירו הנראה שתעמוד עמי לערב. י"א: דדווקא לחבירו, אבל לגוי - אסור, לפי שהוא(א) [עושה] לדעת אותה [אמירה]. ואינו נראה, דהא שרינן ליה הכא משו' דדבור אסור והרהור מותר, [א"כ] ל"ש גוי ל"ש ישראל. מ"ר: **ודיבור** מי אסור. פי': מן התורה. דהא מדשרינן דיבור של מצוה - מכלל דמדאורייתא שרי: **ואמר** ר"א פוסקין צדקה לעניים בשבת. וא"ת: מה צריך לאתויי(ב) הא ה"ל לאתויי מילתייהו דבית הלל [בפי"ז] (בתוספתא), דתני: אין פוסקים צדקה אפי' להשיא יתום ויתומה, ואין משדכין על התינוקות ליארס בו - דברי בית שמאי. ובית הלל מתירין. וי"ל: דניחא ליה לאתויי מילתא דרבי אלעזר, דמהתם לא הוה שמעינן פסיקת צדקה לעניים. דהא לא שרי בית הלל אלא להשיא יתום ויתומה: ואין

[דף ו.]

[כתובות סג. ועיין שם ובאבות דר"נ פ"ו]

[וע"ע תוס' בכורות נח. ד"ה חוץ ותוס' ב"ב קיג. ד"ה ומטו ותוס' פסחים קיב. ד"ה לוה]

רבינו חננאל

נמשכה ערלתו וכו': [מתני'] לא ישכור פועלים בשבת ולא יאמר לחבירו שכור לי פועלים: **גמ'** ואקשינן עלה מ"ש הוא ומ"ש חבירו. ובא רב פפא לאוקמיה למתני' בחבירו גוי. רב אשי אמר אפילו תימא בחבירו ישראל הא קמ"ל דלשכור פועלים הוא דלא יאמר לו אבל אומר לו הנראה שתעמוד עמי לערב כלומר אסור שיאמר לו לערב לך לשכור לי פועלים או כיוצא בו. אבל אם יאמר לו הא נראה שתעמוד עמי לערב ובדעתו שיאמר לו לערב לך לשכור לי פועלים או עשה לי מלאכה כך וכך מותר כר' יהושע בן קרחה. ואמר ר' יוחנן הלכתא כר' יהושע בן קרחה ודייק ר' יוחנן ואמר טעמיה דר' יהושע בן קרחה דיבור בפירוש' אסור אבל הרהור מותר דכתיב ממצוא חפצך ודבר דבר. ואקשינן עליה והא הוא דאמר בכל מקום מותר להרהר חוץ ממרחץ ובית הכסא כו' ואמאי לא אמרינן הכא נמי הרהור מותר. ומפרקינן האי קרא מיבעי ליה לאסור אפילו ערותו של גוי דאשכחנן קרא דאמר וערות אביהם לא ראו. ואקשי' תוב ודבור מי אסור והביאו ה' שמועות אחת שאפילו דבור אמ' מותר בשבת. ואלו הן חשבונות ופוסקין צדקה לעניים ומפקחין פיקוח רבים. והולכין לבתי כנסיות ולבתי מדרשות לפקח על עסקי רבים והולכין לבתי טאטראות ולבתי קרקסאות לפקח על עסקי רבים. ותנא משדכין על התינוקות ליארס. ועל התינוק ללמדו ספר וללמדו אמנות. ומפרקי' אלא אמר קרא ממצוא חפצך ודבר דבר חפצך אסורין כדבור חפצי שמים מותרין. ואלו כולן חפצי שמים הן: חשבונות של מלך. פירוש מילך אורחים ובא הלך לאיש העשיר כלומר מותר לאדם לחשב אורחים הקרואים להסב אצלו בסעודה וכדתנן מונה אדם את אורחיו ואת פרפריותיו פי' חשבונות של מה בכך כמו שיחשב אדם חשבון כגון חיילות המלך כך וכך אלף וכיוצא בו אומ' לו מה בכך. כלומר מה הנאה יש לך ומה צורך לך בזה כגון אלו מותר בשבת. וזה שאומרים מחשבין חשבונות

עין משפט נר מצוה

כב א מיי' פכ"ג מהל' שבת הלכה יב סמג לאוין סה טור שו"ע או"ח סימן שז סעיף ב:

כג ב ג מיי' פכ"ד שם הלכה ג סמג שם טור שו"ע או"ח סימן שו סעיף א וסי' שז סעיף ח:

כד ד מיי' פ"ו שם הל"א סמג שם:

כה ה מיי' פכ"ד שם הל"ד וסמג שם טור שו"ע או"ח סימן שז סעיף ז:

כו ו מיי' פ"ג מהלכות ק"ש הלכה טז סמג עשין יח טור שו"ע או"ח סימן עה סעיף ד:

כז ז ח ט י מיי' פכ"ד מהלכות שבת הל"ה סמג לאוין סה טוש"ע או"ח סימן שו סעיף ו:

כח כ מיי' פכ"ד מהל' שבת הל"א סמג שם טור שו"ע או"ח סימן שז סעיף ז:

מסורת הש"ס

ורבו יתירה הוספת לי - דניאל ד; וגם את חית השדה - ירמיהו כז; ממצוא חפצך - ישעיהו נח; והיה מחניך קדוש - דברים כג; ולא יראה בך ערות דבר - שם; אשר בשר חמורים בשרם - יחזקאל כג; וערות אביהם לא ראו - בראשית ט.

[עי' תוס' לקמן ע"ב ד"ה ואין]

[עירובין סז: גיטין ח: ב"ק פ: ב"מ ל.]

[לעיל קכא.]

לעיל קיג:

[ברכות כ:]

שם כד: לעיל מ: קידושין לג. ע"ז מד: זבחים קב.

ברכות כה: ע"ש

[נ"ל יונתן]

[פסחים ח. יומא פב.]

[כתובות ה.]

[תוספ' פי"ח]

[נ"ל מילך פי' אורחי' כדכתי' ויבא הלך כלומר מותר אדם לחשב אורחיו הקרואים. ערוך ערך חשב]

לעיל קיג.

הגהות הב"ח

(א) תוס' ד"ה אומר וכו' לפי שהוא רוצה לדעת אותה מלאכה ואינו: (ב) ד"ה ואמר רבי אלעזר וכו' וא"ת מה צריך לאתויי מילתא דרבי אלעזר ה"ל לאתויי:

גליון הש"ס

גמ' חבר גוי. עי' סוכה דף לט ע"א תוס' ד"ה הלוקח ועי' מג"א סימן תק ס"ק ג:

גי' רש"ל דאמר

עין משפט
נר מצוה

[שייך לע"א במשנה]

כט א טור שו"ע או"ח סימן שז סעיף ז:

ל ב ג מיי' פכ"ד מהלכו' שבת הלכה ג סמג שם טוש"ע או"ח סימן שז סעיף ח ט:

לא ד מיי' שם הלכה ה סמג שם טור שו"ע או"ח סימן שו סעיף ג:

[בש"ס ליתא אבל בעין יעקב מצאתי ע"ש]

לב ה מיי' פכ"ט מהל' שבת הלכה ה סמג עשין כט טור שו"ע או"ח סימן רצט סעיף י:

לג ו מיי' שם הלכה ופ"ב מהלכות תפלה הלכה יב סמג שם טוש"ע או"ח סי' רצד סעיף א:

לד ז מיי' פכ"ט מהל' שבת הל"ג סמג שם טוש"ע או"ח סימן רצט סעיף י:

מסורת הש"ס

***ואין** מחשיכין על התחום לשכור פועלים ולהביא פירות. משמע דוקא על התחום, אבל בתוך התחום – מחשיכין לשכור פועלי' ולהביא פירו'. וקשה לרבי: דבסוף פ' "בכל מערבין" (עירובין דל"ח:) תניא: לא יהלך אדם לתוך שדהו לידע מה צריכה. כיוצא בו, לא יטייל אדם על פתח מדינה כדי שיכנס למרחץ מיד! ואומר רבי: דהתם מינכרא מילתא, דאינו מטייל אלא ליכנס למרחץ מיד אחר השבת, שעל פתח מדינה רגילים להיות מרחצאות. כדאמרי' בפ"ק *דמגילה (דף ו:): (ג) ה' מאות מעלות עשן חוץ לחומה. אבל הכא אין הוכחה כ"כ בתוך התחום המחשיך לשכור פועלים ולהביא פירות, וכי האי גוונא משני התם. מ"ר:

אבל מחשיך הוא לשמור ומביא פירות בידו. מתוך פירוש הקונטרס משמע לשמור חוץ לתחום. וכן משמע פשט המשנה. וקשה לרבי מהא דאמר שמואל בגמ': מותר לאדם לומר לחבירו לכרך פלוני אני הולך למחר. ופריך, תנן: אין מחשיכין על התחום לשכור פועלים כו'. והשתא מתניתין גופיה תיקשי ליה, דמוכחא מילתא כוותיה דשמואל, מדקתני בסיפא: כלל אמר אבא שאול, כל שאני זכאי באמירתו – יכול אני להחשיך עליו. וקא מפרש בגמ' דמה שמותר לומר – מותר להחשיך. וא"כ, מדשרינן להחשיך לשמור חוץ לתחום – אלמא שרי למימר חוץ לתחום אני הולך למחר, דהא בהא תליא, והיינו כשמואל. ואיני יודע מאי קשיא; דאי לאו דשמואל – מתני' אתיא שפיר, דה"א: אין לך דבר שלא יהא מותר לאדם לומר על עצמו, ואפי' אשכור פועלים למחר או אבנה בנין זה יכול לומר בשבת, דהוה אמינא דווקא לחבירו אסור לומר שכור לי פועלים למחר – דמהני אמירתו. אבל על עצמו יכול לומר כל מה שירצה, דלא מהני אמירתו. וכי תלי אבא שאול ההחשכה(ג) – ה"מ באמירה לחבירו, דיש אסורה ויש מותרת. אבל אם איתא לדשמואל – פריך שפיר, דאסר כל אמירות אפילו על עצמו, אלא דווקא לכרך פלוני אני הולך למחר. משום טעמא דשאם יש שם בורגנין – הולך. והשתא פריך: כיון דאי לאו האי טעמא הוה אסרת ליה, אלא משום האי טעמא דווקא שרית ליה, א"כ מתני' נמי תשתרי להביא פירות, שאם יש מחיצות מביא. נ"ל:

לכרך פלוני אני הולך. תימה: מאי איריא הוא, אפילו לחבירו נמי יכול לומר: לך לי לכרך פלוני למחר מהאי טעמא, דקאמר *מדשרי שמואל לקמן לומר לחבירו שמור לי פירות שבתחומך אפילו בשבת – כ"ש שיכול לומר שמור לי למחר. ואין לפרש דשאני התם שהן בתחומו, אבל אין יכול לומר לחבירו שמור לי פירות שחוץ לתחומך – דנראה הוא שאפילו זה יכול לומר, מכיון שמותר להחשיך. וי"ל: דלא נקט שמואל דוקא לכרך פלוני אני הולך – דהוא הדין לחבירו יכול לומר: לך לי לכרך פלוני למחר:

בשלמא קש במחובר משכחת לה. ה"נ הו"מ למימר מטעם מוקצה, דהא אינו ראוי למאכל בהמה, כדאמר לעיל (דף קמא.): הקש שע"ג המטה לא ינענעו כו'. אלא רבותא קאמר, דאפילו במחובר משכחת לה: **במחובר** משכחת לה. אומר רבי: דלאו משום תלישה נקט לה, דאע"ג שמחובר לארץ – אין בו איסור תלישה, כיון שיבש אינו יונק מן הארץ, כדמוכח בחולין פרק "העור והרוטב" (דף קכז: ושם), דאמר: תאנים שלמקו באביהן – מטמאין טומאת אוכלין, והתולש ממנה בשבת – חייב חטאת. דווקא למקו, אבל יבשו – לא. וכן משמע בכל הסוגיא דיבשו הן ועוקציהן – מטמא טומאת אוכלין, ואין דינו כלל כמחובר. והא דקאמר הכא: במחובר משכחת לה – היינו משום איסור "יפוי קרקע", כדאמר לעיל: התולש עולשין בשבת חייב חטאת, בפרק "הבונה" (לעיל דף קג.). והא דפריך בפרק "המוצא תפילין" (עירובין דף ק:) אאילן יבש: הא קא נתרי פירי, משמע שיש ביבש איסור תלישה – אומר רבי: דמיירי התם ביבשו הן ולא עוקציהן: **בתיבנא** סריא. והא דאמר לקמן פרק "מי שהחשיך" (דף קנה:) מפרכין תבן ואספסתא לפני בהמה ומוקי לה בתבנא סריא, משמע דחזי לבהמה! אומר רבי: דמיירי כגון דלא סרי' כולי האי: **אלא** מת מאי ניהו להביא לו ארון ותכריכין. תימה: אמאי לא קאמר למיגז ליה אסא שהיו רגילין להביא אסא למת כדאשכחן בנדה (דף לז.) דשוור אסא מערסא לערסא! וי"ל: ע"כ צ"ל ארון ותכריכין, כדקתני במתני' בהדיא. מ"ר:

ושל מה בכך – מותר לחושבן. ורמינהו: חושבין חשבונות שאינן צריכין, ואין מחשבין חשבונות שצריכין בשבת. כיצד, אומר אדם לחבירו: כך וכך פועלים(א) הוצאתי על שדה זו, כך וכך דינרין הוצאתי על דירה זו. אבל לא יאמר לו: כך וכך הוצאתי, וכך וכך אני עתיד להוציא! ולטעמיך, קשיא לך היא גופא! אלא, [א]הא דאיכא אגרא דאגירא גביה, הא – דליכא אגרא דאגירא גביה.§ "אין מחשיכין".§ תנו רבנן: מעשה בחסיד אחד שנפרצה לו פרץ בתוך שדהו, ונמלך עליה לגודרה, ונזכר ששבת הוא, *ונמנע אותו חסיד ולא גדרה. ונעשה לו נס, ועלתה בו צלף וממנה היתה פרנסתו ופרנסת אנשי ביתו. א"ר יהודה אמר שמואל: [ב]מותר לאדם לומר לחבירו "לכרך פלוני אני הולך למחר", שאם יש בורגנין – הולך. תנן: אין מחשיכין על התחום לשכור פועלים ולהביא פירות. בשלמא לשכור פועלים – דבשבת לא מצי אגר, אלא להביא פירות – לימא: שאם יש שם מחיצות – מביא! [ג]משכחת לה בפירות המחוברים. והתני ר' אושעיא: אין מחשיכין על התחום להביא תבן וקש; בשלמא קש – משכחת לה במחובר. אלא תבן, היכי משכחת לה? בתיבנא סריא. ת"ש: *[ד]מחשיכין על התחום לפקח על עסקי כלה ועל עסקי המת. על עסקי כלה ומת – אין, על עסקי אחר – לא. בשלמא אחר דומיא דכלה משכחת לה: למיגזא ליה אסא. אלא מת מאי ניהו? להביא לו ארון ותכריכין – וקתני: מת – אין, אבל אחר – לא. ואמאי? לימא: שאם יש שם מחיצו' – מביא! מת נמי משכחת לה – *למיגזא ליה גלימא.§ "אבל מחשיכין".§ ואע"ג דלא אבדיל?! והאמר רבי אליעזר בן אנטיגנוס משום רבי אליעזר בן יעקב: [ה]אסור לו לאדם שיעשה חפציו קודם שיבדיל! וכי תימא – דאבדיל בתפלה, והאמר רב יהודה אמר שמואל: *[ו]המבדיל בתפלה צריך שיבדיל על הכוס. וכי תימא – דאבדיל על הכוס, כוס בשדה מי איכא?! תרגמא רבי נתן בר אמי קמיה דרבא: בין הגיתות שנו. א"ל ר' אבא לרב אשי: [ז]במערבא אמרינן הכי: "המבדיל בין קודש לחול", ועבדינן צורכין. אמר רב אשי: כי הוינא בי רב כהנא הוה אמר: "המבדיל בין קודש לחול" ומסלתינן סילתי.§ כלל אמר אבא שאול כל שאני וכו'.§ (איבעיא להו): אבא שאול אהייא? אילימא ארישא קאי "אין מחשיכין על התחום לשכור פועלים להביא פירות", האי

לקמן קנז.

ושל מה בכך. כגון שכבר היו לצורך, אלא שעברו. כגון: כך וכך הוצאתי בבנין זה: חשבונות שעברו. לקמן מוקי לה דלא עברו לגמרי, שעדיין שכר הפועלים עליו שלא נתנו להן. ושל מה בכך – שעברו לגמרי, ואין שכר פועלים עליו: כך וכך הוצאתי. אלמא: עברו – מותרין: תקשי לך היא גופא. ברייתא קמייתא רישא קתני שעברו אסורין, וסיפא קתני של מה בכך מותרין – דהיינו עברו: צלף. אילן גדול הוא, ובעל ענפים הרבה, ושלשה מיני אוכל יש בפירותיו: אביונות קפריסין ולולבין: שאם יש בורגנין. מע' אמה לע' אמה – הולך אפי' בשבת, שהכל חשוב כעיר אחת, וכל העיר כד' אמות, כדאמרינן בעירובין (דף נה.). וכיון דהוא דבר שיש לו היתר על ידי תקנה בשבת – מותר לאומרו אפילו במקום שאין שם היתר: המחוברים. שא"א לתקנן בשבת ע"י שום תקנה: קש. זנבות השבולים, אסטרלי"א: בתיבנא סריא. שאפי' יש מחיצות אינו מביא, משום דמוקצה הוא: על עסקי כלה ומת אין. דאפלי שמים הן. אבל על עסקי אחר, אפי' דומיא דכלה – לא: בשלמא אחר דומיא דכלה משכחת לה. דאסור להחשיך, כגון לחתוך מן המחובר: למיגז לה אסא. דעבדו לה גננא דאסא לכלתא: אלא עסקי מת מאי היא. הבאה דארון ותכריכין, ואמאי לאחר לא? לימא: הואיל ואם יש שם מחיצות מביא: למיגז ליה גלימא. לתקן לו תכריכין, דאין היתר לדבר היום כלל: ואע"ג דלא אבדיל. אסיפא דמתני' מתמה, דקתני ומביא פירות בידו לקוצצן מן המחובר בלא הבדלה: בין הגיתות שנו. דאיכא כוס בשדה: המבדיל בין קודש לחול. להיכרא בעלמא, ללוות את המלך: ועבדינן צורכין. ואחר כך אנו מברכין על הכוס ברכה גמורה דהבדלה. וכ"ש דאי אבדיל בתפלה מותר לעשות צרכיו, וחוזר ומבדיל על הכוס: ומסלתינן סילתי. חוטבין עצים: אהייא. קאי, ומשוי כללא: אי נימא ארישא. דקתני ת"ק לאיסורא, וקאתי אבא שאול לשווייה בה כללא. א"כ דכללא לאיסורא, ה"ל למימר בהדיא: כל שאינו זכאי באמירה, כגון [illegible] – אינו רשאי להחשיך, מיבעי ליה: אלא לי פועלים או הבא לי פירות למוצאי שבת

רבינו חננאל

חשבונות שאין צריכין ואין מחשבין חשבונות שצריכין. כיצד אומר אדם לחבירו כך וכך פועלין כך וכך דינרין הוצאתי על שדה זו. אבל לא יאמר כך הוצאתי וכך אני עתיד להוציא. ואוקימנא אם נשאר עליו שכירות במה שעבד אסור לומר לו ואפילו כך הוצאתי שרצונו ליחשב ולידע סכום הנשאר עליו והן חשבונות שצריכין ואסור. אמר רב יהודה אמר שמואל מותר לאדם לומר לחבירו לכרך פלוני אני הולך למחר שאם יש בורגנין הולך אפילו בשבת. תנן אין מחשיכין על התחום לשכור פועלין ולהביא פירות הדא משנה היא וקשיא אקשיאו בהא. ומקשינן בשלמא לשכור פועלין היינו טעמא דאין מחשיכין על התחום ובשבת אסור לאוגורי פועלין אלא פירות נימא שאם יש מחיצות מותר להביאו ומותר למחשיך ולהביאם. ומפרקינן הא דתני אין מחשיכין להביא פירות הפירות מחוברין שאסו' לחותכן בשבת ועוד אקשינן מדתני ר' אושעיא ומפרקינן בתיבנא חדיא דלא חזי ותוב אמרינן ת"ש מחשיכין על התחום לפקח על עסקי כלה ועל עסקי המת כו'. ומפרקינן לפקח על עסקי כלה למיגז לה אסא לבי גננא על עסקי המת נמי למיגר ליה גלימא לתפור לו תכריכין והללו דמשום מצוה התירו רבנן. הא אחר כגון דברים הללו אסור. אבל מחשיך הוא לשמור ומביא פירות בידו ואקשינן ואע"ג דלא אבדיל כלומר עושה מלאכה קודם הבדלה והאמר ר' אלעזר וכו' אסור לעשות מלאכה קודם הבדלה. ואם יש לומר זה שמביא פירות התפלל הבדיל בתפלתו והאמר שמואל המבדיל בתפלה צריך שיבדיל על הכוס ואוקימנא מן הגיתות שנו. כלומר בשעת הגיתות מצוי בשדה בימי הבציר יין והבדיל על הכוס. וסלקא שמעתא שאסור לעשות מלאכה עד שהבדיל ואפילו לא אמר אלא המבדיל בין קודש לחול דיו. דהא רב אשי דהוא בתרא אמר כי הוינן בי רב כהנא הוה אמרינן המבדיל בין קודש לחול ואפכינן סלתי כלומר היינו מתעסקין במלאכה ולא [בא] רב אשי למעט אלא שאינו צריך לומר הבדלות. כאשר חלקו בפרק ערבי פסחים אבל צריך להזכיר ברכה בשם ומלכות דלית גרעה מברכת הפירות וברכת המצות. וכן הלכה: כלל אמר אבא שאול. כל שאני זכאי באמירתו רשאי אני להחשיך עליו. והוצרכנו לדקדק לידע באיזה בבא דמתניתין אמר אבא שאול כלל

[עי' בט"ז סי' ש"ז ס"ק י"ד פירוש על זה]

הגהות הב"ח

(א) גמ' כך וכך פועלים השכרתי על שדה: (ב) תום' ד"ה ואין וכו' כדאמרינן פרק קמא דמגילה שלשת אלפים בי בני היה בו ולכל אחד וא' ה' מאות חלונות מעלות עשן: (ג) ד"ה אבל וכו' וכי תלי אבא שאול ההחשכה באמירה ה"מ:

ביצה ו. [ערוך גרס למיגד פי' לחתוך וי"א לתפור]

[ברכות לג. ע"ש פסחים קה: ע"ש וקף קז.]

ועוד מדשרי כנ"ל

האי "כל שאני זכאי באמירתו רשאי אני בחשיכתו"? "כל שאיני זכאי באמירתו איני רשאי בחשיכתו" מיבעי ליה! אלא אסיפא קאי: "אבל מחשיך הוא לשמור ומביא פירות בידו", האי "כל שאני זכאי בחשיכתו רשאי אני באמירתו" מיבעי ליה! לעולם אסיפא קאי, ואבא שאול אהא קאי; דאמר רב יהודה אמר שמואל: [א]מותר לאדם לומר לחבירו: שמור לי פירות שבתחומך, ואני אשמור לך פירות שבתחומי. וקאמר אבא שאול לת"ק: מי לא מודית דמותר אדם לומר לחבירו "שמור לי פירות שבתחומך ואני אשמור לך פירות שבתחומי"? ואימא: כל שאני זכאי באמירתו – רשאי אני להחשיך עליו, 'כלל' לאתויי מאי? לאתויי הא, דת"ר: *אין [ב]מחשיכין על התחום להביא בהמה. *[ג]היתה עומדת חוץ לתחום – קורא לה והיא באה. כלל אמר אבא שאול: [ד]כל שאני זכאי באמירתו – רשאי אני להחשיך עליו. ומחשיכין לפקח על עסקי כלה ועל עסקי המת להביא לו ארון ותכריכין. ואומרים לו: לך למקום פלוני, ואם לא מצאת במקום פלוני – הבא ממקום פלוני. לא מצאת במנה – הבא במאתים. ר' יוסי ברבי יהודה אומר: [ה]ובלבד שלא יזכיר לו סכום מקח.§

מתני' *מחשיכין על התחום לפקח על עסקי כלה ועל עסקי המת להביא לו ארון ותכריכים. [ו]גוי שהביא חלילין בשבת – לא יספוד בהן ישראל, אא"כ באו ממקום קרוב. עשו לו ארון וחפרו לו קבר – יקבר בו ישראל. ואם בשביל ישראל – לא יקבר בו עולמית.§

גמ' מאי ממקום קרוב? רב אמר: ממקום קרוב ממש, ושמואל אמר: [ז]חיישינן שמא (א)חוץ לחומה לנו[א]. דיקא מתניתין כוותיה דשמואל, דקתני: "עשה לו ארון וחפר לו קבר יקבר בו ישראל" אלמא: מספיקא שרי, הכא נמי – מספיקא שרי, *[ח]ותניא כוותיה[ב] דרב(ב): *עיר שישראל וגוים דרים בה, והיתה בה מרחץ המרחצת בשבת. אם רוב גוים – לערב רוחץ בה מיד, אם רוב ישראל – ימתין עד כדי שיחמו חמין. מחצה על מחצה – *(אסור, וימתין) עד כדי שיחמו חמין. ר' יהודה אומר: באמבטי קטנה, אם יש בה רשות – רוחץ בה מיד. מאי "רשות"? אמר רב יהודה אמר רב יצחק בריה דרב יהודה: אם יש בה אדם חשוב, שיש לו עשרה עבדים שמחממין לו י' קומקומין בבת אחת באמבטי קטנה – מותר לרחוץ בה מיד.§ [ט]"עשו לו ארון וחפרו לו קבר וכו'".§ אמאי? הכא נמי ימתין בכדי שיעשו! אמר עולא: [י]בעומד באסרטיא. תינח קבר, ארון מאי איכא למימר? א"ר אבהו: [כ]במוטל על קברו.§

מתני' [ל]עושין כל צרכי המת: סכין ומדיחין אותו, ובלבד שלא יזיז בו אבר. שומטין את הכר מתחתיו, ומטילין אותו על החול בשביל[עד] שימתין

רש"י

אלא אסיפא קאי. דקאמר ת"ק להיתרא: אבל מחשיך הוא לשמור. ואתא איהו ושווייה ביה כללא, להביא כל כיוצא בהן: האי כל שאני זכאי להחשיך עליו זכאי אני באמירתו מיבעי ליה.(ג) דהיתר דחשיכה תנן, והיתר דאמירה לא תנן, והיכי תלי תניא בדלא תניא? לעולם אסיפא קאי. כדקאמרת. ודקשיא לך אמירה מהיכא קאמר ליה להיתרא, דתלי בה החשכה – אהא קאי, דאמר רב יהודה כו'. אלמא: זכאי אני באמירתו. ואבא שאול ות"ק כולהו פשיטא להו הא דשמואל. וקאמר ליה אבא שאול לת"ק: מי לא מודית בהא, שאתה מתיר להחשיך, דמותר הוא לומר כדשמואל. אלמא, הואיל ומותר לומר – מותר להחשיך. הלכך, אמאי נקטת החשכה לשמור לחודא? שוי כללא למילתא, ואימא: כל שאני זכאי באמירתו רשאי אני להחשיך עליו. דש"מ הך, וש"מ מת וכלה, דהא נמי זכאי באמירתו הוא, כדמפרש לקמן. והלכך, מחשיכין עליו. וסיפא דמתני' דקתני מחשיכין על התחום לפקח על עסקי כלה – אבא שאול היא: כלל אמר אבא שאול כו'. והאי נמי זכאי באמירתו, כדקתני סיפא: ואומר לו "לך למקום פלוני": סכום מקח. מנה ומאתים:

מתני' גוי שהביא חלילין בשבת. בשביל ישראל: לא יספוד בהן ישראל. לעולם. וקנסא הוא, משום דמוכחא מילתא דבשבילו הובאו, דאין דרך להביא חלילין אלא בשביל מת: ממקום קרוב. בתוך התחום: עשו לו ארון. בשביל גוי או למכור: **גמ'** רב אמר ממקום קרוב ממש. כלומר: שידוע לנו בירור הדבר דממקום קרוב באו, שראינום שהיו בביתו: ושמואל אמר חיישינן שמא חוץ לחומה לנו. אפילו הביא מחוץ לעיר אנו תולין להתיר, ואומרים: שמא בתוך התחום לנו ערב שבת, וסופדין בהן במוצ"ש מיד. וחיישינן נמי אמרינן לקולא, כדאמרי' במס' חגיגה (דף טו.) גבי בתולה שעיברה: חיישינן שמא באמבטי עיברה, ומותרת לכהונה. ולשמואל הכי קאמר מתני': לא יספוד בהן ישראל, אא"כ יש לתלות שבאו ממקום קרוב. ולאפוקי בידוע דמחוץ לתחום באו: ה"ג: דיקא מתני' כוותיה דשמואל ותניא כוותיה דרב: יקבר בו ישראל. דתלינן מספיקא שמא לצורך גוי נעשה: תניא כוותיה דרב. דספיקא אסור, דקתני: מחצה על מחצה ימתין בכדי שיחמו חמין. וא"ת: בכדי שיחמו חמין מיהא שרי, והכא תני לא יספוד בהן, משמע לעולם – הכא מוכחא מילתא, אבל במרחץ לא מוכחא מילתא כולי האי, הואיל ואיכא גוים: באמבטי קטנה. שיש לתלות ולומר משחשיכה הוחמה על ידי עבדים וקומקמין הרבה: אם יש בה רשות. אדם חשוב שליט: רוחץ בה. ישראל מיד, דיש לומר משחשיכה הוחמו חמין לאותו גוי. לישנא אחרינא גרסינן: תניא כוותיה דשמואל. ולא גרסי' דייקא מתני' כו' עד מספיקא שרי. ומייתי סייעתא לשמואל מדרבי יהודה, דתלינן לקולא. ורישא לא קשיא ליה, כיון דמחצה על מחצה ודאי בשביל ישראל. וגוים הוחמו, שהרי לא לאדם אחד לבדו הוחמו, דנימא ספיקא לגוי ספק לישראל. ולשון זה נראה לי עיקר. ורבותי נמי לא גרסי לעיל להא דקתני עשה גוי את הארון, עד מספיקא שרי. ומיהו, לא מפרשי לה כדפרישית: ימתין בכדי שיעשו. נהי דלא מוכחא מילתא, מיהו י"ל שמא בשביל ישראל נעשה: בעומד. הקבר באיסרטיא, שאין דרך ישראל ליקבר שם. דודאי לא נעשה בשביל ישראל: ארון מאי איכא למימר. להוכיח דלא בשביל ישראל נעשה: במוטל. הארון: על קברו. של גוי באיסרטיא, דמוכח דלשם אותו קבר נעשה הארון: **מתני'** ומדיחין. במים: שלא יזיז בו אבר. לא יגביה לו ידו או רגלו או ריסי עיניו: שימתין

תוספות

האי כל שאני רשאי בחשיכתו רשאי אני באמירתו מיבעי ליה. תימה: הא דכי פריך לעיל, האי כל שאיני רשאי באמירתו איני רשאי בחשיכתו מיבעי ליה. מכלל, דאי הוה תנן הכי – הוה אתי שפיר, אע"ג דתלי חשיכה באמירה! וי"ל: התם שאני, דלא הוה תלי תניא בדלא תניא, דאמירה נמי תנינא לעיל: לא יאמר אדם לחבירו שכור לי פועלים. אבל השתא, תלי תניא בדלא תניא – דהיתר אמירה לא תניא, אבל היתר החשכה תניא:

לעולם אסיפא קאי(ז) דאמר רב יהודה אמר שמואל מותר אדם לומר לחבירו שמור לי פירות שבתחומך. אע"פ שהוא אינו יכול לילך לשומרן – יכול לומר לחבירו לשמרן. ומתניתין הכי קאמר: כל שאני זכאי באמירתו, כגון לפקח על עסקי כלה ועל עסקי מת, ויכול לומר לחבירו לעשות למחר – רשאי אני להחשיך עליו, וכ"ש מה שאני זכאי לומר לעשות היום, כמו שמור לי פירות שבתחומך אע"פ שאיני רשאי לילך שם היום – דמותר להחשיך עליו:

אין מחשיכין על התחום להביא בהמה. יש ספרים דגרסי מחשיכים. לפי שאם יש שם בורגנים הולך ומביאה ובתוספתא גרס אין מחשיכין. וי"ל: דאיירי בבהמה שאינה יכולה לבא ברגליה, כגון טלה קטן, אא"כ ישאוהו בכתף. שאפילו יש מחילות – אינו רשאי להביא, דאסור לטלטל בעלי חיים שהם מוקצים:

גוי שהביא חלילים בשבת לא יספוד בהן ישראל. לא כפי' הקונטרס שפירש עולמית, מדפריך בגמרא גבי עשה גוי ארון וחפר לו קבר יקבר בו ישראל, אמאי? הכא נמי, נימא ימתין בכדי שיעשו. ואמאי קאמר נמי אי לאו דקאי אחלילים, על כן נראה דלא יספוד בהן ישראל – היינו עד כדי שיבואו. דסתם חלילים אין מביאין אותן לשם אדם אחד, אלא לשם כמה בני אדם:

אא"כ באו ממקום קרוב. תימה לרבי: מה מהני שבאו ממקום קרוב, הלא הביאם דרך רה"ר! ומה לי ארון וקבר שנעשו בשבת, ומה לי חלילים שהובאו דרך רה"ר? וי"ל: דהביא ממקום קרוב לא מהני כל כך הבאתו: **דיקא** מתניתין כוותיה דשמואל כו' יקבר בו ישראל אלמא מספיקא שרי. תימה: היכי (ה)מוכיחנא מינה דמספיקא שרי? והא מוקמ' לה בעומד באיסרטיא דודאי לצורך גוי נעשה! מיהו, אומר רבי דל"ג ליה להא דקתני עשו לו ארון כו', ול"ג נמי בסמוך(ו) ת"כ, גם בפי' הקונט' ל"ג, אלא ה"ג: דיקא נמי ממתני', עיר שישראל וגוים דרים בה כו'. ומשנה היא במסכת מכשירין (פ"ב משנה ה): ר' יהודה אומר אם יש בה רשות – רוחץ בה מיד. אלמא תלינן להתיר, כמו כן גבי חלילין יש לתלות בהיתר, ולומר חוץ לחומה לנו. מ"ר:

עין משפט נר מצוה

לה א (מיי' פכ"ד מהל' שבת) סמג לאוין סה טוש"ע או"ח סימן שז סעיף י:
לו ב מיי' שם הלכה ג סמג שם טוש"ע או"ח סימן שו סעיף א:
לז ג מיי' שם טור שו"ע שם סעיף ב:
לח ד ה מיי' שם הל"ה טוש"ע שם סעיף ג וסימן שז סעיף ח:
לט ו ז מיי' פ"ו מהל' שבת הל"ו סמג שם טוש"ע או"ח סימן שכה סעיף טו:
מ ח מיי' שם הלכה ז טוש"ע שם סעיף טז:
מא ט י ב מיי' שם הל' ה טור שו"ע שם סעיף יד:
מב ל מיי' פכ"ו מהל' שבת הלכה כ סמג שם טוש"ע או"ח סימן שיא סעיף ז:

לעיל קכב. ע"ש מכשירין פ"ב מ"ה ע"ש

נ"ל ימתין [וכ"ה במשנה]

מסורת הש"ס

(תוספתא פי"ח)

(לעיל נג:)

לעיל קנ:

[נ"ל דרב]

הגהות הב"ח

(א) גמ' חוץ לחומה לנו אמר רבא דיקא מתני': (ב) שם ותניא כותיה דרב דת"ר עיר: (ג) רש"י ד"ה האי כל וכו' דהיתרא דהחשכה תנן: (ד) תום' ד"ה לעולם אסיפא קאי ואבא שאול אהא קאי דאמר רב יהודה: (ה) ד"ה דיקא וכו' היכי מוכח מינה: (ו) בא"ד ול"ג נמי בסמוך דתנו רבנן גם בפ"ה ל"ג ליה אלא ה"ג:

הגהות הגר"א

[א] גמ' (דיקא מתני' כו' עד ה"נ מספיקא שרי) תא"מ: [ב] שם כוותיה דרב נ"ל דשמואל:

רבינו חננאל

כלל זה. ואמרינן אם על רישא דקתני אין מחשיכין על התחום לשכור פועלין וכו'. כל (שאני) [שאיני] זכאי בחשיכתו (אני) [איני] זכאי באמירתו היה לו לומר כי אין מחשיכין אמרה משנתנו בפירוש ומכללו נלמד האמירה כלומר מאחר שאין לי להחשיך בתחום לשכור פועלין כן אין לי לומר לחבירו השכר לי פועלין עם חשכה. אלא אסיפא. אבל מחשיך הוא לשמור וכו' כלומר כשם שמותר לו להחשיך כך מותר לו לומר לחבירו החשיך והביא לי פירות האי כל שאיני זכאי בחשיכתו זכאי אני באמירתו היה לו לומר ואוקימנא כדרב פפא דאמר מותר לאדם לומר לחבירו שמור לי פירות שבתחומך וכו' כלומר כשם שאני זכאי לומר לחבירו שמור לי פירות שבתחומך כך מותר לי לשמר לי פירות שבתחומי. ולהחשיך עליו ואמרינן עוד ולמה ליה כלל לתנייה בהדיא ופרקינן כלל להביא הא דת"ר מחשיכין על התחום להביא בהמה היתה עומדת חוץ לתחום קורא לה והיא באה. ולפקח על עסקי כלה ועל עסקי המת להביא לו ארון ותכריכין אומרים לו לך למקום פלוני לא מצאת במקום פלוני הבא ממקום פלוני לא מצאת במאה הבא במאתים ובלבד שלא יזכור את הדמים. ר' יוסי ב"ר יהודה [אומר] ובלבד שלא יזכור לי סכום המקח: **מתני'** מחשיכין על התחום. עד אא"כ באו ממקום קרוב. מאי ממקום קרוב רב אמר קרוב ממש. ושמואל אמר חיישינן שמא חוץ לחומה לנו. *)ופירוש לן מרן דברי שמואל הללו והיאך מתני' דייקא כוותיה ומה טעם חלילים שהביאם גוי בשבת שלא יספוד בהם ישראל ולמה לא ימתין בכדי שיביאו או דלמא משום דלא ידעינן מהיכן באו ועוד המותר לספוד בהן ביום ראשון ובשאר ימי החול או לאו מה פירק לו הלא אפילו אם המת מונח בדרך צריך להמתין בכדי שיחפור בקבר והדר קושיין בדובתיה וכן בארון ליסברה לן מרן. ועוד אם הדברים הללו על עיר שרובן ישראל הם או לא. כי אם רובן גוים למה צריך להמתין והלא לענין מרחץ אמרו מותר לרחוץ בה מיד ושמואל אמר חיישינן שמא חוץ

*) נראה דזה הוא שאלה לרבינו וצ"ל יפרש לן מרן (ואולי שאל מאת רב האי גאון) והתשובה חסרה בה ובאמת שאלת החכם היא חצי תשובה.

עין משפט נר מצוה

מג א מיי' פכ"ו מהל' שבת הלכה כ סמג שם טוש"ע או"ח סימן שיא סעיף ז:

מד ב מיי' פ"ד מהלכות אבל הלכה ה סמג עשין ב טוש"ע יו"ד סי' שלט סעיף א:

מה ג סמג עשין עט:

מו ד מיי' פ"י מהלכות תשובה הלכה א:

מז ה מיי' פ"י מהלכות מתנות עניים הל"ב [וכה' עבדים פ"ט הל"ח] טוש"ע יו"ד סימן רמז סעיף ג:

רש"י

שימתין. שלא יסריח מחמת חום הסדין והכרים: קושרין את הלחי. של מת, שהיה פיו הולך ונפתח, קושרין את לחייו כדי שלא יפתח פיו יותר: ולא שיעלה. להסגר ממה שנפתח, דהיינו מזיז אבר, אלא שלא יוסיף ליפתח: סומכין אותה בספסל. שהרי תורת כלי עליו: לא שתעלה. דהוה ליה בונה: גמ' ואמר לו אין סכין. אלמא: דבר האסור לטלטל אסור לסוך: קרקע בקרקע מיחלף. כלומר: ההוא לאו משום טלטול הוא, אלא משום אשוויי גומות. ואע"ג דמרחץ רצפת אבנים הוא, וליכא למיחש לאשוויי גומות – מיחלף מיהא בקרקע אחר: כל צרכי המת לאתויי מאי. דלא תנן: כלי מיקר. שמביאים קרירות, כגון זכוכית: ואף שלמה אמר בחכמתו. שכריסו של מת נופחת ונבקעת: זה חוט השדרה. שהוא כמין חבל, ולבן ככסף: זו אמה. שהוא מעין של תולדה, כמו "גלת מים" (יהושע טו): זה פרש. וגלגל – לשון גלל (יחזקאל ד): אל הבור. שנופל לתוך פיו: כחגים. כתענוגים: מתני' אין מעצמין. את עיניו בשבת, אפילו אחר יציאת הנפש, דמזיז בו אבר: שופך דמים. כדמפרש בברייתא בגמ', שבטורח מועט מקרב מיתתו: גמ' ואוחז בשני גודלי רגליו. עוצרן באצבעותיו: וחתכם. לשון חיותכם: אריה אבי תרי לא נפיל. להורגן, כדכתי' "ומוראכם" תרי, וכתיב "על כל חית הארץ" – ואפי' ארי: כדרמי בר אבא. דנקנסה עליו מיתה, ונדמה לארי כבהמה: נמשל. מי שחיה מושלת בו, בידוע שכבהמה נדמה: עשה. צדקה: עד שאתה מוצא. למי לעשות: ומצוי לך. ממון: ועודך בידך. עודך ברשותך, קודם שתמות: לא זכות. לא דבר לזכות בו, שכולם עשירים: ולא חובה. לאמץ לב ולקפוץ יד: על מדה זו. שלא יבא לידי עניות, דדבר המזומן הוא לבא או עליו או על בנו או על בן בנו: ונתן לך רחמים. שתרחם על הבריות: זו פדחת. המצח, שהוא חלק ומזהיר יותר מכל הפרצוף: זה חוטם. שהוא תואר פני אדם: זו נשמה. כדכתיב: "נר אלהים נשמת אדם" (משלי כ): הלסתות. לחיים: ושבו העבים. חשכת עינים יבא ויכסה המאור, אחר שירבה בבכיה בזקנותו מחמת תשות כח, וצרות רבות עליו: מרווח. מאור עינים: אפילו מליא. כחלא בעיניו, כמכחול גדול: כאביסנא של גרדאי. כובד של גרדיים, אינשוכל"ש בלע"ז: אוקומי.(ב) המאור מוקים שלא יחשיך יותר ממה שהוא: מאי קמ"ל. בהא דאמר אפי' כאביסנא דגרדאי: אלים. עב: מכוחלא. עץ שהוא מכניס בשפופרת ונותן בעיניו, וקורין לו מכחול: תיכלא ועיורא. שיכול בנים ועיורון: הדמעה. של בכי. מתוך אבל וצרה: של

תורה אור

שימתין. קושרין את הלחי, לא שיעלה – אלא שלא יוסיף. *וכן קורה שנשברה – סומכין אותה בספסל או בארוכות המטה, לא שתעלה אלא שלא תוסיף.§ גמ' *והאמר רב יהודה אמר שמואל: מעשה בתלמידו של רבי מאיר שנכנס אחריו לבית המרחץ, ביקש להדיח קרקע, אמר לו: אין מדיחין. לסוך קרקע – אמר לו: אין סכין!° קרקע בקרקע – מחלפא, מת בקרקע לא מיחלף. "כל" לאתויי מאי? לאתויי הא דת"ר: מביאין כלי מיקר וכלי מתכות ומניחין על כריסו, כדי שלא(א) תפוח. ופוקקין את נקביו כדי שלא תיכנס בהן הרוח. ואף שלמה אמר בחכמתו: °"עד *שלא ירתק חבל הכסף" – זה חוט השדרה, "ותרוץ גולת הזהב" – זה אמה, "ותשבר כד על המבוע" – זה הכרס, "ונרוץ הגלגל אל הבור" – זה פרש. וכן הוא אומר: °"וזריתי פרש על פניכם פרש חגיכם". אמר רב הונא ואמרי לה אמר רב חגא: אלו בני אדם שמניחין דברי תורה, ועושין כל ימיהם כחגים. אמר רבי לוי אמר רב פפי א"ר יהושע: לאחר שלשה ימים כריסו נבקעת ונופלת לו על פניו, ואומרת לו: "טול מה שנתת בי".§ מתני' אין(א) מעצמין את המת בשבת, ולא בחול עם יציאת נפש. והמעצים עם יציאת הנפש – הרי זה שופך דמים.§ גמ' תנו רבנן: המעצמו עם יציאת הנפש – הרי זה שופך דמים. משל לנר שכבה והולכת, אדם מניח אצבעו עליה – מיד כבתה. תניא, *רשב"ג אומר: הרוצה שיתעצמו עיניו של מת – נופח לו יין בחוטמו, ונותן שמן בין ריסי עיניו, ואוחז בשני גודלי רגליו – והן מתעצמין מאליהן. תניא, רשב"ג אומר: תינוק בן יומו חי – מחללין עליו את השבת, דוד מלך ישראל מת – אין מחללין עליו את השבת. תינוק בן יומו חי מחללין עליו את השבת, *אמרה תורה: חלל עליו שבת אחד, כדי שישמור שבתות הרבה. דוד מלך ישראל מת – אין מחללין עליו – כיון שמת אדם, בטל מן המצות. והיינו *דא"ר יוחנן: °"במתים חפשי" כיון שמת אדם – נעשה חפשי מן המצות. ותניא, ר' שמעון בן אלעזר אומר: תינוק בן יומו חי – אין צריך לשומרו מן החולדה ומן העכברים, אבל עוג מלך הבשן מת – צריך לשומרו מן החולדה ומן העכברים, שנאמר: °"ומוראכם וחתכם יהיה", כל זמן שאדם חי – אימתו מוטלת על הבריות, כיון שמת – בטלה אימתו. אמר רב פפא: *נקיטינן, אריה אבי תרי – לא נפיל. הא קא חזינן דנפיל! ההוא כדרמי בר אבא, דאמר רמי בר אבא: *אין חיה שולטת באדם עד שנדמה לו כבהמה; שנאמר: °"אדם ביקר בל ילין נמשל כבהמות נדמו". אמר רבי חנינא: אסור לישן בבית יחידי, וכל הישן בבית יחידי אחזתו לילית. ותניא, רשב"א אומר: עשה עד שאתה מוצא ומצוי לך ועודך בידך, ואף שלמה אמר בחכמתו: °"וזכור את בוראיך בימי בחורותיך עד [אשר] (ש) לא יבאו ימי הרעה" – אלו ימי הזקנה. "והגיעו שנים אשר תאמר אין לי בהם חפץ" – אלו ימי המשיח, שאין בהם לא זכות ולא חובה. ופליגא דשמואל, *דאמר שמואל: אין בין העולם הזה לימות המשיח אלא שיעבוד מלכיות בלבד, שנא': °"כי לא יחדל אביון מקרב הארץ". תניא, ר' אלעזר הקפר אומר: לעולם יבקש אדם רחמים על מדה זו, שאם הוא לא בא – בא בנו, ואם בנו לא בא – בן בנו בא, שנאמר: °"כי בגלל הדבר הזה", תנא דבי ר' ישמעאל: גלגל הוא שחוזר בעולם. א"ר יוסף: נקיטינן, האי צורבא מרבנן לא מיעני – והא קא חזינן דמיעני! אם איתא דמיעני, אהדורי אפתחא לא מיהדר. אמר לה רבי חייא לדביתהו: כי אתי עניא – אקדימי ליה ריפתא, כי היכי דלקדמו לבנך. אמרה ליה: מילט קא לייטת להו?! אמר לה: קרא קא כתיב: "כי בגלל הדבר הזה", ותנא דבי ר' ישמעאל: גלגל הוא שחוזר בעולם, תניא *ר' גמליאל ברבי אומר: °"ונתן לך רחמים ורחמך והרבך" *כל המרחם על הבריות – מרחמין עליו מן השמים, וכל שאינו מרחם על הבריות – אין מרחמין עליו מן השמים. °"עד אשר לא תחשך השמש והאור" – זו פדחת והחוטם, "והירח" – זו נשמה, "והכוכבים" – אלו הלסתות, "ושבו העבים אחר הגשם" – זו מאור עיניו של אדם, שהולך אחר הבכי. אמר שמואל: האי דמעתא, עד ארבעין שנין – הדרא, מכאן ואילך – לא הדרא. ואמר רב נחמן: האי כוחלא, עד ארבעין שנין – מרווח, מכאן ואילך – אפילו מליא *כאביסנא דגירדאי – אוקומי מוקים, ארווחי לא מרווח. מאי קא משמע לן – דכמה דאלים מכוחלא טפי מעלי. ר' חנינא שכיבא ליה ברתיה, לא הוה קא בכי עלה. אמרה ליה דביתהו: תרנגולתא אפיקת מביתך?! אמר לה: תרתי, תכלא ועיורא?! סבר לה כי הא דאמר רבי יוחנן משום רבי יוסי בן קצרתה: *שש דמעות הן, שלש יפות ושלש רעות. של עשן ושל בכי ושל

מקורות בגליון: קהלת יב; מלאכי ב; תהלים פח; בראשית ט; תהלים מט; קהלת יב; דברים טו; שם; שם יג; קהלת יב

מסורת הש"ס: לעיל מג. | לעיל מ: | בס"י איתא ר"ש בן אלעזר | [יומא פה:] | לעיל ל. [נדה סא. ע"ש] | [עי' פרש"י בעירובין ה. ד"ה והאמר פירוש ע"ש] [סנהדרין לח. ע"ש] | ברכות לד: לעיל סג. פסחים סח. סנהדרין צא: צט. | [תוספתא דב"ק פ"ט] | [ביצה לב: ע"ש] | [גי' הערוך כאכסנא] | [אדר"נ פמ"א]

הגהות הב"ח

(א) גמ' שלא יהא תפוח: (ב) רש"י ד"ה אוקומי. מוקים המאור שלא:

בקרא אשר לא

גליון הש"ס

גמ' קרקע בקרקע מיחלפא. כה"ג לעיל דף כט ע"ב ועי' בתוספות שם ד"ה גזירה:

א) [גי' הערוך אין מאמצין כו' וכל המאמץ כו' פירוש סותמין עיני המת לאחר המיתה כדי שלא יהיו עיניו פתוחות כענין שנאמר ויוסף ישית ידו על עיניך ע"כ ועי' לעיל דף עז: איבעיא להו מאמצין תנן או מעמצין וכו' ואשר ע"כ ברור לטעות הוא שהקדימו בדפוס נ' קודם למ' במשנה ובברייתא דהכא וגם בפרש"י דהכא אמנם ברי"ף והרא"ש הגירסא במשנה ובברייתא על נכון המ' קודם לנ' וכ"א במשנה שבמשניות וכפי' הרב וכתב התוי"ט אין מאמצין כמו עוצם עיניו כו'].

רבינו חננאל

חוץ לחומה לנו ואע"ג דאיסורא הוא וקיי"ל הלכתא כרב באיסורי הכא הלכתא כשמואל דדיקא מתניתין כותיה דתנן במס' מכשירין עיר של ישראל וגוים דרין בתוכה והיתה בה מרחץ המרחצת בשבת אם רוב גוים מותר לרחוץ בה מיד אם רוב ישראל ימתין עד בכדי שיחמו חמין. מחצה על מחצה ימתין בכדי שיחמו חמין. ר' יהודה אומר באמבטי קטנה ואם יש רשות רוחץ בה מיד. ומפרש רב יצחק בריה דרב יהודה מאי רשות כגון אדם חשוב שיש לו עשרה עבדים שמחממין לו עשרה קומקמין בבת אחת מותר לרחוץ מיד: **עשו** לו ארון וחפרו לו קבר יקבר בהן ישראל ומקשינן אמאי והא ישראל וגוי כמחצה על מחצה דמי ימתין בכדי שיעשו ומפרק עולא כגון בגוי מת המוטל באיסטרטא דמוכחא מלתא שזה הקבר לזה הגוי נחפר שדומה לרוב גוים שאין צריך להמתין בכדי שיעשו תוב אקשינן תינח קבר ארון מאי ופריק ר' אבהו בארון המוטל על הקבר שנמצא הארון בקבר*) דאילו דברי ר"מ נסבייה בדרך גררה. בפרק כירה בענין דברים של (חול) [קדש] אסור לאומרם (בלשה"ק) [בלשון חול] אלא אם הוא לאפרושי מאיסורא כגון זה שא"ר מאיר לתלמידיו אין מדיחין ואין סכין בלשה"ק אבל הרואה שסכין ומדיחין המת לא יתיר הדחה וסיכה בקרקע ולפיכך התיר ר"מ הדחת המת וסיכתו ולא גזר סיכת המת והדחתו מפני סיכת מרחץ והדחתו. כל צרכי המת כלל זה להביא הא דת"ר מביאין כלי מיקר וכלי מתכות ומניחין לו על כרסו בשבת שלא תפוח. ופוקקין נקביו בשביל שלא תכנס בהן הרוח ואף שלמה אמר בחכמתו עד אשר לא ירתק חבל הכסף וגו' ופשוטה היא: **אין** מאמצין את המת בשבת וכו'. פי' מאמצין סותמין את עיני המת. ת"ר המאמץ עם יציאת נפש אפילו בחול הרי זה שופך דמים משל לנר שכבה כו'. תניא ר"ש בן אלעזר אומר תינוק בן יומו חי מחללין עליו את השבת שעומד ומשמר שבתות הרבה. דוד מלך ישראל מת אין מחללין עליו את השבת

*) נראה דחסר כאן איזה תיבות ושייך להא דמקשינן כאן בגמ' והאמר ריב"ש מעשה בתלמידו של ר"מ.

וְשֶׁל בֵּית הַכִּסֵּא – רָעוֹת, שֶׁל סַם וְשֶׁל שְׂחוֹק וְשֶׁל פֵּירוֹת – יָפוֹת. °"בַּיּוֹם שֶׁיָּזוּעוּ שׁוֹמְרֵי הַבַּיִת וְהִתְעַוְּתוּ וגו'". "בַּיּוֹם שֶׁיָּזוּעוּ שׁוֹמְרֵי הַבַּיִת" – אֵלּוּ הַכְּסָלִים וְהַצְּלָעוֹת, "וְהִתְעַוְּתוּ אַנְשֵׁי הֶחָיִל" – אֵלּוּ שׁוֹקַיִם, "וּבָטְלוּ הַטּוֹחֲנוֹת" – אֵלּוּ שִׁינַּיִם, "וְחָשְׁכוּ הָרוֹאוֹת בָּאֲרוּבּוֹת" – אֵלּוּ עֵינַיִם. א"ל קֵיסָר לְר' יְהוֹשֻׁעַ בֶּן חֲנַנְיָה: מ"ט לָא אָתֵית לְבֵי אָבִידָן? א"ל: טוּר תְּלַג סַחֲרוּנִי גְּלִידִין, כַּלְבוֹהִי לָא נָבְחִין, טַחֲנוֹהִי לָא טוֹחֲנִין. בֵּי רַב אָמְרִי: אַדְּלָא אֲבֵידְנָא בָּחֵישְׁנָא. *תַּנְיָא, רַבִּי יוֹסֵי בַּר קִיסְמָא אוֹמֵר: טָבָא תְּרֵי מִתְּלָת, וַוי לָהּ לַחֲדָא דְּאָזְלָא וְלָא אָתְיָא. מַאי הִיא? א"ר חִסְדָּא: יַנְקוּתָא. כִּי אֲתָא רַב דִּימִי אֲמַר: יַנְקוּתָא – כְּלִילָא דְּוַורְדָּא, סִבוּתָא – כְּלִילָא *דְּחִילְפָא. תָּנָא מִשְּׁמֵיהּ דְּרַבִּי מֵאִיר: דּוּק בְּכָבֵי וְתִשְׁכַּח בְּנִיגְרֵי, שֶׁנֶּאֱמַר: °"וַנִּשְׂבַּע לֶחֶם וַנִּהְיֶה טוֹבִים וְרָעָה לֹא רָאִינוּ". א"ל שְׁמוּאֵל לְרַב יְהוּדָה: *שִׁינָּנָא, שְׁרֵי שַׂקָּךְ וְעַיֵּיל לַחְמָךְ. עַד אַרְבְּעִין שְׁנִין – מֵיכְלָא מַעֲלֵי, מִכָּאן וְאֵילָךְ – מִשְׁתֵּי מַעֲלֵי. א"ל הַהוּא גּוֹזָאָה לְר' יְהוֹשֻׁעַ בֶּן קָרְחָה: מֵהָכָא לְקַרְחִינָא כַּמָּה הָוֵי? א"ל: כְּמֵהָכָא לְגוֹזַנְיָא. א"ל צְדוֹקִי: בַּרְחָא קַרְחָא בְּאַרְבָּעָה. אֲמַר לֵיהּ: *עִיקָּרָא שְׁלִיפָא בִּתְמָנְיָא. חַזְיֵיהּ דְּלָא סָיֵים מְסָאנֵיהּ, א"ל: דְּעַל סוּס – מֶלֶךְ, דְּעַל חֲמוֹר – בֶּן חוֹרִין, וּדְמַנְעֲלֵי בְּרִיגְלוֹהִי – בַּר אִינִישׁ, דְּלָא הָא וְלָא הָא – דַּחֲפִיר וּקְבִיר טָב מִינֵּיהּ. א"ל: גּוֹזָא גּוֹזָא, תְּלָת אָמְרַתְּ לִי תְּלָת שְׁמַעְתְּ; הַדְרַת פָּנִים – זָקָן, שִׂמְחַת לֵב – אִשָּׁה, °"נַחֲלַת ה' – בָּנִים" – בָּרוּךְ הַמָּקוֹם שֶׁמְּנָעֲךָ מִכּוּלָּם. א"ל: קַרְחָא מַצְוַויְנָא! אֲמַר לֵיהּ: עִיקָּרָא שְׁלִיפָא תּוֹכֵחָה! א"ל רַבִּי לְר' שִׁמְעוֹן בֶּן חֲלַפְתָּא: מִפְּנֵי מָה לֹא הִקְבַּלְנוּ פָּנֶיךָ בָּרֶגֶל, כְּדֶרֶךְ שֶׁהִקְבִּילוּ אֲבוֹתַי לַאֲבוֹתֶיךָ? א"ל: סְלָעִים נַעֲשׂוּ גְּבוֹהִים, קְרוֹבִים נַעֲשׂוּ רְחוֹקִים, מִשְׁתַּיִם נַעֲשׂוּ שָׁלֹשׁ, מֵשִׂים שָׁלוֹם בַּבַּיִת בָּטֵל.§ °"וְסֻגְּרוּ דְלָתַיִם בַּשּׁוּק וגו'" – אֵלּוּ נְקָבָיו שֶׁל אָדָם, "בִּשְׁפַל קוֹל הַטַּחֲנָה" – בִּשְׁבִיל קוּרְקְבָן שֶׁאֵינוֹ טוֹחֵן, "וְיָקוּם לְקוֹל הַצִּפּוֹר" – שֶׁאֲפִילּוּ צִפּוֹר מְנַעַרְתּוֹ מִשְּׁנָתוֹ, "וְיִשַּׁחוּ כָּל בְּנוֹת הַשִּׁיר" – שֶׁאֲפִילּוּ (*קוֹל שִׁירִים וְשִׁירוֹת) דּוֹמוֹת עָלָיו כְּשׁוּחָה. וְאַף בַּרְזִילַּי הַגִּלְעָדִי אָמַר לְדָוִד: °"בֶּן שְׁמֹנִים שָׁנָה אָנֹכִי הַיּוֹם הַאֵדַע בֵּין טוֹב לְרָע" – מִכָּאן שֶׁדַּעוֹתָן שֶׁל זְקֵנִים מִשְׁתַּנּוֹת, "אִם יִטְעַם עַבְדְּךָ אֶת אֲשֶׁר אֹכַל וְאֶת אֲשֶׁר אֶשְׁתֶּה" – מִכָּאן שֶׁשִּׂפְתוֹתֵיהֶן שֶׁל זְקֵנִים מִתְרַפְּטוֹת, "אִם אֶשְׁמַע עוֹד בְּקוֹל שָׁרִים וְשָׁרוֹת" – מִכָּאן שֶׁאָזְנֵיהֶם שֶׁל זְקֵנִים מִתְכַּבְּדוֹת. אָמַר רַב: בַּרְזִילַּי הַגִּלְעָדִי שַׁקְרָא הֲוָה, דְּהַהִיא אַמְתָא דַּהֲוְיָא בֵּי רַבִּי בַּת תִּשְׁעִין וְתַרְתֵּין שְׁנִין, וַהֲוַת טָעֲמָא קִידְרָא. רָבָא אָמַר: בַּרְזִילַּי הַגִּלְעָדִי שָׁטוּף בְּזִמָּה הֲוָה, אוְכָל הַשָּׁטוּף בְּזִמָּה – *זִקְנָה קוֹפֶצֶת עָלָיו. תַּנְיָא, רַבִּי יִשְׁמָעֵאל בְּרַבִּי יוֹסֵי אוֹמֵר: *תַּלְמִידֵי חֲכָמִים, כָּל זְמַן שֶׁמַּזְקִינִין – חָכְמָה נִתּוֹסֶפֶת בָּהֶם, שֶׁנֶּאֱמַר: °"בִּישִׁישִׁים חָכְמָה וְאוֹרֶךְ יָמִים תְּבוּנָה". וְעַמֵּי הָאָרֶץ, כָּל זְמַן שֶׁמַּזְקִינִין – טִפְּשׁוּת נִתּוֹסֶפֶת בָּהֶן, שֶׁנֶּאֱמַר: °"מֵסִיר שָׂפָה לְנֶאֱמָנִים וְטַעַם זְקֵנִים יִקָּח". "גַּם מִגָּבֹהַּ יִרָאוּ" – שֶׁאֲפִילּוּ גַּבְשׁוּשִׁית קְטַנָּה דּוֹמָה עָלָיו כְּהָרֵי הָרִים, "וְחַתְחַתִּים בַּדֶּרֶךְ" – בְּשָׁעָה שֶׁמְּהַלֵּךְ בַּדֶּרֶךְ נַעֲשׂוּ(א) לוֹ *תְּוָהִים. "וְיָנֵאץ הַשָּׁקֵד" – זוֹ קְלִיבוּסֶת, "וְיִסְתַּבֵּל הֶחָגָב" – אֵלּוּ עֲגָבוֹת, "וְתָפֵר הָאֲבִיּוֹנָה" – זוֹ חֶמְדָּה. רַב כָּהֲנָא הֲוָה פָּסֵיק סִידְרָא קַמֵּיהּ דְּרַב, כִּי מְטָא לְהַאי קְרָא נָגֵיד וְאִתְנַח. אָמַר: ש"מ בְּטֵל לֵיהּ חֶמְדֵּיהּ דְּרַב. אָמַר רַב כָּהֲנָא: מַאי דִּכְתִיב °"כִּי הוּא אָמַר וַיֶּהִי" – זוֹ אִשָּׁה, "הוּא צִוָּה וַיַּעֲמֹד" – אֵלּוּ בָּנִים. תָּנָא: אִשָּׁה חֵמֶת מְלֵאָה צוֹאָה, וּפִיהָ מָלֵא דָּם – וְהַכֹּל רָצִין אַחֲרֶיהָ. °"כִּי הֹלֵךְ הָאָדָם אֶל בֵּית עוֹלָמוֹ" א"ר יִצְחָק: *מְלַמֵּד שֶׁכָּל צַדִּיק וְצַדִּיק נוֹתְנִין לוֹ מָדוֹר לְפִי כְּבוֹדוֹ. מָשָׁל לְמֶלֶךְ שֶׁנִּכְנַס הוּא וַעֲבָדָיו לָעִיר, כְּשֶׁהֵן נִכְנָסִין – כּוּלָּן בְּשַׁעַר אֶחָד נִכְנָסִין, כְּשֶׁהֵן לָנִין – כָּל אֶחָד וְאֶחָד נוֹתְנִין לוֹ מָדוֹר לְפִי כְּבוֹדוֹ. וְאָמַר רַבִּי יִצְחָק: מַאי דִּכְתִיב °"כִּי הַיַּלְדוּת וְהַשַּׁחֲרוּת הָבֶל" דְּבָרִים שֶׁאָדָם עוֹשֶׂה בְּיַלְדוּתוֹ – מַשְׁחִירִים פָּנָיו לְעֵת זִקְנָתוֹ. *וְאָמַר רַבִּי יִצְחָק: קָשָׁה רִימָּה לַמֵּת כְּמַחַט בִּבְשַׂר הַחַי, שֶׁנֶּאֱמַר: °"אַךְ בְּשָׂרוֹ עָלָיו יִכְאָב". אָמַר רַב חִסְדָּא: נַפְשׁוֹ שֶׁל אָדָם מִתְאַבֶּלֶת עָלָיו כָּל שִׁבְעָה, שֶׁנֶּאֱ': "וְנַפְשׁוֹ עָלָיו תֶּאֱבָל", וּכְתִיב: °"וַיַּעַשׂ לְאָבִיו אֵבֶל שִׁבְעַת יָמִים". אָמַר רַב יְהוּדָה: במֵת שֶׁאֵין לוֹ מְנַחֲמִין הוֹלְכִין י' בְּנֵי אָדָם וְיוֹשְׁבִין בִּמְקוֹמוֹ. הַהוּא דִּשְׁכִיב בְּשַׁבָּבוּתֵיהּ דְּרַב יְהוּדָה לָא הָווּ לוֹ מְנַחֲמִין, כָּל

תורה אור: קהלת יב | ירמיהו מד | תהלים קכז | קהלת יב | שמואל ב יט | איוב יב | שם | תהלים לג | קהלת יב | קהלת יא | איוב יד | בראשית נ

שֶׁל בֵּית הַכִּסֵּא. מִתּוֹךְ יִסּוּרִין: שֶׁל פֵּירוֹת. כְּגוֹן רֵיחַ חַרְדָּל: הַכְּסָלִים. ליפלאנק"ש: וְהַצְּלָעוֹת. שֶׁהֵן שׁוֹמְרִין בְּנֵי הַמֵּעַיִים, וְחִיּוּתוֹ שֶׁל אָדָם, וְסוֹגְרִין בַּעֲדָם: אֵלּוּ שׁוֹקַיִים. שֶׁכֹּחוֹ שֶׁל אָדָם נִסְמָךְ עֲלֵיהֶם: לְבֵי אָבִידָן. מָקוֹם הֶעָשׂוּי לְהִתְוַוכֵּחַ שָׁם צְדוֹקִים וּבַיְיתּוֹסִים עִם יִשְׂרָאֵל בְּמִקְרָאוֹת: טוּר תַּלַג. הָהָר נַעֲשָׂה שֶׁלֶג, כְּלוֹמַר: רֹאשִׁי לָבָן: סַחֲרוּנֵי גְּלִידִין. סְבִיבוֹתָיו שֶׁל הָר מְלֵאוֹ קֶרַח, כְּלוֹמַר: שְׂפָמִי וּזְקָנִי הִלְבִּינוּ: כַּלְבוֹהִי לָא נָבְחִין. קוֹלִי אֵינוֹ נִשְׁמָע: טַחֲנוֹהִי. הַשִּׁינַּיִם: אַדְּלָא אֲבֵידְנָא בַּחֵישְׁנָא. אַחַר מַה שֶּׁלֹּא אָבַד מִמֶּנִּי אֲנִי מְפַשְׁפֵּשׁ, מֵרוֹב זִקְנָה אֲנִי הוֹלֵךְ שָׁחוּחַ וּמְנַעֲנֵעַ, וְנִרְאֶה כְּמִי שֶׁמְּבַקֵּשׁ דִּינָר הָאָבוּד לוֹ: תַּרְתֵּי טָבָא מִתְּלָת. טוֹבִים ב' הָרַגְלַיִם שֶׁל יְמֵי בַּחֲרוּת מִג' שֶׁל זִקְנָה, שֶׁצָּרִיךְ מִשְׁעֶנֶת עִם רַגְלָיו: וַוי לַהּ. חֲבָל עָלֶיהָ, כְּלוֹמַר: יֵשׁ לוֹ לְהִתְאוֹנֵן וְלִצְעוֹק: וַוי הַהוֹלֶכֶת וְאֵינָהּ חוֹזֶרֶת: כְּלִילָא דְּוַורְדָּא. נֵזֶר שֶׁל וֶורֶד: חִילְפֵי. אורטיא"ש: דּוּק בְּכָבֵי וְתִשְׁכַּח בְּנִיגְרֵי. אֱכוֹל הַרְבֵּה וְתִמְצָא הָאֲכִילָה בִּפְסִיעוֹתֶיךָ, שֶׁיֶּחֱזַק כֹּחֲךָ. דּוּק – כְּמוֹ "אָכְלָה מַדֱּקָה" (דניאל ז), לְשׁוֹן כּוֹסֵס: שְׁרֵי שַׂקָּךְ. פְּתַח פִּיךָ: גּוֹזָא. סָרִיס, וּצְדוֹקִי הָיָה: מֵהָכָא לְקַרְחִינָא כַּמָּה הָוֵי. כַּמָּה מַהֲלָךְ יֵשׁ מִכָּאן עַד הַקֵּרֵחַ, וּלְהַקְנִיטוֹ עַל קָרַחְתּוֹ נִתְכַּוֵּון: כְּמֵהָכָא לְגוֹזַנְיָא. כְּמוֹ שֶׁמִּכָּאן עַד הַסָּרִיס: אֲמַר לֵיהּ צְדוֹקִי בַּרְחָא קַרְחָא בְּאַרְבָּעָה. שֶׁהַקֵּרֵחַ לָקוּחַ בְּאַרְבַּע – בַּרְחָא קַרְחָא הוּא עֵז, עַל שֵׁם שֶׁאֵינוֹ מְלוּבָּשׁ בְּצֶמֶר כְּרָחֵל קָרוּי קַרְחָא: אֲמַר לֵיהּ. רַבִּי יְהוֹשֻׁעַ: עִיקָּרָא שְׁלִיפָא. שֶׂה שֶׁבֵּיצָיו עֲקוּרִים וּנְתוּקִין לוֹקְחִין בִּשְׁמֹנָה: חַזְיֵיהּ. צְדוֹקִי לְרַבִּי יְהוֹשֻׁעַ דְּלָא סָיֵים מְסָאנֵיהּ: קַרְחָא מַצְוַויְנָא. אַתָּה הַקֵּרֵחַ בִּמְרִיבָה אַתָּה בָּאתָ עִמָּדִי?! בִּתְמִיָּה: אֲמַר לוֹ רַבִּי יְהוֹשֻׁעַ עִיקָּרָא שְׁלִיפָא תּוֹכֵחָה. אַתָּה הַסָּרִיס לְהַקְנִיטֵנִי וּלְהִתְוַוכֵּחַ עִמִּי בָּאתָ: לֹא הִקְבַּלְנוּ פָּנֶיךָ. לֹא הִקְבַּלְתָּ פָּנַי, וְדֶרֶךְ עֲנָוָה קָאָמַר לֵיהּ: סְלָעִים. קְטַנִּים, נַעֲשׂוּ גְּבוֹהִים, שֶׁנִּזְקַנְתִּי: קְרוֹבִים. נִדְמִין לִי כִּרְחוֹקִים: שְׁתַּיִם נַעֲשׂוּ לִי שָׁלֹשׁ. שֶׁצָּרִיךְ אֲנִי מִשְׁעֶנֶת: מֵשִׂים שָׁלוֹם בַּבַּיִת. אֵבֶר תַּשְׁמִישׁ: לִישָּׁנָא אַחֲרִינָא: קְרוֹבִים נַעֲשׂוּ רְחוֹקִים. מֵרוֹב חֻלְשׁוּת שֶׁל אָדָם כְּשֶׁמַּזְקִין, צָרִיךְ לְהַרְחִיק רַגְלָיו זֶה מִזֶּה: שֶׁאֵינוֹ טוֹחֵן. שֶׁאֵין בְּנֵי מֵעָיו טוֹחֲנִין אֲכִילָתוֹ: קוּרְקְבָן. הוּא הַמֵּסֶס, שֶׁקּוֹרִין ליגפי"ל: כָּל בְּנוֹת הַשִּׁיר. כָּל קוֹלוֹת שֶׁל שִׁיר הָוְיָין לֵיהּ שׁוּחָה: שֶׁדַּעְתָּן שֶׁל זְקֵנִים מִשְׁתַּנּוֹת. דִּכְתִיב: "הַאֵדַע בֵּין טוֹב לְרָע", וּבִזְקֵנָה מְרוּבָּה קָאָמַר: מִתְרַפְּטוֹת. מִתְבַּקְּעוֹת. כְּמוֹ "מִנְעָל הַמְרוּפָּט" (לעיל דף קמא:): מִתְכַּבְּדוֹת. כְּמוֹ "וְאָזְנָיו הַכְבֵּד" (ישעיה ו): שָׁטוּף. כְּמוֹ "סוּס שׁוֹטֵף בַּמִּלְחָמָה" (ירמיה ח) – לָהוּט אַחַר הַדָּבָר וְרוֹדֵף: וְטַעַם זְקֵנִים יִקָּח. וְע"כ, מְדַקְדְּקֵי קְרָאֵי אַהֲדָדֵי, חַד מְתוּקָּם בַּחֲכָמִים וְחַד בְּזִקְנֵי הַשּׁוּק: מִגָּבוֹהַּ יִירָאוּ. יְרֵאִים הֵם הַזְּקֵנִים מִגַּבְשׁוּשִׁית שֶׁבַּדְּרָכִים, וְאוֹמְרִים גְּבוֹהִים הֵם: תְּוָהִים. פְּחָדִים: וְיָנֵאץ הַשָּׁקֵד. אִילָן שֶׁל שְׁקֵדִים יָצִיץ, וְיִהְיוּ בּוֹלְטִין נִצָּיו שֶׁלּוֹ: זוֹ קְלִיבוּסֶת. עֶצֶם שֶׁל הנק"א שֶׁהַיָּרֵךְ תָּקוּעַ בּוֹ בּוֹלֵט וְיוֹצֵא מֵרוֹב תָּשׁוּת כֹּחוֹ: וְיִסְתַּבֵּל הֶחָגָב. דּוֹמֶה עָלָיו כְּסֵבֶל, מַשָּׂא כָּבֵד: וְתָפֵר הָאֲבִיּוֹנָה. תִּבָּטֵל הַתַּאֲוָה, חֶמְדַּת תַּשְׁמִישׁ: פָּסֵיק סִידְרָא. מְסַדֵּר פָּרָשִׁיּוֹת שֶׁל פְּסוּקִים: נָגֵיד וְאִיתְנַח. רַב: חֶמְדֵּיהּ. תַּאֲוָתוֹ: זוֹ אִשָּׁה. אִם לֹא עַל פִּי גְּזֵרַת הַמֶּלֶךְ לֹא הָיְתָה רְאוּיָה לְהִתְאַוּוֹת לָהּ, שֶׁהִיא כְּחֵמֶת מְלֵאָה מִיאוּס וְהַכֹּל רָצִים אַחֲרֶיהָ: מָדוֹר לְפִי כְבוֹדוֹ. מִדְּלָא כְּתִיב אֶל בֵּית הָעוֹלָם – ש"מ כָּל אֶחָד וְאֶחָד לְבֵית הַמּוּכָן לוֹ: בְּשַׁעַר אֶחָד. אַף כָּאן הַכֹּל מֵתִים בְּעִנְיָן אֶחָד: שֶׁאָדָם עוֹשֶׂה בְּיַלְדוּתוֹ. רוֹב תַּשְׁמִישׁ: מַשְׁחִירִים פָּנָיו. מַתִּישׁ כֹּחוֹ: שֶׁאֵין לוֹ מְנַחֲמִים. אֵין לוֹ אֲבֵלִים שֶׁיְּהוּ צְרִיכִין לְנַחֲמוֹ: בִּמְקוֹמוֹ. בַּמָּקוֹם שֶׁמֵּת שָׁם:

מס' ד"א זוטא פ"י

[פי' מיני קמשונים ערוך]

[נ"ל איקא עי' בערוך]

[נ"ל קול שרים ושרות]

[תענית ה:]

[קנים ספ"ג ע"ש וכמפרש]

[תרגום של ויחרד ותוה ערוך]

עי' מ"ר ויקרא פ' י"ח

[ב"מ פג:]

ברכות יח: לעיל יג:

[לעיל נה. ברכות לו. עירובין נז. חגיגה טו: ר"ה כו: כתובות יב: יד. נג. קדושין לב. גיטין עח: ב"ק יז. טו: לו: ב"ב קנג: ע"ז מג: סנהדרין פ: כריתות יט: נדה יג. יז. כה:]

הגהות הב"ח

(א) גמ' נעשה לבו תוהים תוהים ויגאץ השקד:

מח א מיי' פ"ד מהלכות דעות הל"ט טוש"ע או"ח סימן רמ סעיף יד:

מט ב מיי' פי"ג מהל' אבל הלכה ד סמג עשין ב טוש"ע יו"ד סי' שעו סעיף ג [וברב אלפס מו"ק פ"ג דף כ"ז:] וברא"ש שם סימן פ"ט:

רבינו חננאל

השבת לפי שבטל מן המצות והיינו דא"ר יוחנן מאי דכתיב במתים חפשי כיון שמת אדם נעשה חפשי מן המצות: **א"ל** קיסר לר' יהושע מ"ט לא אתית לבי אבידן. פי' בי אבידן בית שמתקבצין שם החכמים ונושאין ונותנין בדיני כל אומה ולשון השיבו ר' יהושע טור תלג סחרנוהי גלידין כלבוהי לא נבחין טחנוהי לא טחנן בבי רב אמרי (או לא או דן פי' בו) [אדלא אבדן בחשנא] ופירושו ההר כסהו שלג ודומה האדם להר כלומר ראשו כיסתו השיבה. וסביבותיה שהן הלחיים נעשו גלידין והוא הקרח שנקרא גליד. והגרון והלשון אינן מרימין קול. ככי שהן השניים אינן טוחנין המאכל. אדלא אבדן בחשנא. כלומר הזקן שאינו מביט מה שבפניו מתיירא שמא יכה ראשו באבן או בכיוצא בה וממשש בידו ונראה בדבר שאבד לו וזהו כמין משל ממשש הזקן מה שלא אבד. טבי תרי מתלת. פי' יותר הוא טוב המהלך על ב' רגליו מן הזקן שצריך משען כגון מקל או שבט להישען עליו והוא כמו רגל שלישי. חבל על דאזלא ולא אתיא. פי' הבחרות הולכת כשמזקין האדם ואינה חוזרת אליו. ינקותא כלילא. דוורדי הבחרות כתר של וורד ריחו נודף ושל זקנה כתר של חילף שריחו מאוס. דוק בבכי ותשכח בנגרי. בשניים כלומר אכול כדי שיהיה לך כח להלך ברגליך. א"ל ההוא גאזא חתוך (הערוה) [הביצים] והוא סרים א"ל ר' יהושע בן קרחה מהכא לקרחוניא כמה. ביקש להודיעו שהוא קרח והן ביר לו דברים כמו יהושע כמו הכא לגזוניא כלומר אתה גזוי. עוד אמר ליה ברחא קרחא בארבע. פי' (או) [עור] כבש גדול בד' כספים. השיבו ר' יהושע הדברים מוכיחין שגם אלו דברי הסרים הם שבקשו להודיעו כי השלוף ביוקר יותר מן הקרח. ילמדנו רבינו איקא שליפא בתמניא. פי' עור תיש נתוק ביצים בשמונה כספים. שמבקשין אותו לעשותו נודות של שמן. חזייה דלא מסיים מסאניה. פירוש ראהו יחף כו'. א"ל קרחה מצוי. פי' א"ל קרחה מריבה סחרחר. כדכתיב הן לריב ומצה וגו' השיבו ר' יהושע תיש נתוק תוכחה אינם דברי ריב אלא דברי תוכחה. מפני מה לא הקבלנו פניך. למה לא באת אלינו להתראות פנים: מיכן ששפתותיהן של זקנים מתרפטות. פי' מתרפטות משתרבבות והוא מתרופפות אינם מתאמצת להסתם הפה בחזקה. גבשושית פי' גב קטן של עפר. קליבוסת פירוש מן הפקוקלות ומפורש באלו טרפות. תרבא דאקליבוסתא. יתפר האביונה. זו חמדה (כמו) [כי] בטלה ממנו תאות אשה. פי' טלוניתא כמו על שאין בה ממש. גשיה שם ידו עליו מלשון נגששה:

רב נסים גאון

אמר ליה סלעים נעשין גבוהים כמו שנאמר אח"כ שאפילו גבשושית קטנה דומה עליו כהררי הרים ושאר הענין פירשוהו במקצת ההגדה וכך אמרו רחוקים נעשו קרובים אילין עיניא דחוון מרחוק אף מקרוב ליתנון חמאן קרובים נעשו רחוקים אילין אודניא דהוון שמעין בחד זמן כדו אף בחמשה זימנין ליתנון שמעין ב' נעשו ג' חוטרא ותרין ריגליא משים שלום בבית בטל זו תאוה שהיא מעלה שלום

תורה אור

כל יומא הוה דבר רב יהודה בי עשרה, ויתבי בדוכתיה. לאחר שבעה ימים איתחזי ליה בחילמיה דרב יהודה, ואמר ליה: *תנוח דעתך שהנחת את דעתי. א"ר אבהו: [א]כל שאומרים בפני המת יודע, עד שיסתם הגולל. פליגי בה רבי חייא ור"ש ברבי; חד אמר: עד שיסתם הגולל, וחד אמר: עד שיתעכל הבשר. מאן דאמר עד שיתעכל הבשר – דכתיב °"אך בשרו עליו יכאב ונפשו עליו תאבל". מאן דאמר עד שיסתם הגולל – דכתיב: °"וישוב העפר על הארץ כשהיה וגו'". ת"ר: °"והרוח תשוב אל האלהים אשר נתנה" – תנה לו כמו שנתנה לך בטהרה – אף אתה בטהרה. משל למלך ב"ו שחלק בגדי מלכות לעבדיו. פקחין שבהן קיפלום והניחום בקופסא, טפשים שבהן הלכו ועשו בהן מלאכה. לימים ביקש המלך את כליו, פקחין שבהן החזירום לו כשהן מגוהצין, טפשין שבהן החזירום לו כשהן מלוכלכין. שמח המלך לקראת פקחין, וכעס לקראת טפשין. על פקחין אמר: ינתנו כלי לאוצר, והם ילכו לבתיהם לשלום. ועל טפשין אמר: כלי ינתנו לכובס, והן יתחבשו בבית האסורים. אף הקב"ה, על גופן של צדיקים אומר: °"יבא שלום ינוחו על משכבותם" ועל נשמתן הוא אומר: °"והיתה נפש אדוני צרורה בצרור החיים"*. על גופן של רשעים הוא אומר: °"אין שלום אמר ה' לרשעים" ועל נשמתן הוא אומר: °"ואת נפש אויביך יקלענה בתוך כף הקלע". תניא, ר' אליעזר אומר: נשמתן של צדיקים גנוזות תחת כסא הכבוד, שנאמר: "והיתה נפש אדני צרורה בצרור החיים", ושל רשעים *זוממות והולכות, [*ומלאך אחד עומד בסוף העולם ומלאך אחר עומד בסוף העולם, ומקלעין נשמתן זה לזה], שנא': "ואת נפש אויביך יקלענה בתוך כף הקלע". א"ל רבה לר"נ: של בינונים מאי? א"ל: *איכא[א] שכיבנא לא אמרי לכו האי מילתא. הכי אמר שמואל: אלו ואלו לדומה נמסרין, הללו – יש להן מנוח, הללו – אין להן מנוח. אמרו (ליה) [לה] מרי: עתידים צדיקים דהוו עפרא, דכתיב: °"וישוב העפר על הארץ כשהיה". הנהו קפולאי דהוו קפלי בארעא דרב נחמן, *)נחר בהו רב אחאי בר יאשיה. אתו ואמרו ליה לרב נחמן: נחר בן גברא. אתא ואמר ליה: מאן ניהו מר? אמר ליה: אנא אחאי בר יאשיה. א"ל: ולאו אמר רב מרי: עתידי צדיקי דהוו עפרא? א"ל: ומני מרי, דלא ידענא ליה! א"ל: והא קרא כתיב: "וישוב העפר על הארץ כשהיה"? אמר ליה: דאקרייך קהלת לא אקרייך משלי, דכתיב: °"ורקב עצמות קנאה" כל מי שיש לו קנאה בלבו – עצמותיו מרקיבים, כל שאין לו קנאה בלבו – אין עצמותיו מרקיבים. גששיה, חזייה דאית ביה מששא. אמר ליה: ליקום מר לגוויה דביתא! אמר ליה: גלית אדעתך דאפילו נביאי לא קרית, דכתיב: °"וידעתם כי אני ה' בפתחי *את קברותיכם". א"ל: והכתיב °"כי עפר אתה ואל עפר תשוב"! א"ל: ההוא – שעה אחת קודם תחיית המתים. א"ל ההוא מינא לר' אבהו: אמריתו "נשמתן של צדיקים גנוזות תחת כסא הכבוד". אובא טמיא היכא אסקיה לשמואל *בנגידא? א"ל: התם בתוך שנים עשר חדש הוה. דתניא: כל י"ב חדש גופו קיים, ונשמתו עולה ויורדת. לאחר י"ב חדש הגוף בטל, ונשמתו

*) [עי' פירושו ברש"י גיטין סח. ד"ה נחר].

רש"י

כל יומא. ז' ימי אבילות: גולל. הוא כיסוי שנותנים על ארונו: ונפשו עליו תאבל. כל זמן שיש לו בשר, יש לו לנפש צד חיות להבין: וישוב העפר. גופו קרוי עפר, ומשוב אל הארץ כשהיה – מיד והרוח תשוב, שאין בו רוח עוד: אשר נתנה. קרא יתירה הוא לידרש: הוי זהיר שתשיבנה אליו כמה שנתנה לך, נקייה בלי עון: כלי ינתנו לאוצר. להצניען, אף זו תינתן תחת כסא הכבוד: לכובס. ללבנן, אף זו לגיהנם לצורפם שם: בבית האסורים. בחשך, בלא אורה ושלוה: כף הקלע. רצב הרצועה שנותן האבן לתוכה לקלע, עשויה כעין כף: בצרור החיים וגו'. "את ה' אלהיך" – עמו בכסאו: זוממות. כמו "בזממא דפרזלא" (לעיל דף נא:) – חבושות בבית הסוהר: אלו ואלו. רשעים ובינונים: לדומה. מלאך הממונה על הרוחות: דהוו עפרא. אפילו צדיקים נרקבים ונעשים אפר: קפולאי. חופרים: נחר בהו[ב] רבי אחאי. שהיה נקבר שם: דלא ידענא ליה. ואיני חש לדבריו: מי שיש לו קנאה. ותחרות על חבירו: עצמותיו מרקיבים. ועליו נאמר: "וישוב אל העפר": ליקום מר לגוויה.[ג] יבא אדוני לבית: בפתחי. בהעלותי. עד שיעלנו הקדוש ברוך הוא מקברותינו, אין לנו רשות לעלות: והא כתיב ואל עפר תשוב. והאי ליכא למימר ברשעים לחודייהו, דכל קללותיו של אדה"ר כל דורותיו שוין בהן: אובא טמיא. בעלת אוב שמשתמש בעצמות. טמיא בלשון ארמי עצמות, וכן פירש רב האי בפירושו של טהרות: בית שהוא מלא טמיא – מלא עצמות*: בנגידא. כן קורין למכשפות של אוב בלשון ארמי: אס

תוספות

עד שיסתם הגולל. בכל מקום מפרש רש"י דגולל הוא כיסוי ארונו של מת, ודופק – דף שנתון מצידו, ונקרא דופק על שם שהמת דופק שם. כמו: חתיכה גופה תיהוי סימן, אי לאדפקא אי דלאטמא, בפרק "אלו מציאות" (ב"מ דף כג:). שנקרא דופק לפי שהנשימה דופקת. ואין נראה לר"ת, מדאמר בברכות פרק "מי שמתו" (דף יט: ושם): מדלגים היינו ע"ג ארונות לקראת מלכי אומות העולם. ואי ארון היינו גולל ודופק – היאך היו מדלגין עליו? והלא גולל ודופק מטמאין באהל, כדאמר בחולין בפרק "העור והרוטב" (דף קכו:): גולל ודופק מטמא במגע ובאהל, ואינו מטמא במשא! ועוד: דאמר בעירובין (דף טו:): כל דבר שיש בו רוח חיים אין עושין אותו לא גולל לקבר ולא דופן לסוכה ולא לחי למבוי. ואי כפי' הקונט', וכי דרך לעשות כיסוי ארון מבעלי חיים? ועוד, בפרק "בהמה המקשה" (חולין עב.) מרבינן[ד] דופק דמטמא מדכתיב: "על פני השדה", ולפי' הקונטרס הוא מונח בקרקע – דהיינו ארון, ולא על פני השדה! ועוד, דתנן במס' אהלות בפ"ב (משנה ד): דופק דופקים טהור. ואי כפירוש הקונטרס, וכי דרך להניח שני קרשים מימין המת? ופירש ר"ת: דגולל היינו אבן גדולה שעל ארונו של מת שקורין מצבה, וגוללין אותה שם הקרובי' לסימן. ולשון גולל נופל באבן, כדכתיב (בראשית כט): "וגללו את האבן" "וגולל אבן אליו תשוב" (משלי כו). ודופק הם שתי אבני' שנותנין[ה], אחת לראשו ואחת לרגליו לציון. ופעמים שעדיין האבן אינה מוכנת לשום שם – נותנין שם בהמה או שום דבר לסימן, עד שימצאו אבן. והיינו דתנן בעירובין (דף טו.) לדבר שיש בו רוח חיים אין עושין כו'. ובההיא דמדלגין היינו ע"ג ארונות – שלא היה שם לא גולל ולא דופק, ומחמת המת לא היינו מיטמאים כדמפרש התם, שהיה ברוב ארונות[ו] חלל טפח. ומרבי נמי שפיר גולל ודופק מ"על פני השדה". והא דקאמר דופק דופקים – פעמים שמניחים הגולל ע"ג שתי אבנים, ועוד מניחין לראש הגולל אבן אחת ולסופו אבן אחרת. ולא תקשה לר' יהושע דאמר בפרק קמא דכתובות (דף ד: ושם): מאימתי חל אבילות – משיסתם הגולל, במקום שאין גולל מתי חל? די"ל: מכי אהדרי אפייהו מקברא, כדאמר במו"ק (ד' כב.) בהנהו דלא אזלי בתר שכבא – מנו מכי אהדרי אפייהו. ויש דוחין ראיה של ר"ת: דמאי דמייתי ראיה מדמדלגין היינו – אף על פי שהגולל מטמא באהל מ"מ יכולין היינו לדלג, ולטמא עצמנו בגולל. דהא תניא[א]: כל טומאה שאין הנזיר מגלח עליה – אין כהן מוזהר עליו. וגולל ודופק אין הנזיר מגלח עלייהו, כדתנן במסכת נזיר פרק "כ"ג" (דף נד.)! ואמר ר"ת: דמשבשתא היא דמסכת שמחות, דהא התלמוד ערוך דרביעית דם אין הנזיר מגלח עליו, כדתנן התם בנזיר, *וכהן מוזהר. ואם הברייתא בהתלמוד – הוה פריך עלה ומשבש לה, כדאשכחינן בכמה דוכתין דמשבש להו. ואפילו הויא מתרצתא – אכתי היאך מדלגין? הלא מחמת המת היו מיטמאים, והגולל ודופק לא היו חוצצין! ומה שהביא ראיה מעירובין – יש דוחין, דאע"פ שאין רגילות לעשות כסוי ארון מבעלי חיים – כמה דברים אשכחן דלא שכיחי ומיירי בהו התלמוד, להראות לנו הדין, ודרוש וקבל שכר. כדאמרי' ב"בהמה המקשה" (חולין דף ע.): בלעתו חולדה והוציאתו, והכניסתו והקיאתו, ויצא מאליו מהו? הדביק שני רחמים ויצא מזה ונכנס לזה מהו? ואף על פי שזה לא יהיה לעולם. ועוד מקשינן לפירוש ר"ת: מדתני בהדיא בתוספתא דאהלות בפרק "אמר רבי יהודה": שתי אבנים גדולות שעשאן גולל לקבר, המאהיל על גבי שתיהן – טמא. ניטלה אחת מהן – המאהיל על גבי שנייה טהור, מפני שיש לטומאה דרך שתצא. ומה דרך שתצא שייך לפירוש ר"ת? ובערוך פירש בענין אחר בערך גלל, וכפירושו יתכן מה שבתוספתא*:

א) [במס' שמחות פ"ד הל' כ"א ע"ש].

עין משפט נר מצוה

נ א סמג עשין דרבנן ב:

רב נסים גאון

שלום בין איש לאשתו **אלו** ואלו נמסרין לדומה הללו יש להן מנוח והללו אין להן מנוח. בפרק כל ישראל יש להם חלק (סנהדרין דף לד) גרסינן א"ר יוחנן אותו מלאך שהוא ממונה על הרוחות דומה שמו וכבר הזכרנו אותו בברכות:

סליק שואל אדם

גליון הש"ס

גמ' על גופן של רשעים הוא אומר אין שלום אמר אלהי כנ"ל: שם כל מי שיש לו קנאה בלבו. עי' ב"ב דף יז ע"א תוס' ד"ה שבעה:

[נ"ל את ה' אלקיך על כו']

זוממת והולכת שנאמר ואת נפש כו' פי' לדייק מדלא אמרה יקלענה בכף הקלע ואמר בתוך כף הקלע משמע שהיא חבושה וכבושה בתוך כף הקלע ואינה יוצאת ממנו ומלאך ממלאכי חבלה מקלע אותה רצועה לכאן ולכאן וזהו לשון זוממות

[נ"ל את קברותיכם ובהעלותי אתכם מקברותיכם עמי וכ"ה בע"י וכזה תבין פרק ר"ה בפתחי בהעלותי עד שיעלנו וכו']

מסורת הש"ס

[פסחים לב: יומא סו: סנהדרין ל: מנחות מה. ק.]

רשב"ם ב"ב קיט: ד"ה רבי חנניה [קהלת יב]

ראה רש"י ברכות נט. ד"ה אוכא

שמואל א כה

גי' רש"ל לא משמע כן מפי' רש"י שפי' שהן חבושין ולגי' זו אינן חבושי' ואולי מצא גי' כזו אבל גי' רש"י אינו כן מ"כ

משלי יד

בראשית ג

[ערוך ערך בנגידא פי' בכישוף]

[דף נד.]

[וע"ע תוספות ברכות יט: ד"ה מדלגין ותוס' סוכה כג. ד"ה ולא ותוס' כתובות ד: ד"ה עד ותוס' סנהדרין מז: ד"ה משיסתום]

הגהות הב"ח

(א) גמ' איכא שכיבנא. נ"ב כלומר אי שכיבנא: (ב) רש"י ד"ה נחר בהו גער בהו רבי אחאי: (ג) ד"ה ליקום מר לגויה דביתא יבא: (ד) תוס' ד"ה עד שיסתום וכו' מרבינן גולל ודופק דמטמא: (ה) בא"ד שנותנין אחת לראשו. נ"ב פי' לראשו ולרגליו של גולל וכן הוא בתוספות פ"ק דכתובות דף ד' וע"ש בפרק מי שמתו בדף יט: (ו) בא"ד ברוב ארונות שלהם חלל טפח:

וְנִשְׁמָתוֹ עוֹלָה וְשׁוּב אֵינָהּ יוֹרֶדֶת. אָמַר רַב יְהוּדָה בְּרֵיהּ דְּרַב שְׁמוּאֵל בַּר* שֵׁילַת מִשְּׁמֵיהּ דְּרַב: מֵהֶסְפֵּדוֹ שֶׁל אָדָם נִיכָּר אִם בֶּן הָעוה"ב הוּא אִם לָאו. אִינִי, וְהָאָמַר לֵיהּ רַב לְרַב שְׁמוּאֵל בַּר שֵׁילַת: אַחֵים בְּהֶסְפֵּידָא, דְּהָתָם קָאֵימְנָא! לָא קַשְׁיָא, הָא – דְּמִחַמּוּ לֵיהּ וְאַחֵים, הָא – דְּמִחַמּוּ לֵיהּ וְלָא אַחֵים. א"ל אַבַּיֵי לְרַבָּה: כְּגוֹן מָר, דְּסָנוּ לֵיהּ כּוּלְּהוּ פּוּמְבְּדִיתָאֵי, מַאן אַחֵים הֶסְפֵּידָא? א"ל: מִיסְתַּיָּא אַתְּ וְרַבָּה בַּר רַב חָנָן. בְּעָא מִינֵּיהּ רַבִּי אֶלְעָזָר מֵרַב: אֵיזֶהוּ בֶּן הָעוה"ב? א"ל: °"וְאָזְנֶיךָ תִּשְׁמַעְנָה דָּבָר מֵאַחֲרֶיךָ לֵאמֹר זֶה הַדֶּרֶךְ לְכוּ בוֹ כִּי תַאֲמִינוּ וְכִי תַשְׂמְאִילוּ". ר' חֲנִינָא אָמַר: כֹּל שֶׁדַּעַת *רַבּוֹתֵינוּ נוֹחָה הֵימֶנּוּ. °"וְסָבְבוּ בַשּׁוּק הַסּוֹפְדִים". בְּנֵי גָלִילָא אָמְרִי: עֲשֵׂה דְּבָרִים לְפָנֵי מִטָּתְךָ, בְּנֵי יְהוּדָה אָמְרִי: עֲשֵׂה דְּבָרִים לְאַחַר מִטָּתְךָ. וְלָא פְּלִיגֵי, *מָר כִּי אַתְרֵיהּ וּמָר כִּי אַתְרֵיהּ. תְּנַן הָתָם, רַבִּי אֱלִיעֶזֶר אוֹמֵר*: אשׁוּב יוֹם אֶחָד לִפְנֵי מִיתָתְךָ. שָׁאֲלוּ תַּלְמִידָיו אֶת ר"א: וְכִי אָדָם יוֹדֵעַ אֵיזֶהוּ יוֹם יָמוּת? אָמַר לָהֶן: וְכָל שֶׁכֵּן, יָשׁוּב הַיּוֹם שֶׁמָּא יָמוּת לְמָחָר, וְנִמְצָא כָּל יָמָיו בִּתְשׁוּבָה. וְאַף שְׁלֹמֹה אָמַר בְּחָכְמָתוֹ: °"בְּכָל עֵת יִהְיוּ בְגָדֶיךָ לְבָנִים וְשֶׁמֶן עַל רֹאשְׁךָ אַל יֶחְסָר". א"ר יוֹחָנָן בֶּן זַכַּאי: מָשָׁל לְמֶלֶךְ שֶׁזִּימֵּן אֶת עֲבָדָיו לִסְעוּדָה, וְלֹא קָבַע לָהֶם זְמַן. פִּיקְחִין שֶׁבָּהֶן קִישְּׁטוּ אֶת עַצְמָן וְיָשְׁבוּ עַל פֶּתַח בֵּית הַמֶּלֶךְ, אָמְרוּ: כְּלוּם חָסֵר לְבֵית הַמֶּלֶךְ? טִיפְּשִׁין שֶׁבָּהֶן הָלְכוּ לִמְלַאכְתָּן, אָמְרוּ: כְּלוּם יֵשׁ סְעוּדָה בְּלֹא טוֹרַח? בְּפִתְאוֹם בִּיקֵּשׁ הַמֶּלֶךְ אֶת עֲבָדָיו. פִּיקְחִין שֶׁבָּהֶן נִכְנְסוּ לְפָנָיו כְּשֶׁהֵן מְקוּשָּׁטִין, וְהַטִּיפְּשִׁים נִכְנְסוּ לְפָנָיו כְּשֶׁהֵן מְלוּכְלָכִין. שָׂמַח הַמֶּלֶךְ לִקְרַאת פִּיקְחִים, וְכָעַס לִקְרַאת טִיפְּשִׁים. אָמַר: הַלָּלוּ שֶׁקִּישְּׁטוּ אֶת עַצְמָן לִסְעוּדָה – יֵשְׁבוּ וְיֹאכְלוּ וְיִשְׁתּוּ, הַלָּלוּ שֶׁלֹּא קִישְּׁטוּ עַצְמָן לִסְעוּדָה – יַעַמְדוּ וְיִרְאוּ. חַתְנוֹ שֶׁל ר"מ מִשּׁוּם ר"מ אָמַר: אַף הֵן נִרְאִין כִּמְשַׁמְּשִׁין. אֶלָּא, אֵלּוּ וָאֵלּוּ יוֹשְׁבִין, הַלָּלוּ – אוֹכְלִין, וְהַלָּלוּ – רְעֵבִין, הַלָּלוּ שׁוֹתִין וְהַלָּלוּ צְמֵאִים, שֶׁנֶּאֱמַר:(א) °"כֹּה אָמַר ה' הִנֵּה עֲבָדַי יֹאכֵלוּ וְאַתֶּם תִּרְעָבוּ הִנֵּה עֲבָדַי יִשְׁתּוּ וְאַתֶּם תִּצְמָאוּ הִנֵּה עֲבָדַי יָרֹנּוּ מִטּוּב לֵב וְאַתֶּם תִּצְעֲקוּ מִכְּאֵב לֵב". ד"א: "בְּכָל עֵת יִהְיוּ בְגָדֶיךָ לְבָנִים" – אֵלּוּ צִיצִית, "וְשֶׁמֶן עַל רֹאשְׁךָ אַל יֶחְסָר" – אֵלּוּ תְּפִילִּין.§

הדרן עלך שואל

*מִי בשֶׁהֶחְשִׁיךְ(ה) בַּדֶּרֶךְ – נוֹתֵן כִּיסוֹ לְגוֹי, גוְאִם אֵין עִמּוֹ גּוֹי – מַנִּיחוֹ עַל הַחֲמוֹר. דהִגִּיעַ לֶחָצֵר הַחִיצוֹנָה – נוֹטֵל אֶת הַכֵּלִים הַנִּיטָּלִין בַּשַּׁבָּת, וְשֶׁאֵינָן נִיטָּלִין בַּשַּׁבָּת – מַתִּיר הַחֲבָלִים, וְהַשַּׂקִּין נוֹפְלִין מֵאֵילֵיהֶם.§ **גמ'** מַאי טַעְמָא שָׁרוּ לֵיהּ רַבָּנַן לְמֵיתַב כִּיסֵיהּ לְגוֹי? קִים לְהוּ לְרַבָּנַן הדְּאֵין אָדָם מַעֲמִיד עַצְמוֹ עַל מָמוֹנוֹ, אִי לָא שָׁרֵית לֵיהּ – אָתֵי לְאִיתּוּיֵי ד' אַמּוֹת בִּרה"ר. אָמַר רָבָא: ודַּוְקָא כִּיסוֹ, אֲבָל מְצִיאָה – לָא. פְּשִׁיטָא, "כִּיסוֹ" תְּנַן! מַהוּ דְּתֵימָא: הוּא הַדִּין אֲפִילּוּ מְצִיאָה, וְהַאי דְּקָתָנֵי כִּיסוֹ – אוֹרְחָא דְּמִילְּתָא קָתָנֵי, קמ"ל. וְלָא אֲמַרַן אֶלָּא זדְּלָא אָתֵי לִידֵיהּ, אֲבָל אָתֵי לִידֵיהּ – כְּכִיסֵיהּ דָּמֵי. אִיכָּא דְּאָמְרִי; בָּעֵי רָבָא: מְצִיאָה הַבָּאָה לְיָדוֹ מַהוּ? כֵּיוָן דְּאָתְאָ לִידֵיהּ – כְּכִיסֵיהּ דָּמֵי, אוֹ דִּילְמָא: כֵּיוָן דְּלָא טָרַח בַּהּ – לָאו כְּכִיסֵיהּ דָּמֵי? תֵּיקוּ.§ "אֵין עִמּוֹ גּוֹי".§ טַעְמָא, דְּאֵין עִמּוֹ גּוֹי, הָא יֵשׁ עִמּוֹ גּוֹי – לְגוֹי יָהֵיב לֵיהּ. מַאי טַעְמָא? חחֲמוֹר אַתָּה מְצוּוֶּה עַל שְׁבִיתָתוֹ, גּוֹי – אִי אַתָּה מְצוּוֶּה עַל שְׁבִיתָתוֹ. חֲמוֹר וְחֵרֵשׁ שׁוֹטֶה וְקָטָן – טאַחֲמוֹר מַנַּח לֵיהּ, לְחֵרֵשׁ שׁוֹטֶה וְקָטָן לָא יָהֵיב לֵיהּ. מ"ט – הָנֵי אָדָם, הַאי – לָאו אָדָם. יחֵרֵשׁ וְשׁוֹטֶה – לְשׁוֹטֶה, כשׁוֹטֶה וְקָטָן – לְשׁוֹטֶה. אִיבַּעְיָא לְהוּ: לחֵרֵשׁ וְקָטָן מַאי? אַלִּיבָּא דר"א לָא תִּיבָּעֵי לָךְ, דְּתַנְיָא, *ר' יִצְחָק אוֹמֵר מִשּׁוּם ר' *)אֱלִיעֶזֶר: תְּרוּמַת חֵרֵשׁ לֹא

*) [שם איתא אלעזר]

רש"י

אם בן עוה"ב הוא. שאם כשר היה הכל בוכין עליו ומורידין דמעות ומספרים שבחו: אחים בהספידא דהתם קאימנא. בשעת מיתתי התחמם בהספד שלי, שיתחממו ויכמרו רחמי העומדים ויבכו: דהתם קאימנא. בשעת הספד, ואשמע איך תתחמם. אלמא, איצטריך לרב לאזהוריה אהספדא, וכיון דרב גברא רבה ובן העולם הבא, למה ליה לאזהוריה? הא אמר מהספידו ניכר: הא דמחממין ליה. להספידא ואחים כו' לעולם חמומי בעי, שאין בני אדם נכמרים כל כך על זקן. ומיהו, לאדם חסיד כי מחממו בהספידא – מחממי, ובכו כולהו. ולמי שאינו חסיד כל כך – מחממו ליה ולא מחממו: דסנו ליה כולהו פומבדיתאי. משום דמוכח להו במילי דשמיא(ב). ובני פומבדיתאי רמאין הן, כדאמרינן בשחיטת חולין (חולין קכז.): פומבדיתאי לוייך – שני אושפיזך: ואזניך תשמענה דבר מאחריך לאמר זה הדרך לכו בה(ג). מאחרי מטתך כשתמות, תשמע כשיאמרו: זה הדרך שהלך בה זה לכו בה, מובטח שהוא בן העוה"ב: נוחה הימנו. דעתם נוחה עליהם ממה ששומעין עליו ורואין בו: עשה דברים. שיאמרו לפני מטתך בהספדך: לאחר מטתך. היא היא, אלא שבגליל היו הספדנין לפני המטה, וביהודה לאחר המטה: וכ"ש. שמפני שאינו יודע איזה יום ימות(ד), וטובה תשובה יום אחד לפני מיתתו, נמצא כל ימיו בתשובה יהיו: בגדיך לבנים. נשמתך טהורה ונקיה: כלום חסר בית המלך. בתמיה. הכל מוכן, ושמא יבהילנו לבא פתאום, ואנו צריכין ליכנס לסעודה מקושטין: כלום יש סעודה בלא טורח. עדיין יצטרכו לטרוח לצורכי סעודה של בית המלך, ויש לנו שהות הרבה להתקשט: יעמדו ויראו. ואף לעוה"ב, לצדיקים יושבים ואוכלים, ורשעים עומדים ורואים: ר"מ אומר. אין עומדין ורואין, שא"כ אף הם היו נראים מן הקרואים ולשמש, שכן דרך המשרתים עומדים, ואין כאן בושה: זה ציצית. שמלובן הבגד: אלו תפילין. שהם שם משמן טוב, דכתיב: "וראו כל עמי הארץ כי שם" וגו', ותנא: ר"א הגדול אומר, אלו תפילין שבראש (ברכות דף ו.):

הדרן עלך שואל

מי שהחשיך(ו). נותן כיסו לגוי. מבעוד יום: ואם אין עמו. הא יש עמו – לגוי עדיף, כדמפרש בגמרא: לחצר החיצונה. של עיר, שהוא מקום המשתמר ראשון, ובא לפרק מן החמור: נוטל. בידו מעליו כלים הניטלין בשבת. ושאין ניטלין – מתיר החבלים של אוכף שהן קשורים בהן והשקין נופלין: **גמ'** מאי טעמא שרי ליה למיתב לגוי. והרי הוא שלוחו לישאנו בשבת: מעמיד עצמו. מלהציל ממונו: דוקא כיסו. דכיון דטרח בה, שע"י טורח הוא משתכר – חייס עלה, ואי לא שרית ליה הא – אתי לאיתויי: ולא אמרן. דמציאה לא, אלא דלא אתיא לידיה קודם שתחשך, ולא הגביהה ולא זכה בה: האי אדם. ויש במינו שחייב במצות, ואתי לאיחלופי: לשוטה. יהיב, דלית ליה דעת כלל. אבל חרש – דעתא קלישתא אית ליה, כדאמרי' ביבמות (דף קיג.): לא

תוספות

ונשמתו עולה ושוב אינה יורדת. אף על פי כן כשהיא רוצה היא יורדת, כי ההיא דלעיל דרבי אחי בר יאשיה, וכההיא מעשה דר' בנאה ד"חזקת הבתים" (ב"ב דף נח. ושם) דהוה מציין מערתא, כי מטא למערתא דאברהם אדינו אשכחיה לאליעזר עבד אברהם דקאי אבבא, אמר ליה: מאי קא עביד אברהם כו'. אמר ליה: ניעול וניחי כו'. אע"פ שנשמתו היתה גנוזה מתחת כסא הכבוד. מ"ר:

הדרן עלך שואל

מי שהחשיך כו' חרש שוטה וקטן. אע"ג דאמר לעיל בפרק "כל כתבי" (דף קכא.) גבי קטן שבא לכבות דקטן העושה לדעת אביו אסור – מיהו הכא לא איירי כגון דעביד הקטן עקירה והנחה, אלא כדאמרינן לקמן גבי חמור: כשהיא מהלכת מניחו עליה, וכשהיא עומדת נוטל הימנה. מ"ר: כי

עין משפט נר מצוה

נא א מיי' פ"ז מהלכות תשובה הלכה ב:

א ב מיי' פ"ו מהלכות שבת הלכה כב סמג לאוין סה טוש"ע או"ח סי' רסו סעיף א וסעיף ח וסימן שמט סעיף ה:

ב ג מיי' פ"כ שם הלכה ו סמג שם טוש"ע או"ח סי' רסו סעיף ב:

ג ד מיי' פכ"א שם הל' י סמג שם טוש"ע שם סעיף ט:

ד ה מיי' פ"ו שם הלכה כב סמג שם:

ה ו ז מיי' שם ופ"כ שם הלכה ז סמג שם טוש"ע שם סעיף א:

ו ח מיי' פ"כ שם הלכה ו סמג שם טוש"ע שם סעיף א:

ז ט מיי' שם הלכה ז טוש"ע שם סעיף ג:

ח י מיי' שם טוש"ע שם סעיף ד:

ט כ ל מיי' שם טוש"ע שם סעיף ה:

רבינו חננאל

איזה בן עולם הבא כל שדעת רבותיו נוחה הימנו כך שמעתא דא סלקא:

הדרן עלך שואל אדם

פרק כד מי שהחשיך בדרך נותן כיסו לגוי וכו' ואוקי' למתניתין דאין מעמיד עצמו על ממונו והתירו לו לתת כיסו לגוי בשביל שלא ישאנו הוא בעצמו. ובא רבא ודקדק ואמר דוקא כיסו אבל מציאה דלא אתא לידיה לא התירו לו לתתו לגוי ובמציאה דאתאי לידיה ללישנא בתרא עלתה בתיקו. וכל תיקו דאיסורא לחומרא והלכתא כרבא דאוקמא (לידיה) [למתני'] בכיסו ממש. אין עמו גוי מניחו על חמור דייקינן מינה בעת שמצויין ביחד גוי וחמור לגוי יהיב ליה מפני שאינו מצווה על שביתתו של גוי ולכן לא התירו לו לתת כיסו על החמור שהוא מצווה על שביתתו אלא אם אין שם גוי אלא חמור. וישראל חרש או שוטה או קטן אינו נותן כיסו לאחד מהן אלא נותן כיסו על החמור ולעולם לגרוע שבהן נותן כגון חרש ושוטה לשוטה נותן שוטה וקטן לשוטה נותן והשוטה גרוע בבני אדם שאין הפרש בין אדם לבהמה אלא הדעת והתבונה וזה כיון שאין לו דעת כבהמה חשוב:

מסורת הש"ס

נ"א שילא וכן לקמן

[נ"ל רבותיו וכ"א ברי"ף והרא"ש]

[פסחים ג. וש"נ]

[אבות פ"ב מ"י]

[לעיל יז:]

[יבמות קיג.]

הגהות הב"ח

(א) גמ' שנא' לכן כה אמר: (ב) רש"י ד"ה דסנו וכו' דבני פומבדיתאי: (ג) ד"ה אזניך וכו' לכו בו מאחרי: (ד) ד"ה וכ"ש שמפני וכו' ימות שישוב בתשובה:

פרק כד

(ה) במשנה מי שהחשיך לו בדרך: (ו) רש"י ד"ה מי שהחשיך לו נותן:

גליון הש"ס

גמרא בני גלילא אמרי עשה דברים לפני מטתך. מסכת שמחות פ"ג ה"ז:

מראי מקומות לפסוקים: ישעיהו ל; קהלת יב; שם ט; ישעיהו סה

גמרא

– לא תֵצֵא לְחוּלִּין, מִפְּנֵי שֶׁהוּא סָפֵק. כִּי תִּיבָּעֵי לָךְ – אַלִּיבָּא דְּרַבָּנַן, דִּתְנַן*: חֲמִשָּׁה לֹא יִתְרוֹמוּ, וְאִם תָּרְמוּ אֵין תְּרוּמָתָן תְּרוּמָה. אֵלּוּ הֵן: חֵרֵשׁ שׁוֹטֶה וְקָטָן, וְהַתּוֹרֵם אֶת שֶׁאֵינוֹ שֶׁלּוֹ, *וְגוֹי שֶׁתָּרַם אֶת שֶׁל יִשְׂרָאֵל אֲפִילּוּ בִּרְשׁוּתוֹ – אֵין תְּרוּמָתוֹ תְּרוּמָה. מַאי, לְחֵרֵשׁ יָהֵיב לֵיהּ – דְּקָטָן אָתֵי לִכְלַל דַּעַת, אוֹ דִילְמָא: לְקָטָן יָהֵיב לֵיהּ, דְּחֵרֵשׁ אָתֵי לְאַחְלוּפֵי בְּגָדוֹל פִּיקֵּחַ? אִיכָּא דְּאָמְרִי: לְחֵרֵשׁ יָהֵיב לֵיהּ, אִיכָּא דְּאָמְרִי: לְקָטָן יָהֵיב לֵיהּ. אֵין שָׁם לֹא גּוֹי וְלֹא חֲמוֹר וְלֹא חֵרֵשׁ וְלֹא שׁוֹטֶה וְלֹא קָטָן, מַאי? אָמַר רַבִּי יִצְחָק: עוֹד אַחֶרֶת הָיְתָה, וְלֹא רָצוּ חֲכָמִים לְגַלּוֹתָהּ. מַאי "עוֹד אַחֶרֶת הָיְתָה" – *מוֹלִיכוֹ פָּחוֹת פָּחוֹת מִד' אַמּוֹת. אַמַּאי לֹא רָצוּ חֲכָמִים לְגַלּוֹתָהּ – מִשּׁוּם °"כְּבוֹד אֱלֹהִים הַסְתֵּר דָּבָר וּכְבוֹד מְלָכִים חֲקוֹר דָּבָר". וְהָכָא, מַאי "כְּבוֹד אֱלֹהִים" אִיכָּא? דִּילְמָא אָתֵי לְאַתּוֹיֵי ד' אַמּוֹת בִּרְה"ר. תַּנְיָא, *ר"א אוֹמֵר: בּוֹ בַּיּוֹם גָּדְשׁוּ סְאָה. ר' יְהוֹשֻׁעַ אוֹמֵר: בּוֹ בַּיּוֹם מָחֲקוּ סְאָה. תַּנְיָא, מָשָׁל דְּר"א, לְמָה הַדָּבָר דּוֹמֶה – לְקוּפָּה מְלֵאָה קִישּׁוּאִין וְדִילּוּעִין, אָדָם נוֹתֵן לְתוֹכָהּ חַרְדָּל – וְהִיא מַחֲזֶקֶת. מָשָׁל דְּר' יְהוֹשֻׁעַ, לְמָה הַדָּבָר דּוֹמֶה – לַעֲרֵיבָה מְלֵאָה דְּבַשׁ, נוֹתֵן לְתוֹכָהּ רִימּוֹנִים וֶאֱגוֹזִים – וְהִיא מְקִיאָה. אָמַר מָר: אֵין עִמּוֹ גּוֹי – מַנִּיחוֹ עַל הַחֲמוֹר. וַהֲלֹא מְחַמֵּר, וְרַחֲמָנָא אָמַר: °"לֹא תַעֲשֶׂה כָל מְלָאכָה"! א"ר אַדָּא בַּר אַהֲבָה: מַנִּיחוֹ עָלֶיהָ כְּשֶׁהִיא מְהַלֶּכֶת. וְהָא אִי אֶפְשָׁר דְּלָא קָיְימָא לְהַשְׁתִּין מַיִם וּלְהַטִּיל גְּלָלִים, וְאִיכָּא עֲקִירָה וְהַנָּחָה! כְּשֶׁהִיא מְהַלֶּכֶת – מַנִּיחוֹ עָלֶיהָ, כְּשֶׁהִיא עוֹמֶדֶת – נוֹטְלוֹ הֵימֶנָּה. אִי הָכִי, אֲפִילּוּ חֲבֵרוֹ נָמֵי! אָמַר רַב פַּפָּא: כֹּל שֶׁבְּגוּפוֹ חַיָּיב חַטָּאת – בַּחֲבֵרוֹ פָּטוּר אֲבָל אָסוּר, כֹּל שֶׁחֲבֵרוֹ פָּטוּר אֲבָל אָסוּר – בַּחֲמוֹרוֹ מוּתָּר לְכַתְּחִלָּה. א"ר אַדָּא בַּר אַהֲבָה: הָיְתָה חֲבִילָתוֹ מוּנַּחַת לוֹ עַל כְּתֵיפוֹ – רָץ תַּחְתֶּיהָ עַד שֶׁמַּגִּיעַ לְבֵיתוֹ. דַּוְקָא רָץ, אֲבָל קַלֵּי קַלֵּי – לָא. מַאי טַעְמָא? כֵּיוָן דְּלֵית לֵיהּ הֶיכֵּרָא – אָתֵי לְמֵיעְבַּד עֲקִירָה וְהַנָּחָה, סוֹף סוֹף, כִּי מָטָא לְבֵיתֵיהּ אִי אֶפְשָׁר דְּלָא קָאֵי פּוּרְתָּא, וְקָמְעַיֵּיל מֵרְשׁוּת הָרַבִּים לרה"י! דְּזָרֵיק לֵיהּ כִּלְאַחַר יָד. אָמַר רָמֵי בַּר חָמָא: *הַמְחַמֵּר אַחַר בְּהֶמְתּוֹ בַּשַּׁבָּת, בְּשׁוֹגֵג – חַיָּיב חַטָּאת, בְּמֵזִיד – חַיָּיב סְקִילָה. מַאי טַעְמָא? אָמַר *רָבָא: דְּאָמַר קְרָא "לֹא תַעֲשֶׂה כָל מְלָאכָה אַתָּה וּבְהֶמְתֶּךָ" בְּהֶמְתּוֹ דּוּמְיָא דִּידֵיהּ, מָה הוּא – בְּשׁוֹגֵג חַיָּיב חַטָּאת, בְּמֵזִיד חַיָּיב סְקִילָה, אַף בְּהֶמְתּוֹ נָמֵי, בְּשׁוֹגֵג – חַיָּיב חַטָּאת, בְּמֵזִיד – חַיָּיב סְקִילָה. אָמַר רָבָא: שְׁתֵּי תְּשׁוּבוֹת בַּדָּבָר; חֲדָא, דִּכְתִיב: °"תּוֹרָה אַחַת יִהְיֶה לָכֶם לָעוֹשֶׂה בִּשְׁגָגָה וְהַנֶּפֶשׁ אֲשֶׁר תַּעֲשֶׂה בְּיָד רָמָה" *הוּקְשָׁה כָּל הַתּוֹרָה כּוּלָּהּ לַעֲ"ז, מָה ע"ז – דְּעָבֵיד מַעֲשֶׂה בְּגוּפֵיהּ, ה"נ – עַד דְּעָבֵיד מַעֲשֶׂה בְּגוּפֵיהּ. וְעוֹד, *תְּנַן: הַמְחַלֵּל אֶת הַשַּׁבָּת בְּדָבָר שֶׁחַיָּיבִין עַל שִׁגְגָתוֹ חַטָּאת וְעַל זְדוֹנוֹ *סְקִילָה, מִכְּלָל דְּאִיכָּא מִידֵּי דְּאֵין חַיָּיבִין עַל שִׁגְגָתוֹ חַטָּאת וְלֹא עַל זְדוֹנוֹ סְקִילָה. וּמַאי נִיהוּ, לָאו דִּמְחַמֵּר? לָא, *תְּחוּמִין וְאַלִּיבָּא דְּר"ע, וְהַבְעָרָה אַלִּיבָּא דְּר' יוֹסֵי.

רַב

רש"י

לא תצא לחולין. וְהָוְיָא תְּרוּמָה לֶאֱסוֹר לְזָרִים, וְיַחֲזוֹר וְיִתְרוֹם הַפִּקֵּחַ אַחֶרֶת: שהוא ספק. אִי דַּעַת גְּלוּלָה הִיא אִי לָא, וּלְר' יִצְחָק וַדַּאי לְקָטָן יָהֵיב לֵיהּ דְּלָאו בַּר מִצְוֹת הוּא, וְלָא לְחֵרֵשׁ דְּסָפֵק חַיָּיב בְּמִצְוֹת הוּא: אליבא דרבנן. דְּאָמְרִי לָאו דַּעְתָּא גְּלִילָא הִיא, וּלְעִנְיַן מִצְוֹת הֲרֵי הוּא כְּקָטָן: ותורם את שאינו שלו. בְּלָא רְשׁוּת, דִּכְתִיב (דברים יד): "תְּבוּאַת זַרְעֶךָ", וְחֵרֵשׁ שׁוֹטֶה וְקָטָן דִּכְתִיב: "אֲשֶׁר יִדְּבֶנּוּ לִבּוֹ" – שֶׁיֵּשׁ לוֹ לֵב לְהִתְנַדֵּב, בְּתַלְמוּד יְרוּשַׁלְמִי: אפילו ברשות. דִּשְׁלִיחוּת מֵהֵיכָא אִתְרַבֵּי – מִ"כֵּן תָּרִימוּ גַם אַתֶּם", "גַּם" – לְרַבּוֹת שְׁלוּחֲכֶם; וּמָה אַתֶּם בְּנֵי בְרִית – אַף שְׁלוּחֲכֶם בְּנֵי בְרִית: עוד אחרת היתה. תַּקָּנָה לַכִּיס לְהַצִּילוֹ: ואמאי לא רצו לגלותה. לְהַעֲלִים דִּבְרֵי תוֹרָה: כבוד אלהים הסתר דבר. מוּתָּר לְהַסְתִּיר דִּבְרֵי תוֹרָה לִכְבוֹד שָׁמַיִם: וכבוד מלכים חקור דבר. אֵין לְהַסְתִּיר לִכְבוֹד עוֹשֶׁר אָדָם וַחֲשִׁיבוּתוֹ, אֶלָּא שֵׁב וְתַחְקְרֵהוּ: בו ביום גדשו סאה. בַּיּוֹם שֶׁעָלוּ לַעֲלִיַּית חֲנַנְיָה בֶּן חִזְקִיָּה וְגָזְרוּ י"ח דָּבָר, וְזוֹ אַחַת מֵהֶן הָיְתָה, כִּדְאָמְרִינַן בְּפ"ק (דף יז:): נוֹתֵן כִּיסוֹ לַגּוֹי – בּוֹ בַּיּוֹם גָּזְרוּ שֶׁלֹּא יוֹלִיכֶנּוּ פָּחוֹת פָּחוֹת מִד"א אִם יֵשׁ שָׁם גּוֹי. אוֹתוֹ יוֹם הִרְבּוּ סְיָיג לַתּוֹרָה, בְּמִדָּה גְּדוּשָׁה וְיָפָה מָדְדוּ, לְהַרְבּוֹת גָּדֵר בְּיִשְׂרָאֵל: מחקו סאה. בְּמִדָּה מְחוּקָה מָדְדוּ בּוֹ בַּיּוֹם, שֶׁהִרְבּוּ לִגְזוֹר יוֹתֵר מִדַּאי וְאֵין יְכוֹלִין לַעֲמוֹד בִּגְזֵירָתָם, וּמִתּוֹךְ כָּךְ עוֹבְרִין עַל דִּבְרֵי תוֹרָה. נִמְצֵאת מִדָּתָם מְחוּקָה מְטֻפִּיפָתָהּ, וְטוֹב הָיָה לָהֶם לִהְיוֹת מִדָּתָם טְפוּפָה וְלֹא תָּבֹא לִידֵי מְחַק מֵרוֹב גּוֹדְשָׁהּ: והיא מחזקת. אֶת הַחַרְדָּל, שֶׁנּוֹפֵל הַחַרְדָּל בֵּין הַקִּישּׁוּאִין. אַף כָּאן יָפֶה תִּקְּנוּ, וְהוֹסִיפוּ דָּבָר הַמִּתְקַיֵּים: והיא מקיאה. אֶת הַדְּבַשׁ שֶׁהָיָה בָּהּ רִאשׁוֹן. אַף אֵלּוּ, ע"י גְּזֵירָתָם גָּרְמוּ לַעֲבוֹר, דְּשֶׁמָּא לֹא יַאֲמִין אֶת הַגּוֹי, וְהֵם לֹא הִתִּירוּ לְהוֹלִיכוֹ פָּחוֹת פָּחוֹת מֵאַרְבַּע, וְאָדָם אֵינוֹ מַעֲמִיד עַצְמוֹ עַל מָמוֹנוֹ – וְאָתֵי לְאִיתּוּיֵי ד' אַמּוֹת: והלא מחמר. מַנְהִיג חֲמוֹר טְעוּנָה קָרוּי מְחַמֵּר: ורחמנא אמר לא תעשה כל מלאכה אתה ובהמתך. וְאֵיזוֹהִי סְתָם מְלָאכָה הָעֲשׂוּיָה עַל יְדֵי שְׁנֵיהֶם – זוֹ הִיא, שֶׁהִיא טְעוּנָה וְהוּא מְחַמֵּר: מניחו עליה כשהיא מהלכת. לְאַחַר שֶׁנֶּעֶקְרָה לָלֶכֶת, דְּלָאו עֲקִירָה הִיא, כִּדְאָמַר בְּפ"ק (דף ג.) גַּבֵּי הִטְעִינוֹ חֲבֵרוֹ אוֹכָלִין וּמַשְׁקִין. וְכֵיוָן דְּאָדָם לָא מִיחַיַּיב בָּהּ חַטָּאת כִּי הַאי גַּוְונָא – כָּאן מוּתָּר. דְּהָכָא נָמֵי מְלָאכָה כְּתִיב, וְהָא לָאו מְלָאכָה הִיא: וקאתי למיעבד עקירה והנחה. כְּשֶׁחוֹזֶרֶת וְנֶעֱקֶרֶת לָלֶכֶת אַחַר הֲטָלַת מַיִם אוֹ גְּלָלִים: נוטלו הימנה. וּלְאַחַר שֶׁתַּחֲזוֹר וְתַעֲקוֹר רֶגֶל, יַנִּיחֶנּוּ: אי הכי אפילו על חברו. יָכוֹל לַעֲשׂוֹת כֵּן, כֵּיוָן דְּלָאו אִיסּוּרָא דְּאוֹרַיְיתָא הִיא, גַּבֵּי כִּיס שָׁרֵי: כל שבגופו חייב חטאת. כִּי עָבֵיד לֵיהּ אִיהוּ כּוּלֵּיהּ, כְּגוֹן מַעֲבִיר ד' אַמּוֹת בִּרְה"ר, אֲפִי' עֲקָרוֹ מִן הָאָרֶץ דֶּרֶךְ הֲלִיכָתוֹ – חַיָּיב, דְּהָא אִיכָּא עֲקִירַת חֵפֶץ בְּיָדַיִם. וְלֹא בָּעֵינַן עֲמִידָה אֶלָּא בְּטָעוּן וְעוֹמֵד מִבְּעוֹד יוֹם, אוֹ כְּשֶׁהִטְעִינוֹ חֲבֵירוֹ, דְּלָא עָקַר לֵיהּ לְהַאי חֵפֶץ. אֲבָל הָכָא – הָא עָקַר לֵיהּ. הִלְכָּךְ, כִּי עָבֵיד לֵיהּ חַבְרֵיהּ – הָוֵי לֵיהּ שְׁנַיִם שֶׁעֲשָׂאוּהָ, וְאָסוּר מִדְּרַבָּנַן, וְלָא שְׁרִיוּהָ גַּבֵּי כִּיס: מונחת לו על כתיפו. מִבְּעוֹ"י, וְקָדַשׁ עָלָיו הַיּוֹם: רץ תחתיה. וְכָל כַּמָּה דְּלָא עָמַד לָפוּשׁ אֵין כָּאן עֲקִירָה לְאִיסּוּר: קלי קלי. מְעַט מְעַט, כְּלוֹמַר בְּנַחַת: למיעבד עקירה והנחה. כְּלוֹמַר דְּזִימְנִין דְּקָאֵי וְלָאו אַדַּעְתֵּיהּ. אֲבָל רָץ הֶיכֵּרָא אִיכָּא: כלאחר יד. שֶׁלֹּא כְּדֶרֶךְ זְרִיקָה, כְּגוֹן מִכְּתֵיפָיו וּלְאַחוֹרָיו: בשוגג. בִּמְלָאכָה שֶׁהוּא עוֹשֶׂה לְבַדּוֹ: אף בהמתו. אַף מְלָאכָה שֶׁעוֹשֶׂה עַל יְדֵי בְּהֶמְתּוֹ, דְּהַיְינוּ מְחַמֵּר אַחַר חֲמוֹר טְעוּנָה: חדא דכתיב תורה אחת יהיה לכם וגו' עד דעביד מעשה בגופיה. כִּדְכְתִיב "לָעוֹשֶׂה בִּשְׁגָגָה", וְהָכָא לָא קָא עָבֵיד *מְלָאכָה אֶלָּא דִּבּוּר בְּעָלְמָא, שֶׁמַּנְהִיג בְּקוֹל – הֲרֵי דִּבְשׁוֹגֵג אֵינוֹ חַיָּיב קָרְבָּן: ועוד. דְּקָאָמְרַתְּ נָמֵי בְּמֵזִיד חַיָּיב סְקִילָה – קַשְׁיָא, דִּתְנַן בְּסַנְהֶדְרִין (דף נג.) גַּבֵּי נִסְקָלִים: הַמְחַלֵּל אֶת הַשַּׁבָּת נִסְקָל, אִם חִלְּלוֹ בְּדָבָר שֶׁחַיָּיבִים עַל שִׁגְגָתוֹ חַטָּאת וְעַל זְדוֹנוֹ סְקִילָה: מכלל דאיכא. חִילּוּל דְּאֵין חַיָּיבִין עַל שִׁגְגָתוֹ חַטָּאת, וְלֹא עַל זְדוֹנוֹ סְקִילָה: ואליבא דר"ע. דְּאָמַר *דְּאוֹרַיְיתָא נִינְהוּ, וְהָוֵי מְחַלֵּל. וּמִיהוּ, אֵין חַיָּיבִין לֹא עַל שִׁגְגָתוֹ חַטָּאת כו': אליבא דר' יוסי. דְּאָמַר בְּפֶרֶק "כְּלָל גָּדוֹל" (לעיל דף ע.): הַבְעָרָה לְלָאו יָצָאת:

רַב

תוספות

כי תבעי לך אליבא דרבנן. הכא משמע דהלכה כרבנן, ובמסכת יבמות פרק "חרש" (דף קיג.) משמע דהלכה כר"א, דסבירא ליה לרב חייא בר אשי (*ומר) שמואל כוותיה. מ"ר: דחרש אתי לאיחלופי בגדול פקח. תימה: א"כ לעיל נמי, אמאי קאמר שוטה וקטן לשוטה? הא אמרינן אתא לאיחלופי בגדול פקח: בו ביום גדשו סאה כו' נותן לתוכה חרדל והיא מחזקת. ה"נ כשגזרו י"ח דבר היתה חסרה גזירה זו של נותן כיסו לגוי, עד שגזרו עליה ומלאו הסאה לגמרי כמו שנתנו חרדל לתוכה: ר' יהושע אומר: בו ביום מחקו סאה כו' נותן לתוכה אגוזים ורמונים והיא מקיאה. כמו כן, קודם שגזרו על נתינת כיס לגוי היו מותרין להוליכו פחות פחות מד' אמות, מתוך כך אתי לאיתויי ד' אמות – כעריבה שהיתה מקיאה, עד שהסירו האגוזים והרמונים. ואחר שהסירו האגוזים והרמונים – שוב לא הקיאה יותר. כך, כשגזרו ליתן כיסו לגוי אסרו נמי להוליך פחות פחות מד' אמות. והשתא ר"א ורבי יהושע שניהם לשבח, ולא כפירוש הקונטרס, דפירש דרבי יהושע דאמר שלא עשו היטב, שהרבו לגזור יותר מדאי – דלא משמע הכי בירושלמי בפ"ק דמכילתין, דאמר התם, אמר ליה ר"א: אלו היתה חסרה ומלאה – יאות, חבית שהיא מלאה אגוזים כל מה שאתה נותן לתוכה שומשמין היא מחזקת. א"ל ר' יהושע: אלו היתה מליאה וחסרוה – יאות, חבית שהיא מלאה שמן כל מה שאתה נותן לתוכה מים היא מפזרת השמן. מ"ר: ואדרבה, נ"ל שהירו' קשה לו דלא שייך למימר גבי מים כמו שמפר"י גבי נותן לתוכה אגוזים ורמונים: סוף סוף כי מטי לביתיה א"א דלא קאי וקא מעייל מרשות הרבים לרשות היחיד. תימה: כדשרינן להוליכו פחות פחות מד' אמות, תקשי ליה נמי הכי: ואמרי

עין משפט נר מצוה

[נ"ל אמר]

י א מיי' פ"ד מהלכות תרומות הלכה ב סמג עשין קלד טוש"ע י"ד סימן שלא סעיף ל:

יא ב מיי' פ"כ מהלכות שבת הלכה ז סמג לאוין סה טוש"ע א"ח סי' רסו סעיף ז:

יב ג מיי' שם הלכה ו טוש"ע שם סעיף ב:

יג ד מיי' פי"ג שם הלכה יב:

יד ה ו מיי' פי"ג מהל' שבת הלכה ט סמג לאוין סה טוש"ע א"ח סי' רסו סעיף יא:

טו ז מיי' פ"א שם הלכה א ב:

רבינו חננאל

בזמן שאין עמו נכרי ולא חמור אלא חרש וקטן לאיזה מהן יתן כיסו יש מהן שאומר לחרש יש מהן שאומר לקטן ואם עשה כאחד מהן עשה. ואם אין עמו נכרי ולא חמור ולא חרש ולא שוטה ולא קטן. א"ר יצחק יש שם דרך להתיר לו להביאו במקום הראוי לשמירה והוא הבאתו פחות פחות מד' אמות ולא רצו חכמים לגלותה ואמרי' אמאי לא רצו חכמים לגלותה ואמרו גזירה דלמא אתו לאתויי ד' אמות ברה"ר. תניא ר' אליעזר אומר בו ביום גדשו סאה פי' בו ביום שהושיבו את רבי אלעזר בן עזריה בראש גדשו סאה. מדת הסאה ששת קבין והיא מחוקה הוסיפו רבותינו כמה דברים מדבריהם כגון הגדישה שהיא יתירה על העיקר והדברים שהוסיפו מהן להיתר ומהן לאיסור והכל להיות העיקר שמור ומוזהר והוא כמו זה ששנינו נותן כיסו התירו לו לתתו לנכרי שלא יביאהו בעצמו ויחלל את השבת. זה וכיוצא בו. ולאיסור כל גזירות שגזרו מקצת מן היתר המותר לעשות גדר לנשאר שהוא אסור מן התורה. ורבי יהושע אומר בו ביום מחקו סאה פי' העמידו כל דבר על עיקרו לא פחתו ולא הוסיפו. אלא התירו העיקר המותר מן [illegible]. שאלו באו להוסיף מדבריהן חוששין שמא יפסדו גם דברי תורה שהן העיקר שיבוא אדם להרהר ולומר כשם שזה אינו מן התורה אלא מדרבנן גם זולתי זה יש מן המצות האחרות מדרבנן כמותן ובאו לגדור נמצאו פורצים: אמר מר [אין] עמו נכרי מניחו על החמור ואקשינן עלה והלא מחמר הוא ורחמנא אמר לא תעשה כל מלאכה. ואוקימנא כדתנא כשהיא מהלכת מניחו עליה. כשהיא עומדת נוטלו הימנה. אי הכי חבירו נמי שרי ולמה חמור ולא אמר חבירו ופירק רב פפא כל שבגופו חייב חטאת בחבירו פטור אבל אסור פי' כל מלאכה שהעושה חייב חטאת כגון טוענת משוי ד' אמות ברה"ר אם יטעון חבירו פטור אבל אסור ואם יטעון בהמתו מותר לכתחלה ובלבד שלא תהא עקירה והנחה וזה שאמר רב אדא בר אהבה היתה חבילה מונחת בין כתיפו רץ תחתיה עד שמגיע לביתו מדדייקינן למימריה דווקא רץ ומפרקינן לטעמי' ש"מ הלכתא כוותיה ותו דליכא מאן דפליג עליה ופירוש' דזריק לה כלאחר יד לאו שמכניסה ומפרקה אלא מהלך בריצה וכשמגיע לפתחו מחזיר אחוריו כלפי פתח החצר ופניו לחוץ וזורק החבילה מעל כתיפו בחצר דרך הפתח ע"י ריצה בלא עמידה וזה פי' דזריק לה כלאחר יד שזורקה שלא כדרך מפרק ומכנס חבילות: אמר רמי בר חמא המחמר אחר בהמתו בשבת בשוגג חייב חטאת. במזיד חייב סקילה. פי' המחמר המנהיג בהמתו ועליה משוי חייב ודמי המנהיג בהמה טעונה משאוי כנושא משאוי על כתיפו מדכתיב לא תעשה כל מלאכה אתה ובהמתך הקיש בהמתו לו. והשיב רבא ב' תשובות בדבר חדא דכתיב תורה אחת יהיה לכם לעושה בשגגה. והנפש אשר תעשה ביד רמה הוקשה כל התורה לע"ז וכו' דעביד מעשה בגופה ופשוטה היא ומפורשת בפרק כלל גדול ועוד תנן המחלל את השבת בדבר שחייבין על שגגתו חטאת ועל זדונו סקילה מאי לאו מכלל דאיכא מידי דאין חייבין לא על שגגתו חטאת ולא על זדונו סקילה ומאי נינהו מחמר ופריק ליה דלמא בתחומין

רב נסים גאון

פרק מי שהחשיך תניא ר' אליעזר אומר בו ביום גדשו סאה ר' יהושע אומר בו ביום מחקו סאה זה היום הוא היום שנסמך בו ר' אלעזר בן עזריה בישיבה כמו שאמרו בברכות בפרק תפלת השחר (דף כח) תנא עדיות בו ביום תיקנום וכל בו ביום דאמרינן ההוא יומא איתמר וי"ח דבר שגזרו בו ביום באותו היום נאמרו אחת מהן מי שהחשיך בדרך חסב מא*) שדחו ביציאות השבת (דף יז) ולפיכך אמר בכאן בו ביום גדשו סאה נתכוונו בדבר זה למה שהוסיפו מן הגזירות שהזכירום: תחומין ואליבא דר' עקיבא. עיקר דברי ר' עקיבא במסכת סוטה (פרק כשם דף כז) וכבר פירשנו דבר זה במה שעבר הבערה ואליבא דר'

*) פירושו לפי מה.

מסורת הש"ס / תורה אור

תרומות פ"א מ"א יבמות קיג. | גיטין נג. | [ע"ז ע. ועיין תוספ' עירובין נז: ד"ה רבי שמעון] | [תוספתא פ"א] | [ע"ז טו.] | [נ"ל רבה] | [מכות יג: לעיל סט.] | סנהדרין סו. ע"ש | בסנהדרין הגי' כרת | [לעיל סט. וש"נ] | ס"א מעשה | סוטה כז:

משלי כה | שמות כ | במדבר טו

רַב זְבִיד מַתְנֵי הָכִי, אָמַר רָמִי בַּר חָמָא: הַמְחַמֵּר אַחַר בְּהֵמָה בַּשַּׁבָּת, בְּשׁוֹגֵג – אֵינוֹ חַיָּיב חַטָּאת, בְּמֵזִיד – חַיָּיב סְקִילָה. מְתִיב רָבָא: *הַמְחַלֵּל אֶת הַשַּׁבָּת בְּדָבָר שֶׁחַיָּיבִין עַל שִׁגְגָתוֹ חַטָּאת – חַיָּיבִין עַל זְדוֹנוֹ סְקִילָה. הָא אֵין חַיָּיבִין עַל שִׁגְגָתוֹ חַטָּאת – אֵין חַיָּיבִין עַל זְדוֹנוֹ סְקִילָה! מִי קָתָנֵי "הָא אֵין חַיָּיבִין כו'"? הָכִי קָאָמַר: דָּבָר שֶׁחַיָּיבִין עַל שִׁגְגָתוֹ חַטָּאת – חַיָּיבִין עַל זְדוֹנוֹ סְקִילָה, וְיֵשׁ דָּבָר שֶׁאֵין חַיָּיבִין עַל שִׁגְגָתוֹ חַטָּאת – וְחַיָּיבִין עַל זְדוֹנוֹ סְקִילָה, וּמַאי נִיהוּ – מְחַמֵּר. רָבָא אֲחוּהּ דְּרַב מָרִי בַּר רָחֵל, (א)וְאָמְרִי לַהּ אֲבוּהּ דְּרַב מָרִי בַּר רָחֵל. לְלִישָּׁנָא בָּתְרָא קַשְׁיָא, הָא דְּרַב *אַכְשְׁרֵיהּ לְרַב מָרִי בַּר רָחֵל וּמַנְיֵיהּ בְּפוּרְסֵיהּ דְּבָבֶל. דִּילְמָא תְּרֵי מָרִי בַּר רָחֵל הֲווּ. הֲוָה מַתְנֵי לַהּ לְהָא שְׁמַעְתֵּיהּ מִשְּׁמֵיהּ דְּרַבִּי יוֹחָנָן לִפְטוֹר; אָמַר רַבִּי יוֹחָנָן: [א]הַמְחַמֵּר אַחַר בְּהֶמְתּוֹ בַּשַּׁבָּת – פָּטוּר מִכְּלוּם. בְּשׁוֹגֵג לָא מִחַיַּיב חַטָּאת – דְּהוּקְשָׁה כָּל הַתּוֹרָה כּוּלָּהּ לַעֲ"ז. בְּמֵזִיד נַמִי לָא מִיחַיַּיב – דִּתְנַן: *הַמְחַלֵּל אֶת הַשַּׁבָּת בְּדָבָר שֶׁחַיָּיבִין עַל שִׁגְגָתוֹ חַטָּאת(ב) וְעַל זְדוֹנוֹ סְקִילָה. הָא אֵין חַיָּיבִין עַל שִׁגְגָתוֹ חַטָּאת – אֵין חַיָּיבִין עַל זְדוֹנוֹ סְקִילָה. בְּלָאו נַמִי לָא מִיחַיַּיב, דַּהֲוָה לֵיהּ לָאו שֶׁנִּיתַּן לְאַזְהָרַת מִיתַת ב"ד, וְכָל [א] *לָאו שֶׁנִּיתַּן לְאַזְהָרַת מִיתַת ב"ד – אֵין לוֹקִין עָלָיו. וַאֲפִילּוּ

רַב זְבִיד מַתְנֵי. לְהָא דְּרָמִי בַּר חָמָא הָכִי: אֵינוֹ חַיָּיב חַטָּאת. דְּיָלְפִינַן מֵעֲ"ז דְּעַד דְּעָבֵיד מַעֲשֶׂה בְּגוּפֵיהּ: אֲבָל בְּמֵזִיד חַיָּיב סְקִילָה. מֵהֶיקֵּישָׁא דְּ"אַתָּה וּבְהֶמְתֶּךָ" דִּלְעֵיל: מִי קָתָנֵי. הָךְ דִּיּוּקָא דְּדַיְיקִינַן הָא אֵין חַיָּיב כו', דִּילְמָא הָכִי קָאָמַר: הַמְחַלֵּל בְּדָבָר שֶׁחַיָּיבִין עַל שִׁגְגָתוֹ חַטָּאת – [חַיָּיבִים עַל זְדוֹנוֹ סְקִילָה], הָא דָּבָר שֶׁאֵין חַיָּיבִים עַל שִׁגְגָתוֹ חַטָּאת – יֵשׁ מֵהֶן שֶׁחַיָּיבִין עַל זְדוֹנוֹ סְקִילָה, וְיֵשׁ שֶׁאֵין חַיָּיבִין. וּמַאי נִיהוּ דְּחַיָּיבִין [עַל זְדוֹנוֹ] סְקִילָה וְאֵין חַיָּיבִין עַל שִׁגְגָתוֹ חַטָּאת – מְחַמֵּר: וְאָמְרִי לַהּ אֲבוּהּ דְּרַב מָרִי בַּר רָחֵל. ל"ג. דַּאֲבוּהּ דְּרַב מָרִי אִיסּוּר גִּיּוֹרָא שְׁמֵיהּ. וּמַאן דְּגָרֵס לֵיהּ גָּרֵס בָּתְרֵיהּ הָכִי: לְהָךְ לִישָּׁנָא בַּתְרָא קַשְׁיָא הָךְ דְּרַב אַכְשְׁרֵיהּ לְרַב מָרִי בַּר רָחֵל וּמַנְיֵיהּ בְּפוּרְסֵי דְּבָבֶל. וְהָךְ מִילְּתָא בְּמַסֶּכֶת יְבָמוֹת הִיא (דף מה:). בְּפוּרְסֵי – בְּלַעַ"ז מנסטר"ל, הֵן שׁוֹטְרִים. וְאַף עַל גַּב דְּאָמַר מָר: כָּל מְשִׂימוֹת שֶׁאַתָּה מֵשִׂים לֹא יְהוּ אֶלָּא מִקֶּרֶב אַחֶיךָ – הַאי, כֵּיוָן דְּאִמּוֹ מִיִּשְׂרָאֵל, "מִקֶּרֶב אַחֶיךָ" קָרֵינַן בֵּיהּ: לְאַזְהָרַת מִיתַת בֵּית דִּין. דִּשְׁאָר מְלָאכוֹת דְּשַׁבָּת נַמִי מֵהַאי קְרָא נָפְקָא לְהוּ אַזְהָרָה. הִלְכָּךְ, לְאַזְהָרַת מִיתַת בֵּית דִּין נִיתַּן, דְּלֹא עָנַשׁ מִיתָה אֶלָּא אִם כֵּן הִזְהִיר. הִלְכָּךְ: עִיקַּר אַזְהָרָתוֹ לִמְקוֹם שֶׁיֵּשׁ בּוֹ מִיתָה אֲתָאי, וְלֹא לְמַלְקוֹת: וַאֲפִילּוּ

ואמרי לה רבא אבוה דרב מרי בר רחל. לא גרסינן ליה, דהא מוכח ביבמות דאבוה דרב מרי גר הוה דאמר ב"החולץ" (יבמות מה: ושם): רב אכשריה לרב מרי בר רחל ומנייה אפורסיה דבבל. וקאמר: כיון דאמו מישראל, 'מקרב אחיך' קרינן ביה. וליכא למימר דרבא אבוה דרב מרי נמי גר הוה, דאם כן הוה ליה למימר רבא גיורא, כדאמר התלמוד בעלמא איסור גיורא. ועוד דאביו של רב מרי בר רחל משמע בבבא בתרא פרק "מי שמת" (דף קמט. ושם) דהיינו איסור גיורא, דאמרינן: איסור גיורא הוה ליה תריסר אלפי זוזי בי רבא ורב מרי בריה הורתו שלא בקדושה ולידתו בקדושה הוה. אע"ג דהתם לא גרסינן רב מרי בר רחל בריה דומה הוא שאותו היה. מיהו, אי אמרינן שהוא היה רב מרי בר רחל – צריכא למימר דאיסור גיורא בא על רחל בת מר שמואל קודם שנתגייר. דהא קאמר התם דהורתו שלא בקדושה הוה. ורחל בת מר שמואל היתה, כדאמר בכמה דוכתין רב מרי בר רחל בת מר שמואל. ואמרינן בכתובות (דף כג.) דבנתיה דמר שמואל אישתביין – ושמא אז בא עליה. ואף על גב דאתו לקמיה דר"ח ואמרו נשביתי וטהורה אני – לאו כולהו אמרו הכי. מיהו, תימה: אי רב מרי בריה דאיסור גיורא היינו ההוא דיבמות – איך חי איסור כל כך מימות רב עד רבא? והא רב יהודה תלמידו של רב ואמרינן בקדושין (דף עב:): יום שמת רב יהודה נולד רבא, ואפילו רב מרי בנו כבר היה גדול בתורה הרבה בימי רב מדמנייה אפורסיה דבבל ורב מרי נמי איך יתכן שחי כ"כ. ונראה כפירוש ר"ח דגרסינן ביבמות דרב אשי אכשריה לרב מרי בר רחל. ואע"ג דביום שמת רבא נולד רב אשי, יכול להיות שהיה רב מרי קטן בימי רבא, ובימי רב אשי כבר היה גדול בתורה וזקן, ומינהו אפורסייה דבבל. וכן ודאי נראה, דיש בספרים רבים שכתוב בהם בשמעתא(ג) לאמרי לה והקשה דרב אשי אכשריה לרב מרי בר רחל, ומשני: תרי רב מרי הוו. ופירוש הוא שנכתב בספרים. מ"ר*: **בלאו** נמי לא מיחייב דה"ל לאו שניתן לאזהרת מיתת ב"ד. תימה לר"י: מה בכך? מ"מ ילקה על לאו ד"לא תעשה כל מלאכה", דכיון שבא להזהיר על מחמר, ובמחמר ליכא מיתה אע"פ שבא להזהיר נמי על שאר מלאכות דשייך בהו מיתה, מכל מקום יש לו ללקות. כדאשכחן בבבא קמא (דף עד: ושם) דפליגי ר' יוחנן ור"א התם בעדים שהוכחשו בנפש ולבסוף הוזמו, דחד אמר: נהרגין, וחד אמר: אין נהרגין. ואמרינן נמי, תסתיים דר' אלעזר דאמר אין נהרגין, דאמר ר"א: עדים שהוכחשו בנפש – לוקין. ואי ס"ד ר"א דאמר נהרגין – אמאי לוקין? הוה ליה לאו שניתן לאזהרת מיתת ב"ד; אלא ש"מ ר"א דאמר אין נהרגין, תסתיים. אלמא משום דאין נהרגין כשהוכחשו בתחילה – לוקין. ואע"ג דבעלמא ניתן לאו ד"לא תענה" לאזהרת מיתת ב"ד היכא דהוזמו תחילה. ועוד תימה לר"י: דכל לאוין שבעולם שניתנו לאזהרת מיתת ב"ד יהיו לוקין עליהם כשלא התרו בהם למיתה אלא למלקות, מההוא טעמא דלא ניתנו באותה שעה לאזהרת מיתת ב"ד. ונראה לר"י: דשאני לאו ד"לא תענה" דגלי ביה קרא דניתן למלקות, כדאשכחן גבי עדות בן גרושה, כדמפקינן בריש מסכת מכות (דף ב: ושם)(ד) מ"והרשיעו את הרשע והיה אם בן הכות הרשע". וכיון דכתב בלא תענה מלקות בהדיא, אע"ג דניתן לאזהרת מיתת ב"ד – אית לן לאוקמי בכל מילי דלא מצי אתי לידי מיתה. ומהאי טעמא נמי אתי שפיר הא דאמר במכות בגמרא: מעידין אנו את איש פלוני שהוא חייב לחבירו מאתים זוז ונמצאו זוממים – לוקין ומשלמין דברי ר' מאיר, וחכמים אומרים: כל המשלם אינו לוקה. דקאמר: בשלמא לרבנן "כדי רשעתו" – משום רשעה אחת אתה מחייבו כו'. וקשה לר"י: ל"ל למימר טעמא דרבנן משום "כדי רשעתו"? תיפוק ליה דרבנן מוקמי "לא תענה" לאזהרה לעדים זוממין ולא למלקות, כדמוכח התם על משנת מעידים אנו את איש פלוני שחייב מלקות ארבעים! וקשה לר"י נמי: היכי מצי למימר לרבנן דלאזהרה דעדים זוממים הוא דאתא, ולא למלקות, הא בהזמה דגלות ובן גרושה מודו רבנן דאיכא מלקות! ולמאי דפרישית אתי שפיר, דכי היכי דלא אתי לידי מיתה או לידי מלקות ע"י כאשר זמם – לוקה משום "לא תענה" כיון דהתם לא צריך קרא ד"לא תענה" לאזהרה לכאשר זמם – משום הכי לקי במעידים אנו בפלוני שהוא בן גרושה, או שחייב גלות. ואתי נמי שפיר הא דתלי טעמא דרבנן התם משום "כדי רשעתו". דאי לאו משום כדי רשעתו – היו לוקין משום לא תענה, אפי' לרבנן. דאע"ג דסבירא להו דלא תענה אזהרה לכאשר זמם הוא דאתא, דלא ענש כאשר זמם אלא אם כן הזהיר, והוי כלאו שניתן לאזהרת מיתת ב"ד שלא נכתב למלקות אלא לאזהרת מיתה – ה"מ דוקא כשחייב מלקות מכאשר זמם, כגון: מעידים אנו באיש פלוני שחייב מלקות, אבל כשאין חייבים מכאשר זמם אלא ממון – לא מבעי התם "לא תענה" לאזהרה ד"כאשר זמם" – הוו מודו רבנן דלוקין משום "לא תענה" כמו דבן גרושה וגלות, אי לאו משום כדי רשעתו. וא"ת: למאי דפירש דאי לאו דגלי קרא בהדיא מלקות בלא תענה מ"והצדיקו את הצדיק" לא הוה מחייבינן ביה, משום דניתן לאזהרת מיתת ב"ד – אם כן הא דמפיק עולא דעדים זוממים לוקין מ"והצדיקו את הצדיק" בריש מכות, ופריך עלה: תיפוק ליה מ"לא תענה"! ומשני: משום דהוה ליה לאו שאין בו מעשה. אמאי לא משני: משום דהוה ליה לאו שניתן לאזהרת מיתת ב"ד! ותירץ: דההוא שנויא לא הוה אתי אלא לרבנן, דלר' מאיר איכא תרי לאוי: חד לאזהרה "כאשר זמם" היכא דזמם מיתה או מלקות, וחד למילקי עליה. ולהכי ניחא טפי למימר טעמא דלאו שאין בו מעשה, לאוקמא מילתא בין לרבנן בין לרבי מאיר. דמתניתין דמכות, אע"ג דטעמא דלאו שאין בו תעשה, נמי לא אתי לר"י. ולמאי דפי' איצטריך "והצדיקו" למלקות אפי' למאן דמחייב בלאו שאין בו מעשה. ועוד היה רגיל לתרץ: כיון ד"לא תענה" סתם כתיב – אכל מילי קאי, ולהכי מיחייב מלקות כאילו נכתב אבן גרושה ואגלות וכאילו נכתב לא תענה שקר בממון ולבן גרושה וגלות שאז לא היה הנכתב לממון ניתן לאזהרה כאשר זמם – ולכך היה ראוי ללקות עליו. והכי נמי השתא אע"פ שזה לא היה ראוי ללקות על אותו הניתן לאזהרת מיתה, אפי' כשאינו יכול לבא לידי מיתה – עכשיו יש ללקות עליו כל זמן שלא יוכל לבא לידי מיתה, הואיל ונכתב על מיתה וממון ביחד סתם – וניתן להלקות עליו בהזמת מיתה נמי ניתן ללקות כל זמן שלא יוכל לבא לידי מיתה. ולפי טעם זה לא היה יכול לתרץ בריש מכות: משום דהוה ליה לאו שניתן לאזהרת מיתת ב"ד, כי פריך: ותיפוק ליה משום "לא תענה", דאע"פ שניתן לאזהרת מיתה יש ללקות עליו – הואיל ונכתב סתם על מיתה ודברים אחרים, כדפרישית. ולפי לשון זה לא אתי דרשה ד"והצדיקו" אלא למאן דאית ליה לאו שאין בו מעשה אין לוקין עליו, כדמשני בריש מכות. אבל קשה: דבכל התלמוד חשיב לאו דשבת ניתן לאזהרת מיתת ב"ד, ואמאי? הא קאי נמי אלאו דמחמר, ואההיא דאיסי (לעיל דף ו:) דליכא מיתה! וי"ל, כיון דכתיב: "כל העושה בו מלאכה יומת" – משמע סתם מלאכה דשבת היינו שבמיתה, ולהכי לא משמע לאו דמלאכה דאיסי. אבל לאו ד"לא תענה" משמע שאר דברים שאין בהן מיתה ומלקות. וכן לאו דמחמר ד"לא תעשה כל מלאכה אתה ובהמתך" משמע אשאר חיובי שבת טפי ממחמר, מדכתיב "אתה" כדקאמר הכא. א"נ: מדכתיב "לא תעשה" ולא כתיב "לא תעשו". והוצאה נמי, אע"ג דנפקא מ"אל יצא" (עירובין יז:) בהדי תחומין דבמלקות אין לוקין עליו, אפי' לא התרו בו למיתה – דכל סתם הוצאה דשבת איתא בקרא ד"ויכלא העם מהביא". ותירוץ ראשון נראה לר"י עיקר. מ"ר: והא

עין משפט נר מצוה

טז א מיי' פ"כ מהלכות שבת הלכה א:

[טז] [א] [מיי' פ"ח מהלכות סנהדרין הלכה ב]:

רבינו חננאל

ואליבא דרבי עקיבא דסבר תחומין דאורייתא ועיקרו בסוטה פרק כשם שהמים בודקין אותו וחייב לאו כדכתי' אל יצא איש ממקומו ביום השביעי והבערה אליבא דר' יוסי דתניא הבערה ללאו יצאת דברי ר' יוסי ר' נתן אומר לחלק יצאת רב זביד מתני הכי אמר רמי בר חמא המחמר אחר בהמתו בשבת בשוגג פטור במזיד חייב סקילה ואקשי עליה רבא המחלל את השבת בדבר שחייבין על שגגתו חטאת חייבין על זדונו סקילה הא אין חייבין על שגגתו חטאת אין חייבין על זדונו סקילה ופריק ופשוטה היא. רבא אחוה דרב מרי בר רחל (או') [ואמרי לה] כי רבא הוא אבוה דרב מרי בר רחל והוא מישראל קשיא ליה הא דרב אשי דאכשריה דכיון דאימיה מישראל מקרב אחיך קרינא ביה מכלל שלא היה אביו מישראל אלא אמו. ומפורש בפרק החולץ ליבמתו. ומפרקי' דלמא תרי רב מרי בר רחל וזה אביו מישראל וכן תירוץ שמועה זו רבא אבוה דרב מרי בר רחל: **א"ר** יוחנן המחמר אחר בהמתו בשבת פטור מכלום בשוגג לא מחייב חטאת (והוקשה) [דהוקשה] כל התורה כולה לע"ז במזיד נמי לא מחייב (חטאת) [סקילה]. דתנן בפרק ארבע מיתות נמסרו לבית דין [המחלל את השבת וכו'] ואוקימנא התם בתחומין ואליבא דר"ע בהבערה ואליבא דר' יוסי*) דתנן המחלל את השבת בדבר שחייבין על שגגתו חטאת חייבין על זדונו סקילה הא אין חייבין על שגגתו חטאת אין חייבין על זדונו סקילה לאו נמי לא מיחייב דהוי לאו שניתן לאזהרת מיתת ב"ד וכל לאו שניתן לאזהרת מיתת ב"ד אין לוקין

*) נראה דנתחלפו השורות בכאן וכן צ"ל דתנן בפרק ד' מיתות נמסרו לב"ד המחלל את השבת בדבר שחייבין על שגגתו חטאת חייבין על זדונו סקילה הא אין חייבין על שגגתו חטאת אין חייבין על זדונו סקילה ואוקימנא התם בתחומין ואליבא דר"ע בהבערה אליבא דר"י לאו נמי וכו'.

רב נסים גאון

דרבי יוסי גרסי לה בפרק כלל גדול (דף ע) הבערה ללאו יצאת דברי רבי יוסי:

מסורת הש"ס

[ברייתא היא ועי' תוס' לעיל ו: סד"ה הא קמ"ל]

[יבמות מה: ע"ש]

[סנהדרין סו. ע"ש]

[עירובין יז: ב"ק עד: סנהדרין פז: מכות יג: שבועות ז.]

[עי' תוספות ב"מ עג: ד"ה רב]

גליון הש"ס

תוס' ד"ה בלאו נמי וכו' בסה"ד נראה לר"י עיקר. עיין סנהדרין דף סג ע"א בתוספות ד"ה משום דהוי:

הגהות הב"ח

(א) גמ' רבא אחוה דרב מרי בר רחל (ואמרי לה רבא אבוה דרב וכו' תרי רב מרי בר רחל הוו) תא"מ. ונ"ב ס"א אין זה וכן רש"י ותוספות לא גרסי ליה: (ב) שם על שגגתו חטאת חייבים על זדונו סקילה: (ג) תוס' ד"ה ואמרי לה וכו' בשמעתא לאמרי לה וקשיא הא דרב אשי: (ד) ד"ה בלאו וכו' בריש מס' מכות מוהצדיקו את הצדיק והרשיעו את:

שייך אחר ד"ה בחיבור

יז א ב ג מיי' פכ"א מהלכות שבת הלכה י סמג לאוין סה טוש"ע א"ח סי' רסו סעיף ט:

יח ד ה מיי' שם טוש"ע שם וסימן שה סעיף יח:

יט ו מיי' פ"ד מהלכות סוכה הלכה ו טוש"ע א"ח סי' תרכח סעיף ג:

וַאֲפִי' לְמ"ד לוֹקִין לִיכְתּוֹב רַחֲמָנָא "לֹא תַעֲשֶׂה כָל מְלָאכָה וּבְהֶמְתֶּךָ", "אַתָּה" לָמָּה לִי? הוּא נִיהוּ דְּמִיחַיַּיב, בְּהֶמְתּוֹ – לָא מִיחַיַּיב.§ "הִגִּיעַ לֶחָצֵר הַחִיצוֹנָה".§ אָמַר *רַב הוּנָא: הָיְתָה בְּהֶמְתּוֹ טְעוּנָה כְּלֵי זְכוּכִית – מֵבִיא כָּרִים וּכְסָתוֹת וּמַנִּיחַ תַּחְתֶּיהָ, וּמַתִּיר הַחֲבָלִים וְהַשַּׂקִּין נוֹפְלִים. וְהָאֲנַן תְּנַן: נוֹטֵל אֶת הַכֵּלִים הַנִּיטָּלִין בַּשַּׁבָּת! אכִּי קָאָמַר רַב הוּנָא – בְּקַרְנֵי דְּאוּמָּנָא, דְּלָא חַזְיָא לֵיהּ. וְהָא קָא מְבַטֵּל כְּלִי מֵהֵיכָנוֹ! בבִּשְׁלִיפֵי זוּטְרֵי. מֵיתִיבִי: הָיְתָה בְּהֶמְתּוֹ טְעוּנָה *טֶבֶל וַעֲשָׁשִׁיּוֹת – מַתִּיר אֶת הַחֲבָלִים וְהַשַּׂקִּין נוֹפְלִין, וְאע"פ שֶׁמִּשְׁתַּבְּרִין. הָתָם בְּכוּלְסָא. דַּיְקָא נַמִי, דְּקָתָנֵי דּוּמְיָא דְּטֶבֶל. מָה טֶבֶל – דְּלָא חֲזֵי לֵיהּ, אַף הָכָא נַמִי – לָא חֲזֵי לֵיהּ. וּמַאי אע"פ שֶׁמִּשְׁתַּבְּרִין – גמַהוּ דְּתֵימָא: *לְהֶפְסֵד מוּעָט נַמִי חָשְׁשׁוּ, קמ"ל. תַּנְיָא, ר"ש בֶּן יוֹחַי אוֹמֵר: דהָיְתָה בְּהֶמְתּוֹ טְעוּנָה שְׁלִיף שֶׁל תְּבוּאָה – מַנִּיחַ רֹאשׁוֹ תַּחְתֶּיהָ, וּמְסַלְּקוֹ לְצַד אַחֵר, וְהוּא נוֹפֵל מֵאֵלָיו. חֲמוֹרוֹ שֶׁל רַבָּן גַּמְלִיאֵל הָיְתָה טְעוּנָה דְּבַשׁ וְלֹא רָצָה לְפוֹרְקָהּ עַד מוֹצָאֵי שַׁבָּת, לְמוֹצָאֵי שַׁבָּת מֵתָה. וְהָאֲנַן תְּנַן: נוֹטֵל כֵּלִים הַנִּיטָּלִין! כְּשֶׁהִדְבִּישׁ. *)הִדְבִּישׁ לְמַאי חֲזֵי? לִכְתִיתָא דְּגַמְלֵי. וְיַתִּיר חֲבָלִים וְיִפְּלוּ שַׂקִּין! מִיצְטְרוּ זִיקֵי. וְיָבִיא כָּרִים וּכְסָתוֹת וְיַנִּיחַ תַּחְתֵּיהֶן! מְטַנְּפִי, *וְקָמְבַטֵּל כְּלִי מֵהֵיכָנוֹ. הוְהָאִיכָּא צַעַר בַּעֲלֵי חַיִּים! קָסָבַר: *צַעַר בַּעֲלֵי חַיִּים דְּרַבָּנַן. אַבַּיֵי אַשְׁכַּחֵיהּ לְרַבָּה דְּקָא מְשַׁפְשֵׁף לֵיהּ לִבְרֵיהּ אַגַּבָּא דַּחֲמָרָא. א"ל: קָא מִשְׁתַּמֵּשׁ מָר בְּבַעֲלֵי חַיִּים! א"ל: צְדָדִין הֵן, וּצְדָדִין לָא גָּזְרוּ בְּהוּ רַבָּנַן. מְנָא תֵּימְרָא – דִּתְנַן: מַתִּיר(א) חֲבָלִים וְהַשַּׂקִּין נוֹפְלִין. מַאי לָאו בְּחִבּוּר *גּוּוַלְקֵי, דְּהָווּ לְהוּ צְדָדִין, וּצְדָדִין לָא גְּזַרוּ בְּהוּ רַבָּנַן. לָא, בְּחִבּוּר אַגַּלְוָוקֵי, דְּלָא הָווּ צְדָדִין. אִי נַמִי, בְּלַכְתָּא. אֵיתִיבֵיהּ: *שְׁתַּיִם בִּידֵי אָדָם וְאַחַת בְּאִילָן – כְּשֵׁרָה, וְאֵין עוֹלִין לָהּ בְּיו"ט. מַאי לָאו – דְּדָחֵק בֵּיהּ בְּאִילָן, דְּהָווּ לְהוּ צְדָדִין *וּצְדָדִין אֲסוּרִין! לָא, דְּכַפְיֵיהּ לְאִילָן וְאַנַּח סִיכּוּךְ עִילָּוֵיהּ, (ב)דְּקָמִשְׁתַּמֵּשׁ בְּאִילָן. א"ה, אֵימָא סֵיפָא: שָׁלֹשׁ בִּידֵי אָדָם וְאַחַת בְּאִילָן – כְּשֵׁרָה, וְעוֹלִין לָהּ בְּיו"ט. וְאִי דְּכַפְיֵיהּ לְאִילָן – אַמַּאי עוֹלִין לָהּ בְּיו"ט? וְאֶלָּא מַאי – צְדָדִין אֲסוּרִין? סוֹף סוֹף, אַמַּאי עוֹלִין לָהּ בְּיו"ט? אֶלָּא: הָתָם בְּגַוְוזָא פַּרְסַכְנָא, דְּאִילָן גּוּפֵיהּ דּוֹפֶן בְּעָלְמָא הוּא דְּשַׁוְיֵיהּ. דַּיְקָא נַמִי, דְּקָתָנֵי, זֶה הַכְּלָל: וכָּל(ג) אִילּוּ שֶׁיִּנָּטֵל הָאִילָן וִיכוֹלָה לַעֲמוֹד – עוֹלִין לָהּ בְּיו"ט, ש"מ. לֵימָא כְּתַנָּאֵי: אֵין עוֹלִין לָהּ בְּיו"ט. *רשב"א אוֹמֵר מִשּׁוּם ר"מ: עוֹלִין לָהּ בְּיו"ט. מַאי לָאו, בְּהָא קָמִיפַּלְגִי; דְּמ"ס: צְדָדִין אֲסוּרִין, וּמָר סָבַר: מוּתָּרִין? אָמַר אַבַּיֵי: לָא, דְּכ"ע צְדָדִין אֲסוּרִין, וְהָכָא בְּצִדֵּי צְדָדִין קָמִיפַּלְגִי; מ"ס: צִדֵּי צְדָדִין אֲסוּרִין, וּמ"ס: צִדֵּי צְדָדִין מוּתָּרִין. רָבָא אָמַר: מַאן דְּאָסַר בִּצְדָדִין – אָסַר נַמִי בְּצִדֵּי צְדָדִין, מַאן דְּשָׁרֵי בְּצִדֵּי צְדָדִין – שָׁרֵי נַמִי בִּצְדָדִין. אֵיתִיבֵיהּ רַב מְשַׁרְשְׁיָא לְרָבָא: נָעַץ

יָתֵד

סוכה כב:

*) [עי' רש"י ב"מ לח. הדביש ובפרש"י סנהדרין קח. ד"ה מדביש]

והא מבטל כלי מהיכנו. פירשנו למעלה בפרק "כירה" (דף מג.): *שתים בידי אדם ואחת באילן. בסוכה בפ"ב (דף כב: ושם) תנן: העושה סוכתו בראש האילן. יש לפרש בשני ענינים: העושה סוכתו בראש האילן – כגון שהסכך של סוכה על גבי האילן, והאילן סומך אותה, שאין יכול לעלות על אותו סכך אלא אם כן ישתמש באילן, שרגילין היו לתת כליהן על הסכך. א"נ יש לפרש: שהתקרה סמוכה באילן, שבנאה בגובה ותחתיה על האילן. דהשתא, כל שעה שהוא מהלך בסוכה – משתמש באילן: **בחיבור** גוולקי. שני שקין אחד בימין החמור ואחד משמאלו, ובראש כל אחד מן השקין רצועה אחת, וקושרין אותן שתי הרצועות יחד, ועכשיו מונח הקשר כנגד גבו של החמור והשקין מכבידין לכאן ולכאן. ואי אפשר להתיר הקשר אם לא יגביהו השקין מעט, ונסמכין שתי השקין בכריסו של החמור, והוו להו כצדדים:

למטה

וַאֲפִי' לְמ"ד דְּלוֹקִין. בְּמַסֶּכֶת מַכּוֹת (דף יג:), הָכָא אֲפִי' לָאו לֵיכָּא. דְּאִי לְאַזְהוֹרֵי אַמְּלָאכָה שֶׁעַל יָדוֹ וְע"י בְּהֶמְתּוֹ אָתָא, כְּגוֹן מְחַמֵּר – לִיכְתּוֹב: "לֹא תַעֲשֶׂה כָּל מְלָאכָה וּבְהֶמְתְּךָ", מַאי אַתָּה? – מַשְׁמַע: אַתָּה לְבַדְּךָ, וּבְהֶמְתְּךָ לְבַדָּהּ: בְּהֶמְתּוֹ. בִּמְלָאכָה הַנַּעֲשֵׂית ע"י בְּהֶמְתּוֹ לָא מִיחַיַּיב לָאו גָּמוּר לִלְקוֹת עָלָיו: טְעוּנָה כְּלֵי זְכוּכִית. שֶׁאֵין נִיטָּלִין בְּיָדוֹ לְהַנִּיחָן לָאָרֶץ: וְהָאֲנַן תְּנַן נוֹטֵל אֶת הַכֵּלִים הַנִּיטָּלִין. וּכְלֵי זְכוּכִית נִיטָּלִין הֵן, וְלָמָּה לִי מַתִּיר אֶת הַחֲבָלִים? דְּאוּמָּנֵי. מַקִּיז דָּם, שֶׁאֵין רְאוּיִין בְּשַׁבָּת לִכְלוּם, לְפִי שֶׁמְּאוּסִים: וְהָא(ד) מְבַטֵּל כְּלִי. כָּרִים וּכְסָתוֹת, כְּשֶׁמַּנִּיחָן תַּחַת דָּבָר שֶׁאֵין נִיטָּל, מְבַטְּלָן מֵהֵיכָנָן, דְּשׁוּב לֹא יִטְּלֵם מִשָּׁם, וְדָמֵי לְסוֹתֵר: בִּשְׁלִיפֵי זוּטְרֵי. מַשּׂוֹאוֹת קְטַנִּים, שֶׁשּׁוֹמֵט הַכַּר מִתַּחְתֵּיהֶם וְנוֹפְלִין עַל הַכַּר הַשֵּׁנִי, וְכֵן עַד שֶׁמַּגִּיעָן לָאָרֶץ: עֲשָׁשִׁיּוֹת שֶׁל זְכוּכִית. מש"ש בְּלַע"ז. וְאַע"פ שֶׁהָעֲשָׁשִׁיּוֹת מִשְׁתַּבְּרִין, אַלְמָא: אָסוּר לְהַנִּיחַ כָּרִים וּכְסָתוֹת תַּחְתֵּיהֶן: בְּכוּלְסָא. חֲתִיכוֹת רְחָבוֹת שֶׁל זְכוּכִית שֶׁאֵינָם כֵּלִים, וְעוֹשִׂין מֵהֶן חַלּוֹנוֹת. וְכֵיוָן דְּלֵיכָּא פְּסֵידָא בִּשְׁבִירָתָן וְסוֹפָן לְהֵחָתֵךְ בַּחֲתִיכוֹת קְטַנּוֹת – לָא שָׁרוּ לְהָבִיא כָּרִים וּלְהַנִּיחַ תַּחְתֵּיהֶן: [טֶבֶל לָא חֲזֵי לֵיהּ. דְּמוּקְצֶה הוּא, וַאֲפִילּוּ לְכֹהֲנִים לָא חֲזֵי]: וּמַאי אַף עַל פִּי שֶׁמִּשְׁתַּבְּרִין. הָא לֵיכָּא פְּסֵידָא: מַהוּ דְּתֵימָא לְהֶפְסֵד מוּעָט נַמִי חָשְׁשׁוּ. וְיָבִיא כָּרִים וְיַנִּיחַ תַּחְתֵּיהֶם, דְּהָא וַדַּאי אִי אֶפְשָׁר בְּלֹא הֶפְסֵד מוּעָט, שֶׁגִּילּוּלוֹת נִיתָּזִין בִּשְׁבִירָתָן שֶׁאֵינָם רְאוּיִן לִכְלוּם: שְׁלִיף. מַשּׂוֹי שֶׁל תְּבוּאָה שֶׁל טֶבֶל: וְהָא אֲנַן תְּנַן כו'. וּדְבַשׁ נִיטָּל בְּשַׁבָּת, וְאַמַּאי לֹא רָצָה לְפוֹרְקָהּ? כְּשֶׁהִדְבִּישׁ. הֶחֱמִיץ: לְמַאי חֲזֵי. וְאַמַּאי אַיְיתֵי רַבָּן גַּמְלִיאֵל: לִכְתִיתָא דְּגַמְלֵי. לְכָתִית שֶׁל גְּמַלִּים רדויי"שדוד"א: וְיַתִּיר הַחֲבָלִים וְיִפְּלוּ שַׂקִּים. דְּהָכִי תְּנַן בְּמַתְנִיתִין בְּדָבָר שֶׁאֵינוֹ נִיטָּל. וּמְשַׁנֵּי: מִצְטְרוּ זִיקֵי – נִבְקָעִים הַנּוֹדוֹת בִּנְפִילָתָן לָאָרֶץ: מְטַנְּפִי. בְּדָבָר הַנִּשְׁפָּךְ עֲלֵיהֶם, וְקָא מְבַטֵּל כְּלִי מֵהֵיכָנוֹ, דְּשׁוּב אֵין רְאוּיִין לוֹ בַּיּוֹם לִכְלוּם: וְהָא אִיכָּא צַעַר בַּעֲלֵי חַיִּים. וְלֵיתֵי דְּאוֹרַיְיתָא וְלִידְחֵי דְּרַבָּנַן, בִּיטּוּל כְּלִי מֵהֵיכָנוֹ: קָסָבַר. ר"ג: צַעַר בַּעֲלֵי חַיִּים דְּרַבָּנַן. וּפְלוּגְתָּא הִיא בְּ"אֵלּוּ מְצִיאוֹת" (ב"מ לב:): דִּמְשַׁפְשֵׁף לִבְרֵיהּ אַגַּבָּא דַּחֲמָרָא. בְּשַׁבָּת לְשַׁעֲשֵׁעַ הַתִּינוֹק: קָא מִשְׁתַּמֵּשׁ מָר בְּבַעֲלֵי חַיִּים. וּתְנַן (ביצה דף לו:): לֹא רוֹכְבִין עַל גַּבֵּי בְּהֵמָה, וְה"ה לְכָל תַּשְׁמִישׁ: צְדָדִין. שֶׁאֵינוֹ מַרְכִּיבוֹ עָלָיו, אֶלָּא מְשַׁפְשְׁפוֹ עַל צִדֵּי גַבּוֹ, וְאֵין זֶה דֶּרֶךְ תַּשְׁמִישׁוֹ, וְרַבָּנַן לֹא גָּזְרוּ בָּהּ: מַאי לָאו בְּחִבּוּר גּוּוַלְקֵי. דְּהָווּ לְהוּ צְדָדִין. גּוּוַלְקֵי = עשקנ"ש. חִבֵּר גּוּוַלְקֵי – שַׂקַּיִם מְחוּבָּרוֹת יַחַד בִּרְצוּעוֹת, וּמַרְכִּיבִין עַל הַחֲמוֹר זוֹ מִכָּאן וְזוֹ מִכָּאן. וְצָרִיךְ לְסַלְּקָן יַחַד וְלִיקָּרֵב אֵצֶל הַחֲמוֹר, וּמְשַׁפְשֵׁף עַצְמוֹ וְנִשְׁעָן גּוּפוֹ בְּצִדֵּי הַחֲמוֹר: בְּחִבּוּר אַגַּלְוָוקֵי. שַׂקַּיִם שֶׁאֵין מְחוּבָּרוֹת יַחַד אֶלָּא עַל יְדֵי טַבַּעַת מַתֶּכֶת שֶׁבְּרֹאשׁ הָרְצוּעָה וְזוֹ מַסְמֵר קָטָן, כְּעֵין שֶׁעוֹשִׂין לַחֶבֶק שֶׁקּוֹרִין לינגל"א, שֶׁאֵינוֹ צָרִיךְ אֶלָּא לְנַתֵּק: נוֹעֵץ וְהַמַּסְמֵר יוֹצֵא, וְהֵן מִתְנַתְּקוֹת זוֹ מִזּוֹ: אִי נַמִי בְּלַכְתָּא. כְּעֵין שֶׁעוֹשִׂין לְדַרְדּוּר יַיִן, שֶׁיֵּשׁ בָּהֶן טַבָּעוֹת שֶׁל חֶבֶל לְכָל אֶחָד וְאֶחָד וּמַכְנִיס טַבַּעַת בְּטַבַּעַת, וְנוֹטֵל עֵץ כָּפוּף קָטָן וּמַכְנִיסוֹ בַּפְּנִימִי וְשׁוּב אֵינוֹ יוֹצֵא מֵחֲבֵרוֹ. וּכְשֶׁבָּא לְסַלְּקוֹ – מוֹשֵׁךְ הָעֵץ אֵלָיו, וְהֵן מִתְנַתְּקִין זֶה מִזֶּה וְנוֹפְלִין: שְׁתַּיִם בִּידֵי אָדָם וְאַחַת בְּאִילָן. גַּבֵּי סוּכָּה תְּנַן, שֶׁכְּשֵׁרָה בְּג' דְּפָנוֹת. וְאִם עָשָׂה שְׁתַּיִם כְּהִלְכָתָן וְהַשְּׁלִישִׁי עָשָׂה בָּאִילָן – כְּשֵׁרָה. דְּפָנוֹת לָא אִיכְפַּת לָן אִם מְחוּבָּרוֹת הֵם. וה"ה אִם כּוּלָּן נִקְבָּעוֹת בָּאִילָן. וְהָא דְּנָקַט: שְׁתַּיִם בִּידֵי אָדָם – רְבוּתָא אַשְׁמוּעִינַן, דַּאֲפִילּוּ הָכִי אֵין עוֹלִין לָהּ לֶאֱכוֹל וְלִישַׁן בְּאוֹתָהּ סוּכָּה בְּיו"ט, מִפְּנֵי שֶׁסְּכָכָהּ קָשׁוּר בְּדוֹפְנֶיהָ וְנִשְׁעָן עָלֶיהָ וְהוּא מִשְׁתַּמֵּשׁ עַל סְכָכָהּ וְנוֹתֵן כֵּלָיו, וְנִמְצָא מִשְׁתַּמֵּשׁ בָּאִילָן. כָּל כְּנִיסָה דְּסוּכָּה נָקִיט בִּלְשׁוֹן עֲלִיָּיה בְּמַסֶּכֶת סוּכָּה, לְפִי שֶׁרוּבָּן עוֹשִׂין סוּכּוֹתֵיהֶן בְּרֹאשׁ גַּגָּן, דִּכְמָה דּוּכְתִּין תְּנַן בָּהּ הָכִי:א) אֵין מַטְרִיחִין אוֹתוֹ לַעֲלוֹת.ב) אָמַר לָהֶם: "הַעֲלוּ לַסּוּכָּה" *"אֲבָל מוֹרִיד הוּא אֶת הַכֵּלִים", וְכֵן הַרְבֵּה: מַאי לָאו דְּדָחֵק בֵּיהּ בְּאִילָן. וְאוֹתֵיב בֵּיהּ קָנִים שֶׁל דְּפָנוֹת בִּנְקָבִים שֶׁנִּקֵּב הַרְבֵּה בְּגוּפוֹ שֶׁל אִילָן, וְסִיכֵּךְ שׁוּב עַל אוֹתָן דְּפָנוֹת, ומ"מ אֵין כָּאן תַּשְׁמִישׁ אֶלָּא בְּצִדֵּי אִילָן: דְּכַפְיֵיהּ לְאִילָן. לַעֲנָפָיו הָעֶלְיוֹנִים הִטָּה לְצַד אִילָן אַחֵר, וְכֵן שֶׁל זֶה לָזֶה, וּקְשָׁרָן אֵלּוּ עִם אֵלּוּ, וּמֵהֶן נַעֲשָׂה הַדּוֹפֶן: אַמַּאי עוֹלִין לָהּ בְּיו"ט. הֲרֵי הַסְּכָךְ נִשְׁעָן עָלָיו, וְהוּא מִשְׁתַּמֵּשׁ בּוֹ: ה"ג: אֶלָּא מַאי צְדָדִין אֲסוּרִין סוֹף סוֹף אַמַּאי עוֹלִין לָהּ בְּיו"ט אֶלָּא הָתָם בְּגַוְוזָא פַּרְסַכְנָא שֶׁאִילָן גּוּפֵיהּ דּוֹפֶן בְּעָלְמָא שַׁוְיֵיהּ. גַּוְוזָא פַּרְסַכְנָא = אִילָן שֶׁעֲנָפִים הַרְבֵּה יוֹצְאִין מִגְּדָדִין וּמִתְפַּשְּׁטִין לְכָאן וּלְכָאן, וְשַׁוְיֵהּ דּוֹפֶן בְּעָלְמָא לַסּוּכָּה, וְלֹא סָמַךְ הַסְּכָךְ עֲלֵיהֶן. וּלְהָכִי נָקַט גַּוְוזָא פַּרְסַכְנָא וְלָא שְׁבַקֵיהּ כִּדְקָא ס"ד בִּדְכַפְיֵיהּ, וְלִישְׁנֵי כְּגוֹן דְּלָא סָמַךְ הַסְּכָךְ עָלֶיהָ – מִשּׁוּם דְּכֵיוָן דְּדוֹפֶן רְבִיעִי הוּא שֶׁאֵינוֹ צָרִיךְ לַסּוּכָּה, דְּהָא בְּג' כְּשֵׁרָה, וְהַסְּכָךְ נַמִי לֹא סָמַךְ עָלֶיהָ – לֹא טָרַח לְמֶעֱבַד לוֹ דּוֹפֶן, לְהָכִי אוֹקְמָא בְּגַוְוזָא פַּרְסַכְנָא, וּמִמֵּילָא הוּא בְּלֹא טִרְחָא: מַאי לָאו בְּהָא קָמִיפַּלְגִי כו'. וּכְגוֹן דְּדָחַק בָּאִילָן, וּמוֹתִיב קָנִים בִּגְדָדִין וְסִיכֵּךְ עֲלֵיהֶן, דַּהֲוָה לֵיהּ מִשְׁתַּמֵּשׁ בִּגְדָדִין כְּשֶׁמִּשְׁתַּמְּשִׁין עַל יְדֵי סְכָכָהּ. דְּאִי לָאו בְּהָא פְּלִיגִי – בְּמַאי מוּקְמָא פְּלוּגְתַּיְיהוּ? דְּהָא כּוּלֵּי עָלְמָא סָבְרֵי אָסוּר לְהִשְׁתַּמֵּשׁ בָּאִילָן: אָמַר אַבַּיֵי. א"נ בְּהָכִי פְּלִיגִי – לֵיכָּא לְמֵימַר דִּסְבִירָא לֵיהּ (לת"ק*) צְדָדִין מוּתָּרִין, דְּהָנֵי לָאו צְדָדִין נִינְהוּ, אֶלָּא צִדֵּי צְדָדִים,ג) שֶׁהַקָּנִים הַנְּתוּנִים בַּנְּקָבִים צְדָדִין, וְהַסִּיכּוּךְ הַנָּתוּן עַל גַּבָּן צִדֵּי צְדָדִים, וּבְצִדֵּי צְדָדִים פְּלִיגִי:

א) [ברייתא סוכה כט.] ב) [שם כו:] ג) ס"א שהגזע צדדים והקנים הנתונים בנקבים צדי צדדים וגי' שלפנינו עיקר רש"ל.

יָתֵד

[ועמ"ש תוס' לעיל מג. ד"ה כבר]

[ע' תוס' שם. ד"ה טבלן]

[פסחים טו: כ: נה. ביצה לו. ב"ק קיז. ב"מ לח:]

[לעיל מג. וש"נ]

[ב"מ לב: וש"נ]

[פי' שקים ערוך ועי' בערך חבר פי' באריכות]

[עירובין לג.]

[תוספתא סוכה פ"א]

[סוכה מח.]

[נ"ל לר' מאיר וכן גורסין לרשב"א]

הגהות הב"ח

(א) גמ' ומנא תימרא דתנן מתיר החבלים: (ב) שם דקמשתמש באילן: (ג) שם זה הכלל כל שאילו ינטל האילן: (ד) רש"י ד"ה והא קא מבטל כלי מהיכנו כרים:

רבינו חננאל

עליו ואפי' למאן דאמר לוקין א"כ לכתוב קרא לא תעשה כל מלאכה ובהמתך אתה למה לי אלא לומר לך כל מלאכה ניהו דכי עביד מיחייב בבהמתו לא מיחייב. והלכתא כר' יוחנן דהא דרמי ליתא דרבא אהדר עליה ופריק לטעמיה. ואע"ג דפריק לנפשיה לא שבקינן דברי רבא וסמכינן אשנייה: **הגיע** לחצר החיצונה נוטל הכלים וכו'. אמר רב הונא היתה בהמתו טעונה כלי זכוכית מביא כרים וכסתות ומתיר הכלים והשקין נופלים ואקשינן עלה והתנן נוטל את הכלים הניטלין בשבת וכלי זכוכית ניטלין בשבת ולמה אין ניטלין בפני עצמן. ופריק רב הונא מי סברת הא דאמרי' היתה [בהמתו] טעונה כלי זכוכי' כבוסות ואשישות קאמינא דשרי לטלטלן בשבת קאמר בקרני (דאוני) [דאומנא] קאימנא שמוצצין בהן הדם שאסור לטלטלן ולמה אסור לטלטלן והא קיי"ל דדבר שמלאכתו לאיסור אפי' לצורך גופו ומקומו שרי. תוב אקשי' עליה הא אמרת מביא כרים וכסתות ומניח תחת משאוי הבהמה כדי שיפלו כלי זכוכית הללו על דבר רך שלא ישברו והלא אסור להשתמש באותן הכרים והכסתות כל זמן שאלו כלי זכוכית עליהן ואינו יכול לישן בהם והנה מבטל כלי מהיכנו ופריק רב אשי בשליפי זוטרי. פי' שמנער את הכר או את הכסת מעט והן נופלות כי הא דתנן מעות שעל הכר מנער את הכר והן נופלות. ואקשינן עליה היתה בהמתו טעונה עששיות מתיר חבלים והשקין נופלים. ואע"פ שמשתברין ופריק רב הונא אלו חעששיות אינן כלי זכוכית עשוין אלא פולסא פי' חתיכות גדולות כדכתיב ברזל עשות ורוצה להכניסם לבור לעשות מהן כלי זכוכית והלכתא כרב הונא דאע"ג דאיתותב הא שני לה ושנוייא שינויין אינון דהא מתרץ לה מאן דמותבה ואמרינן דיקא נמי דקתני דומיא דטבל מה טבל דלא חזו ליה פי' אלא אחר שיתקנן אף האי נמי לא חזי ליה. והא דתניא רבי שמעון בן יוחי אומר היתה בהמתו טעונה שליף של תבואה מכנים ראשו תחתיו ומסלקו לצד אחר הלכתא כוותיה שאינו מפרק אלא מכבידו לצד אחר ונופל מעצמו ובאנו להקשות ממשנתנו אדרבן גמליאל שהיתה חמורו טעונה דבש דלא רצה לפרק חמורו. והא אנן תנן נוטל את הכלים הניטלין בשבת וזה הדבש הוא ראוי לאכילה היה לו לנוטלו ומפרקינן דבש זה הדביש פי' הופסד כדמפרש בפרק המפקיד. ותוב היה לו להתיר החבלים ומעצמו יפלו השקין. ופרקי' חייש דלמא כשיפלו השקין בקרקע מצטרו זיקו ופי' מתבקעין הנודות שהדבש בהן כדכתיב וילכו ויצטירו. ותוב אקשינן עליה היה לו להביא כ ויניח תחתיהן ויפלו השקין בהן ולא יתבקעו דהכי שרי למעבד כרב הונא ופרקי' אם יפלו זיקי אילין על הכסתות נמצא מבטל כלי מהיכנו ואם תאמר ינערם ויטול הכסתות כמו שאמרנו למעלה אע"פ ראויין להשתמש בהן היום דקא מיטנפי עוד אקשינן עליה ולמה הניח חמורו טעונה הא איכא צער ב"ח ופריק רשב"ג צער בעלי חיים דרבנן. אביי אשכחיה לרבה דקא משפשף לבריה אגבה דחמרא. כדאמרינן ואם מבערב ישפשף כלומר יוליך ויביא ידו על גופו שיוסר מעליו טינוף הקרי כן רבא היה מעלה ומוריד בנו כעין שפשוף ע"ג החמור מן הצד לא על שדרו של חמור כדרך רכיבה אלא היה החמור והתינוק ומתגדר ונחית ואביו מחזיק בו ומחזיקו שלא יפול לארץ. א"ל אביי משתמש מר בבעלי חיים. כלומר המשתמש בב"ח עובר משום הא דתנן ולא רוכבין על גבי בהמה השיבו רבה אינו שדרו של

רב נסים גאון

ואפי' למאן דאמר לוקין. כלו' שר' ישמעאל סבר כי לאו שניתן לאזהרת [מיתת] ב"ד לוקין עליו ור"ע סבר לאו שניתן לאזהרת [מיתת] ב"ד אין לוקין עליו: **והא** קא מבטל כלי מהיכנו. כבר פירשנו בפ' מפנין שעיקרו בפרק

יָתֵד בָּאִילָן וְתָלָה בָּהּ כַּלְכָּלָה, לְמַעְלָה מֵעֲשָׂרָה טְפָחִים – אֵין עֵירוּבוֹ עֵירוּב, לְמַטָּה מִי' טְפָחִים – עֵירוּבוֹ עֵירוּב. טַעְמָא – דְּנָעַץ יָתֵד בָּאִילָן, הָא לֹא נָעַץ – אֲפִילּוּ לְמַטָּה מִי' טְפָחִים אֵין עֵירוּבוֹ עֵירוּב. וְהָא הַאי תַּנָּא, דְּקָאָסַר בִּצְדָדִין וְקָשָׁרֵי בִּצְדֵי צְדָדִין! אָמַר רַב פַּפָּא: הָכָא בְּכַלְכָּלָה דְּחוּקָה עָסְקִינַן, דְּבַהֲדֵי דְּשָׁקֵיל לֵיהּ לְעֵירוּב – קָמָנֵיד לֵיהּ לָאִילָן, וְקָמִשְׁתַּמֵּשׁ בָּאִילָן גּוּפֵיהּ. א וְהִלְכְתָא: *צְדָדִין – אֲסוּרִין, צְדֵי צְדָדִין – מוּתָּרִין. אֲמַר רַב אַשִׁי: הַשְׁתָּא דְּאָמְרַתְּ "צְדָדִין אֲסוּרִין", הַאי דַּרְגָּא דְּמַדְלָא – לָא לִינָחֵיהּ אִינִישׁ אַדִּיקְלָא, דַּהֲווּ לְהוּ צְדָדִין. אֶלָּא לִינָחֵיהּ אַגַּוָּואזֵי לְבַר מִדִּיקְלָא, וְכִי סָלֵיק – לָא לִינַח כַּרְעֵיהּ אַגַּוָּואזֵי, אֶלָּא לִיתְנַח אַקְּנִין.§

מתני' מַתִּירִין פְּקִיעֵי עָמִיר לִפְנֵי בְּהֵמָה, וּמְפַסְפְּסִין אֶת הַכִּיפִּין, אֲבָל לֹא אֶת(א) הַזִּירִין. אֵין מְרַסְּקִין לֹא אֶת הַשַּׁחַת וְלֹא אֶת הֶחָרוּבִין לִפְנֵי בְהֵמָה, בֵּין דַּקָּה וּבֵין גַּסָּה. רַבִּי יְהוּדָה מַתִּיר בְּחָרוּבִין לַדַּקָּה.§

גמ' אָמַר רַב הוּנָא: הֵן הֵן פְּקִיעִין, הֵן הֵן כִּיפִּין. פְּקִיעִין – תְּרֵי, כִּיפִּין – תְּלָתָא(ב), זִירִין – דְּאַרְזֵי. וְה"ק: מַתִּירִין פְּקִיעֵי עָמִיר לִפְנֵי בְהֵמָה וּמְפַסְפְּסִין, וְהוּא הַדִּין לְכִיפִּין. אֲבָל לֹא אֶת הַזִּירִין – לֹא לְפַסְפֵּס וְלֹא לְהַתִּיר. אָמַר רַב חִסְדָּא: מַאי טַעְמָא דְּרַב הוּנָא – קָא סָבַר: לְמִטְרַח בְּאוּכְלָא – טָרְחִינַן, לְשַׁוּוֹיֵי אוּכְלָא – לָא מְשַׁוֵּינַן. רַב יְהוּדָה אָמַר: הֵן הֵן פְּקִיעִין, הֵן הֵן זִירִין. פְּקִיעִין – תְּרֵי, זִירִין – תְּלָתָא. כִּיפִּין – דְּאַרְזֵי. וְה"ק: ב מַתִּירִין פְּקִיעֵי עָמִיר לִפְנֵי בְהֵמָה, אֲבָל פַּסְפּוּסֵי – לֹא. וְכִיפִּין – פַּסְפּוּסֵי נַמִי מְפַסְפְּסִינַן, אֲבָל לֹא הַזִּירִין לְפַסְפֵּס[א] אֶלָּא לְהַתִּיר. אָמַר רָבָא: מַאי טַעְמָא דְּרַב יְהוּדָה – קָסָבַר: ג שַׁוּוֹיֵי אוּכְלָא – מְשַׁוֵּינַן, מִטְרַח בְּאוּכְלָא – לָא טָרְחִינַן. תְּנַן: ד אֵין מְרַסְּקִין אֶת הַשַּׁחַת וְאֶת הֶחָרוּבִין לִפְנֵי בְהֵמָה, בֵּין דַּקָּה וּבֵין גַּסָּה. מַאי לָאו – חָרוּבִין דּוּמְיָא דְּשַׁחַת, מַה שַּׁחַת – דְּרַכִּיכֵי, אַף חָרוּבִין – דְּרַכִּיכֵי, אַלְמָא: לָא טָרְחִינַן בְּאוּכְלָא, וּתְיוּבְתֵּיהּ דְּרַב הוּנָא! אָמַר לָךְ רַב הוּנָא: לָא, שַׁחַת דּוּמְיָא דְּחָרוּבִין; מָה חָרוּבִין – דְּאַקּוּשֵׁי, אַף שַׁחַת – דְּאַקּוּשֵׁי. הֵיכִי מַשְׁכַּחַת לָהּ – בְּעִילֵּי זוּטְרֵי. ת"ש: רַבִּי יְהוּדָה מַתִּיר בְּחָרוּבִין לַדַּקָּה. לַדַּקָּה – אִין, לַגַּסָּה – לָא. אִי אָמְרַתְּ בִּשְׁלָמָא ת"ק סָבַר: מִיטְרַח בְּאוּכְלָא לָא טָרְחִינַן, שַׁוּוֹיֵ מְשַׁוֵּינַן. הַיְינוּ דְּקָא אָמַר ר' יְהוּדָה(ג): הֶחָרוּבִין לַדַּקָּה נַמִי שַׁוּוֹיֵ אוּכְלָא הוּא. אֶלָּא אִי אָמְרַתְּ ת"ק סָבַר: שַׁוּוֹיֵ אוּכְלָא לָא מְשַׁוֵּינַן, מִיטְרַח בְּאוּכְלָא מְטָרְחִינַן, רַבִּי יְהוּדָה(ד) דְּמַתִּיר בְּחָרוּבִין לַדַּקָּה, כָּל שֶׁכֵּן לַגַּסָּה! מִי סָבְרַתְּ "דַּקָּה" דַּקָּה מַמָּשׁ? מַאי דַּקָּה – גַּסָּה(ה), וּמַאי קָרֵי לָהּ דַּקָּה – דְּדַיְיקָא בְּאוּכְלָא. הָא מִדְּקָתָנֵי רֵישָׁא "בֵּין דַּקָּה וּבֵין גַּסָּה" – מִכְּלַל דְּרַבִּי יְהוּדָה "דַּקָּה" דַּקָּה מַמָּשׁ קָאָמַר! קַשְׁיָא. תָּא שְׁמַע: *מְחַתְּכִין אֶת

רש"י

יָתֵד. נֶגֶר: וְתָלָה בָּהּ כַּלְכָּלָה. וְנָתַן בָּהּ עֵירוּבוֹ, וְהוּא נִתְכַּוֵּין לִשְׁבּוֹת לְמַטָּה תַּחַת הָאִילָן: לְמַטָּה מִי' טְפָחִים. אִם הַכַּלְכָּלָה בְּתוֹךְ י' לָאָרֶץ – עֵירוּבוֹ עֵירוּב, דְּהוּא וְעֵירוּבוֹ בִּרה"ר. אֲבָל לְמַעְלָה מִי', וּסְתָם כַּלְכָּלָה רְחָבָה אַרְבָּעָה – הָוְיָא לָהּ כַּלְכָּלָה רְשׁוּת הַיָּחִיד, וְהוּא נִתְכַּוֵּין לִשְׁבּוֹת בִּרְשׁוּת הָרַבִּים, וְאֵינוֹ יָכוֹל לִיטְּלוֹ שָׁם וּלְאָכְלוֹ, וְכֵיוָן דְּאֵינָהּ סְעוּדָה הָרְאוּיָה לוֹ – אֵינוֹ קוֹנֶה שְׁבִיתָה עַל יָדָהּ: טַעְמָא דְּנָעַץ יָתֵד. דְּכִי שָׁקֵיל לְעֵירוּבוֹ מִשְׁתַּמֵּשׁ בְּצִדֵּי צְדָדִין, אֲבָל לֹא נָעַץ יָתֵד אֶלָּא קְשָׁרָהּ בְּצִדֵּי אִילָן – לֹא: הָכָא בְּכַלְכָּלָה דְּחוּקָה. שֶׁפִּיהָ צַר, וּקְצָרָה הִיא, וּמַכְנִיס יָדוֹ לְתוֹכָהּ בְּדוֹחַק. הִלְכָּךְ, אִי מַמָּשׁ הֲוָה קָטַר לָהּ בְּצִדֵּי אִילָן, כִּי שָׁקֵיל לֵיהּ לְעֵירוּבֵיהּ מָנֵיד לֵיהּ לְאִילָן. הִלְכָּךְ, כִּי אִיכָּא יָתֵד הוּא דְּשָׁרֵי, וְאִי לָא – לָא: הַאי דַּרְגָּא דְּמַדְלָא. סוּלָּם שֶׁעוֹלִין בּוֹ לְסוּכַּת נוֹטְרִים שֶׁעוֹשִׂין ע"ג קוּנְדֵּיסִין גְּבוֹהִין, וְהִיא סְמוּכָה לְאִילָן: לָא לִינָחֵיהּ. רֹאשׁ הַסּוּלָּם אַדִּיקְלָא, לֹא יִסְמוֹךְ רֹאשׁ הַסּוּלָּם לְצַד דֶּקֶל, דְּכִי סָלֵיק מִשְׁתַּמֵּשׁ בִּצְדָדִין: אֶלָּא לִינָחֵיהּ אַגַּוָּואזֵי לְבַר מִדִּיקְלָא. יִתְקַע יָתֵד בְּצִדֵּי הָאִילָן וְיִסְמוֹךְ הַסּוּלָּם עָלָיו, דַּהֲוָה לֵיהּ יָתֵד לִצְדָדִים, וְסוּלָּם לְצִדֵּי צְדָדִין: וְכִי סָלֵיק לָא לִינַח כַּרְעֵיהּ עַל הַיָּתֵד אֶלָּא אַקְּנָיָא. עַל שְׁלִיבוֹת הַסּוּלָּם, אוֹ קָנִים הַיּוֹצְאִים מֵהַקּוּנְדֵּיסִין: **מתני'** פְּקִיעֵי עָמִיר. קַשִּׁין שֶׁל שִׁבֳּלִים (שֶׁאוֹתָם) שֶׁאוֹגְדִים, מַתִּירִין אוֹתָם שֶׁיְּהוּ נוֹחִין לִבְהֵמָה לְאוֹכְלָהּ: מְפַסְפְּסִין. שֶׁכֵּן דֶּרֶךְ שֶׁמְּפַזְּרִים לִבְהֵמָה הָעֲשָׂבִים, וְיָפִין לָהּ לְאוֹכְלָן. שֶׁכְּשֶׁהֵן דְּחוּקִין מִתְחַמְּמִין, וְאֵינָהּ מְרִיחָה רֵיחָהּ כָּל כָּךְ, וְקָלָה בָּהֶן: אֶת הַכִּיפִּין. מְפָרֵשׁ בַּגְּמָרָא, וְכֵן זִירִין: אֵין מְרַסְּקִין. אֵין מְחַתְּכִין: שַׁחַת. עֵשֶׂב שֶׁל תְּבוּאָה, וְהוּא אַסְפַּסְתָּא. וּמִשּׁוּם דְּטִירְחָא דְּלָא צָרִיךְ הוּא: רַבִּי יְהוּדָה מַתִּיר בְּחָרוּבִין לַדַּקָּה. שֶׁשִּׁינֶּיהָ דַּקּוֹת, וְקָשִׁין לָהּ: **גמ'** הֵן הֵן פְּקִיעִין הֵן הֵן כִּיפִּין. כּוּלָּן קַשִּׁין שֶׁל שִׁבֳּלִין הֵן. מִיהוּ, פְּקִיעִין תְּרֵי, שֶׁאֵינָן קְשׁוּרִין אֶלָּא בִּשְׁנֵי רָאשִׁים: כִּיפִּין תְּלָת. קְשׁוּרִין ג' [אֲגוּדִים]: זִירִין דְּאַרְזָא. עֲנָפִים לַחִין שֶׁל אֶרֶז שֶׁמְּזָרְדִין אוֹתָם, וּבְעוֹדָם לַחִין רְאוּיִין לִבְהֵמָה. וְרוֹב בְּנֵי אָדָם מַנִּיחִין אוֹתָם לָעֵצִים: וְה"ק מַתִּירִין פְּקִיעֵי עָמִיר וּמְפַסְפְּסִין. דְּכֵיוָן דִּמֵעִיקָּרָא אוּכְלָא נִינְהוּ – מוּתָּר לִטְרוֹחַ בָּהֶן לְהַכְשִׁירָם לְמַתְקָן לָהּ. וְאֶת הַכִּיפִּין אַף הֵן מַתִּירִין. וּמְפַסְפְּסִין, וְאע"ג דִּנְפִישׁ טִרְחַיְיהוּ. אֲבָל לֹא הַזִּירִין, לֹא לְפַסְפֵּס וְלֹא לְהַתִּיר – דְּכֵיוָן דְּמֵעִיקָּרָא סְתָמַיְיהוּ לָאו אוּכְלָא, וְהַשְׁתָּא הוּא דִּמְשַׁוֵּי לְהוּ אוּכְלָא – ה"ל אוֹלוּדֵי אוּכְלָא בְּשַׁבָּת: מִיטְרַח בְּאוּכְלָא. בְּדָבָר שֶׁתְּחִילָּתוֹ אוֹכֶל קוֹדֶם תִּיקּוּן זֶה – טָרְחִינַן וּמַכְשְׁרִינַן לְיִיפּוּתָן לָהּ: הֵן הֵן פְּקִיעִין הֵן הֵן זִירִין. שְׁנֵיהֶן בְּקַשִּׁים שֶׁל שִׁבֳּלִים, וּמַה שֶּׁהִתִּיר בָּזֶה הִתִּיר בָּזֶה. וּדְקָתָנֵי: אֲבָל לֹא הַזִּירִין – אַפִּסְפּוּס קָאֵי: וְה"ק מַתִּירִין פְּקִיעֵי עָמִיר. דְּכָל זְמַן שֶׁהוּא קָשׁוּר לָאו אוּכְלָא הוּא, וּמַתִּירוֹ לְשַׁוּוֹיֵי אוּכְלָא, וּמִשּׁוּם צַעַר בְּהֵמָה שָׁרֵי, אֲבָל פִּסְפּוּס – לָא, דְּסַגִּי לֵיהּ בְּהַתָּרָה וְאִיתְעֲבִיד אוּכְלָא, וּפִסְפּוּסֵיהּ לְתַעֲנוּג בְּעָלְמָא הוּא, וּמִטְרַח בְּאוֹכֶל בְּדָבָר שֶׁהוּא כְּבָר אוֹכֶל בְּלֹא תִּיקּוּן זֶה – לָא טָרְחִינַן. וּמְפַסְפְּסִין אֶת הַכִּיפִּין דְּאַרְזָא – דִּבְלָאו פִּסְפּוּס לָא הָוֵי אוּכְלָא, אֲבָל לֹא אֶת הַזִּירִין לְפַסְפֵּס, אֶלָּא לְהַתִּיר שְׁלֹשָׁה אוֹגְדֵיהֶן כִּפְקִיעִין – דְּהַתָּרַת אוֹגְדֵיהֶן שַׁוּוֹיֵי אוּכְלָא הוּא: אֵין מְרַסְּקִין. סֵיפָא דְּמַתְנִיתִין הִיא, וְחַד טַעְמָא: דְּרַכִּיכֵי. כְּגוֹן חָרוּבִין לַחִין, דִּרְאוּיִין לְמַאֲכַל בְּהֵמָה בְּלֹא רִיסּוּק, וְרִיסּוּק דִּידְהוּ לְתַעֲנוּג בְּעָלְמָא: דְּאַקּוּשֵׁי. קָשִׁין, כְּגוֹן שֶׁיָּבְשׁוּ: בְּעִילֵּי זוּטְרֵי. עֲיָירִים קְטַנִּים, שֶׁאַף הַשַּׁחַת קָשֶׁה לָהֶם, וּצְרִיכָה רִיסּוּק לְשַׁוּוֹיֵי אוּכְלָא: לַדַּקָּה אִין. דַּהֲוָה לֵיהּ שַׁוּוֹיֵי אוּכְלָא: לַגַּסָּה לָא. דַּהֲוָה לֵיהּ מִטְרַח בְּאוּכְלָא: אִי אָמְרַתְּ בִּשְׁלָמָא. שָׁמַע רַבִּי יְהוּדָה לְת"ק דְּקָאָמַר מִיטְרַח בְּאוּכְלִין אָסוּר, וְאֵין מְרַסְּקִין בִּרְכִיכֵי קָאָמַר, אֲבָל שַׁוּוֹיֵי אוּכְלָא שָׁרֵי – הַיְינוּ דְּקָאָמַר לֵיהּ רַבִּי יְהוּדָה חָרוּבִין לַדַּקָּה לֵית לָן לְמֵיסַר, דְּשַׁוּוֹיֵי אוּכְלָא הוּא, וְאע"ג דְּרַכִּיכֵי. אֶלָּא אִי אָמְרַתְּ קָסָבַר ת"ק מִיטְרַח בְּאוּכְלָא שָׁרֵי, שַׁוּוֹיֵ אוּכְלָא אָסוּר, וְאֵין מְרַסְּקִין דְּקָאָמַר בִּדְאַקּוּשֵׁי קָאָמַר – דְּשַׁוּוֹיֵי אוּכְלָא הָוֵי: רַבִּי יְהוּדָה מַתִּיר בְּחָרוּבִין לַדַּקָּה. בִּתְמִיָּה: הָא כָּל שֶׁכֵּן דְּלַגַּסָּה לְמִיטְרַח בְּאוּכְלָא הוּא, וְשָׁרֵי. הָכִי ה"ל לְמִיתְנֵי: וְר' יְהוּדָה מַתִּיר בְּחָרוּבִין לַגַּסָּה, דַּהֲוָה לֵיהּ מִיטְרַח בְּאוּכְלָא. וְהָא לֵיכָּא לְמֵימַר דְּר' יְהוּדָה מַפִּיךְ, דְּשַׁוּוֹיֵ אוּכְלָא שָׁרֵי, מִיטְרַח בְּאוּכְלָא אֲסִיר – דְּהָא ת"ק בִּדְאַקּוּשֵׁי קָאָמַר, וְגַבֵּי גַּסָּה נַמִי שַׁוּוֹיֵי אוּכְלָא הוּא, וְה"ל לְמִיתְנֵי: וְרַבִּי יְהוּדָה מַתִּיר סְתָמָא בֵּין דַּקָּה בֵּין גַּסָּה. וְעוֹד, הֲוָה לֵיהּ לְמִישְׁרֵי נַמִי זִירִין לְהַתִּיר וּלְפַסְפֵּס, דְּשַׁוּוֹיֵי אוּכְלָא נַמִי הוּא: דְּדַיְיקָא. כּוֹסֶסֶת יָפֶה וּמְדַקֶּקֶת אוֹכְלִין בְּפִיהָ: וְהָא מִדְּקָתָנֵי רֵישָׁא בֵּין דַּקָּה בֵּין גַּסָּה שְׁמַע מִינָּהּ דַּקָּה מַמָּשׁ. וְרַבִּי יְהוּדָה אַת"ק קָאֵי:

תוספות

למטה מי' טפחים עירובו עירוב. קשה: אמאי עירובו עירוב? והא כרמלית הוא, כיון שרחבה ארבעה ואסור לטלטל לרה"ר! וי"ל: אין כרמלית בכלים, כדפירש בקונטרס בפ"ק דמכילתין (דף ח.) גבי היתה קופתו מונחת כו'. אי נמי כרבי, דאמר: *כל דבר שהוא משום שבות – לא גזרו עליו בין השמשות: **אמר** רב פפא הכא בכלכלה דחוקה עסקינן. מדמשני רב פפא הכי, משמע דסבירא ליה לצדדין מותרין, ורב אשי משמע בסמוך דסבר דאסורין, מדאמר רב אשי בסמוך: השתא דאמרת לצדדין אסורין. וקשה לי: הא איפכא שמעינן להו במסכת חגיגה בפ"ב (דף יז. ושם), דאמר רב פפא: שמע מינה לצדדין אסורין, דאי סלקא דעתך לצדדין מותרים – נסמוך ארישא דלצדדין נינהו. רב אשי אמר: אפילו תימא לצדדין מותרין, כל דלהדי גבה כגבה דמי*: **והלכתא** צדדין אסורין צדי צדדין מותרין. ותימה לרבי: אמאי לא חשיב הני בהדי יע"ל קג"ם דהלכה כאביי (בבבא מציעא דף כב:), דאמר רבא: מאן דאסר בצדדין – אסר נמי בצדי צדדין, ואביי אמר: בצדדין כולי עלמא לא פליגי [דאסור], ובצדי צדדין פליגי: **רב** יהודה אמר הן הן פקיעין כו' וה"ק: מתירים פקיעי עמיר כו'. פירש בקונטרס דהתרת פקיעים הויא שווי אוכלא. וצריך לפרש(ו) נמי בהא דרב יהודה חשיב התרת פקיעין שווי אוכלא, ורב הונא לא חשיב לה שווי אוכלא מדשרי לה. ואין נראה לרבינו תם לאפלוגינהו בהכי; אלא: לתרווייהו לא הויא התרת פקיעי עמיר לא שויא אוכלה ולא מיטרח באוכלא, דלא שייך טורח בהתרה ולהכי שריא לתרווייהו. מ"ר: אין

[illegible] באילן הוי רק שבות ול"ג בה"ש. אח"כ ראיתי שתמה כן בתשובת מעיל צדקה סימן ט' ולענ"ד י"ל דנ"מ בעי"ש שחל להיות ביו"ט והניח עירוב בערב יו"ט בכלכלה זו שיהיה עירוב ליו"ט ושבת. ולפי דב' קדושות הן צריך [illegible] ביה"ש דקודם שבת ובזה אם לא נעץ יתד לא מהני עירובו לשבת דבה"ש אינו יכול ליטול עירובו דהא בממנ"פ אסור אי הוי יום והוא יו"ט או לילה והוא שבת אסור בשימוש במחובר אבל בנעץ יתד דמגו טלטול מכרמלית לרה"ר ליכא איסור תורה ביו"ט ובה"ש מותר דמשום שבות לא גזרינן בה"ש דדלמא עדיין יום וליכא איסור תורה:

רבינו חננאל

חמור אלא בצידי החמור אני משפשף (ויגדלן) [וצדדין] לא גזרו בהו רבנן מדתנן מתיר החבלים והשקין נופלין מאי לאו בחבר גואלקי ולא גזרו בהו רבנן פי' חבר גואלקי כשטוענין הבהמה מביאין שק וטוענין אותו מצד אחד ושק האחר מצד השני ומביא חבל וקושרן ומחברן (ומשרכבן) [ומשכיבן] בצדי הבהמה וכשמבקשין לפרק משאוי מגביה השקין לרפרף קשר החבל להיות נוח להתיר ומתיר ומניח השקין והן יורדין מצדי הבהמה ויורדין לארץ נמצא מגביה ומוריד השקין בצידי החמור כאשר אני מגביה ע"ג החמור והוא יורד בדרך שפשוף אמר לך אביי אינו אומר מתיר החבלים בחבר גואלקי אלא באבר גואלקי כדתנן כיצד מאברין את העדים ומפרשינן ליה מלשון אבר כן מוסיף כמין אבר בגואלקי והוא למעלה כדאמרי' בפ' לא יחפור (ב"ב כד:) באברוורי הוו יתבי פי' אברוורי למעלה מן המשאוי כגון שהיה צד המשאוי האחד כבד והשני קל ורצינו להשוות המשאוי שלא יהיה *) מטרטן ומוסיף על הצד הקל דבר להשוות המשקל שלא יהיה אחד מהן מכריע ועליו אמרה משנתנו מתיר החבלים והשקין נופלים שהקשר למעלה הוא. ואין צריך להגביה שק ולא להוריד אלא כשמתיר החבר נופלין אבר גואלקי נמצאו גואלקי על צידי בהמה ואם זה על גואלקי נמצא אבר זה צדי צדדין אי נמי בגואלקי דגואלקי עצמו אינן קשורין בחבלים אלא כמנהג שהי' לאורחים המהלכים בדרכים שעושין בראש השקין כמין קרסים ולולאות מן החבלים ומכנים הלולאות בקרסים אי נמי לולאות בלבד ומכנים בהן עץ ומחברן וכשרוצה לפרקן מושך העץ ההוא והן נופלים ונקרא עץ ההוא לכתא ואינו מגיע לצדדין ואותו האבר נמי שמוסיפין על המשאוי הוא צדדי צדדין והוא מותר אבל הצדדין אסורין. ועוד אקשי ליה אביי לרבה הא ב' בידי אדם ואחת באילן כו' ופריק רבה התם דכפייה לאילן וסיכך על גביו שנמצא משתמש באילן עצמו. תוב אקשינן עליה מסיפא דקתני ג' בידי אדם ואחת באילן כשרה ועולין לה ביו"ט ואי כפייה לאילן וסיכך ע"ג אמאי עולין לה ביו"ט הא משתמש באילן ואסור ופריק ליה התם ופרסי כאנא פי' גיהא ופרסיכנא תרתב מאבקא**) ועלה דייקינן זה הכלל כל שינטל האילן ויכולה לעמוד עולין לה ביו"ט כו' סברי לה כגון דחק באילן ונתן הנסרין שהן הסכך באותה החקיקה והן הצדדין זה אוסר להשתמש בצדדין וזה מתיר אמר אביי כולי עלמא צדדין אסורין והכא בצידי צדדין פליגי פי' כגון דחק באילן ונתן באותה החקיקה עץ חזק כמין קורה ושם ראשי הנסרים שהן הסכך על אותו העץ הנתון כמין קורה שנמצא העץ הוא צדדי האילן והנסרים הנתונין על גביו צדדי צדדין רבא א' צדדין וצדדי צדדין דינם אחד האוסר בצדדין אוסר גם בצידי צדדין והמתיר צדדי צדדין גם בצדדין מתיר ובא רב משרשיא לאותובי לרבה דאמר המותר בצידי צדדין גם בצדדין מתיר הא דתניא נעץ יתד באילן ותלה בו כלכלה למטה מעשרה עירובו עירוב למטה מי' טפחים אין עירובו עירוב. ודייקינן מינה טעמא דנעץ יתד באילן ותלה בו כלכלה פי' דהוה לה יתד בצידי האילן והכלכלה צידי צדדין ולפיכך למטה מעשרה טפחים עירובו עירוב אבל אם לא נעץ יתד ותלה בו אלא תלה באמירי האילן אפילו למטה מעשרה אין עירובו עירוב דהוה לי' צדדין הדר נתברר כי זה

*) עיין ערך אבכורי. **) פה הדברים משובשים בכ"י ומעוה לתקנם ועי' בערוך ערך גז האחרון.

עין משפט נר מצוה

כ א מיי' פכ"א מהל' שבת הלכה ט סמג לאוין סה טוש"ע א"ח סימן שם סעיף יח:

כא ב ג מיי' פכ"א מהל' שבת הל' יח טוש"ע א"ח סי' שכד סעיף ז:

כב ד מיי' שם טוש"ע שם סעיף ח:

מסורת הש"ס

[לעיל ח:] [חגיגה טז:] [ועי' תוספות חגיגה יז. ד"ה רב אשי דלא מקשה אלא לדרב אשי אדרב אשי וכתבו תירוץ לזה] לקמן קנו:

הגהות הב"ח

(א) במשנה את הכיפין אבל לא את הזירין אין: (ב) גמ' כיפין תלתא זרדין דארזי וכו' אבל לא את הזירין לא ליפספס וכו' למטרח באוכלא טרחינן לשווי אוכלא לא משוינן וכו' הן הן זרדין פקיעין תרי זרדין תלתא וכו' ואת הכיפין: (ג) שם היינו דקא אמר ר' יהודה החרובין לדקה נמי שווי אוכלא הוא: (ד) שם מאי דקה גסה ואמאי קרי: (ה) תום' ד"ה ר' יהודה וכו' וצריך לפרש דפליגי נמי בהא:

הגהות הגר"א

[א] גמ' לפספס אלא להתיר. נ"ב גירסת הרי"ף ולא להתיר ונכון מאד:

רב נסים גאון

בפרק כירה (דף מג) ופירשנו בו החלוקה בצער בעלי חיים דאורייתא או דרבנן בפרק אלו מציאות (דף לג):

גליון הש"ס

גמ' והלכתא צדדים אסורין. עיין עירובין דף לג ע"א תוס' ד"ה למטה מי' וכו' וכר' וכו'. ותמוה לתוס' דאפי' לא נעץ

רש"י

את הדלועין. המלושין, ולא אמרינן מוקצין הן לבהמה, דמאכל אדם הן: אשוני. קשין: א"נ. כלבים דקאמר – בגורייתא זוטרי, דכל נבלה קשה להן: ומערבין. התבן והאספסתא יחד, והבהמה אוכלת התבן בשביל האספסתא: תבן בתיבנא סריא. דלא חזיא, והשתא משוי לה אוכלא. והאי סריא – לאו סריא לגמרי, דההיא לטינא קיימא, ואסורה לטלטל: מתני' אין אובסין. מאכילין אותו הרבה על כרחו, ותוחבין לו בגרונו. ובגמרא מפרש לשון אובסין – עושין לה כמין אבוס בתוך מעיה: ולא דורסין. שדורס לה בתוך גרונה את השעורין. ומיהו, לא הוי כל כך כמו אובסין: אבל מלעיטין. מפרש בגמרא: אין מאמירין. מפרש בגמרא: מהלקטין. מפרש בגמרא: אין נותנין מים לפני דבורים. מפרש טעמא בגמרא, אי משום דאין מזונותיהן עליו – שיוצאין ואוכלין בשדה, אי משום דמיא באגמא שכיחא להו: הרדיסאות. על שם מקומן, וניזונין בתוך הבית: גמ' כי האי גוונא. שיאכילנה כל כך שירחיבו מעיה כאבוס: אטעינה כורא. על גבה למזונות לדרך, לבד אחר משאות: למקום שאינה יכולה להחזיר. שתוחבו לה לפנים מבית הבליעה: בכלי. בתרווד: דספי בידים. תוחבו לתוך פיו: אלא יוני שובך וכו'. בתמיה: ואמאי לא, מאי טרחא איכא? אלא לאו כו'. ומדמהלקטין דמתניתין למקום שאינה יכולה להחזיר נמי שרי, שמע מינה מלעיטין דעגלים וגמלים – למקום שאינה יכולה להחזיר, ושרי. אלא דגבי בהמה קרי ליה הלעטה, וגבי עופות קרי ליה הילקוט. ועל כרחך אין מאמירין דקאמר – בכלי הוא: לעולם מהלקטין דספי ליה בידים. ולמקום שיכולה להחזיר: אין מזונותן עליך. דשכיחי להו בדברא: חזיר אין מזונותן עליך. דארור יהודי *שיגדל חזירים: מתני' נמי דיקא. דאפילו שדי קמייהו נמי לא: דשכיחי באגמא. אבל מזונות לא שכיחי להו: שמזונותיו מועטין. שאין אדם חס עליו לתת לו מזונות הרבה: כמה תשהה במעיו. דהכלב שאכל בשר מת ומת הכלב בבית, תוך ג' ימים מטמא באהל. אבל בחייו לא מטמא, דטומאה בלועה בבעלי חיים לא מיטמא, כדאמר ב"בהמה המקשה" (חולין דף עא:): שמע מינה. מדקאמר שהקפיד הקדוש ברוך הוא על מזונותיו: משח אודניה. מעט כמות אזנו, וחוטרא בתריה – יכהו במקל מיד, שלא יהא מרגילו אצלו: אבל במתא לא. ליתיב ליה מידי, אי לאו דידיה הוא: משום דאתי למיעבד, ... ויפסידו: לית דעתיר מחזירא. שכל מאכל ראוי לו, ומוצא לאכול, ואף מאכילין לו הרבה: כוותיה דרב יהודה. שהמראה למקום שאינו יכול להחזיר: פוקם את פיה. נותן חכה לתוך פיה שלא תוכל לסגור פיה: ומאכילה כרשינין ומים בבת אחת. והמים מבליעין הכרשינין לתוך בית בליעתה על כרחה: מאכילה מעומד. נותן לתוך פיה, וכל זמן שאינו מרבילה אינו יכול לתחוב כל כך, ויכול להחזירה: מתניתין מני. דקתני נותן מים לתוך המורסן, דנתינת מים לא זהו גיבולו: אפי' רבי יוסי מודה. דזהו גיבולו: קלי. קמח של תבואה שנתייבשה כשהן קליות בתנור, ואותו קמח לעולם מתוק. והוא *קמחא דאבשונא, ועושין ממנו שתיתא משמן ומים ומלח שמערבין בו:

תוספות

אין אובסין את הגמל וכו'. והא דאמרינן בעירובין פרק "עושין פסין" (דף כ: ושם): גמל שראשו ורובו מבפנים אובסין אותו מבפנים – הך אביסה לאו היינו אביסה ממש. דהא אמרינן הכא אין אובסין כו'. והאי אביסה – היינו הלעטה, וכן פירש רבינו שמואל: אלא קמח דבר גיבול הוא. פירשתי לעיל בפ"ק (דף יח. ושם*): מהו

גמרא

תורה אור

[א]את הדלועין לפני הבהמה, [ב]ואת הנבלה לפני הכלבים. מאי לאו, דלועין דומיא דנבלה; מה נבלה – דרכיכא, אף דלועין – דרכיכי, אלמא: טרחינן באוכלא, ותיובתא דרב יהודה! אמר לך רב יהודה: לא, נבלה דומיא דדלועין; מה דלועין – [ג]דאשוני, אף נבלה – דאשונא. והיכי משכחת לה – בבשר פילי. א"נ: בגורייאתא זוטרי. תא שמע, דתני רב חנן מנהרדעא: *מפרכינן תבן ואספסתא ומערבין. אלמא: טרחינן באוכלא! תבן – בתיבנא סריא, אספסתא – בעילי זוטרי.§ **מתני'** אין אובסין את הגמל, ולא דורסין, אבל מלעיטין. ואין מאמירין את העגלים, אבל מלעיטין. ומהלקטין לתרנגולין, ונותנין מים למורסן, אבל לא גובלין, ואין נותנין מים לפני דבורים ולפני יונים שבשובך, אבל נותנין לפני אווזין ותרנגולין, ולפני יוני הרדיסיות.§ **גמ'** מאי "אין אובסין"? אמר רב יהודה: [ד]אין עושין לה אבוס בתוך מעיה. מי איכא כי האי גוונא? אין, וכדאמר רב ירמיה מדיפתי: לדידי חזי לי ההוא טייעא דאכלא כורא, *ואטעינא כורא.§ "אין מאמירין".§ איזו היא המראה ואיזו היא הלעטה? אמר רב יהודה: [ה]המראה – למקום שאינה יכולה להחזיר, הלעטה – למקום שיכולה להחזיר. רב חסדא אמר: אידי ואידי למקום שאינה יכולה להחזיר, והמראה – בכלי, הלעטה – ביד. מתיב רב יוסף: *[ו]מהלקטין לתרנגולין, ואין צריך לומר שמלקיטין. ואין מלקיטין ליוני שובך וליוני עלייה, ואין צריך לומר שאין מהלקטין. מאי "מהלקטין" ומאי "מלקיטין"? אילימא "מהלקטין" – דספי ליה בידים, "מלקיטין" – דשדי ליה(א) קמייהו, מכלל דיוני שובך ויוני עלייה מישדא קמייהו נמי לא?! אלא לאו: "מהלקטין" – למקום שאינה יכולה להחזיר, "מלקיטין" – למקום שיכולה להחזיר, מכלל – דהמראה בכלי, ותיובתא דרב יהודה! אמר לך רב יהודה: לעולם "מהלקטין" – דספי ליה בידים, "מלקיטין" – דשדי ליה קמייהו. ודקא קשיא לך: יוני שובך ויוני עלייה למישדא קמייהו נמי לא?! הני מזונותן עליך, והני – אין מזונותן עליך. כדתניא: [ז]נותנין מזונות לפני כלב, ואין נותנין מזונות לפני חזיר. ומה הפרש בין זה לזה, זה – מזונותיו עליך וזה – אין מזונותיו עליך. אמר רב אשי: מתניתין נמי דיקא: [ח]"אין נותנין מים לפני דבורים ולפני יונים שבשובך אבל נותנין לפני אווזין ולפני תרנגולין ולפני יוני הרדיסיות" מ"ט? לאו [ט]משום דהני מזונותן עליך והני אין מזונותן עליך? ולטעמיך, מאי איריא מיא, אפילו חיטי ושערי נמי לא! אלא שאני מיא דשכיחי באגמא. דרש רבי יונה אפיתחא דבי נשיאה, מאי דכתיב: °(*"יודע) צדיק דין דלים" יודע הקב"ה בכלב שמזונותיו מועטין, לפיכך שוהה אכילתו במעיו ג' ימים. *כדתנן: [י]כמה תשהה אכילתו במעיו ויהא טמא – בכלב – ג' ימים מעת לעת, ובעופות ובדגים – כדי שתפול לאור ותשרף. אמר רב המנונא, שמע מינה: אורח ארעא למשדא אומצא לכלבא. וכמה? אמר רב מרי: משח אודניה, וחוטרא אבתריה. הני מילי – בדברא, אבל במתא – לא, דאתא למסרך. אמר רב פפא: לית דעניא מכלבא, ולית דעתיר מחזירא. תניא כוותיה דרב יהודה: *[כ]איזו היא המראה ואיזו היא הלעטה? המראה – מרביצה ופוקם את פיה ומאכילה כרשינין ומים בבת אחת, הלעטה – מאכילה מעומד ומשקה מעומד, ונותנין כרשינין בפני עצמן ומים בפני עצמן.§ "מהלקטין לתרנגולין כו'".§ אמר אביי: אמריתה קמיה דמר, מתניתין מני? ואמר לי: ר' יוסי בר יהודה היא, דתניא: *אחד נותן את הקמח ואחד נותן לתוכו מים – האחרון חייב, דברי רבי. *ר' יוסי בר יהודה אומר: אינו חייב עד שיגבל. דילמא עד כאן לא קאמר רבי יוסי בר יהודה התם – אלא קמח דבר גיבול הוא, אבל מורסן דלאו בר גיבול הוא – אפילו רבי יוסי בר יהודה מודה? לא סלקא דעתך, דתניא בהדיא: אין נותנין מים למורסן, דברי רבי. ר' יוסי בר יהודה אומר: [ל]נותנין מים למורסן. ת"ר: אין גובלין את הקלי וי"א גובלין. *מאן י"א? א"ר חסדא: רבי

משלי כט

עין משפט נר מצוה

כג א מיי' פכ"א מהל' שבת הלכה יח סמג לאוין סה טוש"ע א"ח סימן שכד סעיף ו:
כד ב ג מיי' שם טוש"ע שם סעיף ז:
כה ד ה מיי' שם הלכה לה טוש"ע שם סע"ט:
כו ו מיי' שם והלכה לו טוש"ע שם סעיף י:
כז ז ח ט מיי' שם טוש"ע שם סעיף יא:
כח י מיי' פ"כ מהלכות טומאת מת הלכה ז:
כט כ מיי' פכ"א מהלכ' שבת הלכה לה:
ל ל מיי' פכ"א מהלכות שבת הלכה לד טוש"ע א"ח סי' שכד סע"ג:

רבינו חננאל

זה התנא אוסר בצדדין ומתיר בצידי צדדין. ופריק רב פפא אליבא דרבא הכא בכלכלה דחוקה וכו'. ודברי רב פפא פשוטין הן ומפקינן בה והלכתא צדדין אסורין צדדי צדדין מותרין: **דרגא** דמדלא סולם העשוי לעלות בו בערסל והוא (שכתוב) [שת"י] כמלונה במקשה [כערסל]. והוא מלונה לשומרי פירות ודקדק רב אשי מזו ההלכה שאסור להניח סולם על הדקל ולעלות בו שנמצא משתמש בצידי האילן ואסור. ופירוש שאם יחקוק באילן ויניח באותה חקיקה גואזי שהן עצים ויניח באותו העצים הסולם נמצא הסולם נתון בעצים כמין הכלכלה ביתד ושרי וגם אסור להניח רגלי העולה באותה סולם בעצים הנעוצין באילן מפני שהן צדדין והצדדין אסורין. וכי אינו מותר לו להשתמש ולעלות אלא בקנים שהן מעלות הסולם והן שליבותיו שהן ודאי צדדי צדדין: [מתני'] מתירין פקיעי עמיר כו'. פי' פקיעי אגודות כדתנן פקעת גמי בא רב הונא לפרש משנתנו ואמר הפקיעין והכיפין שניהם אגודות קשורות הן. אלא הפקיעין ב' אגודות כפקיע והכפין ג' אגודות בכף זירין דארזי כשמתגזאין ומתקשין נקראין דארזי והן אחד אחד ואינן נאגדין באגודה. ואם אגדן בחזקתן עומדין ותרצה רב הונא למתניתין הכי מתירין פקיעי עמיר לפני בהמה ומפספסין פי' מפספסין מפרכין כעין פיתות (לרכבן לייתות) [לרכבן] לאכלה ומצינו בתלמוד א"י שאמרו בענין (תינוק פתילה) מפספסין ופי' מחרכין כדכתיב ושער ראשיהון לא התחרך ונראין הדברים שהחריכה מרככת כעין הפתיתה דהוא מעין פסיסה. כדאמרינן בידות האוכלין שכססן לגורן וכשם שמתירין ומפספסין הפקיעין הוא הדין לכפין אבל הזירין לא יפספס ולא להתיר אם נקשרו ובא רב חסדא ופי' טעמא דרב הונא ואמר שהעמידו למשנתנו שמתירין ומפספסין הפקיעין והכפין שהן מקודם אוכל ויכולין להיאכל כמות שהן וכן ההתרה והפספום לא להוסיף להם אלא הכשר לאכילה בלבד דייקינן מדבריו הללו דקסבר מותר למיטרח באוכל ומוסיף לו הכשר אבל אם אין יכול להיאכל כגון הזירין שהן דארזי אלא אחרי התר ופספוס אסור וזהו לשוויי אוכלי לא משוינן ורב יהודה חלק על רב הונא לדברי רבה דאוקמינהו לדברי רב יהודה שוויה אוכלא לא משווינן ואמר רבה מדתרצה למתניתין שהפקיעין [והזירין שניהן אגודות מפספס למה הן מיהו הפקיעין שתים באגודה והעמירין ג' מותר להתיר הפקיעין שקשרן מתירן] ואם לא יתירם אינן נאכלין בטוב ושלש אין קשרן אמיץ ונאכלין וכיון שיכולים להיאכל קסבר אטרוחי באכילה טרחינן ואם יש לומר מניין לנו ראיה שיש הפרש בין ב' לג' שאלו קישרם אמיץ יותר מאלו מצאנו לדבריהן שאומרים נימה אחת קשורה חוצצת ג' אין חוצצת ב' איני יודע פי' ג' אינן חוצצת שאין קשרן מתחזק והמים באים בתוכו לפיכך אינן חוצצין אבל הכפים שהן דידי והן קשין כמו שאמרנו למעלה מפספסין כדי לשוותם אוכל וכ"ש שמתירין ובאנו להקשות לרב הונא מסיפא דהא מתניתין דקתני אין מרסקין את השחת ולא את החרובין ופשוטה היא. ופריק רב הונא לא שהחרובין רכין הן כמות שהן (שהדות) [שהדתאה] שהן רכין ויכולין להיאכל אין מרסקין אותן אלמא לא מטרחינן באוכלא אלא שחת דומיא חרובין דאשיני פירוש יבישין וקשין ואין יכולין להיאכל אף שחת כמותן שנתייבש ונתקשה ואינו אוכל והריסוק משווייהו אוכל ומתניתין כוותי דאמרי שוויי אוכלא לא משווינן ואזו היא בהמה לאכול השחת אלא אחרי ריסוק ואמרנו בעילי זוטרי פי' עיירים קטנים. ותוב אקשינן על רב הונא מדרב יהודה נשמע לרבנן לאו ר' יהודה מתיר בחרובין לדקה לדקה [אין] לגסה לא מכלל דרבנן סברי להיאכל כמות שהן לא טרחינן לדחוקינהו להו דמטרח באוכלא לא טרחינן. וא"ל רב יהודה לת"ק התינח לגסה שיכולה לאכול כמות שהיא בלא ריסוק אלא לדקה שאינה יכולה לאוכלה כמות שהיא בלא אוכלא הוא ושוי דאם נאמר כי ת"ק סבר מטרח טרחינן שוויי אוכלא לא משוינן וריסוק זה שוויי אוכלא לדקה ולגסה הוא ואסור וא"ל ר' יהודה לדקה אוכלא הוא ומיטרח באוכל שרי ואם הוא או לגסה ולא היה צריך לומר אלא ר' יהודה מתיר סתם בין לדקה בין לגסה. ועלתה בקשיא לרב הונא וחזרנו להקשות על רב יהודה דתנן מחתכין את הדלועין לפני הבהמה ואת הנבלה לפני הכלבים ופשוטה היא וכן הא דתני רב חנן מנהרדעא מפריכין תבן ואספסתא ומערבין אלמא טרחינן באוכלא ופריק גם זו ואע"ג דרוב סוגיא דשמעתא כרב הונא ריחשא הא איתותב ולא אשכח לה בה קושיא ותוב רב יהודה ורבה רישי מתיבתא הוו דאמרינן האי שיפורא מעיקרא בי רב יהודה ולבסוף בי רבה וחלכתא כוותיה ומשוינן אוכלא ולא קא טרחינן באוכלא מכלל דרב הונא לא הוה ריש אמרינן כי הוו מפטרי רבנן מבי רב הונא הוו פיישי כו' ואמרינן ואמרי במערבא קמא לה מתיבתא דהונא בבלאה: [מתני'] אין אובסין את הגמל כו'. פי' אובסין מפטמין כדכתיב וברבורים אבוסים את הגמל הרבה כרב ירמיה דאמר אנא חזיתיה לההוא טייעא דאכלא כו' כורא ואטענה כורא וכן הלכה דאסור לפטם בהמה בשבת ולא אפילו עופות. אין ממרים את העגלים אבל מלעיטין איזו היא הלעטה. אמר רב יהודה המראה למקום שאינה יכולה להחזיר. פי' המראה שמוריד בידו המאכל בבלעו של עגלים במקום שאינו יכול להחזירו מתוך בלעו אבל חשוב הוא כבלוע כגון זה אסור להלעוטי כדכתיב הלעיטני וגו' לתת המאכל בחך שלו מותר וזה וזה ביד. ורב חסדא אמר אידי ואידי למקום שאין יכול להחזיר והמראה בכלי והלעטה ביד ואותביה רב יוסף לרב יהודה מהלקטין לתרנגולין ואין

מסורת הש"ס

[נ"ל מפרכין וכן העתיקו תוס' לעיל קנ: וכן בתוס']
[ב"ב יט: ד"ה כתיבנא] [ועי' תוס' ב"מ פ: ד"ה פסק]
[תוספתא פי"ח]
[סוטה מט:]
[ובקרא כתיב יודע חסר וי"ו]
[אהלות פי"א מ"ז]
[תוספתא' עי"ו]
לעיל יח.
[לעיל יח. אית' רבי יוסי]
[ועי' מ"ש תוס' ב"ב נג: ד"ה מאן]
[פסחים לט:]

הגהות הב"ח

(א) גמ' דשדי ליה קמייהו אלא דיוני שובך:

גליון הש"ס

גמרא מאי לאו דלועין. כעין זה בב"מ דף קט ע"ב ועיין שיטה מקובצת שם ד"ה כ"ה:

רַבִּי יוֹסֵי בְּר' יְהוּדָה הִיא. וְהנ"מ – הוּא אדִּמְשַׁנֵּי. הֵיכִי מְשַׁנֵּי? א"ר חִסְדָּא: עַל ביָד עַל יָד. *וְשָׁוִין שֶׁבּוֹחֲשִׁין אֶת הַשָּׁתִית בַּשַּׁבָּת וְשׁוֹתִים זִיתוֹם הַמִּצְרִי. וְהָאָמְרַתְּ "אֵין גּוֹבְלִין"! ל"ק, הָא – גבְּעָבָה, הָא – בְּרַכָּה. וְהָנֵי מִילֵּי – הוּא דִּמְשַׁנֵּי. הֵיכִי מְשַׁנֵּי? אָמַר רַב יוֹסֵף: בַּחוֹל נוֹתֵן אֶת הַחוֹמֶץ וְאח"כ נוֹתֵן אֶת הַשָּׁתִית, דבַּשַּׁבָּת – נוֹתֵן אֶת הַשָּׁתִית וְאח"כ נוֹתֵן אֶת הַחוֹמֶץ. לֵוִי בְּרֵיהּ דְּרַב הוּנָא בַּר חִיָּיא אַשְׁכַּחֵיהּ לְגַבָּלָא דְּבֵי *נְשֵׁיהּ דְּקָא גָּבֵיל וְסָפֵי לֵיהּ לְתוֹרֵיהּ, בְּטַשׁ בֵּיהּ. *אֲתָא אֲבוּהּ אַשְׁכַּחֵיהּ, א"ל: הָכִי אָמַר אֲבוּהָ דְּאִמָּךְ מִשְּׁמֵיהּ דְּרַב, וּמַנּוּ – רַבִּי יִרְמְיָה בַּר אַבָּא: גּוֹבְלִין וְלֹא מַסְפִּין. וּדְלָא לָקֵיט בְּלִישָּׁנֵיהּ – מְהַלְקִטִין לֵיהּ. וְה"מ – הוּא דִּמְשַׁנֵּי. הֵיכִי מְשַׁנֵּי? אָמַר רַב יֵימַר בַּר שְׁלַמְיָא מִשְּׁמֵיהּ דְּאַבַּיֵי: שְׁתִי וָעֵרֶב. וְהָא לָא מְעָרֵב שַׁפִּיר! אָמַר רַב יְהוּדָה: מְנַעֲרוֹ לַכְּלִי. כְּתִיב אַפִּינְקְסֵיהּ דִּזְעֵירִי: אֲמָרִית קֳדָם רַבִּי, וּמַנּוּ – רַבִּי חִיָּיא, מַהוּ לְגַבֵּל? אָמַר: אָסוּר. מַהוּ לְפָרֵק? אָמַר: מוּתָּר. אָמַר רַב [*מְנַשְּׁיָא]: חַד קַמֵּי חַד, תְּרֵי קַמֵּי תְּרֵי – שַׁפִּיר דָּמֵי, תְּלָתָא קַמֵּי תְּרֵי – אָסוּר. רַב יוֹסֵף אָמַר: קַב וַאֲפִילּוּ קַבַּיִים. עוּלָּא אָמַר: כּוֹר וַאֲפִילּוּ כּוֹרַיִים. כְּתִיב אַפִּינְקְסֵיהּ דְּלֵוִי: אֲמָרִית קֳדָם רַבִּי, וּמַנּוּ – רַבֵּינוּ הַקָּדוֹשׁ, עַל דַּהֲווּ גָּבְלִין שְׁתִיתָא בְּבָבֶל, וַהֲוָה צָוַח רַבִּי, וּמַנּוּ – רַבֵּינוּ הַקָּדוֹשׁ, עַל דַּהֲווּ גָּבְלִין שְׁתִיתָא, וְלֵית דְּשָׁמַע לֵיהּ, וְלֵית חֵילָא בִּידֵיהּ לְמֵיסַר – מִדְּרַבִּי יוֹסֵי בְּר' יְהוּדָה. כְּתִיב אַפִּינְקְסֵיהּ דְּרַבִּי יְהוֹשֻׁעַ בֶּן לֵוִי: הַאי מַאן דִּבְחַד בְּשַׁבָּא – יְהֵי גְּבַר וְלָא חֲדָא בֵּיהּ. מַאי "[וְלָא חֲדָא בֵּיהּ]"? אִילֵימָא וְלָא חַד לְטִיבוּ – וְהָאָמַר רַב אַשִׁי: אֲנָא בְּחַד בְּשַׁבָּא הֲוַאי! אֶלָּא – לָאו חֲדָא לְבִישׁוּ, וְהָאָמַר רַב אַשִׁי: אֲנָא וְדִימִי בַּר קַקּוּזְתָּא הֲוֵין בְּחַד בְּשַׁבָּא, אֲנָא – מֶלֶךְ, וְהוּא – הֲוָה רֵישׁ גַּנָּבֵי! אֶלָּא: אִי כּוּלֵּי לְטִיבוּ, אִי כּוּלֵּי לְבִישׁוּ. (מַאי טַעְמָא – דְּאִיבְרוּ בֵּיהּ אוֹר וְחוֹשֶׁךְ)? הַאי מַאן דִּבְתְרֵי בְּשַׁבָּא – יְהֵי גְּבַר רַגְזָן. מ"ט – מִשּׁוּם דְּאִיפְּלִיגוּ בֵּיהּ מַיָּא. הַאי מַאן דִּבְתְלָתָא בְּשַׁבָּא – יְהֵי גְּבַר עָתִיר, וְזַנַּאי יְהֵא. מ"ט – מִשּׁוּם דְּאִיבְרוּ בֵּיהּ עֲשָׂבִים. הַאי מַאן דְּבְאַרְבְּעָה בְּשַׁבָּא – יְהֵי גְּבַר חַכִּים *)וְנָהִיר, מ"ט – מִשּׁוּם דְּאִיתְלוּ בֵּיהּ מְאוֹרוֹת. הַאי מַאן דִּבְחַמְשָׁה בְּשַׁבָּא – יְהֵי גְּבַר גּוֹמֵל חֲסָדִים. מ"ט – מִשּׁוּם דְּאִיבְרוּ בֵּיהּ דָּגִים וְעוֹפוֹת. הַאי מַאן דִּבְמַעֲלֵי שַׁבְּתָא – יְהֵי גְּבַר חַזְרָן, אָמַר ר"נ בַּר יִצְחָק: חַזְרָן בְּמִצְוֹת. הַאי מַאן דִּבְשַׁבְּתָא יְהֵי – בְּשַׁבְּתָא יָמוּת, עַל דְּאַחִילוּ עֲלוֹהִי יוֹמָא רַבָּא דְּשַׁבְּתָא. אָמַר רָבָא בַּר רַב שֵׁילָא: וְקַדִּישָׁא רַבָּא יִתְקְרֵי. אָמַר לְהוּ רַבִּי חֲנִינָא: פּוּקוּ אֱמָרוּ לֵיהּ לְבַר לֵיוָאי: לֹא מַזַּל יוֹם גּוֹרֵם, אֶלָּא מַזַּל שָׁעָה גּוֹרֵם. הַאי מַאן דִּבְחַמָּה(א) יְהֵי גְּבַר זִיוְתָן, יְהֵי אָכֵיל מִדִּילֵיהּ וְשָׁתֵי מִדִּילֵיהּ, וְרָזוֹהִי גַּלְיָין. אִם גָּנֵיב – לָא מַצְלַח. הַאי מַאן דְּבְכוֹכַב נוֹגַהּ יְהֵי גְּבַר עָתִיר וְזַנַּאי יְהֵי, מ"ט – מִשּׁוּם דְּאִיתְיְלִיד בֵּיהּ נוּרָא. הַאי מַאן דְּבְכוֹכָב יְהֵי גְּבַר נָהִיר וְחַכִּים, מִשּׁוּם דְּסָפְרָא דְּחַמָּה הוּא. הַאי מַאן דִּבְלְבָנָה יְהֵי גְּבַר סָבֵיל מַרְעִין, בָּנֵאי וְסָתֵיר, סָתֵיר וּבָנֵאי, אָכֵיל דְּלָא דִּילֵיהּ וְשָׁתֵי דְּלָא דִּילֵיהּ, וְרָזוֹהִי כַּסְיָין, אִם גָּנַב – מַצְלַח. הַאי מַאן דִּבְשַׁבְּתַאי יְהֵי גְּבַר מַחְשְׁבָתֵיהּ בְּטֵלִין, וְאִית דְּאָמְרִי: כׇּל דְּמַחְשְׁבִין עֲלֵיהּ בְּטֵלִין. הַאי מַאן דְּבְצֶדֶק יְהֵי גְּבַר צַדְקָן, אָמַר ר"נ בַּר יִצְחָק: וְצַדְקָן בְּמִצְוֹת. הַאי מַאן דְּבְמַאְדִּים יְהֵי גְּבַר אָשֵׁיד דְּמָא. א"ר אַשִׁי: אִי אוּמָּנָא, אִי גַּנָּבָא, אִי טַבָּחָא, אִי מוֹהֲלָא. אָמַר רַבָּה: אֲנָא בְּמַאְדִּים הֲוַאי! אָמַר אַבַּיֵי: מָר נָמֵי עָנֵישׁ וְקָטֵיל. אִיתְּמַר, רַבִּי חֲנִינָא אוֹמֵר: מַזַּל מַחְכִּים, מַזַּל מַעֲשִׁיר, וְיֵשׁ מַזָּל לְיִשְׂרָאֵל. רַבִּי יוֹחָנָן אָמַר: אֵין מַזָּל לְיִשְׂרָאֵל. וְאָזְדָא רַבִּי יוֹחָנָן לְטַעְמֵיהּ, *דְּא"ר יוֹחָנָן: מִנַּיִין שֶׁאֵין מַזָּל לְיִשְׂרָאֵל – שֶׁנֶּאֱמַר: °"כֹּה אָמַר ה' אֶל דֶּרֶךְ הַגּוֹיִם אַל תִּלְמָדוּ וּמֵאוֹתוֹת הַשָּׁמַיִם אַל תֵּחָתּוּ כִּי יֵחַתּוּ הַגּוֹיִם מֵהֵמָּה", *הֵם יֵחַתּוּ, וְלֹא יִשְׂרָאֵל. וְאַף רַב סָבַר אֵין מַזָּל לְיִשְׂרָאֵל, דְּאָמַר רַב יְהוּדָה אָמַר רַב: מִנַּיִין שֶׁאֵין מַזָּל לְיִשְׂרָאֵל – שֶׁנֶּאֱמַר: *°"וַיּוֹצֵא אוֹתוֹ הַחוּצָה". אָמַר אַבְרָהָם לִפְנֵי הקב"ה: רבש"ע °"בֶּן בֵּיתִי יוֹרֵשׁ אוֹתִי". אָמַר לוֹ: לָאו, °"כִּי אִם אֲשֶׁר יֵצֵא מִמֵּעֶיךָ". אָמַר לְפָנָיו: רבש"ע, נִסְתַּכַּלְתִּי בְּאִיצְטַגְנִינוּת שֶׁלִּי וְאֵינִי רָאוּי לְהוֹלִיד בֵּן. אָמַר לֵיהּ: צֵא מֵאִיצְטַגְנִינוּת שֶׁלְּךָ, שֶׁאֵין מַזָּל לְיִשְׂרָאֵל. מַאי דַּעְתִּיךְ – דְּקָאֵי

*) [פי' זכרך ערוך].

רש"י

רַבִּי יוֹסֵי בַּר יְהוּדָה הִיא. (דְּאִי רַבִּי לָא מְהַנֵּי לֵיהּ שִׁינּוּי, דִּמְנַתִּינַת מַיִם מִיחַיַּיב אֲפִילּוּ בְּמִידֵי דְּלָאו בַּר גִּיבּוּל, כִּדְאָמְרִינַן גַּבֵּי מוּרְסָן. אֲבָל לְרַבִּי יוֹסֵי בַּר יְהוּדָה) דְּאָמַר עַד שֶׁיְּגַבֵּל – הָכָא גּוֹבְלִין כִּלְאַחַר יָד, כִּדְמְפָרֵשׁ וְאָזֵיל. וְהנ"מ הוּא דְּקָא מְשַׁנֵּי: שֶׁבּוֹחֲשִׁין. בְּתַרְוָוד, דְּהַיְינוּ גּוֹבְלִין: וְשׁוֹתִים זִיתוֹם הַמִּצְרִי. דִּבְלָאו רְפוּאָה נָמֵי מַשְׁקֶה הוּא, דִּתְנַן: כׇּל הַמַּשְׁקִין שׁוֹתֶה אָדָם לִרְפוּאָה (לעיל דף קט:): בְּעָבָה. אֵין גּוֹבְלִין, בְּרַכָּה – בּוֹחֲשִׁין, שֶׁאֵין זוֹ לִישָׁה: בַּחוֹל נוֹתֵן הַחוֹמֶץ כו'. כְּלוֹמַר: כֵּן דַּרְכּוֹ בַּחוֹל: לְגַבָּלָא דְּבֵי נָשֵׁיהּ. שׁוֹמֵר בְּהֵמוֹת אָבִיו וּמְגַבֵּל מַאֲכָלָן: דְּקָא גָּבֵיל. מוּרְסָן ע"י שִׁינּוּי: בְּטַשׁ בֵּיהּ. דְּהָא לְכוּלֵּי עָלְמָא "אֲבָל לֹא גּוֹבְלִין" תְּנַן: גּוֹבְלִין. מוּרְסָן ע"י שִׁינּוּי, כִּדְמְפָרֵשׁ וְאָזֵיל, וְהוּא דְּקָא מְשַׁנֵּי: וְלֹא מַסְפִּין. לְתוֹרֵי, אֵין מַאֲמִירִין אוֹתָן: וּדְלָא לָקֵיט בְּלִישָּׁנֵיהּ. עֵגֶל קָטָן שֶׁעֲדַיִין לֹא לוֹמֵד לֶאֱכוֹל: וְהָנֵי מִילֵּי. דַּאֲמַרַן, דְּמוּתָּר לְגַבֵּל מוּרְסָן: שְׁתִי וָעֵרֶב. פַּעַם אַחַת מוֹלִיךְ הַמַּקֵּל שְׁתִי, וּפַעַם אַחַת עֵרֶב: מְנַעֲרוֹ לַכְּלִי. וְהוּא מִתְעָרֵב מֵאֵלָיו: אַפִּינְקְסֵיהּ. לוּחוֹת קְשׁוּרוֹת זוֹ עִם זוֹ, כְּאוֹתָן שֶׁל סוֹחֲרִים: מַהוּ לְפָרֵק. לָתֵת מִתּוֹךְ כְּלִי שֶׁלִּפְנֵי בְּהֵמָה זוֹ, וְלָתֵת לִפְנֵי חֲבֶרְתָּהּ: חֲדָא קַמֵּי חֲדָא. מִילְּתָא בְּאַפֵּי נַפְשָׁהּ הִיא. אַחַת מִדָּה שֶׁרְגִילִין לָתֵת לִפְנֵי בְּהֵמָה מוּתָּר לָתֵת לְפָנֶיהָ בַּשַּׁבָּת, וְכֵן תַּרְתֵּי קַמֵּי תַּרְתֵּי הָאוֹכְלוֹת בְּאֵבוּס אֶחָד: אֲבָל תְּלָתָא קַמֵּי תַּרְתֵּי. הוֹאִיל וּבְחוֹל לָא יָהֵיב לְהוּ כִּי הַאי – הָוֵי טִרְחָא דְּלָא צָרִיךְ, וכ"ש תַּרְתֵּי קַמֵּי חֲדָא: אֲמָרִית קַמֵּיהּ רַבִּי. רַבִּי לֵוִי מִשְׁתָּעֵי, דְּהוּא אֲמַר קֳדָם רַבִּי עַל הָנָךְ אִינָשֵׁי דְּגָבְלִין שְׁתִיתָא: מִדְּר' יוֹסֵי בַּר יְהוּדָה. בַּר פְּלוּגְתֵּיהּ דְּהֲוָה שָׁרֵי לְעֵיל אַף בְּעָבָה וְעַל יְדֵי שִׁינּוּי, וְהָיוּ נוֹהֲגִין כְּמוֹתוֹ: הַאי מַאן דִּבְחַד בְּשַׁבָּא. הַנּוֹלָד בְּאֶחָד בַּשַּׁבָּת: יְהֵא גְּבַר וְלָא חֲדָא בֵּיהּ. יְהֵא אָדָם שָׁלֵם, בְּמִדָּה אַחַת יְהֵא, וְלֹא אַחַת בּוֹ מִמִּדָּה אַחֶרֶת. וּלְקַמָּן מְפָרֵשׁ לָהּ וְאָזֵיל: וְהוּא רֵישׁ גַּנָּבֵי. דְּמַאן דִּבְחַד בְּשַׁבָּא יְהֵא רֹאשׁ, כְּמוֹ שֶׁהַיּוֹם רֹאשׁ לְמַעֲשֵׂה בְרֵאשִׁית. מִיהוּ, שְׁמַע מִינָּהּ דְּנוֹלָדִים בּוֹ צַדִּיקִים וּרְשָׁעִים: דְּאִיפְּלִיגוּ מַיָּא. כָּךְ הוּא יִבָּדֵל מִכׇּל אָדָם: זַנַּאי. נוֹאֵף: דְּאִיבְרוּ בֵּיהּ עֲשָׂבִים. דִּכְתִי' (בראשי' א): "תַּדְשֵׁא הָאָרֶץ", וְהוּא דָּבָר שֶׁפָּרֶה וְרָבֶה מְאֹד וּמְמַהֵר לִגְדֹּל וְלִצְמוֹחַ, דְּהוּא עִנְיַן פְּרִיצוּת, אשווי"א בְּלַע"ז. [ל"א]: דְּלָא כְּתִיב "לְמִינֵהוּ" בַּעֲשָׂבִים כַּשְּׁוּוִיִּים, (וְעוֹד) שֶׁיּוֹצְאִין בְּעִרְבּוּבְיָא וְיוֹנְקִין זוֹ מִזּוֹ: וְנָהִיר. זִיוְתָן: דְּאִיתְלוּ בֵּיהּ מְאוֹרוֹת. וּכְתִיב: "וְתוֹרָה אוֹר": דְּאִיבְרוּ בֵּיהּ דָּגִים וְעוֹפוֹת. שֶׁאֵין טוֹרְחִין לֶאֱכוֹל, אֶלָּא נִיזּוֹנִים בְּחַסְדּוֹ שֶׁל הקב"ה: חַזְרָן. מְחַזֵּר אַחַר מִצְוֹת: חַזְרָן בְּמִצְוֹת. שֶׁכֵּן דֶּרֶךְ ע"ש לְחַזֵּר אַחַר מִצְוַת שַׁבָּת: וְקַדִּישָׁא רַבָּה יִתְקְרֵי. שֶׁיְּהֵא פָּרוּשׁ וְקָדוֹשׁ, דִּכְתִיב (שמות כ): "וַיְקַדְּשֵׁהוּ": אֲמַר לְהוּ רַבִּי חֲנִינָא. לְתַלְמִידִים שֶׁקָּרְאוּ פִּנְקָסוֹ שֶׁל ר' יְהוֹשֻׁעַ: מַזַּל שָׁעָה. ז' מַזָּלוֹת הֵן הַמְשַׁמְּשִׁין אֶת הַשָּׁעוֹת – חנכ"ל שצ"ם. חַמָּה – הַיְינוּ חַמָּה מַמָּשׁ, וְהוּא אֶחָד מִן הַמַּזָּלוֹת. וְכֵן לְבָנָה. וְהַשְּׁאָר הָוְויָן כּוֹכָבִים: זִיוְתָן. כַּשֶּׁמֶשׁ הַמֵּאִיר: אָכֵיל מִדִּילֵיהּ. כַּשֶּׁמֶשׁ שֶׁאֵינוֹ מַסִּיג גְּבוּל רֵעֵהוּ לִמְשׁוֹל בַּלַּיְלָה: וְרָזוֹהִי גַּלְיָין. אֵין לוֹ רְשׁוּת לְכַסּוֹת סוֹדוֹ וְנִסְתָּרוֹתָיו, אֶלָּא כַּשֶּׁמֶשׁ הַזֶּה שֶׁהוּא פּוּמְבֵּי לַכֹּל: דְּתָלֵי בֵּיהּ נוּרָא. אֵשׁ תָּלוּי בְּאוֹתוֹ מַזָּל, יֵצֶר שֶׁל תַּשְׁמִישׁ בּוֹעֵר כַּתַּנּוּר: מַזַּל כּוֹכָב. הוּא סוֹפֵר שֶׁל מַזַּל חַמָּה, לִכְתּוֹב דֶּרֶךְ הִילּוּכוֹ וּתְקוּפוֹתָיו, וּמָלוּי אֶצְלוֹ תָּמִיד: סָבֵיל מַרְעִין. כִּלְבָנָה זוֹ(ב), שֶׁמִּתְנַוְּונָה וְהוֹלֶכֶת: בָּנֵאי וְסָתֵיר. כִּלְבָנָה זוֹ שֶׁגְּדֵילָה וּמִתְמַעֶטֶת: אָכֵיל לָא דִּילֵיהּ. כַּלְּבָנָה הַמַּסֶּגֶת גְּבוּל הַחַמָּה, לִמְשׁוֹל אַף בַּיּוֹם: וְרָזוֹהִי כַּסְיָין. כַּלְּבָנָה שֶׁאֵינָהּ מְאִירָה: דְּבְשַׁבְּתַאי. מַזַּל כּוֹכָב שֶׁשְּׁמוֹ שַׁבְּתַאי: בְּטֵלִין. כְּמוֹ "לֹא יִשְׁבּוֹתוּ" (בראשית ח): צַדְקָן בְּמִצְוֹת. לְדָקָה לַעֲנִיִּים דְּקָרֵי לֵיהּ מִצְוָה (בְּכׇל לְשׁוֹן אַגָּדָה: גַּנָּבָא. לִיסְטִים הַהוֹרֵג נְפָשׁוֹת: אוּמָּנָא. מַקִּיז דָּם: עָנֵישׁ. בְּנֵי אָדָם הָעוֹבְרִין עַל דְּבָרָיו: מַזַּל מַחְכִּים. לְפִי הַמַּזָּל הִיא הַחׇכְמָה, כִּדְאָמַר דְּבְחַמָּה נָהִיר וְחַכִּים וְיֵשׁ מַזָּל לְיִשְׂרָאֵל שֶׁאֵין תְּפִלָּה וּצְדָקָה מְשַׁנָּה אֶת הַמַּזָּל: אֵין מַזָּל לְיִשְׂרָאֵל. דְּעַל יְדֵי תְּפִלָּה וּזְכוּת מִשְׁתַּנֶּה מַזָּלוֹ לְטוֹבָה: אִיצְטַגְנִינוּת. חׇכְמַת הַמַּזָּלוֹת: צֵא מֵאִיצְטַגְנִינוּתְךָ. הַיְינוּ דִּכְתִיב: "וַיּוֹצֵא אוֹתוֹ הַחוּצָה" – חוּץ מֵאִיצְטַגְנִינוּתוֹ: דְּקָאֵי

תוספות

מהו לפרק. פירש בקונטרס: לפרק מלפני בהמה זו וליתן לפני אחרת, וכן פירש בערוך בערך פרק. וקשה לר"י: דהיינו מתניתין גבי בהמה (לעיל דף קמ:)! ונראה לר"י: לפרק – היינו להריק המים וגם המורסן מכלי אל כלי שתגבל היטב. ובערוך פירש כמה לשונות:

אין מזל לישראל. והא דאמר רבא בשילהי מו"ק (דף כח. ושם): בני חיי ומזוני – לאו בזכותא תליא מילתא, אלא במזלא תליא מילתא. מכל מקום על ידי זכות גדול משתנה. אבל פעמים שאין המזל משתנה, כדאמר ביבמות פרק "החולץ" (דף נ. ושם): זכה – מוסיפין לו, לא זכה – פוחתין לו, (דאין מזל לישראל): כלדאי

רבינו חננאל

ואין צ"ל שמלקטין כו' ופריק רב יהודה הכי לעולם פי' מתניתא דאמר כך היא מהלקטין דספו ליה בידיה והיא פחותה מהלעטה שאמרנו ומלקטין שמשליך לפניה שעורים וכיוצא בהן דברים שהן מאכל לעופות. ואין משליכין מאכל לפני יוני שובך ויוני [עליה] לפי שאינן [בני] תרבות ואין מזונותן עליך וכי [הא] דתניא נותנין מזונות לפני הכלב ואין נותנין מזונות לפני חזיר ומה הפרש בין זה לזה כלב מזונותיו עליך חזיר אין מזונותיו עליך ובא רב אשי לסייע דברי רב יהודה ולומר שנויא דשני שינויא היא מדוקיא דמתניתין דקתני אין נותנין מים לפני דבורים ולפני יונים שבשובך אבל נותנים לפני אווזים ותרנגולים ולפני יונים הרדוסיית מ"ט לאו משו' דהני מזונותיו עליך והני אין מזונותיו עליך ולא עמדו דברי רב אשי והלכה כרב יהודה דתניא כוותיה דתניא איזו היא המראה ואיזו היא הלעטה המראה מרביצה ופוקס את פיה ומאכילה כרשינין ומים בבב"א. הלעטה מאכילה מעומד ומשקה מעומד ונותן לה כרשינין בפ"ע ומים בפ"ע: מהלקטין לתרנגולים ונותנין מים למורסן אבל לא גובלין אוקימנא לר' יוסי ב"ר יהודה דתניא אחד נותן את הקמח ואחד נותן לתוכו מים האחרון חייב דברי ר' ור' יוסי בר יהודה אומר עד שיגבל אלמא אמרינן [דנתינת מים זהו גיבולו]

ממאי דלמא עד כאן לא קאמר ר' יוסי ב"ר יהודה עד שיגבל אלא בקמח דבר גיבול הוא. אבל מורסן דלאו בר גיבול הוא אפי' ר' יוסי ב"ר יהודה מודי שנתינת מים למורסן אסור שזהו גיבולו ואשכחנן תניא בהדיא אין נותנין מים למורסן דברי ר' [ר'] יוסי ב"ר יהודה אומר נותנים מים למורסן ואע"ג דבבל מקום הלכתא כרבי מחבירו הכא הלכה כר' יוסי דתנינן מתניתין סתמא כוותיה. ותוב מהא דכתוב אפינקסיה דלוי אמרית קדם רבינו הקדוש והוא רבי עד דהוו גבלין שתיתא בבבל והוא צווח רבי דלית דשמע ליה ולית חילא בידיה למיסר מדר' יוסי ב"ר יהודה מהא נמי שמעינן דהלכתא כר' יוסי ב"ר יהודה דהוא בר פלוגתיה לא אסר ונפק עובדא כוותיה: ת"ר אין גובלין את הקליא וי"א גובלין ואמרינן מאן י"א ואמר רב חסדא ר' יוסי ב"ר יהודה היא והוא דמשני היכי משני אמר רב חסדא על יד על יד פי' מעט מעט מדמתרץ רב חסדא אליבא דר' יוסי ב"ר יהודה הלכתא

עין משפט נר מצוה

לא א ב ג ד מיי' שם הלכה לג סמג שם טוש"ע א"ח סימן שכא סעיף יד:

מסורת הש"ס

רש"ל מ"ז

ברכות לח.

[נ"ל נשא ועמ"ש תוספו' לעיל כג: ד"ה דבי]

[עי' תוספות חולין ז. ד"ה מכניס וכו' דגרסי רב מנשה]

ר"מ מוחק זה

ירמיהו י

[סוכה נט.]

[סוכה כט.]

[נדרים לב.]

בראשית טו שם שם

הגהות הב"ח

(א) גמ' מאן דבחמה יהא כו'. נ"ב תחלת סדר הליכתן שצ"ם חנכ"ל [וכאן נקט חנכ"ל שצ"ם] לפי סדר סימני הימים חל"ס כנג"ש נקט חמה בריש והדר נקט נוגה וכו' לפי סדר [השעות והמזלות כשתחיל ממזל חמה שהוא משמש בתחלת יום א' נמצא סדר השעות] חנכ"ל שצ"ם וחוזר חלילה כדאיתא ברש"י ס"פ מפנין וע"ש: (ב) רש"י ד"ה סביל וכו' זו שמתמעטה והולכת:

גליון הש"ס

גמרא אתא אבוה אשכחיה. עי' לעיל דף כג ע"ב תוס' ד"ה דבי נשא: רש"י ד"ה אכיל דלא דיליה כלבנה המסגת. עיין דבר נחמד בזה בכתנות אור לבעל פמ"א בפ' בראשית:

עין משפט
נר מצוה

לב א טוש"ע י"ד סימן רמז סעיף ז:
לג ב טוש"ע א"ח סימן כ סעיף ו:
לד ג ד מיי' פכ"א מהלכות שבת הל' יח סמג שם טוש"ע א"ח סימן שכל סעיף ו ז:
לה ה מיי' פ"ב מהלכות י"ט הלכה טז סמג לאוין עה:

כלדאי. בכולה סוגיא משמע דהיינו חוזים בכוכבים. ולא כמו שפירש"י ב"ערבי פסחים" (דף קיג:), מניין שאין שואלין בכלדאים שנאמר: "תמים תהיה וגו'" ופירש: דהיינו אוב. ועוד קשה, דבהדיא כתיב: "אל תפנו וגו'". ובספרי דרש, מנין שאין שואלין בגורלות – שנאמר: "תמים תהיה", וגורל וחוזה בכוכבים חדא מילתא היא:

רבי יהודה אומר אם לא היתה נבלה מע"ש כו'. תימה: היכי מוכח בפסחים פרק "מקום שנהגו" בסופו (דף נו: ושם), ובפ"ק דביצה (דף ו: ושם) מהך מתניתין דמוכן לאדם לא הוי מוכן לכלבים? לעולם מוכן לאדם הוי מוכן לכלבים, והכא היינו טעמא דאסירא לכלבים – משום דהואי מוקצה מחמת איסור, שלא היתה ראויה חיה (לא) לאדם (ולא לכלבים)! ותירץ ר"י: דיש דברים ראויים ליתן לפני הכלבים חיים, כגון עופות וכיוצא בהן. הלכך, אי לאו דמוכן לאדם לא הוי מוכן לכלבים – הוה שריא ליתן לכלבים. וה"ר יצחק בן הר"ר מאיר גריס במתני': אם לא היתה נבלה מעיו"ט – אסורה. השתא אתי שפיר בפשיטות, דמוכן שפיר לאדם, ואינו מוקצה מחמת איסור. ולא נהירא לי; דבריש ביצה (דף ג.) דייק מינה דגבי שבת סתם לה תנא כר"ש, אלמא: גבי שבת מיתניא! וה"ר פורת מפרש: דממשנה יתירה דייק, דה"ל למתני: "אם לא היתה נבלה מע"ש אסורה" ותו לא, דמאי נ"ל "לפי שאינה מן המוכן"? אלא להכי תני לה: דאפילו הוי מוכן לאדם לגמרי, שלא היה מוקצה מחמת איסור – לא הוי מוכן לכלבים. מ"ר:

ושמואל אמר הלכה כר"ש. תימה לר"י: תרתי דשמואל למה לי? דתיפוק ליה מההיא דכרכי דזוזי, ועז לחלבה ורחל לגיזתה דשילהי פ"ק (דף יט: ושם) ותירץ ר"י: דמוקצה דהתם קיל ממוקצה דהכא:

תרגמא זעירי בבהמת קדשים. תימה לר"י: היכי מוכח מהכא דס"ל כר"ש? ע"כ איצטריך לאוקמה בבהמת קדשים, כדמוכח פרק "אין לדין" (ביצה דף כז:), משום דמתני' נמי דיקא, דקתני עלה: ולא שחלה [illegible] קדשים, אף בהמה דקדשים. ומכח האי דיוקא פריך התם למר בר אמימר, דאמר: מודה היה ר"ש בבעלי חיים שמתו שאסורין. ודחיק ר"י לתרץ: דהכי קים ליה להתלמוד שלא פירש זעירי כן אלא משום דבעי לאוקמה כר"ש. מ"ר:

והא א"ר יוחנן הלכה כסתם משנה ותנן אין מבקעין כו'. תימה לר"י: היכי מוכח מהכא דלא ס"ל כר"ש? דהיא ודאי כרבי יהודה, דשמא אית ליה לרבי יוחנן מיגו דאיתקצאי לבין השמשות איתקצאי לכולי יומא. וקורה שנשברה, אפילו לר"ש, איתקצאי בין השמשות קודם שבירתה. דהואי מוקצה מחמת חסרון כיס דמודה ביה ר"ש. אבל במתניתין לא איתקצאי בין השמשות, דלית ליה ההיא מוקצה מה שהיא עומדת לאדם. והיה רוצה רבי לתרץ: דאי אית ליה לר' יוחנן מיגו דאיתקצאי – היה אוסר ודאי לטלטל בהמה שנתנבלה בשבת, שהרי נהי שהיתה ראויה לכלבים[ג] בלא שחיטה, כדפירשית לעיל – מיהו לטלטל היתה אסורה, דכולי עלמא מודו דבעלי חיים הם מוקצים. הוה לן למימר: מיגו דאיתקצאי. ודנתי לפני רבי: כיון שהיא ראויה לכלבים, משום שהיא מוקצה לטלטל – אין לנו לאוסרה לטלטל נבלה בשבת מידי דהוה אפירות הנושרין, דתלינן טעמא בריש ביצה (דף ג.) שמא יעלה ויתלוש, ומשום מוקצה לא אסירי לטלטל, כיון דחזו לעורבים בעודן מחוברין, אע"פ [ג]שבעת חבורן היו אסורין לטלטל. ותירץ רבי: דמסתמא מתניתין בכל ענין איירי, בין אותן שראויין לכלבים בעודן חיים בין שאינן ראויין לכלבים, דבכולהו שרי ר"ש, ואכולהו קאי רבי יוחנן דאמר: הלכה כרבי שמעון דמתניתין, ולא למחצה. אלמא: לית ליה מיגו דאיתקצאי. מ"ר:

והא אמר רבי יוחנן הלכה כסתם משנה. בריש ביצה (דף ג.) אמרינן גבי שבת דסתם לן תנא כר"ש משמע דחשיב לסתמא דמתני' סתמא. אמר רבי: לאו משום סתמא קאמר, דודאי לא חשיב כסתמא כיון דבמתניתין נמי פליג רבי יהודה, וסתמא לאו דוקא – אלא חשיב כרבים. מ"ר*):

*) [ועי' תוספות ביצה ב: ד"ה גבי שבת].

דְקָאֵי צֶדֶק בְּמַעֲרָב, מְהַדְרְנָא וּמוֹקְמִינָא לֵיהּ בְּמִזְרָח. וְהַיְינוּ דִּכְתִיב: °"מִי הֵעִיר מִמִּזְרָח צֶדֶק יִקְרָאֵהוּ לְרַגְלוֹ". וּמִדִּשְׁמוּאֵל נַמִי, אֵין מַזָּל לְיִשְׂרָאֵל. דִּשְׁמוּאֵל וְאַבְלֵט הֲווּ יָתְבִי, וַהֲווּ קָאָזְלִי הָנָךְ אֱינָשֵׁי לְאַגְמָא. א"ל אַבְלֵט לִשְׁמוּאֵל: הַאי גַּבְרָא אָזֵיל וְלָא אָתֵי, טָרֵיק לֵיהּ חִיוְיָא וּמָיֵית. א"ל שְׁמוּאֵל: אִי בַּר יִשְׂרָאֵל הוּא – אָזֵיל וְאָתֵי. אַדְּיָתְבִי אָזֵיל וְאָתֵי. קָם אַבְלֵט, שַׁדְיֵיהּ לְטוּנֵיהּ אַשְׁכַּח בֵּיהּ חִיוְיָא דִּפְסִיק וּשְׁדֵי בְּתַרְתֵּי גּוּבֵי. א"ל שְׁמוּאֵל: מַאי עֲבַדְתְּ? א"ל: כָּל יוֹמָא הֲוָה מְרַמֵּינַן רִיפְתָּא בַּהֲדֵי הֲדָדֵי וְאָכְלִינַן. הָאִידָּנָא הֲוָה אִיכָּא חַד מִינַּן דְּלָא הֲוָה לֵיהּ רִיפְתָּא, הֲוָה קָא מִיכְסִף. אֲמִינָא לְהוּ: אֲנָא קָאֵימְנָא וְאָרְמֵינָא. כִּי מְטַאי לְגַבֵּיהּ שְׁוַאי נַפְשַׁאי כְּמַאן דִּשְׁקִילִי מִינֵּיהּ, כִּי הֵיכִי דְּלָא לִיכְסִיף. א"ל: מִצְוָה עֲבַדְתְּ! אנְפַק שְׁמוּאֵל וְדָרַשׁ: °"וּצְדָקָה תַּצִּיל מִמָּוֶת" וְלֹא מִמִּיתָה מְשׁוּנָּה, אֶלָּא מִמִּיתָה עַצְמָהּ. וּמִדְּר"ע נַמִי, אֵין מַזָּל לְיִשְׂרָאֵל. דְּר"ע הֲוְיָא לֵיהּ בְּרַתָּא, אָמְרִי לֵיהּ כַּלְדָּאֵי: הַהוּא יוֹמָא דְּעָיְילָה לְבֵי גְּנָנָא – טָרֵיק לַהּ חִיוְיָא וּמֵיתָא. הֲוָה דְּאִיגָא אַמִּילְּתָא טוּבָא. הַהוּא יוֹמָא שְׁקַלְתָּה לְמַכְבַּנְתָּא, דַּצְתָּא בְּגוּדָא, אִיתְרַמֵּי אִיתֵיב בְּעֵינֵיהּ דְּחִיוְיָא. לְצַפְרָא כִּי קָא שָׁקְלָה לַהּ – הֲוָה קָא סָרֵיךְ וְאָתֵי חִיוְיָא בַּתְרָהּ. אֲמַר לַהּ אֲבוּהָ: מַאי עֲבַדְתְּ? אֲמָרָה לֵיהּ: בְּפַנְיָא אֲתָא עַנְיָא, קָרָא אַבָּבָא, וַהֲווּ טְרִידִי כּוּלֵּי עָלְמָא בִּסְעוּדְתָא, וְלֵיכָּא דִּשְׁמַעֵיהּ. קָאֵימְנָא, שְׁקַלְתִּי (א)*לְרִיסְתְּנַאי דִּיהָבִית לִי, יְהַבְתֵּיהּ נִיהֲלֵיהּ. אֲמַר לַהּ: מִצְוָה עֲבַדְתְּ! נְפַק ר"ע וְדָרַשׁ: "וּצְדָקָה תַּצִּיל מִמָּוֶת" וְלֹא מִמִּיתָה מְשׁוּנָּה, אֶלָּא מִמִּיתָה עַצְמָהּ. וּמִדְּר"נ בַּר יִצְחָק נַמִי, אֵין מַזָּל לְיִשְׂרָאֵל. דְּאִימֵּיהּ דְּר"נ בַּר יִצְחָק אָמְרִי לַהּ כַּלְדָּאֵי: בְּרִיךְ גַּנָּבָא הָוֵה. לָא שַׁבְקָתֵיהּ גַּלּוֹיֵי רֵישֵׁיהּ. אֲמָרָה לֵיהּ: בכַּסֵּי רֵישָׁךְ, כִּי הֵיכִי דְּתֶיהֱווּ עֲלָךְ אֵימְתָא דִּשְׁמַיָּא, וּבָעֵי רַחֲמֵי. לָא הֲוָה יָדַע אַמַּאי קָאָמְרָה לֵיהּ. יוֹמָא חַד יָתֵיב קָא גָּרֵיס תּוּתֵי דִּיקְלָא, נְפַל גְּלִימָא מֵעִילָּוֵיהּ רֵישֵׁיהּ דְּלֵי עֵינֵיהּ חֲזָא לְדִיקְלָא, אַלְמֵיהּ יִצְרֵיהּ, סְלֵיק פַּסְקֵיהּ לְקִיבּוּרָא בְּשִׁינֵּיהּ.§

מתני' *גמְחַתְּכִין אֶת הַדִּלּוּעִין לִפְנֵי הַבְּהֵמָה, דוְאֶת הַנְּבֵלָה לִפְנֵי הַכְּלָבִים, רַבִּי יְהוּדָה אוֹמֵר: אִם לֹא הָיְתָה נְבֵלָה מֵעֶרֶב שַׁבָּת – אֲסוּרָה, לְפִי שֶׁאֵינָהּ מִן הַמּוּכָן.§

גמ' אִיתְּמַר (ער"ל שח"ז סִימָן) אָמַר עוּלָּא: הֲלָכָה כְּרַבִּי יְהוּדָה. (*וּשְׁמוּאֵל אָמַר: הֲלָכָה כְּר"ש). וְאַף רַב סָבַר הֲלָכָה כְּרַבִּי יְהוּדָה מִדִּכְרָכֵי דְּזוּזֵי *דְּרַב אָסַר וּשְׁמוּאֵל שָׁרֵי וְאַף לֵוִי סָבַר הֲלָכָה כְּרַבִּי יְהוּדָה. כִּי הָא דְּלֵוִי כִּי הֲווּ מַיְיתִי טְרֵיפְתָּא לְקַמֵּיהּ בְּיוֹמָא טָבָא לָא הֲוָה חָזֵי לַהּ אֶלָּא כִּי יָתֵיב *אַקִּילְקַלִּיתָא. דַּאֲמַר: דִּילְמָא לָא מִתַּכְשְׁרָא, וַאֲפִילּוּ לִכְלָבִים לָא חַזְיָא. וּשְׁמוּאֵל אָמַר: הֲלָכָה כְּרַבִּי שִׁמְעוֹן. וְאַף זְעֵירִי סָבַר הֲלָכָה כְּר"ש דִּתְנַן: *בְּהֵמָה שֶׁמֵּתָה – לֹא יְזִיזֶנָּה מִמְּקוֹמָהּ, וְתַרְגְּמָא זְעֵירִי: הבִּבְהֶמַת קָדָשִׁים, אֲבָל בְּחוּלִּין – שַׁפִּיר דָּמֵי. וְאַף רַבִּי יוֹחָנָן אָמַר: הֲלָכָה כְּר"ש. וּמִי א"ר יוֹחָנָן הָכִי? *וְהָא א"ר יוֹחָנָן: הֲלָכָה כִּסְתָם מִשְׁנָה, וּתְנַן: אֵין

תורה אור
ישעיהו מא: מִי הֵעִיר מִמִּזְרָח
משלי י: וּצְדָקָה תַּצִּיל מִמָּוֶת

דְּקָאֵי צֶדֶק. שֶׁהוּא מַזָּל שֶׁלְּךָ: **בְּמַעֲרָב.** שֶׁהוּא מָקוֹם מְלוּכָן, וְאֵין רָאוּי לְהוֹלִיד. כָּךְ מָצָאתִי בְּתַלְמוּד רַבֵּינוּ הַלֵּוִי: **בְּמִזְרָחוֹ.** שֶׁהוּא מָקוֹם חוֹם: **צֶדֶק.** הקב"ה קְרָאוֹ לַהֲבִיאוֹ לַמִּזְרָח: **לְרַגְלוֹ.** בִּשְׁבִילוֹ: **אַבְלֵט.** שֵׁם חָכָם, גּוֹי הָיָה וְחוֹזֶה בַּכּוֹכָבִים: **אָזֵיל וְאָתֵי.** דְּאֵין מַזָּל לְיִשְׂרָאֵל, וְיוֹעִיל לוֹ תְּפִלָּה: **בְּתַרְתֵּי גּוּבֵי.** בִּשְׁתֵּי חֲתִיכוֹת, שֶׁקְּצָצוֹ עִם הַקָּנִים בְּלֹא יוֹדֵעַ: **מְרַמֵּינַן בַּהֲדֵי.** מְטִילִין פַּת [לַסַּל] לְכָל הַחֲבוּרָה כְּאֶחָד, וְאוֹכְלִין יַחַד, וְהָאֶחָד גּוֹבֶה מִכּוּלָּן: **אֲנָא קָאֵימְנָא וּמַרְמֵינָא.** אֲגַבֶּה וְאָשִׂים בַּסַּל: **שְׁוַאי נַפְשַׁאי כְּמַאן דִּשְׁקִילִי מִינֵּיהּ.** עָשִׂיתִי עַצְמִי כְּגוֹבֶה מִמֶּנּוּ, וְנָתַתִּי מִשֶּׁלִּי חֶלְקוֹ: **לֹא מִמִּיתָה מְשׁוּנָּה.** וּמִיהוּ, מִיתָה הֲגוּנָה יָמוּת. אֶלָּא מִמִּיתָה עַצְמָהּ מַצֶּלֶת וְנוֹתֶנֶת חַיִּים: **כַּלְדָּאֵי.** חוֹזִים בַּכּוֹכָבִים: **דַּצְתָּא.** תְּחָבַתָּהּ: **לְמַכְבַּנְתָּא.** [אִישְׁפִּינְגְלֵי"ז בְּלַע"ז], נוּשְׁקָא שֶׁל זָהָב שֶׁיֵּשׁ כְּמוֹ טַס בְּרֹאשָׁהּ: **רִיסְתְּנַאי.** אמנשטריישו"ן: **וּבָעֵי רַחֲמֵי.** בַּקֵּשׁ רַחֲמִים שֶׁלֹּא יִשְׁלוֹט בְּךָ יֵצֶר הָרָע: **קִיבּוּרָא.** אֶשְׁכּוֹל תְּמָרִים, וְהַדֶּקֶל לֹא שֶׁלּוֹ הָיָה: **מתני' אֶת הַדִּלּוּעִין.** הַתְּלוּשִׁין. וּמִיהוּ, סְתָמָן לָאו לְמַאֲכַל בְּהֵמָה קַיְימִי אֶלָּא לְאָדָם: **וְאֶת הַנְּבֵלָה.** שֶׁנִּתְנַבְּלָה הַיּוֹם, וּבֵין הַשְּׁמָשׁוֹת הָיְתָה עוֹמֶדֶת לְאָדָם, וְאֲפִ"ה מְחַתְּכִין: **גמ' כְּר"ש.** דְּלֵית לֵיהּ מוּקְצֶה: **מִדִּכְרָכֵי דְּזוּזֵי.** מַחְלָלוֹת הָעֲשׂוּיוֹת לִסְפִינוֹת לְכַסּוֹת פְּרַקְמַטְיָא שֶׁבְּתוֹכָן. זוּזֵי סְפִינוֹת בִּלְשׁוֹן אֲרַמִּי, כָּךְ מָצָאתִי בִּתְשׁוּבַת הַגְּאוֹנִים: **כִּי הֲווּ מַיְיתִי טְרֵיפְתָּא לְקַמֵּיהּ.** בְּהֵמָה שֶׁנּוֹלַד בָּהּ סְפֵק טְרֵפוֹת, וּצְרִיכָה לְהוֹרָאַת חָכָם: **אַקִּילְקִילְתָּא.** °עַל הָאַשְׁפָּה, שֶׁאִם יַרְאֶנָּה טְרֵיפָה – יַנִּיחֶהָ שָׁם: **וַאֲפִילּוּ לִכְלָבִים לָא חַזְיָא.** דְּנִשְׁחֲטָה הַיּוֹם, וְלֹא יוּכְלוּ לְטַלְטֵל, כְּרַבִּי יְהוּדָה: **תַּרְגְּמָא זְעֵירִי.** בְּמַסֶּכֶת בֵּיצָה – בְּבֶהֱמַת קָדָשִׁים, דַּאֲסוּרָה בַּהֲנָאָה, וְלָא חַזְיָא לִכְלָבִים. הָא דְּחוּלִּין – שַׁפִּיר דָּמֵי לְהַאֲכִילָהּ לִכְלָבִים:

רבינו חננאל

הלכתא כוותיה ונתברר שהלכה כר' יוסי ב"ר יהודה שנותנין מים למורסן וגובלין את הקליא מעט מעט. **ושוין** שבוחשין את השתית בשבת. פי' השתית היא שתיתא דאמור רבנן בביצה מברכין (דף ל"ח ע"א) ודברי הכל מותר לבחוש בשבת והוא נתינת השתית שהוא הקליא בכלי ואחר כך יתן בו חומץ ויערבנו שתי וערב בתרווד או כיוצא בו כלי הניטל בשבת וינער אח"כ את הכלי לכלי אחר אבל לא יערבנו כדרך מריסה שמריץ התרווד סביבות כל הכלי שבתוכו השתית אלא שתי וערב בלבד. והני מילי דבחיש בה רכה אבל לבוחשה עבה גיבול הוא ואסור. ואקשינן עלה היכי אמרת דשוין שבוחשין את השתית ומי שרי והא אמרת רישא אין גובלין את הקליא. כלומר ת"ק וי"א (אסור) [מתיר] גיבול הקליא וקתני סיפא דשוין שבוחשין את הקליא מכלל דאפי' [ת"ק] שרי ומפרקי' ל"ק הא דתני אין גובלין בעבה וסיפא דקתני ושוין שבוחשין ברכה והוא דמשני ממעשה דחול שדרכו בחול נותן החומץ ואחר כך הקמח ובשבת ישנה יתן השתית ואחר כך יתן החומץ ואפילו נתינת מים למורסן בעין גיבול בשנוי שרי כדאמרי משמיה דרב ירמיה בר אבא גובלין ולא מספין ודלא לקיט בלשניה מלקיטין והני מילי גיבול בשנוי והוא עירוב שתי וזרר וויזור חרלי אל כלי אחר אבל מירום בעין טוחן ברחים של יד שמסבב ומוליך ומביא אסור. אמרו לו לרבי חנינא מהו לגבל אמר להו אסור לפרק מאי אמר [להו] מות' ולמה לא פירש מהו לפרק ומהו חד קמי חדא ותרי קמי תרתי כו' שראיתי בין הגאונים חילוקם בפירושם והלכתא כעולא דאמר אפילו כור אפילו כוריים שרי ואפילו לשלשה ועוד ובלבד ע"י שנוי כאשר פירשנו למעלה ושאר השמועה פשוטה היא: **אבלט** שהיה רבן שמואל אומר גוי הוא דאמרינן בפרק אין מעמידין בהמה בפונדקאות של גוים שמואל ואבלט הוו יתבי כו': **מתני'** מחתכין את הדלועין לפני הבהמה ואת הנבלה לפני הכלבים. רבי יהודה אומר אם לא היתה נבלה מע"ש אסורה: **אתמר** ע'ר'ל' אמר הלכה כר' יהודה. פי' ע'ר'ל' סימן שמות החכמים דאמרו דהלכה כר' יהודה והם ע'ולא ור'ב ול'וי אילו שלשתן כר' יהודה עולא בפירוש אמר הלכה כר' יהודה רב מכלל חלוקתו על שמואל בבראכי דזוגי פי' מחצלאות הכרוכות זוגות זוגות העומדות לתפירה דרב אסר להתירן ולישב בהן שהן לסחורה מוקצות הן מכלל דסבר הלכתא כר' יהודה לוי נמי מכללא דכי הוו מייתי טרפה לקמיה דלוי ביו"ט לא הוה חזי ליה אלא אקיקלתא סבר דלמא לא מכשרא ואפילו לכלבים לא חזי שמעינן מינה דכר' יהודה סבירא ליה דאמר לפי שאינה מן המוכן: ש'ז'ח' סימן והן שמואל זעירי ור' יוחנן: שמואל ור' יוחנן בהדיא אמרי הלכתא כר' שמעון זעירי מכללא מדחזינן ליה לזעירי דמתרגם להא דתנן בהמה שמתה לא יזיזנה ממקומה

מסורת הש"ס

[גירסת הערוך לדסתנא פי' חלק]
ביצה כז: חולין יד.
לעיל יט:
[ע' פרש"י ב"ק כח. ובע"ז כח. ד"ה ניקרא]
ביצה כז:
[לעיל מו. וש"נ]

גליון הש"ס
רש"י ד"ה אקלקילתא על האשפה. אשפות ירים אביון (תהלים קלג) תרגום מקלקלתא מרים תקוכה רש"י ע"ג דף כח ע"א ד"ה ויקרא: תוס' ד"ה תרגמא וכו' דהכי קים ליה. עיין לעיל דף יט ע"ב תוספ' ד"ה הא לן וש"נ:

הגהות הב"ח
(א) גמרא שקלתיה לריסתנאי. נ"ב פירוש חלק סעודה שלי וע' בברכות דף מב: (ב) תוס' ד"ה והא א"ר יוחנן וכו' ראויה לכלבים בע"ש כדפי' לעיל: (ג) בא"ד אע"פ שבשעת חבורן:

[א]אֵין מְבַקְּעִין עֵצִים מִן הַקּוֹרוֹת, וְלֹא מִן הַקּוֹרָה שֶׁנִּשְׁבְּרָה בְּיו"ט! רַבִּי יוֹחָנָן, הַהוּא – כְּרַבִּי יוֹסֵי בַּר יְהוּדָה מַתְנֵי לָהּ. תָּא שְׁמַע: [ב]מַתְחִילִין בַּעֲרֵימַת הַתֶּבֶן, אֲבָל לֹא בְּעֵצִים שֶׁבַּמּוּקְצֶה! הָתָם *[ג]בְּאַרְזֵי וְאַשּׁוּחֵי, דְּמוּקְצֶה מֵחֲמַת חֶסְרוֹן כִּיס אֲפִילּוּ רַבִּי שִׁמְעוֹן מוֹדֶה. ת"ש: *[ד]אֵין מַשְׁקִין [ה]וְשׁוֹחֲטִין אֶת הַמִּדְבָּרִיּוֹת, אֲבָל מַשְׁקִין וְשׁוֹחֲטִין אֶת הַבַּיְיתוֹת! ר' יוֹחָנָן סְתָמָא אַחֲרִינָא אַשְׁכַּח, *"ב"ש אוֹמְרִים: מַגְבִּיהִין מֵעַל הַשֻּׁלְחָן עֲצָמוֹת וּקְלִיפִּין, וּב"ה אוֹמְרִים: מְסַלֵּק אֶת הַטַּבְלָה כּוּלָּהּ וּמְנַעֲרָהּ". וְא"ר נַחְמָן: אָנוּ אֵין לָנוּ אֶלָּא ב"ש כְּרַבִּי יְהוּדָה, וּב"ה כְּר"ש. פְּלִיגִי בָּהּ רַב אַחָא וְרָבִינָא, חַד אָמַר: בְּכָל הַשַּׁבָּת כּוּלָּהּ הֲלָכָה כְּר"ש, לְבַר מִמּוּקְצֶה מֵחֲמַת מִיאוּס, וּמַאי נִיהוּ – *נֵר יָשָׁן. וְחַד אָמַר: בְּמוּקְצֶה מֵחֲמַת מִיאוּס נַמִי הֲלָכָה כְּר"ש, לְבַר מִמּוּקְצֶה מֵחֲמַת אִיסּוּר וּמַאי נִיהוּ – נֵר שֶׁהִדְלִיקוּ בָּהּ בְּאוֹתָהּ שַׁבָּת. אֲבָל *מוּקְצֶה מֵחֲמַת חֶסְרוֹן כִּיס – אֲפִילּוּ ר"ש מוֹדֶה, דִּתְנַן: *כָּל הַכֵּלִים נִיטָּלִין בַּשַּׁבָּת, חוּץ מִמַּסָּר הַגָּדוֹל וְיָתֵד שֶׁל מַחֲרֵישָׁה.§

מתני' *מְפִירִין נְדָרִים בַּשַּׁבָּת, וְנִשְׁאָלִין לִנְדָרִים שֶׁהֵן לְצוֹרֶךְ הַשַּׁבָּת. וּפוֹקְקִין אֶת הַמָּאוֹר, וּמוֹדְדִין אֶת הַמַּטְלִית, וּמוֹדְדִין אֶת הַמִּקְוֶה. וּמַעֲשֶׂה בִּימֵי אָבִיו שֶׁל רַבִּי צָדוֹק וּבִימֵי אַבָּא שָׁאוּל בֶּן בָּטְנִית, שֶׁפָּקְקוּ אֶת הַמָּאוֹר בְּטָפִיחַ, [ה] וְקָשְׁרוּ אֶת הַמְּקֵידָה בְּגֶמִי לֵידַע אִם יֵשׁ בַּגִּיגִית פּוֹתֵחַ טֶפַח אִם לָאו. *וּמִדִּבְרֵיהֶם לָמַדְנוּ, שֶׁפּוֹקְקִין וּמוֹדְדִין וְקוֹשְׁרִין בַּשַּׁבָּת.§

גמ' *אִיבַּעְיָא לְהוּ: [ו]הֲפָרָה – בֵּין לְצוֹרֶךְ וּבֵין שֶׁלֹּא לְצוֹרֶךְ; [ז]וּשְׁאֵלָה – לְצוֹרֶךְ – אִין, שֶׁלֹּא לְצוֹרֶךְ – לָא. וּמִשּׁוּם הָכִי קָפַלְגִינְהוּ מֵהֲדָדֵי – אוֹ דִּילְמָא: הֲפָרָה נַמִי, לְצוֹרֶךְ – אִין, שֶׁלֹּא לְצוֹרֶךְ – לָא. וְהָא דְּקָא פָּלֵיג לְהוּ מֵהֲדָדֵי – מִשּׁוּם דַּהֲפָרָה אֵין צָרִיךְ ב"ד, וּשְׁאֵלָה צְרִיכָה ב"ד? ת"ש, דְּתָנֵי זוּטֵי דְּבֵי רַב פַּפָּא: מְפִירִין נְדָרִים בַּשַּׁבָּת לְצוֹרֶךְ הַשַּׁבָּת. לְצוֹרֶךְ הַשַּׁבָּת – אִין, שֶׁלֹּא לְצוֹרֶךְ הַשַּׁבָּת – לָא. לִישָּׁנָא אַחֲרִינָא, אִיבַּעְיָא לְהוּ: "לְצוֹרֶךְ" אַתַּרְוַיְיהוּ קָתָנֵי, וְשֶׁלֹּא לְצוֹרֶךְ – לָא, אַלְמָא: הֲפָרַת נְדָרִים מֵעֵת לְעֵת. אוֹ דִּילְמָא: כִּי קָתָנֵי לְצוֹרֶךְ – אַשְּׁאֵלָה הוּא דְּקָתָנֵי, אֲבָל הֲפָרַת נְדָרִים – אֲפִילּוּ שֶׁלֹּא לְצוֹרֶךְ. אַלְמָא: הֲפָרַת נְדָרִים כָּל הַיּוֹם. תָּא שְׁמַע; דְּתָנֵי רַב זוּטֵי דְּבֵי רַב פַּפִּי. מְפִירִין נְדָרִים בַּשַּׁבָּת לְצוֹרֶךְ הַשַּׁבָּת. לְצוֹרֶךְ הַשַּׁבָּת – אִין, שֶׁלֹּא לְצוֹרֶךְ הַשַּׁבָּת – לָא. אַלְמָא: הֲפָרַת נְדָרִים מֵעֵת לְעֵת. א"ר אַשִׁי, וְהָאֲנַן *תְּנַן: [ח]הֲפָרַת נְדָרִים כָּל הַיּוֹם, וְיֵשׁ בַּדָּבָר לְהָקֵל וּלְהַחְמִיר. כֵּיצַד? נָדְרָה לֵילֵי שַׁבָּת – מֵיפֵר לֵילֵי שַׁבָּת וְיוֹם הַשַּׁבָּת עַד שֶׁתֶּחְשַׁךְ, נָדְרָה עִם חֲשֵׁכָה – מֵיפֵר עַד שֶׁלֹּא תֶּחְשַׁךְ, שֶׁאִם לֹא הֵפֵר מִשֶּׁחֲשֵׁכָה – אֵינוֹ יָכוֹל לְהָפֵר. תַּנָּאֵי הִיא, דְּתַנְיָא: *הֲפָרַת נְדָרִים כָּל הַיּוֹם, ר' יוֹסֵי בַּר יְהוּדָה וְרַבִּי אֶלְעָזָר בְּרַבִּי שִׁמְעוֹן אָמְרוּ: מֵעֵת לְעֵת.§ "וְנִשְׁאָלִים לִנְדָרִים".§ *אִיבַּעְיָא לְהוּ: כְּשֶׁלֹּא הָיָה לוֹ פְּנַאי, אוֹ דִּלְמָא: אֲפִילּוּ הָיָה לוֹ פְּנַאי? תָּא שְׁמַע: דְּאִזְדַּקִּיקוּ לֵיהּ רַבָּנַן לְרַב זוּטְרָא בְּרֵיהּ דְּרַב זֵירָא, [ט]וְשָׁרוּ לֵיהּ נִדְרֵיהּ וְאַף עַל גַּב דַּהֲוָה לֵיהּ פְּנַאי.§ "שֶׁפָּקְקוּ אֶת הַמָּאוֹר בְּטָפִיחַ וְקָשְׁרוּ אֶת הַמְּקֵידָה בְּגֶמִי".§ אָמַר רַב יְהוּדָה אָמַר רַב: הֵילְקֵטִי קְטַנָּה הָיְתָה בֵּין שְׁנֵי בָּתִּים, [וְטוּמְאָה הָיְתָה שָׁם]. וְגִיגִּית

רש"י

אין מבקעין עצים מן הקורות. קוֹרָה שֶׁל הַקּוֹרוֹת הַמּוּקְצוֹת וּסְדוּרוֹת לְבִנְיָן: **ולא מן קורה.** הַיְשָׁנָה שֶׁנִּשְׁבְּרָה הַיּוֹם, וּמֵהַשְׁתָּא לְהַסָּקָה קָיְימָא, וַאפ"ה – אָסוּר, הוֹאִיל וּבֵין הַשְּׁמָשׁוֹת לָא אִיתְכַּן לְהָכִי: **מתחילין.** לְהַסִּיק בַּעֲרֵימַת הַתֶּבֶן. קָא סָלְקָא דַּעְתָּךְ דְּתִיבְנָא סָרְיָא, דִּסְתָמֵיהּ לְהַסָּקָה: **אבל לא בעצים שבמוקצה.** שֶׁהִכְנִיס בָּרְחָבָה שֶׁאֲחוֹרֵי בֵּיתוֹ וְהִקְצָם לִימוֹת הַסְּתָיו. מוּקְצֶה – רְחָבָה שֶׁאֲחוֹרֵי בָּתִּים, שֶׁהִקְצָה אֲחוֹרֵי בֵּיתוֹ לְהַכְנִיס שָׁם דָּבָר לָאוֹצָר: **בארזי ואשוחי.** אֶרֶז זָכָר וְאֶרֶז נְקֵבָה שֶׁעוֹמְדִין לְבִנְיָן: **משקין.** אוֹרְחָא דְּמִילְּתָא נָקַט, מִשּׁוּם סִירְכָא דְּמַשְׁכָא, שֶׁתְּהֵא נוֹחָה לְהַפְשִׁיט: **מדבריות.**(א) שֶׁרוֹעוֹת בָּאֲפָר תָּמִיד, וְלָנוֹת בְּתוֹךְ הַתְּחוּם: **סתמא אחרינא.** בֵּית הִלֵּל חָשֵׁיב כִּסְתָמָא: **כל הכלים ניטלין.** וַאֲפִי' מְלַאכְתָּן לְאִיסּוּר, וְרַבִּי שִׁמְעוֹן הִיא: **חוץ מן המסר הגדול.** מְגֵירָה שֶׁהִיא לָאוּמָנִין לָקוֹץ בָּהּ עֵצִים. וּמוּקְצֶה מֵחֲמַת חֶסְרוֹן כִּיס הוּא, שֶׁלֹּא יִשְׁתַּבְּרוּ חֲרִיצִים, שֶׁהוּא עָשׂוּי כְּסַכִּין מָלֵא פְּגִימוֹת: **ויתד של מחרישה.** הַחוֹפֵר אֶת הַקַּרְקַע, קולטר"א בְּלַע"ז:

מתני' מפירין. בַּעַל לְאִשְׁתּוֹ: **ונשאלין.** לְחָכָם: **שהן לצורך השבת.** כְּגוֹן שֶׁנָּדַר שֶׁלֹּא לֶאֱכוֹל [הַיּוֹם]: **ופוקקין את המאור.** כְּרַבָּנַן דְּאָמְרִי (לעיל דף קכה:): פּוֹקְקִין פְּקָק הַחַלּוֹן: **ומודדין את המקוה.** בְּמִדָּה, שֶׁיְּהֵא שָׁם עָמוֹק שָׁלֹשׁ אַמּוֹת מַיִם וְרוֹחַב אַמָּה עַל אַמָּה: **ואת המטלית.**(ב) שֶׁתְּהֵא שָׁלֹשׁ עַל שָׁלֹשׁ אֶצְבָּעוֹת, כְּגוֹן אִם הָיְתָה טְמֵאָה וְנָגְעָה בְּטָהֳרוֹת: **בטפיח.** פַּךְ שֶׁל חֶרֶס(ג). וַחֲבֵירוֹ בְּפִי"ז (דף קכה:): זְמוֹרָה שֶׁהִיא קְשׁוּרָה בְּטָפִיחַ מְמַלְּאִין בָּהּ בַּשַּׁבָּת: **מקידה.** כְּלִי חֶרֶס: **לידע אם יש בגיגית פותח טפח.** בַּגְּמָרָא מְפָרֵשׁ לָהּ: **וקושרין.** קֶשֶׁר שֶׁאֵינוֹ שֶׁל קַיָּימָא, אֲפִילּוּ לְכַתְּחִילָּה: **ומודדין.** לְהִתְלַמֵּד עַל דְּבַר הוֹרָאָה:

גמ' איבעיא לְהוּ הֲפָרָה. דְּמַתְנִיתִין, בֵּין לְצוֹרֶךְ [בֵּין שֶׁלֹּא לְצוֹרֶךְ] הַשַּׁבָּת. דְּגַבֵּי הֲפָרָה "בְּיוֹם שָׁמְעוֹ" כְּתִיב (במדבר ל), וְאִם לֹא מֵיפֵר הָאִידָּנָא – שׁוּב אֵינוֹ מֵיפֵר: **ושאלה לצורך אין שלא לצורך לא.** דְּיָכוֹל לִישָּׁאֵל לְמָחָר, וּמִשּׁוּם הָכִי מַפְלִיג לְהוּ מֵהֲדָדֵי, וְלָא קָתָנֵי מְפִירִין וְנִשְׁאָלִין לִנְדָרִים שֶׁהֵן לְצוֹרֶךְ הַשַּׁבָּת, דְּלָא קָאֵי לְצוֹרֶךְ אֶלָּא אַשְּׁאֵלָה: **בית דין.** חָכָם: **הכי גרסי': ל"א איבעיא להו** (במסכת נדרים עז.) **לצורך** אַתַּרְוַיְיהוּ קָאֵי. אַהֲפָרָה וְאַשְּׁאֵלָה. אֲבָל הֲפָרָה שֶׁלֹּא לְצוֹרֶךְ – לֹא. אַלְמָא: הֲפָרַת נְדָרִים מֵעֵת לְעֵת, וְזֶה שֶׁשָּׁמַע בַּשַּׁבָּת יָכוֹל לְהָפֵר מִשֶּׁתֶּחְשַׁךְ בְּתוֹךְ מֵעֵת לְעֵת שֶׁל שְׁמִיעָה, הִלְכָּךְ שֶׁלֹּא לְצוֹרֶךְ לָא שָׁרֵינַן בַּשַּׁבָּת: **כל היום.** עַד שֶׁתֶּחְשַׁךְ וְתוּ לָא, וַאֲפִילּוּ שָׁמַע סָמוּךְ לַחֲשֵׁיכָה. הִלְכָּךְ: אֲפִי' שֶׁלֹּא לְצוֹרֶךְ, *שֶׁאִם לֹא יָפֵר עַכְשָׁיו – לֹא יָפֵר עוֹד: **לצורך השבת.** אַלְמָא: הֲפָרַת נְדָרִים מֵעֵת לְעֵת שֶׁל שְׁמִיעָה, הִלְכָּךְ: שֶׁלֹּא לְצוֹרֶךְ(ד) לֹא, מִדְּלָא שָׁרֵי אֶלָּא לְצוֹרֶךְ: **להקל ולהחמיר.** כְּלוֹמַר, פְּעָמִים שֶׁיֵּשׁ שָׁהוּת גָּדוֹל, וּפְעָמִים שֶׁאֵינוֹ אֶלָּא מְעַט: **איבעיא להו.** הָא דְּקָתָנֵי נִשְׁאָלִין לִנְדָרִים שֶׁהֵן לְצוֹרֶךְ: **כשלא היה לו פנאי.** לִשָּׁאֵל מֵעֶרֶב שַׁבָּת קָאָמַר, אוֹ אֲפִילּוּ כְּשֶׁהָיָה לוֹ פְּנַאי: **הילקטי קטנה.** שְׁבִיל קָטָן בֵּין שְׁנֵי בָּתִּים:

תוספות

אין משקין ושוחטין את המדבריות. הוה מלי למימר דהני כגרוגרות ולמוקין דמיין, כדאמר בפרק "כירה" (לעיל דף מה:): **לבר** ממוקצה מחמת איסור. וכגון איסור דדחייה בידים, כגון נר שהדליקו באותו שבת, כדפירשתי בפ"ק בסופו:

והלכתא מעת לעת. לא גרס בפירוש ר"ח, דבנדרים משמע דלית הלכתא הכי, דאמר בפרק "נערה המאורסה" (כתובות דף עו:): אין הלכה כאותו הזוג. מ"ר:

הלקטי קטנה. מפרש בקונטרס שביל קטן היתה בין שני בתים, והגיגית סדוקה מונחת על גבן, והמת מוטל בהלקטי תחת הגיגית נגד הסדק. וקשרו המקידה לידע אם יש בסדק פותח טפח. ולהאי פירושא קשה לר"י: דאפי' אין בסדק פותח טפח, כיון שהמת נגדו – לא חשבינן לה כמאהיל על המת, כיון שאין [זה] דרך מאהיל(ה). כדמוכח במסכת אהלות (פ"י מ"ה), ומייתי לה בסוף פרק קמא דסוכה (דף יח. ושם): אין בארובה פותח טפח והמת בבית, מה שבבית כנגד ארובה – טהור. המת כנגד ארובה – מה שבבית טהור. וכיון שהמת היה נגד הסדק, מה היה להם לקשור המקידה? ועוד פירש: שלפני מות המת פקקו המאור בטפיח. ולא הבין רבי לפירושו, הלא אותו מת לא היה מת שלם שהרי לא ידעו אם למעלה הימנו היה פותח טפח, והמת היה כולו תחת הסדק. אלא ודאי כזית מן המת היה, וא"כ לא היה לו לומר "לפני מות המת" אלא "לפני שבא כזית מן המת לשם". ומיהו, יתכן לומר שהמת היה כולו מוטל תחת הגיגית שלא כנגד הסדק, והגיגית היתה סדוקה באמצע מראשה לסופה. ואילו היה באותו סדק על פני כולו פותח טפח – לא היתה טומאה עוברת, דלא חשיב כאהל אחד. אבל אין בו פותח טפח – כאלו אין כאן סדק, וחשיב כאהל אחד, ומביא את הטומאה לבית. וקושיא ראשונה מכל מקום במקומה עומדת. ונראה כפירוש ר"ח; דמפרש דהלקטי היינו תל המתלקט, ואותה הלקטי היתה בין שני בתים, והמת היה בבית אחד. ואותה הגיגית היתה למעלה מן התל עד לתקרה. ואותה הגיגית לא היתה טמאה, שהרי בטלה שם. ואם לא היתה סדוקה – לא היה הבית אחר טמא. אלא הגיגית היתה סדוקה מלדה. והשתא אתי שפיר, דקתני סדוקה – לפי שהיא מלדה. אבל לפירוש הקונטרס לא אתי שפיר, דכיון דפירש שהסדק למעלה מן הגיגית – היה לו לומר פתוחה ולא סדוקה. אבל לפר"ח אתי שפיר, שהסדק היה מן הצד וקשרו את המקידה לידע אם יש פותח טפח. ויש לנו לומר שאותו חור היה עשוי לתשמיש, דחור העשוי לתשמיש שיעורו בפותח טפח. ואם היה פותח טפח הבית אחר טמא, ואם לאו – טהור. ומיהו קשה לר"י לפירוש ר"ח: דלא הוה ליה למימר "על גבן" אלא "על גבה". מ"ר: בלוונא

עין משפט נר מצוה

לו א מיי' פ"ב מהלכות יו"ט הלכה יב סמג לאוין עה טוש"ע א"ח סימן תקא סעיף א:

לז ב ג מיי' שם הלכה יא וסמג שם טוש"ע א"ח סי' תקיח סעיף ו:

לח ד מיי' שם הלכה יז סמג שם טוש"ע א"ח סימן תצז סעיף ב:

לט ה מיי' שם הלכה ב וסמג שם טוש"ע א"ח סי' תצ סעיף ג:

[ביצה מ. לעיל מה:]

[ה] [טוש"ע א"ח סימן שיז סעיף א]:

מ ו מיי' פכ"ד מהלכות שבת הלכה ו ופי"ג מהלכות נדרים הלכה ח וסמג לאוין סה טוש"ע א"ח סימן שמא סעיף א וטוש"ע י"ד סימן רלד סעיף כד:

מא ז מיי' פכ"ד מהל' שבת הלכה ו וסמג שם ומיי' פ"ו מהלכות שבועות הלכה ו סמג לאוין סה רסח טוש"ע שם וטוש"ע י"ד סי' רכח סעיף ג:

מב ח מיי' פי"ב מהל' נדרים הלכה טו סמג לאוין רמב טוש"ע י"ד סימן רלד סעיף כא:

מג ט מיי' פכ"ד מהל' שבת הלכה ו ופ"ו מהלכות שבועות הלכה ו סמג לאוין סה ולאוין רמב טוש"ע א"ח סימן שמא סעיף א וטוש"ע י"ד סימן רכח סעיף ג:

מסורת הש"ס

ביצה ב: לא. · [שם כט:] · [פי' עצי ארזים וברושים ערוך] · [לעיל קמג. ביצה ב.] · [לעיל מד.] · [ביצה לט.] · [לעיל קכב: עירובין לה.] · לעיל מו: נדרים עז. · לעיל קכו: · [נדרים עז. ע"ש] · נדרים עו: · [שבת זו נמי רש"ל] · [נדרים עו: עז.] · שם עז. · גי' רש"ל

הגהות הב"ח

(א) רש"י ד"ה מדבריות וכו' תמיד הס"ד ואח"כ מה"ד בייתות שרועות חוץ לתחום ובאות ולנות בתוך התחום: (ב) ד"ה ואת המטלית לידע אם יש בה שלש על שלש: (ג) ד"ה בטפיח פך של חרס (וחבירו וכו' בשבת) תא"מ ונ"ב הג"ה היא: (ד) ד"ה לצורך השבת וכו' שלא לצורך הס"ד ואח"כ מה"ד והאנן תנן במס' נדרים הס"ד: (ה) תום' ד"ה הלקטי וכו' שאין דרך מאהיל בכך כדמוכח:

סליק מסכת שבת בס"ד

רבינו חננאל

ממקומה דבבהמת קדשים [מיירי] מכלל דחולין שרי כר' [שמעון] דלית ליה מוקצה. ומקשינן על ר' יוחנן וכי סבר רבי יוחנן הלכה כרבי שמעון והא אמר ר' יוחנן הלכה כסתם משנה ותנן אין מבקעים עצים מן הקורות ולא מן הקורה שנשברה ומפרקינן האי כר' יוסי ב"ר יהודה מתני לה רבי יוחנן ולית סתמא. ואמרינן תוב ת"ש מתחילין בערימת התבן אבל לא בעצים שבמוקצה ומפרקינן התם בארזי ואשכחי [ואשוחי] דמוקצה מחמת חסרון כיס. דאפילו ר' שמעון מודה. פי' ארזי ואשוחי עצי ארזים וברושים העשויין לקורות שאין דעתו של אדם עליהן להסיקן תחת תבשילו וגמר והקצה אותן. ואמרינן תוב אין משקין ושוחטין את המדבריות אבל משקין ושוחטין הבייתות והנה סתמא כר' יהודה ורבי יוחנן סבירא ליה הלכתא כסתם משנה קשיא הלכתא אהלכתא ומפרקינן ר' יוחנן סתמא אחרינא אשכח בה"א מגביהין מעל השלחן עצמות וקליפין בש"א מסלק את הטבלא כולה ומנערה. ואמר רב נחמן אנו אין לנו אלא ב"ש כר' יהודה וב"ה כר' שמעון והלכתא כר' שמעון וכדפסק ר' יוחנן פליגי בה רב אחא ורבינא הד אמר בכולה שבת הלכתא כר' שמעון בר ממוקצה מחמת מיאוס. וחד אמר במוקצה [מחמת] מיאוס נמי הלכתא כוותיה לבר ממוקצה מחמת איסורו כגון הנר שהדליקו בה באותה שבת וכיוצא בו אבל

רב נסים גאון

מפירין נדרים בשבת. אמרו [בתוספתא פ' י"ח] מפני מה נדרי שבת מפירין אותן בשבת שאם חשיכה ולא הפר אינו יכול להפר ורבי יוסי ב"ר יהודה ורבי אלעזר ברבי שמעון שאמרו הפרת נדרים מעת לעת אין הלכה כמותם כדגרסינן בנדרים בפרק נערה המאורסה (דף עו) אלא אמר רבי שמעון בן פזי אין הלכה כאותו הזוג לוי סבר למיעבד עובדא כי האי זוגא אמר ליה רב הכי אמר רב ביבי אין הלכה כאותו הזוג ואע"פ שהתירו הפרת נדרים בשבת ביארו בדבר זה תנאי והוא שאמרו לא יאמר אדם לאשתו מופר ליכי כדרך שאומר בחול אלא אומר לה [טלי ואכלי] טלי ושתי והנדר בטל מאליו א"ר יוחנן וצריך שיבטל בלבו תניא בית שמאי אומרים מבטל בלבו ובערב בחול מוציא בשפתיו וב"ה אומרים אחד זה ואחד זה מבטל בלבו ואינו צריך להוציא בשפתיו תמצאנו עוד בפרק נערה המאורסה (דף עז): אם